Programme for International Student Assessment

Learning for Tomorrow's World

First Results from PISA 2003

OECD
ORGANISATION FOR ECONOMIC CO-OPERATION AND DEVELOPMENT

ORGANISATION FOR ECONOMIC CO-OPERATION AND DEVELOPMENT

Pursuant to Article 1 of the Convention signed in Paris on 14th December 1960, and which came into force on 30th September 1961, the Organisation for Economic Co-operation and Development (OECD) shall promote policies designed:

- to achieve the highest sustainable economic growth and employment and a rising standard of living in member countries, while maintaining financial stability, and thus to contribute to the development of the world economy;
- to contribute to sound economic expansion in member as well as non-member countries in the process of economic development; and
- to contribute to the expansion of world trade on a multilateral, non-discriminatory basis in accordance with international obligations.

The original member countries of the OECD are Austria, Belgium, Canada, Denmark, France, Germany, Greece, Iceland, Ireland, Italy, Luxembourg, the Netherlands, Norway, Portugal, Spain, Sweden, Switzerland, Turkey, the United Kingdom and the United States. The following countries became members subsequently through accession at the dates indicated hereafter: Japan (28th April 1964), Finland (28th January 1969), Australia (7th June 1971), New Zealand (29th May 1973), Mexico (18th May 1994), the Czech Republic (21st December 1995), Hungary (7th May 1996), Poland (22nd November 1996), Korea (12th December 1996) and the Slovak Republic (14th December 2000). The Commission of the European Communities takes part in the work of the OECD (Article 13 of the OECD Convention).

Publié en français sous le titre :
Apprendre aujourd'hui, réussir demain – Premiers résultats de PISA 2003
Originalfassungen veröffentlicht unter dem Titel:
Lernen für die Welt von morgen – Erste Ergebnisse von PISA 2003

Foreword

Compelling incentives for individuals, economies and societies to raise levels of education have been the driving force for governments to improve the quality of educational services. The prosperity of countries now derives to a large extent from their human capital, and to succeed in a rapidly changing world, individuals need to advance their knowledge and skills throughout their lives. Education systems need to lay strong foundations for this, by fostering knowledge and skills and strengthening the capacity and motivation of young adults to continue learning beyond school.

All stakeholders – parents, students, those who teach and run education systems as well as the general public – need to be informed on how well their education systems prepare students for life. Many countries monitor students' learning in order to provide answers to this question. Assessment and evaluation – coupled with appropriate incentives – can motivate students to learn better, teachers to teach more effectively and schools to become more supportive and productive environments. Comparative international analyses can extend and enrich the national picture by providing a larger context within which to interpret national results. They can provide countries with information to judge their areas of relative strength and weakness and to monitor progress. They can also stimulate countries to raise aspirations. And they can provide evidence to direct national policy, for schools' curricula and instructional efforts and for students' learning.

In response to the need for cross-nationally comparable evidence on student performance, the Organisation for Economic Co-operation and Develoment (OECD) launched the Programme for International Student Assessment (PISA) in 1997. PISA represents a commitment by governments to monitor the outcomes of education systems in terms of student achievement on a regular basis and within an internationally accepted common framework. It aims to provide a new basis for policy dialogue and for collaboration in defining and implementing educational goals, in innovative ways that reflect judgements about the skills that are relevant to adult life. The first PISA assessment was conducted in 2000. Focusing on reading literacy, PISA 2000 revealed wide differences in the extent to which countries succeed in enabling young adults to access, manage, integrate, evaluate and reflect on written information in order to develop their potential and further expand their horizon. For some countries, the results were disappointing, showing that their 15-year-olds' performance lagged considerably behind that of other countries, sometimes by the equivalent of several years of schooling and sometimes despite high investments in education. PISA 2000 also highlighted significant variation in the performance of schools and raised concerns about equity in the distribution of learning opportunities.

How have things changed since 2000? This report presents first results from the PISA 2003 assessment, which focused on mathematics. It shows that average performance in the group of the 25 OECD countries for which data can be compared has increased in one of the two content areas of mathematics that was measured in both 2000 and 2003,[1] while performance in science, reading and the other comparable area of mathematics has essentially remained unchanged. However, performance changes have been uneven across OECD countries. Finland, the top performing country in the PISA 2000 reading assessment, has maintained its high level of reading performance while further improving its performance in mathematics and science, placing it now on a par with the East Asian countries, whose performance in mathematics and science had been previously unmatched. By contrast, in Mexico, the lowest performing OECD country in the 2000 assessment, the pressure to expand the still limited access to secondary education (OECD, 2004a) may have been one of the factors contributing to lower performance in 2003 in all three assessment areas.

However, the report goes well beyond an examination of the relative standing of countries in mathematics, science and reading. It also looks at a wider range of educational outcomes that include students' motivation to learn, their beliefs about themselves and their learning strategies. Furthermore, it examines how performance varies between the genders and between socio-economic groups. It also provides insights into some of the factors that are associated with the development of knowledge and skills at home and at school, and into how these factors interact and what the implications are for policy development. Most importantly, the report sheds light on countries that succeed in achieving high performance standards while at the same time providing an equitable distribution of learning opportunities. Results in these countries pose challenges for other countries by showing what it is possible to achieve.

The report is the product of a collaborative effort between the countries participating in PISA, the experts and institutions working within the framework of the PISA Consortium, and the OECD. The report was drafted by the OECD Directorate for Education, principally by Andreas Schleicher, Claudia Tamassia and Miyako Ikeda, with advice and analytic support from Raymond Adams, Cordula Artelt (who developed the model underlying Chapter 3), Alla Berezner, Jude Cosgrove, John Cresswell, Donald Hirsch, Yuko Nonoyama, Christian Monseur, Claudia Reiter, Wolfram Schulz, Ross Turner and Sophie Vayssettes. Chapters 4 and 5 also draw on analytic work undertaken in the context of PISA 2000 by Jaap Scheerens and Douglas Willms. The PISA assessment instruments and the

1. In 2003, mathematics was assessed in detail and results are reported on four content scales. In 2000, a minor assessment of mathematics was reported on only one scale, but the assessment covered two content areas of the PISA mathematics framework, namely *space and shape* and *change and relationships* (see OECD, 2001a). To allow for comparisons with results from PISA 2003, separate reporting scales were retrospectively constructed for the 2000 results in these two content areas.

data underlying the report were prepared by the PISA Consortium, under the direction of Raymond Adams at the Australian Council for Educational Research.

The development of the report was steered by the PISA Governing Board that is chaired by Ryo Watanabe (Japan). Annex C of the report lists the members of the various PISA bodies as well as the individual experts and consultants who have contributed to this report and to PISA in general.

The report is published on the responsibility of the Secretary-General of the OECD.

Ryo Watanabe
Chair of the PISA Governing Board

Barry McGaw
Director for Education, OECD

Table of Contents

LIST OF BOXES

LIST OF FIGURES

LIST OF TABLES

Introduction

PISA – AN OVERVIEW

In 2003, the OECD's Programme for International Student Assessment (PISA) conducted its second three-yearly survey of student knowledge and skills. This report summarises the results.

PISA seeks to assess how well 15-year-olds are prepared for life's challenges.

PISA seeks to measure how well young adults, at age 15 and therefore approaching the end of compulsory schooling, are prepared to meet the challenges of today's knowledge societies. The assessment is forward-looking, focusing on young people's ability to use their knowledge and skills to meet real-life challenges, rather than merely on the extent to which they have mastered a specific school curriculum. This orientation reflects a change in the goals and objectives of curricula themselves, which are increasingly concerned with what students can do with what they learn at school, and not merely whether they can reproduce what they have learned.

PISA is a collaborative effort by governments to monitor student progress in a global framework...

Key features driving the development of PISA have been:

- its policy orientation, with design and reporting methods determined by the need of governments to draw policy lessons;
- the innovative "literacy" concept that is concerned with the capacity of students to apply knowledge and skills in key subject areas and to analyse, reason and communicate effectively as they pose, solve and interpret problems in a variety of situations;
- its relevance to lifelong learning, which does not limit PISA to assessing students' curricular and cross-curricular competencies but also asks them to report on their own motivation to learn, their beliefs about themselves and their learning strategies;
- its regularity, which will enable countries to monitor their progress in meeting key learning objectives; and
- its breadth of geographical coverage and collaborative nature, with the 49 countries that have participated in a PISA assessment so far and the 11 additional countries that will join the PISA 2006 assessment representing a total of one third of the world population and almost nine-tenths of the world's gross domestic product (GDP).[1]

...with leading experts producing valid cross-country assessments.

PISA is the most comprehensive and rigorous international programme to assess student performance and to collect data on student, family and institutional factors that can help to explain differences in performance. Decisions about the scope and nature of the assessments and the background information to be collected are made by leading experts in participating countries, and are steered jointly by their governments on the basis of shared, policy-driven interests. Substantial efforts and resources are devoted to achieving cultural and linguistic breadth and balance in the assessment materials. Stringent quality assurance mechanisms are applied in translation, sampling and data collection.

Figure 1.1 ■ **A map of PISA countries**

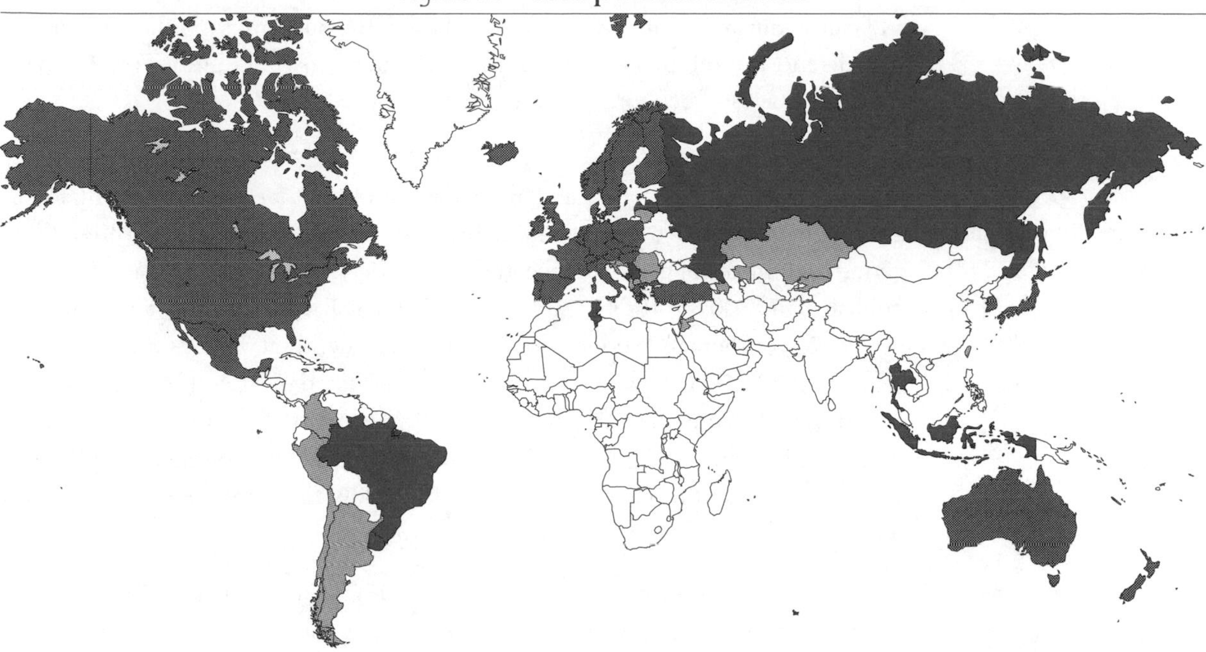

OECD countries

Australia
Austria
Belgium
Canada
Czech Republic
Denmark
Finland
France
Germany
Greece
Hungary
Iceland
Ireland
Italy
Japan
Korea
Luxembourg
Mexico
Netherlands
New Zealand
Norway
Poland
Portugal
Slovak Republic
Spain
Sweden
Switzerland
Turkey
United Kingdom
United States

Partner countries in PISA 2003

Brazil
Hong Kong-China
Indonesia
Latvia
Liechtenstein
Macao-China
Russian Federation
Serbia and Montenegro
Thailand
Tunisia
Uruguay

Partner countries in other PISA assessments

Albania
Argentina
Azerbaijan
Bulgaria
Chile
Colombia
Croatia
Estonia
Israel
Jordan
Kazakhstan
Kyrgyz Republic
Lithuania
Macedonia
Peru
Qatar
Romania
Slovenia
Chinese Taipei

As a consequence, the results of PISA have a high degree of validity and reliability, and can significantly improve understanding of the outcomes of education in the world's most developed countries, as well as in a growing number of countries at earlier stages of economic development.

PISA 2003 was carried out in 41 countries, most of which also administered PISA 2000; the focus shifted from reading in 2000 to mathematics in 2003.

The first PISA survey was conducted in 2000 in 32 countries (including 28 OECD member countries) and repeated in 11 further partner countries in 2002. Two-thirds of the assessment focused on reading, with the other third giving a summary of performance in mathematics and science. First results were published in 2001 (OECD, 2001a) and 2003 (OECD, 2003c), and followed by a series of thematic reports looking in more depth at various aspects of the results.[2] PISA 2003, reported on here, was conducted in 41 countries, including all 30 OECD countries (Figure 1.1). It included an in-depth assessment of mathematics and assessments with less detail in science, reading and problem solving. In the next three-yearly survey, PISA 2006, the primary focus will be on science, and it will return to reading in 2009.[3]

PISA was created by the OECD countries but is now used by a growing number of countries.

Although PISA was originally created by the OECD governments in response to their own needs, it has now become a major policy tool for many other countries and economies as well. PISA is playing an increasing policy role in regions around the world, and the survey has now been conducted or is planned in partner countries in Southeast Asia (Hong Kong-China, Indonesia, Macao-China, Chinese Taipei and Thailand), Eastern Europe (Albania, Bulgaria, Croatia, Estonia, Latvia, Lithuania, the Former Yugoslav Republic of Macedonia, Romania, The Russian Federation, Serbia[4] and Slovenia), the Middle East (Jordan, Israel and Qatar), South America (Argentina, Brazil, Chile, Colombia, Peru and Uruguay) and North Africa (Tunisia). Across the world, policy makers use PISA findings to:

- gauge the literacy skills of students in their own country in comparison with those of the other participating countries;
- establish benchmarks for educational improvement, for example, in terms of the mean scores achieved by other countries or their capacity to provide high levels of equity in educational outcomes and opportunities; and
- understand relative strengths and weaknesses of their education system.

National interest in PISA is illustrated by the many reports produced in participating countries and by the numerous references to the results of PISA in public debates and the media throughout the world (see *www.pisa.oecd.org* for examples).

This report looks at student performance in PISA 2003 and at factors associated with success.

The initial results of PISA 2003 are presented in two volumes. This report is the first volume; it summarises the performance of students in PISA 2003 and uses the information gathered to analyse what factors may help to promote success in education. The second volume, *Problem Solving for Tomorrow's World – First Measures of Cross-Curricular Competencies from PISA 2003* (OECD, 2004d), reports on the new assessment of cross-curricular problem solving, and the *PISA 2003 Technical Report* (OECD, forthcoming) explains the methodology underlying PISA.

In addition to reporting the performance of students, schools and countries in mathematics, science and reading, this report uses background information on students, schools and education systems to examine a range of factors associated with different levels of performance. By revealing patterns of student proficiency in different countries alongside information about the characteristics and experiences of students, PISA provides a powerful tool to improve understanding of what promotes success in education. The remainder of this chapter looks in turn at:

- what PISA measures (overall and within each assessment area), the methods that were employed and the target population that is involved;
- what is distinctive about PISA 2003, including the extent to which the repeat of the survey allows comparisons over time; and
- how the report is organised.

WHAT PISA MEASURES AND HOW

A framework and conceptual underpinning for each assessment area in PISA was developed by international experts from participating countries and following consultation, agreed upon by governments of the participating countries (OECD, 1999a and OECD, 2003e). The framework starts with the concept of "literacy", which is concerned with the capacity of students to apply knowledge and skills and to analyse, reason and communicate effectively as they pose, solve and interpret problems in a variety of situations.

PISA builds on an internationally agreed framework for assessment that measures "literacy"...

The concept of literacy used in PISA is much broader than the historical notion of the ability to read and write. It is measured on a continuum, not as something that an individual either does or does not have. It may be necessary or desirable for some purposes to define a point on a literacy continuum below which levels of competence are considered inadequate, but the underlying variability is important. A literate person has a range of competencies and there is no precise dividing line between a person who is fully literate and one who is not.

...in the broad sense of a continuum of student competencies.

The acquisition of literacy is a lifelong process – taking place not just at school or through formal learning, but also through interactions with peers, colleagues and wider communities. Fifteen-year-olds cannot be expected to have learned everything they will need to know as adults, but they should have a solid foundation of knowledge in areas such as reading, mathematics and science. In order to continue learning in these subject areas and to apply their learning to the real world, they also need to understand fundamental processes and principles and to use these flexibly in different situations. It is for this reason that PISA assesses the ability to complete tasks relating to real life, depending on a broad understanding of key concepts, rather than limiting the assessment to the possession of subject-specific knowledge.

These are acquired throughout life, applied to real situations...

As well as assessing competencies in the three core assessment areas, PISA aims to progressively examine competencies across disciplinary boundaries. PISA 2000 made a start by asking students about motivation and other aspects of their attitudes towards learning, their familiarity with computers and,

...and not restricted to subject disciplines, but considering broader learner characteristics and skills.

Box 1.1 ■ Key features of the PISA 2003 assessment

Content

- The survey covers mathematics (the main focus in 2003), reading, science and problem solving. PISA considers student knowledge in these areas not in isolation but in relation to students' ability to reflect on their knowledge and experience and to apply them to real world issues. The emphasis is on the mastery of processes, the understanding of concepts, and the ability to function in various situations within each assessment area.
- PISA integrates the assessment of subject-specific knowledge with cross-curricular competencies. In PISA 2003, as in 2000, students assessed their own characteristics as learners. The 2003 survey also introduced the first assessment of wider student competencies – assessing problem-solving abilities.

Methods

- Each participating student spent two hours carrying out pencil-and-paper tasks.
- Questions requiring students to construct their own answers were combined with multiple-choice items. Items were typically organised in units based on a written passage or graphic, of the kind that students might encounter in real life.
- A total of six-and-a-half hours of assessment items was included, with different students taking different combinations of the assessment items. Three-and-a-half hours of testing time was in mathematics, with one hour each for reading, science and problem solving.
- Students answered a questionnaire that took about 30 minutes to complete and focused on their background, their learning habits and their perceptions of the learning environment, as well as on their engagement and motivation.
- School principals completed a questionnaire about their school that included demographic characteristics as well as an assessment of the quality of the learning environment at school.

Outcomes

- A profile of knowledge and skills among 15-year-olds in 2003.
- Contextual indicators relating performance results to student and school characteristics.
- A knowledge base for policy analysis and research.
- A first estimate of change in student knowledge and skills over time, between the assessments in 2000 and 2003.

Sample size

- Well over a quarter of a million students, representing about 23 million 15-year-olds in the schools of the 41 participating countries, were assessed on the basis of scientific probability samples.

Future assessments

- The PISA 2006 assessment will focus on science and PISA 2009 will return to a focus on reading.
- Part of future assessments will require students to use computers, expanding the scope of the skills that can be tested and reflecting the importance of information and computer technology (ICT) as a medium in modern societies.

under the heading "self-regulated learning", aspects of their strategies for managing and monitoring their own learning. In PISA 2003, these elements were further developed and complemented with an assessment of problem-solving knowledge and skills. In subsequent PISA surveys, further cross-curricular competencies, as well as the use of information technologies, will play a growing role.

Literacy in PISA: what is measured

Each PISA domain can be defined in three dimensions.

The assessment areas covered by PISA are defined in terms of:

- the *content* or *structure* of knowledge that students need to acquire in each assessment area (*e.g.*, familiarity with mathematical concepts);
- the *processes* that need to be performed (*e.g.*, pursuing a certain mathematical argument); and
- the *situations* in which students encounter mathematical problems and relevant knowledge and skills are applied (*e.g.*, making decisions in relation to one's personal life, or understanding world affairs).

Details of what is covered under mathematics, science and reading are considered in Chapters 2 and 6, and further elaborated in *The PISA 2003 Assessment Framework: Mathematics, Reading, Science and Problem Solving Knowledge and Skills* (OECD, 2003e). Figure 1.2 summarises the core definition of each area of literacy and how the three dimensions are developed in each case.

The PISA instruments: how measurement takes place

Students had to read texts and answer questions about them.

As in PISA 2000, the assessment instruments in PISA 2003 were developed around units of assessment – a series of texts followed by a number of questions on various aspects of each text, aiming to make tasks as close as possible to those encountered in the real world.

In many cases, the responses were in their own words, which required careful, and often multiple, marking…

The questions varied in format, but across the assessment areas of mathematics, science and reading about 50 per cent of the questions required students to construct their own responses, either by providing a brief answer from a wide range of possible answers (short-response items) or by constructing a longer response (open-constructed response items), allowing for the possibility of divergent, individual responses and opposing viewpoints. Partial credit was provided for partially correct or less sophisticated answers, with all of these items marked by experts. To ensure consistency in the marking process, many of the more complex items were marked independently by up to four markers. In addition, a sub-sample of student responses from each country was marked by an independent panel of centrally trained expert markers in order to verify that the marking process was carried out in equivalent ways across countries. The results show that consistent marking was achieved across countries (for details on the marking process see Annex A7 and the *PISA 2003 Technical Report* (OECD, forthcoming).

Figure 1.2 ■ **Summary of the assessment areas in PISA 2003 covered in this volume**

Assessment area	Mathematics	Science	Reading
Definition and its distinctive features	"The capacity to identify and understand the role that mathematics plays in the world, to make well-founded judgements and to use and engage with mathematics in ways that meet the needs of that individual's life as a constructive, concerned and reflective citizen" (OECD, 2003e). Related to wider, functional use of mathematics, engagement requires the ability to recognise and formulate mathematical problems in various situations.	"The capacity to use scientific knowledge, to identify scientific questions and to draw evidence-based conclusions in order to understand and help make decisions about the natural world and the changes made to it through human activity" (OECD, 2003e). Requires understanding of scientific concepts, an ability to apply a scientific perspective and to think scientifically about evidence.	"The capacity to understand, use and reflect on written texts in order to achieve one's goals, to develop one's knowledge and potential, and to participate in society" (OECD, 2003e). Much more than decoding and literal comprehension, reading involves understanding and reflection, and the ability to use reading to fulfil one's goals in life.
Content dimension	Clusters of relevant mathematical areas and concepts: • quantity; • space and shape; • change and relationships; and • uncertainty.	Areas of scientific knowledge and concepts, such as: • biodiversity; • forces and movement; and • physiological change.	The form of reading materials: • continuous materials including different kinds of prose such as narration, exposition, argumentation; and • non-continuous texts including graphs, forms, lists.
Process dimension	"Competency clusters" define skills needed for mathematics: • reproduction (simple mathematical operations); • connections (bringing together ideas to solve straightforward problems); and • reflection (wider mathematical thinking). In general these are associated with tasks of ascending difficulty, but there is overlap in the rating of tasks in each cluster.	The ability to use scientific knowledge and understanding, to acquire, interpret and act on evidence: • describing, explaining and predicting scientific phenomena; • understanding scientific investigation; and • interpreting scientific evidence and conclusions.	Type of reading task or process: • retrieving information; • interpreting texts; and • reflection and evaluation of texts. The focus of PISA is on reading to learn, rather than learning to read, and hence students are not assessed on the most basic reading skills.
Situation dimension	Situations vary according to their distance from individuals' lives. In order of closeness: • personal; • educational and occupational; • local and broader community; and • scientific.	The context of science, focusing on uses in relation to: • life and health; • the Earth and the environment; and • technology.	The use for which the text constructed: • private (*e.g.*, a personal letter); • public (*e.g.*, an official document); • occupational (*e.g.*, a report); • educational (*e.g.*, school related reading).

A further 12 per cent of the test was based on students constructing their own responses, but based on a very limited range of possible responses (closed-constructed response items), which were scored as either correct or incorrect. The remaining items were asked in multiple-choice format, in which students either made one choice from among four or five given alternatives or a series of choices by circling one of two optional responses (for example "yes" or "no", or "agree" or "disagree") in relation to each of a number of different propositions or statements (complex multiple-choice items).

...and in others, they answered more closed questions with fewer possible answers.

The total assessment time of 390 minutes of testing was organised in different combinations of test booklets with each individual being tested for 120 minutes. The time devoted to the assessment of mathematics was 210 minutes (54 per cent of the total) and each of the other assessment areas, namely reading, science and problem solving were assessed through 60 minutes of material. Thus, only a summary profile of reading and scientific skills will be presented in this report. For more information on the PISA assessment instruments see Annex A6.

Each student spent two hours being tested.

The PISA student population

In order to ensure the comparability of the results across countries, PISA needs to assess comparable target populations. Differences between countries in the nature and extent of pre-primary education and care, in the age of entry to formal schooling, and in the structure of the education system do not allow school grades to be defined so that they are internationally comparable. Valid international comparisons of educational performance must, therefore, define their populations with reference to a target age. PISA covers students who are aged between 15 years 3 months and 16 years 2 months at the time of the assessment, regardless of the grade or type of institution in which they are enrolled and of whether they are in full-time or part-time education. The use of this age in PISA, across countries and over time, allows the performance of students shortly before they complete compulsory education to be compared in a consistent way.

PISA assesses students aged 15 who are still at school, regardless of grade or institution...

As a result, this report is able to make statements about the knowledge and skills of individuals born in the same year and still at school at 15 years of age, but having differing educational experiences, both within and outside school. The number of school grades in which these students are to be found depends on a country's policies on school entry and promotion. Furthermore, in some countries, students in the PISA target population represent different education systems, tracks or streams.

Stringent technical standards were established for the definition of national target populations. PISA excludes 15-year-olds not enrolled in educational institutions. In the remainder of this report "15-year-olds" is used as a shorthand to denote the PISA student population. Coverage of the target population of 15-year-olds within education is very high compared with other international surveys: relatively few schools were ineligible for participation, for example because of geographically remoteness or because their students had special needs.

...and only small parts of the target population were left out...

In 24 out of the 41 participating countries, the percentage of school-level exclusions amounted to less than 1 per cent, and to less than 3 per cent in all countries except Mexico (3.6 per cent), Switzerland (3.4 per cent), the United Kingdom (3.4 per cent) and the partner countries Latvia (3.8 per cent) and Serbia (5.3 per cent). When accounting for the exclusion within schools of students who met certain internationally established criteria,[5] the exclusion rates increase slightly. However, they remain below 2 per cent in 19 participating countries, below 4 per cent in 29 participating countries, below 6 per cent in all but two countries and below 8 per cent in all countries (Annex A3). This high level of coverage contributes to the comparability of the assessment results. For example, even assuming that the excluded students would have systematically scored worse than those who participated, and that this relationship is moderately strong, an exclusion rate in the order of 5 per cent would likely lead to an overestimation of national mean scores of less than 5 score points.[6] Moreover, in most cases the exclusions were inevitable. For example, in New Zealand 2.3 per cent of the students were excluded because they had less than one year of instruction in English (often because they were foreign fee-paying students) and were therefore not able to follow the instructions of the assessment.

...with sufficiently large scientific samples to allow for valid comparisons.

The specific sample design and size for each country was designed to maximise sampling efficiency for student-level estimates. In OECD countries, sample sizes ranged from 3 350 students in Iceland to 30 000 students in Mexico. This selection of samples was monitored internationally and accompanied by rigorous standards for the participation rate to ensure that the PISA results reflect the skills of 15-year-old students in participating countries.

WHAT IS DIFFERENT ABOUT THE PISA 2003 SURVEY?

It establishes a detailed understanding of student performance in mathematics

PISA 2003 reports for the first time proficiency levels for mathematics...

With over half of the assessment time devoted to mathematics, PISA 2003 can report in much greater detail on mathematics performance than was the case in PISA 2000. As well as calculating overall performance scores, it also becomes possible to report separately on different content areas of mathematics and to establish conceptually grounded proficiency levels on each performance scale that relate student scores to what students are able to do.

...showing how well students perform in various mathematical content areas.

However, the basis for these scales is different for mathematics than for reading. In the case of the latter, the main distinction was by the *process* dimension – students receive scores for how well they could perform three different types of reading tasks (retrieval, interpretation, and reflection and evaluation). In the case of mathematics the main distinction is by *content* areas (quantity, space and shape, change and relationships, and uncertainty). This reporting of mathematical outcomes allows policy makers to see the way different mathematical competencies have been built up in relation to four broad content areas of mathematics. In this way, the link between teaching and learning methods

and approaches, on the one hand, and the curriculum content priorities and emphases in different countries, on the other, is clearly exposed.

It deepens exploration of cross-curricular competencies

One of the most important innovations of PISA is to assess characteristics of students in ways that go beyond curriculum areas, but also consider their broader characteristics as learners. PISA 2000 took a first step in this direction by asking students about aspects of their motivation, self-concept and learning strategies. PISA 2003 continues to do this, but makes an important advance in assessing directly a generic student competency that crosses curricular areas – problem solving. The design and implementation of an instrument of this kind, valid across cultures, marks an important advance in international student assessment. The second volume examines the results of this part of PISA 2003.

PISA 2003 for the first time directly assesses a cross-curricular student competency: problem solving.

It introduces new background information about students and schools

The background questionnaires completed by students and school principals provide essential information for PISA's analysis. In the 2003 survey, these questionnaires have been refined and deepened. In particular:

Students and principals are asked new questions, about mathematics attitudes and about educational careers.

- They explore in greater depth than in 2000 the organisation of schools and the instructional process. This is so especially in relation to mathematics – with students, for example, being asked about their attitudes towards mathematics instruction, in ways that shed light on important motivational issues.
- An optional part of the student questionnaire was introduced to collect information on educational careers. This allows student performance to be set in the context of prior experiences of students within the school system.

It allows for comparison of change over time

A central characteristic of PISA is its role as a monitoring instrument. Every three years, it measures student knowledge and skills in reading literacy, mathematics and science. The basic survey design remains constant, to allow comparability from one three-year cycle to the next. In the long term, this will allow countries to see the effects of policy changes and improvement in educational standards on wider student skills, and how change in educational outcomes compares to international benchmarks.

PISA will eventually show trends in performance...

The second survey, in 2003, offers a first glimpse of these changes over time. In mathematics, only two of the four content areas used in the 2003 survey were also used in 2000. However, for each of the two common areas, it was possible to calculate what the 2000 results would have been on the newly-established scale, with the mean performance of OECD students set at 500 for 2003.

...and some comparisons can already be made between the 2000 and 2003 results.

While the results do provide a basis for comparisons over time, several limitations need to be borne in mind in the interpretation of change between 2000 and 2003:

These should be interpreted with caution, however...

- First, since data are only available from two points in time, it is not possible to assess to what extent the observed differences are indicative of longer-term trends.
- Second, while the overall approach to measurement used by PISA is consistent across cycles, small refinements continue to be made, so it would not be prudent to read too much into small changes in results. Furthermore, errors from sampling as well as measurement error are inevitably introduced when assessments are linked through a limited number of common assessment tasks over time. To account for the latter, the confidence band for comparisons over time has been widened correspondingly and only changes that are indicated as statistically significant in this report should be considered.
- Third, some countries need to be excluded from comparisons between 2000 and 2003 for methodological reasons. Among OECD countries, the Slovak Republic and Turkey joined PISA only for the 2003 assessment. The 2000 sample for the Netherlands had not met the PISA response rate standards and mean scores for the Netherlands were therefore not reported for PISA 2000. In Luxembourg, the assessment conditions were changed in substantial ways between the 2000 and 2003 assessments in order to reduce linguistic barriers for students and the results are therefore not comparable. The 2003 sample for the United Kingdom does not meet the PISA response rate standards and mean scores for the United Kingdom should therefore not be compared with those in PISA 2000 (Annex A3).

...not least because educational change takes many years.

- Finally, education systems do not change overnight. Many reforms take time to implement, so there is an inevitable gap between a policy decision and change in the classroom. Once teaching has changed, the effect on an individual student will also take time. Finally, PISA measures student competencies on the eve of completion of compulsory education, which reflect the *cumulative* influence of 8-10 years of schooling, not just mastery of the curriculum of the grades in which 15-year-olds are enrolled.

ORGANISATION OF THE REPORT

Following this introductory chapter, the next four chapters consider the mathematics results for 2003, and use them to analyse a range of factors associated with performance. Chapter 6 extends the analysis to science and reading.

The report starts by profiling mathematics performance...

- Chapter 2 gives a profile of student performance in mathematics. The chapter begins with setting the results in the context of how mathematics is defined, measured and reported, and then examines what students are able do in mathematics. Since results vary in important ways across the four content areas of mathematics examined in PISA 2003, the analysis is done separately for each content area before a summary picture is presented at the end. Any comparison of the outcomes of education systems needs to account for countries' social and economic circumstances and the resources that they devote to education. To address this, the final part of the chapter interprets the results within countries' economic and social contexts.

- Chapter 3 broadens the range of learning outcomes by looking, in turn, at student motivation to learn mathematics, their beliefs about themselves, and their learning strategies. It then examines how various aspects of students' attitudes to learning and their learning behaviour relate to each other and to student performance; analyses how these relationships differ across countries; and explores the distribution of relevant characteristics among different students, across and within countries.

...then considers how these results relate to student attitudes and behaviours...

- Chapter 4 starts by examining the performance gaps shown in Chapter 2 more closely and, in particular, the extent to which the overall variation in student performance relates to differences in the results achieved by different schools. The chapter then looks at how socio-economic background relates to student performance. Building on this, the chapter considers the policy implications of these findings, and discusses how different policy strategies aimed at improving equity in the distribution of learning opportunity are likely to be appropriate in different countries.

...how they vary across schools and socio-economic groups, with implications for equity strategies...

- Chapter 5 makes a first step towards identifying how school resources, policies and practices interact with home background and influence student performance.

...and the role of school factors.

- Chapter 6 considers student performance in reading and science in 2003, and how it has changed since 2000.

The report concludes with results for reading and science.

A technical annex addresses the construction of the questionnaire indices, discusses sampling issues, documents quality assurance procedures and the process followed for the development of the assessment instruments, and provides data on the reliability of marking. Finally, the annex provides the data tables underlying the various chapters. Many of the issues covered in the technical annex are elaborated in greater detail in the *PISA 2003 Technical Report* (OECD, forthcoming).

Finally, a further report, *Problem Solving for Tomorrow's World – First Measures of Cross-Curricular Competencies from PISA 2003* (OECD, 2004d), considers the results of the assessment of students' problem-solving abilities.

Notes

1. The combined population of all countries (excluding Chinese Taipei) that participate in the PISA 2000, 2003 or 2006 assessments amounts to 32 per cent of the 2002 world population. The GDP of these countries amounts to 87 per cent of the 2002 world GDP. The data on GDP and population sizes were derived from the U.N. World Development Indicators database.

2. Themes of international thematic reports have included: *Reading for Change – Performance and Engagement Across Countries* (OECD, 2002b), *Learners for Life – Student Approaches to Learning* (OECD, 2003b), *Student Engagement at School – A Sense of Belonging and Participation* (OECD, 2003d), and *What Makes School Systems Perform* (OECD, 2004c).

3. The framework for the PISA 2006 assessment has been finalised and preparations for the implementation of the assessment are currently underway. Governments will decide on subsequent PISA assessments in 2005.

4. For the country Serbia and Montenegro, data for Montenegro are not available. The latter accounts for 7.9 per cent of the national population. The name "Serbia" is used as a shorthand for the Serbian part of Serbia and Montenegro.

5. Countries were permitted to exclude up to 2.5 per cent of the national desired target population within schools if these students were: *i)* considered in the professional opinion of the school principal or of other qualified staff members, to be educable mentally retarded or who had been defined as such through psychological tests (including students who were emotionally or mentally unable to follow the general instructions given in PISA); *ii)* permanently and physically disabled in such a way that they could not perform in the PISA assessment situation (functionally disabled students who could respond were to be included in the assessment); or *iii)* non-native language speakers with less than one year of instruction in the language of the assessment (for details see Annex A3).

6. If the correlation between the propensity of exclusions and student performance is 0.3, resulting mean scores would likely be overestimated by 1 score point if the exclusion rate is 1 per cent, by 3 score points if the exclusion rate is 5 per cent, and by 6 score points if the exclusion rate is 10 per cent. If the correlation between the propensity of exclusions and student performance is 0.5, resulting mean scores would be overestimated by 1 score point if the exclusion rate is 1 per cent, by 5 score points if the exclusion rate is 5 per cent, and by 10 score points if the exclusion rate is 10 per cent. For this calculation, a model was employed that assumes a bivariate normal distribution for the propensity to participate and performance. For details see the *PISA 2000 Technical Report* (OCED 2002d).

READERS' GUIDE

Data underlying the figures

The data referred to in Chapters 2 to 6 of this report are presented in Annex B1 and, with additional detail, on the web site *www.pisa.oecd.org*. Five symbols are used to denote missing data:

- *a* The category does not apply in the country concerned. Data are therefore missing.
- *c* There are too few observations to provide reliable estimates (*i.e.,* there are fewer than 3 per cent of students for this cell or too few schools for valid inferences). However, these statistics were included in the calculation of cross-country averages.
- *m* Data are not available. These data were collected but subsequently removed from the publication for technical reasons.
- *w* Data have been withdrawn at the request of the country concerned.
- *x* Data are included in another category or column of the table.

Calculation of international averages

An OECD average was calculated for most indicators presented in this report. In the case of some indicators, a total representing the OECD area as a whole was also calculated:

- The ***OECD average*** takes the OECD countries as a single entity, to which each country contributes with equal weight. For statistics such as percentages of mean scores, the OECD average corresponds to the arithmetic mean of the respective country statistics. In contrast, for statistics relating to variation, the OECD average may differ from the arithmetic mean of the country statistics because it not only reflects variation within countries, but also variation that lies between countries.
- The ***OECD total*** takes the OECD countries as a single entity, to which each country contributes in proportion to the number of 15-year-olds enrolled in its schools (see Annex A3 for data). It illustrates how a country compares with the OECD area as a whole.

In this publication, the OECD total is generally used when references are made to the stock of human capital in the OECD area. Where the focus is on comparing performance across education systems, the OECD average is used. In the case of some countries, data may not be available for specific indicators or specific categories may not apply. Readers should, therefore, keep in mind that the terms ***OECD average*** and ***OECD total*** refer to the OECD countries included in the respective comparisons. All international averages include data for the United Kingdom, even where these data, for reasons explained in Annex A3, are not shown in the respective data tables.

Rounding of figures

Because of rounding, some figures in tables may not exactly add up to the totals. Totals, differences and averages are always calculated on the basis of exact numbers and are rounded only after calculation.

All standard errors in this publication have been rounded to two decimal places. Where the value 0.00 is shown, this does not imply that the standard error is zero, but that it is smaller than 0.005.

Reporting of student data

The report usually uses "15-year-olds" as shorthand for the PISA target population. In practice, this refers to students who were aged between 15 years and 3 (complete) months and 16 years and 2 (complete) months at the beginning of the assessment period and who were enrolled in an educational institution, regardless of the grade level or type of institution, and of whether they were attending full-time or part-time (for details see Annex A3).

Reporting of school data

The principals of the schools in which students were assessed provided information on their school's characteristics by completing a school questionnaire. Where responses from school principals are presented in this publication, they are weighted so that they are proportionate to the number of 15-year-olds enrolled in the school.

Abbreviations used in this report

The following abbreviations are used in this report:

GDP Gross Domestic Product
ISCED International Standard Classification of Education
PPP Purchasing Power Parity
SD Standard deviation
SE Standard error

Further documentation

For further information on the PISA assessment instruments and the methods used in PISA, see the *PISA 2000 Technical Report* (OECD, 2002d) and the PISA Web site (*www.pisa.oecd.org*).

A Profile of Student Performance in Mathematics

INTRODUCTION

The PISA 2000 results raised issues about student performance both across and within countries…

Since 1997, OECD governments have collaborated to monitor the outcomes of education in terms of student performance on a regular basis and within an internationally agreed common framework. The first PISA assessment, carried out in 2000, revealed wide differences in the extent to which countries succeed in equipping young adults with knowledge and skills in reading, mathematics and science. For some countries, the results were disappointing, showing that their 15-year-olds' performance lagged considerably behind that of other countries (and perhaps their own expectations) sometimes by the equivalent of several years of schooling[1] and in certain cases despite high investments in education. PISA 2000 also highlighted significant variation in the performance of schools and raised concerns about equity in the distribution of learning opportunities.

…and while the overall results in 2003 have changed only slightly, country differences continue to evolve.

Among the 25 OECD countries for which performance can be compared between 2000 and 2003, average mathematics performance increased in one of the two content areas measured in both surveys. For the other mathematical content area, as well as for science and reading, average performance among OECD countries has remained broadly unchanged. However, performance has changed in different ways across OECD countries. Finland, the top performing country in the PISA 2000 reading assessment, has maintained its high level of reading performance while improving its performance in mathematics and science.[2] This now places Finland on a par in mathematics and science with the previously unmatched East Asian countries. By contrast, in Mexico, the lowest performing OECD country in the 2000 assessment, the pressure to expand the still limited access to secondary education[3] may have been one of the factors putting strains on educational quality, with performance in the 2003 assessment lower in all three assessment areas.

This chapter reports results in mathematics, the main focus in PISA 2003…

This chapter presents in detail the results from the PISA 2003 mathematics assessment. Mathematics is the main focus of PISA 2003, and accounted for over half of all assessment time. This allowed mathematics performance to be assessed more thoroughly than in PISA 2000, and for its measurement to be refined.

- The chapter begins by setting the results in the context of how mathematics is defined, measured and reported. It considers a series of key questions. What is meant by "mathematical literacy"? In what ways is this different from other ways of thinking about mathematical knowledge and skills? Why is it useful to think of mathematical competencies in this way, and how can the results be interpreted?
- In the second part, the chapter examines student performance in mathematics. Since results vary in important ways across the four content areas of mathematics examined in PISA 2003, the analysis is described separately for each content area before a summary picture is presented at the end.
- In as much as it is important to take the socio-economic context of schools into account when comparing school performance, any comparison of the

outcomes of education systems needs to account for countries' economic circumstances and the resources that they devote to education. To address this, the third part of the chapter interprets the results within countries' economic and social contexts.

Chapter 3 continues the analysis of student outcomes by examining a wider range of student characteristics that relate to performance in mathematics and that can be considered important educational outcomes in their own right, including students' motivation to learn mathematics, their beliefs about themselves and their learning strategies in mathematics. Later, Chapter 6 extends the reporting of student outcomes in PISA 2003 by looking at performance in reading and science.

...while further chapters report other outcomes: student approaches to learning and performance in reading and science.

THE PISA APPROACH TO ASSESSING MATHEMATICS PERFORMANCE

How mathematics is defined

For much of the last century, the content of school mathematics and science curricula was dominated by the need to provide the foundations for the professional training of a small number of mathematicians, scientists and engineers. With the growing role of science, mathematics and technology in modern life, however, the objectives of personal fulfilment, employment and full participation in society increasingly require that all adults – not just those aspiring to a scientific career – be mathematically, scientifically and technologically literate.

Today, all adults need a solid foundation in mathematics to meet their goals.

PISA therefore starts with a concept of mathematical literacy that is concerned with the capacity of students to analyse, reason and communicate effectively as they pose, solve and interpret mathematical problems in a variety of situations involving quantitative, spatial, probabilistic or other mathematical concepts. *The PISA 2003 Assessment Framework: Mathematics, Reading, Science and Problem Solving Knowledge and Skills* (OECD, 2003e) through which OECD countries established the guiding principles for comparing mathematics performance across countries in PISA, defines mathematical literacy as "...an individual's capacity to identify and understand the role that mathematics plays in the world, to make well-founded judgements and to use and engage with mathematics in ways that meet the needs of that individual's life as a constructive, concerned and reflective citizen" (OECD, 2003e).

PISA defines a form of mathematical literacy...

When thinking about what mathematics might mean for individuals, one must consider both the extent to which they possess mathematical knowledge and understanding, and the extent to which they can activate their mathematical competencies to solve problems they encounter in life. PISA therefore presents students with problems mainly set in real-world situations. These are crafted in such a way that aspects of mathematics would be of genuine benefit in solving the problem. The objective of the PISA assessment is to obtain measures of the extent to which students presented with these problems can activate their mathematical knowledge and competencies to solve such problems successfully.

...that requires engagement with mathematics...

...going beyond the mastery of mathematical techniques conventionally taught at school.

This approach to mathematics contrasts with a traditional understanding of school mathematics which is often narrower. In schools, mathematical content is often taught and assessed in ways that are removed from authentic contexts – *e.g.*, students are taught the techniques of arithmetic, then given an arithmetic computation to complete; they are shown how to solve particular types of equations, then given further similar equations to solve; they are taught about geometric properties and relationships, then given a theorem to prove. Having learned the relevant concepts, skills and techniques, students are typically given contrived mathematical problems that call for the application of that knowledge. The mathematics required is usually obvious. Students have either mastered the techniques needed, or they have not. The usefulness of mathematics in the real world may be given little attention.

Assessment of such functional use of mathematics can influence how it is taught.

Outside school, real-life problems and situations for which mathematical knowledge may be useful often do not present themselves in such familiar forms. The individual must translate the situation or problem into a form that exposes the relevance and usefulness of mathematics. If students are unpractised at such a process, the potential power of mathematics to help deal with the situations and problems of their life may not be fully realised. The PISA approach to assessing mathematics was therefore designed to place the real-life use of mathematical knowledge and skills closer to the centre of a concept of mathematics learning. The intention is to encourage an approach to teaching and learning mathematics that gives strong emphasis to the processes associated with confronting problems in real-world contexts, making these problems amenable to mathematical treatment, using the relevant mathematical knowledge to solve problems, and evaluating the solution in the original problem context. If students can learn to do these things, they will be better equipped to make use of their mathematical knowledge and skills throughout life. They will be mathematically literate.

How mathematics is measured

PISA measures mathematics performance in three dimensions: mathematical content, the processes involved and the situations in which problems are posed.

Students' mathematics knowledge and skills were assessed according to three dimensions relating to: the mathematical content to which different problems and questions relate; the processes that need to be activated in order to connect observed phenomena with mathematics and then to solve the respective problems; and the situations and contexts that are used as sources of stimulus materials and in which problems are posed.

Content

Tasks are divided into four areas of mathematical content.

PISA draws its mathematical content from broad content areas (OECD, 2003e). Taking account of the research literature on this subject, and following an in-depth consensus building process among OECD countries on what would be an appropriate basis to compare mathematics performance internationally, the assessment was established around four content areas:

- *Space and shape* relates to spatial and geometric phenomena and relationships, often drawing on the curricular discipline of geometry. It requires looking for similarities and differences when analysing the components of shapes and recognising shapes in different representations and different dimensions, as well as understanding the properties of objects and their relative positions.

- *Change and relationships* involves mathematical manifestations of change as well as functional relationships and dependency among variables. This content area relates most closely to algebra. Mathematical relationships are often expressed as equations or inequalities, but relationships of a more general nature (*e.g.,* equivalence, divisibility and inclusion, to mention but a few) are relevant as well. Relationships are given a variety of different representations, including symbolic, algebraic, graphic, tabular and geometric representations. Since different representations may serve different purposes and have different properties, translation between representations is often of key importance in dealing with situations and tasks.
- *Quantity* involves numeric phenomena as well as quantitative relationships and patterns. It relates to the understanding of relative size, the recognition of numerical patterns, and the use of numbers to represent quantities and quantifiable attributes of real-world objects (counts and measures). Furthermore, quantity deals with the processing and understanding of numbers that are represented in various ways. An important aspect of dealing with quantity is quantitative reasoning, which involves number sense, representing numbers, understanding the meaning of operations, mental arithmetic and estimating. The most common curricular branch of mathematics with which quantitative reasoning is associated is arithmetic.
- *Uncertainty* involves probabilistic and statistical phenomena and relationships, that become increasingly relevant in the information society. These phenomena are the subject of mathematical study in statistics and probability.

Together, the four content areas cover the range of mathematics 15-year-olds need as a foundation for life and for further extending their horizon in mathematics. The concepts can be related to traditional content strands such as arithmetic, algebra or geometry and their detailed sub-topics that reflect historically well-established branches of mathematical thinking and that facilitate the development of a structured teaching syllabus.

These relate to strands of the school curriculum…

The PISA mathematics assessment sets out to compare levels of student performance in these four content areas, with each area forming the basis of a scale reported later in this chapter. By reporting separately on student performance in each of four areas of mathematics, PISA recognises that different school systems choose to give different emphases in constructing their national curricula. Reporting in this way allows different school systems to situate their national priorities in relation to the choices made by other countries. It also allows different school systems to assess to what extent the level and growth of mathematical knowledge occur uniformly across these conceptually distinguishable assessment areas.

…so performance reported separately on each content area can be related to countries' curricular choices.

The first panel of Table A6.1 shows the breakdown by mathematical content area of the 85 test items used in the PISA 2003 assessment (Annex A6).

Process

To solve real-world problems, students must first transform them into a mathematical form, then perform mathematical operations, retranslate the result into the original problem and communicate the solution.

The PISA mathematics assessment requires students to confront mathematical problems that are based in some real-world context, where the students are required to identify features of the problem situation that might be amenable to mathematical investigation, and to activate the relevant mathematical competencies to solve the problem. In order to do so they need to engage in a multi-step process of "mathematisation": beginning with a problem situated in reality, students must organise it according to mathematical concepts. They must identify the relevant mathematical concepts, and then progressively trim away the reality in order to transform the problem into one that is amenable to direct mathematical solution, by making simplifying assumptions, by generalising and formalising information, by imposing useful ways of representing aspects of the problem, by understanding the relationships between the language of the problem and symbolic and formal language needed to understand it mathematically, by finding regularities and patterns and linking it with known problems or other familiar mathematical formulations and by identifying or imposing a suitable mathematical model.

This requires a number of different skills, which can be grouped in three categories...

Once the problem has been turned into a familiar or directly amenable mathematical form, the student's armoury of specific mathematical knowledge, concepts and skills can then be applied to solve it. This might involve a simple calculation, or using symbolic, formal and technical language and operations, switching between representations, using logical mathematical arguments, and generalising. The final steps in the mathematisation process involve some form of translation of the mathematical result into a solution that works for the original problem context, a reality check of the completeness and applicability of the solution, a reflection on the outcomes and communication of the results, which may involve explanation and justification or proof.

Various competencies are required for such mathematisation to be employed. These include: *thinking and reasoning; argumentation; communication; modelling; problem posing and solving; representation; and using symbolic, formal and technical language and operations*. While it is generally true that these competencies operate together, and there is some overlap in their definitions, PISA mathematics tasks were often constructed to call particularly on one or more of these competencies. The cognitive activities that the above mentioned competencies encompass were organised in PISA within three *competency clusters* that are labelled: the *reproduction cluster*, the *connections cluster*, and the *reflection cluster*. These groupings have been found to provide a convenient basis for discussing the way in which different competencies are invoked in response to the different kinds and levels of cognitive demands imposed by different mathematical problems.

...those involving familiar mathematical processes and computations...

- The *reproduction cluster* is called into play in those items that are relatively familiar, and that essentially require the reproduction of practised knowledge, such as knowledge of facts and of common problem representations, recognition of equivalents, recollection of familiar mathematical objects and properties, performance of routine procedures, application of standard algorithms and technical skills, manipulation of expressions containing symbols and formulae in a familiar and standard form, and carrying out straight-forward computations.

- The *connections cluster* builds on reproduction to solve problems that are not simply routine, but that still involve somewhat familiar settings or extend and develop beyond the familiar to a relatively minor degree. Problems typically involve greater interpretation demands, and require making links between different representations of the situation, or linking different aspects of the problem situation in order to develop a solution.

...those involving a degree of interpretation and linkages...

- The *reflection cluster* builds further on the connections cluster. These competencies are required in tasks that demand some insight and reflection on the part of the student, as well as creativity in identifying relevant mathematical concepts or in linking relevant knowledge to create solutions. The problems addressed using the competencies in this cluster involve more elements than others, and additional demands typically arise for students to generalise and to explain or justify their results.

...and those involving deeper insights and reflection.

The second panel in Table A6.1 shows the breakdown by competency cluster of the 85 test items used in the PISA 2003 assessment (Annex A6). A more detailed description of these competency clusters and the ways in which the individual competencies operate in each of these clusters is described in *The PISA 2003 Assessment Framework: Mathematics, Reading, Science and Problem Solving Knowledge and Skills* (OECD, 2003e).

Situation

As in PISA 2000, students were shown various pieces of written material, and for each were asked a series of questions. The stimulus material represented a situation that students could conceivably confront, and for which activation of their mathematical knowledge, understanding or skill might be required or might be helpful in order to analyse or deal with the situation. There were of four sorts of situations: personal, educational or occupational, public and scientific.

PISA mathematics tasks are set in a range of contexts, relating to...

- *Personal situations* directly relate to students' personal day-to-day activities. These have at their core the way in which a mathematical problem immediately affects the individual and the way the individual perceives the context of the problem. Such situations tend to require a high degree of interpretation before the problem can be solved.

...day-to-day activities...

- *Educational or occupational* situations appear in a student's life at school, or in a work setting. These have at their core the way in which the school or work setting might require a student or employee to confront some particular problem that requires a mathematical solution.

...school and work situations...

- *Public situations relating to the local and broader community* require students to observe some aspect of their broader surroundings. These are generally situations located in the community that have at their core the way in which

...the wider community...

students understand relationships among elements of their surroundings. They require the students to activate their mathematical understanding, knowledge and skills to evaluate aspects of an external situation that might have some relevant consequences for public life.

...and scientific or explicitly mathematical problems.

- *Scientific situations* are more abstract and might involve understanding a technological process, theoretical situation or explicitly mathematical problem. The PISA mathematics framework includes in this category relatively abstract mathematical situations with which students are frequently confronted in a mathematics classroom, consisting entirely of explicit mathematical elements and where no attempt is made to place the problem in some broader context. These are sometimes referred to as "intra-mathematical" contexts.

These situations differ in terms of how directly the problem affects students' lives...

These four situation types vary in two important respects. The first is in terms of the distance between the student and the situation – the degree of immediacy and directness of the problem's impact on the student. Personal situations are closest to students, being characterised by the direct perceptions involved. Educational and occupational situations typically involve some implications for the individual through their daily activities. Situations relating to the local and broader community typically involve a slightly more removed observation of external events in the community. Finally, scientific situations tend to be the most abstract and therefore involve the greatest separation between the student and the situation. The PISA assessment assumes that students need to be able to handle a range of situations, both close to and distant from their immediate lives.

...and also in the extent to which the mathematical aspects are explicit.

There are also differences in the extent to which the mathematical nature of a situation is apparent. A few of the tasks refer only to mathematical objects, symbols or structures, and make no reference to matters outside the mathematical world. However, PISA also encompasses problems that students are likely to encounter in their lives in which the mathematical elements are not stated explicitly. The assessment thus tests the extent to which students can identify mathematical features of a problem when it is presented in a non-mathematical context and the extent to which they can activate their mathematical knowledge to explore and solve the problem and to make sense of the solution in the context or situation in which the problem arose.

The third panel of Table A6.1 shows the breakdown by situation type of the 85 test items used in the PISA 2003 assessment (Annex A6).

A more detailed description of the conceptual underpinning of the PISA 2003 assessment as well as the characteristics of the test itself can be found in *The PISA 2003 Assessment Framework: Mathematics, Reading, Science and Problem Solving Knowledge and Skills* (OECD, 2003e).

How the PISA tests were constructed

Experts developed tasks designed to cover the PISA framework...

Assessment items were constructed to cover the different dimensions of the PISA assessment framework described above. During the process of item development, experts from participating countries undertook a qualitative

analysis of each item, and developed descriptions of aspects of the cognitive demands of each item. This analysis included judgements about the aspects of the PISA mathematics framework that were relevant to the item. A short description was then developed that captured the most important demands placed on students by each particular item, particularly the individual competencies that were called into play (*PISA 2003 Technical Report*, OECD, forthcoming).

...some requiring open answers that were scored by expert markers in a process involving intra-country and inter-country reliability checks...

The items had a variety of formats. In many cases, students were required to construct a response in their own words to questions based on the text given. Sometimes they had to write down their calculations in order to demonstrate some of the methods and thought processes they used in producing an answer. Other questions required students to write an explanation of their results, which again exposed aspects of the methods and thought processes they had employed to answer the question. These open-constructed response items could not easily be machine-scored; rather they required the professional judgement of trained markers to assign the observed responses to defined response categories. To ensure that the marking process yielded reliable and cross-nationally comparable results, detailed guidelines and training contributed to a marking process that was accurate and consistent across countries. In order to examine the consistency of this marking process in more detail within each country and to assess the consistency in the work of the markers, a subsample of items in each country was rated independently by four markers. The PISA Consortium then assessed the reliability of these markings. Finally, to verify that the marking process was carried out in equivalent ways across countries, an inter-country reliability study was carried out on a subset of items. In this process, independent marking of the original booklets was undertaken by trained multilingual staff and compared to the ratings by the national markers in the various countries. The results show that very consistent marking was achieved across countries (Annex A7; *PISA 2003 Technical Report*, OECD, forthcoming).

...but computers could mark tasks with a more limited set of possible responses...

For other items requiring students to construct a response, evaluation of their answers was restricted to the response itself rather than an explanation of how it was derived. For many of these closed constructed-response items, the answer given was in numeric or other fixed form, and could be evaluated against precisely defined criteria. Such responses generally did not require expert markers, but could be analysed by computer.

...including those where students had to choose from stated options.

Items that required students to select one or more responses from a number of given possible answers were also used. This format category includes both standard multiple-choice items, for which students were required to select one correct response from a number of given response options; and complex multiple-choice items, for which students were required to select a response from given optional responses to each of a number of propositions or questions. Responses to these items could be marked automatically.

Table A6.1 shows the breakdown by item format type of the 85 test items used in the PISA 2003 assessment (Annex A6).

Students were given credit for each item that they answered with an acceptable response. In the development of the assessment, extensive field trials were carried out in all participating countries in the year prior to the assessment to identify and anticipate the widest possible range of student responses. These were then assigned to distinct categories by the item developers to determine marks. In some cases, where there is clearly a correct answer, responses can be easily identified as being correct or not. In other cases a range of different responses might be regarded as being correct. In yet other cases, a range of different responses can be identified and among those some are clearly better than others. In such cases it is often possible to define several response categories that are ordered in their degree of correctness – one kind of response is clearly best, a second category is not quite as good but is better than a third category, and so on. In these cases partial credit could be given.

How the PISA tests were designed, analysed and scaled

Each student was given a subset from a broad pool of mathematics tasks…

In total, 85 mathematics items were used in PISA 2003. These tasks, and also those in reading, science and problem solving, were arranged into half-hour clusters. Each student was given a test booklet with four clusters of items – resulting in two hours of individual assessment time. These clusters were rotated in combinations that ensured that each mathematics item appeared in the same number of test booklets, and that each cluster appeared in each of the four possible positions in the booklets.

…and their performance was established on a scale…

Such a design makes it possible to construct a scale of mathematical performance, to associate each assessment item with a point score on this scale according to its difficulty and to assign each student a point score on the same scale representing his or her estimated ability. This is possible using techniques of modern item response modelling (a description of the model can be found in the *PISA 2003 Technical Report*, OECD, forthcoming).

The relative ability of students taking a particular test can be estimated by considering the proportion of test items they answer correctly. The relative difficulty of items in a test can be estimated by considering the proportion of test takers getting each item correct. The mathematical model employed to analyse the PISA data was implemented through iterative procedures that simultaneously estimate the probability that a particular person will respond correctly to a given set of test items, and the probability that a particular item will be answered correctly by a given set of students. The result of these procedures is a set of estimates that allows the creation of a continuous scale representing mathematical literacy. On this continuum it is possible to estimate the location of individual students, thereby seeing what degree of mathematical literacy they demonstrate, and it is possible to estimate the location of individual test items, thereby seeing what degree of mathematical literacy each item embodies.[4]

Once the difficulty of individual items was given a rating on the scale, student performance could be described by giving each student a score according to

the hardest task that they could be predicted to perform. This does not mean that students will *always* be able to perform items at or below the difficulty level associated with their own position on the scale, and *never* be able to do harder items. Rather, the ratings are based on probability. As illustrated in Figure 2.1, students have a relatively high probability[5] of being able to complete items below their own rating (with the probability rising for items further down the scale), but are relatively unlikely to be able to complete those items further up.

...with a score of 500 representing average OECD performance.

To facilitate the interpretation of the scores assigned to students, the scale was constructed to have an average score among OECD countries of 500 points, with about two-thirds of students across OECD countries scoring between 400 and 600 points.[6]

Students were grouped in six levels of proficiency, plus a group below Level 1...

In a manner similar to the reporting of the PISA 2000 reading assessment, which presented results in proficiency levels, student scores in mathematics in 2003 were grouped into six proficiency levels. The six proficiency levels represented groups of tasks of ascending difficulty, with Level 6 as the highest and Level 1 as the lowest. The grouping into proficiency levels was undertaken on the

Figure 2.1 ■ **The relationship between items and students on a proficiency scale**

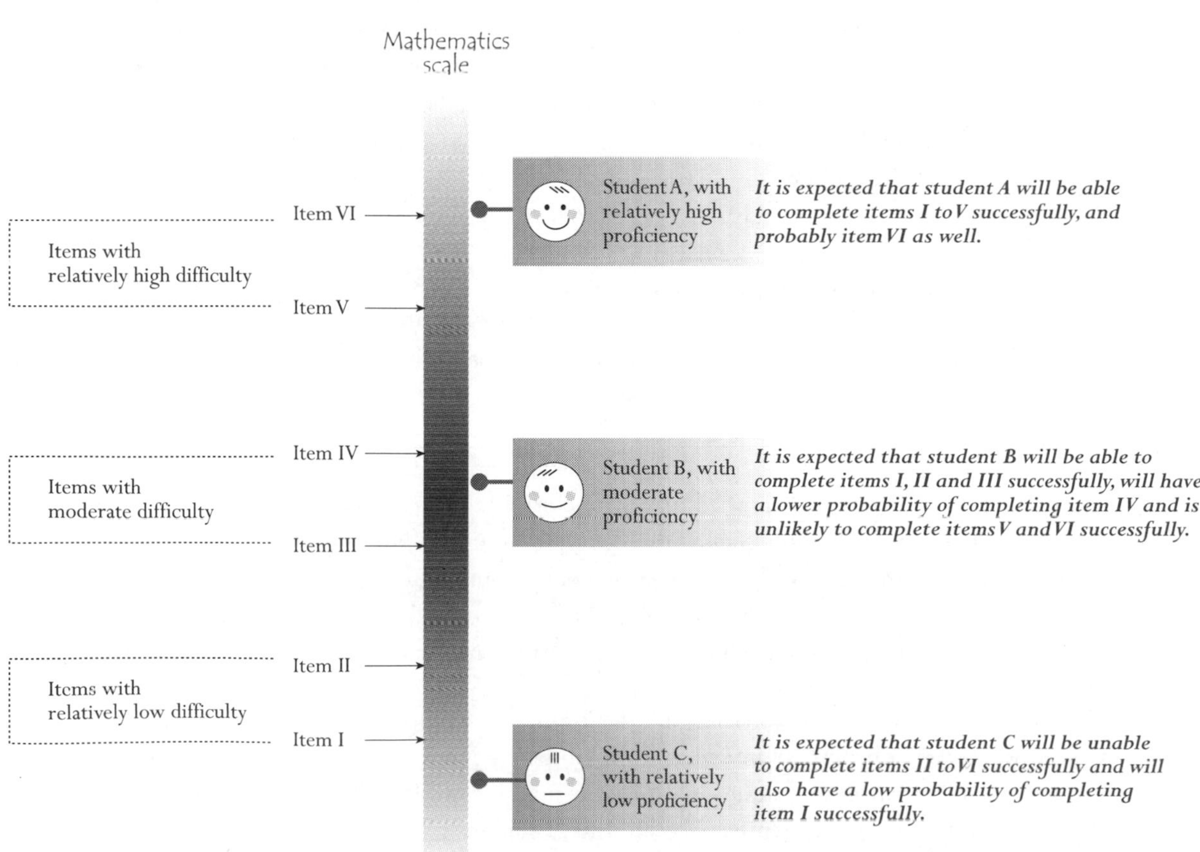

basis of substantive considerations relating to the nature of the underlying competencies. Students with below 358 score points on any of the mathematics scales were classified as below Level 1. Such students, representing 11 per cent of students on average across OECD countries, were not necessarily incapable of performing any mathematical operation. However, they were unable to utilise mathematical skills in the situations required by the easiest PISA tasks.

...with each proficiency level relating to a specific set of mathematical competencies.

Proficiency at each of these levels can be understood in relation to descriptions of the kind of mathematical competency that a student needs to attain them. These are summarised in Figure 2.2. In fact, these descriptions represent a synthesis of the proficiency descriptions for each of the content areas of mathematics, which are given later in this chapter when discussing results in each content area. The progression through these levels, in terms of the ways in which the individual mathematical processes change as levels increase is shown in Annex A2.

The creation of the six proficiency levels leads to a situation where students with a range of scores on a continuous scale are grouped together into each single band. PISA applies an easy-to-understand criterion to assigning students to levels: each student is assigned to the highest level for which they would be expected to answer correctly the majority of assessment items. Thus, for example, in a test composed of items spread uniformly across Level 3 (with difficulty ratings of 483 to 544 score points), all students assigned to that level would expect to get at least 50 per cent of the items correct. Someone at the bottom of the level (scoring 483 points) would be expected to get close to 50 per cent of the items correct; someone in the middle or near the top of the level would get a higher percentage of items correct. For this to be true, a student scoring 483 needs to have a 50 per cent chance of completing an item in the middle of Level 3 (rated 513 score points) and thus have a greater than 50 per cent chance of getting right an item rated at their score, 483 points. This latter probability needs to be 62 per cent to fulfil these conditions.

How results are reported

PISA 2003 mathematics results are reported on four scales relating to the content areas described above. Performance is also reported on an overall mathematics scale.

The mathematics tasks can be mapped according to difficulty...

Figure 2.3 shows a map with a sample of items from the PISA 2003 assessment, with the items shown in detail in Figures 2.4a-c, Figures 2.7a-b, Figures 2.10a-b and Figures 2.13a-c. For each of the four content areas, the selected items and item scores (*i.e.,* full or partial credit) have been ordered according to their difficulty, with the most difficult of these scores at the top, and the least difficult at the bottom.

...with the easiest tasks tending to require mainly reproduction skills and the hardest ones reflection.

The characteristics of the items shown in the map provide the basis for a substantive interpretation of performance at different levels on the scale. Patterns emerge that make it possible to describe aspects of mathematics that are consistently associated with various locations along the literacy continuum shown by the map. For example, among the small sample of items in Figure 2.3,

Figure 2.2 ■ **Summary descriptions for the six levels of proficiency in mathematics**

Level	WHAT STUDENTS CAN TYPICALLY DO
6	At Level 6, students can conceptualise, generalise, and utilise information based on their investigations and modelling of complex problem situations. They can link different information sources and representations and flexibly translate among them. Students at this level are capable of advanced mathematical thinking and reasoning. These students can apply this insight and understanding, along with a mastery of symbolic and formal mathematical operations and relationships, to develop new approaches and strategies for attacking novel situations. Students at this level can formulate and precisely communicate their actions and reflections regarding their findings, interpretations, arguments, and the appropriateness of these to the original situations.
5	At Level 5, students can develop and work with models for complex situations, identifying constraints and specifying assumptions. They can select, compare, and evaluate appropriate problem-solving strategies for dealing with complex problems related to these models. Students at this level can work strategically using broad, well-developed thinking and reasoning skills, appropriately linked representations, symbolic and formal characterisations, and insight pertaining to these situations. They can reflect on their actions and can formulate and communicate their interpretations and reasoning.
4	At Level 4, students can work effectively with explicit models for complex concrete situations that may involve constraints or call for making assumptions. They can select and integrate different representations, including symbolic ones, linking them directly to aspects of real-world situations. Students at this level can utilise well-developed skills and reason flexibly, with some insight, in these contexts. They can construct and communicate explanations and arguments based on their interpretations, arguments and actions.
3	At Level 3, students can execute clearly described procedures, including those that require sequential decisions. They can select and apply simple problem-solving strategies. Students at this level can interpret and use representations based on different information sources and reason directly from them. They can develop short communications reporting their interpretations, results and reasoning.
2	At Level 2, students can interpret and recognise situations in contexts that require no more than direct inference. They can extract relevant information from a single source and make use of a single representational mode. Students at this level can employ basic algorithms, formulae, procedures or conventions. They are capable of direct reasoning and making literal interpretations of the results.
1	At Level 1, students can answer questions involving familiar contexts where all relevant information is present and the questions are clearly defined. They are able to identify information and to carry out routine procedures according to direct instructions in explicit situations. They can perform actions that are obvious and follow immediately from the given stimuli.

Figure 2.3 ■ **A map of selected mathematics items**

Level	Space and shape	Change and relationships	Quantity	Uncertainty
	Figures 2.4a-c	Figures 2.7a-b	Figures 2.10a-b	Figures 2.13a-c
6	**CARPENTER** *Question 1 (687)*	**WALKING** *Question 5 – Score 3 (723)*		**ROBBERIES** *Question 15 – Score 2 (694)*
668.7				
5		**WALKING** *Question 5 – Score 2 (666)* **WALKING** *Question 4 (611)*		**TEST SCORES** *Question 6 (620)*
606.6				
4		**WALKING** *Question 5 – Score 1 (605)* **GROWING UP** *Question 8 (574)*	**EXCHANGE RATE** *Question 11 (586)* **SKATEBOARD** *Question 13 (570)* **SKATEBOARD** *Question 14 (554)*	**ROBBERIES** *Question 15 – Score 1 (577)* **EXPORTS** *Question 18 (565)*
544.4				
3	**NUMBER CUBES** *Question 3 (503)*	**GROWING UP** *Question 7 – Score 2 (525)*	**SKATEBOARD** *Question 12 – Score 2 (496)*	
	OECD average = 500			
482.4				
2	**STAIRCASE** *Question 2 (421)*		**SKATEBOARD** *Question 12 – Score 1 (464)* **EXCHANGE RATE** *Question 10 (439)*	**EXPORTS** *Question 17 (427)*
420.4				
1		**GROWING UP** *Question 7 – Score 1 (420)*	**EXCHANGE RATE** *Question 9 (406)*	
358.3				
Below Level 1				

the easiest items are all from the *reproduction* competency cluster. This reflects the pattern observed with the full set of items. It is also seen from the full set of PISA items that those items characterised as belonging to the *reflection* cluster tend to be the most difficult. Items in the *connections* cluster tend to be of intermediate difficulty, though they span a large part of the proficiency spectrum that is analysed through the PISA assessment. The individual competencies defined in the mathematics framework operate quite differently at different levels of performance, as predicted by the assessment framework.

The easiest tasks require straightforward mathematical operations in familiar contexts…

Near the bottom of the scale, items set in simple and relatively familiar contexts require only the most limited interpretation of the situation, as well as direct application of well-known mathematical knowledge in familiar situations. Typical activities are reading a value directly from a graph or table, performing a very simple and straightforward arithmetic calculation, ordering a small set of numbers correctly, counting familiar objects, using a simple currency exchange rate, identifying and listing simple combinatorial outcomes. For example, Question 9 from the unit *Exchange Rate* (Figure 2.10a) presents students with a simple rate for exchanging Singapore dollars (SGD) into South African rand (ZAR), namely 1 SGD = 4.2 ZAR. The question requires students to apply the rate to convert 3000 SGD into ZAR. The rate is presented in the form of a familiar equation, and the mathematical step required is direct and reasonably obvious. In examples 9.1 and 9.2 from the unit *Building Blocks* (OECD, 2003e), students were presented with diagrams of familiar three-dimensional shapes composed of small cubes, and asked to count (or calculate) the number of the small cubes used to make up the larger shapes.

…and tasks of medium difficulty require more transformation into mathematical form…

Around the middle of the scale, items require substantially more interpretation, frequently of situations that are relatively unfamiliar or unpractised. They often demand the use of different representations of the situation, including more formal mathematical representations, and the thoughtful linking of those different representations in order to promote understanding and facilitate analysis. They often involve a chain of reasoning or a sequence of calculation steps, and can require students to express reasoning through a simple explanation. Typical activities include interpreting a set of related graphs; interpreting text, relating this to information in a table or graph, extracting the relevant information and performing some calculations; using scale conversions to calculate distances on a map; and using spatial reasoning and geometric knowledge to perform distance, speed and time calculations. For example, the unit *Growing Up* (Figure 2.7b) presents students with a graph of the average height of young males and young females from the ages of ten to 20 years. Question 7 from *Growing Up* asks students to identify the period in their life when females are on average taller than males of the same age. Students have to interpret the graph to understand exactly what is being displayed. They also have to relate the graphs for males and females to each other and determine how the specified period is shown then accurately read the relevant values from the horizontal scale. Question 8 from the unit *Growing Up* invites students to give a written explanation as to how the

graph shows a slowdown in the growth rate for girls after a particular age. To answer this question successfully, students must understand how the growth rate is displayed in such a graph, identify what is changing at the specified point in the graph in comparison to an earlier period and clearly articulate their explanation in words.

...while difficult tasks are more complex and require greater interpretation of unfamiliar problems.

Towards the top of the scale, items are displayed that typically involve a number of different elements, and require even higher levels of interpretation. Situations are typically unfamiliar, hence requiring some degree of thoughtful reflection and creativity. Questions usually demand some form of argument, often in the form of an explanation. Typical activities involved include: interpreting complex and unfamiliar data; imposing a mathematical construction on a complex real-world situation; and using mathematical modelling processes. At this part of the scale, items tend to have several elements that need to be linked by students, and their successful negotiation typically requires a strategic approach to several interrelated steps. For example, Question 15 from the unit *Robberies* (Figure 2.13a) presents students with a truncated bar graph showing the number of robberies per year in two specified years. A television reporter's statement interpreting the graph is given. Students are asked to consider whether or not the reporter's statement is a reasonable interpretation of the graph, and to give an explanation as to why. The graph itself is somewhat unusual, and requires some interpretation. The reporter's statement must be interpreted in relation to the graph. Then, some mathematical understanding and reasoning must be applied to determine a suitable meaning of the phrase "reasonable interpretation" in this context. Finally, the conclusion must be articulated clearly in a written explanation. Fifteen-year-old students typically find such a sequence of thought and action quite challenging.

Another example presented in the PISA assessment framework, example 3.2 in the unit *Heartbeat* (OECD, 2003e), presents students with mathematical formulations of the relationship between a person's recommended maximum heart rate and their age, in the context of physical exercise. The question invites students to modify the formulation appropriately under a specified condition. They have to interpret the situation, the mathematical formulations, the changed condition, and construct a modified formulation that satisfies the specified condition. This complex set of linked tasks also proved to be very demanding for 15-year-olds.

Thus, difficulty rises with the amount of interpretation, representation, complex processing and argumentation required of students.

Based on the patterns observed when the full item set is investigated in this way, it is possible to characterise growth along the PISA mathematics scale by referring to the ways in which mathematical competencies are associated with items located at different points along the scale.

The ascending difficulty of mathematics items is associated with:

- The kind and degree of interpretation and reflection needed, including the nature of demands arising from the problem context; the extent to which the mathematical demands of the problem are apparent or to which students must

impose their own mathematical construction on the problem; and the extent to which insight, complex reasoning and generalisation are required.

- The kind of representation skills that are necessary, ranging from problems where only one mode of representation is used to problems where students have to switch between different modes of representation or to find appropriate modes of representation themselves.
- The kind and level of mathematical complexity required, ranging from single-step problems requiring students to reproduce basic mathematical facts and perform simple computation processes through to multi-step problems involving more advanced mathematical knowledge, complex decision-making, information processing, problem-solving and modelling skills.
- The kind and degree of mathematical argumentation that is required, ranging from problems where no argumentation is necessary at all, through to problems where students may apply well-known arguments, to problems where students have to create mathematical arguments or to understand other people's argumentation or judge the correctness of given arguments or proofs.

WHAT STUDENTS CAN DO IN FOUR AREAS OF MATHEMATICS

By looking at how students performed on the four scales, alongside examples of the tasks associated with those content areas of mathematics, it is possible to provide a profile of what PISA shows about students' mathematical abilities. For two of these areas – *change and relationships* and *space and shape*, it is also possible to compare mathematical performance in 2003 with that measured in PISA 2000.

Student performance can be summarised on four scales, relating to space and shape, change and relationships, quantity, and uncertainty phenomena.

Student performance on the mathematics/space and shape scale

A quarter of the mathematical tasks given to students in PISA are related to spatial and geometric phenomena and relationships. Figures 2.4a-c show three sample tasks from this category: one at Level 2, one at Level 3 and one at Level 6.

The knowledge and skills required to reach each level are summarised in Figure 2.5. In PISA 2003, only a small proportion of 15-year-olds – 5 per cent overall in the combined OECD area[7] – can perform the highly complex tasks required to reach Level 6. However, more than 15 per cent of the students in Korea and the PISA partner country Hong Kong-China, and more than 10 per cent of the students in Belgium, the Czech Republic, Japan and Switzerland as well as the partner country Liechtenstein (Figure 2.6a) perform at Level 6. In contrast, in Greece, Mexico and Portugal, as well as in the partner countries Brazil, Indonesia, Serbia,[8] Thailand, Tunisia and Uruguay, less than 1 per cent reach Level 6 (Table 2.1a).

In most countries under 10 per cent of students can perform the hardest space and shape tasks...

A quarter or more of students fail to reach Level 2 in Greece, Hungary, Ireland, Italy, Luxembourg, Mexico, Norway, Poland, Portugal, Spain, Turkey and the United States as well as in the partner countries Brazil, Indonesia, Latvia, the Russian Federation, Serbia, Thailand, Tunisia and Uruguay.

...but in 12 OECD countries at least 25 per cent can only perform very simple tasks.

Figure 2.4a ■ **A sample of mathematics items used in PISA for the space and shape scale: Unit CARPENTER**

CARPENTER

A carpenter has 32 metres of timber and wants to make a border around a garden bed. He is considering the following designs for the garden bed.

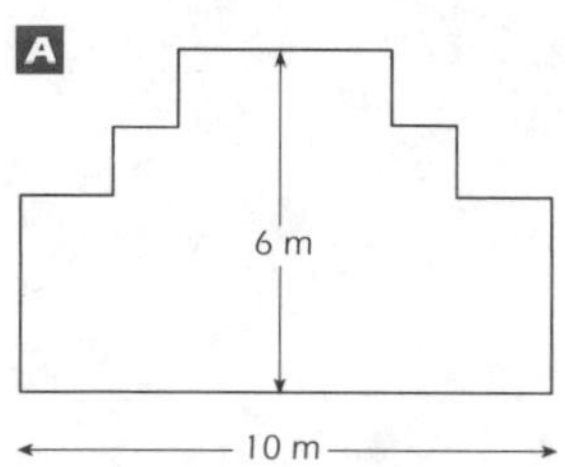

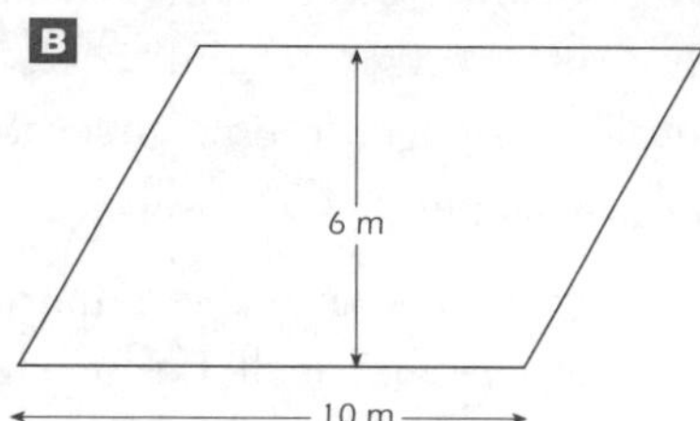

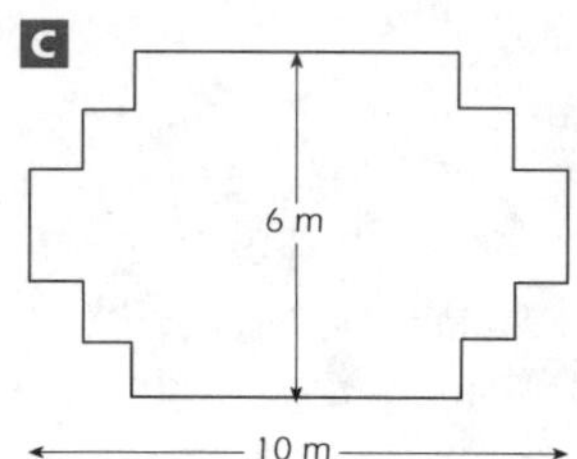

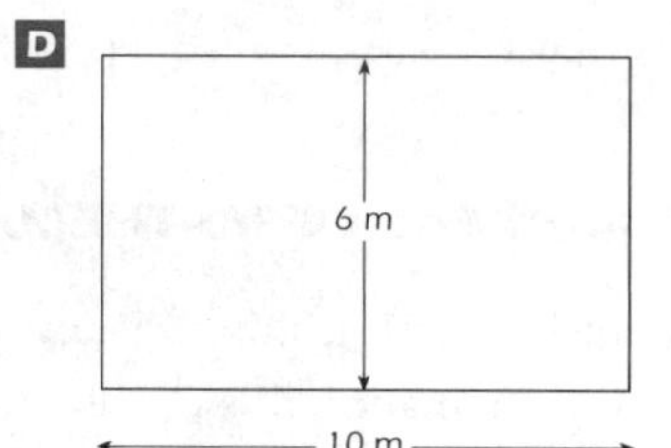

QUESTION 1

Circle either "Yes" or "No" for each design to indicate whether the garden bed can be made with 32 metres of timber.

Garden bed design	Using this design, can the garden bed be made with 32 metres of timber?
Design A	*Yes / No*
Design B	*Yes / No*
Design C	*Yes / No*
Design D	*Yes / No*

Score 1 (687)
Answers which indicate Yes, No, Yes, Yes, in that order.

This complex multiple-choice item is situated in an educational context, since it is the kind of quasi-realistic problem that would typically be seen in a mathematics class, rather than being a genuine problem likely to be met in an occupational setting. While not regarded as typical, a small number of such problems have been included in the PISA assessment. However, the competencies needed for this problem are certainly relevant and part of mathematical literacy. This item illustrates Level 6 with a difficulty of 687 score points. The item belongs to the space and shape content area, and it fits the connections competency cluster – as the problem is non-routine. The students need the competence to recognise that for the purpose of solving the question the two-dimensional shapes A, C and D have the same perimeter, therefore they need to decode the visual information and see similarities and differences. The students need to see whether or not a certain border-shape can be made with 32 metres of timber. In three cases this is rather evident because of the rectangular shapes. But the fourth is a parallelogram, requiring more than 32 metres. This use of geometrical insight and argumentation skills and some technical geometrical knowledge makes this item illustrate the Level 6.

Level
6
668.7
5
606.6
4
544.4
3
482.4
2
420.4
1
358.3
Below 1

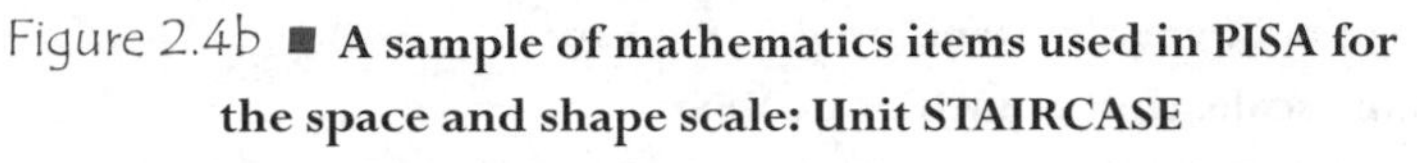
Figure 2.4b ■ **A sample of mathematics items used in PISA for the space and shape scale: Unit STAIRCASE**

STAIRCASE

The diagram below illustrates a staircase with 14 steps and a total height of 252 cm:

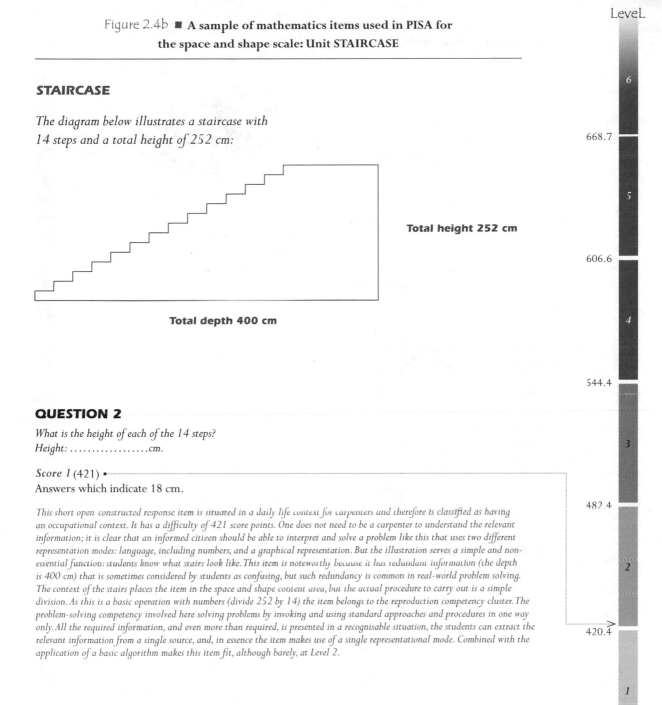

Total height 252 cm

Total depth 400 cm

QUESTION 2

What is the height of each of the 14 steps?
Height: ....cm.

Score 1 (421)
Answers which indicate 18 cm.

This short open constructed response item is situated in a daily life context for carpenters and therefore is classified as having an occupational context. It has a difficulty of 421 score points. One does not need to be a carpenter to understand the relevant information; it is clear that an informed citizen should be able to interpret and solve a problem like this that uses two different representation modes: language, including numbers, and a graphical representation. But the illustration serves a simple and non-essential function: students know what stairs look like. This item is noteworthy because it has redundant information (the depth is 400 cm) that is sometimes considered by students as confusing, but such redundancy is common in real-world problem solving. The context of the stairs places the item in the space and shape content area, but the actual procedure to carry out is a simple division. As this is a basic operation with numbers (divide 252 by 14) the item belongs to the reproduction competency cluster. The problem-solving competency involved here solving problems by invoking and using standard approaches and procedures in one way only. All the required information, and even more than required, is presented in a recognisable situation, the students can extract the relevant information from a single source, and, in essence the item makes use of a single representational mode. Combined with the application of a basic algorithm makes this item fit, although barely, at Level 2.

Level
6
668.7
5
606.6
4
544.4
3
482.4
2
420.4
1
358.3
Below 1

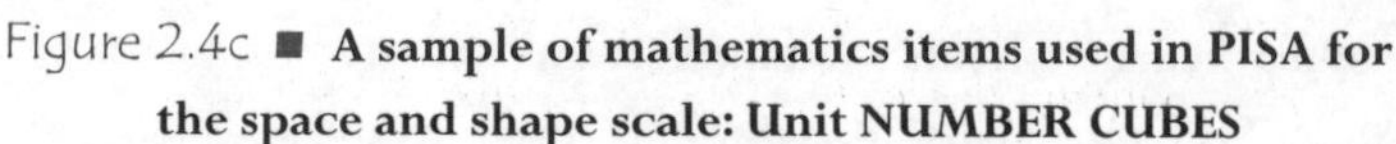

Figure 2.4c ■ **A sample of mathematics items used in PISA for the space and shape scale: Unit NUMBER CUBES**

NUMBER CUBES

On the right, there is a picture of two dice.
Dice are special number cubes for which the following rule applies:
"The total number of dots on two opposite faces is always seven."

QUESTION 3

You can make a simple number cube by cutting, folding and gluing cardboard. This can be done in many ways. In the figure below you can see four cuttings that can be used to make cubes, with dots on the sides.

Which of the following shapes can be folded together to form a cube that obeys the rule that the sum of opposite faces is 7? For each shape, circle either "Yes" or "No" in the table below.

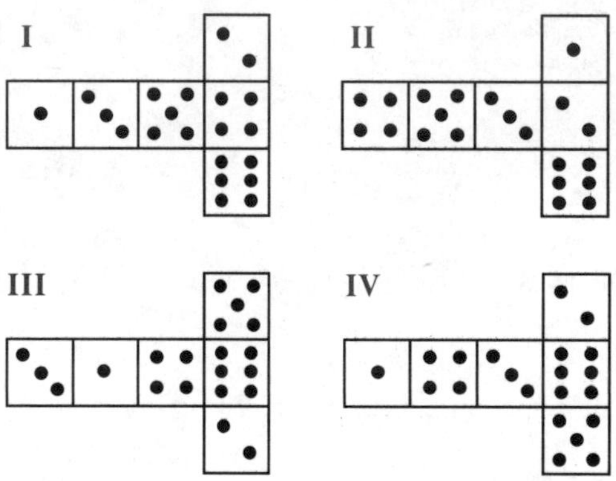

Shape	Obeys the rule that the sum of opposite faces is 7?
I	Yes / No
II	Yes / No
III	Yes / No
IV	Yes / No

Score 1 (503)
Answers which indicate No, Yes, Yes, No, in that order.

This complex multiple-choice item is situated in a personal context. It has a difficulty of 503 score points. Many games that children encounter during their education, whether formal or informal, use number cubes. The problem does not assume any previous knowledge about this cube, but an understanding of the rule of its construction: two opposite sides have a total of seven dots. This construction rule emphasises a numerical aspect, but the problem posed requires some kind of spatial insight or mental visualisation technique. These competencies are an essential part of mathematical literacy as students live in three-dimensional space, and often are confronted with two-dimensional representations. Students need to mentally imagine how the four plans of number cubes, if reconstructed into a 3-D number cube, obey the numerical construction rule. Therefore the item belongs to the space and shape content area. The problem is not routine: it requires the encoding and spatial interpretation of two-dimensional objects, interpretation of the connected three-dimensional object, interpreting back-and-forth between model and reality, and checking certain basic quantitative relations. This leads to a classification in the connections competency cluster. The item requires spatial reasoning skills within a personal context with all the relevant information clearly presented in writing and with graphics. The item illustrates Level 3.

Level
6
668.7
5
606.6
4
544.4
3
482.4
2
420.4
1
358.3
Below 1

Figure 2.5 ■ **Summary descriptions of six levels of proficiency on the mathematics/space and shape scale**

Level	General competencies students should have at each level	Specific tasks students should be able to do
6	*5% of all students across the OECD area can perform tasks at Level 6 on the space and shape scale*	
	Solve complex problems involving multiple representations and often involving sequential calculation processes; identify and extract relevant information and link different but related information; use reasoning, significant insight and reflection; and generalise results and findings, communicate solutions and provide explanations and argumentation	– Interpret complex textual descriptions and relate these to other (often multiple) representations – Use reasoning involving proportions in non-familiar and complex situations – Show significant insight to conceptualise complex geometric situations or to interpret complex and unfamiliar representations – Identify and combine multiple pieces of information to solve problems – Devise a strategy to connect a geometrical context with known mathematical procedures and routines – Carry out a complex sequence of calculations, for example volume calculations or other routine procedures in an applied context, accurately and completely – Provide written explanations and arguments based on reflection, insight and generalisation of understanding
5	*15% of all students across the OECD area can perform tasks at least at Level 5 on the space and shape scale*	
	Solve problems that require appropriate assumptions to be made, or that involve working with assumptions provided; use well-developed spatial reasoning, argument and insight to identify relevant information and to interpret and link different representations; work strategically and carry out multiple and sequential processes	– Use spatial/geometrical reasoning, argument, reflection and insight into two- and three-dimensional objects, both familiar and unfamiliar – Make assumptions or work with assumptions to simplify and solve a geometrical problem in a real-world setting, *e.g.,* involving estimation of quantities in a real-world situation, and communicate explanations – Interpret multiple representations of geometric phenomena – Use geometric constructions – Conceptualise and devise multi-step strategies to solve geometrical problems – Use well-known geometrical algorithms but in unfamiliar situations, such as Pythagoras' theorem, and calculations involving perimeter, area and volume
4	*30% of all students across the OECD area can perform tasks at least at Level 4 on the space and shape scale*	
	Solve problems that involve visual and spatial reasoning and argumentation in unfamiliar contexts; link and integrate different representations; carry out sequential processes; apply well-developed skills in spatial visualisation and interpretation	– Interpret complex text to solve geometric problems – Interpret sequential instructions and follow a sequence of steps – Interpretation using spatial insight into non–standard geometric situations – Use a two–dimensional model to work with 3-D representations of unfamiliar geometric situation – Link and integrate two different visual representations of geometric situations Develop and implement a strategy involving calculation in geometric situations – Reason and argue about numeric relationships in a geometric context – Perform simple calculations (*e.g.,* multiply multi-digit decimal number by an integer, apply numeric conversions using proportion and scale, calculate areas of familiar shapes)

Level	General competencies students should have at each level	Specific tasks students should be able to do
3	***51% of all students across the OECD area can perform tasks at least at Level 3 on the space and shape scale***	
	Solve problems that involve elementary visual and spatial reasoning in familiar contexts; link different representations of familiar objects; use elementary problem solving skills (devising simple strategies); apply simple algorithms	– Interpret textual descriptions of unfamiliar geometric situations – Use basic problem–solving skills, such as devising a simple strategy – Use visual perception and elementary spatial reasoning skills in a familiar situation – Work with a given familiar mathematical model – Perform simple calculations such as scale conversions (using multiplication, basic proportional reasoning) – Apply routine algorithms to solve geometric problems (*e.g.,* calculate lengths within familiar shapes)
2	***71% of all students across the OECD area can perform tasks at least at Level 2 on the space and shape scale***	
	Solve problems involving a single mathematical representation where the mathematical content is direct and clearly presented; use basic mathematical thinking and conventions in familiar contexts	– Recognise simple geometric patterns – Use basic technical terms and definitions and apply basic geometric concepts (*e.g.,* symmetry) – Apply a mathematical interpretation of a common-language relational term (*e.g.,* "bigger") in a geometric context – Create and use a mental image of an object, both two- and three-dimensional – Understand a visual two-dimensional representation of a familiar real-world situation – Apply simple calculations (*e.g.,* subtraction, division by two-digit number) to solve problems in a geometric setting
1	***87% of all students across the OECD area can perform tasks at least at Level 1 on the space and shape scale***	
	Solve simple problems in a familiar context using familiar pictures or drawings of geometric objects and applying counting or basic calculation skills	– Use a given two-dimensional representation to count or calculate elements of a simple three-dimensional object

This level has been chosen to align country performance in Figure 2.6a as it represents a baseline level of mathematics proficiency on the PISA scale at which students begin to demonstrate the kind of literacy skills that enable them to actively use mathematics as stipulated by the PISA definition: at Level 2, students demonstrate the use of direct inference to recognise the mathematical elements of a situation, are able to use a single representation to help explore and understand a situation, can use basic algorithms, formulae and procedures, and make literal interpretations and apply direct reasoning. In Finland, more than 90 per cent of students perform at or above this threshold.

The great majority of students, 87 per cent, can at least complete the easiest space and shape tasks required to reach Level 1 (Table 2.1a). However, this also varies greatly across countries.

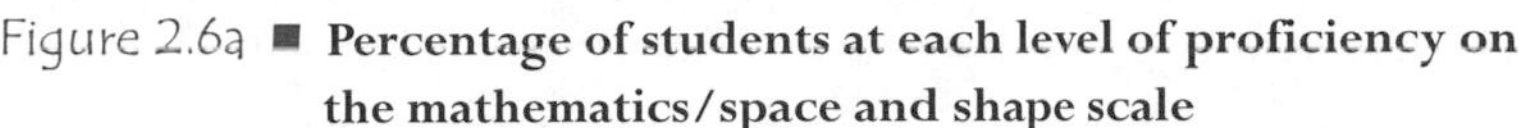

Figure 2.6a ■ **Percentage of students at each level of proficiency on the mathematics/space and shape scale**

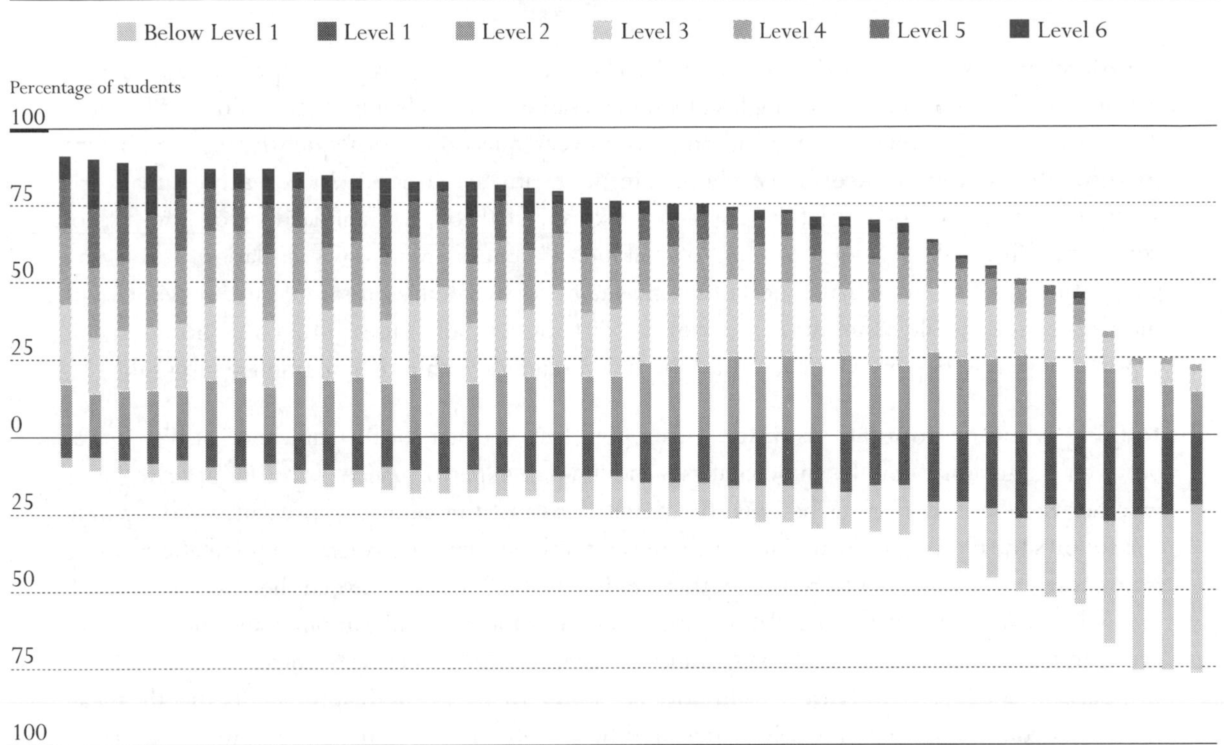

Countries are ranked in descending order of percentage of 15-year-olds in Levels 2, 3, 4, 5 and 6.
Source: OECD PISA 2003 database, Table 2.1a.

One way to summarise student performance and to compare the relative standing of countries on the mathematics/space and shape scale is by way of their mean scores. This is shown in Figure 2.6b. As discussed in Box 2.1, when interpreting mean performance, only those differences between countries that are statistically significant should be taken into account. The figure shows those pairs of countries where the difference in their mean scores is sufficient to say with confidence that the higher performance by sampled students in one country holds for the entire population of enrolled 15-year-olds. A country's performance relative to that of the countries listed along the top of the figure can be seen by reading across each row. The colours indicate whether the average performance of the country in the row is either lower than that of the comparison country, not statistically significant different, or higher. When making multiple comparisons, *e.g.*, when comparing the performance of one country with that of all other countries,

An overall mean score of country performance can be compared, but in some cases country differences are not statistically significant…

Box 2.1 ■ **Interpreting sample statistics**

Standard errors and confidence intervals. The statistics in this report represent *estimates* of national performance based on samples of students rather than the values that could be calculated if every student in every country had answered every question. Consequently, it is important to know the degree of uncertainty inherent in the estimates. In PISA 2003, each estimate has an associated degree of uncertainty, which is expressed through a standard error. The use of confidence intervals provides a means of making inferences about the population means and proportions in a manner that reflects the uncertainty associated with sample estimates. Under the usually reasonable assumption of a normal distribution, and unless otherwise noted in this report, there is a 95 per cent chance that the true value lies within the confidence interval.

Judging whether populations differ. This report tests the statistical significance of differences between the national samples in percentages and in average performance scores in order to judge whether there are differences between the populations that the samples represent. Each separate test follows the convention that, if in fact there is no real difference between two populations, there is no more than a 5 per cent probability that an observed difference between the two samples will erroneously suggest that the populations are different as the result of sampling and measurement error. In the figures and tables showing multiple comparisons of countries' mean scores, multiple comparison significance tests are also employed that limit to 5 per cent the probability that the mean of a given country will erroneously be declared to be different from that of any other country, in cases where there is in fact no difference (Annex A4).

a more cautious approach is required: only those comparisons indicated by the upward and downward pointing symbols should be considered statistically significant for the purpose of multiple comparisons.[9] Figure 2.6b also shows which countries perform above, at or below the OECD average. Results from the United Kingdom were excluded from this and similar comparisons, because the data for England did not comply with the response rate standards which OECD countries had established to ensure that PISA yields reliable and internationally comparable data (Annex A3).

...so one can only say within a range where each country ranks, with Hong Kong-China, Japan and Korea performing strongest.

For the reasons explained in Box 2.1 it is not possible to determine the exact rank order position of countries in the international comparisons. However, Figure 2.6b shows the range of rank order positions within which the country mean lies with 95 per cent probability. Results are shown both for the OECD countries and all countries that participated in PISA 2003, including both OECD and partner countries. For example, while the mean score for the partner country Hong Kong-China is the highest on the mathematics/space and shape scale followed by the scores from Japan and Korea, it is important to note that they are not statistically different from each other. Because of sampling errors, it is not possible to say which country's rank lies first, but it is possible to say with 95 per cent confidence that Japan, Korea and Hong Kong-China lie between first and third positions of all countries.

Figure 2.6b ■ Multiple comparisons of mean performance on the mathematics/space and shape scale

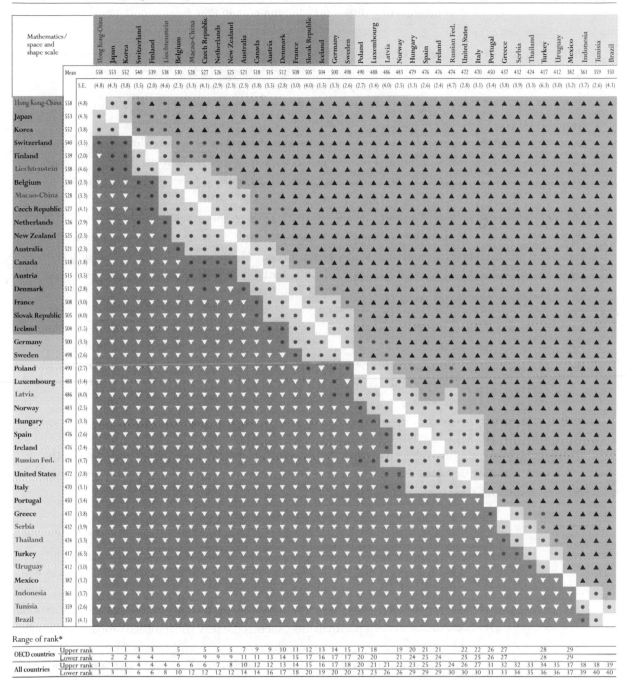

Mathematics/ space and shape scale	Mean	S.E.	Hong Kong-China	Japan	Korea	Switzerland	Finland	Liechtenstein	Belgium	Macao-China	Czech Republic	Netherlands	New Zealand	Australia	Canada	Austria	Denmark	France	Slovak Republic	Iceland	Germany	Sweden	Poland	Luxembourg	Latvia	Norway	Hungary	Spain	Ireland	Russian Fed.	United States	Italy	Portugal	Greece	Serbia	Thailand	Turkey	Uruguay	Mexico	Indonesia	Tunisia	Brazil
	Mean		558	553	552	540	539	538	530	528	527	526	525	521	518	515	512	508	505	504	500	498	490	488	486	483	479	476	476	474	472	470	450	437	432	424	417	412	382	361	359	350
		S.E.	(4.8)	(4.3)	(3.8)	(3.5)	(2.0)	(4.6)	(2.3)	(3.3)	(4.1)	(2.9)	(2.3)	(2.3)	(1.8)	(3.5)	(2.8)	(3.0)	(4.0)	(1.5)	(3.3)	(2.6)	(2.7)	(1.4)	(4.0)	(2.5)	(3.3)	(2.6)	(2.4)	(4.7)	(2.8)	(3.1)	(3.4)	(3.8)	(3.9)	(3.3)	(6.3)	(3.0)	(3.2)	(3.7)	(2.6)	(4.1)
Hong Kong-China	558	(4.8)		●	●	●	▲	●	▲	▲	▲	▲	▲	▲	▲	▲	▲	▲	▲	▲	▲	▲	▲	▲	▲	▲	▲	▲	▲	▲	▲	▲	▲	▲	▲	▲	▲	▲	▲	▲	▲	▲
Japan	553	(4.3)	●		●	●	●	●	▲	▲	▲	▲	▲	▲	▲	▲	▲	▲	▲	▲	▲	▲	▲	▲	▲	▲	▲	▲	▲	▲	▲	▲	▲	▲	▲	▲	▲	▲	▲	▲	▲	▲
Korea	552	(3.8)	●	●		●	●	●	▲	▲	▲	▲	▲	▲	▲	▲	▲	▲	▲	▲	▲	▲	▲	▲	▲	▲	▲	▲	▲	▲	▲	▲	▲	▲	▲	▲	▲	▲	▲	▲	▲	▲
Switzerland	540	(3.5)	●	●	●		●	●	●	●	●	●	▲	▲	▲	▲	▲	▲	▲	▲	▲	▲	▲	▲	▲	▲	▲	▲	▲	▲	▲	▲	▲	▲	▲	▲	▲	▲	▲	▲	▲	▲
Finland	539	(2.0)	▽	●	●	●		●	●	●	●	▲	▲	▲	▲	▲	▲	▲	▲	▲	▲	▲	▲	▲	▲	▲	▲	▲	▲	▲	▲	▲	▲	▲	▲	▲	▲	▲	▲	▲	▲	▲
Liechtenstein	538	(4.6)	●	●	●	●	●		●	●	●	●	●	▲	▲	▲	▲	▲	▲	▲	▲	▲	▲	▲	▲	▲	▲	▲	▲	▲	▲	▲	▲	▲	▲	▲	▲	▲	▲	▲	▲	▲
Belgium	530	(2.3)	▽	▽	▽	●	●	●		●	●	●	●	●	▲	▲	▲	▲	▲	▲	▲	▲	▲	▲	▲	▲	▲	▲	▲	▲	▲	▲	▲	▲	▲	▲	▲	▲	▲	▲	▲	▲
Macao-China	528	(3.3)	▽	▽	▽	●	●	●	●		●	●	●	●	●	●	▲	▲	▲	▲	▲	▲	▲	▲	▲	▲	▲	▲	▲	▲	▲	▲	▲	▲	▲	▲	▲	▲	▲	▲	▲	▲
Czech Republic	527	(4.1)	▽	▽	▽	●	●	●	●	●		●	●	●	●	●	●	▲	▲	▲	▲	▲	▲	▲	▲	▲	▲	▲	▲	▲	▲	▲	▲	▲	▲	▲	▲	▲	▲	▲	▲	▲
Netherlands	526	(2.9)	▽	▽	▽	●	▽	●	●	●	●		●	●	●	●	▲	▲	▲	▲	▲	▲	▲	▲	▲	▲	▲	▲	▲	▲	▲	▲	▲	▲	▲	▲	▲	▲	▲	▲	▲	▲
New Zealand	525	(2.3)	▽	▽	▽	▽	▽	●	●	●	●	●		●	●	●	▲	▲	▲	▲	▲	▲	▲	▲	▲	▲	▲	▲	▲	▲	▲	▲	▲	▲	▲	▲	▲	▲	▲	▲	▲	▲
Australia	521	(2.3)	▽	▽	▽	▽	▽	▽	●	●	●	●	●		●	●	●	▲	▲	▲	▲	▲	▲	▲	▲	▲	▲	▲	▲	▲	▲	▲	▲	▲	▲	▲	▲	▲	▲	▲	▲	▲
Canada	518	(1.8)	▽	▽	▽	▽	▽	▽	▽	●	●	●	●	●		●	●	●	●	▲	▲	▲	▲	▲	▲	▲	▲	▲	▲	▲	▲	▲	▲	▲	▲	▲	▲	▲	▲	▲	▲	▲
Austria	515	(3.5)	▽	▽	▽	▽	▽	▽	▽	●	●	●	●	●	●		●	●	●	●	▲	▲	▲	▲	▲	▲	▲	▲	▲	▲	▲	▲	▲	▲	▲	▲	▲	▲	▲	▲	▲	▲
Denmark	512	(2.8)	▽	▽	▽	▽	▽	▽	▽	▽	●	▽	▽	●	●	●		●	●	●	●	▲	▲	▲	▲	▲	▲	▲	▲	▲	▲	▲	▲	▲	▲	▲	▲	▲	▲	▲	▲	▲
France	508	(3.0)	▽	▽	▽	▽	▽	▽	▽	▽	▽	▽	▽	▽	●	●	●		●	●	●	●	▲	▲	▲	▲	▲	▲	▲	▲	▲	▲	▲	▲	▲	▲	▲	▲	▲	▲	▲	▲
Slovak Republic	505	(4.0)	▽	▽	▽	▽	▽	▽	▽	▽	▽	▽	▽	▽	●	●	●	●		●	●	●	●	▲	▲	▲	▲	▲	▲	▲	▲	▲	▲	▲	▲	▲	▲	▲	▲	▲	▲	▲
Iceland	504	(1.5)	▽	▽	▽	▽	▽	▽	▽	▽	▽	▽	▽	▽	▽	●	●	●	●		●	●	▲	▲	▲	▲	▲	▲	▲	▲	▲	▲	▲	▲	▲	▲	▲	▲	▲	▲	▲	▲
Germany	500	(3.3)	▽	▽	▽	▽	▽	▽	▽	▽	▽	▽	▽	▽	▽	▽	●	●	●	●		●	●	●	●	▲	▲	▲	▲	▲	▲	▲	▲	▲	▲	▲	▲	▲	▲	▲	▲	▲
Sweden	498	(2.6)	▽	▽	▽	▽	▽	▽	▽	▽	▽	▽	▽	▽	▽	▽	▽	●	●	●	●		●	▲	●	▲	▲	▲	▲	▲	▲	▲	▲	▲	▲	▲	▲	▲	▲	▲	▲	▲
Poland	490	(2.7)	▽	▽	▽	▽	▽	▽	▽	▽	▽	▽	▽	▽	▽	▽	▽	▽	●	▽	●	●		●	●	●	●	▲	▲	●	▲	▲	▲	▲	▲	▲	▲	▲	▲	▲	▲	▲
Luxembourg	488	(1.4)	▽	▽	▽	▽	▽	▽	▽	▽	▽	▽	▽	▽	▽	▽	▽	▽	▽	▽	●	▽	●		●	●	●	▲	▲	●	▲	▲	▲	▲	▲	▲	▲	▲	▲	▲	▲	▲
Latvia	486	(4.0)	▽	▽	▽	▽	▽	▽	▽	▽	▽	▽	▽	▽	▽	▽	▽	▽	▽	▽	●	●	●	●		●	●	●	●	●	●	●	▲	▲	▲	▲	▲	▲	▲	▲	▲	▲
Norway	483	(2.5)	▽	▽	▽	▽	▽	▽	▽	▽	▽	▽	▽	▽	▽	▽	▽	▽	▽	▽	▽	▽	●	●	●		●	●	●	●	●	●	▲	▲	▲	▲	▲	▲	▲	▲	▲	▲
Hungary	479	(3.3)	▽	▽	▽	▽	▽	▽	▽	▽	▽	▽	▽	▽	▽	▽	▽	▽	▽	▽	▽	▽	●	●	●	●		●	●	●	●	●	▲	▲	▲	▲	▲	▲	▲	▲	▲	▲
Spain	476	(2.6)	▽	▽	▽	▽	▽	▽	▽	▽	▽	▽	▽	▽	▽	▽	▽	▽	▽	▽	▽	▽	▽	▽	●	●	●		●	●	●	●	▲	▲	▲	▲	▲	▲	▲	▲	▲	▲
Ireland	476	(2.4)	▽	▽	▽	▽	▽	▽	▽	▽	▽	▽	▽	▽	▽	▽	▽	▽	▽	▽	▽	▽	▽	▽	●	●	●	●		●	●	●	▲	▲	▲	▲	▲	▲	▲	▲	▲	▲
Russian Fed.	474	(4.7)	▽	▽	▽	▽	▽	▽	▽	▽	▽	▽	▽	▽	▽	▽	▽	▽	▽	▽	▽	▽	●	●	●	●	●	●	●		●	●	▲	▲	▲	▲	▲	▲	▲	▲	▲	▲
United States	472	(2.8)	▽	▽	▽	▽	▽	▽	▽	▽	▽	▽	▽	▽	▽	▽	▽	▽	▽	▽	▽	▽	▽	▽	●	●	●	●	●	●		●	▲	▲	▲	▲	▲	▲	▲	▲	▲	▲
Italy	470	(3.1)	▽	▽	▽	▽	▽	▽	▽	▽	▽	▽	▽	▽	▽	▽	▽	▽	▽	▽	▽	▽	▽	▽	●	●	●	●	●	●	●		▲	▲	▲	▲	▲	▲	▲	▲	▲	▲
Portugal	450	(3.4)	▽	▽	▽	▽	▽	▽	▽	▽	▽	▽	▽	▽	▽	▽	▽	▽	▽	▽	▽	▽	▽	▽	▽	▽	▽	▽	▽	▽	▽	▽		●	▲	▲	▲	▲	▲	▲	▲	▲
Greece	437	(3.8)	▽	▽	▽	▽	▽	▽	▽	▽	▽	▽	▽	▽	▽	▽	▽	▽	▽	▽	▽	▽	▽	▽	▽	▽	▽	▽	▽	▽	▽	▽	●		●	●	●	▲	▲	▲	▲	▲
Serbia	432	(3.9)	▽	▽	▽	▽	▽	▽	▽	▽	▽	▽	▽	▽	▽	▽	▽	▽	▽	▽	▽	▽	▽	▽	▽	▽	▽	▽	▽	▽	▽	▽	▽	●		●	●	▲	▲	▲	▲	▲
Thailand	424	(3.3)	▽	▽	▽	▽	▽	▽	▽	▽	▽	▽	▽	▽	▽	▽	▽	▽	▽	▽	▽	▽	▽	▽	▽	▽	▽	▽	▽	▽	▽	▽	▽	●	●		●	●	▲	▲	▲	▲
Turkey	417	(6.3)	▽	▽	▽	▽	▽	▽	▽	▽	▽	▽	▽	▽	▽	▽	▽	▽	▽	▽	▽	▽	▽	▽	▽	▽	▽	▽	▽	▽	▽	▽	▽	●	●	●		●	▲	▲	▲	▲
Uruguay	412	(3.0)	▽	▽	▽	▽	▽	▽	▽	▽	▽	▽	▽	▽	▽	▽	▽	▽	▽	▽	▽	▽	▽	▽	▽	▽	▽	▽	▽	▽	▽	▽	▽	▽	▽	●	●		▲	▲	▲	▲
Mexico	382	(3.2)	▽	▽	▽	▽	▽	▽	▽	▽	▽	▽	▽	▽	▽	▽	▽	▽	▽	▽	▽	▽	▽	▽	▽	▽	▽	▽	▽	▽	▽	▽	▽	▽	▽	▽	▽	▽		▲	▲	▲
Indonesia	361	(3.7)	▽	▽	▽	▽	▽	▽	▽	▽	▽	▽	▽	▽	▽	▽	▽	▽	▽	▽	▽	▽	▽	▽	▽	▽	▽	▽	▽	▽	▽	▽	▽	▽	▽	▽	▽	▽	▽		●	●
Tunisia	359	(2.6)	▽	▽	▽	▽	▽	▽	▽	▽	▽	▽	▽	▽	▽	▽	▽	▽	▽	▽	▽	▽	▽	▽	▽	▽	▽	▽	▽	▽	▽	▽	▽	▽	▽	▽	▽	▽	▽	●		●
Brazil	350	(4.1)	▽	▽	▽	▽	▽	▽	▽	▽	▽	▽	▽	▽	▽	▽	▽	▽	▽	▽	▽	▽	▽	▽	▽	▽	▽	▽	▽	▽	▽	▽	▽	▽	▽	▽	▽	▽	▽	●	●	

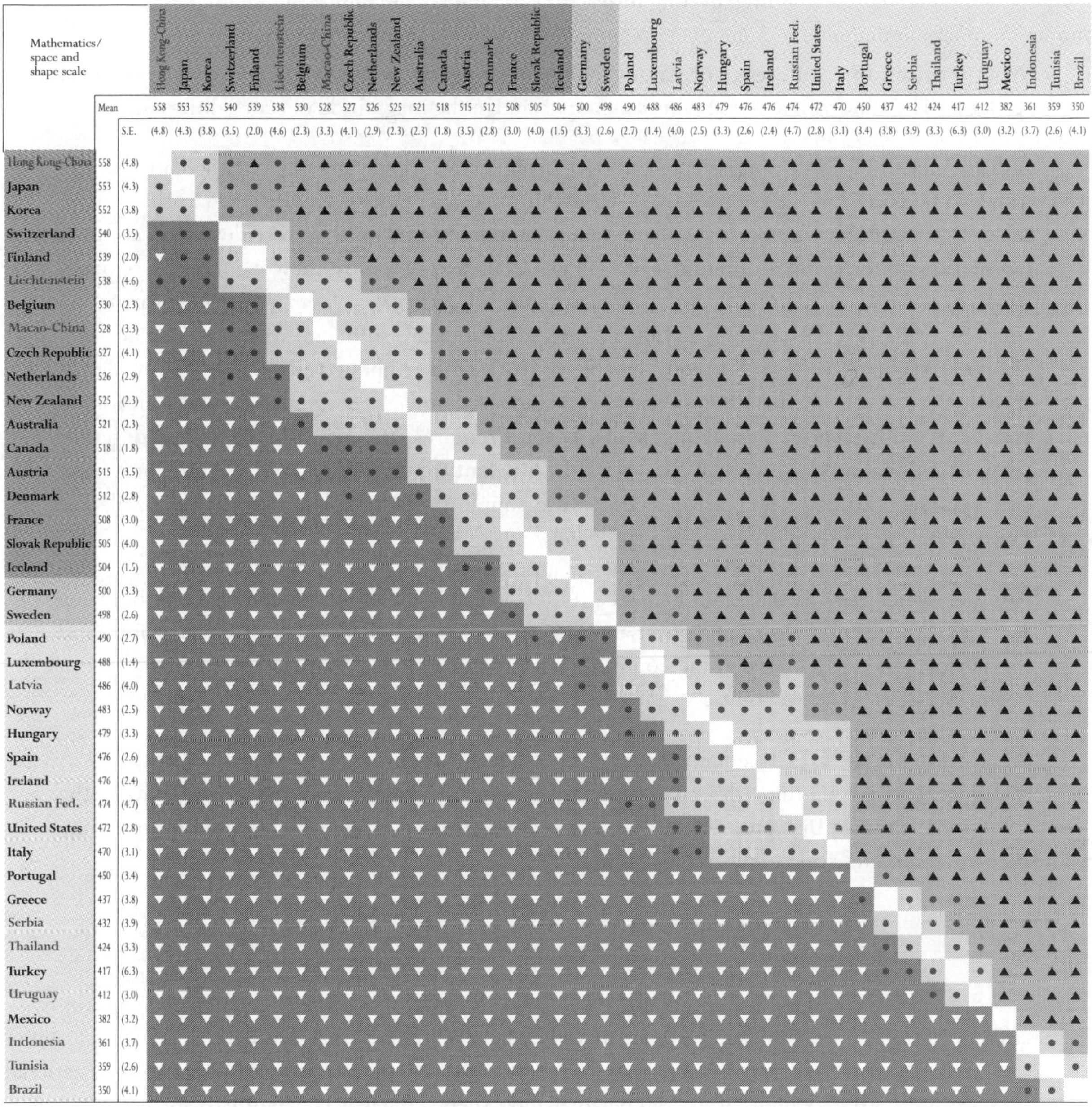

Range of rank*

		Hong Kong-China	Japan	Korea	Switzerland	Finland	Liechtenstein	Belgium	Macao-China	Czech Republic	Netherlands	New Zealand	Australia	Canada	Austria	Denmark	France	Slovak Republic	Iceland	Germany	Sweden	Poland	Luxembourg	Latvia	Norway	Hungary	Spain	Ireland	Russian Fed.	United States	Italy	Portugal	Greece	Serbia	Thailand	Turkey	Uruguay	Mexico	Indonesia	Tunisia	Brazil
OECD countries	Upper rank		1	1	3	3		5		5	5	5	7	9	9	10	11	12	13	14	15	17	18		19	20	21	21		22	22	26	27			28		29			
	Lower rank		2	2	4	4		7		9	9	9	11	11	13	14	15	17	16	17	17	20	20		21	24	25	24		25	25	26	27			28		29			
All countries	Upper rank	1	1	1	4	4	4	6	6	6	7	8	10	12	12	13	14	15	16	17	18	20	21	21	22	23	25	25	24	26	27	31	32	32	33	34	35	37	38	38	39
	Lower rank	3	3	3	6	6	8	10	12	12	12	12	14	14	16	17	18	20	19	20	20	23	23	26	26	29	29	29	30	30	30	31	33	34	35	36	36	37	39	40	40

* Because data are based on samples, it is not possible to report exact rank order positions for countries. However, it is possible to report the range of rank order positions within which the country mean lies with 95 per cent likelihood.

Instructions:

Read across the row for a country to compare performance with the countries listed along the top of the chart. The symbols indicate whether the average performance of the country in the row is lower than that of the comparison country, higher than that of the comparison country, or if there is no statistically significant difference between the average achievement of the two countries.

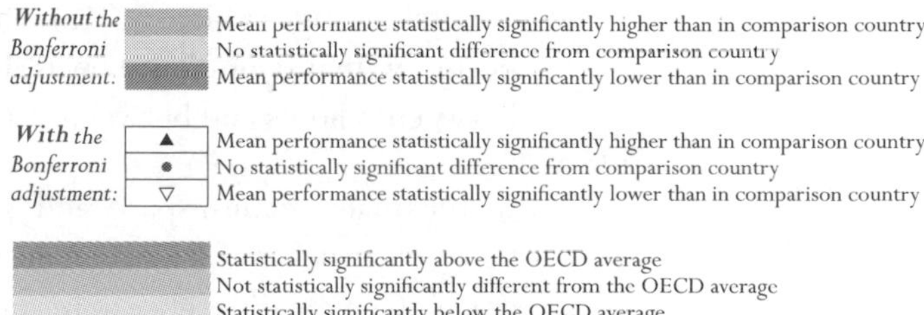

Source: OECD PISA 2003 database.

Box 2.2 ■ **Interpreting differences in PISA scores: how large a gap?**

What is meant by a difference of, say, 50 points between the scores of two different groups of students? The following comparisons can help to judge the magnitude of score differences.

A difference of 62 score points represents one proficiency level on the PISA mathematics scales. This can be considered a comparatively large difference in student performance in substantive terms: for example, with regard to the thinking and reasoning skills that were described above in the section on the process dimension of the PISA 2003 assessment framework, Level 3 requires students to make sequential decisions and to interpret and reason from different information sources, while direct reasoning and literal interpretations are sufficient to succeed at Level 2. Similarly, students at Level 3 need to be able to work with symbolic representations, while for students at Level 2 the handling of basic algorithms, formulae, procedures and conventions is sufficient. With regard to modelling skills, Level 3 requires students to make use of different representational models, while for Level 2 it is sufficient to recognise, apply and interpret basic given models. Students at Level 3 need to use simple problem-solving strategies, while for Level 2 the use of direct inferences is sufficient.

Another benchmark is that the difference in performance on the mathematics scale between the OECD countries with the highest and lowest mean performance is 159 score points, and the performance gap between the countries with the third highest and the third lowest mean performance is 93 score points.

Finally, for the 26 OECD countries in which a sizeable number of 15-year-olds in the PISA samples were enrolled in at least two different grades, the difference between students in the two grades implies that one school year corresponds to an average of 41 score points on the PISA mathematics scale (Table A1.2, Annex A1).[10]

However, since about 90 per cent of performance variation occurs within countries, country averages give only part of the picture.

Finally, it needs to be taken into account that average performance figures mask significant variation in performance within countries, reflecting different levels of performance among many different student groups. As in previous international studies of student performance, such as the IEA Third International Mathematics and Science Study (TIMSS) conducted in 1995 and 1999 and the IEA Trends in Mathematics and Science Study (TIMSS) conducted in 2003, only about one-tenth of the variation in student performance on the overall mathematics scale lies between countries and can, therefore, be captured through a comparison of country averages (Table 5.21a). The remaining variation in student performance occurs within countries, that is, between education systems and programmes, between schools and between students within schools.

In the mathematics/space and shape scale, performance also varies notably between males and females, and more so than in the three other mathematics scales. Gender differences are most clearly visible at the top end of the scale:

on average across countries, 7 per cent of males reach Level 6, while only 4 per cent of females do so and in the Czech Republic, Japan, Korea, the Slovak Republic, Switzerland and the partner country Liechtenstein, the gender gap is around 6 percentage points or larger (Table 2.1b).

Males outperform females in this area of mathematics in most countries, particularly at the top end of the scale.

Nevertheless, in most countries the differences are not large when comparing them over the entire proficiency spectrum.[11] Across the combined OECD area, males perform on average 16 score points higher than females on the mathematics/space and shape scale and they outperform females in all countries except Iceland, where females outperform males. The difference in favour of males reaches more than 35 score points, equivalent to half a proficiency level in mathematics, in the Slovak Republic and in partner country Liechtenstein. However, the overall differences in favour of males are not statistically significant in seven of the participating countries, namely Finland, Japan, the Netherlands and Norway and in the partner countries Hong Kong-China, Serbia and Thailand (Table 2.1c).

Comparison of these results with PISA 2000 must be made with caution…

It is also possible to estimate how much performance on the mathematics/space and shape scale has changed since the last PISA survey in 2000. However, such differences need to be interpreted with caution. Firstly, since data are only available from two points in time, it is not possible to assess to what extent the observed differences are indicative for longer-term trends. Second, while the overall approach to measurement used by PISA is consistent across cycles, small refinements continue to be made, so it would not be prudent to read too much into small changes in results at this stage. Furthermore, sampling and measurement error limit the reliability of comparisons of results over time. Both types of error inevitably arise when assessments are linked through a limited number of common items over time. To account for the effects of such error, the confidence band for comparisons over time has been broadened correspondingly.[12]

…and show little change on average, improvements in four OECD countries and a decline in two.

With these caveats in mind, the following comparisons can be made. On average across OECD countries, performance on the mathematics/space and shape scale has remained broadly similar among the 25 OECD countries for which data can be compared (in 2000, the OECD average was 494 score points whereas in 2003 it was 496 score points). However, when examining performance changes in individual countries, the pattern is uneven (Figures 2.6c and 2.6d, and Table 2.1c and Table 2.1d). In Belgium and Poland, mean performance increases amounted to between 28 and 20 score points, respectively, roughly equivalent to a half grade-year difference in student performance among OECD countries (Box 2.2). The Czech Republic and Italy, as well as the partner countries Brazil, Indonesia, Latvia and Thailand, have also seen significant performance increases in the mathematics/space and shape scale, while performance in Iceland and Mexico declined. In Mexico, this may have been partly attributable to the strong emphasis on increasing participation rates in secondary schools across the country.[13,14] In the remaining countries, there was no statistically significant change in the mean score at the 95 per cent confidence level.

Figure 2.6c ■ **Comparisons between PISA 2003 and PISA 2000 on the mathematics/space and shape scale**

Significance levels	2003 higher than 2000	2003 lower than 2000	No statistically significant difference
90 % confidence level	+	–	o
95 % confidence level	++	– –	
99 % confidence level	+++	– – –	

Differences observed in the mean and percentiles

	5th	10th	25th	Mean	75th	90th	95th
OECD countries							
Australia	o	o	o	o	o	o	o
Austria	o	o	o	o	o	o	o
Belgium	+	o	++	+++	+++	+++	+++
Canada	o	o	o	o	o	o	o
Czech Republic	++	++	++	++	+	o	o
Denmark	---	---	---	-	o	o	o
Finland	++	+	o	o	o	o	o
France	o	o	o	o	o	++	o
Germany	o	o	o	+	+	o	o
Greece	o	o	o	o	--	--	--
Hungary	o	o	o	o	o	+	++
Iceland	---	---	---	--	o	o	o
Ireland	o	o	o	o	o	o	o
Italy	o	o	+	++	++	++	+
Japan	o	o	o	o	o	o	o
Korea	o	o	o	+	o	o	o
Mexico	-	--	--	--	--	-	-
New Zealand	o	o	o	o	o	o	o
Norway	o	o	o	o	o	o	o
Poland	+++	+++	+++	++	o	o	o
Portugal	+++	+++	++	o	o	o	o
Spain	o	o	o	o	o	o	o
Sweden	o	o	o	o	--	--	--
Switzerland	o	o	o	o	o	o	o
United States	o	o	o	o	o	+	+
OECD total	o	o	o	o	o	o	o
OECD average	o	o	o	o	o	o	o
Partner countries							
Brazil	+++	+++	+++	+++	+	o	o
Hong Kong-China	o	o	o	+	+++	+	o
Indonesia	+++	+++	+++	+++	o	o	o
Latvia	+++	+++	+++	+++	++	+	o
Liechtenstein	o	o	o	o	o	o	o
Russian Federation	o	o	o	o	o	o	o
Thailand	+++	+++	++	++	o	o	o

Source: OECD PISA 2003 and PISA 2000 databases, Tables 2.1c and 2.1d.

But it is not just changes in mean scores that are of interest…

Changes in mean performance scores are typically used to assess improvements in the quality of schools and education systems. However, as noted above, mean performance does not provide a full picture of student performance and can mask significant variation within an individual class, school or education system. Moreover, countries aim not only to encourage high performance but also to minimise internal disparities in performance. Both parents and the public at large are aware of the seriousness of low performance and the fact that school-leavers who lack fundamental skills face poor employment prospects. Having a high proportion of students at the lower end of the mathematics scale may give rise to concern that a large proportion of tomorrow's workforce and voters will lack the skills required for the informed judgements that they will need to make.

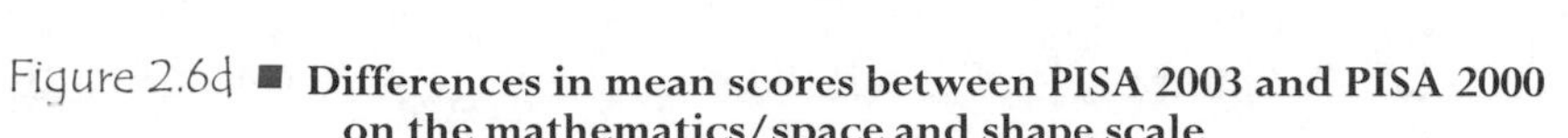

Figure 2.6d ■ **Differences in mean scores between PISA 2003 and PISA 2000 on the mathematics/space and shape scale**

Only countries with valid data for both 2003 and 2000

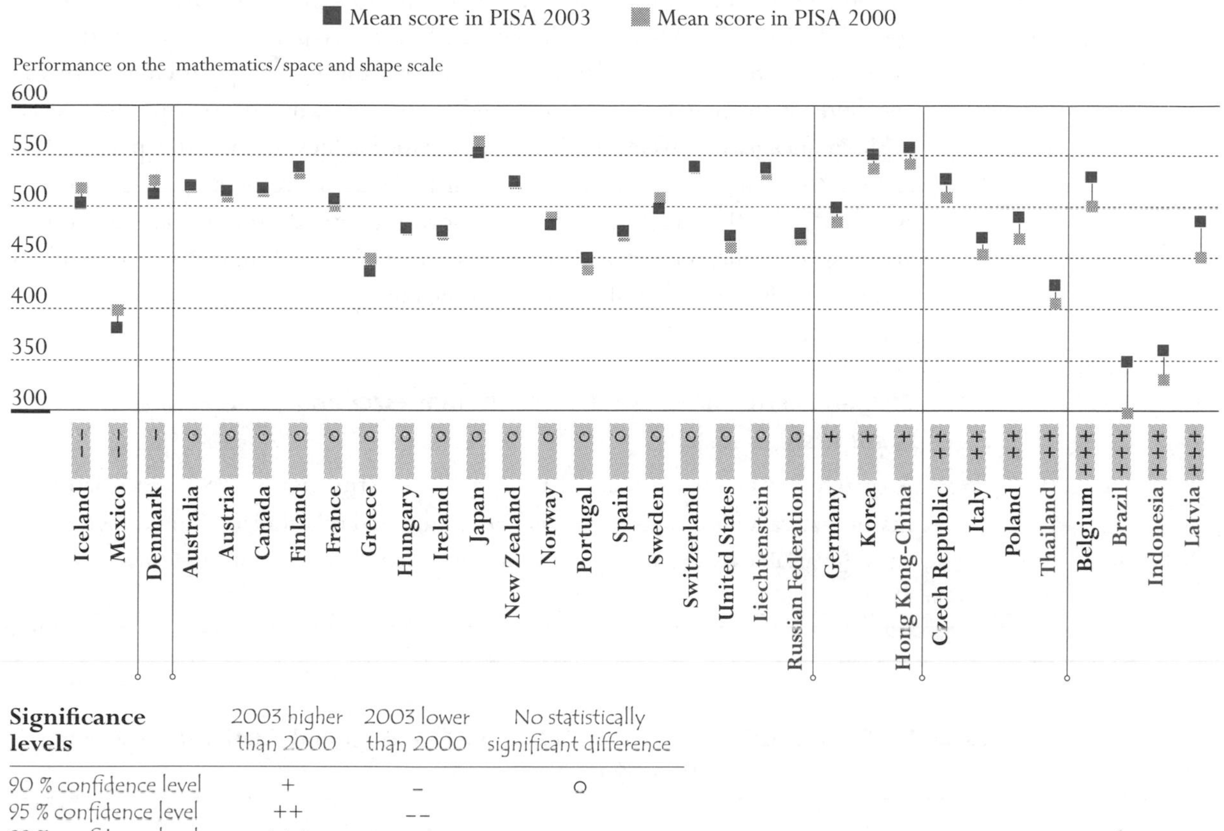

Significance levels	2003 higher than 2000	2003 lower than 2000	No statistically significant difference
90 % confidence level	+	–	O
95 % confidence level	++	– –	
99 % confidence level	+++	– – –	

Countries are ranked in ascending order of the difference between PISA 2003 and PISA 2000 performances.
Source: OECD PISA 2003 and PISA 2000 databases, Tables 2.1c and 2.1d.

...since some change is driven by a particular part of the ability range.

It is, therefore, important to examine the observed performance changes in more detail. As seen in Figure 2.6c some of the observed changes have not necessarily involved an even rise or fall in performance across the ability range. In some countries, performance across the ability range has widened or narrowed over a three-year period, as changes in one part of the ability range are not matched by changes in others.

Improvements in Belgium and Italy have been driven by higher-ability students...

In Belgium, for example, the 28 point rise in average performance on the mathematics/space and shape scale has mainly been driven by improved performance in the top part of the performance distribution – as is visible in the increase in scores at the 75th, 90th and 95th percentiles – while little has changed at the lower end of the distribution (Figures 2.6c and 2.6d, and Tables 2.1c and 2.1d). A similar picture, though less pronounced, emerges for Italy. As a result, in these two countries overall performance increased but the gap between the better and poorer performers has widened.

...whereas in Poland and the Czech Republic overall performance increased because lower-performing students tended to catch up.

In contrast, for Poland, the rise in average performance on the mathematics/space and shape scale is attributable mainly to an increase in performance at the lower end of the performance distribution (*i.e.*, 5th, 10th and 25th percentiles). Consequently, in 2003 fewer than 5 per cent of students fell below performance standards that had not been reached by the bottom 10 per cent of Polish students in 2000. As a result, Poland succeeded in raising the average performance of 15-year-olds on the mathematics/space and shape scale while narrowing the overall performance gap between the lower and higher achievers over this period; this change that may well be associated with the massive reform of the schooling systems in 1999, which now provide more integrated educational structures. To a lesser extent, this pattern also holds for the Czech Republic, the remaining country with a substantial increase in average performance (Figures 2.6c-d, Table 2.1c and Table 2.1d).

Student performance on the mathematics/change and relationships scale

A quarter of the mathematical tasks given to students in PISA are related to mathematical manifestations of change, functional relationships and dependency among variables. Figures 2.7a-b show tasks at all six levels in this category:

Figure 2.7a ■ **A sample of mathematics items used in PISA for the change and relationships scale: Unit WALKING**

WALKING

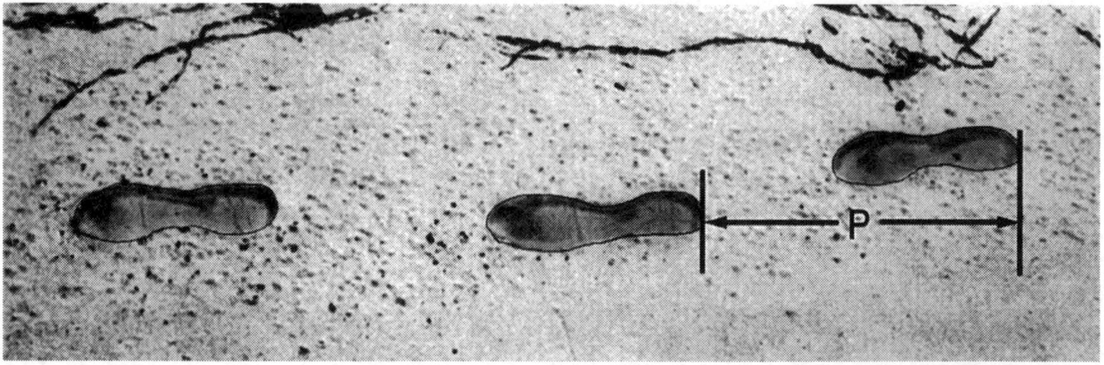

The picture shows the footprints of a man walking. The pacelength P is the distance between the rear of two consecutive footprints.

For men, the formula, $\frac{n}{P} = 140$, *gives an approximate relationship between n and P where:*

n = number of steps per minute, and
P = pacelength in metres.

Level

WALKING

QUESTION 5

Bernard knows his pacelength is 0.80 metres. The formula applies to Bernard's walking.

Calculate Bernard's walking speed in metres per minute and in kilometres per hour. Show your working out.

Score 3 (723)

Answers which indicate correctly metres/minute (89.6) and km/hour (5.4). Errors due to rounding are acceptable.

Score 2 (666)

Answers which are incorrect or incomplete because:

- They were not multiplied by 0.80 to convert from steps per minute to metres per minute.
- They correctly showed the speed in metres per minute (89.6 metres per minute) but the conversion to kilometres per hour was incorrect or missing.
- They were based on the correct method (explicitly shown) but with other minor calculation error(s).
- They indicated only 5.4 km/hr, but not 89.6 metres per minute (intermediate calculations not shown).

Score 1 (605)

Answers which give $n = 140 \times .80 = 112$ but no further working out is shown or incorrect working out from this point.

This open-constructed response item is situated in a personal context. The coding guide for this item provides for full credit, and two levels of partial credit. The item is about the relationship between the number of steps per minute and pacelength. It follows that it fits the change and relationships content area. The mathematical routine needed to solve the problem successfully is substitution in a simple formula (algebra), and carrying out a non-routine calculation. To solve the problem, students first calculate the number of steps per minute when the pace-length is given (0.8 m). This requires substitution into and manipulation of the expression: $n/0.8 = 140$ leading to: $n = 140 \times 0.8$ which is 112 steps per minute. The next question asks for the speed in m/minute which involves converting the number of steps to a distance in metres: $112 \times 0.80 = 89.6$ metres; so his speed is 89.6 m/minute. The final step is to transform this speed into km/h - a more commonly used unit of speed. This involves relationships among units for conversions which is part of the measurement domain. Solving the problem also requires decoding and interpreting basic symbolic language, and handling expressions containing symbols and formulae. The problem, therefore, is rather a complex one involving formal algebraic expression and performing a sequence of different but connected calculations that need understanding of transforming formulas and units of measures. The lower level partial credit part of this item belongs to the connections competency cluster and with a difficulty of 605 score points it illustrates the top part of Level 4. The higher level of partial credit illustrates the upper part of Level 5, with a difficulty of 666 score points. Students who score the higher level of partial credit are able to go beyond finding the number of steps per minute, making progress towards converting this into the more standard units of speed asked for. However, their responses are either not entirely complete or not fully correct. Full credit for this item illustrates the upper part of Level 6, as it has a difficulty of 723 score points. Students who score full credit are able to complete the conversions and provide a correct answer in both of the requested units.

QUESTION 4

If the formula applies to Heiko's walking and Heiko takes 70 steps per minute, what is Heiko's pacelength? Show your work.

Score 1 (611)

Answers which indicate p = 0.5 m or p = 50 cm or p = $^1/_2$ (unit not required).

This open-constructed response item is situated in a personal context. It has a difficulty of 611 score points, just 4 points beyond the boundary with Level 4. Everyone has seen his or her own footsteps printed in the sand at some moment in life, most likely without realising what kind of relations exist in the way these patterns are formed, although many students will have an intuitive feeling that if the pace-length increases, the number of steps per minute will decrease, other things equal. To reflect on and realise the embedded mathematics in such daily phenomena is part of acquiring mathematical literacy. The item is about this relationship: number of steps per minute and pacelength. It follows that it fits the change and relationships content area. The mathematical content could be described as belonging clearly to algebra. Students need to solve the problem successfully by substitution in a simple formula and carrying out a routine calculation: if $n/p = 140$, and $n = 70$, what is the value of p? The students need to carry out the actual calculation in order to get full credit. The competencies needed involve reproduction of practised knowledge, the performance of routine procedures, application of standard technical skills, manipulation of expressions containing symbols and formulae in standard form, and carrying out computations. Therefore the item belongs to the reproduction competency cluster. The item requires problem solving by making use of a formal algebraic expression. With this combination of competencies, and the real-world setting that students must handle, it illustrates Level 5, at the lower end.

6
668.7
5
606.6
4
544.4
3
482.4
2
420.4
1
358.3
Below 1

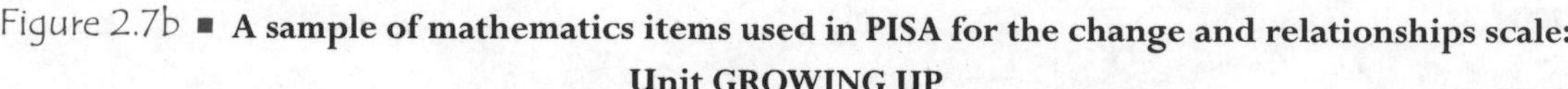

Figure 2.7b ■ **A sample of mathematics items used in PISA for the change and relationships scale: Unit GROWING UP**

GROWING UP

In 1998 the average height of both young males and young females in the Netherlands is represented in this graph.

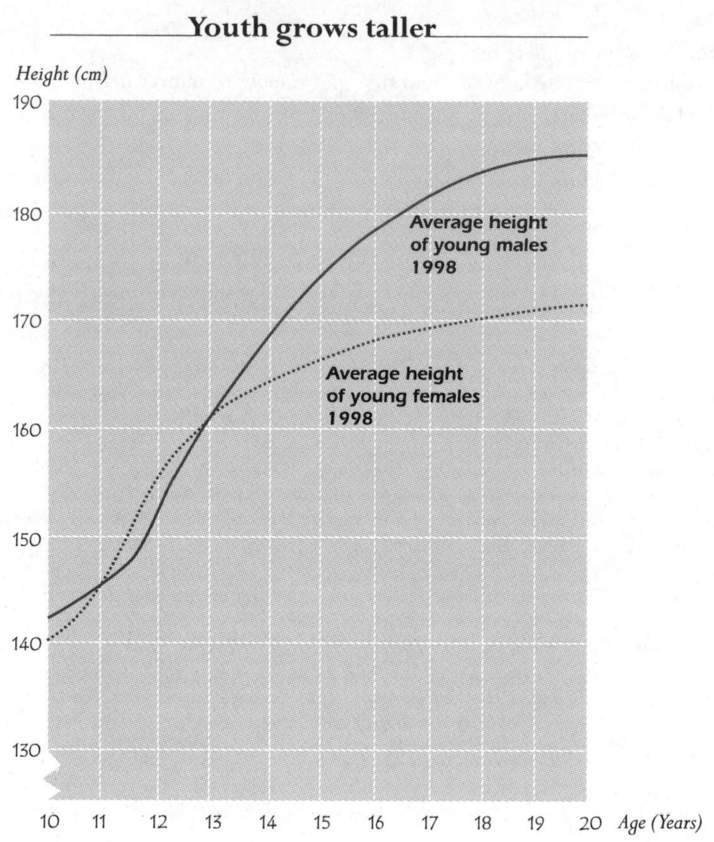

GROWING UP

QUESTION 8

Explain how the graph shows that on average the growth rate for girls slows down after 12 years of age.

Score 1 (574)

Correct answers which refer to the "change" of the gradient of the graph for females, either by explicitly referring to the reduced steepness of the curve from 12 years onwards, using daily-life or mathematical language, or implicitly by using the actual amount of growth before 12 years and after 12 years of age.

This open-constructed response item has a difficulty of 574 score points (Level 4). The focus of the item is on the relationship between age and height, which means that it belongs to the change and relationships content area. Solving the problem involves the interpretation and decoding of familiar representations of well known mathematical objects. But there is a rather complex concept in this item, the concept of "decreasing growth", which is a combination of "growing" and "slowing down", to use the language of the item. In mathematical terms: the graphs become less steep and the slope (or gradient) decreases. The graphs indicate that this diminished growth rate starts at around age 12. The communication of this observation is central to the question for the students. The expression of their answers ranges from daily life language to more mathematical language about the reduced steepness, or they compare the actual growth in centimetres per year. Thus the mathematical content can be described as evaluating the characteristics of a data set represented in a graph, and noting and interpreting the different slopes at various points of the graphs. In competency terms, the item represents a situation that is not routine but involves familiar settings and demands the linking of different ideas and information – it therefore belongs to the connections competencies cluster. The item requires mathematical insight and some reasoning and communication of the results of this process, within the explicit models of growth.

QUESTION 7

According to this graph, on average, during which period in their life are females taller than males of the same age?

Score 2 (525)

Answers which indicate the correct interval, from 11-13 years or state that girls are taller than boys when they are 11 and 12 years old (this answer is correct in daily-life language, because it means the interval from 11 to 13).

Score 1 (420)

Other subsets of (11, 12, 13), not included in the full credit section.

This item, with its focus on age and height means that it lies in the change and relationships content area - it has a difficulty of 420 (Level 1). The mathematical content can be described as belonging to the data domain because the students are asked to compare characteristics of two data sets, interpret these data sets and draw conclusions. The competencies needed to successfully solve the problem are in the reproduction cluster and involve the interpretation and decoding of reasonably familiar and standard representations of well known mathematical objects. Students need thinking and reasoning competencies to answer the question: "Where do the graphs have common points?" and the argumentation and communication competencies to explain the role these points play in finding the desired answer. Students who score partial credit are able to show that their reasoning and/or insight was well directed, but they fail in coming up with a full, comprehensive answer. They properly identify ages like 11 and/or 12 and/or 13 as being part of an answer but fail to identify the continuum from 11 to 13 years. The item provides a good illustration of the boundary between Level 1 and Level 2. The full credit response to this item illustrates Level 3, as it has a difficulty of 525 score points. Students who score full credit are not only able to show that their reasoning and/or insight is well directed, but they also come up with a full, comprehensive answer. Students who solve the problem successfully are adept at using graphical representations, making conclusions and communicating their findings.

QUESTION 6

Since 1980 the average height of 20-year-old females has increased by 2.3 cm, to 170.6 cm. What was the average height of a 20-year-old female in 1980?

Answer: .... cm

Score 1 (477)

Answers which indicate 168.3 cm (unit already given).

This closed-constructed response item is situated in a scientific context: the growth curves of young males and females over a period of ten years. It has a difficulty of 477 score points. Science uses graphical representation frequently, for example as in this item to represent changes in height in relation to the age. Because of the focus on these aspects this item is classified as belonging to the change and relationships area. The mathematics content is basic. Translating the question into a mathematical context and carrying out a basic arithmetic operation: subtraction (170.6 – 2.3). This places it in the reproduction competency cluster: the thinking and reasoning required involves the most basic form of questions ("How much is the difference?"); the same holds for the argumentation competency: the students just need to follow a standard quantitative process. An added complexity is the fact that the answer can be found by ignoring the graph altogether – an example of redundant information. Summarising, the item requires that students can extract the relevant information from a single source (and ignoring the redundant source) and make use of a single representational mode and can employ a basic subtraction algorithm. Therefore the item illustrates Level 2.

Level	Score boundary
6	
	668.7
5	
	606.6
4	
	544.4
3	
	482.4
2	
	420.4
1	
	358.3
Below 1	

A small minority of students can perform the very hardest change and relationships tasks…

The precise competencies required to reach each level are given in Figure 2.8. As with the mathematics/space and shape scale, 5 per cent of students in the combined OECD area can perform Level 6 tasks. Thirty-two per cent of students in the OECD area, but half of the students in Korea, the Netherlands, and the partner country Hong Kong-China, and just under half of the students in Belgium, Finland and the partner country Liechtenstein, and Finland, reach at least Level 4.

Figure 2.8 ■ **Summary descriptions of six levels of proficiency on the mathematics/change and relationships scale**

Level	General competencies students should have at each level	Specific tasks students should be able to do
6	*5% of all students across the OECD area can perform tasks at Level 6 on the change and relationships scale*	
	Use significant insight, abstract reasoning and argumentation skills and technical knowledge and conventions to solve problems and to generalise mathematical solutions to complex real-world problems	– Interpret complex mathematical information in the context of an unfamiliar real-world situation – Interpret periodic functions in a real-world setting, perform related calculations in the presence of constraints – Interpret complex information hidden in the context of an unfamiliar real-world situation – Interpret complex text and use abstract reasoning (based on insight into relationships) to solve problems – Insightful use of algebra or graphs to solve problems; ability to manipulate algebraic expressions to match a real-world situation – Problem solving based on complex proportional reasoning – Multi-step problem-solving strategies involving the use of formulae and calculations – Devise a strategy and solve the problem by using algebra or trial-and-error – Identify a formula which describes a complex real-world situation, generalise exploratory findings to create a summarising formula – Generalise exploratory findings in order to carry out calculations – Apply deep geometrical insight to work with and generalise complex patterns – Conceptualise complex percentage calculations – Coherently communicate logical reasoning and arguments
5	*15% of all students across the OECD area can perform tasks at least at Level 5 on the change and relationships scale*	
	Solve problems by making advanced use of algebraic and other formal mathematical expressions and models; link formal mathematical representations to complex real-world situations; use complex and multi-step problem-solving skills, reflect on and communicate reasoning and arguments	– Interpret complex formulae in a scientific context – Interpret periodic functions in a real-world setting, perform related calculations – Use advanced problem-solving strategies – Interpret and link complex information – Interpret and apply constraints – Identify and carry out a suitable strategy – Reflect on the relationship between an algebraic formula and its underlying data – Use complex proportional reasoning, *e.g.,* related to rates – Analyse and apply a given formula in a real-life situation – Communicate reasoning and argument
4	*32% of all students across the OECD area can perform tasks at least at Level 4 on the change and relationships scale*	
	Understand and work with multiple representations, including explicit mathematical models of real-world situations to solve practical problems; employ considerable flexibility in interpretation and reasoning, including in unfamiliar contexts, and communicate the resulting explanations and arguments	– Interpret complex graphs, and read one or multiple values from graphs – Interpret complex and unfamiliar graphical representations of real-world situations – Use multiple representations to solve a practical problem – Relate text-based information to a graphic representation and communicate explanations – Analyse a formula describing a real-world situation – Analyse three-dimensional geometric situations involving volume and related functions

Level	General competencies students should have at each level	Specific tasks students should be able to do
		– Analyse a given mathematical model involving a complex formula – Interpret and apply word formulae, and manipulate and use linear formulae that represent real-world relationships – Carry out a sequence of calculations involving percentages, proportions, addition or division
3	*54% of all students across the OECD area can perform tasks at least at Level 3 on the change and relationships scale*	
	Solve problems that involve working with multiple related representations (a text, a graph, a table, a formula), including some interpretation, reasoning in familiar contexts, and communication of argument	– Interpret unfamiliar graphical representations of real-world situations – Identify relevant criteria in a text – Interpret text in which a simple algorithm is hidden and apply that algorithm – Interpret a text and devise a simple strategy – Link and connect multiple related representations (*e.g.,* two related graphs, text and a table, a formula and a graph) – Use reasoning involving proportions in various familiar contexts and communicate reasons and argument – Apply a text-given criterion or situation to a graph – Use a range of simple calculation procedures to solve problems, including ordering data, time difference calculations and linear interpolation
2	*73% of all students across the OECD area can perform tasks at least at Level 2 on the change and relationships scale*	
	Work with simple algorithms, formulae and procedures to solve problems; link text with a single representation (a graph, a table, a simple formula); use interpretation and reasoning skills at an elementary level	– Interpret a simple text and link it correctly to graphical elements – Interpret a simple text that describes a simple algorithm and apply that algorithm – Interpret a simple text and use proportional reasoning or a calculation – Interpret a simple pattern – Interpret and use reasoning in a practical context involving a simple and familiar application of motion, speed and time relationships – Locate relevant information in graph, and read values directly from a graph – Correctly substitute numbers to apply a simple numeric algorithm or simple algebraic formula
1	*87% of all students across the OECD area can perform tasks at least at Level 1 on the change and relationships scale*	
	Locate relevant information in a simple table or graph; follow direct and simple instructions to read information directly from a simple table or graph in a standard or familiar form; perform simple calculations involving relationships between two familiar variables	– Make a simple connection of text to a specific feature of a simple graph and read off a value from the graph – Locate and read a specified value in a simple table – Perform simple calculations involving relationships between two familiar variables

...and about one in four cannot perform more than the very simplest tasks.

Seventy-three per cent of students in the combined OECD area perform at least at Level 2, the level that was chosen to align the results in Figure 2.9a. It represents, as explained above, a baseline level of mathematics proficiency on the PISA scale at which students begin to demonstrate the kind of literacy skills that enable them to actively use mathematics as stipulated by the PISA definition (Table 2.2a). However in Greece, Italy, Luxembourg, Mexico, Norway, Poland, Portugal, Spain, Turkey and the United States as well as in the partner countries Brazil, Indonesia, Latvia, the Russian Federation, Serbia, Thailand, Tunisia and Uruguay a quarter or more of students fail to reach this threshold.

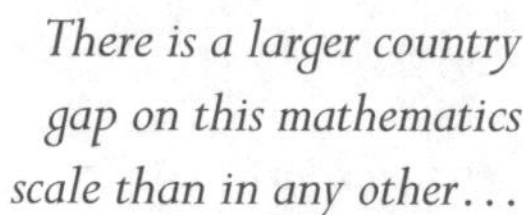

There is a larger country gap on this mathematics scale than in any other...

Among the various mathematics scales, the change and relationships scale shows the largest gap in mean performance between high and low performing countries – 214 score points or more separate the Netherlands at half a standard deviation above the OECD average from Brazil, Indonesia and Tunisia at more than one and a half standard deviations below the OECD average (Figure 2.9b).

...and again, the overall performance can be compared across countries, with the Netherlands, Finland, Korea and Hong Kong-China the strongest.

Figure 2.9b gives a summary of overall student performance in different countries on the change and relationships scale, in terms of the mean student score, and shows, with 95 per cent probability, the range of rank order positions within which the country mean lies. As explained before, it is not possible to determine the exact rank order position of countries in the international comparisons. However, it can be concluded that the Netherlands' position is between first and third among all countries that participated in PISA 2003, indistinguishable from Korea which can be found between the first and fourth ranks.

Figure 2.9a ■ **Percentage of students at each level of proficiency on the mathematics/change and relationships scale**

Below Level 1 | Level 1 | Level 2 | Level 3 | Level 4 | Level 5 | Level 6

Percentage of students

100, 75, 50, 25, 0, 25, 50, 75, 100

Netherlands, Finland, Korea, Canada, Hong Kong-China, Australia, Liechtenstein, Japan, New Zealand, France, Ireland, Belgium, Macao-China, Czech Republic, Switzerland, Iceland, Denmark, Sweden, Germany, Austria, Hungary, Slovak Republic, Norway, United States, Latvia, Luxembourg, Poland, Spain, Russian Fed., Portugal, Italy, Greece, Uruguay, Serbia, Turkey, Thailand, Mexico, Brazil, Tunisia, Indonesia

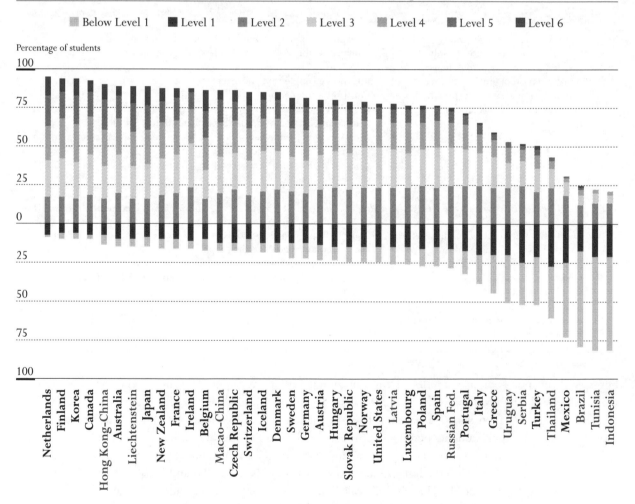

Countries are ranked in descending order of percentage of 15-year-olds in Levels 2, 3, 4, 5 and 6.

Source: OECD PISA 2003 database, Table 2.2a.

Figure 2.9b ■ Multiple comparisons of mean performance on the mathematics/change and relationships scale

Mathematics/ change and relationships scale	Mean	S.E.	Netherlands	Korea	Finland	Hong Kong-China	Liechtenstein	Canada	Japan	Belgium	New Zealand	Australia	Switzerland	France	Macao-China	Czech Republic	Iceland	Denmark	Germany	Ireland	Sweden	Austria	Hungary	Slovak Republic	Norway	Latvia	Luxembourg	United States	Poland	Spain	Russian Fed.	Portugal	Italy	Greece	Turkey	Serbia	Uruguay	Thailand	Mexico	Tunisia	Indonesia	Brazil
Mean			551	548	543	540	540	537	536	535	526	525	523	520	519	515	509	509	507	506	505	500	495	494	488	487	487	486	484	481	477	468	452	436	423	419	417	405	364	337	334	333
S.E.			(3.1)	(3.5)	(2.2)	(4.7)	(3.7)	(1.9)	(4.3)	(2.4)	(2.4)	(2.3)	(3.7)	(2.6)	(3.5)	(3.5)	(1.4)	(3.0)	(3.7)	(2.4)	(2.9)	(3.6)	(3.1)	(3.5)	(2.6)	(4.4)	(1.2)	(3.0)	(2.7)	(2.8)	(4.6)	(4.0)	(3.2)	(4.3)	(7.6)	(4.0)	(3.6)	(3.4)	(4.1)	(2.8)	(4.6)	(6.0)
Netherlands	551	(3.1)		●	●	●	●	▲	●	▲	▲	▲	▲	▲	▲	▲	▲	▲	▲	▲	▲	▲	▲	▲	▲	▲	▲	▲	▲	▲	▲	▲	▲	▲	▲	▲	▲	▲	▲	▲	▲	▲
Korea	548	(3.5)	●		●	●	●	●	●	●	▲	▲	▲	▲	▲	▲	▲	▲	▲	▲	▲	▲	▲	▲	▲	▲	▲	▲	▲	▲	▲	▲	▲	▲	▲	▲	▲	▲	▲	▲	▲	▲
Finland	543	(2.2)	●	●		●	●	●	●	●	▲	▲	▲	▲	▲	▲	▲	▲	▲	▲	▲	▲	▲	▲	▲	▲	▲	▲	▲	▲	▲	▲	▲	▲	▲	▲	▲	▲	▲	▲	▲	▲
Hong Kong-China	540	(4.7)	●	●	●		●	●	●	●	●	●	●	▲	▲	▲	▲	▲	▲	▲	▲	▲	▲	▲	▲	▲	▲	▲	▲	▲	▲	▲	▲	▲	▲	▲	▲	▲	▲	▲	▲	▲
Liechtenstein	540	(3.7)	●	●	●	●		●	●	●	●	▲	▲	▲	▲	▲	▲	▲	▲	▲	▲	▲	▲	▲	▲	▲	▲	▲	▲	▲	▲	▲	▲	▲	▲	▲	▲	▲	▲	▲	▲	▲
Canada	537	(1.9)	▽	●	●	●	●		●	●	▲	▲	▲	▲	▲	▲	▲	▲	▲	▲	▲	▲	▲	▲	▲	▲	▲	▲	▲	▲	▲	▲	▲	▲	▲	▲	▲	▲	▲	▲	▲	▲
Japan	536	(4.3)	●	●	●	●	●	●		●	●	●	●	▲	●	▲	▲	▲	▲	▲	▲	▲	▲	▲	▲	▲	▲	▲	▲	▲	▲	▲	▲	▲	▲	▲	▲	▲	▲	▲	▲	▲
Belgium	535	(2.4)	▽	●	●	●	●	●	●		●	●	●	▲	▲	▲	▲	▲	▲	▲	▲	▲	▲	▲	▲	▲	▲	▲	▲	▲	▲	▲	▲	▲	▲	▲	▲	▲	▲	▲	▲	▲
New Zealand	526	(2.4)	▽	▽	▽	●	●	▽	●	●		●	●	●	●	●	▲	▲	▲	▲	▲	▲	▲	▲	▲	▲	▲	▲	▲	▲	▲	▲	▲	▲	▲	▲	▲	▲	▲	▲	▲	▲
Australia	525	(2.3)	▽	▽	▽	●	▽	▽	●	●	●		●	●	●	●	▲	▲	▲	▲	▲	▲	▲	▲	▲	▲	▲	▲	▲	▲	▲	▲	▲	▲	▲	▲	▲	▲	▲	▲	▲	▲
Switzerland	523	(3.7)	▽	▽	▽	●	▽	▽	●	●	●	●		●	●	●	▲	●	●	▲	▲	▲	▲	▲	▲	▲	▲	▲	▲	▲	▲	▲	▲	▲	▲	▲	▲	▲	▲	▲	▲	▲
France	520	(2.6)	▽	▽	▽	▽	▽	▽	▽	▽	●	●	●		●	●	▲	●	●	▲	▲	▲	▲	▲	▲	▲	▲	▲	▲	▲	▲	▲	▲	▲	▲	▲	▲	▲	▲	▲	▲	▲
Macao-China	519	(3.5)	▽	▽	▽	▽	▽	▽	●	▽	●	●	●	●		●	●	●	●	●	●	▲	▲	▲	▲	▲	▲	▲	▲	▲	▲	▲	▲	▲	▲	▲	▲	▲	▲	▲	▲	▲
Czech Republic	515	(3.5)	▽	▽	▽	▽	▽	▽	▽	▽	●	●	●	●	●		●	●	●	●	●	●	▲	▲	▲	▲	▲	▲	▲	▲	▲	▲	▲	▲	▲	▲	▲	▲	▲	▲	▲	▲
Iceland	509	(1.4)	▽	▽	▽	▽	▽	▽	▽	▽	▽	▽	▽	▽	●	●		●	●	●	●	●	▲	▲	▲	▲	▲	▲	▲	▲	▲	▲	▲	▲	▲	▲	▲	▲	▲	▲	▲	▲
Denmark	509	(3.0)	▽	▽	▽	▽	▽	▽	▽	▽	▽	▽	●	●	●	●	●		●	●	●	●	▲	▲	▲	▲	▲	▲	▲	▲	▲	▲	▲	▲	▲	▲	▲	▲	▲	▲	▲	▲
Germany	507	(3.7)	▽	▽	▽	▽	▽	▽	▽	▽	▽	▽	●	●	●	●	●	●		●	●	●	●	●	▲	▲	▲	▲	▲	▲	▲	▲	▲	▲	▲	▲	▲	▲	▲	▲	▲	▲
Ireland	506	(2.4)	▽	▽	▽	▽	▽	▽	▽	▽	▽	▽	▽	▽	●	●	●	●	●		●	●	●	●	▲	▲	▲	▲	▲	▲	▲	▲	▲	▲	▲	▲	▲	▲	▲	▲	▲	▲
Sweden	505	(2.9)	▽	▽	▽	▽	▽	▽	▽	▽	▽	▽	▽	▽	●	●	●	●	●	●		●	●	●	▲	▲	▲	▲	▲	▲	▲	▲	▲	▲	▲	▲	▲	▲	▲	▲	▲	▲
Austria	500	(3.6)	▽	▽	▽	▽	▽	▽	▽	▽	▽	▽	▽	▽	▽	●	●	●	●	●	●		●	●	●	●	▲	●	▲	▲	▲	▲	▲	▲	▲	▲	▲	▲	▲	▲	▲	▲
Hungary	495	(3.1)	▽	▽	▽	▽	▽	▽	▽	▽	▽	▽	▽	▽	▽	▽	▽	▽	●	●	●	●		●	●	●	●	●	●	▲	●	▲	▲	▲	▲	▲	▲	▲	▲	▲	▲	▲
Slovak Republic	494	(3.5)	▽	▽	▽	▽	▽	▽	▽	▽	▽	▽	▽	▽	▽	▽	▽	▽	●	●	●	●	●		●	●	●	●	●	●	●	▲	▲	▲	▲	▲	▲	▲	▲	▲	▲	▲
Norway	488	(2.6)	▽	▽	▽	▽	▽	▽	▽	▽	▽	▽	▽	▽	▽	▽	▽	▽	▽	▽	▽	●	●	●		●	●	●	●	●	●	▲	▲	▲	▲	▲	▲	▲	▲	▲	▲	▲
Latvia	487	(4.4)	▽	▽	▽	▽	▽	▽	▽	▽	▽	▽	▽	▽	▽	▽	▽	▽	▽	▽	▽	●	●	●	●		●	●	●	●	●	▲	▲	▲	▲	▲	▲	▲	▲	▲	▲	▲
Luxembourg	487	(1.2)	▽	▽	▽	▽	▽	▽	▽	▽	▽	▽	▽	▽	▽	▽	▽	▽	▽	▽	▽	▽	●	●	●	●		●	●	●	●	▲	▲	▲	▲	▲	▲	▲	▲	▲	▲	▲
United States	486	(3.0)	▽	▽	▽	▽	▽	▽	▽	▽	▽	▽	▽	▽	▽	▽	▽	▽	▽	▽	▽	●	●	●	●	●	●		●	●	●	▲	▲	▲	▲	▲	▲	▲	▲	▲	▲	▲
Poland	484	(2.7)	▽	▽	▽	▽	▽	▽	▽	▽	▽	▽	▽	▽	▽	▽	▽	▽	▽	▽	▽	▽	●	●	●	●	●	●		●	●	▲	▲	▲	▲	▲	▲	▲	▲	▲	▲	▲
Spain	481	(2.8)	▽	▽	▽	▽	▽	▽	▽	▽	▽	▽	▽	▽	▽	▽	▽	▽	▽	▽	▽	▽	▽	●	●	●	●	●	●		●	●	▲	▲	▲	▲	▲	▲	▲	▲	▲	▲
Russian Fed.	477	(4.6)	▽	▽	▽	▽	▽	▽	▽	▽	▽	▽	▽	▽	▽	▽	▽	▽	▽	▽	▽	▽	●	●	●	●	●	●	●	●		●	▲	▲	▲	▲	▲	▲	▲	▲	▲	▲
Portugal	468	(4.0)	▽	▽	▽	▽	▽	▽	▽	▽	▽	▽	▽	▽	▽	▽	▽	▽	▽	▽	▽	▽	▽	▽	▽	▽	▽	▽	▽	●	●		●	▲	▲	▲	▲	▲	▲	▲	▲	▲
Italy	452	(3.2)	▽	▽	▽	▽	▽	▽	▽	▽	▽	▽	▽	▽	▽	▽	▽	▽	▽	▽	▽	▽	▽	▽	▽	▽	▽	▽	▽	▽	▽	●		●	▲	▲	▲	▲	▲	▲	▲	▲
Greece	436	(4.3)	▽	▽	▽	▽	▽	▽	▽	▽	▽	▽	▽	▽	▽	▽	▽	▽	▽	▽	▽	▽	▽	▽	▽	▽	▽	▽	▽	▽	▽	▽	●		●	●	▲	▲	▲	▲	▲	▲
Turkey	423	(7.6)	▽	▽	▽	▽	▽	▽	▽	▽	▽	▽	▽	▽	▽	▽	▽	▽	▽	▽	▽	▽	▽	▽	▽	▽	▽	▽	▽	▽	▽	▽	▽	●		●	●	●	▲	▲	▲	▲
Serbia	419	(4.0)	▽	▽	▽	▽	▽	▽	▽	▽	▽	▽	▽	▽	▽	▽	▽	▽	▽	▽	▽	▽	▽	▽	▽	▽	▽	▽	▽	▽	▽	▽	▽	●	●		●	●	▲	▲	▲	▲
Uruguay	417	(3.6)	▽	▽	▽	▽	▽	▽	▽	▽	▽	▽	▽	▽	▽	▽	▽	▽	▽	▽	▽	▽	▽	▽	▽	▽	▽	▽	▽	▽	▽	▽	▽	▽	●	●		●	▲	▲	▲	▲
Thailand	405	(3.4)	▽	▽	▽	▽	▽	▽	▽	▽	▽	▽	▽	▽	▽	▽	▽	▽	▽	▽	▽	▽	▽	▽	▽	▽	▽	▽	▽	▽	▽	▽	▽	▽	●	●	●		▲	▲	▲	▲
Mexico	364	(4.1)	▽	▽	▽	▽	▽	▽	▽	▽	▽	▽	▽	▽	▽	▽	▽	▽	▽	▽	▽	▽	▽	▽	▽	▽	▽	▽	▽	▽	▽	▽	▽	▽	▽	▽	▽	▽		▲	▲	▲
Tunisia	337	(2.8)	▽	▽	▽	▽	▽	▽	▽	▽	▽	▽	▽	▽	▽	▽	▽	▽	▽	▽	▽	▽	▽	▽	▽	▽	▽	▽	▽	▽	▽	▽	▽	▽	▽	▽	▽	▽	▽		●	●
Indonesia	334	(4.6)	▽	▽	▽	▽	▽	▽	▽	▽	▽	▽	▽	▽	▽	▽	▽	▽	▽	▽	▽	▽	▽	▽	▽	▽	▽	▽	▽	▽	▽	▽	▽	▽	▽	▽	▽	▽	▽	●		●
Brazil	333	(6.0)	▽	▽	▽	▽	▽	▽	▽	▽	▽	▽	▽	▽	▽	▽	▽	▽	▽	▽	▽	▽	▽	▽	▽	▽	▽	▽	▽	▽	▽	▽	▽	▽	▽	▽	▽	▽	▽	●	●	

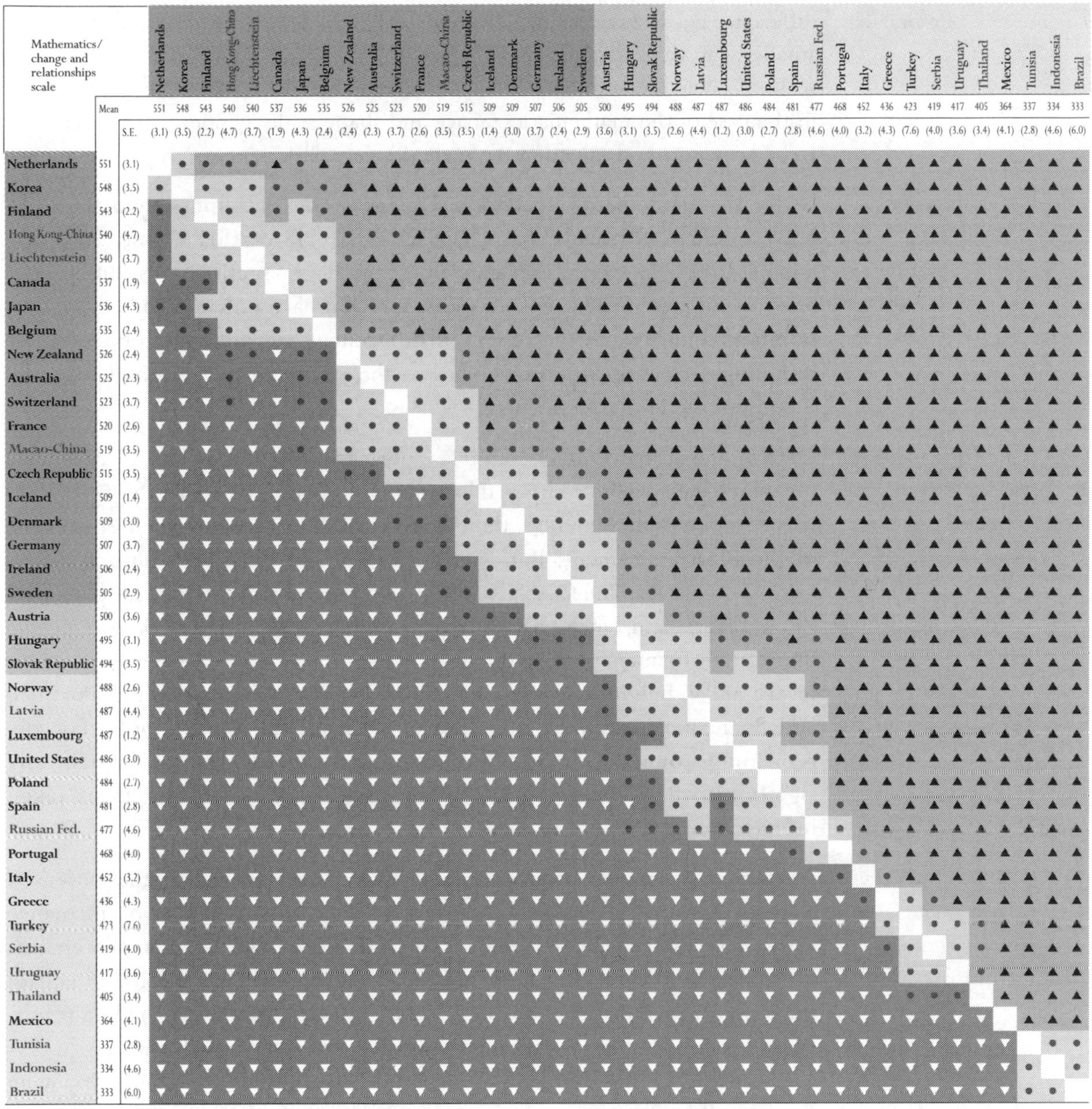

Range of rank*

		Netherlands	Korea	Finland	Hong Kong-China	Liechtenstein	Canada	Japan	Belgium	New Zealand	Australia	Switzerland	France	Macao-China	Czech Republic	Iceland	Denmark	Germany	Ireland	Sweden	Austria	Hungary	Slovak Republic	Norway	Latvia	Luxembourg	United States	Poland	Spain	Russian Fed.	Portugal	Italy	Greece	Turkey	Serbia	Uruguay	Thailand	Mexico	Tunisia	Indonesia	Brazil
OECD countries	Upper rank	1	1	2			4	3	4	7	7	7	8		10	11	11	11	12	12	14	17	17	19		20	20	20	21		25	26	27	27				29			
	Lower rank	2	3	4			6	7	6	9	10	11	11		14	15	16	17	17	17	19	20	21	23		23	24	24	24		25	26	28	28				29			
All countries	Upper rank	1	1	2	2	2	4	3	5	8	9	9	10	10	12	14	14	14	15	15	17	20	20	22	21	23	23	23	25	26	29	31	32	32	33	33	35	37	38	38	38
	Lower rank	3	4	6	8	8	8	9	8	12	12	13	14	14	17	18	19	20	20	20	22	23	24	27	28	27	28	29	29	30	30	31	33	35	35	35	36	37	40	40	40

* Because data are based on samples, it is not possible to report exact rank order positions for countries. However, it is possible to report the range of rank order positions within which the country mean lies with 95 per cent likelihood.

Instructions:

Read across the row for a country to compare performance with the countries listed along the top of the chart. The symbols indicate whether the average performance of the country in the row is lower than that of the comparison country, higher than that of the comparison country, or if there is no statistically significant difference between the average achievement of the two countries.

Without the Bonferroni adjustment:
- Mean performance statistically significantly higher than in comparison country
- No statistically significant difference from comparison country
- Mean performance statistically significantly lower than in comparison country

With the Bonferroni adjustment:
- ▲ Mean performance statistically significantly higher than in comparison country
- ● No statistically significant difference from comparison country
- ▽ Mean performance statistically significantly lower than in comparison country

- Statistically significantly above the OECD average
- Not statistically significantly different from the OECD average
- Statistically significantly below the OECD average

Source: OECD PISA 2003 database.

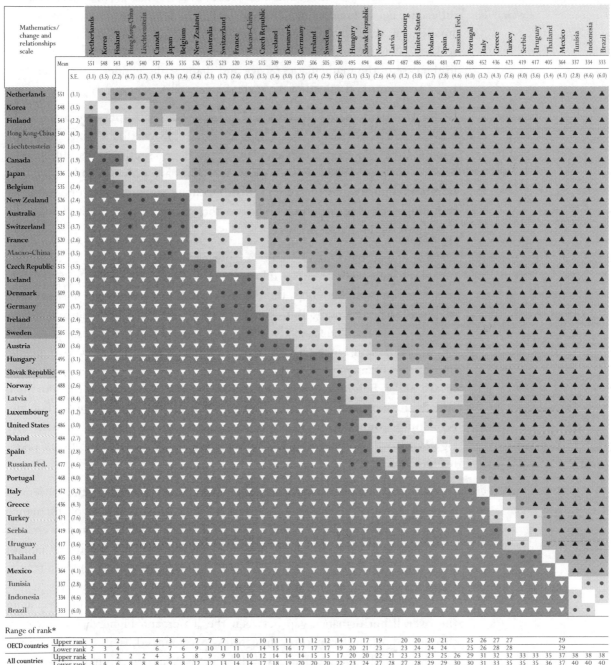

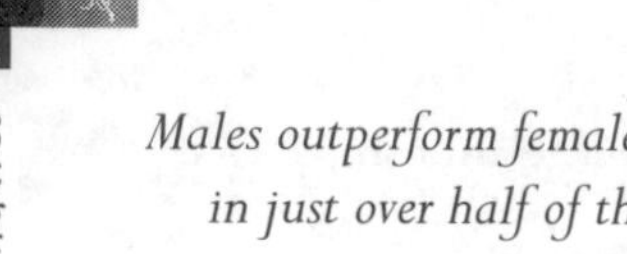

Males outperform females in just over half of the countries.

Males outperform females in 17 OECD countries and four partner countries, but generally only by small amounts (Table 2.2c).[15] The average performance difference between males and females is only 10 score points, that is, a somewhat smaller gap than the difference found for the mathematics/space and shape scale. Only in Iceland do females perform higher than males. Nevertheless, as in the case of the mathematics/space and shape scale, gender differences tend to be larger at the top end of the scale (Table 2.2b).

Results on this scale can also be compared, with caution, to PISA 2000…

As for the mathematics/space and shape scale, it is also possible to estimate how much performance has changed since PISA 2000 (Table 2.2c and Table 2.2d). However, as explained in the preceding section, these differences need to be interpreted with caution since data are only available from two points in time, while the observed differences are not only influenced by sampling error but are also subject to the uncertainty associated with the linking of the two assessments.

…showing that performance in change and relationships tasks rose overall, but unevenly…

On average across OECD countries, performance among the 25 countries for which data can be compared has increased from 488 score points in 2000 to 499 score points in 2003, the biggest overall change observed in any area of the PISA assessment. But again, changes have been very uneven across OECD countries. The Czech Republic and Poland and the partner countries Brazil, Latvia and Liechtenstein have seen increases of 31 to 70 score points in mean performance – equivalent to between half and one PISA proficiency level – and in Belgium, Canada, Finland, Germany, Hungary, Korea, Portugal and Spain increases were still between 13 and 22 score points. For the remaining countries, the differences cannot be considered statistically significant when both measurement and assessment linkage errors are taken into account.[16]

..again driven in some countries by improvements among lower ability students…

As with the mathematics/space and shape scale, some of the observed changes have not necessarily involved an even rise or fall of performance across the ability range (Figures 2.9c and 2.9d). The large improvements in Poland have been driven by improved performance at the lower end of the performance distribution (*i.e.,* 5th, 10th and 25th percentiles). As a result, Poland succeeded in significantly raising the average performance of 15-year-olds in the mathematics/change and relationships scale and narrowing the overall performance gap between the lower and higher achievers over this period. A similar picture, though less pronounced, is also evident in the Czech Republic and Hungary as well as in the partner countries Latvia and Liechtenstein. Also Greece and Switzerland as well as in the partner country the Russian Federation have seen notable improvements at the lower end of the distribution, but these were not sufficient to lead to a statistically significant improvement in mean performance.

…but for others by higher ability students.

In contrast, in Canada, Finland, Germany, Italy, Korea, Portugal and Sweden, improvements in performance have mainly been driven by improved performance in the top part of the performance distribution, as shown in the increase in scores at the 75th, 90th and 95th percentiles, while less has changed at

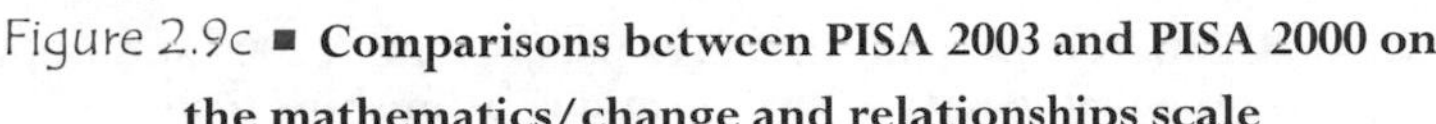

Figure 2.9c ■ **Comparisons between PISA 2003 and PISA 2000 on the mathematics/change and relationships scale**

Significance levels	2003 higher than 2000	2003 lower than 2000	No statistically significant difference
90 % confidence level	+	-	o
95 % confidence level	++	--	
99 % confidence level	+++	---	

	Differences observed in the mean and percentiles						
	5th	10th	25th	Mean	75th	90th	95th
OECD countries							
Australia	o	o	o	o	o	o	o
Austria	o	o	o	o	o	o	o
Belgium	+++	+	+	+++	+++	+++	+
Canada	++	++	++	+++	+++	+++	+++
Czech Republic	+++	+++	+++	+++	+++	++	+
Denmark	++	+	o	o	o	o	o
Finland	o	+	o	++	+++	+++	+++
France	o	o	o	o	o	o	o
Germany	++	+	++	+++	+++	+++	+++
Greece	+++	++	o	o	o	-	---
Hungary	+++	+++	+++	++	o	o	o
Iceland	o	o	o	o	o	o	o
Ireland	o	o	o	o	o	+	o
Italy	o	o	o	o	o	++	+++
Japan	o	o	o	o	o	o	o
Korea	o	o	o	+++	+++	+++	+++
Mexico	o	o	o	o	o	o	o
New Zealand	o	o	o	o	o	o	o
Norway	o	o	o	o	o	o	o
Poland	+++	+++	+++	+++	o	o	o
Portugal	+	+	+	+++	+++	++	+++
Spain	+	+	++	++	+	o	o
Sweden	o	o	o	o	o	++	++
Switzerland	+++	+++	++	+	o	o	o
United States	o	o	o	o	o	o	o
OECD total	o	o	o	o	o	o	o
OECD average	+++	+++	+	++	++	++	++
Partner countries							
Brazil	+++	+++	+++	+++	+++	+++	+++
Hong Kong-China	o	-	o	o	o	o	o
Indonesia	---	---	---	o	o	+++	+++
Latvia	+++	+++	+++	+++	+	o	o
Liechtenstein	++	++	+++	+++	o	o	o
Russian Federation	+++	+++	++	o	o	-	-
Thailand	---	---	---	--	o	+++	+++

Source: OECD PISA 2003 and PISA 2000 databases, Tables 2.2c and 2.2d.

the lower end of the distribution. In some of these countries, disparities among students have grown. In the 2000 assessment, for example, Korea showed the smallest variation in student performance in mathematics. By contrast, in the 2003 assessment variation is now at the OECD average level (Figure 2.9c, Figure 2.9d, Table 2.2c and Table 2.2d).

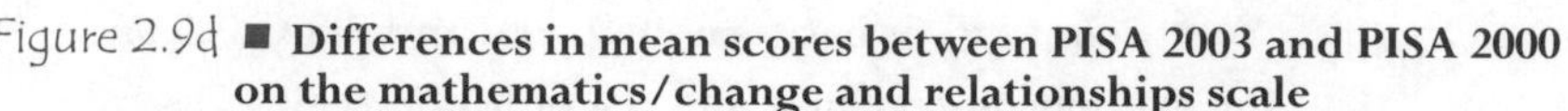

Figure 2.9d ■ **Differences in mean scores between PISA 2003 and PISA 2000 on the mathematics/change and relationships scale**

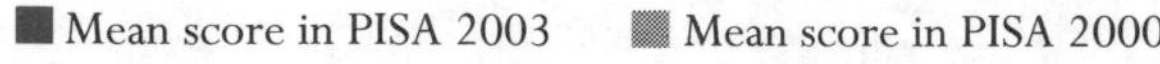

Only countries with valid data for both PISA 2003 and PISA 2000

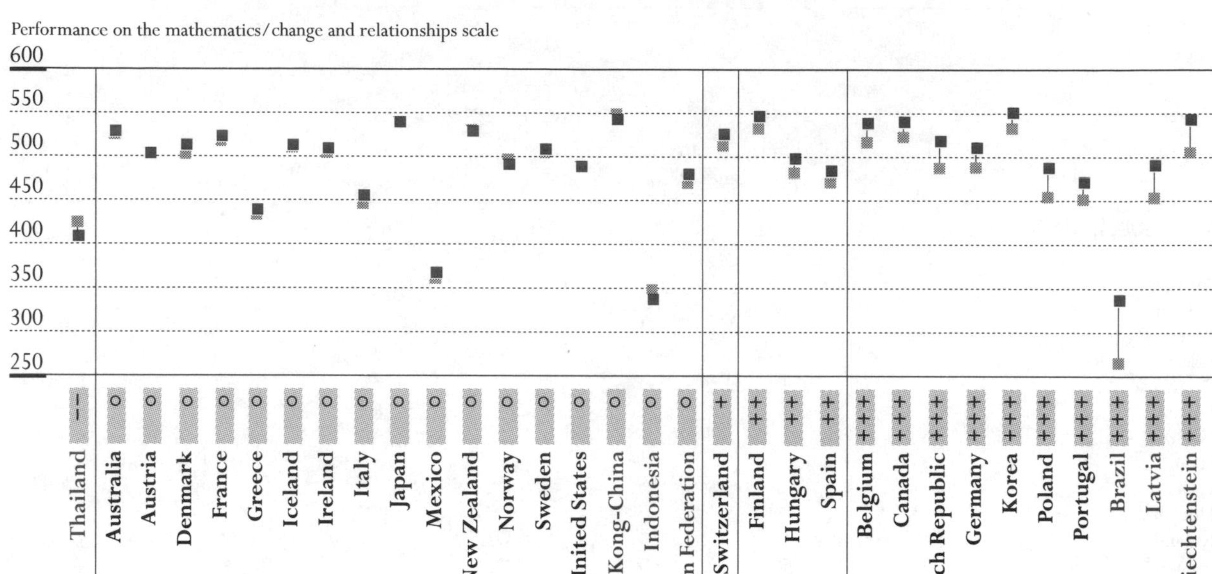

Significance levels	2003 higher than 2000	2003 lower than 2000	No statistically significant difference
90 % confidence level	+	–	o
95 % confidence level	++	– –	
99 % confidence level	+++	– – –	

Countries are ranked in ascending order of the difference between PISA 2003 and PISA 2000 performances.
Source: OECD PISA 2003 and PISA 2000 databases, Tables 2.2c and 2.2d.

Student performance on the mathematics/quantity scale

A quarter of the mathematical tasks given to students in PISA related to numeric phenomena and quantitative relationships and patterns. Figures 2.10a-b show tasks at Levels 1-4 in this category:

Four per cent of students in the OECD area can perform the hardest quantity tasks…

The precise competencies required to reach each level are explained in Figure 2.11. Slightly fewer students than for the previous two scales, at 4 per cent in the combined OECD area, can perform at Level 6 tasks. Slightly more, at 74 per cent, can perform at Level 2 (Table 2.3a). However, in Greece, Italy, Mexico, Portugal, Turkey and the United States, as well as in the partner countries Brazil, Indonesia, the Russian Federation, Serbia, Thailand, Tunisia and Uruguay, a quarter or more of students fail to reach this Level 2 threshold (Figure 2.12a).

Figure 2.10a ■ **A sample of mathematics items used in PISA for the quantity scale: Unit EXCHANGE RATE**

Level	Score
6	
	668.7
5	
	606.6
4	
	544.4
3	
	482.4
2	
	420.4
1	
	358.3
Below 1	

EXCHANGE RATE

Mei-Ling from Singapore was preparing to go to South Africa for 3 months as an exchange student. She needed to change some Singapore dollars (SGD) into South African rand (ZAR).

QUESTION 11

During these 3 months the exchange rate had changed from 4.2 to 4.0 ZAR per SGD.

Was it in Mei-Ling's favour that the exchange rate now was 4.0 ZAR instead of 4.2 ZAR, when she changed her South African rand back to Singapore dollars? Give an explanation to support your answer.

Score 1 (586)

Answers which indicate 'Yes', with adequate explanation.

This open-constructed response item is situated in a public context and has a difficulty of 586 score points. As far as the mathematics content is concerned students need to apply procedural knowledge involving number operations: multiplication and division, which along with the quantitative context, places the item in the quantity area. The competencies needed to solve the problem are not trivial: students need to reflect on the concept of exchange rate and its consequences in this particular situation. The mathematisation required is of a rather high level although all the required information is explicitly presented: not only is the identification of the relevant mathematics somewhat complex, but also the reduction to a problem within the mathematical world places significant demands on the student. The competency needed to solve this problem can be described as using flexible reasoning and reflection. The thinking and reasoning competency, the argumentation competency in combination with the problem-solving competency all include an element of reflectiveness on the part of the student about the process needed to solve the problem. Explaining the results requires some communication skills as well. Therefore the item is classified as belonging to the reflection cluster. The combination of familiar context, complex situation, non-routine problem, the need for reasoning and insight and a communication demand places the item in Level 4.

QUESTION 10

On returning to Singapore after 3 months, Mei-Ling had 3 900 ZAR left. She changed this back to Singapore dollars, noting that the exchange rate had changed to:
1 SGD = 4.0 ZAR

How much money in Singapore dollars did Mei-Ling get?

Score 1 (439)

Answers which indicate 975 SGD (unit not required).

This short-constructed response item is situated in a public context. It has a difficulty of 439 score points. The mathematics content is restricted to a basic operation: division. This places the item in the quantity area, and more specifically: operations with numbers. Regarding the competencies required, a limited form of mathematisation is needed: understanding a simple text, in which all the required information is explicitly presented. But students also need to recognise that division is the right procedure to go with, which makes it less trivial than Exchange Rate Question 1, and shows the most basic form of the thinking and reasoning competency. Thus the competency needed to solve this problem can be described as performance of a routine procedure and/or application of a standard algorithm. Therefore the item is classified as belonging the reproduction competency cluster. The combination of familiar context, clearly defined question, and rather routine procedure that includes some decision-making places the item in Level 2.

QUESTION 9

Mei-Ling found out that the exchange rate between Singapore dollars and South African rand was:
1 SGD = 4.2 ZAR

Mei-Ling changed 3000 Singapore dollars into South African rand at this exchange rate.

How much money in South African rand did Mei-Ling get?

Score 1 (406)

Answers which indicate 12 600 ZAR (unit not required).

This short constructed response item is situated in a public context. It has a difficulty of 406 score points. Experience in using exchange rates may not be common to all students, but the concept can be seen as belonging to skills and knowledge for intelligent citizenship. The mathematics content is restricted to one of the four basic operations: multiplication. This places the item in the quantity area, and more specifically: operations with numbers. As far as the competencies are concerned, a very limited form of mathematisation is needed: understanding a simple text, and linking the given information to the required calculation. All the required information is explicitly presented. Thus the competency needed to solve this problem can be described as performance of a routine procedure and/or application of a standard algorithm. Therefore the item is classified as belonging the reproduction competency cluster. The combination of familiar context, clearly defined question, and routine procedure places the item in Level 1.

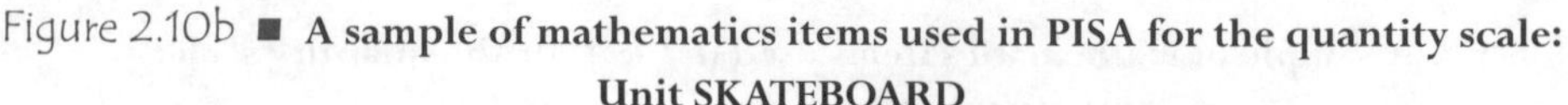

Figure 2.10b ■ **A sample of mathematics items used in PISA for the quantity scale: Unit SKATEBOARD**

SKATEBOARD

Eric is a great skateboard fan. He visits a shop named SKATERS to check some prices.

At this shop you can buy a complete board. Or you can buy a deck, a set of 4 wheels, a set of 2 trucks and a set of hardware, and assemble your own board.

The prices for the shop's products are:

Product	***Price in zeds***	
Complete skateboard	82 or 84	
Deck	40, 60 or 65	
One set of 4 wheels	14 or 36	
One set of 2 trucks	16	
One set of hardware (bearings, rubber pads, bolts and nuts)	10 or 20	

SKATEBOARD

QUESTION 13

The shop offers three different decks, two different sets of wheels and two different sets of hardware. There is only one choice for a set of trucks.

How many different skateboards can Eric construct?

A. 6
B. 8
C. 10
D. 12

Score 1 (570)

The correct answer is option D.

This multiple-choice item is situated in the personal context and has a difficulty of 570 score points (Level 4). All the required information in this item is explicitly presented and the mathematics involves the basic routine computation: 3 x 2 x 2 x 1. However, if students do not have experience with such combinatorial calculations, their strategy might involve a systematic listing of the possible combinations. There are well-known algorithms for this (such as a tree diagram). The strategy to find the number of combinations can be considered as common, and routine. It involves following and justifying standard quantitative processes, including computational processes, statements and results. Therefore, the item can be classified as belonging to the reproduction competency cluster. The computation involved fits in the quantity content area. In order to be successful the students have to accurately apply an algorithm, after correctly interpreting text in combination with a table. This adds to the complexity of the situation.

QUESTION 14

Eric has 120 zeds to spend and wants to buy the most expensive skateboard he can afford.

How much money can Eric afford to spend on each of the 4 parts? Put your answer in the table below.

Part	Amount (zeds)
Deck	
Wheels	
Trucks	
Hardware	

Score 1 (554)

Answers which indicate 65 zeds on a deck, 14 on wheels, 16 on trucks and 20 on hardware.

This short constructed response item is also in the personal context. and illustrates the lower part of Level 4, (554 score points) The item fits in the quantity content area as the students are asked to compute what is the most expensive skateboard you can buy for 120 zeds. The task, however, is not straightforward as there is no standard procedure or routine algorithm available. As far as the competencies needed, the problem solving skill here involves a more independent approach and students may use different strategies in order to find the solution, including trial and error. The setting of this problem can be regarded as familiar. Students have to look at the table with prices, make combinations and do some computation. This places the item within the connections competency cluster. A strategy that will work with this problem is to first use all the higher values, and then adjust the answer, working the way down until the desired maximum of 120 zeds is reached. Thus, students need some reasoning skills in a familiar context, they have to connect the question with the data given in the table, apply a non-standard strategy and carry out routine calculations.

QUESTION 12

Eric wants to assemble his own skateboard. What is the minimum price and the maximum price in this shop for self-assembled skateboards?

(a) Minimum price: ....zeds.
(b) Maximum price: ....zeds.

Score 2 (496)

Answers which indicate both the minimum (80) and the maximum (137) prices.

Score 1 (464)

Answers which indicate only the minimum (80) or the maximum (137) prices.

This short constructed response item is in a personal context because skateboards tend to be part of the youth culture. The students are asked to find a minimum and maximum price for the construction of a skateboard. The partial credit response has a difficulty of 464 score points (Level 2) - this is when the students answer the question by giving either the minimum or the maximum, but not both. To solve the problem the students have to find a strategy, which is fairly simple because the strategy that seems trivial actually works: the minimum cost is based on the lower numbers and the maximum, on the larger numbers. The remaining mathematics content is execution of a basic operation. The addition: 40 + 14 + 16 + 10 = 80, gives the minimum, while the maximum is found by adding the larger numbers: 65 + 36 + 16 + 20 = 137. The strategy, therefore, is the reproduction of practised knowledge in combination with the performance of the routine addition procedure - this item belongs to the reproduction competency cluster and the quantity content area. The full credit response, when students give both the minimum and the maximum, has a difficulty of 496 score points and illustrates Level 3.

Level: 6 — 668.7 — 5 — 606.6 — 4 — 544.4 — 3 — 482.4 — 2 — 420.4 — 1 — 358.3 — Below 1

Figure 2.11 ■ **Summary descriptions of six levels of proficiency on the mathematics/quantity scale**

Level	**General competencies students should have at each level**	**Specific tasks students should be able to do**
6	*4% of all students across the OECD area can perform tasks at Level 6 on the quantity scale*	
	Conceptualise and work with models of complex mathematical processes and relationships; work with formal and symbolic expressions; use advanced reasoning skills to devise strategies for solving problems and to link multiple contexts; use sequential calculation processes; formulate conclusions, arguments and precise explanations	– Conceptualise complex mathematical processes such as exponential growth, weighted average, as well as number properties and numeric relationships – Interpret and understand complex information, and link multiple complex information sources – Use advanced reasoning concerning proportions, geometric representations of quantities, combinatorics and integer number relationships – Interpret and understand formal mathematical expressions of relationships among numbers, including in a scientific context – Perform sequential calculations in a complex and unfamiliar context, including working with large numbers – Formulate conclusions, arguments and precise explanations – Devise a strategy (develop heuristics) for working with complex mathematical processes
5	*13% of all students across the OECD area can perform tasks at least at Level 5 on the quantity scale*	
	Work effectively with models of more complex situations to solve problems; use well-developed reasoning skills, insight and interpretation with different representations; carry out sequential processes; communicate reasoning and argument	– Interpret complex information about real-world situations (including graphs, drawings and complex tables) – Link different information sources (such as graphs, tabular data and related text) – Extract relevant data from a description of a complex situation and perform calculations – Use problem-solving skills (*e.g.*, interpretation, devising a strategy, reasoning, systematic counting) in real-world contexts that involve substantial mathematisation – Communicate reasoning and argument – Make an estimation using daily life knowledge – Calculate relative and/or absolute change
4	*31% of all students across the OECD area can perform tasks at least at Level 4 on the quantity scale*	
	Work effectively with simple models of complex situations; use reasoning skills in a variety of contexts, interpret different representations of the same situation; analyse and apply quantitative relationships; use a variety of calculation skills to solve problems	– Accurately apply a given numeric algorithm involving a number of steps – Interpret complex text descriptions of a sequential process – Relate text-based information to a graphic representation – Perform calculations involving proportional reasoning, divisibility or percentages in simple models of complex situations – Perform systematic listing and counting of combinatorial outcomes – Identify and use information from multiple sources – Analyse and apply a simple system – Interpret complex text to produce a simple mathematical model

Level	General competencies students should have at each level	Specific tasks students should be able to do
3	*53% of all students across the OECD area can perform tasks at least at Level 3 on the quantity scale*	
	Use simple problem-solving strategies including reasoning in familiar contexts; interpret tables to locate information; carry out explicitly described calculations including sequential processes	– Interpret a text description of a sequential calculation process, and correctly implement the process – Use basic problem-solving processes (devise a simple strategy, look for relationships, understand and work with given constraints, use trial and error, simple reasoning) – Perform calculations including working with large numbers, calculations with speed and time, conversion of units (*e.g.,* from annual rate to daily rate) – Interpret tabular information, locate relevant data from a table – Conceptualise relationships involving circular motion and time – Interpret text and diagrams describing a simple pattern
2	*74% of all students across the OECD area can perform tasks at least at Level 2 on the quantity scale*	
	Interpret simple tables to identify and extract relevant information; carry out basic arithmetic calculations; interpret and work with simple quantitative relationships	– Interpret a simple quantitative model (*e.g.,* a proportional relationship) and apply it using basic arithmetic calculations – Interpret simple tabular data, link textual information to related tabular data – Identify the simple calculation required to solve a straight-forward problem – Perform simple calculations involving the basic arithmetic operations, as well as ordering numbers
1	*88% of all students across the OECD area can perform tasks at least at Level 1 on the quantity scale*	
	Solve problems of the most basic type in which all relevant information is explicitly presented, the situation is straight forward and very limited in scope, the required computational activity is obvious and the mathematical task is basic, such as a simple arithmetic operation	– Interpret a simple, explicit mathematical relationship, and apply it directly using a calculation – Read and interpret a simple table of numbers, total the columns and compare the results

Figure 2.12b gives a summary of overall student performance in different countries on the quantity scale, in terms of mean student scores as well as the range of rank order positions within which the country mean lies with 95 per cent probability. Finland shows the highest mean score among OECD countries on the mathematics/quantity scale but the partner country Hong Kong-China performs at a similarly high level, within the range of the first and third position.

...in which Finland and Hong Kong-China show the highest performance.

Figure 2.12a ■ **Percentage of students at each level of proficiency on the mathematics/quantity scale**

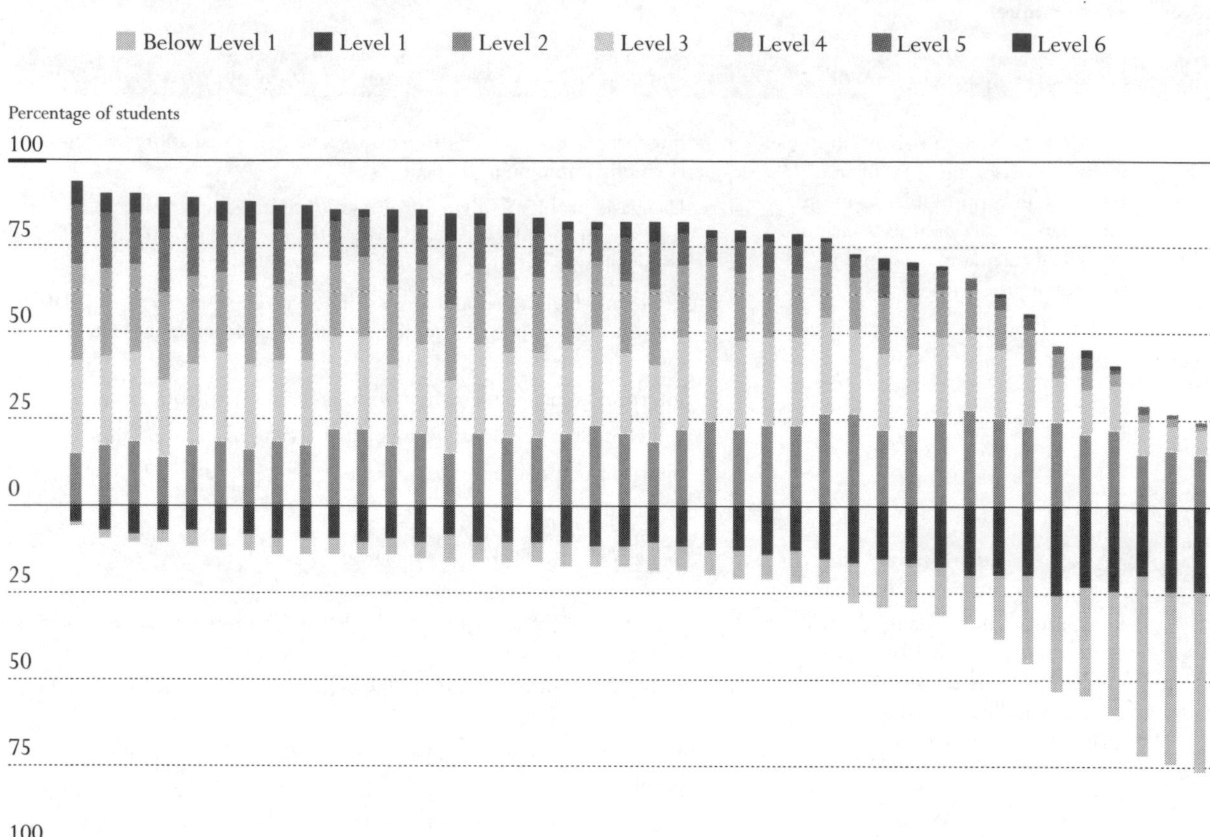

Countries are ranked in descending order of percentage of 15-year-olds in Levels 2, 3, 4, 5 and 6.
Source: OECD PISA 2003 database, Table 2.3a.

In these tasks males' advantage is particularly small.

Consistent with what was found in the other scales, males show an advantage also in the quantity scale, but gender differences here tend to be even smaller than for the mathematics/space and shape and change and relationships scales discussed above. The distributions of males and females by level are relatively similar, with a few more males than females at the top end of the scale (Table 2.3b). Sixteen countries show differences in favour of males.[17] Again, Iceland is the only country where females perform statistically above males (Table 2.3c).

It is not possible to compare student performance in 2000 and 2003 on this scale, since the PISA 2000 assessment did not include this content in its assessment.

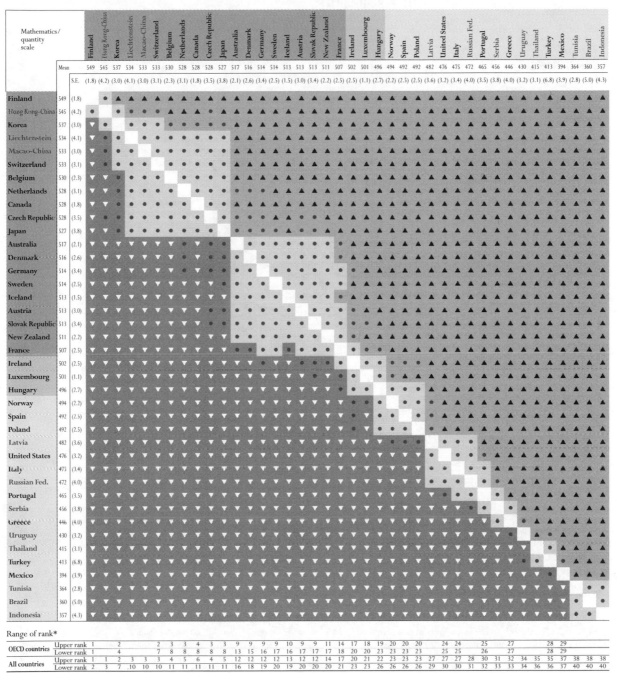

Figure 2.12b ■ Multiple comparisons of mean performance on the mathematics/quantity scale

Mathematics/ quantity scale	Mean	S.E.	Finland	Hong Kong-China	Korea	Liechtenstein	Macao-China	Switzerland	Belgium	Netherlands	Canada	Czech Republic	Japan	Australia	Denmark	Germany	Sweden	Iceland	Austria	Slovak Republic	New Zealand	France	Ireland	Luxembourg	Hungary	Norway	Spain	Poland	Latvia	United States	Italy	Russian Fed.	Portugal	Serbia	Greece	Uruguay	Thailand	Turkey	Mexico	Tunisia	Brazil	Indonesia
	Mean		549	545	537	534	533	533	530	528	528	528	527	517	516	514	514	513	513	513	511	507	502	501	496	494	492	492	482	476	475	472	465	456	446	430	415	413	394	364	360	357
		S.E.	(1.8)	(4.2)	(3.0)	(4.1)	(3.0)	(3.1)	(2.3)	(3.1)	(1.8)	(3.5)	(3.8)	(2.1)	(2.6)	(3.4)	(2.5)	(1.5)	(3.0)	(3.4)	(2.2)	(2.5)	(2.5)	(1.1)	(2.7)	(2.2)	(2.5)	(2.5)	(3.6)	(3.2)	(3.4)	(4.0)	(3.5)	(3.8)	(4.0)	(3.2)	(3.1)	(6.8)	(3.9)	(2.8)	(5.0)	(4.3)
Finland	549	(1.8)		●	▲	▲	▲	▲	▲	▲	▲	▲	▲	▲	▲	▲	▲	▲	▲	▲	▲	▲	▲	▲	▲	▲	▲	▲	▲	▲	▲	▲	▲	▲	▲	▲	▲	▲	▲	▲	▲	▲
Hong Kong-China	545	(4.2)	●		●	●	●	●	▲	▲	▲	●	▲	▲	▲	▲	▲	▲	▲	▲	▲	▲	▲	▲	▲	▲	▲	▲	▲	▲	▲	▲	▲	▲	▲	▲	▲	▲	▲	▲	▲	▲
Korea	537	(3.0)	▼	●		●	●	●	●	●	●	●	●	▲	▲	▲	▲	▲	▲	▲	▲	▲	▲	▲	▲	▲	▲	▲	▲	▲	▲	▲	▲	▲	▲	▲	▲	▲	▲	▲	▲	▲
Liechtenstein	534	(4.1)	▼	●	●		●	●	●	●	●	●	●	▲	▲	▲	▲	▲	▲	▲	▲	▲	▲	▲	▲	▲	▲	▲	▲	▲	▲	▲	▲	▲	▲	▲	▲	▲	▲	▲	▲	▲
Macao-China	533	(3.0)	▼	●	●	●		●	●	●	●	●	●	▲	▲	▲	▲	▲	▲	▲	▲	▲	▲	▲	▲	▲	▲	▲	▲	▲	▲	▲	▲	▲	▲	▲	▲	▲	▲	▲	▲	▲
Switzerland	533	(3.1)	▼	●	●	●	●		●	●	●	●	●	▲	▲	▲	▲	▲	▲	▲	▲	▲	▲	▲	▲	▲	▲	▲	▲	▲	▲	▲	▲	▲	▲	▲	▲	▲	▲	▲	▲	▲
Belgium	530	(2.3)	▼	▼	●	●	●	●		●	●	●	●	▲	▲	▲	▲	▲	▲	▲	▲	▲	▲	▲	▲	▲	▲	▲	▲	▲	▲	▲	▲	▲	▲	▲	▲	▲	▲	▲	▲	▲
Netherlands	528	(3.1)	▼	▼	●	●	●	●	●		●	●	●	●	●	●	▲	▲	▲	▲	▲	▲	▲	▲	▲	▲	▲	▲	▲	▲	▲	▲	▲	▲	▲	▲	▲	▲	▲	▲	▲	▲
Canada	528	(1.8)	▼	▼	●	●	●	●	●	●		●	●	▲	▲	▲	▲	▲	▲	▲	▲	▲	▲	▲	▲	▲	▲	▲	▲	▲	▲	▲	▲	▲	▲	▲	▲	▲	▲	▲	▲	▲
Czech Republic	528	(3.5)	▼	●	●	●	●	●	●	●	●		●	●	●	●	▲	▲	●	●	▲	▲	▲	▲	▲	▲	▲	▲	▲	▲	▲	▲	▲	▲	▲	▲	▲	▲	▲	▲	▲	▲
Japan	527	(3.8)	▼	▼	●	●	●	●	●	●	●	●		●	●	●	●	▲	●	●	▲	▲	▲	▲	▲	▲	▲	▲	▲	▲	▲	▲	▲	▲	▲	▲	▲	▲	▲	▲	▲	▲
Australia	517	(2.1)	▼	▼	▼	▼	▼	▼	▼	●	▼	●	●		●	●	●	●	●	●	●	●	▲	▲	▲	▲	▲	▲	▲	▲	▲	▲	▲	▲	▲	▲	▲	▲	▲	▲	▲	▲
Denmark	516	(2.6)	▼	▼	▼	▼	▼	▼	▼	●	▼	●	●	●		●	●	●	●	●	●	●	▲	▲	▲	▲	▲	▲	▲	▲	▲	▲	▲	▲	▲	▲	▲	▲	▲	▲	▲	▲
Germany	514	(3.4)	▼	▼	▼	▼	▼	▼	▼	●	▼	●	●	●	●		●	●	●	●	●	●	●	▲	▲	▲	▲	▲	▲	▲	▲	▲	▲	▲	▲	▲	▲	▲	▲	▲	▲	▲
Sweden	514	(2.5)	▼	▼	▼	▼	▼	▼	▼	▼	▼	▼	●	●	●	●		●	●	●	●	●	▲	▲	▲	▲	▲	▲	▲	▲	▲	▲	▲	▲	▲	▲	▲	▲	▲	▲	▲	▲
Iceland	513	(1.5)	▼	▼	▼	▼	▼	▼	▼	▼	▼	▼	▼	●	●	●	●		●	●	●	●	▲	▲	▲	▲	▲	▲	▲	▲	▲	▲	▲	▲	▲	▲	▲	▲	▲	▲	▲	▲
Austria	513	(3.0)	▼	▼	▼	▼	▼	▼	▼	▼	▼	●	●	●	●	●	●	●		●	●	●	●	▲	▲	▲	▲	▲	▲	▲	▲	▲	▲	▲	▲	▲	▲	▲	▲	▲	▲	▲
Slovak Republic	513	(3.4)	▼	▼	▼	▼	▼	▼	▼	▼	▼	●	●	●	●	●	●	●	●		●	●	●	●	▲	▲	▲	▲	▲	▲	▲	▲	▲	▲	▲	▲	▲	▲	▲	▲	▲	▲
New Zealand	511	(2.2)	▼	▼	▼	▼	▼	▼	▼	▼	▼	▼	▼	●	●	●	●	●	●	●		●	●	▲	▲	▲	▲	▲	▲	▲	▲	▲	▲	▲	▲	▲	▲	▲	▲	▲	▲	▲
France	507	(2.5)	▼	▼	▼	▼	▼	▼	▼	▼	▼	▼	▼	●	●	●	●	●	●	●	●		●	●	●	▲	▲	▲	▲	▲	▲	▲	▲	▲	▲	▲	▲	▲	▲	▲	▲	▲
Ireland	502	(2.5)	▼	▼	▼	▼	▼	▼	▼	▼	▼	▼	▼	▼	▼	●	▼	▼	●	●	●	●		●	●	●	●	●	▲	▲	▲	▲	▲	▲	▲	▲	▲	▲	▲	▲	▲	▲
Luxembourg	501	(1.1)	▼	▼	▼	▼	▼	▼	▼	▼	▼	▼	▼	▼	▼	▼	▼	▼	▼	●	▼	●	●		●	●	▲	▲	▲	▲	▲	▲	▲	▲	▲	▲	▲	▲	▲	▲	▲	▲
Hungary	496	(2.7)	▼	▼	▼	▼	▼	▼	▼	▼	▼	▼	▼	▼	▼	▼	▼	▼	▼	▼	▼	●	●	●		●	●	●	▲	▲	▲	▲	▲	▲	▲	▲	▲	▲	▲	▲	▲	▲
Norway	494	(2.2)	▼	▼	▼	▼	▼	▼	▼	▼	▼	▼	▼	▼	▼	▼	▼	▼	▼	▼	▼	▼	●	●	●		●	●	●	▲	▲	▲	▲	▲	▲	▲	▲	▲	▲	▲	▲	▲
Spain	492	(2.5)	▼	▼	▼	▼	▼	▼	▼	▼	▼	▼	▼	▼	▼	▼	▼	▼	▼	▼	▼	▼	●	▼	●	●		●	●	▲	▲	▲	▲	▲	▲	▲	▲	▲	▲	▲	▲	▲
Poland	492	(2.5)	▼	▼	▼	▼	▼	▼	▼	▼	▼	▼	▼	▼	▼	▼	▼	▼	▼	▼	▼	▼	●	▼	●	●	●		●	▲	▲	▲	▲	▲	▲	▲	▲	▲	▲	▲	▲	▲
Latvia	482	(3.6)	▼	▼	▼	▼	▼	▼	▼	▼	▼	▼	▼	▼	▼	▼	▼	▼	▼	▼	▼	▼	▼	▼	▼	●	●	●		●	●	●	▲	▲	▲	▲	▲	▲	▲	▲	▲	▲
United States	476	(3.2)	▼	▼	▼	▼	▼	▼	▼	▼	▼	▼	▼	▼	▼	▼	▼	▼	▼	▼	▼	▼	▼	▼	▼	▼	▼	▼	●		●	●	●	▲	▲	▲	▲	▲	▲	▲	▲	▲
Italy	475	(3.4)	▼	▼	▼	▼	▼	▼	▼	▼	▼	▼	▼	▼	▼	▼	▼	▼	▼	▼	▼	▼	▼	▼	▼	▼	▼	▼	●	●		●	●	▲	▲	▲	▲	▲	▲	▲	▲	▲
Russian Fed.	472	(4.0)	▼	▼	▼	▼	▼	▼	▼	▼	▼	▼	▼	▼	▼	▼	▼	▼	▼	▼	▼	▼	▼	▼	▼	▼	▼	▼	●	●	●		●	●	▲	▲	▲	▲	▲	▲	▲	▲
Portugal	465	(3.5)	▼	▼	▼	▼	▼	▼	▼	▼	▼	▼	▼	▼	▼	▼	▼	▼	▼	▼	▼	▼	▼	▼	▼	▼	▼	▼	▼	●	●	●		●	▲	▲	▲	▲	▲	▲	▲	▲
Serbia	456	(3.8)	▼	▼	▼	▼	▼	▼	▼	▼	▼	▼	▼	▼	▼	▼	▼	▼	▼	▼	▼	▼	▼	▼	▼	▼	▼	▼	▼	▼	▼	●	●		●	▲	▲	▲	▲	▲	▲	▲
Greece	446	(4.0)	▼	▼	▼	▼	▼	▼	▼	▼	▼	▼	▼	▼	▼	▼	▼	▼	▼	▼	▼	▼	▼	▼	▼	▼	▼	▼	▼	▼	▼	▼	▼	●		●	▲	▲	▲	▲	▲	▲
Uruguay	430	(3.2)	▼	▼	▼	▼	▼	▼	▼	▼	▼	▼	▼	▼	▼	▼	▼	▼	▼	▼	▼	▼	▼	▼	▼	▼	▼	▼	▼	▼	▼	▼	▼	▼	●		▲	●	▲	▲	▲	▲
Thailand	415	(3.1)	▼	▼	▼	▼	▼	▼	▼	▼	▼	▼	▼	▼	▼	▼	▼	▼	▼	▼	▼	▼	▼	▼	▼	▼	▼	▼	▼	▼	▼	▼	▼	▼	▼	▼		●	▲	▲	▲	▲
Turkey	413	(6.8)	▼	▼	▼	▼	▼	▼	▼	▼	▼	▼	▼	▼	▼	▼	▼	▼	▼	▼	▼	▼	▼	▼	▼	▼	▼	▼	▼	▼	▼	▼	▼	▼	▼	●	●		●	▲	▲	▲
Mexico	394	(3.9)	▼	▼	▼	▼	▼	▼	▼	▼	▼	▼	▼	▼	▼	▼	▼	▼	▼	▼	▼	▼	▼	▼	▼	▼	▼	▼	▼	▼	▼	▼	▼	▼	▼	▼	▼	●		▲	▲	▲
Tunisia	364	(2.8)	▼	▼	▼	▼	▼	▼	▼	▼	▼	▼	▼	▼	▼	▼	▼	▼	▼	▼	▼	▼	▼	▼	▼	▼	▼	▼	▼	▼	▼	▼	▼	▼	▼	▼	▼	▼	▼		●	●
Brazil	360	(5.0)	▼	▼	▼	▼	▼	▼	▼	▼	▼	▼	▼	▼	▼	▼	▼	▼	▼	▼	▼	▼	▼	▼	▼	▼	▼	▼	▼	▼	▼	▼	▼	▼	▼	▼	▼	▼	▼	●		●
Indonesia	357	(4.3)	▼	▼	▼	▼	▼	▼	▼	▼	▼	▼	▼	▼	▼	▼	▼	▼	▼	▼	▼	▼	▼	▼	▼	▼	▼	▼	▼	▼	▼	▼	▼	▼	▼	▼	▼	▼	▼	●	●	

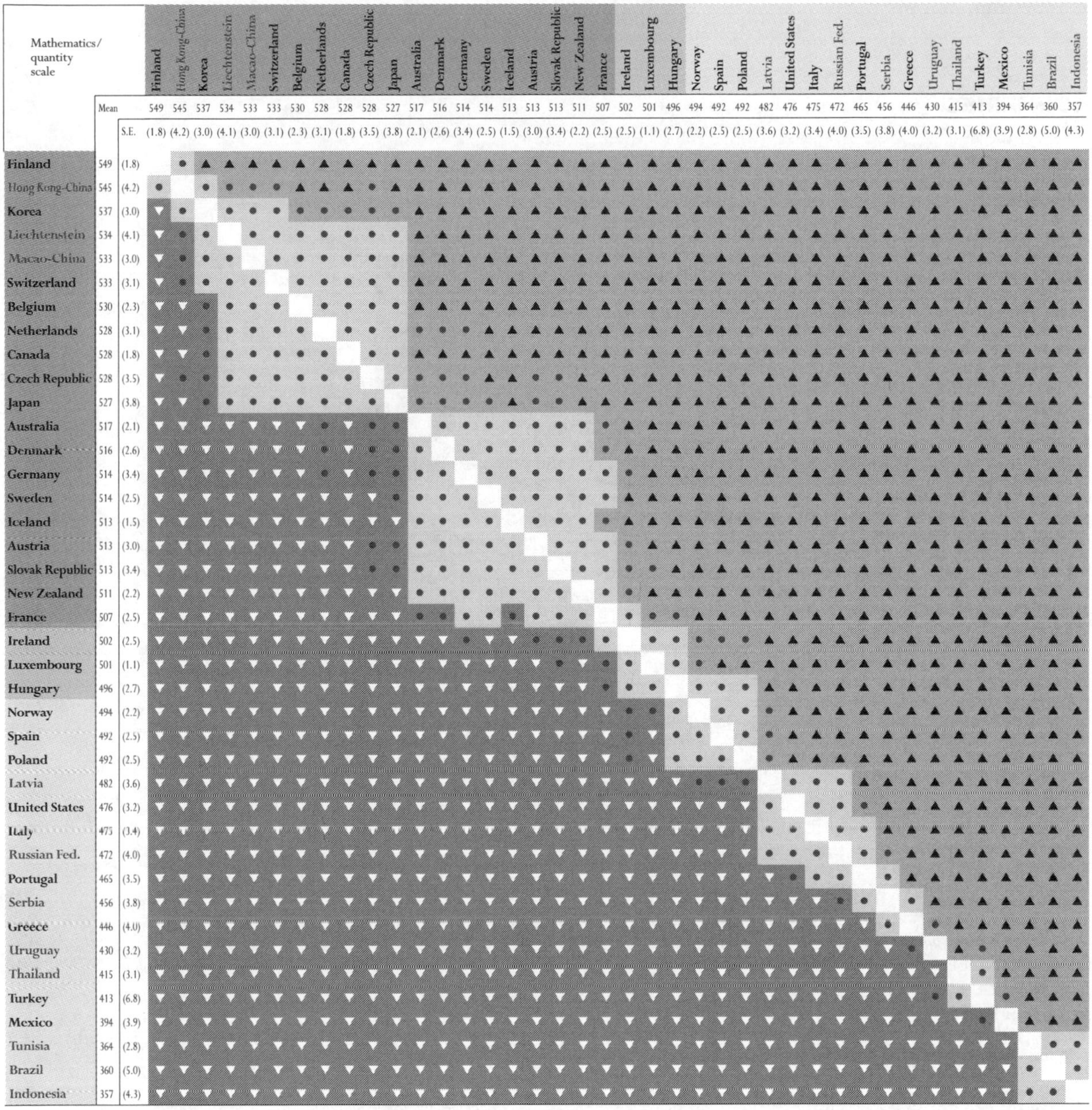

Range of rank*

		Finland	Hong Kong-China	Korea	Liechtenstein	Macao-China	Switzerland	Belgium	Netherlands	Canada	Czech Republic	Japan	Australia	Denmark	Germany	Sweden	Iceland	Austria	Slovak Republic	New Zealand	France	Ireland	Luxembourg	Hungary	Norway	Spain	Poland	Latvia	United States	Italy	Russian Fed.	Portugal	Serbia	Greece	Uruguay	Thailand	Turkey	Mexico	Tunisia	Brazil	Indonesia
OECD countries	Upper rank	1		2			2	3	3	4	3	3	9	9	9	9	10	9	9	11	14	17	18	19	20	20	20		24	24		25		27			28	29			
	Lower rank	1		4			7	8	8	8	8	8	13	15	16	17	16	17	17	17	18	20	20	23	23	23	23		25	25		26		27			28	29			
All countries	Upper rank	1	1	2	3	3	3	4	5	6	4	5	12	12	12	12	13	12	12	14	17	20	21	22	23	23	23	27	27	27	28	30	31	32	34	35	35	37	38	38	38
	Lower rank	2	3	7	10	10	10	11	11	11	11	11	16	18	19	20	19	20	20	20	21	23	23	26	26	26	26	29	30	30	31	32	33	33	34	36	36	37	40	40	40

* Because data are based on samples, it is not possible to report exact rank order positions for countries. However, it is possible to report the range of rank order positions within which the country mean lies with 95 per cent likelihood.

Instructions:

Read across the row for a country to compare performance with the countries listed along the top of the chart. The symbols indicate whether the average performance of the country in the row is lower than that of the comparison country, higher than that of the comparison country, or if there is no statistically significant difference between the average achievement of the two countries.

Without the Bonferroni adjustment:
- Mean performance statistically significantly higher than in comparison country
- No statistically significant difference from comparison country
- Mean performance statistically significantly lower than in comparison country

With the Bonferroni adjustment:
- ▲ Mean performance statistically significantly higher than in comparison country
- ● No statistically significant difference from comparison country
- ▽ Mean performance statistically significantly lower than in comparison country

- Statistically significantly above the OECD average
- Not statistically significantly different from the OECD average
- Statistically significantly below the OECD average

Source: OECD PISA 2003 database.

Figure 2.13a ■ **A sample of mathematics items used in PISA for the uncertainty scale: Unit ROBBERIES**

ROBBERIES

A TV reporter showed this graph and said:

"The graph shows that there is a huge increase in the number of robberies from 1998 to 1999."

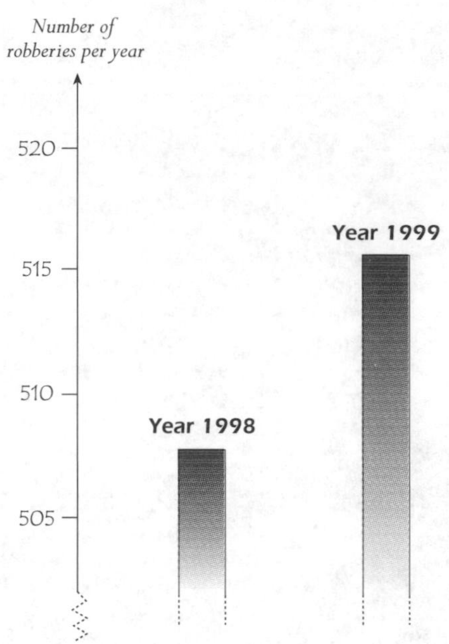

QUESTION 15

Do you consider the reporter's statement to be a reasonable interpretation of the graph? Give an explanation to support your answer.

Score 2 (694) ▪

Answers which indicate "No, not reasonable" and focus on the fact that only a small part of the graph is shown, or contain correct arguments in terms of ratio or percentage increase, or refer to requirement of trend data before a judgement can be made.

Score 1 (577) ▪

Answers which indicate "No, not reasonable" but explanation lacks detail (focuses ONLY on an increase given by the exact number of robberies, but does not compare with the total) or with correct method but with minor computational errors.

This open-constructed response item is situated in a public context. The graph as presented in the stimulus of this item actually was derived from a real graph with a similarly misleading message as the one here. The graph seems to indicate, as the TV reporter said: "a huge increase in the number of robberies". The students are asked if the statement fits the data. It is very important to look through data and graphs as they are frequently presented in the media in order to participate effectively in society. This constitutes an essential skill in mathematical literacy. Quite often designers of graphics use their skills (or lack thereof) to let the data support a pre-determined message, often with a political context. This is an example. The item involves the analysis of a graph and data interpretation, placing it in the uncertainty area. The reasoning and interpretation competencies required, together with the communication skills needed, are clearly belonging to the connections competency cluster. The competencies that are essential for solving this problem are understanding and decoding of a graphical representation in a critical way, making judgments and finding appropriate argumentation based on mathematical thinking and reasoning (although the graph seems to indicate quite a big jump in the number of robberies, the absolute number of increase in robberies is far from dramatic; the reason for this paradox lies is the inappropriate cut in the y-axis) and proper communication of this reasoning process.

A partial credit response illustrates Level 4 with a difficulty of 577 points. In this case students typically indicate that the statement is not reasonable, but fail to explain their judgment in appropriate detail. This means here that the reasoning only focuses on an increase given by an exact number of robberies in absolute terms, but not in relative terms. Communication is critical here, since one will always have answers that are difficult to interpret in detail. An example: "an increase from 508 to 515 is not large" might have a different meaning from "an increase of around 10 is not large". The first statement shows the actual numbers, and thus the intended meaning of the answer might be that the increase is small because of the large numbers involved, while this line of reasoning does not apply to the second answer. In this kind of response, students use and communicate argumentation based on interpretation of data; therefore it illustrates Level 4.

A full credit response illustrates Level 6 with a difficulty score of 694 score points. In the case of full credit the students indicate that the statement is not reasonable, and explain their judgment in appropriate detail. This means here that the reasoning not only focuses on an increase given by an exact number of robberies in absolute terms, but also in relative terms. The question requires students to use and communicate argumentation based on interpretation of data, using some proportional reasoning in a statistical context, and in a not-too-familiar situation. Therefore it illustrates Level 6.

Level
6
668.7
5
606.6
4
544.4
3
482.4
2
420.4
1
358.3
Below 1

Level

Figure 2.13b ■ **A sample of mathematics items used in PISA for the uncertainty scale: Unit TEST SCORES**

TEST SCORES

The diagram shows the results on a science test for two groups, labelled as Group A and Group B.

The mean score for Group A is 62.0 and the mean for Group B is 64.5. Students pass this test when their score is 50 or above.

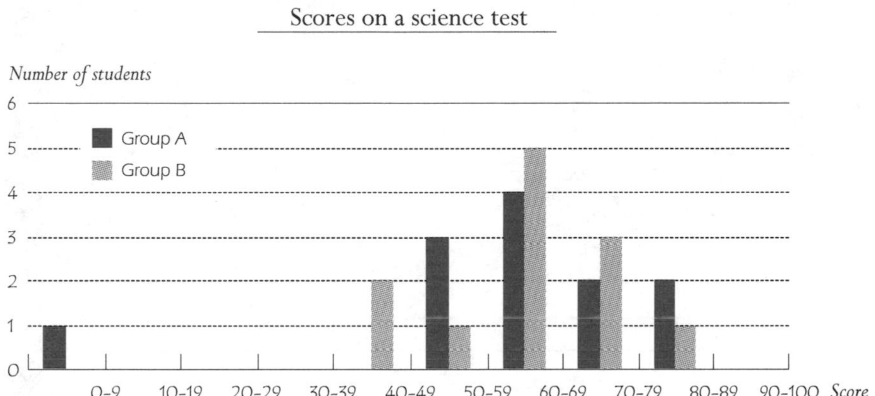

QUESTION 16

Looking at the diagram, the teacher claims that Group B did better than Group A in this test.

The students in Group A don't agree with their teacher. They try to convince the teacher that Group B may not necessarily have done better.

Give one mathematical argument, using the graph that the students in Group A could use.

Score 1 (620)

Answers which present a valid argument. Valid arguments could relate to the number of students passing, the disproportionate influence of the outlier, or the number of students with scores in the highest level.

This open-constructed response item is situated in an educational context. It has a difficulty of 620 score points. The educational context of this item is one that all students are familiar with: comparing test scores. In this case a science test has been administered to two groups of students: A and B. The results are given to the students in two different ways: in words with some data embedded and by means of two graphs in one grid. The problem is to find arguments that support the statement that Group A actually did better than Group B, given the counter-argument of one teacher that Group B did better – on the grounds of the higher mean for Group B. It will be clear that the item falls into the content area of uncertainty. Knowledge of this area of mathematics is essential in the information society, as data and graphical representations play a major role in the media and in other aspects of our daily experience. The connections cluster, in which this item is classified, includes competencies that not only build on those required for the reproduction cluster (like encoding and interpretation of simple graphical representations) but also require reasoning and insight in a particular mathematical argument. Actually the students have a choice of at least three arguments here. The first one is that more students in Group A pass the test; a second one is the distorting effect of the outlier in the results of Group A; and finally Group A has more students that scored 80 or over. Another important competency needed is explaining matters that include relationships. From this it follows that the item belongs to the connections cluster. Students who are successful have applied statistical knowledge in a problem situation that is somewhat structured and where the mathematical representation is partially apparent. They also need reasoning and insight to interpret and analyse the given information, and they must communicate their reasons and arguments. Therefore the item clearly illustrates Level 5.

6
668.7
5
606.6
4
544.4
3
482.4
2
420.4
1
358.3
Below 1

Figure 2.13c ■ **A sample of mathematics items used in PISA for the uncertainty scale: Unit EXPORTS**

Level
6
668.7
5
606.6
4
544.4
3
482.4
2
420.4
1
358.3
Below 1

EXPORTS

The graphics show information about exports from Zedland, a country that uses zeds as its currency.

Total annual exports from Zedland in millions of zeds, 1996-2000

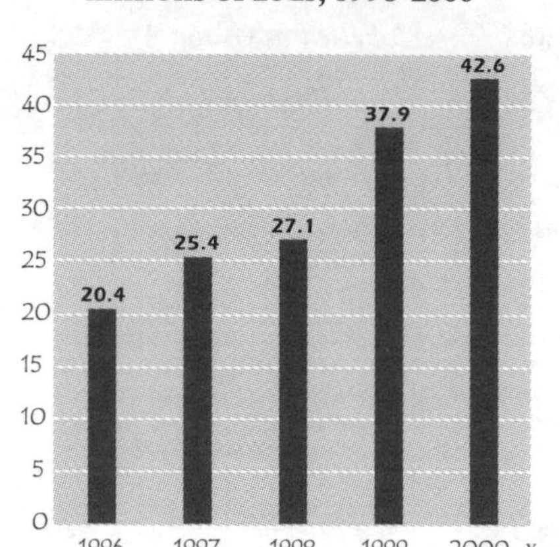

Distribution of exports from Zedland in 2000

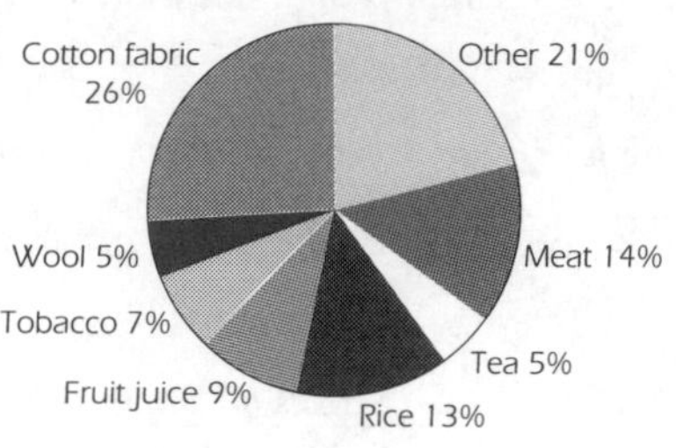

QUESTION 18

What was the value of fruit juice exported from Zedland in 2000?

A. 1.8 million zeds.
B. 2.3 million zeds.
C. 2.4 million zeds.
D. 3.4 million zeds.
E. 3.8 million zeds.

Score 1 (565)

The correct answer is E. 3.8 million zeds.

This multiple-choice item is situated in a public context. It has a difficulty of 565 score points. The data-handling processes involved with this item place it in the uncertainty area. The mathematical content consists of reading data from two graphs: a bar chart and a pie chart, comparing the characteristics of the two graphics, and combining data from the two graphs in order to be able to carry out a basic number operation resulting in a numerical answer. Students need to combine the information of the two graphics in a relevant way. The mathematisation process needed here has distinct phases: decoding the different standard representations by looking at the total of annual exports of 2000 (42.6 million zeds) and at the percentage of this total coming from fruit juice exports (9%). It is this activity and the process of connecting these numbers by an appropriate numerical operation (9% of 42.6) that places this item in the connections competency cluster. It is the more complex concrete situation, containing two related graphical representations, the insight needed to connect and combine them and the application of the appropriate basic mathematical routine in the relevant way that makes this item fit into Level 4.

QUESTION 17

What was the total value (in millions of zeds) of exports from Zedland in 1998?

Answer:

Score 1 (427)

Answers which indicate 27.1 million zeds or 27 100 000 zeds or 27.1 (unit not required). Rounding to 27 also accepted.

This closed-constructed response item is situated in a public context. It has a difficulty of 427 score points. The knowledge society relies heavily on data, and data are often represented in graphics. The media use graphics often to illustrate news articles and make points more convincingly. Reading and understanding this kind of information therefore is an essential component of mathematical literacy. The mathematical content is restricted to reading data from a bar graph or pie chart. Exploratory data analysis is the area of mathematics to which this item belongs, and therefore fits the content area uncertainty. The representation competency is needed to solve this problem: decoding and interpreting a familiar, practised standard representation of a well known mathematical object – following the written instructions, deciding which of the two graphs is relevant and locating the correct information in that graph. This is a routine procedure and therefore the item belongs to the reproduction competency cluster. This item illustrates interpreting and recognising situations in contexts that require no more than direct inference, which is a key feature of Level 2.

Student performance on the mathematics/uncertainty scale

Four per cent of students in the OECD area can perform the hardest uncertainty tasks…

A quarter of the mathematical tasks given to students in PISA related to probabilistic and statistical phenomena and relationships. Figures 2.13a-c shows examples of tasks in Levels 2, 4, 5 and 6 in this category.

The particular competencies required to reach each level are given in Figure 2.14. Only 4 per cent of students in the combined OECD area – but 13 per cent in the partner country Hong Kong-China – can perform Level 6 tasks. Thirty-one per cent of the combined student population in the OECD perform at least at Level 4, but this figure is more than 50 per cent in Finland, the Netherlands and the partner country Hong Kong-China (Table 2.4a).

Figure 2.14 ■ **Summary descriptions of six levels of proficiency on the mathematics/uncertainty scale**

Level	General competencies students should have at each level	Specific tasks students should be able to do
6	*4% of all students across the OECD area can perform tasks at Level 6 on the uncertainty scale*	
	Use high-level thinking and reasoning skills in statistical or probabilistic contexts to create mathematical representations of real-world situations; use insight and reflection to solve problems, and to formulate and communicate arguments and explanations	– Interpret and reflect on real-world situations using probability knowledge and carry out resulting calculations using proportional reasoning, large numbers and rounding – Show insight into probability in a practical context – Use interpretation, logical reasoning and insight at a high level in an unfamiliar probabilistic situation – Use rigorous argumentation based on insightful interpretation of data – Employ complex reasoning using statistical concepts – Show understanding of basic ideas of sampling and carry out calculations with weighted averages, or using insightful systematic counting strategies – Communicate complex arguments and explanations
5	*13% of all students across the OECD area can perform tasks at least at Level 5 on the uncertainty scale*	
	Apply probabilistic and statistical knowledge in problem situations that are somewhat structured and where the mathematical representation is partially apparent. Use reasoning and insight to interpret and analyse given information, to develop appropriate models and to perform sequential calculation processes; communicate reasons and arguments	– Interpret and reflect on the outcomes of an unfamiliar probabilistic experiment – Interpret text using technical language and translate to an appropriate probability calculation – Identify and extract relevant information, and interpret and link information from multiple sources (*e.g.,* from text, multiple tables, graphs) – Use reflection and insight into standard probabilistic situations – Apply probability concepts to analyse a non-familiar phenomenon or situation – Use proportional reasoning and reasoning with statistical concepts – Use multistep reasoning based on data – Carry out complex modelling involving the application of probability knowledge and statistical concepts (*e.g.,* randomness, sample, independence) – Use calculations including addition, proportions, multiplication of large numbers, rounding, to solve problems in non-trivial statistical contexts – Carry out a sequence of related calculations – Carry out and communicate probabilistic reasoning and argument

Level	General competencies students should have at each level	Specific tasks students should be able to do
4	*31% of all students across the OECD area can perform tasks at least at Level 4 on the uncertainty scale*	
	Use basic statistical and probabilistic concepts combined with numerical reasoning in less familiar contexts to solve simple problems; carry out multi-step or sequential calculation processes; use and communicate argumentation based on interpretation of data	– Interpret text, including in an unfamiliar (scientific) but straight-forward context – Show insight into aspects of data from tables and graphs – Translate text description into appropriate probability calculation – Identify and select data from various statistical graphs and carry out basic calculation – Show understanding of basic statistical concepts and definitions (probability, expected value, randomness, average) – Use knowledge of basic probability to solve problems – Construct a basic mathematical explanation of a verbal real-world quantitative concept ("huge increase") – Use mathematical argumentation based on data – Use numerical reasoning – Carry out multi-step calculations involving the basic arithmetic operations, and working with percentage – Draw information from a table and communicate a simple argument based on that information
3	*54% of all students across the OECD area can perform tasks at least at Level 3 on the uncertainty scale*	
	Interpret statistical information and data, and link different information sources; basic reasoning with simple probability concepts, symbols and conventions and communication of reasoning	– Interpret tabular information – Interpret and read from non-standard graphs – Use reasoning to identify probability outcomes in the context of a complex but well-defined and familiar probability experiment – Insight into aspects of data presentation, *e.g.,* number sense; link related information from two different tables; link data to suitable chart type – Communicate common-sense reasoning
2	*75% of all students across the OECD area can perform tasks at least at Level 2 on the uncertainty scale*	
	Locate statistical information presented in familiar graphical form; understand basic statistical concepts and conventions	– Identify relevant information in a simple and familiar graph – Link text to a related graph, in a common and familiar form – Understand and explain simple statistical calculations (*e.g.,* the average) – Read values directly from a familiar data display, such as a bar graph
1	*90% of all students across the OECD area can perform tasks at least at Level 1 on the uncertainty scale*	
	Understand and use basic probabilistic ideas in familiar experimental contexts	– Understand basic probability concepts in the context of a simple and familiar experiment (*e.g.,* involving dice or coins) – Systematic listing and counting of combinatorial outcomes in a limited and well-defined game situation

Seventy-five per cent of OECD students can at least function at the baseline Level 2. However, a quarter or more of students fail to reach this threshold in Greece, Italy, Mexico, Portugal, the Slovak Republic and Turkey as well as in the partner countries Brazil, Indonesia, Latvia, the Russian Federation, Serbia, Thailand, Tunisia and Uruguay (Figure 2.15a and Table 2.4a).

...and again a quarter are capable only of the simplest tasks.

Figure 2.15b gives a summary of overall student performance in different countries on the uncertainty scale. Performance is presented in terms of mean student scores as well as, with 95 per cent probability, the range of rank order positions within which the country mean lies. Hong Kong-China and the Netherlands show the strongest performance on the mathematics/uncertainty scale, and can be found between the first and second, and first and third rank order positions, respectively, among all participating countries.

In uncertainty tasks, Hong Kong-China and the Netherlands are strongest overall.

Figure 2.15a ■ **Percentage of students at each level of proficiency on the mathematics/uncertainty scale**

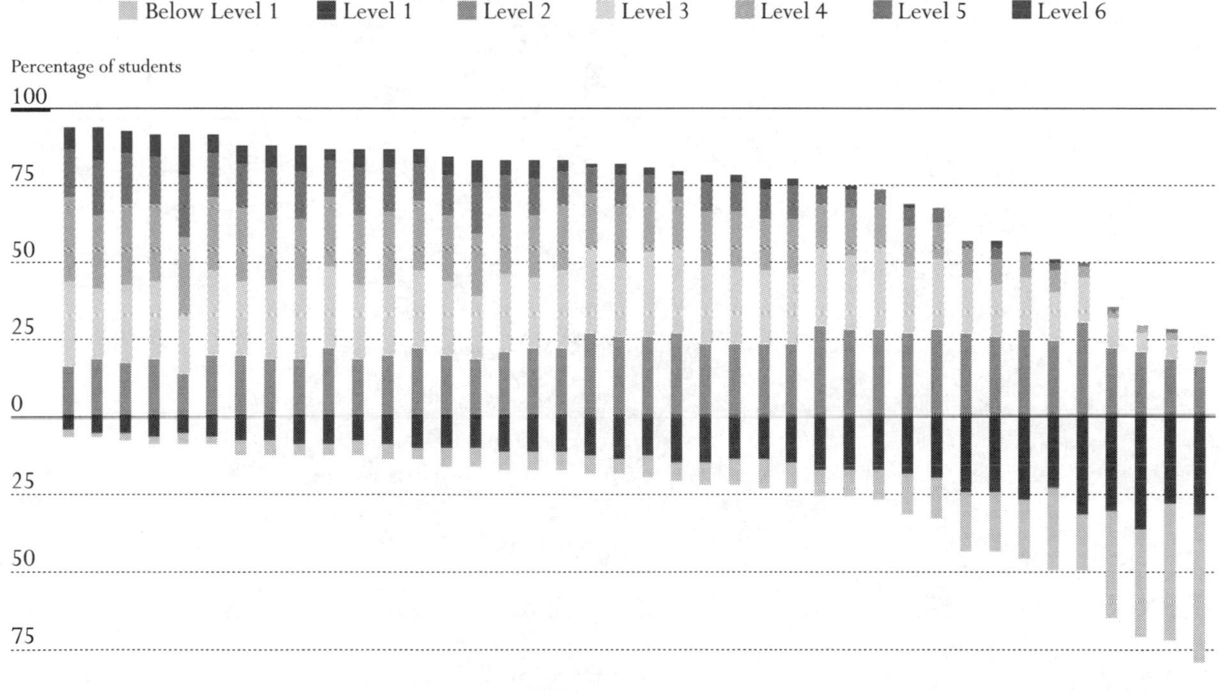

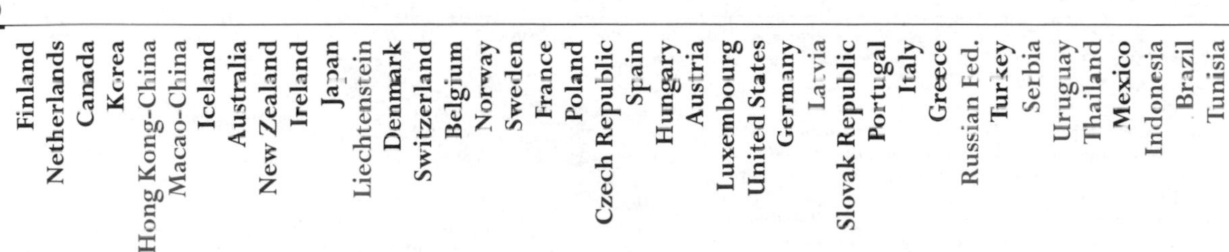

Countries are ranked in descending order of percentage of 15-year-olds in Levels 2, 3, 4, 5 and 6.
Source: OECD PISA 2003 database, Table 2.4a.

Figure 2.15b ■ Multiple comparisons of mean performance on the mathematics/uncertainty scale

Mathematics/ uncertainty scale	Mean	S.E.	Hong Kong-China	Netherlands	Finland	Canada	Korea	New Zealand	Macao-China	Australia	Japan	Iceland	Belgium	Liechtenstein	Ireland	Switzerland	Denmark	Norway	Sweden	France	Czech Republic	Austria	Poland	Germany	Luxembourg	United States	Hungary	Spain	Slovak Republic	Latvia	Portugal	Italy	Greece	Turkey	Russian Fed.	Serbia	Thailand	Uruguay	Mexico	Indonesia	Brazil	Tunisia
Mean			558	549	545	542	538	532	532	531	528	528	526	523	517	517	516	513	511	506	500	494	494	493	492	491	489	489	476	474	471	463	458	443	436	428	423	419	390	385	377	363
S.E.			(4.6)	(3.0)	(2.1)	(1.8)	(3.0)	(2.3)	(3.2)	(2.2)	(3.9)	(1.5)	(2.2)	(3.7)	(2.6)	(3.3)	(2.8)	(2.6)	(2.7)	(2.4)	(3.1)	(3.1)	(2.3)	(3.3)	(1.1)	(3.0)	(2.6)	(2.4)	(3.2)	(3.3)	(3.4)	(3.0)	(3.5)	(6.2)	(4.0)	(3.5)	(2.5)	(3.1)	(3.3)	(2.9)	(3.9)	(2.3)
Hong Kong-China	558	(4.6)		●	●	▲	▲	▲	▲	▲	▲	▲	▲	▲	▲	▲	▲	▲	▲	▲	▲	▲	▲	▲	▲	▲	▲	▲	▲	▲	▲	▲	▲	▲	▲	▲	▲	▲	▲	▲	▲	▲
Netherlands	549	(3.0)	●		●	●	●	▲	▲	▲	▲	▲	▲	▲	▲	▲	▲	▲	▲	▲	▲	▲	▲	▲	▲	▲	▲	▲	▲	▲	▲	▲	▲	▲	▲	▲	▲	▲	▲	▲	▲	▲
Finland	545	(2.1)	●	●		●	●	▲	▲	▲	▲	▲	▲	▲	▲	▲	▲	▲	▲	▲	▲	▲	▲	▲	▲	▲	▲	▲	▲	▲	▲	▲	▲	▲	▲	▲	▲	▲	▲	▲	▲	▲
Canada	542	(1.8)	▽	●	●		●	●	●	▲	●	▲	▲	▲	▲	▲	▲	▲	▲	▲	▲	▲	▲	▲	▲	▲	▲	▲	▲	▲	▲	▲	▲	▲	▲	▲	▲	▲	▲	▲	▲	▲
Korea	538	(3.0)	▽	▽	●	●		●	●	●	●	●	▲	●	▲	▲	▲	▲	▲	▲	▲	▲	▲	▲	▲	▲	▲	▲	▲	▲	▲	▲	▲	▲	▲	▲	▲	▲	▲	▲	▲	▲
New Zealand	532	(2.3)	▽	▽	▽	●	●		●	●	●	●	●	●	▲	▲	▲	▲	▲	▲	▲	▲	▲	▲	▲	▲	▲	▲	▲	▲	▲	▲	▲	▲	▲	▲	▲	▲	▲	▲	▲	▲
Macao-China	532	(3.2)	▽	▽	▽	●	●	●		●	●	●	●	●	▲	▲	▲	▲	▲	▲	▲	▲	▲	▲	▲	▲	▲	▲	▲	▲	▲	▲	▲	▲	▲	▲	▲	▲	▲	▲	▲	▲
Australia	531	(2.2)	▽	▽	▽	▽	●	●	●		●	●	●	●	▲	▲	▲	▲	▲	▲	▲	▲	▲	▲	▲	▲	▲	▲	▲	▲	▲	▲	▲	▲	▲	▲	▲	▲	▲	▲	▲	▲
Japan	528	(3.9)	▽	▽	▽	●	●	●	●	●		●	●	●	●	●	●	▲	▲	▲	▲	▲	▲	▲	▲	▲	▲	▲	▲	▲	▲	▲	▲	▲	▲	▲	▲	▲	▲	▲	▲	▲
Iceland	528	(1.5)	▽	▽	▽	▽	●	●	●	●	●		●	●	▲	●	▲	▲	▲	▲	▲	▲	▲	▲	▲	▲	▲	▲	▲	▲	▲	▲	▲	▲	▲	▲	▲	▲	▲	▲	▲	▲
Belgium	526	(2.2)	▽	▽	▽	▽	▽	●	●	●	●	●		●	●	●	●	▲	▲	▲	▲	▲	▲	▲	▲	▲	▲	▲	▲	▲	▲	▲	▲	▲	▲	▲	▲	▲	▲	▲	▲	▲
Liechtenstein	523	(3.7)	▽	▽	▽	▽	●	●	●	●	●	●	●		●	●	●	●	●	▲	▲	▲	▲	▲	▲	▲	▲	▲	▲	▲	▲	▲	▲	▲	▲	▲	▲	▲	▲	▲	▲	▲
Ireland	517	(2.6)	▽	▽	▽	▽	▽	▽	▽	▽	●	▽	●	●		●	●	●	●	●	▲	▲	▲	▲	▲	▲	▲	▲	▲	▲	▲	▲	▲	▲	▲	▲	▲	▲	▲	▲	▲	▲
Switzerland	517	(3.3)	▽	▽	▽	▽	▽	▽	▽	▽	●	●	●	●	●		●	●	●	●	▲	▲	▲	▲	▲	▲	▲	▲	▲	▲	▲	▲	▲	▲	▲	▲	▲	▲	▲	▲	▲	▲
Denmark	516	(2.8)	▽	▽	▽	▽	▽	▽	▽	▽	●	▽	●	●	●	●		●	●	●	▲	▲	▲	▲	▲	▲	▲	▲	▲	▲	▲	▲	▲	▲	▲	▲	▲	▲	▲	▲	▲	▲
Norway	513	(2.6)	▽	▽	▽	▽	▽	▽	▽	▽	▽	▽	▽	●	●	●	●		●	●	●	▲	▲	▲	▲	▲	▲	▲	▲	▲	▲	▲	▲	▲	▲	▲	▲	▲	▲	▲	▲	▲
Sweden	511	(2.7)	▽	▽	▽	▽	▽	▽	▽	▽	▽	▽	▽	●	●	●	●	●		●	●	▲	▲	▲	▲	▲	▲	▲	▲	▲	▲	▲	▲	▲	▲	▲	▲	▲	▲	▲	▲	▲
France	506	(2.4)	▽	▽	▽	▽	▽	▽	▽	▽	▽	▽	▽	▽	●	●	●	●	●		●	●	▲	▲	▲	▲	▲	▲	▲	▲	▲	▲	▲	▲	▲	▲	▲	▲	▲	▲	▲	▲
Czech Republic	500	(3.1)	▽	▽	▽	▽	▽	▽	▽	▽	▽	▽	▽	▽	▽	▽	▽	●	●	●		●	●	●	●	●	●	●	▲	▲	▲	▲	▲	▲	▲	▲	▲	▲	▲	▲	▲	▲
Austria	494	(3.1)	▽	▽	▽	▽	▽	▽	▽	▽	▽	▽	▽	▽	▽	▽	▽	▽	▽	●	●		●	●	●	●	●	●	▲	▲	▲	▲	▲	▲	▲	▲	▲	▲	▲	▲	▲	▲
Poland	494	(2.3)	▽	▽	▽	▽	▽	▽	▽	▽	▽	▽	▽	▽	▽	▽	▽	▽	▽	▽	●	●		●	●	●	●	●	▲	▲	▲	▲	▲	▲	▲	▲	▲	▲	▲	▲	▲	▲
Germany	493	(3.3)	▽	▽	▽	▽	▽	▽	▽	▽	▽	▽	▽	▽	▽	▽	▽	▽	▽	▽	●	●	●		●	●	●	●	▲	▲	▲	▲	▲	▲	▲	▲	▲	▲	▲	▲	▲	▲
Luxembourg	492	(1.1)	▽	▽	▽	▽	▽	▽	▽	▽	▽	▽	▽	▽	▽	▽	▽	▽	▽	▽	●	●	●	●		●	●	●	▲	▲	▲	▲	▲	▲	▲	▲	▲	▲	▲	▲	▲	▲
United States	491	(3.0)	▽	▽	▽	▽	▽	▽	▽	▽	▽	▽	▽	▽	▽	▽	▽	▽	▽	▽	●	●	●	●	●		●	●	▲	▲	▲	▲	▲	▲	▲	▲	▲	▲	▲	▲	▲	▲
Hungary	489	(2.6)	▽	▽	▽	▽	▽	▽	▽	▽	▽	▽	▽	▽	▽	▽	▽	▽	▽	▽	●	●	●	●	●	●		●	●	▲	▲	▲	▲	▲	▲	▲	▲	▲	▲	▲	▲	▲
Spain	489	(2.4)	▽	▽	▽	▽	▽	▽	▽	▽	▽	▽	▽	▽	▽	▽	▽	▽	▽	▽	●	●	●	●	●	●	●		▲	▲	▲	▲	▲	▲	▲	▲	▲	▲	▲	▲	▲	▲
Slovak Republic	476	(3.2)	▽	▽	▽	▽	▽	▽	▽	▽	▽	▽	▽	▽	▽	▽	▽	▽	▽	▽	▽	▽	▽	▽	▽	▽	●	▽		●	●	●	▲	▲	▲	▲	▲	▲	▲	▲	▲	▲
Latvia	474	(3.3)	▽	▽	▽	▽	▽	▽	▽	▽	▽	▽	▽	▽	▽	▽	▽	▽	▽	▽	▽	▽	▽	▽	▽	▽	▽	▽	●		●	●	●	▲	▲	▲	▲	▲	▲	▲	▲	▲
Portugal	471	(3.4)	▽	▽	▽	▽	▽	▽	▽	▽	▽	▽	▽	▽	▽	▽	▽	▽	▽	▽	▽	▽	▽	▽	▽	▽	▽	▽	●	●		●	●	▲	▲	▲	▲	▲	▲	▲	▲	▲
Italy	463	(3.0)	▽	▽	▽	▽	▽	▽	▽	▽	▽	▽	▽	▽	▽	▽	▽	▽	▽	▽	▽	▽	▽	▽	▽	▽	▽	▽	●	●	●		●	●	▲	▲	▲	▲	▲	▲	▲	▲
Greece	458	(3.5)	▽	▽	▽	▽	▽	▽	▽	▽	▽	▽	▽	▽	▽	▽	▽	▽	▽	▽	▽	▽	▽	▽	▽	▽	▽	▽	▽	●	●	●		●	▲	▲	▲	▲	▲	▲	▲	▲
Turkey	443	(6.2)	▽	▽	▽	▽	▽	▽	▽	▽	▽	▽	▽	▽	▽	▽	▽	▽	▽	▽	▽	▽	▽	▽	▽	▽	▽	▽	▽	▽	▽	●	●		●	●	●	▲	▲	▲	▲	▲
Russian Fed.	436	(4.0)	▽	▽	▽	▽	▽	▽	▽	▽	▽	▽	▽	▽	▽	▽	▽	▽	▽	▽	▽	▽	▽	▽	▽	▽	▽	▽	▽	▽	▽	▽	▽	●		●	●	▲	▲	▲	▲	▲
Serbia	428	(3.5)	▽	▽	▽	▽	▽	▽	▽	▽	▽	▽	▽	▽	▽	▽	▽	▽	▽	▽	▽	▽	▽	▽	▽	▽	▽	▽	▽	▽	▽	▽	▽	●	●		●	●	▲	▲	▲	▲
Thailand	423	(2.5)	▽	▽	▽	▽	▽	▽	▽	▽	▽	▽	▽	▽	▽	▽	▽	▽	▽	▽	▽	▽	▽	▽	▽	▽	▽	▽	▽	▽	▽	▽	▽	●	●	●		●	▲	▲	▲	▲
Uruguay	419	(3.1)	▽	▽	▽	▽	▽	▽	▽	▽	▽	▽	▽	▽	▽	▽	▽	▽	▽	▽	▽	▽	▽	▽	▽	▽	▽	▽	▽	▽	▽	▽	▽	▽	▽	●	●		▲	▲	▲	▲
Mexico	390	(3.3)	▽	▽	▽	▽	▽	▽	▽	▽	▽	▽	▽	▽	▽	▽	▽	▽	▽	▽	▽	▽	▽	▽	▽	▽	▽	▽	▽	▽	▽	▽	▽	▽	▽	▽	▽	▽		●	●	▲
Indonesia	385	(2.9)	▽	▽	▽	▽	▽	▽	▽	▽	▽	▽	▽	▽	▽	▽	▽	▽	▽	▽	▽	▽	▽	▽	▽	▽	▽	▽	▽	▽	▽	▽	▽	▽	▽	▽	▽	▽	●		●	▲
Brazil	377	(3.9)	▽	▽	▽	▽	▽	▽	▽	▽	▽	▽	▽	▽	▽	▽	▽	▽	▽	▽	▽	▽	▽	▽	▽	▽	▽	▽	▽	▽	▽	▽	▽	▽	▽	▽	▽	▽	●	●		●
Tunisia	363	(2.3)	▽	▽	▽	▽	▽	▽	▽	▽	▽	▽	▽	▽	▽	▽	▽	▽	▽	▽	▽	▽	▽	▽	▽	▽	▽	▽	▽	▽	▽	▽	▽	▽	▽	▽	▽	▽	▽	▽	●	

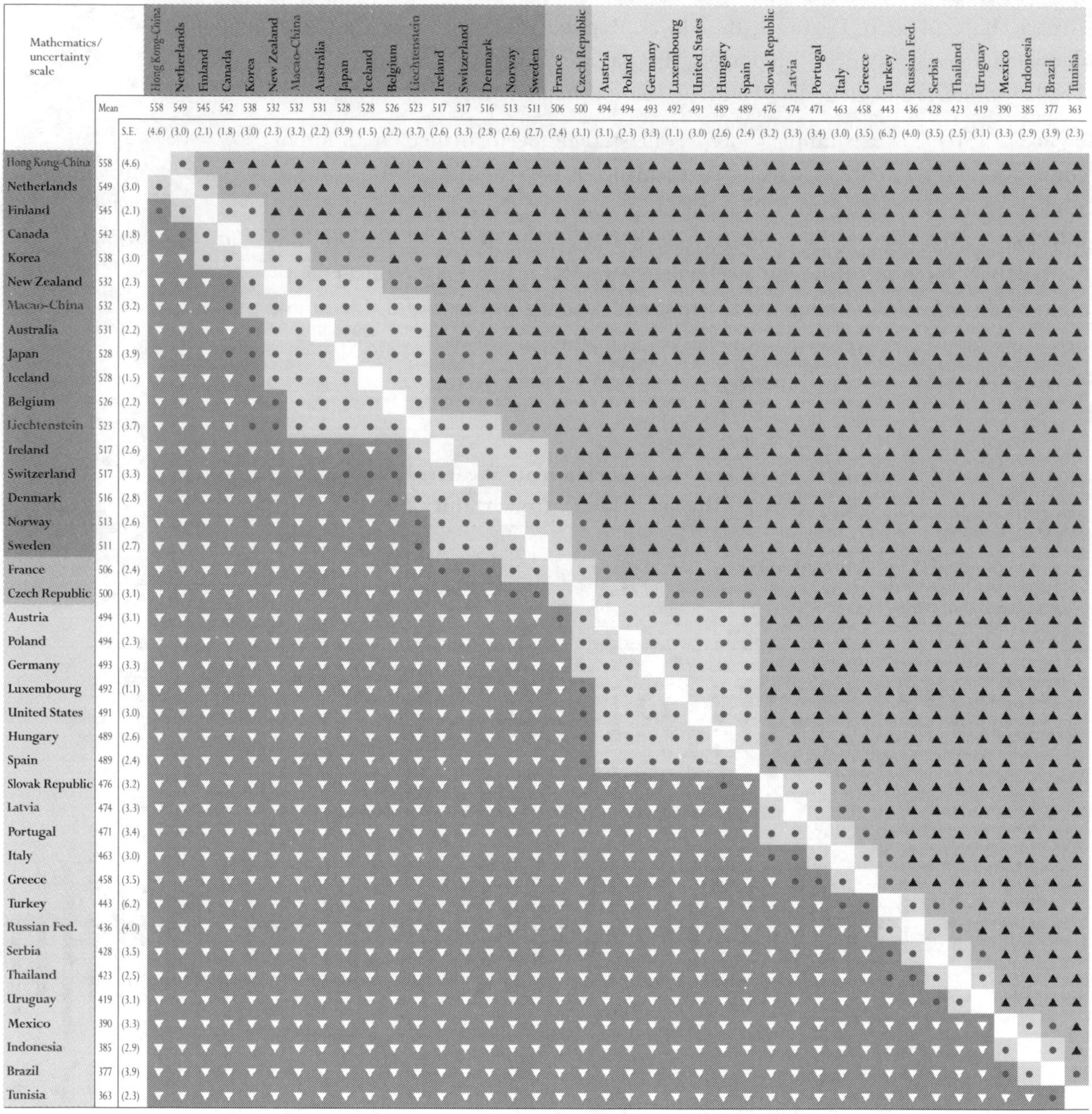

Range of rank*

		Hong Kong-China	Netherlands	Finland	Canada	Korea	New Zealand	Macao-China	Australia	Japan	Iceland	Belgium	Liechtenstein	Ireland	Switzerland	Denmark	Norway	Sweden	France	Czech Republic	Austria	Poland	Germany	Luxembourg	United States	Hungary	Spain	Slovak Republic	Latvia	Portugal	Italy	Greece	Turkey	Russian Fed.	Serbia	Thailand	Uruguay	Mexico	Indonesia	Brazil	Tunisia
OECD countries	Upper rank		1	1	2	2	4		4	5	6	6		10	10	10	10	11	14	15	16	16	16	17	17	18	18	24		24	25	26	28					29			
	Lower rank		2	3	4	5	8		8	9	9	9		13	14	14	14	15	16	18	23	22	23	22	23	23	23	25		26	27	27	28					29			
All countries	Upper rank	1	1	2	3	4	5	5	6	6	7	8	8	12	12	12	13	14	17	18	19	19	19	20	20	21	21	27	27	27	29	30	32	32	33	34	35	37	37	38	40
	Lower rank	2	3	4	5	7	10	11	10	12	11	12	14	16	17	17	17	18	19	21	26	25	26	25	26	26	26	29	29	30	31	31	33	34	35	36	36	38	39	39	40

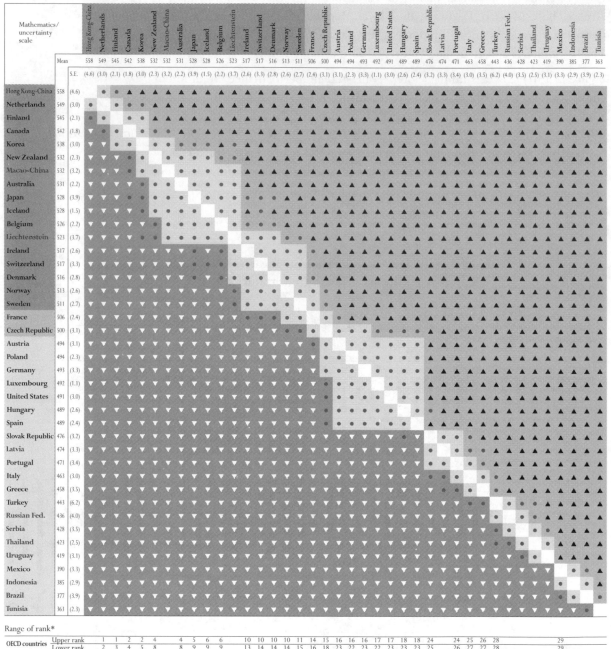

* Because data are based on samples, it is not possible to report exact rank order positions for countries. However, it is possible to report the range of rank order positions within which the country mean lies with 95 per cent likelihood.

Instructions:

Read across the row for a country to compare performance with the countries listed along the top of the chart. The symbols indicate whether the average performance of the country in the row is lower than that of the comparison country, higher than that of the comparison country, or if there is no statistically significant difference between the average achievement of the two countries.

Without the Bonferroni adjustment:
- Mean performance statistically significantly higher than in comparison country
- No statistically significant difference from comparison country
- Mean performance statistically significantly lower than in comparison country

With the Bonferroni adjustment:
- ▲ Mean performance statistically significantly higher than in comparison country
- ● No statistically significant difference from comparison country
- ▽ Mean performance statistically significantly lower than in comparison country

Statistically significantly above the OECD average
Not statistically significantly different from the OECD average
Statistically significantly below the OECD average

Source: OECD PISA 2003 database.

Consistent with what was found in the other scales, males also show an advantage in the uncertainty scale, particularly at the top end of the distribution (Tables 2.4b and 2.4c). Males outperformed females in 23 OECD countries and six partner countries but differences tend to be small,[18] with an advantage of 11 score points for the combined OECD area. Only in Iceland and the partner country Indonesia did females again outperform males.

Males are slightly ahead of females in the great majority of OECD countries.

It is not possible to compare student performance in 2000 and 2003 on this scale, since the PISA 2000 assessment did not covered this area in its assessment.

OVERALL PERFORMANCE IN MATHEMATICS

The relative strengths and weaknesses of countries in different areas of mathematical content

Comparing performance results in the different content areas of mathematics allows an assessment of the relative strengths and weaknesses of countries. It is not appropriate to compare numerical scale scores directly between the different content areas of mathematics. Nevertheless, it is possible to determine the relative strengths of countries in the different content areas of mathematics on the basis of their relative rank-order positions on the respective scales (Annex A2; Figure A2.1).[19] The values in parenthesis represent mean scores for the space and shape, change and relationships, and the quantity and uncertainty scales, respectively.

In some countries, students show marked differences in their relative performance in different areas of mathematics…

- Student performance on the *space and shape* scale stands out in Japan (553, 536, 527, 528) where it is stronger than on the other three scales, and in Canada (518, 537, 528, 542) and Ireland (476, 506, 502, 517) where the relative standing of these countries is weaker than in the other scales.
- Student performance on the *change and relationships* scale stands out in France (508, 520, 507, 506) while students in the partner countries Hong Kong-China (558, 540, 545, 558) and Macao-China (528, 519, 533, 532) show a lower relative standing on this scale.
- On the *quantity* scale, students in Finland (539, 543, 549, 545) show their strongest performance, while students in New Zealand (525, 526, 511, 532) show their weakest performance on this scale.
- On the *uncertainty* scale, students perform more strongly than on other scales in Greece (437, 436, 446, 458), Iceland (504, 509, 513, 528), Ireland (476, 506, 502, 517), New Zealand (525, 526, 511, 532) and Norway (483, 488, 494, 513). They show a lower relative standing on this scale in Belgium (530, 535, 530, 526), the Czech Republic (527, 515, 528, 500), Germany (500, 507, 514, 493), the Slovak Republic (505, 494, 513, 476) and Switzerland (540, 523, 533, 517) as well as in the partner countries Liechtenstein (538, 540, 534, 523) and the Russian Federation (474, 477, 472, 436).

...and while seven OECD countries have very similar results across content areas, 11 show especially great differences...

The relative standing of some countries, most notably Greece, Italy, Korea, Mexico, Portugal, Spain and Turkey, is very similar across the four mathematics content areas. By contrast, in Austria, Canada, the Czech Republic, France, Germany, Ireland, Japan, New Zealand, Norway, the Slovak Republic and Switzerland, performance differences among the scales are particularly large and may warrant attention in curriculum development and implementation. For example, among OECD countries, the Slovak Republic ranks around fourteenth (twelfth to seventeenth) and thirteenth (ninth to seventeenth) for the space and shape and quantity scales, but around twenty-fourth (twenty-fourth to twenty-fifth) in the uncertainty scale. Similarly, the Czech Republic ranks around seventh (fifth to ninth) on the space and shape scale and around fifth (third to eighth) on the quantity scale but around sixteenth (fifteenth to eighteenth) on the uncertainty scale. New Zealand ranks around sixth (fourth to eighth) and seventh (fifth to ninth) on the uncertainty and space and shape scales, but around sixteenth (eleventh to seventeenth) on the quantity scale. Switzerland ranks third (third to fourth) and fourth (second to seventh) on the space and shape and quantity scales only twelfth (tenth to fourteenth) on the uncertainty scale.

...and in some cases this makes overall mathematics performance seem somewhat lower than in the narrower assessment in 2000.

For some countries – most notably Japan – the relative standing in the content areas that were also assessed in 2000 remained broadly similar while performance was lower on the quantity and uncertainty scales that were newly introduced in 2003. While it would thus be wrong to conclude that mathematics performance in these countries has declined, the results do suggest that the introduction of new content areas in the assessment – quantity and uncertainty (essentially because these are valued and considered important by member countries in the OECD) – sheds a slightly different light on the overall performance of these countries in 2003.

A summary picture of mathematics performance

A combined mathematics scale shows performance across the four content areas...

While the relative performance of countries in the four content areas of mathematics is of importance for policy makers as it provides insight into potential strengths and weaknesses of the intended curricula and the effectiveness with which these are delivered, it is also possible to construct a combined performance scale covering performance across the four content areas. Results from this comparison are presented in Figure 2.16a, which shows the percentage of students performing against the international benchmarks defined by the PISA proficiency levels.

...indicating that the top third of students perform at least at Level 4, but the bottom quarter lack all but the basic skills at Level 1...

The results show that about a third of students in OECD countries perform at the top three levels of the mathematics scale (Table 2.5a), but that this figure varies widely in both OECD and the partner countries: half or more of 15-year-olds perform at least at Level 4 in Finland and Korea as well as in the partner country Hong Kong-China. However, only 3 per cent perform at Level 4 in Mexico, with an even lower percentage in the partner countries Indonesia and Tunisia. In most OECD countries, at least three quarters of students perform at or above Level 2. Nevertheless, in Italy, Portugal and the United States over a quarter of students are unable to complete tasks at Level 2. In Greece over a third of students fail

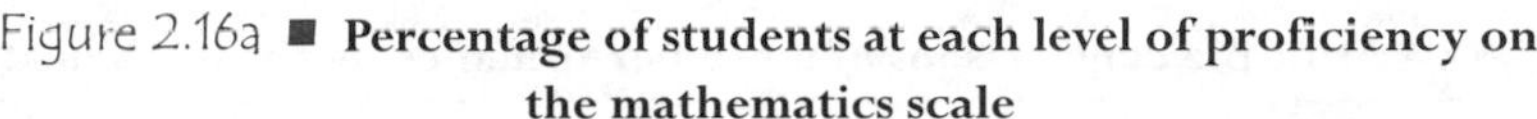

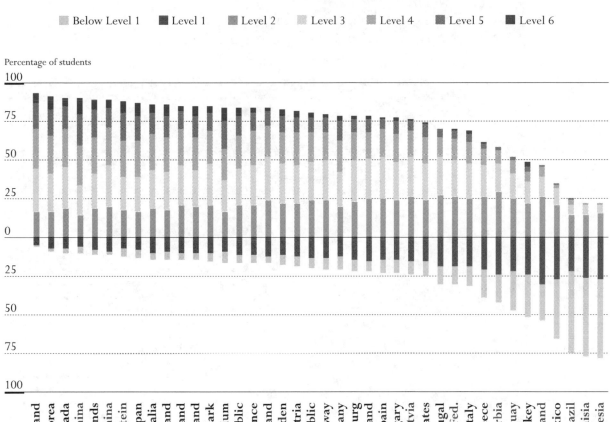

Figure 2.16a ■ **Percentage of students at each level of proficiency on the mathematics scale**

Countries are ranked in descending order of percentage of 15-year-olds in Levels 2, 3, 4, 5 and 6.
Source: OECD PISA 2003 database, Table 2.5a.

to attain Level 2, and in Mexico and Turkey the majority of students do not achieve this level. These students fail to demonstrate consistently that they have baseline mathematical skills, such as the capacity to use direct inference to recognise the mathematical elements of a situation, use a single representation to help explore and understand a situation, use basic algorithms, formulae and procedures, and the capacity to make literal interpretations and apply direct reasoning (Table 2.5a).

...and these can be combined to compare overall mathematics performance in countries.

Figure 2.16b gives a summary of overall student performance in different countries on the mathematics scale, presented in terms of the mean student score. As discussed in Box 2.1, when interpreting mean performance, only those differences between countries that are statistically significant should be taken into account. The figure therefore shows those pairs of countries where the difference in their mean

Figure 2.16b ■ Multiple comparisons of mean performance on the mathematics scale

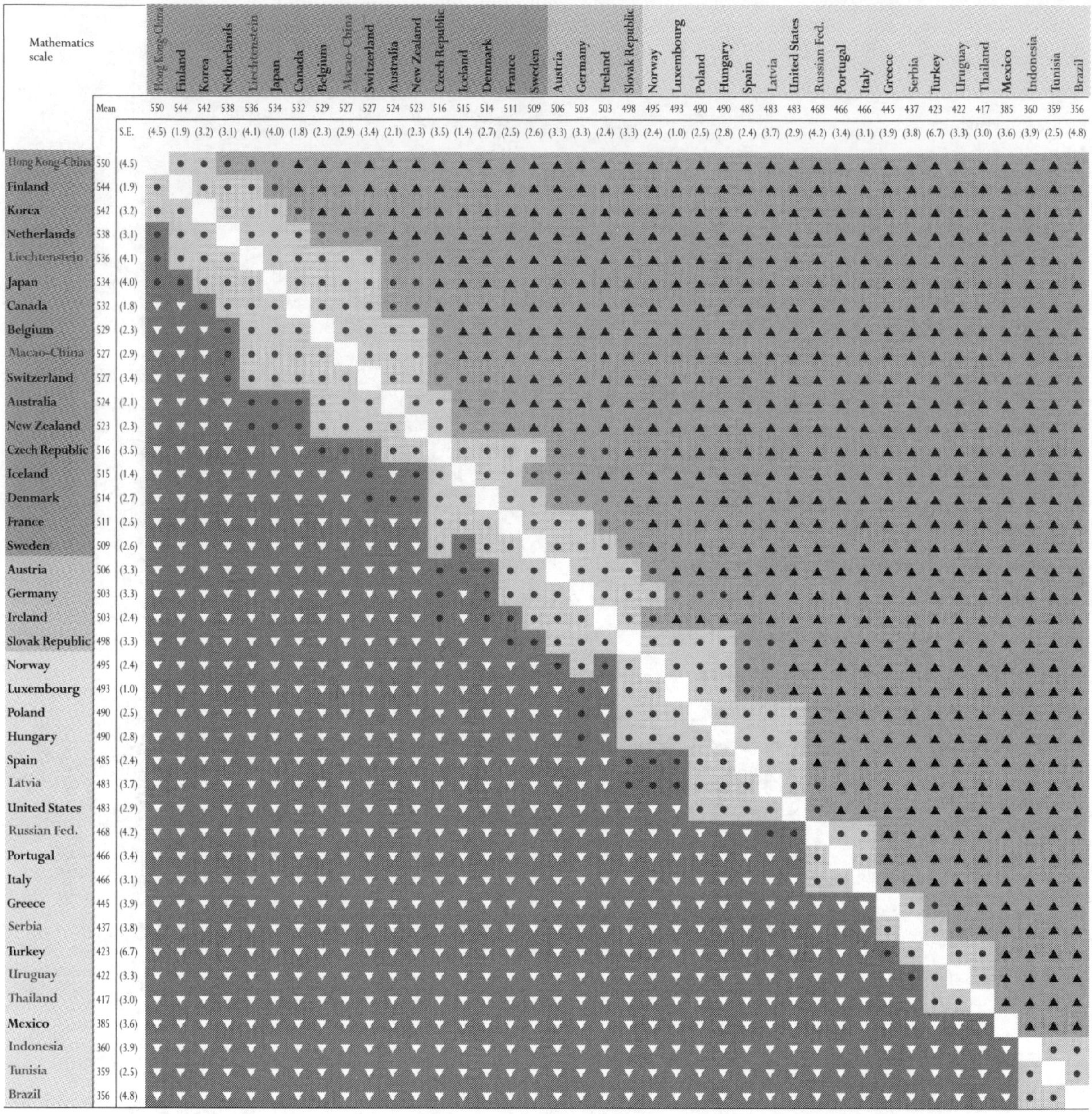

Mathematics scale	Mean	S.E.	Range of rank: OECD countries – Upper rank	OECD countries – Lower rank	All countries – Upper rank	All countries – Lower rank
Hong Kong-China	550	(4.5)			1	3
Finland	544	(1.9)	1	3	1	4
Korea	542	(3.2)	1	4	1	5
Netherlands	538	(3.1)	1	5	2	7
Liechtenstein	536	(4.1)			2	9
Japan	534	(4.0)	2	7	3	10
Canada	532	(1.8)	4	7	5	9
Belgium	529	(2.3)	4	8	5	10
Macao-China	527	(2.9)			6	12
Switzerland	527	(3.4)	4	9	6	12
Australia	524	(2.1)	7	9	9	12
New Zealand	523	(2.3)	7	10	9	13
Czech Republic	516	(3.5)	9	14	12	17
Iceland	515	(1.4)	10	13	13	16
Denmark	514	(2.7)	10	14	13	17
France	511	(2.5)	11	15	14	18
Sweden	509	(2.6)	12	16	15	19
Austria	506	(3.3)	13	18	16	20
Germany	503	(3.3)	14	18	17	21
Ireland	503	(2.4)	15	18	17	21
Slovak Republic	498	(3.3)	16	21	19	24
Norway	495	(2.4)	18	21	21	24
Luxembourg	493	(1.0)	19	21	22	24
Poland	490	(2.5)	19	23	22	26
Hungary	490	(2.8)	19	23	22	27
Spain	485	(2.4)	22	24	25	28
Latvia	483	(3.7)			25	28
United States	483	(2.9)	22	24	25	28
Russian Fed.	468	(4.2)			29	31
Portugal	466	(3.4)	25	26	29	31
Italy	466	(3.1)	25	26	29	31
Greece	445	(3.9)	27	27	32	33
Serbia	437	(3.8)			32	34
Turkey	423	(6.7)	28	28	33	36
Uruguay	422	(3.3)			34	36
Thailand	417	(3.0)			34	36
Mexico	385	(3.6)	29	29	37	37
Indonesia	360	(3.9)			38	40
Tunisia	359	(2.5)			38	40
Brazil	356	(4.8)			38	40

* Because data are based on samples, it is not possible to report exact rank order positions for countries. However, it is possible to report the range of rank order positions within which the country mean lies with 95 per cent likelihood.

Instructions:

Read across the row for a country to compare performance with the countries listed along the top of the chart. The symbols indicate whether the average performance of the country in the row is lower than that of the comparison country, higher than that of the comparison country, or if there is no statistically significant difference between the average achievement of the two countries.

Without the Bonferroni adjustment:
- Mean performance statistically significantly higher than in comparison country
- No statistically significant difference from comparison country
- Mean performance statistically significantly lower than in comparison country

With the Bonferroni adjustment:
- ▲ Mean performance statistically significantly higher than in comparison country
- ● No statistically significant difference from comparison country
- ▽ Mean performance statistically significantly lower than in comparison country

- Statistically significantly above the OECD average
- Not statistically significantly different from the OECD average
- Statistically significantly below the OECD average

Source: OECD PISA 2003 database.

scores is sufficient to say with confidence that the higher performance by sampled students in one country holds for the entire population of enrolled 15-year-olds. A country's performance relative to that of the countries listed along the top of the figure can be seen by reading across each row. The colour-coding indicates whether the average performance of the country in the row is either lower than that of the comparison country, not statistically different, or higher. When making multiple comparisons, *e.g.* when comparing the performance of one country with that of all other countries, an even more cautious approach is required, and only those comparisons that are indicated by the upward or downward pointing symbols should be considered statistically significant for the purpose of multiple comparisons. Figure 2.16b also shows which countries perform above, at or below the OECD average.

It is only possible to present a range of ranks for each country...

For the reasons explained in Box 2.1, it is also not possible to determine the exact rank order position of countries in the international comparisons. However, Figure 2.16b shows, with 95 per cent probability, the range of rank order positions within which the country mean lies, both for the group of OECD countries and for all countries that participated in PISA 2003.

...but within-country differences are critical, including some regional differences that can be measured...

Mean performance scores are typically used to assess the quality of schools and education systems. However, it has been noted above that mean performance does not provide a full picture of student performance and can mask significant variation within an individual class, school or education system. The performance variation among schools is examined more closely in Chapter 4. To capture variation between education systems and regions within countries, some countries have also undertaken the PISA assessment at sub-national levels. Where such results are available, these are presented in Annex B2. For some countries, such sub-national differences are very large. For example, mean scores on the mathematics scale for the Flemish community in Belgium are higher than those in the best-performing OECD countries, Finland and Korea. In contrast, the results from the French community are at the OECD average level.

...so it is useful to look at how each country's scores are distributed around their mean...

Figure 2.17 sheds further light on the performance distribution within countries. This analysis needs to be distinguished from the examination of the distribution of student performance across the PISA proficiency levels discussed above. Whereas the distribution of students across proficiency levels indicates the proportion of students in each country that can demonstrate a specified level of knowledge and skills, and thus compares countries on the basis of *absolute* benchmarks of student performance, the analysis below focuses on the *relative* distribution of scores, *i.e.*, the *gap* that exists between students with the highest and the lowest levels of performance *within* each country. This is an important indicator of the equality of educational outcomes in mathematics.

...revealing that each country has students both with very low and very high performance...

The gradation bars in the figure show the range of performance in each country between the 5th percentile (the point below which the lowest-performing 5 per cent of the students in a country score) and the 95th percentile (the point below which 95 per cent of students perform or, alternatively, above which the 5 per cent highest-performing students in a country score). The density of the bar

Figure 2.17 ■ **Distribution of student performance on the mathematics scale**

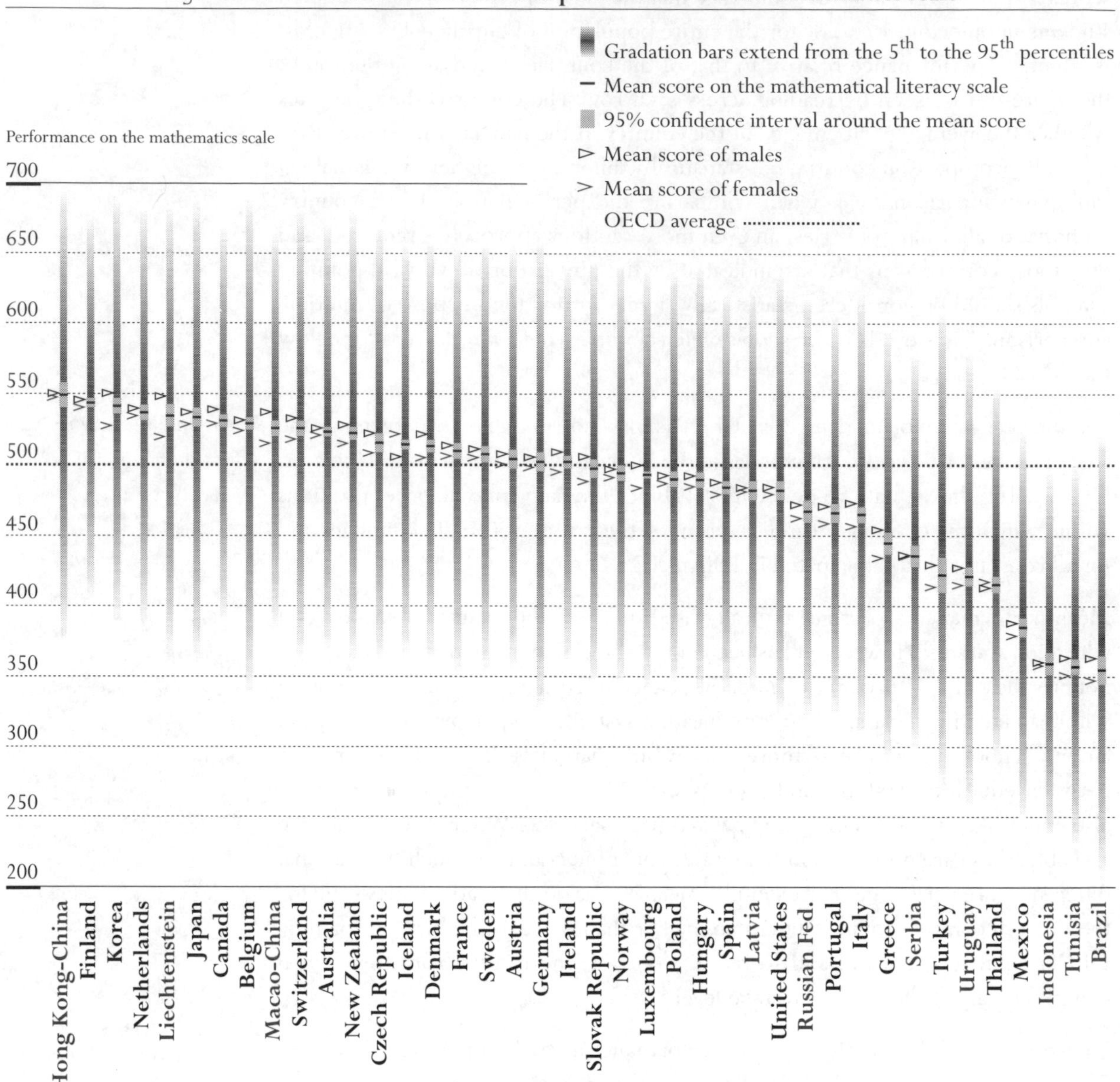

Source: OECD PISA 2003 database, Table 2.5c.

represents the proportion of students performing at the corresponding scale points. The solid, horizontal black line near the middle shows the mean score for each country (*i.e.,* the subject of the discussion in the preceding section) and is located inside a shaded box that shows its confidence interval. The figure shows that there is wide variation in overall student performance on the mathematics scale within countries. The middle 90 per cent of the population shown by the length of the bars exceeds by far the range between the mean scores of the highest and lowest performing countries. In almost all OECD countries, this group includes some students proficient at Level 5 and others not proficient above Level 1. In the majority of countries, the range of performance among the middle half of the students exceeds the magnitude of two proficiency levels, and in Belgium and Germany it is around 2.4 proficiency levels. This suggests that educational programmes, schools or teachers need to cope with a wide range of student knowledge and skills.

...and that the middle half of students vary in performance...

In addition, Table 2.5c identifies the 25th and 75th percentiles, *i.e.,* the scale points that mark the bottom and top quarters of performers in each country. To what extent are differences in student performance a reflection of a natural distribution of ability and, therefore, difficult to influence through changes in public policy? It is not easy to answer such a question with data from PISA alone, not least because differences between countries are influenced by the social and economic context in which education and learning take place. Nonetheless, several findings suggest that public policy can play a role:

...by more in some countries than others.

- First, the amount of within-country variation in performance in mathematics varies widely between OECD countries. For instance, the difference between the 75th and 25th percentiles ranges from less than 120 score points on the mathematics scale in Canada, Finland, Ireland and Mexico to more than 140 score points in Belgium and Germany. In Belgium, this difference can be explained, at least partially, by the difference in performance between the Flemish and French communities (Annex B2).

Countries with similar levels of average performance show considerable variation in disparities of student performance ...

- Second, countries with similar levels of average performance show a considerable variation in disparity of student performance. For example, Germany and Ireland both score near the OECD average but, while Ireland shows one of the narrowest distributions, the difference between the 75th and 25th percentiles in Germany is among the widest. Similarly, towards the lower end of the scale, Italy and Portugal show similar levels of average performance, but Portugal shows much less performance variation than Italy. And among the top performing countries, Finland displays much less performance variation than Korea or the Netherlands.

...with some high-performing countries managing to limit performance gaps.

- Third, it is evident from a comparison between the range of performance within a country and its average performance that wide disparities in performance are not a necessary condition for a country to attain a high level of overall performance. As an illustration, Canada, Denmark, Finland, Iceland and Korea all have above-average performance but below-average differences between the 75th and 25th percentiles (Table 2.5c).

Gender differences in mathematics

Previous sections have examined how performance differs among males and females in the different mathematical content areas. This section draws this information together.

Females have made great progress in reducing their historic educational disadvantage, and are ahead in many respects...

Policy-makers have given considerable priority to issues of gender equality, with particular attention being paid to the disadvantages faced by females. Undeniably, significant progress has been achieved in reducing the gender gap in formal educational qualifications. Younger women today are far more likely to have completed a tertiary qualification than women 30 years ago: in 18 of the 29 OECD countries with comparable data, more than twice as many women

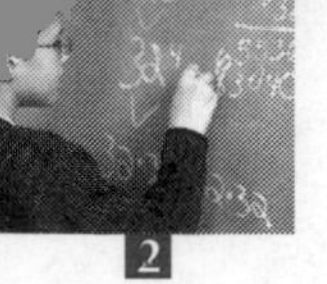

aged 25 to 34 have completed tertiary education than women aged 55 to 64 years. Furthermore, university-level graduation rates for women now equal or exceed those for men in 21 of the 27 OECD countries for which data are comparable (OECD, 2004a).

...yet males continue to do better at the tertiary level in mathematics and associated disciplines...

However, in mathematics and computer science, gender differences in tertiary qualifications remain persistently high: the proportion of women among university graduates in mathematics and computer science is only 30 per cent, on average, among OECD countries. In Austria, Belgium, Germany, Hungary, Iceland, the Netherlands, Norway, the Slovak Republic and Switzerland this share is only between 9 and 25 per cent (OECD, 2004a).

...suggesting that schools still have work to do in nurturing performance and interest among females.

Much therefore remains to be done to close the gender gap in mathematics and related fields in tertiary education and evidence suggests that action in this area needs to be targeted at youth and, indeed, children (Box 2.3). At age 15, many students are approaching major transitions from education to work, or to further education. Their performance at school, and their motivation and attitudes towards mathematics, can have a significant influence on their further educational and occupational pathways. These, in turn, can have an impact not only on individual career and salary prospects, but also on the broader effectiveness with which human capital is developed and utilised in OECD economies and societies.

Box 2.3 ■ **Changes in gender differences in mathematics and science performance between lower and upper levels of educational systems**

In 1994-95, the IEA Third International Mathematics and Science Study (TIMSS) revealed statistically significant gender differences in mathematics among fourth-grade students in only three out of the 16 participating OECD countries (Japan, Korea and the Netherlands). In all cases the gender gap favoured males. However, the same study showed statistically significant gender differences in mathematics at the grade-eight level in six of the same 16 OECD countries, all in favour of males. And finally, in the last year of upper secondary schooling, gender differences in mathematics literacy performance in the TIMSS assessment were large and statistically significant in all participating OECD countries, except Hungary and the United States (again, all in favour of males). A similar and even more pronounced picture emerged in science (Beaton *et al.,* 1996; Mullis *et al.,* 1998).

Although the groups of students assessed at the different grade levels were not made up of the same individuals, the results suggest that gender differences in mathematics and science become more pronounced and pervasive in many OECD countries at higher grade levels.

Despite this general tendency, TIMSS also showed that some countries were managing to contain the growth in gender disparities at higher grade levels (OECD, 1996; OECD, 1997).

In this regard, it is striking how closely the broader gender patterns in later career and occupational choices are already mirrored in the mathematics performance of 15-year-old males and females as observed by PISA. And as shown in Chapter 3, gender differences are even more pronounced in the attitudes and approaches towards mathematics shown by 15-year-old males and females. Gender patterns in mathematics performance are fairly consistent across OECD countries (Figure 2.18). Overall, the gender differences appear to be largest in the mathematics/space and shape scale, where performance differences between males and females are visible for all OECD countries except Finland, Norway,

PISA confirms that by age 15, gender differences are visible in most countries, with males performing better, particularly at the high end of the performance distribution.

Figure 2.18 ■ **Gender differences in student performance in mathematics**
Differences in PISA scale scores

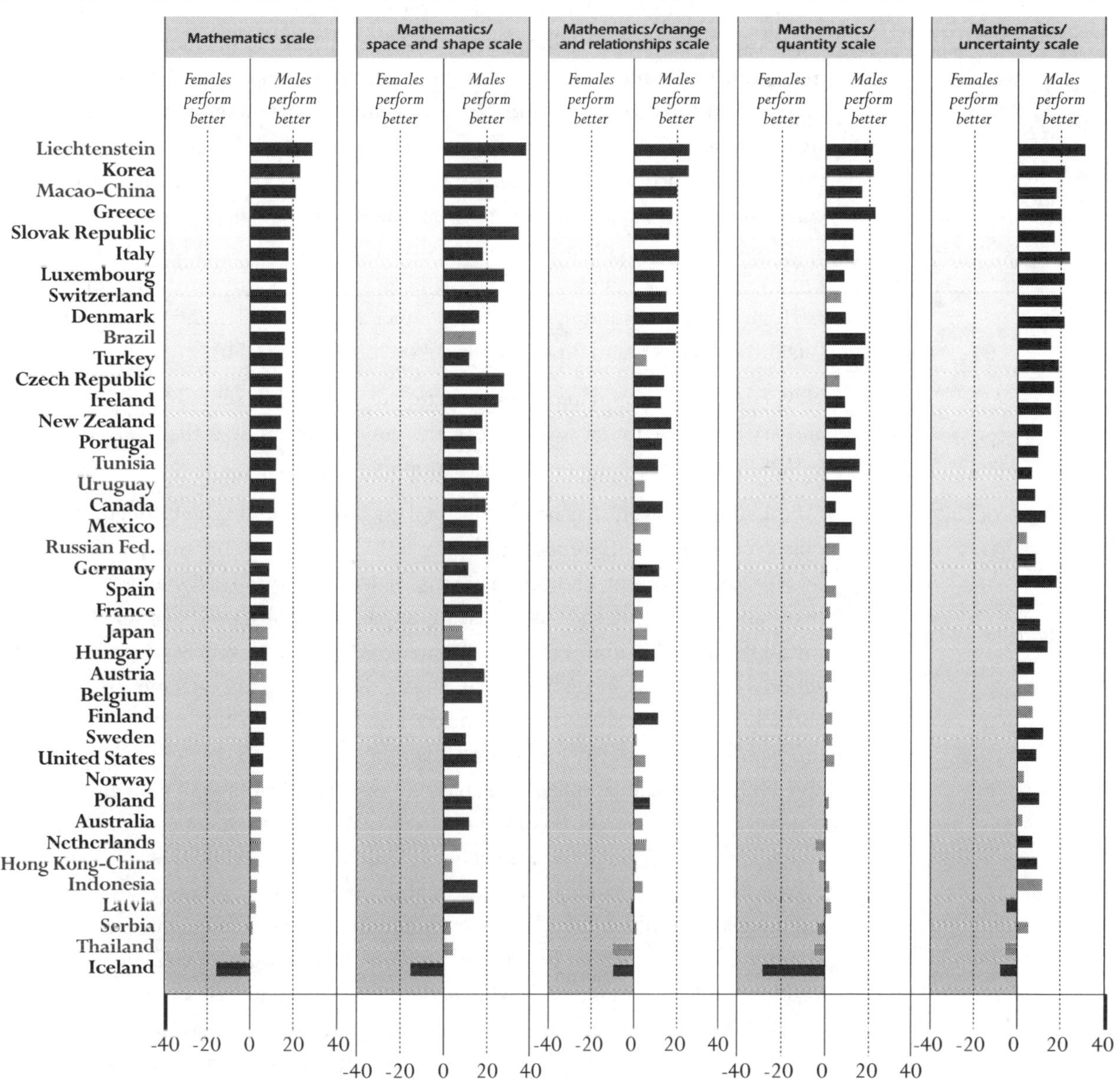

Note: Gender differences that are statistically significant are marked in darker colour (see Annex A4).
Source: OECD PISA 2003 database, Tables 2.5c, 2.1c, 2.2c, 2.3c and 2.4c.

the Netherlands and Japan. Gender differences are similarly important in the mathematics/uncertainty scale, where performance differences are visible for 24 out of the 30 OECD countries. Finally, gender differences tend to be larger at the top end of the performance distribution.

While, overall, the gender gap tends to be small,

Iceland is the only OECD country where females consistently perform better than males do. In Australia, Austria, Belgium, Japan, the Netherlands, Norway and Poland, as well as in the partner countries Hong Kong-China, Indonesia, Latvia, Serbia, and Thailand gender differences on the overall mathematics scale are not statistically significant. For the other countries with visible differences, the advantage of males varies widely. In Canada, Denmark, Greece, Ireland, Korea, Luxembourg, New Zealand, Portugal and the Slovak Republic and in the partner countries Liechtenstein, Macao-China and Tunisia, males outperform females in all four content areas, in some of these cases by notable amounts. In contrast, in Austria, Belgium, the United States and the partner country Latvia males outperform females only on the mathematics/space and shape scale, and in Japan, the Netherlands and Norway only on the mathematics/uncertainty scale (Table 2.5c). The percentages of males and females at the lower end of the scale are not consistent across countries. For example, in Iceland, 7 per cent more males than females perform at or below Level 1 while in Greece and Turkey 6 per cent more females than males perform at or below Level 1. On the top end of the scale, in virtually all countries more males than females perform at Level 6 and in the case of Japan and partner country Liechtenstein, this difference is 5 and 7 per cent respectively (Table 2.5b).

Nevertheless, as noted in previous sections, gender differences tend to be small, and are certainly much smaller than the gender differences that were observed by PISA 2000 in the area of reading literacy.[20]

...much larger differences are observed within individual schools...

One issue, however, that needs to be taken into account when interpreting the observed gender differences is that males and females, in many countries at least, make different choices in terms of the schools, tracks and educational programmes they attend. Table 2.5d compares the observed gender difference for all students (column 1) with estimates of gender differences observed within schools (column 2) and estimates of gender differences once various programme and school characteristics have been accounted for. In most countries, the gender differences are larger within schools than they are overall. In Belgium, Germany and Hungary, for example, males have an overall advantage of 8, 9 and 8 score points, respectively, on the mathematics scale, but the average gap increases to 26, 31 and 26 points within schools. In these countries, this is a reflection of the fact that females attend the higher performing, academically oriented tracks and schools at a higher rate than males. If the programme and school characteristics measured by PISA are taken into account,[21] then the estimated gender differences increase even further in many countries (column 3). This leads to an underestimation of the gender differences that are observed within schools. In other words, in these countries more females attend schools and tracks with higher average performance but, within these schools and tracks, they tend to perform lower than males.

From a policy perspective – and for teachers in classrooms – gender differences in mathematics performance, therefore, warrant continued attention. This is the case even if the advantage of males over females within schools and programmes is overshadowed to some extent by the tendency of females to attend higher performing school programmes and tracks.

...with clear implications for teachers...

The significant advantage of males in many countries on at least some of the areas of mathematical content may also be the result of the broader societal and cultural context or of educational policies and practices. Whatever the cause, they suggest that countries are having differing success at eliminating gender gaps, and that males typically remain better at mathematics.

...and perhaps for society more generally.

At the same time, some countries do appear to provide a learning environment that benefits both genders equally, either as a direct result of educational efforts or because of a more favourable societal context or both. The wide variation in gender gaps among countries suggests that the current differences are not the inevitable outcomes of differences between young males and females and that effective policies and practices can overcome what were long taken to be inevitable outcomes of differences between males and females in interests, learning styles and, even, in underlying capacities.

Such differences are not inevitable: some countries avoid them.

THE SOCIO-ECONOMIC CONTEXT OF COUNTRY PERFORMANCE

In as much as it is important to take socio-economic background into account when comparing the performance of any group of students, a comparison of the outcomes of education systems needs to account for countries' economic circumstances and the resources that countries can devote to education. This is done in the following analysis by adjusting the mathematics scale for various social and economic variables at the country level. At the same time such adjustments are always hypothetical and therefore need to be examined with caution. In a global society, the future economic and social prospects of both individuals and countries remains dependent on the results they actually achieve, not on the performance that might result if they were to operate under average social and economic conditions.

One can also adjust country performance to account for socio-economic differences.

The relative prosperity of some countries allows them to spend more on education, while other countries find themselves constrained by a relatively lower national income. Figure 2.19 displays the relationship between national income as measured by the gross domestic product (GDP) per capita and the average mathematics performance of students in the PISA assessment in each country. The GDP values represent GDP per capita in 2002 at current prices, adjusted for differences in purchasing power between OECD countries (Table 2.6). The figure also shows a trend line that summarises the relationship between GDP per capita and mean student performance in mathematics. It should be borne in mind, however, that the number of countries involved in this comparison is small and that the trend line is therefore strongly affected by the particular characteristics of the countries included in this comparison.

The case for doing so is confirmed by a correlation between national income and mathematics performance, accounting for roughly a fifth of country differences.

Figure 2.19 ■ **Student performance and national income**
Relationship between performance in mathematics and GDP per capita, in US dollars, converted using purchasing power parities (PPPs)

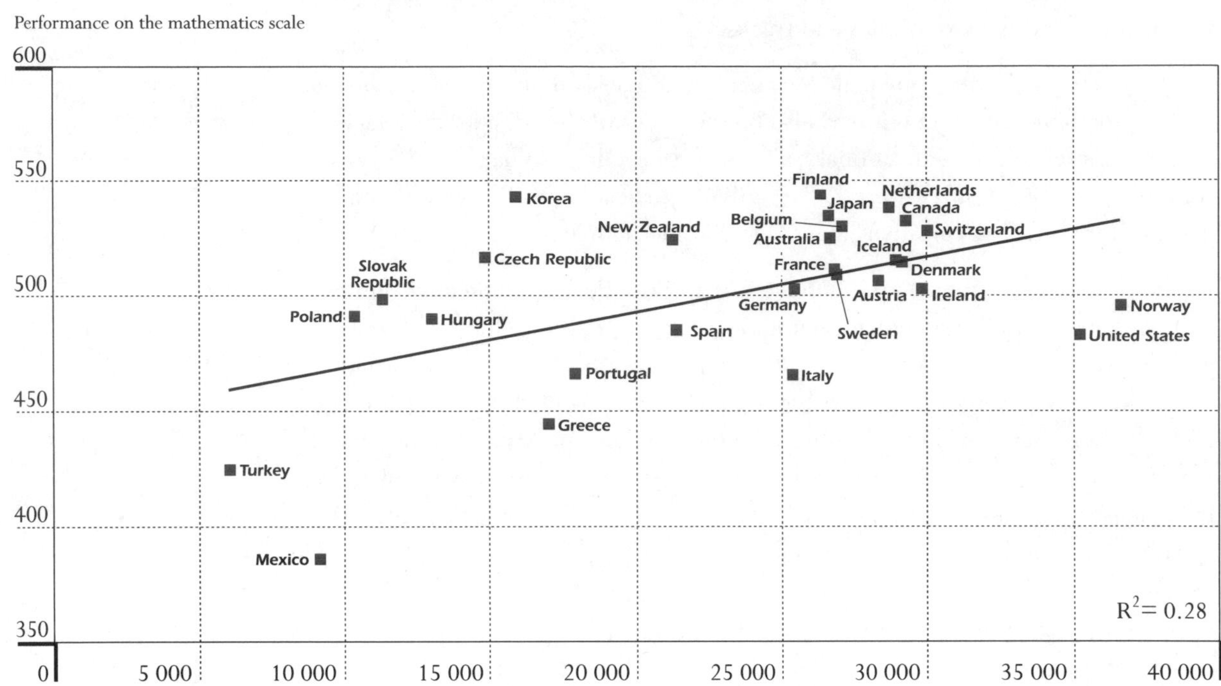

Source: OECD PISA 2003 database, Table 2.6.

The scatter plot suggests that countries with higher national income tend to perform better in mathematics. In fact, the relationship suggests that 28 per cent of the variation between countries' mean scores can be predicted on the basis of their GDP per capita.[22]

There are countries that do better or worse than predicted by their national income.

Countries close to the trend line are where the predictor GDP per capita suggests that they would be. Examples include Austria, Denmark, Germany, Hungary and Sweden. For instance, Sweden outperforms Hungary in mathematics to an extent that one would predict from the difference in their GDP per capita, as shown in Figure 2.19. However, the fact that countries deviate from the trend line also suggests that the relationship is not deterministic and linear. Countries above the trend line have higher average scores on the PISA mathematics assessment than would be predicted on the basis of their GDP per capita (and on the basis of the specific set of countries used for the estimation of the relationship). Countries below the trend line show lower performance than would be predicted from their GDP per capita.

Obviously, the existence of a correlation does not necessarily mean that there is a causal relationship between the two variables; there are, indeed, likely to be many other factors involved. Figure 2.19 does suggest, however, that countries with higher national income are at a relative advantage. This should be taken into

account, in particular, in the interpretation of the performance of countries with comparatively low levels of national income. For some countries, an adjustment for GDP per capita makes a substantial difference to their relative standing internationally. For example, following such an adjustment, Hungary and Poland would move around ten rank order positions upwards on the mathematics scale (490 to 514 and 490 to 521 score points respectively), and the Czech Republic (516 to 536 score points), Portugal (466 to 479 score points) and New Zealand (523 to 528 score points) still by between two and seven positions. Conversely, Austria (506 to 493 score points), Denmark (514 to 500 score points), Norway (495 to 463 score points) and Switzerland (527 to 510 score points) would move between four and six rank positions downwards, given that their performance falls well below what their national levels of income predict.

Adjusting also for adults' educational attainment creates an even greater correction.

One can further extend the range of contextual variables to be considered further. Given the close interrelationship established in Chapter 4 between student performance and parental levels of educational attainment, an obvious contextual consideration concerns differences in levels of adult educational attainment among the OECD countries. Table 2.6 shows the percentage of the population in the age group 35-44 years that have attained upper secondary and tertiary levels of education. This age group roughly corresponds to the age group of parents of the 15-year-olds assessed in PISA that have attained the upper secondary and tertiary levels of education. If these variables are included in the adjustment in addition to GDP per capita, Poland and Portugal would move upwards by around 16 rank positions (490 to 526 and 466 to 521 score points respectively). Both Poland and Portugal would thus be included in the group of the 10 countries with the highest performance relative to their GDP per capita and levels of adult educational attainment. Conversely, Canada (532 to 510 score points), Denmark (514 to 496 score points), Finland (544 to 525 score points), Germany (503 to 484 score points), Japan (534 to 506 score points), Norway (495 to 459 score points) and Sweden (509 to 487 score points) would move downwards by between 5 and 9 positions, given that their GDP per capita and levels of adult educational attainment would predict far higher levels of student performance than they actually attain. Although combining adult attainment with GDP results in a closer relationship with student performance than when GDP is considered alone, the relationship remains far from deterministic and linear as the model underlying the adjustment assumes. The results therefore need to be interpreted with caution.

Another perspective results from considering how much money countries devote to education…

While GDP per capita reflects the potential resources available for education in each country, it does not directly measure the financial resources actually invested in education. Figure 2.20 compares countries' actual spending per student, on average, from the beginning of primary education up to the age of 15, with average student performance across the three assessment areas. Spending per student is approximated by multiplying public and private expenditure on educational institutions per student in 2002 at each level of education by the theoretical duration of education at the respective level, up to the age of 15.[25] The results are expressed in United States dollars (USD) using purchasing power parities (OECD, 2004a).

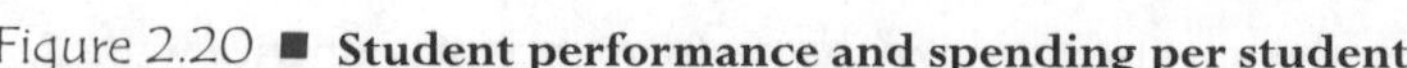

Figure 2.20 ■ **Student performance and spending per student**

Relationship between performance in mathematics and cummulative expenditure on educational institutions per student between the ages of 6 and 15 years, in US dollars, converted using purchasing power parities (PPPs)

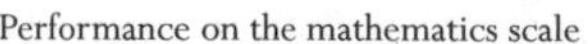

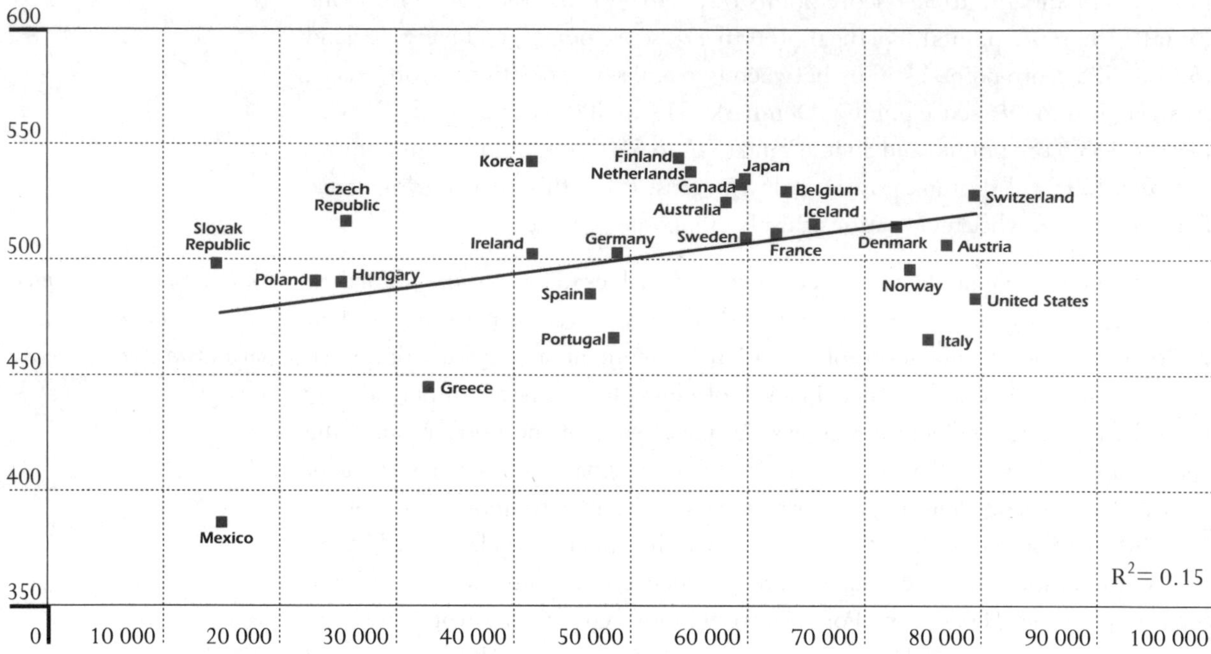

Source: OECD PISA 2003 database, Table 2.6.

...which shows a positive relationship between spending per student and mean mathematics performance...

Figure 2.20 shows a positive relationship between spending per student and mean mathematics performance (see also Table 2.6). As expenditure per student on educational institutions increases, so also does a country's mean performance. However, expenditure per student explains merely 15 per cent of the variation in mean performance between countries.

...but also that high spending levels do not guarantee high performance.

Deviations from the trend line suggest that moderate spending per student cannot automatically be equated with poor performance by education systems. Spending per student between the ages of six and 15 years in the Czech Republic is roughly one-third of, and in Korea roughly one-half of, spending levels in the United States, but while both the Czech Republic and Korea are among the top ten performers in PISA, the United States performs below the OECD average. Similarly, Spain and the United States perform almost equally well, but while the United States spends roughly USD 80 000 per student between the ages of six and 15 years, in Spain this figure is merely USD 47 000. Countries that perform significantly higher than would be expected from their spending per

student alone include Australia, Belgium, Canada, the Czech Republic, Finland, Japan, Korea and the Netherlands. Countries that perform significantly below the level of performance predicted from spending per student include Greece, Italy, Mexico, Norway, Portugal, Spain and the United States. In summary, the results suggest that, while spending on educational institutions is a necessary prerequisite for the provision of high-quality education, spending alone is not sufficient to achieve high levels of outcomes.

IMPLICATIONS FOR POLICY

Mathematics plays a central role for the success of individuals and societies …

For much of the past century, the content of school mathematics curricula was dominated by the need to provide the foundations for the professional training of a small number of mathematicians, scientists and engineers. With the growing role of science, mathematics and technology in modern life, however, the objectives of personal fulfilment, employment and full participation in society increasingly require that all adults, not just those aspiring to a scientific career, should be mathematically, scientifically and technologically literate. The performance of a country's best students in mathematics and related subjects may have implications for the role that the country will play in tomorrow's advanced technology sector, and for its overall international competitiveness. Conversely, deficiencies among lower-performing students in mathematics can have negative consequences for individuals' labour-market and earnings prospects and for their capacity to participate fully in society.

…so most countries attach great importance to securing high performance standards in mathematics throughout their education system…

Not surprisingly, policy-makers and educators alike attach great importance to mathematics education. Addressing the increasing demand for mathematical skills requires excellence throughout education systems, and it is therefore essential to monitor how well countries provide young adults with fundamental skills in this area.

…but some continue to see wide differences in the performance of their students.

The wide disparities in student performance in mathematics within most countries, evident from the analysis in this chapter, suggest that excellence throughout education systems remains still a remote goal and that countries need to serve a wide range of student abilities, including those who perform exceptionally well and also those most in need. At the same time, the analysis has shown that wide disparities in performance are not a necessary condition for a country to attain a high level of overall performance. Indeed, some of the best-performing countries have achieved their results while displaying a modest gap between their stronger and weaker performers.

Relative strengths and weaknesses in various areas of mathematics may lead countries to re-examine curricular priorities.

Performance does not only vary widely among students, but in many countries it also varies between different areas of mathematical content. Such variation may be related to differences in curricular emphases as well as to the effectiveness with which curricula are delivered in different content areas. While countries need to make curricular choices based on their national context and priorities, examining these choices in the light of what other countries consider important can provide a broader frame of reference for national educational policy development.

Gender differences are visible in most countries, with males performing better, particularly at the high end of the performance distribution…

This chapter has shown differences between the performance of males and females in many countries, with the advantage for males being largest in the mathematics/space and shape and the uncertainty scales. Much remains to be done to close the gender gap in mathematics and related fields and evidence suggests that action in this area needs to be targeted at youth and, indeed, children. Their performance at school, and their motivation and attitudes in different subject areas, can have a significant influence on their further educational and occupational pathways. These, in turn, may have an impact not only on individual career and salary prospects, but also on the broader effectiveness with which human capital is developed and utilised in OECD economies and societies. However, the wide variation in gender gaps among countries suggests that the current differences are not the inevitable outcomes of education and that effective policies and practices can overcome what were long taken to be the fixed outcomes of differences in interests, learning styles and even underlying capacities between males and females.

…and, while overall gender differences are often small, the gender gaps which teachers face in classrooms are often considerable.

In most countries, the gender differences are larger within schools than they are overall, reflecting that females tend to attend the higher performing, academically oriented tracks and schools at a higher rate than males but, within these, often perform significantly below males. From a policy perspective – and for teachers in classrooms – gender differences in mathematics performance, therefore, warrant continued attention.

Differences in the overall performance of countries do matter, and cannot be explained only by spending.

Finally, although the variation in student performance within countries is many times larger than the variation between countries, significant differences between countries in the average performance of students should not be overlooked. Particularly in subject areas such as mathematics and science, these differences may raise questions about some countries' future competitiveness. Not all of the variation in the performance of countries in mathematics can be explained by spending on education. Although the analyses have revealed a positive association between the two, they also suggest that while spending on educational institutions is a necessary prerequisite for the provision of high-quality education, spending alone is not sufficient to achieve high levels of outcomes. Other factors, including the effectiveness with which resources are invested, also play a crucial role.

Underperformance matters greatly for individuals, especially where they fail to complete secondary education, reducing their job prospects…

Does mathematics performance on the PISA assessment matter for the future? It is difficult to assess to what extent performance and success in school is predictive of future success. However, what OECD data show is that individuals who have not completed an upper secondary qualification – still roughly one in five on average across OECD countries, despite significant progress over the last generation – face significantly poorer labour-market prospects. For example, labour force participation rates rise steeply with educational attainment in most OECD countries (OECD, 2004a). With very few exceptions, the participation rate for graduates of tertiary education is markedly higher than that for upper secondary graduates which, in turn, is markedly higher than that for individuals without an upper secondary qualification. The gap in male participation rates is particularly wide between upper secondary graduates, and those without an upper secondary qualification and the labour force participation rate for women with less than upper secondary attainment is particularly low.

...and also their earnings prospects, which tend to be strongly affected by whether they obtain upper secondary and tertiary qualifications...

Similarly, education and earnings are positively linked, with upper secondary education representing a threshold in many countries beyond which additional education attracts a particularly high premium (OECD, 2004a). In all countries, graduates of tertiary-level education earn substantially more than upper secondary graduates. It is possible to contrast, on the one hand, the advantages of education for individuals in terms of higher average earnings, lower risks of unemployment and the public subsidies they receive during their studies with, on the other hand, the costs that individuals incur when studying, in terms of the tuition fees they need to pay, earnings lost during their studies or higher tax rates later in life. The annual rate of return on the investment that individuals incur when completing a tertiary degree is higher than real interest rates, and often significantly so, ranging for males from around 7% in Italy and Japan to 17% in the United Kingdom. Even when public investment in education is included, there is still a positive and significant social return to tertiary education in all countries with comparable data.

...while for society as a whole, education can boost productivity and strengthen citizenship.

In addition, international comparisons show a pivotal role that education plays in fostering labour productivity, and by implication economic growth – not just as an input linking aggregate output to the stock of productive inputs, but also as a factor strongly associated with the rate of technological progress. The estimated long-run effect on economic output of one additional year of education in the combined OECD area is in the order of between 3 and 6 per cent (OECD, 2004a). Finally, the importance of mathematics for citizenship in the modern world should not be overlooked.

Fifteen-year-olds have many chances ahead of them, but those who do well early on are more likely to continue learning...

Obviously, learning does not end with compulsory education and modern societies provide various opportunities for individuals to upgrade their knowledge and skills throughout their lives. However, at least when it comes to job-related continuing education and training, on average across OECD countries, about three times as many training hours are invested in employees with a tertiary qualification, as in employees without an upper secondary qualification (OECD, 2000a and 2000b). Thus, initial education combines with other influences to make job-related training beyond school least likely for those who need it most.

...so poor performance at age 15 causes justifiable concern.

This underlines why a solid foundation of knowledge and skills at school is fundamental for the future success of individuals and societies and the importance of providing opportunities for adults who need to improve their basic levels of literacy in reading, mathematics and science in order to be able to engage in relevant learning throughout their lives. It is in that sense that the results from PISA give rise to concern in many countries.

Notes

1. See Box 2.2 for an explanation.
2. In mathematics, the improvement is statistically significant at the 95 per cent confidence level only for one of the two scales with comparable data.
3. In Mexico, the net enrolment rate of 15-year-olds increased from 51.6 per cent in the 1999-2000 school year to 56.1 per cent in the 2002-03 school year (*Source*: OECD education database).
4. Further technical details on the methods used to estimate student ability and item difficulty, and to form the scale, are provided in the *PISA 2003 Technical Report* (OECD, forthcoming).
5. To be more precise, students were placed at a point on the scale at which they had a 62 per cent chance of answering a question correctly. This is not an arbitrary number: its derivation is related to the definition of proficiency levels, as explained later in this section.
6. Technically, the mean score for student performance in mathematics across OECD countries was set at 500 score points and the standard deviation at 100 score points, with the data weighted so that each OECD country contributed equally. Note that this anchoring of the scale was implemented for the combination of the four scales. The average mean score and standard deviation of the individual mathematics scales can therefore differ from 500 and 100 score points.
7. Results for the combined OECD area are represented in the tables by the ***OECD total.*** The OECD total takes the OECD countries as a single entity, to which each country contributes in proportion to the number of 15-year-olds enrolled in its schools. It illustrates how a country compares with the OECD area as a whole. By contrast, the ***OECD average***, that is also referred to in this report, is the mean of the data values for all OECD countries for which data are available or can be estimated. The OECD average can be used to see how a country compares on a given indicator with a typical OECD country. The OECD average does not take into account the absolute size of the student population in each country, *i.e.,* each country contributes equally to the average. In this publication, the OECD total is generally used when references to the stock of human capital in the OECD area are made. Where the focus is on comparing performance across education systems, the OECD average is used.
8. For the country Serbia and Montenegro, data for Montenegro are not available. The latter accounts for 7.9 per cent of the national population. The name "Serbia" is used as a shorthand for the Serbian part of Serbia and Montenegro.
9. Although the probability that a particular difference will falsely be declared to be statistically significant is low (5 per cent) in each single comparison, the probability of making such an error increases when several comparisons are made simultaneously. It is possible to make an adjustment for this which reduces to 5 per cent the maximum probability that differences will be falsely declared as statistically significant at least once among all the comparisons that are made. Such an adjustment, based on the Bonferroni method, has been incorporated into the multiple comparison charts in this volume, as indicated by the arrow symbols.
10. Column 1 in Table A1.2 estimates the score point difference that is associated with one school year. This difference can be estimated for the 26 OECD countries in which a sizeable number of 15-year-olds in the PISA samples were enrolled in at least two different grades. Since 15-year-olds cannot be assumed to be distributed at random across the grade levels, adjustments had to be made for contextual factors that may relate to the assignment of students to the different grade levels. These adjustments are documented in columns 2 to 7 of the table. While it is possible to estimate the typical performance difference among students in two adjacent grades net of the effects of selection and contextual factors, this difference cannot automatically be equated with the progress that students have made over the last school year but should be interpreted as a lower bound of the progress achieved. This is not only because different students were assessed but also because the contents of the PISA assessment was not expressly designed to match what students had learned in the preceding school year but was designed more broadly to assess the cumulative outcome of learning in school up to age 15. For example, if the curriculum of the grades in which 15-year-olds are enrolled mainly in covers other material than that assessed by PISA (which, in turn, may have been included in earlier school years) then the observed performance difference will underestimate student progress. Accurate measures of student progress can only be obtained through a longitudinal assessment design that focuses on content.
11. When measured in terms of effect sizes (for an explanation of the concept and its interpretation see Box 3.3), these are greater than 0.2 only in Canada, Ireland, Luxembourg, Korea, the Slovak Republic, Spain and Switzerland as well as in the partner countries Liechtenstein, Uruguay and Macao-China. In all countries except Liechtenstein the effect sizes remain below 0.3.

12. See Annex A8 for an explanation of the methods employed to establish the link between the PISA 2000 and 2003 assessments.

13. Luxembourg also shows a significant performance difference. However, the results are not comparable because of changes in assessment conditions. In PISA 2000, students in Luxembourg were given one assessment booklet, with the languages chosen by the students one week prior to the assessment. In practice, however, familiarity with the language of assessment became an important barrier for a significant proportion of students in PISA 2000. In 2003, students were each given one assessment booklet in both languages of instruction and could choose their preferred language immediately prior to the assessment. This provided for assessment conditions that are better comparable with those in countries that have only one language of instruction and results in a fairer assessment of the true performance of students in mathematics, science, reading and problem-solving. As a result of this change in procedures, the assessment conditions and hence the assessment results for Luxembourg cannot be compared between 2000 and 2003. Results for 2000 have therefore been excluded for Luxembourg from this report.

14. In the United States, large standard errors in 2000 may account at least in part for the fact that the United States score is not statistically significantly different between 2000 and 2003.

15. When measured in terms of effect sizes (for an explanation of the concept and its interpretation see Box 3.3), these are greater than 0.2 only in Denmark, Italy and Korea as well as the partner countries Liechtenstein and Macao-China. In all countries the effect sizes remain below 0.3.

16. Also, Luxembourg shows a large performance difference between the 2000 and 2003 results, but – as explained previously – this may be largely due to the modified assessment conditions that allowed students to choose their preferred language from among the two official languages of instruction.

17. When measured in terms of effect sizes (for an explanation of the concept and its interpretation see Box 3.3), these are greater than 0.2 only in Greece, Korea and the partner country Liechtenstein. In all countries the effect sizes remain below 0.3.

18. When measured in terms of effect sizes (for an explanation of the concept and its interpretation see Box 3.3), these are greater than 0.2 only in Denmark, Greece, Korea, Italy, Luxembourg, Switzerland, and the partner countries Liechtenstein and Macao-China. In all countries the effect sizes remain below 0.3.

19. The relative probability of a country assuming each rank-order position on each scale is determined from the country mean scores, their standard errors and the covariance between the performance scales of the two assessment areas. From this it can be concluded whether, with a probability of 95 per cent, a country would rank statistically significantly higher, not statistically differently, or statistically significantly lower on one scale than on the other scale. For details on the methods employed see the *PISA 2003 Technical Report* (OECD, forthcoming).

20. When measured in terms of effect sizes (for an explanation of the concept and its interpretation see Box 3.3), gender differences on the mathematics scale are greater than 0.2 only in Greece, Korea and the partner countries Liechtenstein and Macao-China. In all countries the effect sizes remain below 0.3.

21. A list of the school factors and an explanation of the model used is given in Chapter 5.

22. For the 30 OECD countries included in this comparison, the correlation between mean student performance in mathematics and GDP per capita is 0.43. The explained variation is obtained as the square of the correlation.

23. Cumulative expenditure for a given country is approximated as follows: let $n(0)$, $n(1)$ and $n(2)$ be the typical number of years spent by a student from the age of six up to the age of 15 years in primary, lower secondary and upper secondary education. Let $E(0)$, $E(1)$ and $E(2)$ be the annual expenditure per student in US dollars converted using purchasing power parities in primary, lower secondary and upper secondary education, respectively. The cumulative expenditure is then calculated by multiplying current annual expenditure E by the typical duration of study n for each level of education i using the following formula:

$$CE = \sum_{i=0}^{2} n(i) * E(i)$$

Estimates for $n(i)$ are based on the International Standard Classification of Education (ISCED) (OECD, 1997).

Student Learning: Attitudes, Engagement and Strategies

INTRODUCTION

Schools need to maintain and develop children's positive disposition to learning...

Most children come to school ready and willing to learn. How can schools foster and strengthen this predisposition and ensure that young adults leave school with the motivation and capacity to continue learning throughout life? Without the development of these attitudes and skills, individuals will not be well prepared to acquire the new knowledge and skills necessary for successful adaptation to changing circumstances.

...help students acquire the skills to manage their own learning...

In school, teachers manage much of students' learning. However, learning is enhanced if students can manage it themselves; moreover, once they leave school, people have to manage most of their own learning. To do this, they need to be able to establish goals, to persevere, to monitor their learning progress, to adjust their learning strategies as necessary and to overcome difficulties in learning. Students who leave school with the autonomy to set their own learning goals and with a sense that they can reach those goals are better equipped to learn throughout their lives.

...foster students' interest in and positive attitudes towards the subjects they learn...

A genuine interest in school subjects is important as well. Students with an interest in a subject like mathematics are likely to be more motivated to manage their own learning and develop the requisite skills to become effective learners of that subject. Hence, interest in mathematics is relevant when considering the development of effective learning strategies for mathematics. In contrast, anxiety about learning mathematics can act as a barrier to effective learning. Students who feel anxious about their ability to cope in mathematics learning situations may avoid them and thus lose important career and life opportunities.

...and strengthen student engagement with school more generally.

Finally, the majority of students' learning time is spent in school and as such the climate of the school is important for the creation of effective learning environments. If a student feels alienated and disengaged from the learning contexts in school, his or her potential to master fundamental skills and concepts and develop effective learning skills is likely to be reduced.

To shed light on this, PISA assessed student approaches to learning...

A comprehensive assessment of how well a country is performing in education must therefore look at these cognitive, affective and attitudinal aspects in addition to academic performance. To this end, PISA 2003 establishes a broader profile of what students are like as learners at age 15, one that includes students' learning strategies and some of the non-cognitive outcomes of schooling that are important for lifelong learning: their motivation, their engagement and their beliefs about their own capacities. Since the focus of PISA 2003 was on mathematics, most of these issues were analysed in the context of mathematics as well.

...and this chapter gives a profile of...

This chapter reports and analyses these results. It seeks to provide a better understanding of how various aspects of students' attitudes to learning and their learning behaviour relate to each other and to student performance, it observes how these relationships differ across countries, and it explores the distribution of relevant characteristics among students, schools and countries. After summarising existing evidence and explaining how students' characteristics as learners are measured and reported in 2003, the chapter analyses in turn:

- *Students' engagement with mathematics and school*. This is related both to their own interest and enjoyment and to external incentives. Subject motivation is often regarded as the driving force behind learning, but the analysis extends the picture to students' more general attitudes towards school including students' sense of belonging at school.

...students' engagement with mathematics and school...

- *Students' beliefs about themselves*. This includes students' views about their own competence and learning characteristics in mathematics, as well as attitudinal aspects, which have both been shown to have a considerable impact on the way they set goals, the strategies they use and their performance.

...students' beliefs about themselves as learners...

- *Students' anxiety in mathematics*, which is common among students in many countries and is known to affect performance.

...their anxiety in mathematics...

- *Students' learning strategies*. This considers what strategies students use during learning. Also of interest is how these strategies relate to motivational factors and students' self-related beliefs as well as to students' performance in mathematics.

...and student learning strategies.

The chapter places considerable emphasis on comparing approaches to learning for males and females. Although Chapter 2 has shown gender differences in student performance in mathematics to be moderate, this chapter shows that there are marked differences between males and females in their interest in and enjoyment of mathematics, their self-related beliefs, as well as their emotions and learning strategies related to mathematics. An important reason why these additional dimensions warrant policy attention is that research shows them to influence decisions about enrolment in school tracks or study programmes and courses where mathematics is an important subject. These decisions may, in turn, shape students' post-secondary education and career choices.

It also examines gender differences in student approaches to learning, which can influence future learning and career paths.

When interpreting the analyses reported in this chapter, three caveats need to be borne in mind. First, constructs such as interest in and enjoyment of mathematics and the use of particular types of learning strategies are based on students' self-reports, and not on direct measures. To measure directly whether students actually adopt certain approaches to learning, one would need to examine their actions in specific situations. This requires in-depth interview and observation methods of a type that cannot be applied in a large-scale survey like PISA (Artelt, 2000; Boekaerts, 1999; Lehtinen, 1992). While PISA collects information on the extent to which students generally adopt various learning strategies that have been shown to be important for successful learning outcomes, such necessary preconditions for successful learning do not guarantee that a student will actually regulate his or her learning on specific occasions. However, by looking at such characteristics and at students' views on how they see themselves, one can obtain a good indication of whether a student is likely to regulate his or her own learning, and this is the approach taken by PISA. At the centre of this approach is the hypothesis that students who approach learning with confidence, with strong motivation and with a range of learning strategies at their disposal are more likely to be successful learners. This hypothesis has been borne out by the research referred to in Box 3.1.

Bear in mind that the characteristics discussed in this chapter are self-reported...

...that cultural differences make cross-country comparison of some of the learner characteristics difficult...

Second, students across countries may vary with respect to how they perceive and respond to the questionnaire items on which the constructs are based. This is quite understandable since the survey asks students to make subjective assessments about things such as how hard they work, while at the same time students perceive their attitudes and behaviour within a frame of reference shaped by their school and culture. It cannot be taken for granted, for example, that a student who says that he or she works hard has characteristics comparable to a student in another country who says the same: cultural factors can influence profoundly the way in which such responses are given. This is emphasised by research showing that self-reported characteristics are vulnerable to problems of comparability across cultures (*e.g.,* Heine *et al.,* 1999; van de Vijver and Leung, 1997; Bempechat, *et al.,* 2002) and has been confirmed by analyses of students' responses in PISA. Analyses of PISA 2000 data (OECD, 2003b) as well as PISA 2003 data have shown that for some of the student characteristics measured in PISA, most notably their self-beliefs and their sense of belonging at school, valid cross-country comparisons can be made. In these cases, similar relationships between self-reported characteristics and student performance within and across countries indicate that the characteristics being measured are comparable across countries. In contrast, for other measures – most notably interest in mathematics, instrumental motivation, the use of elaboration and control strategies – cross-country comparisons are more difficult to make.

...though not impossible...

Nevertheless, even where cross-country comparisons of student reports are problematic, it is often still possible to compare the distribution of a particular characteristic among students within different countries. Thus, for example, while the average level of instrumental motivation in two countries may not be comparable in absolute terms, the way in which student scores on a scale of instrumental motivation are distributed around each country's average can be compared in building up country profiles of approaches to learning. Differences among subgroups within countries as well as structural relationships between students' approaches to learning and their performance on the combined PISA mathematics test will therefore be the main focus of the results presented here.

...and that, while analyses of associations raise questions of causality, these remain difficult to answer.

Third, while analyses of associations raise questions of causality, these remain difficult to answer. It may be, for example, that good performance and attitudes towards learning are mutually reinforcing. Alternatively, it could be that students with higher natural ability both perform well and use particular learning strategies. Other factors, such as home background or differences in the schooling environment, may also play a part. However, research has identified some measurable learning characteristics of students that are associated with the tendency to regulate learning, as well as with better performance. Research has also shown that learning is more likely to be effective where a student plays a proactive role in the learning process – for example drawing on strong motivation and clear goals to select an appropriate learning strategy.[1] These are the basis for this chapter.

Existing evidence on student approaches to learning and how it frames PISA's approach

Evidence from earlier research has played an important role in the construction of the PISA measures on learner characteristics, both in terms of establishing which aspects of students' learning approaches are important and in terms of developing accurate measures of those approaches.

PISA draws on existing research…

Research on effective student approaches to learning has focused on understanding what it is for a student to regulate his or her own learning. This focus derives both from the direct evidence (Box 3.1) that such regulation yields benefits in terms of improved student performance and also from the assumption (albeit not presently backed by strong research) that lifelong learning is reliant on self-regulation. The latter view is increasingly important in analysis of educational outcomes. For example, a large conceptual study on *Defining and Selecting Competencies,* carried out by the Swiss Federal Statistical Office in collaboration with the OECD, identified three key categories of the broader outcomes of schooling. One of these, personal skills, was defined in terms of "the ability to act autonomously" (Rychen and Salganik, 2002).[2]

…that has focused on how students regulate their own learning.

Although there have been varying definitions of self-regulated learning, it is generally understood to involve students being motivated to learn, selecting appropriate learning goals to guide the learning process using appropriate knowledge and skills to direct learning and consciously selecting learning strategies appropriate to the task at hand.

Self-regulated learning involves motivation and the ability to adopt appropriate goals and strategies…

Box 3.1 ■ **Students who regulate their learning perform better**

There is a broad literature on the effects of self-regulated learning on scholastic achievement. Students who are able to regulate their learning effectively are more likely to achieve specific learning goals. Empirical evidence for such positive effects of regulating one's learning and using learning strategies stems from:

- Experimental research (*e.g.,* Willoughby and Wood, 1994);
- Research on training (*e.g.,* Lehtinen, 1992; Rosenshine and Meister, 1994); and
- Systematic observation of students while they are learning (*e.g.,* Artelt, 2000) including studies that ask students to think aloud about their own awareness and regulation of learning processes (*e.g.,* Veenman and van Hout-Wolters, 2002).

Research demonstrates the importance of a combination of such factors in a particular learning episode (*e.g.*, Boekaerts, 1999). Students must be able to draw simultaneously on a range of resources. Some of these resources are concerned with knowledge about how to process information (cognitive resources) and awareness of different available learning strategies (metacognitive resources). Learners may be aware of appropriate learning strategies, but not put them into use (Flavell and Wellman, 1977). Therefore, students also need motivational resources that contribute to their readiness, for example, to define their own goals, interpret success and failure appropriately, and translate wishes into intentions and plans (Weinert, 1994).

...as well as the interaction between what students know and can do and their dispositions.

Self-regulated learning thus depends on the interaction between what students know and can do on the one hand, and on their motivation and dispositions on the other. PISA's investigation of student approaches to learning is therefore based on a model combining these two broad elements. They interact strongly with each other. For example, students' motivation to learn has a profound impact on their choice of learning strategies because, as shown below, some strategies require a considerable degree of time and effort to implement (Hatano, 1998).

Studies investigating how students actually regulate learning and use appropriate strategies have found particularly strong associations between approaches to learning and performance. Less direct but easier to measure, students' attitudes and behaviours associated with self-regulated learning – such as their motivation and tendency to use certain strategies – are also associated with performance, albeit generally less strongly.

Measuring whether students are likely to adopt effective approaches to learning

PISA considered student characteristics that make positive approaches to learning more likely...

Following the principle described above – that certain characteristics make it more likely that students will approach learning in beneficial ways – PISA examined a number of such characteristics and asked students several questions about each of them in the context of mathematics. These categories came under the four broad elements of motivation, self-related beliefs, emotional factors and learning strategies. Figure 3.1 sets out the characteristics being investigated, giving a brief rationale for their selection, based on previous research, as well as examples of exactly what students were asked. The full set of questions is shown in Annex A1.

...based on reasonably reliable self-reports.

To what extent can one expect an accurate self-assessment by 15-year-olds of their learning approaches? Evidence from selected countries shows that by the age of 15, students' knowledge about their own learning and their ability to give valid answers to questionnaire items have developed considerably (Schneider, 1996). It can thus be assumed that the data provide a reasonable picture of student learning approaches.

Figure 3.1 ■ **Characteristics and attitudes of students as learners in mathematics**

Category of characteristics and rationale	Student characteristics used to construct a scale to report results
A. Motivational factors and general attitudes towards school Motivation is often considered the driving force behind learning. One can distinguish motives deriving from external rewards for good performance such as praise or future prospects and internally generated motives such as interest in subject areas (Deci and Ryan, 1985). Students' more general attitudes towards school and their sense of belonging at school were also considered both as predictors for learning outcomes and as important outcomes of schooling in themselves.	**1.** ***Interest in and enjoyment of mathematics.*** Students were asked about their interest in mathematics as a subject as well as their enjoyment of learning mathematics. Interest in and enjoyment of a subject is a relatively stable orientation that affects the intensity and continuity of engagement in learning situations, the selection of strategies and the depth of understanding. **2.** ***Instrumental motivation in mathematics.*** Students were asked to what extent they are encouraged to learn by external rewards such as good job prospects. Longitudinal studies (*e.g.*, Wigfield *et al.*, 1998) show that such motivation influences both study choices and performance. **3.** ***Attitudes toward school.*** Students were asked to think about what they had learned at school in relation to how the school had prepared them for adult life, given them confidence to make decisions, taught them things that could be useful in their job or been a waste of time. **4.** ***Sense of belonging at school.*** Students were asked to express their perceptions about whether their school was a place where they felt like an outsider, made friends easily, felt like they belonged, felt awkward and out of place or felt lonely.
B. Self-related beliefs in mathematics Learners form views about their own competence and learning characteristics. These have considerable impact on the way they set goals, the strategies they use and their achievement (Zimmerman, 1999). Two ways of defining these beliefs are: in terms of how well students think that they can handle even difficult tasks – self-efficacy (Bandura, 1994); and in terms of their belief in their own abilities – self-concept (Marsh, 1993). These two constructs are closely associated with one another, but nonetheless distinct. Self-related beliefs are sometimes referred to in terms of self-confidence, indicating that such beliefs are positive. In both cases, confidence in oneself has important benefits for motivation and for the way in which students approach learning tasks.	**5.** ***Self-efficacy in mathematics.*** Students were asked to what extent they believe in their own ability to handle learning situations in mathematics effectively, overcoming difficulties. This affects students' willingness to take on challenging tasks and to make an effort and persist in tackling them. It thus has a key impact on motivation (Bandura, 1994). **6.** ***Self-concept in mathematics.*** Students were asked about their belief in their own mathematical competence. Belief in one's own abilities is highly relevant to successful learning (Marsh, 1986), as well as being a goal in its own right.

C. Emotional factors in mathematics Students' avoidance of mathematics due to emotional stress is reported to be widespread in many countries. Some research treats this construct as part of general attitudes to mathematics, though it is generally considered distinct from attitudinal variables.	**7.** ***Anxiety in mathematics.*** Students were asked to what extent they feel helpless and under emotional stress when dealing with mathematics. The effects of anxiety in mathematics are indirect, once self-related cognitions are taken into account (Meece *et al.,* 1990).
D. Student learning strategies in mathematics Learning strategies are the plans students select to achieve their goals: the ability to do so distinguishes competent learners who can regulate their learning (Brown *et al.,* 1983). Cognitive strategies that require information processing skills include, but are not limited to, memorisation and elaboration. Metacognitive strategies, entailing conscious regulation of one's own learning, are measured in the concept of control strategies.	**8.** ***Memorisation / rehearsal strategies.*** Students were asked about their use of learning strategies for mathematics that involve representations of knowledge and procedures stored in memory with little or no further processing.
	9. ***Elaboration strategies.*** Students were asked about their use of learning strategies for mathematics that involve connecting new material to prior learning. By exploring how knowledge learned in other contexts relates to new material students acquire greater understanding than through simple memorisation.
	10. ***Control strategies.*** Students were asked about their use of learning strategies for mathematics that involve checking what one has learned and working out what one still needs to learn, allowing learners to adapt their learning to the task at hand. These strategies are used to ensure that one's learning goals are reached and are at the heart of the approaches to learning measured by PISA.

STUDENTS' ENGAGEMENT WITH LEARNING IN MATHEMATICS AND SCHOOL MORE GENERALLY

This section examines four aspects of student engagement with mathematics and school and relates these to performance.

This section describes four constructs collected from students in PISA 2003 that are related to a positive disposition to school and learning and then proceeds to report how these variables relate to achievement. Two of the constructs are specific to learning in mathematics (interest in and enjoyment of mathematics or intrinsic motivation, and instrumental or external motivation), while two relate to more general engagement with schooling (attitude towards school and sense of belonging at school). As well as being related thematically, these variables are related to each other empirically – *i.e.* there are strong associations between them.

Interest in and enjoyment of mathematics

Intrinsic motivation shows whether students have interest which encourages them to study hard.

Motivation and engagement can be regarded as the driving forces of learning. They can also affect students' quality of life during their adolescence and can influence whether they will successfully pursue further educational or labour market opportunities. In particular, given the importance of mathematics for students' future lives, education systems need to ensure that students have

Box 3.2 ■ **Interpreting the PISA indices**

The measures are presented as indices that summarise student responses to a series of related questions constructed on the basis of previous research (Annex A1). The validity of comparisons across countries was explored using structural equation modelling. In describing students in terms of each characteristic (*e.g.,* interest in mathematics), scales were constructed on which the average OECD student (*e.g.,* the student with an average level of interest) was given an index value of zero, and about two-thirds of the OECD student population are between the values of -1 and 1 (*i.e.,* the index has a standard deviation of 1). Negative values on an index do not necessarily imply that students responded negatively to the underlying questions. Rather, a student with a negative score responded less positively than students on average across OECD countries. Likewise, a student with a positive score responded more positively than the average in the OECD area. As each indicator is introduced below, a diagram shows more precisely which scores are associated with particular responses.

Wherever standard deviations are reported, these refer to the standard deviation of the distribution in the OECD area.

Box 3.3 ■ **Comparing the magnitude of differences across countries**

Sometimes it is useful to compare differences in an index between groups, such as males and females, across countries. A problem that may occur in such instances is that the distribution of the index varies across countries. One way to resolve this is to calculate an effect size that accounts for differences in the distributions. An effect size measures the difference between, say, the interest in mathematics of male and female students in a given country, relative to the average variation in interest in mathematics scores among male and female students in the country.

An effect size also allows a comparison of differences across measures that differ in their metric. For example, it is possible to compare effect sizes between the PISA indices and the PISA test scores.

In accordance with common practices, effect sizes less than 0.20 are considered small in this volume, effect sizes in the order of 0.50 are considered medium, and effect sizes greater than 0.80 are considered large. Many comparisons in this chapter consider differences only if the effect sizes are equal to or great than 0.20, even if smaller differences are still statistically significant.

For detailed information on the construction of the indices, see Annex A1.

both the interest and the motivation to continue learning in this area beyond school. Interest in and enjoyment of particular subjects, or *intrinsic motivation*, affects both the degree and continuity of engagement in learning and the depth of understanding reached. This effect has been shown to operate largely independently of students' general motivation to learn (see also the last section of this chapter). For example, a student who is interested in mathematics and therefore tends to study diligently may or may not show a high level of

general learning motivation, and vice versa. Hence, an analysis of the pattern of students' interest in mathematics is important. Such an analysis can reveal significant strengths and weaknesses in attempts by education systems to promote motivation to learn in various subjects among different sub-groups of students.

Students feel much less positive overall about mathematics than reading...

In PISA 2000, which focussed on reading, students felt generally positive about reading. In contrast, students in PISA 2003 (as well as in PISA 2000) expressed less enthusiasm for mathematics. For example while, on average across OECD countries, about half of the students report being interested in the things they learn in mathematics, only 38 per cent agree or strongly agree with the statement that they do mathematics because they enjoy it.

Less than one-third report looking forward to their mathematics lessons. In fact, in countries such as Belgium, Finland, France, Korea, Iceland, Italy, Latvia, the Netherlands, Portugal, Serbia[3] and Spain fewer than half as many students who report an interest in the things they learn in mathematics, say that they look forward to their mathematics lessons (Figure 3.2).

...and it is important to understand reasons for this and how negative attitudes to mathematics can be avoided.

It is, of course, well established that intrinsic motivation tends to be lower at later stages of schooling and students seem often to lose interest in and enjoyment of mathematics after primary education. This is partly an effect of increasing differentiation of students' interests and their investment of time as they grow older. However, to what extent is lower interest in mathematics an inevitable outcome, and to what extent a consequence of the ways in which schooling takes place and mathematics is taught? One way to examine this is to explore how educational systems vary in this respect and to what extent any observed differences among schools within countries in student motivation relate to differences in educational policies and practices.

A standardised scale shows the strength of students' interest and enjoyment.

Students' reports of their interest in and enjoyment of mathematics can be represented on an index constructed so that the average score across OECD countries is 0 and two-thirds score between 1 and -1. A positive value on the index indicates that students report interest in and enjoyment of mathematics higher than the OECD average. A negative value indicates an interest lower than the OECD average (Box 3.2).[4]

While this kind of measure cannot be easily compared across cultures...

The OECD averages mask significant differences among countries. For example, in the Czech Republic, Hungary and Japan 40 per cent or less of students agree or strongly agree that they are interested in the things they learn in mathematics, while more than two-thirds of students in France, Mexico and Portugal, as well as in the PISA partner countries Brazil, Indonesia, the Russian Federation, Thailand, Tunisia, and Uruguay agree or strongly agree with this statement. This being said, research in PISA 2000 pointed out that it is difficult to interpret the meaning of absolute values on the index of interest in and enjoyment of mathematics across countries and cultures (Figure 3.2 and Table 3.1).

Nevertheless, even if absolute index values are difficult to compare across countries, it is reasonable to compare how closely student interest in and enjoyment of mathematics relate to student performance within each country. While the results from PISA 2003 do not necessarily show that countries with "more interested" students achieve, on average, better mathematics results (in fact, students in one of the best performing countries, Japan, report the lowest interest in and enjoyment of mathematics), the results do show that, within each country, students with greater interest in and enjoyment of mathematics tend to achieve better results than those with less interest in and enjoyment of mathematics. However, the strength of this relationship varies by country.

...it is possible to examine how student motivation relates to mathematics performance...

Table 3.1 shows in more detail the relationship between students' interest in and enjoyment of mathematics and mathematics performance. This is done by dividing students into four groups according to their value on the index. The average mathematics score of students in each of the four groups is shown for each country. When comparing across countries how well students in the top quarter and the bottom quarter of the index perform in mathematics, readers should bear in mind that the overall level of interest in mathematics itself varies between countries, so that these score differences should be interpreted with respect to each country mean. The third panel of Figure 3.2 summarises the relationship between interest in and enjoyment of mathematics and mathematics performance. The length of the bar shows the increase in mathematics scores per unit (*i.e.,* one OECD standard deviation) of the index of interest in and enjoyment of mathematics. The values to the right of the bar show the percentage of variance in mathematics performance that is explained by the index of interest in and enjoyment of mathematics. On average across OECD countries, the increase is equal to 12 score points. But the increase ranges from a negligible or very modest impact in Austria, Hungary, Luxembourg, Mexico, the United States and the partner countries Indonesia, Liechtenstein, Serbia, Thailand and Tunisia to between 27 and 36 score points, or roughly half a proficiency level in mathematics or the equivalent of the performance difference corresponding to a year of schooling,[5] in Denmark, Finland, Japan, Korea, Norway, Sweden and the partner country Hong Kong-China. Finland, Japan and Korea stand out because their average performance in mathematics is high but students do not express strong interest in mathematics. Nevertheless, the performance gap within these countries between students who express greater or lesser interest is also high, with the PISA index of interest in and enjoyment of mathematics explaining 11 per cent of the variance in mathematics performance in Finland and 8 per cent in Japan.

...and this comparison reveals that the association is much stronger in some countries than in others.

As noted before, the causal nature of this relationship may well be complex and is difficult to discern. Interest in the subject and performance may be mutually reinforcing and may also be affected by other factors, such as the social backgrounds of students and their schools. Indeed, as shown later in Table 3.12, the relationship between intrinsic motivation and student performance in mathematics diminishes considerably or even becomes negligible in most

Even though interest in mathematics cannot be clearly said to cause better performance, it is of value in its own right.

Figure 3.2 ■ **Students' interest in and enjoyment of mathematics**

	Percentage of students agreeing or strongly agreeing with the following statements:				Percentage of explained variance in student performance
	I enjoy reading about mathematics.	I look forward to my mathematics lessons.	I do mathematics because I enjoy it.	I am interested in the things I learn in mathematics.	
Tunisia	76	63	67	82	1.0
Indonesia	78	65	74	70	0.5
Thailand	70	66	69	84	0.1
Mexico	64	50	45	87	0.4
Brazil	52	47	61	80	1.4
Turkey	60	50	58	65	3.0
Denmark	48	47	59	65	8.8
Uruguay	40	51	48	70	2.2
Russian Fed.	28	41	41	69	1.3
Hong Kong-China	37	45	52	51	9.2
Portugal	35	27	47	69	1.9
Macao-China	34	35	45	43	4.2
New Zealand	35	41	39	56	1.3
Switzerland	24	41	52	60	1.2
Poland	40	30	40	54	2.5
Greece	46	27	44	50	6.7
Liechtenstein	22	41	52	54	0.1
Sweden	49	30	35	53	8.4
Italy	31	28	47	60	1.0
Latvia	26	22	41	55	1.8
Germany	21	40	43	55	1.4
France	31	24	47	67	4.9
United States	32	40	34	51	0.7
Slovak Republic	27	34	33	58	1.2
Australia	28	37	36	51	3.5
Canada	31	34	36	52	5.8
Ireland	29	32	33	48	3.8
Serbia	29	20	35	48	0.2
Spain	32	20	37	61	5.1
Iceland	33	24	38	49	8.6
Korea	29	22	31	44	15.5
Belgium	23	23	33	54	1.9
Norway	26	29	34	50	16.2
Czech Republic	10	30	31	40	3.9
Netherlands	20	20	35	46	2.1
Hungary	18	24	27	40	0.9
Finland	18	20	25	45	11.2
Luxembourg	21	30	33	43	0.6
Austria	20	31	28	41	1.0
Japan	13	26	26	32	7.9
OECD average	*31*	*31*	*38*	*53*	*1.5*
United Kingdom[1]	30	35	34	49	1.9

1. Response rate too low to ensure comparability (see Annex A3).
Source: OECD PISA 2003 database, Table 3.1.

countries when other learner characteristics are accounted for. However, whatever the nature of this relationship, a positive disposition towards mathematics remains an important educational goal in its own right.

It is of concern that in most countries males are statistically significantly more interested in mathematics than females, and in half of the countries this difference is very substantial.

While the preceding chapter showed that differences in the mathematics performance of males and females in at least two of the four mathematics scales tend to be small or moderate, it is noteworthy that, with the exception of Iceland, Ireland, Portugal, Spain and the partner countries the Russian Federation and Thailand, males express significantly higher interest in and enjoyment of mathematics than females, and particularly so in Austria, Germany, Switzerland and the partner country Liechtenstein (Table 3.1). As an example, on average across OECD countries, 37 per cent of males (compared with 25 per cent of females) agree or strongly agree with the statement that they enjoy reading about mathematics. As an even more extreme example, in Switzerland 33 per cent of males compared with just 13 per cent of females report enjoying reading about mathematics (for data see *www.pisa.oecd.org*). When gender differences on the PISA index of interest in and enjoyment of mathematics are converted into effect sizes (Figure 3.14 and Table 3.16), 21 of the 41 countries participating in PISA show effect sizes equal to or greater than 0.20, which can be interpreted as relevant to educational policy (Box 3.3). In contrast, gender differences in mathematics performance that exceed effect sizes of 0.20 only exist in Greece, Korea and the Slovak Republic and in the partner countries Liechtenstein and Macao-China (Table 3.16, Box 3.3).

This is of concern for policy as these data reveal inequalities between the genders in the effectiveness with which schools and societies promote motivation and interest in mathematics.

Instrumental motivation

Most students believe that success in mathematics will help them in their future work and study…

Beyond a general interest in mathematics, how do 15-year-olds assess the relevance of mathematics to their own life and what role does such external motivation play with regard to their mathematics performance? Among OECD countries 75 per cent of 15-year-olds agree or strongly agree with the statements that making an effort in mathematics is worth it because it will help them in the work that they want to do later on. Seventy-eight per cent of 15-year-olds agree or strongly agree that learning mathematics is important because it will help them with the subjects that they want to study further on in school. Sixty-six per cent of them agree or strongly agree that mathematics is an important subject because they need it for what they want to study later on. And 70 per cent agree or strongly agree that they will learn many things in mathematics that will help them get a job (see first panel of Figure 3.3a).

…but in some countries only half have such attitudes, a notable finding despite difficulties with comparability.

Nevertheless, significant proportions of students disagree or disagree strongly with such statements. There is also considerable cross-country variation in self-reported instrumental motivation. Only half of the students in Japan and Luxembourg agree or strongly agree that making an effort in mathematics is

Figure 3.3a ■ Students' instrumental motivation in mathematics

Percentage of students agreeing or strongly agreeing with the following statements:

	Making an effort in mathematics is worth it because it will help me in the work that I want to do later.	Learning mathematics is important because it will help me with the subjects that I want to study further on in school.	Mathematics is an important subject for me because I need it for what I want to study later on.	I will learn many things in mathematics that will help me get a job.	Percentage of explained variance in student performance
Mexico	95	94	82	91	0.3
Tunisia	84	82	82	81	3.1
Thailand	96	93	94	93	0.6
Brazil	89	86	81	88	2.4
Indonesia	94	90	95	89	0.3
Denmark	91	88	75	83	4.3
Iceland	83	85	79	78	4.0
New Zealand	85	89	77	82	2.2
Uruguay	83	83	71	84	0.2
Portugal	82	89	80	80	3.5
Canada	80	87	73	79	5.4
Turkey	81	86	79	66	1.5
Australia	83	87	74	79	3.0
United States	81	82	73	83	2.0
Norway	82	82	75	73	10.1
Ireland	80	85	66	75	0.7
Latvia	82	84	68	79	3.6
Finland	73	87	74	76	8.5
Poland	79	87	79	79	2.4
Sweden	71	86	67	73	5.3
Czech Republic	74	81	74	77	1.0
Russian Fed.	77	70	68	72	1.9
Macao-China	79	85	71	65	0.1
Germany	73	79	48	72	0.0
Switzerland	76	75	52	66	0.1
Liechtenstein	77	70	51	59	0.4
Slovak Republic	76	81	64	77	0.3
Greece	74	72	63	70	2.6
Spain	76	79	63	68	5.1
France	73	74	65	62	2.4
Hungary	79	71	69	67	0.5
Hong Kong-China	74	82	70	63	4.9
Italy	69	76	66	65	0.7
Serbia	73	73	54	60	0.1
Netherlands	70	71	63	61	0.4
Belgium	66	65	56	57	1.1
Luxembourg	52	61	51	53	0.0
Korea	57	60	58	46	12.0
Austria	64	51	36	56	0.2
Japan	49	43	41	47	6.2
OECD average	***75***	***78***	***66***	***70***	***0.7***
United Kingdom[1]	83	87	65	77	1.1

1. Response rate too low to ensure comparability (see Annex A3).
Source: OECD PISA 2003 database, Table 3.2a.

worth it, because it will help them in the work they want to do (Figure 3.3a). Similarly, the percentage of students that agree or strongly agree that they will learn many things in mathematics that will help them get a job is only around 46 per cent in Japan and Korea and also less than 60 per cent in Austria, Belgium and Luxembourg (it is 70 per cent on average across the OECD). Among the partner countries, this figure is equal to or more than 60 per cent. While the difficulties of comparing student responses on this index across cultures are acknowledged, the magnitude of these observed differences warrants attention.

While the links between instrumental motivation and mathematics performance are often weak...

As in the case of interest in and enjoyment of mathematics, countries can be compared on an index that summarises the different questions about instrumental motivation in mathematics (see *www.pisa.oecd.org* for the item map and Table 3.2a and Figure 3.3a for data). The third panel of Figure 3.3a shows the relationship between student instrumental motivation in mathematics and mathematics performance, measured in terms of the increase in mathematics performance associated with a one unit (one standard deviation) increase on the PISA index of instrumental motivation (Table 3.2a).

... in some countries students who are instrumentally motivated typically expect to stay in education for longer, and it is noteworthy...

Although the results show that the relationship between performance and instrumental motivation is much weaker than with intrinsic motivation (*i.e.*, interest in and enjoyment of mathematics), instrumental or extrinsic motivation has been found to be an important predictor for course selection, career choice and performance (Eccles, 1994).

Obviously, the choices that the 15-year-olds assessed in PISA 2003 will make in their future lives cannot be known. However, PISA asked 15-year-olds what education level they expect to attain. In most countries, levels of instrumental motivation are higher among students aspiring to at least completing educational programmes that provide access to tertiary education. This relationship is stronger still if the students expect to complete a tertiary programme, as is shown in the first panel of Figure 3.3b (Table 3.2b). However, this pattern is not universal, as shown in the second panel of the same figure.

...that in countries where female 15-year-olds show the lowest levels of instrumental motivation, relatively fewer women graduate from university with degrees in mathematics or computer science.

Last but not least, it is also noteworthy that in the countries where the difference in instrumental motivation between males and females is largest, namely in Austria, Germany, the Netherlands and Switzerland, the share of women graduating from university-level tertiary programmes in mathematics or computer science is below the OECD average and in some of these countries it is significantly below this benchmark (OECD, 2004a).[6] This observation supports the hypothesis that instrumental motivation in different subject matter areas, combined with other influences, is predictive of the future labour market and career choice of students. These differences are even more striking as Table 3.3 shows that, overall, females have higher expectation toward their future occupations than males. In the combined OECD area, 89 per cent of females, but only 76 per cent of males expect to hold a white-collar occupation by the age of 30.

Figure 3.3b ■ **Students' instrumental motivation in mathematics and their educational expectations**

Females ▲ Mean index of intrumental motivation in mathematics for females expecting to complete a university-level programme (ISCED Level 5A and 6)

— Mean index of intrumental motivation in mathematics for females expecting to complete an upper secondary programme providing access to university-level programmes (ISCED 3A and 4)

■ Mean index of intrumental motivation in mathematics for females expecting to complete lower secondary education (ISCED Level 2)

Males △ Mean index of intrumental motivation in mathematics for males expecting to complete a university-level programme (ISCED Level 5A and 6)

— Mean index of intrumental motivation in mathematics for males expecting to complete an upper secondary programme providing access to university-level programmes (ISCED 3A and 4)

□ Mean index of intrumental motivation in mathematics for males expecting to complete lower secondary education (ISCED Level 2)

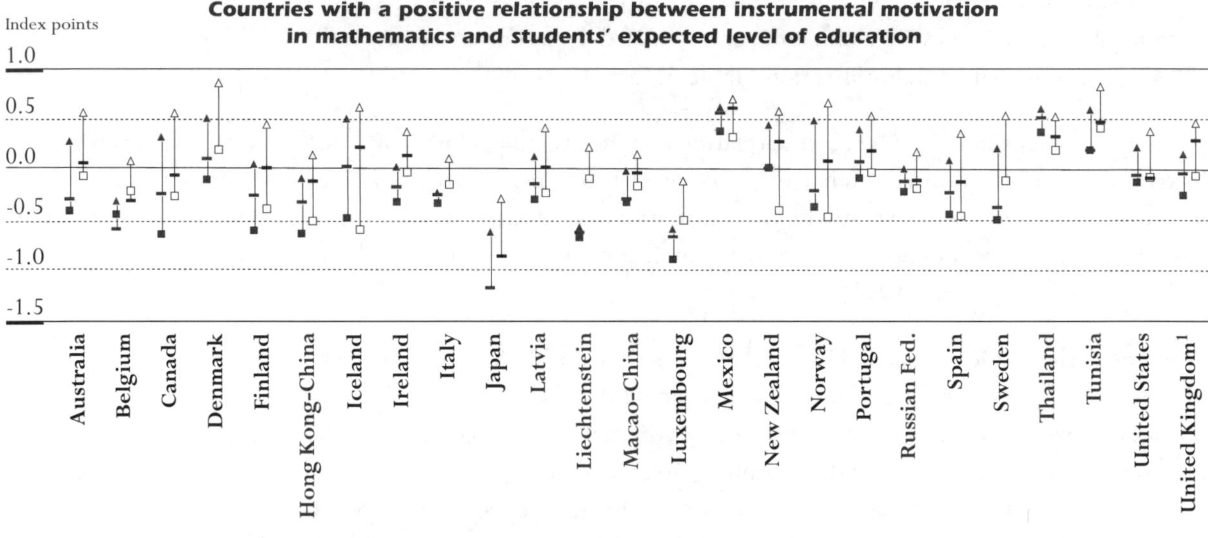

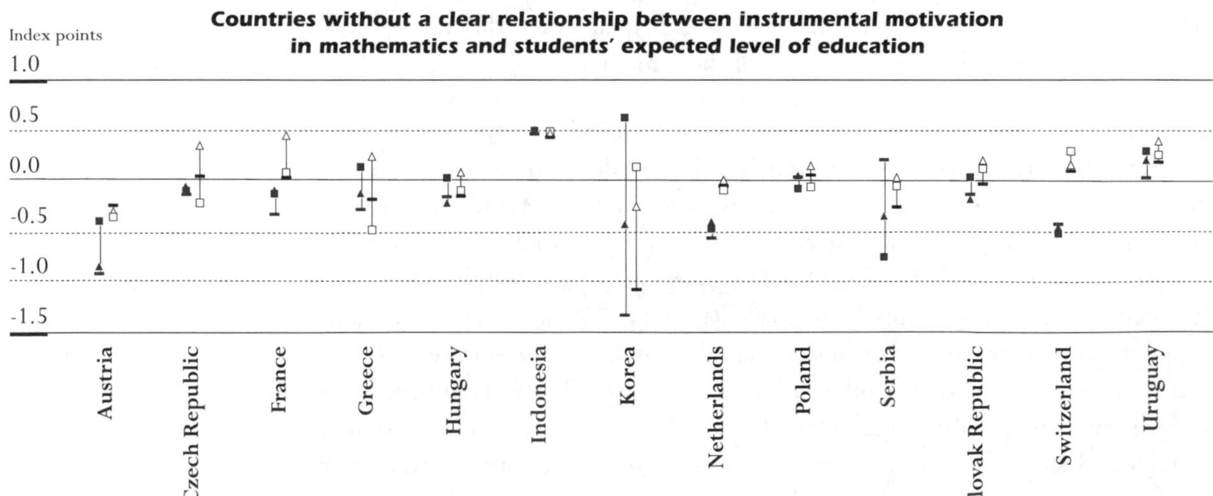

1. Response rate too low to ensure comparability (see Annex A3).
Source: OECD PISA 2003 database, Table 3.2b.

Students' perception of how well school has prepared them for life

In general, most students think that school has prepared them well for life…

All education systems aspire not just to transmit subject knowledge but also to prepare students well for life in general. The views of the majority of 15-year-olds suggest that education systems are quite successful in this respect. Typical students in the OECD area disagree with the statement that school has done little to prepare them for adult life when they leave school. They also disagree or strongly disagree that school has been a waste of time. In contrast, they agree that school helped give them confidence to make decisions and agree that school has taught them things which could be useful in a job.

…but nevertheless substantial minorities disagree.

Nevertheless, a significant minority of students, 8 per cent on average across OECD countries, consider school a waste of time and an average of 32 per cent consider that school has done little to prepare them for life. In Germany, Hungary, Luxembourg, Mexico, Turkey and, among the partner countries, in Hong Kong-China, Liechtenstein, Macao-China and Uruguay, those agreeing or strongly agreeing that school has done little to prepare them for life exceeds 40 per cent (see first panel of Figure 3.4). This suggests that there is room for improvement in general attitudes towards schooling for 15 year-olds.

As in the case of interest in and enjoyment of mathematics, an index summarises results in different countries for the questions about attitudes towards school (see *www.pisa.oecd.org* for the item map and Table 3.4 for data).

Although in each school some students feel let down, in certain schools much more of them do than in others…

To what extent are the attitudes of students towards school an attribute of the educational programmes or the schools that they attend? This question is difficult to answer. However, the last two columns in Figure 3.4 show that, in some countries at least, students' attitudes vary greatly from one school to another. The first of these two columns shows the average level of students' attitudes towards schools in one of the schools with the lowest such attitudes, defined as the school below which only 5 per cent of schools report more negative attitudes. The last column shows the average level of students' attitudes towards school in a school where attitudes are higher than in 95 per cent of the other schools. Together, the two columns thus provide an indication of the range of student attitudes among schools. While differences in these attitudes among students within schools tend to be much larger than differences across schools, the latter are nonetheless significant. In most countries, attitudes in schools where they are most positive tend to be around a standard deviation higher than where they are the most negative. Hence, although students within schools differ far more than schools do in this respect, there are considerable differences between schools in many countries. This is most notably the case in Austria, Greece, Hungary, Iceland, Italy, Mexico, Turkey and the United States as well as in the partner countries Brazil and the Russian Federation.

…but no school can be complacent…

In contrast, schools in Finland, Japan, Korea, the Netherlands and the partner country Hong Kong-China differ less with regard to attitudes towards school.

Figure 3.4 ■ Students' attitudes towards school

Index of attitudes towards school

Average index
Top quarter
Bottom quarter
Average index for females
Average index for males

Index points: -2.5, -1.5, -0.5, 0, 0.5, 1.5, 2.5

	Percentage of students agreeing or strongly agreeing with the following statements:						
	School has done little to prepare me for adult life when I leave school.	School has been a waste of time.	School helped give me confidence to make decisions.	School has taught me things which could be useful in a job.	Percentage of explained variance in student performance	Attitudes towards school in one of the schools with the most negative attitudes[1]	Attitudes towards school in one of the schools with the most positive attitudes[2]
Tunisia	25	6	90	90	1.4	0.2	1.2
Indonesia	18	2	95	95	0.5	0.1	1.2
Brazil	30	2	90	90	0.0	-0.2	1.5
Mexico	45	5	93	93	7.6	-0.9	1.1
Thailand	39	5	95	95	1.0	-0.8	1.3
Portugal	26	4	86	86	1.1	-0.5	0.7
Australia	23	6	84	84	2.4	-0.2	0.7
Latvia	17	4	83	83	1.0	-0.1	0.9
Russian Fed.	19	5	86	86	0.3	-0.3	1.1
Serbia	27	7	82	82	0.1	-0.3	0.8
France	25	7	68	68	0.6	m	m
Spain	33	7	79	79	0.2	-0.4	0.6
Ireland	26	7	79	79	0.7	-0.3	0.5
Turkey	44	8	84	84	0.1	-1.0	0.9
Austria	29	8	64	64	0.1	-0.5	1.5
Finland	21	7	79	79	2.0	-0.2	0.5
Uruguay	41	6	87	87	0.0	-0.4	0.8
New Zealand	30	8	81	81	2.3	-0.7	0.6
United States	31	10	79	79	0.6	-0.7	0.8
Greece	39	6	78	78	1.5	-0.3	1.1
Canada	26	9	74	74	0.8	-0.6	0.7
Slovak Republic	28	6	78	78	1.0	-0.4	0.6
Switzerland	37	9	65	65	0.0	-0.5	0.6
Sweden	31	7	66	66	2.2	-0.5	0.7
Iceland	27	10	63	63	3.4	-0.6	0.8
Czech Republic	31	6	73	73	0.1	-0.5	0.6
Denmark	32	7	72	72	0.5	-0.6	0.5
Italy	34	6	74	74	0.3	-0.7	0.9
Germany	43	7	56	56	0.9	-0.5	0.4
Liechtenstein	43	9	62	62	0.9	c	c
Poland	32	11	76	76	0.1	-0.8	0.4
Belgium	32	11	63	63	0.1	-0.7	0.3
Netherlands	23	11	65	65	0.1	-0.6	0.2
Norway	37	11	64	64	2.9	-0.7	0.5
Hungary	46	6	66	66	0.3	-1.0	0.8
Luxembourg	49	10	53	53	1.0	-0.7	0.2
Korea	28	10	66	66	0.0	-0.6	0.1
Macao-China	46	9	70	70	0.1	-0.7	0.4
Japan	33	10	52	52	0.1	-1.0	-0.2
Hong Kong-China	53	13	66	66	1.1	-0.8	-0.1
OECD average	*32*	*8*	*72*	*72*	*0.0*	*-0.6*	*0.7*
United Kingdom[3]	26	6	78	78	1.9	-0.5	0.6

1. This is the school at the 5th percentile. In only 5% of schools are attitudes towards school more negative.
2. This is the school at the 95th percentile. Attitudes towards school are more positive than in 95% of the other schools.
3. Response rate too low to ensure comparability (see Annex A3).
Source: OECD PISA 2003 database, Table 3.4.

However, what is equally clear from the analysis is that poor attitudes towards school are not confined to a small number of schools. Indeed, there are few schools in any country in which this cannot be considered an issue. In two countries, Japan and the partner country Hong Kong-China, even in the 5 per cent of schools with the most positive student attitudes towards school, school means fall below the OECD average.

...as poor attitudes towards school are not confined to a small number of schools.

A relationship between students' attitude to school and student achievement is not evident from the data. Nonetheless, the promotion of positive attitudes to school is worthwhile given that it has been shown to relate to other important outcomes relevant to learning for life.

Gender differences in attitude to school are statistically significant in all countries except in Korea and New Zealand and in the partner countries Hong Kong-China, Liechtenstein and Macao-China. Females generally report far more positive attitudes towards school.

Attitudes to school are generally more positive among female students.

Students' sense of belonging at school

Beyond students' perception of how well school has prepared them for life, their overall sense of belonging at school is also important. For most students, school is central to their daily life. They view schooling as essential to their long-term well-being, and this attitude is reflected in their participation in academic and non-academic pursuits. These students tend to have good relations with school staff and with other students – they feel that they belong at school. However, some youths do not share this sense of belonging, and do not believe that academic success will have a strong bearing on their future. These feelings and attitudes may result in their becoming disaffected with school (Finn, 1989; Jenkins, 1995). They may withdraw from school activities, and in some cases participate in disruptive behaviour and display negative attitudes towards teachers and other students. Meeting the needs of students who have become disaffected from school is a major challenge facing teachers and school administrators.

Students who feel they do not belong at school face serious risks...

Much of the research on students' sense of belonging at school has been concerned with its relationship to student performance. This chapter also examines this issue. However, in addition, students' sense of belonging at school can be seen as a disposition towards learning, working with others and functioning in a social institution. It is known that students who have behavioural problems tend to be disaffected with school (Offord and Waters, 1983). In some countries, longitudinal studies that have followed young people with behavioural problems into adulthood have found that nearly one half of them continue to suffer from psychological and social difficulties as adults (Offord and Bennett, 1994). Thus, the sense of belonging at school can be, for some students, indicative of economic or educational success and long term health and well being. As such, this perception deserves to be treated alongside academic performance as an important outcome of schooling. Moreover, the sense of belonging at school should not be considered an unalterable trait of individuals, stemming

...and this can affect not just academic performance but other aspects of students' lives as well.

solely from students' experiences at home, but as entailing perceptions that can be affected by teachers and parents, as well as shaped by school policy and practice.

Typically, students in OECD countries have a positive sense of belonging at school…

Students' sense of belonging at school was measured by asking them about their feelings about school as a place. Overall, students in the OECD report a positive sense of belonging at their school. On average across OECD countries, 81 per cent of the students agree or strongly agree that their school is a place where they feel like they belong. Eighty-nine per cent agree or strongly agree that their school is a place where they make friends easily. Ninety per cent disagree or strongly disagree that they feel awkward and out of place, and 93 per cent disagree or strongly disagree that school is a place where they feel like an outsider or left out of things (Figure 3.5).

…but in some countries, relatively large numbers have a low sense of belonging at school…

Nevertheless, there is considerable variation across countries, which is most readily apparent when student views are summarised on an index (see *www.pisa.oecd.org* for the item map and Table 3.5a for data). Students in Austria, Germany, Iceland, Luxembourg, Norway, Spain, Sweden and Switzerland and in the partner countries Liechtenstein and Uruguay report the highest sense of belonging at school. In contrast, the lowest sense of belonging at school is reported by students in Belgium, the Czech Republic, France, Japan, Korea, Poland, the Slovak Republic and Turkey, and in the partner countries Hong Kong-China, Indonesia, Latvia, Macao-China, the Russian Federation and Thailand. For example, while in Sweden 5 per cent of students report that school is a place where they feel awkward and out of place, more than three times this proportion report that feeling in Belgium, Japan and the partner country Tunisia (Figure 3.5).

…and even in some countries where overall students have a high sense of belonging at school, significant proportions feel negative.

Within countries, there is still more variation with regard to students' sense of belonging at school than between countries. It is noteworthy that in some of the countries where students, overall, express a strong sense of belonging at school, including Austria, Germany, Luxembourg, Norway and Sweden, this is not because there are exceptionally few students reporting a low sense of belonging at school. Rather, this is because the quarter of students at the top end report a particularly strong sense of belonging at school.

In 20 of the 41 participating countries, males and females report similar levels of sense of belonging at school. However, there are some notable exceptions, with females in Australia, Belgium, Canada, Hungary, Ireland, Japan, Mexico, Poland and Turkey and in the partner countries in Hong Kong-China, Indonesia, Latvia, the Russian Federation and Thailand, reporting a higher sense of belonging at school. In contrast, the reverse is true in Finland, Korea, Spain, Sweden and the partner country Uruguay.

Students' answers are, of course, likely to depend on their cultural context, their own social confidence and their feelings about school. However, analyses of the PISA data (mentioned in the introduction) support the use of the overall

Figure 3.5 ■ Students' sense of belonging at school

	Percentage of students agreeing or strongly agreeing with the following statements						Index of sense of belonging at school			
	School is a place where:									
	I feel like an outsider (or left out of things).	I make friends easily.	I feel like I belong.	I feel awkward and out of place.	Other students seem to like me.	I feel lonely.	Index points	Percentage of explained variance in student performance	Students' sense of belonging in one of the schools with the lowest levels[1]	Students' sense of belonging in one of the schools with the highest levels[2]
Austria	6	90	89	9	78	7		0.1	-0.3	1.3
Sweden	5	88	81	5	91	7		0.0	-0.5	0.8
Uruguay	7	90	93	7	93	7		0.1	-0.3	0.9
Germany	6	86	87	12	70	6		0.0	-0.3	0.7
Norway	6	90	85	9	91	7		0.0	-0.3	1.0
Luxembourg	8	89	73	10	91	7		0.5	-0.2	0.5
Spain	4	91	85	9	92	5		0.1	-0.3	0.6
Liechtenstein	7	86	91	11	70	8		1.0	c	c
Switzerland	7	88	82	12	78	6		0.8	-0.4	0.9
Iceland	10	85	89	11	90	10		0.0	-0.4	0.7
Brazil	7	91	92	11	92	7		0.3	0.1	0.7
Portugal	6	93	93	12	91	5		2.8	-0.5	0.5
Hungary	9	88	91	7	89	7		1.1	-1.1	0.8
Ireland	6	91	88	8	95	5		0.4	-0.3	0.4
Mexico	10	88	92	10	89	11		2.6	-0.9	1.0
Italy	5	92	85	6	91	6		0.1	-0.8	1.0
Australia	8	91	88	9	95	6		0.1	-0.6	0.4
Greece	6	91	91	8	92	7		0.3	-0.6	0.5
Serbia	10	93	88	10	92	8		0.0	-0.3	0.5
Canada	9	90	81	11	94	8		0.0	-0.5	0.6
Denmark	5	88	69	12	92	6		0.1	-0.5	0.8
New Zealand	8	91	86	11	94	7		0.1	-0.4	0.5
Finland	6	88	89	9	87	6		0.0	-0.3	0.3
Netherlands	4	92	77	8	93	3		0.4	-0.4	0.3
Tunisia	10	88	58	18	89	11		0.2	-0.4	0.3
Slovak Republic	8	92	85	12	91	7		0.1	-0.6	0.5
Poland	8	88	76	10	93	8		0.6	-0.6	0.3
France	8	92	45	13	93	7		0.0	m	m
Latvia	5	89	92	9	72	9		1.5	-0.7	0.1
Czech Republic	10	89	77	7	87	7		1.3	-0.7	0.3
Belgium	8	89	56	16	92	6		0.3	-0.8	0.1
Thailand	6	95	95	15	80	11		1.6	-1.0	0.7
Russian Fed.	6	88	92	15	51	9		1.2	-0.8	0.4
Indonesia	4	98	68	11	83	7		0.3	-0.7	0.1
Korea	8	79	76	9	45	7		1.0	-0.8	0.4
Turkey	14	88	75	11	41	25		3.1	-1.2	-0.2
Japan	6	77	80	18	69	30		1.3	-1.0	-0.2
Hong Kong-China	18	88	68	10	77	12		1.3	-0.9	-0.3
Macao-China	16	84	65	14	72	15		0.3	-0.9	-0.3
OECD average	*7*	*89*	*81*	*10*	*86*	*8*		*0.1*	*-0.7*	*0.6*
United Kingdom[3]	7	91	85	9	95	6		0.0	-0.3	0.6

Legend: *Average index*; ► *Top quarter*; ● *Bottom quarter*; ▌ *Average index for females*; ▌ *Average index for males*

Index points: -2.5 -1.5 -0.5 0 0.5 1.5 2.5

1. This is the school at the 5th percentile. In only 5% of schools is students' sense of belonging at school lower.
2. This is the school at the 95th percentile. Students' sense of belonging at school is higher than in 95% of the other schools.
3. Response rate too low to ensure comparability (see Annex A3).
Source: OECD PISA 2003 database, Table 3.5a.

response to these questions as an indicator of whether students feel that they belong in the school environment. Thus, unlike in the case of previous indicators reported in this chapter, students' reports of their sense of belonging at school produce an indicator that can be validly compared across countries.

To what extent are students who feel that they do not belong concentrated in particular schools within each country? This question is important for education policy, since it helps establish the extent to which disaffection is associated with features of the school system itself or the way it interacts with students and schools in particular circumstances.

Most variation in the sense of belonging at school is found within schools…

The last two columns of Figure 3.5 give some indication of the between-school differences in each country by showing the range of school averages of students' sense of belonging at school. The first of these two columns shows the average sense of belonging in a school where such attitudes are among the lowest, defined as a school below which students' sense of belonging is lower only in 5 per cent of other schools. The last column shows the school average where students' sense of belonging at school is higher than in 95 per cent of other schools.

…suggesting that strategies only targeted at certain schools will not be able to address the problem fully.

Differences in the sense of belonging at school among students within schools – as shown by the range from the 5th to the 95th percentiles – tend to be much larger than differences among schools (in most countries, between-school differences explain only around 4 per cent of the overall variation). Therefore, no school is immune from this problem, and a strategy that is only targeted at certain schools will not be able to address the problem fully. However, in countries such as Austria, Denmark, Hungary, Italy, Mexico, Norway, Switzerland, and the partner countries Liechtenstein and Thailand, students' sense of belonging at school differs considerably between schools. By contrast, between-school differences in students' sense of belonging at school are negligible in Finland, Ireland, Japan, and the Netherlands and in the partner countries Hong Kong-China and Macao-China.

As with attitudes to school, a low sense of belonging at school is thus not confined to small numbers of schools in each country. In Japan and Turkey and in the partner countries Hong Kong-China and Macao-China even in the 5 per cent of schools with the most positive student perception of sense of belonging at school, school means fall below the OECD average.

In some countries students in vocational streams seem to feel they belong at school less than those in general streams.

Determining the extent of this variation across schools is important for at least two reasons. In countries where there is considerable variation among schools, it may be more efficient to target certain schools for intervention, whereas if the prevalence is fairly uniform across most schools in a country, then more universal policies are likely to be more effective. The second reason is that if there is considerable variation among schools in the prevalence of disaffected students, then it may be possible to discern whether particular school factors are related to students' sense of belonging at school, thereby providing some direction for what kinds of interventions might be most effective. It is beyond

the scope of this initial report to examine such school factors but one issue worth noting is significant variation in students' sense of belonging at school between different types of school programmes in some countries (Table 3.5b). For example, in Austria and the Netherlands and in the partner countries Indonesia and Serbia students' sense of belonging at school is considerably weaker in programmes geared towards vocational studies than in academically oriented programmes. Similarly, students' sense of belonging at school in programmes designed to provide direct access to the labour market, tends to be lower than in academically oriented programmes, most notably in Belgium, the Czech Republic, Greece, Hungary, Japan, Korea and the Netherlands and in the partner country Serbia.

The relationship between students' sense of belonging at school and their performance can be interpreted differently …

While, as noted above, students' sense of belonging at school is an important outcome of schooling, it is also important to examine how it relates to their performance. A common explanation of engagement is that it precedes academic outcomes, and that when students become disengaged from school, their academic performance begins to suffer. This may be the case for some students. However, an equally plausible model is that a failure to succeed in academic work at school results in student disaffection and the withdrawal from school activities. A third model is that a range of other factors, including individual, family and school factors, jointly influence both engagement and academic outcomes. It may also be that the causal relationships differ, depending on students' academic ability and family and school contexts. In addition, these explanations are not incompatible with one another. An understanding of the causal mechanisms associated with engagement and academic achievement is central to educational policy in that it affects decisions about when and how to intervene.

…but the fact that the strongest associations with performance are for whole schools rather than for individuals suggests that influences operate at the school level.

PISA cannot determine the causal relationships underlying students' sense of belonging at school and their performance (or vice versa). However, it can provide an indication of how strong the relationships are at age 15. The relationship between sense of belonging at school and mathematics performance can be examined both at the level of individual students and at the level of schools (Table 3.5c). At the student level, the relationship tends to be weak, which suggests that performance and sense of belonging at school are markedly different outcome measures. By contrast, in most countries, the sense of belonging at school that students have in particular schools tends to be more closely related to the average performance level of that school. In particular, in Japan, Mexico and Turkey and in the partner country Hong Kong-China, schools with high average levels of sense of belonging at school also tend to have high average levels of performance.

Students' sense of belonging at the school level – mirroring students' shared experience – is more likely to reflect features of the school that are relevant for students' sense of belonging at school. Thus, schools that provide the basis for students to feel engaged and to experience a sense of belonging at school tend to have better overall performance than schools where students on average feel awkward and out of place.

This may indicate that it is not just underachieving students who may need help…

This finding has a number of implications for educational policy and practice. The weak correlations at the student level suggest that teachers and guidance counsellors are likely to encounter students who have a very low sense of belonging at school but whose performance in academic subjects is average or above average.

…and that schools that focus on helping students fit in are not doing so at the expense of academic performance.

The moderately strong school-level correlations between students' sense of belonging at school and their mathematics performance mean that schools where students tend to have a strong sense of belonging also tend to have high levels of academic performance. The design of PISA does not allow the inference that efforts to increase students' sense of belonging at school are likely to lead to better academic performance. However, the results suggest that efforts to increase students' sense of belonging at school will not usually be harmful to academic performance, and *vice versa*. In fact, the relationship might be mutually reinforcing.

STUDENTS' BELIEFS ABOUT THEMSELVES

PISA also looked at students' belief in their abilities, at their ability to tackle difficult tasks and at their anxiety in mathematics.

Autonomous learning requires both a critical and a realistic judgement of the difficulty of a task as well as the ability to invest enough energy to accomplish it. Learners form views about their own competences and learning characteristics. These views have been shown to have considerable impact on the way they set goals, the strategies they use and their performance. Two ways of defining these beliefs are in terms of students' beliefs in their own academic abilities (self-concept) and of how much students believe in their own ability to handle tasks effectively and overcome difficulties (self-efficacy). A third dimension relates to emotional factors, such as feelings of helplessness and emotional stress when dealing with mathematics. All three dimensions were investigated by PISA.

This section examines these three aspects of students' beliefs about themselves as learners in mathematics. It then analyses how these aspects relate to performance in mathematics.

Students' self-concept in mathematics

Students who believe in their abilities make successful learners…

Students' academic self-concept is both an important outcome of education and a powerful predictor of student success. Belief in one's own abilities is highly relevant to successful learning (Marsh, 1986). It can also affect other factors such as well-being and personality development, factors that are especially important for students from less advantaged backgrounds.

… but two-thirds of students find some of their mathematics work too difficult and half say they do not learn mathematics quickly…

When 15-year-olds are asked about their views of their mathematical abilities, the picture that emerges is, however, less positive than students' self-concept in reading, which was examined in PISA 2000 (OECD, 2001a). On average across OECD countries, 67 per cent of students disagree or strongly disagree that in their mathematics class, they understand even the most difficult work. Countries vary with respect to the response patterns. For example, for the aforementioned question, percentages disagreeing or strongly disagreeing range

from around 84 per cent or more in Japan and Korea to 57 per cent or less in Canada, Mexico, Sweden and the United States. Similarly, on average across OECD countries, roughly half of the students disagree or strongly disagree that they learn mathematics quickly. But while in Japan and Korea, as well as in the partner country Thailand, more than 62 per cent of students disagree or strongly disagree, the proportion is only around 40 per cent of students in Denmark and Sweden (Figure 3.6, but note that results are reported in terms of students' agreement with the respective statements rather than disagreement, as in this text).

...while a third of males and half of females think they are no good at mathematics.

For most of these questions, comparatively large gender differences are apparent. For example, while on average across OECD countries, 36 per cent of males agree or strongly agree that they are simply not good at mathematics, the average for females is 47 per cent. In Italy, Japan, Korea, Norway, Poland, Portugal and Spain and in the partner countries Brazil, Hong Kong-China, Indonesia, Macao-China, Thailand, Tunisia and Turkey, between 50 and 70 per cent of females agree or strongly agree with this statement (for data, see *www.pisa.oecd.org*).

Self-concept in mathematics is summarised in a cross-nationally comparable index...

Countries can be compared on an index that summarises the different questions about students' self-concept in mathematics. As before, the index is constructed with the average score across OECD countries set at 0 and two-thirds scoring between 1 and -1 (see *www.pisa.oecd.org* for the item map). Results for individual countries are displayed in the second panel of Figure 3.6. Countries are here ranked by their mean levels of self-concept in mathematics, with lines connecting the mean of the bottom and top quarters of the distribution in each country. The mean index by gender is shown in this figure as well as in Table 3.6.

...showing country differences together with considerable gender differences in each country...

The comparison shows that students in Canada, Denmark, Germany, Mexico, New Zealand, the United States and the partner country Tunisia have the greatest confidence in their mathematics abilities. Students in Japan and Korea and in the partner country Hong Kong-China have the lowest self-concept. In almost all countries, there is considerable variation between males and females and in all countries males tend to show statistically significantly higher levels of self-concept in mathematics than females. This is particularly so in Denmark, Germany, Luxembourg, the Netherlands and Switzerland and in the partner country Liechtenstein (Table 3.6). Nevertheless, some caution is warranted when comparing index values on this measure across countries.

...and substantial differences in performance among students who are more and less confident in their mathematics abilities.

The third panel of Figure 3.6 also shows that, within countries, students' self-concept in mathematics is closely related to their performance on the PISA 2003 mathematics assessment. An increase of one index point on the scale of self-concept in mathematics corresponds, on average across OECD countries, to 32 score points on the mathematics performance scale, which is about half a proficiency level (Table 3.6).

Besides a moderately strong association between individual students' performance and their self-concept in mathematics, it is perhaps even more important that the

Figure 3.6 ■ Students' self-concept in mathematics

Average index; Top quarter; Bottom quarter; Average index for females; Average index for males

Index of self-concept in mathematics — Index points: -2.5, -1.5, -0.5, 0, 0.5, 1.5, 2.5

Change in mathematics performance per unit of the index of self-concept in mathematics — Score point difference: -60, -40, -20, 0, 20, 40, 60

	Percentage of students agreeing or strongly agreeing with the following statements: I am just not good at mathematics.	I get good marks in mathematics.	I learn mathematics quickly.	I have always believed that mathematics is one of my best subjects.	In my mathematics class, I understand even the most difficult work.	Percentage of explained variance in student performance
United States	36	72	58	44	44	14.6
Denmark	30	70	60	48	34	27.6
Canada	34	63	58	41	43	19.9
Mexico	48	65	50	44	45	5.4
Tunisia	52	53	54	54	39	7.6
Germany	36	59	57	36	42	7.1
New Zealand	33	71	56	40	38	17.0
Switzerland	34	61	57	37	40	6.9
Australia	32	65	56	38	38	16.8
Liechtenstein	35	65	59	35	41	6.5
Russian Fed.	37	50	46	42	42	10.5
Sweden	34	59	60	31	44	24.4
Greece	43	63	59	44	24	16.6
Indonesia	68	64	47	57	36	0.3
Austria	36	59	55	33	39	8.9
Luxembourg	38	61	55	35	37	5.3
Brazil	51	61	48	33	41	4.3
Iceland	46	55	55	41	39	26.4
Poland	52	59	50	37	31	21.6
Serbia	37	45	55	38	27	8.9
Turkey	59	53	55	46	30	11.0
Uruguay	46	55	50	40	32	12.9
Finland	40	56	54	33	38	33.0
Italy	50	56	51	36	40	7.1
Netherlands	38	62	54	33	29	6.1
Belgium	38	62	51	30	28	4.8
Ireland	38	60	49	32	29	14.1
Slovak Republic	44	58	48	28	26	16.1
Thailand	68	44	38	45	35	1.8
Czech Republic	38	55	46	30	21	15.8
Latvia	39	44	46	24	25	16.7
Hungary	45	42	42	33	24	6.6
France	39	48	47	26	28	10.3
Norway	45	48	47	31	30	31.6
Portugal	53	47	46	27	32	15.4
Spain	51	47	45	31	31	13.2
Macao-China	50	29	45	26	28	11.7
Hong Kong-China	57	25	45	32	30	12.1
Korea	62	36	34	30	16	21.4
Japan	53	28	25	27	10	4.1
OECD average	***42***	***57***	***51***	***35***	***33***	***10.8***
United Kingdom[1]	34	68	53	38	38	14.4

1. Response rate too low to ensure comparability (see Annex A3).

Source: OECD PISA 2003 database, Table 3.6.

data reveal a similarly strong association at school levels. This suggests that schools in which students tend to have a strong self-concept in mathematics also tend to have high levels of mathematics performance. Note, however, that countries with high average self-concept in mathematics are not necessarily countries with high mean mathematics scores.

At one level, it is not surprising that students who perform well in PISA also tend to have high opinions of their abilities. However, as explained in Box 3.4, self-concept must be seen as much more than simply a mirror of student performance. Rather, it can have a decisive influence on the learning process. Whether students choose to pursue a particular learning goal is dependent on their appraisal of their abilities and potential in a subject area and on their confidence in being able to achieve this goal even in the face of difficulties. The latter aspect of self-related beliefs is the subject of the following section.

This is not just because able students are more confident, but also because confident students are more likely to adopt certain learning goals.

Box 3.4 ■ **Do students' beliefs about their abilities simply mirror their performance?**

One issue that arises when asking students what they think of their own abilities, especially in terms of whether they can perform verbal and mathematical tasks (which are also assessed directly in PISA), is whether this adds anything of importance to what we know about their abilities from the assessment. In fact, both prior research and the PISA results give strong reasons for assuming that confidence helps to drive learning success, rather than simply reflecting it. In particular:

- Research about the learning process has shown that students need to believe in their own capacities before making necessary investments in learning strategies that will help them to higher performance (Zimmerman, 1999). This finding is also supported by PISA: Figure 3.7 suggests that the belief in one's efficacy is a particularly strong predictor of whether a student will control his or her learning.
- Much more of the observed variation in student levels of self-related beliefs occurs within countries, within schools and within classes than would be the case if self-confidence merely mirrored performance. That is to say, in any group of peers, even those with very low levels of mathematics performance, the stronger performers are likely to have relatively high self-confidence, indicating that they base this on the norms they observe around them. This illustrates the importance of one's immediate environment in fostering the self-confidence that students need in order to develop as effective learners.
- PISA 2000 showed that students reporting that they are good at verbal tasks do not necessarily also believe that they are good at mathematical tasks, despite the fact that PISA 2000 revealed a high correlation between performance on these two scales. Indeed, in most countries there was, at most, a weak and in some cases negative correlation between verbal and mathematical self-concept (OECD, 2003b). This can again be explained by the assertion that students' ability judgements are made in relation to subjective standards which are in turn based on the contexts they are in. Thus, some students who are confident in reading may be less confident in mathematics partly because it is a *relative* weak point in relation to their own overall abilities and partly because they are more likely than weak readers to have peers who are good mathematicians.

The picture remains, of course, largely descriptive and it will require further analysis to examine to what extent self-related beliefs in general, and self-concept in mathematics in particular, are related to factors such as instructional practices and teacher feedback.

Students' confidence in overcoming difficulties in mathematics

Successful learners are not only confident of their abilities, They also believe that investment in learning can make a difference and help them to overcome difficulties.

Successful learners are not only confident of their abilities. They also believe that investment in learning can make a difference and help them to overcome difficulties – that is, they have a strong sense of their own efficacy. By contrast, students who lack confidence in their ability to learn what they judge to be important and to overcome difficulties are exposed to failure, not only at school, but also in their adult lives. Self-efficacy goes beyond how good students think they are in subjects such as mathematics. It is more concerned with the kind of confidence that is needed for them to successfully master specific learning tasks. It is therefore not simply a reflection of a student's abilities and performance, but has also been shown to enhance learning activity, which in turn improves student performance.

Such self-efficacy can be described by a cross-nationally comparable index, that reveals differences between and within countries.

Students' confidence in overcoming difficulties in particular mathematics tasks can be compared through an index of self-efficacy in mathematics. This summarises the different questions about students' confidence in solving certain calculations in mathematics. The index is constructed, with the average score across OECD countries set at 0 and with two-thirds scoring between 1 and -1 (*i.e.,* a standard deviation of 1) (see *www.pisa.oecd.org* for the item map). Evidence from PISA 2000 and PISA 2003 suggests that the index values of self-efficacy in mathematics can be reasonably compared across countries (OECD, 2003b). Results for individual countries are displayed in the first panel of Figure 3.7, where countries are ranked by their mean levels of self-efficacy in mathematics, with lines connecting the mean of the bottom and top quarters of the distribution in each country. On average, students in Greece, Japan, Korea and Mexico and in the partner countries Brazil, Indonesia, Thailand and Tunisia express the least self-efficacy in mathematics whereas students in Canada, Hungary, the Slovak Republic, Switzerland and the United States express comparatively stronger degrees of self-efficacy. However, within each country there is considerable variation, with the top quarter of students in most countries expressing strong confidence in handling specific tasks related to mathematics. Variation is particularly large in Canada, Iceland, Luxembourg, Norway, Switzerland, Turkey and the United States as seen by the difference between the mean index for the top and the bottom quarters.

The link between self-efficacy and performance in mathematics is particularly strong…

Figure 3.7 shows that students' self-efficacy in mathematics is even more closely related to student performance on the PISA 2003 mathematics assessment than self-concept in mathematics. In fact, self-efficacy is one of the strongest predictors of student performance, explaining, on average across OECD countries, 23 per cent of the variance in mathematics performance, and more than 30 per cent in the Czech Republic, Hungary, Japan, Korea, Norway, the Slovak Republic, Sweden and the partner country Hong Kong-China. Even when accounting for other learner characteristics, such as anxiety in mathematics, interest in and

Figure 3.7 ■ Students' self-efficacy in mathematics

Index of self-efficacy in mathematics (Index points: -2.5, -1.5, -0.5, 0, 0.5, 1.5, 2.5) — Average index; Top quarter; Bottom quarter; Average index for females; Average index for males

Change in mathematics performance per unit of the index of self-efficacy in mathematics (Score point difference: -60, -40, -20, 0, 20, 40, 60)

	Percentage of explained variance in student performance
Liechtenstein	28.0
Slovak Republic	34.8
Hungary	31.0
Switzerland	29.8
United States	27.4
Canada	28.9
Austria	24.6
Czech Republic	31.0
Germany	25.8
Hong Kong-China	31.0
Luxembourg	21.8
Australia	27.3
Macao-China	19.3
Poland	29.9
Iceland	25.3
Sweden	31.8
Uruguay	15.8
New Zealand	27.1
France	25.4
Serbia	11.4
Ireland	28.0
Spain	19.4
Belgium	17.7
Norway	30.4
Portugal	28.1
Denmark	27.4
Russian Fed.	19.0
Netherlands	20.8
Italy	20.8
Latvia	24.8
Finland	27.5
Turkey	25.7
Mexico	9.5
Greece	18.4
Tunisia	13.7
Indonesia	1.1
Brazil	9.4
Korea	33.2
Thailand	10.2
Japan	34.3
OECD average	*22.7*
United Kingdom[1]	30.1

1. Response rate too low to ensure comparability (see Annex A3).
Source: OECD PISA 2003 database, Table 3.7.

enjoyment of mathematics or the use of control strategies, sizeable effects sizes remain for virtually all countries (Table 3.12).

...and in no country does the quarter of students with the least efficacy in mathematics reach the OECD average level of performance.

Looked at differently, an OECD average increase of one index point on the scale of self-efficacy in mathematics corresponds to 47 score points – just over the equivalent of one school year – in mathematics performance (Table 3.7 and Box 2.2). Not even in the best-performing OECD countries does the quarter of students who believe least in their own learning efficacy perform at or above the OECD average mathematics score. In contrast, in all but five OECD countries, students in the third quarter on the index of self-efficacy in mathematics score above the OECD average, while students in the top quarter score above the average performance of Finland, the highest scoring OECD country overall, in all but six OECD countries (Table 3.7). In fact, in some of the best performing countries, including the Czech Republic, Japan, Korea and Switzerland, the quarter of students with least self-efficacy face a three to four times higher probability of performing in the bottom quarter on the mathematics assessment than students reporting average self-efficacy.

Much of the difference between schools' performances is associated with the differing self-efficacy of their students...

The association between mathematics efficacy and mathematics performance is not only strong at the student level. In most countries there is also a clear tendency for students in lower performing schools to have less confidence in their abilities to overcome difficulties. In fact, across the OECD, 23 per cent of the mathematics performance differences among schools can be explained by the average levels of students' self-efficacy in mathematics at school (Figure 3.7). This indicates that further research, perhaps with longitudinal studies, is warranted to identify the school and student factors associated with high efficacy, and to investigate whether attempts to increase efficacy also result in increases in achievement.

...and not least, self-efficacy in mathematics is a positive outcome in itself, beyond its effect on performance.

Finally, and as stated above, students' views about their abilities to handle challenges in mathematics effectively should not only be considered a predictor of student performance. These views should be considered an important outcome in their own right, having as they do a key impact on students' motivation and use of control strategies (Table 3.13).

STUDENTS' ANXIETY IN MATHEMATICS

Most 15-year-olds worry to a certain extent about having difficulties in mathematics, although only a minority get very nervous when doing mathematics problems...

Some students' less favourable disposition towards mathematics may be a consequence of earlier failures. Indeed, a considerable proportion of 15-year-olds in PISA report feelings of helplessness and emotional stress when dealing with mathematics (Table 3.8 and Figure 3.8). On average among OECD countries, half of 15-year-old males and more than 60 per cent of females report that they often worry that they will find mathematics classes difficult and that they will get poor marks (for data see *www.pisa.oecd.org*). On the other hand, fewer than 30 per cent of students across the OECD agree or strongly agree with statements indicating that they get very nervous doing mathematics problems, get very tense when they have to do mathematics homework or feel helpless when doing a mathematics problem (see first panel in Figure 3.8).

Figure 3.8 ■ Students' anxiety in mathematics

Percentage of students agreeing or strongly agreeing with the following statements:

Index of anxiety in mathematics

Change in mathematics performance per unit of the index of anxiety in mathematics

Average index

Top quarter

Bottom quarter

Average index for females

Average index for males

Index points: -2.5, -1.5, -0.5, 0, 0.5, 1.5, 2.5

Score point difference: -60, -40, -20, 0, 20, 40, 60

	I often worry that it will be difficult for me in mathematics classes.	I get very tense when I have to do mathematics homework.	I get very nervous doing mathematics problems.	I feel helpless when doing a mathematics problem.	I worry that I will get poor marks in mathematics.	Percentage of explained variance in student performance	Students' anxiety in mathematics in one of the schools with the lowest levels[1]	Students' anxiety in mathematics in one of the schools with the highest levels[2]
Tunisia	80	65	48	39	79	1.8	0.3	1.0
Brazil	70	45	48	43	90	12.1	0.2	1.2
Thailand	64	54	67	45	75	1.6	-0.5	0.8
Mexico	77	45	49	27	87	8.6	-0.2	0.9
Japan	69	52	42	35	66	2.1	-0.1	0.8
Korea	79	33	44	44	78	4.8	-0.1	0.8
France	61	53	39	37	75	6.4	m	m
Turkey	64	50	41	46	68	11.7	-0.6	1.0
Indonesia	79	39	48	37	66	1.1	0.0	0.7
Uruguay	64	36	38	26	83	12.7	-0.2	0.8
Italy	70	28	44	44	72	8.6	-0.1	0.9
Spain	66	36	40	31	77	6.9	-0.1	0.7
Serbia	63	45	43	32	63	13.7	-0.4	0.8
Macao-China	68	32	39	37	63	9.7	-0.3	0.7
Hong Kong-China	68	29	33	35	72	7.9	-0.2	0.6
Greece	69	35	44	38	52	12.4	-0.2	0.9
Portugal	75	22	30	35	67	10.7	-0.2	0.8
Russian Fed.	58	39	32	24	72	14.4	-0.3	0.6
Latvia	62	33	26	24	73	17.6	-0.3	0.5
Belgium	57	28	32	29	69	5.6	-0.3	0.7
Ireland	60	30	26	26	60	13.2	-0.3	0.5
Slovak Republic	58	25	40	28	53	16.7	-0.6	0.5
Poland	61	30	35	31	57	24.0	0.7	0.4
Hungary	62	19	22	29	62	10.1	-0.7	1.0
Luxembourg	58	29	32	30	61	9.8	-0.5	0.4
Canada	54	32	26	24	58	16.0	-0.6	0.5
Czech Republic	52	20	32	29	51	16.8	-0.6	0.5
Australia	53	28	22	20	58	12.4	-0.3	0.3
Norway	47	37	20	31	58	24.5	-1.2	0.9
New Zealand	52	24	21	21	56	19.2	0.6	0.5
United States	56	34	26	23	47	15.7	-0.5	0.7
Iceland	50	19	17	28	59	15.9	-0.7	0.5
Germany	53	30	24	23	47	11.6	-0.7	0.3
Austria	56	30	22	24	44	9.8	-1.3	0.5
Switzerland	48	26	19	25	47	10.1	-0.9	0.3
Finland	50	7	15	26	51	19.7	-0.6	0.0
Liechtenstein	47	19	13	22	51	11.0	c	c
Netherlands	36	7	16	17	44	4.9	-0.8	0.0
Denmark	34	26	15	17	41	26.5	-1.1	0.2
Sweden	32	14	11	17	46	19.9	-0.9	0.1
OECD average	*57*	*29*	*29*	*29*	*59*	*12.7*	*-0.7*	*0.7*
United Kingdom[3]	47	28	25	22	58	11.8	-0.6	0.4

1. This is the school at the 5th percentile. In only 5% of schools is students' anxiety in mathematics lower.
2. This is the school at the 95th percentile. Students' anxiety in mathematics is higher than in 95% of the other schools.
3. Response rate too low to ensure comparability (see Annex A3).
Source: OECD PISA 2003 database, Table 3.8.

...but country-differences are great: for example, half of students in some countries but only a few in others get tense when doing mathematics homework.

There is considerable cross-country variation in the degree to which students feel anxiety when dealing with mathematics, with students in France, Italy, Japan, Korea, Mexico, Spain, and Turkey reporting feeling most concerned and students in Denmark, Finland, the Netherlands and Sweden least concerned (see second panel in Figure 3.8). For example, more than half of the students in France and Japan report that they get very tense when they have to do mathematics homework, but only 7 per cent of students in Finland and the Netherlands report this. It is noteworthy that Finland and the Netherlands are also two of the top performing countries.

More than two-thirds of the students in Greece, Italy, Japan, Korea, Mexico and Portugal report that they often worry that it will be difficult for them in mathematics classes, whereas only about one-third of students in Denmark or Sweden fall into this category. Among the participating partner countries, students in Brazil, Indonesia, Thailand, Tunisia and Uruguay report feeling more anxiety in dealing with mathematics, with students in Liechtenstein feeling the least anxiety. For example, more than half of students in Thailand and Tunisia report that they get very tense when they have to do mathematics homework. More than two-thirds of the students in Brazil, Hong Kong-China, Indonesia, Macao-China and Tunisia report that they often worry that they will find mathematics classes difficult.

Students with high levels of mathematics anxiety tend to perform worse in mathematics...

As is to be expected, anxiety in mathematics is negatively related to student performance. A one-point increase on the PISA index of anxiety in mathematics corresponds, on average across OECD countries, to a 35-point drop in the mathematics score, which is just over half a proficiency level (see the third panel in Figure 3.8 and Table 3.8). Students in the bottom quarter of the index of anxiety in mathematics are half as likely to be among the bottom quarter of performers compared to the average student. This negative association remains even if other learner characteristics – such as students' interest in and enjoyment of mathematics, self-efficacy in mathematics and use of control strategies – are accounted for (Table 3.12).

...and students in lower-performing schools tend to be more anxious.

As was the case with self-efficacy, the association between anxiety in mathematics and mathematics performance is not only strong at student levels. In most countries, there is also a clear tendency for students in lower performing schools to report higher levels of anxiety in mathematics (Table 3.15), with 7 per cent of the performance variance among schools explained by the average levels of students' anxiety in mathematics at school.

The fact that males are less anxious about mathematics than females, and students in some countries less anxious than in others, suggests that this is a problem that can be addressed.

The statistically significantly higher levels of anxiety in mathematics reported among females (apparent in all countries except Poland) are of particular concern for education policy, most notably in Austria, Canada, Denmark, Finland, France, Germany, Luxembourg, the Netherlands, Norway and Switzerland. Females also reported higher levels of anxiety in mathematics than males in all partner countries except Serbia (Table 3.8 and Figure 3.8).

The importance of further research in this area is underlined by the strong prevalence of anxiety in mathematics among 15-year-olds in general, and females in particular, coupled with the finding that in countries such as Denmark, Sweden and the Netherlands students report much lower levels of anxiety in mathematics. The positive experiences of the latter group of countries, which also perform well in mathematics overall, suggest that the issue can be managed successfully and raise questions about how these countries are addressing the issue through the organisation of schooling and instructional delivery.

STUDENTS' LEARNING STRATEGIES

As students are active participants in the learning process, constructing meaning in ways shaped by their own prior knowledge and new experiences…

Students do not passively receive and process information. They are active participants in the learning process, constructing meaning in ways shaped by their own prior knowledge and new experiences. Students with a well-developed ability to manage their own learning are able to choose appropriate learning goals, to use their existing knowledge and skills to direct their learning, and to select learning strategies appropriate to the task in hand. While the development of these skills and attitudes has not always been an explicit focus of teaching in schools, it is increasingly being explicitly identified as a major goal of schooling and should, therefore, also be regarded as a significant outcome of the learning process. This is particularly so as, once students leave school, they need to manage most of their learning for themselves. To do this they must be able to establish goals, persevere, monitor their progress, adjust their learning strategies as necessary and overcome difficulties in learning. Therefore, while understanding and developing strategies that will best enhance their learning will be a benefit for students at school, even larger benefits are likely to accrue when they learn with less support in adult life.

…PISA also sought to capture different types of learning strategy.

This section describes three constructs collected from students in PISA 2003 that are related to the control of learning strategies in general (metacognitive strategies that involve planning, monitoring and regulation); memorisation strategies (*e.g.,* learning key terms or repeated learning of material); and elaboration strategies (*e.g.,* making connections to related areas or thinking about alternative solutions).

Controlling the learning process

Effective learners monitor their own learning by checking that they are meeting their learning goals…

Good learners can manage their own learning and apply an arsenal of learning strategies in an effective manner. Conversely, students who have problems learning on their own often have no access to effective strategies to facilitate and monitor their learning, or fail to select a strategy appropriate to the task in hand. Control strategies through which students can monitor their learning by, for example, checking what they have learned and working out what they still need to learn, form an important component of effective approaches to learning as they help learners to adapt their learning as needed.

…and most students say they do this to some degree…

When asked questions about their approaches to monitoring their learning in mathematics and relating this to their learning goals, 87 per cent of the 15-year-olds

in the OECD countries agree or strongly agree that when they study for a mathematics test they try to work out what are the most important parts to learn. Seventy-three per cent of them agree or strongly agree that when they study mathematics they make themselves check to see if they remembered the work they had already done. Eighty-six per cent agree or strongly agree that when they study mathematics they try to figure out which concept they still have not understood properly. Sixty-nine per cent agree or strongly agree that when they cannot understand something in mathematics they always search for more information to clarify the problem. And 75 per cent of 15-year-olds agree that when they study mathematics they start by working out exactly what they need to learn (Figure 3.9).

Students can be compared on an index that summarises the different questions about the use of control strategies (see *www.pisa.oecd.org* for the item map and Table 3.9 for data). However, analyses of the PISA 2000 data suggest that absolute values of countries on this index cannot be easily compared because of cultural differences in student response behaviour. Nevertheless, it is legitimate to compare how closely student control strategies relate to student performance in each country and how differences between males and females (or other groups) within each country vary across countries (Table 3.9). It is also noteworthy that females report significantly more use of control strategies in mathematics than males in 22 of 30 OECD countries.

...but the association with performance, though substantial in some countries, tends to be weak overall.

The relationship between the reported use of control strategies and student performance in mathematics tends to be relatively weak, with one unit on the index corresponding to around 6 score points on the mathematics scale, on average across OECD countries (Table 3.9). This is different from the case of reading in PISA 2000, where the use of control strategies was strongly related to reading performance, with one unit on the index corresponding to a reading performance difference of 16 score points (Table 4.5 and OECD, 2001a). As suggested later in this chapter, students who are anxious about mathematics may use control strategies to help them more than those who are confident, so that while such strategies help individuals raise their performance, they are not on average used more by people who perform better. For these reasons, schools may still need to give more explicit attention to allowing students to manage and control their learning, with the aim to help them develop effective strategies, not only to support their learning at school but also to provide them with the tools to manage their learning later in life.

It is also noteworthy that the relationship between the use of control strategies in mathematics and mathematics performance varies widely between countries. In Korea, for example, which has a comparatively low mean score on the control strategies index (-0.49), the relationship between the index and student performance is strong, with one unit on the index corresponding to 38 score points on the mathematics scale. In Australia, Japan, Norway, Portugal, Turkey and the partner country Hong Kong-China, one unit corresponds to between 14 and 27 score points. In contrast, in other countries the relationship is not statistically significant or even slightly negative.

Figure 3.9 ■ Effective learning: Control strategies

Percentage of students agreeing or strongly agreeing with the following statements:

- A: When I study for a mathematics test, I try to work out what are the most important parts to learn.
- B: When I study mathematics, I make myself check to see if I remember the work I have already done.
- C: When I study mathematics, I try to figure out which concepts I still have not understood properly.
- D: When I cannot understand something in mathematics, I always search for more information to clarify the problem.
- E: When I study mathematics, I start by working out exactly what I need to learn.

Index of control strategies (Index points: -2.5, -1.5, -0.5, 0, 0.5, 1.5, 2.5) — Average index; Top quarter; Bottom quarter; Average index for females; Average index for males

Change in mathematics performance per unit of the index of control strategies (Score point difference: -60, -40, -20, 0, 20, 40, 60)

	A	B	C	D	E	Percentage of explained variance in student performance
Tunisia	91	80	86	88	83	2.3
Brazil	93	92	91	91	86	0.1
Austria	86	81	91	70	84	0.2
Serbia	90	83	90	87	85	0.4
Mexico	95	83	93	80	85	0.7
Indonesia	95	96	91	88	89	0.1
Germany	90	71	89	66	88	0.7
Greece	89	85	90	79	79	0.5
Turkey	88	85	85	61	86	2.7
Liechtenstein	85	60	89	72	81	2.1
Italy	90	76	91	83	85	0.1
Uruguay	91	79	88	72	78	0.0
Switzerland	89	63	89	72	80	0.1
France	91	72	87	78	78	0.8
Portugal	91	86	85	77	88	3.8
Luxembourg	83	78	84	66	71	0.4
Slovak Republic	91	79	90	78	83	0.2
Macao-China	87	77	91	65	89	0.7
Canada	87	75	87	74	77	2.4
Hungary	90	76	88	76	78	0.2
Czech Republic	84	82	93	80	80	0.0
Australia	89	77	86	69	79	2.4
United States	86	72	83	74	79	0.1
Iceland	89	73	84	58	76	0.3
Ireland	90	75	86	69	76	0.2
Spain	84	79	84	66	82	2.0
Poland	91	80	86	75	79	0.2
Thailand	94	82	85	74	76	0.6
New Zealand	88	77	86	69	73	1.1
Belgium	85	71	85	67	80	0.0
Hong Kong-China	87	76	89	64	82	6.0
Russian Fed.	87	74	86	71	71	0.0
Denmark	84	68	86	78	57	0.2
Norway	87	61	78	66	59	2.3
Latvia	84	67	84	71	66	0.3
Netherlands	86	59	82	58	81	0.0
Sweden	79	57	84	72	41	0.0
Finland	88	46	82	48	59	1.2
Korea	75	60	75	56	47	16.0
Japan	81	65	76	50	26	3.2
OECD average	*87*	*73*	*86*	*69*	*75*	*0.0*
United Kingdom[1]	89	77	86	65	75	0.9

1. Response rate too low to ensure comparability (see Annex A3).

Source: OECD PISA 2003 database, Table 3.9.

Figure 3.10 ■ Effective learning: Memorisation strategies

Percentage of students agreeing or strongly agreeing with the following statements:

Index of memorisation strategies

Average index
Top quarter
Bottom quarter
Average index for females
Average index for males

Index points: -2.5, -1.5, -0.5, 0, 0.5, 1.5, 2.5

Change in mathematics performance per unit of the index of memorisation strategies

Score point difference: -60, -40, -20, 0, 20, 40, 60

	I go over some problems in mathematics so often that I feel as if I could solve them in my sleep.	When I study mathematics, I try to learn the answers to problems off by heart.	In order to remember the method for solving a mathematics problem, I go through examples again and again.	To learn mathematics, I try to remember every step in a procedure.	Percentage of explained variance in student performance
Mexico	41	82	68	92	0.1
Indonesia	68	52	88	79	3.6
Brazil	30	62	88	88	4.1
Thailand	48	90	71	85	0.0
Tunisia	43	52	81	78	0.7
United States	42	67	70	83	0.0
Greece	29	60	75	81	0.1
Australia	30	64	71	80	0.9
Canada	33	58	70	83	0.5
Uruguay	46	42	82	62	0.4
Hungary	44	30	74	89	0.5
Poland	36	62	71	78	0.2
New Zealand	31	66	70	74	0.2
Slovak Republic	60	32	59	82	0.9
Ireland	28	57	77	75	0.3
Turkey	44	30	78	75	0.0
Spain	31	40	76	85	0.7
Austria	43	29	70	78	5.1
Italy	30	32	79	84	1.2
Macao-China	36	55	69	53	1.8
Iceland	26	55	62	72	0.0
Russian Fed.	24	50	63	71	0.0
Luxembourg	42	27	72	73	1.1
Czech Republic	40	34	62	75	1.7
Serbia	33	24	84	68	4.3
France	25	37	70	82	0.0
Germany	42	34	61	68	5.1
Sweden	33	56	63	61	2.2
Belgium	28	36	71	76	0.7
Portugal	27	43	66	74	0.4
Norway	31	41	61	79	6.7
Latvia	19	40	71	74	0.0
Hong Kong-China	34	47	64	56	0.4
Netherlands	41	34	61	61	1.4
Switzerland	32	33	54	74	3.9
Finland	26	44	54	72	0.6
Denmark	19	45	50	69	0.9
Liechtenstein	36	27	50	61	17.7
Korea	30	34	61	52	3.6
Japan	21	27	45	62	1.9
OECD average	***34***	***45***	***66***	***75***	***0.2***
United Kingdom[1]	30	63	70	76	1.6

1. Response rate too low to ensure comparability (see Annex A3).
Source: OECD PISA 2003 database, Table 3.10.

Memorisation and elaboration strategies

Memorisation strategies (*e.g.,* learning of facts or rehearsal of examples) are important in many tasks, but they commonly only lead to verbatim representations of knowledge, with new information being stored in the memory with little further processing. Where the learner's goal is to be able to retrieve the information as presented, memorisation is an appropriate strategy. But such learning by rote rarely leads to deep understanding. In order to achieve understanding, new information must be integrated into a learner's prior knowledge base. Elaboration strategies (*e.g.,* exploring how the material relates to things one has learned in other contexts, or asking how the information might be applied in other contexts) can be used to reach this goal.

Students may need to memorise information, but only where this is integrated with prior knowledge does this bring deeper understanding…

Students in PISA 2003 were asked separate questions on their use of memorisation and elaboration strategies in the field of mathematics. On the basis of their responses, indices were created for each of these learning strategies. As ever, any conclusions need to be drawn with reference to the cultural and educational contexts and analyses in both PISA 2000 and PISA 2003. This suggests that it remains difficult to compare absolute values on both of these indices across countries and cultures (Table 3.10 and Table 3.11).

…so PISA looked at memorisation and elaboration strategies.

With regard to the use of memorisation strategies in the OECD countries, 66 per cent of the 15-year-old students agree or strongly agree that in order to remember the method for solving a mathematics problem they go through examples repeatedly. Seventy-five per cent of them agree or strongly agree that to learn mathematics they try to remember every step in a procedure. However, 65 per cent disagree or strongly disagree that when they study for mathematics they try to learn the answers to problems by heart (Figure 3.10).

Most students memorise procedures but report to not simply learn answers by heart…

With regard to the use of elaboration strategies in OECD countries, 53 per cent of 15-year-olds agree or strongly agree that they think how the mathematics they have learnt can be used in everyday life. Sixty-four per cent agree or strongly agree that they try to understand new concepts in mathematics by relating them to things they already know. Sixty per cent disagree or strongly disagree that when they are solving a mathematics problem they often think about how the solution might be applied to other interesting questions. And 56 per cent of 15-year-olds disagree or strongly disagree that when learning mathematics they try to relate the work to things they have learnt in other subjects.

…and most relate new concepts to what they know, but do not reflect on them more widely.

HOW LEARNER CHARACTERISTICS RELATE TO EACH OTHER AND INFLUENCE PERFORMANCE

Previous sections in this chapter have examined different learner characteristics individually. This section now considers how different learner characteristics interrelate and how each of these learner characteristics relate to student performance, after accounting for the effect of the others.

Examining these learner characteristics together…

Figure 3.11 ■ Effective learning: Elaboration strategies

Percentage of students agreeing or strongly agreeing with the following statements:

	When I am solving mathematics problems, I often think of new ways to get the answer.	I think how the mathematics I have learned can be used in everyday life.	I try to understand new concepts in mathematics by relating them to things I already know.	When I am solving a mathematics problem, I often think about how the solution might be applied to other interesting questions.	When learning mathematics, I try to relate the work to things I have learnt in other subjects.	Percentage of explained variance in student performance
Tunisia	74	79	78	85	72	1.8
Mexico	78	89	84	67	71	0.0
Brazil	78	83	85	68	57	1.3
Thailand	64	90	81	74	75	0.3
Indonesia	74	86	82	71	43	0.0
Turkey	68	60	72	57	68	0.4
Serbia	60	62	78	62	54	0.4
Slovak Republic	65	69	80	43	67	0.0
Uruguay	64	66	72	52	52	0.2
Greece	50	75	71	56	52	0.8
Poland	52	64	80	46	59	0.3
United States	56	55	70	48	52	0.6
Portugal	64	53	73	60	41	0.9
Russian Fed.	32	68	68	48	57	0.1
New Zealand	54	60	67	43	47	0.5
Czech Republic	33	77	76	38	49	1.1
Latvia	44	72	75	38	49	0.2
Spain	55	63	63	44	44	1.3
Canada	53	52	64	43	47	0.5
Denmark	47	57	66	42	47	1.0
Australia	53	55	65	41	44	0.0
Macao-China	56	54	65	40	38	2.4
Italy	54	51	64	43	44	0.2
Hong Kong-China	58	51	63	43	40	4.1
Sweden	48	61	64	33	41	0.9
Switzerland	44	47	66	37	45	0.4
Iceland	38	57	65	38	38	0.0
France	45	47	52	48	44	0.0
Liechtenstein	44	44	70	35	41	1.4
Hungary	34	56	65	31	38	0.2
Ireland	41	49	60	33	36	0.1
Finland	43	51	62	27	40	3.1
Norway	35	59	58	35	37	0.8
Belgium	44	36	58	40	40	1.0
Luxembourg	54	40	44	37	34	1.0
Netherlands	40	27	56	36	41	0.1
Austria	41	41	60	29	40	0.3
Germany	36	42	56	27	36	0.4
Korea	40	34	55	27	21	9.1
Japan	42	12	52	21	15	2.4
OECD average	*49*	*53*	*64*	*40*	*44*	*0.3*
United Kingdom[1]	52	52	67	38	47	0.2

1. Response rate too low to ensure comparability (see Annex A3).
Source: OECD PISA 2003 database, Table 3.11.

Associations between different student characteristics make it difficult to separate out the effect of any single one of them when it comes to predicting performance. For example, students who say that they are interested in mathematics are also more likely to perform well, to believe in their own efficacy and to exert effort and persistence, factors that have also been shown to be associated with strong performance. To what extent is being interested in mathematics a predictor, in itself, of good performance and to what extent can the high performance of students who are interested in mathematics be explained by the fact that they also tend to have these other positive attributes? By building a model of the multiple interactions among these variables, it is possible to separate out the impact of each – effectively looking at the association between, say, mathematics interest and performance while controlling for other measured characteristics. This makes it possible to distinguish a separate effect for each variable (Figure 3.11).

...makes it possible to distinguish the separate influence of each on performance.

The model used here to analyse these effects considers a selection of the measures used by PISA to measure students' interest in mathematics and their anxiety in mathematics, alongside students' use of control strategies and their mathematics performance.[7] The model operates on the basis that students' interest in mathematics and low levels of anxiety are drivers which initiate investment in learning activity, with the adoption of particular strategies, represented in the model by students' tendency to control their own learning. The model then seeks to predict students' performance in mathematics from students' interest in mathematics, their absence of anxiety in mathematics and the frequency with which students report the use of control strategies.

Figure 3.12 shows the measured average degree of association for each of the relationships, with results for individual countries shown in Table 3.12.[8] These are different from the individual associations between the various characteristics

Figure 3.12 ▪ **Individual factors associated with control strategies and performance, when accounting for other factors**

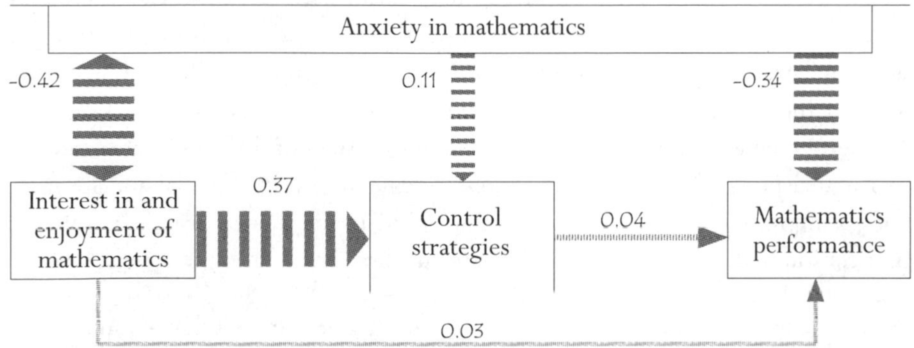

Note: The width of each arrow is proportional to the regression coefficient, shown in each box, a measure of the association between the factors (however, the proportion of explained variance cannot be calculated from the coefficient for a single variable, since several variables are looked at simultaneously). The directions of the arrows in this diagram indicate a suggested effect, rather than a demonstrated causal link.

Source: OECD PISA 2003 database, Tables 3.12, 3.13 and 3.14.

and performance shown in previous sections because they now separate out the specific effect by accounting for interrelationships with the other variables. The following results emerge from this analysis.

This analysis shows that students who are less anxious perform better regardless of other characteristics...

First, the various aspects of student anxiety in mathematics closely affect performance, over and above associations with other learner characteristics. The strength of the influence is shown by the width of each arrow. The results show that students with an absence of anxiety about mathematics perform strongly in mathematics, regardless of other aspects of their attitudes or behaviour. When other factors are taken into account, students' interest in and enjoyment of mathematics have on average no clear association with performance.

...that anxiety and interest in and enjoyment of mathematics are closely interrelated...

This does not mean, however, that interest in and enjoyment of mathematics do not matter: the fact that students with these characteristics are more likely to use effective learning strategies clearly contradicts such an interpretation. Rather, the strong negative association between interest in and enjoyment of mathematics and anxiety in mathematics suggests that these two factors work together: As indicated by the associations between anxiety in mathematics and interest in and enjoyment of mathematics in Figure 3.12, students who are anxious about doing mathematics tend not to be interested in or enjoy mathematics. The associations between the two learner characteristics on the left side of the model are rather consistent across countries (Table 3.14) and thus seem to illustrate a universal pattern of relationships.

... that while control strategies are not directly associated with performance, they are linked to interest and anxiety...

An impact of control strategies on performance, once other learner characteristics are accounted for, is not measurable. This is not because controlling one's learning does not help performance, but rather because a large amount of the variation in the degree to which students control their learning is associated with variation in their interest in and enjoyment of mathematics as well as in their anxiety in mathematics.

...and that students often seem to use control strategies as a response to anxiety.

It is clear from the above that while the separate effects of individual student characteristics on student performance and on the use of control strategies are not always large, measurement of the overall effect is different from the sum of these individual associations, because several factors may combine to have an influence. The modelling process allows the combined effect of several characteristics to be measured by considering the percentage of variation in, for example, student performance that could be explained by the combined association with related factors. These results are shown in Figure 3.13.

Additionally, the low but positive association between students' anxiety in mathematics and their self-reported control strategies – most obvious in Belgium, Luxembourg, the Netherlands and Spain as well as in Latvia and Liechtenstein among the partner countries (Table 3.13) – shows that control strategies are not only used by students who are highly motivated, but also used by students who are anxious about mathematics. Students who are anxious (and often low performing as indicated by the negative effect on mathematic performance)

Figure 3.13 ■ **The combined explanatory power of student learning characteristics on mathematics performance and control stategies**

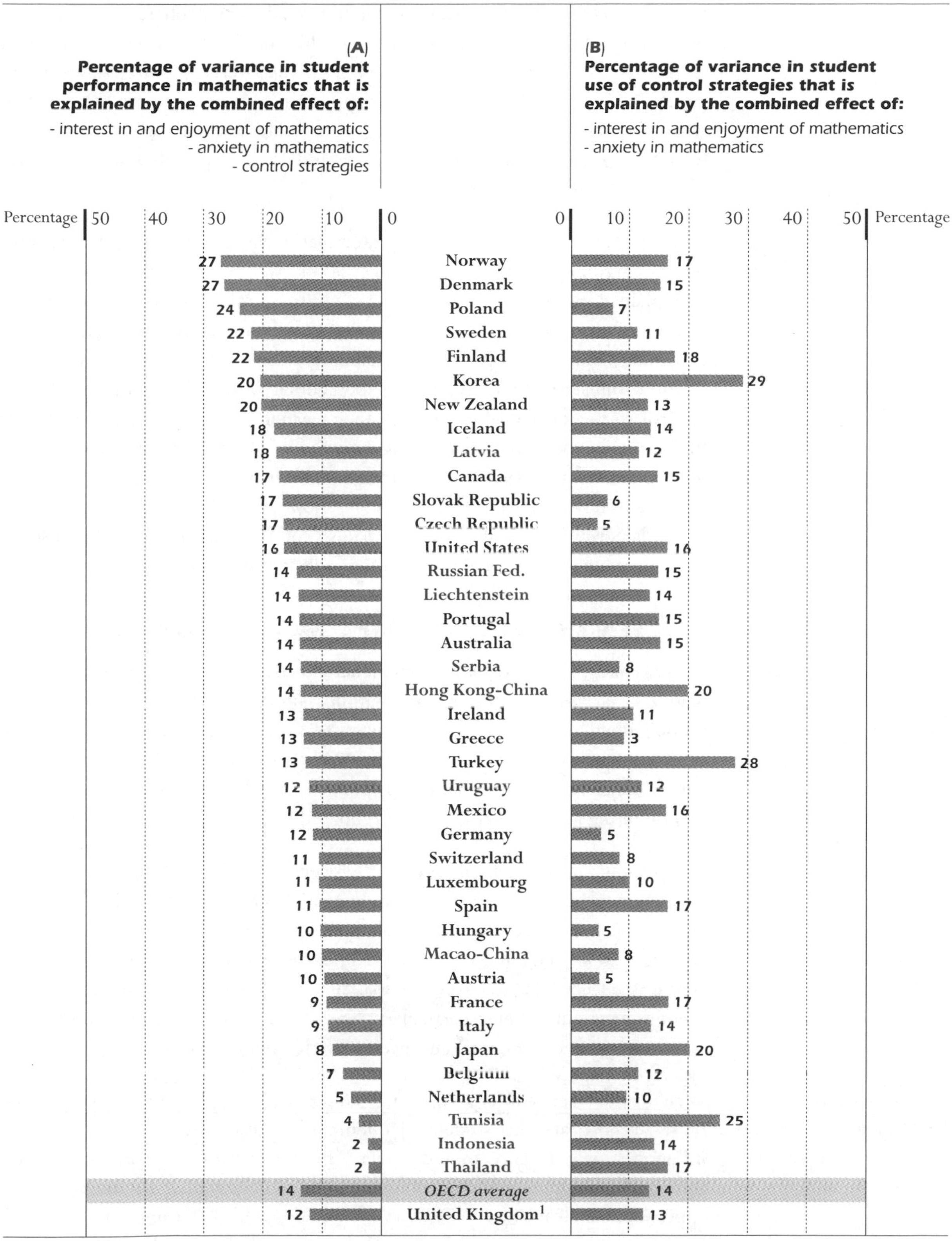

(A) Percentage of variance in student performance in mathematics that is explained by the combined effect of: - interest in and enjoyment of mathematics - anxiety in mathematics - control strategies		(B) Percentage of variance in student use of control strategies that is explained by the combined effect of: - interest in and enjoyment of mathematics - anxiety in mathematics
27	Norway	17
27	Denmark	15
24	Poland	7
22	Sweden	11
22	Finland	18
20	Korea	29
20	New Zealand	13
18	Iceland	14
18	Latvia	12
17	Canada	15
17	Slovak Republic	6
17	Czech Republic	5
16	United States	16
14	Russian Fed.	15
14	Liechtenstein	14
14	Portugal	15
14	Australia	15
14	Serbia	8
14	Hong Kong-China	20
13	Ireland	11
13	Greece	3
13	Turkey	28
12	Uruguay	12
12	Mexico	16
12	Germany	5
11	Switzerland	8
11	Luxembourg	10
11	Spain	17
10	Hungary	5
10	Macao-China	8
10	Austria	5
9	France	17
9	Italy	14
8	Japan	20
7	Belgium	12
5	Netherlands	10
4	Tunisia	25
2	Indonesia	14
2	Thailand	17
14	*OECD average*	14
12	United Kingdom[1]	13

Percentage (A axis: 50 40 30 20 10 0; B axis: 0 10 20 30 40 50)

1. Response rate too low to ensure comparability (see Annex A3).
Source: OECD PISA 2003 database.

seem to regulate their learning by an increased use of control strategies, which can be a highly effective approach given their specific needs. On the other hand, students who are more capable might not need such deliberate self-control, since information processing happens smoothly and thus they report using these to use strategies less frequently. Looking at the overall picture, as shown in Figure 3.12, such a differential (but adaptive) use of strategies can help explain why students who use control strategies most do not necessarily have higher than average performance, even though such strategies can help individuals with particular needs to perform better.

This analysis shows strong interrelationships between learner characteristics and mathematics performance.

Overall, Figure 3.13 shows strong interrelationships between learner characteristics and mathematics performance. Similarly, when looking at the amount of explained variance for students' use of control strategies, the two predictors, namely interest in and enjoyment of mathematics and anxiety in mathematics, explain around 30 per cent of the variance in Korea and Turkey and the partner country Tunisia (OECD average 14 per cent). Although the PISA index of control strategies may also capture other learner characteristics, control over the learning process is an important outcome in its own right, particularly in a lifelong learning context where autonomous learning is becoming increasingly important. It suggests that in all countries, adopting an effective learning strategy depends not just on having cognitive tools (knowing how to learn) but also on having certain attitudes and dispositions (wanting to learn).

HOW LEARNER CHARACTERISTICS VARY ACROSS SCHOOLS

PISA shows fewer differences among schools in learner characteristics than in performance...

How do the overall patterns in learner characteristics vary among schools? A high degree of variation between schools within countries would indicate that certain schools stand out and suggest that it is possible to influence the development of students' approaches to learning through schooling and targeted interventions. Table 3.15 examines the relative proportions of variation between schools in several of the learner characteristics reported in this chapter.

The results suggest that differences between schools in students' reported characteristics are far less pronounced than the differences within schools. For the eight characteristics considered in Table 3.15, on average across OECD countries, variation among schools accounts for less than 15 per cent of the overall variation among students. This may suggest that, in most countries, comparatively few schools stand out as being particularly likely to have students who report being well-motivated, confident and using effective learning strategies.

...but this may be because students describe their characteristics relative to those of their peers.

Such results must be interpreted with caution, though, given that they are based on self-reports and that students' judgements about themselves can be strongly influenced by reference to their peers. In the case of some characteristics, this might disguise important between-school differences in students' real approaches to learning. For example, it is possible that some students with hard-working classmates understate the amount of effort and persistence they put in, compared to students with less hard-working classmates, even though

it is the absolute amount of effort that matters to school success. This makes it hard to identify schools with relatively hard-working pupils overall. On the other hand, in other respects, students' perceptions relative to their peers are an important part of the picture. For example, even if students' perceptions of not being good at mathematics are linked to the high mathematics abilities of others in the school, rather than to an absolute weakness in the subject, this lack of confidence is still an important aspect of their approach to learning that may hold them back.

Nevertheless, the high variation within each school shows that even successful schools have issues to address.

The finding that individual schools do not vary greatly in the profile of students' self-reported approaches to learning has, nevertheless, important implications, even if it does *not* imply that all schools are similar with regard to the learner characteristics of their intake. What it does highlight is the large variation in learner characteristics among students within schools. The large proportion of within-school variation underlines the importance for teachers to be able to engage constructively with heterogeneity not only in student abilities but also in their approaches to learning. Even in schools that are performing well there are students who lack confidence and motivation and who are not inclined to set and monitor their own learning goals.

A SUMMARY PICTURE OF GENDER DIFFERENCES IN LEARNER CHARACTERISTICS

Various gender differences can be compared in standardised form...

Previous sections of this chapter have examined gender differences separately for the various learner characteristics. Figure 3.14 summarises the information on gender differences for student attitudes, anxiety, strategies and cognitions related to mathematics and relates the results to the observed performance differences in mathematics. All results are expressed as effect sizes, so that results can be compared across the different measures and across countries, with an effect size of 0.20 used as a criterion to establish differences that warrant attention by policy makers (Box 3.3).

...showing that males and females approach the learning of mathematics differently...

A first striking finding is that while gender differences in student performance tend to be modest (see first bar in Figure 3.14) there are marked differences between males and females in their interest in and enjoyment of mathematics as well as in their self-related beliefs, emotions and learning strategies related to mathematics.

...with males showing higher motivation, particularly in some countries.

Figure 3.14 shows that in 21 countries males express stronger levels of interest in and enjoyment of mathematics than females, with an average effect size of 0.21, and with effect sizes greater than 0.50 in Switzerland as well as in the partner country Liechtenstein. Gender differences in instrumental motivation in mathematics tend to be even greater (the average effect size is 0.24) than in interest in mathematics, suggesting that males may be more motivated to learn because they believe that mathematics will help them in their later careers.

Figure 3.14 ■ **Gender differences in mathematics and other learning characteristics as measured by effect sizes**

Performance in mathematics
Males perform better in mathematics in 5 countries

Instrumental motivation in mathematics
Males report greater instrumental motivation in mathematics in 25 countries

Interest in and enjoyment of mathematics
Males report greater interest in and enjoyment of mathematics in 21 countries

Higher for females | *Higher for males*

Australia
Austria
Belgium
Canada
Czech Republic
Denmark
Finland
France
Germany
Greece
Hong Kong-China
Hungary
Iceland
Indonesia
Ireland
Italy
Japan
Korea
Latvia
Liechtenstein
Luxembourg
Macao-China
Mexico
Netherlands
New Zealand
Norway
Poland
Portugal
Russian Fed.
Serbia
Slovak Republic
Spain
Sweden
Switzerland
Thailand
Tunisia
Turkey
United States
Uruguay
OECD average
United Kingdom[1]

-0.8 -0.4 0 0.4 0.8
Effect size

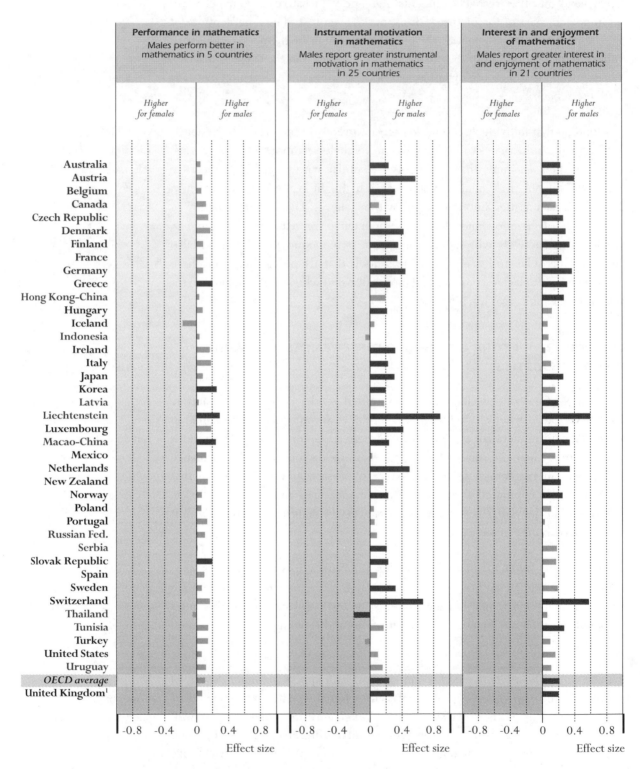

Note: Effect sizes equal to or greater than 0.20 are marked in darker colour (see Annex A4).

1. Response rate too low to ensure comparability (see Annex A3).

Source: OECD PISA 2003 database, Table 3.16.

Figure 3.14 (continued-1) ■ **Gender differences in mathematics and other learning characteristics as measured by effect sizes**

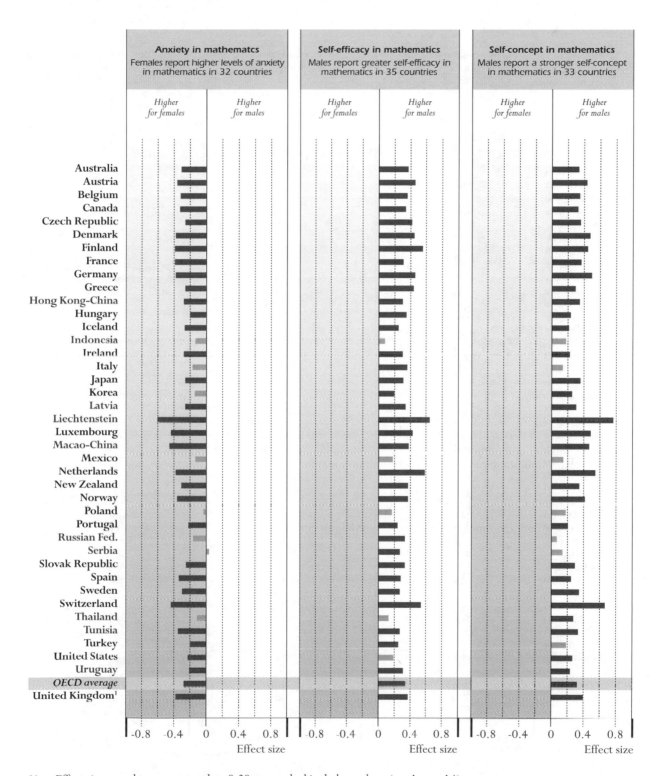

Note: Effect sizes equal to or greater than 0.20 are marked in darker colour (see Annex A4).

1. Response rate too low to ensure comparability (see Annex A3).

Source: OECD PISA 2003 database, Table 3.16.

Figure 3.14 (continued-2) ■ **Gender differences in mathematics and other learning characteristics as measured by effect sizes**

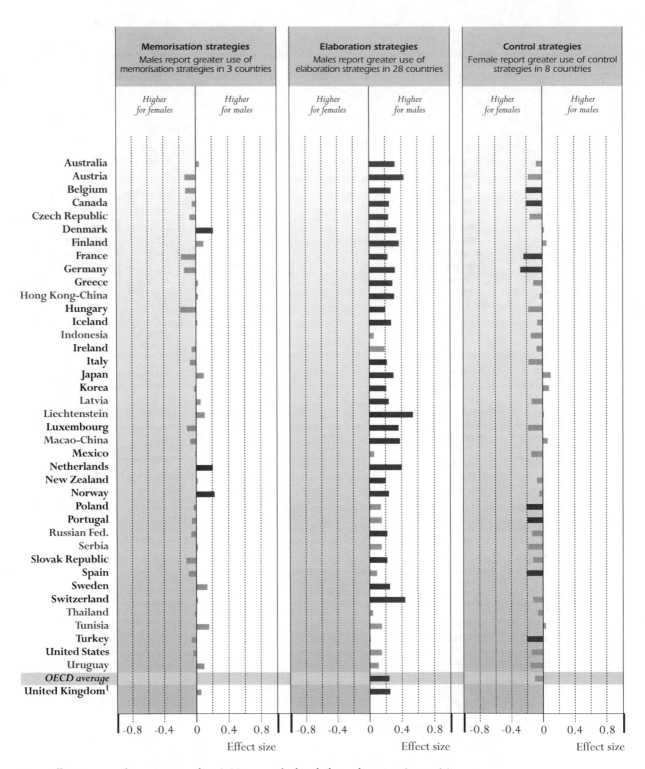

Note: Effect sizes equal to or greater than 0.20 are marked in darker colour (see Annex A4).

1. Response rate too low to ensure comparability (see Annex A3).

Source: OECD PISA 2003 database, Table 3.16.

Males also show greater confidence in mathematics, relative to females, than one might expect from relatively small differences in performance...

Beyond the observed discrepancy between gender difference in actual performance (which are comparatively small) and gender differences in student intrinsic and extrinsic motivation (which tend to be much larger), a similar picture also emerges also when looking at students' mathematics-related self-efficacy beliefs, self-concepts and anxiety. Again, although females often do not perform at a level much lower than males, they tend to report lower mathematics-related self-efficacy than males in almost all countries, with the strongest effects in Finland, the Netherlands, and Switzerland, as well as in the partner country Liechtenstein. Similar results emerge for students' self-concept in mathematics, where males tend to have a more positive view of their abilities than do females in most countries.

...while in most countries females feel more anxious.

Finally, females experience significantly more feelings of anxiety, helplessness and stress in mathematics classes than males in 32 of 40 countries. There are statistically significantly higher levels of anxiety among females in Austria, Denmark, Finland, France, Germany, Luxembourg, the Netherlands, Norway, Spain and Switzerland, as well as in the partner countries Liechtenstein, Macao-China and Tunisia.

This suggests that schools need to promote interest in and confidence about mathematics among females.

Taken together, the difference between males and females in performance in mathematics, on the one hand, and anxiety and attitudes towards the subject, on the other, are highly relevant for policy makers, as these data reveal inequalities between the genders in the effectiveness with which schools and societies promote motivation and interest. The data also reveal a difference in the level of anxiety in mathematics. The results raise questions as to how the gender gap can be reduced and how to reach a high level of overall performance through the organization of schooling and instructional delivery.

In some countries, females are more likely to control their learning and males to elaborate new knowledge.

With respect to students' use of learning strategies, gender differences are less pronounced. Nevertheless, while gender patterns in the use of memorisation strategies are not widely apparent,[9] in 28 of the 40 countries with available data, males consistently report using elaboration strategies more often than females. Conversely, in 8 countries, females report using control strategies more often than males. This suggests that females are more likely to adopt a self-evaluating perspective during the learning process. Females might benefit from training in the use of elaboration strategies, while males, on the other hand, might benefit from more general assistance in planning, organising and structuring learning activities. Similar results have been reported on the basis of the PISA 2000 data, where the same learning strategies were measured for reading (OECD, 2003b).

These gender differences are relevant for students' futures, not just their performance at school.

Although these data reflect the attitudes and behaviour of 15-year-olds, the patterns observed may well be predictive of those appearing later in their educational and occupational careers. As mentioned before, significant progress has been achieved in reducing the gender gap in formal educational qualifications over the last generation and university-level graduation rates for women now equal or exceed those for men in 21 of the 27 OECD countries for which

comparable data exist (OECD, 2004a). However, in mathematics and computer science, gender differences in tertiary qualifications remain persistently high: the proportion of women among university graduates in mathematics and computer science is only 30 per cent, on average, among OECD countries, and in Austria, Belgium, Germany, Hungary, Iceland, the Netherlands, Norway, the Slovak Republic and Switzerland it is only between 9 and 25 per cent.

IMPLICATIONS FOR POLICY

The results from this chapter suggest that students are most likely to initiate high quality learning, using various strategies, if they are well motivated, not anxious about their learning and believe in their own capacities.

Well-motivated and confident students invest well in their own learning…

Students' motivation, their positive self-related beliefs as well as their emotions also affect their use of learning strategies. There are good grounds for this: high quality learning is time and effort-intensive. It involves control of the learning process as well as the explicit checking of relations between previously acquired knowledge and new information, the formulation of hypotheses about possible connections and the testing of these hypotheses against the background of the new material. Learners are only willing to invest such effort if they have a strong interest in a subject or if there is a considerable benefit, in terms of high performance, with learners motivated by the external reward of performing well. Thus, students need to be willing to learn how to learn. From the perspective of teaching this implies that effective ways of learning – including goal setting, strategy selection and the control and evaluation of the learning process – can and should be fostered by the educational setting and by teachers.

…and teachers can help those with weaker approaches to adopt effective learning strategies…

Research on ways of instructing students in learning strategies has shown that the development of learning expertise is dependent not only on the existence of a repertoire of cognitive and metacognitive information-processing abilities but also on the readiness of individuals to define their own goals, to be proactive, to interpret success and failure appropriately, to translate wishes into intentions and plans and to shield learning from competing intentions. A repertoire of strategies combined with other attributes that foster learning develops gradually through the practices of teachers who model learning behaviour, through activities aimed at building a scaffolding structure of learning for the student and through analysis of the reasons for academic success and failure. During the process of becoming effective and self-regulated learners, students need assistance and feedback, not only on the results of their learning, but also on the learning process itself. In particular, the students with the weakest approaches to learning need professional assistance to become effective and self-regulated learners.

…which requires a building of their motivation and confidence.

The links between students' self-related beliefs in mathematics and learning behaviours in mathematics suggest that motivation and self-confidence are indispensable to outcomes that will foster lifelong learning. The combined effect of motivation and self-confidence on control strategies suggests that teaching

a student how to learn autonomously is unlikely to work without strong motivation and self-confidence as a basis.

Teachers in all schools, not just low-performing ones, need to help students become stronger learners…

The finding that the profile of students' self-reported approaches to learning varies much more within schools than among schools also has policy implications, even if it does not imply that all schools are similar with regard to the learner characteristics of their intake. What it does highlight is the large variation in learner characteristics among students in each school. This underlines the importance for schools and teachers to be able to engage constructively with heterogeneity not only in student abilities but also in their characteristics as learners and their approaches to learning. It will not be sufficient to operate on the principle that a rising tide raises all ships, since even in well-performing schools there are students who lack confidence and motivation and who are not inclined to set and monitor their own learning goals.

…and should pay particular attention to females, whose lack of self-confidence and motivation in mathematics exceeds their lower performance.

Another striking finding of the analysis is that while females generally do not perform much below males in mathematics, they consistently report much lower interest in and enjoyment of mathematics, lower self-related beliefs and much higher levels of helplessness and stress in mathematics classes. This finding is highly relevant for policy makers, as it reveals inequalities between the genders in the effectiveness with which schools and societies promote motivation and interest and – to an even greater extent – help students overcome anxiety towards different subject areas. These patterns may well be predictive of gender differences appearing later in the educational and occupational careers of males and females. They raise questions as to how the gender gap can be reduced and a high level of overall performance reached through the organisation of schooling and instructional delivery.

Thus, schools must not just instruct students but also address their learning approaches.

Overall, the results suggest that education systems need to invest in approaches that address aspects of attitudes and learning behaviours and to consider this as a goal that is as central to the mission of education systems as cognitive instruction. This may have implications for the initial training of teachers, as well as for the continuous professional development of teachers.

Notes

1. This research is summarised in Box 3.1 below and further described in OECD (2003b).
2. The other two categories related to the interactive use of tools in the widest possible sense and social skills, defined in terms of successful participation in socially heterogeneous groups.
3. For the country Serbia and Montenegro, data for Montenegro are not available. The latter accounts for 7.9 per cent of the national population. The name "Serbia" is used as a shorthand for the Serbian part of Serbia and Montenegro.
4. To illustrate the meaning of the international scores on the index, question-by-score maps have been constructed that relate the index value to typical student responses to the questions that were asked. These question-by-score maps can be found at *www.pisa.oecd.org*.
5. See Box 2.2 in Chapter 2 for an explanation of how scores are translated into years of schooling.
6. The share of females completing a university-level qualification (tertiary Type A) in mathematics or computer science in 2002 was 30 per cent on average across OECD countries with available data and 19 per cent in Austria, 23 per cent in Germany, 16 per cent in the Netherlands and 19 per cent in Switzerland. Luxembourg also shows large gender differences in instrumental motivation but since tertiary institutions awarding Type A qualifications in mathematics and science do not exist in Luxembourg, no comparison about gender differences can be made (OECD, 2004a).
7. The variables selected for the purpose of this model are as follows: The use of *control strategies in mathematics* is used to illustrate how learning strategies are associated with performance. Thinking about what one needs to learn and relating this to learning goals is a particularly important aspect of regulating one's own learning, which prior research has shown to have a particularly close association with performance. The link between motivation and performance is illustrated *by interest in and enjoyment of mathematics*, one of the motivational characteristics measured. *Anxiety in mathematics* or students' feelings of helplessness and stress when dealing with mathematics has been shown to have a negative effect on performance. Instead of processing task relevant cognitions, students with a high degree of anxiety are often occupied by task-irrelevant cognitions and emotional stress. Both lead to reduced capacity for actually dealing with the tasks at hand and therefore to lower performance.
8. The degree of association is measured by the multiple regression coefficients in the model. These coefficients vary between 1 or -1 (indicating a perfect positive or negative relationship) and 0 (indicating that there is no relationship)
9. Effect sizes exceed 0.2 only in Denmark, the Netherlands and Norway.

How Student Performance Varies between Schools and the Role that Socio-economic Background Plays in This

INTRODUCTION

Nine-tenths of the student performance variation in PISA is within countries, and this chapter looks at…

Chapter 2 considered how well students in different countries perform in mathematics at age 15. The analyses reveal considerable variation in the relative standing of countries in terms of their students' capacity to put mathematical knowledge and skills to functional use. However, the analyses also suggest that differences between countries represent only about one-tenth of the overall variation in student performance in the OECD area.[1]

…how much of that variation is associated with performance differences among schools and with socio-economic groups…

Variation in student performance within countries can have a variety of causes, including the socio-economic backgrounds of students and schools; the ways in which teaching is organised and delivered in classes; the human and financial resources available to schools; and system-level factors such as curricular differences and organisational policies and practices.

This chapter starts by examining more closely the performance gaps shown in Chapter 2. It considers, in particular, the extent to which overall variation in student performance relates to differences in the results achieved by different schools. Next, it looks at how socio-economic background relates to student performance. In so doing, it describes the socio-economic gradients that relate students' performance in mathematics to their backgrounds. The chapter then considers these two phenomena in combination (between-school differences in performance and the impact of socio-economic background). In order to examine how socio-economic background is interrelated with equity in the distribution of learning opportunities.

…as well as at policy approaches for raising performance and improving equity in the distribution of learning opportunities.

Finally, the chapter considers the policy implications of these findings, discussing why different policy strategies are likely to be appropriate in different countries, according to the extent to which low performance is concentrated in particular schools and particular socio-economic groups.

Chapter 5 takes the analysis further by examining school resources, policies and practices that are associated with school performance as measured by PISA.

The overall impact of home background on student performance tends to be similar for mathematics, reading and science in PISA 2003.[2] Therefore, to simplify the presentation and avoid repetition, the chapter limits the analysis to student performance in mathematics, and it considers the combined mathematics scale rather than examining the four mathematics scales separately.

SECURING CONSISTENT STANDARDS FOR SCHOOLS: A PROFILE OF BETWEEN- AND WITHIN-SCHOOL DIFFERENCES IN STUDENT PERFORMANCE

School performance differences can arise from the separation of students…

Catering for the needs of a diverse student body and narrowing the gaps in student performance represent formidable challenges for all countries. The approaches that countries have chosen to address these demands vary. Some countries have comprehensive school systems with no, or only limited institutional differentiation.

They seek to provide all students with similar opportunities for learning by requiring each school and teacher to provide for the full range of student abilities, interests and backgrounds. Other countries respond to diversity by grouping students through tracking or streaming, whether between schools or between classes within schools, with the aim of serving students according to their academic potential and/or interests in specific programmes. And in many countries, combinations of the two approaches occur.

...but even comprehensive systems can see variation linked, for example, to geography and school quality.

Even in comprehensive school systems, there may be significant variation in performance levels between schools, due to the socio-economic and cultural characteristics of the communities that are served or to geographical differences (such as between regions, provinces or states in federal systems, or between rural and urban areas). Finally, there may be differences between individual schools that are more difficult to quantify or describe, part of which could result from differences in the quality or effectiveness of the instruction that those schools deliver. As a result, even in comprehensive systems, the performance levels attained by students may still vary across schools.

How do the policies and historical patterns that shape each country's school system affect and relate to the variation in student performance between and within schools? Do countries with explicit tracking and streaming policies show a higher degree of overall disparity in student performance than countries that have non-selective education systems? Such questions are particularly relevant to countries that observe large variation in overall mathematics performance (Table 4.1a).

Total variation in student performance is over a third greater in some countries than others...

Figure 4.1 shows considerable differences in the extent to which mathematics competencies of 15-year-olds vary within each country (Table 4.1a). The total length of the bars indicates the observed variance in student performance on the PISA mathematics scale. Note that the values in Figure 4.1 are expressed as percentages of the average variance between OECD countries in student performance on the PISA mathematics scale, which is equal to 8 593 units.[3] A value larger than 100 indicates that variance in student performance is greater in the corresponding country than on average among OECD countries. Similarly, a value smaller than 100 indicates below-average variance in student performance. For example, the variance in student performance in Finland, Ireland and Mexico as well as in the PISA partner countries Indonesia, Serbia,[4] Thailand and Tunisia is more than 15 per cent below the OECD average variance. By contrast, in Belgium, Japan and Turkey as well as in the partner countries Brazil, Hong Kong-China and Uruguay, variance in student performance is 15 per cent above the OECD average level.[5]

...and how much of that variation is across different schools varies greatly.

For each country, a distinction is made between the variance attributable to differences in student results attained by students in different schools (between-school differences) and that attributable to the range of student results within schools (within-school differences).[6] In Figure 4.1, the length of the bars to the left of the central line shows between-school differences, and also serves to order countries in the figure. The length of the bars to the right of the central

Figure 4.1 ■ **Variance in student performance between schools and within schools on the mathematics scale**

Expressed as a percentage of the average variance in student performance in OECD countries

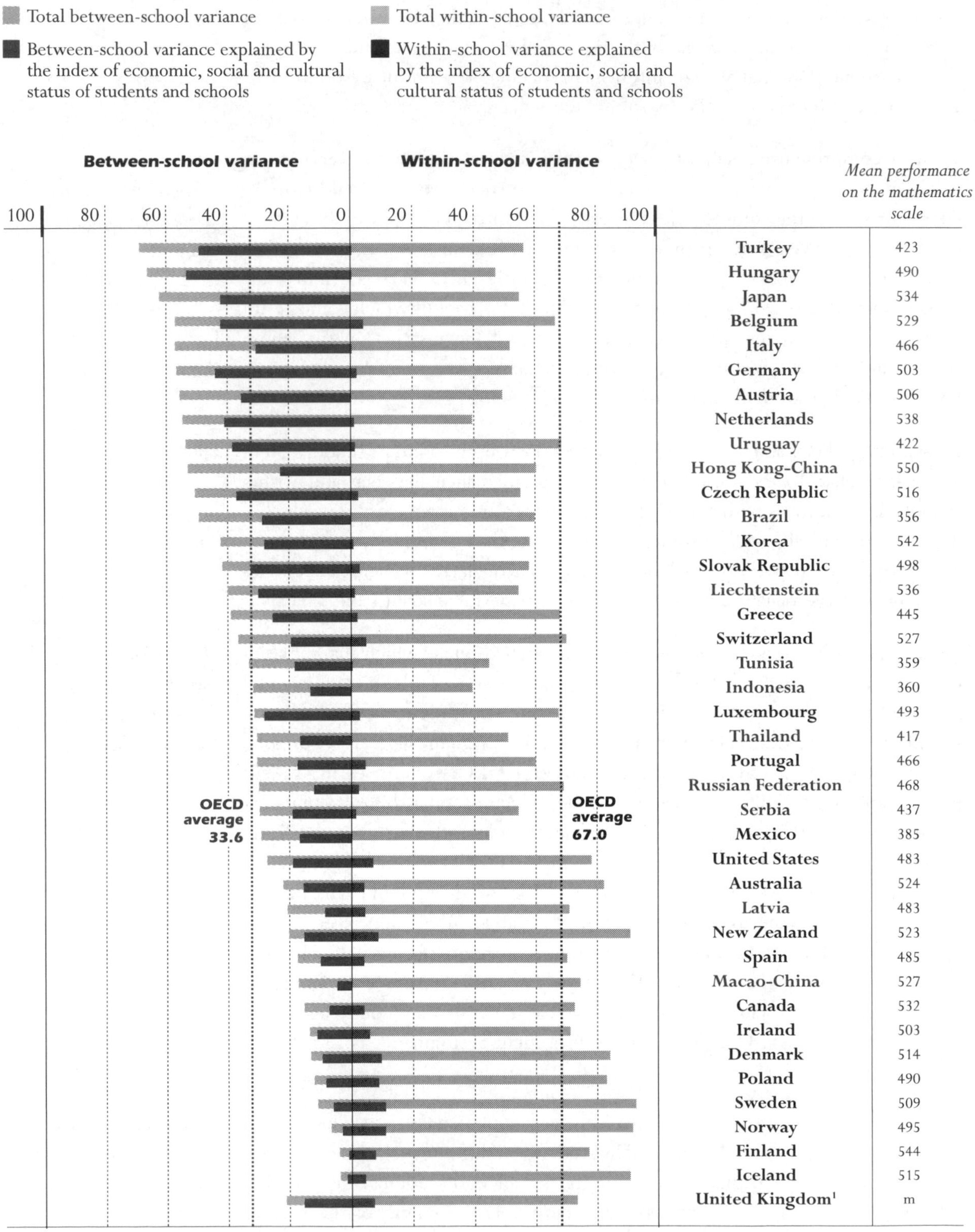

	Mean performance on the mathematics scale
Turkey	423
Hungary	490
Japan	534
Belgium	529
Italy	466
Germany	503
Austria	506
Netherlands	538
Uruguay	422
Hong Kong-China	550
Czech Republic	516
Brazil	356
Korea	542
Slovak Republic	498
Liechtenstein	536
Greece	445
Switzerland	527
Tunisia	359
Indonesia	360
Luxembourg	493
Thailand	417
Portugal	466
Russian Federation	468
Serbia	437
Mexico	385
United States	483
Australia	524
Latvia	483
New Zealand	523
Spain	485
Macao-China	527
Canada	532
Ireland	503
Denmark	514
Poland	490
Sweden	509
Norway	495
Finland	544
Iceland	515
United Kingdom[1]	m

1. Response rate too low to ensure comparability (see Annex A3).
Source: OECD PISA 2003 database, Table 4.1a.

line shows the within-school differences. Therefore, longer segments to the left of the central line indicate greater variation in the mean performance of different schools while longer segments to the right of the central line indicate greater variation among students within schools.

On average, there is half as much variance between schools as within them…

As shown in Figure 4.1, while all countries show considerable within-school variance, in most countries variance in student performance between schools is also considerable. On average across OECD countries, differences in the performance of 15-year-olds between schools account for 34 per cent of the OECD average between-student variance.

…but in some countries the between-school variance is twice the OECD average…

In Hungary and Turkey, variation in performance between schools is particularly large and is about twice the OECD average between-school variance. In Austria, Belgium, the Czech Republic, Germany, Italy, Japan and the Netherlands, as well as in the partner countries Hong Kong-China and Uruguay, the proportion of between-school variance is still over one-and-a-half times that of the OECD average level (see column 3 in Table 4.1a). Where there is substantial variation in performance between schools and less variation between students within schools, students tend to be grouped in schools in which other students perform at levels similar to their own. This may reflect school choices made by families or residential location, as well as policies on school enrolment or the allocation of students to different curricula. To capture variation between education systems and regions within countries, some countries have undertaken the PISA assessment at regional levels. Where such results are available, these are presented in Annex B2.

…while in others it is only a tenth and student differences are contained within schools.

The proportion of between-school variance is around one-tenth of the OECD average level in Finland and Iceland, and half or less in Canada, Denmark, Ireland, Norway, Poland, Sweden and in the partner country Macao-China. In these countries performance is largely unrelated to the schools in which students are enrolled (Table 4.1a). This suggests that the learning environment is similar in the ways that it affects the performance of students.

In some countries, parents can rely on high and consistent performance standards across schools in the entire education system.

It is noteworthy that Canada, Denmark, Finland, Iceland, Ireland, Norway, Sweden and the partner country Macao-China also perform well or at least above the OECD average level. Parents in these countries can be less concerned about school choice in order to enhance their children's performance, and can be confident of high and consistent performance standards across schools in the entire education system.

Socio economic intake affects school differences, but so do differences in the value added by different schools…

While some of the variance between schools is attributable to the socio-economic background of students entering the school, some of it is also likely to reflect certain structural features of schools and schooling systems, particularly in systems where students are tracked by ability. Some of the variance in performance between schools may also attributable to the policies and practices of school administrators and teachers. In other words, there is an added value associated with attending a particular school.

...and in some of the best-performing countries, all schools seem to add roughly equal value.

It is important to note that some, though not all, high performing countries also show low or modest levels of between-school variance. This suggests that securing similar student performance among schools, perhaps most importantly by identifying and reforming poorly performing schools, is a policy goal that is both important in itself and compatible with the goal of high overall performance standards.

Performance variation among schools has been reduced in a few countries...

For most countries, these results are similar to those observed in the PISA 2000 assessment. However, there are some notable exceptions. For instance, in Poland, the move towards a more integrated education system since 1999 – as a consequence of which institutional differentiation now occurs mainly after the age of 15 – may have contributed to the observed dramatic reduction in the between-school variation in performance of 15-year-olds between schools.

...most significantly in Poland, where performance standards among the lowest performing students have markedly increased.

Between-school variance in Poland fell from more than half of the overall performance variance in Poland in 2000 (see column 9 in Table 4.1b) to just 13 per cent in 2003 (see column 13 in Table 4.1a).[7] Simultaneously, the average performance of 15-year-olds in Poland is now significantly higher in both mathematical content areas for which comparable trend data are available, and the overall performance gap between the lower and higher achievers is narrower than it was in 2000. As noted in Chapter 2, the increase in average mathematics performance is thus mainly attributable to an increase in performance at the lower end of the performance distribution (*i.e.,* the 5th, 10th and 25th percentiles). This has occurred to such an extent that in 2003 fewer than 5 per cent of students fell below the performance standards that 10 per cent of Polish students had failed to attain in 2000 (Chapter 2, Table 2.1c, Table 2.1d, Table 2.2c and Table 2.2d). Performance differences among schools were also lower in other countries in 2003: for example, in Belgium, Greece and Mexico, the proportion of national variation in student performance attributable to between-school variance decreased by 8-10 percentage points.[8] In contrast, in Indonesia and Italy, the proportion of variance that lies between schools increased by more than 10 percentage points (see column 13 in Table 4.1 and column 9 in Table 4.1b).

THE QUALITY OF LEARNING OUTCOMES AND EQUITY IN THE DISTRIBUTION OF LEARNING OPPORTUNITIES

To understand what lies behind school differences, one must look at how socio-economic factors affect performance, how much this explains school differences, and how this relates to equity in learning opportunities.

Understanding why some schools show better performance results than others is an important key to school improvement. It requires an analysis that examines, in each country, the effects of student and school factors on both student performance within schools and student performance across schools. As a first step towards such an analysis, this section examines the interrelationship between student performance and socio-economic background, as measured by the PISA index of economic, social and cultural status. In a second step, the section then estimates the proportion of the variance in student performance between schools that is attributable to students' socio-economic backgrounds. In a third step, the section relates the findings to questions about equity in the distribution of learning opportunities.

Students come from a variety of socio-economic and cultural backgrounds. As a result, schools need to provide appropriate and equitable opportunities for a diverse student body. The relative success with which they do this is an important criterion for judging the performance of education systems. Identifying the characteristics of poorly performing students and schools can also help educators and policy-makers determine priorities for policy. Similarly, identifying the characteristics of high performing students and schools can assist policy-makers in promoting high levels of overall performance.

A key objective of schools is to compensate for differences in student backgrounds, which exert a powerful influence.

The results from PISA 2003 show that poor performance in school does not automatically follow from a disadvantaged home background. However, home background remains one of the most powerful factors influencing performance. The nature and extent of this influence is described in the following paragraphs.

Parental occupational status, which is often closely interrelated with other attributes of socio-economic status, has a strong association with student performance (Table 4.2a). The average performance gap in mathematics between students in the top quarter of the PISA index of occupational status (whose parents have occupations in fields such as medicine, university teaching and law) and those in the bottom quarter (with occupations such as small-scale farming, truck-driving and serving in restaurants), amounts to an average of 93 score points, or more than one-and-a-half proficiency levels in mathematics.[9] Expressed differently, one standard deviation (*i.e.,* 16.4 units) on the PISA index of occupational status is associated with an average performance difference of 34 score points. Even when taking into account the fact that parental occupational status is interrelated with other socio-economic background factors and looking at the unique contribution of occupational status alone, an average score difference remains of 21 score points (see column 2 in Table 4.2).

The quarter of students whose parents have the best jobs are one-and-a-half proficiency levels ahead of those with the lowest-status jobs...

In Belgium, France, Germany, Hungary, Luxembourg, the Slovak Republic and the partner country Liechtenstein, differences in performance are particularly large. In these countries, students whose parents have the highest-status jobs score on average about as well as the average student in Finland, the best-performing country in PISA 2003 across mathematics, reading and science. In contrast, students whose parents have the lowest-status jobs score little higher than students in the lowest performing OECD countries. Looked at differently, in Belgium, Germany, Luxembourg and the partner country Liechtenstein, students in the lowest quarter of the distribution of parental occupations are 2.3 times or more likely to be among the bottom quarter of performers in mathematics (see column 11 in Table 4.2a).

...but in some countries, the gap is much larger than in others.

Parental education (Table 4.2b and Table 4.2c) may also be of significant educational benefit for children. The relationship between mothers' educational attainments and students' performance in mathematics is shown to be positive and significant in all participating countries.[10] The gap in mathematics performance between students whose mothers have completed upper secondary education and those whose mothers have not is on average 50 score points, and reaches around

A student's predicted score is one proficiency level higher if his or her mother completed secondary education than if she did not...

60 score points or more in Germany, Mexico, the Slovak Republic, Switzerland, Turkey and the partner country Brazil. In fact, in Germany, the students whose mothers or fathers did not complete upper secondary education are three times more likely to be in the bottom quarter of mathematics performers than the average student (Table 4.2b and Table 4.2c).

...and higher still if she completed tertiary education.

On average across OECD countries, a mother's tertiary education adds another 24 score points to the student's advantage in mathematics (Table 4.2b). Even when controlling for the influence of other socio-economic factors, each year of additional formal education of parents[11] adds an average of 5 score points (see column 3 in Table 4.2).

In addition to their own level of education, which is of course less amenable to policy, parents' support for their children's education is widely deemed to be an essential element of success at school. When parents interact and communicate well with their children, they can offer encouragement, demonstrate their interest in their children's progress, and generally convey their concern for how their children are faring, both in and out of school. Indeed, PISA 2000 demonstrated the important relationship between parental involvement and children's academic success. It also suggested that educational success may be related to patterns of communication between parents and children (OECD, 2001a). An important objective for public policy may therefore be to support parents, particularly those whose own educational attainment is limited, in order to facilitate their interactions both with their children and with their children's schools in ways that enhance their children's learning. PISA 2006 will further examine these questions, and will also include a new international option of a parents' questionnaire.

The separate influence of cultural capital is almost as strong as that of parental occupation.

Possessions and activities related to "classical" culture (*e.g.,* classic literature, books of poetry or works of art) also tend to be closely related to performance (Table 4.2d). The possession of the kind of cultural capital on which school curricula often tend to build, and which examinations and tests assess, appears closely related to student performance in mathematics. While advantages of cultural possessions are related to other home background characteristics, their effects in isolation are generally strong. Even when controlling for other socio-economic background factors, one unit on the PISA index of cultural possessions is associated with an average score difference of 12 score points on the PISA mathematics scale, an association that is almost as strong as the association with parental occupation (see column 4 in Table 4.2).

A single parent may find it harder to support students' learning, and in some countries, students with single parents are much more likely to be among the lowest performers...

As noted above, the family environment can help to promote academic performance. Parents may read to young learners, assist them with homework and, in some countries, volunteer to help in schools. For older students, a supportive family environment can also be helpful with respect to homework, encouragement, and attendance at meetings with teachers or school administrators. Providing and maintaining such an environment may be difficult when students live in a single-parent family, where parents often find themselves having to cope with the dual responsibility of work and their children's education. For some countries, the PISA results suggest a large performance gap for students from single-parent families (Table 4.2e). In Belgium, Ireland, the Netherlands, Sweden and the United States students from single-parent families are 1.5 times or more likely to be among the bottom quarter of mathematics performers than the average student that lives with both parents.

...even controlling for other factors, which points to a need for extra support.

Even when controlling for the influence of other socio-economic factors, an average gap of 18 score points remains between students from single parent and other types of families. This gap is between 25 and 30 score points in Belgium, Ireland and the United States (see column 5 in Table 4.2).

Evidence that children in families with two parents perform better might seem to be discouraging for single-parent families. However, evidence of disadvantage is a starting point for the development of policy. The issue is how to facilitate effective home support for children's learning in ways that are relevant to the circumstances of single parents. Strategic allocation of parental time to activities with the greatest potential effect will increase efficiency where time is limited. Policy questions for education systems and individual schools when interacting with parents relate to the kind of parental engagement that should be encouraged. Obviously, education policies in this area need to be examined in conjunction with policies in other areas, such as those relating to welfare and the provision of childcare.

In some countries, a significant proportion of 15-year-olds have immigrant backgrounds and some do not speak the local language at home...

Finally, over recent decades, most OECD countries have experienced increased migration, much of it of people whose home language is not the language of instruction in the schools that their children attend. One can consider the situation of these groups by looking successively at first-generation students (those born in the country but with parents born outside), non-native students (themselves born abroad) and students who speak a language at home most of the time which is different from any of the official languages of the country where they live.

...and those with immigrant parents typically perform significantly lower.

In countries in which first-generation students represent at least 3 per cent of the students assessed in PISA 2003, a comparison of the mathematics performance of first-generation students with that of native students tends to show large and statistically significant differences in favour of native students. This is the case in all countries except Australia, Canada and the partner countries Latvia, Liechtenstein, Macao-China and Serbia (Table 4.2f). The results are broadly similar to those revealed by PISA 2000 for reading literacy.

This is cause for concern where such students are most numerous...

Concern about such differences is especially justified in those countries where significant performance gaps are combined with comparatively large percentages of first-generation students, such as France, Germany, Luxembourg, the Netherlands, Switzerland and the United States.

...and particularly where they have experienced the same curriculum as others born in the country.

In Germany, the country with the largest such disparities, the performance gap amounts to 93 score points on the mathematics scale, equivalent to an average performance difference of over two grade levels (Box 2.2). These are troubling differences because both groups of students were born in the country where the

assessment took place and, presumably, had experienced the same curriculum that the national education system offers to all students. Despite whatever similarities there might be in their educational histories, something about being a first-generation student leads to a relative disadvantage in these countries (a disadvantage which is reduced – but does not disappear – when controlling for socio-economic background, as discussed below).

As one would expect, non-native students tend to lag even further behind native students than do first-generation students, with the largest performance gap, 109 score points, found in Belgium (Table 4.2f and Figure 4.2).

Figure 4.2 ■ **Place of birth and student performance**

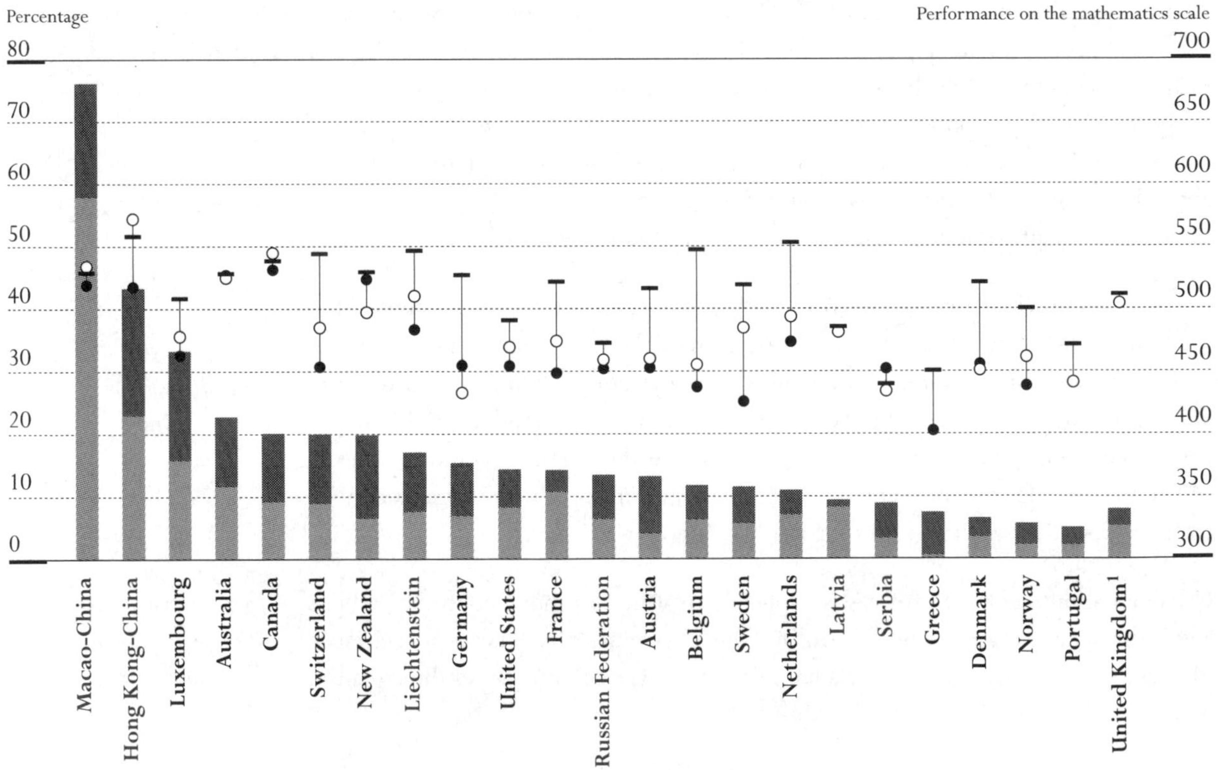

Note: Only countries with at least 3 per cent of students in at least one of these categories.
1. Response rate too low to ensure comparability (see Annex A3).
Source: OECD PISA 2003 database, Table 4.2f.

The nature of the educational disadvantage experienced by students who have an ethnic minority background and/or are the children of migrants is substantially influenced by the circumstances from which they come. Educational disadvantage in the country of origin can be magnified in the country of adoption even though, in absolute terms, their educational performance might have been raised. These students may be academically disadvantaged either because they are immigrants entering a new education system or because they need to learn a new language in a home environment that may not facilitate this learning. In either case, they may be in need of special or extra attention. Focused help in the language of instruction is one policy option that is often adopted for such students. For example, students who do not speak the language of assessment at home in Belgium, Germany, the Netherlands and Switzerland are at least 2.5 times more likely to be in the bottom quarter of mathematics performance (Table 4.2g). More generally, being a non-native student or speaking a language at home that is different from the language of assessment have a negative impact on mathematics performance of, on average across OECD countries, 19 and 9 score points respectively (Table 4.2).

Both the difficulties of adapting to a new system and language difficulties can play a part in performance…

Nevertheless, the results show that some countries appear to be more effective in minimising the performance disadvantage for students with a migration background. The most impressive example is the partner country Hong Kong-China. Here, 23 per cent of students have parents born outside Hong Kong-China and another 20 per cent of students were born outside Hong Kong-China themselves (though many of them come from mainland China). And yet, all three student groups – whether non-native students, first-generation students, or students who speak at home a language that is different from the language of assessment – score well above the OECD average. Also, a large performance difference between first-generation and non-native students suggests that for students for whom there was sufficient time for the education system to integrate them, this has occurred successfully. Australia and Canada are other examples of countries with large immigrant populations and strong overall student performance. However, the profile of these countries' immigrant populations differs substantially from that in most other participating countries, so that comparisons are difficult to make. In particular, the fact that in these countries there is virtually no performance difference between native students and foreign-born students – with many of the foreign-born students likely to have been educated at least for some years in their country of origin – suggests that many students enter the system with already strong levels of performance. This is very different, for example, from the situation in Belgium, the Netherlands, Sweden and Switzerland. This contrast becomes even clearer when the separate impact of the language spoken at home is also taken into account (Table 4.2).

…but in some countries, students seem to succeed in overcoming these difficulties.

When interpreting performance gaps between native students and those with a migrant background, it is important to account for differences among countries in terms of such factors as the national origin as well as the socio-economic, educational and linguistic background of immigrant populations.

Country comparisons need to take account of different characteristics of immigrant populations.

Figure 4.3 ■ **Home language and student performance**

Percentage of students who speak a language at home most of the time that is different from the language of assessment, from other official languages or from other national dialects (left scale)

■ Percentage of students who speak a language at home most of the time that is different from the language of assessment, from other official languages or from other national dialects

Performance of students on the mathematics scale, by language group (right scale)

– Mean performance on the mathematics scale of students who speak a language at home most of the time that is the same as the language of assessment, other official languages or other national dialects

○ Mean performance on the mathematics scale of students who speak a language at home most of the time that is different from the language of assessment, from other official languages or from other national dialects

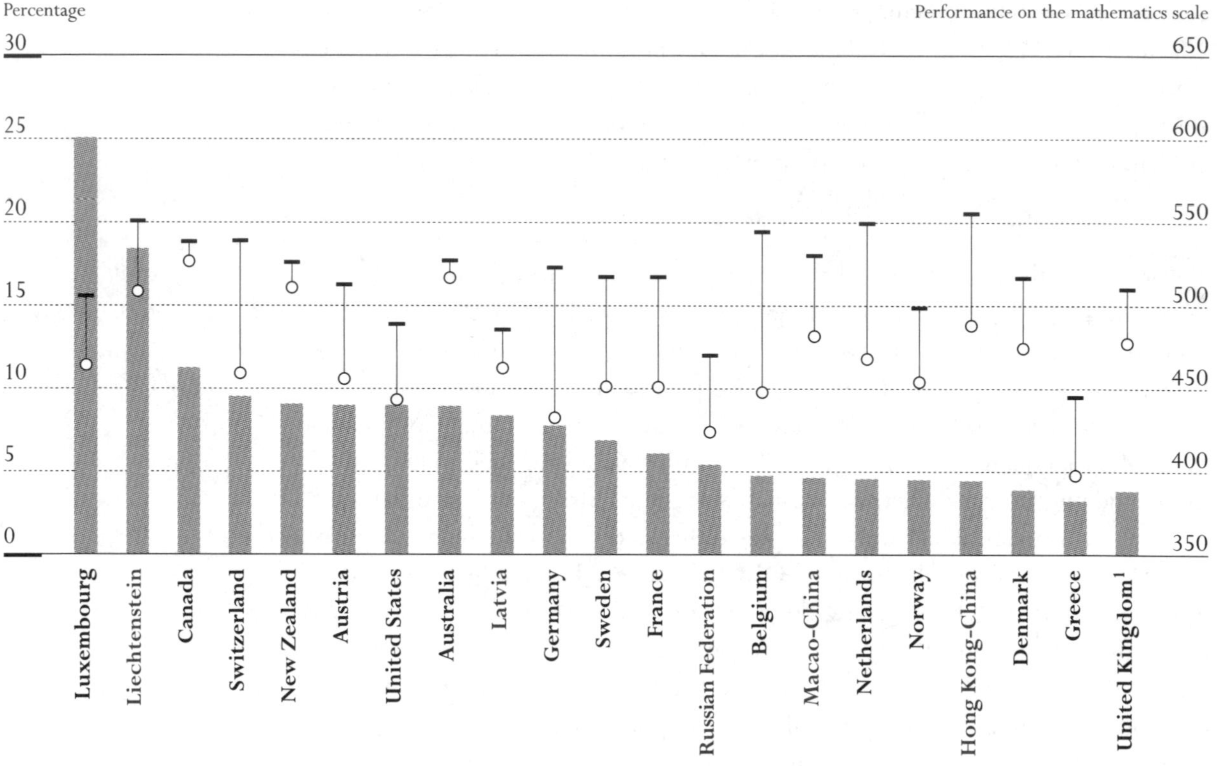

Note: Only countries with at least 3 per cent of students in this category.

1. Response rate too low to ensure comparability (see Annex A3).

Source: OECD PISA 2003 database, Table 4.2g.

The composition of immigrant populations, in turn, is shaped by immigration policies and practices and the criteria used to decide who will be admitted into a country vary considerably across countries (OECD, 2003f). While some countries tend to admit relatively large numbers of immigrants each year and often with a low degree of selectivity, other countries have much lower and often more selective migrant inflows. In addition, the extent to which the social, educational and occupational status of potential immigrants is taken into account in immigration and naturalisation decisions differs across countries. As a result, immigrant populations tend to have more advantaged backgrounds in some countries than in others.

Research shows that the proportion of students with a migration background does not relate to the extent to which these students are more or less successful than their peers from native families (Stanat, 2004). Thus, the size of immigrant populations alone does not seem to explain international variations in the performance gap between these student groups. By contrast, the degree to which students with a migrant background are disadvantaged in terms of their socio-economic and educational background has been shown to relate to their relative performance levels, as observed in the countries participating in PISA 2000 (Stanat, 2004). PISA 2003 confirms these findings. Figure 4.4 shows that in countries where the educational and socio-economic status of immigrant families is comparatively low, the performance gaps between students with and without migrant backgrounds tends to be larger.

The size of the immigrant population apparently has no effect, its socio-economic composition does.

To gauge the extent to which between-country differences in the relative performance of students with a migration background can be attributed to the composition of their immigrant populations, an adjustment for the socio-economic background of students can be made. As was already apparent in Figure 4.2,

Controlling for this factor reduces and in some cases eliminates the migration effect.

Figure 4.4 ■ **Student performance differences and socio-economic background differences by students' immigrant background**

Relationship between differences in mathematics performance between native students and students with immigrant background and socio-economic background differences between these two groups of students

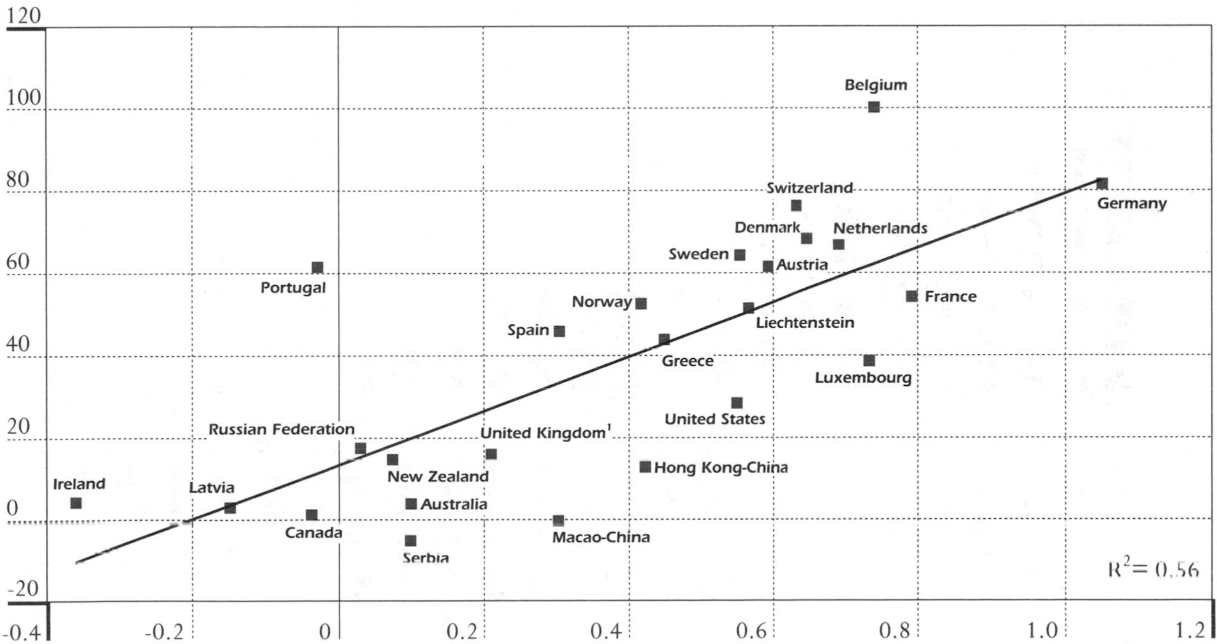

1. Response rate too low to ensure comparability (see Annex A3).
Source: OECD PISA 2003 database, Table 4.2f.

the statistically significant performance gap between native students, on the one hand, and first generation as well as non-native students, on the other, varies across the OECD countries from almost 100 points in Belgium to 42 points in Luxembourg and the United States, and no statistically significant differences in Australia, Canada and New Zealand. After students' socio-economic background, as measured by the PISA index of economic, social and cultural status, is taken into account, the performance gap between native students and students from families with a migration background is reduced considerably in most countries. This is shown in Figure 4.5 and Table 4.2h. In Belgium, for example, the difference decreases from 100 to 60 points and in Germany from 81 to 35 points. In the United States, the performance gap is reduced such that it is no longer statistically significant.[12]

Yet there remain big differences between the relative performance of immigrants in different countries…

At the same time, the magnitude of the performance gap between immigrant and native students continues to vary considerably, even when their socio-economic and educational background is taken into account. Countries like Belgium and Switzerland continue to be among those exhibiting the largest disparities between students with migrant backgrounds and those from native families.

Figure 4.5 ■ **Differences in mathematics performance associated with students' immigrant background**

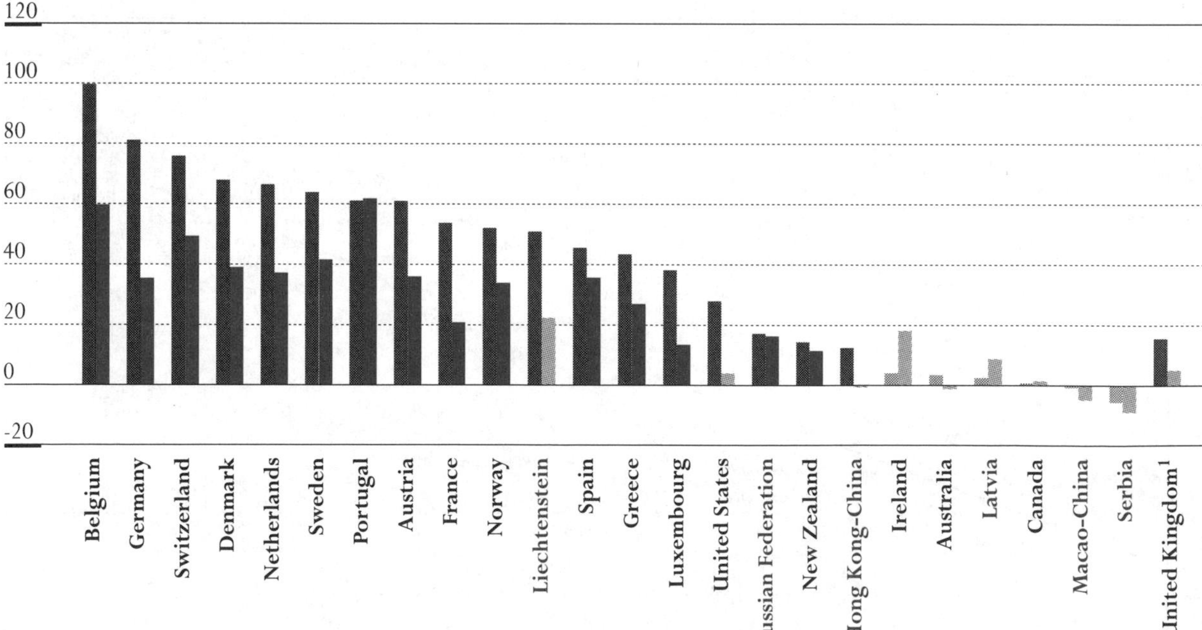

Note: This figure shows data for countries with more than 3 per cent of students in the aggregated category of non-native and first-generation students.

1. Response rate too low to ensure comparability (see Annex A3).

Source: OECD PISA 2003 database, Table 4.2h.

Figure 4.6 ■ **Differences in mathematics performance associated with students' immigrant background and home language**

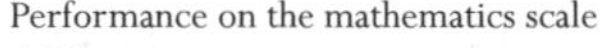

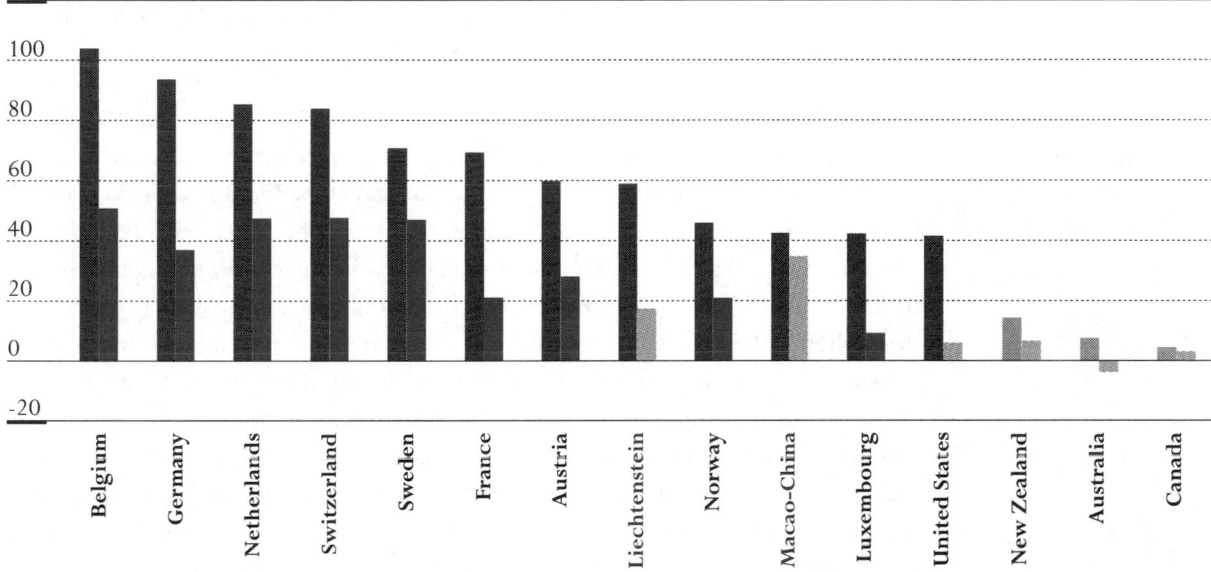

Note: Only countries with at least 3 per cent of students in this category.
Source: OECD PISA 2003 database, Table 4.2h.

This suggests that, in addition to the composition of countries' immigrant populations, other factors determine between-country differences in immigrant students' relative school success.

...and even after controlling for language background, such country differences remain.

One such factor might be the language background of immigrants in the different countries. The extent to which immigrants have to overcome language barriers varies considerably across countries. In countries with colonial histories, for example, many immigrants already speak the official language of the country at the time of their arrival. Using the language that students speak at home as a proxy, Figure 4.6 shows the between-country differences that result when this factor is accounted for. Taking this factor into account slightly reduces the between-country variation in mathematics performance differences. Statistically significant differences range from 42 score points for the United States to 104 score points in Belgium. When socio-economic background is also accounted for, the between-country variation becomes even smaller but continues to remain substantial, ranging from 9 score points in Luxembourg to 51 score points in Belgium.

The separate and collective influence of the various home background factors can be measured…

Figure 4.7 summarises, for each country, the degree to which various features of home background are associated with mathematics performance. These features are: parental occupational status; parents' level of education converted into years of schooling; possessions related to "classical" culture; family structure; students' nationality and that of their parents; and the language spoken at home. Since these features tend to be associated with each other – for example a student whose parents are better educated is also likely to have parents in higher-status occupations – the graph displays the influence of these features together and shows the variance in student performance explained by each feature once the influence of the others has been accounted for. The final bar in Figure 4.7 shows the variance explained by all six factors together (Table 4.2).

…showing that home background makes a substantial contribution to student differences.

Overall across the OECD countries, the combined influence of this set of student-level socio-economic variables explains 17 per cent of the variance in mathematics performance, ranging from less than 10 per cent in Canada, Iceland and the partner countries Indonesia, Macao-China and the Russian Federation, to more than 20 per cent in Belgium, Germany, Hungary and Portugal (see the last column in Table 4.2). These findings have potentially important implications for policy-makers. Skills in mathematics are an important foundation for lifelong learning and enhance future opportunities for employment and earnings. As a consequence, countries in which the relationship between socio-economic background and student performance is strong do not fully capitalise on the skill potential of students from disadvantaged backgrounds. Human capital may thus be wasted and intergenerational mobility from lower to higher socio-economic status limited. The poorer performing students will almost certainly be the ones least likely to obtain the employment opportunities that offer the promise of economic mobility. This is a loss not just for individuals, but also for societies increasingly dependent on the many effects of human capital.

National research sometimes shows that home background influences student development throughout childhood…

Achieving an equitable distribution of learning outcomes without losing high performance standards thus represents an important challenge. Analyses at the national level have often been discouraging. For example, using longitudinal methods, researchers who have tracked children's vocabulary development have found that growth trajectories for children from differing socio-economic backgrounds begin to differ early on (Hart and Risely, 1995) and that when children enter school the impact of socio-economic background on both cognitive skills and behaviour is already well established. Furthermore, during the primary and middle school years, children whose parents have low incomes and low levels of education, or are unemployed or working in low-prestige occupations, are less likely to do well in academic pursuits, or to be engaged in curricular and extra-curricular school activities than children growing up in advantaged socio-economic contexts (Datcher, 1982; Finn and Rock, 1997; Johnson *et al.*, 2001; Voelkl, 1995).

…and that schools seem to make little difference.

National research also suggests that schools appear to make little difference in overcoming the effects of disadvantaged home backgrounds. Indeed, it has sometimes been argued that if school systems become more inclusive –

Figure 4.7 ■ **Effect of student-level factors on student performance in mathematics**

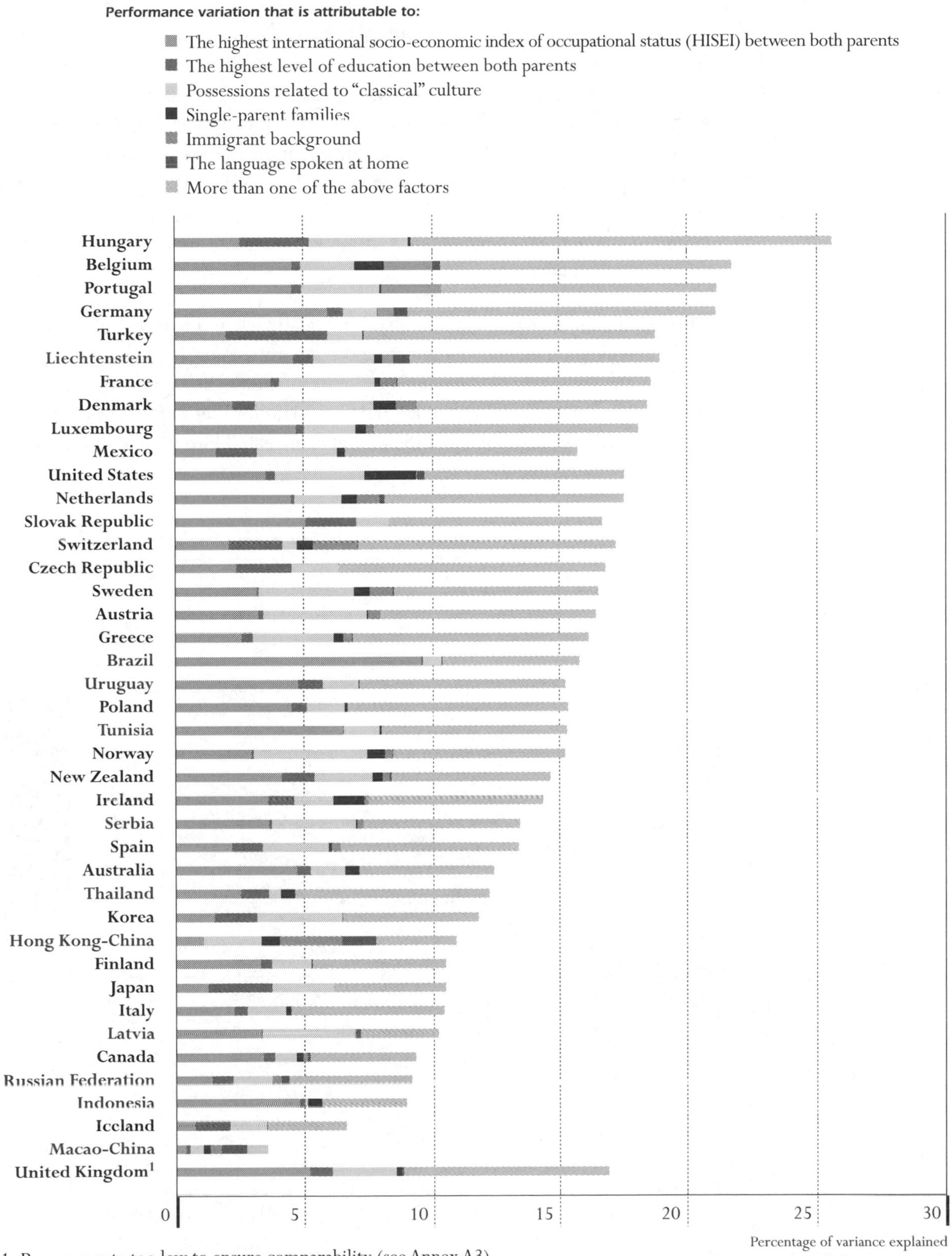

1. Response rate too low to ensure comparability (see Annex A3).

Source: OECD PISA 2003 database, Table 4.2.

for example, by increasing the proportion of young people who complete secondary school – then quality is bound to suffer.

The international perspective of PISA, however, indicates that it is possible to attain socio-economic equity at a high level of overall educational quality.

The international evidence from PISA is more encouraging. It is the case that in all countries, students with more advantaged home backgrounds tend to have higher PISA scores. However, the comparisons of the relationship between student performance and the various aspects of socio-economic background examined above show that some countries simultaneously demonstrate high average quality and relatively high equality of outcomes among students from different socio-economic backgrounds. Thus, wide disparities in student performance are not a necessary condition for a country to attain a high level of overall performance.

This can be analysed by using an overall index of home background…

This finding can be examined more systematically when the different economic, social and cultural aspects of background are combined into a single index, as is done in the following discussion. This index includes the highest International Socio-Economic Index of Occupational Status (ISEI) of the parents or guardians, the highest level of education of the parents converted into years of education,[13]

Figure 4.8 ■ **Relationship between student performance in mathematics and socio-economic background for the OECD area as a whole**

Note: Each dot represents 538 students from the OECD area.
Source: OECD PISA 2003 database.

an index of the educational resources in the home,[14] and the number of books at home. The index is referred to in the following text as the PISA index of economic, social and cultural status, or simply, at times, the students' socio-economic background (see Annex A1).

...which can be mapped against performance...

Figure 4.8 depicts the relationship between student performance and the student index of economic, social and cultural status, for the combined OECD area. The figure describes how well students from differing socio-economic backgrounds perform on the PISA mathematics scale. This relationship is affected both by how well education systems are performing and the extent of dispersion of the economic, social and cultural factors that make up the index (Box 4.1).

...with a gradient indicating socio-economic equity of school outcomes.

An understanding of this relationship, referred to as the *socio-economic gradient,* is a useful starting point for analysing the distribution of educational opportunities. From a school policy perspective, understanding the relationship is also important because it indicates how equitably the benefits of schooling are being shared among students from differing socio-economic backgrounds, at least in terms of student performance.

Box 4.1 ■ **How to read Figure 4.8**

Each *dot* on this graph represents 538 15-year-old students in the combined OECD area. Figure 4.8 plots their performance in mathematics against their economic, social and cultural status.

The *vertical axis* shows student scores on the mathematics scale, for which the mean is 500. Note that since the standard deviation was set at 100 when the PISA scale was constructed, about two-thirds of the dots fall between 400 and 600. The different shaded areas show the six proficiency levels in mathematics.

The *horizontal axis* shows values on the PISA index of economic, social and cultural status. This has been constructed to have a mean of 0 and a standard deviation of 1, so that about two-thirds of students are between +1 and –1.

The *dark line* represents the international socio-economic gradient, which is the best-fitting line showing the association between mathematics performance and socio-economic status across OECD countries.

Since the focus in the figure is not on comparing education systems but on highlighting a relationship throughout the combined OECD area, each student in the combined OECD area contributes equally to this picture – *i.e.,* larger countries, with more students in the PISA population, such as Japan, Mexico and the United States, influence the international gradient line more than smaller countries such as Iceland or Luxembourg.

This shows that students with progressively more advantaged socio-economic backgrounds perform progressively better in mathematics, on average…

Figure 4.8 points to several findings:

- Students from more advantaged socio-economic backgrounds generally perform better. This finding, already noted above, is shown by the upward slope of the gradient line.
- A given difference in socio-economic status is associated with a gap in student mathematics performance that is roughly the same throughout the distribution – *i.e.,* the marginal benefit of extra socio-economic advantage neither diminishes nor rises by a substantial amount as this advantage grows. This is shown by the fact that the socio-economic gradient is nearly a straight line. The gradient is, however, not exactly straight: in fact, the relationship between the index of economic, social and cultural status and performance in mathematics is slightly stronger for students with lower levels of socio-economic status than for those with higher levels.[15]

…but also that many students perform much better or worse than predicted.

- The relationship between student performance and the index of economic, social and cultural status is not deterministic, in the sense that many disadvantaged students shown on the left of the figure score well above what is predicted by the international gradient line while a sizeable proportion of students from privileged home backgrounds perform below what their home background would predict. For any group of students with matched backgrounds, there is thus a considerable range of performance.

The strength of this relationship differs across countries.

To what extent is this relationship an inevitable outcome of socio-economic differences as opposed to an outcome that is amenable to public policy? One approach to answering this question lies in examining to what extent countries succeed in moderating the relationship between socio-economic background and student performance. For each country, Figure 4.9 displays the relationship between student performance on the mathematics scale and the index of economic, social and cultural status separately. Figure 4.9A and Figure 4.9B highlight countries with mathematics performance statistically significantly above the OECD average; Figure 4.9C and Figure 4.9D highlight countries with mathematics performance not statistically different from the OECD average; and Figure 4.9E and Figure 4.9F highlight countries with mathematics performance statistically significantly below the OECD average.

There are countries in which students tend to perform well, irrespective of their socio-economic background…

Countries with above-average mathematics performance and with an impact of socio-economic background not different from the OECD average are shown by the black lines in Figure 4.9A. Countries with above-average mathematics performance and a weaker-than-average relationship between performance and socio-economic background, indicated by a red line in Figure 4.9B, succeed in achieving high overall performance with modest socio-economic disparities. In countries with above-average mathematics performance and a stronger-than-average relationship with socio-economic background, indicated by a dashed black line in Figure 4.9B, high performance levels are mainly due to very high performance standards among students from advantaged socio-economic backgrounds.

4

Figure 4.9 ■ **Relationship between student performance in mathematics and socio-economic background**

Countries in which the impact of socio-economic background is not statistically different from the OECD average impact
OECD average
Countries in which the impact of socio-economic background is statistically significantly ABOVE the OECD average impact
Countries in which the impact of socio-economic background is statistically significantly BELOW the OECD average impact
Performance
700
600
500
400
300
-3 -2 -1 0 1 2 3
Level 6
Level 5
Level 4
Level 3
Level 2
Level 1
Below Level 1
A. Countries with mean performance above the OECD average and with an impact of socio-economic background not statistically significantly different from the OECD average impact
1. Liechtenstein
2. Korea
3. Netherlands
4. Switzerland
5. New Zealand
6. Czech Republic
7. France
8. Denmark
9. Sweden
B. Countries with mean performance above the OECD average and with an impact of socio-economic background above or below the OECD average impact
1. Belgium
2. Hong Kong-China
3. Macao-China
4. Finland
5. Canada
6. Japan
7. Australia
8. Iceland
C. Countries with mean performance not statistically significantly different from the OECD average and with an impact of socio-economic background not statistically significantly different from the OECD average impact
1. Austria
2. Ireland
D. Countries with mean performance not statistically significantly different from the OECD average and with an impact of socio-economic background above or below the OECD average impact
1. Germany
2. Slovak Republic
E. Countries with mean performance below the OECD average and with an impact of socio-economic background not statistically significantly different from the OECD average impact
1. Poland
2. Luxembourg
3. United States
4. Turkey
5. Portugal
6. Greece
7. Serbia
8. Uruguay
9. Mexico
10. Brazil
11. Tunisia
F. Countries with mean performance below the OECD average and with an impact of socio-economic background above or below the OECD average impact
1. Hungary
2. Spain
3. Norway
4. Latvia
5. Russian Federation
6. Italy
7. Thailand
8. Indonesia
Index of economic, social and cultural status

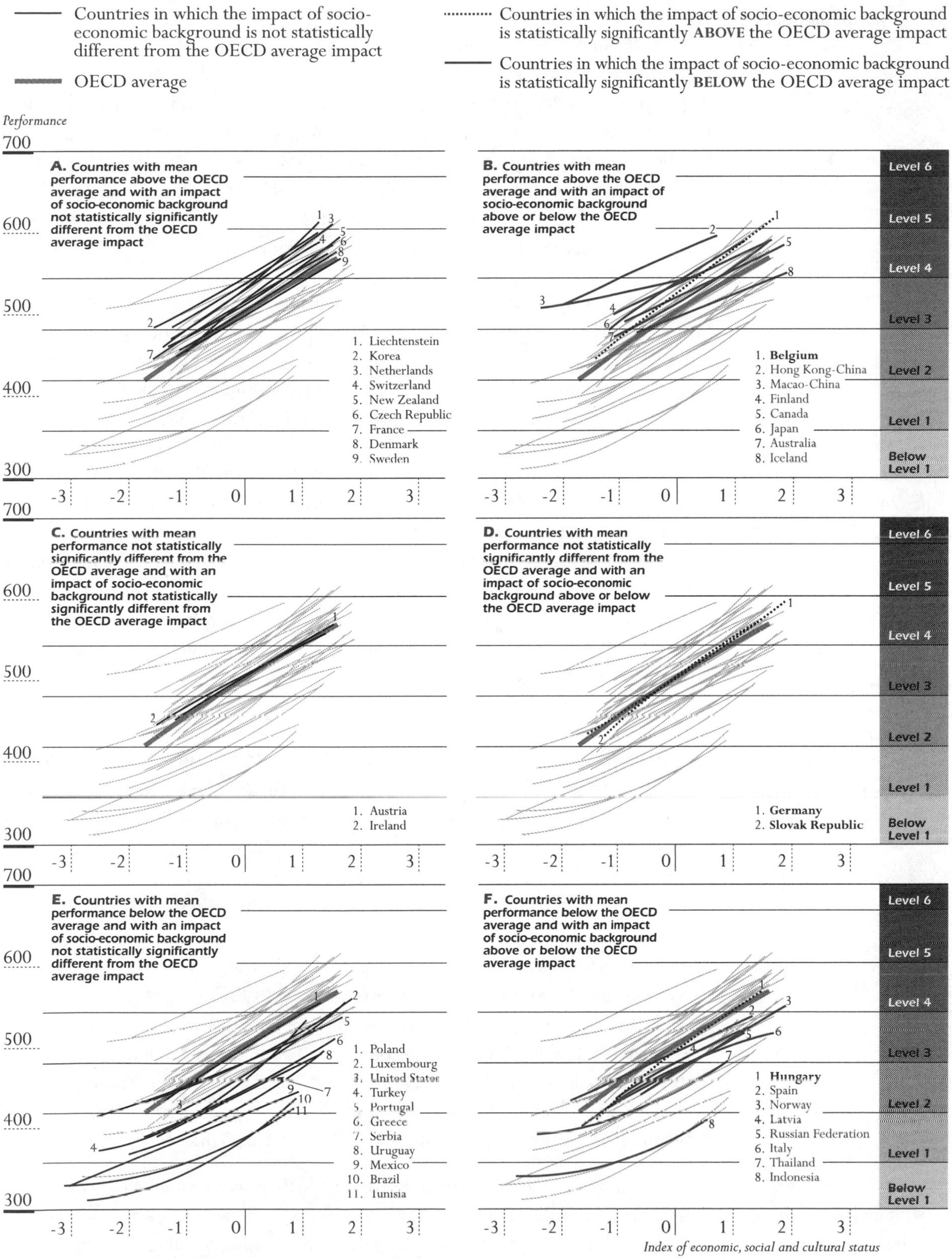

Source: OECD PISA database, 2003.

…as well as countries with below-average performance and large socio-economic disparities.

Countries with below-average mathematics performance and with an impact of socio-economic background not different from the OECD average are shown by the black lines in Figure 4.9E. Countries with below-average performance and a weaker-than-average relationship with socio-economic background are indicated by a red line in Figure 4.9F. While, in these countries, the impact of socio-economic disparities on student performance is comparatively small, this is mainly because students from both advantaged and disadvantaged socio-economic backgrounds perform comparatively poorly. Finally countries with below-average performance and stronger-than-average relationships with socio-economic background are indicated by a dashed black line in Figure 4.9F. In these countries, socio-economic disparities are large and overall performance is poor.

Countries in which performance is not statistically significantly different from the average and the strength of the relationship between socio-economic background and performance is also not different from the OECD average are shown with a black line in Figure 4.9C, while countries with a stronger or weaker than average relationship are shown in Figure 4.9D by the dashed black lines.

The gradient can be described in terms of…

In describing Figure 4.9 and the equivalent distribution of performance in each country as shown in Table 4.3a, several aspects of the gradient should be noted, including how strongly socio-economic background predicts performance, how well students with average background perform, how much difference it makes to have stronger or weaker socio-economic background, and how wide are the socio-economic differences in the student population. More specifically, the features of the relationship between socio-economic background and performance can be described in terms of:

…how much of the performance variation is explained by student background…

- The *strength of the relationship between mathematics performance and socio-economic background*. This refers to how much individual student performance varies above and below the gradient line. This can be seen for the combined OECD area in Figure 4.8 by the dispersion of dots above and below the line. For individual countries, column 3 of Table 4.3a gives the explained variance, a statistic that summarises the strength of the relationship by indicating the proportion of the observed variation in student scores that can be attributed to the relationship shown by the gradient line. If this number is low, relatively little of the variance in student performance is associated with students' socio-economic background; if it is high, the reverse is the case. On average across OECD countries, 17 per cent of the variance in student performance in mathematics within each country is associated with the PISA index of economic, social and cultural status.[16] However, this figure ranges from 7 per cent or less in Iceland and in the partner countries Hong Kong-China, Indonesia and Macao-China to more than 22 per cent in Belgium, Germany, Hungary, the Slovak Republic and Turkey.

…how well a student with an internationally average socio-economic background performs…

- The *level of the gradient lines* in Figure 4.9 – their average height – is given in column 2 of Table 4.3a. This shows the average mathematics score reached by those students in each country that have an economic, social and cultural background equal to the average across OECD countries. The level of a gradient for

a country can be considered an indication of what would be the overall level of performance of the education system if the economic, social and cultural background of the student population were identical to the OECD average.

- The *slope of the gradient line* is an indication of the extent of inequality in mathematics performance attributable to socio-economic factors (see column 4 in Table 4.3a) and is measured in terms of how much difference one unit on the socio-economic background scale makes to student performance in mathematics. Steeper gradients indicate a greater impact of economic, social and cultural status on student performance, *i.e.,* more inequality. Gentler gradients indicate a lower impact of socio-economic background on student performance, *i.e.,* more equality. It is important to distinguish the slope from the strength of the relationship. For example, Germany and Japan show a similar slope with one unit of difference on the socio-economic background scale corresponding, on average, to 47 and 46 score points, respectively, on the mathematics performance scale. However, in Japan, there are many more exceptions to this general trend so that the relationship only explains 12 per cent of the performance variation, while in Germany student performance follows the levels predicted by socio-economic background more closely, with 23 per cent of the performance variation explained by socio-economic background. On average across OECD countries, the slope of the gradient is 42 (see note 16). This means that students' scores on the mathematics scale are, on average in OECD countries, 42 score points higher for each extra unit on the index of economic, social and cultural status. The unit on the index of economic, social and cultural status is one standard deviation, meaning that about two-thirds of the OECD student population score within a range of two units. In the case of Poland, for example, which has a gradient very close to the OECD average, the average mathematics score of students with socio-economic scores one unit below average is 445, similar to the average score of a Greek student, and the average mathematics score of students one unit above the socio-economic status mean is 535, *i.e.,* similar to the average performance of Japan.

...the amount of difference that socio-economic background makes, on average, to performance...

- The *length of the gradient lines* is determined by the range of socio-economic scores for the middle 90 per cent of students (between the 5th and 95th percentiles) in each country (see column 5c in Table 4.3a), as well as by the slope. Columns 5a and 5b in Table 4.3a show the 5th and the 95th percentiles of the PISA index of economic, social and cultural status spanned by the gradient line. The length of the gradient line indicates how widely the student population is dispersed in terms of socio-economic background. Longer projections of the gradient lines represent a wider dispersion of socio-economic background in the student population within the country in question.

...and the range of backgrounds experienced by students in each country.

Figure 4.9 and Table 4.3a point to several findings:

In some countries, a given difference in socio-economic background makes over twice as much difference to predicted performance than in others.

- First, countries vary in the strength and slope of the relationship between socio-economic background and student performance. The figure not only shows countries with relatively high and low levels of performance on the mathematics scale, but also countries which have greater or lesser degrees

of inequality in performance among students from different socio-economic backgrounds. It is worth emphasising the considerable extent of this difference. Consider two students. One is from a less advantaged background, say, one standard deviation below the OECD average on the PISA index of economic, social and cultural status and the other from a relatively privileged background, say, one standard deviation above the OECD average on the PISA index of economic, social and cultural status. The predicted performance gap between these two students varies between countries by a factor of over two. Column 4 in Table 4.3a can be used to calculate this difference. The mathematics score point difference shown in this column is associated with a one standard deviation change in the PISA index of economic, social and cultural status – the two students in this example are separated by two standard deviations. This means that in Iceland this gap is 56 score points but in Belgium and Hungary it is 110 score points, equivalent to two proficiency levels (in each case double the gradient slope, *i.e.,* comparing students two standard deviations apart). The figure also shows clearly that high performance does not have to come at the expense of inequality, as some of the countries with the highest levels of performance have relatively gentle gradients.

Some countries need to cope with a much wider range of student backgrounds.

- Second, the range of the index of economic, social and cultural status spanned by the gradient lines varies widely between countries. Figure 4.9 shows that the range of backgrounds of the middle 90 per cent of the student population spans less than 2.5 index points on the index in Japan, Norway and the partner countries Latvia and the Russian Federation, but around 4 index points or more in Mexico, Portugal and the partner country Tunisia. These figures show that some countries' education systems need to cope with students from a wider range of socio-economic backgrounds than others (see column 5 in Table 4.3a).

In most countries, an advantaged socio-economic background shows benefits for performance to equal degrees along a continuum, but in some the greatest gains are at the lower end and in others at the high end.

- Third, the gradients for many countries are roughly linear, that is, each increment on the index of economic, social and cultural status is associated with a roughly constant increase in performance on the mathematics scale. One might have expected that the gradients would be steep at low levels of economic, social and cultural status, and then level off at higher status levels, signalling that above a certain level of socio-economic background there would be progressively less advantage in terms of student performance. Indeed, the gradients follow this pattern in some countries, namely the Czech Republic, Hungary, Italy and the Slovak Republic (with column 8 in Table 4.3a showing statistically significant negative values). However, in Australia, Germany, Luxembourg, New Zealand, Turkey and the United States and the partner countries Brazil, Indonesia, Liechtenstein, Thailand, Tunisia and Uruguay the gradients display the opposite pattern – they are relatively gentle at low levels of socio-economic status, and become steeper at higher levels (with column 8 in Table 4.3a showing statistically significant positive values). In these countries, among the more advanced group of students, home background makes a greater difference to student performance in mathematics. In other words, the greater the socio-economic advantage, the greater the advantage it has in terms of student performance.

In the remaining 24 countries in PISA, these effects are small and not statistically significant. The finding that in all countries gradients tend to be linear, or only modestly curved across the range of economic, social and cultural status, has an important policy implication. Many socio-economic policies are aimed at increasing resources for the most disadvantaged, either through taxation or by targeting benefits and socio-economic programmes to certain groups. The PISA results suggest that it is not easy to establish a low economic, social and cultural status baseline, below which performance sharply declines. Moreover, if economic, social and cultural status is taken to be a surrogate for the decisions and actions of parents aimed at providing a richer environment for their children – such as taking an interest in their school work – then these findings suggest that there is room for improvement at all levels on the socio-economic continuum. The fact that it is difficult to discern a baseline, however, does not imply that differentiated student support is not warranted. Targeted efforts can be very effective in reducing disparities, as shown, for example, in successful efforts by many countries to close gender gaps in student performance.

Figure 4.10 ■ **Performance in mathematics and the impact of socio-economic background**

Average performance of countries on the PISA mathematics scale and the relationship between performance and the index of economic, social and cultural status

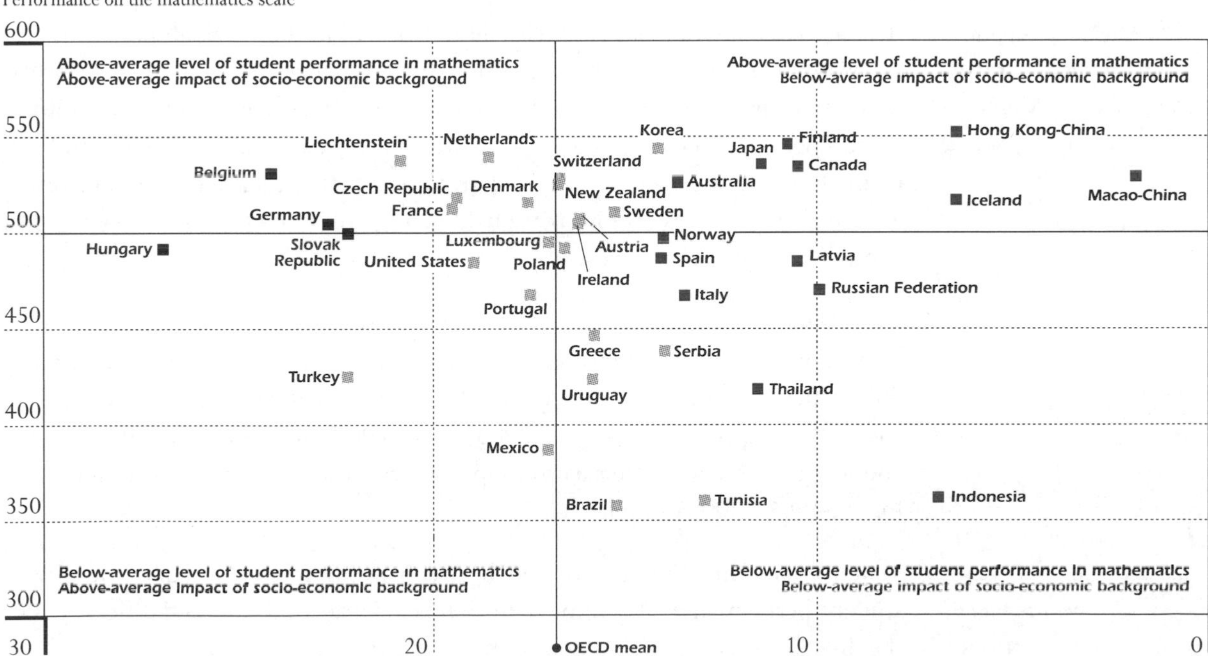

Note: OECD mean used in this figure is the arithmetic average of all OECD countries.
Source: OECD PISA 2003 database, Table 4.3a.

Comparing the strength of the socio-economic gradient with average student performance…

Figure 4.10 summarises the findings by contrasting average performance in mathematics (as shown on the vertical axis) with the strength of the relationship between socio-economic background and mathematics performance (as shown on the horizontal axis). The latter can be viewed as an indicator of equity in the distribution of learning opportunities, with perfect equity being defined by a situation in which students' performance is unrelated to their socio-economic background. Canada, Finland, Japan and the partner country Hong Kong-China, represented in the upper right quadrant of the figure, are examples of countries that display high levels of student performance in mathematics and, at the same time, a below-average impact of economic, social and cultural status on student performance. By contrast, Hungary and Turkey, displayed in the lower left quadrant, are examples of countries with below-average student performance in mathematics and an above-average impact of socio-economic background on performance. Belgium, the Czech Republic and the Netherlands are examples of countries characterised by high average performance levels but in which performance is comparatively strongly related to socio-economic background. Finally, Italy, Norway and Spain are countries in which average performance in mathematics is below the OECD average but not strongly related to student background. Although Mexico and Turkey show below average performance in mathematics associated with an average impact of socio-economic background, it is important to note that because only around half of 15-year-olds in these countries are enrolled in school (the smallest proportion among all participating countries, see Table A3.1) and thus represented in PISA, the impact of socio-economic background on the mathematics performance of 15-year-olds is probably underestimated.

…shows that quality and equity do not need to be considered as competing policy objectives.

The figure highlights that countries differ not just in their overall performance, but also in the extent to which they are able to reduce the association between socio-economic background and performance. PISA suggests that maximising overall performance and securing similar levels of performance among students from different socio-economic backgrounds can be achieved simultaneously. The results suggest therefore that quality and equity need not be considered as competing policy objectives.

The results mirror those observed in PISA 2000 for mathematics. However, some countries are exceptions to this similarity: in Australia and the United States the relationship between student performance and socio-economic background appears weaker in 2003, and in Belgium, Italy and the partner country Liechtenstein the relationship appears stronger in 2003 (see Table 4.3b for the PISA 2000 results).[17]

The differing overall socio-economic composition of countries puts their performance in a different light.

When comparing the relationship between socio-economic background and student performance, it is important to take into account marked differences in the distribution of socio-economic characteristics between countries. Table 4.3a presents key characteristics of the distribution of the PISA index of economic, social and cultural status in 2003. As noted before, PISA's socio-economic index was constructed such that roughly about two-thirds of the OECD student population are between the values of -1 and 1, with an average score of 0 (*i.e.,* the mean for

the combined student population from participating OECD countries is set to 0 and the standard deviation is set to 1). Countries with negative mean indices (see column 6 in Table 4.3a), most notably Mexico, Portugal, Turkey and the partner countries Brazil, Hong Kong-China, Indonesia, Macao-China, Thailand and Tunisia, are characterised by a below-average socio-economic background and thus face far greater overall challenges in addressing the impact of socio-economic background. This makes the high performance achieved by students in Hong Kong-China and Macao-China all the more impressive. However, it also places a different perspective on the observed below-average performance of the remaining countries mentioned. In fact, a hypothetical adjustment that assumes an average index of economic, socio-economic and cultural status across OECD countries would result in an increase of mathematics performance in Turkey from 423 to 468 score points, the observed performance level in Portugal. Portugal's average performance would, in turn, change from 466 to 485 score points, which is almost on a par with the observed performance level of Spain and the United States. Such adjusted scores are shown in column 2 in Table 4.3a. In contrast, in countries such as Canada, Iceland, Norway and the United States, which operate in much more favourable socio-economic conditions, adjusting for this advantage would lower their scores considerably. Obviously, such an adjustment is entirely hypothetical – countries operate in a global market place where actual, rather than adjusted, performance is all that counts. Moreover, the adjustment does not take into consideration the complex cultural context of each country. However, in the same way that proper comparisons of the quality of schools focus on the added value that schools provide (accounting for the socio-economic intake of schools when interpreting results), users of cross-country comparisons need to keep in mind the differences among countries in economic, social and educational circumstances.

It is not only the average socio-economic background but the range of socio-economic backgrounds found among students that affects the challenges education systems face…

The challenges that education systems face depend not just on the average socio-economic background of a country. They also depend on the distribution of socio-economic characteristics within countries. Such heterogeneity in socio-economic characteristics can be measured by the standard deviation, within each country, of student values on the PISA index of economic, social and cultural status (see column 7 in Table 4.3a). The greater this socio-economic heterogeneity in the family background of 15-year-olds, the greater the challenges for teachers, schools and the entire education system. In fact, many of the countries with below-average socio-economic status, most notably Mexico, Portugal, Turkey and the partner country Tunisia, also face the difficulty of significant heterogeneity in the socio-economic background of 15-year-olds.

…and that can compound the effect of the steepness of the socio economic gradient.

Even countries with average levels of socio economic background differ widely in the socio-economic heterogeneity of their populations. For example, both France and Japan have a level in the PISA index of economic, social and cultural status that is near the OECD average. However, while Japan has the most homogeneous distribution of socio-economic characteristics among OECD countries, France has a comparatively wide variation. Similarly, among

the countries with the highest overall levels of socio-economic status, Canada, Iceland, Norway and Sweden show a narrow range in distribution of socio-economic characteristics, whereas the United States shows comparatively large socio-economic disparities.

As a result, the impact of the gradient on student performance is larger in socio-economically more heterogeneous populations.

In countries in which the student population is very heterogeneous, similar socio-economic gradients will have a much larger impact on the performances gap than in countries that have socio-economically more homogeneous student populations. For example, Germany and Poland have socio-economic gradients with similar slopes: *i.e.,* in both countries a given socio-economic difference is associated with a similar difference in performance. Since the distribution of socio-economic characteristics is much more heterogeneous in Germany than in Poland, the performance gap among students in the top and bottom quarters of the PISA index of economic, social and cultural background is much larger in Germany than in Poland (Table 4.4).

Some countries have over ten times as many students as others with backgrounds that would put them in the least advantaged one-sixth of OECD students.

Countries with a low average level of socio-economic background and a wide distribution of socio-economic characteristics face particular challenges in meeting the needs of disadvantaged students, even more so if the distribution of socio-economic background characteristics is skewed towards disadvantage, as indicated by a positive index of skewness in Table 4.3a (see column 9). For example, in Mexico and Turkey, as well as in the partner countries Indonesia, Thailand and Tunisia, more than half of all students come from a socio-economic background below that experienced by the least advantaged 15 per cent of students in OECD countries (see column 10 in Table 4.3a). By contrast, in Canada, Iceland and Norway, less than 5 per cent of students have a socio-economic background below that of the least advanced 15 per cent of all OECD students.

SOCIO-ECONOMIC DIFFERENCE, SCHOOL DIFFERENCE AND THE ROLE THAT EDUCATION POLICY CAN PLAY IN MODERATING THE IMPACT OF SOCIO-ECONOMIC DISADVANTAGE

While education systems cannot alter students' backgrounds, schools can potentially moderate their impact.

Many of the factors of socio-economic disadvantage are not directly amenable to education policy, at least not in the short term. For example, the educational attainment of parents can only gradually improve, and average family wealth depends on the long-term economic development of a country as well as the development of a culture which promotes individual savings. The importance of socio-economic disadvantage, and the realisation that aspects of such disadvantage only change over extended periods of time, give rise to a vital question for policy-makers: to what extent can schools and school policies moderate the impact of socio-economic disadvantage on student performance? The overall relationship between socio-economic background and *student* performance provides an important indicator of the capacity of education systems to provide equitable learning opportunities. However, from a policy perspective, the relationship between socio-economic background and *school* performance is even more important as it indicates how equity is interrelated with systemic aspects of education.

Figure 4.1 reveals large differences among countries in the extent to which student performance varies among schools. Table 4.1a takes this further by showing the between-school and within-school components of variation in student performance that are attributable to students' socio-economic background. In other words, it looks at the strength of the relationship between socio-economic background and student performance both within and between schools. It is evident that there are marked differences among countries in the percentage of within-school variation that can be attributed to socio-economic background. At the same time, in most countries, this percentage is considerably smaller than the between-school performance differences that can be attributed to socio-economic background.

The relationship between performance and socio-economic background tends to be stronger at school than at student levels...

Belgium, the Czech Republic, Germany, Hungary and the partner country Uruguay are countries in which schools differ considerably in their socio-economic intake even though, within schools, student populations tend to have a comparatively homogeneous socio-economic background. In Belgium, the Czech Republic, Germany, Hungary, the Slovak Republic and the United States and the partner country Uruguay, the between-school variance in student performance that is attributable to students' socio-economic background accounts for more than 12 per cent of the OECD average between-student variance (see columns 5 and 6 in Table 4.1a) and for Belgium, Germany and Hungary this figure rises to over 40 per cent if the additional effect of the whole school's socio-economic composition on each student's performance is taken into account as well (see columns 7 and 8 in Table 4.1a). By contrast, within schools, socio-economic background in each of these three countries accounts for less than 5 per cent of the performance variance (see column 6 in Table 4.1a).

...particularly in those countries in which schools differ in their socio-economic intake...

Canada, Finland, Iceland, Japan, Mexico, Norway and Sweden and the partner countries Hong Kong-China, Indonesia and Macao-China are among the countries in which the socio-economic background of individual students accounts for 5 per cent or less of performance variance across schools (see columns 5 and 6 in Table 4.1a). However, Japan stands out in this group of countries in that the picture changes significantly once the socio-economic intake of schools as a whole is taken into account. When the additional effect of the whole school's socio-economic composition on each student's performance is taken into account, the percentage of explained variance in school performance rises from around 3 per cent of the OECD average variance in student performance to 42 per cent (see columns 5 and 7 in Table 4.1a).

...but there are other countries where schools differ mainly for reasons unrelated to student background.

An examination is needed of how within-school and between-school variance is attributable to socio-economic background. This is required in order to understand which policies might help to simultaneously increase overall student performance and moderate the impact of socio-economic background (*i.e.*, to raise and flatten a country's socio-economic gradient line). The following section examines the impact of socio-economic difference on student performance, as measured by the socio-economic gradient. To this end, the gradient for a

To understand this further, one needs to consider both how student background influences performance within a school...

country can be broken down into two parts: a *within-school* gradient and a *between-school* gradient. The *within-school* gradient describes how students' socio-economic background is related to their performance within a common school environment. The *between-school* gradient describes how schools' average level of performance is related to the average economic, social and cultural status of their student intake.[18]

...and how schools' performances differ according to the socio-economic background of their intakes.

Figure 4.13 at the end of this chapter shows the average performance, and the socio-economic composition of the student intake, for each school in the PISA sample. Socio-economic composition is measured by the mean PISA index of economic, social and cultural status in the school. Each dot in the chart represents one school, with the size of the dot proportionate to the number of 15-year-olds enrolled in the school. This shows first that in some countries students are highly segregated along socio-economic lines, whether because of residential segregation, economic factors or selection within the school system.

Figure 4.11 ■ **Effects of students' and schools' socio-economic background on student performance in mathematics**

Differences in performance on the mathematics scale associated with half a student-level standard deviation on the index of economic, social and cultural status

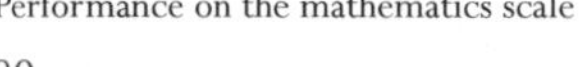

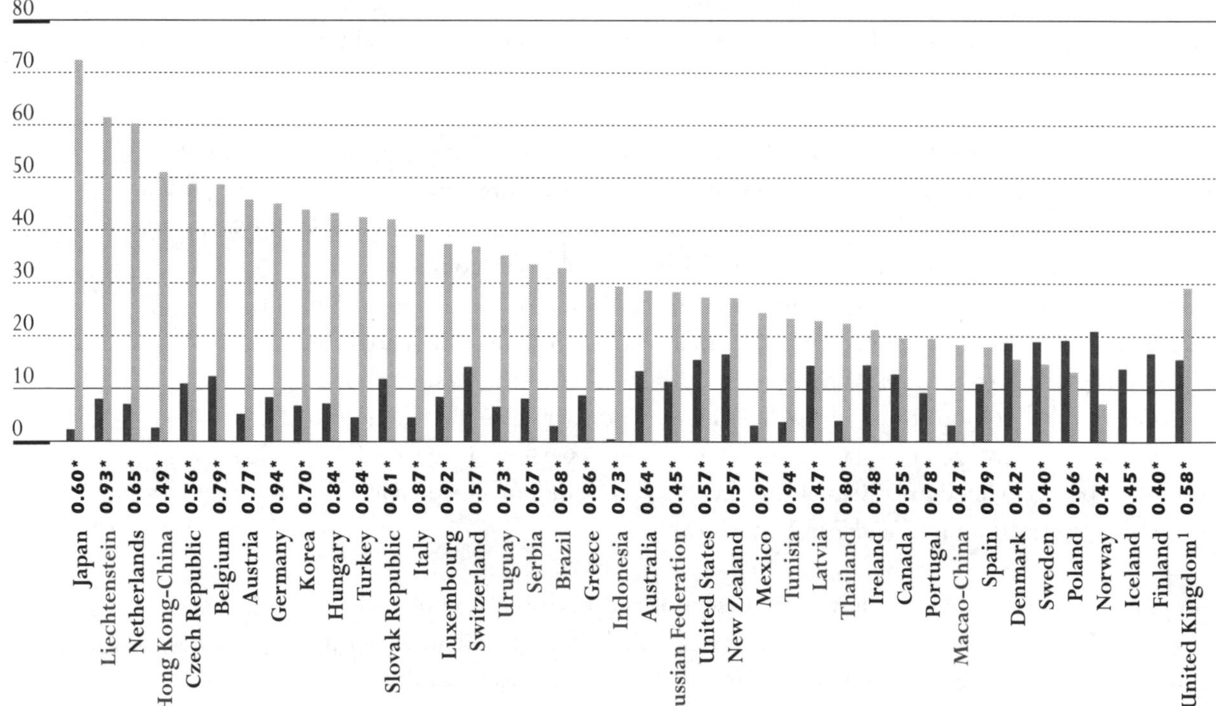

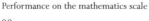

* Interquartile range of the school-level average mean index of economic, social and cultural status.
1. Response rate too low to ensure comparability (see Annex A3).
Source: OECD PISA 2003 database, Table 4.5 (Half values of Columns 2 and 7 respectively).

The figure also shows the overall gradient between socio-economic background and student performance (black line) (which was already shown in Figure 4.9). Finally, the figure displays the between-school gradient (thick dashed black line) and the average within-school gradient (thin dashed black line). Schools above the between-school gradient line (thick dashed black line) perform better than would be predicted by their socio-economic intake. Schools below the between-school gradient line perform below their expected value.

The gradients shown here indicate performance differences associated with a fixed amount of difference in socio-economic background.

Figure 4.11 compares the slopes of within-school and between-school gradients across countries that are shown at the end of this chapter. The slopes represent, respectively, the gap in predicted scores of two students within a school separated by a fixed amount of socio-economic background, and the gap in predicted scores of two students with identical socio-economic backgrounds attending different schools where the average background of their fellow-students is separated by the same fixed amount. The slopes were estimated with a multi-level model that included the PISA index of economic, social and cultural status at the student and school levels. The lengths of the bars in Figure 4.11 indicate the differences in scores on the PISA mathematics scale that are associated with a difference of half of an international standard deviation on the PISA index of economic, social and cultural status for the individual student (red bar) and for the average of the student's school (grey bar). Half a student-level standard deviation was chosen as the benchmark for measuring performance gaps because this value describes realistic differences between schools in terms of their socio-economic composition: on average across OECD countries, the difference between the 75th and 25th quartiles of the distribution of the school mean index of economic, social and cultural status is 0.77 of a student-level standard deviation. This value ranges from 0.42 standard deviations or less in Denmark, Finland, Norway and Sweden to 0.90 or more standard deviations in Germany, Luxembourg and Mexico and in the partner countries Liechtenstein and Tunisia (see column 11 in Table 4.5).

The results show that the effect of the school's socio-economic intake counts for more than an individual's own socio-economic background.

In almost all countries, and for all students, the relatively long grey bars in Figure 4.11 indicate the clear advantage in attending a school whose students are, on average, from more advantaged socio-economic backgrounds. Regardless of their own socio-economic background, students attending schools in which the average socio-economic background is high tend to perform better than when they are enrolled in a school with a below-average socio-economic intake. In the majority of OECD countries the effect of the average economic, social and cultural status of students in a school – in terms of performance variation across students – far outweighs the effects of the individual student's socio-economic background.

Relatively socio-economically advantaged schools confer well over half a proficiency level of performance advantage over the range measured here, and in some countries much more…

All of this is perhaps not surprising, but the magnitude of the differences is striking. In Austria, Belgium, the Czech Republic, Germany, Hungary, Japan, Korea, the Netherlands, the Slovak Republic and Turkey, as well as in the partner countries Hong Kong-China and Liechtenstein, the effect on student performance of a school's average economic, social and cultural status is very substantial. In these countries, half a unit on the index of economic, social and cultural status at the school level is equivalent to between 40 and 72 score points

(half of the value shown in column 7 in Table 4.5). Consider the case of two hypothetical students in any of these countries, living in families with average socio-economic background, as measured by the index of economic, social and cultural status. One student attends a school in a socio-economically advantaged area, in which the mean index of economic, social and cultural status of the school's intake is a quarter of a (student-level) standard deviation above the OECD average. Most of this student's peers will therefore come from families that are more affluent than his or her own. The other student attends a school in a more disadvantaged area: the school's mean economic, social and cultural background is a quarter of a standard deviation below the OECD average, so that the student comes from a more affluent family than his or her peers. Figure 4.11 indicates that the first student would be likely to have a much higher mathematics performance than the second student, by between 40 and 72 score points depending on the country in this list.

Socio-economic differences at student levels are much less predictive for performance than the schools' socio-economic context. Consider the case of two students in the same country living in families whose different economic, social and cultural status give them scores on the index a quarter of a student-level standard deviation above and a quarter below the mean. If these students attend the same school, with an average socio-economic profile, they would have a much smaller gap in their predicted performance of a mere 2 score points in Japan and 12 score points in Belgium and the Slovak Republic (half of the value shown in column 2 in Table 4.5).

...although these differences must be interpreted in the context of how much socio-economic background actually varies in school averages.

In the interpretation of Figure 4.11, it needs to be borne in mind that differences in the averages of schools' socio-economic backgrounds are naturally smaller than comparable differences between individual students, given that every school's intake is mixed in terms of socio-economic variables. To aid in the interpretation, the typical range of the average socio-economic status of schools has been added to Figure 4.11.

Various influences potentially lie behind the effect of socio-economic intake, including the learning climate, teaching quality and peer interaction...

The manner in which students are allocated to schools within a district or region, or to classes and programmes within schools, can have implications for the contextual effect, in terms of the teaching and learning conditions in schools that are associated with educational outcomes. A number of studies have found that schools with a higher average socio-economic status among their student intake tend to have several advantages. They are likely to have fewer disciplinary problems, better teacher-student relations, higher teacher morale, and a general school climate that is oriented towards higher performance. Such schools also often have a faster-paced curriculum. Talented and motivated teachers are more likely to be attracted to schools with higher socio-economic status, and less likely to transfer to another school or to leave the profession. Some of the contextual effect associated with high socio-economic status may also stem from peer interactions that occur as talented students work with each other. The potential influence of such classroom and school factors is examined further in Chapter 5.

Some of the contextual effect might also be due to factors which are not accounted for in PISA. For example, the parents of a student attending a more socio-economically advantaged school may, on average, be more engaged in the student's learning at home. This may be so even though their socio-economic background is comparable to that of the parents of a student attending a less-privileged school. Another caveat is relevant to the previously mentioned example of the two hypothetical students of similar ability, who attended schools with different average socio-economic intakes. This relates to the fact that because no data on the students' earlier achievement are available from PISA, it is not possible to infer ability and motivation. Therefore, it is also not possible to determine whether and to what extent the school background directly or indirectly determines students' performance (for example, indirectly through a process of student selection or self-selection).

...as well as harder-to-measure influences including parental engagement and prior student ability and motivation.

Two different messages emerge about the ways to increase both quality and equality. On the one hand, socio-economic segregation may bring benefits for the advantaged that will enhance the performance of the elite and, perhaps as a consequence, overall average performance. On the other hand, segregation of schools is likely to decrease equality. However, there is strong evidence that this dilemma can be resolved from countries that have achieved both high quality and high equality. Just how other countries might match this record is the key question. Moving all students to schools with higher socio-economic status is a logical impossibility and the results shown in Figure 4.11 should not lead to the conclusion that transferring a group of students from a school with a low socio-economic intake to a school with a high socio-economic intake would automatically result in the gains suggested by Figure 4.11. That is, the estimated contextual effects shown in Figure 4.11 are descriptive of the distribution of school performance, and should not necessarily be interpreted in a causal sense.

In any attempt to develop education policy in the light of the above findings, there needs to be some understanding of the nature of the formal and informal selection mechanisms that contribute to between-school socio-economic segregation, and the effect of this segregation on students' performance. In some countries, socio-economic segregation may be firmly entrenched through residential segregation in major cities, or by a large urban/rural socio-economic divide. In other countries, structural features of the education system tend to stream or track students from different socio-economic contexts into programmes with different curricula and teaching practices (see also Chapter 5). The policy options are either to reduce socio-economic segregation or to mitigate its effects.

Socio-economic segregation may be due to geographic factors or to structural features of the educational system.

IMPLICATIONS FOR POLICY

Home background influences educational success, and experiences at school often appear to reinforce its effects. Although PISA shows that poor performance in school does not automatically follow from a disadvantaged socio-economic background, socio-economic background does appear to be a powerful influence on performance.

Experiences at school too often reinforce rather than mitigate home background.

This could be because privileged children are better able to take advantage of education or because schools find them easier to nurture…

This represents a significant challenge for public policy striving to provide learning opportunities for all students irrespective of their socio-economic backgrounds. National research evidence from various countries has often been discouraging. Schools have appeared to make little difference. Either because privileged families are better able to reinforce and enhance the effect of schools, or because schools are better able to nurture and develop young people from privileged backgrounds, it has often appeared that schools reproduce existing patterns of privilege, rather than bringing about a more equitable distribution of outcomes.

Figure 4.12 ■ **Performance-targeted, socio-economically targeted, compensatory and universal policies**

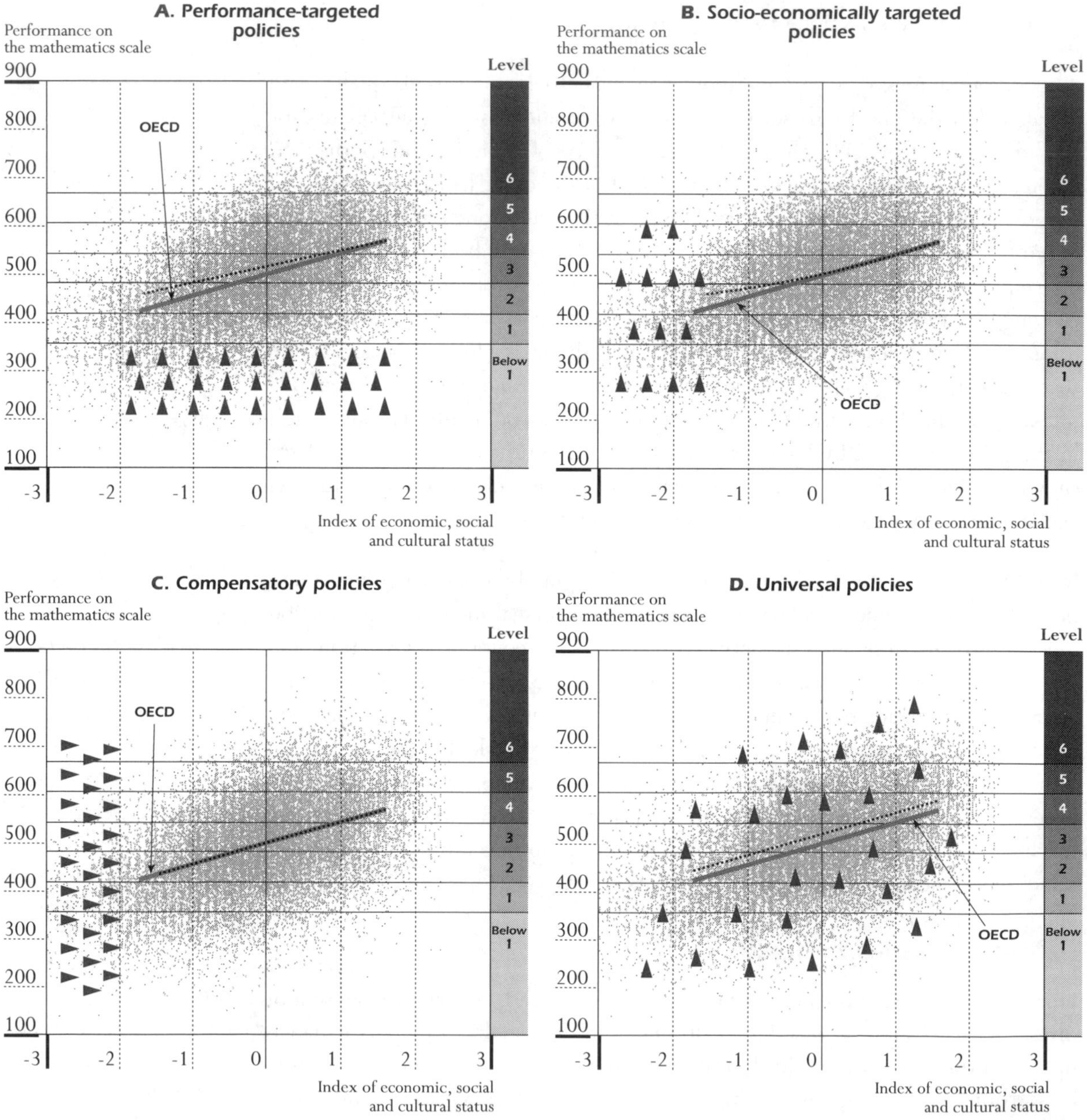

Source: OECD PISA 2003 database.

The international comparative perspective that emerges from PISA is more encouraging. While all countries show a clear positive relationship between home background and educational outcomes, some countries demonstrate that high average quality and equality of educational outcomes can go together.

...yet some countries combine greater equity with high performance.

This chapter has identified a set of indicators that, taking an internationally comparative perspective, can help policy makers to identify strategies aimed at raising performance and improving equity in the distribution of educational opportunities. Although all policy choices need to be defined within the respective national socio-economic, economic and educational contexts, international comparisons can provide some indication as to the kinds of policy that may be most effective. To assess their potential impact on raising performance and improving equity, policies can be classified as follows (Willms, 2004).

Policies trying to live up to these international benchmarks can take several forms...

- *Performance-targeted policies* provide a specialised curriculum or additional instructional resources for particular students based on their levels of academic performance. For example, some schooling systems provide early prevention programmes that target children who are deemed to be at risk of school failure when they enter early childhood programmes or school, while other systems provide late prevention or recovery programmes for children who fail to progress at a normal rate during the first few years of elementary school. Some performance-targeted programmes aim to provide a modified curriculum for students with high academic performance, such as programmes for gifted students. More generally, policies that involve the tracking or streaming of students into different types of programmes could be considered performance-targeted as they strive to match curriculum and instruction to students' academic ability or performance. Grade repetition is also sometimes considered a performance-targeted policy, because the decision to have a student repeat a grade is usually based mainly on school performance. However, in many cases grade repetition does not entail a modified curriculum or additional instructional resources and therefore does not fit the definition of a performance-targeted policy used here. Figure 4.12a illustrates the intended impact of this type of policy. This figure builds on Figure 4.8 and shows student performance on the vertical axis and students' socio-economic background on the horizontal axis. The focus of performance-targeted policies is at the lower end of the performance scale, irrespective of the socio-economic background of students (indicated by upward-moving arrows at the lower end of the vertical axis in the chart, irrespective of students' positions on the horizontal axis). The solid line in Figure 4.12a indicates the currently observed slope of the relationship between socio-economic background and student performance whereas the dotted line indicates the slope that would result from successfully implemented policies of this type.

...some try to help students with low performance by providing them with extra instructional resources...

- *Socio-economically targeted policies* provide a specialised curriculum or additional instructional resources for students from disadvantaged socio-economic backgrounds. An example is the Head Start pre-school programme in the United States for children from disadvantaged socio-economic backgrounds,

...some help students from less advantaged backgrounds...

although there is a wide range of programmes that target at risk children and young persons. Some approaches select students on the basis of a risk factor other than socio-economic background, such as whether the student is a recent immigrant, a member of an ethnic minority, or living in a low-income community. The important distinction is that these programmes select students based on the family's socio-economic background rather than on their cognitive ability. Figure 4.12b illustrates the intended impact of this type of policy (indicated by the upward-moving arrows), as well as its intended outcome (indicated by the dotted gradient line). The focus is at the lower end of the socio-economic scale, irrespective of student performance (indicated by upward-moving arrows at the left end of the horizontal axis in the chart, irrespective of students' positions on the performance scale).

...or with economic resources helping to improve their circumstances.

- *Compensatory policies* provide additional economic resources to students from disadvantaged socio-economic backgrounds. These policies could be considered a subset of the previously mentioned policies that use socio-economic targeting, as they target students from disadvantaged socio-economic backgrounds, rather than students with low cognitive performance. However, the emphasis is on improving the economic circumstances of students from poor families, rather than on providing a specialised curriculum or additional educational resources. The provision of free lunch programmes for students from poor families is an example. More generally, and in many countries, the provision of transfer payments to poor families is the one of the primary policy levers at the national level. The distinction between compensatory policies and socio-economically-targeted policies is not always clear. For example, some jurisdictions have compensatory funding formulas that allocate educational funds to schools differentially, based on schools' socio-economic intake. In some sense this is a compensatory policy, but it could also be considered a socio-economically targeted policy in as much as the intention is to provide additional educational resources to students with disadvantaged socio-economic backgrounds. Figure 4.12c illustrates the intended impact of this type of policy (indicated by arrows pointing towards the right end of the socio-economic scale, irrespective of students' positions on the performance scale) as well as the intended outcome (indicated by the dotted gradient line).

Others try to raise performance for everyone...

- *Universal policies* strive to increase the educational performance of all children through reforms that are applied equally across the schooling system. Generally, universal policies are aimed at altering the content and pace of the curriculum, improving instructional techniques, or improving the learning environment in schools and classrooms. Some jurisdictions responded to PISA 2000 results by introducing major school reforms, introducing full-day schooling, altering the school-entry age, or increasing the time spent on language classes. These are all universal policies. Many universal policies strive to improve children's learning environments by changing the structural features of schools. There has also been an effort to increase parents' involvement in schooling in several ways, including greater involvement at home and greater participation in school governance. Many universal policies are directed at changing teacher practice or aim at increasing the accountability of schools and schooling systems through the assessment of student performance. The underlying belief is that increased accountability will motivate administrators and teachers to improve the learning environment of schools and classrooms and provide better instruction. Figure 4.12d illustrates the intended impact of this type of policy as well as its intended outcome (indicated by the dotted gradient line).

- Finally, *inclusive policies* strive to include marginalised students into mainstream schools and classrooms. Inclusive practices often concentrate on including students with disabilities in regular classrooms, rather than segregating them in special classes or schools. This report considers inclusive policies to broadly encompass reforms aimed at including any type of student who may be segregated, whether with disabilities, students from ethnic minorities, or students from disadvantaged socio-economic backgrounds. Some inclusive policies try to reduce between-school socio-economic segregation by means such as redrawing school catchment boundaries, amalgamating schools, or creating magnet schools in areas with low socio-economic status.

...while yet others aim at integrating disadvantaged students, including through a reduction in socio-economic segregation.

A question that often confronts school administrators is whether efforts to improve student performance should be targeted mainly at those with low performance or low socio-economic background. The overall slope of the socio-economic gradient, together with the proportion of performance variation explained by socio-economic background, are useful indicators for assessing this question. Countries with relatively flat gradients are likely to find performance-based policies more effective in raising performance among students. Conversely, countries with steep socio-economic gradients might find some combination of performance-targeted and socio-economically-targeted policies more effective. For example, as noted earlier, Canada, Finland, Iceland, Italy, Luxembourg, Mexico, Portugal and Spain, as well as the partner countries Indonesia, Hong Kong-China, Macao-China, Thailand and Tunisia, are characterised by gradients that are flatter than that at the OECD average level (Table 4.3a). In these countries, a relatively smaller proportion of their low-performing students come from disadvantaged backgrounds and also school performance is largely unrelated to a school's socio-economic intake. Thus, by themselves, policies that specifically target students from disadvantaged backgrounds would not address the needs of many of the country's low-performing students. Moreover, if the goal is to ensure that most students achieve some minimum level of performance, socio-economically targeted policies in these countries would be providing services to a sizeable proportion of students who have high performance levels.

In deciding between policy approaches targeted at socio-economic disadvantage and at low student performance, countries with relatively gradual socio-economic gradients may see more benefit from the latter.

By contrast, in countries where the impact of socio-economic background on student performance is strong, socio-economically targeted policies would direct more of the resources towards students who are likely to require these services. As an illustration, compare Finland and Germany in Figure 4.13. By focusing on the left area of the chart, socio-economically-targeted policies would exclude many schools and students in Finland with comparatively low performance but

Targeting socio-economic disadvantage might be more effective, however, in countries where low performance and disadvantaged background are more closely associated...

from advantaged backgrounds shown in the bottom right area of the graph. By contrast, performance targeted policies would reach most of the lower-performing students and schools. In Germany, where the relationship between socio-economic background and student performance is much stronger, socio-economically-targeted interventions are likely to have a much stronger impact, as a much larger proportion of students and schools are located in the lower-left quadrant of the figure.

...although in countries with steep gradients, such targeting will still not benefit many students if the strength of the effect is low.

However, the case for socio-economically-targeted policies can still be over-stated for countries with steep socio-economic gradients. In countries with steep socio-economic gradients, but where the variation explained by socio-economic background is only moderate, there tends to be a sizeable group of poorly performing students with higher socio-economic background. In most cases, socio-economically targeted policies are directed at the students from families with very low socio-economic background. For example, for the Czech Republic, as one shifts vertically in Figure 4.13 to the left – *i.e.,* as one focuses on lower levels of socio-economic background – the proportion of schools and students with low levels of performance which is not covered by these policies increases. Thus, in such situations socio-economically-targeted policies are likely to miss a large proportion of students who have relatively poor performance.

Improvement strategies can focus on individual students or on schools, depending on the extent to which performance varies among schools...

Performance-targeted policies can be classified into two types: those aimed at improving the overall performance of low-performing schools, and those aimed at improving the performance of low-performing students within schools. The proportion of performance variation between schools, described at the beginning of this chapter (Table 4.1a), can provide a useful indicator in judging the appropriateness of particular policy approaches.

...with some countries needing to focus on the problem of low-performing schools and others facing mainly within-school differences.

If there is little performance variation between schools, as in Canada, Denmark, Finland, Iceland, Ireland, Norway, Poland or Sweden, then within-school policies aimed at improving the performance of low-performing students are likely to be more effective. By contrast, in countries such as Austria, Belgium, the Czech Republic, Germany, Hungary, Italy, Japan, the Netherlands and Turkey and the partner countries Brazil and Hong Kong-China, large performance differences between schools would suggest that policies target low-performing schools, at least within each type of school where the education system is stratified.

In some countries, greater concentrations of disadvantaged students suggest a stronger case for targeting socio-economic disadvantage.

Two variables – the skewness of the distribution of socio-economic background, as a within-country measure of disadvantage, and the proportion of students in each country that are in the lowest sixth of the international distribution of socio-economic background – help to assess the appropriateness of compensatory policies that seek to meet the needs of students from disadvantaged families by compensating for their economic circumstances (see columns 9 and 10 in Table 4.3a). Among OECD countries, the value for skewness is -0.31 (indicating that the socio-economic background of 15-year-olds is skewed towards socio-economic advantage). Among the partner countries the value is 0.16 (indicating

that the socio-economic background of 15-year-olds is skewed towards socio-economic disadvantage). And in some of the lower-income partner countries (but also in the Czech Republic, Poland, Portugal and Turkey), skewness is more than 1.5 times this number. These figures indicate a greater need for compensatory policies in some low-income countries. As previously noted, however, this kind of policy by itself – like socio economically targeted policies – cannot substantially raise and level socio-economic gradients. Such a policy is likely to be most effective if implemented alongside universal, as well as performance and socio-economically-targeted, strategies.

In countries with greater socio-economic segregation across schools, overall differences by socio-economic background tend to be larger...

Table 4.5 also provides an inclusion index (see column 12) (Willms, 2004). The smaller the index value, the more schools are segregated by socio-economic background. The larger the index value, the less schools are segregated by socio-economic background.[19] Across countries, the relationship between average performance and the inclusion index is positive. This suggests that countries with greater socio-economic inclusion tend to have higher overall performance. Furthermore, the relationship between the socio-economic gradients and the index of socio-economic inclusion in OECD countries is negative, indicating that countries with greater socio-economic inclusion tend to have flatter gradients. Taken together, these results suggest that more inclusive schooling systems have both higher levels of performance and fewer disparities among students from differing socio-economic backgrounds. In some countries, socio-economic segregation can be deeply entrenched due to economic divides between urban and rural areas, as well as residential segregation in cities. However, segregation can also stem from educational policies that stream children into certain kinds of programmes early in their school careers (see also Chapter 5).

...and in these countries some schools may need more resources to compensate, whereas in other countries any improvements will need to be found within schools.

To increase quality and equity (*i.e.,* to raise and flatten the gradient) in such countries would require specific attention to between-school differences. Reducing the socio-economic segregation of schools would be one strategy, while allocating resources differentially to schools and programmes and seeking to provide students with differentiated and appropriate educational opportunities are others. In countries where the inclusion index is low, it is important to understand how the allocation of school resources within a country is related to the socio economic intake of its schools. In other countries, there is relatively little socio-economic segregation between schools – *i.e.,* schools tend to be similar in their average socio-economic intake. In these countries, quality (the level) and equality (the slope of the gradient) are mainly affected by the relationship between student performance and the socio-economic background of individual students within each school. To increase quality and equality in these countries will require actions that predominantly focus within schools. Reducing the segregation within schools of students of differing economic, social and cultural status would be one strategy, and might require a review of classroom streaming practices. More direct assistance for poorly performing students may also be needed. In these countries, it is important to understand how the allocation of resources within schools is related to the socio-economic characteristics of their students.

Policy considerations need to take account of long-term influences on 15-year-olds' performance…

Finally, when considering the information furnished by PISA, policy analysts tend to focus their attention on the schooling system, particularly on features of the secondary system. This is natural, as PISA is an assessment of students at age 15. Indeed, the analyses pertaining to school effectiveness presented in this report are based on data describing school offerings at the late primary or secondary levels. However, PISA is not an assessment of what young people learned during their previous year at school, or even during their secondary school years. It is an indication of the learning development that has occurred since birth. A country's results in PISA depend on the quality of care and stimulation provided to children during infancy and the pre-school years, and on the opportunities children have to learn both in school and at home during the elementary and secondary school years.

…and to take a broad view, including the early childhood years and families.

Improving quality and equity therefore require a long-term view and a broad perspective. For some countries, this may mean taking measures to safeguard the healthy development of young children, or improving early childhood education. For others, it may mean socio-economic reforms that enable families to provide better care for the children. But in many, it can mean efforts to increase socio-economic inclusion and improve school offerings.

Figure 4.13 ■ **Relationship between school performance and schools' socio-economic background**

Note: Each symbol represents one school in the PISA sample, with the size of the symbols proportional to the number of 15-year-olds enrolled.
Source: OECD PISA 2003 database.

Figure 4.13 (continued-1) ■ **Relationship between school performance and schools' socio-economic background**

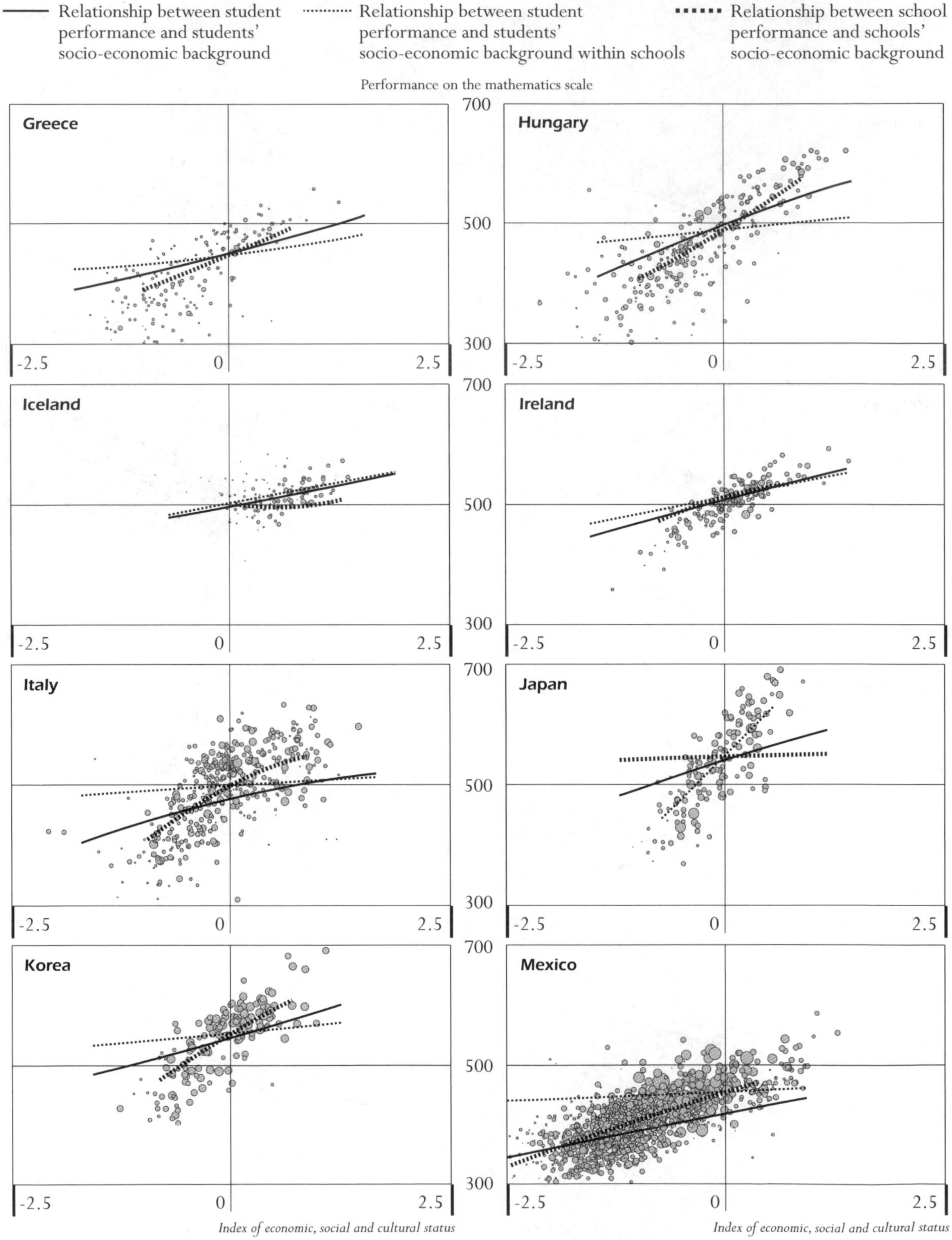

Note: Each symbol represents one school in the PISA sample, with the size of the symbols proportional to the number of 15-year-olds enrolled.
Source: OECD PISA 2003 database.

Figure 4.13 (continued-2) ■ **The relationship between school performance and schools' socio-economic background**

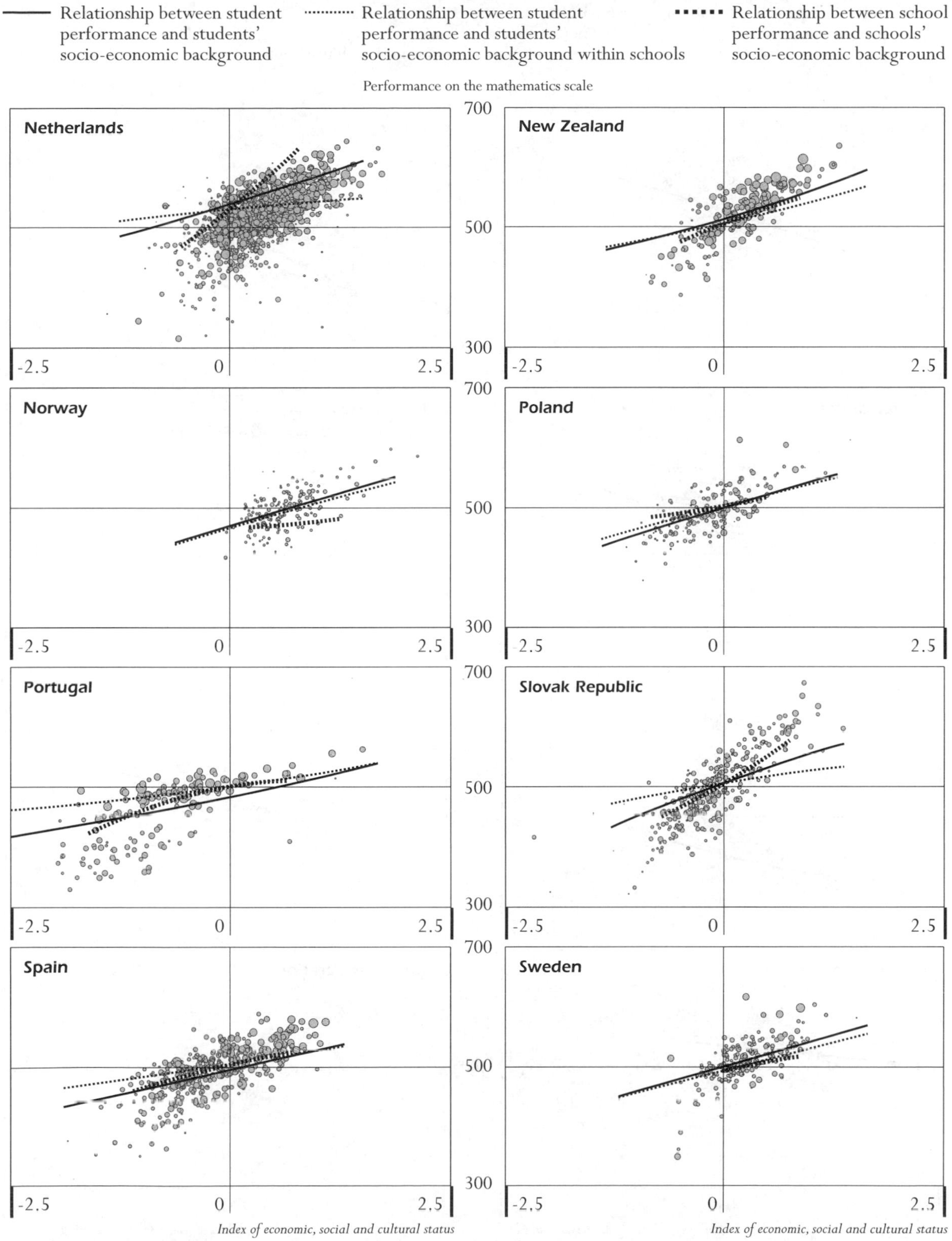

Note: Each symbol represents one school in the PISA sample, with the size of the symbols proportional to the number of 15-year-olds enrolled.
Source: OECD PISA 2003 database.

Figure 4.13 (continued-3) ■ **Relationship between school performance and schools' socio-economic background**

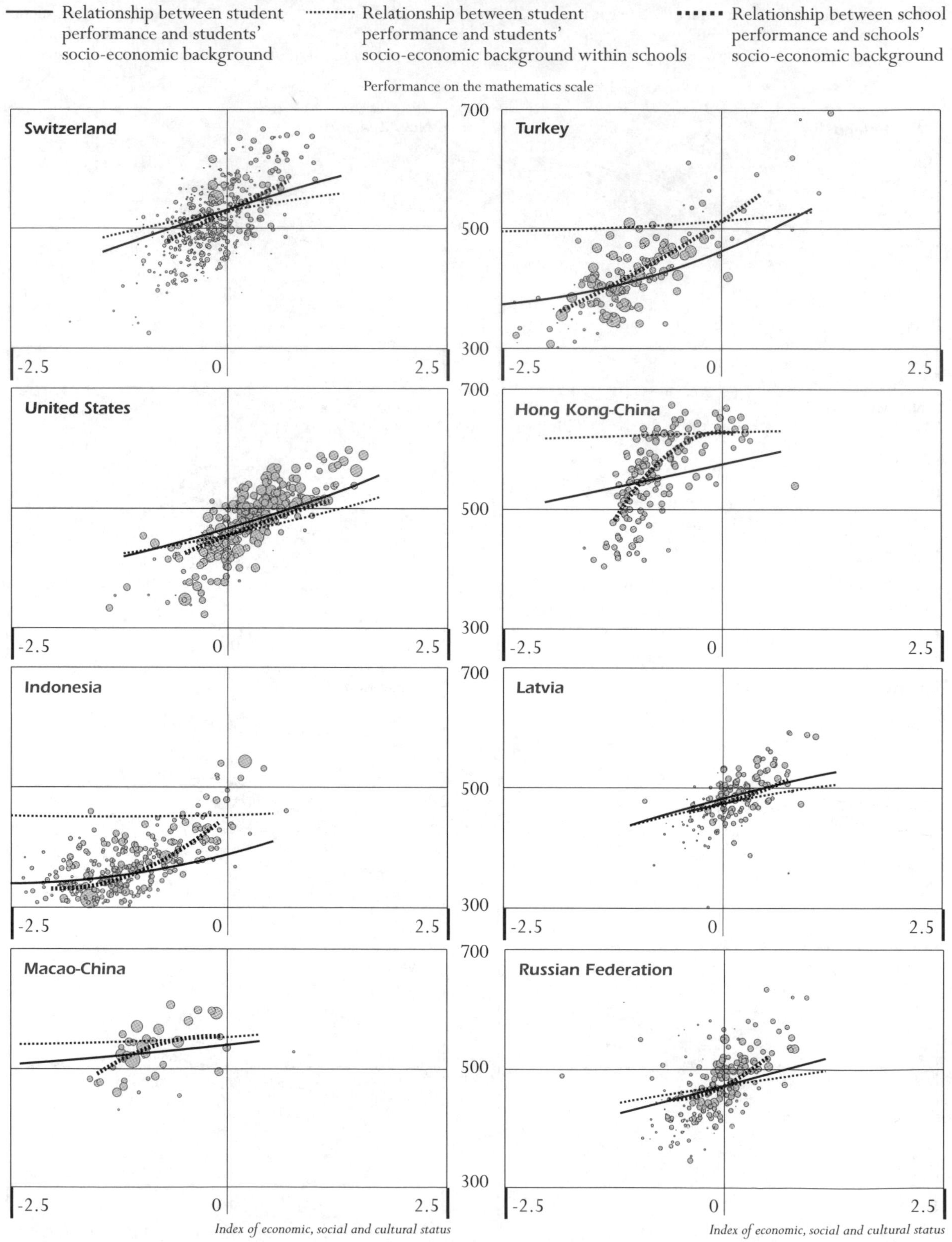

Note: Each symbol represents one school in the PISA sample, with the size of the symbols proportional to the number of 15-year-olds enrolled.
Source: OECD PISA 2003 database.

Figure 4.13 (continued-4) ■ **Relationship between school performance and schools' socio-economic background**

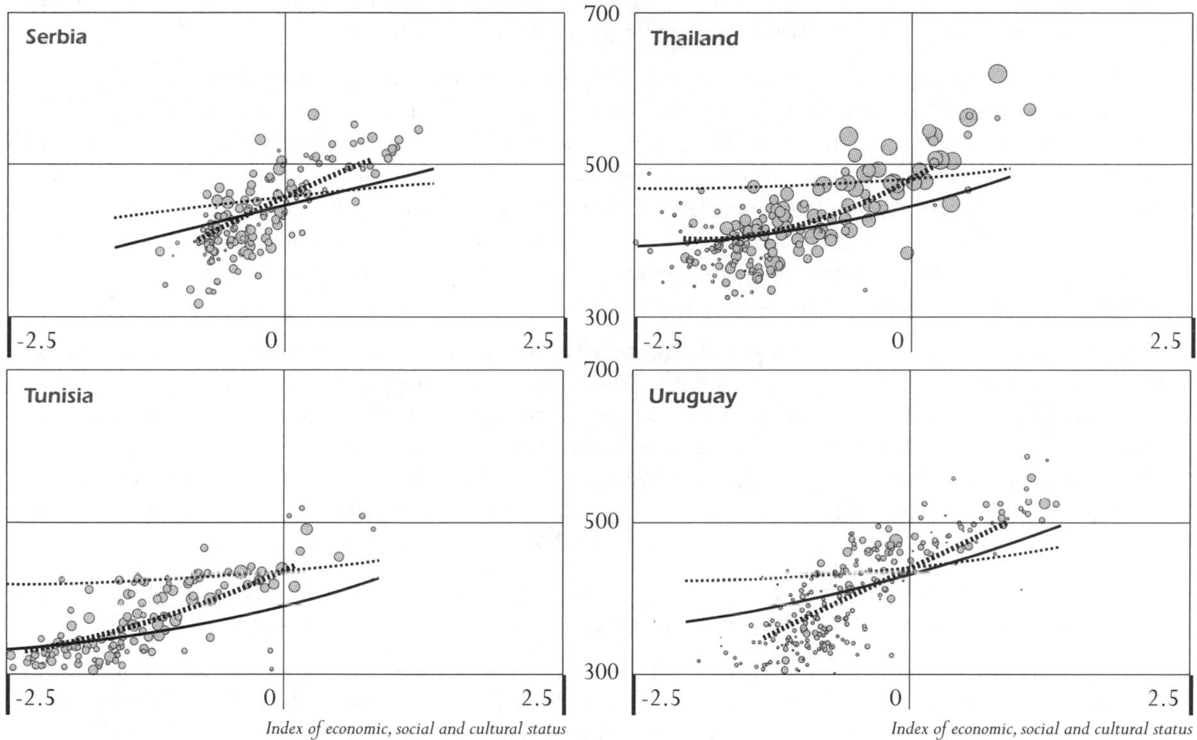

Note: Each symbol represents one school in the PISA sample, with the size of the symbols proportional to the number of 15-year-olds enrolled.
Source: OECD PISA 2003 database.

Notes

1. Performance differences between countries account for 10 per cent of the overall observed variance of student performance in mathematics, while performance differences between schools within countries account for 28 per cent and performance differences between students within schools account for 61 per cent of the overall variance (Table 5.21a)

2. While the overall relationship between socio-economic background and student performance tends to be similar across the areas of mathematics, science and reading, it varies for some countries. For example, for the Czech Republic, Hungary, Korea and the partner countries Brazil, Tunisia and Uruguay, the proportion of science performance variation that is explained by the PISA index of economic, social and cultural status lies between 3.0 and 5.8 percentage points lower than for mathematics while in Germany it lies 3.2 percentage points higher in science. Similarly, for the Czech Republic, Greece, Hungary, Korea, the Netherlands, Portugal and Spain and for the partner countries Brazil, Tunisia and Uruguay the proportion of reading performance that is explained by the PISA index of economic, social and cultural status lies between 3.1 and 6.7 percentage points lower than for mathematics while in Austria it is 5.0 percentage points higher in reading (see *www.pisa.oecd.org*).

3. Variation is expressed by statistical variance. This is obtained by squaring the standard deviation referred to in Chapter 2. The statistical variance rather than the standard deviation is used for this comparison to allow for the decomposition of the components of variation in student performance. For reasons explained in the *PISA 2003 Technical Report*, and most importantly because the data in this table only account for students with valid data on their socio-economic background, the variance may differ from the square of the standard deviation shown in Chapter 2. The *PISA 2003 Technical Report* also explains why, for some countries, the sum of the between-school and within-school variance components differs slightly from the total variance. The average is calculated over the OECD countries included in the table.

4. For the country Serbia and Montenegro, data for Montenegro are not available. The latter accounts for 7.9 per cent of the national population. The name "Serbia" is used as a shorthand for the Serbian part of Serbia and Montenegro.

5. The OECD average level is calculated simply as the arithmetic mean of the respective country values. This average differs from the square of the OECD average standard deviation shown in Chapter 2, since the latter includes the performance variation among countries whereas the former simply averages the within-country performance variation across countries.

6. Note that these results are also influenced by differences in how schools are defined and organised within countries and by the units that were chosen for sampling purposes. For example, in some countries some of the schools in the PISA sample were defined as administrative units (even if they spanned several geographically separate institutions, as in Italy; in others they were defined as those parts of larger educational institutions that serve 15-year-olds; in others they were defined as physical school buildings; and in yet others they were defined from a management perspective (*e.g.*, entities having a principal). The *PISA 2003 Technical Report* (OECD, forthcoming) provides an overview of how schools were defined. Note also that, because of the manner in which students were sampled, the within-school variation includes variation between classes as well as between students.

7. In all countries, the changes between 2000 and 2003 are very similar for both mathematics scales for which trend data can be estimated. For the purpose of this comparison, results are only shown for the overall mathematics scale, even though the PISA 2000 data did not include two of the four mathematical content areas.

8. In Belgium, some of this difference may be attributable to changes in the ways in which schools were defined for the purposes of sampling in PISA.

9. Father's or mother's occupation was used for this comparison, whichever was higher on the PISA socio-economic index of occupational status.

10. Mother's level of education was used for this comparison because the literature shows it to have the strongest relationship with student performance. However, the relationship tends to be similar when fathers' education is considered, with an OECD average performance gap of 40 score points between students whose fathers completed secondary education from students whose fathers did not (Table 4.2c).

11. For this comparison, the education levels of mothers and fathers were jointly examined and whichever was higher was then related to student performance. In order to obtain a continuous metric that can be used in a regression, levels of education were converted into years of schooling, using the conversion table shown in Table A1.1.

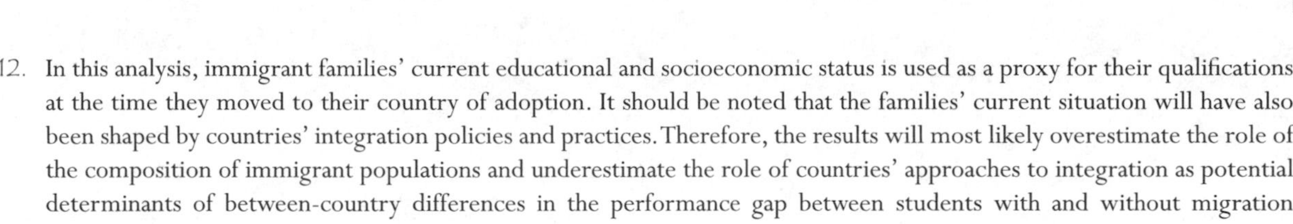

12. In this analysis, immigrant families' current educational and socioeconomic status is used as a proxy for their qualifications at the time they moved to their country of adoption. It should be noted that the families' current situation will have also been shaped by countries' integration policies and practices. Therefore, the results will most likely overestimate the role of the composition of immigrant populations and underestimate the role of countries' approaches to integration as potential determinants of between-country differences in the performance gap between students with and without migration backgrounds.

13. For the methodology used for the conversion see Annex A1.1.

14. The measure of home educational resources is constructed based on students' reports on having at their home a desk to study at, a room of their own, a quiet place to study, a computer they can use for school work, educational software, a link to the Internet, their own calculator, classic literature, books of poetry; works of art (*e.g.*, paintings); books to help with their school work, and a dictionary.

15. These results were based on dividing the distribution of the index of economic, social and cultural status into quartiles and examining the correlation in each quartile with mathematics performance. The following results were obtained: *i)* for the lowest quartile: 0.336 (0.014) for the OECD total and 0.297 (0.009) for the OECD average, and *ii)* for the highest quartile: 0.179 (0.012) for the OECD total and 0.147 (0.007) for the OECD average.

16. The percentage of variance explained on average across OECD countries and the average slope across countries are different from the OECD average and total shown in Table 4.3a since the latter also reflect the between-country differences.

17. In PISA 2000, the index of economic, social and cultural status included a component on family wealth. Since analyses of the PISA 2003 data suggest that the data on family wealth is difficult to compare across countries and cultures due to the nature of the underlying questions, the family-wealth component was excluded from the index. Even though the influence of the family-wealth component on the index was small, for the purpose of the comparison over time the PISA 2000 index was re-calculated with the family-wealth component excluded as well. For this reason, the results for 2000 published in this report differ slightly from those published in 2001.

18. The decomposition is a function of the between-school slope, the average within-school slope, and η^2, which is the proportion of variation in socio-economic background that is between schools. The statistic η^2 can be considered a measure of segregation by socio-economic background (Willms & Paterson, 1995), which theoretically can range from zero for a completely desegregated system in which the distribution of socio-economic background is the same in every school, to one for a system in which students within schools have the same level of socio-economic background, but the schools vary in their average socio-economic background. One can also think of the term, $1 - \eta^2$, as an index of socio-economic inclusion, which would range from zero for a segregated schooling system to one for a fully desegregated schooling system. The overall gradient is related to the within- and between-school gradients through the segregation and inclusion indices: $\beta_t = \eta^2 \times \beta_b + (1 - \eta^2) \times \beta_w$ where β_t is the overall gradient, β_b is the between-school gradient, and β_w is the average within-school gradient.

19. More specifically, the index is defined as one minus the proportion of variation in the PISA index of economic, social and cultural status that lies between schools, as explained in note 18.

The Learning Environment and the Organisation of Schooling

INTRODUCTION

What can schools do in the face of the fixed influence of student background?

Chapter 4 showed the considerable impact that socio-economic background can have on student performance and, by implication, on the distribution of educational opportunities. At the same time, many of the factors of socio-economic disadvantage are not directly amenable to education policy, at least not in the short term. For example, the educational attainment of parents can only gradually improve, and average family wealth depends on the long-term economic development of a country as well as on the development of a culture which promotes individual savings. The importance of socio-economic disadvantage, and the realisation that aspects of such disadvantage only change over extended periods of time, give rise to a vital question for policy makers: what can schools and school policies do to raise performance and promote equity?

This chapter builds on previous results showing that a school's characteristics can make a difference…

Building on the results from PISA 2000, which suggested that students and schools perform better in a climate characterised by high expectations, the readiness of students to invest effort, the enjoyment of learning, a positive disciplinary climate and good teacher-student relations, this chapter examines policy levers and school-level characteristics that are often thought to be conducive to raising levels of student performance and achieving a more equitable distribution of educational opportunities.

…and examines policy levers that are often thought to be conducive to raising student performance and fostering equity.

However, studies like PISA can address such questions only up to a point, both because many important contextual factors cannot be captured by international comparative surveys of this kind, and because such surveys do not examine processes over time to allow cause and effect to be firmly established.

The analysis builds on what is known about effective school improvement…

The school factors that were examined by PISA were selected on the basis of three strands of research:

…including studies on effective teaching and instruction…

- Studies on effective teaching and instruction, which tend to focus on classroom management and teaching strategies, such as students' opportunity to learn, time on task, monitoring performance at classroom levels, approaches to teaching and differentiation practices.

…school effectiveness studies…

- School effectiveness studies, which focus on organisational and managerial characteristics of schools, such as school and classroom climate, achievement orientation, school autonomy and educational leadership, evaluation strategies and practices, parental involvement and staff development.

…and studies relating to economic production functions.

- Studies of economic factors relating to production functions, which focus on resource inputs – such as school size; student/teaching staff ratios; the quality of schools' physical infrastructures and of their educational resources; teacher experience, training and compensation – and how these translate into educational outcomes.

The questions asked by PISA of students and school principals sought a balanced representation of aspects in each of these three areas, concentrating on those aspects having received support in earlier empirical research. However, no data on student opportunities to learn were available to offer insights into effective instruction and time on task.[1] Furthermore, no data were obtained from teachers, thus inferences on teaching and learning can only be made indirectly from the perspective of students and school principals.

The chapter starts from students' direct experience in classrooms, and then moves on to broader characteristics of their schools and school systems...

Research has shown that factors that are closest to the students' actual learning tend to have the strongest impact on learning outcomes (*e.g.*, Wang *et al.*, 1993), whereas the influence of factors more remote from the classroom tends to be more difficult to assess. The chapter therefore moves from more proximate to more distant factors by:

- beginning with an examination of school climate and the learning environment in classes and at school;
- then turning to reviewing the relationship between various school policies and practices and student performance;
- next looking at the impact of school resources on student and school performance;
- and finally examining aspects of the structure of education systems, in particular the nature and degree of stratification and institutional differentiation in participating countries.

...taking account of how these factors interact with each other and with socio-economic background...

Since many factors within each of these categories are closely interrelated, each section concludes with an examination of the joint impact of the factors examined in that section.

It is also important to consider the extent to which differences in the performance of schools are associated with socio-economic factors. As shown in Chapter 4, socio-economic factors play a role both at the level of individual students and through the aggregate context they provide for learning at schools, for example, students from more advantaged backgrounds may choose better schools or create better schooling conditions, by establishing an environment that is more conducive to learning. Each of the following sections therefore also considers the interrelationship between school factors and students' socio-economic background.

...and concludes with identifying the unique influence of each factor.

The concluding section then looks at all of the factors in combination and seeks to determine the unique contribution each of the observed factors makes to school performance, after all other factors have been taken into account. This is used as the basis for drawing policy lessons from international comparisons.

Box 5.1 ■ **Interpreting the data from schools and their relationship to student performance**

Several of the indices summarise the responses of students or school principals to a series of related questions. The questions were selected from larger constructs on the basis of theoretical considerations and previous research. Structural equation modelling was used to confirm the theoretically expected dimensions of the indices and to validate their comparability across countries. For this purpose, a model was estimated separately for each country and, collectively, for all OECD countries. For detailed information on the construction of the indices, see Annex A1.

The PISA 2003 indices are based on students' and school principals' accounts of the learning environment and organisation of schools, and of the social and economic contexts in which learning takes place. The indices rely on self-reports rather than on external observations and may be influenced by cross-cultural differences in response behaviour. For example, students' self-perceptions of classroom situations may only imperfectly reflect the actual classroom situation or students may choose to respond differently from their actual perceptions because certain responses may be more socially desirable than others.

Several limitations of the information collected from principals should be taken into account in the interpretation of the data:

- First, on average only 270 principals were surveyed in each OECD country and in five countries less than 150 principals were surveyed.
- Second, although principals are able to provide information about their schools, generalising from a single source of information for each school (and then matching that information with students' reports) is not straightforward. Most importantly, students' performance in each of the assessment areas depends on many factors, including all the education that they have received in earlier years, not just the period in which they have interacted with their current teachers.
- Third, principals may not be the most appropriate source of information for some information related to teachers, *e.g.,* teachers' morale and commitment.
- Fourth, the learning environment in which 15-year-olds find themselves and that is examined by PISA may only be partially predictive of the learning environment that shaped educational experiences of the 15-year-olds earlier in their schooling career, particularly in education systems where students progress through different types of educational institutions at the pre-primary, primary, lower secondary and upper secondary levels. To the extent that the current learning environment of 15-year-olds differs from that in their earlier school years, the contextual data collected by PISA become an imperfect proxy for the cumulative learning environments of students and their effect on learning outcomes is therefore likely to be underestimated.
- Fifth, the definition of the school in which students are taught is not straightforward in some countries, because 15-year-olds may be in different school types that vary in their level of education or their programme destination.

Despite these caveats, the information from the school questionnaire can be instructive as it provides unique insights into the ways in which national and sub-national authorities implement their educational objectives.

Where information based on reports from school principals is presented in this report, it has been weighted so that it reflects the number of 15-year-olds enrolled in each school.

Unless otherwise noted, comparisons of student performance in this chapter refer to the performance of students on the combined mathematics scale.

THE LEARNING ENVIRONMENT AND SCHOOL CLIMATE

The learning environment and climate is reported by students and school principals.

This section examines school climate and the learning environment in classrooms and at school. It looks at students' perceptions of the degree of individual support that they receive from their teachers, as well as at their perceptions of student-teacher relations and the disciplinary climate at school. The picture also includes the views of school principals on student and teacher behaviour as well as students' and teachers' morale at their school.

Students' perceptions of individual support from their teachers

Countries' strategies to support students vary...

Raising performance levels critically relies on effective support systems that provide professional advice and assistance to students, teachers and school management. Countries pursue different strategies to this end (OECD, 2004c). Some seek primarily to address heterogeneity in the student body with services directed towards students on a needs basis, including services for students requiring special educational or social assistance, or educational and career counselling. Some relate to networks between individual schools and between schools and other institutions aimed at facilitating performance improvement of teachers and schools. Yet others relate to the school system as a whole and often include external agencies. Some countries provide independent professional support structures while others have integrated support systems into school administration, school inspection or the academic sector.

...but fostering individual support by teachers for learning is a central element in most approaches.

The individual support students receive from their teachers for their learning is a central element in any approach to support. Research on school effectiveness, in particular, suggests that students (particularly those with a low level of performance) benefit from teaching practices that demonstrate teachers' interest in the progress of their students, give the clear message that all students are expected to attain reasonable performance standards and show a willingness to help all students to meet these standards. It is this aspect of student support that was examined by PISA 2003.

In order to examine the extent to which such practices are common in different countries, students were asked to indicate the frequency with which teachers in their mathematics lessons show an interest in every student's learning, give students extra help when they need it, help students with their learning, continue to teach until students understand and give students an opportunity to express opinions.[2]

Depending on the country, a majority or only a minority of students feel supported by their teachers…

Results from PISA 2003 suggest that the strength of teachers' efforts to support students individually in their learning is – at least in the eyes of students – mixed, with considerable variation across countries. While in Iceland, Mexico, Portugal, Sweden, Turkey and the United States as well as in the PISA partner countries Brazil, the Russian Federation, Thailand, Tunisia and Uruguay two-thirds of students report that teachers show an interest in every student's learning in every or at least most mathematics lessons, this is only 43 per cent in Germany and Greece (OECD average 58 per cent) (Figure 5.1 and Table 5.1b).

…and substantial numbers feel they do not get the help they need.

In fact, in Germany, Greece and Luxembourg, 18 per cent of students report that their teachers in their mathematics lessons never or hardly ever show an interest in every student's learning (for data, see *www.pisa.oecd.org*). Across the OECD countries, an average of only 66 per cent of students report that teachers generally give extra help when students need it and only 62 per cent report that teachers in their mathematics lesson continue teaching until students understand.

An overall index …

Student responses to these various questions can be summarised on an index of teacher support. Values above the OECD average, which is set at 0, indicate higher than average student perceptions that teachers are supportive in their mathematics lessons, while negative values indicate that students' perceptions of teachers' supportiveness is below average.[3]

…shows that students' perceptions of how much support they get from their teachers varies greatly across countries.

A comparison of this index across countries shows that students in Australia, Canada, Denmark, Iceland, Mexico, New Zealand, Portugal, Sweden, Turkey and the United States and in the partner countries Brazil, Indonesia, the Russian Federation, Thailand, Tunisia and Uruguay report the most positive perceptions of their teachers' supportiveness for individual learning in mathematics classes. By contrast, students in Austria, Germany, Japan, Luxembourg and the Netherlands report the least degree of individual support from teachers in their mathematics lessons. From the data available, there is no way of assessing the extent to which these results reflect true differences in teachers' attitudes and practices – within and between countries – rather than differences in students' subjective perceptions, since students in each country applied their own judgement. Despite this caveat, some of the differences between countries are so large that they merit attention (Figure 5.1 and Table 5.1a).

Within some countries, but not others, there is substantial variation also across schools…

In some countries, there is also important variation in students' perceptions of teacher support across schools. The last two columns in Figure 5.1 provide an indication of the variation between schools in this respect: 5 per cent of 15-year-olds are enrolled in schools where teacher support is perceived to be worse than indicated by the first column, and 5 per cent are enrolled in schools where teacher support is perceived to be better than indicated by the second column. In Austria, the Czech Republic, Hungary, Italy, Mexico, the Slovak Republic and the United States, as well as in the partner countries Liechtenstein and Uruguay, student perceptions of teacher support vary substantially among schools, which can be seen by the large difference of the school level index of teacher support between

Figure 5.1 ■ **Teacher support in mathematics**

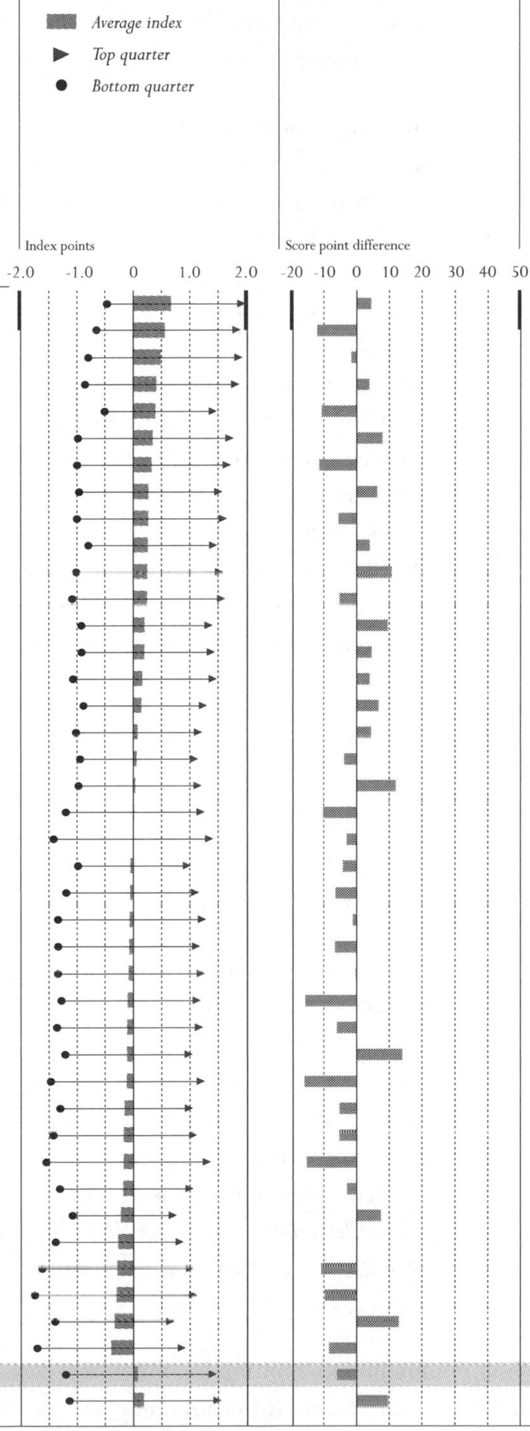

	Percentage of students reporting that the following happens in every or most mathematics lessons:					Index of teacher support	Change in mathematics performance per unit of the index of the teacher support			
	The teacher shows an interest in every student's learning	The teacher gives extra help when students need it.	The teacher helps students with their learning	The teacher continues teaching until the students understand.	The teacher gives students an opportunity to express opinions.	Index points (-2.0 to 2.0)	Score point difference (-20 to 50)	Percentage of explained variance in student performance	Students' view of teacher support in one of the schools with the lowest levels[1]	Students' view of teacher support in one of the schools with the highest levels[2]
Thailand	85	77	88	83	79			0.2	0.0	1.4
Brazil	81	71	86	81	76			1.4	0.0	1.5
Mexico	81	68	78	70	73			0.0	-0.1	1.5
Turkey	77	74	82	68	70			0.1	-0.1	1.1
Indonesia	64	66	81	78	81			1.0	0.0	0.9
United States	69	78	84	71	63			0.8	-0.6	1.1
Uruguay	77	51	81	75	73			1.5	-0.4	1.2
Canada	63	80	86	71	62			0.5	-0.3	1.0
Portugal	67	73	82	71	67			0.4	-0.2	1.0
Russian Fed.	67	74	80	67	71			0.1	-0.2	1.0
Australia	64	78	85	72	63			1.3	-0.2	0.8
Tunisia	71	62	77	70	62			0.4	-0.3	0.7
Iceland	66	69	89	78	59			0.9	-0.4	0.9
Sweden	69	70	87	71	62			0.2	-0.4	0.9
New Zealand	63	77	84	68	59			0.2	-0.4	0.9
Denmark	57	68	85	73	69			0.4	-0.4	0.9
Finland	54	77	86	61	62			0.2	-0.5	0.6
Latvia	51	72	82	63	64			0.1	-0.2	0.7
Hong Kong-China	62	67	74	68	60			1.1	-0.4	0.4
Switzerland	55	73	67	61	69			1.0	-0.6	0.7
Ireland	62	62	75	68	50			0.1	-0.6	0.7
Macao-China	60	57	68	64	57			0.2	-0.4	0.4
Greece	43	62	74	59	71			0.4	-0.6	0.8
Spain	65	48	72	65	60			0.0	-0.7	0.6
Liechtenstein	55	72	63	60	66			0.4	c	c
Hungary	54	64	72	55	62			0.0	-0.9	1.3
Slovak Republic	57	58	65	52	60			2.7	-0.8	1.0
Belgium	49	65	66	64	53			0.3	-0.6	0.7
Norway	55	60	81	60	58			1.9	-0.6	0.6
Italy	57	49	70	61	61			3.3	-0.7	1.0
Czech Republic	47	75	59	51	57			0.3	-1.1	0.5
France	48	63	66	62	50			0.3	w	w
Serbia	53	49	54	51	55			4.4	-0.9	0.6
Poland	51	61	62	55	55			0.1	-0.7	0.5
Korea	58	56	79	40	49			0.4	-0.6	0.2
Netherlands	49	66	49	60	54			0.0	-0.8	0.3
Germany	43	59	59	54	53			1.4	-0.8	0.5
Luxembourg	53	61	49	57	59			1.5	-1.1	0.2
Japan	50	62	73	50	47			1.2	-0.9	0.0
Austria	49	59	45	51	52			0.9	-1.2	0.6
OECD average	*58*	*66*	*73*	*62*	*59*			*0.2*	*-0.7*	*0.9*
United Kingdom[3]	63	75	83	73	57			1.2	-0.3	0.8

Legend: Average index; ► Top quarter; ● Bottom quarter

1. This is the school at the 5th percentile. In only 5% of schools is the index of teacher support more negative.
2. This is the school at the 95th percentile. The index of teacher support is more positive than in 95% of the other schools.
3. Response rate too low to ensure comparability (see Annex A3).
Source: OECD PISA 2003 database, Table 5.1a and Table 5.1b.

the 95th and the 5th percentile, suggesting that problems in this respect relate to specific schools and school types and, therefore, that targeted policy strategies might be most effective to raise perceived teacher support. By contrast, in Korea and Japan, and the partner countries Hong Kong-China, Indonesia and Macao-China, differences between schools in perceived teacher support are much less pronounced, shown by the small between-school differences, suggesting that a perceived lack of teacher support is more of a general issue for the education system.

…and in some cases statistically significant gender differences in both directions.

In some countries, there are also sizeable gender differences in students' perceptions of teacher support, such as in Austria, Germany, and Switzerland, and in the partner countries Liechtenstein and Serbia,[4] where females report particularly low levels of teacher support in their mathematics lessons while the opposite happens in Portugal, Turkey and the United States and in the partner country Thailand.

It is hard to measure, however, how much benefit support brings to performance, since teachers may support weaker students more.

To the extent that teachers typically use more supportive practices for weaker students or for classes attended by a majority of less able students, the correlation between support and performance would be expected to be negative. At the same time, to the extent that the encouragement offered is effective, one would expect that performance would be higher in classes that receive more support than in other classes. As might be anticipated from this, the relationship is mixed and generally weak,[5] and it requires further research and analysis to establish how teacher support affects students' and schools' success.

Student-related factors affecting the school climate for mathematics

School principals and students were both asked about the school climate…

The school and student context questionnaires in PISA included questions that allow for the identification and comparison of students' and principals' perceptions of factors that affect schools' climate for learning, as it related to attitudes and behaviour of students.

Principals were asked to indicate the extent to which learning is hindered by such factors as student absenteeism, the use of alcohol or illegal drugs and disruption of classes by students. They were also asked to assess student morale, with questions such as whether students enjoy being in school, work with enthusiasm, take pride in their school, value academic achievement, are co-operative and respectful, etc. Students, in turn, were asked how frequently certain disruptive situations occur in their mathematics classes. For example, students indicated the frequency with which "students cannot work well", "there is noise and disorder", and "at the start of class, more than five minutes are spent doing nothing" in their mathematics classes.

…and despite different country contexts, overall patterns are similar.

Such data should be interpreted with some caution, though. Students and principals in different countries, or even in different schools, do not necessarily apply the same criteria when considering the school climate. For example, principals in countries with generally low absenteeism may consider a modest level of absenteeism in their school to be a major cause of disciplinary problems, whereas principals in countries with higher levels of absenteeism may see things differently. Similarly, students are likely to consider the disciplinary climate with reference to their own experiences in other classes or schools, rather than with reference to some objective standard or national average. Despite these problems of interpretation, many of the patterns revealed by PISA 2003 are strikingly similar across countries.

Absenteeism and disruptive behaviour are the two problems most frequently cited by principals…

In most OECD countries, principals identify student absenteeism as the most frequent student-related obstacle to learning: on average, 48 per cent of 15-year-olds are enrolled in schools whose principals identify this as hindering learning by 15-year-olds either to some extent or a lot. Disruptive behaviour is the next most frequently indicated obstacle to learning, mentioned by an average of 40 per cent. This is followed by students skipping classes, mentioned by 30 per cent; students' use of alcohol or illegal drugs, mentioned by 10 per cent; and students' intimidation or bullying of other students, mentioned by 15 per cent (Figure 5.2 and Table 5.2b).

…while students report noise and disorder as the most frequent discipline-related problem.

From the students' perspective, having noise and disorder is the most frequently reported disciplinary problem in their mathematics lessons, with 36 per cent of students reporting that this happens in every lesson or at least in most lessons. On average across OECD countries, more than a quarter of students report that in every lesson or at least in most lessons, students do not start working for a long time after lessons begin and a third of students report that the teacher must wait a long time for students to quieten down or that students don't listen to what the teacher says (Figure 5.3and Table 5.3b).

Overall indices summarise the responses of principals and students, and show different countries' strengths and weaknesses.

These averages indicate common tendencies throughout the OECD but disguise considerable variation within and between OECD countries. To examine how countries differ, summary indices were constructed using data from both principals and students. In the case of students' reports of disciplinary climate, the higher the value *above* zero, the more positive an education system's climate in mathematics classes in the opinion of students. On the school-level index, values *above* zero reflect a positive perception of the disciplinary climate on the part of school principals, *i.e.,* the view that learning is perceived to be hindered by the various factors mentioned in this index to less than the OECD average level. By contrast, values *below* zero reflect the opinion that the school climate (on the school-level index) and discipline (on the student-level index) are less than the OECD average in each case (Table 5.2a and Table 5.3a).

The climate in Japan is rated high and in Greece low by both students and principals…

When the views of students are compared through a summary index of disciplinary climate, students in Austria, Germany, Ireland, Japan and the partner countries Latvia and Russian Federation give the most positive picture of disciplinary climate whereas students in Greece, Luxembourg, Norway and the partner country Brazil report the greatest problems (Figure 5.3 and Table 5.3a). According to the views of principals, the strongest climate is in Japan, Korea and the partner country Uruguay, and the weakest in the partners countries Indonesia, the Russian Federation and Tunisia, with Canada, Greece and New Zealand weakest among OECD countries.

Figure 5.2 ■ **Student-related factors affecting the school climate**

Chart columns (graphical): **Index of student-related factors affecting school climate** (Average index; Top quarter; Bottom quarter; Index points, -4 to 3) and **Change in mathematics performance per unit of the index of student-related factors affecting school climate** (Score point difference, -20 to 50).

	Percentage of students in schools where the principals agree or strongly agree that the following hinders students learning: Student absenteeism.	Disruption of classes by students.	Students skipping classes.	Students lacking respect for teachers.	Student use of alcohol or illegal drugs.	Students intimidating or bullying other students.	Percentage of explained variance in student performance	Principal's view on student-related factors affecting school climate in one of the schools with the most negative climate[1]	Principal's view on student-related factors affecting school climate in one of the schools with the most positive climate[2]
Korea	17	18	13	23	13	13	8.7	-1.7	2.6
Uruguay	58	12	42	17	7	11	3.4	-1.5	2.6
Japan	39	13	23	32	1	7	22.4	-1.3	1.8
Belgium	34	26	21	18	7	14	17.7	-1.5	1.8
Hong Kong-China	27	31	21	28	18	25	2.8	-3.6	2.6
Hungary	56	42	26	14	6	8	6.4	-1.7	2.6
Slovak Republic	61	40	a	12	4	5	3.1	-1.2	1.7
Thailand	45	19	19	8	2	4	0.0	-0.8	2.6
Denmark	39	42	14	13	1	7	0.7	-0.8	1.8
Mexico	44	27	32	13	8	24	1.4	-1.3	1.8
Czech Republic	65	36	24	16	2	2	2.0	-1.0	1.4
Iceland	38	62	28	22	5	25	0.3	-1.3	2.6
Italy	68	41	63	17	1	8	6.3	-1.3	1.8
Switzerland	27	52	11	17	19	24	0.5	-1.3	1.4
Spain	44	59	38	34	5	13	4.6	-1.5	1.8
Australia	52	37	20	22	6	24	4.9	-1.3	1.8
Austria	53	38	43	17	9	15	1.0	-1.3	1.8
Poland	47	40	45	21	10	8	0.1	-1.3	1.8
Germany	35	51	25	22	9	24	14.7	-2.2	1.4
Sweden	48	50	28	25	5	17	0.5	-1.3	1.4
Finland	56	39	34	12	4	7	0.4	-1.0	1.0
Latvia	79	24	57	14	11	8	0.1	-1.3	1.4
Portugal	61	35	50	16	3	9	0.6	-1.5	1.4
Luxembourg	39	45	25	16	9	15	1.4	-1.3	1.0
Norway	37	74	20	35	3	12	0.0	-1.0	1.0
Brazil	51	44	45	30	21	26	4.6	-1.9	1.8
Netherlands	43	43	30	28	7	22	12.0	-1.3	1.0
United States	69	27	36	22	21	14	2.7	-1.5	1.4
Ireland	63	47	21	23	24	21	1.6	-1.7	1.4
Turkey	70	46	45	37	22	32	2.0	-2.5	1.8
Greece	66	52	46	47	31	23	1.2	-2.9	1.8
New Zealand	63	41	38	24	20	15	2.2	-1.7	1.4
Canada	65	34	58	25	32	18	2.0	-1.7	1.8
Macao-China	62	54	51	56	39	32	0.3	-3.6	2.6
Serbia	90	45	82	34	24	12	2.1	-1.9	1.0
Russian Fed.	90	41	86	49	41	41	2.5	-3.6	1.4
Tunisia	84	78	67	58	45	43	0.5	-3.6	1.0
Indonesia	80	79	72	69	67	64	0.2	-3.6	1.4
OECD average	*48*	*40*	*30*	*22*	*10*	*15*	*3.6*	*-1.5*	*1.8*
United Kingdom[3]	m	m	m	m	m	m	10.3	-1.7	1.8

1. This is the school at the 5th percentile. In only 5% of schools is the school climate more negative.
2. This is the school at the 95th percentile. The school climate is more positive than in 95% of the other schools.
3. Response rate too low to ensure comparability (see Annex A3).
Source: OECD PISA 2003 database, Table 5.2a and Table 5.2b.

Figure 5.3 ■ **Students' views on the disciplinary climate in their mathematics lessons**

	Percentage of students reporting that the following happens in every or in most of their mathematics lessons					Index of disciplinary climate in mathematics	Change in mathematics performance per unit of the index of disciplinary climate in mathematics			
	Students don't listen to what the teacher says.	There is noise and disorder.	The teacher has to wait a long time for students to quieten down.	Students cannot work well.	Students don't start working for a long time after the lesson begins.	Average index / Top quarter / Bottom quarter (Index points: -2.0, -1.0, 0, 1.0, 2.0)	(Score point difference: -20, -10, 0, 10, 20, 30, 40, 50)	Percentage of explained variance in student performance	Students' views on disciplinary climate in one of the schools with the most negative disciplinary climate[1]	Students' views on disciplinary climate in one of the schools with the most positive disciplinary climate[2]
Russian Fed.	22	16	18	19	15			6.2	-0.2	1.6
Japan	19	17	14	25	15			9.3	-0.3	1.2
Latvia	27	20	20	18	21			2.9	-0.3	1.5
Germany	22	25	32	26	26			5.0	-0.6	1.0
Ireland	32	32	25	19	21			4.5	-0.3	0.9
Liechtenstein	26	28	33	28	25			10.3	c	c
Austria	31	27	33	27	30			5.9	-0.7	1.3
Hungary	28	28	30	22	19			4.6	-1.3	1.1
Hong Kong-China	21	17	19	19	20			4.7	-0.4	0.6
United States	32	34	26	19	27			7.9	-0.6	1.0
Korea	27	a	19	18	21			1.8	-0.4	0.9
Poland	33	27	30	21	22			2.3	-0.5	1.3
Switzerland	28	33	32	26	31			3.5	-0.8	1.0
Macao-China	18	15	17	21	20			2.5	-0.3	0.5
Indonesia	25	32	37	22	30			1.6	-0.5	0.8
Belgium	28	37	34	19	33			5.9	-0.8	0.9
Canada	29	39	28	18	31			3.7	-0.6	0.8
Portugal	28	35	30	22	27			5.8	-0.7	0.4
Mexico	29	27	26	24	34			4.1	-0.9	0.9
Thailand	22	27	32	23	28			5.6	-0.7	1.0
Australia	34	42	32	20	27			5.3	-0.6	0.6
Czech Republic	36	34	34	25	25			3.3	-0.9	0.8
Uruguay	32	37	32	24	31			3.4	-0.9	1.1
Spain	30	35	36	24	35			3.6	-0.7	0.7
Sweden	26	36	33	20	28			2.2	-0.6	0.9
Denmark	32	43	28	20	27			1.1	-0.7	0.7
Tunisia	26	37	36	33	52			1.5	-0.6	0.3
Serbia	33	32	28	27	28			3.7	-0.5	0.6
Slovak Republic	39	34	34	25	28			1.8	-0.9	0.8
Italy	37	42	39	25	33			1.8	-1.1	0.6
Turkey	24	33	35	31	31			7.1	-0.8	0.7
Netherlands	27	42	36	19	39			1.7	-0.7	0.5
France	33	46	38	25	42			2.2	a	a
Finland	36	48	35	19	32			1.3	-0.8	0.5
Iceland	31	41	36	25	26			1.5	-0.9	0.9
New Zealand	38	47	37	23	31			3.5	-0.7	0.7
Luxembourg	35	48	43	39	35			2.8	-0.5	0.2
Greece	35	43	35	29	39			1.5	-0.8	0.3
Norway	34	41	36	28	36			1.2	-0.7	0.8
Brazil	35	38	38	30	63			3.5	-0.9	0.1
OECD average	*31*	*36*	*32*	*23*	*29*			*0.2*	*-0.8*	*0.9*
United Kingdom[3]	m	m	m	m	m			9.1	-0.7	0.7

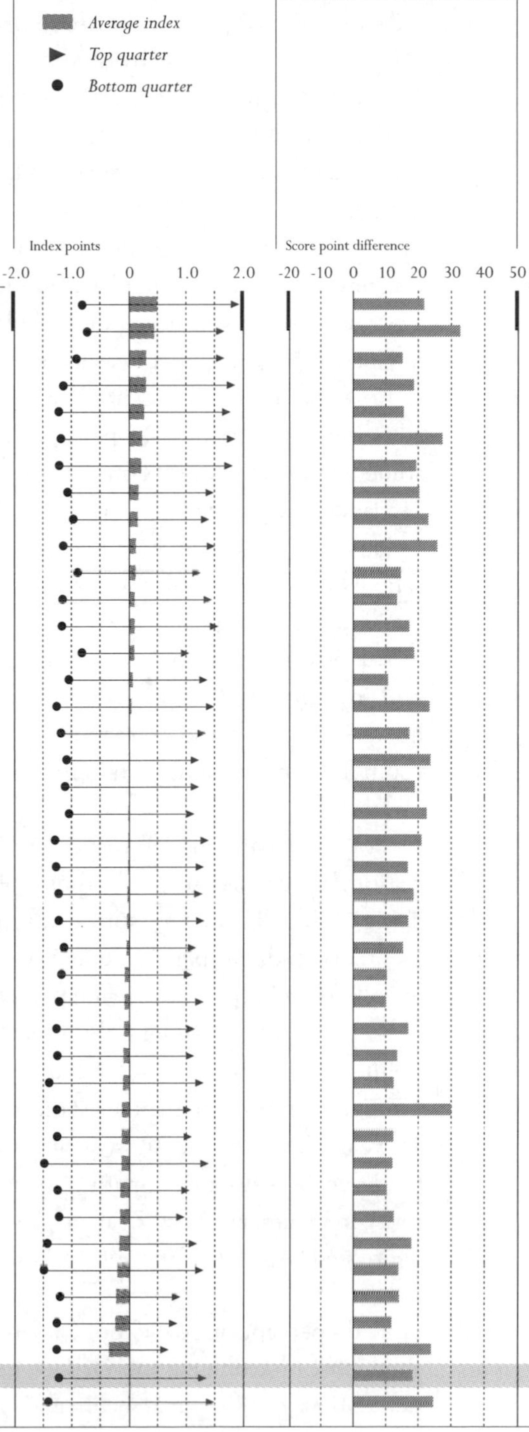

1. This is the school at the 5th percentile. In only 5% of schools is the disciplinary climate in mathematics more negative.
2. This is the school at the 95th percentile. The disciplinary climate in mathematics is more positive than in 95% of the other schools.
3. Response rate too low to ensure comparability (see Annex A3).
Source: OECD PISA 2003 database, Table 5.3a and Table 5.3b.

...but even countries with high overall ratings show room for improvement.

However, even in countries that compare relatively well internationally with regard to their perceived school climate, responses from principals do not suggest the absence of problems. Consider, for example, Japan and Korea, the two countries with the highest scores on the index that summarises principals' perceptions of student-related factors affecting school climate. In Japan, 39 per cent of 15-year-olds are enrolled in schools where principals report that learning is hindered to some or a great extent by student absenteeism (OECD average 48 per cent), 13 per cent of the students are in schools whose principals report that learning is hindered by disruption of classes by students (OECD average 40 per cent), 23 per cent of them indicate that learning is hindered by students skipping classes (OECD average 30 per cent), 32 per cent indicate that learning is hindered by students' lack of respect for teachers (OECD average 22 per cent), and 7 per cent indicate that learning is hindered by students intimidating or bullying other students (OECD average 15 per cent). The use of alcohol and illegal drugs is not considered a problem in Japan (1 per cent, OECD average 10 per cent). Similarly, 17 per cent of students in Korea are enrolled in schools where principals identify student absenteeism as a hindrance to learning, 18 per cent are in schools where disruption of classes by students is seen as a problem, 13 per cent are in schools where students' skipping of classes is identified as a problem, 23 per cent are in schools where students lacking respect for teachers is seen as a problem, 13 per cent of students are in schools where principals indicate that students use of alcohol and illegal drugs (up by 11 percentage points since 2000) is a hindrance to learning and 13 per cent of students are in schools where principals indicate that students intimidating or bullying other students (up by 10 percentage points since 2000) is an obstacle that hinders learning to some extent or a lot (Table 5.2b). This suggests that there is room for improvement even in the countries with the fewest problems.

Disciplinary problems appear to have worsened in some countries, while others saw improvements.

Overall the patterns of responses from students and school principals are reasonably consistent with those observed in PISA 2000 (Table 5.2b and Table 5.3b).[6] However, some differences are noteworthy. For example, in Denmark and the partner country Indonesia, the percentage of 15-year-olds enrolled in schools whose principals reported that learning was hindered to some extent or a lot by student absenteeism increased by more than 20 percentage points. In contrast, in Finland and Greece such problems are now much less frequently reported than was the case in 2000. Similarly, the percentage of 15-year-olds enrolled in schools whose principals reported that learning is hindered by students disrupting classes increased by 10 percentage points or more in Denmark, New Zealand, Poland and the partner country Indonesia, but decreased by similar amounts in Finland, Luxembourg and Portugal.

In schools where the reported climate is stronger, students tend to perform better.

How do perceptions of school climate relate to student performance? Figure 5.3 shows that, on average across OECD countries, one unit on the PISA index of student perceptions of disciplinary climate is associated with an increase in mathematics performance of 18 score points, and between 20 and 33 score points in Australia, Belgium, Hungary, Japan, Portugal, Turkey and the United States and in the partner countries Brazil, Hong Kong-China, Liechtenstein, the Russian Federation

and Thailand. The association between school principals' perceptions of student-related factors affecting school climate and student performance tends to be of similar magnitude. The questions of how these relationships operate, and what contextual and mediating factors may affect them, remain beyond the scope of this initial report and will require further research and analysis. At the cross-country level, there is a tendency for countries with more positive principals' perceptions of school climate to perform better, but the relationship explains only around 5 per cent of the cross-country variation in student performance in OECD countries and is thus not statistically significant. The situation is similar with regard to students' perception of disciplinary climate.

Teacher-related factors affecting the general school climate

Principals also reported on whether teachers' attitudes, behaviour and relationships with students affect learning…

Principals were also asked questions about their perceptions of teacher-related factors affecting the school climate. In particular, principals were asked to indicate the extent to which they perceived learning in their schools to be hindered by such factors as the teachers' low expectations of students, poor student-teacher relations, absenteeism among teachers, staff resistance to change, teachers not meeting individual students' needs, and students not being encouraged to achieve their full potential. The responses were combined to create a composite index of teacher-related factors affecting school climate. Positive values reflect principals' perceptions that teacher-related factors affecting school climate hinder learning to a lesser extent, and negative values that school principals believe teachers' behaviour to hinder learning to a greater extent compared to the OECD average.

…and although the picture was positive overall, in a minority of cases there are problems.

On average across OECD countries, school principals give a fairly positive picture of teacher-related factors affecting the school climate. Nevertheless, an average of 33 per cent of 15-year-olds are enrolled in schools whose principals consider that learning is hindered to some extent or a lot by teachers not meeting the needs of individual students. Less frequently mentioned obstacles to effective learning included staff resisting change (26 per cent), students not being encouraged to achieve their full potential (23 per cent), teachers low expectations of students (22 per cent), teacher absenteeism (19 per cent) and poor student-teacher relations (17 per cent) (Table 5.4b and Figure 5.4).

Teacher-related factors affecting school climate can also be compared across countries…

When the responses of principals are summarised on an index of principals' perceptions of teacher-related factors, school principals in Denmark, Hungary, Iceland, Korea, Poland, the Slovak Republic and Switzerland provide the most positive picture with regard to teacher-related factors affecting the school climate (shown by large positive index values), while principals in the Netherlands and Turkey, and in the partner countries Indonesia, Macao-China and Tunisia tend to report more problems (shown by large negative index values) (Table 5.4a).

…and the results show considerable variations both across and within countries.

In some countries, most notably in Canada, Greece, Hungary, Iceland, Italy, Korea, Mexico, Poland, Spain and Turkey, as well as in the partner countries Brazil, Hong Kong-China, Indonesia, Macao-China, the Russian Federation,

Figure 5.4 ■ Teacher-related factors affecting the school climate

Index of teacher-related factors affecting school climate: ▬ Average index; ► Top quarter; ● Bottom quarter (Index points: -4 -3 -2 -1 0 1 2 3)

Change in mathematics performance per unit of the index of teacher-related factors affecting school climate (Score point difference: -20 -10 0 10 20 30 40 50)

	Percentage of students in schools where the principals agree or strongly agree that the following things hinder students learning									
	Teachers' low expectations of students.	Poor student-teacher relations.	Teachers not meeting individual students' needs.	Teacher absenteeism.	Staff resisting change.	Teachers being too strict with students.	Students not being encouraged to achieve their full potential.	Percentage of explained variance in student performance	Principal's view on teacher-related factors affecting school climate in one of the schools with the most negative climate[1]	Principal's view on teacher-related factors affecting school climate in one of the schools with the most positive climate[2]
Slovak Republic	17	7	10	19	8	6	12	0.2	-0.9	1.7
Denmark	9	5	19	14	16	3	7	0.2	-0.6	2.5
Switzerland	8	11	21	5	23	3	11	2.0	-0.9	1.7
Hungary	9	17	23	21	4	12	23	0.2	-1.8	2.5
Poland	12	10	19	10	10	5	19	0.1	-1.1	2.5
Korea	32	14	28	11	17	8	27	1.5	-1.8	2.5
Iceland	14	8	39	32	13	1	11	0.1	-1.1	2.5
Belgium	8	9	22	22	27	3	15	1.5	-1.1	2.1
Spain	21	10	21	13	27	7	21	0.4	-1.1	2.5
Latvia	13	15	25	7	12	6	24	0.1	-0.9	2.5
Austria	16	9	21	14	17	7	22	0.0	-1.1	1.7
Czech Republic	9	7	13	23	10	10	20	0.4	-0.9	1.7
Brazil	28	19	27	27	24	13	28	0.6	-1.8	2.5
Sweden	12	11	33	16	31	2	16	0.2	-1.1	1.7
Finland	7	14	35	20	13	6	16	0.0	-1.1	1.3
Italy	12	34	28	10	37	13	25	0.4	-1.1	2.5
Canada	11	12	33	8	33	8	16	0.7	-1.3	2.5
Thailand	38	13	37	12	10	26	17	0.6	-1.3	2.5
Germany	10	14	31	23	25	3	23	0.1	-1.1	1.3
United States	24	14	32	13	34	5	13	1.8	-1.1	1.3
Ireland	30	15	47	30	28	9	21	1.1	-1.3	1.3
Australia	31	15	48	16	34	7	19	2.9	-1.1	1.3
New Zealand	40	18	46	8	23	6	24	2.6	-1.3	1.7
Japan	32	23	34	4	42	21	37	13.3	-1.5	1.7
Serbia	33	21	45	20	41	20	44	0.5	-1.5	1.7
Mexico	41	24	35	27	40	27	46	1.0	-1.8	2.5
Greece	45	41	43	40	31	23	29	0.8	-3.4	2.5
Luxembourg	9	29	56	5	19	14	37	0.2	-1.3	0.6
Norway	20	22	72	24	35	4	24	0.0	-1.3	1.3
Hong Kong-China	43	24	44	21	31	20	40	0.4	-3.0	1.3
Portugal	44	16	45	30	44	2	35	0.2	-1.5	1.3
Uruguay	50	22	34	64	41	21	47	0.2	-2.0	2.5
Russian Fed.	52	45	40	51	38	56	42	1.9	-2.6	1.3
Netherlands	39	20	56	46	60	18	40	1.6	-1.8	0.6
Turkey	61	58	46	37	46	34	63	0.3	-2.4	1.3
Macao-China	59	44	60	37	48	45	56	0.2	-2.7	2.5
Tunisia	84	66	75	74	45	45	60	0.2	-3.0	0.6
Indonesia	75	73	76	78	61	72	74	0.0	-4.2	1.3
OECD average	*22*	*17*	*33*	*19*	*26*	*9*	*23*	*0.9*	*-1.5*	*2.5*
United Kingdom[3]	m	m	m	m	m	m	m	3.7	-1.5	1.7

1. This is the school at the 5th percentile. In only 5% of schools are teacher-related factors affecting school climate more negative.
2. This is the school at the 95th percentile. Teacher-related factors affecting school climate are more positive than in 95% of the other schools.
3. Response rate too low to ensure comparability (see Annex A3).
Source: OECD PISA 2003 database, Table 5.4a and Table 5.4b.

Thailand, Tunisia and Uruguay, schools vary considerably in school principals' perceptions of teacher-related factors affecting school climate. To the extent that school principals' perceptions reflect the reality in schools, this suggests that in these countries, staff problems might be localised and targeted policy strategies might be appropriate. The last two columns in Figure 5.4 provide an indication of the variation among schools in teacher-related factors affecting school climate: 5 per cent of 15-year-olds are enrolled in schools where teacher-related factors have been rated worse than the value shown in the first column, and 5 per cent are in schools where teacher-related factors have been rated better than the value shown in the second column. The larger the difference between these two figures, the more variation there is between schools in principals' perceptions of teacher-related factors affecting the school climate.

As one would expect, in most countries the relationship between school principals' perceptions of teacher-related factors affecting school climate and mathematics performance tends to be positive, *i.e.*, the greater the concern with teacher-related factors affecting school climate, the lower the student performance in mathematics. However, in most countries, the relationship is not very strong.

Also at the cross-country level, there is a tendency for countries with more positive principals' perceptions of teacher-related factors affecting school climate to perform better, but the relationship explains only 14 per cent of the cross-country variation in student performance among OECD countries and is thus not statistically significant.

In most countries, the picture remained similar from the one observed in 2000.

In most countries, the views school principals offered on teacher-related factors affecting general school climate in the PISA 2003 survey were fairly similar to those observed in the PISA 2000 survey. However, there are some exceptions (Table 5.4b). Notably in Greece, school principals viewed teacher-related factors affecting school climate more positively in 2003 than in 2000. For example, in Greece, the proportion of 15-year-olds enrolled in schools where principals reported learning to be hindered to some extent or a lot by poor student-teacher relations dropped significantly from 62 per cent to 41 per cent.[7] Similarly, for the questions relating to students not being encouraged to achieve their full potential, teacher absenteeism, teachers not meeting individual students' needs, the drop amounted to 32, 27 and 24 percentage points, respectively. In contrast, views of school principals were more negative in 2003 in at least three of the four aspects in Canada, the Czech Republic, Denmark, Japan, and New Zealand as well as in the partner countries Hong Kong-China and Indonesia.

For example, in Japan the proportion of 15-year-olds enrolled in schools whose principals report learning to be hindered to some extent or a lot by staff resisting change increased significantly from 19 per cent in 2000 to 42 per cent in 2003. Similarly, for the questions relating to teachers being

too strict with students, and teachers not meeting individual students' needs Japanese school principals reported an increase of 17 and 14 percentage points, respectively. Such figures need, however, to be interpreted with regard to the context in which schools operate. For example, in countries where a higher percentage of school principals report that staff are resisting change, this could simply reflect the fact that between 2000 and 2003 significant changes and reforms affecting teachers' work were introduced that pose new challenges for teachers. In contrast, a low percentage of school principals reporting that staff are resisting change might be a reflection of limited change in the education system (Table 5.4b).

Principals generally provide a positive assessments of teachers' morale and commitment...

In addition to questions on teacher-related factors affecting school climate, school principals were asked to provide their views on teachers' morale and commitment. To do so, they were asked to indicate how strongly they agreed or disagreed with the following statements concerning the teachers in their school: "teachers work with enthusiasm", "teachers take pride in this school" and "the morale of teachers in this school is high". Overall, school principals have very positive views on teachers' morale. The percentage of 15-year-olds enrolled in schools where school principals agree or strongly agree that teachers' morale is high in their school was lower than 80 per cent only in Italy, Portugal and Spain. Similarly, Greece, Italy, Portugal, the Slovak Republic and Turkey, and the partner countries Brazil and Serbia were countries where less than 85 per cent of 15-year-olds are enrolled in schools whose principals report that teachers work with enthusiasm. In all participating countries around 80 per cent or more of 15-year-olds are enrolled in schools whose principals report that teachers take pride in their school and value academic achievement (Figure 5.5 and Table 5.5b).

From the responses, an index of principals' perceptions of teachers' morale and commitment was created, with an OECD country average of zero and a standard deviation of one, with higher index values indicating greater perceived morale and commitment. Austria, Denmark, Finland, Iceland, Sweden and the partner country Indonesia have the highest positive values indicating, in the opinion of principals, high morale and commitment among their teachers. In contrast, principals in Italy, Korea and Portugal and in the partner countries Macao-China and Serbia report comparatively low levels of morale and commitment of their teachers (Figure 5.5 and Table 5.5a).

...while they tended to rate students' morale and enthusiasm somewhat lower than that of teachers.

School principals' perceptions of students' morale, as measured by the index of principals' perceptions of students' morale and commitment, tended to be lower than their perceptions of teachers' morale and commitment (Table 5.6a). For example, the percentage of 15-year-olds enrolled in schools whose principals report that students work with enthusiasm was, on average across OECD countries, 17 per cent lower than the corresponding percentage for teachers and in the Czech Republic, Germany, Hungary, Luxembourg, Poland and Spain, students' ratings lagged behind those of teachers by 30 percentage points or more (Table 5.5b and Table 5.6b).

Figure 5.5 ■ Teachers' morale and commitment

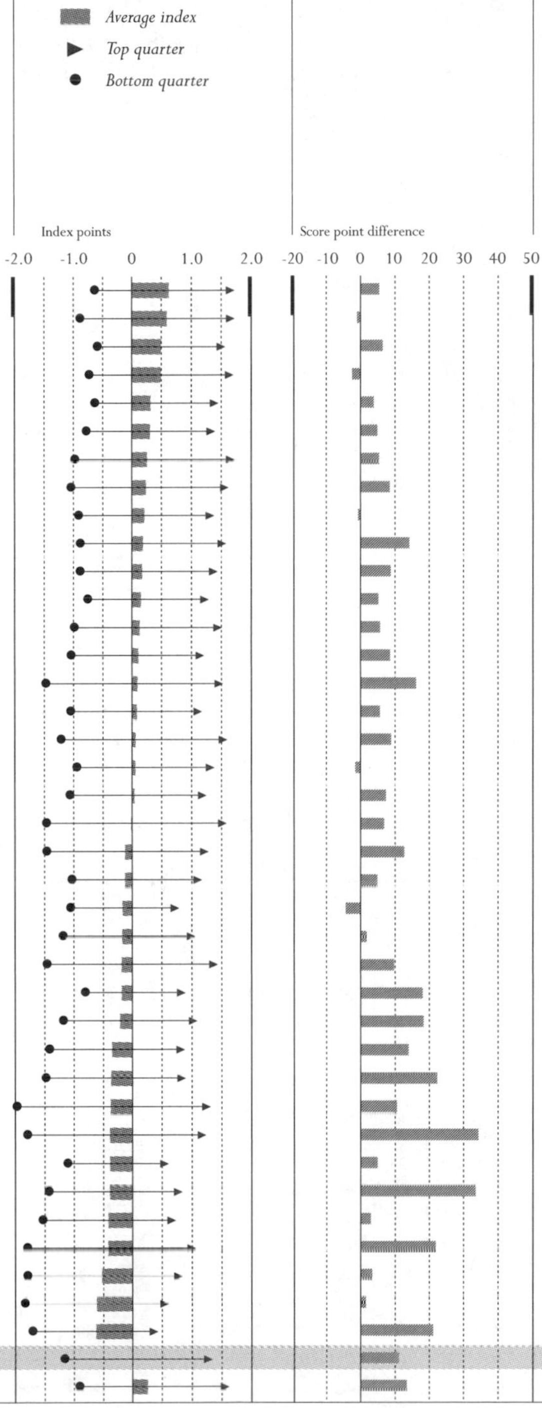

	Percentage of students in schools where the principals agree or strongly agree with the following statements about the teachers in the school				Index of teachers' morale and commitment	Change in mathematics performance per unit of the index of teachers' morale and commitment			
	The morale of teachers in this school is high.	Teachers work with enthusiasm.	Teachers take pride in this school.	Teachers value academic achievement.	Index points	Score point difference	Percentage of explained variance in student performance	Principal's view on teachers' morale and commitment in one of the schools with the lowest levels[1]	Principal's view on teachers' morale and commitment in one of the schools with the highest levels[2]
Iceland	99	99	98	99			0.3	-0.6	1.7
Indonesia	98	94	96	99			0.0	-1.4	1.7
Sweden	99	100	96	99			0.3	-0.6	1.7
Austria	98	99	97	99			0.1	-0.6	1.7
Denmark	99	100	99	98			0.1	-0.6	1.7
Finland	98	96	96	99			0.3	-0.6	1.7
Ireland	88	97	95	99			0.4	-1.8	1.7
United States	88	95	96	99			0.9	-1.8	1.7
Switzerland	94	99	94	98			0.0	-1.4	1.7
Australia	90	97	98	100			2.1	-1.4	1.7
New Zealand	91	98	98	97			0.7	-1.4	1.7
Latvia	99	98	98	96			0.2	-1.4	1.7
Canada	88	95	97	99			0.4	-1.4	1.7
Hungary	96	87	96	100			0.7	-1.4	1.7
Greece	87	84	87	99			4.0	-2.2	1.7
Poland	81	97	95	99			0.3	-1.4	1.7
Tunisia	93	90	95	92			1.4	-1.8	1.7
Norway	98	95	91	100			0.0	-1.4	1.7
Germany	97	96	90	97			0.4	-1.4	1.7
Mexico	91	90	87	92			0.9	-1.8	1.7
Brazil	90	83	94	94			1.9	-1.8	1.7
Uruguay	98	91	95	98			0.2	-1.4	1.7
Czech Republic	96	86	97	99			0.1	-1.8	1.0
Slovak Republic	98	82	94	99			0.0	-1.5	1.7
Thailand	89	87	92	91			1.8	-2.2	1.7
Netherlands	98	100	97	97			2.0	-1.4	1.7
Russian Fed.	93	87	97	98			3.1	-1.8	1.7
Spain	79	90	93	97			2.0	-1.8	1.7
Hong Kong-China	86	95	87	95			4.3	-1.8	1.0
Turkey	82	81	85	84			1.6	-2.8	1.7
Japan	90	94	80	75			15.6	-1.8	1.7
Luxembourg	92	92	86	100			0.1	-1.8	1.0
Belgium	87	93	95	91			7.2	-1.8	1.7
Portugal	71	85	97	99			0.1	-1.8	1.0
Korea	80	93	85	87			6.3	1.8	1.7
Serbia	87	65	85	95			0.2	2.2	1.0
Italy	75	81	87	94			0.0	-2.2	1.0
Macao-China	82	97	83	92			4.3	-2.2	1.0
OECD average	*87*	*90*	*90*	*93*			*1.2*	***-1.8***	***1.7***
United Kingdom[3]	m	m	m	m			2.1	1.4	1.7

Index of teachers' morale and commitment: Average index; Top quarter; Bottom quarter. Index points: -2.0, -1.0, 0, 1.0, 2.0.

Change in mathematics performance: Score point difference: -20, -10, 0, 10, 20, 30, 40, 50.

1. This is the school at the 5th percentile. In only 5% of schools is teachers' morale and commitment lower.
2. This is the school at the 95th percentile. Teachers' morale and commitment is higher than in 95% of the other schools.
3. Response rate too low to ensure comparability (see Annex A3).
Source: OECD PISA 2003 database, Table 5.5a and Table 5.5b.

Figure 5.6 ■ Students' morale and commitment

Percentage of students in schools where the principals agree or strongly agree with the following statements about the students in the school | Index of students' morale and commitment (Index points; Average index, Top quarter, Bottom quarter; scale -4 to 3) | Change in mathematics performance per unit of the index of students' morale and commitment (Score point difference; scale -20 to 50)

	Students enjoy being in school.	Students work with enthusiasm.	Students take pride in this school.	Students value academic achievement.	Students are co-operative and respectful.	Students value the education they can receive in this school.	Students do their best to learn as much as possible.	Percentage of explained variance in student performance	Principal's view on students' morale and commitment in one of the schools with the lowest levels[1]	Principal's view on students' morale and commitment in one of the schools with the highest levels[2]
Indonesia	98	96	99	99	99	99	94	0.0	-0.5	2.6
Thailand	99	88	98	99	100	99	95	0.4	-0.9	2.6
Australia	99	90	94	90	98	96	85	6.1	-1.2	2.6
Canada	99	94	94	94	97	95	90	2.4	-1.2	2.6
New Zealand	100	92	96	90	97	96	84	1.8	-1.5	2.6
United States	99	89	95	92	96	94	84	3.3	-1.5	1.4
Mexico	95	89	96	90	88	88	83	1.1	-1.2	2.6
Ireland	99	83	94	93	98	93	84	3.2	-1.2	1.6
Tunisia	98	76	94	84	85	82	78	0.4	-1.8	2.6
Japan	99	76	81	78	90	82	67	21.1	-2.2	2.6
Sweden	98	88	85	93	97	90	85	1.3	-1.2	2.6
Iceland	100	93	95	89	95	86	73	0.2	-1.5	1.6
Denmark	99	93	95	87	93	95	84	1.6	-1.2	2.0
Austria	97	85	90	82	93	91	72	4.2	-1.5	1.6
Brazil	94	84	92	77	87	88	66	4.4	-1.5	1.4
Finland	99	90	87	94	97	90	64	0.9	-1.2	1.4
Greece	78	65	89	90	93	86	60	4.5	-2.2	1.6
Macao-China	97	75	94	97	97	96	55	4.2	-1.5	1.6
Poland	97	65	96	95	89	87	71	0.4	-1.5	1.4
Switzerland	98	80	79	92	96	90	77	1.8	-1.5	1.4
Italy	79	64	88	96	86	95	67	2.5	-1.5	1.4
Portugal	100	76	95	88	91	86	60	1.2	-1.8	1.1
Russian Fed.	98	57	97	89	88	98	81	4.2	-1.5	1.1
Korea	86	65	81	73	93	81	70	15.1	-1.8	2.6
Turkey	88	57	89	75	89	87	64	5.4	-2.2	2.0
Norway	100	77	82	91	94	87	69	0.1	-1.5	1.1
Netherlands	95	87	86	90	89	91	67	7.6	-1.5	1.1
Hong Kong-China	99	71	86	75	94	95	57	17.1	-1.8	1.4
Latvia	100	72	99	95	91	96	39	1.4	-1.2	1.1
Uruguay	91	71	90	78	93	86	53	0.1	-1.5	1.4
Belgium	99	76	87	77	92	89	68	10.3	-1.8	0.8
Slovak Republic	89	59	89	93	88	91	35	1.9	-1.8	0.8
Czech Republic	91	49	92	94	93	86	51	1.5	-1.2	0.8
Hungary	93	53	93	59	84	90	32	9.4	-1.8	1.1
Spain	97	54	92	77	81	89	35	6.1	-1.5	0.8
Germany	99	63	71	63	88	88	40	3.8	-1.8	1.1
Luxembourg	100	40	88	81	93	94	45	6.0	-1.5	0.0
Serbia	45	40	74	69	69	87	39	2.9	-2.8	1.1
OECD average	*92*	*73*	*86*	*83*	*89*	*87*	*65*	*3.3*	*-1.5*	*1.6*
United Kingdom[3]	m	m	m	m	m	m	m	5.0	-1.5	2.6

1. This is the school at the 5th percentile. In only 5% of schools is students' morale and commitment lower.
2. This is the school at the 95th percentile. Students' morale and commitment is higher than in 95% of the other schools.
3. Response rate too low to ensure comparability (see Annex A3).
Source: OECD PISA 2003 database, Table 5.6a and Table 5.6b.

The relationship between school principals' perceptions of teachers' morale and commitment and their students' scores in mathematics literacy tends to be weak. However, there are countries where the association is stronger, most notably Belgium, Japan and Korea, where it explains between 6 and 15 per cent of the performance variation (Table 5.5a). A stronger relationship is found between school's principals' perceptions of students' morale and commitment. In these same countries, students' morale and commitment explains between 20 and 21 per cent of the performance variation (Table 5.6a). At the cross-country level, the relationship between principals' perception of teachers' morale and commitment and student performance tends to be weak as well, and there is no cross-country relationship between school principals' perception of students' morale and commitment and country performance.

The combined effect of school climate factors

Since the various factors of school climate that were described above are interrelated, it is not possible to estimate the total impact of school climate on student performance by simply adding these factors up. Only a joint examination of the various factors of school climate makes it possible to estimate their collective impact on student and school performance.

The joint effect of these climate factors on performance can be identified…

In such an analysis, it is also important to consider the extent to which differences in the performance of schools are associated with socio-economic factors. As shown in Chapter 4, socio-economic factors play a role both at the level of individual students and through the aggregate context they provide for learning in schools, for example, if students from more advantaged backgrounds choose better schools or because they actively create better schooling conditions, by creating a learning climate that is more conducive to learning. To examine this, the following analysis takes into account both the individual socio-economic background of students, as measured by the PISA index of economic, social and cultural status, and the socio-economic intake of the school, as measured by the average PISA index of economic, social and cultural status for the school.

…but one also needs to take account the fact that more advantaged students may attend schools with better climates.

This leads to the question of how to account for the influence of socio-economic factors in interpreting the PISA results. One approach is to examine the impact of school factors after an adjustment for socio-economic differences. Such an adjustment allows a comparison of schools that are operating in similar socio-economic contexts. However, the net effects resulting from such an adjustment is likely to understate the true effect of school climate because some of the performance differences are jointly attributable to school factors and socio-economic status, as is, for example, the case when socio-economically advantaged students create a school climate that is more conducive to learning.

This can be done by considering climate factors after controlling for socio-economic differences…

Conversely, the interpretation of the school factors without an adjustment for socio-economic factors may overstate their importance and ignores differences in the socio-economic composition of schools. That said, the unadjusted gross effects may give a more realistic picture of the choices that parents face if

…but this underestimates the way in which school climate and social background interact.

they wish to select a school for their children. Parents and other stakeholders, for example, are naturally most interested in the overall performance results of schools, including any effects that are conferred by the socio-economic intake of schools, whereas the added value that schools provide may only be a secondary consideration for them.

In fact, the PISA results show that most of the influence of climate factors is felt in combination with socio-economic factors…

The following analysis incorporates both aspects. When socio-economic background at student and school levels as well as the school climate factors assessed by PISA are considered jointly, 46 per cent of the performance variation among schools is attributable to socio-economic background (see column 1 in Table 5.7), 5 per cent to the school climate factors net of socio-economic factors (see column 2 in Table 5.7), and 22 per cent to the combined influence of socio-economic background and school climate (see column 3 in Table 5.7), on average across OECD countries.[8]

…as, for example, when better-off families manage to help create schools with a better learning climate.

It is apparent from this that socio-economic factors seem to reinforce the impact school climate has on school performance in important ways, perhaps because students from more advantaged socio-economic backgrounds bring with them a higher level of discipline and more positive perceptions of school values, or perhaps because parental expectations of good classroom discipline and strong teacher commitment are higher in schools with advantaged socio-economic intake. Conversely, disadvantaged schools may experience less parental pressure towards enforcing effective disciplinary practices or making sure that absent or unmotivated teachers are replaced. Thus, a large joint influence of socio-economic background and school climate should be of concern for policy makers seeking to ensure that all schools have committed teachers and an orderly climate, irrespective of their socio-economic intake.

In some countries nearly half of variation in performance across schools is accounted for by the joint effect of student background and school climate.

In this regard, it is noteworthy that in some countries the joint influence of socio-economic background and school climate is much larger than at the OECD average level. For example, the net effect of school climate on student performance explains only between 1.4 and 7.5 per cent of the performance variation among schools in Australia, Belgium, Germany, Japan, Korea, the Netherlands and Spain, but when the socio-economic context of students and schools is considered as well, the resulting gross effect increases to between 29 per cent in Spain and 49 per cent in Belgium, with these seven countries having the highest values among OECD countries. Figure 5.7 illustrates the relative magnitude of the three effects in a multilevel model.

Obviously, results on the extent to which performance variation among schools is accounted for by school factors needs to be interpreted in the context of how much performance varies among schools in the first place. For example, among the seven countries examined here, in Australia and Spain schools differ much less in their performance than schools in Belgium, Germany, Japan, Korea and the Netherlands. As a result, even if the share of the performance variation among schools that is accounted for by disciplinary climate socio-economic context is comparatively large in Australia and Spain, its total impact on student

performance is much smaller than in Belgium, Germany, Japan, Korea and the Netherlands. To aid in the interpretation of the results, Figure 5.7 also indicates the magnitude of performance differences among schools in each country.

Figure 5.7 ■ **Impact of school climate on school performance in mathematics**

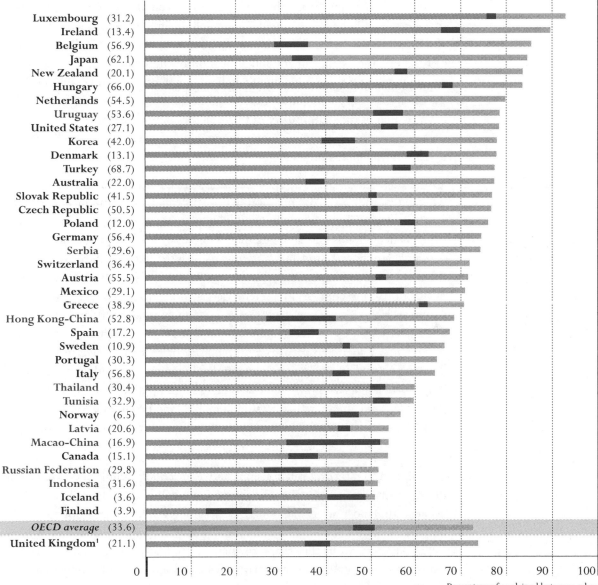

Note: The numbers in the brackets indicate between-school variance expressed as a percentage of the average variance in student performance across OECD countries.

1. Response rate too low to ensure comparability (see Annex A3).

Source: OECD PISA 2003 database, Table 5.7.

SCHOOL POLICIES AND PRACTICES

This section takes the discussion further, by examining school policies and practices through which schools often seek to make a difference.

PISA asked principals about a range of policies and practices that may influence student performance.

Although PISA was able to capture only a limited range of school policies and practices that could be easily quantified by school principals and compared across countries, it provides information on school admittance policies and policies used to group students; the use of assessments at school and the nature of the instruments used to that end, such as standardised assessments, teacher-developed tests, teachers' judgemental ratings; offerings of enrichment and remedial instruction and other mathematics-related activities organised by the school; and the involvement of the school in various aspects of decision making, including aspects relating to resource management, such as the hiring of teachers, the establishment and allocation of the school budget, and aspects relating to content and instruction, such as course content and courses offered, the choice of textbooks and assessment policies. The section concludes with an examination of the joint impact of these factors on performance.

School admittance policies

In some countries most 15-year-olds are in schools that use academic selection; in others only a small minority.

To assess academic selectivity of education systems, school principals were asked to what extent they give consideration, when students are admitted to their school, to students' academic records (including placement tests), recommendations from feeder schools and students' needs or desires for a specific programme.[9] Among these criteria, students' academic records tended to be the most frequently reported one. However, whereas in Austria, the Czech Republic, Hungary, Japan, Korea, Luxembourg, the Netherlands and Switzerland and in the partner countries Hong Kong-China, Indonesia, Macao-China, and Serbia, more than half of 15-year-olds are enrolled in schools whose principals report that consideration of students' academic records is a prerequisite or at least of high priority when deciding on student admittance, in Australia, Denmark, Finland, Greece, Ireland, Italy, Portugal, Spain and Sweden, it is less than 10 per cent (OECD average 25 per cent). Students' needs or desires for a specific programme follow with an OECD average of 21 per cent and recommendations from feeder schools follow with an OECD average of 13 per cent (Table 5.8 and Figure 5.8).

It is difficult to interpret relationships between schools' admittance policies and their performance, because more selective schools may perform better simply because they do not accept poorly performing students, and not necessarily because they provide better services. A discussion on this is therefore deferred to the last section in this chapter where the effect of academic selectivity is considered after other indicators of policies and practices have been accounted for. At the cross-country level, the prevalence of some of the attributes of academic selectivity, including the use of students' academic record or recommendations from feeder schools tend to be positively related to country performance, but only weakly and not statistically significantly so, with between 6 and 10 per cent of the cross-country performance variation explained.

Figure 5.8 ■ **School admittance policies**

Percentage of students in schools where the principals consider the following as a prerequisite or a high priority for admittance at their school

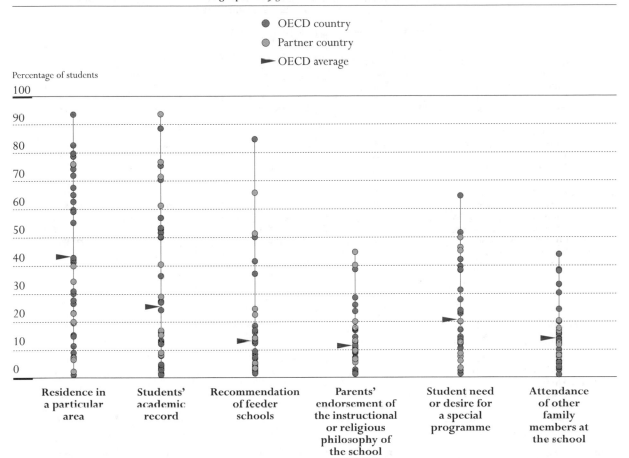

Source: OECD PISA 2003 database, Table 5.8.

Assessment policies and practices

The way student progress is monitored and assessed can influence performance…

The shift in public and governmental concern away from mere control over the resources and content of education toward a focus on outcomes has, in many countries, driven the establishment of standards for the quality of the work of educational institutions. Approaches range from the definition of broad educational goals up to the formulation of concise performance expectations in well-defined subject areas. Such performance standards can only work if their implementation is consistently monitored. Not surprisingly therefore, assessments of student performance are now common in many OECD countries – and often the results are widely reported and used in public debate as well as by those concerned with school improvement. However, the rationale for assessments and the nature of the instruments used to this end vary widely within and across countries. Methods employed in OECD countries include standardised as well as teacher-developed tests and teachers' judgemental ratings.

Figure 5.9 ■ **Methods of assessment and mathematics performance**

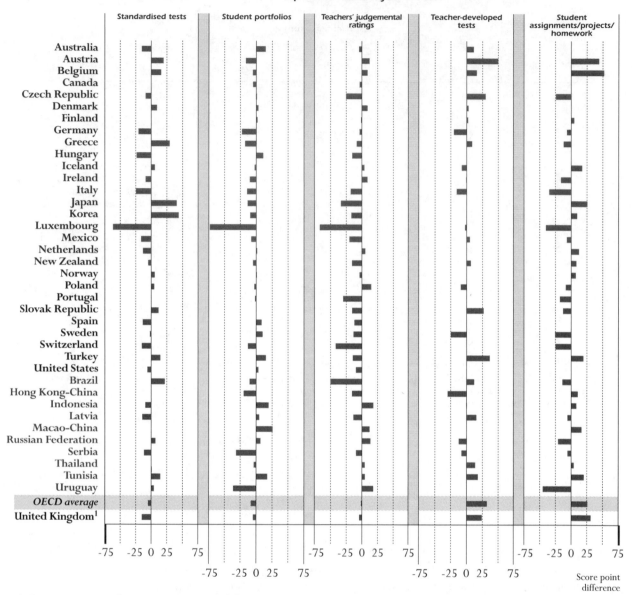

Performance differences in mathematics between schools where the principals report having used the following methods of assessment at least three times a year and those who report two times a year or less

Standardised tests | Student portfolios | Teachers' judgemental ratings | Teacher-developed tests | Student assignments/projects/homework

Australia, Austria, Belgium, Canada, Czech Republic, Denmark, Finland, Germany, Greece, Hungary, Iceland, Ireland, Italy, Japan, Korea, Luxembourg, Mexico, Netherlands, New Zealand, Norway, Poland, Portugal, Slovak Republic, Spain, Sweden, Switzerland, Turkey, United States, Brazil, Hong Kong-China, Indonesia, Latvia, Macao-China, Russian Federation, Serbia, Thailand, Tunisia, Uruguay, *OECD average*, United Kingdom[1]

-75 -25 0 25 75

Score point difference

1. Response rate too low to ensure comparability (see Annex A3).
Source: OECD PISA 2003 database, Table 5.9.

...and while a quarter of students are tested frequently, a quarter never undergo standardised assessment.

On average across OECD countries, 23 per cent of 15-year-olds are enrolled in schools where standardised tests are used at least three times per year and in Korea, New Zealand and the partner country Tunisia, this is the case for more than half the students (Table 5.9). By contrast, an equal proportion report never using standardised assessments for 15-year-olds and in Austria, Belgium, Germany and Switzerland this is the case for half or more of 15-year-olds (see *www.pisa.oecd.org* for data).

Student portfolios are another form of assessment that, on average across OECD countries, tends to be more frequently used than standardised assessments. On average across OECD countries, 43 per cent of school principals report that student portfolios are used at least three times per year to assess 15-year-olds and in Denmark, Iceland, Japan, Mexico, Spain and the partner country Brazil this applies to between 75 and 96 per cent (Table 5.9).

Portfolio assessment is used more frequently…

Even more frequently used to assess 15-year-olds are teachers' judgemental ratings, which on average across OECD countries are applied to 75 per cent of students enrolled at least three times per year. Finally, 92 per cent of students are in schools that report using teacher-developed tests to assess 15-year-olds (Table 5.9).

…and teacher judgements more often still.

It is difficult to relate the use of assessments to learning outcomes at the national level, not only because such assessments differ widely in nature and quality, but also because assessment policies and practices are often applied differentially across school and programme types. However, for the use of teacher-developed tests there is a tendency for schools in which these assessments are applied more frequently to perform better. For example, on average across OECD countries, students in schools that report using teacher-developed tests two times or less per year scored an average of 471 points on the mathematics scale and those in schools where teacher-developed tests are used three times or more per year scored at 503 score points (Table 5.9).

Students who are set teacher-developed tests more frequently tend to perform better…

The picture is more mixed for the use of standardised tests. The frequency with which standardised tests are used tends to be positively related with school performance in Greece, Japan and Korea, while a negative relationship is observed in Italy, Luxembourg, the Netherlands and the partner country Latvia. For the use of teachers' judgemental ratings and student portfolios the relationship tends to be weaker and no clear pattern emerges. It is difficult to shed light on this with the limited information that PISA provides, and an examination how the use of different assessment instruments can contribute to raising performance levels requires further research and analysis. At the cross-country level, the relationship between the frequency of the use of the various assessment practices and country performance is mixed as well, with only a more frequent use of teacher-developed tests and student assignments/projects/homework showing a clear positive relationship with country performance.

…but the effect of other assessment forms is less clear-cut.

There is considerable debate as to how results from assessments can best be harnessed to raise educational aspirations, establish transparency over educational objectives and content, and provide a reference framework for teachers to understand and foster student learning. Some countries see assessments primarily as tools to provide feedback to individual students, to reveal best practices and to identify shared problems in order to encourage teachers and schools to improve and develop more supportive and productive learning environments. Others extend their purpose to support contestability of public services or market-mechanisms in the allocation of resources,

Some countries see tests mainly as tools for teachers, others as ways of making them more widely accountable…

e.g., by making comparative results of schools publicly available to facilitate parental choice or by having funds following students.

...and PISA reveals large differences in the degree to which results from tests are used to compare schools...

The PISA data confirm these differences in objectives and strategies. On average across OECD countries, 40 per cent of 15-year-olds are enrolled in schools that report using assessments to compare the performance of their school with that of other schools. However, while in Belgium, Denmark, Ireland, Luxembourg and the partner country Uruguay this is 10 per cent or less and in Germany, Greece, Japan, Spain, Switzerland and the partner country Macao-China it is still only between 12 and 17 per cent, in Hungary, New Zealand, the United States and the partner country Indonesia more than 70 per cent of 15-year-olds are enrolled in schools who report using assessments for such benchmarking (Figure 5.10). Similarly, in Hungary, Iceland, New Zealand, Poland, Sweden and the United States more than 70 per cent of 15-year-olds are enrolled in schools that use assessments to compare the school to performance levels at district or national levels, while this is only between 6 and 12 per cent in Austria, Belgium, Greece and the partner country Macao-China (Table 5.10 and Figure 5.10). In some of these countries, corresponding instruments simply do not exist so that students cannot compare themselves, even if they wish to do so.[10]

...and in the extent to which they are used to judge teachers...

The use of assessments for making judgements of teachers' effectiveness varies across countries. On average across OECD countries, 44 per cent of 15-year-olds are enrolled in schools reporting such practices, but this ranges from only 4 and 11 per cent in Denmark and Germany to more than 80 per cent in Japan and in the partner countries Indonesia and Latvia, and reaches 99 per cent of students in the Russian Federation.

...even if some monitoring functions are more common among countries.

More frequent uses of assessments relate to monitoring schools' progress (OECD average 69 per cent), making decisions about students' retention or promotion (OECD average 79 per cent) or to inform parents about their children's progress. With the exception of Denmark and the partner country Tunisia, at least 85 per cent of 15-year-olds are enrolled in schools that use assessment for this purpose (OECD average 95 per cent).

How do these policies and practices influence student performance? Again, this is difficult to answer, most notably because the use of results from assessments is often closely interrelated with other school policies and practices (see the last section in this chapter), but also because the relationship with performance is quite different across OECD countries. In Belgium, Japan, Korea, the Netherlands and the partner country Indonesia, for example, schools that compare assessment results with the performance at district or national level perform better – by between 20 and 50 score points – than those who do not and, at the OECD average level, a statistically significant performance advantage of 9 score points remains for countries that use assessment for this purpose (Table 5.10). In contrast, a statistically significant negative relationship exists in Luxembourg. On average across OECD countries, an advantage also emerges for schools that use assessment results to make decisions about students' retention

or promotion and those that use assessments to inform parents about their child's progress. However, here also the picture is uneven across countries.

Figure 5.10 ■ **Percentage of students in schools where the principals report using assessment results for the following purposes**

Results based on reports from school principals and reported proportionate to the number of 15-year-olds enrolled in the school

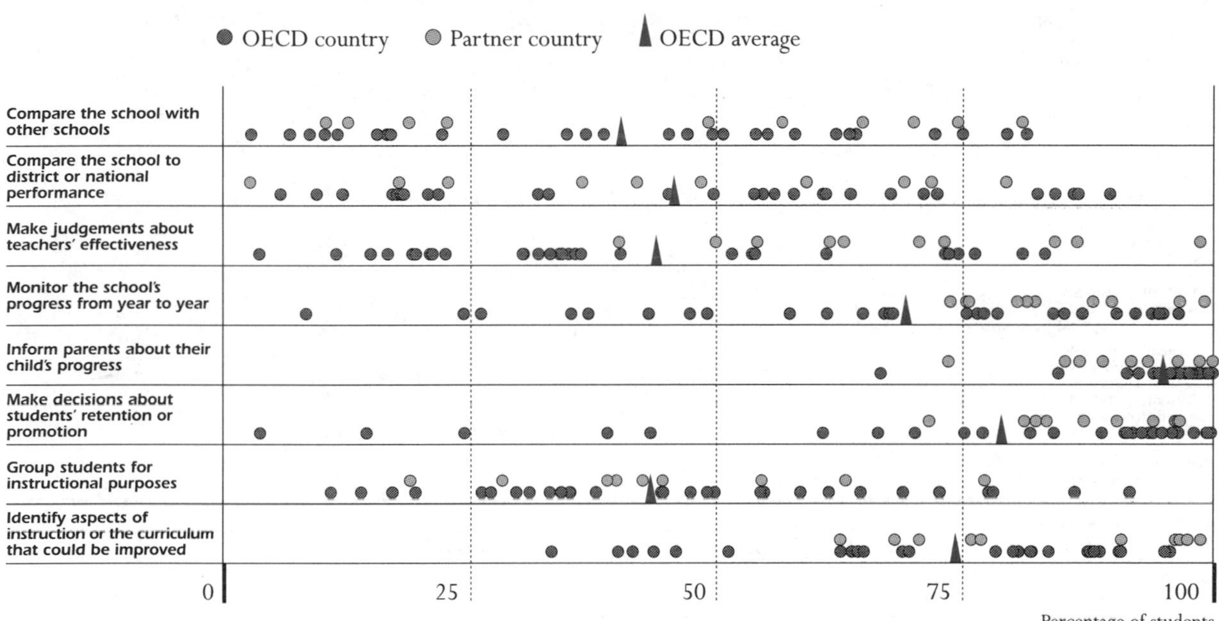

Source: OECD PISA 2003 database, Table 5.10.

Approaches to school management

Improved autonomy can help school management, but some fear it could reinforce privilege.

Increased autonomy over a wide range of institutional operations, with the objective to raise performance levels through devolving responsibility to the frontline and encouraging responsiveness to local needs, has been a main aim of the restructuring and systemic reform since the early 1980s. This has involved enhancing the decision-making responsibility and accountability of principals and, in some cases, the management responsibilities of teachers or department heads. Nonetheless, while school autonomy may stimulate responsiveness to local requirements, it is sometimes seen as creating mechanisms for choice favouring groups in society that are already advantaged.

PISA asked about where a range of responsibilities lie…

In order to gauge the extent to which school staff have a say in decisions relating to school policy and management, principals were asked to report whether teachers, department heads, the principal or an appointed or elected board had responsibility for appointing teachers, dismissing teachers, establishing teachers' starting salaries, determining teachers' salary increases, formulating school budgets, allocating budgets within the school, establishing student disciplinary policies, establishing student assessment policies, approving students for admittance to school, choosing which textbooks to use, determining course content and deciding which courses were offered.

Figure 5.11 ■ **Involvement of schools in decision-making**

Percentage of students in schools where the principals report that schools have responsibility for the following aspects of school policy and management

Source: OECD PISA 2003 database, Tables 5.11a and 5.11b.

Figure 5.11 shows the percentage of students enrolled in schools whose principals have responsibility for various aspects of school management.[11]

...and results show that schools tend to have little control over teacher salaries...

Unlike private sector enterprises, Table 5.11a shows that schools in most countries have little say in the establishment of teachers' starting salaries. Except for Hungary, Mexico, the Netherlands, the Slovak Republic, Sweden, the United States and the partner countries Indonesia, Latvia, Macao-China and the Russian Federation, less than one-third of 15-year-olds are enrolled in schools whose principals report that schools have some responsibility for the establishment of teachers' starting salaries (OECD average 26 per cent). The scope to reward teachers financially, once they have been hired, is also limited. Only in the Czech Republic, the Netherlands, Sweden and the United States and in the partner countries Macao-China and Thailand are more than two-thirds of the students enrolled in schools that report having some responsibility for determining teachers' salary increases (OECD average 27 per cent).

...but more, and in some countries increasingly so, over hiring of teachers.

There appears to be greater flexibility for schools with regard to the appointment and dismissal of teachers. On average across OECD countries, 56 per cent of 15-year-olds are enrolled in schools whose principals report to have some responsibility for the dismissal of teachers. In Belgium, the Czech Republic, Hungary, Iceland,

the Netherlands, New Zealand, Poland, the Slovak Republic, Sweden, Switzerland and the United States and in the partner countries Hong Kong-China, Latvia, Macao-China, the Russian Federation and Serbia, this figure is more than 80 per cent. In fact, Austria, Germany, Greece, Luxembourg, Portugal, Turkey and the partner country Tunisia are the only countries where more than 90 per cent of 15-year-olds are enrolled in schools whose principals report that the school has no responsibility for the dismissal of teachers. In most countries, school involvement is slightly greater in the appointment than in the dismissal of teachers. On average across OECD countries, 64 per cent of 15-year-olds are enrolled in schools whose principals report having some responsibility for the appointment of teachers. This is an area where some countries have seen changes since 2000, with, for example, the percentage of schools with responsibility in this area in Germany increasing from 10 in 2000 to 18 in 2003.

Schools control course content in most cases…

With the exception of Canada, Germany, Ireland, Norway, Portugal, Switzerland, Turkey and the partner countries Serbia, Tunisia and Uruguay, the majority of 15-year-olds are enrolled in schools reporting to play a role in determining course content (OECD average 67 per cent) and, with the exception of Norway, Poland, Switzerland, Turkey and the partner countries Serbia, Tunisia and Uruguay, this is also the case with regard to course offerings.

…but school control over budgets varies greatly across countries.

The roles that schools play in the formulation of their budgets also vary significantly. While in Austria, Germany and Luxembourg 15 per cent or less of schools report some responsibility in this area, it is more than 80 per cent in Australia, Belgium, the Czech Republic, Finland, Hungary, Mexico, Portugal, the Slovak Republic, Spain, Sweden, the United States and the partner country Thailand and more than 90 per cent in Denmark, Iceland, Korea, the Netherlands and New Zealand and in the partner countries Hong Kong-China and Indonesia (OECD average 71 per cent). With the exception of Mexico, Turkey and partner country Uruguay, virtually all 15-year-olds are in schools that report having some responsibility for decisions concerning how money is spent (OECD average 95 per cent).

Schools also play a key role in the choice of textbooks, admissions and assessment.

Finally, most principals report that disciplinary policies, the choice of textbooks and admissions are areas where schools have some responsibility. Assessment is also an area where most schools appear to have some responsibility. However, in most OECD countries, the majority of 15-year-olds are enrolled in schools whose principals report that regional or national authorities have a direct influence on decision-making in this area and the figure is 80 per cent or more in Canada, Germany, Greece, Mexico, New Zealand and the United States (for data, see *www.pisa.oecd.org*).

Within countries, the degree of decision making is relatively uniform, so it is hard to spot a relationship with performance…

Does the distribution of decision-making responsibilities affect student performance? In this field, the association between the different aspects of school autonomy and student performance within a given country is often weak. This is understandable because national legislation frequently specifies the distribution of decision-making responsibilities, so there is often little variation within countries.

...but across countries, school autonomy is positively related to performance in some respects.

However, the data suggest that in those countries in which principals report, on average, higher degrees of autonomy in certain aspects of school management the average performance in mathematics tends to be higher, as shown by the cross-country correlations shown in the bottom of Table 5.11. For example, the percentage of schools that have responsibility for allocation of school budgets accounts for 36 per cent of the cross-country performance differences of schools, and with regard to decision-making in appointing and dismissing teachers, course content and course offerings, and disciplinary policies this is still between 9 and 16 per cent.[12] However, as in other analyses of this kind, such correlations cannot be interpreted in a causal sense since many other factors may be at play. Nonetheless, the findings do suggest that school involvement in various areas of decision-making tends, at least at the cross-country level, to be positively associated with mathematics performance.

Several outside stakeholders exercise influence in schools, national and regional authorities the most so...

Important differences among countries emerge in the ways in which stakeholders outside and inside the school are involved in decision-making. Across the four decision-making areas of staffing, budgeting, instructional content and assessment practices, and among the seven stakeholder groups that were considered, school principals report the strongest influence by regional or national education authorities, followed by school governing boards, teacher groups, external examination boards and then by employers in the enterprise sector, parent groups and student groups (Figure 5.12 and Table 5.12).[13]

...but in some countries the influence of national authorities varies greatly across different areas.

The involvement of regional or national education authorities tends to be strong in all four areas. However, there are exceptions. In Hungary, Korea, Norway, Poland and Sweden, for example, only between 11 and 26 per cent of 15-year-olds are enrolled in schools whose school principals report that regional or national authorities exert a direct influence on decisions relating to staffing (OECD average 57 per cent). Similarly, in Germany, Poland, Sweden, Turkey and the partner country Tunisia, the corresponding percentage of decisions relating to budgeting is only between 10 and 25 per cent (OECD average 58 per cent); in Iceland, Korea and Poland the percentage for decisions relating to instructional content is only between 20 and 29 per cent (OECD average 66 per cent); and in Iceland, Italy, Poland and the Slovak Republic, the percentage for decisions relating to assessment practices is only between 13 and 27 per cent (OECD average 53 per cent).

Moreover, in some countries the involvement of regional or national authorities differs substantially across the areas of decision-making. In Sweden, for example, national or regional authorities appear to influence most schools' decisions relating to setting instructional content and monitoring adherence to standards through assessment at 62 per cent, whereas there appears to be little interference with schools on how educational goals are implemented, with only around 10 per cent of 15-year-olds enrolled in schools whose principals report that regional or national authorities exert a direct influence on decisions relating to staffing or budgeting (Figure 5.12).

Figure 5.12 ■ **Involvement of stakeholders in decision-making at school**

Percentage of students across OECD countries in schools where principals report that the stakeholders shown in the figure exert a direct influence on decision-making about the following aspects: staffing, budgeting, instructional content and assessment practices

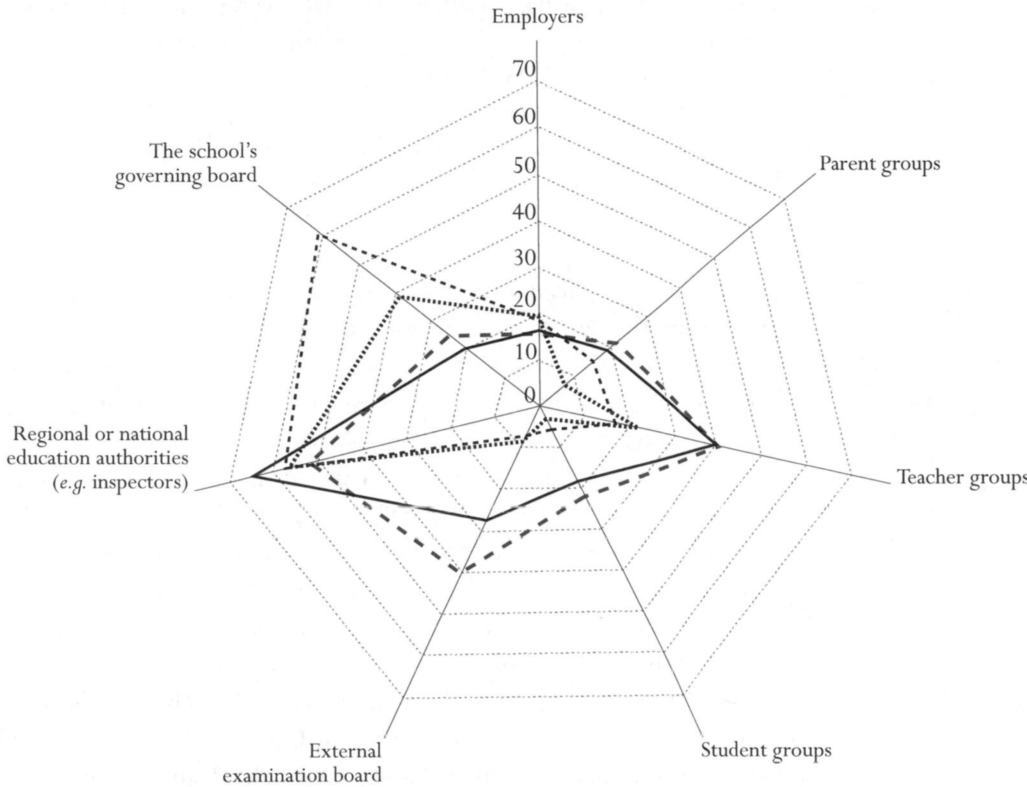

Source: OECD PISA 2003 database, Table 5.12.

Other stakeholders have influence on specific areas: staff or professional organisations for instruction and assessment…

The involvement of teacher groups, such as staff associations, curriculum committees and trade unions tends to be strongest in decisions on instructional content and assessment practices. However, there are wide differences across OECD countries. For example, while in Australia, Denmark, Hungary, the Slovak Republic and the United States and in the partner countries the Russian Federation and Thailand more than two-thirds of 15-year-olds are enrolled in schools whose principals report a direct influence of teacher groups in decisions relating to instructional content, this is 9 per cent or less in Germany, Greece, Iceland and Japan (OECD average 40 per cent). In the areas of assessment practices, staffing and budgeting, the OECD averages are 41, 22 and 17 per cent, respectively (Figure 5.12).

…exam boards on assessment, and sometimes instruction too…

The role of external examination boards is naturally strongest in relation to assessment practices, but in some countries schools also report considerable influence of examination board on matters relating to instructional content.

However, also here countries differ widely. While in Australia, Finland, Ireland, the Netherlands, New Zealand the Slovak Republic, as well as the partner countries Hong Kong-China and Thailand more than three-quarters of 15-year-olds are enrolled in schools whose principals report the involvement of external examination board in decisions relating to assessment practices, in Austria, Germany, Greece, Japan and Sweden such examination boards either do not exist or do not have a significant role (OECD average 40 per cent). In the areas of instructional content, budgeting and staffing, the respective percentages for the OECD averages are 28, 7 and 8.

Only a few countries report strong involvement of employers in decisions relating to the four areas of staffing, budgeting, instructional content and assessment practices.

...and parent groups sometimes in the areas of instructional content and assessment.

The influence of parent groups on decision-making at school tends to be strongest in the areas of instructional content and assessment practices, somewhat less so in budgeting and least in the area of staffing. In Korea, Poland, the Slovak Republic, Sweden and the United States and in the partner countries Hong Kong-China, Macao-China, the Russian Federation and Thailand, between a quarter and two-thirds of 15-year-olds are enrolled in schools whose principals report that parents have a direct influence on instructional content, and this figure reaches 84 and 86 per cent in Finland and Latvia, respectively. In contrast, it is less than 5 per cent in Greece, Ireland, Portugal and Switzerland (OECD average 19 per cent). In Finland, Hungary, Poland and the partner country Latvia, parent groups have a direct influence on decisions relating to assessment practices in the schools where two-thirds or more of the 15-year-olds are enrolled but this is the case in less than 5 per cent of schools in Austria, Japan, Switzerland and the partner country Uruguay (OECD average 22 per cent). Most variability exists with regard to the involvement of parent groups in staffing policies. In Finland, 42 per cent of 15-year-olds are enrolled in schools whose school principals report that parents have a direct influence on decisions relating to staffing, whereas it is less than 1 per cent in the Czech Republic, Iceland, Ireland, Italy, Japan, Luxembourg, Norway, Portugal, the Slovak Republic and Switzerland and in the partner countries Hong Kong-China and Tunisia (OECD average 7 per cent). In the area of budgeting, the OECD average is 15 per cent.

The combined effect of school policies and practices

The effect of these factors can be looked at together, in combination with social background...

As with the school climate variables discussed in the preceding section, the effects of the various school policies and practices on student performance cannot simply be added, since they interrelate. In the following, they are therefore jointly considered. For an examination of school policies and practices, the interaction of these factors with the socio-economic background of students and schools is of importance for policy as well, since such interaction raises questions about equity in the distribution of educational opportunities.

Figure 5.13 ■ **Impact of school policies and practices on school performance in mathematics**

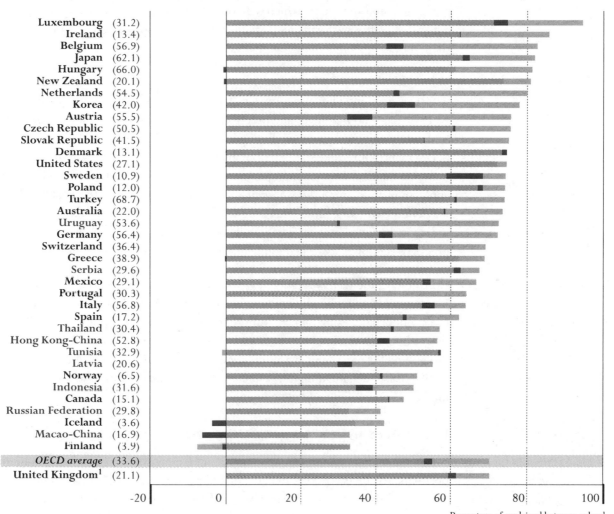

Note: The numbers in the brackets indicate between-school variance expressed as a percentage of the average variance in student performance across OECD countries.

1. Response rate too low to ensure comparability (see Annex A3).

Source: OECD PISA 2003 database, Table 5.13.

...and here again the biggest effects operate in combination with socio-economic difference.

Figure 5.13 presents the results. When socio-economic background at student and school levels as well as the school policies and practices measured by PISA are considered jointly, on average across OECD countries, 53 per cent of the performance variation among schools is attributable to socio-economic background, 2 per cent to the school policies and practices net of socio-economic background factors, and 15 per cent to the combined influence of socio-economic background and school policies and practices.[14] Thus, while the net effect of the school policies and practices observed by PISA on school performance tends to

be small in most countries, the gross effect, which includes an assessment of the interaction of policies and practices with socio-economic background, is sizeable in many countries, most notably in Austria, Belgium, Germany, Korea, the Netherlands and Portugal, as well as in the partner country Uruguay (Table 5.13). As in the preceding section, these results need to be interpreted in the context of the extent to which school performance varies in the first place. Estimates of the performance variation among schools have been included in the figure.

There is only a small net effect...

While the net effect provides an estimate of the impact of school policies and practices over and above the impact of socio-economic background – in other words what school policies and practices add to their intake – they are likely to understate the true effect of these policies and practices because some of the performance differences are attributable to school factors and socio-economic contexts jointly. For example, socio-economically advantaged schools may apply more effective school policies and practices, because the best teachers may choose to work there. This joint effect should be of significant concern for policy makers, as it provides an indication of to what extent school policies and practices reinforce socio-economic disparities in the school system.

...but a larger gross effect shows that students in schools with stronger policies and practices perform better.

Conversely, the interpretation of the gross effect of school policies and practices without an adjustment for socio-economic factors may overstate their importance and ignores differences in the socio-economic conditions that schools face. However, as stated above, the gross effects are often most interesting for parents who are interested primarily in the overall performance results of schools, including any effects that are conferred by the socio-economic intake of schools.

RESOURCES INVESTED IN EDUCATION

Finally PISA looked at the time, staffing and physical resources invested.

This section looks at resource factors that are frequently associated with student performance in the public debate, including time invested in learning, class and school size, and student/teaching staff ratios, perceived deficiencies in the physical infrastructure, perceived staff shortages and the quality of educational resources at school. It also looks at performance differences between public and private schools.

Student time invested in learning

Student learning time is a key resource...

The most valuable resource in the educational process is no doubt student learning time. Policy-makers looking to improve educational outcomes seek to increase or use more effectively the time for which students are engaged in school-related learning.

...and instruction time varies widely across countries...

Instruction in classroom settings comprises the largest part of the public investment in student learning (OECD, 2004b). On average across OECD countries, 15-year-olds report spending 24 hours per school week on learning in classroom settings, but this ranges from 19 to 23 hours in Denmark, Finland, Germany,

Norway, Poland, Sweden, the United States and the partner countries Brazil and Uruguay to between 27 and 30 hours in Austria, Ireland and Korea and in the partner countries Liechtenstein, Thailand and Tunisia (Table 5.14).[15] An average of 3.3 hours of this time are devoted to mathematics classes. Policy decisions on instruction time, *i.e.,* the number of hours that each student spends in organised learning, are closely interrelated with policies on class size, teachers' working hours (teaching time) and the ratios of students to teaching staff. The optimal balance between these factors may vary in different subject areas and at different levels of education.

...and, in some countries, goes well beyond the time that students spend learning in school.

Instruction in classroom settings is, however, only one aspect of student learning time. While in Austria, Belgium, the Czech Republic, Iceland, Japan, Norway, Portugal, Sweden and Switzerland, learning in classroom settings makes up 80 per cent of total school-related learning, students in Greece and the partner country the Russian Federation report spending more than 40 per cent of their time for school-related learning in other ways, including homework or other studies set by their teachers (OECD average 7.5 hours in total of which 3.0 hours for mathematics); by attending out of school classes (OECD average 0.9 hours out of which 0.3 hours for mathematics), remedial classes (OECD average 0.8 hours of which 0.3 for mathematics) or enrichment classes at school (OECD average 0.7 hours of which 0.2 hours for mathematics); by working with a tutor (OECD average 0.5 hours of which more than half for mathematics); or in other forms of study (OECD average 1.6 hours out of which 0.2 for mathematics). Note that these figures refer to school weeks only and that countries differ in the number of weeks per year in which schools are open. To aid the interpretation of the figures, the number of instructional weeks per year has been added to Figure 5.14.

Adding up the various time allocations, students in Korea spend more than 40 hours per school week on school-related learning (Figure 5.14).

Homework accounts for much of out-of-school learning, but it can be hard to measure its effect on performance.

The various forms of learning outside formal classroom settings, of which homework is in most countries the dominant component, increase a student's opportunity to spend time in learning. It should, therefore, be positively related to learning outcomes. However, several factors complicate this relationship. For example, teachers may tend to assign more (or more regular) homework to those students who need it most to improve their performance. Alternatively, slower learners may need more time to complete the same amount of homework. Conversely, students who report spending relatively little time on homework may either be able students who can complete their homework quickly or disengaged students who do not care to spend much time on school activities at home. Finally, students' socio-economic background may influence homework practices, with students from wealthier or better-educated families benefiting potentially from better home learning conditions and assistance with their homework. Similar issues apply for other forms of out-of-school learning, such as remedial or enrichment classes.

The relationship between learning time and learning outcomes is, next to considerations of the effectiveness with which this time is invested, further

Figure 5.14 ■ Student learning time

Students' reports of the average number of hours spent on the following "out-of-school" activities during each school week:

- Homework or other study set by their teachers
- Working with a tutor
- Attending out-of-school classes
- Other study

Students' reports of the average number of hours spent on the following "in-school" activities during each school week:

- Instructional time
- Remedial classes
- Enrichment classes

ALL SUBJECTS — Out of school | In school

MATHEMATICS — Out of school | In school

	Instructional weeks per year
Korea	35.6
Thailand	39.7
Mexico	23.9
Macao-China	39.2
Tunisia	31.9
Ireland	33.1
Hong Kong-China	35.4
Italy	33.5
Turkey	35.7
Austria	36.7
Liechtenstein	39.0
Belgium	36.2
Iceland	36.7
Russian Federation	35.0
Spain	35.4
Greece	34.3
Latvia	34.9
Portugal	35.4
Japan	38.9
France	37.8
Canada	–
Australia	38.6
New Zealand	39.4
United States	36.0
Netherlands	36.0
Hungary	38.1
Luxembourg	36.6
Poland	36.0
Finland	38.3
Switzerland	38.1
Slovak Republic	39.2
Serbia	39.2
Czech Republic	37.1
Germany	41.0
Sweden	39.7
Norway	36.6
Denmark	38.0
Uruguay	39.6
Brazil	33.9
United Kingdom[1]	40.6

30 20 10 0 10 20 30 40
Number of hours per week

30 20 10 0 10 20 30 40
Number of hours per week

1. Response rate too low to ensure comparability (see Annex A3).
Source: OECD PISA 2003 database, Table 5.14.

complicated by the fact that countries vary considerably in how they allocate instruction time over the different levels of education. For example, Sweden invests a significantly larger number of instruction hours in the education of students aged 6 to 7 years than Germany, while the reverse is true in the 12-to-14-year-old age group (OECD, 2004b). As learning outcomes at age 15 are influenced by the cumulative impact of educational opportunities over a student's school career, this variation across grade levels distorts the relationship between learning outcomes at age 15 and instruction hours at age 15, as reported by PISA.

Even pre-school educational investments are relevant, and were asked about in PISA...

Even the time students have invested in education prior to their schooling career may need to be considered when evaluating the impact of learning time on educational outcomes. The importance of early childhood education has been highlighted in much of recent policy dialogue and some research suggests that quality early childhood education and care may contribute to later academic success (OECD, 2001b). However, such research requires longitudinal studies that have not been carried out in many countries. PISA allows this question to be examined only in a retrospective perspective, as students were asked whether and for how long they had attended pre-school programmes. Figure 5.15 shows the student responses and relates these to their performance at age 15.

...and those who had attended pre-school programmes performed on average better at age 15.

In the majority of countries, students who report that they attended pre-school for more than one year show a statistically significant performance advantage in mathematics over those without pre-school attendance; this advantage is between 50 and 107 score points in Belgium, Denmark, France, Germany, Hungary, Mexico, the Netherlands, New Zealand, Switzerland and Turkey as well as in the partner countries Brazil, Hong Kong-China, Liechtenstein and Uruguay. This is shown by the longer bars in light shading in the figure, for shorter and longer pre school programmes, respectively.

In part this can be accounted for by more socially advantaged families having better access to such programmes, yet even controlling for this an association remains...

At the same time, it must be noted that children from socio-economically more advantaged families are, in some countries at least, often more likely to benefit from preschool education, as such families tend to have more of the resources and information needed to enrol their children and to select high-quality programmes. However, PISA allows to account for the socio-economic background of students. The bars in darker shading in Figure 5.15 show the performance advantage of students in mathematics at age 15 who have attended pre-school programmes, net of the effect of socio-economic background, as measured by the PISA index of economic, social and cultural status. As expected, the effect net of socio-economic background tends to be smaller, on average, such that the performance difference between students who have attended pre-school and those who have not is reduced to about half after the adjustment.[16]

...with pre-school participation associated with substantially better results in some countries...

Nevertheless, in more than half of the OECD countries, a considerable effect remains. In Belgium, Denmark, France, Germany, Hungary, Mexico, the Netherlands, Switzerland and Turkey, as well as in the partner countries Brazil, Hong Kong-China, Indonesia, Liechtenstein and Macao China, this effect is also large, varying between 30 and 73 score points.

Figure 5.15 ■ **Pre-school attendance and school success**

	Percentage of students who attended pre-school (ISCED 0) for:	
	One year or less	More than one year
Switzerland	30	67
Liechtenstein	6	91
Turkey	16	8
France	5	94
Belgium	4	94
Hong Kong-China	7	87
Germany	13	83
Denmark	32	66
Hungary	5	94
Brazil	31	45
Mexico	21	66
Netherlands	3	94
Uruguay	21	64
New Zealand	20	72
Indonesia	25	25
Austria	16	80
Sweden	29	60
Tunisia	26	27
Greece	33	62
Poland	52	44
Macao-China	16	80
Canada	45	46
Japan	2	97
Norway	14	78
Australia	47	46
Thailand	21	74
Spain	10	84
Slovak Republic	16	76
Italy	8	87
Luxembourg	9	79
Russian Fed.	10	78
Portugal	17	55
Serbia	34	41
Czech Republic	14	79
United States	87	10
Finland	25	67
Korea	10	87
Ireland	40	32
Iceland	4	89
Latvia	15	56
United Kingdom[1]	26	68

Difference in student performance in mathematics between students who report having attended pre-school (ISCED 0) for more than one year and those without pre-school attendance

Difference in student performance in mathematics between students who report having attended pre-school (ISCED 0) for one year or less and those without pre-school attendance

Note: Countries ranked in descending order of difference in student performance in mathematics between students who have attended pre-school (ISCED 0) for more than one year and those without pre-school attendance.

1. Response rate too low to ensure comparability (see Annex A3).

Source: OECD PISA 2003 database.

In the majority of countries, children from well-off families tend to benefit from pre-school education to a larger extent. However, in Hungary – and to a lesser extent the Czech Republic, France, Germany, Italy, Korea and the Slovak Republic – the performance advantage is larger for students with lower levels of socio-economic backgrounds, and pre-school education may thus have a compensatory effect.[17]

...and in some cases this benefit is especially great for less advantaged students.

Availability and quality of human resources

Teacher shortage

The recruitment and retention of a highly qualified teaching force is a major policy concern in OECD countries. Ageing teacher populations and rising student participation rates continue to put pressure on the demand for teachers in many countries, but aspiring teachers in some countries find that teaching can be unduly stressful, that the profession is under-appreciated, and that salaries are low by comparison with salaries in professions with comparable qualifications (OECD, 2004b).

As the teaching force grows older, it can be difficult to replace it with young recruits...

The PISA school questionnaire provides an opportunity to assess school principals' perspectives of the adequacy of teacher supply and to assess aspects such as perceptions about the quality and availability of teaching staff.

...so PISA asked principals about the extent to which teacher shortages hinder learning...

On average across OECD countries, 22 per cent of 15-year-olds are enrolled in schools whose principals report that their school's capacity is hindered to some extent or even a lot by the availability of qualified mathematics teachers. However this ranges from less than 10 per cent in Austria, Denmark, Finland, Hungary, Korea, Portugal, the Slovak Republic and Switzerland to 41 per cent in New Zealand and to 54, 56, 60 and 84 per cent in Indonesia, Uruguay, Luxembourg and Turkey, respectively. The situation tends to be similar for science and foreign language teachers whereas teacher shortage seems to be less pronounced in the area of language of assessment (Figure 5.16).

...with a quarter of 15-year-olds enrolled in schools whose principals report that this is the case.

Using responses to questions about the extent to which the shortage or inadequacy of teachers in the mathematics, science, language of assessment, foreign language and experienced teachers hinders learning by 15-year-olds, an index of teacher shortage can be constructed, and its effect on student learning can be examined. This index has a mean value of zero for all OECD countries. The larger the value of the index, the greater the perceived impact of teacher shortage on learning, in the opinion of principals. Values above zero indicate a higher-than-average perception that the shortage or inadequacy of teachers hinders learning among 15-year-old students.

Teacher shortages can be compared on an index...

When comparing OECD countries on this index, principals in Belgium, Germany, Greece, Luxembourg, Mexico, the Netherlands, New Zealand and Turkey and in the partner countries Brazil, Indonesia, Macao-China, the Russian Federation, Thailand, Tunisia and Uruguay were the most likely to perceive that a shortage or inadequacy of teachers hindered learning in their schools. By contrast, principals in Austria, Finland, Korea, Portugal and Spain were the least likely to perceive that teacher shortages hinders learning (Table 5.15).

...showing where they are most acute...

Figure 5.16 ■ Teacher shortage

Percentage of students in schools where the principals report that the school's capacity to provide instruction is hindered to some extent or a lot by a shortage or inadequacy of the following:

	qualified mathematics teachers	qualified science teachers	qualified testing language teachers	qualified foreign language teachers	experienced teachers
Turkey	84	77	78	77	80
Indonesia	54	54	48	59	63
Luxembourg	60	13	64	48	59
Uruguay	56	43	28	45	56
Mexico	36	36	37	34	35
Russian Fed.	35	33	31	42	39
New Zealand	41	32	28	26	39
Macao-China	18	27	8	22	56
Thailand	37	34	27	28	24
Belgium	36	26	20	20	45
Greece	30	32	30	33	38
Brazil	33	30	24	40	36
Netherlands	22	26	16	29	46
Tunisia	29	17	6	40	47
Germany	28	41	21	31	17
Australia	30	26	14	40	27
Iceland	29	43	14	15	24
Czech Republic	10	15	6	51	16
Italy	20	19	17	19	23
Sweden	17	22	18	26	20
Poland	15	11	9	50	30
Norway	15	20	11	27	8
Japan	21	21	19	20	37
Latvia	14	12	8	21	13
Slovak Republic	6	10	5	45	16
United States	22	22	6	20	16
Canada	19	18	7	20	16
Hong Kong-China	16	7	10	14	18
Ireland	13	10	5	16	26
Denmark	4	13	4	9	5
Switzerland	9	16	10	12	17
Serbia	10	7	5	24	18
Hungary	7	7	3	13	20
Spain	10	9	10	13	14
Portugal	6	4	5	4	24
Finland	7	4	7	7	9
Austria	6	11	4	7	9
Korea	3	4	1	9	7
OECD average	*22*	*21*	*17*	*26*	*26*
United Kingdom[1]	41	35	28	31	38

1. Response rate too low to ensure comparability (see Annex A3).
Source: OECD PISA 2003 database, Table 5.15.

In the interpretation of these responses, it needs to be borne in mind that teacher shortage was not measured in terms of an internationally comparable unit of measurement, such as the proportion of vacancies per student or the ratio of students to teaching staff, but that the focus of PISA was on the extent to which school principals perceived that the inadequacy of teacher supply hindered learning. For example, some of the countries in which school principals expressed an above-average concern about the negative impact of teacher supply on student learning have comparatively small student/teaching staff ratios and class size (OECD, 2004b). The ratio of students to teaching staff in Greece, for example, where a high proportion of school principals report that teacher shortage hinders learning, is well below the OECD average.

...but this measure relies on principals' perceptions not hard resource comparisons.

Monitoring teacher practices

What these results show is that school principals in many countries are concerned with the supply of qualified teachers. As shown in the first section of this report, in many countries, significant proportions of school principals also consider that learning is hindered by low teacher morale and by teacher-related factors affecting school climate.

To what extent do principals monitor teaching?

As school principals voice concerns about the quality of human resources at their school, what do they do themselves to monitor practices of teachers at school?

On average across OECD countries, 61 per cent of 15-year-olds are enrolled in schools whose principals report that the practices of mathematics teachers were monitored over the preceding year through the principal's or senior staff observations (Table 5.16). In the Czech Republic, Hungary, Korea, New Zealand, Poland, the Slovak Republic, the United States, as well as the partner countries Hong Kong-China, Indonesia, Latvia, Macao-China, the Russian Federation and Uruguay these are more than 90 per cent. By contrast, in Greece, Ireland, Italy, Portugal and Spain, these practices seem much less common, with only between 5 and 16 per cent of school principals reporting such practices. Schools whose principals report monitoring practices of mathematics teachers through principal or senior staff observations perform better in Germany, Luxembourg, Norway, Spain, Switzerland and the partner country Indonesia (OECD average difference 12 score points), but the reverse seems to be the case in Iceland.

In most cases they say that they or their senior colleagues do monitor teacher practices, but in some countries this is rare.

Observations of classes by inspectors or other persons external to the school are a less frequently employed method to monitor the practices of mathematics teachers with, on average across OECD countries, less than a quarter of students being enrolled in schools whose principals report the use of such practices in the preceding year (Table 5.16). The exceptions are Belgium, Korea, New Zealand and Switzerland and the partner countries Indonesia, the Russian Federation, Thailand, Tunisia and Uruguay, where between 48 and 80 per cent of 15-year-olds are enrolled in schools whose school principals report having monitored mathematics teachers in this way in the preceding year. Again, schools reporting

In a minority of countries outsiders monitor classroom performance.

that they use this practice tend to perform better, with an average advantage of 6 score points in OECD countries and statistically significantly better by 20 score points or more in Australia, Luxembourg, Poland, Sweden and the partner country Tunisia. In contrast, the advantage is smaller in other countries and in the cases of Mexico, Switzerland and the United States, even negative.

However, it is not possible to establish causal inferences, particularly as such practices are closely interrelated with other school factors. For example, in some countries the often highly performing independent private schools are not subject to government regulations about inspection practices. As a result, the performance of schools not using such practices may appear higher, even if the influence of such practices on school performance may still be positive, all other things being equal. At the cross-country level, no consistent relationship between the various approaches to monitoring practices of mathematics teachers and country performance is observed.

Monitoring teachers via their students' results is also common, although it remains rare in some countries.

Another way to monitor practices of mathematics teachers lies in looking at the results achieved, as monitored in tests or other forms of student assessments. In many countries, this practice is now fairly common, with an average of 59 per cent of students enrolled in schools whose school principals report this practice having been used over the preceding year. However, countries differ widely in their use of such practices. More than three-quarters of the students in Iceland, Mexico, Poland and the United States and in the partner countries Brazil, Hong Kong-China, Indonesia, Latvia, Macao-China, the Russian Federation, Thailand and Tunisia are enrolled in schools whose principals report having used such practices in the preceding year while in Denmark it is only 13 per cent. Mexico, the Netherlands, Sweden and the partner country Thailand show a performance advantages in schools that use this practice, but the opposite is true for Luxembourg, the United States and the partner country Macao-China.

Finally, around half of students tend, on average across OECD countries, to be enrolled in schools whose principals report monitoring practices of mathematics teachers through teacher peer reviews of lesson plans, assessment instruments or the actual lessons. There is wide variation among countries and no consistent relationship with school performance in this case also.

The quality of schools' physical infrastructure and educational resources

Adequate resources are a necessary but not sufficient condition for effective learning…

Ensuring the availability of a suitable physical infrastructure and an adequate supply of educational resources may not guarantee high performance, but the absence of such an environment could affect learning negatively. Buildings in good condition and adequate amounts of teaching space all contribute to a physical environment that is conducive to learning. Much the same can be said for schools with adequate educational resources, such as computers, library and teaching materials, including textbooks and multimedia resources for learning.

Figure 5.17 ■ Monitoring practices of mathematics teachers

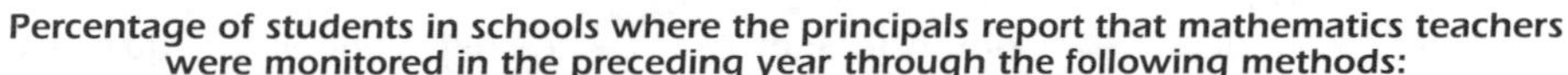

Principal or senior staff observations of lessons

Observations of classes by inspectors or other persons external to the school

Tests or assessments of student achievement

Teacher peer review (of lesson plans, assessment instruments, lessons)

%
100
75
50
25
0
OECD average

Portugal, Ireland, Greece, Spain, Italy, Norway, Finland, Switzerland, Luxembourg, Iceland, Brazil, Japan, Belgium, Netherlands, Sweden, Denmark, Australia, Germany, Mexico, Tunisia, Austria, Canada, Thailand, Serbia, Turkey, Korea, Indonesia, Hong Kong-China, Uruguay, New Zealand, Macao-China, Hungary, Poland, Slovak Republic, Czech Republic, Latvia, United States, Russian Federation, United Kingdom[1]

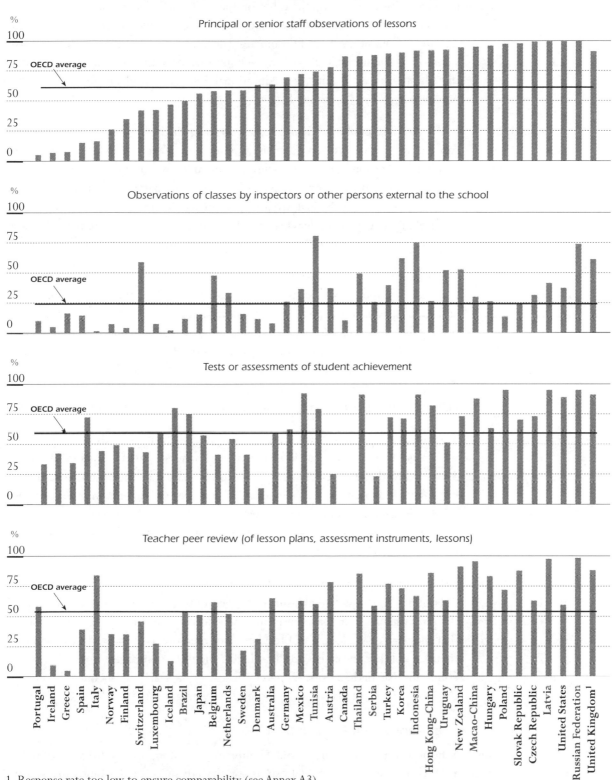

1. Response rate too low to ensure comparability (see Annex A3).
Source: OECD PISA 2003 database, Table 5.16.

...and can be assessed based on whether principals say that their absence hinders learning.

Using principals' responses to a series of questions about the perceived extent to which material and educational resources hinder learning among 15-year-old students, two composite indices were created – one on the quality of the school's physical infrastructure and the other on the quality of educational resources. Like the indices discussed earlier, these indices have an average of zero and a standard deviation of one across OECD countries. The indices were inverted so that positive values on the index reflect a below-average concern among school principals that the physical infrastructure and educational resources available in their schools hinder learning by 15-year-olds.

Physical infrastructure problems are common only in a few OECD countries...

In the Czech Republic and Korea, relatively few principals report that the school's capacity to provide instruction is hindered by a shortage or inadequacy of school buildings and grounds; heating, cooling and lighting systems; or instructional space. In contrast, in Greece, Norway and Turkey and in the partner countries Indonesia and Uruguay, school principals frequently reported that the quality of their school's physical infrastructure hinders learning. However, only in a few countries did these results reveal any relationship with school performance (Table 5.17).[18]

...while shortages of educational resources appear to be a more common problem...

When it comes to the quality of educational resources, such as instructional materials, computers and software for instruction, calculators, library materials, audio-visual resources, and science laboratory equipment and materials, few principals in Australia, Korea, the Netherlands, Switzerland and the United States see their supply or quality hindering instruction. However, in Greece, Mexico, Poland, the Slovak Republic and Turkey – and even more so in the partner countries Brazil, Indonesia, Latvia, the Russian Federation, Serbia, Thailand, Tunisia and Uruguay – these were of concern for many school principals (Table 5.18).

...that is sometimes reflected in school performance.

The relationship with school performance tended to be slightly stronger[19] than with regard to the physical infrastructure of schools, but remains weak (Table 5.18). Nevertheless, in Germany, Italy, Korea and the Netherlands, as well as in the partner country Brazil, the bottom 25 per cent of students in schools whose school principals reported the biggest concerns with educational resources are at least 1.5 times likely to be among the bottom quarter of performers than the remaining students.

However, these measures rely on subjective assessments rather than hard resource measures.

When interpreting these figures, it should be borne in mind that school principals did not provide objective measures of the condition of educational resources and the physical infrastructure, but rather their perceptions of whether they thought that shortage or inadequacy of teachers hindered the learning of 15-year-olds in their school. The measures are therefore difficult to compare across schools and countries. Nevertheless, such perceptions can have an important influence on the work of school principals and therefore warrant attention.

Public and private stakeholders

While schooling remains primarily public, other partners are being brought in.

School education is mainly a public enterprise. Among the 20 OECD countries with comparable data, in only six is the private share of the funds invested in primary and secondary education greater than 10 per cent and in no country does it exceed 20 per cent (OECD, 2004b). Nevertheless, with an increasing variety of educational opportunities, programmes and providers, governments are forging new partnerships to mobilise resources for education and to design new policies that allow the different stakeholders to participate more fully and to share costs and benefits more equitably.

A small number of schools are fully private ...

On average across OECD countries, only 4 per cent of 15-year-olds are enrolled in schools that are privately managed and predominantly privately financed (referred to as government-independent private schools) (Table 5.19). These are schools which principals report to be managed by non-governmental organisations such as churches, trade unions or business enterprises and/or to have governing boards consisting mostly of members not selected by a public agency. At least 50 per cent of their funds come from private sources, such as fees paid by parents, donations, sponsorships or parental fund-raising and other non-public sources.

...but student enrolment in such schools exceeds 10 per cent in just three OECD countries.

There are only a few countries in which such a model of private education is common. Only in Japan (26 per cent), Korea (22 per cent) and Mexico (13 per cent) and in the partner countries Brazil (13 per cent), Indonesia (45 per cent), Macao-China (46 per cent) and Uruguay (14 per cent) is the proportion of students enrolled in independent private schools greater than 10 per cent. By contrast, in many countries the financing of schools by students and their families is considered a potential barrier to student access. In 12 OECD countries for which this type of school exists, 3 per cent or less of 15-year-olds are enrolled in independent private schools.

More commonly, public funds support privately managed institutions...

Private education is not only a way of mobilising resources from a wider range of funding sources, it is sometimes also regarded as a way of making education more cost-effective. Publicly financed schools do not necessarily have to be publicly managed. Instead, governments can transfer funds to public and private educational institutions according to various allocation mechanisms (OECD, 2004b). By making the funding for educational institutions dependent on parents' choosing to enrol their children, governments sometimes seek to introduce incentives for institutions to organise programmes and teaching in ways that better meet diverse student requirements and interests, thus reducing the costs of failure and mismatches. Direct public funding of institutions based on student enrolments or student credit-hours is one model for this. Giving money to students and their families (through, for example, scholarships or vouchers) to spend in public or private educational institutions of their choice is another method.

...and in some cases a majority of schools.

Schools that are privately managed but predominantly financed through the public purse (defined here as government-dependent private schools) are a much more common model of private schooling in OECD countries than are privately financed schools. On average across the OECD countries with comparable data, 13 per cent of 15-year-olds are enrolled in government-dependent private schools and in Ireland, Korea and the Netherlands, it is 58, 36 and 77 per cent, respectively (Table 5.19).[20]

Students in private schools perform much better on average…

How do these institutional arrangements relate to school performance? This question is difficult to answer, not only because student characteristics sometimes differ between public and private schools, but also because in some countries private schools are unevenly spread across different school types, such as general and vocational programmes, which may, in turn, be related to performance. On average across the participating countries included in this comparison, private schools outperform students in mathematics in public schools in ten OECD member countries and three of the partner countries, while public schools outperform private ones only in Japan and Luxembourg and in the partner country Indonesia.[21] The performance advantage of private schools amounts to 33 score points, on average across OECD countries, to between 24 and 46 score points in Canada, Ireland, Korea, the Slovak Republic, Spain, the United States and the partner country Macao-China, to between 55 and 66 score points in Germany, Mexico and New Zealand and to more than 90 score points in the partner countries Brazil and Uruguay.

…but this is influenced by the character of the client group.

In the interpretation of these figures, it is important to recognise that there are many factors that affect school choice. Insufficient family wealth can, for example, be an important impediment to students wanting to attend independent private schools with a high level of tuition fees. Even government-dependent private schools that charge no tuition fees can cater for a different clientele or apply more restrictive transfer or selection practices.

The private school advantage remains after controlling for individual students' backgrounds…

One way to examine this is to adjust for differences in the socio-economic background of students and schools. The results for this are shown in Figure 5.18. Even if the family background of students is accounted for, an average advantage of 24 score points remains for private schools. In fact, the advantage of private schools net of students' family background is between 16 and 19 score points in Ireland, the Slovak Republic and Spain, between 25 and 40 score points in Canada, Germany, Mexico, New Zealand and the partner country Macao-China and more than 50 score points in Brazil and Uruguay.

…but disappears once the effect of the social composition of their schools is controlled for,…

The picture changes, however, when in addition to students' family background also the socio-economic background of schools' intake is taken into account. The impact of this contextual effect, that was discussed in detail already in Chapter 4, on school performance is strong and, once it is accounted for, an advantage of private schools is no longer visible. This suggests that private schools may realise a significant part of their advantage not only from the socio-economic advantage that students bring with them, but even more so because their combined socio-economic intake allows them to create a learning environment that is more conducive to learning.

…although from parents' point of view they may remain an attractive alternative.

That said, while the performance of private schools does not tend to be superior once socio-economic factors have been taken into account, in many countries they still pose an attractive alternative for parents looking to maximise the benefits for their children, including those benefits that are conferred to students through the socio-economic level of schools' intake.

Figure 5.18 ■ **Public and private schools**

	Percentage of students enrolled in public schools	Percentage of students enrolled in private schools: Government-dependent	Percentage of students enrolled in private schools: Government-independent
Luxembourg	86	14	0
Hong Kong-China	93	7	0
Japan	73	1	26
Indonesia	51	4	45
Italy	96	0	4
Switzerland	95	1	4
Finland	93	7	0
Denmark	78	22	0
Czech Republic	93	6	1
Thailand	88	6	6
Sweden	96	4	0
Hungary	89	10	1
Austria	92	7	1
Portugal	94	4	2
United States	94	0	6
Netherlands	23	77	0
Slovak Republic	87	13	0
Korea	42	36	22
Ireland	42	58	1
Spain	64	28	8
Canada	94	4	2
Macao-China	5	49	46
Mexico	87	0	13
New Zealand	95	0	5
Germany	92	7	0
Uruguay	86	0	14
Brazil	87	0	13
OECD average	*80*	*12*	*4*
United Kingdom[1]	94	1	5

1. Response rate too low to ensure comparability (see Annex A3).
Source: OECD PISA 2003 database, Table 5.19.

The combined effect of school resources

The overall school resource effect and its interaction with social background has implications for equity…

As with the school climate variables, the effects of the various school resources that were discussed on student performance cannot simply be added, since they closely interrelate. In the following, they are therefore considered jointly. For an examination of school resources, the interaction of these factors with the socio-economic background of students and schools is of importance for policy development as well, since such interaction raises questions about equity in the distribution of educational resources.

Figure 5.19 ■ **Impact of school resources on school performance in mathematics**

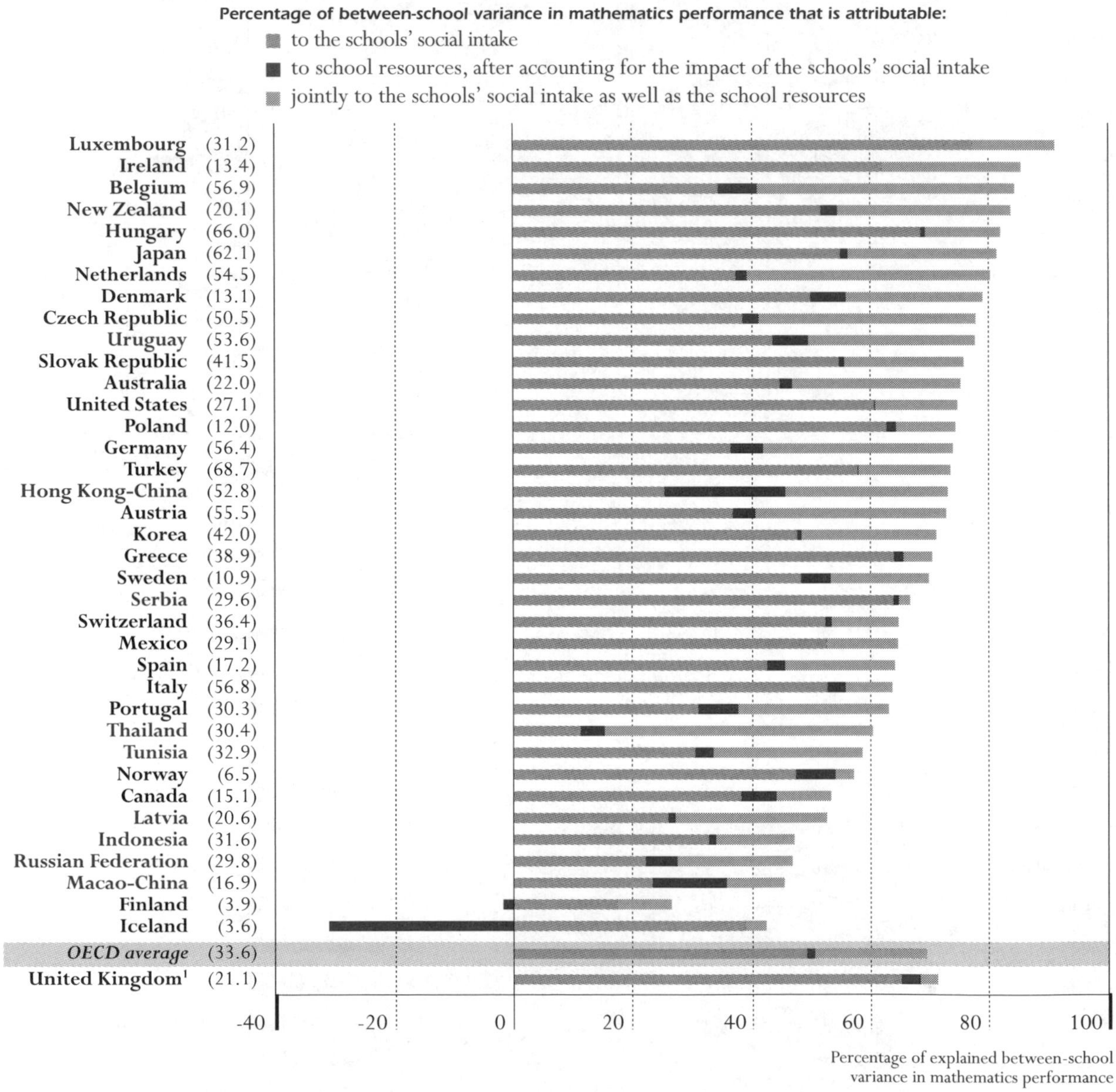

Note: The numbers in the brackets indicate between-school variance expressed as a percentage of the average variance in student performance across OECD countries.

1. Response rate too low to ensure comparability (see Annex A3).

Source: OECD PISA 2003 database, Table 5.20.

Figure 5.19 presents the results. When socio-economic background at student and school levels as well as the school policies and practices measured by PISA are considered jointly, on average across OECD countries, 49 per cent of the performance variation among schools is attributable to socio-economic background, 1 per cent to the school resources, and 19 per cent to the combined influence of socio-economic background and school resources.[22] Thus, while the net effect of the school resources observed by PISA on school performance tends to be small in most countries, the gross effect, (which includes an assessment of how the socio-economic background of students and schools reinforces the distribution of the quality and quantity of educational resources) is sizeable in many countries, most notably in Australia, Austria, Belgium, the Czech Republic, Germany, the Netherlands, New Zealand and the partner countries Thailand and Uruguay (see last column in Table 5.20). In these latter countries, policy makers need to address the fact that school resources appear to reinforce, rather than moderate, socio-economic differences.

...and while there is often little net effect, the combined effect with social background is substantial...

While the net effect provides an estimate of the impact of school resources over and above the impact of socio-economic background – in other words, what schools add to their intake – they are likely to understate the true effect of school resources because some of the performance differences are attributable to school and socio-economic factors jointly as is, for example, the case when socio-economically advantaged students use school resources more effectively or socio-economically more advantaged schools have better access to school resources.

...which suggests that socially advantaged students are getting better access to resources.

Conversely, the interpretation of the gross effect of resources without an adjustment for socio-economic factors may overstate their importance and ignores differences in the socio-economic conditions which schools face. However, as stated above, the gross effects are often most interesting for parents who are interested primarily in the overall performance results of schools, including any effects that are conferred by the socio-economic intake of schools.

WHAT MAKES A DIFFERENCE FOR SCHOOL PERFORMANCE

While the preceding sections examined the influence of three groups of school factors, related to school climate, school policies and practices, and school resources, on school performance and how this interacts with socio-economic background, this section now seeks to integrate various factors from the three groups into a single model, in order to determine the effect of each factor with all others taken into account. This will allow policy makers to make inferences as to their relative importance.

All three groups of school factors can be considered together.

The results of this analysis, first undertaken for the combined OECD student population with countries given equal weight, and then replicated for all participating countries, are shown in Tables 5.21a and 5.21b. Note, however, that several of the school factors that emerge as having a statistically significant

impact on student performance when OECD countries are examined jointly do not show the same relationship within each country. Not included in the model were school factors that already did not have any measurable gross effect.

The combined characteristics of students and schools explain over 70 per cent of school performance differences…

Taken together, the students' characteristics, the socio-economic background of students and schools, the students' and school principals' perceptions of the school climate, the school principals' reports on school policies and practices, and the assessment of the availability and quality of educational resources, as measured by PISA, account for 8 per cent of the variation in the average performance of OECD countries, an average of 71 per cent of the performance variation between schools within countries, and an average of 54 per cent of the performance variation of students within schools (see Model 4 in Table 5.21a).

…within which one can compare the net effect of certain factors…

Where can schools make most of a difference? An analysis of the question of the added value which schools can provide puts the emphasis on the net effects of school factors, *i.e.* the effect of school climate, policies, practices and resources over and above the performance differences between students and schools that are accounted for by their socio-economic background.

…even if this may underestimate the contribution of these factors to school performance.

As explained above, these results are likely to understate the true effect of school climate, school policies and practices and resources on school performance because some of the performance differences are attributable to school and socio-economic factors jointly as is, for example, the case when socio-economically advantaged students create a better learning climate, benefit more from strong school policies and practices, or have better access to school resources. Therefore, although the focus of the following analysis is on the net effects, readers are pointed to instances where the gap between net and gross effects is particularly large.

To assess the influence of school factors, an adjustment can be made for demographic and socio-economic characteristics of individuals…

To examine the net effects of school factors, adjustments were made for the following aspects of the demographic and socio-economic background of students and their families (see Model 2 in Table 5.21a):

- *Economic, social and cultural status.* Parents occupation and education, as well as students' access to home educational and cultural resources, as measured by one unit on the PISA index of economic, social and cultural status, add 24 score points in mathematics performance over and above the effects of the socio-economic variables listed in the following.
- *Students' gender.* Males show a mathematics performance advantage of 15 score points, the remaining socio-economic background factors equal.
- *Students' country of birth.* On average across OECD countries, students who were foreign born perform 12 score points below students born in the country where the PISA assessment took place, even though the latter might still have foreign-born parents, the other socio-economic background factors being equal.

- *Language spoken at home.* Over and above the other socio-economic aspects considered here, speaking a language at home that differs from the language of assessment and from other official languages or national dialects most of the time or always is associated with a mathematics performance disadvantage of 10 score points.
- *Pre-school or early education attendance.* Students who attended pre-school for at least one year, have an 8 score points advantage in mathematics performance, the remaining socio-economic background factors equal.

...as well as the characteristics of whole schools.

As shown in preceding sections, the aggregate social intake of schools can have significant effects over and above students' individual socio-economic backgrounds. To account for this, adjustments were made for this as well. The average PISA index of economic, social and cultural status for all 15-year-olds enrolled in the school (a proxy for the socio-economic intake of the school) makes, with 63 score points on average across OECD countries, the largest contribution over and above students' individual socio-economic backgrounds (see Model 3 in Table 5.21a).

The following discusses the association between school climate, school policies and practices, as well as school resources and school characteristics, on the one hand, and student performance in mathematics, on the other. For each factor, the results show the strength of the association that remains after all other factors examined here as well as the socio-economic background of students and schools have been taken into account (Model 4 in Table 5.21a). In interpreting the results, it needs to be taken into account that some of the school policies and practices are regulated at national or subnational levels, so that there is very limited variation in these within each country. In such cases, the importance of these variables may be underestimated by the models. An example is the decision-making responsibility of schools. Here a within-country relationship with school performance is often not measurable because there tends to be very little variation in the decision-making responsibilities of schools within countries. Nevertheless, as shown above, countries with more decision-making responsibility in some of the aspects of school management tend to perform better overall.

The aspect of school climate that detracts most from student performance is poor student-teacher relations...

Among the school climate variables included in the model,[23] students' concern for poor student-teacher relations has, on average across OECD countries, the strongest negative impact on mathematics performance. On average, students who strongly disagree that they and their peers get along well with most teachers, that most teachers are interested in students' well being, that most teachers really listen to what the students had to say, that if students needed help, they received from their teachers and that most of the teachers treat students fairly show an mathematics performance disadvantage of 74 score points, after socio-economic factors are taken into account (Table 5.21a). However, it needs to be taken into account that the percentage of students reporting such poor student-teacher relations tends to be low, so that the effect is statistically significant only in Australia, Canada, Finland, Mexico, Sweden and the United States, and the partner countries Indonesia and Thailand (Table 5.21b).

...with discipline and student morale having smaller separate effects...

One unit on the PISA index of students' perceptions of disciplinary climate adds, on average across OECD countries, another 27 score points, even after socio-economic factors are taken into account (Table 5.21a). The effect is statistically significant in all countries except Finland, Iceland, Luxembourg, the Netherlands and Sweden, and its size reaches 60 score points or more points in Portugal, Turkey and the partner country Serbia (Table 5.21b).

The effect of teacher and student morale tends to be smaller...

On average across OECD countries, a small positive effect also resulted from principals' perceptions of students' morale and commitment. However, the pattern is mixed and some countries show negative effects. One unit on the PISA index of school principals' perceptions of students' morale and commitment has an effect of 10 score points before an adjustment for socio-economic factors is made (*i.e.,* in Model 5 in Table 5.21a) and 3 score points afterwards (*i.e.,* in Model 4 in Table 5.21a). Statistically significant positive effects are found in Australia, Canada, Finland, Korea, Spain, Sweden and the partner country Hong Kong-China.

...as is the effect of students' sense of belonging at school.

One unit of the index of students' sense of belonging at school has a sizeable effect of 15 score points on student performance before accounting for socio-economic background factors (Table 5.21a). However, once the socio-economic intake of schools is accounted for, the effect is small and no longer statistically significant, signalling that the social composition of schools may play a major role in shaping students' sense of belonging at school. Nevertheless, in some countries – most notably Belgium, Luxembourg, and Switzerland and in the partner countries Indonesia and Latvia – the effect remains large even after accounting for socio-economic characteristics, with one unit of the index of students' sense of belonging at school associated with a performance difference between 20 and 65 score points. Finland and Ireland show a negative effect (Table 5.21b).

Among school policies and practices, the most pronounced effect on performance is exerted by selective admission policies...

Perhaps not surprisingly, among the school policies and practices examined in this comparison, on average across OECD countries, the strongest effects are related to selective admissions policies in schools. Schools in which academic records or feeder school recommendations are of high priority or a prerequisite for student admittance score 12 score points higher (Table 5.21a), and between 15 and 31 score points in the Czech Republic, Finland, Germany, Hungary, Luxembourg, Norway, the Slovak Republic, Sweden and the partner countries Brazil and Latvia (Table 5.21b). However, a negative impact of 17 score points is found in Denmark.

...while avoidance of ability grouping...

On average across OECD countries, avoiding ability grouping in mathematics classes has an overall positive effect on student performance that is equivalent to 9 score points, but this is reduced to 5 score points after accounting for the impact of socio-economic background (Table 5.21a). Given the small proportion of schools reporting that no ability grouping is used in many countries, the effect tends not to be statistically significant at the country level.

Schools' offering of activities to promote student engagement with mathematics, such as mathematics competitions, mathematics clubs or computer clubs related to mathematics, show a positive impact as well, over and above all other factors. Each additional such activity that is offered by schools is associated with an average performance advantage of 7 score points. However, once socio-economic factors are accounted for, only 2 points remain, signalling that schools' offerings of activities to promote the engagement with mathematics depend highly on their socio-economic characteristics (Table 5.21a).

...as well as schools' offerings of activities to promote student engagement with mathematics have smaller positive effects.

Finally, the frequency with which teacher-developed tests are used has a small effect of 1 score point, on average, for each additional time per year such tests are used. However, the effect disappears once socio-economic factors are taken into account. For standardised tests, a small negative effect of -1 score point is observed but also that effect disappears once socio-economic factors are taken into account (Table 5.21a).

Teacher/student staff ratios and class size are often considered important school resource factors. Smaller classes are valued by parents and teachers because they may allow students to receive more individual attention from their teachers and reduce the disadvantage of managing large number of students and their work. However, the predominance of teacher costs in educational expenditure means that reducing class size leads to sharp increases in the costs of education. It is also difficult to examine the relationship between student/teaching staff ratios and class sizes, on the one hand, and student performance on the other. For example, in many countries, there is a tendency for teachers and schools to put weaker students into smaller classes so that these students can receive the necessary attention. In such situations, smaller classes would tend to perform worse, even if reducing class size were conducive to improving performance, all other things being equal. Perhaps because these influences often compensate each other, the model does not detect a statistically significant relationship between student/teaching staff ratios and student performance (Table 5.21a).

In terms of resources, teacher/student ratios are considered important, but PISA does not detect a performance benefit, perhaps because weaker students are often put in small classes.

On average across OECD countries, school size tends to be positively related to school performance, all other things equal. Each 100 additional students are associated with an advantage of 5 score points before socio-economic factors are taken into account and 2 points after (Table 5.21a).

Private schools have a performance advantage of 11 score points, but once socio-economic factors have been taken into account, public schools emerge with an advantage of 7 score points. As noted before, this suggests that private schools may realise a significant part of their advantage because their combined socio-economic intake allows them to create a learning environment that is more conducive to learning (Table 5.21a).

The performance advantage of private schools turns into an advantage for public schools once the socio-economic intake of schools is accounted for.

Schools located in communities with fewer than 3,000 inhabitants have an advantage of 9 score points, after their average socio-economic intake has

Similarly, the disadvantage of schools located in rural areas turns into an advantage once their socio-economic intake is taken into account.

been accounted for (Table 5.21a). This suggests that much of the performance disadvantage that is sometimes observed for rural schools is related to socio-economic factors rather than the quality of educational services provided by these schools. However, this effect varies greatly among countries and is positive in some, most notably in Canada and the United States, and negative in others, most notably Mexico (Table 5.21b).

Educational resources show limited association with performance.

On average across OECD countries, schools' educational resources are also positively associated with school performance, but one unit on the PISA index of the quality of the school's educational resources corresponds to only 2 score points (Table 5.21a).[24] Large effects are only observed for Belgium (6 score points), Italy (10 score points) and the partner country the Russian Federation (8 score points) (Table 5.21b).

Finally, on average across OECD countries, students enrolled in schools where principals reported a high degree of teacher shortage tended to perform lower, although this disadvantage is small once socio-economic factors are taken into account (Table 5.21a).[25] The relationship between perceived teacher shortage and performance was particularly strong in the Czech Republic, where one unit on the teacher-shortage index was associated with a performance drop of 16 score points. For Belgium and Luxembourg a score point differences of 6 and 13 points are observed (Table 5.21b).

Overall, then, each school factor has only a limited separate effect on performance, but contributes to the effect of socio-economic advantage.

The analyses suggest that school and socio-economic background factors closely interact. The combined influence of school and background factors on differences in school performance is not simply the sum of the influence of school factors and that of background factors. This is because many characteristics of schools are closely associated with the characteristics of the families of their students. This means that some of the effect of family background on school results is *mediated* by the school characteristics. Consider, for example, the predicted difference between PISA mathematics scores in two schools whose students have different backgrounds – with a gap of one unit in their average scores on the index of economic, social and cultural status. In total, students at the better-off school are expected to score 63 score points more, on average, across OECD countries (Model 3 in Table 5.21a).

Part of this advantage may be gained from better off students being more likely to attend a school with strong characteristics.

Some of this difference arises because, on average, better-off students attend schools with features associated with better performance – this is the *mediated* portion. It accounts for about 10 of the 63 score points' difference. The remaining effect of student background – that which is not associated with school variables – accounts for 53 score points (Model 4 in Table 5.21a). This 10-point difference can be taken as a measure of the extent to which school systems tend, on average, to reinforce the advantage of those students who already come from advantaged backgrounds. This should be of concern for policy makers seeking to provide equitable learning opportunities for all students.

INSTITUTIONAL DIFFERENTIATION

Education systems can be classified by the degree to which they select and separate students...

As noted in Chapter 4, catering for an increasingly diverse student body and narrowing the gaps in student performance represent formidable challenges for all countries and the approaches that countries have chosen to address these demands vary. Some countries have non-selective school systems that seek to provide all students with similar opportunities for learning by requiring that each school caters for the full range of student performance. Other countries respond to diversity explicitly by forming groups of students through selection either between schools or between classes within schools, with the aim of serving students according to their academic potential and/or interests in specific programmes. Education systems can be located on a continuum ranging from systems with low stratification at system, school and classroom levels to systems that are highly differentiated. Figure 5.20a displays some features of school systems that are relevant in this context.

...and the number of tracks into which they sort students of differing ability helps explain both the degree to which schools differ in their performance...

One device to differentiate among students is the use of different institutions or programmes that seek to group students, in accordance with their performance or other characteristics. Where students are sorted based on their performance, this is often done on the assumption that their talents will develop best in a learning environment in which they can stimulate each other equally well, and that an intellectually homogeneous student body will be conducive to the efficiency of teaching. The measure shown in Figure 5.20a ranges from essentially undivided secondary education until the age of 15 years to systems with four or more school types or distinct educational programmes (Austria, Belgium, the Czech Republic, Germany, Ireland, the Netherlands, the Slovak Republic and Switzerland). Simple cross-country comparisons show that, while the number of school types or distinct educational programmes available to 15-year-olds is not related to average country performance in mathematics (see column 1 and row 7 in Figure 5.20b), it accounts for 39 per cent of the share of the OECD average variation that lies between schools (see column 1 and row 9 in Figure 5.20b).[26]

...as well as the strength of the impact of socio-economic background on learning outcomes.

No less important, it accounts for 26 per cent of the cross-country variation among countries in the strength of the relationship between socio-economic background and student performance (see column 1 and row 10 in Figure 5.20b). In other words, in countries with a larger number of distinct programme types, socio-economic background tends to have a significantly larger impact on student performance such that equity is much harder to realise.

The percentage of 15 year olds in vocational programmes shows similar associations.

A specific aspect of such differentiation is the separate provision of academic and vocational programmes. Vocational programmes differ from academic ones not only with regard to their curriculum, but also in that they generally prepare students for specific types of occupations and, in some cases, for direct entry into the labour market. The picture that emerges when the proportion of students enrolled in vocational educational programmes is related to between-school differences remains very similar to the one that the relationship with the number of school types or programmes reveals (see column 2 in Figure 5.20b).

Figure 5.20a ■ **Structural features of school systems across the OECD countries**

	Number of school types or distinct educational programmes available to 15-year-olds	Proportion of 15-year-olds enrolled in programmes that give access to vocational studies at the next programme level or direct access to the labour market[1]	First age of selection in the education system	Proportion of repeaters among 15-year-olds in:		
				Primary education	Lower secondary education	Upper secondary education
Australia	1	8.9	16	8.1	1.3	m
Austria	4	42.9	10	5.0	4.7	3.9
Belgium	4	22.8	12	16.6	7.7	8.2
Canada	1	a	13	5.8	5.6	0.8
Czech Republic	5	16.9	11	1.9	1.7	0.0
Denmark	1	0.0	16	2.8	0.7	0.0
Finland	1	0.0	16	2.4	0.0	0.0
France	m	9.5	15	15.6	26.7	m
Germany	4	a	10	9.0	14.1	m
Greece	2	19.9	15	0.9	6.3	1.1
Hungary	3	19.6	11	4.3	3.8	3.3
Iceland	1	0.0	16	0.6	0.4	0.0
Ireland	4	17.8	15	13.4	1.2	0.3
Italy	3	m	14	1.6	5.7	8.8
Japan	2	25.4	15	0.0	0.0	0.0
Korea	3	26.7	14	0.3	0.5	0.2
Luxembourg	4	4.6	13	15.1	25.3	m
Mexico	3	5.8	12	22.6	6.3	2.7
Netherlands	4	61.3	12	21.4	9.5	m
New Zealand	1	0.0	16	3.9	1.6	0.8
Norway	1	0.0	16	0.0	0.0	0.0
Poland	3	m	15	2.7	1.9	m
Portugal	3	8.8	15	17.1	16.9	0.2
Slovak Republic	5	2.7	11	1.7	1.3	m
Spain	1	0.0	16	6.5	25.2	m
Sweden	1	0.0	16	3.0	1.0	0.0
Switzerland	4	8.8	15	14.1	8.2	1.3
Turkey	3	m	11	5.1	4.0	9.9
United States	1	0.0	16	8.0	4.2	1.0
OECD average	3	12.6	14	7.2	6.4	2.0
United Kingdom[3]	1	m	16	2.1	0.9	0.7

	Performance on the mathematics scale				Variance expressed as a percentage of the average variance in student performance across OECD countries		
	Mean score	S.E.	Standard deviation	S.E.	Total variance in student performance	Total variance in student performance between schools	Average of the standardised indices[2]
Australia	524	(2.1)	95	(1.5)	105	22	-0.64
Austria	506	(3.3)	93	(1.7)	98	55	1.21
Belgium	529	(2.3)	110	(1.8)	122	57	0.94
Canada	532	(1.8)	87	(1.0)	89	15	-0.24
Czech Republic	516	(3.5)	96	(1.9)	100	51	0.73
Denmark	514	(2.7)	91	(1.4)	96	13	-0.89
Finland	544	(1.9)	84	(1.1)	81	4	-0.90
France	511	(2.5)	92	(1.8)	w	w	0.41
Germany	503	(3.3)	103	(1.8)	108	56	1.15
Greece	445	(3.9)	94	(1.8)	102	39	-0.15
Hungary	490	(2.8)	94	(2.0)	102	66	0.50
Iceland	515	(1.4)	90	(1.2)	95	4	-0.92
Ireland	503	(2.4)	85	(1.3)	84	13	0.25
Italy	466	(3.1)	96	(1.9)	107	57	-0.03
Japan	534	(4.0)	101	(2.8)	116	62	-0.22
Korea	542	(3.2)	92	(2.1)	99	42	0.11
Luxembourg	493	(1.0)	92	(1.0)	98	31	0.74
Mexico	385	(3.6)	85	(1.9)	85	29	0.46
Netherlands	538	(3.1)	93	(2.3)	92	55	1.60
New Zealand	523	(2.3)	98	(1.2)	110	20	-0.85
Norway	495	(2.4)	92	(1.2)	98	6	-0.88
Poland	490	(2.5)	90	(1.3)	95	12	-0.27
Portugal	466	(3.4)	88	(1.7)	89	30	0.14
Slovak Republic	498	(3.3)	93	(2.3)	99	42	0.49
Spain	485	(2.4)	88	(1.3)	91	17	-0.43
Sweden	509	(2.6)	95	(1.8)	103	11	-0.89
Switzerland	527	(3.4)	98	(2.0)	111	36	0.16
Turkey	423	(6.7)	105	(5.3)	127	69	0.76
United States	483	(2.9)	95	(1.3)	105	27	-0.76
OECD average	500	(0.6)	100	(0.4)	100	34	0.00
United Kingdom[3]	m	m	m	m	97	21	-0.91

1. Based on the designation of the study programme (ISCED categories B and C).
2. This average includes the standardised indices of first age of selection, the number of school types or distinct educational programmes available to 15-year-olds, the proportion of grade repeaters at the different levels, and the proportion of 15-year-olds enrolled in programmes that give access to vocational studies at the next programme level or direct access to the labour market.
3. Response rate too low to ensure comparability (see Annex A3).

Source: OECD PISA 2003 database; OECD education database; *Education Policy Analysis* (OECD, 2002e).

Figure 5.20b ■ **Inter-correlation matrix of averages of structural features across the OECD countries**

	Number of school types or distinct educational programmes available to 15-year-olds	Proportion of 15-year-olds enrolled in programmes that give access to vocational studies at the next programme level or direct access to the labour market	First age of selection in the education system	Proportion of repeaters in primary education	Proportion of repeaters in lower secondary education	Proportion of repeaters in upper secondary education	Performance on the mathematics scale – Mean score	Performance on the mathematics scale – Standard deviation	Total variance in student performance between schools	Strength of the relationship between the index of economic, social and cultural background and student performance
Number of school types or distinct educational programmes available to 15-year-olds	1									
Proportion of 15-year-olds enrolled in programmes that give access to vocational studies at the next programme level or direct access to the labour market	**0.50**	1								
First age of selection in the education system	**–0.76**	**–0.52**	1							
Repeaters in primary education	**0.39**	0.27	–0.23	1						
Proportion of repeaters in lower secondary education	0.22	–0.02	–0.11	**0.56**	1					
Proportion of repeaters in upper secondary education	**0.45**	0.22	**–0.53**	0.23	0.27	1				
Performance on the mathematics scale – Mean score	–0.09	0.26	0.23	–0.21	–0.17	–0.40	1			
Performance on the mathematics scale – Standard deviation	0.25	0.19	–0.29	–0.05	–0.06	**0.58**	0.08	1		
Total variance in student performance between schools	**0.62**	**0.63**	**–0.70**	0.15	0.16	**0.65**	–0.14	**0.62**	1	
Strength of the relationship between the index of economic, social and cultural background and student performance	**0.51**	0.24	**–0.53**	0.29	0.17	**0.43**	–0.19	**0.48**	**0.57**	1

Note: Data marked in bold are statistically significant at the 0.05 level (2-tailed). The proportion of explained variance is obtained by squaring the correlations shown in this figure.
Source: OECD PISA 2003 database; OECD education database; *Education Policy Analysis* (OECD, 2002e).

Early selection is also closely associated with school difference and social disparities…

An important dimension of tracking and streaming is the age at which decisions between different school types are generally made, and therefore students and their parents are faced with choices. Such decisions occur very early in Austria and Germany, at around age 10. By contrast, in countries such as New Zealand, Spain and the United States no formal differentiation takes place at least between schools until the completion of secondary education. There is no statistically significant correlation between the age of selection and country mean performance in mathematics. However, the share of the OECD average variation in student performance that lies between students and schools tends to be much higher in countries with early selection policies. In fact, the age of selection accounts for half of the between-school differences (see column 3 and row 9 in Figure 5.20b). While this, in itself, is not surprising because variation in school performance is an intended outcome of stratification, the findings also show that education systems with lower ages of selection tend to show much larger social disparities, with the age of selection explaining 28 per cent of the country average of the strength of the relationship between the PISA index of economic, social and cultural status and student performance in mathematics (see column 3 and row 10 in Figure 5.20b).

...and so is a high prevalence of grade repetition.

Grade repetition can also be considered as a form of differentiation in that it seeks to adapt curriculum content to student performance. The results suggest that countries with high proportions of students who have repeated a grade at the upper secondary level at least once tend to perform worse (with the relationship accounting for around 16 per cent of the variance) (see column 6 and row 7 in Figure 5.20b). Moreover, the frequency of grade repetition at the upper secondary level also accounts for 34 per cent of the OECD average variation that lies between students and 43 per cent of the OECD average variation that lies between schools (see column 6 and rows 8 and 9 in Figure 5.20b). Moreover, countries with higher rates of grade repetition at the upper secondary level also show much larger social disparities, with 19 per cent of the OECD average variation in student performance that lies between schools accounted for by this variable (see column 6 and row 10 in Figure 5.20b). The relationships with grade repetition at primary and lower secondary levels are not statistically significant.

Overall, these results show that differentiation of students is associated with performance differences across schools and across social groups.

It is difficult to define these measures of differentiation in ways that are cross-nationally comparable and interpretable. However, as shown in Figure 5.20b, the various indicators of stratification that have been employed in these comparisons are highly interrelated so that the results do not depend in significant ways on how stratification is measured. The results can be summarised by constructing an index across the various measures of stratification.[27] Relating this index to the PISA performance measures reveals that the more differentiated and selective education systems tend to show not only much larger variation in school performance, but also larger performance differences between students from more and less advantaged family backgrounds. This is true for the various aspects of family background that were measured by PISA, and it remains true even when control variables such as national income are taken into account.

As a result, both overall variation in student performance and performance differences between schools tend to be greater in those countries with explicit differentiation between types of programme and schools at an early age.

Finally, it is noteworthy that the majority of the countries in which students report a comparatively low level of individual support from their teachers are also those with a particularly high degree of institutional differentiation.[28]

There is no clear-cut reason why differentiation should produce these results, but there are several possible explanations...

An explanation for these results is not straightforward. There is no intrinsic reason why institutional differentiation should necessarily lead to greater variation in student performance, or even to greater social selectivity. If teaching homogeneous groups of students is more efficient than teaching heterogeneous groups, this should increase the overall level of student performance rather than the dispersion of scores. However, in homogeneous environments, while high-performing students may profit from the wider opportunities to learn from one another, and stimulate each other's performance, low performers may not be able to access effective models and support.

It may also be that in highly differentiated systems it is easier to move students not meeting certain performance standards to other schools, tracks or streams with lower performance expectations, rather than investing the effort to raise their performance. Finally, it could be that a learning environment that has a greater variety of student abilities and backgrounds may stimulate teachers to use approaches that involve a higher degree of individual attention for students.

...including that highly differentiated systems may make it easer to move students not meeting certain standards to lower performing tracks, rather than investing efforts to raise their performance...

The reason why the age at which differentiation begins is closely associated with social selectivity may be explained by the fact that students are more dependent upon their parents and their parental resources when they are younger. In systems with a high degree of educational differentiation, parents from higher socio-economic backgrounds are in a better position to promote their children's chances than in a system in which such decisions are taken at a later age, and students themselves play a bigger role.

...and that early differentiation may emphasise parental influence at early ages.

The question, of course, remains whether differentiation might still contribute to raising overall performance levels. This question cannot be answered conclusively with a cross-sectional survey such as PISA. Although there is a tendency for the more stratified education systems to perform less well, this tendency is small and not statistically significant.

IMPLICATIONS FOR POLICY

This chapter has identified a range of school characteristics that can have a bearing on learning outcomes and on differences in these outcomes across schools. Taken together, the students' characteristics, the socio-economic background of students and schools, the students' and school principals' perceptions of the school climate, the school principals' reports on school policies and practices, and the assessment of the availability and quality of educational resources, as described in this chapter, account for 54 per cent of the variation in the average performance of OECD countries, an average of 71 per cent of the performance variation between schools within countries, and an average of 8 per cent of the performance variation of students within schools

The incidence of school characteristics known to be conducive to learning vary greatly across schools and countries, raising issues for policy makers

Even though it is not always possible to measure precisely the impact that each of these factors has on student performance, many of the identified differences within and between schools raise critical issues for policy makers. For example, both principals and students have widely differing views about the quality of the learning environment of their schools in different countries and in different schools within each country. These differences have been shown in research to affect whether teaching and learning is effective, as have differences in the ways in which schools are managed. Thus, these results show first and foremost a need to ensure that all schools have a learning climate, a management culture and resources that are compatible with effective teaching and learning.

PISA provides evidence on different relationships between school factors and performance: first, the difference separately attributable to a school characteristic…

As well as describing these school phenomena, PISA goes some way towards measuring their effect on student and school performance, of three kinds.

The first is an effect independent of other school factors and of socio-economic background. For example, in the case of discipline, to what extent can students in a well-disciplined school expect to do better than in one with poor discipline, if the social intake of the two schools are the same, and the schools are similar in terms of school policies, processes and resources. In these terms, PISA identifies few school factors with a substantial effect on performance. Nevertheless, the results suggest that schools can make a difference. Students and schools tend to perform better in a climate characterised by discipline and high levels of student morale and commitment. In contrast, schools with poor student-teacher relationships tend to perform significantly worse. Thus, schools can benefit from emphasising not just instructional techniques but the ways in which teachers relate to students. In addition, schools offering mathematics related activities also tend to perform better and so do schools which tend to avoid grouping students by ability and in which school principals assess the adequacy of teacher supply and educational resources positively.

…second, the effect of the higher-than-average home advantages of students attending schools with certain characteristics…

A second type of effect occurs where the socio-economic composition of schools makes it more likely that those with certain characteristics achieve better results. This part of the effect may have less direct implications for policy makers, since it would be misguided to try to improve a factor because it seems to be associated with performance, when in fact social background is the driving influence. Nevertheless, parents choosing schools may be justified in paying attention to such factors, as they are interested in the overall performance results of schools, including any effects that are conferred by the socio-economic intake of schools.

…and third, the joint effect of school and student background factors, which suggests that policy should focus on helping less advantaged schools improve on several fronts.

A third type of effect, and the most important one identified here, is where socio-economic and school factors are acting together. The analysis in this chapter suggests that socio-economic factors reinforce the impact school climate has on school performance in important ways and this should be of concern for policy makers seeking to ensure that all schools have committed teachers and an orderly climate, irrespective of their socio-economic intake. The effect may arise because students from more advantaged socio-economic backgrounds bring with them a higher level of discipline and more positive perceptions of school values, or perhaps because parental expectations of good classroom discipline and strong teacher commitment are higher in schools with advantaged socio-economic intake. Conversely, disadvantaged schools may experience less parental pressure towards enforcing effective disciplinary practices or making sure that absent or unmotivated teachers are replaced.

Similarly, the analysis has shown that a large proportion of the performance variation among schools is attributable to school policies, practices and resources and socio-economic jointly. Socio-economically advantaged schools may apply more effective school policies and practices, perhaps because the best teachers may choose to work there or they may have access to more and better resources.

All of this shows that the schools attended by advantaged students are themselves advantaged in a wide range of ways, and policies to improve schooling for those from less privileged families need to be similarly wide-ranging. The implication for policy is that there is a need to improve schools attended by students from less advantaged backgrounds, in order to work towards more equitable outcomes.

Such improvements are particularly needed in secondary school systems that differentiate students into different groups, where socio-economic advantage tends to have a greater effect.

This need is all the greater in school systems that separate students early into different school types or tracks, because not only does this type of stratification appear to lead to greater differences among schools, but it is also associated with greater than average socio-economic disparities in learning outcomes. Much of this is related to the different characteristics of the schools that students from different social groups attend in the countries concerned. One way of addressing this phenomenon may be to reduce segregation of social groups, potentially by reducing the degree of stratification of students within the school system. Other approaches seek to strengthen efforts to improve resources, policies, processes and climate in schools attended by students from less advantaged backgrounds. To some extent this may be a more clear-cut task in systems that differentiate than in ones where social segregation exists *de facto,* but where most schools are in principle comprehensive. In the former case, insofar as less advantaged students are concentrated in certain types of school, policies can potentially focus on improving conditions for these types. Yet such change is often not easily engineered, since some of the favourable conditions enjoyed by schools with advantaged intakes are not the product of policy but of behaviour, for example where better-off families put greater pressure on schools to improve, or better teachers are attracted to schools with easier-to-teach students. Only bold interventions are likely to be sufficient to overcome these inequities.

A particular policy message arising from these comparisons is the reinforced evidence showing the value of pre-school education...

Finally, the analysis sheds light on two particular issues that have been central to debates about educational improvement. The first concerns the extent to which educational experiences in early childhood bring long-term benefits. Some studies following the experiences of relatively small groups of students in particular countries have demonstrated that the gains to early childhood learning can be substantial and durable through youth and early adulthood. A wider measure of this effect is harder to obtain, since large-scale international studies tracking students over time are expensive. PISA was only able to rely on self-reports of 15-year-olds about whether they had attended early childhood education. It is therefore striking that in many countries it found a very substantial association between attending pre-school and performing well age 15, even after correcting for the fact that students with more advantaged backgrounds are more likely to do both. In nine OECD countries this effect was particularly great – ranging between half a proficiency level and just over one proficiency level in mathematics (30-73 points). This suggests that preschool investments may have effects that are still marked and widespread across the student population (and in some cases greater for the least advantaged students) 8-10 years into a child's school education.

...while policies to enhance overall performance only by moving funding from public to private institutions are subject to considerable uncertainty.

A second finding with close relevance to the educational debate concerns performance in private schools, including those receiving financial support by government. Overall, although not in every country, students in private schools perform better. However, much of this advantage disappears when the effect of the social background of students attending private schools is taken into account. There remains a statistically significant effect in some countries, but in all but five OECD countries (Canada, Germany, New Zealand, Mexico and Spain) this is less than a quarter of a proficiency level. That is to say, the potential performance gain from supporting children in private schools appears to be only half as great, and seen in fewer countries, than the gain from having at least a year's preschool education, as shown in the previous paragraph. Moreover, the private school advantage disappears entirely if one corrects for the whole school effect of social background – the gain in a student's predicted score associated with having more advantaged peers. There might still be some benefit associated with the school being private and not just its intake – the advantage of having more advantaged peers may be more likely to show through with certain kinds of school policies and approaches experienced in private schools. However, these comparisons show that the association between a school being private and its students doing well is at best tenuous. Thus, any policy to enhance overall performance only by moving funding from public to private institutions is subject to considerable uncertainty.

Notes

1. The reason why no such data were collected is that PISA only provides information on 15-year-olds. Relating data on *current* performance and *current* opportunities to learn would underestimate the extent of the relationship, because student learning outcomes at age 15 are shaped by their cumulative experiences in previous school years as well.

2. The response categories were "every lesson", "most lessons", "some lessons" and "never or hardly ever".

3. Note that students were asked to indicate their perceptions of teachers in their mathematics lessons in a single year of learning. Consequently, results should not be interpreted as a characterisation of all teachers that 15-year-olds have encountered during their years as students.

4. For the country Serbia and Montenegro, data for Montenegro are not available. The latter accounts for 7.9 per cent of the national population. The name "Serbia" is used as a shorthand for the Serbian part of Serbia and Montenegro.

5. On average across OECD countries, the index explains 0.2 per cent of the variation in student performance on the mathematics scale and this exceeds 1 per cent only in 8 OECD countries.

6. When comparing data between 2000 and 2003, it should be borne in mind that in 2000 school principals were asked to report with regard to the situation of 15-year-olds in their school whereas in 2003 school principals were asked to reflect the situation in the entire school in their responses. Similarly, in 2000 students were asked to reflect the situation in their language classes whereas in 2003 they were asked to reflect the situation in their mathematics classes.

7. This overall tendency was determined by averaging the difference between the percentage of school principals who report that learning was hindered to some extent or a lot by the various questions relating to the index in 2003 and 2000.

8. The estimates are based on the combined impact of the socio-economic and climate variables at the school level. Socio-economic context is measured by: the index of economic, social and cultural status, the student's place of birth and the language spoken at their home, the number of books at the student's home, the index of possessions related to "classical" culture in the family home, the student's gender, the school-level average index of economic, social and cultural status, the school location (rural/urban), and the school type (public/private). School climate is measured by: the index of student-teacher relations, the index of student's sense of belonging to school, the index of teacher support, the index of disciplinary climate, the index of students' morale and commitment, the index of teachers' morale and commitment, the index of teacher-related factors affecting school climate, and the index of student-related factors affecting school climate (see Annex A1). The analysis is undertaken for the combined OECD student population, with countries given equal weight. The resulting international model is then applied to each country to estimate the effects at the country level.

9. The response categories for these questions were "prerequisite", "high priority", "considered" and "not considered".

10. Denmark also falls into this category but, in the Danish school questionnaire, the question on assessment was narrowed to proficiency tests only, which may partially contribute to the low figures.

11. Technically, this percentage was derived by subtracting from 100 the weighted percentage of school principals who had checked the response category "not a main school responsibility of the school" for the relevant question.

12. The explained variance is obtained as the square of the cross-country correlation shown in the table.

13. The relative influence of the seven stakeholders was determined by averaging the percentage of 15-year-olds whose school principals report that the stakeholder in question has a direct influence across the four decision-making areas of staffing, budgeting, instructional content and assessment practices.

14. The estimates are based on the combined impact of socio-economic and policy and practice variables at the school level. Socio-economic context is measured by: the index of economic, social and cultural status, the student's place of birth and the language spoken at their home, the number of books at the student's home, the index of possessions related to "classical" culture in the family home, the student's gender, the school-level average index of economic, social and cultural status, the school location (rural/urban), and the school type (public/private). School policies and practices are measured by: academic selectivity of schools, the estimated times per year standardised tests are used, the estimated times per year teacher-developed tests are used, the use of ability grouping for all classes, the school offerings of extension activities, the number of decisions made at the school level regarding staffing and budgeting, and the number of decisions made at the school level regarding curriculum and assessment (see Annex A1). The analysis is undertaken for the combined OECD student population, with countries given equal weight. The resulting international model is then applied to each country to estimate the effects at the country level.

15. Students were asked how many minutes there are, on average, in a class period. They were also asked how many class periods they had spent in their school in the preceding week in total and for mathematics. The figures in the chart were obtained through simple multiplication of the two factors and the assumption is made that the preceding week is typical for an average school week in the school year. The numbers do not reflect differences in the number of instructional weeks in the school year.

16. The reduction is calculated for those countries with statistically significant effects prior to the adjustment.

17. This was estimated by the interaction between the PISA index of economic, social and cultural status and the incidence of pre-school attendance.

18. On average across OECD countries, the PISA index of the quality of the physical infrastructure of schools explains 1 per cent of the variation in mathematics performance.

19. On average across OECD countries, the PISA index of the quality of the educational resources of schools explains 2.5 per cent of the variation in mathematics performance.

20. In PISA, public schools are defined as educational instructional institutions that are controlled and managed directly by a public education authority or agency; or controlled and managed either by a government agency directly or by a governing body (council, committee, etc.), most of whose members were either appointed by a public authority or elected by public

franchise. Private schools are defined as educational instructional institutions that are controlled and managed by a non-governmental organisation (*e.g.*, a church, a trade union or a business enterprise) or if their governing board consisted mostly of members not selected by a public agency.

21. For the comparisons below, government-dependent and government-independent private schools were combined as otherwise the cell sizes in the models would have been too small. Moreover, only countries with at least 3 per cent of students enrolled in private schools have been included in this comparison.

22. The estimates are based on the combined impact of socio-economic and school resource variables. Socio-economic context is measured by: the index of economic, social and cultural status, the student's place of birth and the language spoken at their home, the number of books at the student's home, the index of possessions related to "classical" culture in the family home, the student's gender, the school-level average index of economic, social and cultural status, the school location (rural/urban), and the school type (public/private). School resource variables include: class size, school size, school size squared, the student-teacher ratio, the index of the quality of the school's educational resources, and the index of teacher shortage (see Annex A1). The analysis is undertaken for the combined OECD student population, with countries given equal weight. The resulting international model is then applied to each country to estimate the effects at the country level.

23. These variables included: the PISA index of school principals' perception of the school climate; the PISA index of teacher-student relations; the PISA index of students' sense of belonging to school; the PISA index of disciplinary climate; the PISA index of school principals' perception of student morale and commitment; the PISA index of school principals' perception of teacher morale and commitment; and the PISA index of school principals' perception of teacher behaviour.

24. One unit of the PISA index of the quality of school's educational resources has an effect of 2.4 score points before socio-economic factors are taken into account and 1.7 score point after.

25. One unit of the index of teacher shortage corresponds to 4 point score difference and to 2 score points (which is not statistically significant) after socio-economic factors are taken into account.

26. The proportion of explained variation is obtained by squaring the correlation shown in Figure 5.20b.

27. For the purpose of this analysis, the normalised components were averaged with equal weight, with the measure of the age of selection inverted.

28. In the Czech Republic, Germany, Italy and Luxembourg, for example, at least 51 per cent of students say that their mathematics teachers never show interest in every student's learning or do so only in some lessons (as opposed to most lessons or every lesson), at least 27 per cent of students say that their teachers never or only in some lessons provide an opportunity for students to express their opinions, and 58 per cent or more of students say that their teachers never or only in some lessons help them with their learning. (For a further analysis of the relationship between teacher support and student performance, see OECD, 2001a.)

A Profile of Student Performance in Reading and Science

INTRODUCTION

The 2003 survey provides an update of reading and science performance.

In PISA 2003, the areas of reading and science were given smaller amounts of assessment time than mathematics (the focus of the 2003 assessment), with 60 minutes for each allowing an update on overall performance rather than the kind of in-depth analysis of knowledge and skills shown for mathematics in Chapter 2. This chapter describes how PISA 2003 measures student achievement in reading and science, examines student outcomes in these two areas, and also compares outcomes for PISA 2003 with PISA 2000.

HOW READING LITERACY IS MEASURED IN PISA

PISA measures students' applied ability to deal with written material…

Reading literacy focuses on the ability of students to use written information in situations which they encounter in their life. In PISA, reading literacy is defined as understanding, using and reflecting written texts, in order to achieve one's goals, to develop one's knowledge and potential and to participate in society. This definition goes beyond the traditional notion of decoding information and literal interpretation of what is written towards more applied tasks.

The concept of reading literacy in PISA is defined by three dimensions: the *format* of the reading material, the *type* of reading task or reading aspects, and the *situation* or the use for which the text was constructed.

…through handling different kinds of texts…

The first dimension, the text format, classifies the reading material or texts into continuous and non-continuous texts. Continuous texts are typically composed of sentences that are, in turn, organised into paragraphs. These may fit under larger structures such as sections, chapters and books. Non-continuous texts are organised differently from continuous texts as they require a different reading approach and can be classified according to their format. Outcomes of students on two reading scales based on the form of the text were reported in the PISA 2000 report *Reading for Change – Performance and Engagement across Countries* (OECD, 2002b).

…and performing different types of reading tasks…

The second dimension is defined by the three reading aspects. Some tasks required students to retrieve information – that is, to locate single or multiple pieces of information in a text. Other tasks required students to interpret texts – that is, to construct meaning and draw inferences from written information. The third type of task required students to reflect on and evaluate texts – that is, to relate written information to their prior knowledge, ideas and experiences. In PISA 2000 student performance in these three types of task were each reported on a separate scale. In 2003, however, less assessment time was allocated to reading and results are reported only on a single reading literacy scale that combines the three types of tasks.

…in relation to various situations where reading is needed.

The third dimension, the situation or context, reflects the categorisation of texts based on the author's intended use, the relationship with other persons implicitly or explicitly associated with the text, and the general content. The situations included in PISA and selected to maximise the diversity of content included in the reading literacy assessment were reading for private use (personal), reading for public use, reading for work (occupational) and reading for education.

A full description of the conceptual framework underlying the PISA assessment of reading literacy is provided in *The PISA 2003 Assessment Framework: Mathematics, Reading, Science and Problem Solving Knowledge and Skills* (OECD, 2003e).

STUDENT PERFORMANCE IN READING

PISA 2003 measures reading in the framework established in 2000, using a subset of tasks used in the PISA 2000 assessment...

The principles for the reporting of results in reading are similar to those applied for mathematics (see Chapter 2). However, unlike in mathematics, where the scales were newly established for the 2003 assessment, the PISA 2003 reading scale is anchored to the results of the 2000 assessment. Since reading was the focus of the 2000 assessment, it was possible to fully develop the instrument for measuring reading literacy at that stage, so the PISA 2000 mean of 500 has been established as the benchmark against which future reading performance will be measured. For reading literacy, PISA 2003 uses an identical framework and a subset of items from PISA 2000. To ensure comparability in calculating trends, the 28 reading items used in PISA 2003 are a subset of the 141 items used in 2000. The subset of items was selected taking the relative balance of aspects of the framework into account; for example, in both years, the proportion of items falling into each task classification is similar (see Table A6.2 for the breakdown of items by the various aspects of the framework).

...and reports results on the same scale that was used in 2000.

Therefore, the reading literacy results that are presented in this chapter are based on the reading literacy proficiency scale that was developed for PISA 2000 which had a mean of 500 and a standard deviation of 100 for the 27 OECD countries that participated. The PISA 2003 results include 29 OECD countries – the Slovak Republic and Turkey joined PISA in 2003 and the Netherlands met all technical standards in 2003, while the United Kingdom has been excluded from the results as it failed to reach the technical standards required by PISA 2003. For the 25 OECD countries for which comparable data are available for both the PISA 2000 and 2003 assessments, the average performance has essentially remained unchanged.[1] However, mainly because of the inclusion of new countries in 2003, the overall OECD mean for reading literacy is now 494 score points and the standard deviation is 100 score points.

The scale divides students into five levels of proficiency...

As in 2000, reading scores in 2003 are reported according to five levels of proficiency, corresponding to tasks of varying difficulty. Proficiency levels are defined by tasks sharing common characteristics including conceptual or substantive as well as statistical ones so that tasks within each level meet certain technical specifications (see Chapter 2). Level 5 corresponds to a score of more than 625, Level 4 to scores in the range 553 to 625, Level 3 to scores from 481 to 552, Level 2 to scores from 408 to 480, and Level 1 to scores from 335 to 407.

...according to the difficulty of tasks that they can usually answer correctly...

Students at a particular level not only demonstrate the knowledge and skills associated with that level but also the proficiencies required at lower levels. For example, all students proficient at Level 3 are also proficient at Levels 1 and 2. All students at a given level are expected to answer at least half of the items at that level correctly (see Chapter 2).

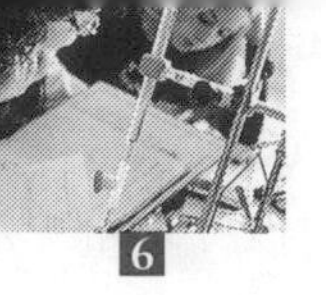

Figure 6.1 ■ **Summary descriptions for the five levels of proficiency in reading literacy**

Level	Retrieving information	Interpreting	Reflecting and evaluating
5	Locate and possibly sequence or combine multiple pieces of deeply embedded information, some of which may be outside the main body of the text. Infer which information in the text is relevant to the task. Deal with highly plausible and/or extensive competing information.	Either construe the meaning of nuanced language or demonstrate a full and detailed understanding of a text.	Critically evaluate or hypothesise, drawing on specialised knowledge. Deal with concepts that are contrary to expectations and draw on a deep understanding of long or complex texts.
	Continuous texts: Analyse texts whose discourse structure is not obvious or clearly marked, in order to discern the relationship of specific parts of the text to its implicit theme or intention. ***Non-continuous texts***: Identify patterns among many pieces of information presented in a display which may be long and detailed, sometimes by referring to information external to the display. The reader may need to realise independently that a full understanding of the section of text requires reference to a separate part of the same document, such as a footnote.		
4	Locate and possibly sequence or combine multiple pieces of embedded information, each of which may need to meet multiple criteria, in a text with familiar context or form. Infer which information in the text is relevant to the task.	Use a high level of text-based inference to understand and apply categories in an unfamiliar context, and to construe the meaning of a section of text by taking into account the text as a whole. Deal with ambiguities, ideas that are contrary to expectation and ideas that are negatively worded.	Use formal or public knowledge to hypothesise about or critically evaluate a text. Show accurate understanding of long or complex texts.
	Continuous texts: Follow linguistic or thematic links over several paragraphs, often in the absence of clear discourse markers, in order to locate, interpret or evaluate embedded information or to infer psychological or metaphysical meaning. ***Non-continuous texts***: Scan a long, detailed text in order to find relevant information, often with little or no assistance from organisers such as labels or special formatting, to locate several pieces of information to be compared or combined.		
3	Locate, and in some cases recognise the relationship between pieces of information, each of which may need to meet multiple criteria. Deal with prominent competing information.	Integrate several parts of a text in order to identify a main idea, understand a relationship or construe the meaning of a word or phrase. Compare, contrast or categorise taking many criteria into account. Deal with competing information.	Make connections or comparisons, give explanations, or evaluate a feature of text. Demonstrate a detailed understanding of the text in relation to familiar, everyday knowledge, or draw on less common knowledge.
	Continuous texts: Use conventions of text organisation, where present, and follow implicit or explicit logical links such as cause and effect relationships across sentences or paragraphs in order to locate, interpret or evaluate information. ***Non-continuous texts***: Consider one display in the light of a second, separate document or display, possibly in a different format, or combine several pieces of spatial, verbal and numeric information in a graph or map to draw conclusions about the information represented.		

Figure 6.1 *(continued)* ■ **Summary descriptions for the five levels of proficiency in reading literacy**

Level	Retrieving information	Interpreting	Reflecting and evaluating
2	Locate one or more pieces of information, each of which may be required to meet multiple criteria. Deal with competing information.	Identify the main idea in a text, understand relationships, form or apply simple categories, or construe meaning within a limited part of the text when the information is not prominent and low-level inferences are required.	Make a comparison or connections between the text and outside knowledge, or explain a feature of the text by drawing on personal experience and attitudes.
	Continuous texts: Follow logical and linguistic connections within a paragraph in order to locate or interpret information; or synthesise information across texts or parts of a text in order to infer the author's purpose. ***Non-continuous texts***: Demonstrate a grasp of the underlying structure of a visual display such as a simple tree diagram or table, or combine two pieces of information from a graph or table.		
1	Locate one or more independent pieces of explicitly stated information, typically meeting a single criterion, with little or no competing information in the text.	Recognise the main theme or author's purpose in a text about a familiar topic, when the required information in the text is prominent.	Make a simple connection between information in the text and common, everyday knowledge.
	Continuous texts: Use redundancy, paragraph headings or common print conventions to form an impression of the main idea of the text, or to locate information stated explicitly within a short section of text. ***Non-continuous texts***: Focus on discrete pieces of information, usually within a single display such as a simple map, a line graph or a bar graph that presents only a small amount of information in a straightforward way, and in which most of the verbal text is limited to a small number of words or phrases.		

Students scoring below 335 score points, *i.e.*, those who do not reach Level 1, are not able to routinely show the most basic skills that PISA seeks to measure. While such performance should not be interpreted to mean that those students have no literacy skills at all, performance below Level 1 does signal serious deficiencies in students' ability to use reading literacy as a tool for the acquisition of knowledge and skills in other areas. Similarly, since Level 5 is also unbounded, some students participating in PISA may demonstrate higher reading skills than those measured by the assessment.

...plus a sixth group made up of those unable to show basic functional reading skills.

The establishment of proficiency levels in reading makes it possible not only to rank students' performance but also to describe what they can do (Figure 6.1). Each successive reading level is associated with tasks of ascending difficulty. The tasks at each level of reading literacy were judged by panels of experts to share certain features and requirements and to differ consistently from tasks at either higher or lower levels. The assumed difficulty of tasks was then validated empirically on the basis of student performance in participating countries.

Tasks in each proficiency level have identifiable features...

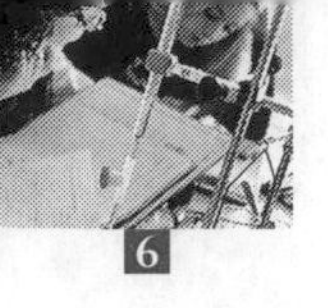

The reading literacy tasks used in PISA 2003 include the three dimensions previously described and have a diverse range of difficulty. Samples of the reading tasks (a total of 45 items) were released after PISA 2000 and can be found in the publication *Sample Tasks from the PISA 2000 Assessment – Reading, Mathematical and Scientific Literacy* (OECD, 2002c). Each item includes an indication of the dimension being assessed, and a description of the knowledge and skills being assessed. These descriptions provide some insight into the range of processes required of students and the proficiencies which they need to demonstrate to reach different reading levels. Further sample tasks can also be found at *www.pisa.oecd.org*.

...with easier tasks requiring basic handling of simple texts...

Even a cursory review of these items reveals that tasks at the lower end of the scale require very different skills from those at the higher end. A more careful analysis of the range of tasks provides some indication of an ordered set of knowledge-construction skills and strategies. For example, the easiest of these tasks require students to locate explicitly stated information according to a single criterion where there is little, if any, competing information in the text, or to identify the main theme of a familiar text, or make a simple connection between a piece of the text and everyday life. In general, the information is prominent in the text and the text itself is less dense and less complex in structure.

...and harder ones involving increasing complexity and less explicit information.

In contrast, harder retrieval tasks require students to locate and sequence multiple pieces of deeply embedded information, sometimes in accordance with multiple criteria. Often there is competing information in the text that shares some features with the information required for the answer. Similarly, with tasks requiring interpretation or reflection and evaluation, those at the lower end differ from those at the higher end in terms of the process needed to answer them correctly, the degree to which the reading strategies required for a correct answer are signalled in the question or the instructions, the level of complexity and familiarity of the text and the quantity of competing or distracting information present in the text.

Figure 6.2 presents an overall profile of proficiency on the reading literacy scale, with the length of the bars showing the percentage of students proficient at each level.

Proficiency at Level 5 (above 625 score points)

The hardest tasks are sophisticated and require critical thinking...

Students proficient at Level 5 on the reading literacy scale are capable of completing sophisticated reading tasks, such as managing information that is difficult to find in unfamiliar texts; showing detailed understanding of such texts and inferring which information in the text is relevant to the task; and being able to evaluate critically and build hypotheses, draw on specialised knowledge, and accommodate concepts that may be contrary to expectations. See Figure 6.1 for a more detailed description.

...measuring the kind of skill needed by high-level knowledge workers.

The proportion of students performing at the highest PISA proficiency levels in participating countries are of interest as today's proportion of students performing at these levels may influence the contribution which that country

Figure 6.2 ■ **Percentage of students at each level of proficiency on the reading scale**

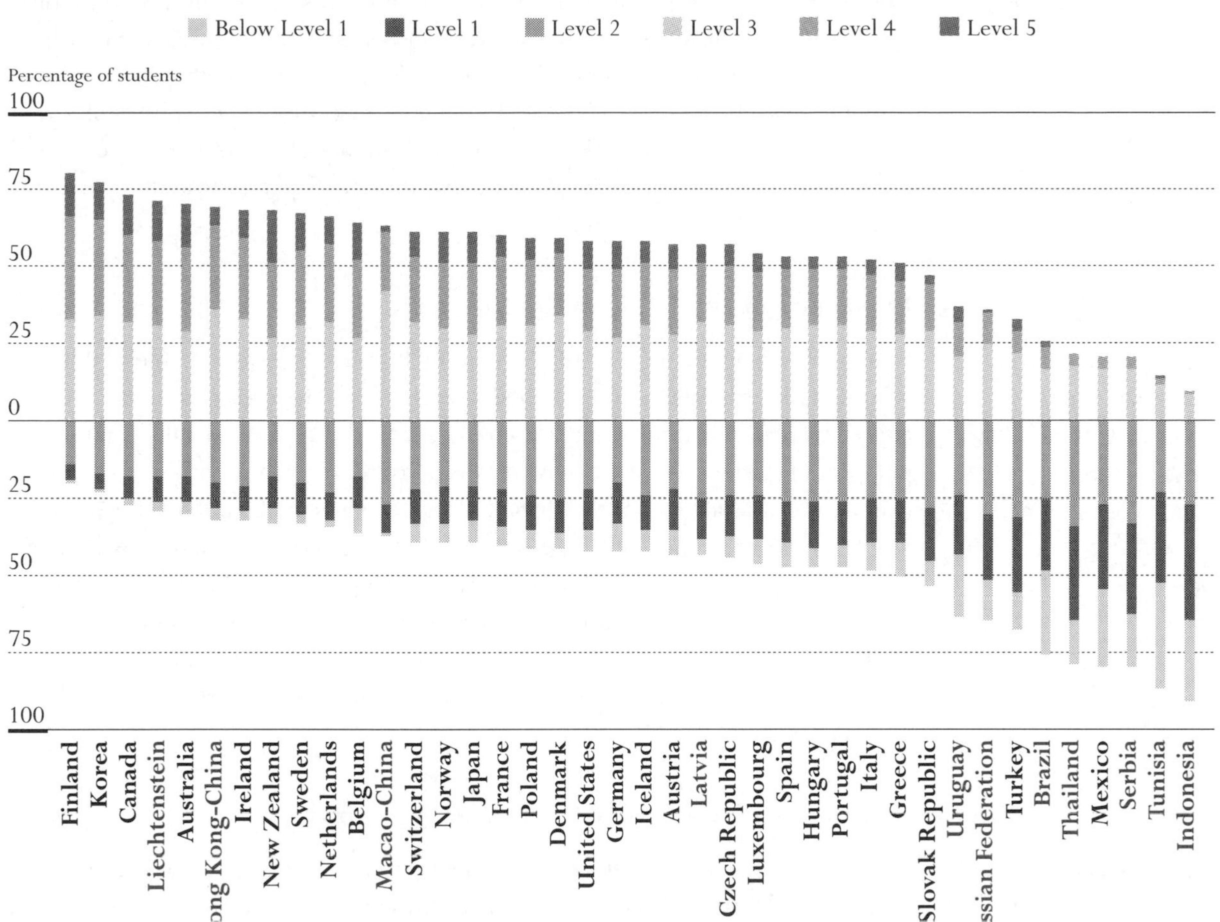

Countries are ranked in descending order of percentage of 15-year-olds in Levels 3, 4 and 5.
Source: OECD PISA 2003 database, Table 6.1.

will make towards the pool of tomorrow's world-class knowledge workers in the global economy.

In the combined OECD area, 8 per cent of the students are at proficiency Level 5. More than 16 per cent of the students in New Zealand and more than 12 per cent of the students in Australia, Belgium, Canada, Finland, Korea and the partner country Liechtenstein are at this level. In contrast, less than 1 per cent of the students in Mexico reach Level 5 and this is also true in the partner countries Indonesia, Serbia,[2] Thailand and Tunisia (Figure 6.2 and Table 6.1).

Having more students at this top level does not always go with having fewer at lower performance levels.

It is important to keep in mind that the proportion of students performing at Level 5 is influenced not only by the overall performance of countries in reading literacy but also by the variation that exists within countries between the students with the highest and the lowest levels of performance. While there is a general tendency for countries with a higher proportion of students scoring

at Level 5 to have fewer students at Level 1 and below, this is not always the case. In Finland, for example, 15 per cent of students reach Level 5 while only 1 per cent are below Level 1. By contrast, in Belgium and New Zealand, which also have high percentages reaching Level 5, a relatively high proportion of students score below Level 1 as well (8 and 5 per cent respectively). Finally, in the partner countries Hong Kong-China and Macao-China, only 6 per cent and 2 per cent, respectively, reach Level 5, while only 3 per cent and 1 per cent, respectively, score below Level 1.

Proficiency at Level 4 (from 553 to 625 score points)

In some countries around 40 per cent of students can at least do difficult tasks at Level 4, but in others very few can.

Students proficient at Level 4 on the reading literacy scale are capable of difficult reading tasks, such as locating embedded information, dealing with ambiguities and critically evaluating a text (Figure 6.1). In the combined OECD area, 28 per cent of students are proficient at Level 4 or above (that is, at Levels 4 and 5) (Figure 6.2 and Table 6.1). Nearly half of the students in Finland and between 40 and 50 per cent or more of those in Australia, Canada, Korea and New Zealand and the partner country Liechtenstein attain at least Level 4. With the exception of Mexico, the Slovak Republic and Turkey, at least one in five students in each OECD country reaches at least Level 4. In addition, fewer than 5 per cent of the students in four of the partner countries – Indonesia, Serbia, Thailand and Tunisia – reach this level.

Proficiency at Level 3 (from 481 to 552 score points)

Most students in OECD countries have at least moderate reading skills…

Students proficient at Level 3 on the reading literacy scale are capable of reading tasks of moderate complexity, such as locating multiple pieces of information, making links between different parts of a text and relating it to familiar everyday knowledge (Figure 6.1). In the combined OECD area, 55 per cent of students are proficient at least at Level 3 (that is, at Levels 3, 4 and 5) on the reading literacy scale (Figure 6.2 and Table 6.1). In 8 of the 30 OECD countries (Australia, Canada, Finland, Ireland, Korea, the Netherlands, New Zealand and Sweden), and in two partner countries (Hong Kong-China and Liechtenstein), between 65 and 80 per cent of 15-year-old students are proficient at least at Level 3. This level is the OECD modal level – that is, the one at which most students are placed at their highest level of proficiency, with 27 per cent in the OECD combined area.

Proficiency at Level 2 (from 408 to 480 score points)

…and in all but two OECD countries, at least 75 per cent can do basic reading tasks.

Students proficient at Level 2 are capable of basic reading tasks, such as locating straightforward information, making low-level inferences of various types, working out what a well-defined part of a text means and using some outside knowledge to understand it (Figure 6.1). In the combined OECD area, 78 per cent of students are proficient at Level 2 or above on the reading literacy scale. In every OECD country except Mexico and Turkey, at least three in four students are at Level 2 or above (Figure 6.2 and Table 6.1).

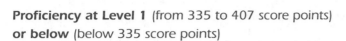

Proficiency at Level 1 (from 335 to 407 score points)
or below (below 335 score points)

Level 1 represents the simplest functional reading tasks…

Reading literacy, as defined in PISA, focuses on the knowledge and skills required to apply reading for learning rather than on the technical skills acquired in learning to read. Since comparatively few young adults in OECD countries have not acquired technical reading skills, PISA does not seek to measure such things as the extent to which 15-year-old students are fluent readers or how well they spell or recognise words. In line with most contemporary views about reading literacy, PISA focuses on measuring the extent to which individuals are able to construct, expand and reflect on the meaning of what they have read in a wide range of texts common both within and beyond school. The simplest reading tasks that can still be associated with this notion of reading literacy are those at Level 1. Students proficient at this level are capable of completing only the simplest reading tasks developed for PISA, such as locating a single piece of information, identifying the main theme of a text or making a simple connection with everyday knowledge (Figure 6.1).

…and those not reaching it may be able to read but have serious problems using reading for learning.

Students performing below 335 score points – that is, below Level 1 – are not likely to demonstrate success on the most basic type of reading that PISA seeks to measure. This does not mean that they have no literacy skills. Nonetheless, their pattern of answers in the assessment is such that they would be expected to solve fewer than half of the tasks in a test made up of items drawn solely from Level 1, and therefore perform below Level 1. Such students have serious difficulties in using reading literacy as an effective tool to advance and extend their knowledge and skills in other areas. Students with literacy skills below Level 1 may therefore be at risk not only of difficulties in their initial transition from education to work, but also of failure to benefit from further education and learning opportunities throughout life.

Although over nine out of ten OECD students can at least perform at Level 1…

In the combined OECD area, 14 per cent of students perform at Level 1, and 8 per cent perform below Level 1, but there are wide differences between countries. In Finland and Korea, only 5 per cent of students perform at Level 1, and 1 per cent below it, but these countries are the exceptions. In all other OECD countries, the percentage of students performing at or below Level 1 ranges from 10 to 52 per cent (Figure 6.2 and Table 6.1). One-quarter of the OECD countries have between 2 and 5 per cent of students performing below Level 1.

…in 11 OECD countries at least one in five are not proficient beyond Level 1.

The OECD countries with 20 per cent or more of students at or below Level 1 are (in descending order): Mexico, Turkey, Greece, the Slovak Republic, Italy, Luxembourg, Germany, Portugal, Spain, Austria and Hungary. This is also the case in the following partner countries (in descending order): Indonesia, Tunisia, Brazil, Serbia, Thailand, Uruguay and the Russian Federation. It is notable that among these countries Germany has the relatively high contrasting figure of close to 10 per cent of its students performing at Level 5.

In addition, between 25 and 34 per cent of students do not reach Level 1 in Mexico and in the partner countries Brazil, Indonesia and Tunisia. These students are routinely unable to show the most basic skills that PISA seeks to measure.

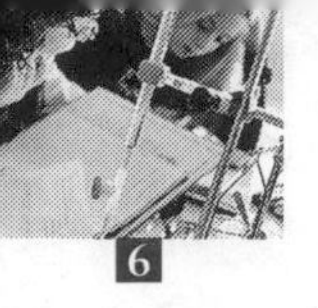

The mean performances of countries in reading

Country performance can be summarised by a mean score…

The discussion above has focused on comparisons of the distribution of student performance between countries. Another way to summarise student performance and to compare the relative standing of countries in reading literacy is by way of their mean scores. Given that high average performance at age 15 is predictive of a highly skilled future workforce, countries with high average performance will have a considerable economic and social advantage.

…but a comparison of country means is only possible where there is a statistically significant difference.

As discussed in Chapter 2, when interpreting mean performance, only those differences between countries which are statistically significant should be taken into account. Figure 6.3 shows those pairs of countries where the difference in their mean scores is sufficient to say with confidence that the higher performance by sampled students in one country holds for the entire population of enrolled 15-year-olds. Read across the row for a country to compare its performance with the countries listed along the top of the figure. The colour-coding indicates whether the average performance of the country in the row is significantly lower than that of the comparison country, not statistically different, or significantly higher.

When making multiple comparisons – for example, when comparing the performance of one country with that of all other countries, an even more cautious approach is required, and only those comparisons that are indicated by the respective symbols in dark shadings should be considered statistically significant for the purpose of multiple comparisons. The figure also shows which countries perform above, at or below the OECD average.

These mean performances span a wide range, with Finnish students doing best overall.

In Finland, performance on the reading literacy scale is above that of any other OECD country. Its country mean, 543 score points, is more than half of a proficiency level above the OECD average of 494 score points in PISA 2003. Other OECD countries with mean performances statistically significantly above the OECD average include Australia, Belgium, Canada, Ireland, Korea, the Netherlands, New Zealand and Sweden. Among the partner countries, Hong Kong-China and Liechtenstein are also part of that group. Eleven OECD countries perform around the OECD average: Austria, the Czech Republic, Denmark, France, Germany, Iceland, Japan, Norway, Poland, Switzerland and the United States. The partner countries Latvia and Macao-China also perform around the OECD average.[3] Among OECD countries, differences are relatively large – 143 score points separate the two extreme performances (*i.e.*, highest and lowest performing countries) – and when the partner countries are considered, this is 150 points.

Within each country, however, the range of performance is even greater, and some countries manage to contain this difference better than others.

Although there are large differences in the mean performance between countries, the variation in performance between students within each country is much larger. One of the major challenges faced by education systems is to encourage high performance while at the same time minimising poor performance. The question of poor performance is particularly relevant to reading literacy because levels of literacy have a significant impact on the welfare of individuals, the state of society and the economic standing of countries in the international arena (OECD, 2003c). Inequality in this context can be examined through the performance distribution as

Figure 6.3 ■ Multiple comparisons of mean performance on the reading scale

Reading scale	Mean	S.E.
Finland	543	(1.6)
Korea	534	(3.1)
Canada	528	(1.7)
Australia	525	(2.1)
Liechtenstein	525	(3.6)
New Zealand	522	(2.5)
Ireland	515	(2.6)
Sweden	514	(2.4)
Netherlands	513	(2.9)
Hong Kong-China	510	(3.7)
Belgium	507	(2.6)
Norway	500	(2.8)
Switzerland	499	(3.3)
Japan	498	(3.9)
Macao-China	498	(2.2)
Poland	497	(2.9)
France	496	(2.7)
United States	495	(3.2)
Denmark	492	(2.8)
Iceland	492	(1.6)
Germany	491	(3.4)
Austria	491	(3.8)
Latvia	491	(3.7)
Czech Republic	489	(3.5)
Hungary	482	(2.5)
Spain	481	(2.6)
Luxembourg	479	(1.5)
Portugal	478	(3.7)
Italy	476	(3.0)
Greece	472	(4.1)
Slovak Republic	469	(3.1)
Russian Fed.	442	(3.9)
Turkey	441	(5.8)
Uruguay	434	(3.4)
Thailand	420	(2.8)
Serbia	412	(3.6)
Brazil	403	(4.6)
Mexico	400	(4.1)
Indonesia	382	(3.4)
Tunisia	375	(2.8)

Range of rank*

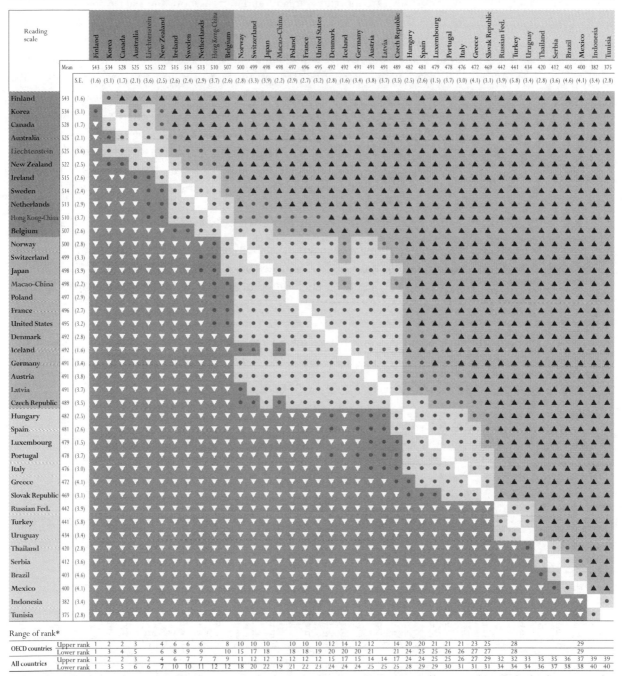

		Finland	Korea	Canada	Australia	Liechtenstein	New Zealand	Ireland	Sweden	Netherlands	Hong Kong-China	Belgium	Norway	Switzerland	Japan	Macao-China	Poland	France	United States	Denmark	Iceland	Germany	Austria	Latvia	Czech Republic	Hungary	Spain	Luxembourg	Portugal	Italy	Greece	Slovak Republic	Russian Fed.	Turkey	Uruguay	Thailand	Serbia	Brazil	Mexico	Indonesia	Tunisia
OECD countries	Upper rank	1	2	2	3		4	6	6	6		8	10	10	10		10	10	10	12	14	12	12		14	20	20	21	21	21	23	25		28					29		
	Lower rank	1	3	4	5		6	8	9	9		10	15	17	18		18	18	19	20	20	20	21		21	24	25	25	26	26	27	27		28					29		
All countries	Upper rank	1	2	2	3	2	4	6	7	7	7	9	11	12	12	12	12	12	12	15	17	15	14	14	17	24	24	25	25	26	27	29	32	32	33	35	35	36	37	39	39
	Lower rank	1	3	5	6	6	7	10	10	11	12	12	18	20	22	19	21	22	23	24	24	24	25	25	25	28	29	29	30	31	31	31	34	34	34	36	37	38	38	40	40

* Because data are based on samples, it is not possible to report exact rank order positions for countries. However, it is possible to report the range of rank order positions within which the country mean lies with 95 per cent likelihood.

Instructions:

Read across the row for a country to compare performance with the countries listed along the top of the chart. The symbols indicate whether the average performance of the country in the row is lower than that of the comparison country, higher than that of the comparison country, or if there is no statistically significant difference between the average achievement of the two countries.

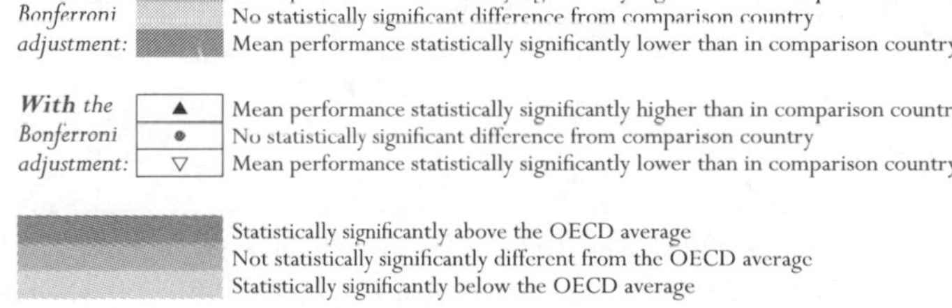

Source: OECD, PISA 2003 database.

seen by the gap in performance between the 5th and the 95th percentiles (Table 6.2). Among OECD countries, Finland and Korea show the narrowest distributions in the OECD with this difference equivalent to 267 score points while at the same time these two countries show the strongest overall performance. From the partner countries, Macao-China has a very narrow distribution with only 220 score points separating the bottom 5th to the top 95th percent of students. Furthermore, in Canada, Denmark, Ireland and the Netherlands and in the partner countries Hong Kong-China, Indonesia, Latvia, Liechtenstein, Serbia and Thailand the performance gaps are below 300 score points. On the other hand, Belgium and Germany show the OECD largest gaps in the performance of students in the middle of the distribution at 362 and 357 score points, which is almost one standard deviation more than in Finland and Korea.

Differences in reading performance between PISA 2000 and PISA 2003

Results from the two PISA surveys should be compared cautiously.

Figure 6.4 shows the overall reading scores for PISA 2000 and 2003 and indicates differences in performance between the two assessments. However, as explained in Chapter 2, such differences need to be interpreted with caution.

Figure 6.4 ■ **Differences in mean scores between PISA 2003 and PISA 2000 on the reading scale**

Only countries with valid data for both 2003 and 2000

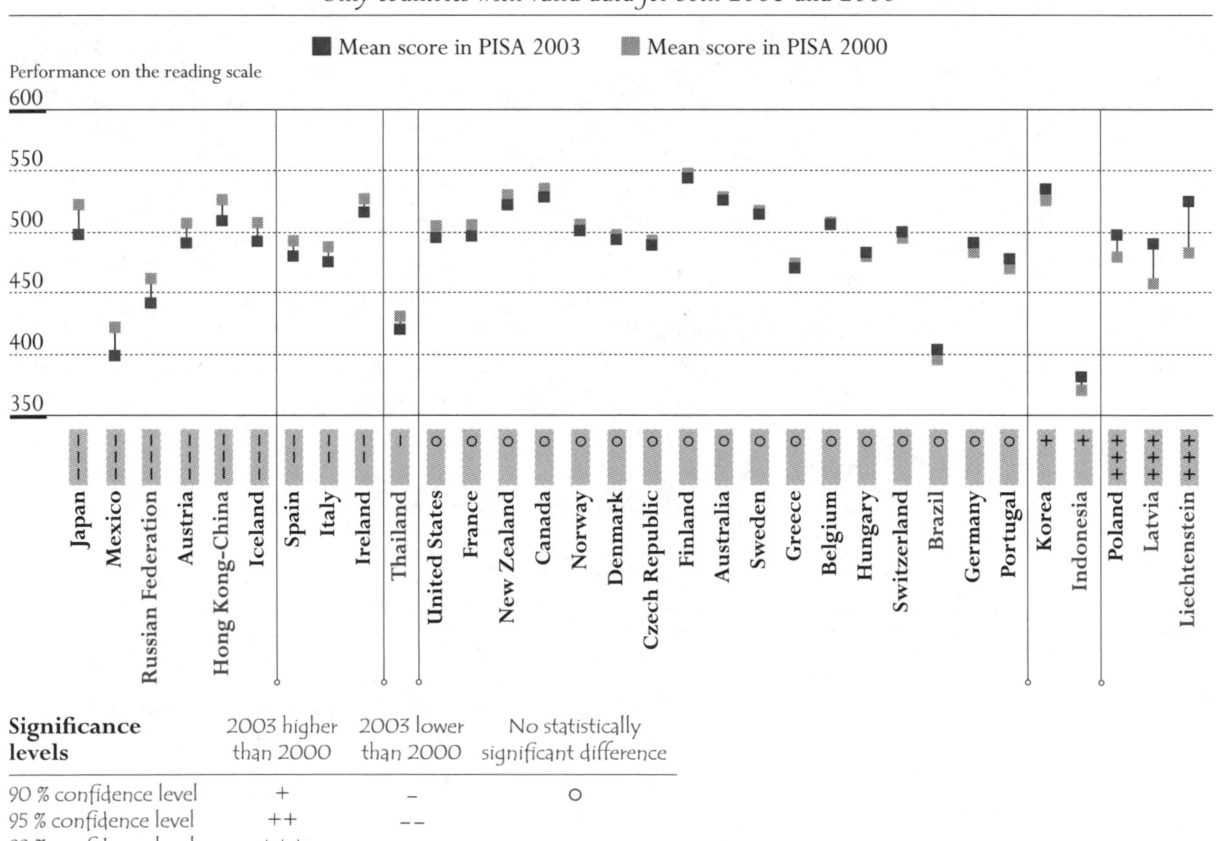

Significance levels	2003 higher than 2000	2003 lower than 2000	No statistically significant difference
90 % confidence level	+	–	o
95 % confidence level	++	– –	
99 % confidence level	+++	– – –	

Countries are ranked in ascending order of the difference between PISA 2003 and PISA 2000 performances.
Source: OECD PISA 2003 database, Table 6.2; OECD PISA 2000 database, Table 2.3a (OECD 2001a).

First of all, since data are only available from two points in time, it is not possible to assess to what extent the observed differences are indicative of longer-term trends. Furthermore, errors from sampling as well as measurement errors are inevitably introduced when sample-based assessments are linked through a limited number of common items over time, which limits the reliability of comparisons of results over time. To account for the latter, the confidence band for comparisons over time has been broadened correspondingly.[4]

The performance of some countries was slightly better, of others slightly worse.

Figure 6.5 shows that, of the 32 countries for which there is comparative data across 2000 and 2003, in eight there is no statistically significant change at any point in the student distribution. For a further 15 countries, there is a decrease in the scores

Figure 6.5 ■ **Comparisons between PISA 2003 and PISA 2000 in reading**

Significance levels	2003 higher than 2000	2003 lower than 2000	No statistically significant difference
90 % confidence level	+	-	O
95 % confidence level	++	--	
99 % confidence level	+++	---	

Differences observed in the mean and percentiles

	5th	10th	25th	Mean	75th	90th	95th
OECD countries							
Australia	O	O	O	O	O	-	-
Austria	---	---	---	---	O	O	O
Belgium	O	O	O	O	O	O	O
Canada	O	O	O	O	--	---	---
Czech Republic	O	O	O	O	O	O	O
Denmark	O	O	O	O	--	---	---
Finland	O	O	O	O	-	--	---
France	--	O	O	O	O	O	O
Germany	O	O	O	O	O	O	O
Greece	O	O	O	O	O	O	O
Hungary	O	O	O	O	O	O	O
Iceland		---	---	---	--	O	O
Ireland	O	O	O	--	---	---	---
Italy	---	---	--	--	O	O	O
Japan	---	---	---	---	O	O	O
Korea	O	O	O	+	+++	+++	+++
Mexico	---	---	---	---	--	O	O
New Zealand	O	O	O	O	-	O	O
Norway	O	O	O	O	O	O	O
Poland	++	+++	+++	+++	O	O	+
Portugal	O	O	O	O	O	O	O
Spain	---	---	--	--	O	O	O
Sweden	O	O	O	O	O	O	O
Switzerland	O	++	O	O	O	O	O
United States	O	O	O	O	O	O	--
OECD total	---	---	---	--	-	O	O
OECD average	O	O	O	O	O	O	O
Partner countries							
Brazil	---	---	O	O	+++	+++	+++
Hong Kong-China	O	O	--	---	---	---	--
Indonesia	O	O	O	+	O	O	O
Latvia	+++	+++	+++	+++	+++	++	+
Liechtenstein	++	+++	+++	+++	+++	++	++
Russian Federation	--	--	--	---	---	---	--
Thailand	O	O	--	-	-	O	O

Source: OECD PISA 2003 database, Table 6.2; OECD PISA 2000 database, Table 2.3a (OECD 2001a).

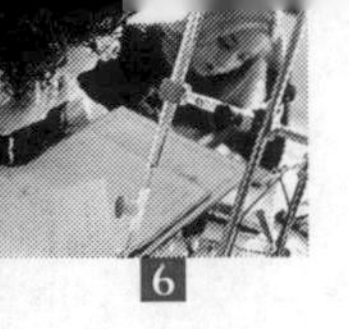

of one or more percentile points, for six countries there is an improvement of one or more points and for only one country the results were mixed.

Poland raised its overall performance through improvements at the lower end of the distribution...

Poland and the partner countries Indonesia, Latvia and Liechtenstein showed markedly higher performance in 2003 than in 2000.[5] In Poland, the overall performance gap between the lower and higher achievers decreased at the same time that the average performance of 15-year-olds increased overall. This rise in overall performance is attributable mainly to an increase in performance at the lower end of the performance distribution (*i.e.,* 5th, 10th and 25th percentiles), in other words, the lowest performing students became better. While in 2000, the lowest 10 per cent of 15-year-olds in Poland scored below 343 score points, in 2003 this changed to 374 score points. The reverse holds for Korea where there was a statistically significant increase in the top half of the distribution between 2000 and 2003 to the extent that only 5 per cent of the students in 2000 reached the performance level that is now reached by the best performing 10 per cent of Korean students. Latvia and Liechtenstein showed increases throughout the distribution.

...whereas in other countries changes at different parts of the performance distribution were insufficient to produce change overall.

Canada, Denmark and Finland showed no measurable overall performance differences between 2000 and 2003. However, in these countries performance at the top end of the distribution (*i.e.,* the 75th, 90th and 95th percentiles) decreased somewhat.

Countries with lower performance in 2003 compared with 2000 include Austria, Iceland, Ireland, Italy, Japan, Mexico and Spain and among the partner countries Hong Kong-China, the Russian Federation and Thailand. For Austria, Iceland, Italy, Japan, and Spain the decline is due to a drop in performance among the 5th, 10th and 25th percentiles (the points under which 5, 10 and 25 per cent of the population score). In other words, in these countries the top end of the distribution performed similarly in 2000 and 2003 but the lower end of the distribution performed markedly lower, making the distribution wider. The Russian Federation is the only country which showed a universal decrease in performance.

Gender differences in reading literacy

Females perform better at reading than males, but to different degrees across countries.

Figure 6.6 shows differences in performance between males and females for reading in PISA 2000 and PISA 2003 (see also Table 6.3 and Table 5.1 in OECD, 2001a). The panel shows a similar picture to what was found in 2000. Females have significantly higher average performance in reading in all countries with the exception of Liechtenstein, with an average OECD gap in reading of 34 score points, equivalent to half a proficiency level (see Chapter 2 and OECD, 2001a). There is variation across countries in the magnitude of this difference: for example, at least 40 score points separate females from males in reading performance in Austria, Finland, Germany, Iceland, Norway and Poland and in the partner countries Serbia and Thailand. The gender difference is particularly high in Iceland where it reaches 58 score points.

Figure 6.6 ■ **Gender differences in reading performance in PISA 2003 and PISA 2000**

Differences in PISA scale scores

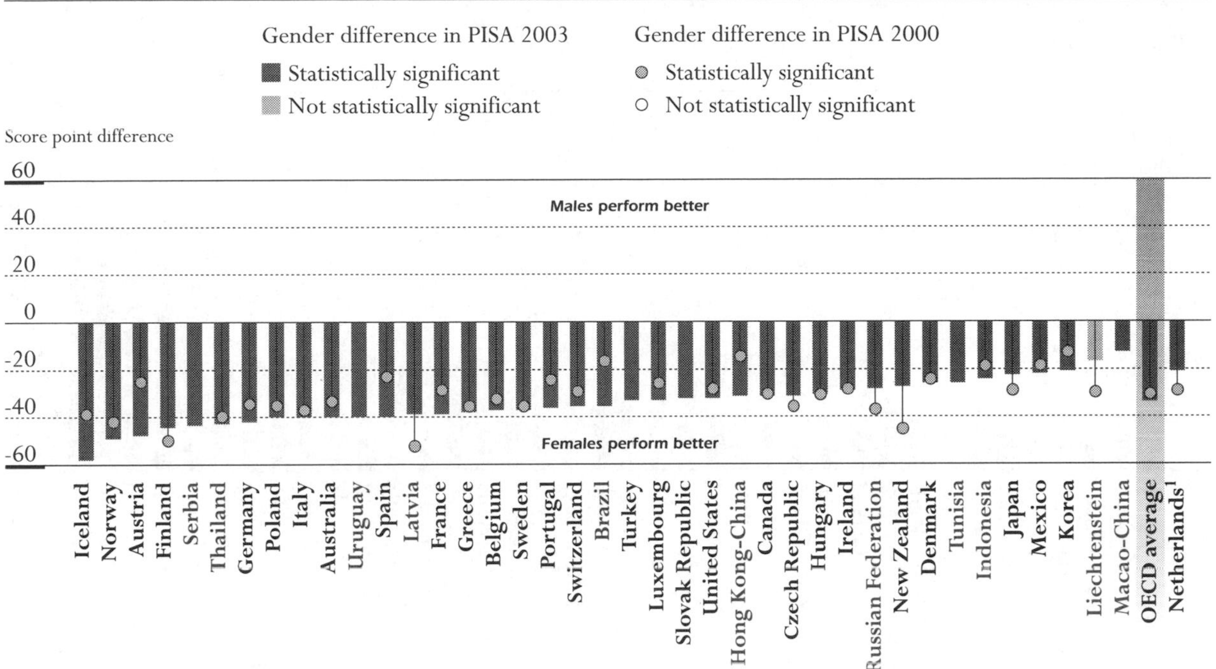

1. The 2000 response rate in the Netherlands was too low to ensure comparability (see Annex A3, OECD 2001a).

Source: OECD PISA 2003 database, Table 6.3; OECD PISA 2000 database, Table 5.1a (OECD 2001a).

For these countries, the average score for females falls within Level 3 while the average score for males falls within Level 2, with the exception of Finland where females score on average within Level 4 while males score on average within Level 3.

The better performance of females in reading and males in mathematics (see Chapter 2) are consistent with results found in other studies for similar age groups.

When the gender gap found in PISA 2003 is compared with the gap found in PISA 2000, they are in general consistent. However, there are some exceptions.

In many countries males are far more likely than females to be among the lowest performers.

One way to understand the gender differences is to examine the extremes of the distribution. Previous studies have also shown that gender differences in performance increase towards the extremes of the distribution of performance and the large gender differences among students with the lowest levels of performance is of concern to policy makers. In all participating countries, except for the partner countries Liechtenstein and Macao-China, males are significantly more likely than females to be among the lowest-performing students. In 12 OECD countries males are at least twice as likely than females to score below 400 score points (*i.e.*, one standard deviation below the OECD average) and in Finland and Iceland they are three times or more as likely (Table 6.4).

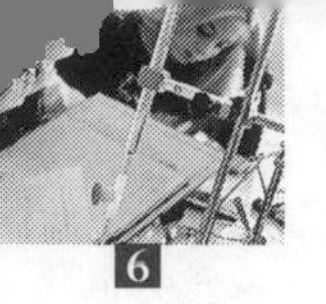

Figure 6.7 ■ **Proportion of males and females among the lowest performers on the reading scale**

Percentage of males and females at or below Level 1

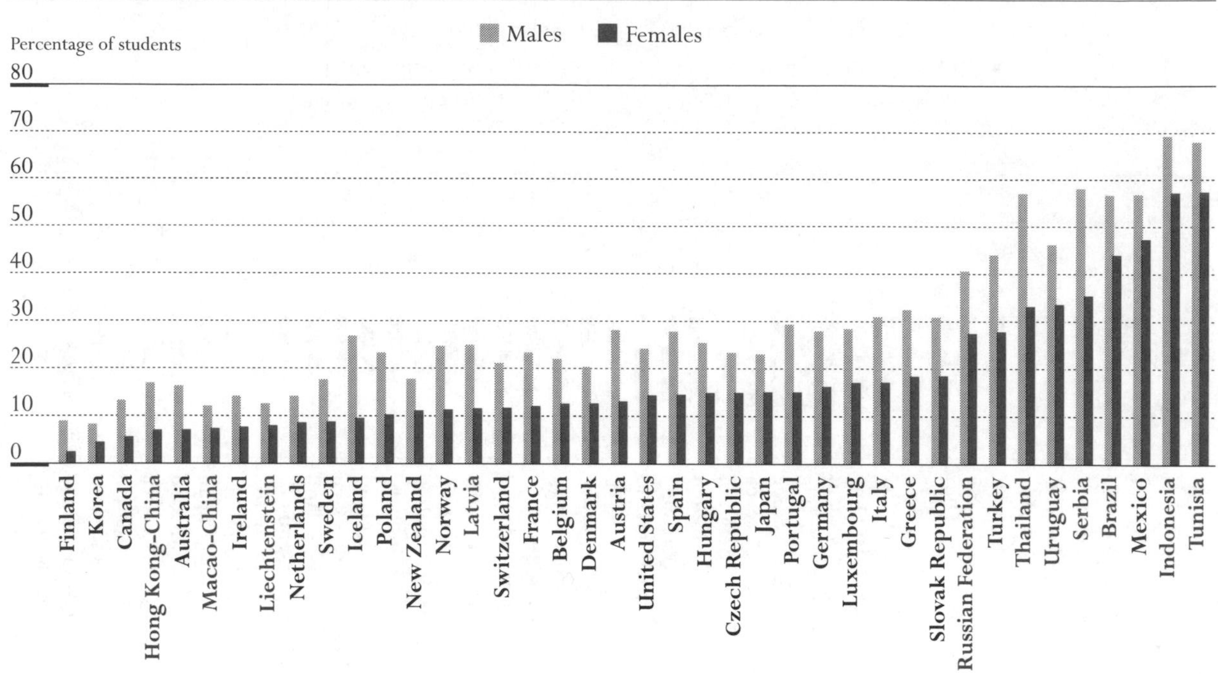

Source: OECD PISA 2003 database, Table 6.5.

Figure 6.7 shows the percentages of males and females scoring at or below Level 1 in reading (Table 6.5). In Iceland, while 10 per cent of females score at or below Level 1, the percentage of males is 27 per cent. In the partner countries Serbia and Thailand, there are at least 20 per cent more males than females at or below Level 1. Among the OECD countries, the smallest differences between the percentages of males and females at lower levels of performance are found in Korea and the Netherlands and in the partner countries, these are found in Liechtenstein and Macao-China.

HOW SCIENCE PERFORMANCE IS MEASURED IN PISA

The science assessment emphasises the application of knowledge…

The emphasis of the PISA 2003 assessment of science is on the application of science knowledge and skills in real-life situations, as opposed to testing particular curricular components. Scientific literacy is defined as the capacity to use scientific knowledge, to identify questions and to draw evidence-based conclusions in order to understand and help make decisions about the natural world and the changes made to it through human activity.

This definition is based on three dimensions: scientific knowledge or concepts, scientific processes and the situations or context in which the knowledge and processes are assessed.

With the limited assessment time that was available for science in 2003, it was not possible to assess all areas of scientific knowledge, so a sample of concepts was assessed. The selection of these concepts from the major scientific fields of physics, chemistry, biological science, and earth and space science was guided by a number of principles. First, the knowledge assessed should be relevant to real life situations. Second, the knowledge assessed should have some enduring relevance to life over the next decade at least. Third, the knowledge required to successfully answer a PISA science item should be related to some important scientific process – that is, it should not be an isolated recall of a piece of information.

. . . focusing on a selection of concepts that are central to science, of enduring relevance and important to real life.

Three main scientific processes are part of the PISA assessment in 2003. The first of these is describing, explaining and predicting scientific phenomena – important facets of the scientific process. Students were given tasks that involved recognising phenomena, giving explanations and making considered judgements as to the impact of these phenomena. The second is understanding scientific investigation, which involves being able to recognise questions and problems that could be solved using scientific methods and what evidence may be needed to achieve this, and may also involve an understanding of the variables that need to be measured and controlled in an experiment. In addition, students were assessed on their ability to communicate these ideas. The third is interpreting scientific evidence and conclusions, which is concerned with the use of scientific findings as evidence for a diverse range of claims and conclusions. Through the media, students are constantly coming into contact with claims made by advertisers, proponents of change and commentators who use scientific evidence as a justification.

Students were required to recognise and explain scientific phenomena, understand scientific investigation and interpret evidence. . .

The third main aspect of the assessment of science in PISA is a consideration of the areas of application. For PISA 2003 these are science in life and health, science in the earth and environment, and science in technology. The range of assessment tasks includes problems that affect people as individuals (such as food and energy use), as members of a local community (such as the location of a power station) or as world citizens (such as global warming).

. . . .with tasks drawn from a range of scientific situations.

Following PISA 2000, two units, which contained eight items, were released to give an indication of the type of problems that students were encountering (OECD, 2002c). These items were replaced with newly created ones which underwent an extensive field trial process to ensure they had similar levels of difficulty as the released items. A sufficient number of items was retained to allow linking to occur between the assessments carried out different times.

The 2003 science assessment overlapped with that used in 2000. . .

Like performance in reading literacy, performance in science was marked in PISA 2000 on a single scale with an average score of 500 score points and a standard deviation of 100 score points. Approximately two-thirds of students across OECD countries scored between 400 and 600 score points. The same scale was used for the PISA 2003 science assessment. The scale measures students' ability to use scientific knowledge (understanding of scientific concepts), to recognise scientific questions and to identify what is involved in scientific investigations (understanding of the nature of scientific investigation), to relate scientific data to claims and conclusions (use of scientific evidence) and to communicate these aspects of science.

. . .and results were reported on the same scale.

Figure 6.8 ■ **A sample of science items used in PISA: Unit DAYLIGHT**

DAYLIGHT

Read the following information and answer the questions that follow.

Today, as the Northern Hemisphere celebrates its longest day, Australians will experience their shortest.

In Melbourne,* Australia, the sun will rise at 7:36 am and set at 5:08 pm, giving nine hours and 32 minutes of daylight.

Compare today to the year's longest day in the Southern Hemisphere, expected on 22 December, when the sun will rise at 5:55 am and set at 8:42 pm, giving 14 hours and 47 minutes of daylight.

The President of the Astronomical Society, Mr Perry Vlahos, said the existence of changing seasons in the Northern and Southern Hemispheres was linked to the Earth's 23-degree tilt.

*Melbourne is a city in Australia at a latitude of about 38 degrees south of the equator.

Item difficulty

690

550

400

Highest

Middle

Lowest

DAYLIGHT

QUESTION 1

Which statement explains why daylight and darkness occur on earth?

A. The earth rotates on its axis.

B. The sun rotates on its axis.

C. The earth's axis is tilted.

D. The earth revolves around the sun.

Score 1 (592)

The correct answer is option A.

This is a multiple-choice item that requires students to be able to relate the rotation of the earth on its axis to the phenomenon of day and night and to distinguish this from the phenomenon of the seasons, which arises from the tilt of the axis of the earth as it revolves around the sun. All four alternatives given are scientifically correct.

QUESTION 2

In the Figure light rays from the sun are shown shining on the earth.

Figure: light rays from the sun

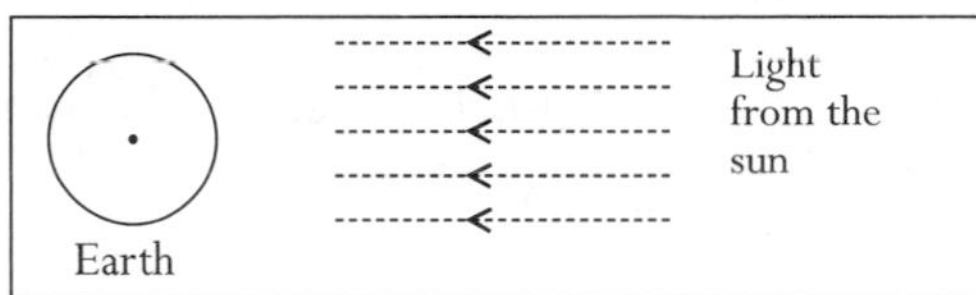

Suppose it is the shortest day in Melbourne.

Show the earth's axis, the Northern Hemisphere, the Southern Hemisphere and the Equator on the figure. Label all parts of your answer.

Score 2 (720)

Answers which include a diagram with the Equator tilted towards the sun at an angle between 10° and 45° and the earth's axis tilted towards the sun within the range 10° and 45° from vertical, and the Northern and or Southern Hemispheres correctly labelled (or one only labelled, the other implied).

Score 1 (667)

Answers which include a diagram with:

- the angle of tilt of earth's axis between 10° and 45°, the Northern and/or Southern Hemispheres correctly labelled (or one only labelled, the other implied), but angle of tilt of the Equator not between 10° and 45°; or the Equator missing.
- the angle of tilt of the Equator between 10° and 45°, the Northern and/or Southern Hemispheres correctly labelled (or one only labelled, the other implied), but angle of tilt of axis not between 10° and 45°; or axis missing.
- the angle of tilt of the Equator between 10° and 45°, and angle of tilt of axis between 10° and 45°, but the Northern and Southern Hemispheres not correctly labelled (or one only labelled, the other implied, or both missing).

This is an open-response item that requires students to create a conceptual model in the form of a diagram showing the relationship between the rotation of the earth on its tilted axis and its orientation to the sun on the shortest day for a city in the southern hemisphere. In addition they had to include in this diagram the position of the equator at a 90-degree angle to the tilted axis. Full credit is obtained if the students correctly place and label all three significant elements – the hemispheres, the tilted axis and the equator. Partial credit is given for a diagram with two of the three elements correctly placed and labelled.

Figure 6.9 ■ **A sample of science items used in PISA: Unit CLONING**

CLONING

Read the newspaper article and answer the questions that follow.

A copying machine for living beings?

Without any doubt, if there had been elections for the animal of the year 1997, Dolly would have been the winner! Dolly is a Scottish sheep that you see in the photo. But Dolly is not just a simple sheep. She is a clone of another sheep. A clone means: "a copy". Cloning means: "copying from a single master copy". Scientists succeeded in creating a sheep (Dolly) that is identical to a sheep that functioned as a master copy.

It was the Scottish scientist Ian Wilmut who designed the "copying machine" for sheep. He took a very small piece from the udder of an adult sheep (sheep 1). From that small piece he removed the nucleus, then he transferred the nucleus into the egg-cell of another (female) sheep (sheep 2). But first he removed from that egg-cell all the material that would have determined sheep 2 characteristics in a lamb produced from that egg-cell. Ian Wilmut implanted the manipulated egg-cell of sheep 2 into yet another (female) sheep (sheep 3). Sheep 3 became pregnant and had a lamb: Dolly.

Some scientists think that within a few years it will be possible to clone people as well. But many governments have already decided to forbid the cloning of people by law.

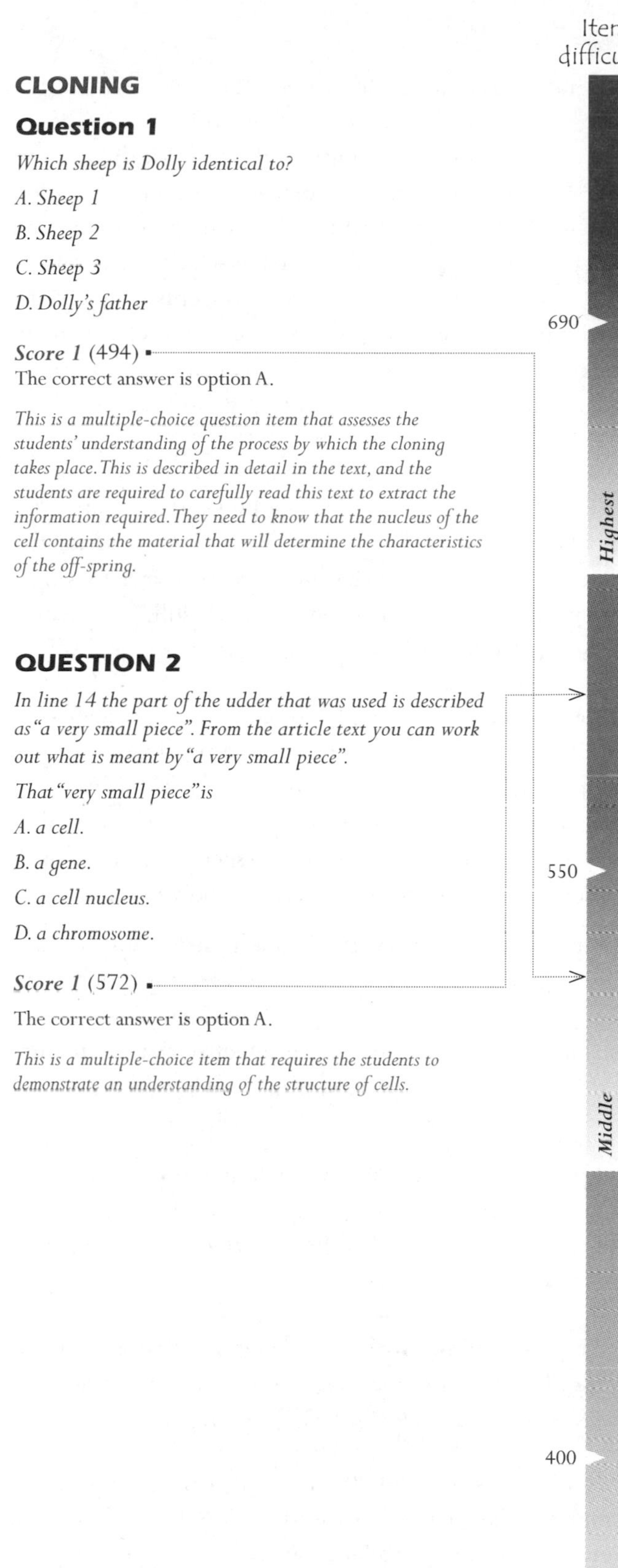

CLONING

Question 1

Which sheep is Dolly identical to?

A. Sheep 1

B. Sheep 2

C. Sheep 3

D. Dolly's father

Score 1 (494)

The correct answer is option A.

This is a multiple-choice question item that assesses the students' understanding of the process by which the cloning takes place. This is described in detail in the text, and the students are required to carefully read this text to extract the information required. They need to know that the nucleus of the cell contains the material that will determine the characteristics of the off-spring.

QUESTION 2

In line 14 the part of the udder that was used is described as "a very small piece". From the article text you can work out what is meant by "a very small piece".

That "very small piece" is

A. a cell.

B. a gene.

C. a cell nucleus.

D. a chromosome.

Score 1 (572)

The correct answer is option A.

This is a multiple-choice item that requires the students to demonstrate an understanding of the structure of cells.

QUESTION 3

In the last sentence of the article it is stated that many governments have already decided to forbid the cloning of people by law.

Two possible reasons for this decision are mentioned below.

Are these reasons scientific reasons?

Circle either "Yes" or "No" for each.

Reason:	**Scientific?**
Cloned people could be more sensitive to certain diseases than normal people.	Yes/No
People should not take over the role of a Creator.	Yes/No

Score 1 (507)

Answers which indicate Yes, No, in that order.

This is a complex multiple-choice item that requires students to show that they can distinguish between statements that are scientifically based and those that are not. One of the aspects of the PISA scientific literacy framework is the notion that students understand scientific investigation and reasoning. The question poses two reasons why governments might forbid human cloning. One of the reasons is concerned with the fact that cloned people might be more susceptible to disease (a reason that could be said to be "scientific"), while the other is statement that people should not take on the role of a Creator (a valid reason for many people, but one which cannot be said to be "scientific"). Full credit is obtained for correctly labelling both statements.

More difficult tasks involve more complex concepts and greater skill requirements, and demand more sophisticated scientific knowledge.

The increasing difficulty of tasks along the scale involves the complexity of the concepts used, the amount of data given, the chain of reasoning required and the precision required in communication. In addition, the level of difficulty is influenced by the context of the information, the format and the presentation of the question. The tasks in PISA require scientific knowledge involving (in ascending order of difficulty): recall of simple scientific knowledge or common scientific knowledge or data; the application of scientific concepts or questions and a basic knowledge of investigation; the use of more highly developed scientific concepts or a chain of reasoning; and knowledge of simple conceptual models or analysis of evidence in order to try out alternative approaches.

Science is not rated at proficiency levels, but it is possible to define characteristics of difficult, medium and easy scientific tasks.

Unlike for reading and mathematics (see Chapter 2), the science scale cannot yet be defined in terms of proficiency levels. This will only be possible from 2006 onwards, when science becomes the main focus of the PISA assessment for the first time and when a full instrument for measuring and reporting science will be developed. However, the criteria for harder and easier tasks can still be described in relation to items associated with different points on the science scale.

- Towards the top end of the science scale (around 690 score points) students are generally able to create or use conceptual models to make predictions or give explanations; to analyse scientific investigations in order to grasp, for example, the design of an experiment or to identify an idea being tested; to compare data in order to evaluate alternative viewpoints or differing perspectives; and to communicate scientific arguments and/or descriptions in detail and with precision.
- At around 550 score points, students are typically able to use scientific concepts to make predictions or provide explanations; to recognise questions that can be answered by scientific investigation and/or identify details of what is involved in a scientific investigation; and to select relevant information from competing data or chains of reasoning in drawing or evaluating conclusions.
- Towards the lower end of the scale (around 400 score points), students are able to recall simple factual scientific knowledge (*e.g.,* names, facts, terminology, simple rules); and to use common scientific knowledge in drawing or evaluating conclusions.

A full description of the conceptual framework underlying the PISA assessment of science is provided in *The PISA 2003 Assessment Framework: Mathematics, Reading, Science and Problem Solving Kowledge and Skills* (OECD, 2003e).

The tasks used for the assessment of science in PISA are quite diverse. Figure 6.8 and Figure 6.9 show examples of the science tasks used in PISA 2003, along with a description of the criteria used to mark students' answers. A more complete set of sample tasks can be found at *www.pisa.oecd.org*. The science assessment was comprised of 35 items divided into 13 units from which 25 items from 10 units were the same as the ones used in 2000 (see Annex A6, Table A6.3 for the breakdown of the items by the various aspects of the framework).

The sample unit *Daylight* provides verbal information on the variation in the length of daylight between the Northern and Southern hemispheres (Figure 6.8). The change of seasons in these hemispheres is also related to the tilt of the earth's axis.

The stimulus for the sample unit, *Cloning*, features an extract from a newspaper article and a photograph of Dolly, the first sheep to be cloned (Figure 6.9). The questions that follow are probing the students' knowledge of the structure of animal cells and scientific methods of investigation.

When taken together, these science units help to illustrate the underlying understanding of science that PISA has adopted in its framework as scientific literacy, in particular the ability to use science knowledge to give explanations.

STUDENT PERFORMANCE IN SCIENCE

The mean performances of countries in science

On average, students did as well in science in 2003 as in 2000, but their results were slightly more spread out.

As previously described in Chapter 2 for the case of mathematics and earlier in this Chapter for reading, the average scores of countries provide an indication of the overall level of performance, keeping in mind that mean scores provide an incomplete picture of performance. As with reading, the outcomes for science are based on the science scale that was developed for PISA 2000 and which had a mean of 500 and a standard deviation of 100. Figure 6.10 shows average performance on the science scale (Table 6.6). The PISA 2003 results include 29 OECD countries – the Slovak Republic and Turkey joined PISA in 2003 and the Netherlands met all technical standards in 2003, while the United Kingdom has been excluded from the results as it failed to reach the technical standards required by PISA 2003.

Four countries had the highest performance and their averages are indistinguishable.

When the 25 OECD countries for which comparable data are available for both the PISA 2000 and 2003 assessments are compared jointly, it is clear that the average performance has remained unchanged (Figure 6.10).[6] However, mainly because of the inclusion of new countries in 2003, the overall OECD mean for science is now 496 score points and the standard deviation is 105 score points.

The gap in performance between the highest and the lowest performing OECD countries is 143 points. That is, while the average scores of the highest performing countries of Finland and Japan is 548 or about half a standard deviation above the OECD average, Mexico's average score of 405 score points is almost one standard deviation below the OECD average.

Finland and Japan have the highest mean scores and rank between first and third on the science scale, but their performance is not statistically significantly different from that in Korea and the partner country Hong Kong-China, who both rank between second and fourth. Other OECD countries that show mean performance in science higher than the OECD average are Australia, Belgium, Canada, the Czech Republic, France, Ireland, the Netherlands, New Zealand, Sweden, Switzerland and among the partner countries Liechtenstein and Macao-China. Countries with performance not statistically different from the OECD average are Germany, Hungary, Poland and the Slovak Republic.[7]

Figure 6.10 ■ Multiple comparisons of mean performance on the science scale

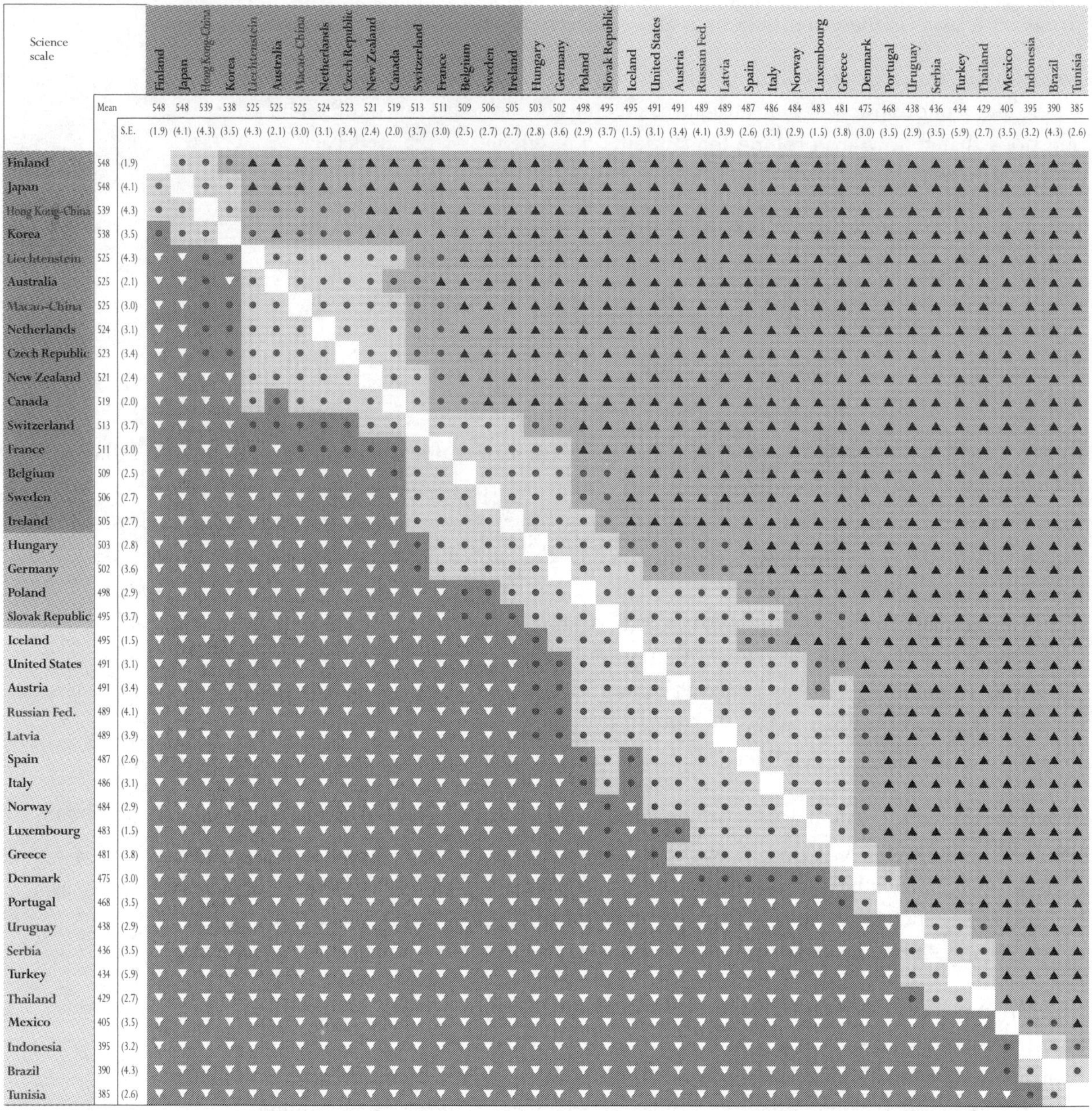

Science scale	Mean	S.E.	Finland	Japan	Hong Kong-China	Korea	Liechtenstein	Australia	Macao-China	Netherlands	Czech Republic	New Zealand	Canada	Switzerland	France	Belgium	Sweden	Ireland	Hungary	Germany	Poland	Slovak Republic	Iceland	United States	Austria	Russian Fed.	Latvia	Spain	Italy	Norway	Luxembourg	Greece	Denmark	Portugal	Uruguay	Serbia	Turkey	Thailand	Mexico	Indonesia	Brazil	Tunisia
	Mean		548	548	539	538	525	525	525	524	523	521	519	513	511	509	506	505	503	502	498	495	495	491	491	489	489	487	486	484	483	481	475	468	438	436	434	429	405	395	390	385
		S.E.	(1.9)	(4.1)	(4.3)	(3.5)	(4.3)	(2.1)	(3.0)	(3.1)	(3.4)	(2.4)	(2.0)	(3.7)	(3.0)	(2.5)	(2.7)	(2.7)	(2.8)	(3.6)	(2.9)	(3.7)	(1.5)	(3.1)	(3.4)	(4.1)	(3.9)	(2.6)	(3.1)	(2.9)	(1.5)	(3.8)	(3.0)	(3.5)	(2.9)	(3.5)	(5.9)	(2.7)	(3.5)	(3.2)	(4.3)	(2.6)
Finland	548	(1.9)		●	●	●	▲	▲	▲	▲	▲	▲	▲	▲	▲	▲	▲	▲	▲	▲	▲	▲	▲	▲	▲	▲	▲	▲	▲	▲	▲	▲	▲	▲	▲	▲	▲	▲	▲	▲	▲	▲
Japan	548	(4.1)	●		●	●	▲	▲	▲	▲	▲	▲	▲	▲	▲	▲	▲	▲	▲	▲	▲	▲	▲	▲	▲	▲	▲	▲	▲	▲	▲	▲	▲	▲	▲	▲	▲	▲	▲	▲	▲	▲
Hong Kong-China	539	(4.3)	●	●		●	●	●	●	●	●	▲	▲	▲	▲	▲	▲	▲	▲	▲	▲	▲	▲	▲	▲	▲	▲	▲	▲	▲	▲	▲	▲	▲	▲	▲	▲	▲	▲	▲	▲	▲
Korea	538	(3.5)	●	●	●		●	▲	●	●	●	▲	▲	▲	▲	▲	▲	▲	▲	▲	▲	▲	▲	▲	▲	▲	▲	▲	▲	▲	▲	▲	▲	▲	▲	▲	▲	▲	▲	▲	▲	▲
Liechtenstein	525	(4.3)	▽	▽	●	●		●	●	●	●	●	●	●	●	▲	▲	▲	▲	▲	▲	▲	▲	▲	▲	▲	▲	▲	▲	▲	▲	▲	▲	▲	▲	▲	▲	▲	▲	▲	▲	▲
Australia	525	(2.1)	▽	▽	●	▽	●		●	●	●	●	●	●	▲	▲	▲	▲	▲	▲	▲	▲	▲	▲	▲	▲	▲	▲	▲	▲	▲	▲	▲	▲	▲	▲	▲	▲	▲	▲	▲	▲
Macao-China	525	(3.0)	▽	▽	●	●	●	●		●	●	●	●	●	●	▲	▲	▲	▲	▲	▲	▲	▲	▲	▲	▲	▲	▲	▲	▲	▲	▲	▲	▲	▲	▲	▲	▲	▲	▲	▲	▲
Netherlands	524	(3.1)	▽	▽	●	●	●	●	●		●	●	●	●	●	▲	▲	▲	▲	▲	▲	▲	▲	▲	▲	▲	▲	▲	▲	▲	▲	▲	▲	▲	▲	▲	▲	▲	▲	▲	▲	▲
Czech Republic	523	(3.4)	▽	▽	●	●	●	●	●	●		●	●	●	●	▲	▲	▲	▲	▲	▲	▲	▲	▲	▲	▲	▲	▲	▲	▲	▲	▲	▲	▲	▲	▲	▲	▲	▲	▲	▲	▲
New Zealand	521	(2.4)	▽	▽	▽	▽	●	●	●	●	●		●	●	●	▲	▲	▲	▲	▲	▲	▲	▲	▲	▲	▲	▲	▲	▲	▲	▲	▲	▲	▲	▲	▲	▲	▲	▲	▲	▲	▲
Canada	519	(2.0)	▽	▽	▽	▽	●	●	●	●	●	●		●	●	●	▲	▲	▲	▲	▲	▲	▲	▲	▲	▲	▲	▲	▲	▲	▲	▲	▲	▲	▲	▲	▲	▲	▲	▲	▲	▲
Switzerland	513	(3.7)	▽	▽	▽	▽	●	●	●	●	●	●	●		●	●	●	●	●	●	▲	▲	▲	▲	▲	▲	▲	▲	▲	▲	▲	▲	▲	▲	▲	▲	▲	▲	▲	▲	▲	▲
France	511	(3.0)	▽	▽	▽	▽	●	▽	●	●	●	●	●	●		●	●	●	●	●	▲	▲	▲	▲	▲	▲	▲	▲	▲	▲	▲	▲	▲	▲	▲	▲	▲	▲	▲	▲	▲	▲
Belgium	509	(2.5)	▽	▽	▽	▽	▽	▽	▽	▽	▽	▽	●	●	●		●	●	●	●	●	●	▲	▲	▲	▲	▲	▲	▲	▲	▲	▲	▲	▲	▲	▲	▲	▲	▲	▲	▲	▲
Sweden	506	(2.7)	▽	▽	▽	▽	▽	▽	▽	▽	▽	▽	▽	●	●	●		●	●	●	●	●	▲	▲	▲	▲	▲	▲	▲	▲	▲	▲	▲	▲	▲	▲	▲	▲	▲	▲	▲	▲
Ireland	505	(2.7)	▽	▽	▽	▽	▽	▽	▽	▽	▽	▽	▽	●	●	●	●		●	●	●	●	▲	▲	▲	▲	▲	▲	▲	▲	▲	▲	▲	▲	▲	▲	▲	▲	▲	▲	▲	▲
Hungary	503	(2.8)	▽	▽	▽	▽	▽	▽	▽	▽	▽	▽	▽	●	●	●	●	●		●	●	●	●	●	●	●	●	▲	▲	▲	▲	▲	▲	▲	▲	▲	▲	▲	▲	▲	▲	▲
Germany	502	(3.6)	▽	▽	▽	▽	▽	▽	▽	▽	▽	▽	▽	●	●	●	●	●	●		●	●	●	●	●	●	●	▲	▲	▲	▲	▲	▲	▲	▲	▲	▲	▲	▲	▲	▲	▲
Poland	498	(2.9)	▽	▽	▽	▽	▽	▽	▽	▽	▽	▽	▽	▽	▽	●	●	●	●	●		●	●	●	●	●	●	●	●	▲	▲	▲	▲	▲	▲	▲	▲	▲	▲	▲	▲	▲
Slovak Republic	495	(3.7)	▽	▽	▽	▽	▽	▽	▽	▽	▽	▽	▽	▽	▽	●	●	●	●	●	●		●	●	●	●	●	●	●	●	●	●	▲	▲	▲	▲	▲	▲	▲	▲	▲	▲
Iceland	495	(1.5)	▽	▽	▽	▽	▽	▽	▽	▽	▽	▽	▽	▽	▽	▽	▽	▽	●	●	●	●		●	●	●	●	●	●	▲	▲	▲	▲	▲	▲	▲	▲	▲	▲	▲	▲	▲
United States	491	(3.1)	▽	▽	▽	▽	▽	▽	▽	▽	▽	▽	▽	▽	▽	▽	▽	▽	●	●	●	●	●		●	●	●	●	●	●	●	●	▲	▲	▲	▲	▲	▲	▲	▲	▲	▲
Austria	491	(3.4)	▽	▽	▽	▽	▽	▽	▽	▽	▽	▽	▽	▽	▽	▽	▽	▽	●	●	●	●	●	●		●	●	●	●	●	●	●	▲	▲	▲	▲	▲	▲	▲	▲	▲	▲
Russian Fed.	489	(4.1)	▽	▽	▽	▽	▽	▽	▽	▽	▽	▽	▽	▽	▽	▽	▽	▽	●	●	●	●	●	●	●		●	●	●	●	●	●	●	▲	▲	▲	▲	▲	▲	▲	▲	▲
Latvia	489	(3.9)	▽	▽	▽	▽	▽	▽	▽	▽	▽	▽	▽	▽	▽	▽	▽	▽	●	●	●	●	●	●	●	●		●	●	●	●	●	●	▲	▲	▲	▲	▲	▲	▲	▲	▲
Spain	487	(2.6)	▽	▽	▽	▽	▽	▽	▽	▽	▽	▽	▽	▽	▽	▽	▽	▽	▽	▽	●	●	●	●	●	●	●		●	●	●	●	●	▲	▲	▲	▲	▲	▲	▲	▲	▲
Italy	486	(3.1)	▽	▽	▽	▽	▽	▽	▽	▽	▽	▽	▽	▽	▽	▽	▽	▽	▽	▽	●	●	●	●	●	●	●	●		●	●	●	●	▲	▲	▲	▲	▲	▲	▲	▲	▲
Norway	484	(2.9)	▽	▽	▽	▽	▽	▽	▽	▽	▽	▽	▽	▽	▽	▽	▽	▽	▽	▽	▽	●	▽	●	●	●	●	●	●		●	●	●	▲	▲	▲	▲	▲	▲	▲	▲	▲
Luxembourg	483	(1.5)	▽	▽	▽	▽	▽	▽	▽	▽	▽	▽	▽	▽	▽	▽	▽	▽	▽	▽	▽	●	▽	●	●	●	●	●	●	●		●	●	▲	▲	▲	▲	▲	▲	▲	▲	▲
Greece	481	(3.8)	▽	▽	▽	▽	▽	▽	▽	▽	▽	▽	▽	▽	▽	▽	▽	▽	▽	▽	▽	●	▽	●	●	●	●	●	●	●	●		●	●	▲	▲	▲	▲	▲	▲	▲	▲
Denmark	475	(3.0)	▽	▽	▽	▽	▽	▽	▽	▽	▽	▽	▽	▽	▽	▽	▽	▽	▽	▽	▽	▽	▽	▽	▽	●	●	●	●	●	●	●		●	▲	▲	▲	▲	▲	▲	▲	▲
Portugal	468	(3.5)	▽	▽	▽	▽	▽	▽	▽	▽	▽	▽	▽	▽	▽	▽	▽	▽	▽	▽	▽	▽	▽	▽	▽	▽	▽	▽	▽	▽	▽	●	●		▲	▲	▲	▲	▲	▲	▲	▲
Uruguay	438	(2.9)	▽	▽	▽	▽	▽	▽	▽	▽	▽	▽	▽	▽	▽	▽	▽	▽	▽	▽	▽	▽	▽	▽	▽	▽	▽	▽	▽	▽	▽	▽	▽	▽		●	●	●	▲	▲	▲	▲
Serbia	436	(3.5)	▽	▽	▽	▽	▽	▽	▽	▽	▽	▽	▽	▽	▽	▽	▽	▽	▽	▽	▽	▽	▽	▽	▽	▽	▽	▽	▽	▽	▽	▽	▽	▽	●		●	●	▲	▲	▲	▲
Turkey	434	(5.9)	▽	▽	▽	▽	▽	▽	▽	▽	▽	▽	▽	▽	▽	▽	▽	▽	▽	▽	▽	▽	▽	▽	▽	▽	▽	▽	▽	▽	▽	▽	▽	▽	●	●		●	▲	▲	▲	▲
Thailand	429	(2.7)	▽	▽	▽	▽	▽	▽	▽	▽	▽	▽	▽	▽	▽	▽	▽	▽	▽	▽	▽	▽	▽	▽	▽	▽	▽	▽	▽	▽	▽	▽	▽	▽	●	●	●		▲	▲	▲	▲
Mexico	405	(3.5)	▽	▽	▽	▽	▽	▽	▽	▽	▽	▽	▽	▽	▽	▽	▽	▽	▽	▽	▽	▽	▽	▽	▽	▽	▽	▽	▽	▽	▽	▽	▽	▽	▽	▽	▽	▽		●	●	▲
Indonesia	395	(3.2)	▽	▽	▽	▽	▽	▽	▽	▽	▽	▽	▽	▽	▽	▽	▽	▽	▽	▽	▽	▽	▽	▽	▽	▽	▽	▽	▽	▽	▽	▽	▽	▽	▽	▽	▽	▽	●		●	●
Brazil	390	(4.3)	▽	▽	▽	▽	▽	▽	▽	▽	▽	▽	▽	▽	▽	▽	▽	▽	▽	▽	▽	▽	▽	▽	▽	▽	▽	▽	▽	▽	▽	▽	▽	▽	▽	▽	▽	▽	●	●		●
Tunisia	385	(2.6)	▽	▽	▽	▽	▽	▽	▽	▽	▽	▽	▽	▽	▽	▽	▽	▽	▽	▽	▽	▽	▽	▽	▽	▽	▽	▽	▽	▽	▽	▽	▽	▽	▽	▽	▽	▽	▽	●	●	

Range of rank*

		Finland	Japan	Hong Kong-China	Korea	Liechtenstein	Australia	Macao-China	Netherlands	Czech Republic	New Zealand	Canada	Switzerland	France	Belgium	Sweden	Ireland	Hungary	Germany	Poland	Slovak Republic	Iceland	United States	Austria	Russian Fed.	Latvia	Spain	Italy	Norway	Luxembourg	Greece	Denmark	Portugal	Uruguay	Serbia	Turkey	Thailand	Mexico	Indonesia	Brazil	Tunisia
OECD countries	Upper rank	1	1		2		4		4	4	4	6	7	9	9	10	10	11	11	14	15	16	17	16			19	19	20	22	21	25	26			28		29			
	Lower rank	2	3		3		7		8	8	8	9	13	13	13	15	15	16	17	19	21	19	23	23			24	25	25	25	26	27	27			28		29			
All countries	Upper rank	1	1	2	2	5	5	5	5	5	6	8	10	12	12	13	13	14	14	17	18	19	20	19	20	20	22	22	24	26	25	30	31	33	33	33	34	37	38	38	39
	Lower rank	3	3	4	4	11	10	10	11	11	11	12	15	16	16	18	18	19	21	22	25	23	27	28	30	29	29	30	30	30	31	32	32	35	36	36	36	37	39	40	40

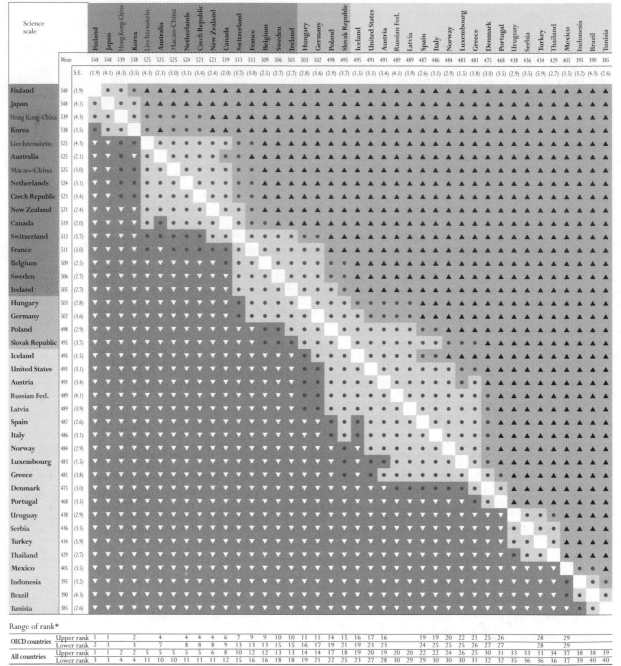

* Because data are based on samples, it is not possible to report exact rank order positions for countries. However, it is possible to report the range of rank order positions within which the country mean lies with 95 per cent likelihood.

Instructions:

Read across the row for a country to compare performance with the countries listed along the top of the chart. The symbols indicate whether the average performance of the country in the row is lower than that of the comparison country, higher than that of the comparison country, or if there is no statistically significant difference between the average achievement of the two countries.

Without the Bonferroni adjustment:
- Mean performance statistically significantly higher than in comparison country
- No statistically significant difference from comparison country
- Mean performance statistically significantly lower than in comparison country

With the Bonferroni adjustment:
- ▲ Mean performance statistically significantly higher than in comparison country
- ● No statistically significant difference from comparison country
- ▽ Mean performance statistically significantly lower than in comparison country

- Statistically significantly above the OECD average
- Not statistically significantly different from the OECD average
- Statistically significantly below the OECD average

Source: OECD, PISA 2003 database.

Figure 6.11 ■ **Differences in mean scores between PISA 2003 and PISA 2000 on the science scale**
Only countries with valid data for both 2003 and 2000

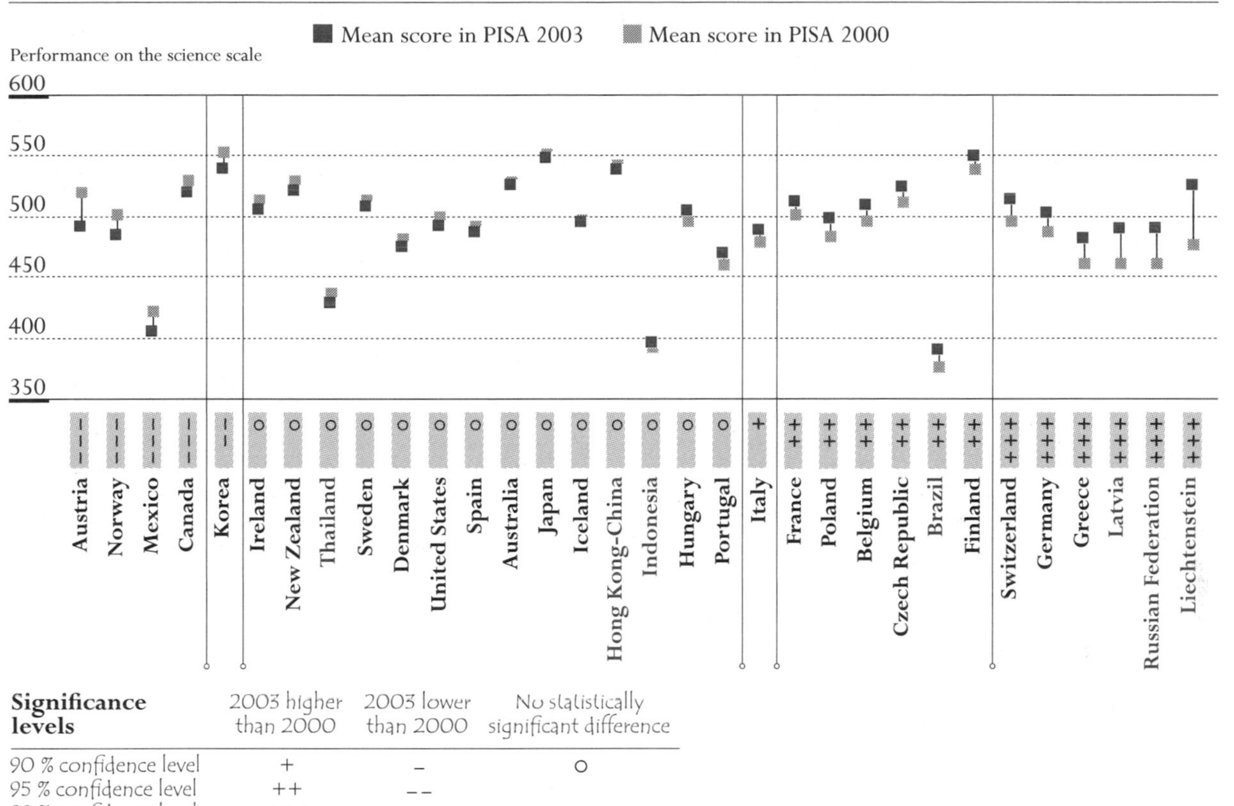

Countries are ranked in ascending order of the difference between PISA 2003 and PISA 2000 performances.
Source: OECD PISA 2003 database, Table 6.6; OECD PISA 2000 database, Table 3.3 (OECD 2001a).

Differences in science performance between PISA 2000 and PISA 2003

Results for the two science surveys should be compared cautiously.

Most of the science items that were used for assessment in 2000 were also used in 2003. This meant that links could be made with any of the new items that were used and, consequently, changes from 2000 to 2003 could be considered. Figure 6.11 shows science scores for PISA 2000 and 2003 for the countries and indicates differences in performance between the two assessments. However, as explained before, such differences need to be interpreted with caution.

Some countries showed improvement, most often driven by higher-ability students…

Thirteen countries, among them nine OECD countries, showed statistically significant increases in overall performance from PISA 2000 to PISA 2003 as indicated by the mean score. These include Belgium, the Czech Republic, Finland, France, Germany, Greece, Italy, Poland and Switzerland as well as the partner countries Brazil, Latvia, Liechtenstein and the Russian Federation. Figure 6.12 shows the differences within each country at the various percentile levels. In Belgium, the Czech Republic, Finland, France, Germany, Italy, Poland and the partner country Brazil the increases tended to be driven by improvements in the upper half of the performance distribution (the 75th, 90th and 95th percentiles), *i.e.*, the better performing students became better.

Figure 6.12 ■ **Comparisons between PISA 2003 and PISA 2000 in science**

Significance levels	2003 higher than 2000	2003 lower than 2000	No statistically significant difference
90 % confidence level	+	–	O
95 % confidence level	++	– –	
99 % confidence level	+++	– – –	

Differences observed in the mean and percentiles

	5th	10th	25th	Mean	75th	90th	95th
OECD countries							
Australia	--	-	O	O	O	O	O
Austria	---	---	---	---	---	---	--
Belgium	+	O	O	++	++	++	++
Canada	---	---	---	---	O	O	O
Czech Republic	O	O	O	++	+++	+++	+++
Denmark	O	O	O	O	O	O	O
Finland	O	O	O	++	+++	+++	+++
France	O	O	O	++	+++	+++	+++
Germany	O	O	O	+++	+++	+++	+++
Greece	O	O	++	+++	+++	+++	+++
Hungary	O	++	+	O	O	O	O
Iceland	--	-	O	O	O	O	+
Ireland	O	O	O	O	O	O	O
Italy	O	O	O	+	+++	+++	+++
Japan	--	--	--	O	+	+++	+++
Korea	---	---	---	--	O	O	++
Mexico	---	---	---	---	O	O	O
New Zealand	O	O	-	O	O	O	O
Norway	---	---	---	---	--	O	O
Poland	O	O	O	++	++	++	+++
Portugal	O	O	O	O	+	+	+
Spain	-	-	O	O	O	O	O
Sweden	---	---	-	O	O	++	+
Switzerland	O	O	+	+++	++	++	++
United States	O	O	O	O	O	O	O
OECD total	---	---	---	-	O	O	++
OECD average	--	--	O	O	O	++	+++
Partner countries							
Brazil	O	O	O	++	++	++	++
Hong Kong-China	O	O	O	O	O	O	O
Indonesia	O	O	O	O	O	O	O
Latvia	+++	+++	+++	+++	+++	+++	++
Liechtenstein	O	O	+++	+++	+++	+++	++
Russian Federation	+++	+++	+++	+++	+++	+++	+++
Thailand	-	--	--	O	O	O	O

Source: OECD PISA 2003 database, Table 6.6 and OECD PISA 2000 database, Table 3.3 (OECD 2001a).

...while science performance fell in a smaller number of countries, most often pulled down by lower-ability students.

Five countries showed a significant decline in performance, namely Austria, Canada, Korea, Mexico and Norway. For Korea, while the top performing 5 per cent of students showed higher performance in 2003, the 25 per cent lowest-performing students performed markedly lower, dragging overall performance down. The picture is similar for Japan and Sweden, but with no difference in average performance.

Gender differences in science

Science showed the smallest average gender differences among all content areas assessed.

As in PISA 2000, science showed the smallest average gender differences among all content areas assessed (Table 6.7 and Figure 6.13), with an OECD average difference between males and females of six score points in favour of males. Statistically significant differences in favour of males are found in Canada,

Denmark, Greece, Korea, Luxembourg, Mexico, New Zealand, Poland, Portugal, Slovak Republic and Switzerland and in the partner countries Liechtenstein and the Russian Federation. On the other hand, females in Finland, Iceland and the partner country Tunisia outperform males.

Another way of looking at the distribution of scores is to examine the percentage of students scoring below 400 score points, *i.e.*, one standard deviation below the OECD mean and the percentage of students scoring above 600 score points – that is, one standard deviation above the OECD mean. This is particularly useful in science given that performance has not been classified by proficiency levels. With around two-thirds of the students scoring between 400 and 600 score points, around one-sixth of students perform at each of these extremes.

As expected from the previous analysis in PISA 2000 which showed a minimal level of gender differences in the results of science, there are also very small differences between the percentage of males and females scoring below 400 score points (less than 5 per cent in either direction for the OECD countries). The same is true for students scoring above 600 score points (Table 6.8).

Figure 6.13 ■ **Gender differences in science performance in PISA 2003 and PISA 2000**
Differences in PISA scale scores

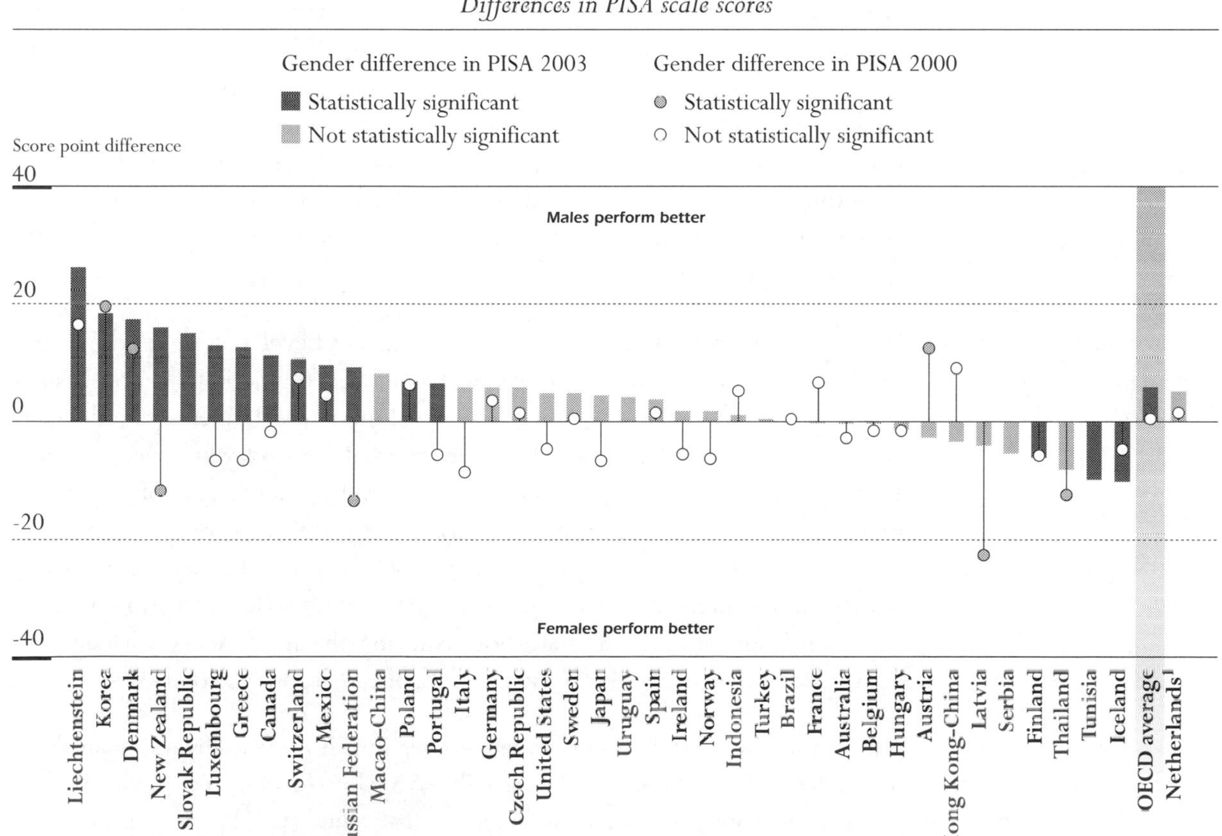

1. The response rate in the Netherlands in 2000 is to low to ensure comparability (see Annex A3, OECD, 2001a).
Source: OECD PISA 2003 database, Table 6.7; OECD (2001a), Table 5.1a.

IMPLICATIONS FOR POLICY

Reading

The results for PISA 2000 show wide differences between countries in the knowledge and skills of 15-year-olds in reading literacy. Differences between countries represent, however, only a fraction of overall variation in student performance, with differences within countries being on average about ten times as great as the variation between country means.

The persistence of a small but significant minority of students unable to perform even simple reading tasks remains of concern…

Catering for such a diverse client base and narrowing the gaps in student performance represents formidable challenges for all countries: An average of 8 per cent of 15-year-olds reach the highest reading level in PISA, demonstrating the ability to complete sophisticated reading tasks, to show detailed understanding of texts and the relevance of their components, and to evaluate information critically and build hypotheses drawing on specialised knowledge. At the other end of the scale, an average of 8 per cent of students do not reach proficiency Level 1. They fail to demonstrate routinely the most basic knowledge and skills that PISA seeks to measure. These students may still be able to read in a technical sense, but they show serious difficulties in applying reading literacy as a tool to advance and extend their knowledge and skills in other areas. Although the proportion of these students is below 2 per cent in three countries, including two OECD countries, and exceeds 10 per cent in only three OECD and seven partner countries, the existence of a small but significant minority of students who, near the end of compulsory schooling, lack the foundation of literacy skills needed for further learning, must be of concern to policy makers seeking to make lifelong learning a reality for all. This is so, in particular, in the face of mounting evidence that continuing education and training beyond school tend to reinforce rather than to mitigate skill differences resulting from unequal success in initial education.

…as does the nearly one in five who can only perform the simplest tasks.

Adding to this proportion of students not reaching Level 1 those who perform only at Level 1, namely those who are capable only of completing the most basic of reading tasks, such as locating a simple piece of information, identifying the main theme of a text or making a simple connection with everyday knowledge, brings the proportion of low performers at or below Level 1 to an average of 19 per cent across OECD countries. Parents, educators, and policy makers in systems with large proportions of students performing at or below Level 1 need to recognise that significant numbers of students are not benefiting sufficiently from available educational opportunities and are not acquiring the necessary knowledge and skills to do so effectively in their further school careers and beyond.

In some higher-performing countries, a wide distribution can be of concern even if most students do comparatively well.

Wide variation in student performance does not, however, always mean that a large part of the student population will have a low level of reading literacy. In fact, in some countries with high average performance, the 25th percentile on the combined reading literacy scale lies well within proficiency Level 2, indicating that students at the 25th percentile are doing reasonably well by international comparative standards. Nevertheless, the variation in the distribution of

student performance in these countries suggests that the students at the 25th percentile may be performing substantially below expected benchmarks of good performance in the countries in question.

The success of some countries in containing student disparities while achieving high overall performance suggests that education policy can make a difference.

To what extent is the observed variation in student performance on the PISA 2003 assessments a reflection of the innate distribution of students' abilities and thus a challenge for education systems that cannot be influenced directly by education policy? The analysis in this chapter has shown not only that the magnitude of within-country disparities in reading literacy varies widely between countries but also that wide disparities in performance are not a necessary condition for a country to attain a high level of overall performance. Although more general contextual factors need to be considered when such disparities are compared between countries, public policy may therefore have the potential to make an important contribution to providing equal opportunities and equitable learning outcomes for all students. Showing that countries differ not just in their mean performance, but also in the extent to which they are able to close the gap between the students with the lowest and the highest levels of performance and to reduce some of the barriers to equitable distribution of learning outcomes is an important finding which has direct relevance for policy makers.

Science

Scientific literacy is today important for individuals and for society…

In an increasingly technological world, literacy is not just about reading, but citizens also need to be scientifically literate. Scientific literacy is important for understanding environmental, medical, economic and other issues that confront modern societies, which rely heavily on technological and scientific advances. Further, the performance of a country's best students in scientific subjects may have implications for the part which that country will play in tomorrow's advanced technology sector, and for its general international competitiveness. Conversely, deficiencies in mathematical and scientific literacy can have negative consequences for individuals' labour-market and earnings prospects and for their capacity to participate fully in society.

…and countries need to be better at spreading scientific skills to more students.

Addressing the increasing demand for scientific skills requires excellence throughout education systems, and it is important to monitor how well countries provide young adults with fundamental skills in this area. However, the wide disparities in student performance on the scientific literacy scale that emerge from the analysis in this chapter suggest that this remains still a remote goal and that countries need to serve a wide range of student abilities, including those who perform exceptionally well but also those most in need.

It is encouraging that gender differences in science are now small.

Gender difference in science, in which males have often been more proficient in past assessments, tend to be much smaller than the difference in favour of females in reading. In fact, in science there is no clear pattern of gender differences, and in most countries gender differences are small. Although it will take time for these results to translate into corresponding participation patterns in higher education as well as occupational structures, this is an encouraging signal.

PISA will assess science performance more thoroughly in 2006.

The 2006 PISA assessment, which will put the main focus on the knowledge, skills and attitudes of 15-year-olds towards science, will reveal to what extent countries are further progressing towards raising science performance, fostering equity in learning opportunities and, perhaps most important of all, developing positive attitudes and dispositions among young adults towards scientific subjects and careers.

Notes

1. For the 25 countries with comparable data in 2000 and 2003, the average performance in 2000 was 501 score points, while the average performance in 2003 was 497 score points. Because of sampling errors and errors associated with the link between the two assessments, the difference is not statistically significant.
2. For the country Serbia and Montenegro, data for Montenegro are not available. The latter accounts for 7.9 per cent of the national population. The name "Serbia" is used as a shorthand for the Serbian part of Serbia and Montenegro.
3. Comparisons of a particular country average score with the OECD average are based on a recomputed OECD average that excludes the data from the country in question. This is done to avoid dependency between the two averages.
4. See Annex A8 for an explanation of the methodology underlying the link between the PISA 2000 and PISA 2003 assessments.
5. In Luxembourg, the assessment conditions were changed in substantial ways between the 2000 and 2003 assessments in order to reduce linguistic barriers for students. For this reasons, results cannot be compared between 2000 and 2003.
6. For the 25 countries with comparable data in 2000 and 2003, average performance was 501 score points in both the 2000 and the 2003 assessments.
7. Comparisons of a particular country's average score with the OECD average are based on a recomputed OECD average that excludes the data from the country in question. This is done to avoid dependency between the two averages.

REFERENCES

Artelt, C. (2000), *Strategisches Lernen,* Waxmann, Münster.

Bandura, A. (1994), *Self-Efficacy: The Exercise of Control,* Freeman, New York.

Beaton, A.E., **M.O. Martin**, **I.V.S. Mullis**, **E.J. Gonzalez**, **T.A. Smith** and **D.L. Kelly** (1996), *Science Achievement in the Middle School Years: IEA's Third International Mathematics and Science Study (TIMSS),* Center for the Study of Testing, Evaluation, and Educational Policy, Boston College, Chestnut Hill, M.A.

Bempechat, J., **N.V. Jimenez** and **B.A. Boulay** (2002), "Cultural-Cognitive Issues in Academic Achievement: New Directions for Cross-National Research", in A.C. Porter and A. Gamoran (eds.), *Methodological Advances in Cross-National Surveys of Educational Achievement,* National Academic Press, Washington, D.C.

Boekaerts, M. (1999), "Self-regulated learning: Where we are today", *International Journal of Educational Research,* Vol. 31, Issue 6, Elsevier Ltd., pp.445-475.

Brown, A.L., **J.D. Bransford**, **R.A. Ferrara** and **J.C. Campione** (1983), "Learning, remembering and understanding", in J. H. Flavell and E. M. Markman (eds.), *Handbook of Child Psychology, Cognitive Development,* New York, Wiley, pp. 77-166.

Datcher, L. (1982), "Effects of Community and Family Background on Achievement", *Review of Economics and Statistics,* Vol. 64, No. 1, The MIT Press, Cambridge, M.A., pp. 32-41.

Deci, E.L. and **R.M. Ryan** (1985), *Intrinsic Motivation and Self-Determination in Human Behavior,* Plenum Press, New York.

Eccles, J. S. (1994), "Understanding women's educational and occupational choice: Applying the Eccles et al. model of achievement-related choices", *Psychology of Women Quarterly,* Vol. 18, Blackwell Publishing, Oxford, pp. 585-609.

Finn, J. (1989), "Withdrawing from school", *Review of Educational Research,* Vol. 59, No. 2, American Educational Research Association , Washington, D.C., pp. 117-142.

Finn, J.D. (1993), *School Engagement & Students At Risk,* National Center for Educational Statistics, Washington, D.C.

Finn, J. and **D.A. Rock** (1997), "Academic success among students at risk for school failure", *Journal of Applied Psychology,* Vol. 82, No. 2, American Psychological Association, Washington, D.C., pp. 221-234.

Flavell, J.H. and **H.M. Wellman** (1977), "Metamemory", in R.V. Kail, Jr. and W. Hagen (eds.), *Perspectives on the Development of Memory and Cognition,* Erlbaum, Hillsdale, N.J., pp. 3-31.

Ganzeboom, H.B.G., **P.M. De Graaf** and **D.J. Treiman** (1992), "A standard international socio-economic index of occupational status", *Social Science Research,* Vol. 21, Issue 1, Elsevier Ltd., pp. 1-56.

Hart, B. and **T.R. Risely** (1995), *Meaningful Differences in the Everyday Experience of Young American Children,* Brookes, Baltimore, M.D.

Hatano, G. (1998), "Comprehension activity in individuals and groups", in M. Sabourin, F. Craik and M. Robert (eds.), *Advances in Psychological Science, Volume 2: Biological and Cognitive Aspects,* Psychology Press/Erlbaum, Hove, pp. 399-417.

Heine, S.J., **Lehman, D.R.**, **Markus, H.R.** and **Kitayama, S.** (1999), "Is there a universal need for positive self regard?", *Psychological Review,* Vol. 106, No. 4, American Psychological Association, Washington, D.C., pp. 766-794.

Jenkins, P. H. (1995), "School delinquency and school commitment", *Sociology of Education,* Vol. 68, American Sociological Association, Washington, D.C., pp. 221-239.

Johnson, M. K., **R. Crosnoe** and **G.H. Elder** (2001), "Students' attachment and academic engagement: The role of race and ethnicity", *Sociology of Education,* Vol. 74, American Sociological Association, Washington, D.C., pp.318-340.

Lehtinen, E. (1992), "Lern- und Bewältigungsstrategien im Unterricht", in H. Mandl and F.H. Friedrich (eds.), *Lern- und Denkstrategien: Analyse und Intervention,* Hogrefe, Göttingen, pp. 125-149.

Rosenshine, B. and **C. Meister** (1994), "Reciprocal teaching: A review of the research", *Review of Educational Research,* Vol. 64, No. 4, American Educational Research Association, Washington, D.C., pp. 479-531.

Marsh, H.W. (1986), "Verbal and math self-concepts: An internal/external frame of reference model", *American Educational Research Journal,* Vol. 23, No. 1, American Educational Research Association , Washington, D.C., pp. 129-149.

Marsh, H.W. (1993), "The multidimensional structure of academic self-concept: Invariance over gender and age", *American Educational Research Journal,* Vol. 30, No. 4, American Educational Research Association , Washington, D.C., pp. 841-860.

Meece, J.L., A. Wigfield and **J.S. Eccles** (1990), "Predictors of math anxiety and its influence on young adolescents' course enrolment intentions and performance in mathematics", *Journal of Educational Psychology,* Vol. 82, No. 1, American Psychological Association, Washington, D.C., pp. 60-70.

OECD (**Organisation for Economic Co-operation and Development**) (1996), *Education at a Glance,* OECD, Paris.

OECD (1997), *Education at a Glance,* OECD, Paris.

OECD (1999a), *Measuring Student Knowledge and Skills – A New Framework for Assessment,* OECD, Paris.

OECD (1999b), *Classifying Educational Programmes: Manual for ISCED-97 Implementation in OECD Countries*, OECD, Paris.

OECD (2000a), *Education at a Glance,* OECD, Paris.

OECD and **Statistics Canada** (2000b), *Literacy in the Information Age,* OECD, Paris and Ottawa.

OECD (2001a), *Knowledge and Skills for Life – First Results from PISA 2000,* OECD, Paris.

OECD (2001b), *Starting Strong - Early Childhood Education and Care,* OECD, Paris.

OECD (2002a*), Manual for the PISA 2000 Database,* OECD, Paris.

OECD (2002b), *Reading for Change – Performance and Engagement across Countries*, OECD, Paris.

OECD (2002c), *Sample Tasks from the PISA 2000 Assessment – Reading, Mathematical and Scientific Literacy,* OECD, Paris.

OECD (2002d), *PISA 2000 Technical Report,* OECD, Paris.

OECD (2002e), *Education Policy Analysis,* OECD, Paris.

OECD (2003a), *Education at a Glance,* OECD, Paris.

OECD (2003b), *Learners for Life – Student Approaches to Learning,* OECD, Paris.

OECD (2003c), *Literacy Skills for the World of Tomorrow – Further Results from PISA 2003,* OECD, Paris.

OECD (2003d), *Student Engagement at School – A Sense of Belonging and Participation,* OECD, Paris.

OECD (2003e), *The PISA 2003 Assessment Framework – Mathematics, Reading, Science and Problem Solving Knowledge and Skills,* OECD, Paris.

OECD (2003f), *Trends in International Migration,* OECD, Paris.

OECD (2004a), *Education at a Glance,* OECD, Paris.

OECD (2004b), *Attracting, Developing and Retaining Effective Teachers,* OECD, Paris.

OECD (2004c), *What Makes School Systems Perform,* OECD, Paris.

OECD (2004d), *Problem Solving for Tomorrow's World – First Measures of Cross-Curricular Competencies,* OECD, Paris.

OECD (forthcoming), *PISA 2003 Technical Report,* OECD, Paris.

OECD and **Statistics Canada** (1995), *Literacy, Economy and Society: Results of the First International Adult Literacy Survey,* OECD, Paris and Ottawa.

Offord, D.R. and **B.G. Waters** (1983), "Socialization and its failure", in M.D. Levine, W.B. Carey, A.C. Crocker and R.T. Gross (eds.), *Developmental-Behavioral Pediatrics,* John Wiley and Sons Inc., New York, pp. 650-682.

Offord, D.R. and **K. Bennett** (1994), "Conduct disorder: Long-term outcomes and intervention effectiveness", *Journal of the American Academy of Child & Adolescent Psychiatry,* Vol. 33, Issue 8, Lippincott Williams & Wilkins, Baltimore, M.D., pp.1069-1078.

Owens, L. and **J. Barnes** (1992), *Learning Preferences Scales,* ACER, Victoria.

Rychen, D.S. and **L.H. Salganik** (eds.) (2002), *Defining and Selecting Key Competencies,* Hogrefe and Huber Publishers, Seattle, W.A.

Schiefele, U., **A. Krapp** and **A. Winteler** (1992), "Interest as a predictor of academic achievement: A meta-analysis of research", in K. A. Renninger, S. Hidi and A. Krapp (eds.), *The Role of Interest in Learning and Development,* Erlbaum, Hillsdale, N.J., pp. 183-212.

Schneider, W. (1996), "Zum Zusammenhang zwischen Metakognition und Motivation bei Lern- und Gedächtnisvorgängen", in C. Spiel, U. Kastner-Koller and P. Deimann (eds.), *Motivation und Lernen aus der Perspektive lebenslanger Entwicklung,* Waxmann, Münster, pp. 121-133.

Schunk, D.H. (1991), *Learning Theories: An Educational Perspective,* Macmillan Publishing Company, New York.

Steen (1990), *On the Shoulders of Giants: New Approaches to Numeracy,* National Academy Press, Washington, DC.

Stanat, P. (2004), "The role of migration background for student performance: an international comparison", paper presented at the 2004 Annual Meeting of the American Educational Research Association (AERA) San Diego, C.A., 12-16 April.

Veenman, M.V. J. and **B.H.A.M. van Hout-Wolters** (2002), "Het meten van metacognitieve vaardigheden", in F. Daems, R. Rymenans and G. Rogiest (eds.), *Onderwijsonderzoek in Nederland en Vlaanderen. Prooceedings van de 29e Onderwijs Research Dagen 2002 te Antwerpen,* Universiteit Antwerpen, Antwerpen, pp. 102-103.

van de Vijver, F. and **K. Leung** (1997), "Methods and data analysis of comparative research", in J. W. Berry, Y., H. Poortinga and J. Pandey (eds.), *Handbook of Cross-Cultural Psychology, Vol. 1 Theory and Method,* Allyn and Bacon, Needham Heights, M.A., pp. 257-300.

Voelkl, K.E. (1995), "School warmth, student participation, and achievement", *Journal of Experimental Education,* Vol. 63, No. 2, HELDREF Publications, Washington, D.C., pp.127-138.

Wang, M., **G. Haertel** and **H. Walberg** (1993), "Toward a knowledge base for school learning", *Review of Educational Research,* Vol. 63, pp. 249-294.

Warm, T.A. (1985), "Weighted maximum likelihood estimation of ability in Item Response Theory with tests of finite length", *Technical Report CGI-TR-85-08,* U.S. Coast Guard Institute, Oklahoma City.

Weinert, F. E. (1994), "Lernen lernen und das eigene lernen verstehen", in K. Reusser and M. Reusser-Weyeneth (eds.), *Verstehen. Psychologischer Prozeß und didaktische Aufgabe,* Huber, Bern, pp. 183-05.

Wigfield, A., **J.S. Eccles** and **D. Rodriguez** (1998), "The development of children's motivation in school context", *Review of Research in Education,* Vol. 23, American Educational Research Association, Washington, D.C. pp. 73-118.

Willms, J. D. (2002), *Vulnerable Children: Findings from Canada's National Longitudinal Survey of Children and Youth,* University of Alberta Press, Edmonton.

Willms, J.D. (2004), "Student Performance and Socio-economic Background", unpublished research, University of New Brunswick.

Willoughby, T. and **E. Wood** (1994), "Elaborative interrogation examined at encoding and retrieval", *Learning and Instruction,* Vol. 4, Issue 2, Elsevier Ltd., pp. 139-149.

Winne, P.H. (2001), "Self-regulated learning viewed from models of information processing", in B.J. Zimmerman and D.H. Schunk (eds.), *Self-regulated learning and academic achievement: theoretical perspectives,* Lawrence Erlbaum Associates, Inc., Mahwah, N.J., pp. 153-189.

Zimmerman, B.J. (1999), "Commentary: toward a cyclically interactive view of self-regulated learning", *International Journal of Educational Research,* Vol. 31, Issue 6, Elsevier Ltd., pp.545-551.

Zimmerman, B. J. and **M. Martinez-Pons** (1990), "Student differences in self-regulated learning: Relating grade, sex and giftedness to self efficacy and strategy use", *Journal of Educational Psychology,* Vol. 82, No. 1, American Psychological Association, Washington, D.C., pp. 51-59.

Annex A

TECHNICAL BACKGROUND

Annex A1: Construction of indices and other derived measures from the student and school context questionnaires

This section explains the indices derived from the student and school context questionnaires that are used in this report.

Several of PISA's measures reflect indices that summarise responses from students or school representatives (typically principals) to a series of related questions. The questions were selected from larger constructs on the basis of theoretical considerations and previous research. Structural equation modelling was used to confirm the theoretically expected behaviour of the indices and to validate their comparability across countries. For this purpose, a model was estimated separately for each country and collectively for all OECD countries.

For a detailed description of other PISA indices and details on the methods see the *PISA 2000 Technical Report* (OECD, 2002d) or the *PISA 2003 Technical Report* (OECD, forthcoming).

Unless otherwise indicated, where an index involves multiple questions and student responses, the index was scaled using a weighted maximum likelihood estimate (WLE) (see Warm, 1985), using a one-parameter item response model, which in the case of items with more than two categories was the Partial Credit Model. The scaling was done in three stages:

- The item parameters were estimated from equal-sized sub-samples of students from each OECD country.
- The estimates were computed for all students and all schools by anchoring the item parameters obtained in the preceding step.
- The indices were then standardised so that the mean of the index value for the OECD student population was zero and the standard deviation was one (countries being given equal weight in the standardisation process).

To illustrate the meaning of the international scores on the index, item maps were constructed that relate the index value to typical student responses to the questions asked. These item maps can be found on the website *www.pisa.oecd.org*. The vertical lines on the maps indicate for each of the index scores at the top of the figure which response a student is most likely to give, with zero representing the average student response across OECD countries.

It is important to note that negative values for an index do not necessarily imply that students responded negatively to the underlying questions. A negative value merely indicates that a group of students (or all students, collectively, in a single country) or principals responded less positively than all students or principals did on average across OECD countries. Likewise, a positive value on an index indicates that a group of students or principals responded more favourably, or more positively, than students or principals did, on average, in OECD countries.

Terms enclosed in brackets < > in the following descriptions were replaced in the national versions of the student and school questionnaires by the appropriate national equivalent. For example, the term <qualification at ISCED level 5A> was translated in the United States into "Bachelor's degree, post-graduate certificate program, Master's degree program or first professional degree program". Similarly the term <classes in the language of assessment> in Luxembourg was translated into "German classes" or "French classes" depending on whether students received the German or French version of the assessment instruments.

For additional information on how these indices were constructed, see the *PISA 2000 Technical Report* (OECD, 2002d) or the *PISA 2003 Technical Report* (OECD, forthcoming).

Student level variables

Student background

Family structure

Students were asked to report who usually lived at home with them. The response categories were then grouped into four categories: *i)* ***single-parent family*** (students who reported living with one of the following: mother, father, female guardian or male guardian); *ii)* ***nuclear family*** (students who reported living with a mother and a father); *iii)* ***mixed family*** (students who reported living with a mother and a guardian, a father and a guardian, or two guardians); and *iv)* ***other response combinations***. Non responses are maintained as missing.

Parental occupations and student expected occupation

Students were asked to report their mothers' and fathers' occupations, and to state whether each parent was in full-time paid work; part-time paid work; not working but looking for a paid job; or "other".

Students were also asked to report on their expected occupation at age 30. The open-ended responses for occupations were then coded in accordance with the International Standard Classification of Occupations (ISCO 1988).

The PISA ***international socio-economic index of occupational status*** (ISEI) was derived from students' responses on parental occupation. The index captured the attributes of occupations that convert parents' education into income. The index was derived by the optimal scaling of occupation groups to maximise the indirect effect of education on income through occupation and to minimise the direct effect of education on income, net of occupation (both effects being net of age). For more information on the methodology, see Ganzeboom *et al.* (1992). The ***highest international socio-economic index of occupational status*** (HISEI) corresponds to the highest ISEI of either the father or the mother.

The variables on students' expected occupation and their fathers' and mothers' occupations were also transformed into four ***socio-economic categories***: *i)* white-collar high-skilled: legislators, senior officials and managers, professionals, technicians and associate professionals; *ii)* white-collar low-skilled: service workers, shop and market sales workers and clerks; *iii)* blue-collar high-skilled: skilled agricultural and fishery workers and craft and related trades workers; and *iv)* blue-collar low-skilled: plant and machine operators and assemblers and elementary occupations.

Index of economic, social and cultural status

The ***index of economic, social and cultural status*** was created to capture wider aspects of a student's family and home background in addition to occupational status and is a variation of the index used in PISA 2000. It was derived from the following variables: *i)* the highest international socio-economic index of occupational status of the father or mother; *ii)* the highest level of education of the father or mother converted into years of schooling (for the conversion of levels of education into years of schooling see Table A1.1); and *iii)* the number of books at home as well as access to home educational and cultural resources, obtained by asking students whether they had at their home: a desk to study at, a room of their own, a quiet place to study, a computer they can use for school work, educational software, a link to the Internet, their own calculator, classic literature, books of poetry, works of art (*e.g.*, paintings), books to help with their school work, and a dictionary. The rationale for the choice of these variables was that socio-economic status is usually seen as being determined by occupational status, education and wealth. As no direct measure on parental wealth was available from PISA, access to relevant household items was used as a proxy. The student scores on the index are factor scores derived from a Principal Component Analysis which are standardised to have an OECD mean of zero and a standard deviation of one.

The Principal Component Analysis was also performed for each participating country to determine to what extent the components of the index operate in similar ways across countries. The analysis revealed that patterns of factor loadings were very similar across countries, with all three components contributing to a similar extent to the index. For the occupational component, the average factor loading was 0.81, ranging from 0.72 to 0.86 across countries. For the educational component, the average factor loading was 0.80, ranging from 0.70 to 0.87 across countries. For the wealth component, the average factor loading was 0.76, ranging from 0.65 to 0.80 across countries. The reliability of the index ranged from 0.56 to 0.77. These results support the cross-national validity of the index of economic, social and cultural status.

The correlation between the average value on the index and the Gross Domestic Product of countries is 0.62 (increasing to 0.69 when Luxembourg is removed).

The index used in PISA 2000 (OECD, 2001) was similar to the one used for PISA 2003. However, some adjustments were made. First of all, only 11 questions on home educational resources were common to both surveys. Second, for the question on parental levels of education no distinction had been made in PISA 2000 between university-level and non-university tertiary education. Where comparisons between 2000 and 2003 data are made, the index for PISA 2000 was recomputed on the basis of a common methodology used for both assessments. Results may therefore differ slightly from those reported in PISA 2000. This being said, the correlation between the PISA 2000 and PISA 2003 indices is very high (R of 0.96). This shows that different methods of computation of the indices did not have a major impact on the results. For more information on this index see the *PISA 2003 Technical Report* (OECD, forthcoming).

Educational level of parents

Parental education is a family background variable that is often used in the analysis of educational outcomes. Indices were constructed using information on the ***educational level of the father***, the ***educational level of the mother***, and the highest

level of education between the two parents, referred to as the ***highest educational level of parents***. Students were asked to identify the highest level of education of their mother and father on the basis of national qualifications, which were then coded in accordance with the International Standard Classification of Education (ISCED 1997, see OECD, 1999b) in order to obtain internationally comparable categories of educational attainment. The resulting categories were: (0) for no education; (1) for the completion of <ISCED Level 1> (primary education); (2) for completion of <ISCED Level 2> (lower secondary education); (3) for the completion of <ISCED Level 3B or 3C> (vocational/pre-vocational upper secondary education, aimed in most countries at providing direct entry into the labour market); (4) for completion of <ISCED Level 3A> (upper secondary education, aimed in most countries at gaining entry into tertiary-type A [university level] education) and/or <ISCED Level 4> (non-tertiary post-secondary); (5) for qualifications in <ISCED 5B> (vocational tertiary); and (6) for completion of<ISCED Level 5A, 6> (tertiary-type A and advanced research programmes).

As noted above, the highest level of educational attainment of the parents was also converted into ***years of schooling*** using the conversion coefficients shown in Table A1.1.

Table A1.1
Levels of parental education converted into years of schooling

		Did not go to school	Completed ISCED Level 1 (primary education)	Completed ISCED Level 2 (lower secondary education)	Completed ISCED Levels 3B or 3C (upper secondary education providing direct access to the labour market or to ISCED 5B programmes)	Completed ISCED Level 3A (upper secondary education providing access to ISCED 5A and 5B programmes)	Completed ISCED Level 5A (university level tertiary education)	Completed ISCED Level 5B (non-university tertiary education)
OECD countries	Australia	0.0	6.5	10.0	11.0	12.0	15.0	14.0
	Austria	0.0	4.0	8.0	9.0	13.0	17.0	15.0
	Belgium	0.0	6.0	8.0	12.0	12.0	16.0	15.0
	Canada	0.0	6.0	9.0	12.0	12.0	17.0	15.0
	Czech Republic	0.0	5.0	9.0	12.0	13.0	16.0	15.0
	Denmark	0.0	6.0	9.0	12.0	12.0	15.0	14.0
	Finland	0.0	6.0	9.0	12.0	12.0	15.0	14.0
	France	0.0	5.0	9.0	11.0	12.0	14.0	14.0
	Germany	0.0	4.0	10.0	11.0	12.0	17.0	15.0
	Greece	0.0	6.0	9.0	11.0	12.0	16.0	16.0
	Hungary	0.0	4.0	8.0	10.0	12.0	15.0	14.0
	Iceland	0.0	7.0	10.0	10.5	14.0	15.5	15.0
	Ireland	0.0	8.0	11.0	12.0	13.0	17.0	15.0
	Italy	0.0	5.0	8.0	11.0	13.0	16.0	15.0
	Japan	0.0	6.0	9.0	10.0	12.0	16.0	14.0
	Korea	0.0	6.0	9.0	12.0	12.0	16.0	14.0
	Luxembourg	0.0	6.0	9.0	12.0	13.0	17.0	17.0
	Mexico	0.0	6.0	9.0	12.0	12.0	16.0	14.0
	Netherlands	0.0	6.0	8.0	12.0	13.0	15.0	13.0
	New Zealand	0.0	6.0	10.0	12.0	13.0	16.0	16.0
	Norway	0.0	7.0	10.0	13.0	13.0	16.0	14.0
	Poland	0.0	6.0	9.0	11.0	12.0	15.0	15.0
	Portugal	0.0	4.0	7.0	12.0	12.0	17.0	15.0
	Slovak Republic	0.0	4.0	9.0	12.0	12.0	16.0	15.0
	Spain	0.0	6.0	10.0	11.0	12.0	15.0	14.0
	Sweden	0.0	6.0	9.0	12.0	12.0	15.0	13.5
	Switzerland	0.0	6.0	9.0	11.0	12.0	15.0	14.0
	Turkey	0.0	4.0	8.0	11.0	11.0	15.0	13.0
	United States	0.0	6.0	9.0	a	12.0	15.0	14.0
Partner countries	Brazil	0.0	7.0	11.0	14.0	14.0	18.0	17.0
	Hong Kong-China	0.0	6.0	9.0	11.0	13.0	17.0	16.0
	Indonesia	0.0	6.0	9.0	12.0	12.0	15.0	16.0
	Latvia	0.0	4.0	9.0	12.0	12.0	16.0	16.0
	Liechtenstein	0.0	6.0	9.0	11.0	12.0	15.0	14.0
	Russian Federation	0.0	4.0	9.0	11.0	11.0	15.0	13.0
	Serbia	0.0	4.0	8.0	11.0	12.0	16.0	14.0
	Thailand	0.0	6.0	9.0	12.0	12.0	16.0	14.0
	Tunisia	0.0	6.0	9.0	11.0	13.0	17.0	15.0
	Uruguay	0.0	6.0	9.0	11.0	12.0	16.0	14.0
	United Kingdom[1]	0.0	6.0	9.0	11.0	12.0	15.0	14.0

1. Response rate too low to ensure comparability (see Annex A3).

Immigration background

The index on ***immigrant background*** was derived from students' responses to questions about whether or not their mother and their father were born in the country of assessment or in another country. The response categories were then grouped into three categories: *i)* "native" students (those students born in the country of assessment or who had at least one parent born in that country); *ii)* "first-generation" students (those born in the country of assessment but whose parents were born in another country); and *iii)* "non-native" students (those born outside the country of assessment and whose parents were also born in another country). For some comparisons, first generation and non native students were grouped together.

Language used at home

Students were asked if the language spoken at home most of the time or always was the language of assessment, another official national language, other national dialect or language, or another language. The index on ***language spoken at home*** distinguishes between students who report using the language of assessment, another official national language, a national dialect or another national language always or most of the time at home and those who report using another language always or most of the time at home.

In most countries, the languages were individually identified and were coded internationally to allow for further research and analysis in this area.

Home educational resources

The PISA index of ***home educational resources*** was derived from students' reports on the availability of the following items in their home: *i)* a dictionary; *ii)* a quiet place to study; *iii)* a desk for study; *iv)* a calculator; and *v)* books to help with school work. Scale construction was done using Item Response Theory (IRT) scaling and positive values indicate higher levels of home educational resources.

Possessions related to "classical" culture in the family home

The PISA index of ***possessions related to "classical" culture in the family home*** was derived from students' reports on the availability of the following items in their home: classic literature (examples were given), books of poetry and works of art (examples were given). Scale construction was performed through IRT scaling and positive values indicate higher levels of cultural possessions.

School climate (students' views)

Attitudes towards school

The PISA index of ***attitudes towards school*** was derived from students' reported agreement with the following statements: *i)* school has done little to prepare me for adult life when I leave school; *ii)* school has been a waste of time; *iii)* school helped give me confidence to make decisions; and *iv)* school has taught me things which could be useful in a job. A four-point scale with the response categories "strongly agree" (=1), "agree" (=2), "disagree" (=3) and "strongly disagree" (=4) was used. As items *iii)* and *iv)* were inverted for scaling, positive values on this index indicate positive attitudes towards school. Scale construction was done using IRT scaling.

Student-teacher relations

The PISA index of ***student-teacher relations*** is derived from students' reported agreement with the following statements: *i)* most teachers are interested in students' well-being; *ii)* students who need extra help, will receive it from their teacher; *iii)* most teachers treat students fairly; *iv)* students get along well with most teachers; and *v)* most teachers really listen to what students have to say. A four-point scale with the response categories "strongly agree", "agree", "disagree" and "strongly disagree" was used. All items were inverted for scaling and positive scores on this index indicate good student-teacher relations at school. This index was constructed using IRT scaling.

Sense of belonging at school

The PISA index of ***sense of belonging at school*** was derived from students' reported agreement that school is a place where: *i)* I feel like an outsider (or left out of things); *ii)* I make friends easily; *iii)* I feel like I belong; *iv)* I feel awkward and out of place; *v)* other students seem to like me; and *vi)* I feel lonely. A four-point scale with the response categories "strongly agree", "agree", "disagree" and "strongly disagree" was used. Items *ii)*, *iii)*, and *v)* are inverted for scaling and positive values indicate positive feelings about the students' school. This index was constructed using IRT scaling.

Self-related cognitions in mathematics

Interest in and enjoyment of mathematics

The PISA index of ***interest in and enjoyment of mathematics*** was derived from students' reported agreement with the following statements: *i)* I enjoy reading about mathematics; *ii)* I look forward to my mathematics lessons; *iii)* I do mathematics because I enjoy it; and *iv)* I am interested in the things I learn in mathematics. A four-point scale with the response categories "strongly agree", "agree", "disagree" and "strongly disagree" was used. All items were inverted for IRT scaling and positive values on this index indicate higher levels of interest in and enjoyment of mathematics. This index was constructed using IRT scaling.

Instrumental motivation in mathematics

The PISA index of ***instrumental motivation in mathematics*** was derived from students' reported agreement with the following statements: *i)* making an effort in mathematics is worth it because it will help me in the work that I want to do later on; *ii)* learning mathematics is important because it will help me with the subjects that I want to study further on in school; *iii)* mathematics is an important subject for me because I need it for what I want to study later on; and *iv)* I will learn many things in mathematics that will help me get a job. A four-point scale with the response categories "strongly agree", "agree", "disagree" and "strongly disagree" was used. All items were inverted for scaling and positive values on this index indicate higher levels of instrumental motivation to learn mathematics. This index was constructed using IRT scaling.

Self-efficacy in mathematics

The PISA index of ***self-efficacy in mathematics*** was derived from students' reported level of confidence with the following calculations: *i)* using a <train timetable>, how long it would take to get from Zedville to Zedtown; *ii)* calculating how much cheaper a TV would be after a 30 per cent discount; *iii)* calculating how many square metres of tiles you need to cover a floor; *iv)* understanding graphs presented in newspapers; solving an equation like 3x + 5 = 17; *v)* finding the actual distance between two places on a map with a 1:10,000 scale; *vi)* solving an equation like 2(x+3) = (x + 3)(x - 3); and *vii)* calculating the petrol consumption rate of a car. A four-point scale with the response categories "very confident", "confident", "not very confident", "not at all confident" was used. All items were inverted for scaling and positive values on this index indicate higher levels of self-efficacy in mathematics. This index was constructed using IRT scaling.

Anxiety in mathematics

The PISA index of ***anxiety in mathematics*** was derived from students' reported agreement with the following statements: *i)* I often worry that it will be difficult for me in mathematics classes; *ii)* I get very tense when I have to do mathematics homework; *iii)* I get very nervous doing mathematics problems; *iv)* I feel helpless when doing a mathematics problem; and *v)* I worry that I will get poor <marks> in mathematics. A four-point scale with the response categories "strongly agree", "agree", "disagree" and "strongly disagree" was used. All items were inverted for scaling and positive values on this index indicate higher levels of mathematics anxiety. This index was constructed using IRT scaling.

Self-concept in mathematics

The PISA index of ***self-concept in mathematics*** is derived from students' level of agreement with the following statements: *i)* I am just not good at mathematics; *ii)* I get good <marks> in mathematics; *iii)* I learn mathematics quickly; *iv)* I have always believed that mathematics is one of my best subjects; and *v)* in my mathematics class, I understand even the most difficult work. A four-point scale with the response categories "strongly agree", "agree", "disagree" and "strongly disagree" was used. Items *ii)*, *iii)*, *iv)*, and *v)* were inverted for scaling and positive values on this index indicate a positive self-concept in mathematics. This index was constructed using IRT scaling.

Learning and instruction

Grade

Data on the grade in which students are enrolled are obtained both from the Student Questionnaire and from the Student Tracking Forms. The relationship between the grade and student performance was estimated through a multilevel model accounting for the following background variables: *i)* the index of economic, social and cultural status; *ii)* the index of economic, social and cultural status squared; *iii)* the school mean of the index of economic, social and cultural status; *iv)* an indicator whether students were foreign-born; *v)* the percentage of non-native students in the school; and *vi)* students' gender.

Table A1.2

A multilevel model to estimate grade effects in mathematics accounting for some background variables

	Grade		Index of economic, social and cultural status		Index of economic, social and cultural status, squared		School mean index of economic, social and cultural status	
	Coeff.	S.E.	Coeff.	S.E.	Coeff.	S.E.	Coeff.	S.E.
Australia	40.7	(1.6)	24.1	(1.1)	1.2	(0.8)	56.9	(3.6)
Austria	34.3	(2.3)	5.2	(1.4)	–0.9	(1.1)	79.1	(6.1)
Belgium	53.7	(1.6)	18.2	(1.0)	0.2	(0.7)	72.3	(4.5)
Canada	53.1	(1.2)	22.7	(0.9)	1.1	(0.6)	25.1	(2.9)
Czech Republic	29.2	(3.2)	22.7	(1.5)	–7.0	(1.2)	99.3	(5.0)
Denmark	44.5	(4.3)	31.4	(1.9)	1.1	(1.4)	29.7	(5.7)
Finland	45.3	(3.0)	32.4	(1.4)	1.9	(1.2)	–0.5	(5.2)
France	a	a	a	a	a	a	a	a
Germany	39.2	(1.6)	10.1	(1.2)	–0.5	(0.8)	81.6	(5.4)
Greece	21.2	(3.0)	17.7	(1.5)	3.4	(1.1)	51.3	(6.0)
Hungary	30.9	(2.0)	11.4	(1.5)	0.7	(1.1)	74.0	(4.5)
Iceland	0.0	a	26.4	(4.1)	3.0	(2.5)	–5.7	(8.0)
Ireland	18.5	(1.6)	29.7	(1.7)	–0.6	(1.2)	40.6	(4.7)
Italy	40.9	(1.7)	4.6	(0.8)	–0.5	(0.6)	70.9	(4.5)
Japan	0.0	a	3.5	(1.7)	–0.8	(1.5)	152.8	(9.3)
Korea	45.6	(13.5)	12.8	(1.5)	0.5	(1.1)	91.3	(7.0)
Luxembourg	41.3	(1.8)	10.9	(1.2)	0.1	(0.8)	59.1	(5.9)
Mexico	a	a	a	a	a	a	a	a
Netherlands	38.7	(1.7)	10.8	(1.2)	0.3	(0.9)	108.9	(7.4)
New Zealand	49.5	(4.2)	30.4	(1.6)	2.4	(1.1)	56.1	(5.8)
Norway	37.9	(19.6)	37.0	(2.7)	1.9	(1.7)	13.0	(6.8)
Poland	76.8	(5.5)	35.9	(1.8)	–0.4	(1.4)	22.6	(4.6)
Portugal	55.9	(1.5)	13.9	(1.0)	2.4	(0.6)	11.7	(2.3)
Slovak Republic	12.3	(3.1)	21.4	(1.2)	–3.5	(1.0)	81.6	(4.7)
Spain	70.0	(1.5)	11.9	(1.0)	0.9	(0.6)	29.7	(3.1)
Sweden	64.7	(6.9)	33.9	(1.8)	2.3	(1.4)	18.8	(5.4)
Switzerland	55.4	(2.0)	19.6	(1.1)	–3.7	(0.9)	43.7	(5.6)
Turkey	21.4	(2.2)	11.2	(1.9)	1.7	(0.8)	76.9	(5.8)
United States	27.0	(2.3)	28.4	(1.7)	3.6	(1.1)	45.2	(5.0)
United Kingdom[1]	12.8	(1.8)	30.2	(1.1)	0.7	(0.9)	57.1	(4.1)

	Non-native students		Percentage of non-native students		Gender – Student is a female		Intercept	
	Coeff.	S.E.	Coeff.	S.E.	Coeff.	S.E.	Coeff.	S.E.
Australia	–3.5	(2.4)	–0.2	(0.1)	–13.1	(1.7)	512	(2.4)
Austria	–28.4	(3.6)	–0.1	(0.2)	–23.2	(2.5)	546	(4.4)
Belgium	–16.1	(3.4)	–0.4	(0.2)	–29.8	(1.8)	562	(3.1)
Canada	–4.2	(1.8)	0.0	(0.1)	–18.3	(1.0)	530	(1.8)
Czech Republic	–0.6	(7.4)	–1.7	(0.8)	–22.7	(2.0)	536	(3.3)
Denmark	–31.0	(6.5)	–0.8	(0.4)	–18.0	(2.8)	521	(3.5)
Finland	–32.3	(6.1)	–0.6	(0.4)	–11.5	(2.0)	550	(2.5)
France	a	a	a	a	a	a	a	a
Germany	–9.9	(3.8)	0.2	(0.3)	–33.6	(2.1)	513	(4.1)
Greece	10.6	(5.0)	–0.1	(0.2)	–26.6	(2.5)	465	(4.3)
Hungary	5.1	(6.3)	–0.5	(0.4)	–26.0	(2.2)	505	(3.2)
Iceland	–16.2	(9.6)	–0.1	(0.6)	5.9	(4.5)	499	(6.0)
Ireland	–5.2	(5.3)	–0.2	(0.3)	–19.7	(3.0)	503	(3.5)
Italy	12.7	(4.3)	0.4	(0.2)	–28.2	(1.6)	513	(2.9)
Japan	18.1	(16.6)	–1.0	(3.0)	–17.0	(2.3)	556	(4.2)
Korea	19.6	(21.7)	–0.9	(2.4)	–16.1	(2.9)	561	(3.6)
Luxembourg	–12.6	(3.0)	–0.5	(0.3)	–29.1	(2.4)	502	(6.4)
Mexico	a	a	a	a	a	a	a	a
Netherlands	–16.3	(4.2)	–0.3	(0.5)	–16.5	(1.9)	519	(4.6)
New Zealand	–6.7	(3.9)	–0.1	(0.2)	–13.9	(3.0)	519	(3.6)
Norway	–31.3	(6.7)	–0.1	(0.3)	–10.5	(2.9)	474	(4.9)
Poland	–47.7	(56.4)	–5.4	(4.5)	–10.2	(2.5)	512	(2.5)
Portugal	–7.3	(4.1)	–0.3	(0.2)	–24.3	(2.0)	526	(2.5)
Slovak Republic	–8.2	(7.9)	–0.8	(1.0)	–26.1	(1.8)	532	(3.0)
Spain	–23.7	(4.0)	–0.5	(0.3)	–20.3	(1.5)	535	(2.3)
Sweden	–41.0	(5.4)	–0.7	(0.2)	–8.9	(2.7)	510	(3.0)
Switzerland	–27.7	(2.6)	–1.1	(0.2)	–28.0	(1.7)	569	(3.3)
Turkey	–21.2	(10.7)	0.2	(1.3)	–21.2	(2.4)	516	(7.3)
United States	–1.4	(5.1)	–0.2	(0.2)	–15.4	(2.5)	480	(3.7)
United Kingdom[1]	–10.4	(4.0)	–0.1	(0.2)	–11.5	(1.8)	511	(2.4)

1. Response rate too low to ensure comparability (see Annex A3).

Table A1.2 presents the results of the multilevel model. Column 1 in Table A1.2 estimates the score point difference that is associated with one grade level (or school year). This difference can be estimated for the 26 OECD countries in which a sizeable number of 15-year-olds in the PISA samples were enrolled in at least two different grades. Since 15-year-olds cannot be assumed to be distributed at random across the grade levels, adjustments had to be made for above-mentioned contextual factors that may relate to the assignment of students to the different grade levels. These adjustments are documented in columns 2 to 7 of the table. While it is possible to estimate the typical performance difference among students in two adjacent grades net of the effects of selection and contextual factors, this difference cannot automatically be equated with the progress that students have made over the last school year but should be interpreted as a lower bound of the progress achieved. This is not only because different students were assessed but also because the contents of the PISA assessment was not expressly designed to match what students had learned in the preceding school year but more broadly to assess the cumulative outcome of learning in school up to age 15. For example, if the curriculum of the grades in which 15-year-olds are enrolled mainly includes material other than that assessed by PISA (which, in turn, may have been included in earlier school years) then the observed performance difference will underestimate student progress.

In order to adjust for between-country variation the ***relative grade index*** indicates whether students are at the modal grade in a country (value of 0), or whether they are below or above the modal grade (-x grades, + x grades).

Expected educational level

In PISA 2003 students were asked about their educational aspirations. Educational levels were classified according to International Standard Classification of Education (OECD, 1999b).

An index on the ***expected educational level*** was developed with the following categories: *i)* did not go to school; *ii)* completed ISCED Level 1 (primary education); *iii)* completed ISCED Level 2 (lower secondary education); *iv)* completed ISCED Levels 3B or 3C (upper secondary education providing direct access to the labour market or to ISCED 5B programmes); *v)* completed ISCED Level 3A (upper secondary education providing access to ISCED 5A and 5B programmes); *vi)* completed ISCED Level 5A (university level tertiary education); and *vii)* completed ISCED Level 5B (non-university level education).

Minutes of mathematics instruction

Students were asked to provide information on the average length in minutes of a class period and the number of class periods devoted to mathematics instruction the last full week. The index of the ***minutes of mathematics instruction*** was calculated by multiplying the median of the students' reported average length of a class period within a schools' study programme by the students' reported number of class periods devoted to mathematics instruction. Note that this index does not account for differences among countries in the number of weeks the school is open.

Learning strategies and preferences in mathematics

Students may develop different types of learning strategies that shape their learning behaviour. Cognitive strategies include *memorisation* (learning key terms, repeated learning of material, *etc.*) and *elaboration* (making connections to related areas, thinking about alternative solutions, *etc.*). *Control strategies* are metacognitive strategies that involve planning, monitoring and regulation.

Learning behaviour is also influenced by the students' preference for learning situations: here, preference for co-operative learning for example, learning in groups, and preference for competitive learning, for example striving to be better than others (Owens and Barnes, 1992) are the most salient aspects. Cognitive and non-cognitive benefits of co-operative goal structures have been investigated in the past.

Learning strategies: memorisation/rehearsal

The PISA index of ***memorisation/rehearsal*** was derived from students' level of agreement with the four following statements: *i)* I go over some problems in mathematics so often that I feel as if I could solve them in my sleep; *ii)* when I study for mathematics, I try to learn the answers to problems off by heart; *iii)* in order to remember the method for solving a mathematics problem, I go through examples again and again; and *iv)* to learn mathematics, I try to remember every step in a procedure. A four-point scale with the response categories "strongly agree", "agree", "disagree" and "strongly disagree" is used. All of these items were inverted for IRT scaling and positive values on this new PISA 2003 index indicate preferences for this learning strategy. This index was constructed using IRT scaling.

Learning strategies: elaboration

The PISA index of ***elaboration*** was derived from students' reported agreement with the following statements: *i)* when I am solving mathematics problems, I often think of new ways to get the answer; *ii)* I think how the mathematics I have learnt can be used in everyday life; *iii)* I try to understand new concepts in mathematics by relating them to things I already know; *iv)* when I am solving a mathematics problem, I often think about how the solution might be applied to other interesting questions; and *v)* when learning mathematics, I try to relate the work to things I have learnt in other subjects. A four-point scale with the response categories "strongly agree", "agree", "disagree" and "strongly disagree" was used. All of these items were inverted for scaling and positive values on this new PISA 2003 index indicate preferences for this learning strategy. This index was constructed using IRT scaling.

Learning strategies: control strategies

The PISA index of ***control strategies*** was derived from students' reported agreement with the following statements: *i)* when I study for a mathematics test, I try to work out what are the most important parts to learn; *ii)* when I study mathematics, I make myself check to see if I remember the work I have already done; *iii)* when I study mathematics, I try to figure out which concepts I still have not understood properly; *iv)* when I cannot understand something in mathematics, I always search for more information to clarify the problem; and *v)* when I study mathematics, I start by working out exactly what I need to learn. A four-point scale with the response categories "strongly agree", "agree", "disagree" and "strongly disagree" was used. All of these items were inverted for scaling and positive values indicate preferences for this learning strategy. This index was constructed using IRT scaling.

Preference for competitive learning situations

The PISA index of ***competitive learning*** was derived from students' reported agreement with the following statements: *i)* I would like to be the best in my class in mathematics; *ii)* I try very hard in mathematics because I want to do better in the exams than the others; *iii)* I make a real effort in mathematics because I want to be one of the best; *iv)* in mathematics I always try to do better than the other students in my class; and *v)* I do my best work in mathematics when I try to do better than others. A four-point scale with the response categories "strongly agree", "agree", "disagree" and "strongly disagree" was used. All of these items were inverted for scaling and positive values on this new PISA 2003 index indicate preferences for competitive learning situations. This index was constructed using IRT scaling.

Preference for co-operative learning situations

The PISA index of ***co-operative learning*** was derived from students' reported agreement with the following statements: *i)* in mathematics I enjoy working with other students in groups; *ii)* when we work on a project in mathematics, I think that it is a good idea to combine the ideas of all the students in a group; *iii)* I do my best work in mathematics when I work with other students; *iv)* in mathematics, I enjoy helping others to work well in a group; and *v)* in mathematics I learn most when I work with other students in my class. A four-point scale with the response categories "strongly agree", "agree", "disagree" and "strongly disagree" was used. All of these items were inverted for scaling and positive values on this new PISA 2003 index indicate preferences for co-operative learning situations. This index was constructed using IRT scaling.

Classroom climate

Teacher support

The PISA index of ***teacher support*** was derived from students' reports on the frequency with which: *i)* the teacher shows an interest in every student's learning; *ii)* the teacher gives extra help when students need it; *iii)* the teacher helps students with their learning; *iv)* the teacher continues teaching until the students understand; and *v)* the teacher gives students an opportunity to express opinions. A four-point scale with the response categories "every lesson", "most lessons", "some lessons" and "never or hardly ever" was used. All items were inverted for scaling and positive values on this PISA 2003 index indicate perceptions of higher levels of teacher support. This index was constructed using IRT scaling.

Disciplinary climate

The PISA index of ***disciplinary climate*** was derived from students' reports on the frequency with which, in their mathematics lessons: *i)* students don't listen to what the teacher says; *ii)* there is noise and disorder; *iii)* the teacher has to wait a long time for students to <quieten down>; *iv)* students cannot work well; and *v)* students don't start working for a long time after the lesson begins. A four-point scale with the response categories "every lesson", "most lessons", "some lessons", and "never or hardly ever" was used. Positive values on this PISA 2000/2003 index indicate perceptions of a more positive disciplinary climate whereas low values indicate a more negative disciplinary climate. This index was constructed using IRT scaling.

School level variables

School characteristics

School size

The school size index contains the total enrolment at school based on the enrolment data provided by the school principal, summing the number of males and females at a school.

Proportion of females enrolled at school

This index of ***proportion of females enrolled at school*** provides the proportion of females at the school based on the enrolment data provided by the school principal, dividing the number of females by the total of males and females at a school.

School type

Schools are classified as either public or private according to whether a private entity or a public agency has the ultimate power to make decisions concerning its affairs. The index of ***school type*** has three categories: *i)* public schools controlled and managed by a public education authority or agency; *ii)* "government-dependent" private schools which principals report to be managed by non-governmental organisations such as churches, trade unions or business enterprises and/or having governing boards consisting mostly of members not selected by a public agency and which receive 50 per cent or more of their core funding from government agencies; and *iii)* "government-independent" private schools controlled by a non-government organisation or with a governing board not selected by a government agency which receive less than 50 per cent of their core funding from government agencies.

Indicators of school resources

Quantity of teaching staff at school

School principals reported the number of full-time and part-time teachers in total, of full-time and part-time teachers fully certified by <the appropriate authority>, of full-time and part-time teachers with an <ISCED 5A> qualification in <pedagogy>. From this an index of ***total student-teacher*** ratio is obtained by dividing the school size by the total number of teachers. The number of part-time teachers contributes 0.5 and the number of full-time teachers contributes 1.0 to the total number of teachers.

Admittance policies and instructional context

Academic selectivity

School principals were asked about admittance policies at their school. Among these policies, principals were asked how much consideration was given to the following factors when students are admitted to the school based on a scale from not considered, considered, high priority or prerequisite: *i)* students' academic record (including placement tests), *ii)* recommendation of feeder schools, *iii)* parents' endorsement of the instructional or religious philosophy of the school, *iv)* student need or desire for a special programme, or *v)* attendance of other family members at the school (past or present), and *vi)* country specific factors. A school was considered to have selective admittance policies if students' academic records or recommendations from a feeder school was a high priority or a pre-requisite for admittance. It was considered a school with non-selective admittance if both factors were not considered for admittance.

Use of assessments

School principals were asked to rate the frequency of the following assessments for 15-year-old students at school: *i)* standardised tests; *ii)* teacher-developed tests; *iii)* teachers' judgemental ratings; *iv)* student <portfolios>; and *v)* student assignments/projects/homework. All five items are recoded into numerical values, which approximately reflect frequency of assessments per year ("never"=0, "1-2 times a year"=1.5, "3-5 times a year"=4, "monthly"=8, "more than once a month"=12). The index *use of assessments* is calculated as the sum of these recoded items and then divided into three categories: *i)* less than 20 times a year; *ii)* 20-39 times a year; and *iii)* more than 40 times a year.

Ability grouping

To determine the extent of ability grouping within schools, school principals were asked to report the extent to which their school organises instruction differently for students with different abilities as *i)* mathematics classes studying similar content, but at different levels of difficulty; or as *ii)* different classes studying different content or sets of mathematics topics

that have different levels of difficulty. An index of *ability grouping between mathematics classes* was derived from assigning schools to one of three categories: *i)* schools with no ability grouping between any classes, *ii)* schools with one of these forms of ability grouping between classes for some classes and *iii)* schools with one of these forms of ability grouping for all classes.

Promotion of mathematics-related activities

School principals were asked to report on the occurrence of the following activities to promote engagement with mathematics at their school: *i)* enrichment mathematics; *ii)* remedial mathematics; *iii)* mathematics competitions; *iv)* mathematics clubs; and *v)* computer clubs (specifically related to mathematics). Schools are considered to offer extension courses when they offer enrichment or remedial mathematics courses – the index of *mathematics extension courses* is simply the number of types of extension courses offered. They are considered to offer other types of mathematics activities when they offer competitions, clubs or computer clubs related to mathematics – the index of *mathematics activities* is simply the number of different types of activities offered at the school.

School management

School principals were asked to report whether teachers, department heads, the school principal, an appointed or elected board or education authorities at a higher level had the main responsibility for: *i)* selecting teachers for hire; *ii)* dismissing teachers; *iii)* establishing teachers' starting salaries; *iv)* determining teachers' salary increases; *v)* formulating school budgets; *vi)* deciding on budget allocations within the school; *vii)* establishing student disciplinary policies; *viii)* establishing student assessment policies; *ix)* approving students for admittance to school; *x)* choosing which textbooks to use; *xi)* determining course content; and *xii)* deciding which courses are offered. The index of ***resource autonomy*** is the number of decisions that relate to school resources that are a school responsibility (items i to vi). The index of ***curricular autonomy*** is the number of decisions that relate to curriculum which are a school responsibility (items viii, x, xi and xii).

School resources

Quality of the school's physical infrastructure

The PISA index of the ***quality of the school's physical infrastructure*** was derived from three items measuring the school principals' perceptions of potential factors hindering instruction at school: *i)* school buildings and grounds; *ii)* heating/cooling and lighting systems; and *iii)* instructional space (*e.g.,* classrooms). A four-point scale with the response categories "not at all", "very little", "to some extent", and "a lot" was used. All items were inverted for scaling and positive values indicate positive evaluations of this aspect. This index was constructed using IRT scaling.

Quality of the school's educational resources

The PISA index of the ***quality of the school's educational resources*** was derived from seven items measuring the school principals' perceptions of potential factors hindering instruction at school: *i)* instructional materials (*e.g.,* textbooks); *ii)* computers for instruction; *iii)* computer software for instruction; *iv)* calculators for instruction; *v)* library materials; *vi)* audio-visual resources; and *vii)* science laboratory equipment and materials. A four-point scale with the response categories "not at all", "very little", "to some extent", and "a lot" was used. All items were inverted for scaling and positive values indicate positive evaluations of this aspect. This index was constructed using IRT scaling.

Teacher shortage

The PISA index on ***teacher shortage*** was derived from items measuring the school principal's perceptions of potential factors hindering instruction at school. These factors are a shortage or inadequacy of: *i)* qualified mathematics teachers; *ii)* qualified science teachers; *iii)* qualified <test language> teachers; *iv)* qualified foreign language teachers; and *v)* experienced teachers. For PISA 2003 these items were administered together with the items on the quality of physical environment and educational resources. A four-point scale with the response categories "not at all", "very little", "to some extent" and "a lot" is used. The items were not inverted for scaling and positive values indicate school principal's reports of teacher shortage at a school. This index was constructed using IRT scaling.

School climate (school principals' views)

School principals' perceptions of teacher morale and commitment

The PISA index of ***teacher morale and commitment*** was derived from items measuring the school principals' perceptions of teachers with the following statements: *i)* the morale of teachers in this school is high; *ii)* teachers work with enthusiasm; *iii)* teachers take pride in this school; and *iv)* teachers value academic achievement. A four-point scale with the response categories "strongly agree", "agree", "disagree" and "strongly disagree" was used. All items were inverted for scaling and the categories "disagree" and "strongly disagree" were combined into one category. Positive values indicate principals' reports of higher levels of teacher morale and commitment. This index was constructed using IRT scaling.

School principals' perceptions of student morale and commitment

The index of ***student morale and commitment*** was derived from items measuring the school principals' perceptions of students at a school with the following statements: *i)* students enjoy being in school; *ii)* students work with enthusiasm; *iii)* students take pride in this school; *iv)* students value academic achievement; *v)* students are co-operative and respectful; *vi)* students value the education they can receive in this school; and *vii)* students do their best to learn as much as possible. The items are, in part, a parallel to those on teacher morale and commitment. A four-point scale with the response categories "strongly agree", "agree", "disagree" and "strongly disagree" was used. All items were inverted for scaling and the categories "disagree" and "strongly disagree" were combined into one category. Positive values indicate principals' reports of higher levels of student morale and commitment. This index was constructed using IRT scaling.

School principals' perceptions of teacher-related factors affecting school climate

The index of ***teacher-related factors affecting school climate*** was derived from items measuring the school principals' reports of potential factors hindering the learning of students at school with the following statements: *i)* teachers' low expectations of students; *ii)* poor student-teacher relations; *iii)* teachers not meeting individual students' needs; *iv)* teacher absenteeism; *v)* staff resisting change; *vi)* teachers being too strict with students; and *vii)* students not being encouraged to achieve their full potential. A four-point scale with the response categories "strongly agree", "agree", "disagree" and "strongly disagree" was used. All items were inverted for scaling and positive values indicate positive evaluations of this aspect. This index was constructed using IRT scaling.

School principals' perceptions of student-related factors affecting school climate

The index of ***student-related factors affecting school climate*** was derived from items measuring the school principals' perceptions of potential factors hindering the learning of students at school with the following statements: *i)* student absenteeism; *ii)* disruption of classes by students; *iii)* students skipping classes; *iv)* students lacking respect for teachers; *v)* students' use of alcohol or illegal drugs; and *vi)* students intimidating or bullying other students. A four-point scale with the response categories "strongly agree", "agree", "disagree" and "strongly disagree" was used. All items were inverted for scaling and positive values indicate positive evaluations of this aspect. This index was constructed using IRT scaling.

Annex A2: Issues relating to the reporting of mathematics performance

The progression through the mathematics proficiency levels

This section illustrates the progression through the six proficiency levels for the PISA mathematics scale, in terms of the ways in which the individual mathematical processes referred to in Chapter 2 play out as proficiency levels increase.

- Students need to use progressively more sophisticated *thinking and reasoning* skills to progress to higher proficiency levels, as follows:
  - At Level 1: Follow direct instructions and take obvious actions.
  - At Level 2: Use direct reasoning and literal interpretations.
  - At Level 3: Make sequential decisions, interpret and reason from different information sources.
  - At Level 4: Employ flexible reasoning and some insight.
  - At Level 5: Use well-developed thinking and reasoning skills.
  - At Level 6: Use advanced mathematical thinking and reasoning.
- For competency in *communication,* students need to progress through the following stages:
  - At Level 1: Follow explicit instructions.
  - At Level 2: Extract information and make literal interpretations.
  - At Level 3: Produce short communications supporting interpretations.
  - At Level 4: Construct and communicate explanations and arguments.
  - At Level 5: Formulate and communicate interpretations and reasoning.
  - At Level 6: Formulate precise communications.
- For *modelling,* the following development is observed as literacy levels increase:
  - At Level 1: Apply simple given models.
  - At Level 2: Recognise, apply and interpret basic given models.
  - At Level 3: Make use of different representational models.
  - At Level 4: Work with explicit models, and related constraints and assumptions.
  - At Level 5: Develop and work with complex models, and reflect on modelling processes and outcomes.
  - At Level 6: Conceptualise and work with models of complex mathematical processes and relationships, and reflect on, generalise and explain modelling outcomes.
- For *problem posing and solving,* students need to progress as follows:
  - At Level 1: Handle direct and explicit problems.
  - At Level 2: Use direct inference.
  - At Level 3: Use simple problem-solving strategies.
  - At Level 4: Work with constraints and assumptions.
  - At Level 5: Select, compare and evaluate appropriate problem-solving strategies.
  - At Level 6: Investigate and model with complex problem situations.
- In the case of the *competency representation,* students need to progress as follows:
  - At Level 1: Handle familiar and direct information.
  - At Level 2: Extract information from single representations.
  - At Level 3: Interpret and use different representations.
  - At Level 4: Select and integrate different representations and link them to real-world situations.
  - At Level 5: Make strategic use of appropriately linked representations.
  - At Level 6: Link different information and representations and translate flexibly among them.
- For *using symbolic, formal and technical language and operations,* students progress as follows:
  - At Level 1: Apply routine procedures.
  - At Level 2: Employ basic algorithms, formulae, procedures and conventions.
  - At Level 3: Work with symbolic representations.
  - At Level 4: Use symbolic and formal characterisations.
  - At Levels 5 and 6: Master symbolic and formal mathematical operations and relationships.

Comparison in performance between the four mathematics scales

Table A2.1, referred to in Chapter 2, shows for each country the comparison between their performances on the four mathematics scales, namely: the mathematics/space and shape scale (referred to below as M1), the mathematics/change and relationships scale (referred to below as M2), the mathematics/quantity scale (referred to below as M3), and the mathematics/uncertainty scale (referred to below as M4). The table shows the relative strengths of country performance on the four scales: *i)* the arrows show the relationship between performance on two scales, pointing to the "stronger" of the two, using a 95 per cent confidence level; *ii)* the circles indicate that the country's relative position on the two scales is not statistically significantly different at the 95 per cent confidence level; and *iii)* the blank cells mean that it is not possible to make any inference between the performances on these scales at the 95 per cent confidence level.

Table A2.1
Comparison of performance between the four mathematics scales

M1: mathematics/space and shape scale	**M2:** mathematics/change and relationships scale	**M3:** mathematics/quantity scale	**M4:** mathematics/uncertainty scale

Country		M1	M2	M3	M4
Australia	M1		∧		∧
	M2	<		<	
	M3		∧		∧
	M4	<		<	
Austria	M1		<		<
	M2	∧		∧	
	M3		<		<
	M4	∧		∧	
Belgium	M1				<
	M2				<
	M3				<
	M4	∧	∧	∧	
Canada	M1		∧	∧	∧
	M2	<		<	
	M3	<	∧		∧
	M4	<		<	
Czech Republic	M1		<		<
	M2	∧		∧	<
	M3		<		<
	M4	∧	∧	∧	
Denmark	M1				
	M2				
	M3				
	M4				
Finland	M1			∧	∧
	M2			∧	
	M3	<	<		<
	M4	<		∧	
France	M1		∧	<	
	M2	<		<	<
	M3	∧	∧		
	M4		∧		
Germany	M1			∧	<
	M2				<
	M3	<			<
	M4	∧	∧	∧	
Greece	M1				∧
	M2				∧
	M3				∧
	M4	<	<	<	
Hungary	M1		∧	∧	
	M2	<		<	<
	M3	<	∧		
	M4		∧		
Iceland	M1				∧
	M2				∧
	M3				∧
	M4	<	<	<	
Ireland	M1		∧	∧	∧
	M2	<		<	∧
	M3	<	∧		∧
	M4	<	<	<	
Italy	M1		<		
	M2	∧		∧	
	M3		<		
	M4				
Japan	M1		<	<	<
	M2	∧		<	<
	M3	∧	∧		
	M4	∧	∧		
Korea	M1				<
	M2				<
	M3				
	M4	∧	∧		
Luxembourg	M1		<		
	M2	∧		∧	
	M3		<		
	M4				
Mexico	M1		○	○	
	M2	○		○	
	M3	○	○		
	M4				
Netherlands	M1		∧		∧
	M2	<		<	
	M3		∧		∧
	M4	<		<	
New Zealand	M1			<	∧
	M2			<	∧
	M3	∧	∧		∧
	M4	<	<	<	
Norway	M1				∧
	M2				∧
	M3				∧
	M4	<	<	<	
Poland	M1		<	<	
	M2	∧			∧
	M3	∧			∧
	M4		<	<	
Portugal	M1		∧		∧
	M2	<			
	M3				∧
	M4	<		<	
Slovak Republic	M1		<		<
	M2	∧		∧	<
	M3		<		<
	M4	∧	∧	∧	
Spain	M1				
	M2			∧	∧
	M3		<		
	M4		<		
Sweden	M1			∧	∧
	M2				
	M3	<			
	M4	<			
Switzerland	M1		<		<
	M2	∧		∧	<
	M3		<		<
	M4	∧	∧	∧	
Turkey	M1				∧
	M2			<	
	M3		∧		∧
	M4	<		<	
United States	M1		∧		∧
	M2	<		<	
	M3		∧		∧
	M4	<		<	
Brazil	M1				∧
	M2				
	M3				
	M4	<			

Hong Kong-China

	M1	M2	M3	M4
M1		<		
M2	∧		∧	∧
M3		<		
M4		<		

Indonesia

	M1	M2	M3	M4
M1				
M2				
M3				∧
M4			<	

Latvia

	M1	M2	M3	M4
M1			<	<
M2				
M3	∧			
M4	∧			

Liechtenstein

	M1	M2	M3	M4
M1				<
M2				<
M3				<
M4	∧	∧	∧	

Macao-China

	M1	M2	M3	M4
M1		<	∧	
M2	∧		∧	∧
M3	<	<		
M4		<		

Russian Federation

	M1	M2	M3	M4
M1				<
M2				<
M3				<
M4	∧	∧	∧	

Serbia

	M1	M2	M3	M4
M1				
M2			∧	
M3		<		<
M4			∧	

Thailand

	M1	M2	M3	M4
M1		<	<	
M2	∧			
M3	∧			
M4				

Tunisia

	M1	M2	M3	M4
M1				<
M2				
M3				<
M4	∧		∧	

Uruguay

	M1	M2	M3	M4
M1		∧	∧	
M2	<			
M3	<			<
M4			∧	

Annex A3: The PISA target population, the PISA samples and the definition of schools

The PISA concept of "yield" and the definition of the PISA target population

PISA 2003 provides an assessment of the cumulative yield of education and learning at a point at which most young adults are still enrolled in initial education.

A major challenge for an international survey is to operationalise such a concept in ways that guarantee the international comparability of national target populations.

Differences between countries in the nature and extent of pre-primary education and care, the age of entry to formal schooling and the institutional structure of educational systems do not allow the definition of internationally comparable grade levels of schooling. Consequently, international comparisons of educational performance typically define their populations with reference to a target age group. Some previous international assessments have defined their target population on the basis of the grade level that provides maximum coverage of a particular age cohort. A disadvantage of this approach is that slight variations in the age distribution of students across grade levels often lead to the selection of different target grades in different countries, or between education systems within countries, raising serious questions about the comparability of results across, and at times within, countries. In addition, because not all students of the desired age are usually represented in grade-based samples, there may be a more serious potential bias in the results if the unrepresented students are typically enrolled in the next higher grade in some countries and the next lower grade in others. This would exclude students with potentially higher levels of performance in the former countries and students with potentially lower levels of performance in the latter.

In order to address this problem, PISA uses an age-based definition for its target population, *i.e.* a definition that is not tied to the institutional structures of national education systems: PISA assesses students who were aged between 15 years and 3 (complete) months and 16 years and 2 (complete) months at the beginning of the assessment period and who were enrolled in an educational institution, regardless of the grade levels or type of institution in which they were enrolled, and regardless of whether they were in full-time or part-time education (15-year-olds enrolled in Grade 6 or lower were excluded from PISA 2003, but, among the countries participating in PISA 2003, such students only exist in significant numbers in Brazil). Educational institutions are generally referred to as ***schools*** in this publication, although some educational institutions (in particular some types of vocational education establishments) may not be termed schools in certain countries. As expected from this definition, the average age of students across OECD countries was 15 years and 8 months, a value which varied by less than 0.2 years between participating countries.

As a result of this population definition, PISA makes statements about the knowledge and skills of a group of individuals who were born within a comparable reference period, but who may have undergone different educational experiences both within and outside schools. In PISA, these knowledge and skills are referred to as the ***yield*** of education at an age that is common across countries. Depending on countries' policies on school entry and promotion, these students may be distributed over a narrower or a wider range of grades. Furthermore, in some countries, students in PISA's target population are split between different education systems, tracks or streams.

If a country's scale scores in reading, scientific or mathematical literacy are significantly higher than those in another country, it cannot automatically be inferred that the schools or particular parts of the education system in the first country are more effective than those in the second. However, one can legitimately conclude that the cumulative impact of learning experiences in the first country, starting in early childhood and up to the age of 15 and embracing experiences both in school and at home, have resulted in higher outcomes in the literacy domains that PISA measures.

The PISA target population did not include residents attending schools in a foreign country.

To accommodate countries that desired grade-based results for the purpose of national analyses, PISA 2003 provided an international option to supplement age-based sampling with grade-based sampling.

Population coverage

All countries attempted to maximise the coverage of 15-year-olds enrolled in education in their national samples, including students enrolled in special educational institutions. As a result, PISA 2003 reached standards of population coverage that are unprecedented in international surveys of this kind.

Table A3.1
PISA target populations and samples

		Population and sample information				
		(1) Total population of 15-year-olds	(2) Total enrolled population of 15-year-olds at grade 7 or above	(3) Total in national desired target population	(4) Total school-level exclusions	(5) Total in national desired target population after all school exclusions and before within-school exclusions
OECD countries	Australia	268 164	250 635	248 035	1 621	246 414
	Austria	94 515	89 049	89 049	321	88 728
	Belgium	120 802	118 185	118 185	561	117 624
	Canada	398 865	399 265	397 520	6 600	390 920
	Czech Republic	130 679	126 348	126 348	1 294	125 054
	Denmark	59 156	58 188	58 188	628	57 560
	Finland	61 107	61 107	61 107	1 324	59 783
	France	809 053	808 276	774 711	18 056	756 655
	Germany	951 800	916 869	916 869	5 600	911 269
	Greece	111 286	108 314	108 314	808	107 506
	Hungary	129 138	123 762	123 762	3 688	120 074
	Iceland	4 168	4 112	4 112	26	4 086
	Ireland	61 535	58 997	58 906	864	58 042
	Italy	561 304	574 611	574 611	2 868	571 743
	Japan	1 365 471	1 328 498	1 328 498	13 592	1 314 906
	Korea	606 722	606 370	606 370	2 729	603 641
	Luxembourg	4 204	4 204	4 204	0	4 204
	Mexico	2 192 452	1 273 163	1 273 163	46 483	1 226 680
	Netherlands	194 216	194 216	194 216	2 559	191 657
	New Zealand	55 440	53 293	53 160	194	52 966
	Norway	56 060	55 648	55 531	294	55 237
	Poland	589 506	569 294	569 294	14 600	554 694
	Portugal	109 149	99 216	99 216	826	98 390
	Slovak Republic	84 242	81 945	81 890	1 042	80 848
	Spain	454 064	418 005	418 005	1 639	416 366
	Sweden	109 482	112 258	112 258	1 615	110 643
	Switzerland	83 247	81 020	81 020	2 760	78 260
	Turkey	1 351 492	725 030	725 030	5 328	719 702
	United Kingdom	768 180	736 785	736 785	24 773	712 012
	United States	3 979 116	3 979 116	3 979 116	0	3 979 116
Partner countries	Brazil	3 618 332	2 359 854	2 348 405	0	2 348 405
	Hong Kong-China	75 000	72 631	72 631	601	72 030
	Indonesia	4 281 895	3 113 548	2 968 756	9 292	2 959 464
	Latvia	37 544	37 138	37 138	1 419	35 719
	Liechtenstein	402	348	348	0	348
	Macao-China	8 318	6 939	6 939	0	6 939
	Russian Federation	2 496 216	2 366 285	2 366 285	23 445	2 342 840
	Serbia	98 729	92 617	92 617	4 931	87 686
	Thailand	927 070	778 267	778 267	7 597	770 670
	Tunisia	164 758	164 758	164 758	553	164 205
	Uruguay	53 948	40 023	40 023	59	39 964

		Population and sample information				
		(6) Percentage of all school-level exclusions	(7) Number of participating students	(8) Weighted number of participating students	(9) Number of excluded students	(10) Weighted number of excluded students
OECD countries	Australia	0.65	12 551	235 591	228	3 612
	Austria	0.36	4 597	85 931	60	1 099
	Belgium	0.47	8 796	111 831	102	1 193
	Canada	1.66	27 953	330 436	1 993	18 328
	Czech Republic	1.02	6 320	121 183	22	218
	Denmark	1.08	4 218	51 741	214	2 321
	Finland	2.17	5 796	57 883	79	725
	France	2.33	4 300	734 579	51	8 158
	Germany	0.61	4 660	884 358	61	11 533
	Greece	0.75	4 627	105 131	144	2 652
	Hungary	2.98	4 765	107 044	62	1 065
	Iceland	0.63	3 350	3 928	79	79
	Ireland	1.47	3 880	54 850	139	1 619
	Italy	0.50	11 639	481 521	188	6 794
	Japan	1.02	4 707	1 240 054	0	0
	Korea	0.45	5 444	533 504	24	2 283
	Luxembourg	0.00	3 923	4 080	66	66
	Mexico	3.65	29 983	1 071 650	34	7 264
	Netherlands	1.32	3 992	184 943	20	1 041
	New Zealand	0.36	4 511	48 638	263	2 411
	Norway	0.53	4 064	52 816	139	1 563
	Poland	2.56	4 383	534 900	75	7 517
	Portugal	0.83	4 608	96 857	84	1 450
	Slovak Republic	1.27	7 346	77 067	109	1 341
	Spain	0.39	10 791	344 372	591	25 619
	Sweden	1.44	4 624	107 104	144	3 085
	Switzerland	3.41	8 420	86 491	194	893
	Turkey	0.73	4 855	481 279	0	0
	United Kingdom	3.36	9 535	698 579	270	15 062
	United States	0.00	5 456	3 147 089	534	246 991
Partner countries	Brazil	0.00	4 452	1 952 253	5	2 142
	Hong Kong-China	0.83	4 478	72 484	8	103
	Indonesia	0.31	10 761	1 971 476	0	0
	Latvia	3.82	4 627	33 643	44	380
	Liechtenstein	0.00	332	338	5	5
	Macao-China	0.00	1 250	6 546	4	13
	Russian Federation	0.99	5 974	2 153 373	35	14 716
	Serbia	5.32	4 405	68 596	15	241
	Thailand	0.98	5 236	637 076	5	563
	Tunisia	0.34	4 721	150 875	1	31
	Uruguay	0.15	5 835	33 775	18	80

Table A3.1 *(continued)*
PISA target populations and samples

	Population and sample information		Coverage indices		
	(11) Within-school exclusion rate (%)	(12) Overall exclusion rate (%)	(13) Coverage index 1: Coverage of national desired population	(14) Coverage index 2: Coverage of national enrolled population	(15) Coverage index 3: Percentage of enrolled population
OECD countries					
Australia	1.51	2.15	0.98	0.97	0.93
Austria	1.26	1.62	0.98	0.98	0.94
Belgium	1.06	1.53	0.98	0.98	0.98
Canada	5.26	6.83	0.93	0.93	1.00
Czech Republic	0.18	1.20	0.99	0.99	0.97
Denmark	4.29	5.33	0.95	0.95	0.98
Finland	1.24	3.38	0.97	0.97	1.00
France	1.10	3.40	0.97	0.93	1.00
Germany	1.29	1.89	0.98	0.98	0.96
Greece	2.46	3.19	0.97	0.97	0.97
Hungary	0.99	3.94	0.96	0.96	0.96
Iceland	1.97	2.59	0.97	0.97	0.99
Ireland	2.87	4.29	0.96	0.96	0.96
Italy	1.39	1.88	0.98	0.98	1.02
Japan	0.00	1.02	0.99	0.99	0.97
Korea	0.43	0.87	0.99	0.99	1.00
Luxembourg	1.59	1.59	0.98	0.98	1.00
Mexico	0.67	4.30	0.96	0.96	0.58
Netherlands	0.56	1.87	0.98	0.98	1.00
New Zealand	4.72	5.07	0.95	0.95	0.96
Norway	2.87	3.39	0.97	0.96	0.99
Poland	1.39	3.91	0.96	0.96	0.97
Portugal	1.47	2.30	0.98	0.98	0.91
Slovak Republic	1.71	2.96	0.97	0.97	0.97
Spain	6.92	7.29	0.93	0.93	0.92
Sweden	2.80	4.20	0.96	0.96	1.03
Switzerland	1.02	4.39	0.96	0.96	0.97
Turkey	0.00	0.73	0.99	0.99	0.54
United Kingdom	2.11	5.40	0.95	0.95	0.96
United States	7.28	7.28	0.93	0.93	1.00
Partner countries					
Brazil	0.11	0.11	1.00	0.99	0.65
Hong Kong-China	0.14	0.97	0.99	0.99	0.97
Indonesia	0.00	0.31	1.00	0.95	0.73
Latvia	1.12	4.89	0.95	0.95	0.99
Liechtenstein	1.46	1.46	0.99	0.99	0.87
Macao-China	0.20	0.20	1.00	1.00	0.83
Russian Federation	0.68	1.66	0.98	0.98	0.95
Serbia	0.35	5.66	0.94	0.94	0.94
Thailand	0.09	1.06	0.99	0.99	0.84
Tunisia	0.02	0.36	1.00	1.00	1.00
Uruguay	0.24	0.38	1.00	1.00	0.74

Note: For a full explanation of the details in this table please refer to the PISA 2003 Technical Report (OECD, forthcoming).

The sampling standards used in PISA permitted countries to exclude up to a total of 5 per cent of the relevant population either by excluding schools or by excluding students within schools. All but seven countries, New Zealand (5.1 per cent), Denmark (5.3 per cent), the United Kingdom (5.4 per cent), Serbia (5.7 per cent),[1] Canada (6.8 per cent), the United States (7.3 per cent) and Spain (7.3 per cent) achieved this standard and in 20 countries the overall exclusion rate was less than 2 per cent. In some of the countries with exclusion rates exceeding 5 per cent, exclusions were inevitable. For example, in New Zealand 2.3 per cent of the students were excluded because they had less than one year of instruction in English, often because they were foreign fee-paying students and were therefore not able to follow the instructions of the assessment. When language exclusions are accounted for (*i.e.,* removed from the overall exclusion rate), Denmark and New Zealand no longer had exclusion rates greater than 5 per cent. For details, see *www.pisa.oecd.org*.

Exclusions within the above limits include:

- *At the school level: i)* schools which were geographically inaccessible or where the administration of the PISA assessment was not considered feasible; and *ii)* schools that provided teaching only for students in the categories defined under "within-school exclusions", such as schools for the blind. The percentage of 15-year-olds enrolled in such schools had to be less than 2.5 per cent of the nationally desired target population (0.5% maximum for *i)* and 2% maximum for *ii)*). The magnitude, nature and justification of school-level exclusions are documented in the *PISA 2003 Technical Report* (OECD, forthcoming).
- *At the student level: i)* students with an intellectual disability; *ii)* students with a functional disability; and *iii)* students with a limited assessment language proficiency. Students could not be excluded solely because of low proficiency or normal discipline problems. The percentage of 15-year-olds excluded within schools had to be less than 2.5 per cent of the nationally desired target population.

1. For the country Serbia and Montenegro, data for Montenegro are not available. The latter accounts for 7.9 per cent of the national population. The name "Serbia" is used as a shorthand for the Serbian part of Serbia and Montenegro.

Table A3.1 describes the target population of the countries participating in PISA 2003. Further information on the target population and the implementation of PISA sampling standards can be found in the *PISA 2003 Technical Report (OECD, forthcoming)*.

- **Column 1** shows the total number of 15-year-olds according to the most recent available information, which in most countries meant the year 2002 as the year before the assessment.
- **Column 2** shows the number of 15-year-olds enrolled in schools in grades 7 or above (as defined above), which is referred to as the ***eligible population.***
- **Column 3** shows the ***national desired target population***. Countries were allowed to exclude up to 0.5 per cent of students *a priori* from the eligible population, essentially for practical reasons. The following *a priori* exclusions exceed this limit but were agreed with the PISA Consortium: Australia excluded 1.04 per cent of its populations from TAFE colleges; France excluded 4.15 per cent of its students in Territoires d'Outre-Mer because they were students in outlying territories not subject to the national education system (students from outlying *departments* were included), as well as eligible students in hospitals or trade chambers; and Indonesia excluded 4.65 per cent of its students from four provinces because of security reasons.
- **Column 4** shows the number of students enrolled in schools that were excluded from the national desired target population either from the sampling frame or later in the field during data collection.
- **Column 5** shows the size of the national desired target population after subtracting the students enrolled in excluded schools. This is obtained by subtracting column 4 from column 3.
- **Column 6** shows the percentage of students enrolled in excluded schools. This is obtained by dividing column 4 by column 3 and multiplying by 100.
- **Column 7** shows the ***number of students participating in PISA 2003***. Note that this number does not account for 15-year-olds assessed as part of additional national options.
- **Column 8** shows the ***weighted number of participating students***, *i.e.,* the number of students in the nationally defined target population that the PISA sample represents.
- Each country attempted to maximise the coverage of PISA's target population within the sampled schools. In the case of each sampled school, all eligible students, namely those 15 years of age, regardless of grade, were first listed. Sampled students who were to be excluded had still to be included in the sampling documentation, and a list drawn up stating the reason for their exclusion. **Column 9** indicates the total number of ***excluded students,*** which is further described and classified into specific categories in Table A3.2. **Column 10** indicates the ***weighted number of excluded students,*** *i.e.,* the overall number of students in the nationally defined target population represented by the number of students excluded from the sample, which is also described and classified by exclusion categories in Table A3.2. Excluded students were excluded based on four categories: *i)* students with an intellectual disability – student has a mental or emotional disability and is cognitively delayed such that he/she cannot perform in the PISA testing situation; *ii)* students with a functional disability – student has a moderate to severe permanent physical disability such that he/she cannot perform in the PISA testing situation; and *iii)* students with a limited assessment language proficiency – student is unable to read or speak any of the languages of the assessment in the country and would be unable to overcome the language barrier in the testing situation. Typically a student who has received less than one year of instruction in the languages of the assessment may be excluded; and *iv)* other – which is a category defined by the national centres and approved by the international centre.
- **Column 11** shows the ***percentage of students excluded within schools.*** This is calculated as the weighted number of excluded students (column 10) divided by the weighted number of excluded and participating students (column 8 plus column 10).
- **Column 12** shows the ***overall exclusion rate*** which represents the weighted percentage of the national desired target population excluded from PISA either through school-level exclusions or through the exclusion of students within schools. It is calculated as the school-level exclusion rate (column 6 divided by 100) plus within-school exclusion rate (column 11 divided by 100) multiplied by 1 minus the school-level exclusion rate (column 6 divided by 100). This result is then multiplied by 100. Seven countries, namely Canada, Denmark, New Zealand, Spain, the United Kingdom, the United States and the partner country Serbia, had exclusion rates higher than 5 per cent (see also *www.oecd.org* for further information on these exclusions). When language exclusions were accounted for (*i.e.,* removed from the overall exclusion rate), Denmark and New Zealand no longer had exclusion rates greater than 5 per cent.
- **Column 13** presents an index of ***the extent to which the national desired target population is covered by the PISA sample.*** Canada, Spain, the United States and the partner country Serbia were the only countries where the coverage is below 95 per cent.

Table A3.2
Exclusions

	Student exclusions (unweighted)					Student exclusions (weighted)				
	(1) Number of excluded students with disabilities (code 1)	(2) Number of excluded students with disabilities (code 2)	(3) Number of excluded students because of language (code 3)	(4) Number of excluded students for other reasons (code 4)	(5) Total number of excluded students	(6) Weighted number of excluded students with disabilities (code 1)	(7) Weighted number of excluded students with disabilities (code 2)	(8) Weighted number of excluded students because of language (code 3)	(9) Weighted number of excluded students for other reasons (code 4)	(10) Total weighted number of excluded students
OECD countries										
Australia	33	133	62	0	228	457	2 443	712	0	3 612
Austria	3	27	30	0	60	62	573	465	0	1 099
Belgium	4	49	49	0	102	64	507	622	0	1 193
Canada	100	1 590	303	0	1 993	874	13 720	3 734	0	18 328
Czech Republic	5	14	2	1	22	106	35	66	11	218
Denmark	9	70	79	56	214	101	768	861	591	2 321
Finland	15	37	20	7	79	138	334	200	53	725
France	9	31	11	0	51	1 227	5 110	1 821	0	8 158
Germany	4	21	30	6	61	768	4 526	5 347	893	11 533
Greece	14	30	31	69	144	289	555	498	1 310	2 652
Hungary	0	55	7	0	62	0	928	138	0	1 065
Iceland	12	45	22	0	79	12	45	22	0	79
Ireland	14	78	16	31	139	152	906	183	377	1 619
Italy	20	99	69	0	188	619	3 655	2 521	0	6 794
Japan	0	0	0	0	0	0	0	0	0	0
Korea	3	21	0	0	24	284	1 999	0	0	2 283
Luxembourg	2	15	45	4	66	2	15	45	4	66
Mexico	7	10	17	0	34	167	1 618	5 479	0	7 264
Netherlands	2	17	1	0	20	154	773	114	0	1 041
New Zealand	29	94	140	0	263	260	880	1 271	0	2 411
Norway	7	90	42	0	139	77	1 019	468	0	1 563
Poland	9	26	3	37	75	894	2 623	310	3 691	7 517
Portugal	14	55	15	0	84	255	929	265	0	1 450
Slovak Republic	16	74	19	0	109	108	913	320	0	1 341
Spain	34	421	136	0	591	1 594	17 246	6 779	0	25 619
Sweden	1	110	33	0	144	18	2 297	769	0	3 085
Switzerland	26	93	75	0	194	127	344	422	0	893
Turkey	0	0	0	0	0	0	0	0	0	0
United Kingdom	23	208	39	0	270	1 146	12 401	1 515	0	15 062
United States	32	431	71	0	534	14 239	201 562	31 190	0	246 991
Partner countries										
Brazil	4	1	0	0	5	1 642	500	0	0	2 142
Hong Kong-China	2	5	1	0	8	26	63	14	0	103
Indonesia	0	0	0	0	0	0	0	0	0	0
Latvia	21	23	0	0	44	148	231	0	0	380
Liechtenstein	1	0	4	0	5	1	0	4	0	5
Macao-China	4	0	0	0	4	13	0	0	0	13
Russian Federation	13	19	3	0	35	4 538	8 969	1 209	0	14 716
Serbia	5	8	2	0	15	78	129	34	0	241
Thailand	4	1	0	0	5	463	100	0	0	563
Tunisia	0	0	1	0	1	0	0	31	0	31
Uruguay	5	9	4	0	18	30	38	12	0	80

Exclusion codes:

Code 1: *Functional disability* – student has a moderate to severe permanent physical disability.

Code 2: *Intellectual disability* – student has a mental or emotional disability and has either been tested as cognitively delayed or is considered in the professional opinion of qualified staff to be cognitively delayed.

Code 3: *Limited assessment language proficiency* – student is not a native speaker of any of the languages of the assessment in the country and has limited proficiency in these languages.

Code 4: *Other* – defined by the national centres and approved by the international centre.

Note: For a full explanation of other details in this table please refer to the PISA 2003 Technical Report (OECD, forthcoming).

- **Column 14** presents an index of ***the extent to which 15-year-olds enrolled in schools are covered by the PISA sample.*** The index measures the overall proportion of the national enrolled population that is covered by the non-excluded portion of the student sample. The index takes into account both school-level and student-level exclusions. Values close to 100 indicate that the PISA sample represents the entire education system as defined for PISA 2003. The index is the weighted number of participating students (column 8) divided by the weighted number of participating and excluded students (column 8 plus column 10), times the nationally defined target population (column 5) divided by the eligible population (column 2) (times 100). The same countries with index 1 below 0.95 also had index 2 below 0.95. In addition, France also had this index below 95 per cent due to the exclusion of Territoires d'Outre Mer. This was consistent with the results from PISA 2000.
- **Column 15** presents an index of ***the percentage of enrolled population.*** This index is the total enrolled population of 15-year-olds (column 2) divided by the total population of 15-year-old students (column 1).

This high level of coverage contributes to the comparability of the assessment results. For example, even assuming that the excluded students would have systematically scored worse than those who participated, and that this relationship is moderately strong, an exclusion rate in the order of 5 per cent would likely lead to an overestimation of national mean scores of less than 5 score points (on a scale with an international mean of 500 score points and a standard deviation of 100 score points). This assessment is based on the following calculations: If the correlation between the propensity of exclusions and student performance is 0.3, resulting mean scores would likely be overestimated by 1 score point if the exclusion rate is 1 per cent, by 3 score points if the exclusion rate is 5 per cent, and by 6 score points if the exclusion rate is 10 per cent. If the correlation between the propensity of exclusions and student performance is 0.5, resulting mean scores would be overestimated by 1 score point if the exclusion rate is 1 per cent, by 5 score points if the exclusion rate is 5 per cent, and by 10 score points if the exclusion rate is 10 per cent. For this calculation, a model was employed that assumes a bivariate normal distribution for the propensity to participate and performance. For details see the *PISA 2003 Technical Report* (OECD, forthcoming).

Sampling procedures and response rates

The accuracy of any survey results depends on the quality of the information on which national samples are based as well as on the sampling procedures. Quality standards, procedures, instruments and verification mechanisms were developed for PISA that ensured that national samples yielded comparable data and that the results could be compared with confidence.

Most PISA samples were designed as two-stage stratified samples (where countries applied different sampling designs, these are documented in the *PISA 2003 Technical Report* (OECD, forthcoming)). The first stage consisted of sampling individual schools in which 15-year-old students could be enrolled. Schools were sampled systematically with probabilities proportional to size, the measure of size being a function of the estimated number of eligible (15-year-old) students enrolled. A minimum of 150 schools were selected in each country (where this number existed), although the requirements for national analyses often required a somewhat larger sample. As the schools were sampled, replacement schools were simultaneously identified, in case a sampled school chose not to participate in PISA 2003.

In the case of Iceland, Liechtenstein and Luxembourg, all schools and all eligible students within schools were included in the sample. However, since not all students in the PISA samples were assessed in all domains, these national samples represent a complete census only in respect of the assessment of mathematical literacy as the major domain.

Experts from the PISA Consortium performed the sample selection process for each participating country and monitored it closely in those countries where they selected their own samples.

The second stage of the selection process sampled students within sampled schools. Once schools were selected, a list of each sampled school's 15-year-old students was prepared. From this list, 35 students were then selected with equal probability (all 15-year-old students were selected if fewer than 35 were enrolled).

Data quality standards in PISA required minimum participation rates for schools as well as for students. These standards were established to minimise the potential for response biases. In the case of countries meeting these standards, it was likely that any bias resulting from non-response would be negligible, *i.e.,* typically smaller than the sampling error.

A minimum response rate of 85 per cent was required for the schools initially selected. Where the initial response rate of schools was between 65 and 85 per cent, however, an acceptable school response rate could still be achieved through the use of replacement schools. This procedure brought with it a risk of increased response bias. Participating countries were, therefore, encouraged to persuade as many of the schools in the original sample as possible to participate. Schools with a student participation rate between 25 and 50 per cent were not regarded as participating schools, but data from these schools were included in the database and contributed to the various estimations. Data from schools with a student participation rate of less than 25 per cent were excluded from the database.

PISA 2003 also required a minimum participation rate of 80 per cent of students within participating schools. This minimum participation rate had to be met at the national level, not necessarily by each participating school. Follow-up sessions were required in schools in which too few students had participated in the original assessment sessions. Student participation rates were calculated over all original schools, and also over all schools whether original sample or replacement schools, and from the participation of students in both the original assessment and any follow-up sessions. A student who participated in the original or follow-up cognitive sessions was regarded as a participant. Those who attended only the questionnaire session were

included in the international database and contributed to the statistics presented in this publication if he or she provided at least a description of his or her father's or mother's occupation.

Table A3.3 shows the response rates for students and schools, before and after replacement.

- **Column 1** shows the ***weighted participation rate of schools before replacement***. This is obtained by dividing column 2 by column 3.
- **Column 2** shows the ***weighted number of responding schools before school replacement*** (weighted by student enrolment).
- **Column 3** shows the ***weighted number of sampled schools before school replacement*** (including both responding and non responding schools) (weighted by student enrolment).
- **Column 4** shows the ***unweighted number of responding schools before school replacement***.
- **Column 5** shows the ***unweighted number of responding and non responding schools before school replacement***.
- **Column 6** shows the ***weighted participation rate of schools after replacement.*** This is obtained by dividing column 7 by column 8. Canada, the United Kingdom and the United States did not meet PISA's requirements for response rates before replacement, which was 85 per cent. The participation rate of Canada before replacement was 79.9 per cent (column 1) reaching 84.4 per cent after replacement, thus short by 3.1 per cent of the required 87.5 per cent. In the United Kingdom, the response rate before replacement was 64.3 (column 1) falling short of the minimum requirement by 0.7 per cent. After replacement, the participation rate increased to 77.4, still short of the final requirement. The United States achieved an initial participation rate of 64.9 before replacement reaching 68.1 after replacement
- **Column 7** shows the ***weighted number of responding schools after school replacement*** (weighted by student enrolment).
- **Column 8** shows the ***weighted number of schools sampled after school replacement*** (including both responding and nonresponding schools) (weighted by student enrolment).
- **Column 9** shows the ***unweighted number of responding schools after school replacement***.
- **Column 10** shows the ***unweighted number of responding and non responding schools after school replacement.***
- **Column 11** shows the ***weighted student participation rate after replacement.*** This is obtained by dividing column 12 by column 13. The United Kingdom was the only country where the student participation rate of 77.9 per cent was below the required 80 per cent.
- **Column 12** shows the ***weighted number of students assessed***.
- **Column 13** shows the ***weighted number of students sampled*** (including both students that were assessed and students who were absent on the day of the assessment).
- **Column 14** shows the ***unweighted number of students assessed***. Note that any students in schools with student response rates less than 50 per cent were not included in these rates (both weighted and unweighted).
- **Column 15** shows the ***unweighted number of students sampled*** (including both students that were assessed and students who were absent on the day of the assessment). Note that any students in schools with student response rates less than 50 per cent were not included in these rates (both weighted and unweighted).

Reporting of data for the United Kingdom in PISA 2003

In order to ensure that PISA yields reliable and internationally comparable data, OECD Member countries agreed on a process for the validation of all national data submissions. As the basis for this process, PISA established technical standards for the quality of datasets which countries must meet in order to be reported in OECD publications. These standards are described in detail in the *PISA 2003 Technical Report* (OECD, forthcoming). One of the requirements is that initial response rates should be 85 per cent at the school level and 80 per cent at the student level. The response rates are reported in Table A3.3.

The United Kingdom fell significantly short of these standards, with a weighted school participation rate before replacement of 64.3 per cent at the school level. As mentioned above, the Technical Standards include an approved procedure through which countries with an initial school-level response rate of at least 65 per cent could improve response rates through the use of designated replacement schools. For the United Kingdom, a school-level response rate of 96 per cent was required, but only 77.4 per cent was achieved after replacement and it was 77.9 per cent at the student level.

Table A3.3
Response rates

		Initial sample – before school replacement					Final sample – after school replacement				
		(1) Weighted school participation rate before replacement (%)	(2) Number of responding schools (weighted by enrolment)	(3) Weighted number of schools sampled (responding and non-responding) (weighted by enrolment)	(4) Number of responding schools (unweighted)	(5) Number of responding and non-responding schools (unweighted)	(6) Weighted school participation rate after replacement (%)	(7) Weighted number of responding schools (weighted by enrolment)	(8) Number of schools sampled (responing and non-responding) (weighted by enrolment)	(9) Number of responding schools (unweighted)	(10) Number of responding and non-responding schools (unweighted)
OECD countries	Australia	86.31	237 525	275 208	301	355	90.43	248 876	275 208	314	355
	Austria	99.29	87 169	87 795	192	194	99.29	87 169	87 795	192	194
	Belgium	83.40	98 423	118 010	248	296	95.63	112 775	117 924	282	296
	Canada	79.95	300 328	375 622	1 040	1 162	84.38	316 977	375 638	1 066	1 162
	Czech Republic	91.38	113 178	123 855	239	262	99.05	122 629	123 811	259	262
	Denmark	84.60	47 573	56 234	175	210	98.32	55 271	56 213	205	210
	Finland	97.39	58 209	59 766	193	197	100.00	59 766	59 766	197	197
	France	88.65	671 417	757 355	162	183	89.24	675 840	757 355	163	183
	Germany	98.06	886 841	904 387	211	216	98.82	893 879	904 559	213	216
	Greece	80.60	82 526	102 384	145	179	95.77	104 859	109 490	171	179
	Hungary	97.32	115 041	118 207	248	262	99.37	117 269	118 012	252	262
	Iceland	99.90	4 082	4 086	129	131	99.90	4 082	4 086	129	131
	Ireland	90.24	52 791	58 499	139	154	92.84	54 310	58 499	143	154
	Italy	97.54	549 168	563 039	398	406	100.00	563 039	563 039	406	406
	Japan	87.12	1 144 942	1 314 227	131	150	95.91	1 260 428	1 314 227	144	150
	Korea	95.89	589 540	614 825	143	149	100.00	614 825	614 825	149	149
	Luxembourg	99.93	4 087	4 090	29	32	99.93	4 087	4 090	29	32
	Mexico	93.98	1 132 315	1 204 851	1 090	1 154	95.45	1 150 023	1 204 851	1 102	1 154
	Netherlands	82.61	161 682	195 725	144	175	87.86	171 955	195 725	153	175
	New Zealand	91.09	48 401	53 135	158	175	97.55	51 842	53 145	171	175
	Norway	87.87	48 219	54 874	175	200	90.40	49 608	54 874	180	200
	Poland	95.12	531 479	558 752	157	166	98.09	548 168	558 853	163	166
	Portugal	99.31	106 174	106 916	152	153	99.31	106 174	106 916	152	153
	Slovak Republic	98.39	406 170	412 829	377	383	100.00	412 777	412 777	383	383
	Spain	78.92	63 629	80 626	223	284	99.08	80 394	81 141	281	284
	Sweden	99.08	112 467	113 511	185	188	99.08	112 467	113 511	185	188
	Switzerland	97.32	77 867	80 011	437	456	98.53	78 838	80 014	444	456
	Turkey	93.29	671 385	719 702	145	159	100.00	719 405	719 405	159	159
	United Kingdom	64.32	456 818	710 203	311	451	77.37	549 059	709 641	361	451
	United States	64.94	2 451 083	3 774 330	249	382	68.12	2 571 003	3 774 322	262	382
Partner countries	Brazil	93.20	2 181 287	2 340 538	213	229	99.51	2 328 972	2 340 538	228	229
	Hong Kong-China	81.89	59 216	72 312	124	151	95.90	69 345	72 312	145	151
	Indonesia	100.00	2 173 824	2 173 824	344	344	100.00	2 173 824	2 173 824	344	344
	Latvia	95.31	33 845	35 509	157	164	95.31	33 845	35 509	157	164
	Liechtenstein	100.00	348	348	12	12	100.00	348	348	12	12
	Macao-China	100.00	6 992	6 992	39	39	100.00	6 992	6 992	39	39
	Russian Federation	99.51	1 798 096	1 806 954	210	211	100.00	1 806 954	1 806 954	211	211
	Serbia	100.00	90 178	90 178	149	149	100.00	90 178	90 178	149	149
	Thailand	91.46	704 344	770 109	163	179	100.00	769 392	769 392	179	179
	Tunisia	100.00	163 555	163 555	149	149	100.00	163 555	163 555	149	149
	Uruguay	93.20	39 773	42 677	233	245	97.11	41 474	42 709	239	245

		Final sample – Students within schools after school replacement				
		(11) Weighted student participation rate after replacement (%)	(12) Number of students assessed (weighted)	(13) Number of students sampled (assessed and absent) (weighted)	(14) Number of students assessed (unweighted)	(15) Number of students sampled (assessed and absent) (unweighted)
OECD countries	Australia	83.31	176 085	211 357	12 425	15 179
	Austria	83.56	71 392	85 439	4 566	6 212
	Belgium	92.17	98 936	106 995	8 796	9 498
	Canada	83.90	233 829	278 714	27 712	31 899
	Czech Republic	89.03	106 645	119 791	6 316	7 036
	Denmark	89.88	45 356	50 464	4 216	4 687
	Finland	92.84	53 737	57 883	5 796	6 235
	France	88.11	581 957	660 491	4 214	4 774
	Germany	92.18	806 312	874 762	4 642	5 040
	Greece	95.43	96 273	100 883	4 627	4 854
	Hungary	92.87	98 996	106 594	4 764	5 132
	Iceland	85.37	3 350	3 924	3 350	3 924
	Ireland	82.58	42 009	50 873	3 852	4 670
	Italy	92.52	445 502	481 521	11 639	12 407
	Japan	95.08	1 132 200	1 190 768	4 707	4 951
	Korea	98.81	527 177	533 504	5 444	5 509
	Luxembourg	96.22	3 923	4 077	3 923	4 077
	Mexico	92.26	938 902	1 017 667	29 734	32 276
	Netherlands	88.25	144 212	163 418	3 979	4 498
	New Zealand	85.71	40 595	47 363	4 483	5 233
	Norway	87.86	41 923	47 715	4 039	4 594
	Poland	81.95	429 921	524 584	4 338	5 296
	Portugal	87.92	84 783	96 437	4 590	5 199
	Slovak Republic	90.61	312 044	344 372	10 791	11 655
	Spain	91.90	70 246	76 441	7 346	7 994
	Sweden	92.61	98 095	105 927	4 624	4 970
	Switzerland	94.70	81 026	85 556	8 415	8 880
	Turkey	96.87	466 201	481 279	4 855	5 010
	United Kingdom	77.92	419 810	538 737	9 265	11 352
	United States	82.73	1 772 279	2 142 288	5 342	6 502
Partner countries	Brazil	91.19	1 772 522	1 943 751	4 452	4 871
	Hong Kong-China	90.20	62 756	69 576	4 478	4 966
	Indonesia	98.09	1 933 839	1 971 476	10 761	10 960
	Latvia	93.88	30 043	32 001	4 627	4 940
	Liechtenstein	98.22	332	338	332	338
	Macao-China	98.02	6 642	6 775	1 250	1 274
	Russian Federation	95.71	2 061 050	2 153 373	5 974	6 253
	Serbia	91.36	62 669	68 596	4 405	4 829
	Thailand	97.81	623 093	637 076	5 236	5 339
	Tunisia	96.27	145 251	150 875	4 721	4 902
	Uruguay	90.83	29 756	32 759	5 797	6 422

The results of a subsequent bias analysis provided no evidence for any significant bias of school-level performance results but did suggest that there was potential non-response bias at student levels. The PISA Consortium concluded that it was not possible to reliably assess the magnitude, or even the direction, of this non-response bias and to correct for this. As a result, it is not possible to say with confidence that the United Kingdom's sample results reliably reflect those for the national population, with the level of accuracy required by PISA. The mean performance of the responding sample of United Kingdom pupils was 508, 507 and 518 score points in mathematics, reading and science *respectively*. In the mathematics subscales the mean performance was 496 score points on the space and shape scale, 513 score points on the change and relationships scale, 520 score points on the uncertainty scale and 499 score points on the quantity scale. If negligible to moderate levels of bias are assumed, the United Kingdom mean performance would lie between 492 and 524 score points on the mathematical literacy scale, between 491 and 523 score points on the reading literacy scale, and between 502 and 534 score points on the scientific literacy scale (for further details see *the PISA* 2003 Technical Report, OECD, forthcoming) . The uncertainties surrounding the sample and its bias are such that scores for the United Kingdom cannot reliably be compared with those of other countries. They can also not be compared with the performance scores for the United Kingdom from PISA 2000.

The results are, however, accurate for many within-country comparisons between subgroups (*e.g.,* males and females) and for relational analyses. The results for the United Kingdom have, therefore, been included in a separate category below the results for the other participating countries. Other data for the United Kingdom that are not reported in this volume are available at *www.pisa.oecd.org* to allow researchers to reproduce the results from the international comparisons.

All international averages and aggregate statistics include the data for the United Kingdom.

It should be noted that Scotland and Northern Ireland carried out an independent sample that met the PISA technical standards. Results for Scotland, including sampling information, are reported in Annex B2 and are fully comparable with results from other OECD countries and with results from PISA 2000.

Definition of schools

PISA 2003

In some countries, sub-units within schools were sampled instead of schools as administrative units and this may affect the estimation of the between-school variance components. In Austria, the Czech Republic, Hungary, Italy and Japan, schools with more than one study programme were split into the units delivering these programmes. In the Netherlands, for schools with both lower and upper secondary programmes, schools were split into units delivering each programme level. In Uruguay and Mexico, schools where instruction is delivered in shifts were split into the corresponding units. In the Flemish part of Belgium, in case of multi-campus schools, implantations (campuses) were sampled whereas in the French part, in case of multi-campus schools the larger administrative units were sampled. In the Slovak Republic, in case of schools with both Slovak and Hungarian as languages of instruction, schools were split into units delivering each language of instruction. For a definition of the sampling units in each country see *www.pisa.oecd.org.*

Annex A4: Standard errors, significance tests and subgroup comparisons

The statistics in this report represent ***estimates*** of national performance based on samples of students rather than values that could be calculated if every student in every country had answered every question. Consequently, it is important to have measures of the degree of uncertainty of the estimates. In PISA, each estimate has an associated degree of uncertainty, which is expressed through a ***standard error***. The use of ***confidence intervals*** provides a way to make inferences about the population means and proportions in a manner that reflects the uncertainty associated with the sample estimates. From an observed sample statistic it can, under the assumption of a normal distribution, be inferred that the corresponding population result would lie within the confidence interval in 95 out of 100 replications of the measurement on different samples drawn from the same population.

In many cases, readers are primarily interested in whether a given value in a particular country is different from a second value in the same or another country, *e.g.*, whether females in a country perform better than males in the same country. In the tables and charts used in this report, differences are labelled as ***statistically significant*** when a difference of that size, smaller or larger, would be observed less than 5 per cent of the time, if there was actually no difference in corresponding population values. Similarly, the risk of reporting as significant if there is, in fact, no correlation between two measures is contained at 5 per cent.

Although the probability that a particular difference will falsely be declared to be statistically significant is low (5 per cent) in each single comparison, the probability of making such an error increases when several comparisons are made simultaneously.

It is possible to make an adjustment for this which reduces to 5 per cent the maximum probability that differences will be falsely declared as statistically significant at least once among all the comparisons that are made. Such an adjustment, based on the Bonferroni method, has been incorporated into the multiple comparison charts in Chapters 2 and 6. The adjusted significance test should be used when the interest of readers is to compare a country's performance with that of all other countries. For comparing a single country with another single country, no adjustment is needed.

For all other tables and charts readers should note that, if there were no real differences on a given measure, then the ***multiple comparison*** in conjunction with a 5 per cent significance level, would erroneously identify differences on 0.05 times the number of comparisons made, occasions. For example, even though the significance tests applied in PISA for identifying gender differences ensure that, for each country, the likelihood of identifying a gender difference erroneously is less than 5 per cent, a comparison showing differences for 30 countries would, on average, identify 1.35 cases (0.05 times 30) with significant gender differences, even if there were no real gender difference in any of the countries. The same applies for other statistics for which significance tests have been undertaken in this publication, such as correlations and regression coefficients.

Throughout the report, significance tests were undertaken to assess the statistical significance of the comparisons made.

Differences in performance between 2003 and 2000

See Annex A8 for notes on the interpretation of differences between the PISA 2003 and PISA 2000 assessments.

Gender differences

Gender differences in student performance or other indices were tested for statistical significance. Positive differences indicate higher scores for males while negative differences indicate higher scores for females. Differences marked in bold in the tables in Annexes B1 and B2 are statistically significant at the 95 per cent confidence level. For examples, see Table 2.1c and Table 3.1, Annex B1.

Performance differences between top and bottom quartiles

Differences in average performance between the top quarter and the bottom quarter on the PISA indices were tested for statistical significance. Figures marked in bold indicate that performance between the top and bottom quarter of students on the respective index is statistically significantly different at the 95 per cent confidence level.

Change in the performance per unit of the index

For many tables in Annex B1, the difference in student performance per unit of the index shown was calculated. Figures in bold indicate that the differences are statistically significantly different from zero at the 95 per cent confidence level.

Relative risk or increased likelihood

The relative risk is a measure of association between an antecedent factor and an outcome factor. The relative risk is simply the ratio of two risks, *i.e.*, the risk of observing the outcome when the antecedent is present and the risk of observing the outcome when the risk is not present. Exhibit 1 presents the notation that is used in the following.

Labels used in a two-way table

p_{11}	p_{12}	$p_{1.}$
p_{21}	p_{22}	$p_{2.}$
$p_{.1}$	$p_{.2}$	$p_{..}$

$p_{..}$ is equal to $\frac{n_{..}}{n_{..}}$, with $n_{..}$ the total number of students and $p_{..}$ is therefore equal to 1, $p_{i.}$, $p_{.j}$ respectively represent the marginal probabilities for each row and for each column. The marginal probabilities are equal to the marginal frequencies divided by the total number of students. Finally, the p_{ij} represent the probabilities for each cell and are equal to the number of observations in a particular cell divided by the total number of observations.

In PISA, the rows represents the antecedent factor with the first row for "having the antecedent" and the second row for "not *having the antecedent*" and the columns represent the outcome with, the first column for "having the outcome" and the second column for "*not having the outcome*". The relative risk is then equal to:

$$RR = \frac{(p_{11} / p_{1.})}{(p_{21} / p_{2.})}$$

Figures in bold in Annex B1 indicate that the relative risk is statistically significantly different from 1 at the 95 per cent confidence level.

Differences in percentages between 2003 and 2000

Where percentages are compared between the PISA 2003 and PISA 2000 samples, differences were tested for statistical significance. Figures in bold in Annex B1 indicate statistically significantly different percentages at the 95 per cent confidence level. When comparing data between 2003 and 2000, it should be borne in mind that in 2000 school principals were asked to report with regard to the situation of 15-year-olds in their school whereas in 2003 school principals were asked to reflect the situation in the entire school in their responses. Similarly, in 2000 students were asked to reflect the situation in their language classes whereas in 2003 they were asked to reflect the situation in their mathematics classes.

Difference in the mathematics performance between public and private schools

Differences in the performance between public and private schools were tested for statistical significance. For this purpose, government-dependent and government-independent private schools were jointly considered. Positive differences represent higher scores for public schools while negative differences represent higher scores for private schools. Figures in bold in Annex B1 indicate statistically significant different scores at the 95 per cent confidence level.

Difference in the mathematics performance between native students and students with an immigrant background

Differences in the performance between native and non-native students were tested for statistical significance. For this purpose, non-native and first-generation students were jointly considered. Positive differences represent higher scores for native students, while negative differences represent higher scores for non-native and first-generation students. Figures in bold in Annex B1 indicate statistically significantly different scores at the 95 per cent confidence level.

Effect sizes

Sometimes it is useful to compare differences in an index between groups, such as males and females, across countries. A problem that may occur in such instances is that the distribution of the index varies across countries. One way to resolve this is to calculate an effect size that accounts for differences in the distributions. An effect size measures the difference between, say,

the self-efficacy in mathematics of male and female students in a given country, relative to the average variation in self-efficacy in mathematics scores among male and female students in the country.

An effect size also allows a comparison of differences across measures that differ in their metric. For example, it is possible to compare effect sizes between the PISA indices and the PISA test scores. For example, see Table 3.16 where gender differences in performance in mathematics are compared with the gender differences in several of the indices.

In accordance with common practices, effect sizes less than 0.20 are considered small in this volume, effect sizes in the order of 0.50 are considered medium, and effect sizes greater than 0.80 are considered large. Many comparisons in this report consider differences only if the effect sizes are equal to or greater than 0.20, even if smaller differences are still statistically significant; figures in bold in Annex B1 indicate values equal to or greater than 0.20. Values smaller than 0.20 but that due to rounding are shown as 0.20 in tables and figures have not been highlighted.

The effect size between two subgroups is calculated as:

$$\frac{m_1 - m_2}{\sqrt{\frac{\sigma_1^2 + \sigma_2^2}{2}}}$$

, *i.e.* the mean difference between the two subgroups, divided by the pooled standard deviation, *i.e.* the root square of the sum of the subgroup variance divided by 2.

Skewness of a distribution

The skewness for the distribution of socio-economic background was calculated. Negative values for the skewness indicate a longer tail of students from disadvantaged socio-economic background while positive values indicate a longer tail of students from advantaged socio-economic backgrounds.

Annex A5: Quality assurance

Quality assurance procedures were implemented in all parts of PISA.

The consistent quality and linguistic equivalence of the PISA assessment instruments were facilitated by providing countries with equivalent source versions of the assessment instruments in English and French and requiring countries (other than those assessing students in English and French) to prepare and consolidate two independent translations using both source versions. Precise translation and adaptation guidelines were supplied, also including instructions for the selection and training of the translators. For each country, the translation and format of the assessment instruments (including test materials, marking guides, questionnaires and manuals) were verified by expert translators appointed by the PISA Consortium (whose mother tongue was the language of instruction in the country concerned and who were knowledgeable about education systems) before they were used in the PISA Field Trial and Main Study. For further information on the PISA translation procedures see the *PISA 2003 Technical Report* (OECD, forthcoming).

The survey was implemented through standardised procedures. The PISA Consortium provided comprehensive manuals that explained the implementation of the survey, including precise instructions for the work of School Co-ordinators and scripts for Test Administrators for use during the assessment sessions. Proposed adaptations to survey procedures, or proposed modifications to the assessment session script, were submitted to the PISA Consortium for approval prior to verification. The PISA Consortium then verified the national translation and adaptation of these manuals.

To establish the credibility of PISA as valid and as unbiased and to encourage uniformity in the administration of the assessment sessions, Test Administrators in participating countries were selected using the following criteria: It was required that the Test Administrator not be the reading, mathematics or science instructor of any students in the sessions he or she would administer for PISA; it was recommended that the Test Administrator not be a member of the staff of any school where he or she would administer PISA; and it was considered preferable that the Test Administrator not be a member of the staff of any school in the PISA sample. Participating countries organised an in-person training session for Test Administrators.

Participating countries were required to ensure that: Test Administrators worked with the School Co-ordinator to prepare the assessment session, including updating student tracking forms and identifying excluded students; no extra time was given for the cognitive items (while it was permissible to give extra time for the student questionnaire); no instrument was administered before the two 1-hour parts of the cognitive session; Test Administrators recorded the student participation status on the student tracking forms and filled in a Session Report Form; no cognitive instrument was permitted to be photocopied; no cognitive instrument could be viewed by school staff before the assessment session; and that Test Administrators returned the material to the national centre immediately after the assessment sessions.

National Project Managers were encouraged to organise a follow-up session when more than 15 per cent of the PISA sample was not able to attend the original assessment session.

National Quality Monitors from the PISA Consortium visited all national centres to review data-collection procedures. Finally, School Quality Monitors from the PISA Consortium visited a sample of 15 schools during the assessment. For further information on the field operations see the *PISA 2003 Technical Report* (OECD, forthcoming).

Marking procedures were designed to ensure consistent and accurate application of the marking guides outlined in the PISA Operations manuals. National Project Managers were required to submit proposed modifications to these procedures to the Consortium for approval. Reliability studies to analyse the consistency of marking were implemented, these are discussed in more detail below.

Software specially designed for PISA 2003 facilitated data entry, detected common errors during data entry, and facilitated the process of data cleaning. Training sessions familiarised National Project Managers with these procedures.

For a description of the quality assurance procedures applied in PISA and the results see the *PISA 2003 Technical Report* (OECD, forthcoming).

Annex A6: Development of the PISA assessment instruments

The development of the PISA 2003 assessment instruments was an interactive process between the PISA Consortium, the various expert committees, the PISA Governing Board and national experts. A panel of international experts led, in close consultation with participating countries, the identification of the range of skills and competencies that were, in the respective assessment domains, considered to be crucial for an individual's capacity to fully participate in and contribute to a successful modern society. A description of the assessment domains – the assessment framework – was then used by participating countries, and other test development professionals, as they contributed assessment materials. The development of this assessment framework involved the following steps:

- development of a working definition for the domain and description of the assumptions that underlay that definition;
- evaluation of how to organise the set of tasks constructed in order to report to policy-makers and researchers on performance in each assessment domain among 15-year-old students in participating countries;
- identification of a set of key characteristics to be taken into account when assessment tasks were constructed for international use;
- operationalisation of the set of key characteristics to be used in test construction, with definitions based on existing literature and the experience of other large-scale assessments;
- validation of the variables, and assessment of the contribution which each made to the understanding of task difficulty in participating countries; and
- preparation of an interpretative scheme for the results.

The frameworks were agreed at both scientific and policy levels and subsequently provided the basis for the development of the assessment instruments. The frameworks are described in *The PISA 2003 Assessment Framework – Mathematics, Reading, Science and Problem Solving Knowledge and Skills* (OECD, 2003e). They provided a common language and a vehicle for participating countries to develop a consensus as to the measurement goals of PISA.

Assessment items were then developed to reflect the intentions of the frameworks and were piloted in a Field Trial in all participating countries before a final set of items was selected for the PISA 2003 Main Study. Tables A6.1-A6-3 show the distribution of PISA 2003 assessment items by the various dimensions of the PISA frameworks.

Due attention was paid to reflecting the national, cultural and linguistic variety among OECD countries. As part of this effort the PISA Consortium used professional test item development teams in several different countries, including Australia, the United Kingdom, the Netherlands and Japan. In addition to the items that were developed by the PISA Consortium teams, assessment material was contributed by participating countries. The Consortium's multi-national team of test developers deemed a substantial amount of this submitted material as appropriate given the requirements laid out by the PISA assessment frameworks. As a result, the item pool included assessment items from Argentina, Australia, Austria, Canada, Czech Republic, Denmark, Finland, France, Germany, Greece, Ireland, Italy, Japan, Korea, the Netherlands, New Zealand, Norway, Portugal, Sweden, Switzerland, and the United States. About one-third of items selected for inclusion in the Field Trial were submitted by participating countries, and about 37 per cent of items selected for the Main Study were from participating countries.

Approximately 232 units comprising about 530 items were included in item bundles for national review, in the mathematics, problem solving and science areas. After the first consultation process, the Field Trial included 115 Mathematics Units with 217 Mathematics Items. Of these Mathematics Units, the stimulus material for 53 came from national contributions, 80 originated with the PISA Consortium, and one unit came from the Third International Mathematics and Science Study (TIMSS).

Each item included in the assessment pool was then rated by each country: for potential cultural, gender or other bias; for relevance to 15-year-olds in school and non-school contexts; and for familiarity and level of interest. A first consultation of countries on the item pool was undertaken as part of the process of developing the Field Trial assessment instruments. A second consultation was undertaken after the Field Trial to assist in the final selection of items for the Main Study.

Following the Field Trial, in which all items were tested in all participating countries, test developers and expert groups considered a variety of aspects in selecting the items for the Main Study: *i)* the results from the Field Trial, *ii)* the outcome of the item review from countries, and *iii)* queries received during the Field Trial marking process. The test developers and expert groups selected a final set of items in October 2002 which, following a period of negotiation, was adopted by participating countries at both scientific and policy levels.

Table A6.1
Distribution of items by the dimensions of the PISA framework for the assessment of mathematics

	Number of items[1]	Number of multiple-choice items	Number of complex multiple-choice items	Number of closed-constructed response items	Number of open-constructed response items	Number of short response items
Distribution of mathematics items by "overarching ideas"						
Space and shape	20	4	4	6	4	2
Change and relationships	22	1	2	4	11	4
Quantity	23	4	2	2	1	14
Uncertainty	20	8	3	1	5	3
Total	*85*	*17*	*11*	*13*	*21*	*23*
Distribution of mathematics items by competency cluster						
Reproduction	26	7	0	7	3	9
Connections	40	5	9	4	9	13
Reflection	19	5	2	2	9	1
Total	*85*	*17*	*11*	*13*	*21*	*23*
Distribution of mathematics items by situations or contexts						
Personal	18	5	3	1	3	6
Educational/Occupational	20	2	4	6	2	6
Public	29	8	2	4	8	7
Scientific	18	2	2	2	8	4
Total	*85*	*17*	*11*	*13*	*21*	*23*

1. One item was eliminated from subsequent analysis: item ID M434Q01.

Table A6.2
Distribution of items by the dimensions of the PISA framework for the assessment of reading

	Number of items	Number of multiple-choice items	Number of complex multiple-choice items	Number of closed-constructed response items	Number of open-constructed response items	Number of short response items
Distribution of reading items by text structure						
Continuous	18	8	1	0	9	0
Non-continuous	10	1	0	4	1	4
Total	*28*	*9*	*1*	*4*	*10*	*4*
Distribution of reading items by type of task (process)						
Retrieving information	7	0	1	3	0	3
Interpreting texts	14	9	0	1	3	1
Reflection and evaluation	7	0	0	0	7	0
Total	*28*	*9*	*1*	*4*	*10*	*4*
Distribution of reading items by text type						
Charts and graphs	2	1	0	0	0	1
Descriptive	3	1	1	0	1	0
Expository	12	6	0	0	6	0
Forms	3	0	0	1	1	1
Maps	1	0	0	0	0	1
Narrative	3	1	0	0	2	0
Tables	4	0	0	3	0	1
Total	*28*	*9*	*1*	*4*	*10*	*4*
Distribution of reading items by context						
Personal	6	2	0	1	3	0
Public	7	1	0	2	3	1
Educational	8	5	0	0	2	1
Occupational	7	1	1	1	2	2
Total	*28*	*9*	*1*	*4*	*10*	*4*

The Main Study included 54 mathematics units with 85 items. Twenty-four of these units originated from material submitted by participating countries. Twenty-eight of the units came from one or other of the Consortium teams, and two originated as TIMSS material. The Main Study instruments also included eight Reading units (28 items), 13 Science units (35 items) and ten Problem Solving units (19 items).

Table A6.3
Distribution of items by the dimensions of the PISA framework for the assessment of science

	Number of items[1]	Number of multiple-choice items	Number of complex multiple-choice items	Number of open-constructed response items	Number of short response items
Distribution of science items by science processes					
Process 1: Describing, explaining and predicting scientific phenomena	17	7	3	6	1
Process 2: Understanding scientific investigation	7	2	2	3	0
Process 3: Interpreting scientific evidence and conclusion	11	4	2	5	0
Total	*35*	*13*	*7*	*14*	*1*
Distribution of science items by science area					
Science in Earth and environment	12	3	2	6	1
Science in life and health	12	5	2	5	0
Science in technology	11	5	3	3	0
Total	*35*	*13*	*7*	*14*	*1*
Distribution of science items by science application[2]					
Structure and property of matter	6	4	2	0	0
Atmospheric change	3	0	0	3	0
Chemical and physical change	1	0	0	1	0
Energy transformations	4	0	1	3	0
Forces and movement	1	1	0	0	0
Form and function	3	1	0	2	0
Physiological change	4	1	1	2	0
Genetic control	2	1	1	0	0
Ecosystems	3	2	0	1	0
The Earth and its place in the universe	7	3	2	1	1
Geographical change	1	0	0	1	0
Total	*35*	*13*	*7*	*14*	*1*

1. One item was eliminated from subsequent analysis: item ID S327Q02.
2. There were no items in PISA 2003 from the categories "human biology" and "biodiversity".

Five item types were used in the PISA assessment instruments:

- ***Open-constructed response items***: in these items, students constructed a longer response, allowing for the possibility of a broad range of divergent, individual responses and differing viewpoints. These items usually asked students to relate information or ideas in the stimulus text to their own experience or opinions, with the acceptability depending less on the position taken by the student than on the ability to use what they had read when justifying or explaining that position. Partial credit was often permitted for partially correct or less sophisticated answers, and all of these items were marked by hand.
- ***Closed-constructed response items***: these items required students to construct their own responses, there being a limited range of acceptable answers. Most of these items were scored dichotomously with a few items included in the marking process.
- ***Short response items***: as in the closed constructed-response items, students were to provide a brief answer, but there was a wide range of possible answers. These items were hand-marked, thus allowing for dichotomous as well as partial credit.
- ***Complex multiple-choice items***: in these items, the student made a series of choices, usually binary. Students indicated their answer by circling a word or short phrase (for example *yes* or *no*) for each point. These items were scored dichotomously for each choice, yielding the possibility of full or partial credit for the whole item.
- ***Multiple-choice items***: these items required students to circle a letter to indicate one choice among four or five alternatives, each of which might be a number, a word, a phrase or a sentence. They were scored dichotomously.

PISA 2003 was designed to yield group-level information in a broad range of content. The PISA assessment of mathematics included material allowing for a total of 210 minutes of assessment time. The reading, science and problem-solving assessments each included 60 minutes of assessment time. Each student, however, sat assessments lasting a total of 120 minutes.

In order to cover the intended broad range of content while meeting the limit of 120 minutes of individual assessment time, the assessment in each domain was divided into clusters, organised into thirteen booklets. There were seven 30-minute mathematics clusters, two 30-minute clusters for each of reading, science and problem solving. In PISA 2003, every student answered mathematics items, and over half the students answered items on reading, science and problem solving.

This assessment design was balanced so that each item cluster appeared four times, once in each of four possible locations in a booklet. Further, each cluster appeared once with each other cluster. The final design, therefore, ensured that a representative sample responded to each cluster of items.

For further information on the development of the PISA assessment instruments and the PISA assessment design, see the *PISA 2003 Technical Report* (OECD, forthcoming).

Annex A7: Reliability of the marking of open-ended items

The process of marking open-ended items was an important step in ensuring the quality and comparability of results from PISA.

Detailed guidelines contributed to a marking process that was accurate and consistent across countries. The marking guidelines consisted of marking manuals, training materials for recruiting markers, and workshop materials used for the training of national markers. Before national training, the PISA Consortium organised training sessions to present the material and train the marking co-ordinators from the participating countries. The latter were then responsible for training their national markers.

For each assessment item, the relevant marking manual described the aim of the question and how to code students' responses to each item. This description included the credit labels – full credit, partial credit or no credit – attached to the possible categories of responses. PISA 2003 also included a system of double-digit coding for the mathematics and science items in which the first digit represented the score and the second digit represented different strategies or approaches that students used to solve the problem. The second digit generated national profiles of student strategies and misconceptions. By way of illustration, the marking manuals also included real examples of students' responses (drawn from the Field Trial) accompanied by a rationale for their classification.

In each country, a sub-sample of assessment booklets was marked independently by four markers and examined by the PISA Consortium. In order to examine the consistency of this marking process in more detail within each country and to estimate the magnitude of the variance components associated with the use of markers, the PISA Consortium conducted an inter-marker reliability study on the sub-sample of assessment booklets. Homogeneity analysis was applied to the national sets of multiple marking and compared with the results of the Field Trial. For details see the *PISA 2003 Technical Report* (OECD, forthcoming).

At the between-country level, an inter-country reliability study was carried out on a sub-set of items. The aim was to check whether the marking given by national markers was of equal severity in each country, both overall and for particular items. In this process, independent marking of the original booklets was undertaken by trained multilingual staff and compared to the ratings by the national markers in the various countries. The results showed that very consistent marks were achieved across countries. The average index of "agreement" in the inter-country reliability study was 92 per cent (out of 71 941 student responses that were independently scored by the international verifiers). "Agreement" meant both cases where the international verifier agreed with at least three of the national markers and cases where the verifier disagreed with the national markers, but the adjudication undertaken by the PISA Consortium's test developers concluded, after reviewing the translated student's answer, that the national markers had given the correct mark. Only 6 countries had rates of agreement lower than 90 per cent (with a minimum of 86 per cent in Spain [Catalonian region]). On average, marking was too harsh in 1.8 per cent of cases and too lenient in 3.1 per cent of cases. The highest per cent of too harsh codes (7.0 per cent) was observed for the science items in Portugal, and the highest per cent of too lenient marks (10.0 per cent) was observed for the science items in Indonesia. A full description of this process and the results can be found in the *PISA 2003 Technical Report* (OECD, forthcoming).

Annex A8: Comparison of results from the PISA 2000 and PISA 2003 assessments

The reading and science reporting scales used for PISA 2000 and PISA 2003 are directly comparable. The value of 500, for example, has the same meaning as it did in PISA 2000 – that is, the mean score in 2000 of the sampled students in the 27 OECD countries that participated in PISA 2000.

This is not the case, however, for mathematics. Mathematics, as the major domain, was the subject of major development work for PISA 2003, and the PISA 2003 mathematics assessment was much more comprehensive than the PISA 2000 mathematics assessment – the PISA 2000 assessment covered just two (*space and shape* and *change and relationships*) of the four areas that are covered in PISA 2003. Because of this broadening in the assessment it was deemed inappropriate to report the PISA 2003 mathematics scores on the same scale as the PISA 2000 mathematics scores.

The PISA 2000 and PISA 2003 assessments of mathematics, reading and science are linked assessments. That is, the sets of items used to assess each of mathematics, reading and science in PISA 2000 and the sets of items used to assess each of mathematics, reading and science in PISA 2003 include a subset of items common to both sets. For mathematics there were 20 items that were used in both assessments, in reading there were 28 items used in both assessments and for science 25 items were used in both assessments. These common items are referred to as link items.

To establish common reporting metrics for PISA 2000 and PISA 2003 the difficulty of these link items, on the two assessment occasions, was compared. Using procedures that are detailed in the *PISA 2003 Technical Report* (OECD, forthcoming), the comparison of the item difficulties on the two occasions was used to determine a score transformation that allows the reporting of the data from the two assessments on a common scale. The change in the difficulty of each of the individual link items is used in determining the transformation.

As each item provides slightly different information about the link transformation it follows that the chosen sample of link items will influence the estimated transformation. This means that if an alternative set of link items had been chosen the resulting transformation would be slightly different. The consequence is an uncertainty in the transformation due to the sampling of the link items, just as there is an uncertainty in values such as country means due to the use of a sample of students.

The uncertainty that results from the link-item sampling is referred to as linking error and this error must be taken into account when making certain comparisons between PISA 2000 and PISA 2003 results. Just as with the error that is introduced through the process of sampling students, the exact magnitude of this linking error can only be estimated. As with sampling errors, the likely range of magnitude for the errors is represented as a standard error. The standard error of linking for the reading scale is 3.74, for the science scale is 3.02, for the mathematics/space and shape scale is 6.01 and for the mathematics/change and relationships scale is 4.84.

Annex B

DATA TABLES

Table 2.1a
Percentage of students at each level of proficiency on the mathematics/space and shape scale

		Proficiency levels													
		Below Level 1 (below 358 score points)		Level 1 (from 358 to 420 score points)		Level 2 (from 421 to 482 score points)		Level 3 (from 483 to 544 score points)		Level 4 (from 545 to 606 score points)		Level 5 (from 607 to 668 score points)		Level 6 (above 668 score points)	
		%	S.E.	%	S.E.	%	S.E.	%	S.E.	%	S.E.	%	S.E.	%	S.E.
OECD countries	Australia	6.1	(0.5)	10.8	(0.6)	18.4	(0.5)	23.0	(0.7)	21.2	(0.7)	13.2	(0.6)	7.3	(0.5)
	Austria	8.0	(0.7)	12.0	(0.8)	18.6	(0.8)	21.4	(0.7)	19.1	(0.9)	12.3	(0.9)	8.5	(0.7)
	Belgium	6.6	(0.5)	10.4	(0.5)	16.7	(0.5)	20.3	(0.7)	20.0	(0.9)	15.7	(0.8)	10.2	(0.5)
	Canada	4.7	(0.4)	10.7	(0.6)	20.4	(0.6)	25.0	(0.5)	21.4	(0.5)	12.1	(0.5)	5.6	(0.4)
	Czech Republic	8.1	(0.9)	10.6	(0.7)	17.0	(0.7)	19.3	(0.7)	18.9	(0.8)	14.4	(0.8)	11.7	(0.8)
	Denmark	7.1	(0.6)	11.2	(0.7)	19.5	(0.7)	23.8	(0.8)	20.0	(0.7)	12.5	(0.7)	5.9	(0.5)
	Finland	2.5	(0.3)	7.3	(0.5)	17.0	(0.7)	25.5	(0.8)	24.6	(0.8)	15.2	(0.6)	7.9	(0.6)
	France	7.7	(0.8)	12.0	(0.7)	19.6	(0.9)	23.4	(1.1)	20.0	(0.8)	12.0	(0.8)	5.1	(0.5)
	Germany	11.1	(0.8)	13.3	(1.0)	18.6	(0.9)	21.2	(0.9)	18.4	(0.8)	11.4	(0.7)	6.0	(0.4)
	Greece	21.3	(1.2)	21.7	(1.0)	24.4	(1.0)	18.7	(0.9)	9.6	(0.7)	3.6	(0.5)	0.8	(0.3)
	Hungary	13.1	(1.0)	17.3	(0.8)	21.8	(0.8)	20.5	(0.7)	14.8	(0.9)	8.0	(0.7)	4.5	(0.6)
	Iceland	6.5	(0.6)	12.1	(0.7)	21.6	(0.8)	26.0	(1.1)	20.5	(0.8)	10.0	(0.6)	3.3	(0.4)
	Ireland	10.7	(0.8)	16.9	(1.1)	25.4	(0.9)	23.0	(1.0)	15.4	(0.8)	6.8	(0.6)	1.8	(0.2)
	Italy	15.1	(1.0)	16.8	(0.9)	22.0	(0.7)	21.1	(0.7)	14.5	(0.6)	7.2	(0.5)	3.3	(0.3)
	Japan	4.2	(0.7)	7.4	(0.8)	13.9	(0.7)	20.0	(0.8)	21.9	(1.0)	18.2	(0.9)	14.3	(1.2)
	Korea	4.8	(0.5)	8.4	(0.6)	14.7	(0.9)	19.7	(0.9)	19.9	(1.0)	16.5	(0.8)	16.0	(1.3)
	Luxembourg	9.5	(0.5)	15.6	(0.6)	23.0	(0.9)	22.6	(1.1)	17.1	(0.7)	8.5	(0.8)	3.6	(0.4)
	Mexico	39.1	(1.6)	27.8	(0.8)	20.6	(0.9)	9.4	(0.7)	2.5	(0.4)	0.5	(0.1)	0.0	(0.0)
	Netherlands	3.7	(0.7)	10.1	(0.8)	18.6	(1.1)	24.9	(1.2)	21.9	(1.1)	14.6	(0.8)	6.2	(0.6)
	New Zealand	5.8	(0.5)	10.8	(0.7)	18.1	(0.8)	21.8	(0.8)	20.7	(0.9)	14.4	(0.7)	8.5	(0.5)
	Norway	11.5	(0.6)	16.1	(0.6)	22.2	(0.9)	22.3	(0.8)	16.4	(0.7)	8.2	(0.5)	3.3	(0.3)
	Poland	10.7	(0.8)	14.9	(0.7)	22.0	(0.9)	22.1	(0.9)	16.4	(0.7)	8.8	(0.5)	5.0	(0.5)
	Portugal	16.4	(1.4)	21.5	(0.8)	26.0	(1.0)	20.2	(1.0)	10.9	(0.7)	4.1	(0.4)	0.9	(0.2)
	Slovak Republic	10.2	(0.9)	13.4	(0.8)	19.0	(0.8)	20.2	(0.8)	17.4	(0.8)	11.6	(0.7)	8.2	(0.7)
	Spain	10.1	(0.8)	16.7	(0.8)	25.5	(0.8)	24.7	(0.8)	15.3	(0.8)	6.0	(0.5)	1.6	(0.3)
	Sweden	7.9	(0.6)	13.4	(0.6)	22.1	(0.8)	24.2	(1.0)	18.2	(0.8)	10.0	(0.6)	4.2	(0.4)
	Switzerland	5.4	(0.5)	8.6	(0.5)	15.7	(0.8)	21.4	(0.9)	21.4	(0.9)	15.9	(0.7)	11.7	(1.1)
	Turkey	28.6	(1.9)	26.0	(1.2)	22.3	(1.2)	12.7	(1.1)	5.8	(1.0)	2.5	(0.7)	2.1	(0.9)
	United States	12.1	(0.8)	18.2	(1.1)	24.7	(1.1)	22.0	(0.9)	14.2	(0.7)	6.5	(0.5)	2.3	(0.3)
	OECD total	*12.8*	*(0.3)*	*15.7*	*(0.3)*	*20.8*	*(0.3)*	*20.5*	*(0.3)*	*15.6*	*(0.2)*	*9.3*	*(0.2)*	*5.2*	*(0.2)*
	OECD average	*10.6*	*(0.2)*	*14.2*	*(0.2)*	*20.4*	*(0.1)*	*21.5*	*(0.2)*	*17.2*	*(0.1)*	*10.4*	*(0.1)*	*5.8*	*(0.1)*
Partner countries	Brazil	54.8	(1.7)	22.7	(1.1)	13.6	(0.9)	6.2	(0.8)	2.0	(0.4)	0.6	(0.2)	0.1	(0.1)
	Hong Kong-China	4.1	(0.7)	7.0	(0.9)	13.2	(1.2)	18.7	(0.9)	21.5	(1.1)	19.9	(0.9)	15.6	(1.0)
	Indonesia	49.7	(1.7)	25.9	(1.2)	15.5	(1.0)	6.6	(0.7)	1.8	(0.4)	0.4	(0.1)	0.1	(0.0)
	Latvia	10.7	(0.9)	15.1	(1.0)	22.4	(0.9)	23.3	(1.1)	16.8	(0.9)	8.2	(0.7)	3.5	(0.5)
	Liechtenstein	5.7	(1.4)	8.1	(1.7)	14.9	(2.8)	21.5	(3.5)	23.2	(4.2)	16.5	(2.6)	10.1	(1.8)
	Macao-China	4.0	(0.7)	9.8	(1.5)	17.6	(2.0)	24.5	(2.0)	23.2	(1.7)	13.7	(1.3)	7.2	(0.9)
	Russian Federation	14.9	(1.0)	16.5	(0.8)	21.9	(0.9)	20.4	(0.8)	14.2	(0.9)	7.7	(0.7)	4.3	(0.6)
	Serbia	21.8	(1.3)	24.4	(1.0)	24.5	(0.8)	16.9	(1.0)	8.6	(0.9)	2.8	(0.5)	0.9	(0.2)
	Thailand	23.4	(1.2)	26.8	(0.9)	24.7	(1.1)	15.4	(0.9)	7.0	(0.6)	2.2	(0.4)	0.5	(0.2)
	Tunisia	49.7	(1.3)	26.0	(1.1)	15.5	(0.7)	6.3	(0.5)	2.1	(0.4)	0.5	(0.1)	0.0	a
	Uruguay	29.3	(1.2)	23.3	(0.9)	22.9	(0.9)	15.2	(0.8)	6.7	(0.5)	2.2	(0.4)	0.4	(0.1)
	United Kingdom[1]	m	m	m	m	m	m	m	m	m	m	m	m	m	m

1. Response rate too low to ensure comparability (see Annex A3).

Table 2.1b

Percentage of students at each level of proficiency on the mathematics/space and shape scale, by gender

Males – Proficiency levels

		Below Level 1 (below 358 score points)		Level 1 (from 358 to 420 score points)		Level 2 (from 421 to 482 score points)		Level 3 (from 483 to 544 score points)		Level 4 (from 545 to 606 score points)		Level 5 (from 607 to 668 score points)		Level 6 (above 668 score points)	
		%	S.E.	%	S.E.	%	S.E.	%	S.E.	%	S.E.	%	S.E.	%	S.E.
OECD countries	Australia	5.8	(0.7)	10.5	(0.8)	17.4	(0.8)	22.0	(1.1)	21.4	(1.0)	13.8	(1.0)	9.0	(0.9)
	Austria	7.6	(0.8)	11.4	(0.8)	17.1	(1.0)	20.5	(1.2)	18.8	(1.3)	13.8	(1.4)	10.7	(1.1)
	Belgium	6.3	(0.7)	9.8	(0.7)	15.4	(0.8)	19.4	(1.0)	19.7	(1.2)	16.8	(1.1)	12.6	(0.8)
	Canada	4.4	(0.4)	9.4	(0.5)	17.8	(1.0)	22.9	(0.9)	22.7	(0.9)	14.9	(0.7)	7.8	(0.7)
	Czech Republic	6.1	(0.8)	9.6	(1.0)	15.6	(1.1)	18.9	(0.9)	19.3	(1.0)	16.0	(0.9)	14.5	(1.2)
	Denmark	6.0	(0.7)	10.1	(0.9)	18.2	(1.2)	24.1	(1.5)	21.2	(1.3)	13.6	(1.1)	6.8	(0.7)
	Finland	2.8	(0.5)	7.6	(0.6)	16.3	(0.8)	24.9	(1.3)	24.3	(0.9)	15.4	(0.7)	8.8	(0.9)
	France	7.6	(1.1)	10.7	(1.0)	17.7	(1.0)	22.7	(1.3)	20.4	(1.2)	14.0	(1.2)	6.8	(0.9)
	Germany	10.6	(1.0)	13.2	(1.2)	17.2	(1.0)	20.8	(1.5)	18.5	(1.1)	12.7	(1.0)	7.0	(0.7)
	Greece	19.5	(1.4)	19.8	(1.4)	23.3	(1.4)	19.9	(1.5)	11.5	(1.3)	4.6	(0.8)	1.3	(0.5)
	Hungary	11.7	(1.0)	16.4	(1.2)	21.4	(1.4)	20.8	(1.5)	15.5	(1.5)	8.7	(1.0)	5.5	(0.8)
	Iceland	8.3	(1.0)	13.2	(1.1)	21.5	(1.5)	25.4	(1.4)	19.0	(1.1)	9.3	(0.8)	3.3	(0.6)
	Ireland	8.6	(0.9)	14.8	(1.3)	24.4	(1.1)	24.0	(1.2)	17.5	(1.1)	8.3	(1.0)	2.5	(0.4)
	Italy	14.3	(1.4)	15.8	(1.2)	20.2	(1.1)	20.8	(1.0)	15.6	(0.9)	8.7	(0.8)	4.7	(0.4)
	Japan	4.5	(0.8)	7.8	(0.9)	13.8	(1.0)	18.3	(1.2)	20.4	(1.5)	18.0	(1.2)	17.3	(2.0)
	Korea	4.3	(0.7)	7.4	(0.8)	13.3	(1.3)	18.2	(1.0)	20.4	(1.0)	17.8	(1.3)	18.6	(1.6)
	Luxembourg	7.8	(0.7)	14.3	(1.0)	20.4	(1.2)	22.2	(1.6)	19.4	(1.2)	10.7	(1.2)	5.3	(0.7)
	Mexico	36.1	(2.0)	27.1	(1.4)	21.5	(1.3)	11.4	(1.0)	3.3	(0.6)	0.6	(0.2)	0.1	(0.0)
	Netherlands	3.3	(0.8)	9.6	(1.2)	17.8	(1.2)	25.5	(1.6)	22.2	(1.6)	14.8	(1.2)	6.9	(0.7)
	New Zealand	5.4	(0.5)	10.2	(0.8)	16.8	(1.1)	20.4	(0.9)	21.0	(1.4)	15.7	(1.1)	10.6	(0.7)
	Norway	11.4	(0.9)	15.6	(0.9)	21.9	(1.1)	21.5	(1.0)	16.7	(0.9)	8.8	(0.7)	4.2	(0.6)
	Poland	10.7	(1.2)	14.0	(1.0)	20.3	(1.3)	21.9	(1.1)	16.8	(1.2)	10.0	(0.8)	6.5	(0.8)
	Portugal	15.9	(1.8)	19.3	(1.0)	24.5	(1.4)	20.8	(1.4)	12.8	(1.1)	5.5	(0.7)	1.2	(0.3)
	Slovak Republic	8.3	(0.9)	11.3	(1.0)	17.4	(1.3)	20.1	(0.9)	18.5	(1.0)	13.4	(1.1)	11.1	(1.0)
	Spain	9.5	(0.9)	15.0	(1.0)	23.6	(1.4)	24.6	(1.2)	17.2	(1.1)	8.0	(0.7)	2.2	(0.5)
	Sweden	7.5	(0.8)	12.5	(1.0)	21.4	(1.3)	24.4	(1.4)	18.7	(1.3)	10.4	(0.8)	5.2	(0.6)
	Switzerland	4.5	(0.5)	7.5	(0.9)	14.3	(1.2)	20.6	(1.3)	21.4	(1.5)	17.1	(1.2)	14.6	(1.6)
	Turkey	27.8	(2.3)	24.1	(1.4)	22.3	(1.5)	13.7	(1.4)	6.6	(1.2)	2.9	(0.8)	2.6	(1.2)
	United States	11.2	(1.0)	16.9	(1.1)	24.2	(1.5)	22.1	(1.3)	14.7	(1.0)	7.8	(0.7)	3.2	(0.5)
	OECD total	*12.0*	*(0.4)*	*14.8*	*(0.4)*	*20.0*	*(0.5)*	*20.3*	*(0.4)*	*16.0*	*(0.3)*	*10.3*	*(0.2)*	*6.6*	*(0.3)*
	OECD average	*9.8*	*(0.2)*	*13.2*	*(0.2)*	*19.2*	*(0.2)*	*21.2*	*(0.2)*	*17.8*	*(0.2)*	*11.5*	*(0.1)*	*7.3*	*(0.1)*
Partner countries	Brazil	52.3	(2.1)	22.1	(1.2)	14.4	(1.3)	7.3	(1.3)	2.7	(0.6)	1.0	(0.3)	0.3	(0.2)
	Hong Kong-China	5.0	(1.0)	6.9	(1.1)	12.6	(1.4)	18.0	(1.1)	20.1	(1.4)	20.0	(1.3)	17.4	(1.6)
	Indonesia	45.7	(2.0)	27.2	(1.9)	17.2	(1.3)	7.2	(0.7)	2.1	(0.4)	0.5	(0.2)	0.1	(0.1)
	Latvia	10.6	(1.4)	13.7	(1.2)	21.5	(1.6)	22.9	(1.7)	17.1	(1.3)	9.5	(1.1)	4.8	(0.8)
	Liechtenstein	5.8	(1.8)	4.5	(2.0)	12.1	(3.4)	21.1	(3.2)	22.6	(4.6)	19.2	(4.8)	14.7	(2.9)
	Macao-China	3.4	(1.0)	9.5	(1.9)	15.5	(1.9)	21.4	(2.6)	24.2	(2.3)	16.5	(1.9)	9.5	(1.7)
	Russian Federation	13.4	(1.3)	15.3	(1.0)	21.0	(1.1)	20.6	(1.2)	14.9	(1.1)	9.1	(1.1)	5.7	(0.8)
	Serbia	22.4	(1.5)	24.6	(1.3)	22.4	(1.1)	16.5	(1.1)	9.3	(1.1)	3.5	(0.7)	1.3	(0.3)
	Thailand	23.5	(1.7)	25.6	(1.7)	24.0	(1.5)	15.9	(1.4)	7.7	(0.9)	2.6	(0.5)	0.6	(0.3)
	Tunisia	46.0	(1.5)	27.0	(1.3)	16.6	(1.0)	7.2	(0.7)	2.6	(0.5)	0.7	(0.2)	0.0	a
	Uruguay	26.1	(1.3)	22.6	(1.5)	23.0	(1.9)	16.8	(1.2)	8.0	(0.8)	2.9	(0.6)	0.8	(0.3)
	United Kingdom[1]	m	m	m	m	m	m	m	m	m	m	m	m	m	m

Females – Proficiency levels

		Below Level 1 (below 358 score points)		Level 1 (from 358 to 420 score points)		Level 2 (from 421 to 482 score points)		Level 3 (from 483 to 544 score points)		Level 4 (from 545 to 606 score points)		Level 5 (from 607 to 668 score points)		Level 6 (above 668 score points)	
		%	S.E.	%	S.E.	%	S.E.	%	S.E.	%	S.E.	%	S.E.	%	S.E.
OECD countries	Australia	6.4	(0.7)	11.0	(0.7)	19.4	(0.9)	24.1	(1.0)	20.9	(1.1)	12.6	(0.7)	5.6	(0.5)
	Austria	8.4	(1.2)	12.7	(1.4)	20.1	(1.2)	22.4	(1.1)	19.3	(1.1)	10.9	(1.2)	6.3	(0.9)
	Belgium	6.9	(0.8)	11.1	(0.7)	18.2	(0.8)	21.4	(0.9)	20.3	(1.0)	14.4	(0.9)	7.6	(0.6)
	Canada	4.9	(0.4)	11.1	(0.8)	21.8	(0.9)	26.7	(0.7)	20.9	(0.7)	10.3	(0.5)	4.2	(0.4)
	Czech Republic	10.1	(1.3)	11.7	(1.1)	18.5	(1.0)	19.7	(1.1)	18.5	(1.6)	12.7	(1.2)	8.8	(0.8)
	Denmark	8.2	(1.0)	12.3	(0.9)	20.7	(1.5)	23.4	(1.3)	18.8	(1.2)	11.5	(0.8)	5.0	(0.6)
	Finland	2.2	(0.4)	6.9	(0.6)	17.8	(0.9)	26.1	(0.9)	24.9	(1.1)	14.9	(0.9)	7.1	(0.6)
	France	7.9	(0.9)	13.2	(1.0)	21.4	(1.2)	24.1	(1.4)	19.6	(1.1)	10.3	(0.9)	3.6	(0.5)
	Germany	11.3	(1.0)	13.4	(1.1)	20.1	(1.2)	21.8	(1.1)	18.3	(1.2)	10.2	(1.0)	5.0	(0.5)
	Greece	22.9	(1.4)	23.3	(1.4)	25.4	(1.3)	17.5	(1.3)	7.8	(0.9)	2.6	(0.5)	0.4	(0.1)
	Hungary	14.6	(1.3)	18.2	(1.1)	22.2	(1.6)	20.2	(1.5)	14.1	(1.0)	7.3	(0.9)	3.5	(0.5)
	Iceland	4.6	(0.6)	10.8	(1.4)	21.7	(1.4)	26.7	(1.4)	22.1	(1.1)	10.7	(0.9)	3.4	(0.5)
	Ireland	13.0	(1.2)	19.0	(1.5)	26.4	(1.4)	22.1	(1.4)	13.3	(1.2)	5.2	(0.8)	1.1	(0.3)
	Italy	15.8	(1.4)	17.8	(1.2)	23.7	(1.1)	21.3	(0.9)	13.6	(0.9)	5.8	(0.7)	1.9	(0.3)
	Japan	3.9	(0.9)	7.1	(1.0)	14.1	(1.1)	21.7	(1.2)	23.2	(1.1)	18.5	(1.2)	11.5	(0.9)
	Korea	5.5	(0.8)	9.7	(1.1)	16.8	(1.3)	22.0	(1.3)	19.2	(1.5)	14.7	(1.2)	12.2	(1.6)
	Luxembourg	11.2	(0.7)	17.0	(1.2)	25.6	(1.1)	23.0	(1.3)	14.8	(1.1)	6.4	(0.8)	2.0	(0.4)
	Mexico	41.9	(1.8)	28.5	(1.3)	19.8	(1.3)	7.6	(0.9)	1.8	(0.3)	0.3	(0.1)	0.0	(0.0)
	Netherlands	4.2	(0.9)	10.7	(1.1)	19.4	(1.4)	24.4	(2.1)	21.7	(1.8)	14.3	(1.1)	5.5	(0.6)
	New Zealand	6.2	(0.8)	11.4	(1.0)	19.5	(1.2)	23.1	(1.1)	20.3	(1.1)	13.1	(0.9)	6.3	(0.6)
	Norway	11.6	(1.0)	16.6	(1.1)	22.6	(1.6)	23.1	(1.1)	16.1	(1.1)	7.5	(0.7)	2.4	(0.5)
	Poland	10.7	(0.9)	15.9	(0.9)	23.7	(1.4)	22.4	(1.1)	16.1	(1.1)	7.7	(0.7)	3.5	(0.5)
	Portugal	16.9	(1.4)	23.5	(1.2)	27.4	(1.2)	19.7	(1.0)	9.1	(0.9)	2.8	(0.4)	0.7	(0.3)
	Slovak Republic	12.1	(1.1)	15.6	(0.9)	20.7	(0.9)	20.4	(1.3)	16.3	(1.1)	9.8	(0.8)	5.2	(0.6)
	Spain	10.7	(0.8)	18.4	(1.0)	27.3	(1.1)	24.9	(1.0)	13.5	(0.9)	4.2	(0.5)	1.1	(0.3)
	Sweden	8.3	(1.0)	14.4	(0.9)	22.7	(1.2)	24.1	(1.4)	17.8	(1.2)	9.5	(0.7)	3.2	(0.6)
	Switzerland	6.4	(0.8)	9.7	(0.9)	17.2	(1.5)	22.2	(1.1)	21.4	(1.1)	14.6	(1.2)	8.6	(1.0)
	Turkey	29.5	(2.2)	28.3	(1.7)	22.2	(1.7)	11.6	(1.3)	4.9	(1.1)	2.1	(0.7)	1.5	(0.7)
	United States	13.1	(1.0)	19.6	(1.3)	25.2	(1.4)	21.9	(1.6)	13.6	(0.8)	5.2	(0.8)	1.4	(0.3)
	OECD total	*13.6*	*(0.4)*	*16.7*	*(0.4)*	*21.6*	*(0.3)*	*20.7*	*(0.4)*	*15.2*	*(0.3)*	*8.3*	*(0.3)*	*3.9*	*(0.2)*
	OECD average	*11.3*	*(0.2)*	*15.2*	*(0.2)*	*21.5*	*(0.3)*	*21.8*	*(0.2)*	*16.6*	*(0.2)*	*9.3*	*(0.2)*	*4.3*	*(0.1)*
Partner countries	Brazil	57.0	(1.9)	23.1	(1.7)	12.9	(1.3)	5.3	(0.7)	1.3	(0.4)	0.4	(0.3)	0.0	a
	Hong Kong-China	3.2	(0.6)	7.1	(1.1)	13.7	(1.5)	19.5	(1.3)	22.9	(1.6)	19.8	(1.5)	13.8	(1.2)
	Indonesia	53.7	(2.0)	24.6	(1.2)	13.9	(1.2)	5.9	(0.9)	1.6	(0.5)	0.3	(0.1)	0.0	(0.0)
	Latvia	10.9	(1.0)	16.3	(1.5)	23.3	(1.2)	23.8	(1.7)	16.4	(1.1)	7.0	(0.9)	2.3	(0.5)
	Liechtenstein	5.6	(2.4)	11.8	(3.5)	17.9	(4.2)	21.9	(6.8)	23.8	(5.4)	13.6	(3.4)	5.3	(2.1)
	Macao-China	4.6	(1.0)	10.0	(2.2)	19.6	(3.1)	27.5	(2.9)	22.1	(2.3)	11.0	(1.5)	5.1	(1.5)
	Russian Federation	16.4	(1.2)	17.7	(1.1)	22.9	(1.3)	20.3	(1.0)	13.5	(1.0)	6.4	(0.8)	2.9	(0.7)
	Serbia	21.3	(1.8)	24.2	(1.4)	26.6	(1.1)	17.4	(1.3)	7.9	(1.0)	2.2	(0.6)	0.6	(0.2)
	Thailand	23.2	(1.4)	27.7	(1.3)	25.4	(1.3)	15.0	(1.2)	6.4	(0.9)	1.9	(0.5)	0.4	(0.2)
	Tunisia	53.2	(1.7)	25.0	(1.6)	14.4	(1.1)	5.5	(0.8)	1.6	(0.4)	0.3	(0.1)	0.0	a
	Uruguay	32.4	(1.5)	23.9	(1.2)	22.9	(1.3)	13.6	(1.0)	5.5	(0.7)	1.5	(0.4)	0.1	(0.1)
	United Kingdom[1]	m	m	m	m	m	m	m	m	m	m	m	m	m	m

1. Response rate too low to ensure comparability (see Annex A3).

Table 2.1c

Mean score, variation and gender differences in student performance on the mathematics/space and shape scale in PISA 2003

		All students				Gender differences					
		Mean score		Standard deviation		Males		Females		Difference (M-F)	
		Mean	S.E.	S.D.	S.E.	Mean score	S.E.	Mean score	S.E.	Score dif.	S.E.
OECD countries	Australia	521	(2.3)	104	(1.7)	526	(3.2)	515	(2.9)	**12**	(3.9)
	Austria	515	(3.5)	112	(1.7)	525	(4.4)	506	(4.3)	**19**	(5.2)
	Belgium	530	(2.3)	111	(1.4)	538	(3.2)	520	(3.3)	**18**	(4.6)
	Canada	518	(1.8)	95	(0.9)	530	(2.1)	511	(2.2)	**20**	(2.5)
	Czech Republic	527	(4.1)	119	(2.3)	542	(4.8)	512	(5.1)	**30**	(5.7)
	Denmark	512	(2.8)	103	(1.6)	521	(3.4)	504	(3.3)	**16**	(3.7)
	Finland	539	(2.0)	92	(1.2)	540	(2.6)	538	(2.4)	2	(3.0)
	France	508	(3.0)	102	(2.0)	517	(4.3)	499	(3.2)	**18**	(4.7)
	Germany	500	(3.3)	112	(1.9)	506	(4.0)	494	(4.0)	**11**	(4.7)
	Greece	437	(3.8)	100	(1.6)	447	(4.7)	428	(3.8)	**19**	(4.0)
	Hungary	479	(3.3)	109	(2.2)	486	(3.8)	471	(3.9)	**15**	(4.0)
	Iceland	504	(1.5)	94	(1.5)	496	(2.4)	511	(2.3)	**–15**	(3.7)
	Ireland	476	(2.4)	94	(1.5)	489	(3.0)	463	(3.4)	**25**	(4.3)
	Italy	470	(3.1)	109	(1.8)	480	(4.7)	462	(4.1)	**18**	(6.3)
	Japan	553	(4.3)	110	(2.9)	558	(6.3)	549	(4.2)	9	(6.3)
	Korea	552	(3.8)	117	(2.5)	563	(5.1)	536	(6.2)	**27**	(8.0)
	Luxembourg	488	(1.4)	100	(1.2)	503	(2.2)	474	(2.0)	**28**	(3.3)
	Mexico	382	(3.2)	87	(1.4)	390	(4.1)	374	(3.5)	**16**	(3.8)
	Netherlands	526	(2.9)	94	(2.3)	530	(3.7)	522	(3.4)	8	(4.3)
	New Zealand	525	(2.3)	106	(1.3)	534	(2.7)	516	(3.3)	**18**	(3.9)
	Norway	483	(2.5)	103	(1.3)	486	(3.1)	479	(3.5)	7	(4.3)
	Poland	490	(2.7)	107	(1.9)	497	(3.2)	484	(3.3)	**13**	(3.7)
	Portugal	450	(3.4)	93	(1.7)	458	(4.2)	443	(3.5)	**15**	(3.5)
	Slovak Republic	505	(4.0)	117	(2.3)	522	(4.7)	487	(4.1)	**35**	(4.5)
	Spain	476	(2.6)	92	(1.4)	486	(3.5)	467	(2.4)	**18**	(3.0)
	Sweden	498	(2.6)	100	(1.7)	503	(3.0)	493	(3.2)	**10**	(3.5)
	Switzerland	540	(3.5)	110	(2.1)	552	(5.3)	526	(3.7)	**25**	(5.6)
	Turkey	417	(6.3)	102	(5.1)	423	(7.6)	411	(6.2)	**12**	(6.0)
	United States	472	(2.8)	97	(1.4)	480	(3.3)	464	(3.1)	**15**	(3.2)
	OECD total	*486*	*(1.0)*	*112*	*(0.7)*	*494*	*(1.4)*	*478*	*(1.3)*	***16***	*(1.6)*
	OECD average	*496*	*(0.6)*	*110*	*(0.4)*	*505*	*(0.8)*	*488*	*(0.8)*	***17***	*(0.9)*
Partner countries	Brazil	350	(4.1)	96	(2.3)	358	(5.2)	343	(4.0)	**15**	(4.1)
	Hong Kong-China	558	(4.8)	111	(2.9)	560	(6.8)	556	(5.0)	4	(6.8)
	Indonesia	361	(3.7)	88	(1.9)	369	(3.7)	353	(4.2)	**16**	(2.9)
	Latvia	486	(4.0)	102	(1.7)	494	(5.2)	480	(3.9)	**14**	(4.2)
	Liechtenstein	538	(4.6)	107	(4.3)	557	(7.9)	518	(7.1)	**39**	(12.1)
	Macao-China	528	(3.3)	97	(3.3)	540	(5.1)	517	(4.3)	**23**	(6.8)
	Russian Federation	474	(4.7)	112	(2.0)	485	(5.8)	464	(5.0)	**21**	(5.0)
	Serbia	432	(3.9)	96	(1.8)	434	(4.3)	431	(4.9)	3	(4.9)
	Thailand	424	(3.3)	90	(1.8)	426	(4.3)	422	(3.8)	5	(4.7)
	Tunisia	359	(2.6)	92	(1.7)	367	(2.8)	351	(3.2)	**16**	(3.0)
	Uruguay	412	(3.0)	101	(1.7)	423	(3.6)	402	(3.4)	**21**	(3.6)
	United Kingdom[1]	m	m	m	m	m	m	m	m	m	m

		Percentiles											
		5th		10th		25th		75th		90th		95th	
		Score	S.E.	Score	S.E.	Score	S.E.	Score	S.E.	Score	S.E.	Score	S.E.
OECD countries	Australia	347	(4.7)	385	(3.8)	450	(3.3)	592	(2.6)	653	(3.1)	687	(3.8)
	Austria	334	(5.5)	371	(5.6)	438	(4.4)	592	(3.8)	661	(5.0)	698	(6.8)
	Belgium	342	(4.9)	382	(4.2)	453	(3.4)	610	(3.1)	670	(2.5)	704	(2.4)
	Canada	361	(3.5)	395	(2.6)	453	(2.0)	583	(2.4)	640	(2.7)	674	(2.8)
	Czech Republic	330	(7.4)	373	(6.9)	445	(4.7)	611	(4.8)	681	(5.2)	721	(5.1)
	Denmark	339	(6.5)	380	(5.5)	444	(3.9)	584	(3.3)	644	(3.9)	677	(4.2)
	Finland	386	(4.1)	421	(3.0)	477	(2.4)	602	(2.4)	658	(3.5)	690	(3.6)
	France	333	(7.6)	374	(5.8)	439	(3.9)	579	(3.4)	638	(4.3)	670	(5.1)
	Germany	310	(5.3)	350	(4.7)	422	(5.0)	579	(4.0)	641	(4.4)	679	(4.9)
	Greece	273	(5.1)	310	(4.4)	371	(4.4)	505	(4.3)	565	(5.1)	601	(6.3)
	Hungary	304	(5.8)	341	(5.0)	404	(3.7)	554	(4.2)	623	(6.4)	665	(6.2)
	Iceland	344	(5.1)	380	(3.5)	441	(2.6)	569	(2.3)	622	(3.0)	654	(3.7)
	Ireland	324	(4.4)	354	(3.6)	412	(3.3)	542	(2.9)	599	(4.5)	632	(4.2)
	Italy	287	(6.2)	329	(5.9)	398	(4.3)	545	(3.3)	610	(3.4)	648	(4.3)
	Japan	366	(6.7)	410	(6.8)	480	(5.1)	629	(4.8)	690	(6.0)	726	(7.6)
	Korea	360	(5.6)	401	(5.1)	472	(4.3)	634	(5.1)	701	(6.9)	742	(7.9)
	Luxembourg	323	(4.1)	360	(2.9)	420	(2.0)	557	(1.9)	618	(3.2)	653	(4.0)
	Mexico	240	(6.4)	269	(5.1)	322	(3.8)	441	(3.6)	494	(4.3)	525	(4.6)
	Netherlands	370	(5.9)	403	(5.5)	461	(4.9)	593	(3.5)	648	(3.5)	678	(4.6)
	New Zealand	350	(5.1)	388	(4.3)	451	(3.3)	600	(2.5)	660	(3.0)	695	(4.0)
	Norway	312	(4.5)	350	(4.0)	412	(2.9)	554	(3.5)	615	(3.9)	652	(3.7)
	Poland	318	(5.0)	355	(4.2)	418	(3.5)	562	(3.4)	628	(3.9)	669	(5.6)
	Portugal	298	(5.7)	331	(5.1)	387	(4.7)	513	(3.6)	572	(4.1)	607	(4.2)
	Slovak Republic	315	(6.4)	356	(6.2)	425	(5.5)	587	(4.2)	657	(4.4)	696	(5.8)
	Spain	324	(4.4)	358	(4.0)	415	(3.0)	539	(3.2)	595	(3.5)	626	(4.8)
	Sweden	334	(5.0)	371	(4.0)	432	(3.5)	566	(3.3)	627	(3.8)	661	(4.3)
	Switzerland	353	(5.8)	397	(5.6)	467	(3.9)	616	(4.6)	678	(5.7)	714	(6.0)
	Turkey	266	(6.0)	297	(5.3)	349	(4.7)	476	(8.0)	548	(14.0)	601	(22.5)
	United States	315	(4.8)	347	(4.2)	404	(3.6)	538	(3.4)	601	(3.6)	637	(4.2)
	OECD total	*304*	*(2.0)*	*342*	*(1.6)*	*408*	*(1.4)*	*563*	*(1.3)*	*632*	*(1.3)*	*672*	*(1.8)*
	OECD average	*315*	*(1.4)*	*354*	*(1.2)*	*421*	*(0.9)*	*572*	*(0.7)*	*639*	*(0.8)*	*677*	*(1.0)*
Partner countries	Brazil	198	(5.5)	229	(4.9)	284	(4.5)	412	(5.3)	475	(6.8)	513	(9.2)
	Hong Kong-China	367	(7.3)	412	(9.6)	485	(7.4)	638	(3.6)	697	(4.6)	729	(4.8)
	Indonesia	219	(5.0)	251	(4.2)	301	(3.9)	418	(5.1)	476	(6.1)	510	(6.6)
	Latvia	318	(6.7)	353	(5.0)	418	(4.6)	555	(4.4)	616	(5.6)	652	(6.3)
	Liechtenstein	354	(16.1)	394	(11.4)	469	(10.5)	613	(9.2)	669	(12.6)	706	(14.3)
	Macao-China	368	(9.5)	402	(10.1)	463	(6.4)	595	(4.7)	652	(7.2)	687	(8.7)
	Russian Federation	289	(6.0)	332	(5.5)	399	(4.9)	549	(5.9)	620	(6.6)	661	(7.5)
	Serbia	280	(4.4)	312	(3.7)	368	(4.3)	495	(4.7)	557	(6.4)	593	(6.0)
	Thailand	283	(4.8)	311	(3.7)	362	(3.3)	483	(4.1)	543	(5.3)	580	(6.8)
	Tunisia	208	(4.0)	242	(3.6)	298	(2.7)	418	(3.2)	476	(4.8)	513	(6.4)
	Uruguay	245	(3.7)	279	(4.5)	343	(4.2)	481	(3.6)	541	(4.2)	576	(6.2)
	United Kingdom[1]	m	m	m	m	m	m	m	m	m	m	m	m

Note: Values that are statistically significant are indicated in bold (see Annex A4).

1. Response rate too low to ensure comparability (see Annex A3).

Table 2.1d

Mean score, variation and gender differences in student performance on the mathematics/space and shape scale in PISA 2000

		All students				Gender differences					
		Mean score		Standard deviation		Males		Females		Difference (M-F)	
		Mean	**S.E.**	**S.D.**	**S.E.**	**Mean score**	**S.E.**	**Mean score**	**S.E.**	**Score dif.**	**S.E.**
OECD countries	Australia	520	(3.1)	101	(2.0)	523	(4.1)	516	(4.7)	8	(6.1)
	Austria	510	(2.8)	106	(1.7)	519	(4.2)	503	(4.4)	**16**	(6.5)
	Belgium	502	(3.1)	104	(1.7)	505	(3.8)	500	(4.0)	4	(4.9)
	Canada	515	(1.5)	99	(1.6)	520	(2.1)	512	(1.7)	**8**	(2.5)
	Czech Republic	510	(3.5)	123	(2.8)	517	(5.6)	504	(3.9)	13	(6.8)
	Denmark	526	(2.6)	88	(1.7)	531	(3.9)	521	(2.9)	**10**	(4.6)
	Finland	533	(2.0)	97	(1.7)	533	(3.5)	533	(2.7)	0	(4.7)
	France	501	(2.7)	96	(2.1)	506	(3.7)	497	(3.0)	**9**	(4.0)
	Germany	486	(3.1)	113	(2.8)	490	(4.3)	482	(5.0)	8	(7.0)
	Greece	450	(4.4)	109	(2.5)	454	(6.6)	448	(4.3)	6	(7.1)
	Hungary	478	(3.3)	99	(1.9)	480	(4.1)	477	(4.5)	3	(5.4)
	Iceland	519	(2.3)	83	(1.9)	517	(3.2)	521	(2.9)	–4	(4.0)
	Ireland	474	(3.2)	96	(1.7)	480	(4.6)	468	(4.1)	**12**	(5.7)
	Italy	455	(3.6)	106	(2.6)	460	(6.2)	450	(3.9)	10	(7.3)
	Japan	565	(5.1)	109	(2.5)	567	(7.0)	562	(5.8)	5	(7.9)
	Korea	538	(3.6)	117	(2.1)	549	(4.8)	525	(5.8)	**23**	(7.8)
	Luxembourg	449	(3.0)	110	(1.9)	455	(4.5)	442	(3.6)	**13**	(5.7)
	Mexico	400	(2.6)	85	(1.6)	404	(4.0)	396	(2.9)	8	(4.6)
	New Zealand	524	(4.0)	114	(2.5)	525	(5.4)	523	(5.7)	2	(7.6)
	Norway	490	(3.1)	104	(1.8)	495	(4.2)	487	(3.5)	8	(4.6)
	Poland	470	(5.5)	123	(3.0)	472	(7.9)	468	(6.5)	5	(9.4)
	Portugal	440	(3.5)	106	(1.7)	448	(4.4)	432	(4.8)	**16**	(5.9)
	Spain	473	(2.6)	96	(1.7)	480	(3.7)	467	(2.9)	**12**	(4.3)
	Sweden	510	(2.6)	106	(1.9)	513	(3.6)	507	(4.3)	7	(5.9)
	Switzerland	539	(3.6)	105	(1.9)	545	(4.8)	534	(4.3)	11	(5.5)
	United Kingdom	505	(2.6)	99	(1.7)	507	(3.7)	503	(3.3)	4	(4.7)
	United States	461	(4.9)	96	(2.3)	465	(5.9)	458	(5.6)	7	(5.9)
	OECD total	*486*	*(1.6)*	*112*	*(1.0)*	*491*	*(2.0)*	*482*	*(1.9)*	*9*	*(2.3)*
	OECD average	*494*	*(0.7)*	*110*	*(0.4)*	*499*	*(1.0)*	*490*	*(0.9)*	*9*	*(1.3)*
Partner countries	Brazil	300	(4.2)	131	(2.3)	315	(5.8)	288	(5.8)	**26**	(7.9)
	Hong Kong-China	543	(3.4)	107	(2.0)	551	(5.0)	535	(4.4)	**16**	(6.5)
	Indonesia	333	(4.7)	109	(2.1)	337	(6.1)	330	(6.0)	7	(7.6)
	Latvia	452	(4.6)	118	(2.1)	455	(5.5)	450	(5.6)	6	(6.1)
	Liechtenstein	533	(9.4)	104	(8.5)	530	(13.7)	539	(13.3)	–9	(19.4)
	Russian Federation	469	(4.9)	114	(2.2)	470	(5.3)	469	(6.1)	1	(5.8)
	Thailand	407	(3.5)	98	(1.9)	406	(4.7)	408	(3.9)	–3	(4.9)
	Netherlands[1]	m	m	m	m	m	m	m	m	m	m

		Percentiles											
		5th		10th		25th		75th		90th		95th	
		Score	**S.E.**	**Score**	**S.E.**	**Score**	**S.E.**	**Score**	**S.E.**	**Score**	**S.E.**	**Score**	**S.E.**
OECD countries	Australia	350	(8.0)	387	(6.6)	454	(6.0)	588	(3.8)	649	(5.6)	684	(5.0)
	Austria	332	(6.8)	368	(3.3)	438	(4.5)	583	(4.2)	646	(6.2)	685	(3.1)
	Belgium	322	(8.2)	367	(7.7)	435	(5.0)	574	(3.0)	631	(3.3)	668	(7.1)
	Canada	349	(4.9)	385	(3.9)	450	(2.3)	584	(1.9)	640	(2.0)	674	(1.8)
	Czech Republic	301	(8.0)	347	(8.0)	427	(3.7)	596	(5.1)	668	(5.4)	714	(6.5)
	Denmark	375	(6.9)	415	(5.5)	468	(3.5)	588	(3.9)	635	(5.1)	666	(5.5)
	Finland	368	(5.3)	405	(4.7)	469	(3.0)	600	(3.4)	656	(4.4)	691	(4.1)
	France	337	(9.3)	378	(3.7)	438	(4.5)	568	(3.1)	621	(3.8)	658	(5.3)
	Germany	300	(4.6)	338	(6.6)	410	(3.9)	565	(3.6)	632	(6.5)	675	(6.3)
	Greece	263	(9.3)	310	(5.8)	378	(7.0)	527	(4.5)	587	(6.1)	629	(7.6)
	Hungary	310	(8.5)	352	(6.0)	411	(4.5)	547	(4.0)	606	(5.3)	642	(4.6)
	Iceland	375	(7.9)	413	(4.1)	463	(3.6)	577	(2.6)	622	(5.1)	655	(6.4)
	Ireland	312	(5.4)	346	(6.1)	411	(5.3)	540	(4.2)	597	(5.4)	629	(4.5)
	Italy	275	(7.8)	315	(4.8)	383	(3.8)	529	(4.1)	590	(5.0)	627	(7.9)
	Japan	377	(8.7)	421	(8.5)	495	(5.7)	641	(4.1)	701	(5.6)	740	(9.0)
	Korea	344	(6.7)	386	(6.4)	463	(5.5)	620	(4.3)	689	(4.0)	726	(6.3)
	Luxembourg	257	(9.5)	307	(5.9)	375	(3.7)	526	(3.5)	584	(5.8)	626	(9.8)
	Mexico	259	(5.7)	292	(4.3)	341	(3.9)	460	(4.5)	510	(5.1)	541	(4.8)
	New Zealand	331	(11.3)	375	(6.3)	449	(6.4)	601	(5.7)	669	(5.7)	707	(5.8)
	Norway	315	(7.7)	353	(6.6)	422	(4.2)	562	(3.7)	625	(5.1)	662	(4.1)
	Poland	265	(9.8)	306	(6.8)	389	(6.9)	557	(6.4)	627	(9.9)	666	(6.3)
	Portugal	262	(7.1)	298	(6.8)	367	(5.2)	514	(3.8)	575	(3.7)	613	(6.3)
	Spain	309	(6.0)	349	(4.8)	409	(3.9)	540	(2.9)	595	(5.1)	629	(5.5)
	Sweden	331	(5.3)	371	(4.5)	442	(5.0)	582	(2.9)	645	(4.5)	681	(6.5)
	Switzerland	360	(6.0)	405	(6.4)	468	(6.2)	612	(5.3)	669	(5.5)	708	(7.9)
	United Kingdom	337	(5.7)	372	(4.8)	440	(3.6)	574	(4.5)	632	(5.1)	665	(3.7)
	United States	299	(8.4)	338	(8.7)	398	(7.2)	530	(5.3)	583	(6.0)	618	(5.9)
	OECD total	*303*	*(2.8)*	*343*	*(2.3)*	*410*	*(2.4)*	*562*	*(2.3)*	*631*	*(2.3)*	*671*	*(2.7)*
	OECD average	*309*	*(1.7)*	*351*	*(1.3)*	*421*	*(1.2)*	*570*	*(1.2)*	*634*	*(1.1)*	*671*	*(1.5)*
Partner countries	Brazil	80	(15.7)	130	(6.8)	211	(4.3)	394	(6.3)	467	(7.3)	516	(7.5)
	Hong Kong-China	362	(5.2)	399	(6.9)	473	(5.4)	616	(3.6)	680	(4.5)	717	(4.3)
	Indonesia	153	(6.7)	191	(6.9)	260	(6.7)	409	(5.0)	475	(8.3)	504	(6.3)
	Latvia	256	(11.0)	303	(8.2)	373	(7.3)	535	(5.6)	597	(5.9)	642	(6.5)
	Liechtenstein	356	(25.4)	397	(17.5)	462	(16.2)	603	(13.9)	666	(18.3)	708	(29.4)
	Russian Federation	276	(7.3)	323	(5.7)	393	(6.9)	549	(6.9)	614	(5.4)	656	(8.1)
	Thailand	243	(5.6)	280	(5.6)	342	(5.7)	474	(5.4)	535	(7.3)	565	(6.9)
	Netherlands[1]	m	m	m	m	m	m	m	m	m	m	m	m

Note: Values that are statistically significant are indicated in bold (see Annex A4).

1. Response rate too low to ensure comparability (see Annex A3).

Table 2.2a

Percentage of students at each level of proficiency on the mathematics/change and relationships scale

		Proficiency levels													
		Below Level 1 (below 358 score points)		Level 1 (from 358 to 420 score points)		Level 2 (from 421 to 482 score points)		Level 3 (from 483 to 544 score points)		Level 4 (from 545 to 606 score points)		Level 5 (from 607 to 668 score points)		Level 6 (above 668 score points)	
		%	S.E.	%	S.E.	%	S.E.	%	S.E.	%	S.E.	%	S.E.	%	S.E.
OECD countries	Australia	4.8	(0.4)	9.5	(0.5)	18.5	(0.6)	23.8	(0.7)	22.9	(0.7)	14.0	(0.6)	6.5	(0.6)
	Austria	8.6	(0.8)	14.1	(0.9)	20.5	(0.9)	22.5	(1.1)	18.8	(1.0)	10.9	(0.8)	4.6	(0.5)
	Belgium	7.6	(0.6)	9.7	(0.6)	14.8	(0.6)	18.2	(0.7)	19.7	(0.7)	17.5	(0.9)	12.4	(0.5)
	Canada	2.9	(0.2)	7.6	(0.4)	17.2	(0.6)	24.9	(0.5)	24.4	(0.6)	15.6	(0.6)	7.3	(0.4)
	Czech Republic	5.7	(0.7)	11.8	(1.0)	20.8	(0.9)	23.5	(0.8)	19.4	(0.8)	12.5	(0.7)	6.4	(0.6)
	Denmark	6.3	(0.6)	11.9	(0.8)	20.4	(1.1)	24.5	(0.9)	20.7	(0.8)	11.4	(0.8)	4.6	(0.5)
	Finland	2.7	(0.3)	7.0	(0.6)	16.1	(0.7)	24.5	(0.9)	24.1	(0.8)	16.7	(0.7)	8.9	(0.5)
	France	6.4	(0.8)	9.5	(0.7)	18.2	(0.7)	23.9	(0.9)	22.2	(0.8)	14.2	(0.7)	5.6	(0.5)
	Germany	9.5	(0.9)	12.6	(0.7)	18.5	(0.9)	20.6	(0.8)	19.6	(0.9)	13.2	(0.8)	6.1	(0.5)
	Greece	23.3	(1.4)	19.9	(0.9)	22.9	(0.8)	18.0	(0.9)	10.8	(0.9)	4.0	(0.5)	1.1	(0.2)
	Hungary	8.4	(0.8)	14.5	(0.7)	22.0	(1.2)	23.5	(1.0)	18.4	(0.8)	9.6	(0.7)	3.6	(0.4)
	Iceland	6.3	(0.4)	12.0	(0.6)	20.2	(0.8)	24.4	(0.8)	21.0	(0.8)	11.9	(0.7)	4.2	(0.4)
	Ireland	5.1	(0.5)	11.2	(0.9)	22.6	(0.8)	27.0	(1.1)	21.6	(0.9)	10.2	(0.6)	2.3	(0.4)
	Italy	18.2	(1.3)	19.2	(0.8)	23.7	(0.8)	20.4	(0.9)	11.8	(0.8)	5.2	(0.4)	1.5	(0.2)
	Japan	6.4	(0.7)	8.5	(0.7)	15.7	(0.8)	20.6	(0.8)	21.1	(1.1)	16.4	(0.8)	11.3	(1.2)
	Korea	3.0	(0.4)	7.0	(0.7)	15.7	(1.0)	22.3	(0.9)	23.6	(1.0)	17.5	(0.9)	10.9	(1.1)
	Luxembourg	10.7	(0.6)	15.3	(0.9)	21.5	(1.1)	22.5	(0.9)	18.1	(1.0)	8.5	(0.6)	3.4	(0.4)
	Mexico	47.2	(1.7)	24.1	(0.8)	17.0	(0.9)	8.6	(0.8)	2.6	(0.4)	0.4	(0.1)	0.1	(0.0)
	Netherlands	1.4	(0.4)	7.2	(0.8)	16.4	(1.2)	22.7	(1.1)	21.8	(1.1)	19.2	(0.9)	11.3	(0.7)
	New Zealand	5.6	(0.6)	10.2	(0.9)	17.5	(0.7)	22.5	(1.0)	22.2	(0.8)	14.0	(0.7)	7.9	(0.5)
	Norway	9.5	(0.7)	15.1	(0.7)	22.8	(1.0)	23.9	(0.8)	17.4	(0.9)	8.3	(0.6)	2.9	(0.4)
	Poland	10.1	(0.8)	16.1	(0.7)	23.6	(0.8)	23.0	(0.9)	16.1	(0.8)	7.9	(0.6)	3.3	(0.3)
	Portugal	13.6	(1.3)	17.5	(1.0)	23.8	(0.9)	22.5	(1.1)	15.1	(0.9)	5.8	(0.5)	1.7	(0.3)
	Slovak Republic	9.7	(0.9)	14.3	(0.9)	21.0	(0.9)	22.4	(0.9)	18.1	(1.0)	10.1	(0.7)	4.4	(0.5)
	Spain	11.3	(0.7)	14.9	(1.0)	22.9	(0.7)	24.0	(0.9)	17.1	(0.6)	7.7	(0.5)	2.0	(0.2)
	Sweden	9.4	(0.6)	12.6	(0.6)	19.6	(0.9)	21.7	(0.9)	18.3	(0.8)	11.6	(0.5)	6.7	(0.6)
	Switzerland	7.6	(0.6)	10.1	(0.6)	17.3	(1.1)	21.3	(1.0)	20.9	(0.8)	13.9	(0.8)	8.8	(0.9)
	Turkey	30.0	(2.0)	21.1	(1.1)	20.1	(1.2)	13.9	(1.2)	7.9	(1.2)	3.8	(0.8)	3.2	(1.2)
	United States	10.4	(0.8)	14.4	(0.7)	22.6	(0.8)	24.3	(0.7)	17.7	(0.8)	8.4	(0.6)	2.2	(0.3)
	OECD total	*12.9*	*(0.3)*	*13.8*	*(0.2)*	*19.8*	*(0.2)*	*21.3*	*(0.3)*	*17.3*	*(0.3)*	*10.2*	*(0.2)*	*4.7*	*(0.2)*
	OECD average	*10.2*	*(0.2)*	*13.0*	*(0.1)*	*19.8*	*(0.1)*	*22.0*	*(0.2)*	*18.5*	*(0.2)*	*11.1*	*(0.1)*	*5.3*	*(0.1)*
Partner countries	Brazil	59.7	(2.0)	16.9	(0.9)	11.4	(0.8)	6.6	(0.8)	3.3	(0.5)	1.2	(0.4)	0.7	(0.3)
	Hong Kong-China	5.6	(0.9)	8.0	(0.8)	14.5	(1.1)	20.6	(1.0)	23.0	(1.0)	18.6	(1.0)	9.8	(0.9)
	Indonesia	59.6	(1.8)	20.2	(0.8)	12.3	(0.8)	5.4	(0.6)	1.9	(0.4)	0.6	(0.2)	0.1	(0.1)
	Latvia	10.6	(1.0)	14.7	(1.1)	22.2	(1.3)	23.5	(1.2)	17.6	(1.2)	8.2	(0.7)	3.2	(0.5)
	Liechtenstein	4.6	(1.1)	10.0	(1.9)	15.1	(2.4)	20.7	(3.0)	20.5	(3.4)	18.6	(2.3)	10.5	(1.6)
	Macao-China	5.2	(1.1)	12.2	(1.3)	18.2	(1.5)	23.4	(1.8)	21.6	(1.8)	13.8	(1.2)	5.7	(1.0)
	Russian Federation	11.8	(1.1)	16.2	(0.9)	23.7	(1.0)	23.5	(0.9)	15.3	(1.1)	6.9	(0.7)	2.6	(0.4)
	Serbia	26.5	(1.6)	24.1	(1.1)	23.5	(0.9)	15.7	(0.9)	7.2	(0.7)	2.5	(0.4)	0.5	(0.1)
	Thailand	31.9	(1.6)	26.4	(1.3)	22.0	(0.9)	12.1	(0.8)	5.3	(0.6)	1.8	(0.4)	0.4	(0.2)
	Tunisia	58.8	(1.2)	20.4	(0.7)	12.9	(0.7)	5.8	(0.4)	1.8	(0.3)	0.4	(0.1)	0.0	
	Uruguay	29.8	(1.3)	19.1	(0.8)	21.6	(1.1)	16.5	(1.0)	8.8	(0.7)	3.4	(0.4)	0.9	(0.2)
	United Kingdom[1]	m	m	m	m	m	m	m	m	m	m	m	m	m	m

1. Response rate too low to ensure comparability (see Annex A3).

Table 2.2b

Percentage of students at each level of proficiency on the mathematics/change and relationships scale, by gender

Males – Proficiency levels

		Below Level 1 (below 358 score points)		Level 1 (from 358 to 420 score points)		Level 2 (from 421 to 482 score points)		Level 3 (from 483 to 544 score points)		Level 4 (from 545 to 606 score points)		Level 5 (from 607 to 668 score points)		Level 6 (above 668 score points)	
		%	S.E.	%	S.E.	%	S.E.	%	S.E.	%	S.E.	%	S.E.	%	S.E.
OECD countries	Australia	5.3	(0.6)	9.9	(0.7)	17.6	(0.8)	22.6	(0.9)	22.2	(0.9)	14.4	(0.9)	8.0	(0.8)
	Austria	9.5	(1.0)	13.6	(1.4)	19.8	(1.3)	21.2	(1.6)	18.3	(1.2)	11.9	(1.1)	5.7	(0.7)
	Belgium	7.8	(0.8)	10.2	(0.9)	14.2	(1.0)	17.0	(0.9)	18.6	(0.9)	17.8	(1.2)	14.3	(0.8)
	Canada	3.2	(0.3)	7.2	(0.5)	15.2	(0.6)	22.5	(0.8)	23.8	(0.8)	18.0	(0.7)	10.1	(0.7)
	Czech Republic	5.0	(0.8)	11.3	(1.1)	20.7	(1.3)	22.4	(1.1)	18.9	(1.1)	14.1	(1.0)	7.6	(0.8)
	Denmark	5.4	(0.7)	10.2	(0.9)	19.0	(1.2)	24.1	(1.1)	22.0	(1.4)	13.4	(1.1)	5.9	(0.7)
	Finland	2.7	(0.5)	7.0	(0.8)	14.9	(0.8)	23.2	(0.9)	23.3	(1.2)	18.0	(1.0)	10.9	(0.8)
	France	7.2	(1.0)	9.6	(1.0)	17.2	(1.0)	22.6	(1.3)	20.7	(1.2)	15.6	(1.0)	7.1	(0.7)
	Germany	8.6	(1.0)	12.4	(1.0)	18.4	(1.1)	19.7	(1.1)	19.5	(1.1)	13.9	(1.0)	7.6	(0.9)
	Greece	21.6	(1.6)	19.0	(1.3)	21.5	(1.1)	18.3	(1.3)	12.7	(1.4)	5.1	(0.7)	1.7	(0.3)
	Hungary	8.1	(0.9)	13.7	(1.0)	21.7	(1.4)	23.1	(1.4)	18.8	(1.2)	10.1	(0.8)	4.5	(0.7)
	Iceland	7.7	(0.8)	13.2	(1.0)	19.6	(1.1)	23.3	(1.4)	20.1	(1.3)	11.2	(0.8)	4.9	(0.8)
	Ireland	4.7	(0.6)	10.3	(1.0)	21.2	(1.2)	26.8	(1.5)	22.5	(1.1)	11.5	(0.8)	3.0	(0.6)
	Italy	16.7	(1.7)	17.8	(1.1)	21.6	(1.0)	20.9	(1.3)	13.7	(1.1)	6.8	(0.6)	2.4	(0.3)
	Japan	7.1	(1.0)	8.8	(0.9)	15.2	(1.1)	18.6	(1.1)	19.9	(1.2)	16.5	(1.5)	13.9	(2.0)
	Korea	2.6	(0.5)	6.2	(0.8)	13.7	(1.1)	20.7	(1.0)	24.4	(1.1)	19.5	(1.2)	12.9	(1.2)
	Luxembourg	10.5	(0.8)	15.2	(1.1)	19.5	(2.1)	20.9	(1.5)	19.1	(1.6)	10.2	(0.9)	4.7	(0.6)
	Mexico	45.9	(2.2)	23.4	(1.3)	17.3	(1.3)	9.5	(1.1)	3.3	(0.5)	0.6	(0.2)	0.1	(0.1)
	Netherlands	0.9	(0.4)	6.8	(1.1)	16.4	(1.9)	23.1	(1.6)	21.9	(1.9)	18.6	(1.3)	12.3	(0.9)
	New Zealand	5.1	(0.6)	9.6	(1.0)	16.6	(0.9)	20.6	(1.2)	23.0	(1.2)	15.1	(0.8)	10.1	(0.7)
	Norway	9.9	(0.8)	14.8	(0.9)	22.1	(1.4)	23.3	(1.1)	17.2	(1.0)	9.1	(0.7)	3.6	(0.6)
	Poland	10.7	(1.1)	15.2	(1.2)	22.4	(1.3)	22.3	(1.1)	16.4	(1.0)	8.8	(0.8)	4.3	(0.5)
	Portugal	14.4	(1.6)	15.6	(1.4)	21.3	(1.2)	21.9	(1.3)	16.8	(1.3)	7.3	(0.7)	2.6	(0.4)
	Slovak Republic	9.1	(1.1)	12.9	(1.1)	20.5	(1.1)	21.6	(1.3)	18.8	(1.3)	11.4	(1.0)	5.7	(0.6)
	Spain	11.8	(0.9)	13.9	(1.2)	21.7	(1.1)	23.0	(1.2)	17.8	(1.0)	9.3	(0.8)	2.5	(0.4)
	Sweden	9.9	(0.9)	12.3	(0.9)	19.4	(1.0)	21.2	(1.5)	18.2	(1.4)	11.8	(0.8)	7.2	(0.8)
	Switzerland	7.0	(0.6)	10.0	(0.8)	16.1	(1.5)	20.8	(1.6)	20.5	(1.0)	14.7	(1.1)	10.8	(1.4)
	Turkey	30.6	(2.6)	19.5	(1.3)	18.8	(1.4)	14.8	(1.4)	8.4	(1.3)	4.2	(0.9)	3.8	(1.4)
	United States	11.0	(1.0)	13.6	(0.9)	21.9	(1.2)	23.2	(1.1)	18.1	(1.0)	9.1	(0.8)	3.1	(0.5)
	OECD total	*12.9*	*(0.5)*	*13.2*	*(0.3)*	*19.0*	*(0.4)*	*20.5*	*(0.4)*	*17.5*	*(0.4)*	*11.0*	*(0.3)*	*5.9*	*(0.3)*
	OECD average	*10.2*	*(0.2)*	*12.4*	*(0.2)*	*18.8*	*(0.2)*	*21.2*	*(0.3)*	*18.7*	*(0.2)*	*12.1*	*(0.2)*	*6.6*	*(0.1)*
Partner countries	Brazil	56.7	(2.4)	16.8	(1.3)	11.8	(1.1)	7.7	(1.0)	4.2	(0.9)	1.6	(0.6)	1.2	(0.5)
	Hong Kong-China	7.1	(1.4)	8.3	(1.1)	13.6	(1.7)	18.7	(1.2)	21.3	(1.6)	19.2	(1.3)	11.8	(1.6)
	Indonesia	58.6	(1.9)	21.1	(1.3)	12.4	(0.9)	5.5	(0.7)	1.8	(0.4)	0.5	(0.2)	0.1	(0.1)
	Latvia	11.3	(1.5)	15.4	(1.4)	21.4	(1.6)	22.7	(1.8)	17.3	(1.5)	7.8	(1.0)	4.0	(0.7)
	Liechtenstein	5.0	(1.9)	7.5	(2.4)	13.1	(2.7)	20.2	(3.4)	19.3	(3.3)	21.2	(3.7)	13.8	(3.1)
	Macao-China	5.3	(1.4)	10.6	(1.8)	17.7	(1.9)	19.8	(2.4)	22.5	(2.9)	16.9	(2.1)	7.2	(1.5)
	Russian Federation	12.5	(1.6)	16.3	(1.1)	22.2	(1.2)	22.5	(1.3)	15.5	(1.2)	7.5	(1.1)	3.4	(0.7)
	Serbia	28.0	(1.7)	23.1	(1.4)	21.4	(1.1)	15.1	(1.0)	8.4	(0.9)	3.2	(0.7)	0.7	(0.2)
	Thailand	35.0	(2.2)	25.4	(1.6)	20.1	(1.1)	11.8	(1.1)	5.4	(0.9)	1.8	(0.5)	0.4	(0.2)
	Tunisia	57.0	(1.4)	20.5	(1.0)	13.1	(0.9)	6.6	(0.6)	2.3	(0.4)	0.5	(0.2)	0.0	
	Uruguay	29.8	(1.6)	18.3	(1.1)	20.9	(1.3)	16.7	(1.2)	9.2	(0.9)	4.0	(0.5)	1.2	(0.4)
	United Kingdom[1]	m	m	m	m	m	m	m	m	m	m	m	m	m	m

Females – Proficiency levels

		Below Level 1 (below 358 score points)		Level 1 (from 358 to 420 score points)		Level 2 (from 421 to 482 score points)		Level 3 (from 483 to 544 score points)		Level 4 (from 545 to 606 score points)		Level 5 (from 607 to 668 score points)		Level 6 (above 668 score points)	
		%	S.E.	%	S.E.	%	S.E.	%	S.E.	%	S.E.	%	S.E.	%	S.E.
OECD countries	Australia	4.3	(0.5)	9.1	(0.7)	19.3	(0.7)	25.0	(1.0)	23.7	(0.8)	13.5	(0.8)	5.0	(0.6)
	Austria	7.7	(1.1)	14.6	(1.3)	21.1	(1.2)	23.8	(1.4)	19.3	(1.4)	10.0	(1.0)	3.5	(0.5)
	Belgium	7.4	(0.8)	9.2	(0.7)	15.5	(0.9)	19.6	(1.1)	20.9	(1.1)	17.1	(1.1)	10.3	(0.7)
	Canada	2.6	(0.3)	7.8	(0.4)	17.7	(0.7)	26.5	(0.8)	25.3	(0.7)	14.5	(0.6)	5.6	(0.4)
	Czech Republic	6.3	(1.0)	12.3	(1.2)	20.9	(1.2)	24.7	(1.3)	19.8	(1.2)	10.9	(0.9)	5.1	(0.6)
	Denmark	7.2	(0.9)	13.6	(1.1)	21.8	(1.5)	24.9	(1.3)	19.4	(1.2)	9.6	(0.9)	3.5	(0.6)
	Finland	2.6	(0.4)	7.0	(0.7)	17.4	(1.1)	25.8	(1.5)	24.9	(1.2)	15.5	(0.8)	6.9	(0.6)
	France	5.7	(0.9)	9.4	(0.9)	19.2	(1.1)	25.0	(1.5)	23.5	(1.3)	13.0	(1.0)	4.3	(0.5)
	Germany	10.0	(1.0)	12.8	(1.1)	18.7	(1.4)	21.6	(1.6)	19.8	(1.3)	12.5	(1.0)	4.6	(0.6)
	Greece	25.0	(1.7)	20.7	(1.2)	24.2	(1.0)	17.7	(1.3)	9.0	(0.9)	2.9	(0.5)	0.5	(0.2)
	Hungary	8.6	(1.0)	15.5	(1.2)	22.5	(1.3)	23.9	(1.3)	17.8	(1.1)	9.1	(1.0)	2.6	(0.4)
	Iceland	4.8	(0.7)	10.6	(1.1)	20.7	(1.2)	25.6	(1.6)	22.0	(1.4)	12.7	(1.1)	3.5	(0.6)
	Ireland	5.4	(0.7)	12.0	(1.2)	23.9	(1.2)	27.3	(1.2)	20.7	(1.3)	8.9	(1.0)	1.6	(0.5)
	Italy	19.5	(1.8)	20.6	(1.2)	25.5	(1.1)	19.9	(1.0)	10.1	(0.9)	3.7	(0.4)	0.7	(0.2)
	Japan	5.8	(0.9)	8.3	(0.9)	16.1	(1.1)	22.5	(1.3)	22.3	(1.7)	16.3	(1.1)	8.8	(0.7)
	Korea	3.5	(0.7)	8.2	(1.1)	18.7	(1.7)	24.7	(1.5)	22.4	(1.7)	14.6	(1.3)	7.9	(1.4)
	Luxembourg	10.9	(0.8)	15.4	(1.1)	23.5	(1.1)	24.1	(1.1)	17.3	(1.0)	6.8	(0.8)	2.1	(0.3)
	Mexico	48.4	(2.0)	24.7	(1.3)	16.7	(1.1)	7.8	(0.9)	2.0	(0.4)	0.3	(0.1)	0.0	(0.0)
	Netherlands	1.9	(0.5)	7.6	(1.1)	16.4	(1.3)	22.2	(1.7)	21.8	(1.5)	19.9	(1.2)	10.2	(1.0)
	New Zealand	6.1	(0.8)	10.8	(1.1)	18.5	(1.2)	24.4	(1.4)	21.4	(1.5)	13.0	(1.0)	5.7	(0.5)
	Norway	9.2	(0.9)	15.5	(1.1)	23.6	(1.4)	24.5	(1.1)	17.5	(1.3)	7.6	(0.9)	2.2	(0.4)
	Poland	9.5	(0.9)	17.0	(1.0)	24.7	(1.0)	23.6	(1.2)	15.8	(1.1)	7.0	(0.7)	2.2	(0.4)
	Portugal	13.0	(1.5)	19.1	(1.3)	26.0	(1.5)	23.1	(1.4)	13.5	(1.0)	4.3	(0.6)	1.0	(0.3)
	Slovak Republic	10.2	(1.0)	15.7	(1.2)	21.6	(1.4)	23.2	(1.1)	17.4	(1.3)	8.7	(0.9)	3.1	(0.6)
	Spain	10.9	(0.8)	15.8	(1.1)	24.1	(1.1)	25.1	(1.1)	16.4	(0.8)	6.2	(0.6)	1.5	(0.4)
	Sweden	8.9	(1.0)	13.0	(0.9)	19.8	(1.5)	22.2	(1.4)	18.5	(1.0)	11.5	(0.8)	6.2	(0.9)
	Switzerland	8.3	(0.8)	10.2	(1.0)	18.5	(1.2)	21.9	(1.2)	21.2	(1.1)	13.1	(1.0)	6.8	(0.8)
	Turkey	29.3	(2.3)	23.1	(1.7)	21.7	(1.7)	12.9	(1.6)	7.3	(1.3)	3.3	(1.0)	2.4	(1.0)
	United States	9.8	(1.1)	15.2	(0.9)	23.2	(1.1)	25.3	(1.3)	17.3	(1.1)	7.7	(0.8)	1.4	(0.3)
	OECD total	*12.9*	*(0.4)*	*14.4*	*(0.4)*	*20.6*	*(0.4)*	*22.0*	*(0.4)*	*17.1*	*(0.4)*	*9.4*	*(0.3)*	*3.5*	*(0.2)*
	OECD average	*10.4*	*(0.2)*	*13.6*	*(0.2)*	*20.8*	*(0.2)*	*22.8*	*(0.2)*	*18.3*	*(0.2)*	*10.1*	*(0.2)*	*4.1*	*(0.1)*
Partner countries	Brazil	62.4	(2.0)	17.0	(1.2)	11.1	(1.1)	5.7	(0.8)	2.6	(0.6)	0.9	(0.5)	0.3	(0.2)
	Hong Kong-China	4.1	(0.7)	7.7	(0.9)	15.4	(1.4)	22.5	(1.9)	24.7	(1.3)	17.9	(1.3)	7.8	(0.8)
	Indonesia	60.6	(2.1)	19.2	(0.9)	12.3	(1.1)	5.3	(0.8)	1.9	(0.5)	0.6	(0.3)	0.1	(0.1)
	Latvia	9.9	(1.1)	14.1	(1.4)	22.9	(1.5)	24.3	(1.6)	17.9	(1.4)	8.5	(0.8)	2.5	(0.5)
	Liechtenstein	4.1	(1.8)	12.7	(2.7)	17.2	(3.9)	21.2	(4.4)	21.7	(5.1)	15.8	(3.6)	7.1	(2.6)
	Macao-China	5.1	(1.3)	13.7	(1.8)	18.7	(2.1)	26.8	(2.3)	20.6	(2.4)	10.9	(1.6)	4.2	(1.1)
	Russian Federation	11.0	(1.1)	16.2	(1.1)	25.3	(1.4)	24.6	(1.2)	15.1	(1.3)	6.2	(0.8)	1.7	(0.5)
	Serbia	25.0	(2.0)	25.1	(1.6)	25.5	(1.6)	16.3	(1.3)	6.1	(1.0)	1.8	(0.4)	0.2	(0.2)
	Thailand	29.4	(1.7)	27.3	(1.5)	23.5	(1.2)	12.3	(1.2)	5.3	(0.6)	1.9	(0.5)	0.4	(0.2)
	Tunisia	60.5	(1.5)	20.3	(0.9)	12.6	(1.0)	4.9	(0.6)	1.3	(0.3)	0.3	(0.2)	0.0	
	Uruguay	29.8	(1.7)	19.8	(1.4)	22.3	(1.6)	16.3	(1.3)	8.3	(0.9)	2.9	(0.5)	0.5	(0.2)
	United Kingdom[1]	m	m	m	m	m	m	m	m	m	m	m	m	m	m

1. Response rate too low to ensure comparability (see Annex A3).

Table 2.2c

Mean score, variation and gender differences in student performance on the mathematics/change and relationships scale in PISA 2003

		All students				Gender differences					
		Mean score		Standard deviation		Males		Females		Difference (M-F)	
		Mean	S.E.	S.D.	S.E.	Mean score	S.E.	Mean score	S.E.	Score dif.	S.E.
OECD countries	Australia	525	(2.3)	98	(1.8)	527	(3.2)	523	(2.8)	4	(3.8)
	Austria	500	(3.6)	102	(1.8)	502	(4.4)	497	(4.4)	5	(5.0)
	Belgium	535	(2.4)	116	(1.6)	539	(3.6)	531	(3.5)	8	(5.1)
	Canada	537	(1.9)	92	(0.9)	546	(2.2)	532	(2.0)	**13**	(2.3)
	Czech Republic	515	(3.5)	100	(1.8)	521	(4.5)	508	(4.0)	**13**	(4.9)
	Denmark	509	(3.0)	98	(1.8)	520	(3.7)	499	(3.3)	**21**	(3.5)
	Finland	543	(2.2)	95	(1.4)	549	(2.8)	537	(2.4)	**11**	(2.8)
	France	520	(2.6)	100	(2.1)	522	(4.0)	518	(3.2)	4	(5.0)
	Germany	507	(3.7)	109	(1.7)	514	(4.3)	502	(4.4)	**12**	(4.4)
	Greece	436	(4.3)	107	(1.7)	445	(5.2)	427	(4.4)	**18**	(4.2)
	Hungary	495	(3.1)	99	(2.1)	499	(3.6)	490	(3.6)	**10**	(3.9)
	Iceland	509	(1.4)	97	(1.2)	505	(2.4)	514	(2.3)	**–10**	(3.8)
	Ireland	506	(2.4)	87	(1.4)	512	(3.0)	500	(3.5)	**13**	(4.4)
	Italy	452	(3.2)	103	(1.9)	463	(4.9)	442	(4.0)	**21**	(6.3)
	Japan	536	(4.3)	112	(3.0)	539	(6.4)	533	(4.3)	6	(6.6)
	Korea	548	(3.5)	99	(2.4)	558	(4.7)	532	(5.8)	**25**	(7.3)
	Luxembourg	487	(1.2)	102	(1.0)	494	(2.5)	480	(1.8)	**14**	(3.7)
	Mexico	364	(4.1)	98	(1.9)	368	(4.9)	360	(4.6)	8	(4.4)
	Netherlands	551	(3.1)	94	(2.0)	554	(3.8)	548	(3.7)	6	(4.3)
	New Zealand	526	(2.4)	103	(1.5)	534	(2.8)	517	(3.4)	**17**	(4.1)
	Norway	488	(2.6)	98	(1.3)	490	(3.2)	486	(3.1)	4	(3.3)
	Poland	484	(2.7)	99	(1.7)	488	(3.1)	481	(3.4)	**8**	(3.6)
	Portugal	468	(4.0)	99	(2.2)	475	(4.8)	462	(4.0)	**13**	(3.8)
	Slovak Republic	494	(3.5)	105	(2.3)	502	(4.1)	486	(3.9)	**16**	(4.2)
	Spain	481	(2.8)	99	(1.4)	485	(3.8)	477	(2.6)	**8**	(3.3)
	Sweden	505	(2.9)	111	(1.9)	506	(3.4)	504	(3.9)	1	(4.3)
	Switzerland	523	(3.7)	112	(2.2)	530	(5.1)	515	(3.9)	**15**	(5.3)
	Turkey	423	(7.6)	121	(5.4)	425	(9.1)	419	(7.4)	6	(7.2)
	United States	486	(3.0)	98	(1.6)	488	(3.4)	483	(3.3)	6	(2.9)
	OECD total	***489***	***(1.2)***	***113***	***(0.8)***	***493***	***(1.4)***	***484***	***(1.4)***	***10***	***(1.5)***
	OECD average	***499***	***(0.7)***	***109***	***(0.5)***	***504***	***(0.8)***	***493***	***(0.8)***	***11***	***(0.9)***
Partner countries	Brazil	333	(6.0)	124	(3.4)	344	(7.3)	324	(5.5)	**20**	(4.7)
	Hong Kong-China	540	(4.7)	106	(2.9)	540	(6.8)	539	(4.8)	1	(7.2)
	Indonesia	334	(4.6)	105	(2.6)	336	(4.4)	332	(5.4)	4	(3.4)
	Latvia	487	(4.4)	101	(1.6)	487	(5.3)	488	(4.3)	1	(4.0)
	Liechtenstein	540	(3.7)	107	(3.8)	552	(7.4)	526	(6.5)	**26**	(12.1)
	Macao-China	519	(3.5)	99	(2.9)	529	(5.0)	509	(4.6)	**20**	(6.6)
	Russian Federation	477	(4.6)	100	(2.1)	479	(6.0)	475	(4.5)	3	(5.1)
	Serbia	419	(4.0)	99	(1.7)	420	(4.5)	418	(4.9)	1	(4.9)
	Thailand	405	(3.4)	93	(2.1)	400	(4.5)	409	(4.0)	–10	(5.1)
	Tunisia	337	(2.8)	103	(1.9)	342	(3.0)	331	(3.3)	**11**	(3.0)
	Uruguay	417	(3.6)	115	(1.7)	420	(4.2)	414	(4.2)	5	(4.4)
	United Kingdom[1]	m	m	m	m	m	m	m	m	m	m

		Percentiles											
		5th		10th		25th		75th		90th		95th	
		Score	S.E.	Score	S.E.	Score	S.E.	Score	S.E.	Score	S.E.	Score	S.E.
OECD countries	Australia	360	(4.9)	398	(3.7)	459	(3.0)	594	(2.7)	648	(3.3)	681	(4.7)
	Austria	331	(6.3)	366	(4.8)	428	(4.4)	572	(4.0)	633	(4.0)	666	(4.6)
	Belgium	332	(5.6)	375	(4.5)	454	(4.0)	623	(2.8)	680	(2.2)	711	(2.4)
	Canada	382	(3.4)	417	(2.6)	474	(2.5)	601	(2.3)	654	(2.7)	685	(2.9)
	Czech Republic	353	(6.4)	388	(5.8)	446	(3.9)	585	(4.6)	647	(5.2)	681	(5.0)
	Denmark	345	(6.0)	382	(4.5)	443	(3.9)	578	(3.2)	634	(3.9)	665	(5.1)
	Finland	387	(5.1)	422	(3.7)	480	(2.6)	609	(2.7)	664	(3.0)	695	(3.2)
	France	345	(7.0)	386	(5.8)	454	(3.8)	591	(2.5)	644	(3.3)	674	(4.2)
	Germany	323	(6.8)	362	(6.4)	430	(4.5)	588	(4.5)	645	(3.9)	678	(3.7)
	Greece	256	(5.8)	296	(5.5)	364	(5.1)	509	(5.6)	572	(4.6)	607	(5.7)
	Hungary	332	(5.5)	367	(5.0)	427	(3.4)	563	(4.2)	623	(5.1)	656	(4.5)
	Iceland	345	(4.1)	382	(3.5)	444	(2.3)	579	(2.4)	633	(2.6)	662	(3.8)
	Ireland	357	(4.4)	393	(4.6)	448	(3.4)	568	(2.8)	618	(2.6)	645	(3.6)
	Italy	281	(6.5)	319	(6.4)	382	(4.6)	522	(3.6)	585	(3.4)	622	(3.6)
	Japan	342	(8.3)	389	(7.0)	462	(5.5)	616	(4.6)	676	(6.6)	709	(7.6)
	Korea	383	(5.8)	420	(5.0)	480	(4.5)	617	(4.3)	674	(5.8)	708	(6.7)
	Luxembourg	315	(4.0)	354	(3.5)	417	(2.2)	559	(1.9)	616	(2.8)	651	(4.5)
	Mexico	199	(6.6)	236	(4.9)	297	(4.5)	432	(5.0)	491	(5.7)	525	(5.2)
	Netherlands	398	(5.3)	426	(4.7)	482	(5.0)	623	(3.8)	675	(2.9)	702	(3.8)
	New Zealand	352	(5.4)	390	(4.9)	456	(3.6)	598	(2.7)	657	(2.9)	691	(3.9)
	Norway	324	(4.7)	360	(4.4)	421	(3.2)	555	(3.4)	613	(3.9)	646	(3.6)
	Poland	323	(5.4)	357	(4.6)	417	(3.1)	552	(3.1)	613	(3.9)	650	(4.9)
	Portugal	301	(7.0)	338	(6.8)	401	(5.6)	537	(4.1)	594	(3.4)	626	(4.7)
	Slovak Republic	320	(7.7)	360	(5.7)	424	(4.8)	568	(3.8)	629	(3.9)	663	(4.7)
	Spain	310	(4.3)	350	(4.2)	416	(3.6)	550	(3.2)	606	(4.0)	637	(3.7)
	Sweden	318	(6.4)	362	(4.2)	431	(3.6)	582	(3.5)	648	(4.5)	684	(5.5)
	Switzerland	329	(5.6)	375	(5.5)	449	(3.7)	599	(4.5)	662	(5.8)	700	(7.3)
	Turkey	238	(9.1)	276	(7.1)	341	(6.7)	496	(10.0)	578	(15.6)	633	(22.9)
	United States	318	(6.5)	355	(4.8)	421	(3.6)	555	(3.3)	610	(3.7)	642	(3.7)
	OECD total	***295***	***(2.5)***	***339***	***(2.2)***	***414***	***(1.6)***	***568***	***(1.4)***	***631***	***(1.3)***	***667***	***(1.5)***
	OECD average	***313***	***(1.5)***	***356***	***(1.2)***	***426***	***(1.0)***	***576***	***(0.7)***	***637***	***(0.8)***	***672***	***(0.9)***
Partner countries	Brazil	140	(7.0)	180	(6.4)	247	(5.9)	414	(6.9)	498	(10.9)	548	(12.0)
	Hong Kong-China	351	(10.6)	397	(8.8)	471	(7.1)	617	(4.3)	668	(4.4)	699	(5.1)
	Indonesia	164	(6.8)	202	(6.4)	263	(4.7)	402	(5.7)	469	(6.9)	509	(8.9)
	Latvia	319	(5.2)	355	(4.8)	419	(5.0)	556	(5.4)	615	(5.5)	649	(6.0)
	Liechtenstein	362	(12.7)	401	(10.2)	467	(7.6)	619	(7.4)	673	(11.5)	705	(13.3)
	Macao-China	356	(10.1)	388	(7.3)	449	(6.2)	590	(5.0)	644	(5.7)	675	(9.0)
	Russian Federation	309	(6.9)	348	(5.8)	411	(5.2)	544	(5.3)	604	(5.3)	641	(6.9)
	Serbia	257	(5.0)	293	(4.7)	353	(4.7)	485	(4.5)	546	(5.3)	582	(7.4)
	Thailand	261	(4.4)	289	(3.9)	341	(3.8)	465	(4.2)	528	(6.1)	568	(7.5)
	Tunisia	169	(4.2)	205	(3.7)	267	(3.7)	405	(4.0)	469	(4.9)	508	(5.3)
	Uruguay	219	(5.3)	262	(4.5)	339	(4.9)	497	(3.8)	561	(4.6)	600	(5.6)
	United Kingdom[1]	m	m	m	m	m	m	m	m	m	m	m	m

Note: Values that are statistically significant are indicated in bold (see Annex A4).

1. Response rate too low to ensure comparability (see Annex A3).

Table 2.2d

Mean score, variation and gender differences in student performance on the mathematics/change and relationships scale in PISA 2000

		All students				Gender differences					
		Mean score		Standard deviation		Males		Females		Difference (M-F)	
		Mean	S.E.	S.D.	S.E.	Mean score	S.E.	Mean score	S.E.	Score dif.	S.E.
OECD countries	Australia	522	(3.2)	95	(1.8)	525	(4.1)	519	(4.6)	6	(5.8)
	Austria	499	(3.1)	97	(2.4)	506	(4.7)	495	(3.9)	11	(6.1)
	Belgium	514	(3.8)	121	(2.8)	516	(5.1)	513	(4.7)	2	(6.1)
	Canada	520	(1.3)	91	(1.1)	523	(1.7)	518	(1.4)	**5**	(1.9)
	Czech Republic	484	(3.0)	114	(1.8)	487	(4.6)	482	(3.5)	4	(5.8)
	Denmark	499	(2.7)	102	(1.9)	505	(3.9)	494	(3.4)	**12**	(5.0)
	Finland	529	(2.1)	92	(1.7)	529	(3.2)	530	(2.7)	–1	(4.1)
	France	515	(2.7)	106	(2.0)	518	(4.3)	511	(3.6)	7	(5.6)
	Germany	485	(2.4)	111	(2.2)	488	(3.9)	483	(3.8)	5	(5.9)
	Greece	430	(5.2)	124	(2.8)	433	(7.9)	428	(5.1)	5	(8.4)
	Hungary	479	(4.1)	115	(2.0)	477	(4.9)	480	(5.3)	–3	(6.2)
	Iceland	507	(2.8)	97	(1.9)	505	(4.3)	511	(3.6)	–5	(5.5)
	Ireland	501	(2.7)	85	(1.6)	504	(4.1)	499	(3.6)	6	(5.4)
	Italy	443	(3.0)	101	(2.7)	444	(5.4)	442	(3.7)	2	(7.1)
	Japan	536	(5.1)	105	(2.5)	538	(6.7)	534	(5.8)	4	(7.1)
	Korea	530	(2.6)	84	(1.4)	537	(3.7)	522	(4.3)	**15**	(6.1)
	Luxembourg	424	(2.6)	111	(2.4)	427	(3.5)	421	(3.8)	6	(5.1)
	Mexico	358	(3.1)	100	(2.5)	361	(4.5)	355	(3.4)	6	(4.8)
	New Zealand	527	(3.0)	100	(1.8)	527	(4.9)	529	(4.1)	–2	(6.6)
	Norway	494	(3.1)	94	(1.9)	497	(3.7)	491	(3.4)	6	(4.0)
	Poland	451	(5.7)	121	(2.9)	451	(7.9)	451	(6.3)	0	(8.7)
	Portugal	448	(3.6)	99	(2.7)	455	(4.2)	443	(4.6)	**12**	(5.3)
	Spain	468	(2.8)	104	(2.0)	475	(4.0)	462	(3.3)	**13**	(4.7)
	Sweden	502	(2.6)	102	(1.8)	504	(3.6)	500	(3.6)	4	(4.8)
	Switzerland	510	(4.8)	125	(2.2)	514	(5.9)	506	(5.7)	8	(6.4)
	United Kingdom	519	(2.2)	92	(1.8)	520	(3.2)	519	(3.2)	1	(4.6)
	United States	486	(6.0)	101	(2.3)	488	(6.7)	483	(6.6)	5	(5.8)
	OECD total	*485*	*(1.6)*	*113*	*(0.9)*	*488*	*(2.0)*	*482*	*(1.9)*	*6*	*(2.1)*
	OECD average	*488*	*(0.7)*	*111*	*(0.5)*	*491*	*(1.0)*	*486*	*(0.9)*	*6*	*(1.2)*
Partner countries	Brazil	263	(4.8)	140	(3.6)	272	(5.4)	255	(6.4)	**17**	(7.1)
	Hong Kong-China	546	(3.0)	99	(1.9)	551	(4.7)	540	(4.1)	12	(6.6)
	Indonesia	345	(3.0)	71	(1.8)	346	(3.7)	344	(3.3)	2	(3.7)
	Latvia	450	(4.7)	124	(2.4)	450	(5.9)	452	(5.8)	–2	(6.6)
	Liechtenstein	502	(12.4)	131	(7.5)	502	(19.7)	506	(17.2)	–4	(26.8)
	Russian Federation	467	(5.5)	121	(2.3)	465	(5.7)	469	(6.6)	–5	(5.6)
	Thailand	421	(2.2)	62	(1.3)	419	(3.2)	422	(2.5)	–3	(3.5)
	Netherlands[1]	m	m	m	m	m	m	m	m	m	m

		Percentiles											
		5th		10th		25th		75th		90th		95th	
		Score	S.E.	Score	S.E.	Score	S.E.	Score	S.E.	Score	S.E.	Score	S.E.
OECD countries	Australia	361	(11.3)	398	(3.7)	463	(3.2)	587	(4.8)	643	(4.8)	674	(6.3)
	Austria	337	(9.3)	374	(5.5)	437	(2.6)	567	(5.9)	620	(6.3)	654	(6.0)
	Belgium	298	(10.5)	356	(9.2)	439	(6.4)	595	(3.2)	661	(5.4)	698	(5.1)
	Canada	365	(4.6)	402	(2.9)	462	(2.3)	583	(2.0)	632	(2.0)	664	(2.1)
	Czech Republic	294	(9.2)	336	(3.6)	412	(6.1)	562	(5.3)	629	(3.3)	667	(4.2)
	Denmark	376	(5.7)	367	(5.7)	434	(3.7)	568	(3.1)	630	(4.7)	663	(6.9)
	Finland	375	(7.6)	410	(2.5)	472	(4.6)	592	(3.6)	645	(2.8)	677	(3.2)
	France	331	(8.0)	376	(6.6)	447	(3.5)	585	(2.7)	648	(4.4)	685	(6.1)
	Germany	293	(8.7)	340	(7.7)	413	(4.1)	562	(3.4)	624	(2.9)	659	(3.7)
	Greece	221	(10.2)	270	(8.1)	350	(6.8)	514	(6.0)	590	(7.4)	630	(8.5)
	Hungary	288	(9.3)	330	(6.7)	401	(4.7)	556	(4.2)	629	(5.8)	667	(7.3)
	Iceland	343	(9.8)	382	(6.7)	446	(4.6)	571	(3.0)	632	(4.2)	667	(6.2)
	Ireland	357	(8.2)	390	(4.0)	447	(5.2)	558	(4.7)	607	(3.1)	636	(4.5)
	Italy	270	(12.0)	312	(6.1)	377	(6.2)	512	(3.5)	568	(3.8)	600	(3.9)
	Japan	355	(9.0)	403	(8.5)	468	(7.3)	608	(5.1)	667	(7.1)	701	(5.8)
	Korea	389	(6.8)	424	(4.8)	475	(3.3)	588	(3.0)	635	(5.7)	667	(5.6)
	Luxembourg	236	(10.0)	278	(6.8)	353	(4.8)	499	(4.6)	565	(6.5)	598	(8.2)
	Mexico	193	(6.8)	228	(7.4)	290	(4.6)	427	(4.0)	486	(4.5)	520	(6.1)
	New Zealand	354	(8.4)	398	(5.8)	465	(5.4)	596	(4.9)	651	(5.5)	682	(5.0)
	Norway	335	(10.7)	372	(4.7)	433	(4.6)	556	(4.1)	611	(4.7)	642	(5.8)
	Poland	251	(16.0)	293	(5.8)	372	(6.3)	537	(8.4)	602	(9.5)	638	(7.9)
	Portugal	279	(10.0)	319	(6.0)	384	(6.1)	516	(3.5)	573	(5.3)	605	(3.8)
	Spain	290	(9.1)	332	(7.0)	401	(4.8)	538	(3.2)	602	(5.5)	637	(6.3)
	Sweden	328	(10.8)	371	(3.7)	435	(4.0)	572	(3.7)	630	(4.0)	664	(6.5)
	Switzerland	297	(9.5)	346	(6.5)	428	(6.2)	593	(4.9)	669	(8.1)	713	(6.5)
	United Kingdom	365	(8.5)	399	(3.5)	459	(2.9)	583	(3.0)	636	(2.8)	666	(5.3)
	United States	314	(13.1)	353	(7.1)	420	(6.8)	554	(8.5)	614	(5.3)	648	(8.4)
	OECD total	*289*	*(2.8)*	*335*	*(2.8)*	*413*	*(2.4)*	*563*	*(1.7)*	*626*	*(1.9)*	*660*	*(2.3)*
	OECD average	*295*	*(2.5)*	*342*	*(2.1)*	*418*	*(1.4)*	*564*	*(0.9)*	*626*	*(1.0)*	*662*	*(1.9)*
Partner countries	Brazil	33	(9.0)	81	(6.2)	166	(6.1)	363	(8.2)	448	(10.1)	492	(13.0)
	Hong Kong-China	371	(8.7)	416	(4.6)	482	(5.2)	614	(4.4)	669	(4.9)	703	(6.2)
	Indonesia	224	(7.3)	255	(4.7)	297	(3.1)	394	(4.1)	435	(5.3)	459	(5.5)
	Latvia	241	(11.3)	289	(8.6)	369	(6.5)	538	(7.3)	613	(5.3)	647	(7.6)
	Liechtenstein	278	(36.8)	331	(31.1)	416	(16.9)	591	(14.9)	666	(25.0)	720	(28.6)
	Russian Federation	260	(9.3)	308	(10.0)	389	(6.1)	548	(6.1)	622	(6.6)	661	(8.9)
	Thailand	321	(6.3)	343	(4.3)	380	(3.2)	462	(3.7)	499	(3.7)	524	(4.6)
	Netherlands[1]	m	m	m	m	m	m	m	m	m	m	m	m

Note: Values that are statistically significant are indicated in bold (see Annex A4).

1. Response rate too low to ensure comparability (see Annex A3).

Table 2.3a
Percentage of students at each level of proficiency on the mathematics/quantity scale

		Proficiency levels													
		Below Level 1 (below 358 score points)		Level 1 (from 358 to 420 score points)		Level 2 (from 421 to 482 score points)		Level 3 (from 483 to 544 score points)		Level 4 (from 545 to 606 score points)		Level 5 (from 607 to 668 score points)		Level 6 (above 668 score points)	
		%	S.E.	%	S.E.	%	S.E.	%	S.E.	%	S.E.	%	S.E.	%	S.E.
OECD countries	Australia	5.5	(0.4)	11.0	(0.5)	19.0	(0.8)	24.3	(0.9)	22.4	(0.6)	12.5	(0.6)	5.2	(0.4)
	Austria	3.7	(0.5)	11.2	(0.9)	20.9	(1.0)	27.2	(1.1)	23.1	(1.0)	11.2	(0.8)	2.8	(0.4)
	Belgium	7.2	(0.6)	8.9	(0.5)	15.1	(0.5)	20.6	(0.6)	22.3	(0.6)	17.5	(0.6)	8.5	(0.5)
	Canada	3.8	(0.3)	8.8	(0.4)	18.1	(0.6)	25.2	(0.6)	23.7	(0.5)	14.4	(0.5)	6.0	(0.3)
	Czech Republic	4.7	(0.7)	9.7	(0.9)	17.2	(0.9)	23.5	(1.0)	23.1	(0.9)	15.0	(0.7)	6.7	(0.6)
	Denmark	4.7	(0.6)	10.4	(0.6)	19.9	(0.8)	26.3	(0.9)	22.7	(0.9)	12.0	(0.7)	4.0	(0.4)
	Finland	1.4	(0.2)	5.0	(0.5)	14.6	(0.7)	26.9	(0.7)	27.3	(0.9)	17.9	(0.7)	7.0	(0.4)
	France	6.7	(0.7)	11.1	(0.8)	20.4	(1.0)	25.4	(1.2)	21.9	(0.8)	11.0	(0.7)	3.5	(0.3)
	Germany	8.5	(0.7)	10.4	(0.8)	17.5	(0.9)	22.0	(1.1)	22.0	(1.2)	14.1	(1.0)	5.5	(0.4)
	Greece	19.0	(1.2)	19.8	(0.9)	25.1	(0.9)	20.0	(0.9)	11.0	(0.8)	4.1	(0.6)	1.0	(0.3)
	Hungary	7.8	(0.7)	13.5	(0.8)	21.6	(0.9)	25.2	(0.9)	19.7	(0.8)	9.7	(0.7)	2.5	(0.3)
	Iceland	6.2	(0.4)	10.9	(0.6)	19.1	(1.1)	24.3	(1.0)	22.5	(0.8)	12.7	(0.7)	4.2	(0.5)
	Ireland	5.6	(0.6)	12.3	(0.9)	23.0	(1.0)	26.9	(1.1)	20.6	(0.8)	9.5	(0.6)	2.2	(0.4)
	Italy	13.7	(1.1)	16.1	(0.7)	22.0	(0.8)	22.4	(0.8)	15.2	(0.8)	7.7	(0.5)	2.8	(0.3)
	Japan	5.7	(0.7)	9.2	(0.8)	16.6	(0.8)	23.1	(1.1)	23.6	(1.0)	15.1	(0.8)	6.7	(0.8)
	Korea	2.6	(0.3)	7.2	(0.7)	17.0	(0.8)	25.2	(0.8)	26.0	(1.0)	15.6	(0.9)	6.4	(0.8)
	Luxembourg	6.5	(0.4)	12.4	(0.8)	21.8	(1.0)	26.2	(1.3)	21.0	(0.8)	9.4	(0.6)	2.7	(0.3)
	Mexico	35.5	(1.8)	25.0	(1.2)	21.4	(1.1)	12.4	(0.8)	4.6	(0.5)	1.0	(0.2)	0.1	(0.1)
	Netherlands	4.1	(0.7)	10.1	(1.0)	18.3	(1.2)	23.0	(1.2)	21.9	(1.1)	15.9	(1.0)	6.7	(0.6)
	New Zealand	6.4	(0.6)	11.9	(0.7)	20.1	(0.7)	23.6	(0.8)	21.2	(0.8)	11.9	(0.6)	5.0	(0.3)
	Norway	7.7	(0.5)	13.8	(0.7)	22.8	(0.9)	25.4	(1.1)	18.8	(0.9)	8.9	(0.6)	2.6	(0.3)
	Poland	7.1	(0.7)	13.5	(0.7)	24.2	(1.0)	27.1	(0.9)	18.7	(0.8)	7.6	(0.6)	1.8	(0.3)
	Portugal	12.9	(1.2)	18.3	(1.1)	25.2	(0.8)	23.4	(1.2)	13.8	(0.8)	5.2	(0.4)	1.2	(0.2)
	Slovak Republic	5.6	(0.7)	10.6	(0.8)	20.0	(0.8)	26.1	(0.9)	21.9	(0.8)	12.3	(0.8)	3.6	(0.4)
	Spain	8.9	(0.7)	13.2	(0.9)	22.5	(0.8)	25.0	(0.7)	18.8	(0.8)	8.8	(0.6)	2.6	(0.3)
	Sweden	4.4	(0.5)	10.3	(0.6)	21.4	(0.8)	27.3	(1.0)	21.6	(0.9)	11.1	(0.8)	3.9	(0.6)
	Switzerland	4.2	(0.4)	8.6	(0.6)	16.0	(0.8)	24.2	(1.0)	24.6	(0.8)	15.7	(0.9)	6.7	(0.9)
	Turkey	32.1	(2.1)	23.1	(1.0)	20.2	(1.1)	12.6	(1.1)	6.5	(1.0)	3.2	(0.7)	2.3	(0.9)
	United States	13.7	(1.0)	15.6	(0.8)	22.0	(0.7)	21.9	(0.8)	16.0	(0.7)	8.1	(0.7)	2.8	(0.4)
	OECD total	*12.3*	*(0.3)*	*14.1*	*(0.3)*	*20.3*	*(0.3)*	*22.0*	*(0.3)*	*17.8*	*(0.3)*	*9.7*	*(0.2)*	*3.7*	*(0.1)*
	OECD average	*8.8*	*(0.2)*	*12.5*	*(0.2)*	*20.1*	*(0.2)*	*23.7*	*(0.2)*	*19.9*	*(0.2)*	*11.0*	*(0.1)*	*4.0*	*(0.1)*
Partner countries	Brazil	51.1	(1.8)	20.7	(1.1)	15.0	(0.8)	8.3	(0.8)	3.4	(0.6)	1.2	(0.3)	0.4	(0.2)
	Hong Kong-China	4.1	(0.7)	7.0	(0.7)	13.7	(1.2)	21.5	(1.3)	25.8	(1.2)	18.7	(0.9)	9.2	(0.7)
	Indonesia	51.5	(1.9)	24.7	(0.9)	14.9	(1.0)	6.1	(0.6)	2.1	(0.5)	0.6	(0.2)	0.1	(0.1)
	Latvia	7.4	(0.9)	15.5	(1.2)	26.4	(1.1)	27.7	(1.2)	16.3	(1.1)	5.5	(0.6)	1.2	(0.3)
	Liechtenstein	4.0	(1.4)	7.6	(1.4)	16.5	(2.9)	24.1	(2.9)	24.8	(2.6)	17.1	(2.4)	6.0	(1.5)
	Macao-China	2.4	(0.6)	8.1	(1.3)	17.8	(1.4)	25.8	(1.7)	25.3	(1.8)	15.6	(1.5)	5.1	(1.1)
	Russian Federation	11.1	(1.0)	16.8	(1.0)	25.8	(0.9)	24.6	(1.0)	14.8	(1.0)	5.6	(0.6)	1.4	(0.3)
	Serbia	13.6	(1.1)	20.6	(1.1)	27.1	(1.2)	22.1	(1.1)	12.3	(1.0)	3.7	(0.6)	0.7	(0.2)
	Thailand	27.7	(1.4)	26.4	(1.2)	23.3	(0.9)	13.7	(0.8)	6.3	(0.6)	2.0	(0.4)	0.6	(0.2)
	Tunisia	49.0	(1.3)	25.2	(1.0)	16.1	(0.9)	7.0	(0.6)	2.2	(0.4)	0.4	(0.2)	0.1	(0.1)
	Uruguay	25.6	(1.1)	19.5	(0.8)	22.1	(0.8)	18.1	(1.2)	10.0	(0.7)	3.7	(0.4)	0.9	(0.2)
	United Kingdom[1]	m	m	m	m	m	m	m	m	m	m	m	m	m	m

1. Response rate too low to ensure comparability (see Annex A3).

Table 2.3b

Percentage of students at each level of proficiency on the mathematics/quantity scale, by gender

Males – Proficiency levels

		Below Level 1 (below 358 score points)		Level 1 (from 358 to 420 score points)		Level 2 (from 421 to 482 score points)		Level 3 (from 483 to 544 score points)		Level 4 (from 545 to 606 score points)		Level 5 (from 607 to 668 score points)		Level 6 (above 668 score points)	
		%	S.E.	%	S.E.	%	S.E.	%	S.E.	%	S.E.	%	S.E.	%	S.E.
OECD countries	Australia	5.9	(0.6)	11.5	(0.6)	18.2	(1.2)	23.8	(1.5)	21.6	(1.1)	12.9	(0.8)	6.0	(0.6)
	Austria	3.9	(0.6)	11.4	(1.1)	20.6	(1.1)	26.0	(1.4)	22.6	(1.4)	12.2	(1.1)	3.3	(0.7)
	Belgium	7.9	(0.8)	9.4	(0.7)	14.6	(0.8)	19.3	(0.8)	21.6	(0.9)	17.6	(0.8)	9.7	(0.6)
	Canada	4.5	(0.4)	8.8	(0.5)	16.6	(0.7)	23.2	(0.7)	23.4	(0.8)	16.1	(0.8)	7.5	(0.5)
	Czech Republic	4.1	(0.7)	9.7	(1.0)	17.5	(1.1)	23.0	(1.1)	22.3	(1.1)	16.0	(1.2)	7.3	(0.8)
	Denmark	4.2	(0.6)	9.9	(0.9)	18.8	(1.2)	26.3	(1.3)	23.8	(1.1)	12.8	(1.0)	4.2	(0.5)
	Finland	1.5	(0.3)	5.5	(0.7)	14.3	(0.9)	25.9	(1.0)	26.5	(1.1)	18.3	(0.8)	8.0	(0.6)
	France	7.3	(1.1)	11.1	(0.9)	19.7	(1.3)	24.5	(1.3)	21.2	(1.0)	12.1	(0.9)	4.1	(0.5)
	Germany	8.8	(1.0)	10.9	(0.9)	17.3	(1.3)	20.7	(1.4)	21.3	(1.8)	14.8	(1.4)	6.2	(0.6)
	Greece	16.9	(1.4)	17.9	(1.1)	24.0	(1.4)	20.7	(1.3)	13.3	(1.1)	5.6	(0.9)	1.6	(0.5)
	Hungary	7.9	(0.8)	13.6	(0.9)	21.6	(1.1)	24.7	(1.2)	19.1	(1.1)	10.0	(0.8)	3.1	(0.5)
	Iceland	8.8	(0.8)	13.0	(0.9)	20.2	(1.6)	23.6	(1.6)	20.1	(1.3)	10.8	(0.9)	3.6	(0.8)
	Ireland	5.1	(0.7)	11.4	(1.2)	22.7	(1.2)	26.6	(1.8)	21.2	(1.3)	10.3	(0.8)	2.7	(0.5)
	Italy	13.4	(1.4)	15.4	(1.0)	20.3	(1.0)	21.9	(1.1)	15.8	(1.2)	9.1	(0.9)	4.0	(0.4)
	Japan	6.4	(1.0)	9.8	(0.9)	16.1	(0.9)	21.3	(1.3)	22.2	(1.3)	15.5	(1.1)	8.5	(1.5)
	Korea	2.4	(0.4)	6.2	(0.8)	15.0	(1.1)	23.8	(1.0)	27.2	(1.4)	17.8	(1.3)	7.6	(0.8)
	Luxembourg	6.3	(0.7)	12.6	(0.9)	21.0	(1.1)	24.0	(1.7)	21.8	(1.7)	10.9	(1.1)	3.4	(0.5)
	Mexico	33.8	(2.1)	24.4	(1.1)	21.1	(1.4)	13.8	(1.1)	5.4	(0.6)	1.3	(0.3)	0.2	(0.1)
	Netherlands	4.0	(0.9)	10.4	(1.2)	19.0	(1.5)	23.1	(1.7)	21.7	(1.4)	15.1	(1.3)	6.7	(0.7)
	New Zealand	6.2	(0.7)	11.5	(0.9)	18.9	(0.9)	22.1	(1.1)	22.2	(1.0)	13.1	(0.9)	6.0	(0.5)
	Norway	8.7	(0.7)	13.5	(0.8)	22.3	(1.3)	24.4	(1.6)	18.5	(1.0)	9.7	(0.9)	3.0	(0.5)
	Poland	8.5	(1.0)	12.8	(0.8)	23.0	(1.4)	25.7	(1.3)	18.9	(1.2)	8.7	(0.8)	2.3	(0.5)
	Portugal	13.2	(1.4)	16.8	(1.4)	23.1	(1.1)	22.7	(1.4)	15.5	(1.1)	6.9	(0.7)	1.8	(0.4)
	Slovak Republic	5.2	(0.9)	10.3	(1.1)	18.9	(1.1)	25.1	(1.3)	22.0	(1.2)	13.9	(1.0)	4.5	(0.6)
	Spain	9.5	(0.9)	12.8	(1.3)	21.5	(1.2)	24.0	(1.0)	19.1	(1.1)	9.9	(0.8)	3.2	(0.4)
	Sweden	4.6	(0.7)	10.1	(0.9)	21.0	(1.2)	26.9	(1.4)	21.6	(1.3)	11.4	(1.1)	4.5	(0.7)
	Switzerland	3.9	(0.5)	8.8	(0.8)	15.8	(1.1)	23.4	(1.7)	24.1	(1.1)	16.1	(1.2)	7.9	(1.2)
	Turkey	30.2	(2.4)	21.5	(1.3)	20.8	(1.5)	13.8	(1.2)	7.1	(1.1)	3.7	(0.9)	2.9	(1.2)
	United States	14.2	(1.2)	14.9	(1.1)	21.4	(1.0)	21.4	(1.1)	15.8	(0.9)	8.8	(0.9)	3.5	(0.5)
	OECD total	*12.4*	*(0.4)*	*13.7*	*(0.4)*	*19.7*	*(0.4)*	*21.4*	*(0.4)*	*17.8*	*(0.4)*	*10.5*	*(0.3)*	*4.5*	*(0.2)*
	OECD average	*8.8*	*(0.2)*	*12.3*	*(0.2)*	*19.5*	*(0.2)*	*23.0*	*(0.3)*	*19.9*	*(0.2)*	*11.8*	*(0.1)*	*4.7*	*(0.1)*
Partner countries	Brazil	48.5	(2.5)	20.3	(1.8)	15.3	(1.1)	9.2	(1.0)	4.2	(1.0)	1.8	(0.6)	0.7	(0.4)
	Hong Kong-China	5.2	(1.1)	7.6	(0.9)	13.4	(1.5)	20.1	(1.8)	24.6	(1.7)	18.8	(1.3)	10.3	(1.2)
	Indonesia	50.6	(2.0)	26.0	(1.5)	14.9	(1.2)	5.8	(0.7)	2.0	(0.4)	0.6	(0.2)	0.1	(0.1)
	Latvia	7.5	(1.2)	16.0	(1.4)	25.7	(1.4)	26.5	(1.6)	16.5	(1.3)	6.1	(0.9)	1.7	(0.4)
	Liechtenstein	5.2	(2.3)	5.8	(2.3)	12.5	(3.5)	23.6	(4.6)	24.9	(3.9)	19.1	(3.1)	8.9	(2.3)
	Macao-China	2.4	(1.1)	7.7	(1.8)	16.0	(2.0)	23.7	(2.8)	25.9	(2.5)	17.7	(2.3)	6.7	(1.8)
	Russian Federation	11.4	(1.4)	16.5	(1.3)	24.4	(1.2)	24.2	(1.3)	15.2	(1.3)	6.6	(0.9)	1.9	(0.5)
	Serbia	15.2	(1.4)	21.1	(1.4)	26.1	(1.4)	19.3	(1.5)	12.8	(1.2)	4.6	(0.8)	0.9	(0.3)
	Thailand	29.0	(1.7)	26.1	(1.3)	22.7	(1.2)	13.3	(1.1)	6.1	(1.0)	2.0	(0.5)	0.7	(0.3)
	Tunisia	45.4	(1.4)	26.5	(1.3)	17.0	(1.3)	7.5	(0.8)	2.9	(0.5)	0.5	(0.2)	0.1	(0.1)
	Uruguay	24.3	(1.5)	18.8	(1.1)	22.0	(1.2)	18.7	(1.5)	10.5	(0.9)	4.3	(0.6)	1.4	(0.3)
	United Kingdom[1]	m	m	m	m	m	m	m	m	m	m	m	m	m	m

Females – Proficiency levels

		Below Level 1 (below 358 score points)		Level 1 (from 358 to 420 score points)		Level 2 (from 421 to 482 score points)		Level 3 (from 483 to 544 score points)		Level 4 (from 545 to 606 score points)		Level 5 (from 607 to 668 score points)		Level 6 (above 668 score points)	
		%	S.E.	%	S.E.	%	S.E.	%	S.E.	%	S.E.	%	S.E.	%	S.E.
OECD countries	Australia	5.0	(0.5)	10.5	(0.7)	19.9	(0.8)	24.8	(0.7)	23.2	(0.8)	12.2	(0.8)	4.4	(0.4)
	Austria	3.4	(0.6)	11.0	(1.3)	21.2	(1.6)	28.4	(1.2)	23.6	(1.3)	10.1	(0.9)	2.3	(0.5)
	Belgium	6.5	(0.8)	8.3	(0.8)	15.6	(0.8)	22.1	(0.8)	23.0	(0.9)	17.4	(0.8)	7.2	(0.6)
	Canada	3.3	(0.3)	8.4	(0.5)	18.2	(0.7)	26.7	(0.7)	24.5	(0.6)	13.6	(0.6)	5.3	(0.5)
	Czech Republic	5.2	(1.1)	9.7	(1.2)	16.9	(1.2)	24.0	(1.4)	23.9	(1.5)	14.1	(1.2)	6.1	(0.7)
	Denmark	5.2	(0.8)	10.9	(0.8)	21.0	(1.1)	26.3	(1.2)	21.6	(1.1)	11.2	(0.8)	3.7	(0.6)
	Finland	1.2	(0.3)	4.4	(0.6)	14.9	(0.8)	27.9	(1.1)	28.2	(1.3)	17.4	(1.0)	5.9	(0.5)
	France	6.1	(0.8)	11.1	(1.1)	21.0	(1.2)	26.2	(1.6)	22.5	(1.2)	10.0	(1.1)	2.9	(0.5)
	Germany	7.9	(0.8)	9.8	(1.2)	17.7	(1.2)	23.5	(1.3)	22.7	(1.1)	13.6	(1.2)	4.7	(0.6)
	Greece	21.0	(1.5)	21.5	(1.3)	26.2	(1.5)	19.3	(1.7)	8.9	(1.0)	2.7	(0.6)	0.5	(0.2)
	Hungary	7.7	(0.9)	13.3	(1.2)	21.7	(1.2)	25.8	(1.4)	20.4	(1.1)	9.3	(0.9)	1.9	(0.4)
	Iceland	3.4	(0.6)	8.7	(1.0)	18.1	(1.1)	25.0	(1.3)	25.2	(1.3)	14.7	(1.0)	4.9	(0.6)
	Ireland	6.0	(0.8)	13.2	(1.0)	23.4	(1.3)	27.1	(1.1)	20.0	(1.4)	8.6	(1.0)	1.8	(0.5)
	Italy	13.9	(1.5)	16.8	(1.0)	23.5	(1.0)	22.9	(1.1)	14.7	(1.0)	6.5	(0.5)	1.8	(0.2)
	Japan	5.1	(0.9)	8.6	(1.1)	17.1	(1.1)	24.8	(1.5)	24.9	(1.3)	14.7	(1.0)	4.9	(0.5)
	Korea	2.8	(0.5)	8.8	(1.2)	20.0	(1.4)	27.1	(1.3)	24.2	(1.4)	12.4	(1.1)	4.7	(1.0)
	Luxembourg	6.7	(0.6)	12.3	(1.1)	22.6	(1.3)	28.3	(1.5)	20.2	(1.2)	7.9	(0.7)	2.0	(0.3)
	Mexico	37.1	(2.1)	25.6	(1.8)	21.7	(1.3)	11.1	(0.9)	3.7	(0.5)	0.7	(0.2)	0.1	(0.0)
	Netherlands	4.2	(0.9)	9.8	(1.2)	17.5	(1.5)	22.9	(1.4)	22.2	(1.3)	16.7	(1.3)	6.7	(0.8)
	New Zealand	6.6	(0.7)	12.2	(1.0)	21.4	(1.2)	25.1	(1.0)	20.1	(1.2)	10.7	(0.9)	4.0	(0.5)
	Norway	6.6	(0.7)	14.1	(1.1)	23.2	(1.2)	26.5	(1.4)	19.1	(1.3)	8.1	(0.8)	2.2	(0.4)
	Poland	5.6	(0.8)	14.2	(1.3)	25.3	(1.3)	28.5	(1.1)	18.5	(1.0)	6.6	(0.7)	1.4	(0.4)
	Portugal	12.6	(1.4)	19.8	(1.4)	27.2	(1.1)	24.0	(1.4)	12.3	(1.0)	3.6	(0.5)	0.6	(0.3)
	Slovak Republic	6.0	(0.9)	10.8	(1.0)	21.1	(1.1)	27.1	(1.1)	21.8	(1.1)	10.5	(1.0)	2.7	(0.5)
	Spain	8.4	(0.6)	13.6	(1.0)	23.5	(1.1)	26.1	(1.1)	18.6	(1.0)	7.8	(0.7)	2.1	(0.3)
	Sweden	4.2	(0.7)	10.4	(0.9)	21.9	(1.3)	27.6	(1.8)	21.7	(1.4)	10.9	(0.9)	3.3	(0.8)
	Switzerland	4.4	(0.6)	8.5	(0.8)	16.2	(0.9)	25.1	(1.2)	25.2	(1.0)	15.2	(1.3)	5.4	(0.7)
	Turkey	34.4	(2.5)	25.0	(1.6)	19.5	(1.4)	11.1	(1.3)	5.9	(1.3)	2.6	(0.8)	1.5	(0.7)
	United States	13.2	(1.0)	16.3	(0.9)	22.7	(1.0)	22.1	(1.1)	16.1	(0.9)	7.3	(0.8)	2.0	(0.5)
	OECD total	*12.2*	*(0.4)*	*14.5*	*(0.4)*	*20.9*	*(0.3)*	*22.6*	*(0.4)*	*17.9*	*(0.3)*	*8.9*	*(0.3)*	*2.9*	*(0.2)*
	OECD average	*8.8*	*(0.2)*	*12.8*	*(0.2)*	*20.7*	*(0.2)*	*24.4*	*(0.2)*	*19.8*	*(0.2)*	*10.2*	*(0.2)*	*3.3*	*(0.1)*
Partner countries	Brazil	53.4	(1.9)	21.0	(1.5)	14.7	(1.0)	7.5	(1.0)	2.7	(0.5)	0.7	(0.3)	0.2	(0.2)
	Hong Kong-China	3.0	(0.6)	6.3	(0.9)	14.0	(1.3)	22.9	(1.4)	27.0	(1.3)	18.7	(1.6)	8.1	(0.9)
	Indonesia	52.5	(2.2)	23.5	(1.2)	14.8	(1.2)	6.4	(0.8)	2.2	(0.7)	0.5	(0.2)	0.1	(0.1)
	Latvia	7.4	(0.9)	15.1	(1.6)	27.0	(1.8)	28.7	(1.5)	16.2	(1.4)	4.9	(0.7)	0.7	(0.2)
	Liechtenstein	2.8	(1.9)	9.4	(2.8)	20.7	(6.0)	24.7	(5.6)	24.6	(4.5)	14.9	(3.4)	3.0	(1.6)
	Macao-China	2.3	(0.7)	8.6	(1.6)	19.5	(2.0)	27.7	(2.5)	24.7	(3.1)	13.6	(2.2)	3.5	(1.0)
	Russian Federation	10.9	(1.1)	17.1	(1.2)	27.2	(1.1)	24.9	(1.3)	14.4	(1.1)	4.6	(0.6)	0.9	(0.3)
	Serbia	12.1	(1.4)	20.1	(1.5)	28.0	(1.5)	24.9	(1.6)	11.7	(1.6)	2.8	(0.6)	0.4	(0.2)
	Thailand	26.7	(1.8)	26.6	(1.7)	23.7	(1.1)	13.9	(1.0)	6.5	(0.8)	2.0	(0.5)	0.6	(0.2)
	Tunisia	52.5	(1.6)	23.9	(1.3)	15.2	(1.1)	6.5	(0.9)	1.6	(0.4)	0.3	(0.2)	0.0	a
	Uruguay	27.0	(1.3)	20.2	(1.4)	22.2	(1.2)	17.6	(1.5)	9.6	(0.9)	3.0	(0.5)	0.4	(0.2)
	United Kingdom[1]	m	m	m	m	m	m	m	m	m	m	m	m	m	m

1. Response rate too low to ensure comparability (see Annex A3).

Table 2.3c
Mean score, variation and gender differences in student performance on the mathematics/quantity scale

		All students				Gender differences					
		Mean score		Standard deviation		Males		Females		Difference (M-F)	
		Mean	**S.E.**	**S.D.**	**S.E.**	**Mean score**	**S.E.**	**Mean score**	**S.E.**	**Score dif.**	**S.E.**
OECD countries	Australia	517	(2.1)	97	(1.5)	518	(2.9)	516	(2.7)	1	(3.7)
	Austria	513	(3.0)	86	(1.7)	515	(3.7)	512	(3.7)	3	(4.2)
	Belgium	530	(2.3)	109	(1.8)	530	(3.3)	529	(3.3)	1	(4.7)
	Canada	528	(1.8)	94	(0.9)	533	(2.2)	528	(1.9)	**5**	(2.2)
	Czech Republic	528	(3.5)	98	(2.1)	531	(4.2)	525	(4.5)	6	(5.1)
	Denmark	516	(2.6)	92	(1.6)	520	(3.2)	511	(2.9)	**9**	(3.1)
	Finland	549	(1.8)	83	(1.1)	550	(2.3)	547	(2.1)	3	(2.3)
	France	507	(2.5)	95	(1.8)	508	(3.8)	506	(2.9)	2	(4.4)
	Germany	514	(3.4)	106	(1.9)	515	(4.2)	514	(3.8)	1	(4.4)
	Greece	446	(4.0)	100	(1.7)	458	(4.9)	435	(4.0)	**23**	(4.0)
	Hungary	496	(2.7)	95	(1.9)	497	(3.3)	495	(3.2)	2	(3.6)
	Iceland	513	(1.5)	96	(1.3)	500	(2.5)	528	(2.3)	**–28**	(3.9)
	Ireland	502	(2.5)	88	(1.3)	506	(3.1)	497	(3.5)	**9**	(4.3)
	Italy	475	(3.4)	106	(2.0)	481	(5.0)	469	(4.4)	13	(6.5)
	Japan	527	(3.8)	102	(2.5)	528	(5.6)	525	(3.7)	3	(5.7)
	Korea	537	(3.0)	90	(1.9)	546	(4.0)	524	(4.9)	**22**	(6.2)
	Luxembourg	501	(1.1)	91	(1.1)	506	(2.2)	497	(1.6)	**9**	(3.2)
	Mexico	394	(3.9)	95	(1.9)	400	(4.8)	388	(4.3)	**12**	(4.5)
	Netherlands	528	(3.1)	97	(2.4)	526	(4.2)	530	(3.6)	–4	(4.7)
	New Zealand	511	(2.2)	99	(1.3)	517	(2.7)	505	(3.2)	**12**	(3.9)
	Norway	494	(2.2)	94	(1.1)	494	(2.8)	494	(2.7)	0	(3.3)
	Poland	492	(2.5)	89	(1.7)	493	(2.9)	491	(3.0)	2	(3.3)
	Portugal	465	(3.5)	94	(1.8)	473	(4.1)	459	(3.7)	**14**	(3.3)
	Slovak Republic	513	(3.4)	94	(2.3)	519	(4.0)	506	(3.6)	**13**	(3.6)
	Spain	492	(2.5)	97	(1.3)	495	(3.6)	490	(2.2)	5	(3.1)
	Sweden	514	(2.5)	90	(1.7)	515	(2.9)	512	(3.2)	3	(3.6)
	Switzerland	533	(3.1)	96	(1.7)	536	(4.4)	529	(3.2)	7	(4.6)
	Turkey	413	(6.8)	112	(5.1)	421	(8.0)	404	(6.6)	**18**	(6.3)
	United States	476	(3.2)	105	(1.5)	478	(3.6)	474	(3.6)	4	(3.4)
	OECD total	*487*	*(1.1)*	*108*	*(0.7)*	*490*	*(1.4)*	*484*	*(1.3)*	6	*(1.5)*
	OECD average	*501*	*(0.6)*	*102*	*(0.4)*	*504*	*(0.8)*	*498*	*(0.8)*	6	*(0.8)*
Partner countries	Brazil	360	(5.0)	109	(3.0)	370	(6.3)	351	(4.8)	**18**	(4.5)
	Hong Kong-China	545	(4.2)	99	(2.6)	544	(6.0)	546	(4.1)	–3	(6.1)
	Indonesia	357	(4.3)	91	(2.4)	359	(4.0)	356	(5.0)	2	(3.1)
	Latvia	482	(3.6)	85	(1.4)	483	(4.4)	480	(3.6)	3	(3.4)
	Liechtenstein	534	(4.1)	93	(4.5)	544	(7.0)	523	(5.6)	**21**	(9.9)
	Macao-China	533	(3.0)	87	(2.3)	542	(4.3)	525	(4.2)	**17**	(6.0)
	Russian Federation	472	(4.0)	92	(1.7)	476	(5.0)	469	(4.2)	6	(4.4)
	Serbia	456	(3.8)	89	(1.6)	455	(4.2)	458	(4.7)	–3	(4.7)
	Thailand	415	(3.1)	93	(2.1)	412	(4.1)	417	(3.8)	–5	(4.9)
	Tunisia	364	(2.8)	88	(2.1)	372	(2.9)	357	(3.3)	**16**	(2.7)
	Uruguay	430	(3.2)	109	(1.6)	436	(3.9)	424	(3.8)	**12**	(4.1)
	United Kingdom[1]	m	m	m	m	m	m	m	m	m	m

		Percentiles											
		5th		10th		25th		75th		90th		95th	
		Score	**S.E.**	**Score**	**S.E.**	**Score**	**S.E.**	**Score**	**S.E.**	**Score**	**S.E.**	**Score**	**S.E.**
OECD countries	Australia	352	(4.3)	390	(3.4)	451	(2.8)	585	(2.3)	639	(2.7)	671	(3.1)
	Austria	370	(4.6)	400	(5.3)	454	(3.5)	574	(3.4)	622	(3.6)	650	(4.1)
	Belgium	332	(7.8)	382	(5.4)	460	(3.4)	610	(2.2)	662	(2.2)	690	(2.4)
	Canada	370	(3.0)	407	(2.8)	466	(2.3)	593	(1.9)	647	(2.6)	677	(2.8)
	Czech Republic	361	(7.3)	398	(6.4)	462	(4.6)	597	(3.4)	651	(3.9)	682	(3.9)
	Denmark	360	(5.4)	395	(3.9)	454	(3.1)	580	(2.9)	632	(3.8)	661	(4.5)
	Finland	409	(3.9)	441	(3.2)	494	(2.4)	607	(2.2)	654	(2.3)	683	(2.8)
	France	341	(7.3)	381	(5.4)	445	(3.6)	574	(2.8)	626	(3.4)	656	(3.8)
	Germany	325	(6.8)	369	(6.4)	445	(4.7)	590	(4.0)	645	(3.2)	673	(3.2)
	Greece	279	(5.0)	316	(4.8)	379	(4.7)	514	(5.0)	573	(5.6)	609	(5.7)
	Hungary	335	(5.7)	371	(5.2)	433	(4.1)	565	(3.3)	616	(3.4)	644	(3.7)
	Iceland	347	(4.0)	386	(3.4)	449	(3.0)	583	(2.2)	633	(2.8)	664	(4.6)
	Ireland	353	(5.3)	388	(4.3)	442	(3.4)	564	(3.0)	615	(3.1)	644	(3.2)
	Italy	297	(6.9)	336	(6.1)	404	(5.0)	548	(3.8)	610	(3.6)	645	(3.4)
	Japan	350	(8.5)	393	(6.5)	462	(5.1)	598	(4.1)	652	(5.3)	682	(6.4)
	Korea	386	(5.1)	421	(4.5)	477	(3.8)	599	(3.6)	650	(4.6)	680	(5.9)
	Luxembourg	345	(3.8)	382	(3.3)	440	(2.3)	565	(2.3)	617	(2.8)	647	(3.6)
	Mexico	237	(6.5)	270	(5.5)	329	(4.7)	460	(4.7)	517	(5.1)	550	(4.8)
	Netherlands	367	(7.0)	400	(6.1)	461	(4.6)	600	(3.2)	651	(3.3)	681	(4.1)
	New Zealand	346	(4.6)	381	(4.2)	443	(3.5)	580	(3.0)	638	(2.5)	669	(3.5)
	Norway	336	(4.0)	372	(4.0)	431	(3.3)	559	(3.2)	614	(2.7)	645	(4.3)
	Poland	342	(5.1)	376	(5.0)	433	(3.4)	553	(2.7)	605	(3.6)	634	(3.8)
	Portugal	308	(7.1)	343	(6.3)	401	(5.0)	529	(3.3)	585	(3.7)	618	(4.0)
	Slovak Republic	352	(7.6)	391	(6.2)	451	(4.7)	578	(3.3)	630	(3.1)	659	(3.6)
	Spain	327	(5.5)	365	(4.6)	429	(3.6)	560	(2.9)	614	(3.2)	645	(4.3)
	Sweden	364	(5.0)	398	(3.6)	454	(2.9)	575	(3.6)	628	(3.8)	659	(5.1)
	Switzerland	366	(4.8)	405	(3.7)	471	(3.8)	599	(3.6)	652	(5.4)	682	(6.3)
	Turkey	242	(6.7)	277	(5.4)	337	(5.6)	481	(8.9)	559	(14.3)	614	(21.3)
	United States	300	(5.9)	337	(5.4)	406	(4.4)	551	(3.3)	611	(3.8)	645	(5.7)
	OECD total	*303*	*(2.5)*	*343*	*(1.9)*	*415*	*(1.6)*	*564*	*(1.1)*	*623*	*(1.2)*	*657*	*(1.5)*
	OECD average	*325*	*(1.4)*	*366*	*(1.2)*	*433*	*(0.9)*	*573*	*(0.6)*	*629*	*(0.7)*	*661*	*(0.8)*
Partner countries	Brazil	188	(5.3)	223	(5.6)	286	(5.0)	432	(6.5)	502	(9.8)	545	(10.6)
	Hong Kong-China	369	(9.2)	413	(7.7)	483	(6.0)	615	(3.6)	665	(3.9)	694	(4.6)
	Indonesia	213	(4.8)	243	(4.6)	295	(4.4)	416	(5.4)	475	(6.9)	514	(9.5)
	Latvia	339	(6.8)	371	(5.4)	426	(4.1)	539	(4.2)	589	(4.5)	618	(4.4)
	Liechtenstein	369	(16.2)	410	(14.3)	474	(7.2)	601	(6.2)	648	(10.6)	675	(11.0)
	Macao-China	388	(7.8)	418	(5.9)	472	(5.6)	594	(4.1)	645	(5.3)	669	(7.6)
	Russian Federation	316	(5.7)	353	(4.8)	411	(4.8)	535	(4.6)	590	(4.5)	622	(4.9)
	Serbia	311	(3.9)	341	(4.4)	396	(4.6)	518	(4.6)	570	(4.7)	602	(5.9)
	Thailand	269	(4.6)	299	(3.5)	351	(3.5)	475	(4.1)	537	(6.0)	576	(6.7)
	Tunisia	225	(3.1)	255	(3.4)	303	(3.2)	422	(3.8)	481	(5.5)	518	(6.4)
	Uruguay	246	(5.4)	286	(4.6)	355	(4.1)	506	(4.0)	566	(3.7)	602	(5.1)
	United Kingdom[1]	m	m	m	m	m	m	m	m	m	m	m	m

Note: Values that are statistically significant are indicated in bold (see Annex A4).

1. Response rate too low to ensure comparability (see Annex A3).

Table 2.4a

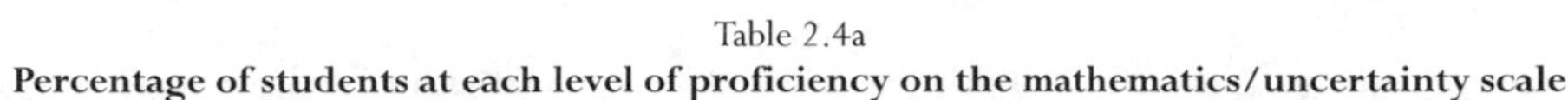

Percentage of students at each level of proficiency on the mathematics/uncertainty scale

		Proficiency levels													
		Below Level 1 (below 358 score points)		Level 1 (from 358 to 420 score points)		Level 2 (from 421 to 482 score points)		Level 3 (from 483 to 544 score points)		Level 4 (from 545 to 606 score points)		Level 5 (from 607 to 668 score points)		Level 6 (above 668 score points)	
		%	S.E.	%	S.E.	%	S.E.	%	S.E.	%	S.E.	%	S.E.	%	S.E.
OECD countries	Australia	4.1	(0.4)	9.0	(0.5)	17.5	(0.6)	23.8	(0.6)	23.0	(0.6)	15.1	(0.5)	7.4	(0.5)
	Austria	7.4	(0.7)	15.2	(1.0)	22.9	(1.3)	24.3	(1.1)	17.9	(1.1)	9.3	(0.7)	3.0	(0.4)
	Belgium	6.2	(0.5)	11.1	(0.5)	17.3	(0.6)	20.4	(0.6)	20.8	(0.6)	15.8	(0.5)	8.4	(0.4)
	Canada	2.0	(0.2)	6.4	(0.4)	16.5	(0.6)	25.6	(0.5)	26.3	(0.6)	16.4	(0.6)	6.8	(0.5)
	Czech Republic	5.2	(0.6)	14.4	(0.8)	24.4	(1.1)	24.2	(1.0)	19.2	(0.9)	9.3	(0.9)	3.3	(0.4)
	Denmark	4.4	(0.6)	10.4	(0.7)	20.8	(0.8)	25.8	(0.8)	22.0	(0.8)	12.6	(0.7)	4.0	(0.4)
	Finland	1.6	(0.2)	5.5	(0.6)	15.4	(0.6)	27.2	(0.8)	27.0	(0.9)	16.4	(0.8)	6.8	(0.6)
	France	6.0	(0.7)	12.3	(0.9)	20.9	(0.8)	25.3	(1.0)	21.7	(0.7)	11.0	(0.6)	2.8	(0.3)
	Germany	8.7	(0.8)	15.2	(0.8)	21.8	(0.9)	22.6	(1.0)	19.0	(0.9)	9.7	(0.8)	2.9	(0.3)
	Greece	12.8	(1.1)	20.4	(1.3)	27.3	(1.0)	23.1	(0.9)	11.8	(0.9)	4.0	(0.6)	0.7	(0.2)
	Hungary	6.0	(0.7)	15.2	(0.9)	26.2	(1.1)	26.5	(0.9)	17.3	(0.9)	7.1	(0.7)	1.6	(0.3)
	Iceland	4.0	(0.4)	8.9	(0.6)	18.8	(0.7)	24.4	(1.1)	22.9	(0.9)	14.8	(0.7)	6.1	(0.5)
	Ireland	3.6	(0.4)	10.2	(0.7)	21.2	(0.9)	26.5	(0.9)	22.0	(0.9)	12.4	(0.7)	4.0	(0.4)
	Italy	13.7	(1.1)	18.9	(0.7)	25.6	(0.7)	22.2	(0.9)	13.0	(0.8)	5.1	(0.4)	1.4	(0.2)
	Japan	4.9	(0.6)	9.1	(0.9)	17.5	(0.8)	23.7	(1.1)	23.5	(1.3)	14.8	(1.0)	6.6	(0.9)
	Korea	2.2	(0.3)	7.2	(0.6)	17.3	(0.8)	25.0	(1.0)	25.7	(0.9)	15.7	(0.8)	6.7	(0.8)
	Luxembourg	8.2	(0.4)	14.6	(0.8)	22.8	(1.0)	24.5	(1.2)	18.2	(0.7)	8.7	(0.6)	2.9	(0.4)
	Mexico	35.3	(1.7)	30.6	(1.3)	21.3	(1.0)	9.5	(0.8)	2.7	(0.4)	0.5	(0.1)	0.0	(0.0)
	Netherlands	1.0	(0.2)	6.7	(0.8)	17.0	(1.0)	23.4	(1.2)	23.2	(1.3)	19.1	(1.1)	9.5	(0.8)
	New Zealand	3.9	(0.5)	9.4	(0.8)	18.0	(1.0)	23.3	(1.0)	22.1	(1.0)	14.6	(0.7)	8.6	(0.5)
	Norway	5.7	(0.6)	11.8	(0.8)	20.6	(0.8)	24.4	(1.2)	20.3	(0.8)	11.6	(0.9)	5.6	(0.4)
	Poland	5.2	(0.6)	13.9	(0.9)	25.7	(1.0)	27.4	(0.9)	18.7	(1.0)	7.5	(0.8)	1.6	(0.3)
	Portugal	9.0	(1.1)	18.4	(1.1)	27.7	(1.0)	25.6	(1.1)	14.5	(1.0)	4.2	(0.4)	0.6	(0.2)
	Slovak Republic	8.6	(1.0)	17.9	(0.8)	26.8	(0.9)	24.1	(0.9)	15.7	(0.8)	5.6	(0.5)	1.2	(0.2)
	Spain	7.1	(0.6)	13.7	(0.7)	25.5	(0.8)	26.9	(0.8)	18.4	(0.7)	6.9	(0.5)	1.5	(0.3)
	Sweden	6.4	(0.5)	11.8	(0.7)	21.5	(0.8)	22.9	(0.8)	19.7	(0.8)	12.1	(0.6)	5.6	(0.5)
	Switzerland	6.3	(0.5)	10.7	(0.7)	19.1	(0.8)	24.0	(0.9)	21.2	(0.8)	12.9	(1.0)	5.8	(0.7)
	Turkey	18.6	(1.5)	25.6	(1.4)	25.3	(1.2)	16.6	(1.3)	8.0	(1.1)	3.4	(0.8)	2.6	(1.1)
	United States	9.0	(0.8)	14.9	(0.7)	22.3	(0.7)	23.6	(0.7)	17.4	(0.8)	9.5	(0.7)	3.2	(0.4)
	OECD total	*9.8*	*(0.3)*	*14.9*	*(0.3)*	*21.5*	*(0.2)*	*22.6*	*(0.3)*	*17.9*	*(0.3)*	*9.7*	*(0.2)*	*3.6*	*(0.2)*
	OECD average	*7.4*	*(0.1)*	*13.3*	*(0.2)*	*21.5*	*(0.2)*	*23.8*	*(0.2)*	*19.2*	*(0.2)*	*10.6*	*(0.1)*	*4.2*	*(0.1)*
Partner countries	Brazil	43.5	(1.9)	29.1	(1.3)	17.0	(0.9)	7.0	(0.7)	2.6	(0.5)	0.7	(0.3)	0.2	(0.1)
	Hong Kong-China	3.3	(0.7)	6.3	(0.7)	12.5	(0.9)	19.3	(0.9)	24.8	(1.2)	21.1	(1.1)	12.7	(1.1)
	Indonesia	35.3	(1.6)	36.7	(1.0)	20.4	(1.1)	6.2	(0.7)	1.3	(0.3)	0.1	(0.1)	0.0	
	Latvia	8.3	(0.8)	17.8	(1.2)	28.1	(1.3)	25.7	(1.2)	14.6	(0.9)	4.5	(0.5)	1.0	(0.2)
	Liechtenstein	5.2	(1.6)	9.5	(2.0)	18.4	(2.3)	23.0	(2.9)	23.8	(3.0)	14.9	(2.5)	5.1	(1.4)
	Macao-China	2.5	(0.6)	7.2	(1.3)	18.9	(1.6)	27.4	(2.0)	23.5	(1.7)	14.9	(1.5)	5.4	(1.0)
	Russian Federation	19.0	(1.4)	24.8	(1.1)	26.3	(1.0)	18.1	(1.0)	8.6	(0.8)	2.7	(0.4)	0.5	(0.1)
	Serbia	20.1	(1.3)	27.3	(1.1)	26.8	(1.1)	17.4	(1.3)	6.7	(0.7)	1.5	(0.3)	0.2	(0.1)
	Thailand	18.1	(1.1)	32.8	(1.0)	29.6	(1.0)	14.1	(0.9)	4.3	(0.5)	1.1	(0.3)	0.1	(0.1)
	Tunisia	47.9	(1.3)	32.3	(1.0)	14.8	(0.9)	4.2	(0.6)	0.8	(0.3)	0.0	(0.0)		
	Uruguay	27.1	(1.3)	23.5	(1.1)	23.5	(1.3)	16.0	(0.8)	7.1	(0.5)	2.4	(0.3)	0.4	(0.1)
	United Kingdom[1]	m	m	m	m	m	m	m	m	m	m	m	m	m	m

1. Response rate too low to ensure comparability (see Annex A3).

Table 2.4b

Percentage of students at each level of proficiency on the mathematics/uncertainty scale, by gender

Males – Proficiency levels

		Below Level 1 (below 358 score points)		Level 1 (from 358 to 420 score points)		Level 2 (from 421 to 482 score points)		Level 3 (from 483 to 544 score points)		Level 4 (from 545 to 606 score points)		Level 5 (from 607 to 668 score points)		Level 6 (above 668 score points)	
		%	S.E.	%	S.E.	%	S.E.	%	S.E.	%	S.E.	%	S.E.	%	S.E.
OECD countries	Australia	4.4	(0.5)	9.2	(0.7)	16.7	(0.8)	22.7	(0.9)	22.2	(0.8)	15.7	(0.7)	9.1	(0.8)
	Austria	7.8	(0.9)	14.6	(1.3)	22.4	(1.3)	22.7	(1.3)	17.7	(1.2)	11.0	(0.9)	3.8	(0.6)
	Belgium	6.3	(0.7)	11.6	(0.8)	16.4	(0.8)	19.2	(0.8)	20.2	(0.9)	16.3	(0.9)	10.0	(0.7)
	Canada	2.4	(0.3)	6.1	(0.4)	14.4	(0.6)	22.5	(0.8)	25.9	(0.7)	19.0	(0.8)	9.7	(0.7)
	Czech Republic	4.2	(0.6)	13.2	(1.0)	23.7	(1.2)	23.7	(1.2)	19.7	(1.2)	11.3	(1.0)	4.1	(0.6)
	Denmark	3.7	(0.6)	8.7	(0.8)	18.7	(1.1)	25.2	(1.1)	23.9	(1.2)	14.7	(1.0)	5.2	(0.7)
	Finland	1.6	(0.3)	5.5	(0.7)	14.2	(0.8)	25.4	(1.0)	26.8	(1.1)	17.9	(1.1)	8.6	(1.0)
	France	6.4	(1.0)	11.4	(1.2)	19.4	(1.2)	24.1	(1.5)	21.9	(1.2)	13.0	(0.9)	3.7	(0.5)
	Germany	7.1	(1.1)	15.0	(1.2)	21.1	(1.2)	21.4	(1.3)	19.8	(1.1)	11.5	(1.0)	4.1	(0.6)
	Greece	11.5	(1.3)	17.8	(1.4)	26.3	(1.4)	23.8	(1.4)	14.1	(1.2)	5.4	(0.8)	1.1	(0.2)
	Hungary	5.9	(0.8)	14.5	(1.0)	25.6	(1.3)	26.3	(1.2)	17.7	(1.3)	7.9	(0.9)	2.1	(0.5)
	Iceland	4.8	(0.6)	10.0	(1.0)	19.4	(1.1)	22.7	(1.7)	22.1	(1.6)	14.4	(1.1)	6.4	(0.7)
	Ireland	3.3	(0.5)	9.2	(1.0)	19.3	(1.3)	26.5	(1.3)	22.7	(1.3)	13.6	(1.0)	5.2	(0.7)
	Italy	12.2	(1.4)	17.1	(1.0)	23.2	(1.0)	23.0	(1.5)	15.1	(1.1)	7.0	(0.6)	2.3	(0.3)
	Japan	5.0	(0.8)	9.1	(0.9)	15.9	(1.1)	21.5	(1.6)	22.8	(2.2)	16.6	(1.4)	9.1	(1.6)
	Korea	2.1	(0.4)	6.3	(0.8)	15.3	(1.1)	23.5	(1.2)	27.1	(1.2)	17.8	(1.1)	8.0	(0.9)
	Luxembourg	7.3	(0.6)	13.5	(0.9)	21.0	(1.4)	22.8	(1.6)	20.3	(1.1)	11.0	(0.9)	4.1	(0.6)
	Mexico	34.8	(2.0)	29.9	(1.3)	21.1	(1.2)	10.2	(1.0)	3.2	(0.5)	0.6	(0.2)	0.0	(0.0)
	Netherlands	0.6	(0.2)	5.9	(1.1)	16.8	(1.4)	23.8	(1.4)	23.1	(1.8)	19.2	(1.6)	10.6	(0.9)
	New Zealand	3.9	(0.6)	9.2	(1.0)	17.1	(1.3)	21.7	(1.4)	22.3	(1.3)	15.4	(1.0)	10.4	(0.7)
	Norway	5.6	(0.6)	11.3	(0.9)	19.8	(1.1)	23.7	(1.5)	19.9	(1.2)	12.8	(1.0)	7.0	(0.6)
	Poland	6.3	(0.9)	14.1	(1.2)	23.4	(1.2)	26.5	(1.1)	18.7	(1.1)	8.8	(0.9)	2.1	(0.4)
	Portugal	9.5	(1.3)	17.6	(1.1)	25.3	(1.4)	24.7	(1.3)	16.4	(1.2)	5.6	(0.7)	0.9	(0.3)
	Slovak Republic	7.8	(1.2)	16.2	(1.3)	25.8	(1.2)	23.9	(1.2)	17.7	(1.3)	6.9	(0.7)	1.7	(0.4)
	Spain	7.5	(0.8)	13.2	(0.9)	23.7	(1.0)	26.2	(1.1)	19.4	(1.2)	8.4	(0.8)	1.8	(0.3)
	Sweden	6.5	(0.7)	10.9	(0.8)	20.6	(1.1)	22.7	(1.0)	19.9	(1.1)	12.6	(0.9)	6.7	(0.7)
	Switzerland	5.4	(0.5)	10.0	(0.9)	17.7	(1.2)	23.3	(1.3)	21.5	(0.9)	14.6	(1.4)	7.7	(1.1)
	Turkey	17.5	(1.8)	23.1	(1.9)	24.5	(1.7)	18.0	(1.7)	9.6	(1.4)	4.1	(1.0)	3.1	(1.4)
	United States	9.9	(1.0)	14.5	(1.0)	21.4	(1.0)	22.7	(1.1)	17.4	(0.9)	10.0	(0.8)	4.1	(0.6)
	OECD total	*9.8*	*(0.4)*	*14.2*	*(0.3)*	*20.3*	*(0.3)*	*21.9*	*(0.4)*	*18.2*	*(0.4)*	*10.9*	*(0.3)*	*4.7*	*(0.2)*
	OECD average	*7.1*	*(0.2)*	*12.6*	*(0.2)*	*20.3*	*(0.2)*	*23.0*	*(0.3)*	*19.7*	*(0.2)*	*11.9*	*(0.2)*	*5.3*	*(0.1)*
Partner countries	Brazil	40.4	(2.2)	28.8	(1.7)	17.6	(1.4)	8.2	(1.1)	3.5	(0.9)	1.1	(0.5)	0.3	(0.3)
	Hong Kong-China	4.1	(1.0)	6.4	(1.0)	11.3	(1.1)	17.6	(1.1)	22.7	(1.4)	22.0	(1.5)	16.0	(1.8)
	Indonesia	36.1	(1.8)	36.9	(1.2)	20.4	(1.2)	5.6	(0.6)	1.0	(0.3)	0.1	(0.1)		
	Latvia	9.0	(1.2)	18.4	(1.6)	26.6	(1.7)	25.2	(1.8)	14.6	(1.2)	4.9	(0.7)	1.3	(0.3)
	Liechtenstein	5.3	(2.3)	6.2	(2.3)	17.1	(3.0)	21.3	(4.1)	22.5	(3.7)	18.9	(3.2)	8.8	(2.6)
	Macao-China	2.9	(1.0)	7.0	(2.0)	16.2	(2.4)	24.6	(2.4)	24.6	(2.3)	17.4	(2.6)	7.3	(1.8)
	Russian Federation	18.9	(1.8)	23.7	(1.3)	25.5	(1.3)	17.9	(1.3)	9.7	(1.2)	3.5	(0.7)	0.8	(0.2)
	Serbia	20.3	(1.5)	26.8	(1.7)	25.3	(1.5)	17.0	(1.4)	8.1	(1.0)	2.1	(0.5)	0.3	(0.2)
	Thailand	20.0	(1.6)	32.4	(1.6)	28.0	(1.7)	14.1	(1.3)	4.4	(0.7)	1.1	(0.3)	0.1	(0.1)
	Tunisia	46.0	(1.8)	32.8	(1.6)	15.1	(1.1)	4.8	(0.7)	1.1	(0.4)	0.1	(0.1)		
	Uruguay	26.5	(1.6)	22.5	(1.9)	23.6	(2.0)	16.1	(1.3)	7.7	(0.7)	3.0	(0.4)	0.7	(0.2)
	United Kingdom[1]	m	m	m	m	m	m	m	m	m	m	m	m	m	m

Females – Proficiency levels

		Below Level 1 (below 358 score points)		Level 1 (from 358 to 420 score points)		Level 2 (from 421 to 482 score points)		Level 3 (from 483 to 544 score points)		Level 4 (from 545 to 606 score points)		Level 5 (from 607 to 668 score points)		Level 6 (above 668 score points)	
		%	S.E.	%	S.E.	%	S.E.	%	S.E.	%	S.E.	%	S.E.	%	S.E.
OECD countries	Australia	3.9	(0.6)	8.8	(0.6)	18.4	(0.7)	25.0	(0.8)	23.8	(0.9)	14.5	(0.8)	5.7	(0.6)
	Austria	7.0	(1.0)	15.9	(1.3)	23.5	(1.9)	25.9	(1.7)	18.0	(1.6)	7.5	(1.0)	2.2	(0.4)
	Belgium	6.0	(0.8)	10.6	(0.8)	18.2	(0.9)	21.7	(1.0)	21.4	(0.8)	15.3	(0.8)	6.6	(0.5)
	Canada	1.7	(0.3)	6.2	(0.5)	16.3	(0.7)	27.8	(0.9)	27.3	(0.8)	15.6	(0.7)	5.0	(0.4)
	Czech Republic	6.1	(0.9)	15.6	(1.5)	25.2	(1.8)	24.7	(1.7)	18.6	(1.1)	7.3	(1.0)	2.5	(0.5)
	Denmark	5.1	(0.9)	12.1	(0.9)	22.7	(1.2)	26.4	(1.5)	20.2	(1.4)	10.6	(0.8)	2.8	(0.4)
	Finland	1.6	(0.3)	5.4	(0.8)	16.7	(1.0)	29.1	(1.1)	27.3	(1.2)	15.0	(1.1)	4.9	(0.5)
	France	5.6	(0.7)	13.0	(1.1)	22.3	(1.0)	26.4	(1.6)	21.6	(1.1)	9.2	(0.9)	2.0	(0.4)
	Germany	10.1	(1.0)	15.4	(1.2)	22.6	(1.5)	24.1	(1.5)	18.3	(1.2)	7.9	(0.9)	1.6	(0.3)
	Greece	14.0	(1.3)	22.8	(1.6)	28.2	(1.4)	22.4	(1.3)	9.6	(1.1)	2.7	(0.7)	0.3	(0.2)
	Hungary	6.2	(0.9)	16.0	(1.5)	26.8	(1.3)	26.7	(1.6)	16.9	(1.1)	6.2	(0.8)	1.1	(0.3)
	Iceland	3.2	(0.5)	7.8	(0.8)	18.2	(1.2)	26.1	(1.4)	23.8	(1.3)	15.2	(1.1)	5.8	(0.8)
	Ireland	4.0	(0.7)	11.3	(1.1)	23.0	(1.3)	26.5	(1.2)	21.3	(1.4)	11.2	(1.2)	2.7	(0.5)
	Italy	15.2	(1.6)	20.6	(1.1)	27.8	(1.2)	21.5	(1.0)	11.0	(0.8)	3.4	(0.4)	0.6	(0.2)
	Japan	4.6	(0.9)	9.0	(1.3)	18.9	(1.2)	25.7	(1.4)	24.2	(1.3)	13.2	(1.0)	4.3	(0.5)
	Korea	2.5	(0.4)	8.6	(1.0)	20.4	(1.5)	27.3	(1.4)	23.7	(1.5)	12.7	(1.2)	4.8	(1.0)
	Luxembourg	9.2	(0.8)	15.7	(1.0)	24.6	(1.4)	26.0	(1.6)	16.2	(1.0)	6.5	(0.8)	1.8	(0.5)
	Mexico	35.7	(1.8)	31.3	(1.7)	21.5	(1.1)	8.9	(1.0)	2.3	(0.5)	0.3	(0.1)	0.0	(0.0)
	Netherlands	1.5	(0.4)	7.6	(1.2)	17.2	(1.3)	23.1	(1.7)	23.2	(1.6)	19.0	(1.1)	8.4	(1.0)
	New Zealand	4.0	(0.7)	9.7	(1.0)	18.9	(1.3)	24.9	(1.3)	21.8	(1.2)	13.8	(0.9)	6.9	(0.8)
	Norway	5.8	(0.8)	12.3	(1.1)	21.4	(1.1)	25.2	(1.6)	20.8	(1.7)	10.5	(1.3)	4.2	(0.6)
	Poland	4.2	(0.6)	13.6	(1.0)	27.9	(1.3)	28.2	(1.1)	18.8	(1.4)	6.2	(0.8)	1.1	(0.3)
	Portugal	8.6	(1.1)	19.1	(1.5)	29.9	(1.4)	26.4	(1.3)	12.8	(1.2)	2.9	(0.4)	0.3	(0.2)
	Slovak Republic	9.5	(1.2)	19.8	(1.3)	27.9	(1.3)	24.3	(1.5)	13.7	(1.0)	4.2	(0.6)	0.6	(0.2)
	Spain	6.8	(0.7)	14.2	(0.8)	27.2	(1.2)	27.6	(1.1)	17.5	(0.8)	5.5	(0.5)	1.2	(0.3)
	Sweden	6.3	(0.8)	12.6	(1.1)	22.3	(1.4)	23.1	(1.4)	19.6	(1.2)	11.5	(0.8)	4.6	(0.7)
	Switzerland	7.3	(0.7)	11.5	(1.1)	20.5	(1.1)	24.7	(1.2)	21.0	(1.3)	11.2	(1.0)	3.7	(0.6)
	Turkey	19.9	(1.9)	28.5	(1.8)	26.3	(2.0)	14.9	(1.4)	6.1	(1.3)	2.5	(0.8)	1.9	(0.8)
	United States	8.2	(0.8)	15.3	(0.9)	23.3	(1.1)	24.6	(1.2)	17.3	(1.0)	9.1	(0.9)	2.3	(0.5)
	OECD total	*9.8*	*(0.3)*	*15.5*	*(0.4)*	*22.6*	*(0.4)*	*23.4*	*(0.4)*	*17.5*	*(0.3)*	*8.6*	*(0.3)*	*2.6*	*(0.2)*
	OECD average	*7.6*	*(0.2)*	*14.1*	*(0.2)*	*22.7*	*(0.2)*	*24.5*	*(0.2)*	*18.6*	*(0.2)*	*9.4*	*(0.2)*	*3.1*	*(0.1)*
Partner countries	Brazil	46.2	(2.2)	29.3	(1.5)	16.4	(1.3)	5.9	(0.9)	1.8	(0.5)	0.4	(0.2)	0.0	
	Hong Kong-China	2.5	(0.5)	6.2	(0.9)	13.8	(1.2)	21.0	(1.3)	26.9	(1.4)	20.2	(1.5)	9.4	(1.0)
	Indonesia	34.5	(1.8)	36.6	(1.3)	20.5	(1.3)	6.7	(0.9)	1.6	(0.5)	0.1	(0.1)	0.0	
	Latvia	7.7	(0.9)	17.2	(1.3)	29.6	(1.7)	26.1	(1.8)	14.5	(1.0)	4.1	(0.7)	0.8	(0.3)
	Liechtenstein	5.1	(1.9)	13.1	(3.0)	19.8	(3.4)	24.8	(3.5)	25.1	(4.1)	10.7	(4.2)	1.4	(1.1)
	Macao-China	2.0	(0.8)	7.5	(1.4)	21.5	(2.3)	30.1	(3.0)	22.6	(2.4)	12.6	(1.8)	3.7	(0.9)
	Russian Federation	19.1	(1.4)	25.8	(1.4)	27.0	(1.4)	18.3	(1.3)	7.6	(0.7)	2.0	(0.5)	0.3	(0.1)
	Serbia	19.9	(1.9)	27.8	(1.6)	28.3	(1.2)	17.8	(1.6)	5.3	(0.9)	0.9	(0.2)	0.1	(0.1)
	Thailand	16.6	(1.2)	33.0	(1.3)	30.9	(1.3)	14.1	(1.1)	4.2	(0.6)	1.1	(0.3)	0.2	(0.1)
	Tunisia	49.8	(1.9)	31.7	(1.8)	14.4	(1.1)	3.6	(0.7)	0.6	(0.2)	0.0			
	Uruguay	27.8	(1.6)	24.5	(1.2)	23.4	(1.4)	15.9	(1.1)	6.6	(0.6)	1.7	(0.4)	0.2	(0.1)
	United Kingdom[1]	m	m	m	m	m	m	m	m	m	m	m	m	m	m

1. Response rate too low to ensure comparability (see Annex A3).

Table 2.4c
Mean score, variation and gender differences in student performance on the mathematics/uncertainty scale

		All students				Gender differences					
		Mean score		Standard deviation		Males		Females		Difference (M-F)	
		Mean	**S.E.**	**S.D.**	**S.E.**	**Mean score**	**S.E.**	**Mean score**	**S.E.**	**Score dif.**	**S.E.**
OECD countries	Australia	531	(2.2)	98	(1.6)	535	(3.0)	527	(2.7)	**7**	(3.7)
	Austria	494	(3.1)	94	(1.7)	498	(3.8)	490	(4.0)	8	(4.6)
	Belgium	526	(2.2)	106	(1.5)	529	(3.2)	522	(3.2)	7	(4.7)
	Canada	542	(1.8)	87	(0.9)	551	(2.2)	538	(1.9)	**13**	(2.3)
	Czech Republic	500	(3.1)	91	(1.7)	509	(3.9)	492	(3.8)	**17**	(4.6)
	Denmark	516	(2.8)	92	(1.6)	527	(3.4)	505	(3.0)	**22**	(3.2)
	Finland	545	(2.1)	85	(1.1)	551	(2.6)	539	(2.3)	**12**	(2.6)
	France	506	(2.4)	92	(1.7)	512	(3.5)	501	(2.8)	**11**	(4.2)
	Germany	493	(3.3)	98	(1.7)	502	(3.9)	484	(3.8)	**18**	(4.0)
	Greece	458	(3.5)	88	(1.5)	469	(4.3)	449	(3.7)	**20**	(3.7)
	Hungary	489	(2.6)	86	(1.8)	493	(3.2)	485	(3.0)	**8**	(3.3)
	Iceland	528	(1.5)	95	(1.4)	524	(2.4)	532	(2.4)	**–8**	(3.8)
	Ireland	517	(2.6)	89	(1.4)	525	(3.2)	509	(3.7)	**15**	(4.6)
	Italy	463	(3.0)	95	(1.7)	475	(4.5)	451	(3.8)	**24**	(5.9)
	Japan	528	(3.9)	98	(2.6)	535	(5.6)	521	(3.8)	**14**	(5.7)
	Korea	538	(3.0)	89	(1.9)	547	(4.1)	525	(5.2)	**22**	(6.6)
	Luxembourg	492	(1.1)	96	(1.0)	503	(2.2)	481	(1.8)	**22**	(3.5)
	Mexico	390	(3.3)	80	(1.5)	392	(3.8)	388	(3.6)	4	(3.5)
	Netherlands	549	(3.0)	90	(2.0)	554	(3.6)	544	(3.7)	**9**	(4.1)
	New Zealand	532	(2.3)	99	(1.3)	538	(2.7)	526	(3.3)	**12**	(3.9)
	Norway	513	(2.6)	98	(1.1)	518	(3.0)	508	(3.2)	**10**	(3.3)
	Poland	494	(2.3)	85	(1.7)	495	(2.8)	492	(2.8)	3	(3.2)
	Portugal	471	(3.4)	83	(1.8)	476	(4.1)	466	(3.5)	**10**	(3.1)
	Slovak Republic	476	(3.2)	87	(1.8)	484	(3.8)	467	(3.4)	**17**	(3.5)
	Spain	489	(2.4)	88	(1.4)	493	(3.3)	485	(2.2)	**8**	(2.8)
	Sweden	511	(2.7)	101	(1.7)	515	(3.2)	506	(3.4)	**9**	(3.7)
	Switzerland	517	(3.3)	100	(2.1)	526	(4.7)	506	(3.7)	**20**	(5.2)
	Turkey	443	(6.2)	98	(5.0)	451	(7.3)	432	(6.1)	**19**	(5.7)
	United States	491	(3.0)	98	(1.5)	493	(3.4)	490	(3.1)	3	(2.8)
	OECD total	*492*	*(1.1)*	*102*	*(0.7)*	*497*	*(1.3)*	*487*	*(1.2)*	***11***	*(1.3)*
	OECD average	*502*	*(0.6)*	*99*	*(0.4)*	*508*	*(0.7)*	*496*	*(0.8)*	***13***	*(0.8)*
Partner countries	Brazil	377	(3.9)	84	(2.7)	385	(4.9)	369	(3.7)	**15**	(3.4)
	Hong Kong-China	558	(4.6)	101	(3.0)	564	(6.6)	552	(4.6)	12	(6.7)
	Indonesia	385	(2.9)	66	(1.5)	382	(2.8)	387	(3.4)	**–5**	(2.4)
	Latvia	474	(3.3)	84	(1.4)	474	(4.2)	474	(3.1)	0	(3.3)
	Liechtenstein	523	(3.7)	96	(3.7)	538	(6.9)	508	(5.6)	**31**	(10.5)
	Macao-China	532	(3.2)	88	(2.6)	541	(4.5)	523	(4.2)	**18**	(5.9)
	Russian Federation	436	(4.0)	90	(1.6)	441	(5.1)	432	(3.9)	**8**	(4.2)
	Serbia	428	(3.5)	83	(1.5)	431	(4.0)	425	(4.2)	5	(4.2)
	Thailand	423	(2.5)	73	(1.8)	420	(3.4)	425	(3.0)	–5	(4.0)
	Tunisia	363	(2.3)	71	(1.7)	367	(2.5)	360	(2.8)	**7**	(2.6)
	Uruguay	419	(3.1)	98	(1.7)	423	(3.9)	415	(3.6)	**8**	(4.1)
	United Kingdom[1]	m	m	m	m	m	m	m	m	m	m

		Percentiles											
		5th		10th		25th		75th		90th		95th	
		Score	**S.E.**	**Score**	**S.E.**	**Score**	**S.E.**	**Score**	**S.E.**	**Score**	**S.E.**	**Score**	**S.E.**
OECD countries	Australia	367	(4.0)	404	(3.5)	464	(2.9)	600	(2.7)	655	(3.1)	686	(3.5)
	Austria	340	(4.4)	372	(4.3)	427	(3.7)	560	(3.8)	618	(4.4)	649	(4.7)
	Belgium	348	(4.9)	383	(4.1)	450	(3.6)	605	(2.4)	661	(2.3)	692	(2.4)
	Canada	397	(3.2)	429	(2.4)	483	(2.1)	602	(2.0)	653	(2.6)	682	(3.1)
	Czech Republic	357	(5.4)	385	(3.9)	436	(3.2)	564	(3.8)	620	(4.2)	652	(4.4)
	Denmark	363	(5.2)	396	(4.9)	454	(3.4)	580	(3.1)	632	(3.6)	661	(4.3)
	Finland	403	(3.4)	437	(4.1)	489	(2.6)	602	(2.4)	652	(3.6)	683	(3.3)
	France	349	(6.0)	384	(4.2)	443	(3.6)	572	(2.6)	622	(3.3)	651	(3.2)
	Germany	331	(5.5)	365	(4.1)	423	(4.0)	564	(3.4)	618	(3.5)	649	(4.0)
	Greece	313	(5.4)	345	(4.4)	398	(3.8)	518	(3.8)	572	(5.0)	605	(5.0)
	Hungary	351	(4.7)	380	(4.3)	430	(3.0)	548	(3.4)	601	(3.6)	631	(4.5)
	Iceland	368	(4.9)	405	(3.4)	463	(2.5)	595	(2.6)	647	(3.2)	678	(3.9)
	Ireland	371	(5.6)	403	(4.5)	456	(3.5)	580	(3.4)	633	(3.4)	661	(3.5)
	Italy	306	(6.4)	339	(5.2)	399	(4.2)	528	(3.0)	585	(3.1)	620	(3.4)
	Japan	359	(7.0)	399	(6.7)	463	(4.9)	597	(4.2)	649	(5.7)	681	(7.5)
	Korea	390	(4.8)	423	(4.0)	477	(4.0)	600	(3.4)	651	(5.0)	682	(5.7)
	Luxembourg	332	(5.0)	369	(2.5)	427	(2.1)	558	(2.2)	615	(2.9)	648	(3.6)
	Mexico	262	(4.7)	289	(3.9)	335	(3.3)	442	(4.4)	494	(5.0)	528	(5.7)
	Netherlands	403	(5.2)	431	(5.1)	483	(5.0)	617	(3.7)	667	(3.6)	693	(3.2)
	New Zealand	368	(5.6)	403	(4.5)	463	(3.1)	601	(2.6)	662	(2.7)	695	(3.6)
	Norway	352	(3.9)	386	(4.2)	445	(3.4)	580	(3.8)	640	(3.9)	675	(3.8)
	Poland	355	(6.1)	387	(4.2)	437	(3.0)	552	(2.7)	603	(3.4)	631	(3.4)
	Portugal	333	(5.8)	363	(5.5)	414	(4.7)	528	(3.2)	578	(2.9)	605	(4.1)
	Slovak Republic	335	(6.0)	364	(5.4)	416	(3.8)	537	(3.6)	589	(3.5)	619	(3.7)
	Spain	340	(5.2)	376	(4.2)	432	(3.0)	549	(3.1)	600	(2.9)	628	(3.9)
	Sweden	345	(5.0)	384	(4.7)	442	(3.4)	581	(3.6)	640	(3.9)	675	(4.8)
	Switzerland	346	(4.6)	384	(3.8)	450	(3.5)	587	(4.2)	642	(5.6)	676	(6.9)
	Turkey	299	(5.0)	328	(4.3)	375	(4.8)	499	(8.2)	571	(13.9)	622	(22.2)
	United States	328	(5.6)	363	(4.8)	424	(3.8)	560	(3.2)	620	(3.5)	654	(5.1)
	OECD total	*323*	*(1.9)*	*359*	*(1.7)*	*421*	*(1.4)*	*564*	*(1.2)*	*623*	*(1.2)*	*657*	*(1.6)*
	OECD average	*339*	*(1.1)*	*374*	*(1.0)*	*434*	*(0.9)*	*571*	*(0.7)*	*629*	*(0.7)*	*662*	*(0.9)*
Partner countries	Brazil	250	(4.2)	276	(3.7)	320	(3.5)	427	(5.0)	485	(7.7)	525	(9.4)
	Hong Kong-China	382	(10.1)	423	(8.3)	493	(6.6)	630	(3.7)	680	(4.3)	709	(4.9)
	Indonesia	281	(4.2)	303	(3.5)	340	(2.7)	426	(3.6)	471	(4.6)	499	(6.2)
	Latvia	337	(5.4)	366	(4.6)	417	(3.9)	530	(4.0)	582	(4.0)	611	(4.8)
	Liechtenstein	356	(20.2)	394	(16.9)	461	(5.8)	594	(6.8)	641	(8.3)	672	(16.6)
	Macao-China	391	(11.8)	421	(7.3)	473	(5.9)	592	(5.1)	644	(5.7)	673	(7.7)
	Russian Federation	293	(4.4)	324	(4.6)	375	(4.2)	496	(4.5)	554	(4.6)	588	(6.3)
	Serbia	294	(4.3)	323	(4.2)	371	(3.6)	485	(4.8)	536	(5.0)	568	(5.3)
	Thailand	310	(3.4)	333	(3.1)	373	(2.5)	468	(3.2)	518	(4.6)	549	(6.3)
	Tunisia	250	(3.5)	276	(2.6)	317	(2.7)	408	(2.8)	453	(4.8)	483	(6.1)
	Uruguay	258	(4.6)	293	(4.4)	352	(3.9)	486	(4.0)	544	(4.2)	581	(5.2)
	United Kingdom[1]	m	m	m	m	m	m	m	m	m	m	m	m

Note: Values that are statistically significant are indicated in bold (see Annex A4).

1. Response rate too low to ensure comparability (see Annex A3).

Table 2.5a

Percentage of students at each level of proficiency on the mathematics scale

	Proficiency levels													
	Below Level 1 (below 358 score points)		Level 1 (from 358 to 420 score points)		Level 2 (from 421 to 482 score points)		Level 3 (from 483 to 544 score points)		Level 4 (from 545 to 606 score points)		Level 5 (from 607 to 668 score points)		Level 6 (above 668 score points)	
	%	S.E.	%	S.E.	%	S.E.	%	S.E.	%	S.E.	%	S.E.	%	S.E.
OECD countries														
Australia	4.3	(0.4)	10.0	(0.5)	18.6	(0.6)	24.0	(0.7)	23.3	(0.6)	14.0	(0.5)	5.8	(0.4)
Austria	5.6	(0.7)	13.2	(0.8)	21.6	(0.9)	24.9	(1.1)	20.5	(0.8)	10.5	(0.9)	3.7	(0.5)
Belgium	7.2	(0.6)	9.3	(0.5)	15.9	(0.6)	20.1	(0.7)	21.0	(0.6)	17.5	(0.7)	9.0	(0.5)
Canada	2.4	(0.3)	7.7	(0.4)	18.3	(0.6)	26.2	(0.7)	25.1	(0.6)	14.8	(0.5)	5.5	(0.4)
Czech Republic	5.0	(0.7)	11.6	(0.9)	20.1	(1.0)	24.3	(0.9)	20.8	(0.9)	12.9	(0.8)	5.3	(0.5)
Denmark	4.7	(0.5)	10.7	(0.6)	20.6	(0.9)	26.2	(0.9)	21.9	(0.8)	11.8	(0.9)	4.1	(0.5)
Finland	1.5	(0.2)	5.3	(0.4)	16.0	(0.6)	27.7	(0.7)	26.1	(0.9)	16.7	(0.6)	6.7	(0.5)
France	5.6	(0.7)	11.0	(0.8)	20.2	(0.8)	25.9	(1.0)	22.1	(1.0)	11.6	(0.7)	3.5	(0.4)
Germany	9.2	(0.8)	12.4	(0.8)	19.0	(1.0)	22.6	(0.8)	20.6	(1.0)	12.2	(0.9)	4.1	(0.5)
Greece	17.8	(1.2)	21.2	(1.2)	26.3	(1.0)	20.2	(1.0)	10.6	(0.9)	3.4	(0.5)	0.6	(0.2)
Hungary	7.8	(0.8)	15.2	(0.8)	23.8	(1.0)	24.3	(0.9)	18.2	(0.9)	8.2	(0.7)	2.5	(0.4)
Iceland	4.5	(0.4)	10.5	(0.6)	20.2	(1.0)	26.1	(0.9)	23.2	(0.8)	11.7	(0.6)	3.7	(0.4)
Ireland	4.7	(0.6)	12.1	(0.8)	23.6	(0.8)	28.0	(0.8)	20.2	(1.1)	9.1	(0.8)	2.2	(0.3)
Italy	13.2	(1.2)	18.7	(0.9)	24.7	(1.0)	22.9	(0.8)	13.4	(0.7)	5.5	(0.4)	1.5	(0.2)
Japan	4.7	(0.7)	8.6	(0.7)	16.3	(0.8)	22.4	(1.0)	23.6	(1.2)	16.1	(1.0)	8.2	(1.1)
Korea	2.5	(0.3)	7.1	(0.7)	16.6	(0.8)	24.1	(1.0)	25.0	(1.1)	16.7	(0.8)	8.1	(0.9)
Luxembourg	7.4	(0.4)	14.3	(0.6)	22.9	(0.9)	25.9	(0.8)	18.7	(0.8)	8.5	(0.6)	2.4	(0.3)
Mexico	38.1	(1.7)	27.9	(1.0)	20.8	(0.9)	10.1	(0.8)	2.7	(0.4)	0.4	(0.1)	0.0	(0.0)
Netherlands	2.6	(0.7)	8.4	(0.9)	18.0	(1.1)	23.0	(1.1)	22.6	(1.3)	18.2	(1.1)	7.3	(0.6)
New Zealand	4.9	(0.4)	10.1	(0.6)	19.2	(0.7)	23.2	(0.9)	21.9	(0.8)	14.1	(0.6)	6.6	(0.4)
Norway	6.9	(0.5)	13.9	(0.8)	23.7	(1.2)	25.2	(1.0)	18.9	(1.0)	8.7	(0.6)	2.7	(0.3)
Poland	6.8	(0.6)	15.2	(0.8)	24.8	(0.7)	25.3	(0.9)	17.7	(0.9)	7.8	(0.5)	2.3	(0.3)
Portugal	11.3	(1.1)	18.8	(1.0)	27.1	(1.0)	24.0	(1.0)	13.4	(0.9)	4.6	(0.5)	0.8	(0.2)
Slovak Republic	6.7	(0.8)	13.2	(0.9)	23.5	(0.9)	24.9	(1.1)	18.9	(0.8)	9.8	(0.7)	2.9	(0.4)
Spain	8.1	(0.7)	14.9	(0.9)	24.7	(0.8)	26.7	(1.0)	17.7	(0.6)	6.5	(0.6)	1.4	(0.2)
Sweden	5.6	(0.5)	11.7	(0.6)	21.7	(0.8)	25.5	(0.9)	19.8	(0.8)	11.6	(0.6)	4.1	(0.5)
Switzerland	4.9	(0.4)	9.6	(0.6)	17.5	(0.8)	24.3	(1.0)	22.5	(0.7)	14.2	(1.1)	7.0	(0.9)
Turkey	27.7	(2.0)	24.6	(1.3)	22.1	(1.1)	13.5	(1.3)	6.8	(1.0)	3.1	(0.8)	2.4	(1.0)
United States	10.2	(0.8)	15.5	(0.8)	23.9	(0.8)	23.8	(0.8)	16.6	(0.7)	8.0	(0.5)	2.0	(0.4)
OECD total	***11.0***	***(0.3)***	***14.6***	***(0.3)***	***21.2***	***(0.3)***	***22.4***	***(0.3)***	***17.6***	***(0.2)***	***9.6***	***(0.2)***	***3.5***	***(0.2)***
OECD average	***8.2***	***(0.2)***	***13.2***	***(0.2)***	***21.1***	***(0.1)***	***23.7***	***(0.2)***	***19.1***	***(0.2)***	***10.6***	***(0.1)***	***4.0***	***(0.1)***
Partner countries														
Brazil	53.3	(1.9)	21.9	(1.1)	14.1	(0.9)	6.8	(0.8)	2.7	(0.5)	0.9	(0.4)	0.3	(0.2)
Hong Kong-China	3.9	(0.7)	6.5	(0.6)	13.9	(1.0)	20.0	(1.2)	25.0	(1.2)	20.2	(1.0)	10.5	(0.9)
Indonesia	50.5	(2.1)	27.6	(1.1)	14.8	(1.1)	5.5	(0.7)	1.4	(0.4)	0.2	(0.1)	0.0	a
Latvia	7.6	(0.9)	16.1	(1.1)	25.5	(1.2)	26.3	(1.2)	16.6	(1.2)	6.3	(0.7)	1.6	(0.4)
Liechtenstein	4.8	(1.3)	7.5	(1.7)	17.3	(2.8)	21.6	(2.5)	23.2	(3.1)	18.3	(3.2)	7.3	(1.7)
Macao-China	2.3	(0.6)	8.8	(1.3)	19.6	(1.4)	26.8	(1.8)	23.7	(1.7)	13.8	(1.6)	4.8	(1.0)
Russian Federation	11.4	(1.0)	18.8	(1.1)	26.4	(1.1)	23.1	(1.0)	13.2	(0.9)	5.4	(0.6)	1.6	(0.4)
Serbia	17.6	(1.3)	24.5	(1.1)	28.6	(1.2)	18.9	(1.1)	8.1	(0.9)	2.1	(0.4)	0.2	(0.1)
Thailand	23.8	(1.3)	30.2	(1.2)	25.4	(1.1)	13.7	(0.8)	5.3	(0.5)	1.5	(0.3)	0.2	(0.1)
Tunisia	51.1	(1.4)	26.9	(1.0)	14.7	(0.8)	5.7	(0.6)	1.4	(0.3)	0.2	(0.1)	0.0	a
Uruguay	26.3	(1.3)	21.8	(0.8)	24.2	(0.9)	16.8	(0.7)	8.2	(0.7)	2.3	(0.3)	0.5	(0.2)
United Kingdom[1]	m	m	m	m	m	m	m	m	m	m	m	m	m	m

1. Response rate too low to ensure comparability (see Annex A3).

Table 2.5b

Percentage of students at each level of proficiency on the mathematics scale, by gender

		Males – Proficiency levels													
		Below Level 1 (below 358 score points)		Level 1 (from 358 to 420 score points)		Level 2 (from 421 to 482 score points)		Level 3 (from 483 to 544 score points)		Level 4 (from 545 to 606 score points)		Level 5 (from 607 to 668 score points)		Level 6 (above 668 score points)	
		%	**S.E.**	**%**	**S.E.**	**%**	**S.E.**	**%**	**S.E.**	**%**	**S.E.**	**%**	**S.E.**	**%**	**S.E.**
OECD countries	Australia	4.6	(0.6)	10.3	(0.8)	17.8	(1.0)	22.7	(1.2)	22.9	(1.1)	14.6	(1.0)	7.0	(0.7)
	Austria	6.1	(1.0)	13.1	(1.0)	20.4	(1.1)	23.3	(1.5)	20.4	(1.3)	11.9	(1.0)	4.8	(0.7)
	Belgium	7.4	(0.8)	9.8	(0.9)	15.1	(0.9)	18.6	(0.8)	20.1	(0.9)	18.1	(1.0)	10.9	(0.7)
	Canada	2.9	(0.4)	7.4	(0.5)	16.1	(0.9)	23.4	(0.9)	25.0	(0.7)	17.6	(0.9)	7.5	(0.8)
	Czech Republic	4.3	(0.7)	10.9	(1.1)	19.8	(1.3)	23.2	(1.1)	20.3	(1.0)	15.0	(1.1)	6.6	(0.7)
	Denmark	3.8	(0.6)	9.6	(0.9)	18.7	(1.3)	26.4	(1.3)	23.5	(1.1)	13.1	(1.0)	4.9	(0.6)
	Finland	1.6	(0.3)	5.8	(0.6)	15.4	(0.8)	25.9	(0.9)	25.4	(1.1)	17.7	(1.1)	8.2	(0.8)
	France	6.1	(1.0)	10.7	(1.0)	18.7	(1.0)	25.1	(1.5)	21.6	(1.5)	13.3	(1.2)	4.6	(0.6)
	Germany	8.9	(1.0)	12.5	(1.0)	18.1	(1.2)	21.4	(1.0)	20.7	(1.3)	13.0	(1.1)	5.3	(0.6)
	Greece	16.4	(1.3)	19.4	(1.3)	24.7	(1.4)	21.0	(1.0)	12.8	(1.2)	4.8	(0.8)	1.0	(0.3)
	Hungary	7.6	(0.8)	14.6	(1.0)	23.6	(1.4)	23.9	(1.3)	18.3	(1.2)	8.6	(0.8)	3.3	(0.6)
	Iceland	6.1	(0.6)	12.1	(0.9)	20.4	(1.2)	25.3	(1.3)	21.0	(1.2)	11.4	(0.9)	3.7	(0.5)
	Ireland	4.2	(0.8)	10.8	(1.1)	22.5	(1.4)	27.8	(1.5)	21.0	(1.6)	10.8	(1.1)	2.9	(0.5)
	Italy	12.5	(1.6)	17.2	(1.6)	22.8	(1.3)	22.7	(1.1)	15.1	(1.1)	7.1	(0.6)	2.5	(0.3)
	Japan	5.2	(0.9)	9.1	(0.9)	15.8	(1.1)	20.2	(1.4)	22.3	(1.4)	16.5	(1.4)	10.9	(1.9)
	Korea	2.3	(0.4)	6.2	(0.8)	14.6	(1.0)	22.3	(1.0)	25.9	(1.4)	18.9	(1.2)	9.7	(1.0)
	Luxembourg	6.8	(0.6)	13.2	(0.8)	21.4	(1.1)	24.8	(1.1)	20.0	(1.1)	10.5	(0.9)	3.4	(0.6)
	Mexico	36.2	(2.1)	26.9	(1.6)	21.6	(1.5)	11.4	(1.0)	3.4	(0.5)	0.5	(0.2)	0.0	(0.0)
	Netherlands	2.2	(0.7)	8.0	(1.2)	18.2	(1.5)	22.9	(1.6)	22.6	(1.7)	18.1	(1.5)	8.0	(0.8)
	New Zealand	4.7	(0.6)	9.9	(0.8)	17.7	(0.9)	21.9	(1.2)	21.9	(1.2)	15.7	(1.0)	8.3	(0.7)
	Norway	7.3	(0.7)	13.3	(0.9)	23.2	(1.2)	23.9	(1.4)	19.1	(1.2)	9.7	(0.8)	3.5	(0.5)
	Poland	7.7	(0.9)	14.9	(0.9)	22.9	(1.1)	24.5	(1.2)	17.9	(1.2)	9.0	(0.9)	3.1	(0.5)
	Portugal	12.0	(1.4)	16.7	(1.1)	24.6	(1.2)	23.9	(1.2)	15.6	(1.6)	5.9	(0.8)	1.3	(0.3)
	Slovak Republic	6.1	(0.9)	12.0	(1.1)	22.0	(1.1)	24.5	(1.3)	20.0	(1.2)	11.4	(0.9)	4.1	(0.6)
	Spain	8.4	(0.9)	14.1	(1.1)	23.3	(1.2)	25.6	(1.5)	18.7	(1.1)	8.0	(1.1)	1.9	(0.4)
	Sweden	5.6	(0.6)	11.1	(0.9)	21.3	(1.1)	25.4	(1.5)	19.4	(1.4)	12.4	(1.0)	4.9	(0.7)
	Switzerland	4.4	(0.5)	9.1	(0.8)	16.5	(1.2)	23.2	(1.5)	22.6	(1.2)	15.2	(1.8)	9.0	(1.3)
	Turkey	26.4	(2.3)	22.9	(1.5)	22.2	(1.3)	14.3	(1.5)	7.5	(1.1)	3.5	(0.9)	3.0	(1.2)
	United States	10.5	(1.0)	14.7	(0.8)	23.2	(1.0)	23.1	(1.4)	16.9	(1.1)	8.9	(0.7)	2.8	(0.5)
	OECD total	*10.9*	*(0.4)*	*14.0*	*(0.3)*	*20.3*	*(0.3)*	*21.7*	*(0.5)*	*17.8*	*(0.4)*	*10.6*	*(0.2)*	*4.6*	*(0.3)*
	OECD average	*8.1*	*(0.2)*	*12.6*	*(0.2)*	*20.0*	*(0.2)*	*22.9*	*(0.2)*	*19.5*	*(0.2)*	*11.8*	*(0.2)*	*5.1*	*(0.1)*
Partner countries	Brazil	51.1	(2.3)	21.4	(1.4)	13.9	(1.1)	8.1	(1.1)	3.6	(0.8)	1.4	(0.6)	0.5	(0.3)
	Hong Kong-China	5.1	(1.1)	6.7	(0.9)	13.0	(0.9)	18.1	(1.0)	23.9	(1.6)	20.4	(1.5)	12.7	(1.5)
	Indonesia	49.2	(2.2)	28.8	(1.3)	15.2	(1.2)	5.1	(0.6)	1.4	(0.4)	0.2	(0.1)	0.0	
	Latvia	8.1	(1.6)	16.3	(1.5)	24.6	(1.4)	25.6	(1.5)	16.1	(1.5)	7.1	(1.0)	2.3	(0.5)
	Liechtenstein	4.7	(1.8)	5.5	(2.2)	15.6	(3.1)	19.6	(3.5)	22.2	(4.9)	21.5	(5.5)	10.8	(2.7)
	Macao-China	2.3	(1.1)	8.5	(1.8)	16.8	(1.7)	23.7	(2.6)	24.7	(3.2)	17.2	(3.3)	6.8	(1.9)
	Russian Federation	11.4	(1.5)	18.4	(1.5)	24.5	(1.6)	22.6	(1.5)	14.1	(1.1)	6.6	(0.9)	2.3	(0.6)
	Serbia	19.2	(1.7)	24.1	(1.4)	26.3	(1.5)	17.5	(1.2)	9.6	(1.0)	2.9	(0.6)	0.4	(0.2)
	Thailand	25.3	(1.7)	29.7	(1.5)	24.5	(1.4)	13.2	(1.3)	5.6	(0.8)	1.5	(0.4)	0.2	(0.1)
	Tunisia	48.2	(1.7)	28.1	(1.4)	15.1	(1.0)	6.3	(0.7)	2.0	(0.4)	0.3	(0.2)	0.0	
	Uruguay	24.7	(1.6)	20.9	(0.9)	24.3	(1.3)	17.4	(1.0)	8.9	(0.8)	3.0	(0.4)	0.8	(0.3)
	United Kingdom[1]	m	m	m	m	m	m	m	m	m	m	m	m	m	m

		Females – Proficiency levels													
		Below Level 1 (below 358 score points)		Level 1 (from 358 to 420 score points)		Level 2 (from 421 to 482 score points)		Level 3 (from 483 to 544 score points)		Level 4 (from 545 to 606 score points)		Level 5 (from 607 to 668 score points)		Level 6 (above 668 score points)	
		%	**S.E.**	**%**	**S.E.**	**%**	**S.E.**	**%**	**S.E.**	**%**	**S.E.**	**%**	**S.E.**	**%**	**S.E.**
OECD countries	Australia	4.0	(0.5)	9.7	(0.7)	19.4	(0.8)	25.3	(0.8)	23.6	(1.0)	13.4	(0.8)	4.5	(0.5)
	Austria	5.1	(0.7)	13.3	(1.2)	22.7	(1.3)	26.5	(1.4)	20.5	(1.4)	9.2	(1.0)	2.7	(0.5)
	Belgium	6.9	(0.8)	8.8	(0.8)	16.9	(0.9)	21.8	(1.0)	22.1	(0.8)	16.7	(0.7)	6.8	(0.5)
	Canada	2.0	(0.3)	7.4	(0.5)	18.7	(0.8)	28.6	(1.2)	25.4	(1.0)	13.6	(0.8)	4.2	(0.4)
	Czech Republic	5.7	(1.1)	12.3	(1.3)	20.4	(1.4)	25.4	(1.4)	21.3	(1.3)	10.8	(1.0)	4.1	(0.5)
	Denmark	5.6	(0.8)	11.8	(0.9)	22.3	(1.1)	26.0	(1.2)	20.4	(1.3)	10.6	(1.0)	3.3	(0.6)
	Finland	1.4	(0.3)	4.9	(0.6)	16.7	(0.8)	29.5	(1.1)	26.9	(1.2)	15.7	(0.8)	5.1	(0.5)
	France	5.2	(0.7)	11.3	(1.0)	21.6	(1.1)	26.6	(1.4)	22.6	(1.1)	10.1	(1.0)	2.5	(0.6)
	Germany	9.2	(1.0)	12.1	(1.0)	19.9	(1.4)	23.9	(1.4)	20.6	(1.2)	11.3	(1.0)	2.9	(0.6)
	Greece	19.1	(1.5)	22.8	(1.5)	27.8	(1.2)	19.4	(1.5)	8.6	(0.8)	2.1	(0.5)	0.2	(0.1)
	Hungary	8.0	(1.1)	15.9	(1.1)	24.0	(1.6)	24.7	(1.3)	18.1	(1.1)	7.7	(1.0)	1.6	(0.4)
	Iceland	2.8	(0.5)	8.8	(0.8)	20.1	(1.4)	26.9	(1.2)	25.5	(1.1)	12.2	(0.9)	3.8	(0.5)
	Ireland	5.2	(0.7)	13.5	(1.3)	24.7	(1.4)	28.2	(1.4)	19.4	(1.2)	7.4	(0.8)	1.6	(0.4)
	Italy	13.9	(1.7)	20.1	(1.3)	26.4	(1.4)	23.1	(1.2)	11.9	(0.8)	3.9	(0.4)	0.7	(0.1)
	Japan	4.3	(0.7)	8.1	(0.9)	16.9	(1.1)	24.5	(1.2)	24.9	(1.6)	15.6	(1.2)	5.7	(0.8)
	Korea	2.7	(0.5)	8.3	(1.0)	19.6	(1.7)	26.7	(1.5)	23.6	(1.5)	13.4	(1.2)	5.7	(1.2)
	Luxembourg	8.0	(0.7)	15.3	(1.1)	24.4	(1.2)	26.9	(1.1)	17.4	(1.1)	6.6	(0.7)	1.4	(0.3)
	Mexico	39.7	(1.9)	28.8	(1.3)	20.2	(1.3)	8.9	(1.1)	2.1	(0.5)	0.2	(0.1)	0.0	(0.0)
	Netherlands	2.9	(0.8)	8.7	(1.2)	17.9	(1.4)	23.0	(1.3)	22.5	(1.5)	18.3	(1.2)	6.6	(0.7)
	New Zealand	5.2	(0.7)	10.4	(1.0)	20.6	(1.2)	24.5	(1.2)	21.8	(1.1)	12.4	(1.0)	5.0	(0.6)
	Norway	6.5	(0.8)	14.5	(1.1)	24.1	(1.5)	26.5	(1.2)	18.7	(1.2)	7.7	(0.7)	1.9	(0.4)
	Poland	5.9	(0.7)	15.5	(1.1)	26.8	(1.0)	26.2	(1.1)	17.5	(1.1)	6.5	(0.8)	1.5	(0.3)
	Portugal	10.6	(1.2)	20.6	(1.3)	29.4	(1.3)	24.1	(1.4)	11.5	(1.0)	3.3	(0.6)	0.4	(0.2)
	Slovak Republic	7.4	(0.9)	14.5	(1.3)	25.0	(1.4)	25.4	(1.5)	17.8	(1.0)	8.1	(0.8)	1.7	(0.3)
	Spain	7.8	(0.7)	15.7	(1.0)	26.1	(1.0)	27.7	(1.1)	16.7	(0.9)	5.1	(0.5)	1.0	(0.3)
	Sweden	5.6	(0.7)	12.3	(0.8)	22.1	(1.0)	25.6	(1.0)	20.2	(1.2)	10.9	(1.0)	3.4	(0.6)
	Switzerland	5.5	(0.6)	10.2	(0.8)	18.6	(1.1)	25.4	(1.2)	22.3	(1.2)	13.1	(1.2)	4.9	(0.9)
	Turkey	29.2	(2.4)	26.6	(1.8)	21.9	(1.7)	12.4	(1.5)	5.8	(1.2)	2.6	(0.8)	1.6	(0.9)
	United States	9.9	(1.0)	16.4	(1.2)	24.6	(1.4)	24.5	(1.1)	16.2	(1.0)	7.2	(0.8)	1.2	(0.1)
	OECD total	*11.1*	*(0.4)*	*15.2*	*(0.4)*	*22.1*	*(0.5)*	*23.1*	*(0.4)*	*17.3*	*(0.4)*	*8.6*	*(0.3)*	*2.5*	*(0.2)*
	OECD average	*8.4*	*(0.2)*	*13.8*	*(0.2)*	*22.1*	*(0.2)*	*24.5*	*(0.2)*	*18.8*	*(0.2)*	*9.5*	*(0.2)*	*2.9*	*(0.1)*
Partner countries	Brazil	55.1	(2.0)	22.3	(1.3)	14.3	(1.0)	5.7	(0.8)	2.0	(0.4)	0.5	(0.2)	0.1	
	Hong Kong-China	2.7	(0.7)	6.3	(0.9)	14.9	(1.6)	21.8	(2.3)	26.1	(1.3)	19.9	(1.6)	8.3	(1.0)
	Indonesia	51.8	(2.2)	26.5	(1.3)	14.3	(1.2)	5.8	(0.9)	1.3	(0.5)	0.2	(0.1)	0.0	
	Latvia	7.2	(1.0)	15.9	(1.3)	26.3	(1.5)	26.9	(1.7)	17.0	(1.3)	5.6	(0.8)	1.1	(0.3)
	Liechtenstein	4.9	(2.4)	9.6	(3.0)	19.2	(3.9)	23.6	(3.7)	24.2	(4.5)	15.0	(3.6)	3.6	(1.8)
	Macao-China	2.4	(0.8)	9.1	(1.7)	22.3	(2.1)	29.8	(2.6)	22.7	(2.2)	10.7	(1.5)	3.0	(0.9)
	Russian Federation	11.4	(1.0)	19.2	(1.4)	28.3	(1.5)	23.6	(1.3)	12.3	(1.1)	4.2	(0.6)	1.0	(0.3)
	Serbia	16.1	(1.7)	24.8	(1.6)	30.9	(1.5)	20.2	(1.5)	6.7	(1.2)	1.3	(0.3)	0.1	(0.1)
	Thailand	22.6	(1.5)	30.6	(1.8)	26.1	(1.4)	14.0	(1.0)	5.1	(0.7)	1.4	(0.5)	0.2	(0.1)
	Tunisia	53.8	(1.7)	25.8	(1.4)	14.3	(1.0)	5.1	(0.9)	0.9	(0.4)	0.2	(0.1)		
	Uruguay	27.7	(1.6)	22.7	(1.3)	24.1	(1.5)	16.1	(1.1)	7.4	(0.9)	1.7	(0.3)	0.2	(0.1)
	United Kingdom[1]	m	m	m	m	m	m	m	m	m	m	m	m	m	m

1. Response rate too low to ensure comparability (see Annex A3).

Table 2.5c

Mean score, variation and gender differences in student performance on the mathematics scale

		All students				Gender differences					
		Mean score		Standard deviation		Males		Females		Difference (M-F)	
		Mean	**S.E.**	**S.D.**	**S.E.**	**Mean score**	**S.E.**	**Mean score**	**S.E.**	**Score dif.**	**S.E.**
OECD countries	Australia	524	(2.1)	95	(1.5)	527	(3.0)	522	(2.7)	5	(3.8)
	Austria	506	(3.3)	93	(1.7)	509	(4.0)	502	(4.0)	8	(4.4)
	Belgium	529	(2.3)	110	(1.8)	533	(3.4)	525	(3.2)	8	(4.8)
	Canada	532	(1.8)	87	(1.0)	541	(2.1)	530	(1.9)	**11**	(2.1)
	Czech Republic	516	(3.5)	96	(1.9)	524	(4.3)	509	(4.4)	**15**	(5.1)
	Denmark	514	(2.7)	91	(1.4)	523	(3.4)	506	(3.0)	**17**	(3.2)
	Finland	544	(1.9)	84	(1.1)	548	(2.5)	541	(2.1)	**7**	(2.7)
	France	511	(2.5)	92	(1.8)	515	(3.6)	507	(2.9)	**9**	(4.2)
	Germany	503	(3.3)	103	(1.8)	508	(4.0)	499	(3.9)	**9**	(4.4)
	Greece	445	(3.9)	94	(1.8)	455	(4.8)	436	(3.8)	**19**	(3.6)
	Hungary	490	(2.8)	94	(2.0)	494	(3.3)	486	(3.3)	**8**	(3.5)
	Iceland	515	(1.4)	90	(1.2)	508	(2.3)	523	(2.2)	**–15**	(3.5)
	Ireland	503	(2.4)	85	(1.3)	510	(3.0)	495	(3.4)	**15**	(4.2)
	Italy	466	(3.1)	96	(1.9)	475	(4.6)	457	(3.8)	**18**	(5.9)
	Japan	534	(4.0)	101	(2.8)	539	(5.8)	530	(4.0)	8	(5.9)
	Korea	542	(3.2)	92	(2.1)	552	(4.4)	528	(5.3)	**23**	(6.8)
	Luxembourg	493	(1.0)	92	(1.0)	502	(1.9)	485	(1.5)	**17**	(2.8)
	Mexico	385	(3.6)	85	(1.9)	391	(4.3)	380	(4.1)	**11**	(3.9)
	Netherlands	538	(3.1)	93	(2.3)	540	(4.1)	535	(3.5)	5	(4.3)
	New Zealand	523	(2.3)	98	(1.2)	531	(2.8)	516	(3.2)	**14**	(3.9)
	Norway	495	(2.4)	92	(1.2)	498	(2.8)	492	(2.9)	6	(3.2)
	Poland	490	(2.5)	90	(1.3)	493	(3.0)	487	(2.9)	6	(3.1)
	Portugal	466	(3.4)	88	(1.7)	472	(4.2)	460	(3.4)	**12**	(3.3)
	Slovak Republic	498	(3.3)	93	(2.3)	507	(3.9)	489	(3.6)	**19**	(3.7)
	Spain	485	(2.4)	88	(1.3)	490	(3.4)	481	(2.2)	**9**	(3.0)
	Sweden	509	(2.6)	95	(1.8)	512	(3.0)	506	(3.1)	**7**	(3.3)
	Switzerland	527	(3.4)	98	(2.0)	535	(4.7)	518	(3.6)	**17**	(4.9)
	Turkey	423	(6.7)	105	(5.3)	430	(7.9)	415	(6.7)	**15**	(6.2)
	United States	483	(2.9)	95	(1.3)	486	(3.3)	480	(3.2)	**6**	(2.9)
	OECD total	*489*	*(1.1)*	*104*	*(0.7)*	*494*	*(1.3)*	*484*	*(1.3)*	*10*	*(1.4)*
	OECD average	*500*	*(0.6)*	*100*	*(0.4)*	*506*	*(0.8)*	*494*	*(0.8)*	*11*	*(0.8)*
Partner countries	Brazil	356	(4.8)	100	(3.0)	365	(6.1)	348	(4.4)	**16**	(4.1)
	Hong Kong-China	550	(4.5)	100	(3.0)	552	(6.5)	548	(4.6)	4	(6.6)
	Indonesia	360	(3.9)	81	(2.1)	362	(3.9)	358	(4.6)	3	(3.4)
	Latvia	483	(3.7)	88	(1.7)	485	(4.8)	482	(3.6)	3	(4.0)
	Liechtenstein	536	(4.1)	99	(4.4)	550	(7.2)	521	(6.3)	**29**	(10.9)
	Macao-China	527	(2.9)	87	(2.4)	538	(4.8)	517	(3.3)	**21**	(5.8)
	Russian Federation	468	(4.2)	92	(1.9)	473	(5.3)	463	(4.2)	**10**	(4.4)
	Serbia	437	(3.8)	85	(1.6)	437	(4.2)	436	(4.5)	1	(4.4)
	Thailand	417	(3.0)	82	(1.8)	415	(4.0)	419	(3.4)	–4	(4.2)
	Tunisia	359	(2.5)	82	(2.0)	365	(2.7)	353	(2.9)	**12**	(2.5)
	Uruguay	422	(3.3)	100	(1.6)	428	(4.0)	416	(3.8)	**12**	(4.2)
	United Kingdom[1]	m	m	m	m	m	m	m	m	m	m

		Percentiles											
		5th		10th		25th		75th		90th		95th	
		Score	**S.E.**	**Score**	**S.E.**	**Score**	**S.E.**	**Score**	**S.E.**	**Score**	**S.E.**	**Score**	**S.E.**
OECD countries	Australia	364	(4.4)	399	(3.4)	460	(2.7)	592	(2.5)	645	(3.0)	676	(3.5)
	Austria	353	(6.6)	384	(4.4)	439	(4.0)	571	(4.2)	626	(4.0)	658	(5.0)
	Belgium	334	(6.5)	381	(4.6)	456	(3.4)	611	(2.5)	664	(2.4)	693	(2.4)
	Canada	386	(3.0)	419	(2.5)	474	(2.2)	593	(2.1)	644	(2.6)	673	(3.4)
	Czech Republic	358	(6.2)	392	(5.7)	449	(4.5)	584	(4.0)	641	(4.3)	672	(4.9)
	Denmark	361	(4.4)	396	(4.5)	453	(3.7)	578	(3.1)	632	(3.7)	662	(4.7)
	Finland	406	(3.8)	438	(2.8)	488	(2.2)	603	(2.3)	652	(2.8)	680	(3.1)
	France	352	(6.0)	389	(5.6)	449	(3.7)	575	(3.0)	628	(3.6)	656	(3.5)
	Germany	324	(6.1)	363	(5.6)	432	(4.7)	578	(3.5)	632	(3.5)	662	(3.6)
	Greece	288	(5.4)	324	(5.1)	382	(4.6)	508	(4.3)	566	(5.3)	598	(5.1)
	Hungary	335	(5.6)	370	(4.2)	426	(3.0)	556	(3.9)	611	(4.7)	644	(4.6)
	Iceland	362	(4.0)	396	(2.7)	454	(2.8)	578	(1.9)	629	(3.0)	658	(3.8)
	Ireland	360	(4.7)	393	(3.2)	445	(3.4)	562	(3.0)	614	(3.6)	641	(3.3)
	Italy	307	(6.4)	342	(5.9)	400	(4.3)	530	(3.0)	589	(3.6)	623	(3.7)
	Japan	361	(8.2)	402	(6.3)	467	(5.4)	605	(4.4)	660	(6.1)	690	(6.6)
	Korea	388	(4.6)	423	(4.5)	479	(3.7)	606	(4.2)	659	(5.4)	690	(6.8)
	Luxembourg	338	(3.9)	373	(2.7)	430	(2.2)	557	(1.9)	611	(3.2)	641	(2.7)
	Mexico	247	(5.4)	276	(4.7)	327	(4.3)	444	(4.5)	497	(4.7)	527	(5.6)
	Netherlands	385	(6.9)	415	(5.8)	471	(5.4)	608	(3.8)	657	(3.2)	683	(3.4)
	New Zealand	358	(4.1)	394	(3.9)	455	(2.9)	593	(2.2)	650	(3.2)	682	(2.9)
	Norway	343	(4.0)	376	(3.4)	433	(2.9)	560	(3.3)	614	(3.6)	645	(3.9)
	Poland	343	(5.8)	376	(3.6)	428	(3.1)	553	(2.9)	607	(3.3)	640	(3.5)
	Portugal	321	(6.3)	352	(5.3)	406	(5.0)	526	(3.5)	580	(3.3)	610	(3.7)
	Slovak Republic	342	(6.9)	379	(5.8)	436	(4.6)	565	(3.8)	619	(3.5)	648	(4.1)
	Spain	335	(5.1)	369	(3.5)	426	(3.0)	546	(3.1)	597	(3.5)	626	(3.7)
	Sweden	353	(5.3)	387	(4.4)	446	(3.0)	576	(3.2)	630	(3.8)	662	(4.8)
	Switzerland	359	(4.8)	396	(4.2)	461	(3.6)	595	(4.9)	652	(5.2)	684	(6.8)
	Turkey	270	(5.8)	300	(5.0)	351	(5.3)	485	(8.5)	560	(14.2)	614	(22.7)
	United States	323	(4.9)	356	(4.5)	418	(3.7)	550	(3.4)	607	(3.9)	638	(5.1)
	OECD total	*315*	*(2.1)*	*352*	*(1.7)*	*418*	*(1.6)*	*563*	*(1.1)*	*622*	*(1.3)*	*655*	*(1.8)*
	OECD average	*332*	*(1.3)*	*369*	*(1.1)*	*432*	*(0.9)*	*571*	*(0.7)*	*628*	*(0.7)*	*660*	*(1.0)*
Partner countries	Brazil	203	(6.0)	233	(5.3)	286	(4.6)	419	(6.2)	488	(9.5)	528	(11.3)
	Hong Kong-China	374	(11.0)	417	(8.0)	485	(6.9)	622	(3.7)	672	(4.1)	700	(4.0)
	Indonesia	233	(5.2)	260	(4.8)	306	(3.5)	412	(4.8)	466	(6.5)	499	(7.7)
	Latvia	339	(5.9)	371	(5.1)	424	(3.9)	544	(4.7)	596	(4.4)	626	(5.0)
	Liechtenstein	362	(19.7)	408	(9.8)	470	(7.6)	609	(7.9)	655	(9.5)	686	(16.4)
	Macao-China	382	(8.8)	414	(6.0)	467	(4.4)	587	(4.0)	639	(5.5)	668	(8.3)
	Russian Federation	319	(5.5)	351	(5.0)	406	(4.8)	530	(5.0)	588	(5.3)	622	(6.1)
	Serbia	299	(4.4)	329	(4.5)	379	(4.0)	493	(4.8)	546	(5.1)	579	(5.3)
	Thailand	290	(4.0)	316	(3.1)	361	(2.9)	469	(3.8)	526	(4.7)	560	(6.4)
	Tunisia	229	(3.8)	256	(3.5)	303	(2.6)	412	(3.6)	466	(4.8)	501	(6.8)
	Uruguay	255	(4.3)	291	(3.8)	353	(4.1)	491	(3.8)	550	(4.4)	583	(4.7)
	United Kingdom[1]	m	m	m	m	m	m	m	m	m	m	m	m

Note: Values that are statistically significant are indicated in bold (see Annex A4).

1. Response rate too low to ensure comparability (see Annex A3).

Table 2.5d

Gender differences in student performance on the mathematics scale after taking student programmes into account

		Gender differences in mathematics performance (M – F)					
		Observed		Within school		After accounting for the programme level and programme destination in which students are enrolled[1]	
		Score dif.	S.E.	Score dif.	S.E.	Score dif.	S.E.
OECD countries	Australia	5	(3.8)	**8**	(2.4)	7	(3.7)
	Austria	8	(4.4)	**17**	(2.6)	**30**	(3.1)
	Belgium	8	(4.8)	**26**	(2.4)	**19**	(3.0)
	Canada	**11**	(2.1)	**12**	(1.8)	**15**	(2.1)
	Czech Republic	**15**	(5.1)	**25**	(2.7)	**29**	(3.9)
	Denmark	**17**	(3.2)	**16**	(3.0)	**17**	(3.2)
	Finland	**7**	(2.7)	**8**	(2.6)	**7**	(2.7)
	France	**9**	(4.2)	**18**	(2.6)	**23**	(2.9)
	Germany	**9**	(4.4)	**31**	(2.6)	**9**	(4.4)
	Greece	**19**	(3.6)	**26**	(2.0)	**29**	(2.3)
	Hungary	**8**	(3.5)	**26**	(2.4)	**21**	(3.2)
	Iceland	**–15**	(3.5)	**–15**	(3.5)	**–15**	(3.5)
	Ireland	**15**	(4.2)	**17**	(3.3)	**19**	(4.0)
	Italy	**18**	(5.9)	**24**	(2.3)	**20**	(5.9)
	Japan	8	(5.9)	**16**	(2.5)	**11**	(5.5)
	Korea	**23**	(6.8)	**16**	(3.5)	**18**	(4.1)
	Luxembourg	**17**	(2.8)	**21**	(2.5)	**26**	(2.6)
	Mexico	**11**	(3.9)	**17**	(2.3)	**16**	(3.9)
	Netherlands	5	(4.3)	**13**	(2.1)	**15**	(2.6)
	New Zealand	**14**	(3.9)	**12**	(3.4)	**15**	(3.9)
	Norway	6	(3.2)	6	(3.2)	**6**	(3.2)
	Poland	6	(3.1)	**6**	(3.0)	6	(3.2)
	Portugal	**12**	(3.3)	**20**	(2.6)	**25**	(2.3)
	Slovak Republic	**19**	(3.7)	**26**	(2.8)	**20**	(3.8)
	Spain	**9**	(3.0)	**11**	(2.7)	**9**	(3.0)
	Sweden	**7**	(3.3)	**7**	(3.1)	**9**	(3.2)
	Switzerland	**17**	(4.9)	**25**	(2.4)	**18**	(4.5)
	Turkey	**15**	(6.2)	**20**	(3.0)	**21**	(6.2)
	United States	**6**	(2.9)	**8**	(2.8)	**10**	(2.7)
	OECD total	*10*	*(1.4)*	*15*	*(1.1)*	*12*	*(1.3)*
	OECD average	*11*	*(0.8)*	*15*	*(0.5)*	*12*	*(0.8)*
Partner countries	Brazil	**16**	(4.1)	**17**	(2.7)	**26**	(3.7)
	Hong Kong-China	4	(6.6)	**17**	(2.8)	6	(6.3)
	Indonesia	3	(3.4)	**9**	(2.7)	**8**	(3.5)
	Latvia	3	(4.0)	**8**	(3.8)	4	(4.2)
	Liechtenstein	**29**	(10.9)	**42**	(7.5)	**28**	(11.0)
	Macao-China	**21**	(5.8)	**23**	(6.8)	**24**	(5.5)
	Russian Federation	**10**	(4.4)	**19**	(2.7)	**17**	(4.4)
	Serbia	1	(4.4)	**22**	(3.1)	**25**	(4.1)
	Thailand	–4	(4.2)	–2	(2.5)	0	(3.8)
	Tunisia	**12**	(2.5)	**23**	(1.9)	**23**	(2.0)
	Uruguay	**12**	(4.2)	**19**	(3.1)	**24**	(3.3)
	United Kingdom[2]	7	(4.9)	**10**	(2.6)	7	(4.7)

Note: Values that are statistically significant are indicated in bold (see Annex A4).

1. Programme level indicates whether the student is enrolled in a lower (ISCED Level 2) or upper (ISCED Level 3) secondary programme. Programme destination indicates the destination of the study programme: A, B or C (see Annex A1).
2. Response rate is too low to ensure comparability (see Annex A3).

Table 2.6
Economic and social indicators and the relationship with performance in mathematics

		Economic and social indicators				Adjusted performance on the mathematics scale			
	Mean performance on the mathematics scale	GDP per capita (In equivalent US dollars using purchasing power parities)[1]	Percentage of the population in the age group 35-44 years that has attained at least upper secondary education[1]	Mean PISA index of economic, social and cultural status (ESCS)	Cumulative expenditure per student between 6 and 15 years (In equivalent US dollars using purchasing power parities)[1]	Mathematics performance adjusted by GDP per capita	Mathematics performance adjusted by GDP per capita and educational attainment	Mathematics performance adjusted by the mean PISA index of economic, social and cultural status (ESCS)	Mathematics performance adjusted by cumulative expenditure per student between 6 and 15 years
OECD countries									
Australia	524	26 685	62	0.23	58 480	516	528	509	520
Austria	506	28 372	82	0.06	77 255	493	487	501	489
Belgium	529	27 096	66	0.15	63 571	520	529	519	522
Canada	532	29 290	86	0.45	59 810	518	510	502	528
Czech Republic	516	14 861	91	0.16	26 000	536	504	505	534
Denmark	514	29 223	81	0.20	72 934	500	496	501	501
Finland	544	26 344	85	0.25	54 373	537	525	528	543
France	511	26 818	68	-0.08	62 731	502	508	516	504
Germany	503	25 453	86	0.16	49 145	498	484	492	505
Greece	445	17 020	58	-0.15	32 990	460	463	455	458
Hungary	490	13 043	79	-0.07	25 631	514	492	495	508
Iceland	515	28 968	62	0.69	65 977	501	517	469	506
Ireland	503	29 821	65	-0.08	41 845	487	500	508	510
Italy	466	25 377	50	-0.11	75 693	460	483	473	450
Japan	534	26 636	94	-0.08	60 004	526	506	539	529
Korea	542	15 916	79	-0.10	41 802	560	541	549	549
Luxembourg	493	w	w	w	w	w	w	w	w
Mexico	385	9 148	26	-1.13	15 312	419	444	461	410
Netherlands	538	28 711	71	0.10	55 416	525	531	531	536
New Zealand	523	21 230	80	0.21	m	528	515	509	m
Norway	495	36 587	91	0.61	74 040	463	459	454	481
Poland	490	10 360	48	-0.20	23 387	521	526	504	510
Portugal	466	17 912	20	-0.63	48 811	479	521	508	468
Slovak Republic	498	11 323	91	-0.08	14 874	527	490	504	523
Spain	485	21 347	46	-0.30	46 774	490	511	505	489
Sweden	509	26 902	87	0.25	60 130	500	487	492	504
Switzerland	527	30 036	85	-0.06	79 691	510	504	530	508
Turkey	423	6 046	25	-0.98	m	465	487	489	m
United States	483	35 179	88	0.30	79 716	454	451	463	465
United Kingdom[2]	m	m	m	m	m	m	m	m	m

1. Source: *Education at a Glance* (OECD, 2004a).
2. Response rate too low to ensure comparability (see Annex A3).

Table 3.1
Index of interest in and enjoyment of mathematics and performance on the mathematics scale, by national quarters of the index
Results based on students' self-reports

		Index of interest in and enjoyment of mathematics															
		All students		Males		Females		Gender difference (M – F)		Bottom quarter		Second quarter		Third quarter		Top quarter	
		Mean index	S.E.	Mean index	S.E.	Mean index	S.E.	Dif.	S.E.	Mean index	S.E.	Mean index	S.E.	Mean index	S.E.	Mean index	S.E.
OECD countries	Australia	0.01	(0.02)	0.12	(0.02)	–0.10	(0.02)	**0.22**	(0.02)	–1.22	(0.01)	–0.26	(0.00)	0.32	(0.01)	1.20	(0.01)
	Austria	–0.28	(0.02)	–0.08	(0.03)	–0.49	(0.02)	**0.42**	(0.04)	–1.60	(0.01)	–0.67	(0.01)	0.02	(0.01)	1.10	(0.02)
	Belgium	–0.17	(0.02)	–0.07	(0.02)	–0.27	(0.02)	**0.20**	(0.03)	–1.44	(0.01)	–0.45	(0.00)	0.17	(0.00)	1.07	(0.01)
	Canada	–0.01	(0.01)	0.08	(0.02)	–0.10	(0.02)	**0.18**	(0.02)	–1.35	(0.01)	–0.34	(0.00)	0.33	(0.00)	1.32	(0.01)
	Czech Republic	–0.19	(0.02)	–0.09	(0.02)	–0.29	(0.02)	**0.21**	(0.03)	–1.21	(0.02)	–0.42	(0.00)	0.03	(0.01)	0.85	(0.01)
	Denmark	0.41	(0.02)	0.56	(0.02)	0.27	(0.02)	**0.29**	(0.03)	–0.85	(0.02)	0.11	(0.01)	0.80	(0.01)	1.59	(0.02)
	Finland	–0.24	(0.02)	–0.09	(0.02)	–0.40	(0.02)	**0.31**	(0.03)	–1.41	(0.01)	–0.49	(0.01)	–0.01	(0.01)	0.94	(0.02)
	France	0.04	(0.02)	0.17	(0.03)	–0.06	(0.02)	**0.23**	(0.03)	–1.24	(0.01)	–0.21	(0.01)	0.41	(0.01)	1.22	(0.01)
	Germany	0.04	(0.02)	0.25	(0.03)	–0.16	(0.03)	**0.41**	(0.04)	–1.38	(0.01)	–0.39	(0.01)	0.41	(0.01)	1.54	(0.02)
	Greece	0.10	(0.02)	0.27	(0.03)	–0.05	(0.03)	**0.32**	(0.03)	–1.20	(0.01)	–0.22	(0.01)	0.42	(0.01)	1.41	(0.02)
	Hungary	–0.21	(0.02)	–0.16	(0.02)	–0.27	(0.02)	**0.11**	(0.03)	–1.33	(0.01)	–0.44	(0.01)	0.01	(0.01)	0.92	(0.01)
	Iceland	–0.11	(0.02)	–0.08	(0.02)	–0.15	(0.03)	0.07	(0.04)	–1.52	(0.01)	–0.48	(0.01)	0.29	(0.01)	1.26	(0.02)
	Ireland	–0.05	(0.02)	–0.03	(0.03)	–0.07	(0.03)	0.04	(0.04)	–1.28	(0.01)	–0.34	(0.01)	0.26	(0.01)	1.16	(0.02)
	Italy	0.07	(0.02)	0.12	(0.03)	0.02	(0.03)	**0.10**	(0.04)	–1.17	(0.01)	–0.21	(0.01)	0.41	(0.01)	1.24	(0.01)
	Japan	–0.39	(0.03)	–0.25	(0.03)	–0.51	(0.03)	**0.26**	(0.04)	–1.68	(0.01)	–0.69	(0.01)	–0.14	(0.01)	0.96	(0.02)
	Korea	–0.12	(0.02)	–0.06	(0.03)	–0.21	(0.03)	**0.16**	(0.04)	–1.41	(0.01)	–0.40	(0.00)	0.14	(0.01)	1.19	(0.02)
	Luxembourg	–0.26	(0.02)	–0.08	(0.02)	–0.43	(0.02)	**0.35**	(0.03)	–1.64	(0.01)	–0.68	(0.01)	0.08	(0.01)	1.21	(0.02)
	Mexico	0.58	(0.02)	0.65	(0.02)	0.52	(0.02)	**0.13**	(0.02)	–0.42	(0.01)	0.35	(0.00)	0.84	(0.00)	1.54	(0.02)
	Netherlands	–0.20	(0.02)	–0.05	(0.03)	–0.35	(0.03)	**0.30**	(0.03)	–1.38	(0.01)	–0.43	(0.01)	0.10	(0.01)	0.93	(0.01)
	New Zealand	0.12	(0.02)	0.23	(0.02)	0.01	(0.03)	**0.22**	(0.04)	–1.11	(0.02)	–0.17	(0.01)	0.46	(0.01)	1.32	(0.01)
	Norway	–0.17	(0.02)	–0.03	(0.03)	–0.30	(0.03)	**0.26**	(0.04)	–1.54	(0.01)	–0.54	(0.01)	0.20	(0.01)	1.23	(0.02)
	Poland	0.11	(0.02)	0.16	(0.02)	0.05	(0.02)	**0.10**	(0.03)	–1.03	(0.02)	–0.20	(0.01)	0.39	(0.01)	1.26	(0.02)
	Portugal	0.16	(0.02)	0.17	(0.03)	0.15	(0.02)	0.02	(0.04)	–0.94	(0.02)	–0.05	(0.01)	0.47	(0.01)	1.16	(0.01)
	Slovak Republic	0.03	(0.02)	0.10	(0.02)	–0.04	(0.02)	**0.14**	(0.03)	–1.01	(0.02)	–0.20	(0.00)	0.26	(0.01)	1.07	(0.01)
	Spain	–0.07	(0.02)	–0.06	(0.02)	–0.08	(0.02)	0.03	(0.03)	–1.34	(0.01)	–0.35	(0.01)	0.26	(0.01)	1.14	(0.01)
	Sweden	0.09	(0.02)	0.18	(0.03)	–0.01	(0.03)	**0.19**	(0.04)	–1.23	(0.01)	–0.21	(0.01)	0.43	(0.01)	1.36	(0.02)
	Switzerland	0.12	(0.02)	0.41	(0.02)	–0.19	(0.02)	**0.60**	(0.03)	–1.22	(0.02)	–0.23	(0.01)	0.49	(0.01)	1.43	(0.02)
	Turkey	0.55	(0.03)	0.60	(0.04)	0.49	(0.04)	**0.10**	(0.04)	–0.85	(0.02)	0.23	(0.01)	0.94	(0.01)	1.89	(0.02)
	United States	0.04	(0.02)	0.13	(0.03)	–0.04	(0.02)	**0.17**	(0.03)	–1.30	(0.01)	–0.29	(0.00)	0.37	(0.01)	1.40	(0.01)
	OECD total	*0.04*	*(0.01)*	*0.14*	*(0.01)*	*–0.05*	*(0.01)*	*0.19*	*(0.01)*	*–1.28*	*(0.00)*	*–0.28*	*(0.00)*	*0.38*	*(0.00)*	*1.34*	*(0.01)*
	OECD average	*0.00*	*(0.00)*	*0.10*	*(0.00)*	*–0.11*	*(0.01)*	*0.21*	*(0.01)*	*–1.29*	*(0.00)*	*–0.31*	*(0.00)*	*0.33*	*(0.01)*	*1.26*	*(0.01)*
Partner countries	Brazil	0.57	(0.02)	0.65	(0.03)	0.50	(0.03)	**0.15**	(0.03)	–0.54	(0.02)	0.31	(0.01)	0.85	(0.01)	1.64	(0.02)
	Hong Kong-China	0.22	(0.02)	0.35	(0.03)	0.10	(0.02)	**0.26**	(0.03)	–0.95	(0.02)	–0.11	(0.01)	0.60	(0.01)	1.37	(0.02)
	Indonesia	0.74	(0.02)	0.76	(0.02)	0.71	(0.02)	**0.05**	(0.02)	–0.14	(0.02)	0.63	(0.01)	0.97	(0.00)	1.48	(0.01)
	Latvia	0.05	(0.02)	0.12	(0.02)	–0.02	(0.02)	**0.14**	(0.03)	–0.87	(0.02)	–0.17	(0.01)	0.27	(0.01)	0.96	(0.01)
	Liechtenstein	0.09	(0.05)	0.39	(0.06)	–0.22	(0.07)	**0.61**	(0.10)	–1.19	(0.04)	–0.27	(0.03)	0.44	(0.02)	1.40	(0.05)
	Macao-China	0.13	(0.03)	0.28	(0.04)	–0.02	(0.04)	**0.30**	(0.06)	–0.92	(0.04)	–0.22	(0.01)	0.40	(0.02)	1.26	(0.03)
	Russian Federation	0.25	(0.02)	0.25	(0.03)	0.25	(0.02)	0.01	(0.03)	–0.72	(0.02)	–0.04	(0.00)	0.48	(0.00)	1.27	(0.01)
	Serbia	–0.06	(0.02)	0.03	(0.03)	–0.14	(0.03)	**0.17**	(0.04)	–1.26	(0.01)	–0.36	(0.00)	0.21	(0.01)	1.17	(0.02)
	Thailand	0.71	(0.01)	0.74	(0.02)	0.70	(0.02)	0.04	(0.02)	–0.17	(0.01)	0.63	(0.01)	0.97	(0.00)	1.43	(0.01)
	Tunisia	0.94	(0.02)	1.08	(0.03)	0.81	(0.03)	**0.27**	(0.03)	–0.44	(0.02)	0.72	(0.01)	1.33	(0.01)	2.16	(0.01)
	Uruguay	0.36	(0.02)	0.41	(0.03)	0.30	(0.03)	**0.11**	(0.04)	–0.93	(0.01)	0.03	(0.01)	0.72	(0.01)	1.61	(0.02)
	United Kingdom[1]	0.00	(0.02)	0.11	(0.02)	–0.09	(0.02)	**0.19**	(0.03)	–1.20	(0.01)	–0.27	(0.00)	0.30	(0.01)	1.19	(0.01)

		Performance on the mathematics scale, by national quarters of the index of interest in and enjoyment of mathematics								Change in the mathematics score per unit of the index of interest in and enjoyment of mathematics		Increased likelihood of students in the bottom quarter of this index scoring in the bottom quarter of the national mathematics performance distribution		Explained variance in student performance (r-squared × 100)	
		Bottom quarter		Second quarter		Third quarter		Top quarter							
		Mean score	S.E.	Mean score	S.E.	Mean score	S.E.	Mean score	S.E.	Effect	S.E.	Ratio	S.E.	%	S.E.
OECD countries	Australia	**502**	(3.3)	517	(2.5)	535	(2.6)	**547**	(3.0)	**18.6**	(1.36)	**1.4**	(0.06)	3.5	(0.49)
	Austria	**495**	(3.9)	503	(3.4)	512	(5.0)	**520**	(5.3)	**8.7**	(1.92)	1.2	(0.08)	1.0	(0.43)
	Belgium	**514**	(3.2)	533	(3.3)	544	(3.4)	**554**	(3.5)	**15.0**	(1.55)	**1.3**	(0.07)	1.9	(0.41)
	Canada	**511**	(2.0)	527	(2.1)	543	(2.8)	**564**	(2.5)	**20.3**	(0.96)	**1.5**	(0.06)	5.8	(0.58)
	Czech Republic	**505**	(3.4)	509	(4.1)	524	(4.8)	**552**	(5.0)	**22.5**	(2.22)	**1.3**	(0.08)	3.9	(0.77)
	Denmark	**478**	(3.3)	505	(3.9)	532	(4.0)	**546**	(4.4)	**27.7**	(1.71)	**1.8**	(0.11)	8.8	(1.11)
	Finland	**511**	(2.6)	536	(2.5)	550	(2.8)	**583**	(3.4)	**30.5**	(1.59)	**1.8**	(0.10)	11.2	(1.11)
	France	**487**	(3.4)	500	(3.1)	526	(4.0)	**537**	(4.1)	**20.9**	(1.76)	**1.6**	(0.10)	4.9	(0.85)
	Germany	**493**	(4.9)	510	(3.9)	521	(4.4)	**524**	(4.7)	**10.2**	(1.67)	**1.2**	(0.09)	1.4	(0.46)
	Greece	**418**	(4.0)	431	(4.9)	459	(4.4)	**476**	(5.4)	**23.7**	(1.88)	**1.5**	(0.09)	6.7	(0.97)
	Hungary	**486**	(3.5)	482	(3.9)	484	(4.3)	**509**	(4.9)	**10.0**	(2.30)	0.9	(0.07)	0.9	(0.42)
	Iceland	**477**	(3.1)	507	(3.6)	531	(3.7)	**547**	(3.2)	**24.5**	(1.44)	**2.0**	(0.11)	8.6	(1.00)
	Ireland	**482**	(3.3)	499	(3.3)	507	(3.6)	**524**	(4.1)	**17.4**	(1.78)	**1.4**	(0.10)	3.8	(0.79)
	Italy	**450**	(3.6)	462	(3.8)	481	(4.4)	**471**	(4.5)	**10.3**	(1.70)	1.1	(0.07)	1.0	(0.35)
	Japan	**494**	(4.7)	531	(4.6)	543	(5.0)	**572**	(5.9)	**27.6**	(2.44)	**1.9**	(0.12)	7.9	(1.21)
	Korea	**500**	(3.9)	520	(4.0)	557	(4.6)	**593**	(3.8)	**36.2**	(1.62)	**2.0**	(0.11)	15.5	(1.05)
	Luxembourg	**485**	(2.6)	489	(3.1)	498	(2.9)	**503**	(3.5)	**6.7**	(1.48)	1.1	(0.06)	0.6	(0.28)
	Mexico	**395**	(4.3)	393	(3.9)	389	(4.6)	**381**	(5.6)	**–6.3**	(2.50)	**0.8**	(0.08)	0.4	(0.29)
	Netherlands	**525**	(4.0)	541	(4.7)	548	(4.0)	**559**	(4.9)	**14.3**	(2.09)	**1.3**	(0.10)	2.1	(0.63)
	New Zealand	**513**	(3.5)	519	(3.3)	533	(4.1)	**534**	(4.0)	**11.4**	(1.72)	1.0	(0.08)	1.3	(0.39)
	Norway	**447**	(3.1)	481	(3.3)	512	(4.0)	**544**	(3.6)	**34.3**	(1.41)	**2.2**	(0.14)	16.2	(1.30)
	Poland	**479**	(3.1)	478	(3.2)	495	(4.0)	**511**	(3.9)	**15.6**	(1.48)	**1.2**	(0.07)	2.5	(0.50)
	Portugal	**452**	(3.7)	462	(3.9)	475	(4.6)	**479**	(5.3)	**14.2**	(2.20)	**1.3**	(0.08)	1.9	(0.59)
	Slovak Republic	**488**	(3.9)	492	(4.5)	504	(4.0)	**513**	(5.1)	**12.1**	(2.26)	**1.3**	(0.09)	1.2	(0.44)
	Spain	**460**	(2.8)	479	(2.8)	494	(3.7)	**511**	(4.1)	**20.4**	(1.61)	**1.5**	(0.10)	5.1	(0.83)
	Sweden	**476**	(2.5)	499	(3.6)	522	(4.1)	**543**	(4.6)	**27.0**	(1.79)	**1.6**	(0.10)	8.4	(1.07)
	Switzerland	**513**	(4.2)	519	(4.6)	538	(4.4)	**538**	(4.2)	**10.4**	(1.47)	**1.2**	(0.08)	1.2	(0.35)
	Turkey	**401**	(4.8)	421	(7.3)	434	(8.8)	**452**	(10.0)	**16.9**	(3.08)	**1.3**	(0.11)	3.0	(1.01)
	United States	**472**	(3.2)	486	(3.9)	484	(4.1)	**494**	(4.9)	**7.8**	(1.47)	1.0	(0.06)	0.7	(0.28)
	OECD total	*483*	*(1.3)*	*492*	*(1.3)*	*495*	*(1.6)*	*494*	*(1.9)*	*5.1*	*(0.72)*	*1.0*	*(0.02)*	*0.3*	*(0.07)*
	OECD average	*486*	*(0.7)*	*498*	*(0.7)*	*509*	*(0.9)*	*515*	*(1.1)*	*11.9*	*(0.45)*	*1.2*	*(0.02)*	*1.5*	*(0.11)*
Partner countries	Brazil	**375**	(4.4)	367	(6.0)	352	(6.0)	**346**	(6.9)	**–13.3**	(2.98)	**0.8**	(0.06)	1.4	(0.64)
	Hong Kong-China	**512**	(6.1)	539	(5.2)	567	(5.8)	**585**	(4.5)	**32.0**	(1.80)	**1.9**	(0.12)	9.2	(0.85)
	Indonesia	**371**	(6.5)	363	(4.1)	361	(3.9)	**351**	(4.7)	**–8.8**	(3.41)	**0.8**	(0.10)	0.5	(0.46)
	Latvia	**475**	(4.5)	474	(4.9)	485	(4.9)	**501**	(6.4)	**15.7**	(2.64)	1.1	(0.08)	1.8	(0.57)
	Liechtenstein	537	(10.9)	528	(10.9)	534	(11.6)	544	(12.1)	2.5	(5.86)	0.7	(0.18)	0.1	(0.42)
	Macao-China	**505**	(7.3)	515	(5.8)	539	(6.7)	**550**	(6.7)	**20.2**	(4.02)	**1.3**	(0.17)	4.2	(1.60)
	Russian Federation	**458**	(4.8)	459	(4.3)	475	(5.2)	**486**	(5.5)	**13.2**	(1.97)	**1.2**	(0.06)	1.3	(0.38)
	Serbia	444	(4.1)	437	(4.1)	447	(5.4)	434	(5.4)	–3.5	(1.97)	0.9	(0.07)	0.2	(0.19)
	Thailand	419	(3.8)	412	(4.0)	412	(3.9)	425	(4.8)	4.0	(2.45)	1.0	(0.07)	0.1	(0.13)
	Tunisia	**350**	(3.6)	359	(3.4)	356	(3.6)	**374**	(3.7)	**8.2**	(1.57)	1.1	(0.08)	1.0	(0.40)
	Uruguay	**413**	(4.6)	414	(4.2)	433	(3.9)	**444**	(5.1)	**14.4**	(1.56)	**1.2**	(0.08)	2.2	(0.47)
	United Kingdom[1]	**492**	(3.8)	503	(3.5)	514	(3.6)	**524**	(3.7)	**13.6**	(1.45)	**1.3**	(0.07)	1.9	(0.43)

Note: Values that are statistically significant are indicated in bold (see Annex A4).
1. Response rate too low to ensure comparability (see Annex A3).

Table 3.2a
Index of instrumental motivation in mathematics and performance on the mathematics scale, by national quarters of the index
Results based on students' self-reports

		Index of instrumental motivation in mathematics														
		All students		Males		Females		Gender difference (M – F)		Bottom quarter		Second quarter		Third quarter		Top quarter	
		Mean index	S.E.	Mean index	S.E.	Mean index	S.E.	Dif.	S.E.	Mean index	S.E.	Mean index	S.E.	Mean index	S.E.	Mean index	S.E.
OECD countries	Australia	0.23	(0.02)	0.34	(0.02)	0.11	(0.02)	**0.23**	(0.02)	–0.99	(0.02)	–0.04	(0.00)	0.42	(0.01)	1.52	(0.01)
	Austria	–0.49	(0.03)	–0.20	(0.03)	–0.78	(0.03)	**0.58**	(0.04)	–1.68	(0.01)	–0.90	(0.01)	–0.26	(0.01)	0.87	(0.01)
	Belgium	–0.32	(0.02)	–0.17	(0.02)	–0.49	(0.02)	**0.32**	(0.03)	–1.54	(0.01)	–0.66	(0.00)	–0.04	(0.00)	0.95	(0.01)
	Canada	0.23	(0.01)	0.30	(0.02)	0.17	(0.02)	**0.13**	(0.02)	–1.09	(0.01)	–0.06	(0.00)	0.50	(0.01)	1.57	(0.00)
	Czech Republic	0.01	(0.02)	0.12	(0.02)	–0.10	(0.03)	**0.22**	(0.03)	–1.05	(0.01)	–0.21	(0.01)	0.15	(0.00)	1.14	(0.01)
	Denmark	0.37	(0.02)	0.57	(0.02)	0.19	(0.02)	**0.38**	(0.03)	–0.77	(0.02)	0.03	(0.00)	0.70	(0.01)	1.54	(0.01)
	Finland	0.06	(0.01)	0.22	(0.02)	–0.10	(0.02)	**0.32**	(0.03)	–1.06	(0.01)	–0.16	(0.01)	0.20	(0.01)	1.27	(0.01)
	France	–0.08	(0.02)	0.11	(0.03)	–0.25	(0.03)	**0.36**	(0.03)	–1.37	(0.02)	–0.44	(0.01)	0.22	(0.01)	1.26	(0.01)
	Germany	–0.04	(0.02)	0.18	(0.02)	–0.26	(0.02)	**0.44**	(0.03)	–1.25	(0.01)	–0.47	(0.01)	0.26	(0.01)	1.30	(0.01)
	Greece	–0.05	(0.02)	0.09	(0.03)	–0.18	(0.03)	**0.27**	(0.03)	–1.31	(0.02)	–0.38	(0.01)	0.22	(0.01)	1.28	(0.01)
	Hungary	–0.11	(0.02)	–0.02	(0.02)	–0.22	(0.02)	**0.19**	(0.02)	–1.18	(0.02)	–0.39	(0.01)	0.10	(0.00)	1.02	(0.01)
	Iceland	0.31	(0.02)	0.34	(0.02)	0.28	(0.03)	0.06	(0.04)	–1.01	(0.02)	0.02	(0.01)	0.63	(0.01)	1.60	(0.01)
	Ireland	0.10	(0.02)	0.25	(0.03)	–0.06	(0.03)	**0.31**	(0.04)	–1.11	(0.02)	–0.15	(0.01)	0.30	(0.01)	1.35	(0.01)
	Italy	–0.15	(0.02)	–0.04	(0.02)	–0.26	(0.03)	**0.21**	(0.03)	–1.32	(0.02)	–0.45	(0.01)	0.10	(0.00)	1.05	(0.01)
	Japan	–0.66	(0.03)	–0.49	(0.04)	–0.81	(0.03)	**0.32**	(0.04)	–1.92	(0.01)	–1.03	(0.00)	–0.39	(0.01)	0.71	(0.02)
	Korea	–0.44	(0.02)	–0.36	(0.02)	–0.55	(0.04)	**0.20**	(0.05)	–1.59	(0.01)	–0.81	(0.01)	–0.15	(0.01)	0.81	(0.02)
	Luxembourg	–0.41	(0.02)	–0.16	(0.03)	–0.64	(0.02)	**0.48**	(0.03)	–1.80	(0.01)	–0.88	(0.01)	–0.09	(0.01)	1.14	(0.02)
	Mexico	0.58	(0.02)	0.59	(0.02)	0.57	(0.02)	0.02	(0.03)	–0.44	(0.01)	0.22	(0.01)	0.94	(0.01)	1.60	(0.01)
	Netherlands	–0.26	(0.02)	–0.04	(0.02)	–0.48	(0.03)	**0.44**	(0.03)	–1.37	(0.02)	–0.52	(0.01)	0.05	(0.00)	0.82	(0.02)
	New Zealand	0.29	(0.02)	0.37	(0.02)	0.21	(0.02)	**0.16**	(0.03)	–0.87	(0.02)	0.02	(0.01)	0.49	(0.01)	1.52	(0.01)
	Norway	0.15	(0.02)	0.27	(0.03)	0.03	(0.03)	**0.24**	(0.04)	–1.16	(0.02)	–0.11	(0.01)	0.41	(0.01)	1.47	(0.01)
	Poland	0.04	(0.02)	0.06	(0.02)	0.02	(0.02)	0.04	(0.03)	–0.95	(0.02)	–0.08	(0.01)	0.10	(0.00)	1.10	(0.02)
	Portugal	0.27	(0.02)	0.30	(0.03)	0.25	(0.02)	0.05	(0.04)	–0.93	(0.02)	0.03	(0.01)	0.47	(0.01)	1.51	(0.01)
	Slovak Republic	–0.05	(0.02)	0.05	(0.02)	–0.15	(0.03)	**0.20**	(0.03)	–1.10	(0.02)	–0.28	(0.01)	0.11	(0.00)	1.08	(0.01)
	Spain	–0.05	(0.02)	0.00	(0.03)	–0.09	(0.03)	**0.09**	(0.03)	–1.35	(0.02)	–0.34	(0.01)	0.21	(0.00)	1.28	(0.01)
	Sweden	0.02	(0.02)	0.17	(0.02)	–0.13	(0.02)	**0.30**	(0.03)	–1.12	(0.02)	–0.30	(0.01)	0.21	(0.01)	1.30	(0.01)
	Switzerland	–0.04	(0.02)	0.30	(0.02)	–0.40	(0.02)	**0.70**	(0.03)	–1.34	(0.01)	–0.47	(0.01)	0.30	(0.01)	1.34	(0.01)
	Turkey	0.23	(0.02)	0.20	(0.03)	0.26	(0.03)	–0.06	(0.04)	–1.04	(0.02)	–0.09	(0.01)	0.54	(0.01)	1.49	(0.01)
	United States	0.17	(0.02)	0.22	(0.02)	0.12	(0.02)	**0.10**	(0.03)	–1.05	(0.02)	–0.07	(0.01)	0.34	(0.01)	1.47	(0.01)
	OECD total	*0.02*	*(0.01)*	*0.11*	*(0.01)*	*–0.08*	*(0.01)*	*0.19*	*(0.01)*	*–1.27*	*(0.01)*	*–0.28*	*(0.00)*	*0.25*	*(0.00)*	*1.35*	*(0.01)*
	OECD average	*0.00*	*(0.00)*	*0.12*	*(0.00)*	*–0.12*	*(0.00)*	*0.25*	*(0.01)*	*–1.26*	*(0.00)*	*–0.30*	*(0.00)*	*0.23*	*(0.01)*	*1.31*	*(0.01)*
Partner countries	Brazil	0.48	(0.02)	0.52	(0.03)	0.44	(0.03)	**0.07**	(0.03)	–0.68	(0.02)	0.14	(0.00)	0.84	(0.01)	1.61	(0.01)
	Hong Kong-China	–0.12	(0.02)	–0.03	(0.03)	–0.20	(0.02)	**0.17**	(0.03)	–1.17	(0.02)	–0.33	(0.01)	0.10	(0.00)	0.94	(0.02)
	Indonesia	0.46	(0.01)	0.44	(0.02)	0.47	(0.02)	–0.04	(0.02)	–0.34	(0.01)	0.10	(0.00)	0.66	(0.01)	1.41	(0.01)
	Latvia	0.07	(0.02)	0.15	(0.02)	0.00	(0.02)	**0.15**	(0.03)	–0.95	(0.01)	–0.17	(0.01)	0.21	(0.01)	1.20	(0.02)
	Liechtenstein	–0.05	(0.04)	0.41	(0.07)	–0.53	(0.06)	**0.94**	(0.09)	–1.31	(0.04)	–0.57	(0.02)	0.32	(0.04)	1.39	(0.03)
	Macao-China	–0.03	(0.03)	0.07	(0.04)	–0.13	(0.03)	**0.20**	(0.05)	–1.06	(0.03)	–0.24	(0.02)	0.13	(0.01)	1.05	(0.03)
	Russian Federation	–0.01	(0.02)	0.04	(0.03)	–0.05	(0.02)	**0.08**	(0.04)	–1.13	(0.01)	–0.30	(0.01)	0.20	(0.01)	1.21	(0.01)
	Serbia	–0.20	(0.03)	–0.09	(0.03)	–0.30	(0.03)	**0.21**	(0.04)	–1.41	(0.02)	–0.53	(0.01)	0.06	(0.00)	1.10	(0.02)
	Thailand	0.49	(0.01)	0.41	(0.02)	0.55	(0.02)	**–0.14**	(0.02)	–0.25	(0.01)	0.10	(0.00)	0.63	(0.01)	1.47	(0.01)
	Tunisia	0.52	(0.02)	0.61	(0.02)	0.43	(0.03)	**0.18**	(0.03)	–0.92	(0.02)	0.28	(0.01)	1.00	(0.01)	1.72	(0.00)
	Uruguay	0.27	(0.02)	0.35	(0.03)	0.20	(0.03)	**0.16**	(0.03)	–0.98	(0.02)	–0.03	(0.01)	0.57	(0.01)	1.53	(0.01)
	United Kingdom[1]	0.12	(0.02)	0.27	(0.02)	0.00	(0.02)	**0.27**	(0.03)	–1.00	(0.01)	–0.16	(0.01)	0.29	(0.01)	1.37	(0.01)

		Performance on the mathematics scale, by national quarters of the index of instrumental motivation in mathematics								Change in the mathematics score per unit of the index of instrumental motivation in mathematics		Increased likelihood of students in the bottom quarter of this index scoring in the bottom quarter of the national mathematics performance distribution		Explained variance in student performance (r-squared × 100)	
		Bottom quarter		Second quarter		Third quarter		Top quarter							
		Mean score	S.E.	Mean score	S.E.	Mean score	S.E.	Mean score	S.E.	Effect	S.E.	Ratio	S.E.	%	S.E.
OECD countries	Australia	**508**	(3.0)	518	(3.1)	527	(3.6)	**548**	(2.9)	**16.9**	(0.91)	**1.3**	(0.04)	3.0	(0.33)
	Austria	511	(3.9)	511	(4.2)	506	(4.8)	503	(4.1)	**–3.7**	(1.60)	**0.8**	(0.06)	0.2	(0.15)
	Belgium	**520**	(3.3)	533	(3.4)	547	(3.1)	**546**	(3.9)	**11.0**	(1.63)	1.1	(0.06)	1.1	(0.33)
	Canada	**513**	(2.4)	528	(2.0)	540	(2.5)	**564**	(2.3)	**19.8**	(0.96)	**1.5**	(0.06)	5.4	(0.54)
	Czech Republic	**513**	(3.9)	518	(4.5)	526	(4.2)	**535**	(4.5)	**10.7**	(1.82)	**1.2**	(0.08)	1.0	(0.35)
	Denmark	**489**	(4.0)	510	(3.8)	522	(4.1)	**540**	(3.8)	**20.9**	(1.77)	**1.5**	(0.11)	4.3	(0.74)
	Finland	**517**	(2.7)	536	(2.5)	548	(2.8)	**579**	(3.4)	**26.9**	(1.70)	**1.5**	(0.08)	8.5	(1.06)
	France	**492**	(3.0)	509	(2.9)	519	(4.4)	**529**	(4.3)	**13.7**	(1.61)	**1.4**	(0.09)	2.4	(0.59)
	Germany	509	(4.3)	512	(4.2)	518	(4.7)	509	(4.8)	1.1	(1.93)	0.9	(0.06)	0.0	(0.06)
	Greece	**428**	(4.1)	438	(4.3)	450	(5.1)	**468**	(4.8)	**14.9**	(1.76)	**1.3**	(0.09)	2.6	(0.58)
	Hungary	**489**	(3.9)	479	(3.8)	487	(3.9)	**506**	(4.9)	**7.9**	(1.90)	0.9	(0.07)	0.5	(0.26)
	Iceland	**494**	(3.5)	509	(3.8)	523	(3.0)	**537**	(3.2)	**17.7**	(1.72)	**1.4**	(0.11)	4.0	(0.78)
	Ireland	**498**	(3.4)	500	(3.8)	501	(4.1)	**514**	(3.5)	**7.7**	(1.45)	1.1	(0.07)	0.7	(0.29)
	Italy	**456**	(3.9)	461	(3.8)	477	(3.8)	**471**	(4.9)	**8.5**	(1.58)	1.0	(0.08)	0.7	(0.27)
	Japan	**500**	(4.9)	534	(4.3)	541	(5.5)	**565**	(5.5)	**23.9**	(2.25)	**1.7**	(0.12)	6.2	(1.04)
	Korea	**504**	(3.8)	527	(3.8)	556	(4.2)	**583**	(4.1)	**32.8**	(1.77)	**2.0**	(0.11)	12.0	(1.05)
	Luxembourg	492	(2.7)	498	(3.3)	494	(2.9)	491	(3.0)	0.0	(1.35)	0.9	(0.06)	0.0	(0.03)
	Mexico	382	(5.4)	388	(4.0)	388	(4.6)	390	(4.9)	**5.4**	(2.44)	1.1	(0.11)	0.3	(0.24)
	Netherlands	**534**	(4.0)	547	(4.5)	546	(4.4)	**546**	(5.1)	**6.1**	(2.00)	1.1	(0.09)	0.4	(0.24)
	New Zealand	**508**	(3.5)	520	(3.7)	525	(3.9)	**546**	(4.2)	**15.6**	(1.81)	**1.2**	(0.08)	2.2	(0.51)
	Norway	**457**	(3.6)	491	(3.0)	503	(3.9)	**534**	(3.8)	**28.5**	(1.49)	**2.0**	(0.11)	10.1	(1.06)
	Poland	**475**	(3.6)	488	(3.4)	491	(4.6)	**510**	(4.1)	**17.0**	(1.82)	**1.4**	(0.09)	2.4	(0.51)
	Portugal	**446**	(4.1)	461	(4.7)	471	(4.6)	**489**	(5.1)	**17.3**	(2.04)	**1.5**	(0.09)	3.5	(0.84)
	Slovak Republic	**492**	(3.6)	495	(4.5)	503	(4.4)	**505**	(4.7)	**6.3**	(1.98)	1.2	(0.09)	0.3	(0.21)
	Spain	**461**	(2.9)	479	(3.0)	494	(3.8)	**511**	(3.6)	**19.4**	(1.39)	**1.5**	(0.09)	5.1	(0.74)
	Sweden	**485**	(2.9)	504	(3.0)	511	(3.6)	**540**	(4.9)	**23.0**	(2.00)	**1.5**	(0.09)	5.3	(0.88)
	Switzerland	529	(5.1)	529	(4.2)	526	(3.9)	525	(3.6)	–2.4	(1.62)	1.1	(0.07)	0.1	(0.09)
	Turkey	**411**	(6.4)	424	(8.2)	434	(7.6)	**441**	(8.9)	**12.9**	(2.39)	1.2	(0.10)	1.5	(0.55)
	United States	**470**	(3.5)	483	(3.6)	482	(4.2)	**503**	(4.2)	**13.6**	(1.52)	**1.2**	(0.06)	2.0	(0.44)
	OECD total	*490*	*(1.4)*	*490*	*(1.3)*	*491*	*(1.6)*	*493*	*(1.8)*	*3.0*	*(0.75)*	*0.9*	*(0.02)*	*0.1*	*(0.04)*
	OECD average	*493*	*(0.8)*	*498*	*(0.9)*	*503*	*(0.8)*	*513*	*(1.0)*	*8.5*	*(0.41)*	*1.1*	*(0.02)*	*0.7*	*(0.07)*
Partner countries	Brazil	**383**	(7.8)	361	(6.0)	349	(4.5)	**343**	(6.3)	**–17.1**	(3.10)	**0.6**	(0.06)	2.4	(0.84)
	Hong Kong-China	**525**	(5.4)	544	(5.7)	557	(6.0)	**576**	(4.6)	**25.9**	(2.25)	**1.5**	(0.10)	4.9	(0.78)
	Indonesia	**362**	(5.6)	370	(4.6)	361	(4.0)	**352**	(4.6)	**–5.6**	(2.78)	1.0	(0.09)	0.3	(0.25)
	Latvia	**466**	(4.2)	475	(4.3)	487	(5.1)	**506**	(5.1)	**19.7**	(2.00)	**1.3**	(0.08)	3.6	(0.69)
	Liechtenstein	540	(10.1)	542	(11.8)	535	(11.6)	527	(11.9)	–5.8	(5.21)	1.1	(0.26)	0.4	(0.69)
	Macao-China	527	(6.4)	525	(6.3)	525	(7.9)	533	(6.6)	3.4	(3.79)	1.0	(0.14)	0.1	(0.26)
	Russian Federation	**456**	(4.3)	459	(4.9)	475	(5.0)	**488**	(5.3)	**13.9**	(1.66)	**1.3**	(0.08)	1.9	(0.44)
	Serbia	443	(4.7)	443	(4.6)	439	(4.7)	434	(5.2)	–3.1	(2.10)	0.9	(0.07)	0.1	(0.19)
	Thailand	**412**	(4.1)	411	(4.0)	419	(3.9)	**426**	(4.6)	**9.1**	(2.56)	1.1	(0.09)	0.6	(0.34)
	Tunisia	**339**	(3.0)	358	(3.1)	356	(3.4)	**386**	(4.0)	**13.8**	(1.41)	**1.4**	(0.07)	3.1	(0.61)
	Uruguay	421	(4.3)	420	(4.5)	425	(4.4)	431	(5.7)	**5.0**	(2.13)	0.9	(0.06)	0.2	(0.20)
	United Kingdom[1]	**500**	(4.2)	502	(3.8)	507	(3.9)	**525**	(3.7)	**10.4**	(1.48)	**1.2**	(0.08)	1.1	(0.33)

Note: Values that are statistically significant are indicated in bold (see Annex A4).
1. Response rate too low to ensure comparability (see Annex A3).

Table 3.2b

Index of instrumental motivation in mathematics by students' expected educational level

Results based on students' self-reports

		All students by expected educational level									
		Students expecting to complete lower secondary education (ISCED Level 2)		Students expecting to complete upper secondary education, not providing access to university-level programmes (ISCED Levels 3B and 3C)		Students expecting to complete upper secondary education, providing access to university-level programmes (ISCED Levels 3A and 4)		Students expecting to complete a non-university tertiary-level programme (ISCED Level 5B)		Students expecting to complete a university-level programme (ISCED Levels 5A and 6)	
		Mean index	S.E.	Mean index	S.E.	Mean index	S.E.	Mean index	S.E.	Mean index	S.E.
OECD countries	Australia	–0.14	(0.08)	–0.01	(0.06)	–0.08	(0.02)	–0.07	(0.04)	0.41	(0.02)
	Austria	–0.37	(0.09)	–0.42	(0.04)	–0.65	(0.04)	–0.25	(0.05)	–0.59	(0.05)
	Belgium	–0.31	(0.05)	–0.48	(0.06)	–0.43	(0.03)	–0.47	(0.03)	–0.12	(0.02)
	Canada	–0.43	(0.15)	–0.33	(0.04)	–0.10	(0.03)	–0.02	(0.02)	0.43	(0.02)
	Czech Republic	–0.16	(0.19)	–0.23	(0.03)	–0.03	(0.03)	0.04	(0.04)	0.12	(0.03)
	Denmark	0.07	(0.04)	0.28	(0.04)	0.30	(0.02)	0.30	(0.04)	0.69	(0.03)
	Finland	–0.48	(0.06)	a	a	–0.11	(0.02)	a	a	0.25	(0.02)
	France	0.00	(0.13)	–0.22	(0.04)	–0.16	(0.03)	–0.13	(0.05)	0.13	(0.04)
	Germany	m	m	m	m	m	m	m	m	m	m
	Greece	–0.23	(0.19)	–0.18	(0.04)	–0.22	(0.05)	–0.17	(0.05)	0.03	(0.03)
	Hungary	–0.07	(0.17)	–0.10	(0.04)	–0.15	(0.03)	–0.16	(0.04)	–0.09	(0.02)
	Iceland	–0.54	(0.17)	–0.11	(0.06)	0.13	(0.02)	0.46	(0.04)	0.56	(0.03)
	Ireland	–0.12	(0.10)	–0.04	(0.06)	0.04	(0.03)	–0.02	(0.05)	0.18	(0.02)
	Italy	–0.20	(0.13)	–0.37	(0.07)	–0.17	(0.03)	–0.35	(0.05)	–0.10	(0.03)
	Japan	a	a	–0.70	(0.07)	–1.01	(0.04)	–0.86	(0.03)	–0.45	(0.03)
	Korea	0.36	(0.36)	–0.92	(0.06)	–1.16	(0.13)	–0.76	(0.03)	–0.33	(0.02)
	Luxembourg	–0.71	(0.08)	–0.30	(0.04)	–0.39	(0.04)	–0.57	(0.05)	–0.36	(0.03)
	Mexico	0.35	(0.06)	0.42	(0.05)	0.59	(0.03)	0.59	(0.03)	0.65	(0.02)
	Netherlands	–0.26	(0.04)	a	a	–0.31	(0.03)	a	a	–0.22	(0.02)
	New Zealand	–0.17	(0.12)	–0.02	(0.04)	0.16	(0.02)	0.36	(0.04)	0.51	(0.02)
	Norway	–0.42	(0.21)	–0.15	(0.04)	–0.04	(0.04)	0.20	(0.03)	0.55	(0.04)
	Poland	–0.06	(0.05)	–0.03	(0.03)	0.05	(0.03)	0.10	(0.03)	0.08	(0.03)
	Portugal	–0.05	(0.05)	0.19	(0.06)	0.13	(0.03)	a	a	0.45	(0.02)
	Slovak Republic	0.09	(0.09)	–0.11	(0.05)	–0.08	(0.02)	–0.04	(0.06)	–0.02	(0.03)
	Spain	–0.45	(0.04)	–0.35	(0.04)	–0.17	(0.04)	–0.08	(0.04)	0.20	(0.03)
	Sweden	–0.25	(0.07)	–0.20	(0.04)	–0.22	(0.03)	–0.01	(0.03)	0.35	(0.03)
	Switzerland	–0.13	(0.05)	0.04	(0.03)	–0.22	(0.03)	0.25	(0.08)	–0.17	(0.05)
	Turkey	m	m	m	m	m	m	m	m	m	m
	United States	–0.10	(0.19)	a	a	–0.08	(0.03)	0.05	(0.04)	0.29	(0.02)
	OECD total	***–0.03***	***(0.02)***	***–0.19***	***(0.02)***	***–0.10***	***(0.01)***	***–0.16***	***(0.02)***	***0.15***	***(0.01)***
	OECD average	***–0.18***	***(0.01)***	***–0.14***	***(0.01)***	***–0.09***	***(0.01)***	***–0.08***	***(0.01)***	***0.13***	***(0.01)***
Partner countries	Brazil	m	m	m	m	m	m	m	m	m	m
	Hong Kong-China	–0.54	(0.13)	–0.43	(0.04)	–0.22	(0.03)	–0.20	(0.04)	0.03	(0.02)
	Indonesia	0.49	(0.06)	0.40	(0.04)	0.45	(0.02)	0.48	(0.03)	0.47	(0.02)
	Latvia	–0.25	(0.07)	–0.07	(0.04)	–0.05	(0.03)	0.10	(0.02)	0.25	(0.03)
	Liechtenstein	–0.38	(0.20)	0.11	(0.09)	–0.30	(0.12)	0.92	(0.24)	–0.15	(0.10)
	Macao-China	–0.21	(0.11)	–0.45	(0.28)	–0.13	(0.05)	–0.06	(0.07)	0.07	(0.04)
	Russian Federation	–0.20	(0.09)	–0.30	(0.05)	–0.11	(0.03)	a	a	0.08	(0.02)
	Serbia	–0.23	(0.57)	–0.18	(0.04)	–0.02	(0.32)	–0.18	(0.04)	–0.21	(0.05)
	Thailand	0.25	(0.05)	0.31	(0.04)	0.42	(0.02)	a	a	0.57	(0.02)
	Tunisia	0.34	(0.07)	0.23	(0.08)	0.35	(0.04)	0.41	(0.06)	0.69	(0.02)
	Uruguay	0.27	(0.06)	0.43	(0.05)	0.12	(0.06)	0.32	(0.05)	0.28	(0.03)
	United Kingdom[1]	–0.13	(0.08)	0.00	(0.03)	0.11	(0.02)	0.20	(0.04)	0.27	(0.04)

1. Response rate too low to ensure comparability (see Annex A3).

Table 3.2b *(continued)*
Index of instrumental motivation in mathematics by students' expected educational level
Results based on students' self-reports

		Male students by expected educational level									
		Students expecting to complete lower secondary education (ISCED Level 2)		Students expecting to complete upper secondary education, not providing access to university-level programmes (ISCED Levels 3B and 3C)		Students expecting to complete upper secondary education, providing access to university-level programmes (ISCED Levels 3A and 4)		Students expecting to complete a non-university tertiary-level programme (ISCED Level 5B)		Students expecting to complete a university-level programme (ISCED Levels 5A and 6)	
		Mean index	S.E.	Mean index	S.E.	Mean index	S.E.	Mean index	S.E.	Mean index	S.E.
OECD countries	Australia	–0.06	(0.09)	0.12	(0.07)	0.07	(0.03)	0.10	(0.05)	0.56	(0.02)
	Austria	–0.35	(0.11)	–0.24	(0.05)	–0.24	(0.06)	0.00	(0.06)	–0.30	(0.07)
	Belgium	–0.21	(0.06)	–0.41	(0.08)	–0.31	(0.03)	–0.22	(0.04)	0.08	(0.03)
	Canada	–0.26	(0.18)	–0.30	(0.05)	–0.05	(0.04)	0.07	(0.03)	0.55	(0.02)
	Czech Republic	–0.21	(0.26)	–0.27	(0.05)	0.05	(0.03)	0.35	(0.07)	0.35	(0.04)
	Denmark	0.20	(0.05)	0.56	(0.05)	0.50	(0.04)	0.50	(0.05)	0.87	(0.05)
	Finland	–0.38	(0.10)	a	a	0.03	(0.03)	a	a	0.46	(0.03)
	France	0.09	(0.17)	–0.12	(0.05)	0.04	(0.05)	0.08	(0.06)	0.45	(0.05)
	Germany	m	m	m	m	m	m	m	m	m	m
	Greece	–0.48	(0.22)	–0.19	(0.05)	–0.18	(0.08)	–0.05	(0.05)	0.25	(0.04)
	Hungary	–0.10	(0.20)	–0.08	(0.05)	–0.15	(0.03)	–0.05	(0.06)	0.09	(0.03)
	Iceland	–0.59	(0.22)	–0.09	(0.07)	0.23	(0.04)	0.51	(0.06)	0.63	(0.05)
	Ireland	–0.02	(0.12)	–0.01	(0.08)	0.15	(0.04)	0.24	(0.07)	0.38	(0.04)
	Italy	–0.14	(0.16)	–0.28	(0.08)	–0.13	(0.03)	–0.14	(0.12)	0.11	(0.04)
	Japan	a	a	–0.59	(0.08)	–0.86	(0.05)	–0.68	(0.07)	–0.29	(0.05)
	Korea	0.14	(0.62)	–0.82	(0.10)	–1.08	(0.15)	–0.70	(0.04)	–0.25	(0.02)
	Luxembourg	–0.50	(0.12)	–0.16	(0.06)	–0.16	(0.06)	–0.12	(0.07)	–0.12	(0.04)
	Mexico	0.32	(0.06)	0.42	(0.05)	0.62	(0.04)	0.57	(0.04)	0.71	(0.03)
	Netherlands	–0.09	(0.04)	a	a	–0.05	(0.05)	a	a	0.00	(0.03)
	New Zealand	–0.40	(0.20)	–0.01	(0.05)	0.29	(0.03)	0.50	(0.06)	0.59	(0.04)
	Norway	–0.47	(0.28)	0.00	(0.05)	0.09	(0.05)	0.46	(0.05)	0.66	(0.06)
	Poland	–0.06	(0.05)	–0.04	(0.03)	0.06	(0.03)	0.23	(0.05)	0.14	(0.04)
	Portugal	–0.03	(0.06)	0.21	(0.09)	0.19	(0.04)	a	a	0.54	(0.03)
	Slovak Republic	0.12	(0.12)	–0.15	(0.05)	–0.03	(0.03)	–0.01	(0.06)	0.19	(0.03)
	Spain	–0.45	(0.06)	–0.34	(0.06)	–0.12	(0.06)	0.03	(0.05)	0.37	(0.04)
	Sweden	–0.09	(0.09)	0.00	(0.05)	–0.11	(0.04)	0.23	(0.04)	0.54	(0.04)
	Switzerland	0.30	(0.07)	0.36	(0.04)	0.10	(0.05)	0.56	(0.07)	0.15	(0.05)
	Turkey	m	m	m	m	m	m	m	m	m	m
	United States	–0.07	(0.26)	a	a	–0.09	(0.04)	0.13	(0.06)	0.39	(0.03)
	OECD total	***0.00***	***(0.03)***	***–0.11***	***(0.02)***	***–0.03***	***(0.02)***	***0.01***	***(0.02)***	***0.25***	***(0.01)***
	OECD average	***–0.08***	***(0.02)***	***–0.03***	***(0.01)***	***0.03***	***(0.01)***	***0.11***	***(0.01)***	***0.27***	***(0.01)***
Partner countries	Brazil	m	m	m	m	m	m	m	m	m	m
	Hong Kong-China	–0.52	(0.15)	–0.38	(0.05)	–0.11	(0.04)	–0.10	(0.05)	0.16	(0.04)
	Indonesia	0.49	(0.11)	0.38	(0.04)	0.43	(0.03)	0.45	(0.04)	0.47	(0.03)
	Latvia	–0.23	(0.07)	0.00	(0.05)	0.03	(0.04)	0.20	(0.04)	0.42	(0.04)
	Liechtenstein	–0.09	(0.29)	0.63	(0.11)	0.17	(0.24)	1.06	(0.19)	0.22	(0.14)
	Macao-China	–0.16	(0.12)	–0.36	(0.35)	–0.03	(0.06)	0.22	(0.13)	0.17	(0.06)
	Russian Federation	–0.18	(0.12)	–0.30	(0.08)	–0.10	(0.03)	a	a	0.19	(0.03)
	Serbia	–0.05	(0.57)	–0.20	(0.05)	–0.25	(0.37)	–0.08	(0.05)	0.03	(0.05)
	Thailand	0.20	(0.06)	0.28	(0.06)	0.33	(0.03)	a	a	0.53	(0.03)
	Tunisia	0.42	(0.09)	0.26	(0.10)	0.47	(0.05)	0.59	(0.08)	0.83	(0.03)
	Uruguay	0.26	(0.07)	0.45	(0.06)	0.19	(0.07)	0.46	(0.06)	0.40	(0.04)
	United Kingdom[1]	–0.06	(0.11)	0.12	(0.03)	0.29	(0.03)	0.39	(0.06)	0.46	(0.05)

		Female students by expected educational level									
		Students expecting to complete lower secondary education (ISCED Level 2)		Students expecting to complete upper secondary education, not providing access to university-level programmes (ISCED Levels 3B and 3C)		Students expecting to complete upper secondary education, providing access to university-level programmes (ISCED Levels 3A and 4)		Students expecting to complete a non-university tertiary-level programme (ISCED Level 5B)		Students expecting to complete a university-level programme (ISCED Levels 5A and 6)	
		Mean index	S.E.	Mean index	S.E.	Mean index	S.E.	Mean index	S.E.	Mean index	S.E.
OECD countries	Australia	–0.41	(0.13)	–0.35	(0.08)	–0.30	(0.03)	–0.22	(0.04)	0.28	(0.02)
	Austria	–0.40	(0.12)	–0.63	(0.05)	–0.92	(0.04)	–0.69	(0.08)	–0.85	(0.05)
	Belgium	–0.45	(0.08)	–0.59	(0.06)	–0.59	(0.04)	–0.66	(0.03)	–0.30	(0.03)
	Canada	–0.65	(0.21)	–0.37	(0.06)	–0.24	(0.07)	–0.12	(0.03)	0.33	(0.02)
	Czech Republic	–0.10	(0.24)	–0.14	(0.06)	–0.14	(0.04)	–0.12	(0.06)	–0.07	(0.04)
	Denmark	–0.10	(0.05)	–0.18	(0.08)	0.10	(0.03)	0.18	(0.05)	0.52	(0.04)
	Finland	–0.61	(0.10)	a	a	–0.26	(0.02)	a	a	0.06	(0.03)
	France	–0.11	(0.19)	–0.32	(0.05)	–0.33	(0.04)	–0.41	(0.06)	–0.09	(0.04)
	Germany	m	m	m	m	m	m	m	m	m	m
	Greece	0.14	(0.27)	–0.16	(0.07)	–0.28	(0.06)	–0.31	(0.06)	–0.14	(0.03)
	Hungary	0.03	(0.29)	–0.16	(0.08)	–0.16	(0.03)	–0.28	(0.06)	–0.23	(0.03)
	Iceland	–0.48	(0.29)	–0.16	(0.12)	0.03	(0.04)	0.41	(0.06)	0.51	(0.03)
	Ireland	–0.32	(0.14)	–0.07	(0.10)	–0.18	(0.05)	–0.25	(0.05)	0.03	(0.03)
	Italy	–0.33	(0.15)	–0.57	(0.12)	–0.23	(0.04)	–0.44	(0.06)	–0.23	(0.03)
	Japan	a	a	–0.88	(0.09)	–1.18	(0.06)	–0.93	(0.04)	–0.61	(0.03)
	Korea	0.62	(0.05)	–1.02	(0.07)	–1.34	(0.16)	–0.86	(0.05)	–0.45	(0.04)
	Luxembourg	–0.89	(0.10)	–0.46	(0.06)	–0.67	(0.05)	–0.93	(0.06)	–0.59	(0.03)
	Mexico	0.38	(0.10)	0.43	(0.11)	0.57	(0.05)	0.61	(0.05)	0.61	(0.03)
	Netherlands	–0.48	(0.05)	a	a	–0.57	(0.04)	a	a	–0.42	(0.04)
	New Zealand	0.01	(0.14)	–0.04	(0.07)	0.01	(0.03)	0.27	(0.04)	0.43	(0.03)
	Norway	–0.37	(0.28)	–0.37	(0.05)	–0.21	(0.06)	0.01	(0.04)	0.47	(0.05)
	Poland	–0.08	(0.10)	0.00	(0.04)	0.03	(0.04)	–0.02	(0.05)	0.04	(0.04)
	Portugal	–0.09	(0.07)	0.16	(0.06)	0.07	(0.05)	a	a	0.39	(0.03)
	Slovak Republic	0.05	(0.13)	–0.04	(0.08)	–0.14	(0.03)	–0.07	(0.10)	–0.19	(0.03)
	Spain	–0.45	(0.08)	–0.36	(0.06)	–0.23	(0.05)	–0.21	(0.05)	0.08	(0.03)
	Sweden	–0.50	(0.11)	–0.44	(0.05)	–0.38	(0.04)	–0.21	(0.03)	0.20	(0.03)
	Switzerland	–0.50	(0.06)	–0.34	(0.03)	–0.44	(0.03)	–0.45	(0.12)	–0.47	(0.06)
	Turkey	m	m	m	m	m	m	m	m	m	m
	United States	–0.13	(0.27)	a	a	–0.07	(0.05)	–0.03	(0.06)	0.21	(0.03)
	OECD total	***–0.07***	***(0.04)***	***–0.31***	***(0.02)***	***–0.18***	***(0.02)***	***–0.30***	***(0.02)***	***0.05***	***(0.01)***
	OECD average	***–0.31***	***(0.02)***	***–0.31***	***(0.02)***	***–0.23***	***(0.01)***	***–0.24***	***(0.01)***	***0.01***	***(0.01)***
Partner countries	Brazil	m	m	m	m	m	m	m	m	m	m
	Hong Kong-China	–0.64	(0.23)	–0.52	(0.07)	–0.33	(0.03)	–0.28	(0.05)	–0.08	(0.03)
	Indonesia	0.50	(0.07)	0.42	(0.05)	0.46	(0.04)	0.53	(0.04)	0.48	(0.03)
	Latvia	–0.30	(0.13)	–0.17	(0.07)	–0.15	(0.05)	0.01	(0.04)	0.14	(0.04)
	Liechtenstein	–0.68	(0.21)	–0.45	(0.10)	–0.63	(0.16)	0.51	(0.72)	–0.59	(0.15)
	Macao-China	–0.33	(0.29)	–0.83	(0.10)	–0.30	(0.07)	–0.24	(0.08)	–0.01	(0.05)
	Russian Federation	–0.22	(0.13)	–0.29	(0.07)	–0.12	(0.04)	a	a	0.00	(0.03)
	Serbia	–0.76	(1.27)	–0.15	(0.06)	0.21	(0.51)	–0.26	(0.05)	–0.36	(0.05)
	Thailand	0.37	(0.09)	0.37	(0.06)	0.51	(0.03)	a	a	0.59	(0.02)
	Tunisia	0.19	(0.13)	0.17	(0.13)	0.19	(0.06)	0.27	(0.07)	0.58	(0.03)
	Uruguay	0.28	(0.08)	0.37	(0.09)	0.02	(0.09)	0.17	(0.06)	0.20	(0.03)
	United Kingdom[1]	–0.26	(0.11)	–0.15	(0.03)	–0.05	(0.03)	0.08	(0.05)	0.14	(0.04)

1. Response rate too low to ensure comparability (see Annex A3).

Table 3.2c
Index of instrumental motivation in mathematics by students' programme destination
Results based on students' self-reports

		All students											
		Programme Type A[1]				Programme Type B[2]				Programme Type C[3]			
		%	S.E.	Mean index	S.E.	%	S.E.	Mean index	S.E.	%	S.E.	Mean index	S.E.
OECD countries	Australia	91.1	(0.6)	0.23	(0.02)	8.9	(0.6)	0.14	(0.03)	a	a	a	a
	Austria	56.8	(1.9)	–0.61	(0.03)	34.1	(1.9)	–0.35	(0.04)	9.2	(0.7)	–0.22	(0.04)
	Belgium	77.1	(1.1)	–0.31	(0.02)	2.1	(0.4)	c	c	20.9	(1.1)	–0.35	(0.03)
	Canada	100.0	(0.0)	0.22	(0.01)	a	a	a	a	a	a	a	a
	Czech Republic	83.1	(1.2)	0.04	(0.02)	0.3	(0.3)	c	c	16.6	(1.2)	–0.15	(0.03)
	Denmark	100.0	(0.0)	0.37	(0.02)	a	a	a	a	a	a	a	a
	Finland	100.0	(0.0)	0.06	(0.01)	a	a	a	a	a	a	a	a
	France	90.5	(0.9)	–0.08	(0.02)	2.1	(0.6)	c	c	7.4	(0.7)	–0.19	(0.07)
	Germany	98.4	(0.2)	–0.04	(0.02)	1.6	(0.2)	c	c	a	a	a	a
	Greece	80.1	(2.2)	–0.03	(0.03)	a	a	a	a	19.9	(2.2)	–0.11	(0.06)
	Hungary	80.4	(0.7)	–0.13	(0.02)	a	a	a	a	19.6	(0.7)	–0.05	(0.04)
	Iceland	100.0	(0.0)	0.31	(0.02)	a	a	a	a	a	a	a	a
	Ireland	82.2	(1.4)	0.12	(0.02)	1.1	(0.3)	c	c	16.7	(1.3)	–0.02	(0.05)
	Italy	99.9	(0.0)	–0.15	(0.02)	a	a	a	a	0.1	(0.0)	c	c
	Japan	74.6	(0.5)	–0.64	(0.03)	0.9	(0.9)	c	c	24.5	(1.0)	–0.72	(0.06)
	Korea	73.3	(0.9)	–0.31	(0.02)	a	a	a	a	26.7	(0.9)	–0.79	(0.03)
	Luxembourg	95.4	(0.1)	–0.41	(0.02)	3.2	(0.1)	–0.27	(0.10)	1.3	(0.1)	c	c
	Mexico	94.2	(1.2)	0.57	(0.02)	a	a	a	a	5.8	(1.2)	0.52	(0.05)
	Netherlands	38.6	(1.8)	–0.31	(0.02)	58.0	(2.0)	–0.22	(0.03)	3.4	(1.4)	0.01	(0.01)
	New Zealand	100.0	(0.0)	0.29	(0.02)	a	a	a	a	a	a	a	a
	Norway	100.0	(0.0)	0.15	(0.02)	a	a	a	a	a	a	a	a
	Poland	100.0	(0.0)	0.04	(0.02)	a	a	a	a	a	a	a	a
	Portugal	91.2	(1.0)	0.27	(0.02)	8.5	(0.9)	0.20	(0.05)	0.3	(0.1)	c	c
	Slovak Republic	97.3	(0.8)	–0.05	(0.02)	1.0	(0.6)	c	c	1.8	(0.5)	c	c
	Spain	100.0	(0.0)	–0.05	(0.02)	a	a	a	a	a	a	a	a
	Sweden	100.0	(0.0)	0.02	(0.02)	a	a	a	a	a	a	a	a
	Switzerland	91.2	(2.8)	–0.04	(0.02)	8.4	(2.8)	–0.08	(0.10)	0.4	(0.2)	c	c
	Turkey	100.0	(0.0)	0.22	(0.02)	a	a	a	a	a	a	a	a
	United States	100.0	(0.0)	0.17	(0.02)	a	a	a	a	a	a	a	a
	OECD total	*86.9*	*(0.2)*	*0.04*	*(0.01)*	*1.8*	*(0.1)*	*–0.12*	*(0.03)*	*11.3*	*(0.2)*	*–0.18*	*(0.02)*
	OECD average	*86.5*	*(0.2)*	*0.03*	*(0.00)*	*4.4*	*(0.2)*	*–0.18*	*(0.02)*	*9.1*	*(0.2)*	*–0.15*	*(0.01)*
Partner countries	Brazil	100.0	(0.0)	0.46	(0.02)	a	a	a	a	a	a	a	a
	Hong Kong-China	100.0	(0.0)	–0.12	(0.02)	a	a	a	a	a	a	a	a
	Indonesia	89.1	(1.2)	0.46	(0.02)	10.9	(1.2)	0.36	(0.04)	a	a	a	a
	Latvia	100.0	(0.0)	0.06	(0.02)	a	a	a	a	a	a	a	a
	Liechtenstein	100.0	(0.0)	–0.05	(0.05)	a	a	a	a	a	a	a	a
	Macao-China	99.0	(0.1)	–0.03	(0.03)	1.0	(0.1)	c	c	a	a	a	a
	Russian Federation	92.5	(2.6)	0.02	(0.02)	a	a	a	a	7.5	(2.6)	–0.26	(0.06)
	Serbia	21.4	(2.6)	–0.29	(0.06)	45.4	(2.5)	–0.14	(0.04)	33.3	(2.4)	–0.18	(0.04)
	Thailand	89.7	(1.4)	0.50	(0.02)	a	a	a	a	10.3	(1.4)	0.38	(0.03)
	Tunisia	100.0	(0.0)	0.52	(0.02)	a	a	a	a	a	a	a	a
	Uruguay	91.9	(1.2)	0.25	(0.02)	4.2	(1.1)	0.60	(0.06)	3.9	(0.5)	0.37	(0.05)
	United Kingdom[4]	0.9	(0.3)	c	c	0.6	(0.1)	c	c	98.5	(0.3)	0.12	(0.02)

1. Type A: General programmes designed to give access to the next level of education.
2. Type B: Programmes designed to give access to vocational studies at the next level of education.
3. Type C: Programmes designed to give direct access to the labour market.
4. Response rate too low to ensure comparability (see Annex A3).

Table 3.2c *(continued)*

Index of instrumental motivation in mathematics by students' programme destination

Results based on students' self-reports

Males

	Programme Type A[1]				Programme Type B[2]				Programme Type C[3]			
	%	S.E.	Mean index	S.E.	%	S.E.	Mean index	S.E.	%	S.E.	Mean index	S.E.
OECD countries												
Australia	90.3	(0.8)	0.35	(0.02)	9.7	(0.8)	0.23	(0.04)	a	a	a	a
Austria	49.0	(2.4)	–0.28	(0.05)	38.6	(2.6)	–0.15	(0.05)	12.4	(1.2)	–0.05	(0.06)
Belgium	74.0	(1.7)	–0.14	(0.02)	2.2	(0.4)	c	c	23.8	(1.7)	–0.23	(0.04)
Canada	100.0	(0.0)	0.29	(0.02)	a	a	a	a	a	a	a	a
Czech Republic	78.4	(1.7)	0.19	(0.02)	0.1	(0.1)	c	c	21.4	(1.7)	–0.17	(0.04)
Denmark	100.0	(0.0)	0.56	(0.02)	a	a	a	a	a	a	a	a
Finland	100.0	(0.0)	0.22	(0.02)	a	a	a	a	a	a	a	a
France	91.2	(1.4)	0.11	(0.03)	2.6	(0.9)	c	c	6.2	(1.2)	0.03	(0.07)
Germany	98.3	(0.8)	0.17	(0.02)	1.7	(0.8)	c	c	a	a	a	a
Greece	76.2	(3.1)	0.13	(0.04)	a	a	a	a	23.8	(3.1)	–0.03	(0.05)
Hungary	76.8	(1.5)	–0.02	(0.02)	a	a	a	a	23.2	(1.5)	–0.03	(0.05)
Iceland	100.0	(0.0)	0.33	(0.02)	a	a	a	a	a	a	a	a
Ireland	85.5	(1.3)	0.26	(0.02)	0.9	(0.3)	c	c	13.6	(1.3)	0.17	(0.08)
Italy	99.9	(0.0)	–0.04	(0.02)	a	a	a	a	0.1	(0.0)	c	c
Japan	71.2	(2.6)	–0.48	(0.04)	1.5	(1.5)	c	c	27.2	(2.5)	–0.55	(0.07)
Korea	75.4	(2.5)	–0.25	(0.02)	a	a	a	a	24.6	(2.5)	–0.69	(0.05)
Luxembourg	93.5	(0.3)	–0.16	(0.03)	4.2	(0.3)	–0.22	(0.11)	2.3	(0.2)	c	c
Mexico	93.7	(1.2)	0.58	(0.03)	a	a	a	a	6.3	(1.2)	0.51	(0.06)
Netherlands	35.4	(2.0)	–0.09	(0.03)	60.8	(2.4)	–0.01	(0.03)	3.9	(1.7)	0.01	(0.02)
New Zealand	100.0	(0.0)	0.37	(0.02)	a	a	a	a	a	a	a	a
Norway	100.0	(0.0)	0.26	(0.03)	a	a	a	a	a	a	a	a
Poland	100.0	(0.0)	0.06	(0.02)	a	a	a	a	a	a	a	a
Portugal	89.6	(1.3)	0.31	(0.03)	10.1	(1.3)	0.21	(0.06)	0.3	(0.1)	c	c
Slovak Republic	96.8	(1.0)	0.05	(0.02)	1.2	(0.7)	c	c	1.9	(0.6)	c	c
Spain	100.0	(0.0)	–0.01	(0.03)	a	a	a	a	a	a	a	a
Sweden	100.0	(0.0)	0.17	(0.02)	a	a	a	a	a	a	a	a
Switzerland	88.6	(5.1)	0.32	(0.03)	11.2	(5.1)	0.13	(0.06)	0.2	(0.2)	c	c
Turkey	100.0	(0.0)	0.19	(0.03)	a	a	a	a	a	a	a	a
United States	100.0	(0.0)	0.22	(0.02)	a	a	a	a	a	a	a	a
OECD total	*86.6*	*(0.4)*	*0.13*	*(0.01)*	*2.1*	*(0.2)*	*0.05*	*(0.03)*	*11.3*	*(0.4)*	*–0.07*	*(0.02)*
OECD average	*85.6*	*(0.3)*	*0.15*	*(0.01)*	*4.9*	*(0.3)*	*0.00*	*(0.02)*	*9.6*	*(0.3)*	*–0.06*	*(0.02)*
Partner countries												
Brazil	100.0	(0.0)	0.49	(0.03)	a	a	a	a	a	a	a	a
Hong Kong-China	100.0	(0.0)	–0.03	(0.03)	a	a	a	a	a	a	a	a
Indonesia	86.7	(2.3)	0.44	(0.02)	13.3	(2.3)	0.39	(0.04)	a	a	a	a
Latvia	100.0	(0.0)	0.15	(0.02)	a	a	a	a	a	a	a	a
Liechtenstein	100.0	(0.0)	0.41	(0.07)	a	a	a	a	a	a	a	a
Macao-China	99.1	(0.3)	0.07	(0.04)	0.9	(0.3)	c	c	a	a	a	a
Russian Federation	88.3	(3.8)	0.08	(0.03)	a	a	a	a	11.7	(3.8)	–0.28	(0.07)
Serbia	14.4	(2.2)	–0.02	(0.06)	40.8	(2.6)	0.00	(0.04)	44.8	(2.8)	–0.19	(0.04)
Thailand	85.7	(2.4)	0.42	(0.02)	a	a	a	a	14.3	(2.4)	0.33	(0.03)
Tunisia	100.0	(0.0)	0.60	(0.02)	a	a	a	a	a	a	a	a
Uruguay	88.0	(1.8)	0.33	(0.03)	6.2	(1.6)	0.64	(0.08)	5.8	(0.9)	0.32	(0.07)
United Kingdom[4]	1.1	(0.6)	c	c	0.8	(0.2)	c	c	98.0	(0.6)	0.26	(0.02)

Females

	Programme Type A[1]				Programme Type B[2]				Programme Type C[3]			
	%	S.E.	Mean index	S.E.	%	S.E.	Mean index	S.E.	%	S.E.	Mean index	S.E.
OECD countries												
Australia	91.9	(0.7)	0.11	(0.02)	8.1	(0.7)	0.03	(0.04)	a	a	a	a
Austria	64.5	(2.6)	–0.87	(0.03)	29.6	(2.6)	–0.62	(0.05)	5.9	(0.6)	–0.57	(0.07)
Belgium	80.3	(1.1)	–0.47	(0.02)	2.0	(0.5)	c	c	17.7	(1.1)	–0.53	(0.04)
Canada	100.0	(0.0)	0.16	(0.02)	a	a	a	a	a	a	a	a
Czech Republic	87.9	(1.8)	–0.10	(0.03)	0.4	(0.4)	c	c	11.7	(1.7)	–0.12	(0.05)
Denmark	100.0	(0.0)	0.18	(0.02)	a	a	a	a	a	a	a	a
Finland	100.0	(0.0)	–0.10	(0.02)	a	a	a	a	a	a	a	a
France	89.9	(1.0)	–0.25	(0.03)	1.7	(0.5)	c	c	8.4	(0.9)	–0.33	(0.09)
Germany	98.7	(0.3)	–0.25	(0.02)	1.3	(0.3)	c	c	a	a	a	a
Greece	83.6	(2.1)	–0.17	(0.03)	a	a	a	a	16.4	(2.1)	–0.22	(0.06)
Hungary	84.4	(1.3)	–0.24	(0.02)	a	a	a	a	15.6	(1.3)	–0.09	(0.04)
Iceland	100.0	(0.0)	0.27	(0.03)	a	a	a	a	a	a	a	a
Ireland	78.8	(2.2)	–0.03	(0.04)	1.4	(0.5)	c	c	19.8	(2.1)	–0.15	(0.05)
Italy	99.9	(0.0)	–0.26	(0.03)	a	a	a	a	0.1	(0.0)	c	c
Japan	77.8	(2.9)	–0.78	(0.03)	0.2	(0.2)	c	c	22.0	(3.0)	–0.92	(0.05)
Korea	70.4	(3.2)	–0.40	(0.04)	a	a	a	a	29.6	(3.2)	–0.90	(0.04)
Luxembourg	97.3	(0.3)	–0.65	(0.02)	2.3	(0.2)	c	c	0.5	(0.1)	c	c
Mexico	94.7	(1.3)	0.56	(0.02)	a	a	a	a	5.3	(1.3)	0.52	(0.09)
Netherlands	42.0	(2.1)	–0.50	(0.03)	55.2	(2.3)	–0.46	(0.04)	2.9	(1.0)	c	c
New Zealand	100.0	(0.0)	0.21	(0.02)	a	a	a	a	a	a	a	a
Norway	100.0	(0.0)	0.03	(0.03)	a	a	a	a	a	a	a	a
Poland	100.0	(0.0)	0.02	(0.02)	a	a	a	a	a	a	a	a
Portugal	92.6	(0.8)	0.25	(0.03)	7.0	(0.8)	0.18	(0.08)	0.3	(0.2)	c	c
Slovak Republic	97.7	(0.8)	–0.15	(0.03)	0.7	(0.4)	c	c	1.6	(0.7)	c	c
Spain	100.0	(0.0)	–0.09	(0.03)	a	a	a	a	a	a	a	a
Sweden	100.0	(0.0)	–0.13	(0.02)	a	a	a	a	a	a	a	a
Switzerland	93.9	(1.3)	–0.40	(0.02)	5.4	(1.1)	–0.56	(0.07)	0.7	(0.3)	c	c
Turkey	100.0	(0.0)	0.25	(0.03)	a	a	a	a	a	a	a	a
United States	100.0	(0.0)	0.12	(0.02)	a	a	a	a	a	a	a	a
OECD total	*87.1*	*(0.4)*	*–0.05*	*(0.01)*	*1.6*	*(0.1)*	*–0.34*	*(0.03)*	*11.3*	*(0.4)*	*–0.29*	*(0.03)*
OECD average	*87.5*	*(0.3)*	*–0.10*	*(0.01)*	*3.9*	*(0.2)*	*–0.40*	*(0.03)*	*8.7*	*(0.2)*	*–0.26*	*(0.02)*
Partner countries												
Brazil	100.0	(0.0)	0.43	(0.02)	a	a	a	a	a	a	a	a
Hong Kong-China	100.0	(0.0)	–0.20	(0.02)	a	a	a	a	a	a	a	a
Indonesia	91.4	(2.3)	0.48	(0.02)	8.6	(2.3)	0.31	(0.08)	a	a	a	a
Latvia	100.0	(0.0)	–0.01	(0.02)	a	a	a	a	a	a	a	a
Liechtenstein	100.0	(0.0)	–0.53	(0.06)	a	a	a	a	a	a	a	a
Macao-China	99.0	(0.2)	–0.13	(0.03)	1.0	(0.2)	c	c	a	a	a	a
Russian Federation	96.6	(1.4)	–0.04	(0.02)	a	a	a	a	3.4	(1.4)	–0.19	(0.09)
Serbia	28.1	(3.2)	–0.43	(0.07)	49.9	(3.2)	–0.26	(0.04)	22.0	(2.7)	–0.16	(0.06)
Thailand	93.0	(1.2)	0.56	(0.02)	a	a	a	a	7.0	(1.2)	0.46	(0.09)
Tunisia	100.0	(0.0)	0.43	(0.03)	a	a	a	a	a	a	a	a
Uruguay	95.5	(0.9)	0.18	(0.03)	2.4	(0.8)	c	c	2.1	(0.4)	c	c
United Kingdom[4]	0.6	(0.1)	c	c	0.5	(0.2)	c	c	98.9	(0.2)	–0.01	(0.02)

1. Type A: General programmes designed to give access to the next level of education.
2. Type B: Programmes designed to give access to vocational studies at the next level of education.
3. Type C: Programmes designed to give direct access to the labour market.
4. Response rate too low to ensure comparability (see Annex A3).

Table 3.3
Percentage of students expecting a certain class of occupations at age 30 and performance on the mathematics and reading scales, by gender
Results based on students' self-reports

Males	Students expecting a white-collar high-skilled occupation						Students expecting a white-collar low-skilled occupation					
			Performance on the mathematics scale		Performance on the reading scale				Performance on the mathematics scale		Performance on the reading scale	
	%	S.E.	Mean score	S.E.	Mean score	S.E.	%	S.E.	Mean score	S.E.	Mean score	S.E.
OECD countries												
Australia	70.1	(1.1)	552	(3.2)	534	(2.9)	8.8	(0.5)	491	(5.9)	474	(6.2)
Austria	53.8	(2.2)	546	(4.1)	511	(4.4)	11.5	(1.7)	470	(8.0)	433	(7.5)
Belgium	60.5	(2.3)	577	(3.0)	536	(3.2)	6.7	(0.6)	492	(11.1)	455	(11.4)
Canada	m	m	m	m	m	m	m	m	m	m	m	m
Czech Republic	54.0	(1.8)	571	(3.8)	516	(3.4)	13.7	(1.5)	472	(5.0)	435	(4.9)
Denmark	m	m	m	m	m	m	m	m	m	m	m	m
Finland	m	m	m	m	m	m	m	m	m	m	m	m
France	67.7	(1.7)	545	(3.8)	509	(3.8)	10.0	(0.8)	476	(8.2)	427	(8.6)
Germany	52.6	(1.8)	560	(4.6)	525	(4.7)	11.9	(1.0)	491	(7.6)	457	(8.9)
Greece	72.0	(1.8)	475	(4.5)	474	(4.7)	10.0	(1.0)	433	(6.3)	435	(9.7)
Hungary	56.1	(2.3)	535	(4.0)	507	(3.6)	12.7	(1.5)	453	(7.9)	431	(8.9)
Iceland	65.3	(1.2)	523	(3.2)	480	(3.2)	11.8	(0.9)	475	(6.5)	441	(7.6)
Ireland	63.5	(1.7)	540	(3.2)	534	(3.2)	7.1	(0.8)	479	(8.7)	478	(8.9)
Italy	69.5	(1.9)	499	(3.8)	481	(4.2)	12.6	(1.5)	423	(8.9)	403	(12.8)
Japan	m	m	m	m	m	m	m	m	m	m	m	m
Korea	79.1	(1.1)	563	(4.1)	537	(3.4)	18.6	(1.0)	521	(5.3)	499	(5.0)
Luxembourg	m	m	m	m	m	m	m	m	m	m	m	m
Mexico	85.6	(1.0)	411	(4.3)	411	(4.6)	3.2	(0.5)	394	(14.8)	398	(16.8)
Netherlands	m	m	m	m	m	m	m	m	m	m	m	m
New Zealand	m	m	m	m	m	m	m	m	m	m	m	m
Norway	m	m	m	m	m	m	m	m	m	m	m	m
Poland	65.8	(1.3)	528	(2.9)	514	(3.1)	7.8	(0.7)	458	(9.4)	450	(8.8)
Portugal	79.8	(1.5)	496	(4.7)	482	(4.5)	7.1	(0.6)	433	(9.0)	424	(11.1)
Slovak Republic	55.5	(2.1)	552	(4.2)	497	(3.7)	14.2	(1.6)	468	(6.4)	423	(7.6)
Spain	m	m	m	m	m	m	m	m	m	m	m	m
Sweden	m	m	m	m	m	m	m	m	m	m	m	m
Switzerland	m	m	m	m	m	m	m	m	m	m	m	m
Turkey	m	m	m	m	m	m	m	m	m	m	m	m
United States	81.4	(0.9)	500	(3.5)	495	(3.6)	6.0	(0.5)	455	(7.4)	447	(9.4)
OECD total	*68.2*	*(0.5)*	*508*	*(1.7)*	*494*	*(1.6)*	*8.0*	*(0.2)*	*471*	*(2.9)*	*451*	*(3.3)*
OECD average	*59.0*	*(0.4)*	*526*	*(1.0)*	*502*	*(1.0)*	*9.2*	*(0.3)*	*471*	*(1.9)*	*447*	*(2.1)*
Partner countries												
Brazil	m	m	m	m	m	m	m	m	m	m	m	m
Hong Kong-China	63.2	(1.7)	591	(5.4)	526	(4.1)	28.1	(1.6)	556	(8.7)	499	(6.5)
Indonesia	72.7	(1.4)	378	(4.3)	384	(3.9)	8.8	(1.0)	360	(7.1)	374	(7.3)
Latvia	66.1	(2.8)	518	(7.9)	506	(7.3)	10.6	(1.4)	431	(13.0)	436	(11.5)
Liechtenstein	m	m	m	m	m	m	m	m	m	m	m	m
Macao-China	64.6	(2.8)	569	(5.8)	517	(5.3)	32.8	(2.7)	528	(8.9)	477	(6.2)
Russian Federation	m	m	m	m	m	m	m	m	m	m	m	m
Serbia	53.8	(2.3)	478	(5.1)	424	(4.3)	8.7	(1.3)	405	(8.4)	374	(8.6)
Thailand	53.5	(1.9)	440	(5.1)	423	(4.4)	26.4	(1.6)	416	(5.1)	397	(5.1)
Tunisia	m	m	m	m	m	m	m	m	m	m	m	m
Uruguay	m	m	m	m	m	m	m	m	m	m	m	m
United Kingdom[1]	68.4	(1.7)	554	(3.0)	532	(3.1)	10.4	(0.9)	500	(8.9)	472	(8.5)

Males	Students expecting a blue-collar high-skilled occupation						Students expecting a blue-collar low-skilled occupation					
			Performance on the mathematics scale		Performance on the reading scale				Performance on the mathematics scale		Performance on the reading scale	
	%	S.E.	Mean score	S.E.	Mean score	S.E.	%	S.E.	Mean score	S.E.	Mean score	S.E.
OECD countries												
Australia	19.9	(0.9)	481	(3.6)	458	(4.5)	1.3	(0.2)	c	c	c	c
Austria	31.2	(2.8)	464	(5.5)	412	(5.7)	3.6	(0.6)	458	(12.2)	415	(15.3)
Belgium	29.4	(2.4)	464	(6.0)	422	(6.6)	3.4	(0.5)	490	(11.2)	442	(13.3)
Canada	m	m	m	m	m	m	m	m	m	m	m	m
Czech Republic	27.9	(2.1)	471	(5.3)	429	(5.6)	4.5	(0.7)	505	(9.2)	455	(9.0)
Denmark	m	m	m	m	m	m	m	m	m	m	m	m
Finland	m	m	m	m	m	m	m	m	m	m	m	m
France	20.5	(1.8)	442	(6.6)	396	(8.8)	1.8	(0.4)	c	c	c	c
Germany	31.3	(1.5)	476	(5.3)	439	(5.7)	4.3	(0.6)	480	(12.6)	445	(15.8)
Greece	16.4	(1.7)	395	(5.7)	391	(7.5)	1.5	(0.3)	c	c	c	c
Hungary	28.7	(2.5)	425	(4.9)	405	(4.9)	2.5	(0.4)	c	c	c	c
Iceland	20.5	(0.9)	481	(5.1)	440	(5.7)	2.5	(0.5)	c	c	c	c
Ireland	27.4	(1.7)	469	(4.7)	457	(5.1)	2.0	(0.4)	c	c	c	c
Italy	15.3	(1.4)	414	(11.5)	394	(11.2)	2.6	(0.4)	c	c	c	c
Japan	m	m	m	m	m	m	m	m	m	m	m	m
Korea	1.4	(0.3)	c	c	c	c	0.9	(0.2)	c	c	c	c
Luxembourg	m	m	m	m	m	m	m	m	m	m	m	m
Mexico	6.7	(0.6)	375	(11.9)	370	(9.9)	4.5	(0.6)	369	(10.9)	379	(11.6)
Netherlands	m	m	m	m	m	m	m	m	m	m	m	m
New Zealand	m	m	m	m	m	m	m	m	m	m	m	m
Norway	m	m	m	m	m	m	m	m	m	m	m	m
Poland	23.3	(1.2)	429	(4.3)	410	(4.7)	3.1	(0.4)	461	(15.0)	445	(14.7)
Portugal	10.4	(1.1)	400	(7.0)	378	(9.1)	2.7	(0.4)	c	c	c	c
Slovak Republic	25.9	(2.2)	440	(5.7)	387	(5.2)	4.4	(0.7)	473	(9.9)	421	(13.1)
Spain	m	m	m	m	m	m	m	m	m	m	m	m
Sweden	m	m	m	m	m	m	m	m	m	m	m	m
Switzerland	m	m	m	m	m	m	m	m	m	m	m	m
Turkey	m	m	m	m	m	m	m	m	m	m	m	m
United States	10.5	(0.8)	458	(6.8)	453	(7.4)	2.1	(0.3)	c	c	c	c
OECD total	*13.4*	*(0.4)*	*450*	*(2.9)*	*426*	*(2.9)*	*10.4*	*(0.2)*	*476*	*(3.5)*	*452*	*(3.6)*
OECD average	*17.5*	*(0.4)*	*450*	*(1.7)*	*419*	*(1.8)*	*14.4*	*(0.2)*	*499*	*(2.0)*	*467*	*(2.0)*
Partner countries												
Brazil	m	m	m	m	m	m	m	m	m	m	m	m
Hong Kong-China	2.3	(0.3)	c	c	c	c	6.3	(0.7)	521	(13.6)	463	(10.7)
Indonesia	7.4	(1.0)	350	(7.9)	364	(8.7)	11.1	(0.9)	340	(7.0)	349	(7.3)
Latvia	19.5	(1.9)	443	(8.4)	431	(9.6)	3.8	(0.7)	452	(19.0)	438	(16.6)
Liechtenstein	m	m	m	m	m	m	m	m	m	m	m	m
Macao-China	1.5	(1.0)	c	c	c	c	1.1	(0.4)	c	c	c	c
Russian Federation	m	m	m	m	m	m	m	m	m	m	m	m
Serbia	31.1	(2.1)	391	(4.6)	353	(4.1)	6.4	(1.1)	417	(8.9)	368	(8.7)
Thailand	11.5	(1.6)	384	(10.8)	370	(9.2)	8.6	(2.1)	387	(15.4)	367	(9.0)
Tunisia	m	m	m	m	m	m	m	m	m	m	m	m
Uruguay	m	m	m	m	m	m	m	m	m	m	m	m
United Kingdom[1]	19.1	(1.4)	474	(6.5)	449	(6.8)	2.0	(0.5)	c	c	c	c

1. Response rate is too low to ensure comparability (see Annex A3).

Table 3.3 *(continued)*

Percentage of students expecting a certain class of occupations at age 30 and performance on the mathematics and reading scales, by gender

Results based on students' self-reports

	Females	Students expecting a white-collar high-skilled occupation						Students expecting a white-collar low-skilled occupation					
				Performance on the mathematics scale		Performance on the reading scale				Performance on the mathematics scale		Performance on the reading scale	
		%	S.E.	Mean score	S.E.	Mean score	S.E.	%	S.E.	Mean score	S.E.	Mean score	S.E.
OECD countries	Australia	81.8	(0.7)	536	(2.6)	562	(2.4)	16.1	(0.7)	468	(4.3)	491	(4.5)
	Austria	63.3	(2.0)	527	(4.4)	546	(4.2)	31.0	(2.0)	454	(4.6)	460	(5.2)
	Belgium	75.1	(1.4)	549	(2.9)	552	(3.0)	22.5	(1.5)	452	(5.3)	459	(6.0)
	Canada	m	m	m	m	m	m	m	m	m	m	m	m
	Czech Republic	63.0	(1.8)	543	(4.0)	537	(3.5)	31.2	(1.5)	465	(4.6)	468	(4.5)
	Denmark	m	m	m	m	m	m	m	m	m	m	m	m
	Finland	m	m	m	m	m	m	m	m	m	m	m	m
	France	71.5	(1.4)	524	(3.4)	533	(3.2)	26.0	(1.5)	455	(4.0)	459	(5.2)
	Germany	69.8	(1.3)	529	(4.0)	543	(3.9)	24.6	(1.3)	462	(5.0)	481	(6.3)
	Greece	81.8	(1.5)	449	(4.0)	502	(4.0)	17.5	(1.6)	380	(6.0)	445	(7.4)
	Hungary	66.1	(1.8)	514	(4.2)	526	(3.7)	27.3	(1.6)	433	(4.9)	451	(5.1)
	Iceland	75.7	(1.3)	534	(2.7)	535	(2.7)	17.3	(1.2)	483	(5.7)	484	(6.6)
	Ireland	77.7	(1.3)	514	(3.1)	552	(3.2)	20.4	(1.3)	441	(4.8)	475	(4.7)
	Italy	80.2	(1.4)	466	(4.8)	506	(4.1)	18.6	(1.4)	419	(5.9)	455	(6.1)
	Japan	m	m	m	m	m	m	m	m	m	m	m	m
	Korea	80.3	(1.4)	541	(5.5)	559	(4.1)	15.8	(1.2)	486	(5.8)	509	(5.9)
	Luxembourg	m	m	m	m	m	m	m	m	m	m	m	m
	Mexico	86.7	(0.9)	398	(3.9)	432	(4.2)	9.5	(0.9)	359	(11.0)	389	(12.8)
	Netherlands	m	m	m	m	m	m	m	m	m	m	m	m
	New Zealand	m	m	m	m	m	m	m	m	m	m	m	m
	Norway	m	m	m	m	m	m	m	m	m	m	m	m
	Poland	78.8	(1.2)	510	(3.0)	539	(3.4)	19.1	(1.1)	436	(5.4)	470	(5.5)
	Portugal	88.3	(0.9)	472	(3.4)	506	(3.5)	10.5	(0.9)	408	(5.6)	446	(7.0)
	Slovak Republic	64.0	(2.0)	522	(3.5)	520	(3.1)	28.8	(1.9)	446	(6.3)	446	(6.0)
	Spain	m	m	m	m	m	m	m	m	m	m	m	m
	Sweden	m	m	m	m	m	m	m	m	m	m	m	m
	Switzerland	m	m	m	m	m	m	m	m	m	m	m	m
	Turkey	m	m	m	m	m	m	m	m	m	m	m	m
	United States	88.9	(0.8)	485	(3.3)	518	(3.3)	9.5	(0.7)	445	(5.9)	477	(6.4)
	OECD total	*74.8*	*(0.4)*	*488*	*(1.8)*	*516*	*(1.8)*	*13.9*	*(0.4)*	*443*	*(2.2)*	*466*	*(2.2)*
	OECD average	*66.5*	*(0.4)*	*503*	*(1.1)*	*526*	*(1.1)*	*17.4*	*(0.3)*	*444*	*(1.6)*	*463*	*(1.4)*
Partner countries	Brazil	m	m	m	m	m	m	m	m	m	m	m	m
	Hong Kong-China	66.0	(1.5)	571	(4.6)	542	(3.7)	29.4	(1.3)	539	(5.4)	520	(4.1)
	Indonesia	75.5	(1.4)	371	(4.8)	405	(4.4)	12.1	(1.1)	363	(7.9)	400	(7.2)
	Latvia	76.8	(2.1)	503	(4.6)	528	(4.9)	20.6	(1.9)	436	(7.0)	472	(6.0)
	Liechtenstein	m	m	m	m	m	m	m	m	m	m	m	m
	Macao-China	69.3	(2.5)	534	(4.9)	518	(5.1)	28.3	(2.5)	512	(7.6)	506	(6.0)
	Russian Federation	m	m	m	m	m	m	m	m	m	m	m	m
	Serbia	75.5	(2.5)	458	(4.2)	452	(3.8)	19.4	(2.3)	392	(5.8)	398	(5.5)
	Thailand	66.3	(1.4)	433	(4.3)	452	(3.7)	27.7	(1.2)	412	(4.8)	434	(3.5)
	Tunisia	m	m	m	m	m	m	m	m	m	m	m	m
	Uruguay	m	m	m	m	m	m	m	m	m	m	m	m
	United Kingdom[1]	78.5	(1.4)	537	(3.2)	544	(3.4)	20.2	(1.3)	460	(5.0)	470	(5.9)

	Females	Students expecting a blue-collar high-skilled occupation						Students expecting a blue-collar low-skilled occupation					
				Performance on the mathematics scale		Performance on the reading scale				Performance on the mathematics scale		Performance on the reading scale	
		%	S.E.	Mean score	S.E.	Mean score	S.E.	%	S.E.	Mean score	S.E.	Mean score	S.E.
OECD countries	Australia	1.6	(0.2)	c	c	c	c	0.5	(0.1)	c	c	c	c
	Austria	2.9	(0.8)	c	c	c	c	2.8	(0.5)	c	c	c	c
	Belgium	2.1	(0.3)	c	c	c	c	0.3	(0.1)	c	c	c	c
	Canada	m	m	m	m	m	m	m	m	m	m	m	m
	Czech Republic	4.8	(0.7)	447	(13.7)	458	(16.6)	1.0	(0.2)	c	c	c	c
	Denmark	m	m	m	m	m	m	m	m	m	m	m	m
	Finland	m	m	m	m	m	m	m	m	m	m	m	m
	France	2.1	(0.5)	c	c	c	c	0.5	(0.2)	c	c	c	c
	Germany	3.9	(0.5)	500	(11.4)	510	(11.4)	1.8	(0.3)	c	c	c	c
	Greece	0.5	(0.1)	c	c	c	c	0.2	(0.1)	c	c	c	c
	Hungary	6.3	(1.2)	431	(10.0)	454	(10.3)	0.2	(0.2)	c	c	c	c
	Iceland	5.5	(0.7)	516	(10.4)	518	(10.8)	1.5	(0.3)	c	c	c	c
	Ireland	1.2	(0.3)	c	c	c	c	0.7	(0.3)	c	c	c	c
	Italy	0.9	(0.2)	c	c	c	c	0.4	(0.1)	c	c	c	c
	Japan	m	m	m	m	m	m	m	m	m	m	m	m
	Korea	0.7	(0.2)	c	c	c	c	3.2	(0.5)	472	(11.2)	486	(11.3)
	Luxembourg	m	m	m	m	m	m	m	m	m	m	m	m
	Mexico	1.1	(0.4)	c	c	c	c	2.6	(0.4)	c	c	c	c
	Netherlands	m	m	m	m	m	m	m	m	m	m	m	m
	New Zealand	m	m	m	m	m	m	m	m	m	m	m	m
	Norway	m	m	m	m	m	m	m	m	m	m	m	m
	Poland	1.7	(0.3)	c	c	c	c	0.4	(0.2)	c	c	c	c
	Portugal	0.8	(0.2)	c	c	c	c	0.4	(0.1)	c	c	c	c
	Slovak Republic	6.1	(0.9)	390	(7.2)	399	(8.4)	1.1	(0.4)	c	c	c	c
	Spain	m	m	m	m	m	m	m	m	m	m	m	m
	Sweden	m	m	m	m	m	m	m	m	m	m	m	m
	Switzerland	m	m	m	m	m	m	m	m	m	m	m	m
	Turkey	m	m	m	m	m	m	m	m	m	m	m	m
	United States	1.5	(0.3)	c	c	c	c	0.1	(0.1)	c	c	c	c
	OECD total	*1.6*	*(0.1)*	*465*	*(6.9)*	*485*	*(8.9)*	*9.6*	*(0.3)*	*467*	*(3.5)*	*487*	*(3.6)*
	OECD average	*2.1*	*(0.1)*	*455*	*(4.4)*	*468*	*(4.9)*	*13.9*	*(0.3)*	*488*	*(1.9)*	*501*	*(2.0)*
Partner countries	Brazil	m	m	m	m	m	m	m	m	m	m	m	m
	Hong Kong-China	0.3	(0.1)	c	c	c	c	4.4	(0.6)	514	(12.5)	500	(10.3)
	Indonesia	2.0	(0.5)	c	c	c	c	10.3	(1.0)	340	(8.2)	375	(7.4)
	Latvia	2.1	(0.6)	c	c	c	c	0.5	(0.3)	c	c	c	c
	Liechtenstein	m	m	m	m	m	m	m	m	m	m	m	m
	Macao-China	0.8	(0.7)	c	c	c	c	1.7	(0.5)	c	c	c	c
	Russian Federation	m	m	m	m	m	m	m	m	m	m	m	m
	Serbia	4.2	(0.9)	377	(11.2)	387	(14.8)	0.9	(0.2)	c	c	c	c
	Thailand	1.5	(0.4)	c	c	c	c	4.5	(0.7)	377	(8.6)	403	(8.3)
	Tunisia	m	m	m	m	m	m	m	m	m	m	m	m
	Uruguay	m	m	m	m	m	m	m	m	m	m	m	m
	United Kingdom[1]	1.0	(0.3)	c	c	c	c	0.2	(0.1)	c	c	c	c

1. Response rate is too low to ensure comparability (see Annex A3).

Table 3.4
Index of attitudes towards school and performance on the mathematics scale, by national quarters of the index
Results based on students' self-reports

		Index of attitudes towards school															
		All students		Males		Females		Gender difference (M – F)		Bottom quarter		Second quarter		Third quarter		Top quarter	
		Mean index	S.E.	Mean index	S.E.	Mean index	S.E.	Dif.	S.E.	Mean index	S.E.	Mean index	S.E.	Mean index	S.E.	Mean index	S.E.
OECD countries	Australia	0.25	(0.01)	0.20	(0.02)	0.31	(0.02)	**–0.10**	(0.03)	–0.97	(0.01)	–0.20	(0.00)	0.48	(0.01)	1.70	(0.01)
	Austria	0.12	(0.02)	0.06	(0.02)	0.17	(0.03)	**–0.11**	(0.03)	–1.16	(0.01)	–0.29	(0.01)	0.45	(0.01)	1.46	(0.02)
	Belgium	–0.19	(0.02)	–0.27	(0.02)	–0.10	(0.02)	**–0.17**	(0.03)	–1.21	(0.01)	–0.52	(0.00)	–0.02	(0.01)	1.01	(0.02)
	Canada	0.06	(0.01)	–0.06	(0.02)	0.17	(0.02)	**–0.23**	(0.02)	–1.14	(0.01)	–0.40	(0.00)	0.28	(0.01)	1.47	(0.02)
	Czech Republic	–0.01	(0.02)	–0.08	(0.02)	0.06	(0.02)	**–0.14**	(0.03)	–1.06	(0.01)	–0.37	(0.00)	0.23	(0.01)	1.14	(0.02)
	Denmark	–0.03	(0.02)	–0.09	(0.03)	0.02	(0.02)	**–0.11**	(0.03)	–1.14	(0.01)	–0.41	(0.01)	0.19	(0.01)	1.23	(0.02)
	Finland	0.11	(0.02)	–0.02	(0.02)	0.24	(0.02)	**–0.26**	(0.03)	–0.97	(0.01)	–0.28	(0.00)	0.34	(0.01)	1.35	(0.02)
	France	0.14	(0.02)	–0.01	(0.03)	0.28	(0.03)	**–0.29**	(0.04)	–1.08	(0.02)	–0.27	(0.01)	0.46	(0.01)	1.45	(0.02)
	Germany	–0.08	(0.02)	–0.16	(0.02)	0.00	(0.02)	**–0.16**	(0.03)	–1.21	(0.01)	–0.47	(0.01)	0.14	(0.01)	1.23	(0.02)
	Greece	0.08	(0.02)	–0.01	(0.02)	0.16	(0.03)	**–0.18**	(0.03)	–1.08	(0.02)	–0.33	(0.01)	0.38	(0.01)	1.34	(0.02)
	Hungary	–0.22	(0.02)	–0.28	(0.02)	–0.16	(0.02)	**–0.12**	(0.02)	–1.16	(0.01)	–0.54	(0.01)	–0.06	(0.01)	0.87	(0.02)
	Iceland	0.00	(0.02)	–0.16	(0.03)	0.17	(0.03)	**–0.33**	(0.05)	–1.29	(0.02)	–0.45	(0.01)	0.32	(0.01)	1.43	(0.02)
	Ireland	0.13	(0.02)	0.02	(0.03)	0.24	(0.03)	**–0.22**	(0.04)	–1.08	(0.02)	–0.30	(0.01)	0.41	(0.01)	1.49	(0.02)
	Italy	–0.06	(0.02)	–0.17	(0.02)	0.05	(0.02)	**–0.22**	(0.03)	–1.13	(0.01)	–0.40	(0.00)	0.19	(0.01)	1.11	(0.01)
	Japan	–0.50	(0.01)	–0.60	(0.02)	–0.42	(0.02)	**–0.18**	(0.03)	–1.48	(0.02)	–0.83	(0.00)	–0.35	(0.01)	0.64	(0.02)
	Korea	–0.37	(0.02)	–0.36	(0.02)	–0.39	(0.02)	0.03	(0.02)	–1.33	(0.01)	–0.68	(0.01)	–0.25	(0.00)	0.77	(0.02)
	Luxembourg	–0.23	(0.02)	–0.32	(0.02)	–0.15	(0.02)	**–0.18**	(0.03)	–1.39	(0.01)	–0.63	(0.01)	–0.02	(0.01)	1.10	(0.02)
	Mexico	0.42	(0.03)	0.31	(0.03)	0.53	(0.03)	**–0.23**	(0.03)	–0.90	(0.02)	–0.01	(0.01)	0.72	(0.01)	1.89	(0.02)
	Netherlands	–0.19	(0.02)	–0.24	(0.03)	–0.15	(0.02)	**–0.09**	(0.03)	–1.06	(0.02)	–0.45	(0.01)	–0.05	(0.01)	0.79	(0.03)
	New Zealand	0.10	(0.02)	0.07	(0.02)	0.12	(0.02)	–0.04	(0.03)	–1.08	(0.01)	–0.35	(0.00)	0.35	(0.01)	1.46	(0.02)
	Norway	–0.21	(0.02)	–0.31	(0.03)	–0.11	(0.03)	**–0.20**	(0.04)	–1.35	(0.02)	–0.55	(0.01)	0.01	(0.01)	1.05	(0.02)
	Poland	–0.12	(0.02)	–0.24	(0.02)	0.00	(0.02)	**–0.24**	(0.03)	–1.27	(0.01)	–0.49	(0.01)	0.02	(0.01)	1.26	(0.02)
	Portugal	0.27	(0.02)	0.12	(0.03)	0.40	(0.03)	**–0.28**	(0.03)	–0.84	(0.01)	–0.11	(0.01)	0.50	(0.01)	1.53	(0.02)
	Slovak Republic	0.03	(0.02)	–0.04	(0.02)	0.11	(0.02)	**–0.15**	(0.03)	–0.98	(0.01)	–0.33	(0.00)	0.24	(0.01)	1.19	(0.02)
	Spain	0.14	(0.02)	–0.01	(0.02)	0.28	(0.02)	**–0.29**	(0.03)	–1.05	(0.01)	–0.27	(0.01)	0.41	(0.01)	1.47	(0.02)
	Sweden	0.02	(0.02)	–0.03	(0.03)	0.07	(0.02)	**–0.10**	(0.03)	–1.10	(0.01)	–0.40	(0.01)	0.27	(0.01)	1.31	(0.02)
	Switzerland	0.03	(0.02)	–0.02	(0.03)	0.08	(0.02)	**–0.11**	(0.03)	–1.19	(0.02)	–0.42	(0.01)	0.35	(0.01)	1.37	(0.02)
	Turkey	0.13	(0.03)	–0.01	(0.04)	0.29	(0.03)	**–0.31**	(0.05)	–1.11	(0.01)	–0.33	(0.01)	0.39	(0.01)	1.56	(0.02)
	United States	0.09	(0.02)	–0.02	(0.03)	0.20	(0.03)	**–0.23**	(0.04)	–1.11	(0.01)	–0.37	(0.00)	0.29	(0.01)	1.55	(0.02)
	OECD total	*0.01*	*(0.01)*	*–0.09*	*(0.01)*	*0.11*	*(0.01)*	*–0.20*	*(0.01)*	*–1.17*	*(0.00)*	*–0.42*	*(0.00)*	*0.22*	*(0.01)*	*1.39*	*(0.01)*
	OECD average	*0.00*	*(0.00)*	*–0.09*	*(0.00)*	*0.09*	*(0.00)*	*–0.18*	*(0.01)*	*–1.15*	*(0.00)*	*–0.41*	*(0.00)*	*0.23*	*(0.01)*	*1.33*	*(0.01)*
Partner countries	Brazil	0.53	(0.02)	0.43	(0.04)	0.61	(0.03)	**–0.18**	(0.05)	–0.73	(0.02)	0.11	(0.01)	0.81	(0.00)	1.92	(0.02)
	Hong Kong-China	–0.52	(0.01)	–0.53	(0.02)	0.51	(0.02)	–0.03	(0.02)	–1.33	(0.01)	–0.78	(0.00)	–0.38	(0.00)	0.41	(0.02)
	Indonesia	0.59	(0.02)	0.55	(0.03)	0.64	(0.02)	**–0.08**	(0.03)	–0.57	(0.01)	0.25	(0.01)	0.80	(0.00)	1.90	(0.02)
	Latvia	0.22	(0.02)	0.10	(0.03)	0.34	(0.03)	**–0.24**	(0.04)	–0.85	(0.01)	–0.11	(0.01)	0.47	(0.01)	1.37	(0.02)
	Liechtenstein	–0.10	(0.05)	–0.06	(0.07)	–0.14	(0.07)	0.09	(0.10)	–1.26	(0.06)	–0.45	(0.02)	0.12	(0.03)	1.21	(0.06)
	Macao-China	–0.37	(0.03)	–0.37	(0.05)	–0.38	(0.03)	0.01	(0.07)	–1.30	(0.03)	–0.65	(0.01)	–0.20	(0.01)	0.66	(0.04)
	Russian Federation	0.19	(0.03)	0.08	(0.03)	0.30	(0.03)	**–0.22**	(0.03)	–0.93	(0.01)	–0.22	(0.00)	0.44	(0.01)	1.48	(0.02)
	Serbia	0.17	(0.02)	0.11	(0.03)	0.23	(0.03)	**–0.13**	(0.04)	–1.02	(0.01)	0.23	(0.01)	0.45	(0.01)	1.50	(0.02)
	Thailand	0.28	(0.02)	0.15	(0.02)	0.38	(0.03)	**–0.23**	(0.03)	–0.72	(0.01)	–0.05	(0.01)	0.52	(0.01)	1.37	(0.03)
	Tunisia	0.72	(0.02)	0.60	(0.03)	0.84	(0.03)	**–0.24**	(0.04)	–0.74	(0.02)	0.37	(0.01)	1.07	(0.01)	2.19	(0.01)
	Uruguay	0.11	(0.02)	0.04	(0.02)	0.18	(0.02)	**–0.15**	(0.02)	–1.02	(0.01)	–0.26	(0.01)	0.39	(0.01)	1.34	(0.02)
	United Kingdom[1]	0.12	(0.02)	0.08	(0.02)	0.16	(0.02)	**–0.08**	(0.03)	–1.11	(0.02)	–0.27	(0.01)	0.39	(0.01)	1.46	(0.02)

		Performance on the mathematics scale, by national quarters of the index of attitudes towards school								Change in the mathematics score per unit of the index of attitudes towards school		Increased likelihood of students in the bottom quarter of this index scoring in the bottom quarter of the national mathematics performance distribution		Explained variance in student performance (r-squared × 100)	
		Bottom quarter		Second quarter		Third quarter		Top quarter							
		Mean score	S.E.	Mean score	S.E.	Mean score	S.E.	Mean score	S.E.	Effect	S.E.	Ratio	S.E.	%	S.E.
OECD countries	Australia	**502**	(3.2)	521	(2.6)	536	(2.3)	**540**	(2.6)	**13.8**	(1.03)	**1.5**	(0.06)	2.4	(0.36)
	Austria	501	(4.2)	517	(4.7)	516	(4.8)	496	(4.5)	–2.7	(1.72)	1.0	(0.06)	0.1	(0.14)
	Belgium	528	(4.0)	544	(3.5)	540	(3.8)	523	(3.9)	**–4.3**	(2.16)	1.1	(0.06)	0.1	(0.14)
	Canada	**524**	(2.4)	536	(2.2)	540	(2.4)	**545**	(2.4)	**7.2**	(1.00)	**1.3**	(0.06)	0.8	(0.21)
	Czech Republic	**516**	(4.6)	522	(4.7)	528	(4.0)	**525**	(3.5)	**3.6**	(1.72)	**1.2**	(0.08)	0.1	(0.11)
	Denmark	**503**	(4.0)	513	(4.3)	526	(3.7)	**520**	(4.4)	**7.0**	(1.78)	**1.3**	(0.08)	0.5	(0.27)
	Finland	**525**	(2.9)	542	(2.4)	553	(2.7)	**558**	(3.4)	**12.5**	(1.50)	**1.5**	(0.07)	2.0	(0.47)
	France	**495**	(3.5)	518	(3.6)	524	(3.8)	**513**	(4.2)	**6.8**	(1.69)	**1.5**	(0.10)	0.6	(0.30)
	Germany	**516**	(4.8)	522	(4.5)	514	(4.8)	**496**	(4.5)	**–9.4**	(1.98)	0.9	(0.06)	0.9	(0.37)
	Greece	**459**	(4.5)	450	(5.1)	443	(5.3)	**431**	(3.7)	**–11.4**	(1.74)	**0.8**	(0.06)	1.5	(0.43)
	Hungary	**496**	(4.7)	493	(4.1)	487	(4.4)	**485**	(4.1)	**–6.5**	(2.28)	**0.9**	(0.07)	0.3	(0.24)
	Iceland	**490**	(3.3)	511	(3.0)	526	(3.2)	**536**	(2.9)	**15.3**	(1.42)	**1.8**	(0.12)	3.4	(0.64)
	Ireland	**491**	(4.0)	499	(4.0)	513	(3.7)	**508**	(3.8)	**6.8**	(1.53)	**1.4**	(0.10)	0.7	(0.31)
	Italy	**467**	(4.1)	472	(3.9)	468	(4.3)	**456**	(3.9)	**–5.6**	(1.73)	1.0	(0.07)	0.3	(0.17)
	Japan	530	(5.0)	533	(5.4)	538	(4.9)	537	(4.7)	2.6	(2.03)	1.1	(0.07)	0.1	(0.09)
	Korea	546	(4.0)	539	(4.0)	540	(4.0)	544	(4.8)	0.2	(1.78)	0.9	(0.06)	0.0	(0.03)
	Luxembourg	**497**	(3.4)	506	(2.9)	497	(3.5)	**476**	(3.0)	**–9.2**	(1.46)	**0.8**	(0.07)	1.0	(0.33)
	Mexico	**353**	(4.7)	385	(4.0)	394	(3.9)	**414**	(4.1)	**21.4**	(1.71)	**2.0**	(0.14)	7.6	(1.10)
	Netherlands	532	(4.6)	547	(4.4)	548	(3.9)	545	(5.2)	3.8	(3.05)	**1.3**	(0.11)	0.1	(0.18)
	New Zealand	**502**	(3.5)	522	(4.0)	529	(3.6)	**545**	(4.2)	**14.6**	(1.70)	**1.4**	(0.08)	2.3	(0.54)
	Norway	**467**	(3.8)	497	(4.0)	512	(3.9)	**510**	(3.9)	**16.3**	(1.80)	**1.6**	(0.10)	2.9	(0.63)
	Poland	489	(4.1)	496	(3.7)	496	(3.5)	483	(3.5)	–3.3	(1.73)	1.1	(0.06)	0.1	(0.14)
	Portugal	**450**	(4.4)	465	(4.0)	475	(4.2)	**475**	(4.7)	**9.5**	(1.73)	**1.5**	(0.11)	1.1	(0.39)
	Slovak Republic	**510**	(4.1)	500	(4.1)	502	(4.2)	**482**	(4.5)	**–10.5**	(1.51)	**0.9**	(0.06)	1.0	(0.27)
	Spain	**477**	(4.2)	484	(2.8)	495	(3.8)	**487**	(3.5)	**4.2**	(1.41)	**1.2**	(0.06)	0.2	(0.16)
	Sweden	**489**	(4.0)	509	(3.6)	515	(4.0)	**526**	(4.4)	**14.3**	(1.65)	**1.4**	(0.09)	2.2	(0.48)
	Switzerland	517	(4.7)	535	(4.4)	536	(4.0)	521	(4.2)	1.1	(1.95)	**1.2**	(0.09)	0.0	(0.07)
	Turkey	426	(11.1)	424	(7.3)	433	(6.4)	414	(7.1)	–3.3	(3.75)	1.1	(0.11)	0.1	(0.27)
	United States	**470**	(4.3)	485	(3.9)	491	(4.3)	**489**	(4.8)	**6.6**	(1.39)	**1.3**	(0.08)	0.6	(0.23)
	OECD total	*489*	*(1.5)*	*495*	*(1.3)*	*494*	*(1.5)*	*484*	*(1.5)*	*–1.8*	*(0.61)*	*1.1*	*(0.02)*	*0.0*	*(0.02)*
	OECD average	*496*	*(0.9)*	*505*	*(0.8)*	*506*	*(0.8)*	*499*	*(0.9)*	*0.9*	*(0.35)*	*1.1*	*(0.01)*	*0.0*	*(0.01)*
Partner countries	Brazil	351	(6.4)	367	(5.6)	358	(5.2)	357	(6.3)	0.8	(1.75)	1.1	(0.09)	0.0	(0.04)
	Hong Kong-China	**539**	(5.6)	545	(5.6)	555	(5.0)	**565**	(5.4)	**13.9**	(2.48)	**1.2**	(0.07)	1.1	(0.36)
	Indonesia	**352**	(5.1)	366	(4.8)	361	(4.3)	**366**	(3.9)	**5.7**	(1.62)	**1.4**	(0.07)	0.5	(0.27)
	Latvia	**471**	(4.8)	482	(4.6)	488	(5.4)	**494**	(4.9)	**9.8**	(1.97)	**1.3**	(0.09)	1.0	(0.38)
	Liechtenstein	537	(11.4)	542	(10.9)	536	(10.2)	532	(11.4)	–9.2	(5.31)	1.1	(0.25)	0.9	(1.05)
	Macao-China	533	(6.3)	522	(7.1)	522	(6.4)	534	(6.2)	2.0	(5.21)	0.9	(0.11)	0.1	(0.25)
	Russian Federation	**461**	(5.4)	467	(4.7)	476	(4.6)	**471**	(4.8)	**4.9**	(1.71)	1.1	(0.07)	0.3	(0.19)
	Serbia	**442**	(4.8)	443	(4.5)	443	(4.8)	**426**	(4.3)	–2.8	(1.50)	1.1	(0.07)	0.1	(0.12)
	Thailand	**404**	(4.4)	417	(4.1)	422	(3.7)	**425**	(4.1)	**9.5**	(2.06)	**1.3**	(0.09)	1.0	(0.47)
	Tunisia	**348**	(3.9)	360	(3.6)	362	(3.4)	**371**	(3.6)	**8.4**	(1.35)	**1.4**	(0.09)	1.4	(0.46)
	Uruguay	418	(5.2)	426	(4.9)	431	(4.7)	419	(4.8)	1.9	(2.16)	1.1	(0.09)	0.0	(0.08)
	United Kingdom[1]	**492**	(3.2)	501	(3.7)	518	(4.2)	**520**	(3.8)	**12.1**	(1.39)	**1.3**	(0.08)	1.9	(0.43)

Note: Values that are statistically significant are indicated in bold (see Annex A4).
1. Response rate too low to ensure comparability (see Annex A3).

Table 3.5a

Index of students' sense of belonging at school and performance on the mathematics scale, by national quarters of the index

Results based on students' self-reports

		Index of students' sense of belonging at school															
		All students		Males		Females		Gender difference (M – F)		Bottom quarter		Second quarter		Third quarter		Top quarter	
		Mean index	S.E.	Mean index	S.E.	Mean index	S.E.	Dif.	S.E.	Mean index	S.E.	Mean index	S.E.	Mean index	S.E.	Mean index	S.E.
OECD countries	Australia	0.04	(0.02)	0.00	(0.02)	0.09	(0.02)	**–0.09**	(0.02)	–1.07	(0.01)	–0.48	(0.00)	0.29	(0.00)	1.43	(0.01)
	Austria	0.44	(0.02)	0.41	(0.03)	0.47	(0.03)	–0.06	(0.04)	–0.98	(0.02)	0.20	(0.01)	0.85	(0.01)	1.71	(0.01)
	Belgium	–0.28	(0.01)	–0.33	(0.02)	–0.23	(0.02)	**–0.10**	(0.03)	–1.30	(0.01)	–0.69	(0.00)	–0.09	(0.01)	0.94	(0.01)
	Canada	0.02	(0.01)	–0.03	(0.02)	0.06	(0.02)	**–0.09**	(0.02)	–1.18	(0.01)	–0.51	(0.00)	0.26	(0.01)	1.50	(0.01)
	Czech Republic	–0.27	(0.01)	–0.27	(0.02)	–0.28	(0.02)	0.01	(0.02)	–1.19	(0.01)	–0.63	(0.00)	–0.11	(0.01)	0.83	(0.01)
	Denmark	0.01	(0.02)	0.01	(0.02)	0.01	(0.02)	0.01	(0.03)	–1.17	(0.01)	–0.37	(0.01)	0.31	(0.01)	1.28	(0.02)
	Finland	–0.02	(0.02)	0.03	(0.02)	–0.07	(0.02)	**0.10**	(0.03)	–1.13	(0.01)	–0.46	(0.00)	0.31	(0.01)	1.22	(0.02)
	France	–0.18	(0.02)	–0.19	(0.03)	–0.17	(0.02)	–0.02	(0.03)	–1.28	(0.01)	–0.58	(0.01)	0.08	(0.01)	1.05	(0.02)
	Germany	0.24	(0.02)	0.24	(0.03)	0.24	(0.02)	0.00	(0.04)	–1.16	(0.02)	–0.08	(0.01)	0.65	(0.01)	1.56	(0.01)
	Greece	0.04	(0.02)	0.03	(0.02)	0.04	(0.02)	–0.01	(0.03)	–1.01	(0.01)	–0.40	(0.01)	0.29	(0.01)	1.27	(0.02)
	Hungary	0.08	(0.02)	0.04	(0.02)	0.13	(0.03)	**–0.09**	(0.03)	–1.08	(0.01)	–0.34	(0.01)	0.34	(0.01)	1.40	(0.02)
	Iceland	0.16	(0.02)	0.19	(0.03)	0.13	(0.03)	0.06	(0.04)	–1.22	(0.02)	–0.30	(0.01)	0.49	(0.01)	1.67	(0.02)
	Ireland	0.08	(0.02)	0.04	(0.02)	0.12	(0.03)	**–0.07**	(0.04)	–1.02	(0.01)	–0.42	(0.01)	0.32	(0.01)	1.43	(0.02)
	Italy	0.05	(0.01)	0.05	(0.02)	0.05	(0.02)	0.01	(0.03)	–1.02	(0.01)	–0.35	(0.01)	0.32	(0.00)	1.25	(0.02)
	Japan	–0.53	(0.02)	–0.59	(0.02)	–0.47	(0.02)	**–0.13**	(0.03)	–1.49	(0.01)	–0.88	(0.00)	–0.41	(0.01)	0.67	(0.02)
	Korea	–0.39	(0.01)	–0.36	(0.02)	–0.43	(0.02)	**0.07**	(0.03)	–1.32	(0.01)	–0.80	(0.00)	–0.20	(0.01)	0.76	(0.02)
	Luxembourg	0.23	(0.02)	0.23	(0.02)	0.22	(0.02)	0.01	(0.03)	–1.14	(0.01)	–0.15	(0.01)	0.58	(0.01)	1.62	(0.02)
	Mexico	0.08	(0.02)	0.02	(0.03)	0.13	(0.02)	**–0.12**	(0.03)	–1.11	(0.01)	–0.44	(0.01)	0.36	(0.01)	1.50	(0.01)
	Netherlands	–0.06	(0.02)	–0.08	(0.02)	–0.04	(0.02)	–0.04	(0.03)	–1.02	(0.01)	–0.45	(0.01)	0.24	(0.01)	1.00	(0.02)
	New Zealand	–0.01	(0.01)	0.00	(0.02)	–0.02	(0.02)	0.02	(0.03)	–1.11	(0.01)	–0.49	(0.01)	0.26	(0.01)	1.31	(0.02)
	Norway	0.24	(0.02)	0.27	(0.03)	0.21	(0.03)	0.06	(0.04)	–1.09	(0.01)	–0.13	(0.01)	0.57	(0.01)	1.60	(0.02)
	Poland	–0.17	(0.02)	–0.20	(0.02)	–0.14	(0.02)	**–0.06**	(0.03)	–1.21	(0.01)	–0.60	(0.00)	0.04	(0.01)	1.10	(0.02)
	Portugal	0.09	(0.02)	0.09	(0.03)	0.10	(0.02)	–0.01	(0.04)	–0.99	(0.01)	–0.31	(0.01)	0.33	(0.01)	1.34	(0.02)
	Slovak Republic	–0.16	(0.01)	–0.16	(0.02)	–0.16	(0.02)	0.00	(0.03)	–1.13	(0.01)	–0.56	(0.00)	0.00	(0.01)	1.05	(0.02)
	Spain	0.20	(0.02)	0.24	(0.02)	0.16	(0.03)	**0.08**	(0.04)	–1.00	(0.01)	–0.21	(0.01)	0.48	(0.01)	1.54	(0.01)
	Sweden	0.25	(0.02)	0.35	(0.02)	0.14	(0.03)	**0.21**	(0.03)	–1.06	(0.02)	–0.10	(0.01)	0.56	(0.00)	1.58	(0.02)
	Switzerland	0.19	(0.03)	0.17	(0.04)	0.22	(0.02)	–0.04	(0.05)	–1.15	(0.02)	–0.18	(0.01)	0.59	(0.01)	1.50	(0.01)
	Turkey	–0.44	(0.02)	–0.48	(0.02)	–0.39	(0.03)	**–0.09**	(0.04)	–1.44	(0.01)	–0.83	(0.00)	–0.26	(0.01)	0.76	(0.02)
	United States	m	m	m	m	m	m	m	m	m	m	m	m	m	m	m	m
	OECD total	*–0.09*	*(0.01)*	*–0.12*	*(0.01)*	*–0.07*	*(0.01)*	*–0.05*	*(0.01)*	*–1.26*	*(0.00)*	*–0.53*	*(0.00)*	*0.18*	*(0.01)*	*1.23*	*(0.01)*
	OECD average	*0.00*	*(0.00)*	*–0.01*	*(0.00)*	*0.01*	*(0.00)*	*–0.02*	*(0.01)*	*–1.17*	*(0.00)*	*–0.46*	*(0.00)*	*0.30*	*(0.00)*	*1.33*	*(0.01)*
Partner countries	Brazil	0.13	(0.02)	0.12	(0.03)	0.14	(0.02)	–0.02	(0.04)	–1.08	(0.02)	–0.38	(0.01)	0.41	(0.01)	1.57	(0.02)
	Hong Kong-China	–0.61	(0.01)	–0.63	(0.02)	–0.58	(0.02)	**–0.06**	(0.02)	–1.38	(0.01)	–0.84	(0.00)	–0.55	(0.00)	0.34	(0.02)
	Indonesia	–0.30	(0.02)	–0.33	(0.02)	–0.28	(0.02)	**–0.05**	(0.02)	–1.10	(0.01)	–0.66	(0.00)	–0.23	(0.01)	0.79	(0.02)
	Latvia	–0.21	(0.02)	–0.25	(0.02)	–0.18	(0.02)	**–0.07**	(0.03)	–1.16	(0.01)	–0.55	(0.01)	–0.01	(0.01)	0.87	(0.02)
	Liechtenstein	0.19	(0.05)	0.14	(0.07)	0.26	(0.08)	–0.12	(0.11)	–1.17	(0.06)	–0.11	(0.02)	0.57	(0.02)	1.50	(0.04)
	Macao-China	–0.61	(0.02)	–0.60	(0.04)	–0.63	(0.03)	0.03	(0.05)	–1.46	(0.02)	–0.87	(0.01)	–0.50	(0.01)	0.38	(0.04)
	Russian Federation	–0.29	(0.02)	–0.31	(0.02)	–0.26	(0.02)	**–0.05**	(0.03)	–1.26	(0.01)	–0.72	(0.00)	–0.13	(0.01)	0.96	(0.02)
	Serbia	0.03	(0.02)	0.02	(0.03)	0.05	(0.02)	–0.03	(0.04)	–1.08	(0.01)	–0.47	(0.00)	0.26	(0.01)	1.42	(0.02)
	Thailand	–0.29	(0.02)	–0.32	(0.03)	–0.26	(0.03)	**–0.07**	(0.03)	–1.11	(0.01)	–0.64	(0.00)	–0.20	(0.01)	0.82	(0.04)
	Tunisia	–0.09	(0.02)	–0.10	(0.03)	–0.08	(0.03)	–0.02	(0.03)	–1.32	(0.01)	–0.54	(0.01)	0.19	(0.01)	1.32	(0.02)
	Uruguay	0.24	(0.01)	0.30	(0.02)	0.18	(0.02)	**0.12**	(0.04)	–1.01	(0.02)	–0.21	(0.01)	0.58	(0.01)	1.61	(0.01)
	United Kingdom[1]	0.08	(0.01)	0.12	(0.02)	0.05	(0.02)	**0.07**	(0.03)	–1.08	(0.01)	–0.37	(0.01)	0.35	(0.01)	1.42	(0.01)

		Performance on the mathematics scale, by national quarters of the index of students' sense of belonging at school								Change in the mathematics score per unit of the index of sense of belonging		Increased likelihood of students in the bottom quarter of this index scoring in the bottom quarter of the national mathematics performance distribution		Explained variance in student performance (r-squared × 100)	
		Bottom quarter		Second quarter		Third quarter		Top quarter							
		Mean score	S.E.	Mean score	S.E.	Mean score	S.E.	Mean score	S.E.	Effect	S.E.	Ratio	S.E.	%	S.E.
OECD countries	Australia	**518**	(3.8)	524	(2.7)	530	(2.9)	**527**	(2.7)	3.1	(1.63)	**1.2**	(0.06)	0.1	(0.12)
	Austria	497	(3.8)	513	(4.4)	515	(4.3)	505	(4.4)	2.9	(1.64)	**1.2**	(0.08)	0.1	(0.11)
	Belgium	**517**	(5.0)	537	(3.9)	543	(3.2)	**539**	(2.8)	**6.3**	(2.18)	**1.3**	(0.08)	0.3	(0.20)
	Canada	534	(2.5)	541	(2.1)	538	(2.5)	532	(2.5)	–1.0	(0.85)	**1.1**	(0.05)	0.0	(0.03)
	Czech Republic	**505**	(4.7)	516	(3.8)	532	(4.5)	**537**	(3.8)	**12.7**	(1.98)	**1.4**	(0.09)	1.3	(0.39)
	Denmark	511	(4.1)	513	(4.1)	522	(4.5)	516	(4.1)	3.1	(1.92)	**1.2**	(0.10)	0.1	(0.14)
	Finland	544	(3.5)	547	(2.7)	547	(3.1)	540	(3.2)	–1.9	(1.37)	1.1	(0.06)	0.0	(0.07)
	France	505	(3.9)	516	(4.5)	515	(4.1)	513	(3.3)	1.2	(1.28)	1.1	(0.08)	0.0	(0.04)
	Germany	509	(4.5)	516	(4.2)	519	(4.3)	504	(5.2)	–1.4	(1.81)	1.1	(0.09)	0.0	(0.07)
	Greece	**433**	(5.1)	446	(4.5)	455	(4.3)	**448**	(5.1)	**5.8**	(1.69)	**1.3**	(0.09)	0.3	(0.18)
	Hungary	**476**	(4.0)	484	(4.2)	500	(4.3)	**501**	(3.5)	**10.0**	(1.63)	**1.4**	(0.08)	1.1	(0.35)
	Iceland	512	(3.7)	518	(3.8)	519	(3.7)	513	(3.8)	0.5	(1.55)	1.1	(0.09)	0.0	(0.04)
	Ireland	**506**	(4.2)	503	(3.6)	511	(3.4)	**492**	(3.6)	**–5.2**	(1.55)	1.0	(0.07)	0.4	(0.22)
	Italy	467	(4.4)	467	(3.9)	469	(3.8)	460	(4.6)	–3.7	(1.92)	1.0	(0.08)	0.1	(0.13)
	Japan	**512**	(4.9)	535	(5.3)	546	(4.6)	**546**	(4.8)	**12.9**	(2.16)	**1.4**	(0.08)	1.3	(0.39)
	Korea	**528**	(4.3)	539	(3.8)	549	(3.7)	**553**	(4.8)	**11.1**	(2.09)	**1.3**	(0.07)	1.0	(0.35)
	Luxembourg	**482**	(3.1)	491	(3.2)	504	(2.7)	**497**	(3.3)	**5.9**	(1.45)	**1.2**	(0.08)	0.5	(0.24)
	Mexico	**363**	(4.3)	383	(3.8)	398	(4.4)	**399**	(4.3)	**13.3**	(1.41)	**1.6**	(0.09)	2.6	(0.51)
	Netherlands	**531**	(4.2)	539	(4.3)	553	(4.4)	**549**	(4.2)	**7.0**	(2.31)	**1.2**	(0.09)	0.4	(0.28)
	New Zealand	515	(4.0)	529	(3.7)	532	(3.2)	523	(3.9)	2.6	(1.51)	**1.3**	(0.07)	0.1	(0.08)
	Norway	492	(3.8)	499	(3.5)	504	(3.9)	490	(3.9)	0.1	(1.57)	**1.2**	(0.07)	0.0	(0.03)
	Poland	**480**	(3.2)	484	(3.6)	499	(4.0)	**499**	(3.8)	**7.7**	(1.51)	**1.3**	(0.07)	0.6	(0.25)
	Portugal	**438**	(4.7)	469	(4.4)	480	(3.8)	**479**	(3.9)	**15.7**	(1.72)	**1.8**	(0.11)	2.8	(0.58)
	Slovak Republic	**489**	(4.0)	495	(3.9)	510	(3.9)	**499**	(4.9)	**3.1**	(1.41)	**1.2**	(0.07)	0.1	(0.08)
	Spain	479	(3.3)	486	(2.6)	494	(3.1)	482	(4.1)	2.4	(1.34)	**1.2**	(0.06)	0.1	(0.10)
	Sweden	506	(3.4)	512	(4.0)	516	(3.4)	505	(4.1)	0.3	(1.57)	**1.2**	(0.08)	0.0	(0.03)
	Switzerland	**512**	(4.8)	523	(3.9)	540	(4.8)	**532**	(4.5)	**8.4**	(1.90)	**1.3**	(0.07)	0.8	(0.36)
	Turkey	**390**	(6.6)	419	(7.0)	444	(8.2)	**442**	(8.0)	**21.0**	(2.87)	**1.7**	(0.14)	3.1	(0.83)
	United States	m	m	m	m	m	m	m	m	m	m	m	m	m	m
	OECD total	*485*	*(1.6)*	*494*	*(1.4)*	*500*	*(1.3)*	*492*	*(1.4)*	*2.0*	*(0.63)*	*1.2*	*(0.02)*	*0.0*	*(0.02)*
	OECD average	*492*	*(1.0)*	*502*	*(0.8)*	*511*	*(0.7)*	*502*	*(0.9)*	*3.5*	*(0.38)*	*1.3*	*(0.02)*	*0.1*	*(0.03)*
Partner countries	Brazil	**346**	(5.2)	360	(5.6)	364	(6.2)	**361**	(6.1)	**4.7**	(1.56)	1.2	(0.08)	0.3	(0.17)
	Hong Kong-China	**531**	(4.6)	547	(4.8)	558	(5.9)	**566**	(5.9)	**16.3**	(2.65)	**1.5**	(0.11)	1.3	(0.44)
	Indonesia	**347**	(4.6)	366	(3.9)	364	(4.8)	**366**	(4.8)	**5.8**	(1.81)	**1.4**	(0.08)	0.3	(0.18)
	Latvia	**469**	(4.5)	479	(4.5)	489	(4.9)	**498**	(4.6)	**13.1**	(1.98)	**1.4**	(0.10)	1.5	(0.43)
	Liechtenstein	517	(11.0)	549	(9.4)	542	(12.3)	538	(9.4)	9.5	(5.05)	1.4	(0.29)	1.0	(1.12)
	Macao-China	517	(7.6)	527	(7.1)	533	(6.8)	533	(7.0)	6.2	(5.24)	1.3	(0.18)	0.3	(0.49)
	Russian Federation	**453**	(5.2)	462	(4.4)	481	(4.9)	**479**	(4.4)	**11.1**	(1.38)	**1.4**	(0.09)	1.2	(0.28)
	Serbia	428	(4.7)	442	(4.7)	451	(4.5)	431	(4.8)	1.0	(1.50)	**1.2**	(0.09)	0.0	(0.05)
	Thailand	**401**	(4.1)	417	(3.6)	421	(3.6)	**429**	(4.2)	**13.0**	(2.14)	**1.4**	(0.09)	1.6	(0.57)
	Tunisia	354	(4.0)	360	(4.6)	360	(3.7)	363	(2.9)	3.0	(1.74)	**1.2**	(0.09)	0.2	(0.18)
	Uruguay	414	(3.7)	422	(4.1)	437	(5.5)	418	(5.1)	**3.4**	(1.55)	**1.2**	(0.08)	0.1	(0.12)
	United Kingdom[1]	507	(4.5)	505	(3.1)	514	(3.8)	505	(3.8)	0.7	(1.29)	1.1	(0.07)	0.0	(0.03)

Note: Values that are statistically significant are indicated in bold (see Annex A4).

1. Response rate too low to ensure comparability (see Annex A3).

Table 3.5b

Index of students' sense of belonging at school by students' programme destination

Results based on students' self-reports

		All students											
		Programme Type A[1]				Programme Type B[2]				Programme Type C[3]			
		%	S.E.	Mean index	S.E.	%	S.E.	Mean index	S.E.	%	S.E.	Mean index	S.E.
OECD countries	Australia	91.1	(0.6)	0.05	(0.02)	8.9	(0.6)	–0.01	(0.04)	a	a	a	a
	Austria	56.8	(1.9)	0.48	(0.03)	34.1	(1.9)	0.38	(0.03)	9.2	(0.7)	0.37	(0.10)
	Belgium	77.1	(1.1)	–0.25	(0.01)	2.1	(0.4)	c	c	20.9	(1.1)	–0.37	(0.04)
	Canada	100.0	(0.0)	0.02	(0.01)	a	a	a	a	a	a	a	a
	Czech Republic	83.1	(1.2)	–0.24	(0.02)	0.3	(0.3)	c	c	16.6	(1.2)	–0.36	(0.04)
	Denmark	100.0	(0.0)	0.01	(0.02)	a	a	a	a	a	a	a	a
	Finland	100.0	(0.0)	–0.02	(0.02)	a	a	a	a	a	a	a	a
	France	90.5	(0.9)	–0.17	(0.02)	2.1	(0.6)	c	c	7.4	(0.7)	–0.19	(0.04)
	Germany	98.4	(0.2)	0.23	(0.02)	1.6	(0.2)	c	c	a	a	a	a
	Greece	80.1	(2.2)	0.07	(0.02)	a	a	a	a	19.9	(2.2)	–0.10	(0.03)
	Hungary	80.4	(0.7)	0.13	(0.02)	a	a	a	a	19.6	(0.7)	–0.12	(0.03)
	Iceland	100.0	(0.0)	0.16	(0.02)	a	a	a	a	a	a	a	a
	Ireland	82.2	(1.4)	0.08	(0.02)	1.1	(0.3)	c	c	16.7	(1.3)	0.08	(0.04)
	Italy	99.9	(0.0)	0.05	(0.01)	a	a	a	a	0.1	(0.0)	c	c
	Japan	74.6	(0.5)	–0.50	(0.02)	0.9	(0.9)	c	c	24.5	(1.0)	–0.60	(0.03)
	Korea	73.3	(0.9)	–0.34	(0.02)	a	a	a	a	26.7	(0.9)	–0.53	(0.02)
	Luxembourg	95.4	(0.1)	0.23	(0.02)	3.2	(0.1)	0.16	(0.09)	1.3	(0.1)	c	c
	Mexico	94.2	(1.2)	0.07	(0.02)	a	a	a	a	5.8	(1.2)	0.16	(0.06)
	Netherlands	38.6	(1.8)	0.05	(0.02)	58.0	(2.0)	–0.13	(0.02)	3.4	(1.4)	–0.04	(0.04)
	New Zealand	100.0	(0.0)	–0.01	(0.01)	a	a	a	a	a	a	a	a
	Norway	100.0	(0.0)	0.23	(0.02)	a	a	a	a	a	a	a	a
	Poland	100.0	(0.0)	–0.17	(0.02)	a	a	a	a	a	a	a	a
	Portugal	91.2	(1.0)	0.09	(0.02)	8.5	(0.9)	0.13	(0.05)	0.3	(0.1)	c	c
	Slovak Republic	97.3	(0.8)	–0.15	(0.01)	1.0	(0.6)	c	c	1.8	(0.5)	c	c
	Spain	100.0	(0.0)	0.20	(0.02)	a	a	a	a	a	a	a	a
	Sweden	100.0	(0.0)	0.24	(0.02)	a	a	a	a	a	a	a	a
	Switzerland	91.2	(2.8)	0.22	(0.02)	8.4	(2.8)	–0.07	(0.17)	0.4	(0.2)	c	c
	Turkey	100.0	(0.0)	–0.44	(0.02)	a	a	a	a	a	a	a	a
	United States	100.0	(0.0)	m	m	a	a	a	a	a	a	a	a
	OECD total	***86.9***	***(0.2)***	***–0.06***	***(0.00)***	***1.8***	***(0.1)***	***–0.06***	***(0.02)***	***11.3***	***(0.2)***	***–0.16***	***(0.01)***
	OECD average	***86.5***	***(0.2)***	***0.01***	***(0.00)***	***4.4***	***(0.2)***	***0.03***	***(0.02)***	***9.1***	***(0.2)***	***–0.13***	***(0.01)***
Partner countries	Brazil	100.0	(0.0)	0.13	(0.02)	a	a	a	a	a	a	a	a
	Hong Kong-China	100.0	(0.0)	–0.61	(0.01)	a	a	a	a	a	a	a	a
	Indonesia	89.1	(1.2)	–0.29	(0.02)	10.9	(1.2)	–0.39	(0.03)	a	a	a	a
	Latvia	100.0	(0.0)	–0.21	(0.02)	a	a	a	a	a	a	a	a
	Liechtenstein	100.0	(0.0)	0.19	(0.05)	a	a	a	a	a	a	a	a
	Macao-China	99.0	(0.1)	–0.61	(0.02)	1.0	(0.1)	c	c	a	a	a	a
	Russian Federation	92.5	(2.6)	–0.28	(0.02)	a	a	a	a	7.5	(2.6)	–0.35	(0.06)
	Serbia	21.4	(2.6)	0.13	(0.04)	45.4	(2.5)	0.01	(0.02)	33.3	(2.4)	0.00	(0.04)
	Thailand	89.7	(1.4)	–0.29	(0.03)	a	a	a	a	10.3	(1.4)	0.26	(0.06)
	Tunisia	100.0	(0.0)	–0.09	(0.02)	a	a	a	a	a	a	a	a
	Uruguay	91.9	(1.2)	0.24	(0.02)	4.2	(1.1)	0.20	(0.06)	3.9	(0.5)	0.21	(0.06)
	United Kingdom[4]	0.9	(0.3)	c	c	0.6	(0.1)	c	c	98.5	(0.3)	0.08	(0.01)

1. Type A: General programmes designed to give access to the next level of education.
2. Type B: Programmes designed to give access to vocational studies at the next level of education.
3. Type C: Programmes designed to give direct access to the labour market.
4. Response rate too low to ensure comparability (see Annex A3).

Table 3.5b *(continued)*

Index of students' sense of belonging at school by students' programme destination

Results based on students' self-reports

Males

		Programme Type A[1]				Programme Type B[2]				Programme Type C[3]			
		%	S.E.	Mean index	S.E.	%	S.E.	Mean index	S.E.	%	S.E.	Mean index	S.E.
OECD countries	Australia	90.3	(0.8)	0.00	(0.02)	9.7	(0.8)	–0.04	(0.05)	a	a	a	a
	Austria	49.0	(2.4)	0.48	(0.04)	38.6	(2.6)	0.32	(0.04)	12.4	(1.2)	0.38	(0.12)
	Belgium	74.0	(1.7)	–0.29	(0.02)	2.2	(0.4)	c	c	23.8	(1.7)	–0.45	(0.04)
	Canada	100.0	(0.0)	–0.03	(0.02)	a	a	a	a	a	a	a	a
	Czech Republic	78.4	(1.7)	–0.22	(0.02)	0.1	(0.1)	c	c	21.4	(1.7)	–0.38	(0.04)
	Denmark	100.0	(0.0)	0.02	(0.02)	a	a	a	a	a	a	a	a
	Finland	100.0	(0.0)	0.03	(0.02)	a	a	a	a	a	a	a	a
	France	91.2	(1.4)	–0.19	(0.03)	2.6	(0.9)	c	c	6.2	(1.2)	–0.19	(0.08)
	Germany	98.3	(0.8)	0.23	(0.03)	1.7	(0.8)	c	c	a	a	a	a
	Greece	76.2	(3.1)	0.08	(0.03)	a	a	a	a	23.8	(3.1)	–0.11	(0.05)
	Hungary	76.8	(1.5)	0.09	(0.03)	a	a	a	a	23.2	(1.5)	–0.13	(0.03)
	Iceland	100.0	(0.0)	0.19	(0.03)	a	a	a	a	a	a	a	a
	Ireland	85.5	(1.3)	0.06	(0.02)	0.9	(0.3)	c	c	13.6	(1.3)	–0.03	(0.07)
	Italy	99.9	(0.0)	0.05	(0.02)	a	a	a	a	0.1	(0.0)	c	c
	Japan	71.2	(2.6)	–0.58	(0.02)	1.5	(1.5)	c	c	27.2	(2.5)	–0.64	(0.03)
	Korea	75.4	(2.5)	–0.32	(0.02)	a	a	a	a	24.6	(2.5)	–0.50	(0.03)
	Luxembourg	93.5	(0.3)	0.23	(0.02)	4.2	(0.3)	0.23	(0.13)	2.3	(0.2)	c	c
	Mexico	93.7	(1.2)	0.01	(0.03)	a	a	a	a	6.3	(1.2)	0.09	(0.08)
	Netherlands	35.4	(2.0)	0.09	(0.03)	60.8	(2.4)	–0.17	(0.03)	3.9	(1.7)	–0.08	(0.06)
	New Zealand	100.0	(0.0)	0.00	(0.02)	a	a	a	a	a	a	a	a
	Norway	100.0	(0.0)	0.26	(0.03)	a	a	a	a	a	a	a	a
	Poland	100.0	(0.0)	–0.20	(0.02)	a	a	a	a	a	a	a	a
	Portugal	89.6	(1.3)	0.09	(0.03)	10.1	(1.3)	0.11	(0.06)	0.3	(0.1)	c	c
	Slovak Republic	96.8	(1.0)	–0.15	(0.02)	1.2	(0.7)	c	c	1.9	(0.6)	c	c
	Spain	100.0	(0.0)	0.24	(0.02)	a	a	a	a	a	a	a	a
	Sweden	100.0	(0.0)	0.35	(0.02)	a	a	a	a	a	a	a	a
	Switzerland	88.6	(5.1)	0.22	(0.02)	11.2	(5.1)	–0.21	(0.18)	0.2	(0.2)	c	c
	Turkey	100.0	(0.0)	–0.48	(0.02)	a	a	a	a	a	a	a	a
	United States	100.0	(0.0)	m	m	a	a	a	a	a	a	a	a
	OECD total	*86.6*	*(0.4)*	*–0.07*	*(0.01)*	*2.1*	*(0.2)*	*–0.12*	*(0.03)*	*11.3*	*(0.4)*	*–0.18*	*(0.02)*
	OECD average	*85.6*	*(0.3)*	*0.01*	*(0.01)*	*4.9*	*(0.3)*	*–0.02*	*(0.03)*	*9.6*	*(0.3)*	*–0.15*	*(0.01)*
Partner countries	Brazil	100.0	(0.0)	0.11	(0.03)	a	a	a	a	a	a	a	a
	Hong Kong-China	100.0	(0.0)	–0.63	(0.02)	a	a	a	a	a	a	a	a
	Indonesia	86.7	(2.3)	–0.32	(0.02)	13.3	(2.3)	–0.38	(0.04)	a	a	a	a
	Latvia	100.0	(0.0)	–0.24	(0.02)	a	a	a	a	a	a	a	a
	Liechtenstein	100.0	(0.0)	0.14	(0.07)	a	a	a	a	a	a	a	a
	Macao-China	99.1	(0.3)	–0.60	(0.04)	0.9	(0.3)	c	c	a	a	a	a
	Russian Federation	88.3	(3.8)	–0.30	(0.02)	a	a	a	a	11.7	(3.8)	–0.39	(0.03)
	Serbia	14.4	(2.2)	0.06	(0.08)	40.8	(2.6)	0.01	(0.03)	44.8	(2.8)	0.00	(0.05)
	Thailand	85.7	(2.4)	–0.32	(0.03)	a	a	a	a	14.3	(2.4)	–0.32	(0.05)
	Tunisia	100.0	(0.0)	–0.10	(0.03)	a	a	a	a	a	a	a	a
	Uruguay	88.0	(1.8)	0.32	(0.03)	6.2	(1.6)	0.22	(0.09)	5.8	(0.9)	0.18	(0.07)
	United Kingdom[4]	1.1	(0.6)	c	c	0.8	(0.2)	c	c	98.0	(0.6)	0.12	(0.02)

Females

		Programme Type A[1]				Programme Type B[2]				Programme Type C[3]			
		%	S.E.	Mean index	S.E.	%	S.E.	Mean index	S.E.	%	S.E.	Mean index	S.E.
OECD countries	Australia	91.9	(0.7)	0.09	(0.02)	8.1	(0.7)	0.04	(0.05)	a	a	a	a
	Austria	64.5	(2.6)	0.48	(0.03)	29.6	(2.6)	0.47	(0.05)	5.9	(0.6)	0.34	(0.12)
	Belgium	80.3	(1.1)	–0.22	(0.02)	2.0	(0.5)	c	c	17.7	(1.1)	–0.25	(0.05)
	Canada	100.0	(0.0)	0.06	(0.02)	a	a	a	a	a	a	a	a
	Czech Republic	87.9	(1.8)	–0.26	(0.02)	0.4	(0.4)	c	c	11.7	(1.7)	–0.32	(0.06)
	Denmark	100.0	(0.0)	0.01	(0.02)	a	a	a	a	a	a	a	a
	Finland	100.0	(0.0)	–0.07	(0.02)	a	a	a	a	a	a	a	a
	France	89.9	(1.0)	–0.16	(0.02)	1.7	(0.5)	c	c	8.4	(0.9)	–0.18	(0.06)
	Germany	98.7	(0.3)	0.24	(0.02)	1.3	(0.3)	c	c	a	a	a	a
	Greece	83.6	(2.1)	0.06	(0.02)	a	a	a	a	16.4	(2.1)	–0.08	(0.04)
	Hungary	84.4	(1.3)	0.17	(0.03)	a	a	a	a	15.6	(1.3)	–0.09	(0.05)
	Iceland	100.0	(0.0)	0.13	(0.03)	a	a	a	a	a	a	a	a
	Ireland	78.8	(2.2)	0.10	(0.03)	1.4	(0.5)	c	c	19.8	(2.1)	0.15	(0.05)
	Italy	99.9	(0.0)	0.05	(0.02)	a	a	a	a	0.1	(0.0)	c	c
	Japan	77.8	(2.9)	–0.44	(0.02)	0.2	(0.2)	c	c	22.0	(3.0)	–0.56	(0.05)
	Korea	70.4	(3.2)	–0.38	(0.02)	a	a	a	a	29.6	(3.2)	–0.55	(0.03)
	Luxembourg	97.3	(0.3)	0.22	(0.03)	2.3	(0.2)	c	c	0.5	(0.1)	c	c
	Mexico	94.7	(1.3)	0.13	(0.03)	a	a	a	a	5.3	(1.3)	0.24	(0.06)
	Netherlands	42.0	(2.1)	0.02	(0.03)	55.2	(2.3)	–0.08	(0.03)	2.9	(1.0)	c	c
	New Zealand	100.0	(0.0)	–0.02	(0.02)	a	a	a	a	a	a	a	a
	Norway	100.0	(0.0)	0.21	(0.03)	a	a	a	a	a	a	a	a
	Poland	100.0	(0.0)	–0.14	(0.02)	a	a	a	a	a	a	a	a
	Portugal	92.6	(0.8)	0.09	(0.03)	7.0	(0.8)	0.16	(0.09)	0.3	(0.2)	c	c
	Slovak Republic	97.7	(0.8)	–0.16	(0.02)	0.7	(0.4)	c	c	1.6	(0.7)	c	c
	Spain	100.0	(0.0)	0.16	(0.03)	a	a	a	a	a	a	a	a
	Sweden	100.0	(0.0)	0.14	(0.03)	a	a	a	a	a	a	a	a
	Switzerland	93.9	(1.3)	0.22	(0.02)	5.4	(1.1)	0.25	(0.13)	0.7	(0.3)	c	c
	Turkey	100.0	(0.0)	–0.39	(0.03)	a	a	a	a	a	a	a	a
	United States	100.0	(0.0)	m	m	a	a	a	a	a	a	a	a
	OECD total	*87.1*	*(0.4)*	*–0.04*	*(0.01)*	*1.6*	*(0.1)*	*0.01*	*(0.03)*	*11.3*	*(0.4)*	*–0.15*	*(0.02)*
	OECD average	*87.5*	*(0.3)*	*0.02*	*(0.01)*	*3.9*	*(0.2)*	*0.10*	*(0.03)*	*8.7*	*(0.2)*	*–0.10*	*(0.02)*
Partner countries	Brazil	100.0	(0.0)	0.14	(0.02)	a	a	a	a	a	a	a	a
	Hong Kong-China	100.0	(0.0)	–0.58	(0.02)	a	a	a	a	a	a	a	a
	Indonesia	91.4	(2.3)	–0.27	(0.02)	8.6	(2.3)	–0.40	(0.06)	a	a	a	a
	Latvia	100.0	(0.0)	–0.19	(0.02)	a	a	a	a	a	a	a	a
	Liechtenstein	100.0	(0.0)	0.25	(0.08)	a	a	a	a	a	a	a	a
	Macao-China	99.0	(0.2)	–0.62	(0.03)	1.0	(0.2)	c	c	a	a	a	a
	Russian Federation	96.6	(1.4)	–0.26	(0.02)	a	a	a	a	3.4	(1.4)	–0.23	(0.19)
	Serbia	28.1	(3.2)	0.17	(0.05)	49.9	(3.2)	0.01	(0.03)	22.0	(2.7)	–0.01	(0.07)
	Thailand	93.0	(1.2)	–0.26	(0.03)	a	a	a	a	7.0	(1.2)	–0.16	(0.12)
	Tunisia	100.0	(0.0)	–0.08	(0.03)	a	a	a	a	a	a	a	a
	Uruguay	95.5	(0.9)	0.18	(0.02)	2.4	(0.8)	c	c	2.1	(0.4)	c	c
	United Kingdom[4]	0.6	(0.1)	c	c	0.5	(0.2)	c	c	98.9	(0.2)	0.05	(0.02)

1. Type A: General programmes designed to give access to the next level of education.
2. Type B: Programmes designed to give access to vocational studies at the next level of education.
3. Type C: Programmes designed to give direct access to the labour market.
4. Response rate too low to ensure comparability (see Annex A3).

Table 3.5c

Student- and school-level correlations between the index of students' sense of belonging at school and student performance and variance in student performances on the mathematics scale explained by the index of students' sense of belonging at school

		Student level				School level	
		Correlation coefficient		Percentage of variance explained		Correlation coefficient	Percentage of variance explained
		r	S.E.	r-squared × 100	S.E.	r	r-squared × 100
OECD countries	Australia	0.03	0.02	0.11	0.12	0.38	14.80
	Austria	0.03	0.02	0.11	0.11	0.01	0.03
	Belgium	0.05	0.02	0.29	0.20	0.42	17.43
	Canada	-0.01	0.01	0.02	0.03	0.09	0.83
	Czech Republic	0.11	0.02	1.26	0.39	0.13	1.82
	Denmark	0.03	0.02	0.11	0.14	0.30	9.38
	Finland	-0.02	0.02	0.05	0.07	-0.10	1.08
	France	0.01	0.01	0.02	0.04	m	m
	Germany	-0.02	0.02	0.03	0.07	0.12	1.47
	Greece	0.06	0.02	0.33	0.18	0.03	0.09
	Hungary	0.11	0.02	1.10	0.35	0.24	5.63
	Iceland	0.01	0.02	0.01	0.04	0.04	0.18
	Ireland	-0.06	0.02	0.37	0.22	-0.22	4.78
	Italy	-0.04	0.02	0.13	0.13	0.12	1.54
	Japan	0.11	0.02	1.26	0.39	0.58	33.64
	Korea	0.10	0.02	1.00	0.35	0.13	2.09
	Luxembourg	0.07	0.02	0.49	0.24	0.07	0.57
	Mexico	0.16	0.02	2.63	0.51	0.62	37.97
	Netherlands	0.07	0.02	0.42	0.28	0.44	19.46
	New Zealand	0.03	0.02	0.07	0.08	-0.02	0.38
	Norway	0.00	0.02	0.00	0.03	-0.03	0.44
	Poland	0.08	0.02	0.64	0.25	0.20	4.10
	Portugal	0.17	0.02	2.79	0.58	0.37	13.75
	Slovak Republic	0.03	0.01	0.09	0.08	0.07	0.62
	Spain	0.03	0.02	0.08	0.10	0.13	1.83
	Sweden	0.00	0.02	0.00	0.03	0.15	2.55
	Switzerland	0.09	0.02	0.80	0.36	0.13	1.75
	Turkey	0.18	0.02	3.15	0.83	0.69	47.60
	United States	m	m	m	m	m	m
	OECD total	*0.02*	*0.01*	*0.03*	*0.02*	*0.24*	*5.75*
	OECD average	*0.04*	*0.00*	*0.12*	*0.03*	*0.19*	*8.02*
Partner countries	Brazil	0.05	0.02	0.25	0.17	-0.04	0.22
	Hong Kong-China	0.12	0.02	1.35	0.44	0.51	25.92
	Indonesia	0.06	0.02	0.32	0.18	0.29	8.23
	Latvia	0.12	0.02	1.46	0.43	0.21	4.66
	Liechtenstein	0.10	0.05	1.02	1.12	0.33	11.24
	Macao-China	0.05	0.05	0.31	0.49	0.38	14.72
	Russian Federation	0.11	0.01	1.15	0.28	-0.05	0.25
	Serbia	0.01	0.02	0.01	0.05	0.09	0.81
	Thailand	0.13	0.02	1.56	0.57	0.30	9.18
	Tunisia	0.04	0.02	0.15	0.18	-0.01	0.03
	Uruguay	0.04	0.02	0.13	0.12	-0.07	0.48
	United Kingdom[1]	0.01	0.01	0.01	0.03	0.10	1.04

1. Response rate too low to ensure comparability (see Annex A3).

Table 3.6

Index of self-concept in mathematics and performance on the mathematics scale, by national quarters of the index

Results based on students' self-reports

		Index of self-concept in mathematics															
		All students		Males		Females		Gender difference (M – F)		Bottom quarter		Second quarter		Third quarter		Top quarter	
		Mean index	S.E.	Mean index	S.E.	Mean index	S.E.	Dif.	S.E.	Mean index	S.E.	Mean index	S.E.	Mean index	S.E.	Mean index	S.E.
OECD countries	Australia	0.13	(0.02)	0.28	(0.02)	–0.03	(0.02)	**0.31**	(0.02)	–1.03	(0.02)	–0.14	(0.00)	0.43	(0.00)	1.26	(0.01)
	Austria	0.07	(0.02)	0.31	(0.03)	–0.17	(0.03)	**0.47**	(0.04)	–1.29	(0.02)	–0.30	(0.01)	0.43	(0.01)	1.44	(0.02)
	Belgium	–0.03	(0.02)	0.14	(0.02)	–0.21	(0.02)	**0.34**	(0.03)	–1.28	(0.01)	–0.30	(0.01)	0.28	(0.00)	1.18	(0.01)
	Canada	0.19	(0.01)	0.37	(0.02)	0.01	(0.02)	**0.36**	(0.02)	–1.19	(0.01)	–0.17	(0.01)	0.53	(0.00)	1.58	(0.01)
	Czech Republic	–0.09	(0.02)	0.07	(0.02)	–0.26	(0.03)	**0.33**	(0.03)	–1.26	(0.01)	–0.36	(0.01)	0.18	(0.01)	1.06	(0.02)
	Denmark	0.24	(0.02)	0.49	(0.02)	0.00	(0.02)	**0.49**	(0.03)	–1.09	(0.02)	–0.06	(0.01)	0.60	(0.01)	1.52	(0.02)
	Finland	0.01	(0.02)	0.25	(0.02)	–0.23	(0.02)	**0.47**	(0.03)	–1.34	(0.02)	–0.33	(0.01)	0.38	(0.01)	1.33	(0.02)
	France	–0.17	(0.02)	0.03	(0.03)	–0.35	(0.02)	**0.38**	(0.03)	–1.51	(0.02)	–0.47	(0.01)	0.21	(0.01)	1.10	(0.02)
	Germany	0.15	(0.02)	0.44	(0.02)	–0.13	(0.03)	**0.56**	(0.04)	–1.30	(0.01)	–0.25	(0.01)	0.53	(0.01)	1.62	(0.01)
	Greece	0.11	(0.02)	0.25	(0.03)	–0.02	(0.02)	**0.27**	(0.03)	–0.97	(0.01)	–0.20	(0.01)	0.37	(0.00)	1.24	(0.01)
	Hungary	–0.15	(0.02)	–0.06	(0.02)	–0.26	(0.02)	**0.20**	(0.03)	–1.19	(0.01)	–0.40	(0.00)	0.06	(0.00)	0.92	(0.01)
	Iceland	0.03	(0.02)	0.16	(0.03)	–0.10	(0.03)	**0.26**	(0.05)	–1.46	(0.02)	–0.36	(0.01)	0.45	(0.01)	1.50	(0.02)
	Ireland	–0.03	(0.02)	0.08	(0.02)	–0.14	(0.03)	**0.21**	(0.03)	–1.20	(0.02)	–0.29	(0.01)	0.26	(0.01)	1.11	(0.02)
	Italy	0.00	(0.02)	0.08	(0.03)	–0.07	(0.02)	**0.14**	(0.03)	–1.26	(0.02)	–0.34	(0.01)	0.34	(0.01)	1.27	(0.02)
	Japan	–0.53	(0.02)	–0.35	(0.03)	–0.70	(0.02)	**0.35**	(0.03)	–1.78	(0.01)	–0.76	(0.01)	–0.24	(0.01)	0.67	(0.02)
	Korea	–0.35	(0.02)	–0.26	(0.03)	–0.49	(0.03)	**0.24**	(0.04)	–1.49	(0.01)	–0.60	(0.00)	–0.12	(0.00)	0.81	(0.01)
	Luxembourg	0.07	(0.02)	0.34	(0.02)	–0.20	(0.02)	**0.54**	(0.03)	–1.35	(0.02)	–0.30	(0.01)	0.45	(0.01)	1.47	(0.02)
	Mexico	0.17	(0.02)	0.24	(0.02)	0.12	(0.02)	**0.12**	(0.02)	–0.79	(0.01)	–0.12	(0.00)	0.39	(0.00)	1.22	(0.02)
	Netherlands	0.00	(0.02)	0.26	(0.03)	–0.28	(0.03)	**0.55**	(0.04)	–1.28	(0.02)	–0.28	(0.01)	0.33	(0.01)	1.22	(0.02)
	New Zealand	0.15	(0.02)	0.31	(0.02)	–0.01	(0.02)	**0.32**	(0.03)	–0.98	(0.02)	–0.11	(0.01)	0.44	(0.01)	1.25	(0.02)
	Norway	–0.18	(0.02)	0.06	(0.03)	–0.41	(0.03)	**0.47**	(0.04)	–1.59	(0.01)	–0.55	(0.01)	0.18	(0.01)	1.25	(0.02)
	Poland	0.03	(0.02)	0.11	(0.02)	–0.05	(0.02)	**0.17**	(0.03)	–1.02	(0.02)	–0.33	(0.00)	0.25	(0.01)	1.21	(0.02)
	Portugal	–0.18	(0.02)	–0.08	(0.02)	–0.28	(0.02)	**0.20**	(0.03)	–1.37	(0.02)	–0.45	(0.00)	0.11	(0.01)	0.98	(0.02)
	Slovak Republic	–0.05	(0.02)	0.07	(0.02)	–0.18	(0.02)	**0.25**	(0.02)	–1.06	(0.01)	–0.33	(0.00)	0.18	(0.00)	1.01	(0.02)
	Spain	–0.19	(0.02)	–0.06	(0.03)	–0.31	(0.03)	**0.25**	(0.03)	–1.47	(0.01)	–0.49	(0.00)	0.15	(0.01)	1.06	(0.01)
	Sweden	0.13	(0.02)	0.30	(0.03)	–0.05	(0.03)	**0.35**	(0.04)	–1.11	(0.01)	–0.20	(0.01)	0.43	(0.01)	1.39	(0.02)
	Switzerland	0.13	(0.02)	0.48	(0.02)	–0.23	(0.02)	**0.72**	(0.03)	–1.21	(0.02)	–0.23	(0.01)	0.49	(0.01)	1.49	(0.01)
	Turkey	0.02	(0.03)	0.10	(0.04)	–0.09	(0.04)	**0.19**	(0.04)	–1.17	(0.02)	–0.35	(0.01)	0.27	(0.01)	1.32	(0.02)
	United States	0.25	(0.02)	0.39	(0.02)	0.11	(0.02)	**0.28**	(0.03)	–1.04	(0.02)	–0.08	(0.01)	0.56	(0.01)	1.58	(0.02)
	OECD total	*0.02*	*(0.01)*	*0.17*	*(0.01)*	*–0.13*	*(0.01)*	*0.30*	*(0.01)*	*–1.25*	*(0.01)*	*–0.30*	*(0.00)*	*0.33*	*(0.01)*	*1.31*	*(0.01)*
	OECD average	*0.00*	*(0.00)*	*0.17*	*(0.00)*	*–0.17*	*(0.00)*	*0.33*	*(0.01)*	*–1.26*	*(0.00)*	*–0.32*	*(0.00)*	*0.30*	*(0.01)*	*1.27*	*(0.01)*
Partner countries	Brazil	0.04	(0.02)	0.20	(0.03)	–0.10	(0.02)	**0.30**	(0.03)	–1.02	(0.02)	–0.27	(0.01)	0.26	(0.01)	1.18	(0.02)
	Hong Kong-China	–0.26	(0.02)	–0.10	(0.03)	–0.42	(0.03)	**0.32**	(0.04)	–1.40	(0.02)	–0.53	(0.00)	–0.02	(0.01)	0.90	(0.02)
	Indonesia	0.11	(0.02)	0.17	(0.02)	0.05	(0.02)	**0.11**	(0.02)	–0.62	(0.01)	–0.15	(0.00)	0.29	(0.01)	0.91	(0.01)
	Latvia	–0.11	(0.02)	0.02	(0.03)	–0.23	(0.02)	**0.25**	(0.03)	–1.09	(0.01)	–0.37	(0.00)	0.13	(0.01)	0.91	(0.02)
	Liechtenstein	0.13	(0.05)	0.52	(0.07)	–0.28	(0.08)	**0.80**	(0.10)	–1.18	(0.06)	–0.21	(0.03)	0.48	(0.02)	1.44	(0.05)
	Macao-China	–0.20	(0.03)	0.02	(0.04)	–0.42	(0.04)	**0.44**	(0.06)	–1.32	(0.03)	–0.48	(0.01)	0.00	(0.01)	1.00	(0.04)
	Russian Federation	0.13	(0.02)	0.15	(0.03)	0.10	(0.02)	**0.05**	(0.02)	–0.77	(0.01)	–0.16	(0.00)	0.31	(0.00)	1.13	(0.01)
	Serbia	0.02	(0.02)	0.09	(0.02)	–0.04	(0.03)	**0.12**	(0.03)	–1.03	(0.02)	–0.25	(0.01)	0.26	(0.01)	1.12	(0.02)
	Thailand	–0.09	(0.01)	0.01	(0.02)	–0.17	(0.02)	**0.18**	(0.03)	–0.82	(0.01)	–0.35	(0.00)	0.10	(0.00)	0.73	(0.01)
	Tunisia	0.15	(0.02)	0.34	(0.03)	–0.04	(0.03)	**0.38**	(0.03)	–1.25	(0.01)	–0.26	(0.01)	0.51	(0.01)	1.60	(0.01)
	Uruguay	0.02	(0.02)	0.14	(0.03)	–0.10	(0.03)	**0.24**	(0.04)	–1.23	(0.02)	–0.33	(0.01)	0.30	(0.01)	1.32	(0.02)
	United Kingdom[1]	0.11	(0.02)	0.31	(0.02)	–0.06	(0.02)	**0.37**	(0.03)	–1.05	(0.01)	–0.16	(0.01)	0.41	(0.00)	1.24	(0.02)

		Performance on the mathematics scale, by national quarters of the index of self-concept in mathematics								Change in the mathematics score per unit of the index of self-concept in mathematics		Increased likelihood of students in the bottom quarter of this index scoring in the bottom quarter of the national mathematics performance distribution		Explained variance in student performance (r-squared × 100)	
		Bottom quarter		Second quarter		Third quarter		Top quarter							
		Mean score	S.E.	Mean score	S.E.	Mean score	S.E.	Mean score	S.E.	Effect	S.E.	Ratio	S.E.	%	S.E.
OECD countries	Australia	**479**	(2.8)	507	(2.2)	537	(3.0)	**579**	(3.1)	**42.3**	(1.40)	**2.0**	(0.07)	16.8	(0.99)
	Austria	**474**	(3.7)	497	(3.7)	511	(4.6)	**549**	(4.3)	**25.7**	(1.75)	**1.7**	(0.10)	8.9	(1.15)
	Belgium	**506**	(3.2)	529	(3.5)	546	(3.4)	**567**	(3.9)	**23.3**	(1.44)	**1.5**	(0.07)	4.8	(0.62)
	Canada	**490**	(2.0)	516	(2.2)	548	(2.5)	**590**	(2.1)	**35.9**	(0.78)	**2.2**	(0.08)	19.9	(0.84)
	Czech Republic	**481**	(3.6)	499	(3.6)	535	(4.2)	**575**	(3.9)	**39.8**	(1.60)	**2.1**	(0.11)	15.8	(1.07)
	Denmark	**456**	(3.0)	493	(3.7)	536	(3.5)	**578**	(3.6)	**46.5**	(1.32)	**2.8**	(0.16)	27.6	(1.32)
	Finland	**488**	(2.2)	517	(2.5)	562	(2.3)	**611**	(3.0)	**45.5**	(1.12)	**2.8**	(0.14)	33.0	(1.40)
	France	**475**	(3.2)	500	(3.4)	523	(3.9)	**552**	(4.0)	**28.3**	(1.71)	**1.9**	(0.12)	10.3	(1.21)
	Germany	**484**	(4.6)	498	(4.3)	516	(4.0)	**551**	(4.6)	**22.7**	(1.51)	**1.4**	(0.08)	7.1	(0.90)
	Greece	**400**	(3.5)	423	(4.5)	464	(4.7)	**498**	(4.5)	**42.6**	(1.88)	**2.0**	(0.12)	16.6	(1.23)
	Hungary	**471**	(3.2)	473	(3.6)	488	(3.7)	**531**	(4.8)	**28.4**	(1.99)	**1.2**	(0.08)	6.6	(0.94)
	Iceland	**461**	(3.0)	489	(3.2)	534	(3.2)	**580**	(2.8)	**39.7**	(1.15)	**2.5**	(0.14)	26.4	(1.26)
	Ireland	**467**	(3.4)	488	(3.4)	513	(3.7)	**546**	(3.9)	**34.4**	(1.77)	**1.9**	(0.14)	14.1	(1.44)
	Italy	**436**	(3.9)	448	(4.0)	476	(3.5)	**505**	(3.5)	**25.3**	(1.43)	**1.5**	(0.08)	7.1	(0.73)
	Japan	**505**	(4.8)	532	(4.7)	545	(4.7)	**558**	(5.4)	**21.2**	(1.96)	**1.6**	(0.10)	4.1	(0.72)
	Korea	**493**	(3.3)	517	(4.1)	555	(3.7)	**604**	(4.1)	**47.3**	(1.89)	**2.3**	(0.13)	21.4	(1.24)
	Luxembourg	**474**	(2.8)	478	(2.8)	498	(2.7)	**526**	(3.0)	**19.1**	(1.35)	**1.4**	(0.08)	5.3	(0.71)
	Mexico	**373**	(3.3)	378	(3.5)	387	(4.3)	**419**	(6.4)	**24.1**	(2.42)	**1.2**	(0.07)	5.4	(1.09)
	Netherlands	**518**	(4.0)	534	(4.0)	549	(4.0)	**574**	(4.1)	**22.2**	(1.75)	**1.5**	(0.10)	6.1	(0.95)
	New Zealand	**476**	(3.5)	510	(3.1)	530	(3.7)	**583**	(3.6)	**44.9**	(1.47)	**2.0**	(0.13)	17.0	(1.06)
	Norway	**435**	(2.3)	470	(2.9)	510	(3.5)	**570**	(3.2)	**46.6**	(1.16)	**2.7**	(0.14)	31.6	(1.51)
	Poland	**451**	(3.2)	464	(3.5)	497	(3.6)	**554**	(3.6)	**46.0**	(1.48)	**1.9**	(0.11)	21.6	(1.28)
	Portugal	**426**	(3.4)	449	(4.6)	478	(3.8)	**513**	(4.4)	**36.8**	(1.53)	**2.1**	(0.13)	15.4	(1.37)
	Slovak Republic	**457**	(4.0)	477	(4.6)	512	(3.0)	**551**	(5.0)	**44.5**	(1.89)	**2.2**	(0.13)	16.1	(1.63)
	Spain	**447**	(2.7)	470	(3.4)	497	(2.9)	**531**	(4.3)	**31.9**	(1.61)	**1.9**	(0.13)	13.2	(1.30)
	Sweden	**458**	(3.0)	487	(3.2)	519	(3.4)	**577**	(4.4)	**47.0**	(1.70)	**2.2**	(0.12)	24.4	(1.47)
	Switzerland	**498**	(3.8)	511	(4.7)	536	(4.4)	**564**	(4.3)	**24.2**	(1.47)	**1.6**	(0.07)	6.9	(0.80)
	Turkey	**387**	(4.5)	409	(5.6)	431	(7.1)	**484**	(11.5)	**34.8**	(4.23)	**1.6**	(0.12)	11.0	(1.77)
	United States	**443**	(3.5)	465	(3.8)	494	(3.6)	**536**	(3.9)	**35.1**	(1.54)	**1.8**	(0.09)	14.6	(1.18)
	OECD total	*465*	*(1.3)*	*474*	*(1.4)*	*494*	*(1.6)*	*532*	*(1.6)*	*25.5*	*(0.65)*	*1.4*	*(0.03)*	*6.4*	*(0.34)*
	OECD average	*467*	*(0.7)*	*482*	*(0.9)*	*509*	*(0.8)*	*550*	*(0.9)*	*32.4*	*(0.37)*	*1.7*	*(0.02)*	*10.8*	*(0.24)*
Partner countries	Brazil	**340**	(4.5)	342	(5.9)	367	(6.7)	**390**	(7.7)	**23.2**	(3.00)	1.2	(0.10)	4.3	(0.98)
	Hong Kong-China	**509**	(5.4)	534	(5.8)	562	(5.6)	**598**	(4.4)	**38.4**	(2.05)	**2.0**	(0.14)	12.1	(1.19)
	Indonesia	367	(5.5)	365	(4.4)	358	(4.0)	357	(5.3)	**–7.0**	(3.36)	**0.8**	(0.08)	0.3	(0.30)
	Latvia	**448**	(3.5)	458	(4.6)	495	(4.1)	**535**	(5.8)	**44.6**	(1.99)	**1.8**	(0.10)	16.7	(1.57)
	Liechtenstein	**516**	(9.9)	520	(11.0)	533	(13.8)	**574**	(9.1)	**24.4**	(4.76)	1.2	(0.27)	6.5	(2.45)
	Macao-China	**498**	(5.8)	507	(6.1)	530	(6.1)	**573**	(6.8)	**32.3**	(3.69)	**1.5**	(0.18)	11.7	(2.50)
	Russian Federation	**435**	(4.7)	449	(4.0)	476	(5.2)	**516**	(5.0)	**39.0**	(2.03)	**1.7**	(0.09)	10.5	(0.98)
	Serbia	**410**	(3.9)	429	(3.6)	450	(4.1)	**474**	(5.4)	**28.4**	(1.85)	**1.7**	(0.11)	8.9	(1.05)
	Thailand	**412**	(3.2)	407	(3.1)	411	(4.1)	**438**	(4.4)	**17.3**	(2.29)	1.0	(0.06)	1.8	(0.48)
	Tunisia	**337**	(2.8)	344	(3.1)	363	(3.5)	**395**	(4.3)	**20.1**	(1.49)	**1.3**	(0.08)	7.6	(0.97)
	Uruguay	**383**	(3.7)	409	(3.7)	436	(4.3)	**474**	(4.3)	**35.0**	(1.53)	**1.9**	(0.09)	12.9	(1.11)
	United Kingdom[1]	**472**	(3.6)	489	(2.9)	514	(3.9)	**560**	(3.2)	**37.7**	(1.49)	**1.8**	(0.10)	14.4	(1.06)

Note: Values that are statistically significant are indicated in bold (see Annex A4).

1. Response rate too low to ensure comparability (see Annex A3).

Table 3.7
Index of self-efficacy in mathematics and performance on the mathematics scale, by national quarters of the index

Results based on students' self-reports

		Index of self-efficacy in mathematics														
		All students		Males		Females		Gender difference (M – F)		Bottom quarter		Second quarter		Third quarter		Top quarter	
		Mean index	S.E.	Mean index	S.E.	Mean index	S.E.	Dif.	S.E.	Mean index	S.E.	Mean index	S.E.	Mean index	S.E.	Mean index	S.E.
OECD countries	Australia	0.10	(0.02)	0.28	(0.03)	–0.09	(0.02)	**0.37**	(0.03)	–0.97	(0.01)	–0.31	(0.00)	0.22	(0.01)	1.47	(0.02)
	Austria	0.16	(0.02)	0.39	(0.03)	–0.07	(0.03)	**0.46**	(0.03)	–1.00	(0.02)	–0.21	(0.01)	0.37	(0.01)	1.48	(0.02)
	Belgium	–0.04	(0.02)	0.12	(0.02)	–0.22	(0.02)	**0.35**	(0.03)	–1.11	(0.02)	–0.40	(0.00)	0.11	(0.00)	1.23	(0.02)
	Canada	0.25	(0.02)	0.44	(0.02)	0.07	(0.02)	**0.37**	(0.03)	–0.93	(0.01)	–0.20	(0.00)	0.42	(0.01)	1.71	(0.02)
	Czech Republic	0.16	(0.02)	0.35	(0.03)	–0.04	(0.02)	**0.39**	(0.03)	–0.88	(0.01)	–0.23	(0.00)	0.34	(0.01)	1.41	(0.02)
	Denmark	–0.07	(0.02)	0.15	(0.02)	–0.27	(0.02)	**0.42**	(0.03)	–1.11	(0.02)	–0.43	(0.00)	0.10	(0.01)	1.17	(0.02)
	Finland	–0.15	(0.02)	0.12	(0.02)	–0.42	(0.02)	**0.53**	(0.03)	–1.21	(0.02)	–0.52	(0.00)	0.01	(0.01)	1.11	(0.02)
	France	–0.01	(0.02)	0.15	(0.04)	–0.15	(0.02)	**0.29**	(0.04)	–1.07	(0.02)	–0.38	(0.00)	0.15	(0.01)	1.28	(0.02)
	Germany	0.15	(0.02)	0.39	(0.03)	–0.07	(0.02)	**0.45**	(0.04)	–0.97	(0.02)	–0.21	(0.01)	0.35	(0.01)	1.44	(0.02)
	Greece	–0.26	(0.02)	–0.06	(0.03)	–0.45	(0.02)	**0.39**	(0.03)	–1.28	(0.02)	–0.56	(0.00)	–0.07	(0.00)	0.86	(0.02)
	Hungary	0.36	(0.02)	0.52	(0.03)	0.17	(0.03)	**0.35**	(0.03)	–0.71	(0.01)	–0.13	(0.00)	0.51	(0.01)	1.75	(0.02)
	Iceland	0.04	(0.02)	0.17	(0.03)	–0.10	(0.03)	**0.28**	(0.04)	–1.24	(0.03)	–0.36	(0.01)	0.23	(0.01)	1.51	(0.02)
	Ireland	–0.03	(0.02)	0.11	(0.02)	–0.17	(0.03)	**0.28**	(0.04)	–1.07	(0.02)	–0.39	(0.00)	0.13	(0.01)	1.22	(0.02)
	Italy	–0.11	(0.02)	0.05	(0.03)	–0.25	(0.02)	**0.30**	(0.03)	–0.99	(0.02)	–0.41	(0.00)	0.00	(0.00)	0.98	(0.02)
	Japan	–0.53	(0.04)	–0.35	(0.05)	–0.69	(0.03)	**0.33**	(0.06)	–1.77	(0.03)	–0.76	(0.00)	–0.30	(0.00)	0.73	(0.04)
	Korea	–0.42	(0.02)	–0.34	(0.03)	–0.54	(0.04)	**0.19**	(0.05)	–1.48	(0.02)	–0.73	(0.00)	–0.29	(0.00)	0.83	(0.03)
	Luxembourg	0.10	(0.02)	0.33	(0.03)	–0.12	(0.02)	**0.45**	(0.03)	–1.07	(0.02)	–0.29	(0.00)	0.27	(0.01)	1.49	(0.02)
	Mexico	–0.22	(0.02)	–0.14	(0.02)	–0.30	(0.03)	**0.15**	(0.03)	–1.15	(0.01)	–0.56	(0.00)	–0.09	(0.00)	0.91	(0.02)
	Netherlands	–0.09	(0.02)	0.17	(0.02)	–0.37	(0.02)	**0.53**	(0.03)	–1.09	(0.03)	–0.42	(0.00)	0.03	(0.01)	1.11	(0.03)
	New Zealand	0.01	(0.02)	0.19	(0.02)	–0.17	(0.02)	**0.36**	(0.03)	–1.02	(0.02)	–0.40	(0.00)	0.11	(0.01)	1.34	(0.02)
	Norway	–0.04	(0.02)	0.15	(0.03)	–0.24	(0.03)	**0.40**	(0.04)	–1.28	(0.02)	–0.43	(0.01)	0.16	(0.01)	1.37	(0.02)
	Poland	0.05	(0.02)	0.12	(0.03)	–0.03	(0.02)	**0.16**	(0.03)	–0.93	(0.01)	–0.34	(0.00)	0.14	(0.01)	1.32	(0.02)
	Portugal	–0.06	(0.02)	0.05	(0.02)	–0.15	(0.03)	**0.20**	(0.03)	–0.95	(0.02)	–0.39	(0.00)	0.05	(0.01)	1.06	(0.02)
	Slovak Republic	0.39	(0.03)	0.55	(0.04)	0.22	(0.03)	**0.33**	(0.04)	–0.73	(0.03)	–0.04	(0.00)	0.60	(0.01)	1.73	(0.02)
	Spain	–0.04	(0.02)	0.09	(0.03)	–0.16	(0.02)	**0.25**	(0.03)	–1.02	(0.02)	–0.33	(0.00)	0.09	(0.00)	1.10	(0.02)
	Sweden	0.03	(0.03)	0.17	(0.03)	–0.10	(0.03)	**0.27**	(0.04)	–1.09	(0.02)	–0.38	(0.00)	0.21	(0.01)	1.39	(0.02)
	Switzerland	0.32	(0.03)	0.59	(0.04)	0.04	(0.03)	**0.55**	(0.04)	–0.84	(0.02)	–0.08	(0.01)	0.56	(0.01)	1.67	(0.02)
	Turkey	–0.18	(0.05)	–0.05	(0.06)	–0.33	(0.05)	**0.28**	(0.05)	–1.42	(0.02)	–0.51	(0.00)	0.00	(0.01)	1.22	(0.05)
	United States	0.27	(0.02)	0.37	(0.03)	0.16	(0.03)	**0.21**	(0.03)	–0.88	(0.02)	–0.18	(0.00)	0.39	(0.01)	1.73	(0.02)
	OECD total	*–0.02*	*(0.01)*	*0.12*	*(0.01)*	*–0.16*	*(0.01)*	*0.28*	*(0.01)*	*–1.15*	*(0.01)*	*–0.39*	*(0.00)*	*0.12*	*(0.00)*	*1.35*	*(0.01)*
	OECD average	*0.00*	*(0.00)*	*0.17*	*(0.01)*	*–0.17*	*(0.01)*	*0.34*	*(0.01)*	*–1.11*	*(0.00)*	*–0.38*	*(0.00)*	*0.15*	*(0.01)*	*1.33*	*(0.01)*
Partner countries	Brazil	–0.38	(0.02)	–0.23	(0.03)	–0.50	(0.03)	**0.27**	(0.03)	–1.34	(0.02)	0.68	(0.00)	–0.23	(0.01)	0.74	(0.03)
	Hong Kong-China	0.11	(0.03)	0.26	(0.04)	–0.04	(0.03)	**0.30**	(0.05)	–1.02	(0.02)	–0.27	(0.00)	0.29	(0.01)	1.44	(0.03)
	Indonesia	–0.31	(0.01)	–0.28	(0.02)	–0.33	(0.02)	**0.05**	(0.02)	–0.95	(0.01)	–0.53	(0.00)	–0.22	(0.00)	0.48	(0.02)
	Latvia	–0.11	(0.03)	0.04	(0.04)	–0.24	(0.02)	**0.28**	(0.03)	–0.95	(0.02)	–0.43	(0.00)	–0.03	(0.01)	0.98	(0.03)
	Liechtenstein	0.53	(0.05)	0.85	(0.07)	0.20	(0.07)	**0.64**	(0.10)	–0.64	(0.04)	0.13	(0.02)	0.77	(0.02)	1.89	(0.07)
	Macao-China	0.08	(0.03)	0.25	(0.05)	–0.09	(0.04)	**0.34**	(0.06)	–0.87	(0.02)	–0.29	(0.01)	0.19	(0.01)	1.28	(0.04)
	Russian Federation	–0.08	(0.02)	0.06	(0.04)	–0.22	(0.02)	**0.28**	(0.03)	–0.97	(0.01)	–0.42	(0.00)	0.00	(0.00)	1.07	(0.03)
	Serbia	–0.02	(0.03)	0.11	(0.03)	–0.14	(0.03)	**0.25**	(0.03)	–1.02	(0.02)	–0.36	(0.00)	0.11	(0.01)	1.18	(0.03)
	Thailand	–0.52	(0.02)	–0.47	(0.02)	–0.57	(0.03)	**0.10**	(0.03)	–1.41	(0.02)	–0.79	(0.00)	–0.33	(0.00)	0.45	(0.02)
	Tunisia	–0.29	(0.02)	0.16	(0.03)	–0.43	(0.03)	**0.27**	(0.03)	–1.41	(0.02)	–0.63	(0.00)	–0.11	(0.01)	0.97	(0.02)
	Uruguay	0.02	(0.02)	0.17	(0.03)	–0.12	(0.02)	**0.29**	(0.03)	–1.01	(0.02)	–0.34	(0.00)	0.17	(0.01)	1.26	(0.02)
	United Kingdom[1]	–0.11	(0.02)	0.09	(0.03)	–0.28	(0.03)	**0.37**	(0.04)	–1.15	(0.02)	–0.53	(0.00)	0.00	(0.01)	1.23	(0.02)

		Performance on the mathematics scale, by national quarters of the index of self-efficacy in mathematics								Change in the mathematics score per unit of the index of self-efficacy in mathematics		Increased likelihood of students in the bottom quarter of this index scoring in the bottom quarter of the national mathematics performance distribution		Explained variance in student performance (r-squared × 100)	
		Bottom quarter		Second quarter		Third quarter		Top quarter							
		Mean score	S.E.	Mean score	S.E.	Mean score	S.E.	Mean score	S.E.	Effect	S.E.	Ratio	S.E.	%	S.E.
OECD countries	Australia	**461**	(2.5)	507	(2.5)	541	(2.2)	**593**	(2.9)	**49.6**	(1.28)	**2.9**	(0.11)	27.3	(1.18)
	Austria	**449**	(3.4)	488	(3.5)	523	(3.4)	**571**	(4.5)	**45.5**	(1.80)	**2.8**	(0.14)	24.6	(1.67)
	Belgium	**471**	(3.5)	526	(3.1)	559	(3.0)	**590**	(2.7)	**45.2**	(1.52)	**2.8**	(0.13)	17.7	(0.98)
	Canada	**475**	(2.0)	516	(2.2)	555	(1.9)	**599**	(1.9)	**43.8**	(0.77)	**3.0**	(0.12)	28.9	(0.99)
	Czech Republic	**454**	(3.7)	502	(3.5)	543	(3.6)	**591**	(3.4)	**55.5**	(1.54)	**3.3**	(0.21)	31.0	(1.30)
	Denmark	**449**	(3.0)	498	(3.2)	536	(3.6)	**579**	(3.5)	**50.8**	(1.80)	**3.3**	(0.16)	27.4	(1.39)
	Finland	**488**	(2.5)	527	(2.3)	559	(2.3)	**606**	(3.0)	**45.9**	(1.41)	**2.9**	(0.16)	27.5	(1.50)
	France	**451**	(3.8)	497	(3.0)	528	(3.6)	**574**	(3.1)	**47.4**	(1.72)	**3.1**	(0.18)	25.4	(1.42)
	Germany	**442**	(3.7)	497	(3.8)	537	(4.1)	**574**	(3.9)	**50.2**	(1.86)	**3.1**	(0.22)	25.8	(1.59)
	Greece	**394**	(3.8)	433	(4.0)	461	(4.0)	**500**	(4.8)	**45.5**	(2.13)	**2.5**	(0.15)	18.4	(1.35)
	Hungary	**420**	(3.5)	471	(3.1)	510	(3.1)	**560**	(3.9)	**52.6**	(1.74)	**3.5**	(0.24)	31.0	(1.58)
	Iceland	**453**	(3.1)	498	(2.7)	537	(2.8)	**577**	(2.6)	**40.2**	(1.33)	**3.1**	(0.19)	25.3	(1.36)
	Ireland	**446**	(2.6)	488	(3.0)	515	(3.1)	**565**	(3.1)	**47.5**	(1.32)	**3.1**	(0.21)	28.0	(1.43)
	Italy	**407**	(4.7)	449	(3.1)	482	(3.0)	**525**	(3.8)	**52.4**	(2.24)	**2.7**	(0.15)	20.8	(1.51)
	Japan	**452**	(4.8)	519	(3.4)	559	(3.2)	**609**	(5.3)	**54.9**	(2.06)	**3.9**	(0.23)	34.3	(2.21)
	Korea	**469**	(3.6)	524	(2.8)	559	(2.8)	**617**	(4.2)	**54.0**	(1.71)	**3.6**	(0.18)	33.2	(1.48)
	Luxembourg	**436**	(2.3)	481	(2.6)	509	(2.6)	**552**	(2.7)	**40.5**	(1.37)	**2.8**	(0.13)	21.8	(1.18)
	Mexico	**353**	(4.0)	376	(3.7)	391	(3.9)	**426**	(4.8)	**30.9**	(2.20)	**1.7**	(0.09)	9.5	(1.20)
	Netherlands	**490**	(4.2)	529	(3.8)	554	(3.8)	**602**	(3.4)	**44.6**	(1.99)	**2.8**	(0.22)	20.8	(1.42)
	New Zealand	**464**	(3.4)	503	(3.2)	535	(3.5)	**597**	(3.0)	**52.0**	(1.44)	**2.4**	(0.14)	27.1	(1.17)
	Norway	**431**	(2.6)	474	(3.3)	516	(2.9)	**565**	(3.6)	**46.8**	(1.49)	**2.9**	(0.17)	30.4	(1.58)
	Poland	**426**	(2.8)	471	(3.2)	505	(3.1)	**562**	(3.0)	**53.3**	(1.98)	**3.1**	(0.17)	29.9	(1.52)
	Portugal	**407**	(4.0)	448	(4.0)	479	(3.5)	**532**	(3.3)	**55.3**	(1.92)	**3.0**	(0.19)	28.1	(1.56)
	Slovak Republic	**424**	(4.3)	479	(3.2)	522	(2.8)	**570**	(2.9)	**55.0**	(1.99)	**4.0**	(0.20)	34.8	(1.61)
	Spain	**434**	(2.6)	470	(2.9)	503	(2.7)	**539**	(3.0)	**42.7**	(1.46)	**2.6**	(0.13)	19.4	(1.00)
	Sweden	**443**	(3.0)	485	(2.8)	528	(3.3)	**583**	(3.6)	**52.8**	(1.65)	**3.1**	(0.19)	31.8	(1.57)
	Switzerland	**456**	(3.1)	505	(3.0)	552	(3.3)	**595**	(5.4)	**53.2**	(2.33)	**3.3**	(0.19)	29.8	(2.27)
	Turkey	**366**	(3.8)	405	(5.1)	432	(6.3)	**503**	(13.5)	**48.6**	(5.07)	**2.2**	(0.20)	25.7	(4.11)
	United States	**425**	(2.9)	457	(2.7)	502	(3.4)	**551**	(3.9)	**46.7**	(1.30)	**2.5**	(0.13)	27.4	(1.38)
	OECD total	*434*	*(1.4)*	*472*	*(1.3)*	*502*	*(1.4)*	*555*	*(1.7)*	*44.4*	*(0.71)*	*2.3*	*(0.05)*	*19.8*	*(0.58)*
	OECD average	*441*	*(0.8)*	*482*	*(0.7)*	*516*	*(0.8)*	*567*	*(0.9)*	*47.2*	*(0.42)*	*2.6*	*(0.03)*	*22.7*	*(0.34)*
Partner countries	Brazil	**318**	(4.3)	348	(4.0)	369	(5.1)	**401**	(9.2)	**35.1**	(4.44)	**1.7**	(0.13)	9.4	(2.15)
	Hong Kong-China	**471**	(5.7)	538	(4.3)	575	(3.5)	**619**	(4.0)	**54.5**	(2.18)	**3.9**	(0.25)	31.0	(1.71)
	Indonesia	**347**	(4.5)	364	(3.8)	363	(4.3)	**371**	(6.1)	**13.6**	(3.70)	1.2	(0.09)	1.1	(0.54)
	Latvia	**428**	(3.1)	465	(4.3)	497	(3.4)	**545**	(4.7)	**53.8**	(2.41)	**2.7**	(0.27)	24.8	(1.88)
	Liechtenstein	**461**	(10.3)	515	(11.0)	566	(9.3)	**600**	(10.2)	**52.9**	(5.46)	**3.2**	(0.52)	28.0	(4.80)
	Macao-China	**478**	(6.1)	517	(6.3)	536	(6.0)	**579**	(6.0)	**43.1**	(3.43)	**2.2**	(0.25)	19.3	(2.91)
	Russian Federation	**418**	(4.6)	453	(4.1)	481	(4.3)	**525**	(5.2)	**47.1**	(2.03)	**2.4**	(0.14)	19.0	(1.39)
	Serbia	**402**	(3.4)	428	(3.5)	452	(4.2)	**478**	(6.1)	**30.7**	(2.48)	**2.0**	(0.13)	11.4	(1.68)
	Thailand	**387**	(2.9)	403	(3.8)	425	(4.0)	**454**	(4.9)	**33.5**	(2.42)	**1.5**	(0.09)	10.2	(1.30)
	Tunisia	**323**	(2.6)	344	(3.2)	368	(2.9)	**406**	(5.4)	**30.9**	(2.29)	**1.9**	(0.11)	13.7	(1.80)
	Uruguay	**375**	(3.6)	411	(3.3)	438	(4.2)	**478**	(4.9)	**41.9**	(1.73)	**2.1**	(0.11)	15.8	(1.10)
	United Kingdom[1]	**446**	(3.1)	484	(3.0)	523	(3.2)	**582**	(3.0)	**51.1**	(1.62)	**3.0**	(0.18)	30.1	(1.35)

Note: Values that are statistically significant are indicated in bold (see Annex A4).
1. Response rate too low to ensure comparability (see Annex A3).

Table 3.8
Index of anxiety in mathematics and performance on the mathematics scale, by national quarters of the index
Results based on students' self-reports

	Index of anxiety in mathematics															
	All students		Males		Females		Gender difference (M – F)		Bottom quarter		Second quarter		Third quarter		Top quarter	
	Mean index	S.E.	Mean index	S.E.	Mean index	S.E.	Dif.	S.E.	Mean index	S.E.	Mean index	S.E.	Mean index	S.E.	Mean index	S.E.
OECD countries																
Australia	–0.05	(0.01)	–0.19	(0.02)	0.09	(0.02)	**–0.28**	(0.02)	–1.13	(0.02)	–0.29	(0.00)	0.21	(0.00)	0.99	(0.01)
Austria	–0.27	(0.02)	–0.47	(0.03)	–0.06	(0.03)	**–0.42**	(0.04)	–1.77	(0.02)	–0.61	(0.01)	0.12	(0.01)	1.18	(0.02)
Belgium	0.09	(0.02)	–0.06	(0.02)	0.24	(0.02)	**–0.30**	(0.02)	–1.09	(0.02)	–0.14	(0.00)	0.36	(0.00)	1.22	(0.01)
Canada	–0.04	(0.01)	–0.23	(0.02)	0.13	(0.02)	**–0.36**	(0.02)	–1.42	(0.02)	–0.30	(0.00)	0.30	(0.00)	1.24	(0.01)
Czech Republic	–0.05	(0.02)	–0.16	(0.02)	0.07	(0.03)	**–0.23**	(0.03)	–1.13	(0.02)	–0.31	(0.00)	0.22	(0.00)	1.05	(0.02)
Denmark	–0.46	(0.02)	–0.66	(0.03)	–0.26	(0.03)	**–0.40**	(0.03)	–1.87	(0.02)	–0.65	(0.01)	–0.10	(0.01)	0.81	(0.02)
Finland	–0.31	(0.01)	–0.49	(0.02)	–0.14	(0.02)	**–0.35**	(0.02)	–1.47	(0.02)	–0.51	(0.00)	–0.02	(0.00)	0.74	(0.01)
France	0.34	(0.02)	0.15	(0.02)	0.51	(0.02)	**–0.35**	(0.03)	–0.81	(0.02)	0.11	(0.01)	0.64	(0.01)	1.43	(0.02)
Germany	–0.25	(0.02)	–0.48	(0.03)	–0.03	(0.03)	**–0.44**	(0.04)	–1.79	(0.02)	–0.59	(0.01)	0.15	(0.01)	1.20	(0.02)
Greece	0.16	(0.02)	0.03	(0.03)	0.28	(0.03)	**–0.25**	(0.03)	–1.06	(0.02)	–0.07	(0.01)	0.51	(0.01)	1.28	(0.01)
Hungary	–0.01	(0.02)	–0.09	(0.02)	0.08	(0.02)	**–0.17**	(0.03)	–1.13	(0.02)	–0.22	(0.01)	0.26	(0.00)	1.06	(0.02)
Iceland	–0.20	(0.02)	–0.34	(0.02)	–0.06	(0.03)	**–0.29**	(0.04)	–1.62	(0.02)	–0.43	(0.01)	0.15	(0.01)	1.08	(0.02)
Ireland	0.07	(0.02)	–0.06	(0.02)	0.20	(0.03)	**–0.27**	(0.03)	–1.06	(0.03)	–0.18	(0.01)	0.32	(0.01)	1.20	(0.02)
Italy	0.29	(0.01)	0.21	(0.02)	0.35	(0.02)	**–0.14**	(0.02)	–0.79	(0.02)	0.08	(0.00)	0.58	(0.00)	1.27	(0.01)
Japan	0.44	(0.02)	0.31	(0.03)	0.57	(0.02)	**–0.26**	(0.03)	–0.76	(0.02)	0.12	(0.01)	0.70	(0.01)	1.73	(0.02)
Korea	0.41	(0.01)	0.37	(0.02)	0.48	(0.02)	**–0.12**	(0.03)	–0.60	(0.01)	0.21	(0.00)	0.64	(0.00)	1.40	(0.02)
Luxembourg	–0.01	(0.02)	–0.26	(0.02)	0.23	(0.02)	**–0.50**	(0.03)	–1.50	(0.02)	–0.30	(0.01)	0.39	(0.01)	1.37	(0.02)
Mexico	0.47	(0.02)	0.42	(0.02)	0.52	(0.02)	**–0.10**	(0.02)	–0.44	(0.02)	0.28	(0.00)	0.70	(0.00)	1.35	(0.01)
Netherlands	–0.38	(0.02)	–0.54	(0.03)	–0.21	(0.02)	**–0.33**	(0.03)	–1.52	(0.02)	–0.51	(0.00)	–0.13	(0.01)	0.64	(0.02)
New Zealand	–0.10	(0.02)	–0.23	(0.02)	0.04	(0.02)	**–0.27**	(0.03)	–1.20	(0.02)	–0.30	(0.00)	0.18	(0.01)	0.94	(0.02)
Norway	–0.05	(0.02)	–0.25	(0.03)	0.14	(0.03)	**–0.39**	(0.04)	–1.45	(0.02)	–0.33	(0.00)	0.31	(0.01)	1.26	(0.02)
Poland	0.04	(0.02)	0.02	(0.02)	0.05	(0.02)	–0.03	(0.03)	–1.17	(0.02)	–0.16	(0.01)	0.37	(0.01)	1.11	(0.02)
Portugal	0.15	(0.02)	0.06	(0.02)	0.24	(0.03)	**–0.18**	(0.03)	–0.90	(0.02)	–0.03	(0.01)	0.40	(0.01)	1.14	(0.02)
Slovak Republic	0.04	(0.02)	–0.06	(0.02)	0.15	(0.02)	**–0.21**	(0.03)	–0.99	(0.02)	–0.21	(0.00)	0.30	(0.00)	1.07	(0.02)
Spain	0.28	(0.01)	0.13	(0.02)	0.42	(0.02)	**–0.29**	(0.03)	–0.79	(0.02)	0.07	(0.01)	0.54	(0.00)	1.30	(0.01)
Sweden	–0.49	(0.02)	–0.64	(0.02)	–0.34	(0.03)	**–0.30**	(0.03)	–1.82	(0.02)	–0.66	(0.01)	–0.17	(0.01)	0.68	(0.01)
Switzerland	–0.29	(0.02)	–0.52	(0.02)	–0.05	(0.03)	**–0.47**	(0.03)	–1.71	(0.02)	–0.56	(0.01)	0.08	(0.01)	1.03	(0.02)
Turkey	0.34	(0.03)	0.25	(0.04)	0.45	(0.04)	**–0.20**	(0.04)	–0.97	(0.02)	0.10	(0.01)	0.68	(0.01)	1.55	(0.02)
United States	–0.10	(0.02)	–0.22	(0.02)	0.03	(0.02)	**–0.25**	(0.03)	–1.51	(0.02)	–0.34	(0.00)	0.26	(0.01)	1.21	(0.02)
OECD total	*0.10*	*(0.01)*	*–0.03*	*(0.01)*	*0.22*	*(0.01)*	***–0.25***	*(0.01)*	*–1.20*	*(0.01)*	*–0.15*	*(0.00)*	*0.43*	*(0.00)*	*1.30*	*(0.01)*
OECD average	*0.00*	*(0.00)*	*–0.14*	*(0.00)*	*0.14*	*(0.00)*	***–0.28***	*(0.01)*	*–1.28*	*(0.00)*	*–0.24*	*(0.00)*	*0.33*	*(0.01)*	*1.19*	*(0.01)*
Partner countries																
Brazil	0.57	(0.02)	0.43	(0.02)	0.69	(0.02)	**–0.25**	(0.02)	–0.36	(0.01)	0.30	(0.00)	0.78	(0.00)	1.57	(0.02)
Hong Kong-China	0.23	(0.02)	0.11	(0.03)	0.36	(0.02)	**–0.25**	(0.03)	–0.86	(0.02)	0.00	(0.00)	0.49	(0.00)	1.31	(0.02)
Indonesia	0.34	(0.01)	0.29	(0.01)	0.38	(0.02)	**–0.09**	(0.02)	–0.47	(0.02)	0.19	(0.00)	0.55	(0.00)	1.09	(0.01)
Latvia	0.12	(0.02)	0.02	(0.02)	0.22	(0.02)	**–0.20**	(0.03)	–0.87	(0.02)	–0.04	(0.00)	0.36	(0.01)	1.04	(0.01)
Liechtenstein	–0.35	(0.05)	–0.64	(0.07)	–0.06	(0.08)	**–0.58**	(0.10)	–1.64	(0.06)	–0.54	(0.02)	–0.02	(0.02)	0.80	(0.05)
Macao-China	0.24	(0.04)	0.00	(0.05)	0.46	(0.04)	**–0.45**	(0.07)	–1.00	(0.05)	–0.03	(0.01)	0.59	(0.01)	1.40	(0.03)
Russian Federation	0.14	(0.01)	0.08	(0.02)	0.21	(0.02)	**–0.13**	(0.02)	–0.85	(0.02)	–0.04	(0.00)	0.40	(0.01)	1.06	(0.01)
Serbia	0.28	(0.03)	0.30	(0.03)	0.26	(0.03)	0.04	(0.04)	–0.92	(0.02)	0.01	(0.01)	0.59	(0.01)	1.44	(0.02)
Thailand	0.49	(0.01)	0.44	(0.02)	0.52	(0.02)	**–0.08**	(0.02)	–0.37	(0.02)	0.29	(0.00)	0.74	(0.00)	1.29	(0.01)
Tunisia	0.62	(0.02)	0.46	(0.02)	0.77	(0.02)	**–0.32**	(0.03)	–0.51	(0.02)	0.39	(0.01)	0.88	(0.00)	1.71	(0.01)
Uruguay	0.30	(0.02)	0.21	(0.02)	0.39	(0.02)	**–0.18**	(0.03)	–0.82	(0.02)	0.09	(0.01)	0.58	(0.01)	1.36	(0.01)
United Kingdom[1]	–0.08	(0.02)	–0.27	(0.02)	0.09	(0.02)	**–0.35**	(0.03)	–1.23	(0.02)	–0.30	(0.00)	0.20	(0.01)	1.02	(0.01)

	Performance on the mathematics scale, by national quarters of the index of anxiety in mathematics								Change in the mathematics score per unit of the index of anxiety in mathematics		Increased likelihood of students in the top quarter of this index scoring in the bottom quarter of the national mathematics performance distribution		Explained variance in student performance (r-squared × 100)	
	Bottom quarter		Second quarter		Third quarter		Top quarter							
	Mean score	S.E.	Mean score	S.E.	Mean score	S.E.	Mean score	S.E.	Effect	S.E.	Ratio	S.E.	%	S.E.
OECD countries														
Australia	**569**	(3.2)	536	(2.4)	515	(2.5)	**483**	(3.3)	**–37.8**	(1.50)	**2.1**	(0.10)	12.4	(0.85)
Austria	**545**	(5.0)	518	(4.1)	496	(4.0)	**470**	(3.7)	**–25.1**	(1.67)	**1.8**	(0.11)	9.8	(1.25)
Belgium	**568**	(3.4)	552	(3.6)	529	(3.2)	**499**	(3.5)	**–26.1**	(1.72)	**1.8**	(0.09)	5.6	(0.71)
Canada	**584**	(2.0)	545	(2.3)	522	(2.4)	**493**	(2.1)	**–32.6**	(0.81)	**2.1**	(0.07)	16.0	(0.72)
Czech Republic	**574**	(3.7)	538	(3.9)	507	(3.8)	**472**	(3.9)	**–42.1**	(1.88)	**2.5**	(0.14)	16.8	(1.15)
Denmark	**578**	(3.5)	532	(3.1)	497	(3.6)	**455**	(3.5)	**–44.6**	(1.50)	**2.8**	(0.16)	26.5	(1.48)
Finland	**594**	(3.1)	556	(2.7)	530	(2.5)	**499**	(2.6)	**–41.9**	(1.53)	**2.3**	(0.11)	19.7	(1.23)
France	**540**	(3.5)	527	(3.6)	502	(3.0)	**482**	(3.8)	**–25.0**	(1.68)	**1.6**	(0.11)	6.4	(0.82)
Germany	**556**	(4.0)	525	(3.7)	497	(4.2)	**471**	(5.1)	**–28.1**	(1.42)	**1.8**	(0.10)	11.6	(1.06)
Greece	**496**	(4.7)	457	(4.5)	424	(4.1)	**408**	(3.5)	**–34.5**	(1.75)	**1.7**	(0.10)	12.4	(1.20)
Hungary	**534**	(4.6)	499	(4.0)	475	(3.5)	**455**	(3.7)	**–33.2**	(1.83)	**1.9**	(0.12)	10.1	(1.09)
Iceland	**568**	(2.8)	526	(3.3)	500	(3.7)	**470**	(3.1)	**–33.4**	(1.36)	**2.1**	(0.12)	15.9	(1.22)
Ireland	**541**	(4.2)	513	(3.8)	495	(4.1)	**465**	(3.0)	**–32.9**	(1.65)	**2.0**	(0.14)	13.2	(1.29)
Italy	**505**	(3.8)	479	(3.6)	451	(3.8)	**431**	(4.0)	**–33.2**	(1.70)	**1.8**	(0.09)	8.6	(0.85)
Japan	**548**	(6.2)	547	(4.4)	531	(4.4)	**514**	(4.7)	**–14.3**	(2.06)	**1.4**	(0.08)	2.1	(0.59)
Korea	**571**	(4.6)	547	(3.9)	530	(4.0)	**521**	(3.4)	**–24.5**	(1.66)	**1.3**	(0.07)	4.8	(0.64)
Luxembourg	**531**	(2.8)	505	(2.9)	482	(2.8)	**458**	(3.2)	**–25.0**	(1.43)	**2.0**	(0.12)	9.8	(1.04)
Mexico	**422**	(6.0)	392	(4.1)	377	(3.2)	**359**	(3.7)	**–34.0**	(2.61)	**1.6**	(0.10)	8.6	(1.32)
Netherlands	**568**	(4.2)	551	(4.5)	541	(4.1)	**515**	(4.3)	**–22.6**	(2.32)	**1.7**	(0.11)	4.9	(0.95)
New Zealand	**581**	(3.0)	539	(3.3)	508	(3.2)	**473**	(4.0)	**–48.0**	(1.56)	**2.2**	(0.15)	19.2	(1.12)
Norway	**558**	(3.5)	513	(3.1)	474	(3.1)	**441**	(2.9)	**–42.1**	(1.22)	**2.4**	(0.15)	24.5	(1.42)
Poland	**554**	(3.4)	503	(3.5)	466	(3.3)	**441**	(2.9)	**–46.4**	(1.53)	**2.4**	(0.14)	24.0	(1.24)
Portugal	**506**	(4.2)	472	(4.1)	458	(4.4)	**431**	(3.9)	**–34.2**	(1.81)	**1.9**	(0.11)	10.7	(1.10)
Slovak Republic	**547**	(4.1)	511	(3.9)	490	(3.1)	**447**	(4.7)	**–44.8**	(1.71)	**2.6**	(0.14)	16.7	(1.40)
Spain	**519**	(4.0)	497	(3.4)	474	(2.9)	**455**	(2.7)	**–26.7**	(1.79)	**1.6**	(0.09)	6.9	(0.88)
Sweden	**568**	(3.3)	520	(3.8)	494	(3.5)	**458**	(3.8)	**–42.8**	(1.69)	**2.3**	(0.14)	19.9	(1.21)
Switzerland	**568**	(5.2)	539	(4.7)	517	(4.1)	**486**	(3.6)	**–28.9**	(1.73)	**1.9**	(0.11)	10.1	(1.03)
Turkey	**484**	(11.5)	433	(6.6)	401	(5.3)	**389**	(5.6)	**–34.6**	(4.01)	**1.6**	(0.11)	11.7	(1.79)
United States	**537**	(4.1)	495	(3.3)	470	(3.8)	**436**	(3.5)	**–34.4**	(1.52)	**2.1**	(0.10)	15.7	(1.21)
OECD total	***537***	*(1.4)*	*502*	*(1.3)*	*474*	*(1.4)*	***452***	*(1.5)*	***–31.9***	*(0.61)*	***1.8***	*(0.04)*	*10.1*	*(0.34)*
OECD average	***550***	*(0.8)*	*515*	*(0.7)*	*486*	*(0.8)*	***458***	*(0.9)*	***–35.3***	*(0.37)*	***2.0***	*(0.02)*	*12.7*	*(0.22)*
Partner countries														
Brazil	**407**	(7.4)	371	(5.8)	342	(4.5)	**317**	(4.5)	**–44.0**	(3.70)	**1.8**	(0.12)	12.1	(1.56)
Hong Kong-China	**592**	(4.5)	560	(5.8)	537	(5.7)	**514**	(5.8)	**–31.5**	(2.37)	**1.8**	(0.13)	7.9	(1.09)
Indonesia	**368**	(5.5)	371	(4.4)	360	(4.2)	**348**	(4.4)	**–13.0**	(2.85)	**1.2**	(0.07)	1.1	(0.46)
Latvia	**538**	(5.3)	493	(4.1)	465	(3.9)	**440**	(3.6)	**–47.3**	(2.27)	**2.2**	(0.14)	17.6	(1.57)
Liechtenstein	**588**	(9.3)	536	(11.3)	517	(10.2)	**500**	(11.0)	**–34.3**	(5.40)	1.6	(0.33)	11.0	(3.16)
Macao-China	**566**	(7.4)	532	(5.9)	511	(5.7)	**501**	(5.7)	**–27.6**	(3.68)	**1.5**	(0.20)	9.7	(2.49)
Russian Federation	**517**	(5.1)	479	(4.9)	454	(4.2)	**425**	(4.2)	**–44.1**	(1.87)	**2.1**	(0.13)	14.4	(1.03)
Serbia	**481**	(4.4)	454	(3.7)	422	(3.6)	**399**	(4.3)	**–31.9**	(1.69)	**2.2**	(0.13)	13.7	(1.22)
Thailand	**435**	(4.3)	417	(3.8)	407	(4.0)	**410**	(3.7)	**–15.2**	(2.26)	1.1	(0.08)	1.6	(0.50)
Tunisia	**374**	(4.2)	362	(3.2)	358	(3.3)	**344**	(3.0)	**–12.4**	(1.68)	1.2	(0.08)	1.8	(0.48)
Uruguay	**474**	(5.0)	435	(4.8)	407	(4.2)	**382**	(3.5)	**–39.7**	(1.97)	**1.9**	(0.11)	12.7	(1.11)
United Kingdom[1]	**551**	(3.2)	517	(3.7)	495	(3.8)	**472**	(3.4)	**–34.0**	(1.51)	**1.8**	(0.09)	11.8	(0.99)

Note: Values that are statistically significant are indicated in bold (see Annex A4).
1. Response rate too low to ensure comparability (see Annex A3).

Table 3.9
Index of control strategies and performance on the mathematics scale, by national quarters of the index
Results based on students' self-reports

	Index of control strategies															
	All students		Males		Females		Gender difference (M – F)		Bottom quarter		Second quarter		Third quarter		Top quarter	
	Mean index	S.E.	Mean index	S.E.	Mean index	S.E.	Dif.	S.E.	Mean index	S.E.	Mean index	S.E.	Mean index	S.E.	Mean index	S.E.
OECD countries																
Australia	0.01	(0.01)	–0.02	(0.02)	0.05	(0.01)	**–0.07**	(0.02)	–1.05	(0.01)	–0.28	(0.00)	0.13	(0.00)	1.24	(0.01)
Austria	0.52	(0.02)	0.42	(0.03)	0.62	(0.03)	**–0.20**	(0.04)	–0.90	(0.03)	0.17	(0.01)	0.90	(0.01)	1.92	(0.02)
Belgium	–0.05	(0.01)	–0.15	(0.02)	0.05	(0.02)	**–0.20**	(0.03)	–1.14	(0.02)	–0.36	(0.00)	0.11	(0.00)	1.18	(0.01)
Canada	0.06	(0.01)	–0.05	(0.02)	0.16	(0.02)	**–0.21**	(0.02)	–1.13	(0.01)	–0.24	(0.00)	0.21	(0.00)	1.39	(0.02)
Czech Republic	0.06	(0.02)	–0.01	(0.02)	0.12	(0.02)	**–0.13**	(0.02)	–0.84	(0.02)	–0.15	(0.01)	0.13	(0.00)	1.09	(0.02)
Denmark	–0.19	(0.01)	–0.18	(0.02)	–0.20	(0.02)	0.01	(0.03)	–1.10	(0.01)	–0.49	(0.00)	–0.04	(0.01)	0.87	(0.02)
Finland	–0.48	(0.01)	–0.46	(0.02)	–0.50	(0.02)	0.04	(0.02)	–1.39	(0.01)	–0.78	(0.00)	–0.30	(0.00)	0.54	(0.02)
France	0.15	(0.02)	0.02	(0.02)	0.27	(0.02)	**–0.25**	(0.03)	–1.06	(0.02)	–0.16	(0.01)	0.33	(0.01)	1.52	(0.02)
Germany	0.38	(0.02)	0.23	(0.02)	0.54	(0.03)	**–0.31**	(0.03)	–0.99	(0.02)	–0.04	(0.01)	0.75	(0.01)	1.81	(0.02)
Greece	0.27	(0.02)	0.21	(0.02)	0.33	(0.02)	**–0.11**	(0.03)	–0.82	(0.02)	–0.05	(0.01)	0.43	(0.01)	1.53	(0.02)
Hungary	0.06	(0.01)	–0.02	(0.02)	0.14	(0.02)	**–0.16**	(0.03)	–0.94	(0.02)	–0.21	(0.01)	0.19	(0.01)	1.19	(0.02)
Iceland	0.00	(0.02)	–0.03	(0.03)	0.04	(0.03)	–0.07	(0.04)	–1.19	(0.02)	–0.34	(0.01)	0.20	(0.01)	1.34	(0.02)
Ireland	–0.01	(0.02)	–0.05	(0.02)	0.02	(0.03)	**–0.07**	(0.03)	–1.05	(0.02)	–0.30	(0.01)	0.14	(0.00)	1.16	(0.02)
Italy	0.21	(0.02)	0.12	(0.03)	0.29	(0.03)	**–0.17**	(0.04)	–0.85	(0.02)	–0.07	(0.01)	0.32	(0.01)	1.46	(0.02)
Japan	–0.54	(0.02)	–0.49	(0.03)	–0.59	(0.03)	**0.10**	(0.04)	–1.71	(0.03)	–0.87	(0.00)	–0.36	(0.01)	0.79	(0.02)
Korea	–0.49	(0.02)	–0.46	(0.03)	–0.53	(0.04)	0.07	(0.05)	–1.63	(0.02)	–0.79	(0.00)	–0.23	(0.01)	0.71	(0.02)
Luxembourg	0.08	(0.02)	–0.03	(0.03)	0.18	(0.02)	**–0.21**	(0.03)	–1.26	(0.02)	–0.30	(0.01)	0.32	(0.01)	1.55	(0.02)
Mexico	0.45	(0.02)	0.37	(0.03)	0.52	(0.03)	**–0.16**	(0.03)	–0.72	(0.01)	0.02	(0.00)	0.63	(0.01)	1.87	(0.02)
Netherlands	–0.27	(0.02)	–0.27	(0.02)	–0.26	(0.02)	–0.01	(0.03)	–1.20	(0.03)	–0.52	(0.01)	–0.09	(0.01)	0.75	(0.02)
New Zealand	–0.03	(0.01)	–0.07	(0.02)	0.01	(0.02)	**–0.08**	(0.03)	–1.10	(0.02)	–0.34	(0.01)	0.10	(0.00)	1.21	(0.02)
Norway	–0.26	(0.02)	–0.28	(0.02)	–0.23	(0.02)	–0.05	(0.03)	–1.37	(0.02)	–0.55	(0.01)	–0.05	(0.01)	0.95	(0.02)
Poland	–0.03	(0.01)	–0.11	(0.02)	0.06	(0.02)	**–0.17**	(0.03)	–0.93	(0.02)	–0.25	(0.01)	0.07	(0.00)	0.99	(0.02)
Portugal	0.14	(0.02)	0.04	(0.03)	0.23	(0.02)	**–0.19**	(0.03)	–0.92	(0.03)	–0.06	(0.01)	0.23	(0.01)	1.32	(0.02)
Slovak Republic	0.07	(0.01)	0.02	(0.02)	0.13	(0.02)	**–0.11**	(0.03)	–0.86	(0.02)	–0.18	(0.01)	0.14	(0.01)	1.18	(0.02)
Spain	–0.02	(0.02)	–0.12	(0.03)	0.09	(0.02)	**–0.21**	(0.03)	–1.16	(0.02)	–0.26	(0.01)	0.15	(0.00)	1.20	(0.02)
Sweden	–0.40	(0.01)	–0.40	(0.02)	–0.40	(0.02)	0.00	(0.03)	–1.36	(0.01)	–0.69	(0.00)	–0.23	(0.01)	0.67	(0.02)
Switzerland	0.19	(0.01)	0.13	(0.02)	0.26	(0.02)	**–0.14**	(0.03)	–1.06	(0.02)	–0.17	(0.01)	0.45	(0.01)	1.55	(0.02)
Turkey	0.26	(0.03)	0.15	(0.04)	0.40	(0.03)	**–0.25**	(0.04)	–1.12	(0.03)	–0.13	(0.01)	0.47	(0.01)	1.82	(0.02)
United States	0.01	(0.02)	–0.07	(0.02)	0.09	(0.02)	**–0.16**	(0.03)	–1.17	(0.02)	–0.29	(0.01)	0.13	(0.00)	1.36	(0.02)
OECD total	***0.01***	***(0.01)***	***–0.06***	***(0.01)***	***0.08***	***(0.01)***	***–0.14***	***(0.01)***	***–1.20***	***(0.01)***	***–0.32***	***(0.00)***	***0.18***	***(0.00)***	***1.37***	***(0.01)***
OECD average	***0.00***	***(0.00)***	***–0.06***	***(0.01)***	***0.06***	***(0.01)***	***–0.12***	***(0.01)***	***–1.16***	***(0.00)***	***–0.32***	***(0.00)***	***0.17***	***(0.01)***	***1.30***	***(0.01)***
Partner countries																
Brazil	0.57	(0.02)	0.51	(0.03)	0.62	(0.02)	**–0.11**	(0.04)	–0.49	(0.02)	0.10	(0.00)	0.76	(0.01)	1.92	(0.02)
Hong Kong-China	–0.07	(0.02)	–0.09	(0.03)	–0.05	(0.02)	–0.04	(0.04)	–1.10	(0.02)	–0.30	(0.01)	0.07	(0.00)	1.05	(0.02)
Indonesia	0.38	(0.02)	0.32	(0.02)	0.45	(0.02)	**–0.13**	(0.02)	–0.49	(0.01)	0.07	(0.00)	0.38	(0.01)	1.57	(0.02)
Latvia	–0.26	(0.01)	–0.32	(0.02)	–0.21	(0.02)	**–0.11**	(0.02)	–1.11	(0.01)	–0.51	(0.01)	–0.07	(0.01)	0.63	(0.02)
Liechtenstein	0.25	(0.06)	0.26	(0.08)	0.25	(0.08)	0.01	(0.11)	–1.17	(0.07)	–0.16	(0.02)	0.63	(0.03)	1.72	(0.07)
Macao-China	0.07	(0.02)	0.09	(0.04)	0.04	(0.03)	0.05	(0.05)	–0.89	(0.03)	–0.23	(0.01)	0.21	(0.01)	1.18	(0.03)
Russian Federation	–0.09	(0.02)	–0.15	(0.02)	–0.04	(0.02)	**–0.12**	(0.03)	–1.05	(0.01)	–0.40	(0.00)	0.07	(0.00)	1.00	(0.02)
Serbia	0.50	(0.02)	0.40	(0.03)	0.61	(0.03)	**–0.21**	(0.04)	–0.80	(0.03)	0.08	(0.00)	0.78	(0.01)	1.96	(0.02)
Thailand	–0.03	(0.02)	–0.06	(0.02)	–0.01	(0.02)	**–0.05**	(0.02)	–0.87	(0.01)	–0.24	(0.01)	0.08	(0.00)	0.92	(0.02)
Tunisia	0.68	(0.02)	0.70	(0.03)	0.67	(0.02)	0.04	(0.03)	–0.80	(0.02)	0.29	(0.01)	1.09	(0.01)	2.15	(0.02)
Uruguay	0.20	(0.02)	0.11	(0.02)	0.28	(0.02)	**–0.17**	(0.03)	–0.90	(0.02)	–0.16	(0.01)	0.34	(0.01)	1.52	(0.02)
United Kingdom[1]	–0.11	(0.01)	–0.11	(0.02)	–0.10	(0.02)	–0.01	(0.02)	–1.08	(0.01)	–0.42	(0.00)	0.06	(0.00)	1.00	(0.02)

	Performance on the mathematics scale, by national quarters of the index of control strategies								Change in the mathematics score per unit of the index of control strategies		Increased likelihood of students in the bottom quarter of this index scoring in the bottom quarter of the national mathematics performance distribution		Explained variance in student performance (r-squared × 100)	
	Bottom quarter		Second quarter		Third quarter		Top quarter							
	Mean score	S.E.	Mean score	S.E.	Mean score	S.E.	Mean score	S.E.	Effect	S.E.	Ratio	S.E.	%	S.E.
OECD countries														
Australia	**503**	(3.4)	523	(2.2)	531	(2.7)	**545**	(3.1)	**15.6**	(1.14)	**1.5**	(0.07)	2.4	(0.35)
Austria	**511**	(4.0)	513	(4.1)	510	(4.5)	**496**	(4.5)	**–4.0**	(1.47)	1.0	(0.06)	0.2	(0.18)
Belgium	532	(4.1)	549	(3.1)	541	(3.3)	527	(3.2)	–1.7	(1.69)	**1.1**	(0.05)	0.0	(0.05)
Canada	**517**	(2.4)	535	(2.2)	540	(2.4)	**553**	(2.7)	**13.2**	(1.13)	**1.5**	(0.06)	2.4	(0.41)
Czech Republic	524	(4.4)	520	(4.0)	522	(3.6)	525	(4.5)	0.4	(2.10)	1.1	(0.07)	0.0	(0.03)
Denmark	511	(3.9)	517	(4.3)	515	(3.8)	519	(4.9)	**4.6**	(2.23)	1.1	(0.09)	0.2	(0.18)
Finland	**533**	(2.7)	547	(2.2)	542	(3.0)	**556**	(3.0)	**11.5**	(1.42)	**1.2**	(0.06)	1.2	(0.31)
France	**496**	(3.7)	516	(4.4)	522	(3.8)	**516**	(3.6)	**7.9**	(1.34)	**1.4**	(0.08)	0.8	(0.29)
Germany	**521**	(4.7)	517	(4.4)	517	(4.3)	**496**	(4.5)	**–7.3**	(1.87)	0.9	(0.06)	0.7	(0.38)
Greece	**434**	(4.8)	447	(5.3)	453	(5.0)	**451**	(4.8)	**6.8**	(1.55)	**1.4**	(0.08)	0.5	(0.22)
Hungary	496	(4.3)	489	(4.2)	487	(3.8)	490	(4.2)	**–4.4**	(1.99)	0.9	(0.08)	0.2	(0.16)
Iceland	**504**	(3.8)	522	(3.7)	518	(3.6)	**519**	(3.4)	**4.5**	(1.66)	**1.3**	(0.09)	0.3	(0.20)
Ireland	**495**	(3.1)	504	(4.1)	510	(4.7)	**505**	(4.0)	**3.9**	(1.54)	1.2	(0.08)	0.2	(0.14)
Italy	457	(4.2)	469	(4.6)	473	(4.0)	464	(4.2)	3.6	(1.87)	**1.2**	(0.08)	0.1	(0.14)
Japan	**504**	(5.2)	541	(4.9)	546	(4.7)	**550**	(5.5)	**17.2**	(2.44)	**1.7**	(0.11)	3.2	(0.80)
Korea	**487**	(4.2)	533	(3.3)	563	(3.5)	**587**	(4.0)	**38.0**	(1.75)	**2.7**	(0.16)	16.0	(1.14)
Luxembourg	**500**	(2.8)	502	(2.6)	492	(2.9)	**484**	(2.9)	**–5.4**	(1.41)	0.9	(0.06)	0.4	(0.24)
Mexico	**375**	(4.8)	389	(3.7)	394	(4.2)	**391**	(4.8)	**7.1**	(1.77)	**1.3**	(0.08)	0.7	(0.36)
Netherlands	538	(4.9)	553	(4.8)	549	(4.8)	536	(4.7)	–1.2	(2.84)	1.2	(0.10)	0.0	(0.09)
New Zealand	**508**	(3.4)	525	(3.3)	527	(3.8)	**539**	(4.1)	**11.1**	(1.85)	**1.3**	(0.09)	1.1	(0.38)
Norway	**473**	(3.7)	502	(3.5)	502	(3.6)	**510**	(3.8)	**14.5**	(1.59)	**1.4**	(0.09)	2.3	(0.51)
Poland	**486**	(4.3)	490	(3.8)	492	(3.9)	**497**	(3.6)	**4.3**	(1.88)	**1.2**	(0.08)	0.2	(0.14)
Portugal	**441**	(4.9)	465	(4.5)	474	(4.2)	**487**	(4.9)	**18.2**	(1.79)	**1.7**	(0.10)	3.8	(0.73)
Slovak Republic	**500**	(4.9)	502	(4.3)	501	(4.2)	**491**	(4.6)	**–4.7**	(1.93)	1.1	(0.07)	0.2	(0.15)
Spain	**464**	(3.6)	491	(3.2)	497	(3.4)	**494**	(3.0)	**12.6**	(1.22)	**1.7**	(0.09)	2.0	(0.42)
Sweden	507	(3.3)	517	(3.7)	511	(4.0)	506	(4.6)	–0.4	(1.95)	1.0	(0.06)	0.0	(0.03)
Switzerland	527	(4.5)	529	(5.4)	533	(4.0)	520	(3.7)	**–2.6**	(1.43)	1.0	(0.06)	0.1	(0.09)
Turkey	**398**	(5.8)	424	(7.0)	445	(9.3)	**440**	(8.6)	**14.4**	(2.15)	**1.6**	(0.11)	2.7	(0.77)
United States	**477**	(3.9)	487	(3.7)	486	(4.0)	**488**	(4.3)	**3.4**	(1.60)	1.1	(0.07)	0.1	(0.13)
OECD total	***489***	***(1.5)***	***496***	***(1.4)***	***492***	***(1.4)***	***488***	***(1.6)***	***–0.5***	***(0.73)***	***1.0***	***(0.03)***	***0.0***	***(0.01)***
OECD average	***498***	***(0.7)***	***506***	***(0.8)***	***503***	***(0.8)***	***500***	***(1.0)***	***6.4***[2]	***m***	***1.1***	***(0.01)***	***0.0***	***(0.01)***
Partner countries														
Brazil	361	(5.5)	362	(5.3)	358	(5.5)	356	(6.5)	–3.4	(1.83)	0.9	(0.07)	0.1	(0.14)
Hong Kong-China	**518**	(5.8)	553	(5.1)	556	(5.8)	**576**	(4.9)	**27.0**	(2.23)	**1.8**	(0.11)	6.0	(0.88)
Indonesia	**350**	(5.5)	370	(4.7)	364	(4.7)	**360**	(4.6)	3.4	(1.88)	**1.3**	(0.09)	0.1	(0.14)
Latvia	492	(4.7)	486	(5.2)	476	(6.0)	482	(5.4)	**–6.2**	(2.52)	1.0	(0.08)	0.3	(0.23)
Liechtenstein	553	(11.3)	541	(9.9)	524	(10.6)	524	(12.7)	**–12.2**	(5.52)	0.7	(0.17)	2.1	(1.77)
Macao-China	518	(7.2)	522	(5.8)	530	(5.9)	538	(6.8)	**8.2**	(3.92)	1.2	(0.14)	0.7	(0.64)
Russian Federation	469	(4.8)	468	(4.5)	464	(5.1)	475	(4.7)	0.5	(1.52)	1.0	(0.06)	0.0	(0.02)
Serbia	**443**	(4.5)	443	(4.6)	446	(4.5)	**426**	(4.4)	**–4.6**	(1.21)	1.0	(0.07)	0.4	(0.19)
Thailand	**412**	(3.8)	417	(4.0)	414	(4.6)	**425**	(4.2)	**8.5**	(2.07)	1.1	(0.07)	0.6	(0.29)
Tunisia	**341**	(2.8)	362	(3.8)	363	(3.5)	**374**	(4.1)	**10.5**	(1.31)	**1.4**	(0.09)	2.3	(0.58)
Uruguay	425	(5.1)	428	(4.2)	427	(4.2)	420	(5.0)	–1.9	(1.94)	1.1	(0.07)	0.0	(0.08)
United Kingdom[1]	**496**	(4.0)	511	(3.5)	511	(3.4)	**517**	(3.5)	**10.1**	(1.68)	**1.4**	(0.08)	0.9	(0.31)

Note: Values that are statistically significant are indicated in bold (see Annex A4).
1. Response rate too low to ensure comparability (see Annex A3).
2. The index of control strategies behaves differently accross countries, so the arithmetic average is used here.

Table 3.10
Index of memorisation strategies and performance on the mathematics scale, by national quarters of the index
Results based on students' self-reports

	Index of memorisation strategies															
	All students		Males		Females		Gender difference (M – F)		Bottom quarter		Second quarter		Third quarter		Top quarter	
	Mean index	S.E.	Mean index	S.E.	Mean index	S.E.	Dif.	S.E.	Mean index	S.E.	Mean index	S.E.	Mean index	S.E.	Mean index	S.E.
OECD countries																
Australia	0.17	(0.01)	0.19	(0.02)	0.14	(0.01)	**0.05**	(0.03)	–0.93	(0.02)	–0.07	(0.00)	0.39	(0.00)	1.29	(0.02)
Austria	0.06	(0.02)	–0.01	(0.03)	0.14	(0.03)	**–0.15**	(0.03)	–1.32	(0.03)	–0.28	(0.01)	0.42	(0.01)	1.43	(0.02)
Belgium	–0.09	(0.01)	–0.14	(0.02)	–0.04	(0.02)	**–0.11**	(0.02)	–1.17	(0.02)	–0.29	(0.00)	0.13	(0.00)	0.97	(0.02)
Canada	0.16	(0.01)	0.14	(0.02)	0.19	(0.02)	**–0.04**	(0.02)	–1.01	(0.01)	–0.10	(0.00)	0.41	(0.00)	1.36	(0.02)
Czech Republic	–0.05	(0.02)	–0.08	(0.02)	–0.02	(0.02)	**–0.06**	(0.03)	–1.05	(0.02)	–0.27	(0.01)	0.16	(0.01)	0.96	(0.02)
Denmark	–0.27	(0.02)	–0.17	(0.03)	–0.37	(0.02)	**0.20**	(0.03)	–1.39	(0.02)	–0.51	(0.00)	–0.01	(0.01)	0.83	(0.02)
Finland	–0.19	(0.01)	–0.15	(0.02)	–0.24	(0.02)	**0.10**	(0.03)	–1.35	(0.02)	–0.40	(0.01)	0.07	(0.01)	0.90	(0.02)
France	–0.06	(0.02)	–0.16	(0.03)	0.03	(0.03)	**–0.18**	(0.03)	–1.30	(0.03)	–0.28	(0.01)	0.17	(0.01)	1.17	(0.02)
Germany	–0.06	(0.02)	–0.14	(0.03)	0.03	(0.03)	**–0.17**	(0.04)	–1.56	(0.02)	–0.37	(0.01)	0.26	(0.01)	1.43	(0.02)
Greece	0.20	(0.02)	0.21	(0.02)	0.18	(0.02)	0.03	(0.03)	–0.88	(0.02)	–0.04	(0.00)	0.39	(0.01)	1.32	(0.03)
Hungary	0.16	(0.02)	0.08	(0.02)	0.25	(0.02)	**–0.17**	(0.03)	–0.89	(0.02)	–0.11	(0.00)	0.37	(0.00)	1.25	(0.02)
Iceland	–0.03	(0.02)	–0.02	(0.03)	–0.05	(0.03)	0.03	(0.04)	–1.34	(0.03)	–0.32	(0.01)	0.21	(0.01)	1.32	(0.03)
Ireland	0.11	(0.02)	0.08	(0.02)	0.13	(0.02)	–0.04	(0.03)	–0.98	(0.02)	–0.13	(0.00)	0.34	(0.00)	1.20	(0.02)
Italy	0.03	(0.02)	0.00	(0.02)	0.06	(0.02)	**–0.07**	(0.03)	–1.01	(0.02)	–0.17	(0.00)	0.22	(0.01)	1.08	(0.02)
Japan	–0.56	(0.02)	–0.51	(0.03)	–0.61	(0.02)	**0.10**	(0.03)	–1.78	(0.03)	–0.74	(0.01)	–0.26	(0.01)	0.54	(0.02)
Korea	–0.35	(0.02)	–0.35	(0.02)	–0.34	(0.03)	–0.01	(0.03)	–1.47	(0.02)	–0.51	(0.01)	–0.05	(0.00)	0.64	(0.01)
Luxembourg	–0.05	(0.02)	–0.11	(0.02)	0.01	(0.02)	**–0.13**	(0.04)	–1.43	(0.03)	–0.32	(0.01)	0.25	(0.01)	1.31	(0.02)
Mexico	0.56	(0.02)	0.55	(0.03)	0.56	(0.02)	–0.01	(0.03)	–0.54	(0.02)	0.19	(0.00)	0.71	(0.01)	1.86	(0.02)
Netherlands	–0.16	(0.02)	–0.07	(0.02)	–0.25	(0.02)	**0.17**	(0.03)	–1.11	(0.03)	–0.37	(0.01)	0.06	(0.01)	0.78	(0.02)
New Zealand	0.13	(0.02)	0.14	(0.02)	0.12	(0.02)	0.02	(0.03)	–0.97	(0.02)	–0.10	(0.00)	0.37	(0.00)	1.22	(0.02)
Norway	–0.12	(0.02)	0.00	(0.03)	–0.25	(0.02)	**0.24**	(0.04)	–1.41	(0.03)	–0.34	(0.01)	0.14	(0.01)	1.12	(0.02)
Poland	0.15	(0.01)	0.13	(0.02)	0.16	(0.02)	–0.02	(0.03)	–0.88	(0.02)	–0.05	(0.00)	0.36	(0.00)	1.15	(0.02)
Portugal	–0.11	(0.02)	–0.14	(0.03)	–0.09	(0.02)	–0.05	(0.03)	–1.27	(0.03)	–0.29	(0.01)	0.17	(0.01)	0.94	(0.02)
Slovak Republic	0.13	(0.01)	0.08	(0.02)	0.18	(0.01)	**–0.11**	(0.02)	–0.87	(0.02)	–0.12	(0.00)	0.34	(0.00)	1.16	(0.02)
Spain	0.07	(0.02)	0.02	(0.02)	0.11	(0.02)	**–0.09**	(0.03)	–1.08	(0.03)	–0.12	(0.00)	0.30	(0.00)	1.18	(0.02)
Sweden	–0.08	(0.02)	–0.01	(0.02)	–0.15	(0.03)	**0.14**	(0.03)	–1.25	(0.02)	–0.32	(0.01)	0.17	(0.01)	1.08	(0.02)
Switzerland	–0.19	(0.02)	–0.18	(0.03)	–0.20	(0.03)	0.03	(0.04)	–1.55	(0.02)	–0.48	(0.01)	0.11	(0.01)	1.16	(0.02)
Turkey	0.10	(0.02)	0.07	(0.03)	0.13	(0.02)	–0.06	(0.03)	–1.09	(0.02)	–0.16	(0.00)	0.37	(0.01)	1.28	(0.03)
United States	0.31	(0.02)	0.29	(0.03)	0.33	(0.02)	–0.05	(0.03)	–0.87	(0.02)	0.04	(0.01)	0.53	(0.01)	1.54	(0.03)
OECD total	*0.07*	*(0.01)*	*0.05*	*(0.01)*	*0.09*	*(0.01)*	*–0.04*	*(0.01)*	*–1.16*	*(0.01)*	*–0.22*	*(0.00)*	*0.33*	*(0.01)*	*1.31*	*(0.01)*
OECD average	*0.00*	*(0.00)*	*–0.01*	*(0.00)*	*0.01*	*(0.00)*	*–0.02*	*(0.01)*	*–1.18*	*(0.01)*	*–0.25*	*(0.00)*	*0.23*	*(0.00)*	*1.19*	*(0.01)*
Partner countries																
Brazil	0.48	(0.02)	0.49	(0.03)	0.48	(0.02)	0.01	(0.03)	–0.50	(0.02)	0.17	(0.01)	0.58	(0.01)	1.68	(0.02)
Hong Kong-China	–0.15	(0.02)	–0.14	(0.03)	–0.17	(0.02)	0.03	(0.03)	–1.26	(0.02)	–0.35	(0.01)	0.10	(0.01)	0.89	(0.02)
Indonesia	0.50	(0.02)	0.50	(0.02)	0.50	(0.02)	0.00	(0.03)	–0.49	(0.01)	0.21	(0.01)	0.69	(0.00)	1.60	(0.02)
Latvia	–0.14	(0.02)	–0.12	(0.02)	–0.16	(0.02)	0.04	(0.03)	–1.01	(0.02)	–0.32	(0.01)	0.06	(0.01)	0.71	(0.02)
Liechtenstein	–0.32	(0.05)	–0.25	(0.09)	–0.38	(0.07)	0.13	(0.12)	–1.76	(0.08)	–0.67	(0.02)	0.05	(0.02)	1.13	(0.07)
Macao-China	–0.03	(0.04)	–0.06	(0.06)	0.00	(0.04)	–0.07	(0.06)	–1.13	(0.05)	–0.26	(0.01)	0.17	(0.01)	1.10	(0.04)
Russian Federation	–0.04	(0.02)	–0.07	(0.03)	–0.01	(0.02)	–0.05	(0.03)	–1.02	(0.02)	–0.28	(0.01)	0.17	(0.01)	0.96	(0.02)
Serbia	–0.05	(0.02)	–0.05	(0.03)	–0.06	(0.03)	0.02	(0.04)	–1.18	(0.03)	–0.33	(0.01)	0.12	(0.01)	1.17	(0.03)
Thailand	0.47	(0.02)	0.46	(0.02)	0.48	(0.02)	–0.01	(0.02)	–0.41	(0.02)	0.27	(0.00)	0.68	(0.01)	1.34	(0.02)
Tunisia	0.43	(0.02)	0.53	(0.03)	0.33	(0.02)	**0.19**	(0.04)	–1.00	(0.02)	0.06	(0.01)	0.72	(0.01)	1.93	(0.02)
Uruguay	0.16	(0.02)	0.21	(0.03)	0.11	(0.02)	**0.10**	(0.03)	–0.99	(0.02)	–0.16	(0.00)	0.40	(0.01)	1.38	(0.02)
United Kingdom[1]	0.11	(0.02)	0.14	(0.03)	0.08	(0.02)	**0.06**	(0.03)	–1.00	(0.02)	–0.12	(0.00)	0.34	(0.00)	1.20	(0.02)

	Performance on the mathematics scale, by national quarters of the index of memorisation strategies								Change in the mathematics score per unit of the index of memorisation strategies		Increased likelihood of students in the bottom quarter of this index scoring in the bottom quarter of the national mathematics performance distribution		Explained variance in student performance (r-squared × 100)	
	Bottom quarter		Second quarter		Third quarter		Top quarter							
	Mean score	S.E.	Mean score	S.E.	Mean score	S.E.	Mean score	S.E.	Effect	S.E.	Ratio	S.E.	%	S.E.
OECD countries														
Australia	**515**	(3.2)	526	(2.6)	527	(2.8)	**535**	(3.2)	**9.7**	(1.29)	**1.2**	(0.04)	0.9	(0.25)
Austria	**535**	(4.3)	516	(3.6)	499	(4.0)	**481**	(4.5)	**–18.5**	(1.72)	**0.7**	(0.06)	5.1	(0.84)
Belgium	**544**	(4.4)	551	(3.0)	540	(3.4)	**517**	(3.3)	**–9.3**	(1.96)	1.0	(0.06)	0.7	(0.30)
Canada	**531**	(2.3)	537	(2.5)	534	(2.1)	**544**	(2.4)	**6.2**	(1.02)	**1.2**	(0.05)	0.5	(0.17)
Czech Republic	**543**	(4.4)	525	(4.6)	513	(3.8)	**511**	(4.4)	**–14.2**	(2.06)	0.9	(0.08)	1.7	(0.47)
Denmark	**506**	(4.3)	516	(3.5)	520	(3.6)	**524**	(3.9)	**9.3**	(1.79)	**1.2**	(0.08)	0.9	(0.36)
Finland	**535**	(2.9)	548	(3.5)	548	(3.0)	**546**	(3.3)	**6.7**	(1.53)	**1.3**	(0.06)	0.6	(0.27)
France	513	(3.7)	520	(3.8)	514	(3.6)	506	(4.0)	–0.9	(1.41)	1.1	(0.07)	0.0	(0.03)
Germany	**543**	(4.3)	521	(4.0)	505	(4.1)	**483**	(4.6)	**–17.9**	(1.46)	**0.7**	(0.05)	5.1	(0.82)
Greece	**454**	(5.7)	446	(4.4)	443	(4.6)	**443**	(4.4)	–2.9	(2.09)	1.0	(0.06)	0.1	(0.12)
Hungary	**500**	(4.1)	489	(3.8)	489	(3.7)	**485**	(3.3)	**–7.3**	(1.88)	0.9	(0.05)	0.5	(0.25)
Iceland	515	(3.5)	519	(4.2)	520	(3.4)	509	(3.1)	–0.7	(1.50)	1.0	(0.08)	0.0	(0.05)
Ireland	**496**	(3.3)	510	(3.7)	503	(4.0)	**506**	(3.7)	**5.0**	(1.74)	**1.2**	(0.08)	0.3	(0.21)
Italy	**479**	(4.2)	470	(4.4)	467	(3.6)	**448**	(4.4)	**–11.8**	(1.97)	**0.8**	(0.06)	1.2	(0.38)
Japan	**513**	(5.9)	541	(4.9)	546	(4.3)	**540**	(5.3)	**13.9**	(2.30)	**1.5**	(0.10)	1.9	(0.62)
Korea	**517**	(4.7)	545	(4.4)	551	(3.9)	**558**	(3.4)	**19.6**	(1.77)	**1.8**	(0.09)	3.6	(0.65)
Luxembourg	**504**	(2.7)	499	(2.8)	496	(2.6)	**480**	(2.7)	**–8.6**	(1.39)	0.9	(0.07)	1.1	(0.36)
Mexico	389	(4.5)	395	(4.3)	386	(3.9)	393	(4.8)	2.0	(1.42)	1.0	(0.09)	0.1	(0.08)
Netherlands	**526**	(4.4)	545	(4.3)	554	(4.0)	**551**	(4.0)	**12.8**	(2.08)	**1.4**	(0.12)	1.4	(0.46)
New Zealand	523	(3.5)	528	(3.4)	525	(3.4)	527	(4.1)	**4.3**	(1.96)	1.0	(0.06)	0.2	(0.16)
Norway	**459**	(3.2)	498	(4.0)	512	(4.7)	**520**	(3.9)	**22.3**	(1.48)	**1.8**	(0.09)	6.7	(0.84)
Poland	**500**	(3.9)	495	(3.4)	482	(3.9)	**489**	(3.4)	**–4.5**	(1.85)	1.0	(0.07)	0.2	(0.15)
Portugal	**477**	(4.8)	473	(4.2)	462	(4.3)	**454**	(5.0)	**–5.4**	(1.87)	1.0	(0.06)	0.4	(0.24)
Slovak Republic	**512**	(4.8)	501	(4.7)	496	(3.2)	**486**	(4.2)	**–10.5**	(1.92)	1.0	(0.07)	0.9	(0.33)
Spain	**477**	(3.4)	494	(3.5)	491	(3.3)	**485**	(3.0)	**7.7**	(1.45)	**1.4**	(0.08)	0.7	(0.29)
Sweden	**493**	(3.4)	508	(3.4)	517	(3.7)	**524**	(4.7)	**14.1**	(1.88)	**1.3**	(0.08)	2.2	(0.62)
Switzerland	**555**	(5.3)	531	(3.9)	521	(4.2)	**502**	(3.7)	**–17.1**	(1.64)	**0.6**	(0.05)	3.9	(0.68)
Turkey	427	(9.1)	435	(8.1)	432	(6.9)	424	(7.0)	1.2	(2.62)	**1.2**	(0.10)	0.0	(0.09)
United States	485	(4.0)	488	(4.0)	484	(4.1)	481	(4.3)	0.3	(1.38)	1.0	(0.07)	0.0	(0.02)
OECD total	*503*	*(1.5)*	*501*	*(1.2)*	*489*	*(1.4)*	*476*	*(1.8)*	*–7.5*	*(0.72)*	*0.9*	*(0.02)*	*0.6*	*(0.11)*
OECD average	*508*	*(0.9)*	*509*	*(0.8)*	*502*	*(0.8)*	*492*	*(0.9)*	*–4.5*	*(0.41)*	*1.0*	*(0.01)*	*0.2*	*(0.04)*
Partner countries														
Brazil	**392**	(7.5)	365	(6.0)	351	(5.4)	**335**	(4.7)	**–21.9**	(2.60)	**0.7**	(0.08)	4.1	(0.87)
Hong Kong-China	545	(6.1)	556	(6.6)	551	(6.5)	551	(5.1)	**6.7**	(2.23)	**1.3**	(0.08)	0.4	(0.26)
Indonesia	**382**	(6.3)	371	(4.8)	356	(3.8)	**341**	(3.8)	**–17.4**	(2.40)	**0.7**	(0.06)	3.6	(0.98)
Latvia	490	(5.0)	487	(4.1)	479	(4.5)	480	(6.3)	–2.5	(3.43)	0.9	(0.09)	0.0	(0.15)
Liechtenstein	**594**	(10.1)	521	(10.8)	541	(12.2)	**485**	(11.4)	**–35.3**	(4.42)	**0.4**	(0.14)	17.7	(3.85)
Macao-China	**543**	(7.2)	532	(7.7)	519	(6.2)	**515**	(6.3)	**–12.3**	(4.18)	0.8	(0.14)	1.8	(1.24)
Russian Federation	468	(4.8)	474	(4.7)	470	(4.9)	469	(5.5)	0.1	(1.71)	1.1	(0.07)	0.0	(0.02)
Serbia	**459**	(4.5)	455	(4.4)	443	(4.4)	**411**	(4.2)	**–17.1**	(1.64)	**0.7**	(0.05)	4.3	(0.81)
Thailand	422	(4.0)	422	(4.6)	411	(3.4)	414	(4.4)	–1.7	(2.50)	0.9	(0.07)	0.0	(0.09)
Tunisia	**351**	(3.8)	362	(4.1)	360	(3.7)	**368**	(3.3)	**5.8**	(1.22)	**1.2**	(0.08)	0.7	(0.32)
Uruguay	**434**	(5.0)	435	(4.5)	426	(4.4)	**415**	(4.7)	**–6.4**	(2.11)	1.0	(0.07)	0.4	(0.29)
United Kingdom[1]	**491**	(3.9)	511	(3.7)	512	(3.5)	**522**	(3.6)	**12.3**	(1.85)	**1.5**	(0.09)	1.6	(0.48)

Note: Values that are statistically significant are indicated in bold (see Annex A4).
1. Response rate too low to ensure comparability (see Annex A3).

Table 3.11
Index of elaboration strategies and performance on the mathematics scale, by national quarters of the index
Results based on students' self-reports

		Index of elaboration strategies														
		All students		Males		Females		Gender difference (M – F)		Bottom quarter		Second quarter		Third quarter		Top quarter	
		Mean index	S.E.	Mean index	S.E.	Mean index	S.E.	Dif.	S.E.	Mean index	S.E.	Mean index	S.E.	Mean index	S.E.	Mean index	S.E.
OECD countries	Australia	0.06	(0.01)	0.20	(0.02)	–0.08	(0.01)	**0.28**	(0.02)	–0.97	(0.01)	–0.24	(0.00)	0.31	(0.00)	1.15	(0.02)
	Austria	–0.27	(0.03)	–0.03	(0.03)	–0.51	(0.03)	**0.48**	(0.04)	–1.68	(0.02)	–0.60	(0.01)	0.08	(0.01)	1.13	(0.02)
	Belgium	–0.17	(0.01)	–0.05	(0.02)	–0.31	(0.02)	**0.26**	(0.02)	–1.33	(0.02)	–0.44	(0.00)	0.07	(0.00)	1.01	(0.02)
	Canada	0.08	(0.01)	0.20	(0.02)	–0.05	(0.02)	**0.25**	(0.02)	–1.09	(0.01)	–0.26	(0.00)	0.34	(0.00)	1.31	(0.02)
	Czech Republic	0.13	(0.01)	0.22	(0.02)	0.04	(0.01)	**0.18**	(0.02)	–0.75	(0.01)	–0.08	(0.00)	0.31	(0.00)	1.04	(0.02)
	Denmark	0.07	(0.01)	0.22	(0.02)	–0.07	(0.02)	**0.29**	(0.03)	–0.92	(0.02)	–0.24	(0.01)	0.30	(0.00)	1.15	(0.02)
	Finland	–0.14	(0.01)	0.02	(0.02)	–0.30	(0.02)	**0.32**	(0.02)	–1.17	(0.02)	–0.38	(0.00)	0.06	(0.01)	0.92	(0.01)
	France	–0.10	(0.02)	0.02	(0.02)	–0.21	(0.02)	**0.23**	(0.03)	–1.34	(0.02)	–0.36	(0.00)	0.18	(0.01)	1.11	(0.02)
	Germany	–0.31	(0.02)	–0.13	(0.03)	–0.49	(0.03)	**0.36**	(0.03)	–1.66	(0.02)	–0.65	(0.01)	–0.04	(0.01)	1.09	(0.02)
	Greece	0.33	(0.02)	0.47	(0.03)	0.20	(0.02)	**0.27**	(0.03)	–0.76	(0.02)	0.03	(0.01)	0.57	(0.01)	1.46	(0.02)
	Hungary	0.10	(0.01)	–0.02	(0.02)	–0.19	(0.02)	**0.17**	(0.03)	–1.07	(0.02)	–0.36	(0.01)	0.08	(0.01)	0.93	(0.02)
	Iceland	–0.06	(0.02)	0.07	(0.03)	–0.21	(0.02)	**0.28**	(0.04)	–1.28	(0.02)	–0.36	(0.01)	0.19	(0.01)	1.19	(0.03)
	Ireland	–0.14	(0.02)	–0.06	(0.02)	–0.22	(0.03)	**0.16**	(0.03)	–1.17	(0.02)	–0.39	(0.01)	0.08	(0.01)	0.93	(0.02)
	Italy	0.04	(0.02)	0.15	(0.03)	–0.07	(0.03)	**0.21**	(0.04)	–1.10	(0.02)	–0.27	(0.00)	0.31	(0.00)	1.21	(0.02)
	Japan	–0.75	(0.02)	–0.58	(0.03)	–0.91	(0.02)	**0.32**	(0.04)	–2.13	(0.03)	–0.97	(0.00)	–0.41	(0.01)	0.50	(0.02)
	Korea	–0.39	(0.02)	–0.31	(0.02)	–0.51	(0.02)	**0.20**	(0.03)	–1.49	(0.02)	–0.63	(0.00)	–0.14	(0.00)	0.68	(0.01)
	Luxembourg	–0.25	(0.02)	–0.03	(0.03)	–0.45	(0.03)	**0.42**	(0.04)	–1.66	(0.02)	–0.60	(0.01)	0.08	(0.01)	1.20	(0.02)
	Mexico	0.85	(0.02)	0.88	(0.03)	0.83	(0.02)	**0.06**	(0.03)	–0.24	(0.02)	0.59	(0.01)	0.98	(0.01)	2.08	(0.02)
	Netherlands	–0.26	(0.02)	–0.09	(0.03)	–0.43	(0.03)	**0.34**	(0.04)	–1.26	(0.02)	–0.50	(0.00)	–0.03	(0.01)	0.77	(0.02)
	New Zealand	0.13	(0.02)	0.22	(0.02)	0.04	(0.03)	**0.18**	(0.03)	–0.89	(0.02)	–0.15	(0.01)	0.35	(0.01)	1.21	(0.02)
	Norway	–0.16	(0.02)	–0.05	(0.03)	–0.28	(0.03)	**0.24**	(0.04)	–1.38	(0.03)	–0.41	(0.01)	0.10	(0.01)	1.03	(0.02)
	Poland	0.25	(0.01)	0.31	(0.02)	0.20	(0.02)	**0.11**	(0.03)	–0.70	(0.02)	0.00	(0.01)	0.45	(0.01)	1.27	(0.02)
	Portugal	0.16	(0.02)	0.23	(0.03)	0.10	(0.02)	**0.14**	(0.04)	–0.97	(0.02)	–0.04	(0.00)	0.45	(0.01)	1.21	(0.02)
	Slovak Republic	0.38	(0.01)	0.47	(0.02)	0.29	(0.02)	**0.18**	(0.03)	–0.55	(0.02)	0.13	(0.00)	0.62	(0.01)	1.33	(0.02)
	Spain	0.09	(0.02)	0.14	(0.02)	0.04	(0.02)	**0.09**	(0.03)	–1.08	(0.02)	–0.17	(0.01)	0.35	(0.00)	1.25	(0.02)
	Sweden	–0.02	(0.02)	0.09	(0.02)	–0.14	(0.03)	**0.23**	(0.03)	–1.07	(0.02)	–0.28	(0.00)	0.23	(0.01)	1.04	(0.02)
	Switzerland	–0.06	(0.02)	0.16	(0.02)	–0.30	(0.02)	**0.46**	(0.03)	–1.31	(0.02)	–0.36	(0.01)	0.22	(0.01)	1.22	(0.02)
	Turkey	0.44	(0.03)	0.44	(0.04)	0.43	(0.03)	0.01	(0.04)	–0.90	(0.03)	0.16	(0.01)	0.71	(0.01)	1.78	(0.02)
	United States	0.18	(0.02)	0.26	(0.03)	0.11	(0.03)	**0.16**	(0.04)	–1.08	(0.02)	–0.13	(0.01)	0.49	(0.01)	1.46	(0.02)
	OECD total	*0.03*	*(0.01)*	*0.13*	*(0.01)*	*–0.06*	*(0.01)*	*0.19*	*(0.01)*	*–1.27*	*(0.01)*	*–0.29*	*(0.00)*	*0.34*	*(0.01)*	*1.34*	*(0.01)*
	OECD average	*0.00*	*(0.00)*	*0.12*	*(0.00)*	*–0.12*	*(0.01)*	*0.23*	*(0.01)*	*–1.19*	*(0.00)*	*–0.31*	*(0.00)*	*0.29*	*(0.01)*	*1.21*	*(0.01)*
Partner countries	Brazil	0.76	(0.02)	0.80	(0.03)	0.72	(0.02)	**0.09**	(0.03)	–0.34	(0.02)	0.43	(0.01)	0.93	(0.00)	2.01	(0.03)
	Hong Kong-China	0.00	(0.02)	0.15	(0.02)	–0.15	(0.02)	**0.30**	(0.03)	–1.14	(0.02)	–0.29	(0.01)	0.31	(0.01)	1.13	(0.02)
	Indonesia	0.52	(0.01)	0.54	(0.02)	0.50	(0.01)	**0.04**	(0.02)	–0.27	(0.01)	0.31	(0.00)	0.68	(0.00)	1.35	(0.02)
	Latvia	0.13	(0.02)	0.22	(0.02)	0.05	(0.02)	**0.17**	(0.02)	–0.73	(0.02)	–0.06	(0.01)	0.33	(0.01)	0.98	(0.02)
	Liechtenstein	–0.10	(0.05)	0.17	(0.07)	–0.39	(0.08)	**0.55**	(0.10)	–1.34	(0.06)	–0.37	(0.02)	0.17	(0.03)	1.15	(0.08)
	Macao-China	0.04	(0.03)	0.22	(0.04)	–0.12	(0.04)	**0.34**	(0.06)	–1.01	(0.03)	–0.26	(0.01)	0.31	(0.01)	1.13	(0.03)
	Russian Federation	0.14	(0.02)	0.24	(0.02)	0.05	(0.02)	**0.18**	(0.03)	–0.83	(0.01)	–0.09	(0.00)	0.35	(0.01)	1.15	(0.02)
	Serbia	0.41	(0.02)	0.49	(0.03)	0.33	(0.03)	**0.16**	(0.04)	–0.83	(0.03)	0.10	(0.01)	0.68	(0.01)	1.70	(0.02)
	Thailand	0.62	(0.02)	0.64	(0.02)	0.61	(0.02)	0.03	(0.02)	–0.22	(0.01)	0.43	(0.00)	0.84	(0.00)	1.44	(0.02)
	Tunisia	0.94	(0.02)	1.02	(0.03)	0.86	(0.02)	**0.16**	(0.03)	–0.35	(0.02)	0.66	(0.01)	1.16	(0.01)	2.27	(0.02)
	Uruguay	0.36	(0.02)	0.42	(0.03)	0.30	(0.02)	**0.11**	(0.03)	–0.80	(0.02)	0.02	(0.01)	0.63	(0.01)	1.59	(0.03)
	United Kingdom[1]	0.04	(0.02)	0.16	(0.02)	–0.06	(0.02)	**0.22**	(0.03)	–0.97	(0.02)	–0.25	(0.00)	0.30	(0.01)	1.10	(0.02)

		Performance on the mathematics scale, by national quarters of the index of elaboration strategies								Change in the mathematics score per unit of the index of elaboration strategies		Increased likelihood of students in the bottom quarter of this index scoring in the bottom quarter of the national mathematics performance distribution		Explained variance in student performance (r-squared × 100)	
		Bottom quarter		Second quarter		Third quarter		Top quarter							
		Mean score	S.E.	Mean score	S.E.	Mean score	S.E.	Mean score	S.E.	Effect	S.E.	Ratio	S.E.	%	S.E.
OECD countries	Australia	**528**	(3.2)	535	(2.8)	521	(2.3)	**518**	(3.1)	–2.1	(1.17)	**0.8**	(0.04)	0.0	(0.04)
	Austria	**511**	(3.7)	513	(4.4)	508	(3.9)	**498**	(5.0)	**–4.1**	(1.59)	**0.8**	(0.06)	0.3	(0.22)
	Belgium	**543**	(3.4)	554	(3.4)	541	(3.5)	**514**	(4.3)	**–10.6**	(1.92)	**0.8**	(0.05)	1.0	(0.36)
	Canada	**532**	(2.2)	538	(2.2)	535	(2.7)	**540**	(2.6)	**6.2**	(1.12)	1.0	(0.04)	0.5	(0.18)
	Czech Republic	**508**	(3.5)	522	(5.1)	528	(4.7)	**534**	(4.0)	**13.0**	(1.75)	**1.2**	(0.08)	1.1	(0.29)
	Denmark	**506**	(3.6)	515	(3.7)	518	(4.1)	**525**	(4.4)	**10.4**	(2.13)	1.1	(0.07)	1.0	(0.41)
	Finland	**526**	(2.5)	542	(2.9)	550	(3.3)	**560**	(3.4)	**16.9**	(1.52)	**1.3**	(0.07)	3.1	(0.55)
	France	513	(3.2)	517	(3.5)	516	(3.8)	506	(4.6)	1.2	(1.69)	0.9	(0.06)	0.0	(0.05)
	Germany	**518**	(4.8)	518	(4.1)	518	(4.0)	**498**	(5.2)	**–5.5**	(1.71)	**0.9**	(0.07)	0.4	(0.26)
	Greece	**435**	(4.3)	448	(4.5)	450	(4.6)	**453**	(5.6)	**8.9**	(1.82)	**1.2**	(0.08)	0.8	(0.33)
	Hungary	**495**	(4.1)	494	(3.8)	489	(4.0)	**483**	(4.8)	**–4.9**	(2.23)	**0.8**	(0.06)	0.2	(0.18)
	Iceland	509	(2.9)	525	(3.3)	519	(4.1)	510	(3.5)	0.1	(1.61)	1.1	(0.08)	0.0	(0.03)
	Ireland	506	(3.6)	512	(3.1)	501	(3.5)	496	(5.0)	–3.1	(2.16)	**0.8**	(0.06)	0.1	(0.15)
	Italy	**473**	(3.5)	469	(3.6)	463	(4.4)	**459**	(4.0)	**–3.9**	(1.46)	**0.7**	(0.05)	0.2	(0.12)
	Japan	**514**	(4.7)	531	(4.2)	548	(5.2)	**548**	(6.7)	**14.4**	(2.39)	**1.4**	(0.09)	2.4	(0.73)
	Korea	**510**	(3.7)	530	(4.0)	551	(3.8)	**579**	(4.4)	**30.0**	(1.64)	**1.7**	(0.10)	9.1	(0.82)
	Luxembourg	**504**	(2.1)	505	(2.5)	491	(3.2)	**477**	(3.4)	**–7.7**	(1.25)	**0.6**	(0.05)	1.0	(0.31)
	Mexico	**397**	(4.4)	390	(4.1)	387	(4.1)	**387**	(4.9)	–1.0	(1.63)	**0.9**	(0.07)	0.0	(0.05)
	Netherlands	**545**	(4.3)	555	(3.9)	544	(4.0)	**533**	(5.5)	–3.5	(2.43)	**0.9**	(0.07)	0.1	(0.17)
	New Zealand	**535**	(3.5)	533	(3.5)	523	(3.8)	**510**	(3.9)	**–8.2**	(2.04)	**0.7**	(0.07)	0.5	(0.27)
	Norway	**484**	(3.3)	501	(3.4)	503	(3.8)	**501**	(3.6)	**8.4**	(1.46)	**1.2**	(0.06)	0.8	(0.30)
	Poland	488	(3.5)	491	(3.1)	492	(4.0)	494	(4.1)	**5.9**	(1.90)	0.9	(0.07)	0.3	(0.20)
	Portugal	**456**	(3.5)	471	(4.1)	464	(5.2)	**474**	(4.8)	**9.2**	(2.07)	**1.1**	(0.06)	0.9	(0.43)
	Slovak Republic	500	(4.7)	500	(3.5)	499	(4.0)	497	(4.7)	0.4	(1.79)	0.9	(0.07)	0.0	(0.02)
	Spain	**472**	(3.5)	489	(3.5)	493	(3.2)	**491**	(3.1)	**10.2**	(1.41)	**1.3**	(0.09)	1.3	(0.38)
	Sweden	**499**	(2.9)	512	(3.6)	513	(3.4)	**517**	(5.3)	**9.8**	(2.18)	**1.2**	(0.08)	0.9	(0.39)
	Switzerland	**535**	(4.0)	534	(4.9)	525	(3.6)	**515**	(4.2)	**–5.9**	(1.42)	**0.8**	(0.05)	0.4	(0.18)
	Turkey	**417**	(5.9)	435	(7.6)	431	(7.9)	**433**	(9.2)	**5.7**	(2.17)	1.2	(0.08)	0.4	(0.29)
	United States	**496**	(3.4)	494	(3.7)	478	(3.8)	**470**	(4.1)	**–7.0**	(1.39)	**0.7**	(0.05)	0.6	(0.24)
	OECD total	*506*	*(1.4)*	*507*	*(1.2)*	*489*	*(1.2)*	*467*	*(1.9)*	*–11.4*	*(0.76)*	*0.7*	*(0.02)*	*1.5*	*(0.19)*
	OECD average	*508*	*(0.8)*	*512*	*(0.7)*	*502*	*(0.8)*	*488*	*(1.2)*	*–5.3*	*(0.43)*	*0.8*	*(0.01)*	*0.3*	*(0.05)*
Partner countries	Brazil	**384**	(6.1)	356	(5.8)	349	(6.0)	**352**	(5.6)	**–12.0**	(2.18)	**0.6**	(0.05)	1.3	(0.50)
	Hong Kong-China	**524**	(5.6)	552	(4.9)	560	(5.8)	**567**	(5.3)	**21.0**	(2.03)	**1.5**	(0.08)	4.1	(0.79)
	Indonesia	356	(5.3)	365	(3.9)	369	(4.8)	359	(4.9)	1.1	(2.50)	1.1	(0.09)	0.0	(0.06)
	Latvia	479	(4.0)	487	(4.9)	484	(5.3)	486	(6.5)	4.8	(3.92)	1.0	(0.08)	0.2	(0.26)
	Liechtenstein	**543**	(9.1)	541	(10.9)	547	(13.0)	**512**	(11.4)	**–11.5**	(5.22)	**0.6**	(0.13)	1.4	(1.28)
	Macao-China	**512**	(6.2)	530	(6.5)	525	(6.5)	**542**	(6.6)	**15.2**	(3.83)	1.2	(0.16)	2.4	(1.19)
	Russian Federation	468	(4.9)	469	(4.5)	467	(5.0)	471	(5.3)	3.4	(1.88)	1.0	(0.05)	0.1	(0.11)
	Serbia	**445**	(4.3)	451	(4.6)	441	(4.3)	**429**	(5.4)	**–5.1**	(1.85)	**0.9**	(0.07)	0.4	(0.31)
	Thailand	**413**	(3.6)	415	(3.8)	418	(3.8)	**423**	(4.4)	**6.9**	(2.24)	1.0	(0.06)	0.3	(0.22)
	Tunisia	**346**	(3.0)	359	(3.6)	363	(4.2)	**373**	(4.1)	**10.4**	(1.34)	**1.3**	(0.08)	1.8	(0.47)
	Uruguay	**434**	(4.3)	435	(4.0)	420	(4.8)	**418**	(5.5)	**–4.4**	(2.14)	**0.8**	(0.06)	0.2	(0.21)
	United Kingdom[1]	**519**	(3.3)	512	(3.9)	505	(3.6)	**500**	(3.4)	**–4.9**	(1.58)	**0.7**	(0.05)	0.2	(0.14)

Note: Values that are statistically significant are indicated in bold (see Annex A4).
1. Response rate too low to ensure comparability (see Annex A3).

Table 3.12
Relationships between selected learner characteristics and student performance in mathematics

		Effect of the index without accounting for the effects of the other learner characteristics shown in the remaining columns (bivariate)						Effect of the index after accounting for the effects of the other learner characteristics shown in the remaining columns (multivariate)					
		Anxiety in mathematics		Interest in and enjoyment of mathematics		Control strategies		Anxiety in mathematics		Interest in and enjoyment of mathematics		Control strategies	
		Effect	S.E.	Effect	S.E.	Effect	S.E.	Effect	S.E.	Effect	S.E.	Effect	S.E.
OECD countries	Australia	**–0.35**	(0.01)	**0.19**	(0.01)	**0.15**	(0.01)	**–0.33**	(0.01)	0.01	(0.02)	**0.10**	(0.01)
	Austria	**–0.31**	(0.02)	**0.10**	(0.02)	**–0.05**	(0.02)	**–0.33**	(0.02)	–0.04	(0.02)	–0.02	(0.02)
	Belgium	**–0.24**	(0.02)	**0.14**	(0.02)	–0.02	(0.02)	**–0.21**	(0.02)	**0.08**	(0.02)	0.00	(0.02)
	Canada	**–0.40**	(0.01)	**0.24**	(0.01)	**0.15**	(0.01)	**–0.38**	(0.01)	0.02	(0.02)	**0.10**	(0.01)
	Czech Republic	**–0.41**	(0.01)	**0.20**	(0.02)	0.00	(0.02)	**–0.40**	(0.02)	0.02	(0.02)	–0.01	(0.02)
	Denmark	**–0.51**	(0.01)	**0.30**	(0.02)	**0.04**	(0.02)	**–0.49**	(0.02)	**0.07**	(0.02)	**–0.07**	(0.02)
	Finland	**–0.44**	(0.01)	**0.33**	(0.02)	**0.11**	(0.01)	**–0.37**	(0.01)	**0.17**	(0.02)	0.00	(0.01)
	France	**–0.25**	(0.02)	**0.22**	(0.02)	**0.09**	(0.02)	**–0.22**	(0.02)	**0.14**	(0.02)	**0.07**	(0.02)
	Germany	**–0.34**	(0.02)	**0.12**	(0.02)	**–0.08**	(0.02)	**–0.36**	(0.02)	**–0.06**	(0.02)	–0.04	(0.02)
	Greece	**–0.35**	(0.02)	**0.26**	(0.02)	**0.07**	(0.02)	**–0.30**	(0.02)	**0.09**	(0.02)	0.01	(0.02)
	Hungary	**–0.32**	(0.02)	**0.09**	(0.02)	**–0.04**	(0.02)	**–0.34**	(0.02)	**–0.06**	(0.03)	–0.02	(0.02)
	Iceland	**–0.40**	(0.02)	**0.29**	(0.02)	**0.05**	(0.02)	**–0.33**	(0.02)	**0.17**	(0.02)	**–0.06**	(0.02)
	Ireland	**–0.36**	(0.02)	**0.20**	(0.02)	**0.04**	(0.02)	**–0.34**	(0.02)	0.04	(0.02)	0.00	(0.02)
	Italy	**–0.29**	(0.01)	**0.10**	(0.02)	0.03	(0.04)	**–0.30**	(0.02)	–0.01	(0.02)	**0.06**	(0.02)
	Japan	**–0.14**	(0.02)	**0.28**	(0.02)	**0.18**	(0.02)	0.03	(0.02)	**0.27**	(0.03)	**0.06**	(0.02)
	Korea	**–0.22**	(0.02)	**0.39**	(0.01)	**0.40**	(0.01)	**–0.04**	(0.02)	**0.23**	(0.02)	**0.27**	(0.02)
	Luxembourg	**–0.31**	(0.02)	**0.08**	(0.02)	**0.07**	(0.02)	**–0.32**	(0.02)	–0.02	(0.02)	–0.03	(0.02)
	Mexico	**–0.29**	(0.02)	**–0.06**	(0.02)	**0.09**	(0.02)	**–0.33**	(0.02)	**–0.17**	(0.03)	**0.16**	(0.02)
	Netherlands	**–0.22**	(0.02)	**0.14**	(0.02)	–0.01	(0.03)	**–0.20**	(0.02)	**0.07**	(0.02)	–0.01	(0.02)
	New Zealand	**–0.44**	(0.01)	**0.11**	(0.02)	**0.11**	(0.02)	**–0.46**	(0.02)	**–0.07**	(0.02)	**0.08**	(0.02)
	Norway	**–0.50**	(0.01)	**0.40**	(0.02)	**0.15**	(0.02)	**–0.40**	(0.02)	**0.19**	(0.02)	0.00	(0.02)
	Poland	**–0.49**	(0.01)	**0.16**	(0.02)	**0.04**	(0.02)	**–0.51**	(0.02)	**–0.06**	(0.02)	0.02	(0.02)
	Portugal	**–0.33**	(0.02)	**0.14**	(0.02)	**0.20**	(0.02)	**–0.32**	(0.02)	–0.04	(0.02)	**0.18**	(0.02)
	Slovak Republic	**–0.41**	(0.02)	**0.11**	(0.02)	**–0.04**	(0.02)	**–0.42**	(0.02)	**–0.04**	(0.02)	–0.01	(0.02)
	Spain	**–0.26**	(0.02)	**0.23**	(0.02)	**0.14**	(0.02)	**–0.25**	(0.02)	**0.10**	(0.02)	**0.14**	(0.02)
	Sweden	**–0.45**	(0.01)	**0.29**	(0.02)	0.00	(0.02)	**–0.39**	(0.02)	**0.14**	(0.02)	**–0.06**	(0.02)
	Switzerland	**–0.32**	(0.02)	**0.11**	(0.02)	**–0.03**	(0.02)	**–0.33**	(0.02)	–0.03	(0.02)	–0.01	(0.02)
	Turkey	**–0.34**	(0.03)	**0.17**	(0.03)	**0.16**	(0.02)	**–0.33**	(0.03)	–0.03	(0.03)	**0.14**	(0.03)
	United States	**–0.40**	(0.02)	**0.09**	(0.02)	**0.04**	(0.02)	**–0.44**	(0.02)	**–0.11**	(0.02)	0.02	(0.02)
	OECD average	*–0.36*	*(0.01)*	*0.12*	*(0.01)*	*0.01*	*(0.01)*	*–0.34*	*(0.01)*	*0.03*	*(0.00)*	*0.04*	*(0.01)*
Partner countries	Brazil	m	m	m	m	m	m	m	m	m	m	m	m
	Hong Kong-China	**–0.28**	(0.02)	**0.30**	(0.01)	**0.25**	(0.02)	**–0.19**	(0.02)	**0.15**	(0.02)	**0.15**	(0.02)
	Indonesia	**–0.10**	(0.02)	**–0.07**	(0.03)	**0.04**	(0.02)	**–0.13**	(0.02)	**–0.13**	(0.03)	**0.08**	(0.02)
	Latvia	**–0.42**	(0.02)	**0.13**	(0.02)	**–0.05**	(0.02)	**–0.42**	(0.02)	–0.01	(0.02)	0.01	(0.02)
	Liechtenstein	**–0.33**	(0.05)	0.03	(0.06)	**–0.14**	(0.06)	**–0.35**	(0.05)	–0.08	(0.06)	–0.07	(0.06)
	Macao-China	**–0.31**	(0.04)	**0.20**	(0.04)	**0.08**	(0.04)	**–0.29**	(0.05)	0.04	(0.04)	0.05	(0.04)
	Russian Federation	**–0.38**	(0.01)	**0.12**	(0.02)	0.00	(0.01)	**–0.38**	(0.02)	0.00	(0.02)	0.02	(0.01)
	Serbia	**–0.37**	(0.02)	–0.04	(0.02)	**0.08**	(0.02)	**–0.39**	(0.02)	**–0.13**	(0.02)	0.01	(0.02)
	Thailand	**–0.13**	(0.02)	0.03	(0.02)	**–0.06**	(0.02)	**–0.14**	(0.02)	**–0.06**	(0.02)	**0.09**	(0.02)
	Tunisia	**–0.14**	(0.02)	**0.10**	(0.02)	**0.15**	(0.02)	**–0.13**	(0.02)	–0.01	(0.02)	**0.15**	(0.02)
	Uruguay	**–0.36**	(0.02)	**0.15**	(0.02)	0.02	(0.02)	**–0.34**	(0.02)	0.01	(0.02)	0.00	(0.02)
	United Kingdom[1]	**–0.34**	(0.01)	**0.14**	(0.02)	**0.10**	(0.02)	**–0.35**	(0.02)	**–0.04**	(0.02)	**0.06**	(0.02)

Note: Values that are statistically significant are indicated in bold (see Annex A4).
1. Response rate too low to ensure comparability (see Annex A3).

Table 3.13
Relationships between selected learner characteristics and student use of control strategies

		Effect of the index without accounting for the effects of the other learner characteristics shown in the remaining columns (bivariate)				Effect of the index after accounting for the effects of the other learner characteristics shown in the remaining columns (multivariate)			
		Anxiety in mathematics		Interest in and enjoyment of mathematics		Anxiety in mathematics		Interest in and enjoyment of mathematics	
		Effect	**S.E.**	**Effect**	**S.E.**	**Effect**	**S.E.**	**Effect**	**S.E.**
OECD countries	Australia	**–0.16**	(0.02)	**0.39**	(0.01)	0.00	(0.02)	**0.39**	(0.02)
	Austria	**0.08**	(0.02)	**0.15**	(0.01)	**0.18**	(0.02)	**0.23**	(0.02)
	Belgium	**0.14**	(0.02)	**0.25**	(0.01)	**0.25**	(0.02)	**0.33**	(0.01)
	Canada	**–0.14**	(0.01)	**0.38**	(0.01)	**0.06**	(0.01)	**0.41**	(0.01)
	Czech Republic	–0.03	(0.02)	**0.20**	(0.02)	**0.08**	(0.03)	**0.24**	(0.02)
	Denmark	**–0.18**	(0.02)	**0.39**	(0.02)	0.04	(0.02)	**0.41**	(0.02)
	Finland	**–0.10**	(0.02)	**0.41**	(0.01)	**0.09**	(0.02)	**0.45**	(0.01)
	France	**0.13**	(0.02)	**0.34**	(0.02)	**0.23**	(0.02)	**0.40**	(0.02)
	Germany	**0.11**	(0.02)	**0.12**	(0.02)	**0.23**	(0.02)	**0.23**	(0.02)
	Greece	**–0.11**	(0.02)	**0.30**	(0.02)	**0.08**	(0.03)	**0.34**	(0.02)
	Hungary	0.02	(0.02)	**0.18**	(0.02)	**0.13**	(0.02)	**0.25**	(0.02)
	Iceland	**–0.15**	(0.02)	**0.37**	(0.02)	0.02	(0.02)	**0.38**	(0.02)
	Ireland	**–0.09**	(0.02)	**0.32**	(0.02)	**0.07**	(0.02)	**0.36**	(0.02)
	Italy	**0.06**	(0.02)	**0.33**	(0.02)	**0.18**	(0.01)	**0.39**	(0.02)
	Japan	**–0.26**	(0.02)	**0.45**	(0.01)	–0.01	(0.03)	**0.45**	(0.02)
	Korea	**–0.26**	(0.02)	**0.54**	(0.01)	0.00	(0.02)	**0.54**	(0.01)
	Luxembourg	**0.12**	(0.02)	**0.23**	(0.02)	**0.24**	(0.02)	**0.32**	(0.02)
	Mexico	0.04	(0.02)	**0.39**	(0.02)	**0.10**	(0.02)	**0.41**	(0.01)
	Netherlands	**0.12**	(0.02)	**0.23**	(0.02)	**0.22**	(0.02)	**0.30**	(0.02)
	New Zealand	**–0.11**	(0.02)	**0.36**	(0.02)	0.02	(0.02)	**0.37**	(0.02)
	Norway	**–0.18**	(0.02)	**0.41**	(0.02)	0.04	(0.03)	**0.43**	(0.02)
	Poland	**–0.07**	(0.02)	**0.26**	(0.02)	**0.05**	(0.02)	**0.29**	(0.02)
	Portugal	**–0.11**	(0.02)	**0.39**	(0.02)	0.02	(0.02)	**0.39**	(0.02)
	Slovak Republic	**0.05**	(0.02)	**0.21**	(0.02)	**0.14**	(0.02)	**0.27**	(0.02)
	Spain	**0.12**	(0.02)	**0.33**	(0.02)	**0.24**	(0.02)	**0.41**	(0.01)
	Sweden	–0.03	(0.02)	**0.31**	(0.02)	**0.14**	(0.02)	**0.38**	(0.02)
	Switzerland	0.02	(0.02)	**0.25**	(0.02)	**0.16**	(0.02)	**0.32**	(0.02)
	Turkey	**–0.14**	(0.03)	**0.52**	(0.01)	**0.10**	(0.02)	**0.57**	(0.02)
	United States	**–0.13**	(0.02)	**0.40**	(0.01)	**0.06**	(0.02)	**0.43**	(0.02)
	OECD average	*–0.05*	*(0.01)*	*0.32*	*(0.01)*	*0.11*	*(0.01)*	*0.37*	*(0.01)*
Partner countries	Brazil	m	m	m	m	m	m	m	m
	Hong Kong-China	**–0.14**	(0.02)	**0.44**	(0.02)	**0.08**	(0.02)	**0.48**	(0.02)
	Indonesia	**–0.07**	(0.03)	**0.38**	(0.02)	0.04	(0.02)	**0.39**	(0.02)
	Latvia	**0.12**	(0.02)	**0.26**	(0.02)	**0.24**	(0.02)	**0.34**	(0.02)
	Liechtenstein	**0.16**	(0.07)	**0.26**	(0.05)	**0.28**	(0.07)	**0.36**	(0.05)
	Macao-China	–0.03	(0.04)	**0.27**	(0.03)	**0.14**	(0.04)	**0.34**	(0.04)
	Russian Federation	0.03	(0.02)	**0.36**	(0.01)	**0.15**	(0.02)	**0.41**	(0.01)
	Serbia	**0.08**	(0.02)	**0.26**	(0.02)	**0.14**	(0.02)	**0.29**	(0.02)
	Thailand	**–0.09**	(0.04)	**0.40**	(0.02)	**0.08**	(0.03)	**0.43**	(0.02)
	Tunisia	**–0.08**	(0.02)	**0.50**	(0.01)	**0.10**	(0.02)	**0.53**	(0.02)
	Uruguay	**0.05**	(0.02)	**0.30**	(0.02)	**0.20**	(0.02)	**0.38**	(0.02)
	United Kingdom[1]	**–0.15**	(0.02)	**0.35**	(0.02)	0.01	(0.02)	**0.36**	(0.02)

Note: Values that are statistically significant are indicated in bold (see Annex A4).
1. Response rate too low to ensure comparability (see Annex A3).

Table 3.14
Correlations between anxiety in mathematics and interest in and enjoyment of mathematics

		Correlation coefficients between anxiety in mathematics and interest in and enjoyment of mathematics	
		Correlation	S.E.
OECD countries	Australia	–0.41	(0.01)
	Austria	–0.42	(0.02)
	Belgium	–0.33	(0.02)
	Canada	–0.50	(0.01)
	Czech Republic	–0.45	(0.02)
	Denmark	–0.53	(0.02)
	Finland	–0.43	(0.01)
	France	–0.26	(0.02)
	Germany	–0.51	(0.02)
	Greece	–0.57	(0.02)
	Hungary	–0.46	(0.02)
	Iceland	–0.45	(0.02)
	Ireland	–0.47	(0.02)
	Italy	–0.32	(0.02)
	Japan	–0.58	(0.01)
	Korea	–0.49	(0.01)
	Luxembourg	–0.37	(0.02)
	Mexico	–0.18	(0.02)
	Netherlands	–0.33	(0.02)
	New Zealand	–0.35	(0.02)
	Norway	–0.54	(0.01)
	Poland	–0.42	(0.02)
	Portugal	–0.34	(0.02)
	Slovak Republic	–0.37	(0.01)
	Spain	–0.29	(0.02)
	Sweden	–0.45	(0.01)
	Switzerland	–0.44	(0.02)
	Turkey	–0.44	(0.03)
	United States	–0.44	(0.02)
	OECD total	*–0.42*	*(0.01)*
Partner countries	Brazil	m	m
	Hong Kong-China	–0.47	(0.02)
	Indonesia	–0.29	(0.03)
	Latvia	–0.34	(0.02)
	Liechtenstein	–0.35	(0.05)
	Macao-China	–0.52	(0.03)
	Russian Federation	–0.31	(0.02)
	Serbia	–0.23	(0.03)
	Thailand	–0.39	(0.02)
	Tunisia	–0.34	(0.02)
	Uruguay	–0.41	(0.02)
	United Kingdom[1]	–0.43	(0.02)

1. Response rate too low to ensure comparability (see Annex A3).

Table 3.15

Percentage of variance in learner characteristics that lies between schools

		Percentage of between-school variance on each index						
		Interest in and enjoyment of mathematics	Instrumental motivation in mathematics	Self-efficacy in mathematics	Anxiety in mathematics	Self-concept in mathematics	Memorisation strategies	Elaboration strategies	Control strategies
OECD countries	Australia	3.9	2.3	10.7	4.9	5.1	4.2	4.3	5.4
	Austria	8.3	16.3	22.1	9.5	10.0	7.3	11.2	6.2
	Belgium	5.7	5.8	15.9	5.9	5.0	6.2	8.4	9.9
	Canada	3.7	3.3	9.6	5.9	6.5	6.1	6.1	8.7
	Czech Republic	4.5	7.7	23.4	10.5	9.0	9.3	7.4	7.5
	Denmark	4.0	2.3	9.9	8.5	7.5	6.9	6.5	7.3
	Finland	4.1	0.9	5.4	4.3	4.4	3.2	3.1	3.6
	France	w	w	w	w	w	w	w	w
	Germany	3.7	4.2	15.6	6.8	5.8	8.5	8.5	6.9
	Greece	3.4	3.0	12.9	6.9	8.6	4.3	4.7	5.0
	Hungary	5.4	3.4	24.9	9.8	9.0	7.8	8.0	6.6
	Iceland	3.0	2.3	3.4	1.6	1.6	1.1	1.4	2.2
	Ireland	1.7	3.3	10.3	6.6	6.7	4.5	5.7	5.3
	Italy	9.7	12.0	17.7	6.0	8.6	7.2	11.9	10.7
	Japan	6.2	8.7	28.6	5.9	5.9	5.5	6.2	7.4
	Korea	8.1	9.0	22.6	4.9	12.7	8.0	8.4	15.9
	Luxembourg	2.5	3.9	6.3	2.1	0.9	1.8	4.1	1.9
	Mexico	8.5	3.1	12.5	9.0	9.7	10.4	10.4	10.0
	Netherlands	3.9	2.8	12.5	7.4	7.3	7.3	8.1	7.5
	New Zealand	6.8	2.3	9.3	7.2	5.9	6.9	8.2	6.1
	Norway	2.8	3.0	8.4	7.4	6.6	5.3	5.9	5.5
	Poland	3.1	2.5	9.1	6.0	5.3	4.0	5.5	4.7
	Portugal	3.0	2.5	13.1	5.9	6.2	5.9	5.2	7.9
	Slovak Republic	5.6	7.7	25.7	9.3	9.8	6.3	8.0	7.5
	Spain	4.0	3.0	10.2	7.2	8.0	5.0	6.2	5.3
	Sweden	3.6	1.8	10.1	6.4	7.2	5.1	5.9	5.9
	Switzerland	3.3	6.0	17.9	7.6	6.3	7.4	6.7	5.9
	Turkey	6.4	4.3	25.3	10.4	10.5	6.0	7.2	8.0
	United States	4.7	2.5	10.8	8.4	8.5	9.0	9.4	8.2
	OECD average	***4.7***	***4.5***	***14.5***	***6.8***	***7.1***	***6.2***	***6.9***	***6.9***
Partner countries	Brazil	m	m	m	m	m	m	m	m
	Hong Kong-China	2.6	2.4	19.1	7.4	7.5	4.5	4.2	7.0
	Indonesia	11.7	5.4	11.4	8.8	15.6	11.2	8.4	8.0
	Latvia	3.8	2.8	10.5	7.1	6.4	5.7	4.8	5.0
	Liechtenstein	5.0	10.3	14.6	-0.2	-0.3	16.5	11.9	1.9
	Macao-China	1.0	0.3	8.5	1.8	6.4	3.6	4.1	4.5
	Russian Federation	6.3	4.6	11.2	8.2	8.6	6.0	6.5	6.2
	Serbia	10.4	9.8	11.0	10.2	7.5	9.8	9.4	8.4
	Thailand	5.0	3.2	12.7	8.5	8.0	7.3	8.0	7.9
	Tunisia	4.6	4.0	13.6	5.8	8.5	4.7	5.4	5.4
	Uruguay	3.8	4.9	11.7	8.9	8.2	6.7	8.6	5.8
	United Kingdom[1]	3.0	3.0	11.9	6.7	6.1	7.7	6.1	6.4

1. Response rate too low to ensure comparability (see Annex A3).

Table 3.16
Gender differences in learner characteristics, measured in terms of effect sizes

		Gender differences in terms of effect sizes for each index							
		Performance in mathematics		Instrumental motivation in mathematics		Interest in and enjoyment of mathematics		Anxiety in mathematics	
		Effect size	S.E.	Effect size	S.E.	Effect size	S.E.	Effect size	S.E.
OECD countries	Australia	0.06	(0.04)	**0.24**	(0.03)	**0.23**	(0.03)	**–0.31**	(0.02)
	Austria	0.08	(0.05)	**0.58**	(0.04)	**0.40**	(0.03)	**–0.36**	(0.03)
	Belgium	0.07	(0.04)	**0.32**	(0.03)	**0.20**	(0.03)	**–0.32**	(0.03)
	Canada	0.13	(0.02)	0.12	(0.02)	0.17	(0.02)	**–0.33**	(0.02)
	Czech Republic	0.16	(0.05)	**0.26**	(0.04)	**0.26**	(0.04)	**–0.26**	(0.03)
	Denmark	0.18	(0.03)	**0.43**	(0.03)	**0.29**	(0.03)	**–0.38**	(0.03)
	Finland	0.09	(0.03)	**0.36**	(0.03)	**0.34**	(0.03)	**–0.39**	(0.02)
	France	0.09	(0.05)	**0.35**	(0.03)	**0.24**	(0.03)	**–0.39**	(0.03)
	Germany	0.09	(0.04)	**0.45**	(0.03)	**0.37**	(0.03)	**–0.38**	(0.03)
	Greece	**0.21**	(0.04)	**0.26**	(0.03)	**0.31**	(0.03)	**–0.26**	(0.03)
	Hungary	0.08	(0.04)	**0.22**	(0.03)	0.12	(0.03)	**–0.20**	(0.04)
	Iceland	–0.17	(0.04)	0.06	(0.04)	0.07	(0.04)	**–0.27**	(0.04)
	Ireland	0.17	(0.05)	**0.32**	(0.04)	0.04	(0.04)	**–0.28**	(0.04)
	Italy	0.19	(0.06)	**0.23**	(0.03)	0.11	(0.04)	–0.17	(0.03)
	Japan	0.08	(0.06)	**0.31**	(0.03)	**0.26**	(0.04)	**–0.26**	(0.03)
	Korea	**0.26**	(0.08)	**0.20**	(0.05)	0.16	(0.04)	–0.14	(0.03)
	Luxembourg	0.19	(0.03)	**0.42**	(0.03)	**0.32**	(0.03)	**–0.44**	(0.02)
	Mexico	0.13	(0.05)	0.03	(0.04)	0.16	(0.03)	–0.13	(0.03)
	Netherlands	0.06	(0.05)	**0.50**	(0.04)	**0.34**	(0.04)	**–0.38**	(0.03)
	New Zealand	0.15	(0.04)	0.17	(0.03)	**0.23**	(0.04)	**–0.31**	(0.03)
	Norway	0.07	(0.04)	**0.23**	(0.04)	**0.25**	(0.04)	**–0.36**	(0.04)
	Poland	0.06	(0.04)	0.05	(0.03)	0.11	(0.03)	–0.03	(0.03)
	Portugal	0.14	(0.04)	0.06	(0.04)	0.03	(0.04)	**–0.22**	(0.04)
	Slovak Republic	**0.20**	(0.04)	**0.23**	(0.03)	0.17	(0.04)	**–0.25**	(0.04)
	Spain	0.10	(0.03)	0.09	(0.03)	0.03	(0.03)	**–0.34**	(0.03)
	Sweden	0.07	(0.03)	**0.32**	(0.03)	0.19	(0.04)	**–0.30**	(0.04)
	Switzerland	0.17	(0.05)	**0.67**	(0.03)	**0.58**	(0.03)	**–0.44**	(0.03)
	Turkey	0.15	(0.06)	–0.06	(0.04)	0.10	(0.04)	**–0.20**	(0.04)
	United States	0.07	(0.03)	0.10	(0.03)	0.16	(0.03)	**–0.23**	(0.03)
	OECD average	*0.11*	*(0.01)*	*0.24*	*(0.01)*	*0.21*	*(0.01)*	*–0.28*	*(0.01)*
Partner countries	Brazil	0.16	(0.04)	m	m	m	m	m	m
	Hong Kong-China	0.04	(0.07)	**0.20**	(0.04)	**0.27**	(0.03)	**–0.28**	(0.04)
	Indonesia	0.04	(0.04)	–0.05	(0.03)	0.08	(0.03)	–0.13	(0.03)
	Latvia	0.03	(0.05)	0.18	(0.04)	**0.20**	(0.04)	**–0.26**	(0.04)
	Liechtenstein	**0.29**	(0.11)	**0.89**	(0.09)	**0.60**	(0.09)	**–0.61**	(0.10)
	Macao-China	**0.25**	(0.07)	**0.24**	(0.06)	**0.34**	(0.07)	**–0.46**	(0.07)
	Russian Federation	0.11	(0.05)	0.09	(0.04)	0.01	(0.04)	–0.16	(0.03)
	Serbia	0.01	(0.05)	**0.21**	(0.04)	0.18	(0.04)	0.04	(0.04)
	Thailand	–0.05	(0.05)	**–0.20**	(0.03)	0.06	(0.03)	–0.11	(0.03)
	Tunisia	0.15	(0.03)	0.17	(0.03)	**0.27**	(0.03)	**–0.35**	(0.03)
	Uruguay	0.12	(0.04)	0.16	(0.03)	0.11	(0.04)	**–0.21**	(0.03)
	United Kingdom[1]	0.07	(0.05)	**0.30**	(0.03)	**0.20**	(0.03)	**–0.38**	(0.03)

		Gender differences in terms of effect sizes for each index									
		Self-efficacy in mathematics		Self-concept in mathematics		Memorisation strategies		Elaboration strategies		Control strategies	
		Effect size	S.E.	Effect size	S.E.	Effect size	S.E.	Effect size	S.E.	Effect size	S.E.
OECD countries	Australia	**0.37**	(0.03)	**0.34**	(0.02)	0.05	(0.03)	**0.32**	(0.02)	–0.08	(0.03)
	Austria	**0.46**	(0.03)	**0.44**	(0.03)	–0.13	(0.03)	**0.43**	(0.04)	–0.18	(0.04)
	Belgium	**0.36**	(0.03)	**0.35**	(0.03)	–0.12	(0.03)	**0.27**	(0.02)	**–0.21**	(0.03)
	Canada	**0.34**	(0.02)	**0.33**	(0.02)	–0.04	(0.02)	**0.25**	(0.02)	**–0.21**	(0.02)
	Czech Republic	**0.42**	(0.04)	**0.36**	(0.03)	–0.07	(0.03)	**0.24**	(0.03)	–0.16	(0.03)
	Denmark	**0.45**	(0.03)	**0.48**	(0.03)	**0.22**	(0.04)	**0.34**	(0.03)	0.02	(0.03)
	Finland	**0.56**	(0.03)	**0.45**	(0.03)	0.10	(0.03)	**0.37**	(0.03)	0.05	(0.03)
	France	**0.31**	(0.04)	**0.37**	(0.03)	–0.18	(0.03)	**0.23**	(0.03)	**–0.24**	(0.03)
	Germany	**0.46**	(0.04)	**0.50**	(0.03)	–0.14	(0.03)	**0.32**	(0.03)	**–0.28**	(0.03)
	Greece	**0.44**	(0.04)	**0.30**	(0.03)	0.03	(0.03)	**0.29**	(0.03)	–0.12	(0.03)
	Hungary	**0.35**	(0.03)	**0.24**	(0.04)	–0.19	(0.03)	**0.20**	(0.03)	–0.18	(0.03)
	Iceland	**0.25**	(0.04)	**0.22**	(0.04)	0.02	(0.04)	**0.27**	(0.03)	–0.07	(0.04)
	Ireland	**0.30**	(0.04)	**0.23**	(0.04)	–0.05	(0.03)	0.19	(0.04)	–0.08	(0.04)
	Italy	**0.36**	(0.04)	0.14	(0.03)	–0.07	(0.03)	**0.22**	(0.04)	–0.18	(0.04)
	Japan	**0.31**	(0.05)	**0.36**	(0.03)	0.10	(0.03)	**0.30**	(0.03)	0.10	(0.04)
	Korea	**0.20**	(0.05)	**0.26**	(0.04)	–0.02	(0.04)	**0.21**	(0.04)	0.08	(0.05)
	Luxembourg	**0.43**	(0.03)	**0.49**	(0.02)	–0.11	(0.03)	**0.36**	(0.04)	–0.19	(0.03)
	Mexico	0.18	(0.03)	0.15	(0.03)	–0.01	(0.03)	0.06	(0.03)	–0.15	(0.03)
	Netherlands	**0.59**	(0.03)	**0.55**	(0.04)	**0.21**	(0.04)	**0.40**	(0.04)	–0.01	(0.04)
	New Zealand	**0.37**	(0.03)	**0.35**	(0.03)	0.02	(0.03)	**0.20**	(0.04)	–0.08	(0.03)
	Norway	**0.37**	(0.04)	**0.42**	(0.03)	**0.23**	(0.03)	**0.24**	(0.04)	–0.05	(0.03)
	Poland	0.17	(0.03)	0.18	(0.03)	–0.03	(0.03)	0.14	(0.03)	**–0.21**	(0.03)
	Portugal	**0.24**	(0.03)	**0.21**	(0.04)	–0.05	(0.04)	0.15	(0.04)	**–0.20**	(0.04)
	Slovak Republic	**0.33**	(0.04)	**0.30**	(0.03)	–0.12	(0.03)	**0.22**	(0.03)	–0.13	(0.03)
	Spain	**0.28**	(0.03)	**0.25**	(0.03)	–0.09	(0.03)	0.09	(0.03)	**–0.21**	(0.03)
	Sweden	**0.27**	(0.04)	**0.35**	(0.04)	0.14	(0.03)	**0.25**	(0.04)	0.00	(0.03)
	Switzerland	**0.54**	(0.04)	**0.67**	(0.03)	0.02	(0.04)	**0.44**	(0.03)	–0.13	(0.03)
	Turkey	**0.25**	(0.05)	0.19	(0.04)	–0.06	(0.03)	0.01	(0.04)	**–0.21**	(0.04)
	United States	0.19	(0.03)	**0.27**	(0.03)	–0.04	(0.03)	0.15	(0.03)	–0.15	(0.03)
	OECD average	*0.34*	*(0.01)*	*0.33*	*(0.01)*	*0.00*	*(0.01)*	*0.24*	*(0.01)*	*–0.11*	*(0.01)*
Partner countries	Brazil	m	m	m	m	m	m	m	m	m	m
	Hong Kong-China	**0.30**	(0.05)	**0.35**	(0.04)	0.03	(0.04)	**0.31**	(0.03)	–0.04	(0.04)
	Indonesia	0.08	(0.04)	0.18	(0.03)	0.00	(0.03)	0.06	(0.03)	–0.15	(0.03)
	Latvia	**0.34**	(0.04)	**0.31**	(0.04)	0.06	(0.04)	**0.24**	(0.03)	–0.14	(0.03)
	Liechtenstein	**0.65**	(0.10)	**0.77**	(0.09)	0.11	(0.10)	**0.54**	(0.10)	0.01	(0.10)
	Macao-China	**0.38**	(0.07)	**0.47**	(0.06)	–0.07	(0.07)	**0.38**	(0.07)	0.06	(0.06)
	Russian Federation	**0.33**	(0.04)	0.07	(0.03)	–0.06	(0.03)	**0.22**	(0.04)	–0.14	(0.03)
	Serbia	**0.27**	(0.04)	0.14	(0.04)	0.02	(0.04)	0.15	(0.04)	–0.19	(0.04)
	Thailand	0.13	(0.04)	**0.28**	(0.04)	–0.02	(0.03)	0.04	(0.03)	–0.07	(0.03)
	Tunisia	**0.27**	(0.03)	**0.34**	(0.03)	0.16	(0.03)	0.15	(0.03)	0.03	(0.03)
	Uruguay	**0.31**	(0.04)	**0.24**	(0.04)	0.10	(0.03)	0.11	(0.03)	–0.17	(0.03)
	United Kingdom[1]	**0.37**	(0.04)	**0.40**	(0.03)	0.06	(0.03)	**0.25**	(0.03)	–0.01	(0.03)

Note: Bold figures represent values that are equal to or greater than 0.2 (see Annex A4).
1. Response rate too low to ensure comparability (see Annex A3).

Table 4.1a

Between-school and within-school variance in student performance on the mathematics scale in PISA 2003

			Variance expressed as a percentage of the average variance in student performance (SP) across OECD countries[1]											
			Total variance in SP expressed as a percentage of the average variance in student performance across OECD countries[3]	Total variance in SP between schools[4]	Total variance in SP within schools	Variance explained by the international index of economic, social and cultural status of students		Variance explained by the international index of economic, social and cultural status of students and schools		Variance explained by students' study programmes		Variance explained by students' study programmes and the international index of economic, social and cultural status		Total variance between schools expressed as a percentage of the total variance within the country[5]
		Total variance in SP[2]				Between-school variance explained	Within-school variance explained	Between-school variance explained	Within-school variance explained	Between-school variance explained	Within-school variance explained	Between-school variance explained	Within-school variance explained	
OECD countries	Australia	9 036	105.1	22.0	82.3	9.0	4.2	15.4	4.3	1.8	2.8	16.7	6.8	21.1
	Austria	8 455	98.4	55.5	49.5	7.6	0.6	35.2	0.5	42.6	0.4	45.3	0.9	52.9
	Belgium	10 463	121.8	56.9	66.7	17.7	4.4	42.0	4.4	49.1	15.8	52.1	17.0	46.0
	Canada	7 626	88.7	15.1	72.6	4.7	4.2	7.1	4.3	2.6	5.0	7.0	8.5	17.3
	Czech Republic	8 581	99.9	50.5	55.2	13.8	2.5	37.0	2.6	34.1	0.2	41.6	2.7	47.8
	Denmark	8 289	96.5	13.1	84.2	7.7	9.7	9.3	9.8	1.6	0.1	9.7	9.9	13.4
	Finland	6 974	81.2	3.9	77.3	0.9	7.9	0.9	7.9	0.0	0.0	0.9	7.9	4.8
	France	w	w	w	w	w	w	w	w	w	w	w	w	w
	Germany	9 306	108.3	56.4	52.6	14.1	2.2	43.8	2.2	47.2	1.1	50.7	3.2	51.7
	Greece	8 752	101.8	38.9	68.1	10.3	2.5	25.2	2.3	28.3	0.0	32.9	2.3	36.3
	Hungary	8 726	101.5	66.0	47.3	15.6	1.0	53.2	0.7	49.0	–0.1	57.1	0.8	58.3
	Iceland	8 123	94.5	3.6	90.9	1.3	4.7	1.3	4.7	0.0	0.0	1.3	4.7	3.8
	Ireland	7 213	83.9	13.4	71.2	7.8	6.0	11.1	6.1	1.4	4.4	11.0	10.0	15.9
	Italy	9 153	106.5	56.8	52.0	6.6	0.7	30.5	0.7	26.0	0.1	34.6	0.7	52.2
	Japan	9 994	116.3	62.1	55.0	3.3	0.1	42.0	0.1	5.2	0.0	42.9	0.1	53.0
	Korea	8 531	99.3	42.0	58.2	7.7	1.1	27.8	1.1	21.5	0.6	31.2	1.6	42.0
	Luxembourg	8 432	98.1	31.2	67.6	9.3	3.0	27.9	2.9	14.8	14.6	27.8	15.7	31.6
	Mexico	7 295	84.9	29.1	44.8	4.2	0.3	16.6	0.4	12.7	0.0	20.8	0.5	39.4
	Netherlands	7 897	91.9	54.5	39.5	8.8	1.3	40.7	1.3	50.8	7.8	51.4	8.4	58.0
	New Zealand	9 457	110.1	20.1	90.9	9.8	8.7	15.2	8.8	0.8	3.1	15.2	11.4	18.1
	Norway	8 432	98.1	6.5	91.7	2.7	11.1	2.9	11.2	0.2	0.1	2.9	11.2	6.6
	Poland	8 138	94.7	12.0	83.1	7.1	8.9	8.2	9.0	0.8	0.1	8.3	9.0	12.6
	Portugal	7 647	89.0	30.3	60.0	9.5	4.8	17.2	4.8	26.5	8.6	28.6	11.6	33.6
	Slovak Republic	8 478	98.7	41.5	58.0	12.9	3.1	32.3	3.1	26.0	0.4	33.6	3.4	41.7
	Spain	7 803	90.8	17.2	70.2	6.4	4.1	9.8	4.2	0.0	0.0	9.8	4.2	19.7
	Sweden	8 880	103.3	10.9	92.8	4.7	11.2	5.8	11.2	1.5	0.6	6.9	11.6	10.5
	Switzerland	9 541	111.0	36.4	70.2	9.4	5.1	19.3	5.1	6.1	1.0	19.8	6.0	34.2
	Turkey	10 952	127.4	68.7	56.5	10.1	0.7	49.0	0.6	42.5	3.1	56.0	3.4	54.9
	United States	9 016	104.9	27.1	78.3	12.1	7.0	18.7	7.2	3.2	2.8	19.2	9.2	25.7
	OECD average	*8 593*	*100.0*	*33.6*	*67.0*	*8.5*	*4.4*	*23.0*	*4.4*	*17.8*	*2.6*	*26.4*	*6.5*	
Partner countries	Brazil	10 000	116.4	49.2	59.8	6.3	0.2	28.6	0.3	18.7	3.6	36.8	3.9	45.1
	Hong Kong-China	9 946	115.7	52.8	60.4	2.6	0.1	22.7	0.2	15.2	4.5	29.4	4.6	46.6
	Indonesia	6 480	75.4	31.6	39.5	0.7	0.0	13.1	0.0	9.1	0.0	15.1	0.0	44.5
	Latvia	7 749	90.2	20.6	71.0	5.3	4.6	8.4	4.6	0.6	1.4	8.3	5.7	22.5
	Liechtenstein	9 816	114.2	39.8	54.6	6.9	1.5	29.9	1.5	4.1	0.7	30.0	2.0	42.2
	Macao-China	7 566	88.1	16.9	74.5	1.4	0.2	4.5	0.2	6.1	7.4	9.1	7.5	18.5
	Russian Federation	8 501	98.9	29.8	69.2	5.6	2.7	11.9	2.6	4.5	2.9	12.6	4.9	30.1
	Serbia	7 146	83.2	29.6	54.5	7.3	1.7	18.9	1.7	17.5	6.8	20.3	7.4	35.2
	Thailand	6 723	78.2	30.4	51.0	5.9	0.4	16.4	0.5	4.8	1.6	17.0	2.0	37.3
	Tunisia	6 707	78.0	32.9	44.9	5.3	0.6	18.1	0.6	25.3	1.8	27.6	2.4	42.3
	Uruguay	9 915	115.4	53.6	68.7	13.0	1.4	38.3	1.5	39.3	2.8	47.6	4.2	43.8
	United Kingdom[6]	8 372	97.4	21.1	73.4	9.5	7.2	15.3	7.5	1.6	1.3	16.0	8.4	22.3

1. The variance components were estimated for all students in participating countries with data on socio-economic background and study programmes. Students in special education programmes were excluded from these analyses.
2. The total variance in student performance is obtained as the square of the standard deviation shown in Chapter 2. The statistical variance in student performance and not the standard deviation is used for this comparison to allow for the decomposition of variance in student performance. For reasons explained in the *PISA 2003 Technical Report*, the sum of the between and within-school variance components may, for some countries, differ slightly from the square of the standard deviation shown in Chapter 2.
3. The sum of the between- and within-school variance components, as an estimate from a sample, does not necessarily add up to the total.
4. In some countries, sub-units within schools were sampled instead of schools and this may affect the estimation of the between-school variance components. In Austria, the Czech Republic, Hungary, Italy and Japan, schools with more than one study programme were split into the units delivering these programmes. In the Netherlands, for schools with both lower and upper secondary programmes, schools were split into units delivering each programme level. In Uruguay and Mexico, schools where instruction is delivered in shifts were split into the corresponding units. In the Flemish part of Belgium, in case of multi-campus schools, implantations (campuses) were sampled whereas in the French part, in case of multi-campus schools the larger administrative units were sampled. In the Slovak Republic, in case of schools with both Slovak and Hungarian as test languages, schools were split into units delivering each language of instruction.
5. This index is often referred to as the intra-class correlation (rho).
6. Response rate too low to ensure comparability (see Annex A3).

Table 4.1b

Between-school and within-school variance in student performance on the mathematics scale in PISA 2000

	Total variance in SP[2]	Variance expressed as a percentage of the average variance in student performance (SP) across OECD countries[1]: Total variance in SP expressed as a percentage of the average variance in student performance across OECD countries[3]	Total variance in SP between schools[4]	Total variance in SP within schools	Variance explained by the international index of economic, social and cultural status of students: Between-school variance explained	Within-school variance explained	Variance explained by the international index of economic, social and cultural status of students and schools: Between-school variance explained	Within-school variance explained	Total variance between schools expressed as a percentage of the total variance within the country[5]
OECD countries									
Australia	8 066	94.8	16.2	77.9	9.9	5.8	11.9	6.4	17.2
Austria	8 481	99.7	59.7	53.4	9.6	0.5	34.6	0.6	52.8
Belgium	11 054	130.0	72.8	60.7	14.9	1.8	46.8	1.9	54.5
Canada	7 104	83.5	14.7	68.3	3.8	4.5	4.9	4.7	17.7
Czech Republic	9 260	108.9	47.6	60.1	14.7	3.3	32.3	3.4	44.2
Denmark	7 195	84.6	12.6	72.7	6.0	6.6	7.2	6.8	14.8
Finland	6 431	75.6	4.9	71.0	0.5	6.1	0.5	6.1	6.4
France	w	w	w	w	w	w	w	w	w
Germany	10 400	122.3	66.1	55.0	16.0	2.0	48.3	2.2	54.6
Greece	11 736	138.0	65.3	76.7	11.8	2.3	31.6	2.3	46.0
Hungary	9 491	111.6	60.3	53.5	16.1	0.8	48.5	0.7	53.0
Iceland	6 979	82.1	4.4	77.8	1.0	4.4	1.0	4.4	5.4
Ireland	6 916	81.3	9.2	72.2	5.3	5.7	6.8	6.0	11.3
Italy	8 079	95.0	41.4	57.3	3.9	0.2	16.9	0.2	41.9
Japan[6]	m	m	m	m	m	m	m	m	m
Korea	7 108	83.6	33.9	50.4	4.6	0.4	20.6	0.4	40.2
Luxembourg	8 269	97.2	22.9	73.8	9.4	4.2	20.8	4.1	23.7
Mexico	6 897	81.1	41.0	41.5	7.4	0.2	24.9	0.1	49.7
New Zealand	9 432	110.9	19.8	91.2	9.7	7.9	13.4	8.1	17.9
Norway	8 359	98.3	8.6	89.7	1.7	8.7	1.7	8.7	8.8
Poland	9 949	117.0	62.8	52.9	6.9	0.4	34.4	0.4	54.3
Portugal	8 263	97.2	28.8	67.2	10.3	3.8	18.1	3.9	30.0
Spain	8 139	95.7	16.7	78.2	8.1	5.3	9.9	5.4	17.6
Sweden	8 638	101.6	7.7	94.0	4.8	7.6	5.6	7.7	7.6
Switzerland	9 886	116.2	45.7	69.3	11.0	3.4	23.4	3.1	39.7
United Kingdom	8 289	97.5	21.5	71.5	9.6	4.9	15.5	5.5	23.1
United States	8 825	103.8	32.8	72.7	16.8	7.7	24.9	7.8	31.1
OECD average	***8 505***	***100.0***	***33.1***	***67.7***	***8.6***	***3.8***	***20.4***	***3.9***	
Partner countries									
Brazil	9 496	111.6	41.8	72.5	16.5	1.0	27.9	2.1	36.5
Hong Kong-China	8 642	101.6	45.7	55.7	2.5	0.2	15.5	0.2	45.1
Indonesia	7 095	83.4	26.1	51.3	1.6	0.1	7.3	0.1	33.7
Latvia	10 614	124.8	33.5	91.7	5.3	1.4	14.2	1.5	26.8
Liechtenstein	9 080	106.8	39.7	52.5	3.0	0.7	17.9	0.6	43.1
Russian Federation	10 772	126.7	45.1	81.3	5.4	2.1	12.9	2.0	35.7
Thailand	6 799	79.9	27.2	54.5	5.2	0.5	11.1	0.6	33.3
Netherlands[7]	m	m	m	m	m	m	m	m	m

1. The variance components were estimated for all students in participating countries with data on socio-economic background and study programmes. Students in special education programmes were excluded from these analyses.
2. The total variance in student performance is obtained as the square of the standard deviation shown in Chapter 2. The statistical variance in student performance and not the standard deviation is used for this comparison to allow for the decomposition of variance in student performance. For reasons explained in the *PISA 2003 Technical Report*, the sum of the between and within-school variance components may, for some countries, differ slightly from the square of the standard deviation shown in Chapter 2.
3. The sum of the between- and within-school variance components, as an estimate from a sample, does not necessarily add up to the total.
4. In some countries, sub-units within schools were sampled instead of schools and this may affect the estimation of the between-school variance components. In Austria, the Czech Republic, Hungary and Italy, schools with more than one study programme were split into the units delivering these programmes. In Brazil, schools where instruction is delivered in shifts were split into the corresponding units. In the French part of Belgium, in case of multi-campus schools, implantations (campuses) were sampled whereas in the Flemish part, in case of multi-campus schools the larger administrative units were sampled.
5. This index is often referred to as the intra-class correlation (rho).
6. Due to high percentages of missing data on socio-economic background, data from Japan are not included in these analyses.
7. Response rate too low to ensure comparability (see Annex A3, OECD 2001a).

Table 4.2
Effects of student-level factors on student performance in mathematics

Score point difference associated with the various factors shown below, after accounting for the other factors

		Intercept		Highest occupational status of parents (SEI scores)		Highest level of parents education (in years of schooling)		Possessions related to the classical culture		Single-parent family		First-generation students (those born in the country of assessment but whose parents were born in another country)		Non-native students (those born outside the country of assessment and whose parents were also born in another country)		Language spoken at home is different from the language of assessment and other national languages or dialects	
		Score	S.E.	Score	S.E.	Score	S.E.	Score	S.E.	Score	S.E.	Score	S.E.	Score	S.E.	Score	S.E.
OECD countries	Australia	530	(1.7)	23.2	(1.2)	3.2	(0.6)	11.1	(1.0)	–17.2	(2.4)	2.8	(3.8)	–2.7	(4.3)	–0.3	(5.1)
	Austria	519	(2.8)	19.2	(2.0)	1.7	(0.7)	19.9	(1.6)	–5.2	(4.1)	–23.8	(10.3)	–35.1	(7.2)	–1.4	(7.7)
	Belgium	559	(1.9)	24.8	(1.7)	2.3	(0.5)	15.6	(1.5)	–29.4	(3.1)	–41.2	(7.9)	–68.4	(11.2)	–31.3	(8.8)
	Canada	533	(1.4)	18.6	(1.2)	2.5	(0.4)	8.3	(1.1)	–10.9	(2.5)	13.2	(4.2)	1.4	(5.5)	–12.6	(5.2)
	Czech Republic	513	(3.0)	21.0	(1.8)	8.4	(1.0)	13.7	(1.5)	0.0	(4.1)	c	c	c	c	c	c
	Denmark	521	(2.2)	16.1	(1.6)	3.6	(0.7)	21.2	(1.6)	–19.9	(3.2)	–39.7	(12.5)	–47.4	(12.7)	7.3	(9.8)
	Finland	544	(1.8)	16.5	(1.4)	2.6	(0.5)	10.5	(1.4)	–3.9	(3.2)	c	c	c	c	c	c
	France	527	(2.1)	20.0	(2.0)	2.2	(0.7)	19.0	(1.8)	–10.2	(4.2)	–18.6	(6.0)	–42.1	(15.0)	–9.8	(9.6)
	Germany	527	(2.9)	26.0	(1.8)	2.5	(0.6)	11.3	(1.7)	–3.7	(5.1)	–37.4	(9.7)	–12.6	(9.3)	–36.0	(9.4)
	Greece	450	(2.9)	18.2	(2.1)	2.2	(0.5)	19.9	(2.1)	–13.6	(4.6)	c	c	–24.8	(8.5)	–8.5	(9.7)
	Hungary	492	(2.6)	20.4	(2.2)	7.8	(0.8)	21.5	(1.9)	–7.5	(3.5)	c	c	c	c	c	c
	Iceland	499	(2.4)	8.2	(1.7)	4.5	(0.6)	13.8	(2.0)	–3.7	(4.6)	c	c	c	c	c	c
	Ireland	515	(2.0)	19.0	(1.8)	3.6	(0.6)	11.0	(1.4)	–25.7	(3.8)	c	c	c	c	c	c
	Italy	474	(2.8)	17.6	(2.0)	2.3	(0.5)	12.7	(1.7)	–12.1	(3.6)	c	c	c	c	c	c
	Japan	540	(4.0)	12.9	(2.6)	7.8	(0.9)	16.8	(2.3)	m	m	c	c	c	c	c	c
	Korea	546	(3.0)	14.9	(2.6)	3.9	(0.5)	18.3	(2.1)	–1.9	(2.9)	c	c	a	a	c	c
	Luxembourg	510	(1.9)	23.7	(2.1)	1.3	(0.4)	13.5	(1.5)	–15.9	(4.5)	–8.3	(6.0)	–19.2	(7.2)	–3.1	(7.4)
	Mexico	425	(3.4)	11.0	(1.4)	2.6	(0.4)	19.1	(2.3)	–9.9	(2.7)	c	c	c	c	c	c
	Netherlands	558	(2.6)	22.3	(1.9)	1.4	(0.8)	13.8	(2.1)	–20.2	(4.5)	–28.7	(9.2)	–46.8	(12.1)	–24.9	(11.2)
	New Zealand	533	(2.3)	21.1	(2.0)	3.5	(0.6)	15.6	(2.0)	–15.7	(4.7)	–20.6	(9.2)	–8.3	(7.0)	–12.6	(8.3)
	Norway	494	(2.7)	19.1	(1.8)	1.5	(0.8)	19.3	(1.4)	–17.0	(3.5)	–22.3	(16.0)	–44.7	(17.5)	8.3	(17.6)
	Poland	499	(2.1)	26.1	(1.9)	4.1	(0.8)	13.2	(2.0)	–9.0	(4.9)	c	c	c	c	c	c
	Portugal	487	(2.3)	23.7	(1.9)	1.1	(0.3)	17.1	(1.8)	–6.3	(3.5)	–35.3	(11.8)	c	c	c	c
	Slovak Republic	498	(2.6)	23.7	(1.8)	6.2	(0.8)	11.1	(1.6)	–2.9	(3.8)	c	c	c	c	c	c
	Spain	497	(2.2)	15.1	(1.4)	2.9	(0.4)	15.5	(1.6)	–8.4	(4.5)	c	c	c	c	c	c
	Sweden	520	(2.1)	18.5	(2.0)	1.1	(0.6)	19.3	(1.9)	–17.3	(3.3)	–4.6	(8.0)	–54.6	(11.2)	–14.1	(10.0)
	Switzerland	554	(3.4)	16.1	(1.6)	5.9	(0.7)	7.8	(1.8)	–18.4	(3.6)	–29.8	(6.0)	–54.7	(6.5)	–8.4	(7.5)
	Turkey	464	(8.5)	19.1	(4.1)	6.1	(0.8)	14.0	(2.8)	–4.8	(4.7)	c	c	c	c	c	c
	United States	494	(2.4)	19.4	(1.5)	2.5	(0.5)	17.4	(1.4)	–29.2	(3.4)	7.2	(6.2)	3.3	(7.0)	–24.8	(6.8)
	OECD total	*506*	*(0.8)*	*18.3*	*(0.6)*	*6.0*	*(0.2)*	*16.0*	*(0.6)*	*–28.6*	*(1.5)*	*3.8*	*(3.3)*	*–9.9*	*(3.2)*	*–17.2*	*(3.4)*
	OECD average	*512*	*(0.5)*	*21.1*	*(0.4)*	*5.0*	*(0.1)*	*12.2*	*(0.3)*	*–18.4*	*(0.8)*	*0.5*	*(2.2)*	*–18.8*	*(2.6)*	*–8.6*	*(2.2)*
Partner countries	Brazil	388	(4.8)	35.3	(3.7)	0.5	(0.5)	9.7	(2.1)	–4.3	(5.8)	c	c	c	c	c	c
	Hong Kong-China	579	(4.4)	14.6	(2.4)	0.5	(0.7)	17.6	(2.4)	–21.0	(4.1)	20.7	(4.4)	–25.4	(4.7)	–54.9	(9.5)
	Indonesia	391	(5.4)	18.8	(2.1)	0.9	(0.5)	3.2	(1.7)	–20.8	(4.6)	c	c	c	c	c	c
	Latvia	476	(3.8)	16.8	(1.9)	0.9	(0.8)	18.6	(1.9)	1.7	(3.8)	–4.2	(5.6)	c	c	–13.1	(7.4)
	Liechtenstein	557	(7.0)	26.4	(7.6)	3.9	(2.9)	16.1	(5.8)	–13.2	(14.6)	–0.6	(24.4)	–22.2	(24.5)	–22.3	(13.2)
	Macao-China	541	(6.9)	7.8	(4.6)	0.9	(0.9)	7.6	(3.6)	–10.4	(8.1)	9.1	(8.2)	–4.7	(10.9)	–40.9	(15.5)
	Russian Federation	466	(3.9)	12.7	(2.0)	6.4	(1.2)	14.2	(1.6)	–0.2	(3.0)	–13.4	(6.8)	–17.6	(5.5)	–22.8	(13.5)
	Serbia	440	(3.3)	18.9	(2.1)	1.4	(0.8)	15.4	(1.6)	–5.4	(4.1)	–3.6	(6.9)	17.4	(6.2)	c	c
	Thailand	453	(4.6)	17.9	(2.1)	3.0	(0.6)	6.2	(1.5)	–14.7	(4.0)	c	c	c	c	a	a
	Tunisia	389	(4.0)	24.1	(2.3)	0.3	(0.4)	12.9	(1.8)	–9.3	(5.2)	c	c	c	c	c	c
	Uruguay	436	(2.8)	22.9	(1.7)	2.9	(0.6)	13.4	(2.0)	–3.7	(3.9)	c	c	c	c	c	c
	United Kingdom[2]	516	(2.2)	22.7	(1.4)	3.6	(0.7)	14.5	(1.4)	–10.3	(3.2)	1.3	(6.6)	c	c	–10.7	(11.4)

Explained variance in student performance (unique,[1] common and total)

		Unique to highest occupational status of parents (HISEI)	Unique to highest level of parents' education	Unique to possessions related to the classical culture	Unique to single parent family	Unique to immigrant background (first-generation or non-native students)	Unique to language spoken at home	Common explained variance (explained by more than one factor)	Total explained variance	
		Percentage	Percentage	Percentage	Percentage	Percentage	Percentage	Percentage	Percentage	S.E.
OECD countries	Australia	4.7	0.5	1.3	0.5	0.0	0.0	5.3	12.4	(0.80)
	Austria	3.3	0.2	4.0	0.0	0.5	0.0	8.5	16.4	(1.60)
	Belgium	4.6	0.3	2.1	1.2	1.9	0.3	11.4	21.7	(1.49)
	Canada	3.4	0.4	0.8	0.2	0.2	0.1	4.1	9.3	(0.75)
	Czech Republic	2.4	2.2	1.8	0.0	c	c	10.5	17.0	(1.47)
	Denmark	2.2	0.9	4.6	0.9	0.8	0.0	9.1	18.5	(1.57)
	Finland	3.3	0.4	1.5	0.0	c	c	5.2	10.8	(1.07)
	France	3.8	0.3	3.7	0.2	0.6	0.0	10.0	18.6	(1.74)
	Germany	5.9	0.6	1.3	0.0	0.6	0.5	12.1	21.1	(1.95)
	Greece	2.6	0.4	3.1	0.4	0.3	0.0	9.3	16.1	(1.89)
	Hungary	2.5	2.7	3.8	0.1	c	c	16.4	25.7	(1.68)
	Iceland	0.7	1.4	1.4	0.0	c	c	3.0	6.7	(0.87)
	Ireland	3.6	1.0	1.5	1.2	0.2	c	6.9	14.4	(1.42)
	Italy	2.3	0.5	1.5	0.2	c	c	5.9	10.4	(1.15)
	Japan	1.2	2.5	2.3	0.0	c	c	4.4	10.6	(1.70)
	Korea	1.5	1.7	3.3	0.0	c	c	5.3	11.9	(1.85)
	Luxembourg	4.7	0.3	2.0	0.4	0.3	0.0	10.4	18.1	(1.27)
	Mexico	1.6	1.6	3.1	0.3	c	c	9.1	17.7	(1.73)
	Netherlands	4.5	0.1	1.8	0.6	0.9	0.2	9.4	17.6	(1.90)
	New Zealand	4.1	1.2	2.2	0.4	0.3	0.1	6.3	14.7	(1.34)
	Norway	3.0	0.1	4.4	0.7	0.3	0.0	6.8	15.2	(1.21)
	Poland	4.5	0.6	1.4	0.1	c	c	8.7	15.4	(1.28)
	Portugal	4.6	0.4	3.0	0.1	2.3	c	10.8	21.2	(2.32)
	Slovak Republic	5.1	1.9	1.3	0.0	c	c	8.4	17.3	(1.57)
	Spain	2.2	1.2	2.5	0.1	0.4	c	7.0	13.4	(1.28)
	Sweden	3.2	0.1	3.7	0.6	0.9	0.1	8.0	16.5	(1.49)
	Switzerland	2.1	2.1	0.6	0.6	1.7	0.0	10.1	17.2	(1.20)
	Turkey	2.0	3.9	1.4	0.0	c	c	11.5	19.5	(3.64)
	United States	3.6	0.4	3.4	2.0	0.0	0.3	7.9	17.6	(1.20)
	OECD total	*2.6*	*3.0*	*2.3*	*1.3*	*0.0*	*0.1*	*10.3*	*19.5*	*(0.58)*
	OECD average	*3.5*	*2.2*	*1.4*	*0.5*	*0.1*	*0.0*	*9.1*	*16.8*	*(0.29)*
Partner countries	Brazil	9.5	0.1	0.7	0.0	c	c	5.4	15.8	(2.57)
	Hong Kong-China	1.0	0.0	2.3	0.7	2.4	1.3	3.1	10.9	(1.32)
	Indonesia	4.8	0.2	0.1	0.5	c	c	3.3	9.1	(1.82)
	Latvia	3.3	0.0	3.6	0.0	0.0	0.2	3.0	10.2	(1.29)
	Liechtenstein	4.6	0.8	2.3	0.3	0.4	0.7	9.8	19.0	(4.10)
	Macao-China	0.4	0.2	0.5	0.3	0.4	1.0	0.8	3.6	(1.45)
	Russian Federation	1.4	0.8	1.5	0.0	0.4	0.3	4.7	9.1	(1.07)
	Serbia	3.6	0.1	3.2	0.1	0.2	c	6.2	13.6	(1.56)
	Thailand	2.5	1.1	0.5	0.5	c	a	7.6	12.2	(1.94)
	Tunisia	6.5	0.0	1.4	0.1	c	c	7.3	15.4	(2.48)
	Uruguay	4.8	0.9	1.4	0.0	c	c	8.1	15.5	(1.68)
	United Kingdom[2]	5.2	0.8	2.5	0.2	0.0	0.0	8.1	16.9	(1.38)

1. Unique variance is the variance explained by each factor in addition to the variance explained by the other factors in the model.
2. Response rate too low to ensure comparability (see Annex A3).

Table 4.2a

International socio-economic index of occupational status (HISEI) and performance on the mathematics scale, by national quarters of the index

Results based on students' self-reports

		International socio-economic index of occupational status (highest of the father's or mother's)										Performance on the mathematics scale, by national quarters of the international socio-economic index of occupational status							
		All students		Bottom quarter		Second quarter		Third quarter		Top quarter		Bottom quarter		Second quarter		Third quarter		Top quarter	
		Mean index	S.E.	Mean index	S.E.	Mean index	S.E.	Mean index	S.E.	Mean index	S.E.	Mean score	S.E.	Mean score	S.E.	Mean score	S.E.	Mean score	S.E.
OECD countries	Australia	52.6	(0.3)	31.6	(0.1)	48.0	(0.07)	58.3	(0.1)	72.5	(0.1)	**489**	(2.8)	520	(2.7)	539	(2.7)	**566**	(2.9)
	Austria	47.1	(0.5)	27.3	(0.2)	40.9	(0.11)	51.4	(0.1)	68.7	(0.3)	**467**	(4.4)	492	(3.7)	524	(3.3)	**548**	(4.4)
	Belgium	50.6	(0.4)	29.0	(0.1)	44.5	(0.13)	56.4	(0.1)	72.4	(0.2)	**482**	(3.7)	527	(3.2)	555	(2.8)	**590**	(3.3)
	Canada	52.6	(0.3)	31.7	(0.1)	47.7	(0.08)	58.1	(0.1)	72.9	(0.2)	**506**	(2.0)	531	(2.3)	544	(2.1)	**569**	(2.8)
	Czech Republic	50.1	(0.3)	32.3	(0.2)	45.7	(0.12)	52.5	(0.1)	69.7	(0.2)	**486**	(4.0)	508	(3.9)	530	(3.9)	**570**	(4.3)
	Denmark	49.3	(0.5)	29.4	(0.2)	44.2	(0.11)	53.2	(0.1)	70.3	(0.3)	**481**	(3.4)	504	(3.6)	525	(3.9)	**554**	(3.5)
	Finland	50.2	(0.4)	28.7	(0.1)	43.4	(0.16)	56.4	(0.1)	72.4	(0.2)	**515**	(2.7)	536	(2.7)	552	(2.9)	**576**	(2.9)
	France	48.7	(0.5)	27.6	(0.2)	42.3	(0.15)	53.6	(0.1)	71.2	(0.3)	**469**	(3.7)	507	(4.2)	525	(3.0)	**557**	(3.8)
	Germany	49.3	(0.4)	29.5	(0.2)	42.6	(0.14)	53.7	(0.1)	71.5	(0.2)	**463**	(4.9)	505	(3.3)	528	(3.8)	**565**	(4.0)
	Greece	46.9	(0.7)	26.9	(0.1)	38.8	(0.13)	51.8	(0.1)	70.3	(0.4)	**409**	(4.3)	435	(3.8)	450	(4.5)	**493**	(5.0)
	Hungary	48.6	(0.3)	30.2	(0.2)	42.3	(0.08)	51.6	(0.1)	70.2	(0.2)	**450**	(3.9)	473	(3.9)	503	(3.4)	**547**	(3.9)
	Iceland	53.7	(0.3)	31.5	(0.2)	48.0	(0.13)	61.7	(0.2)	73.7	(0.2)	**497**	(3.1)	512	(3.2)	519	(3.1)	**538**	(3.1)
	Ireland	48.3	(0.5)	28.5	(0.2)	42.2	(0.11)	52.7	(0.1)	70.0	(0.3)	**471**	(3.9)	496	(3.2)	513	(3.1)	**541**	(3.5)
	Italy	46.8	(0.4)	26.9	(0.2)	40.3	(0.11)	50.6	(0.1)	69.5	(0.4)	**430**	(4.2)	457	(3.9)	478	(3.6)	**502**	(4.1)
	Japan	50.0	(0.3)	33.4	(0.2)	43.9	(0.04)	50.6	(0.1)	72.0	(0.2)	**505**	(5.1)	534	(4.7)	543	(4.4)	**568**	(6.4)
	Korea	46.3	(0.4)	28.9	(0.2)	43.5	(0.09)	49.4	(0.1)	63.5	(0.4)	**511**	(4.4)	547	(3.7)	549	(3.6)	**568**	(6.1)
	Luxembourg	48.2	(0.2)	27.3	(0.2)	42.1	(0.13)	52.8	(0.1)	70.5	(0.2)	**448**	(3.0)	481	(3.0)	509	(2.6)	**542**	(3.1)
	Mexico	40.1	(0.7)	22.2	(0.1)	28.9	(0.04)	42.1	(0.3)	67.3	(0.2)	**357**	(4.8)	374	(3.9)	394	(3.7)	**424**	(4.9)
	Netherlands	51.3	(0.4)	30.9	(0.3)	45.4	(0.15)	56.9	(0.2)	71.8	(0.2)	**502**	(4.3)	535	(3.8)	559	(3.5)	**584**	(3.9)
	New Zealand	51.5	(0.4)	30.1	(0.2)	46.2	(0.12)	56.8	(0.2)	72.7	(0.3)	**485**	(3.8)	514	(3.4)	532	(3.3)	**564**	(3.4)
	Norway	54.6	(0.4)	35.0	(0.2)	49.0	(0.12)	60.6	(0.2)	73.9	(0.2)	**461**	(3.5)	489	(3.6)	507	(3.5)	**533**	(3.5)
	Poland	45.0	(0.3)	26.9	(0.2)	39.5	(0.11)	49.1	(0.1)	64.4	(0.3)	**455**	(3.9)	479	(3.2)	498	(3.3)	**534**	(3.1)
	Portugal	43.1	(0.5)	26.4	(0.1)	33.9	(0.08)	46.6	(0.2)	65.5	(0.5)	**431**	(5.3)	447	(3.4)	481	(3.8)	**511**	(3.8)
	Slovak Republic	48.8	(0.4)	29.3	(0.2)	41.4	(0.1)	53.1	(0.1)	71.5	(0.2)	**457**	(4.2)	484	(3.3)	523	(3.5)	**544**	(3.8)
	Spain	44.3	(0.6)	26.2	(0.1)	35.5	(0.14)	49.3	(0.1)	66.1	(0.4)	**454**	(3.6)	475	(2.8)	496	(3.2)	**519**	(3.3)
	Sweden	50.6	(0.4)	30.4	(0.2)	44.1	(0.14)	56.1	(0.2)	71.9	(0.2)	**477**	(3.7)	501	(3.1)	518	(3.9)	**551**	(4.2)
	Switzerland	49.3	(0.4)	29.4	(0.1)	43.1	(0.14)	53.5	(0.1)	71.1	(0.3)	**487**	(4.1)	524	(4.1)	538	(4.9)	**568**	(3.9)
	Turkey	41.6	(0.7)	23.7	(0.3)	33.6	(0.15)	47.2	(0.1)	61.8	(0.8)	**395**	(5.6)	411	(6.7)	420	(7.5)	**479**	(12.5)
	United States	54.6	(0.4)	32.6	(0.2)	49.9	(0.15)	61.4	(0.1)	74.3	(0.2)	**448**	(3.2)	477	(3.8)	497	(4.0)	**530**	(3.7)
	OECD total	*49.2*	*(0.1)*	*28.1*	*(0.1)*	*42.5*	*(0.07)*	*54.1*	*(0.1)*	*71.9*	*(0.1)*	*440*	*(1.5)*	*490*	*(1.3)*	*506*	*(1.1)*	*536*	*(1.4)*
	OECD average	*48.8*	*(0.1)*	*28.2*	*(0.0)*	*42.3*	*(0.08)*	*53.2*	*(0.1)*	*71.2*	*(0.1)*	*455*	*(0.9)*	*493*	*(0.8)*	*516*	*(0.7)*	*548*	*(0.8)*
Partner countries	Brazil	40.1	(0.6)	21.7	(0.3)	32.4	(0.09)	44.4	(0.2)	62.1	(0.6)	**317**	(4.9)	346	(5.1)	372	(5.3)	**410**	(8.4)
	Hong Kong-China	41.1	(0.4)	25.9	(0.1)	34.9	(0.07)	45.1	(0.1)	58.7	(0.4)	**532**	(5.5)	547	(5.1)	562	(4.1)	**575**	(5.6)
	Indonesia	33.6	(0.6)	16.0	(0.0)	24.1	(0.15)	34.6	(0.3)	59.9	(0.4)	**335**	(4.3)	356	(4.1)	361	(4.5)	**397**	(6.3)
	Latvia	50.3	(0.5)	29.1	(0.2)	44.2	(0.16)	54.8	(0.1)	73.0	(0.3)	**457**	(3.8)	475	(4.3)	494	(4.6)	**514**	(5.0)
	Liechtenstein	50.7	(0.8)	30.8	(0.6)	47.4	(0.52)	55.0	(0.1)	70.0	(0.7)	**482**	(10.3)	530	(11.2)	553	(9.6)	**587**	(11.0)
	Macao-China	39.4	(0.4)	25.8	(0.3)	34.4	(0.12)	41.7	(0.2)	55.9	(0.5)	**522**	(5.2)	523	(6.3)	528	(7.5)	**540**	(7.3)
	Russian Federation	49.9	(0.4)	30.8	(0.2)	40.9	(0.10)	54.2	(0.2)	73.6	(0.2)	**443**	(4.5)	459	(5.3)	473	(4.9)	**501**	(4.7)
	Serbia	48.1	(0.5)	28.3	(0.2)	41.2	(0.12)	51.4	(0.1)	71.4	(0.4)	**406**	(3.7)	426	(3.8)	449	(4.3)	**475**	(5.0)
	Thailand	36.0	(0.4)	22.1	(0.1)	26.7	(0.13)	35.6	(0.1)	59.6	(0.4)	**396**	(3.6)	399	(3.4)	427	(4.0)	**457**	(5.2)
	Tunisia	37.5	(0.6)	18.0	(0.2)	29.2	(0.18)	39.6	(0.2)	63.1	(0.4)	**331**	(3.0)	342	(4.0)	361	(3.8)	**406**	(6.1)
	Uruguay	46.1	(0.5)	25.2	(0.2)	37.8	(0.15)	50.8	(0.1)	70.8	(0.4)	**388**	(4.8)	415	(4.0)	430	(4.2)	**478**	(3.8)
	United Kingdom[1]	49.6	(0.4)	28.5	(0.1)	43.0	(0.14)	55.5	(0.1)	71.6	(0.2)	**469**	(2.9)	500	(3.1)	519	(3.5)	**555**	(3.4)

		Change in the mathematics score per 16.4 units of the international socio-economic index of occupational status		Increased likelihood of students in the bottom quarter of the HISEI index distribution scoring in the bottom quarter of the national mathematics performance distribution		Explained variance in student performance (r-squared × 100)	
		Effect	S.E.	Ratio	S.E.	%	S.E.
OECD countries	Australia	**30.1**	(1.35)	**2.0**	(0.08)	9.6	(0.73)
	Austria	**30.7**	(1.92)	**2.0**	(0.12)	10.6	(1.22)
	Belgium	**39.8**	(1.71)	**2.4**	(0.11)	15.3	(1.16)
	Canada	**24.4**	(1.17)	**1.8**	(0.06)	7.5	(0.66)
	Czech Republic	**37.5**	(1.97)	**1.8**	(0.11)	12.6	(1.19)
	Denmark	**28.9**	(1.71)	**1.7**	(0.11)	9.1	(1.02)
	Finland	**21.7**	(1.29)	**1.7**	(0.08)	7.2	(0.83)
	France	**31.6**	(1.93)	**2.2**	(0.14)	13.0	(1.39)
	Germany	**38.0**	(1.95)	**2.3**	(0.14)	15.5	(1.38)
	Greece	**29.4**	(2.11)	**1.9**	(0.14)	10.5	(1.52)
	Hungary	**40.8**	(2.17)	**2.1**	(0.14)	16.9	(1.51)
	Iceland	**14.4**	(1.51)	**1.5**	(0.10)	2.7	(0.57)
	Ireland	**27.4**	(1.89)	**1.9**	(0.14)	10.0	(1.30)
	Italy	**27.1**	(1.88)	**1.9**	(0.10)	8.3	(1.03)
	Japan	**23.0**	(3.12)	**1.7**	(0.11)	4.4	(1.00)
	Korea	**26.4**	(3.28)	**1.7**	(0.11)	5.5	(1.27)
	Luxembourg	**33.7**	(1.56)	**2.3**	(0.12)	13.8	(1.15)
	Mexico	**23.5**	(1.88)	**1.7**	(0.16)	9.5	(1.38)
	Netherlands	**32.3**	(2.03)	**2.2**	(0.13)	12.6	(1.32)
	New Zealand	**29.4**	(1.65)	**1.9**	(0.13)	9.1	(1.01)
	Norway	**29.2**	(1.62)	**1.8**	(0.11)	8.9	(0.93)
	Poland	**35.2**	(1.82)	**1.8**	(0.12)	12.6	(1.19)
	Portugal	**34.3**	(1.70)	**2.0**	(0.13)	14.8	(1.47)
	Slovak Republic	**33.2**	(1.83)	**2.1**	(0.11)	13.1	(1.20)
	Spain	**25.4**	(1.43)	**1.8**	(0.10)	8.2	(0.90)
	Sweden	**28.7**	(1.79)	**1.8**	(0.11)	9.2	(1.03)
	Switzerland	**30.3**	(1.71)	**2.0**	(0.09)	9.4	(0.96)
	Turkey	**38.1**	(5.87)	**1.4**	(0.12)	11.8	(2.98)
	United States	**30.2**	(1.37)	**2.1**	(0.09)	10.3	(0.88)
	OECD total	*34.0*	*(0.74)*	*2.3*	*(0.05)*	*11.6*	*(0.41)*
	OECD average	*33.7*	*(0.40)*	*2.2*	*(0.02)*	*11.7*	*(0.22)*
Partner countries	Brazil	**39.0**	(3.63)	**1.9**	(0.13)	15.2	(2.55)
	Hong Kong-China	**22.6**	(2.64)	**1.5**	(0.11)	3.6	(0.82)
	Indonesia	**22.0**	(2.35)	**1.6**	(0.12)	8.4	(1.68)
	Latvia	**21.0**	(1.69)	**1.9**	(0.14)	6.0	(0.98)
	Liechtenstein	**41.2**	(5.92)	**2.8**	(0.54)	14.5	(3.40)
	Macao-China	**11.7**	(3.97)	0.9	(0.12)	1.0	(0.68)
	Russian Federation	**21.4**	(1.77)	**1.6**	(0.12)	5.6	(0.85)
	Serbia	**26.0**	(1.86)	**1.8**	(0.12)	9.9	(1.28)
	Thailand	**26.6**	(2.35)	**1.4**	(0.11)	9.5	(1.47)
	Tunisia	**28.3**	(2.56)	**1.6**	(0.13)	13.9	(2.36)
	Uruguay	**31.4**	(1.83)	**1.8**	(0.14)	11.9	(1.28)
	United Kingdom[1]	**31.8**	(1.46)	**2.0**	(0.12)	12.5	(1.08)

Note: Values that are statistically significant are indicated in bold (see Annex A4).

1. Response rate too low to ensure comparability (see Annex A3).

Table 4.2b

Percentage of students and performance on the mathematics, reading and science scales, by highest level of mothers' education

Results based on students' self-reports

		Mothers with completed primary or lower secondary education (ISCED Levels 1 or 2)								Mothers with completed upper secondary education (ISCED Level 3)							
				Performance								Performance					
				Mathematics scale		Reading scale		Science scale				Mathematics scale		Reading scale		Science scale	
		% of students	S.E.	Mean score	S.E.	Mean score	S.E.	Mean score	S.E.	% of students	S.E.	Mean score	S.E.	Mean score	S.E.	Mean score	S.E.
OECD countries	Australia	25.4	(0.5)	507	(3.2)	510	(2.9)	506	(3.0)	34.7	(0.7)	518	(2.7)	515	(2.8)	517	(2.5)
	Austria	14.8	(0.9)	470	(4.9)	441	(5.7)	440	(5.3)	63.4	(0.9)	512	(2.9)	498	(3.3)	498	(3.0)
	Belgium	16.3	(0.6)	496	(4.1)	476	(4.8)	472	(4.6)	37.1	(0.7)	532	(2.4)	512	(2.8)	512	(2.7)
	Canada	8.5	(0.3)	504	(3.0)	503	(3.3)	487	(3.4)	40.2	(0.6)	529	(1.9)	526	(2.0)	514	(2.1)
	Czech Republic	5.1	(0.3)	468	(8.6)	446	(8.0)	478	(10.0)	77.6	(0.9)	516	(2.9)	492	(2.6)	522	(2.8)
	Denmark	18.0	(1.0)	476	(4.2)	457	(4.4)	436	(4.8)	32.0	(0.8)	512	(3.4)	488	(3.5)	471	(4.1)
	Finland	16.5	(0.6)	520	(3.1)	523	(2.8)	527	(3.3)	25.8	(0.6)	538	(3.1)	536	(2.5)	541	(3.0)
	France	28.7	(1.0)	483	(4.6)	467	(5.2)	476	(6.1)	43.5	(0.9)	521	(2.3)	510	(2.4)	524	(3.0)
	Germany	23.4	(1.0)	460	(4.6)	447	(5.0)	450	(4.9)	53.8	(1.1)	527	(3.1)	520	(3.1)	528	(3.2)
	Greece	33.0	(1.6)	415	(3.8)	448	(4.2)	453	(3.7)	40.1	(0.8)	452	(3.4)	480	(4.3)	487	(4.4)
	Hungary	15.5	(0.8)	428	(5.3)	428	(5.6)	448	(5.5)	58.9	(1.0)	485	(2.9)	479	(2.5)	500	(2.8)
	Iceland	33.5	(0.8)	499	(2.7)	482	(2.9)	480	(2.8)	39.3	(0.8)	516	(2.1)	489	(2.6)	492	(2.4)
	Ireland	24.4	(1.3)	476	(3.5)	492	(3.8)	477	(4.2)	47.6	(1.1)	506	(2.5)	519	(2.8)	511	(2.7)
	Italy	41.3	(0.9)	441	(3.9)	450	(4.2)	460	(4.5)	32.8	(0.6)	483	(3.3)	493	(3.2)	504	(3.3)
	Japan	9.6	(0.7)	496	(9.6)	460	(10.4)	510	(9.3)	44.1	(0.9)	524	(4.2)	489	(4.5)	535	(4.5)
	Korea	30.8	(1.0)	512	(3.8)	512	(4.0)	512	(4.4)	47.4	(1.0)	551	(2.9)	541	(2.7)	547	(3.3)
	Luxembourg	28.3	(0.7)	469	(2.7)	453	(3.2)	456	(3.5)	31.2	(0.9)	497	(2.9)	489	(3.3)	492	(3.4)
	Mexico	67.0	(1.7)	371	(3.2)	384	(3.6)	391	(2.9)	11.6	(0.8)	431	(5.8)	453	(7.3)	441	(5.1)
	Netherlands	27.9	(1.0)	532	(5.1)	509	(4.5)	514	(5.7)	43.4	(1.0)	540	(3.0)	516	(2.9)	525	(3.4)
	New Zealand	17.1	(0.6)	487	(4.2)	487	(4.2)	484	(4.6)	46.6	(0.7)	534	(2.9)	534	(3.0)	532	(3.3)
	Norway	8.0	(0.6)	461	(5.4)	470	(6.9)	451	(6.3)	42.5	(0.9)	487	(2.7)	494	(3.6)	477	(3.1)
	Poland	6.4	(0.5)	443	(6.3)	440	(8.2)	442	(8.0)	76.9	(0.7)	484	(2.6)	492	(2.8)	490	(2.9)
	Portugal	62.8	(1.2)	453	(3.3)	468	(3.9)	455	(3.6)	15.6	(0.6)	492	(3.9)	504	(3.8)	491	(3.9)
	Slovak Republic	7.0	(0.8)	419	(9.7)	402	(10.3)	403	(16.9)	75.4	(0.9)	496	(2.8)	468	(2.7)	493	(2.9)
	Spain	46.2	(1.7)	471	(2.7)	470	(2.9)	470	(2.7)	27.5	(0.8)	489	(3.4)	487	(3.5)	492	(3.7)
	Sweden	16.7	(0.8)	473	(4.7)	479	(4.8)	468	(5.4)	30.4	(0.8)	519	(3.2)	525	(3.0)	517	(3.3)
	Switzerland	34.2	(1.0)	491	(3.3)	463	(3.5)	469	(3.9)	44.4	(1.0)	550	(3.0)	523	(3.3)	540	(3.1)
	Turkey	76.7	(1.8)	404	(4.8)	425	(4.4)	417	(4.4)	14.0	(1.1)	477	(8.0)	490	(7.5)	482	(7.2)
	United States	8.9	(0.8)	430	(5.6)	439	(6.6)	439	(6.9)	52.6	(1.0)	478	(2.8)	494	(3.2)	487	(2.9)
	OECD total	*24.5*	*(0.4)*	*436*	*(1.7)*	*440*	*(1.6)*	*444*	*(1.6)*	*44.0*	*(0.4)*	*500*	*(1.0)*	*500*	*(1.2)*	*506*	*(1.1)*
	OECD average	*25.7*	*(0.2)*	*458*	*(1.1)*	*458*	*(1.0)*	*458*	*(1.0)*	*42.8*	*(0.2)*	*508*	*(0.6)*	*501*	*(0.6)*	*508*	*(0.6)*
Partner countries	Brazil	51.8	(1.5)	339	(4.6)	390	(4.3)	373	(3.9)	13.7	(0.8)	411	(6.9)	457	(6.7)	441	(6.3)
	Hong Kong-China	68.0	(1.3)	543	(4.3)	506	(3.5)	534	(4.1)	25.4	(1.1)	571	(6.0)	524	(4.6)	555	(5.7)
	Indonesia	65.7	(1.4)	352	(3.1)	375	(2.9)	387	(2.7)	22.0	(1.1)	387	(5.8)	403	(4.6)	415	(4.7)
	Latvia	2.7	(0.3)	c	c	c	c	c	c	45.5	(1.8)	476	(4.3)	486	(4.0)	481	(4.4)
	Liechtenstein	38.8	(2.7)	517	(8.6)	509	(7.4)	504	(9.0)	42.7	(2.9)	561	(7.2)	552	(6.7)	552	(6.9)
	Macao-China	72.9	(1.2)	525	(3.8)	495	(3.1)	519	(3.9)	22.0	(1.2)	537	(6.0)	508	(5.1)	540	(6.5)
	Russian Federation	1.5	(0.2)	c	c	c	c	c	c	65.1	(1.1)	457	(4.2)	432	(3.9)	478	(4.0)
	Serbia	16.5	(0.9)	397	(4.0)	373	(4.0)	401	(4.3)	44.6	(1.0)	443	(3.9)	420	(3.7)	442	(3.7)
	Thailand	76.0	(1.0)	406	(2.8)	410	(2.5)	418	(2.3)	14.5	(0.6)	438	(4.6)	438	(4.7)	449	(4.5)
	Tunisia	76.2	(1.4)	351	(2.1)	369	(2.6)	379	(2.3)	15.9	(0.9)	383	(5.6)	398	(6.4)	406	(5.3)
	Uruguay	46.6	(1.2)	396	(4.1)	408	(4.9)	413	(3.8)	13.0	(0.5)	439	(4.8)	446	(7.7)	453	(6.0)
	United Kingdom[1]	14.2	(0.7)	481	(4.6)	481	(5.2)	484	(5.4)	54.1	(1.0)	504	(2.8)	504	(2.6)	516	(2.8)

		Mothers with completed tertiary education (ISCED Levels 5 or 6)								Increased likelihood of students whose mothers have not completed upper secondary education scoring in the bottom quarter of the national mathematics performance distribution	
				Performance							
				Mathematics scale		Reading scale		Science scale			
		% of students	S.E.	Mean score	S.E.	Mean score	S.E.	Mean score	S.E.	Ratio	S.E.
OECD countries	Australia	40.0	(0.8)	547	(2.8)	551	(2.9)	550	(2.9)	**1.4**	(0.09)
	Austria	21.8	(0.9)	523	(5.8)	520	(5.6)	516	(5.7)	**1.8**	(0.13)
	Belgium	16.6	(0.8)	563	(2.6)	539	(2.8)	541	(2.7)	**1.9**	(0.11)
	Canada	51.3	(0.7)	550	(2.1)	543	(2.0)	538	(2.3)	**1.7**	(0.10)
	Czech Republic	17.3	(0.8)	571	(5.2)	534	(4.7)	576	(5.0)	**2.0**	(0.21)
	Denmark	50.0	(1.1)	537	(3.1)	515	(2.8)	500	(3.2)	**1.9**	(0.14)
	Finland	57.6	(0.8)	555	(2.1)	555	(1.9)	559	(2.2)	**1.5**	(0.11)
	France	27.8	(1.0)	538	(3.4)	522	(3.8)	545	(4.2)	**1.8**	(0.13)
	Germany	22.8	(0.8)	548	(5.0)	539	(4.9)	558	(5.3)	**3.0**	(0.21)
	Greece	26.9	(1.4)	473	(6.0)	494	(6.3)	510	(5.3)	**1.8**	(0.13)
	Hungary	25.6	(0.9)	542	(4.0)	525	(4.2)	550	(4.5)	**2.5**	(0.18)
	Iceland	27.2	(0.7)	538	(3.1)	514	(3.4)	522	(3.4)	**1.4**	(0.10)
	Ireland	28.0	(1.1)	525	(3.6)	534	(3.8)	526	(3.8)	**1.7**	(0.12)
	Italy	25.9	(0.8)	484	(4.0)	498	(3.8)	509	(4.1)	**1.8**	(0.12)
	Japan	46.2	(0.9)	553	(5.0)	515	(4.3)	568	(4.9)	**1.7**	(0.16)
	Korea	21.8	(1.3)	571	(7.5)	556	(5.9)	563	(7.6)	**1.8**	(0.12)
	Luxembourg	40.5	(0.9)	522	(2.4)	507	(2.6)	511	(2.7)	**1.8**	(0.12)
	Mexico	21.4	(1.1)	411	(5.4)	427	(5.7)	434	(5.4)	**2.1**	(0.29)
	Netherlands	28.7	(1.0)	572	(4.2)	542	(3.9)	562	(4.5)	**1.3**	(0.14)
	New Zealand	36.3	(0.7)	547	(3.1)	545	(3.7)	546	(3.3)	**2.0**	(0.14)
	Norway	49.5	(1.0)	514	(2.9)	518	(3.3)	502	(3.6)	**1.5**	(0.14)
	Poland	16.7	(0.7)	538	(4.0)	541	(4.3)	556	(4.9)	**1.9**	(0.14)
	Portugal	21.7	(1.0)	494	(5.3)	495	(5.9)	495	(5.2)	**1.6**	(0.14)
	Slovak Republic	17.6	(0.7)	515	(4.2)	505	(4.1)	515	(4.4)	**2.6**	(0.25)
	Spain	26.3	(1.4)	514	(3.8)	504	(4.0)	522	(3.8)	**1.6**	(0.11)
	Sweden	52.9	(1.0)	521	(2.9)	527	(2.9)	519	(3.3)	**1.8**	(0.13)
	Switzerland	21.4	(0.9)	547	(6.8)	519	(5.8)	538	(8.6)	**2.1**	(0.11)
	Turkey	9.3	(1.1)	512	(22.8)	509	(18.8)	513	(20.2)	**2.4**	(0.40)
	United States	38.5	(0.9)	507	(3.9)	515	(4.0)	514	(4.1)	**2.0**	(0.17)
	OECD total	*31.5*	*(0.3)*	*522*	*(1.5)*	*517*	*(1.5)*	*530*	*(1.5)*	*2.5*	*(0.06)*
	OECD average	*31.5*	*(0.2)*	*532*	*(0.8)*	*524*	*(0.8)*	*532*	*(0.8)*	*2.2*	*(0.03)*
Partner countries	Brazil	34.5	(1.2)	365	(6.9)	406	(6.0)	399	(5.8)	**1.3**	(0.12)
	Hong Kong-China	6.6	(0.5)	567	(10.2)	521	(8.3)	560	(8.7)	**1.4**	(0.14)
	Indonesia	12.3	(0.7)	362	(9.0)	384	(8.2)	405	(7.5)	**1.2**	(0.10)
	Latvia	51.8	(1.9)	494	(4.4)	498	(4.7)	500	(4.7)	**1.9**	(0.32)
	Liechtenstein	18.6	(1.8)	527	(15.1)	509	(16.4)	520	(17.0)	1.7	(0.37)
	Macao-China	5.0	(0.6)	525	(10.9)	486	(8.0)	545	(12.6)	1.1	(0.16)
	Russian Federation	33.4	(1.2)	494	(4.4)	467	(4.4)	516	(4.9)	**1.6**	(0.30)
	Serbia	38.9	(1.2)	449	(4.6)	420	(4.6)	448	(4.6)	**2.0**	(0.15)
	Thailand	9.5	(0.6)	477	(7.6)	472	(6.7)	493	(6.7)	**1.6**	(0.15)
	Tunisia	7.9	(0.8)	395	(10.9)	393	(11.9)	408	(11.2)	**1.3**	(0.13)
	Uruguay	40.5	(1.0)	449	(4.2)	463	(3.8)	467	(3.6)	**1.8**	(0.15)
	United Kingdom[1]	31.8	(0.9)	539	(3.9)	537	(4.3)	554	(4.3)	**1.6**	(0.12)

Note: Values that are statistically significant are indicated in bold (see Annex A4).

1. Response rate too low to ensure comparability (see Annex A3).

Table 4.2b *(continued)*

Percentage of students and performance on the mathematics, reading and science scales, by highest level of mothers' education

Results based on students' self-reports

		Difference in performance between students whose mother completed upper secondary education and students whose mother completed primary or lower secondary education						Difference in performance between students whose mother completed tertiary education and those whose mother completed upper secondary education					
		Mathematics scale		Reading scale		Science scale		Mathematics scale		Reading scale		Science scale	
		Dif.	S.E.	Dif.	S.E.	Dif.	S.E.	Dif.	S.E.	Dif.	S.E.	Dif.	S.E.
OECD countries	Australia	**10.3**	(2.9)	5.0	(2.8)	**10.4**	(3.0)	**28.9**	(3.6)	**35.9**	(4.1)	**33.6**	(3.7)
	Austria	**41.4**	(5.1)	**56.8**	(6.0)	**57.6**	(5.3)	**11.7**	(4.8)	**22.3**	(4.7)	**18.3**	(4.7)
	Belgium	**35.7**	(3.9)	**35.9**	(3.8)	**39.7**	(4.0)	**31.7**	(2.9)	**27.0**	(3.6)	**29.3**	(3.3)
	Canada	**24.4**	(2.9)	**23.2**	(3.4)	**26.7**	(3.4)	**21.0**	(2.4)	**16.1**	(2.4)	**24.1**	(2.4)
	Czech Republic	**48.7**	(7.9)	**45.8**	(7.4)	**44.7**	(9.1)	**54.3**	(4.7)	**41.4**	(4.5)	**53.1**	(4.8)
	Denmark	**36.0**	(4.7)	**30.7**	(4.9)	**35.2**	(5.9)	**24.9**	(4.0)	**26.9**	(3.7)	**29.2**	(4.6)
	Finland	**18.8**	(3.7)	**13.4**	(3.3)	**13.4**	(4.0)	**17.0**	(3.0)	**18.6**	(2.8)	**18.2**	(3.1)
	France	**38.1**	(4.8)	**43.2**	(5.4)	**47.8**	(6.3)	**16.5**	(3.6)	**11.7**	(4.1)	**20.9**	(4.7)
	Germany	**67.1**	(4.6)	**73.1**	(5.1)	**78.0**	(5.0)	**21.3**	(4.5)	**18.4**	(4.6)	**29.3**	(4.7)
	Greece	**37.6**	(4.2)	**32.4**	(4.6)	**33.7**	(4.6)	**20.6**	(4.6)	**13.9**	(5.7)	**22.9**	(4.9)
	Hungary	**56.9**	(5.6)	**50.7**	(5.9)	**51.6**	(6.0)	**57.7**	(4.1)	**45.7**	(4.1)	**49.9**	(4.2)
	Iceland	**16.5**	(3.6)	7.8	(4.1)	**12.4**	(3.9)	**22.0**	(4.0)	**24.3**	(4.5)	**29.3**	(4.4)
	Ireland	**29.6**	(3.9)	**27.8**	(4.2)	**33.9**	(4.4)	**19.2**	(3.5)	**14.8**	(3.6)	**15.5**	(3.9)
	Italy	**42.4**	(3.7)	**42.6**	(4.1)	**44.8**	(4.5)	1.3	(3.7)	5.4	(4.0)	4.3	(4.1)
	Japan	**28.3**	(9.7)	**29.4**	(10.1)	**25.2**	(9.2)	**28.5**	(4.4)	**25.8**	(4.2)	**33.0**	(4.3)
	Korea	**39.4**	(3.5)	**29.0**	(3.2)	**35.1**	(3.9)	**20.3**	(6.7)	**15.1**	(5.1)	**16.0**	(6.8)
	Luxembourg	**27.6**	(4.2)	**36.2**	(4.7)	**36.5**	(4.8)	**25.5**	(4.3)	**17.5**	(4.8)	**19.4**	(4.9)
	Mexico	**59.8**	(5.8)	**68.2**	(7.3)	**50.1**	(4.9)	**–20.1**	(5.5)	**–25.6**	(6.1)	–7.5	(4.7)
	Netherlands	7.1	(5.2)	6.7	(4.3)	10.9	(5.8)	**32.6**	(4.3)	**25.5**	(4.1)	**36.6**	(4.6)
	New Zealand	**47.2**	(4.5)	**47.7**	(4.7)	**48.8**	(5.3)	**13.3**	(4.3)	**10.4**	(4.3)	**13.2**	(4.4)
	Norway	**25.8**	(5.7)	**24.0**	(7.9)	**26.2**	(6.7)	**27.4**	(3.3)	**24.2**	(3.9)	**25.1**	(3.5)
	Poland	**41.4**	(5.9)	**51.7**	(7.8)	**47.5**	(8.1)	**53.9**	(4.6)	**49.1**	(4.4)	**65.8**	(5.5)
	Portugal	**39.0**	(4.0)	**36.3**	(4.4)	**36.3**	(4.5)	1.7	(5.5)	–8.8	(5.5)	3.2	(5.5)
	Slovak Republic	**76.7**	(9.2)	**66.3**	(9.7)	**89.7**	(16.4)	**48.6**	(4.2)	**36.5**	(4.0)	**51.9**	(4.5)
	Spain	**17.8**	(3.9)	**17.3**	(4.1)	**22.6**	(4.2)	**25.1**	(4.3)	**17.3**	(4.4)	**30.0**	(4.4)
	Sweden	**45.5**	(5.1)	**45.2**	(5.8)	**49.6**	(6.2)	2.6	(3.9)	2.1	(3.7)	1.4	(4.2)
	Switzerland	**58.6**	(2.9)	**59.7**	(3.8)	**70.5**	(4.0)	–2.4	(5.8)	–4.3	(4.8)	–1.6	(8.2)
	Turkey	**72.7**	(7.1)	**64.7**	(7.0)	**64.9**	(6.5)	34.9	(19.5)	19.5	(15.7)	31.1	(17.6)
	United States	**47.4**	(6.1)	**55.0**	(6.2)	**48.5**	(6.7)	**28.9**	(4.0)	**21.4**	(4.3)	**26.2**	(4.3)
	OECD total	***63.6***	***(1.94)***	***59.7***	***(1.67)***	***61.9***	***(1.70)***	***21.9***	***(1.49)***	***17.0***	***(1.46)***	***24.0***	***(1.51)***
	OECD average	***50.6***	***(1.17)***	***43.0***	***(1.06)***	***49.6***	***(1.07)***	***24.0***	***(0.75)***	***22.5***	***(0.74)***	***23.5***	***(0.80)***
Partner countries	Brazil	**71.4**	(6.8)	**66.2**	(6.6)	**67.9**	(6.4)	**–45.4**	(7.5)	**–50.6**	(7.5)	**–42.6**	(6.1)
	Hong Kong-China	**27.6**	(5.0)	**17.6**	(3.9)	**20.8**	(4.8)	–4.0	(9.8)	–2.1	(8.5)	5.3	(9.0)
	Indonesia	**34.8**	(5.0)	**28.7**	(4.4)	**27.4**	(4.5)	**–24.2**	(6.4)	**–19.4**	(6.6)	–10.2	(5.5)
	Latvia	**35.8**	(12.5)	18.8	(13.8)	16.4	(12.4)	**18.6**	(4.1)	**11.2**	(4.7)	**19.2**	(4.6)
	Liechtenstein	**44.2**	(12.4)	**43.0**	(11.4)	**48.8**	(12.6)	–34.0	(18.0)	**–42.7**	(18.8)	–32.6	(18.9)
	Macao-China	11.8	(7.3)	13.0	(6.8)	**21.2**	(8.1)	–11.3	(12.9)	**–22.1**	(9.7)	5.2	(13.0)
	Russian Federation	c	c	c	c	c	c	**37.4**	(3.4)	**35.5**	(3.8)	**37.6**	(4.1)
	Serbia	**46.1**	(4.1)	**47.1**	(4.2)	**40.8**	(5.0)	5.8	(3.8)	–0.4	(4.0)	6.0	(4.1)
	Thailand	**32.0**	(4.3)	**27.6**	(4.1)	**31.2**	(4.2)	**39.5**	(6.4)	**34.4**	(6.1)	**44.1**	(5.8)
	Tunisia	**31.5**	(5.6)	**28.7**	(6.7)	**27.5**	(5.3)	12.2	(8.1)	–5.2	(9.5)	1.7	(8.6)
	Uruguay	**42.3**	(5.3)	**37.6**	(9.3)	**40.0**	(7.1)	**10.8**	(5.2)	**17.3**	(7.5)	**13.6**	(6.3)
	United Kingdom[1]	**23.1**	(4.8)	**23.0**	(5.3)	**31.7**	(5.6)	**35.6**	(3.6)	**33.4**	(3.9)	**38.8**	(3.9)

Note: Values that are statistically significant are indicated in bold (see Annex A4).

1. Response rate too low to ensure comparability (see Annex A3).

Table 4.2c

Percentage of students and performance on the mathematics, reading and science scales, by highest level of fathers' education

Results based on students' self-reports

		Fathers with completed primary or lower secondary education (ISCED Levels 1 or 2)								Fathers with completed upper secondary education (ISCED Level 3)							
				Performance								Performance					
				Mathematics scale		Reading scale		Science scale				Mathematics scale		Reading scale		Science scale	
		% of students	S.E.	Mean score	S.E.	Mean score	S.E.	Mean score	S.E.	% of students	S.E.	Mean score	S.E.	Mean score	S.E.	Mean score	S.E.
OECD countries	Australia	23.8	(0.6)	505	(3.3)	511	(2.8)	504	(3.0)	34.4	(0.5)	516	(2.1)	515	(2.5)	517	(2.3)
	Austria	10.9	(0.7)	471	(5.9)	447	(6.4)	455	(6.4)	50.8	(1.1)	511	(3.9)	497	(4.6)	494	(4.3)
	Belgium	14.9	(0.5)	502	(4.4)	484	(4.9)	482	(4.4)	38.7	(0.8)	536	(2.5)	515	(3.0)	514	(2.8)
	Canada	11.9	(0.4)	511	(2.7)	505	(2.9)	491	(3.2)	39.1	(0.6)	529	(1.7)	527	(1.9)	517	(2.0)
	Czech Republic	3.3	(0.3)	465	(11.5)	446	(11.0)	474	(13.5)	76.5	(0.8)	513	(3.0)	489	(2.6)	519	(2.8)
	Denmark	18.6	(1.0)	486	(4.1)	465	(4.0)	446	(4.6)	43.2	(0.9)	508	(2.9)	487	(3.0)	468	(3.3)
	Finland	21.9	(0.6)	525	(3.0)	523	(3.0)	530	(3.9)	27.1	(0.7)	538	(2.8)	535	(2.6)	541	(3.1)
	France	28.8	(1.0)	489	(4.6)	475	(5.0)	483	(5.3)	40.5	(1.1)	520	(2.5)	508	(2.8)	521	(3.5)
	Germany	19.2	(0.9)	454	(5.4)	441	(5.7)	444	(5.8)	44.5	(0.9)	520	(3.8)	515	(3.8)	520	(3.9)
	Greece	32.8	(1.5)	419	(3.8)	443	(4.2)	453	(4.0)	34.4	(0.9)	450	(3.7)	481	(4.8)	487	(4.2)
	Hungary	9.2	(0.6)	425	(6.5)	426	(7.0)	440	(6.6)	67.8	(1.0)	482	(2.8)	476	(2.5)	497	(2.7)
	Iceland	20.1	(0.6)	497	(3.8)	481	(4.1)	481	(4.2)	50.3	(1.0)	514	(2.3)	491	(2.5)	490	(2.2)
	Ireland	31.4	(0.9)	482	(3.2)	495	(3.6)	480	(3.9)	40.4	(0.9)	507	(2.8)	522	(2.9)	509	(3.0)
	Italy	40.9	(0.9)	442	(3.6)	449	(4.0)	459	(4.1)	33.6	(0.6)	485	(3.4)	493	(3.5)	505	(3.5)
	Japan	16.4	(0.9)	492	(7.0)	454	(7.7)	509	(7.5)	37.3	(0.9)	524	(4.4)	492	(4.7)	537	(4.8)
	Korea	23.6	(0.8)	506	(4.0)	507	(4.4)	504	(4.8)	40.7	(1.1)	541	(3.1)	533	(2.9)	538	(3.5)
	Luxembourg	21.3	(0.7)	461	(3.6)	441	(3.7)	445	(3.7)	35.0	(0.8)	499	(3.0)	490	(2.9)	490	(3.3)
	Mexico	61.7	(1.7)	366	(3.2)	380	(3.7)	389	(2.9)	12.5	(0.6)	426	(4.8)	440	(5.7)	437	(4.7)
	Netherlands	24.4	(1.1)	524	(5.0)	504	(4.8)	508	(5.6)	35.7	(1.2)	541	(3.3)	518	(3.3)	525	(3.9)
	New Zealand	18.1	(0.7)	495	(4.0)	497	(4.2)	490	(4.3)	52.5	(0.9)	529	(2.5)	530	(3.3)	528	(3.0)
	Norway	9.5	(0.6)	473	(5.3)	481	(6.9)	462	(7.2)	41.7	(1.1)	490	(2.8)	491	(3.3)	474	(3.1)
	Poland	8.5	(0.5)	454	(6.7)	459	(6.8)	458	(7.4)	76.9	(0.8)	485	(2.4)	491	(2.9)	490	(2.7)
	Portugal	62.9	(1.3)	456	(3.1)	470	(3.7)	458	(3.5)	17.0	(0.8)	498	(3.5)	510	(4.5)	498	(4.1)
	Slovak Republic	5.1	(0.7)	426	(12.3)	406	(11.6)	410	(22.0)	74.4	(1.0)	490	(3.1)	463	(3.0)	488	(3.2)
	Spain	43.3	(1.5)	469	(2.9)	468	(3.1)	469	(3.1)	26.4	(0.8)	488	(3.0)	485	(3.4)	490	(3.5)
	Sweden	23.9	(0.8)	491	(3.4)	496	(3.5)	484	(3.6)	30.8	(0.9)	520	(3.3)	527	(3.2)	519	(4.6)
	Switzerland	29.5	(1.0)	491	(3.6)	466	(3.6)	471	(3.9)	32.4	(0.8)	542	(2.9)	516	(3.3)	532	(3.0)
	Turkey	58.8	(2.1)	395	(4.2)	418	(4.3)	408	(4.0)	22.7	(1.0)	444	(6.9)	459	(6.6)	453	(5.9)
	United States	11.2	(0.7)	439	(4.7)	451	(5.3)	448	(5.4)	52.0	(1.1)	479	(2.7)	495	(3.2)	490	(3.0)
	OECD total	***24.3***	***(0.4)***	***439***	***(1.6)***	***442***	***(1.6)***	***448***	***(1.5)***	***42.0***	***(0.4)***	***497***	***(1.1)***	***498***	***(1.3)***	***504***	***(1.2)***
	OECD average	***24.4***	***(0.2)***	***460***	***(1.1)***	***461***	***(1.0)***	***461***	***(0.9)***	***42.0***	***(0.2)***	***505***	***(0.6)***	***499***	***(0.7)***	***504***	***(0.7)***
Partner countries	Brazil	51.0	(1.5)	342	(4.6)	393	(4.6)	378	(4.4)	13.8	(0.8)	404	(6.4)	449	(5.8)	432	(6.4)
	Hong Kong-China	64.5	(1.4)	542	(4.4)	505	(3.6)	533	(4.2)	25.4	(1.0)	569	(4.8)	523	(4.0)	554	(4.5)
	Indonesia	55.9	(1.5)	350	(3.2)	372	(2.9)	386	(2.9)	28.0	(1.0)	378	(4.6)	397	(3.7)	407	(3.9)
	Latvia	4.4	(0.5)	451	(7.4)	466	(9.4)	449	(10.3)	50.1	(1.9)	482	(4.0)	492	(4.0)	489	(4.3)
	Liechtenstein	25.3	(2.3)	499	(11.0)	492	(9.8)	481	(12.8)	33.9	(2.8)	534	(8.5)	531	(8.6)	528	(9.8)
	Macao-China	69.7	(1.6)	523	(3.8)	494	(2.8)	520	(3.7)	24.7	(1.5)	541	(6.5)	508	(4.2)	534	(6.2)
	Russian Federation	2.2	(0.2)	c	c	c	c	c	c	68.4	(1.2)	459	(4.3)	431	(4.1)	480	(4.2)
	Serbia	11.5	(0.7)	395	(4.5)	378	(4.6)	403	(4.1)	47.3	(0.9)	437	(3.6)	414	(3.8)	434	(3.7)
	Thailand	70.7	(1.1)	404	(2.8)	409	(2.4)	415	(2.4)	19.5	(0.7)	437	(4.9)	439	(4.4)	449	(4.6)
	Tunisia	63.1	(1.4)	346	(2.2)	364	(2.8)	376	(2.4)	24.2	(0.9)	376	(4.1)	397	(4.7)	397	(4.0)
	Uruguay	48.3	(1.4)	405	(3.8)	412	(4.3)	418	(3.4)	13.0	(0.6)	441	(5.1)	451	(6.2)	454	(4.8)
	United Kingdom[1]	19.1	(0.6)	488	(3.8)	488	(3.5)	493	(4.1)	51.0	(1.0)	506	(2.8)	506	(2.9)	518	(2.9)

		Fathers with completed tertiary education (ISCED Levels 5 or 6)								Increased likelihood of students whose fathers have not completed upper secondary education scoring in the bottom quarter of the national mathematics performance distribution	
				Performance							
				Mathematics scale		Reading scale		Science scale			
		% of students	S.E.	Mean score	S.E.	Mean score	S.E.	Mean score	S.E.	Ratio	S.E.
OECD countries	Australia	41.8	(0.8)	551	(2.8)	553	(2.8)	554	(3.0)	**1.5**	(0.08)
	Austria	38.3	(1.0)	517	(3.9)	507	(4.1)	506	(4.0)	**1.8**	(0.16)
	Belgium	46.4	(0.9)	565	(2.9)	510	(2.9)	543	(3.0)	**1.9**	(0.13)
	Canada	49.0	(0.8)	552	(2.2)	546	(2.0)	541	(2.3)	**1.5**	(0.10)
	Czech Republic	20.2	(0.8)	575	(4.8)	539	(4.4)	581	(4.7)	**2.0**	(0.25)
	Denmark	38.2	(1.2)	549	(3.5)	524	(3.1)	514	(3.9)	**1.8**	(0.14)
	Finland	51.0	(0.9)	560	(2.2)	560	(2.1)	563	(2.4)	**1.5**	(0.12)
	France	30.7	(1.2)	539	(3.7)	521	(3.7)	549	(4.6)	**1.7**	(0.15)
	Germany	36.3	(0.9)	549	(3.8)	537	(3.5)	555	(3.9)	**3.1**	(0.26)
	Greece	32.9	(1.6)	466	(5.8)	493	(5.4)	503	(5.3)	**1.6**	(0.11)
	Hungary	23.0	(1.0)	546	(4.8)	528	(4.5)	555	(5.1)	**2.3**	(0.19)
	Iceland	29.6	(0.9)	534	(2.9)	506	(3.2)	518	(3.3)	**1.4**	(0.11)
	Ireland	28.3	(1.1)	531	(3.8)	539	(3.8)	536	(3.9)	**1.7**	(0.12)
	Italy	25.5	(0.8)	482	(3.8)	499	(3.6)	511	(4.1)	**1.8**	(0.11)
	Japan	46.3	(1.0)	558	(4.8)	520	(4.2)	571	(4.8)	**1.9**	(0.15)
	Korea	35.7	(1.3)	572	(5.6)	557	(4.5)	565	(5.7)	**1.9**	(0.12)
	Luxembourg	43.6	(0.8)	523	(2.2)	510	(2.5)	516	(2.6)	**2.0**	(0.17)
	Mexico	25.8	(1.3)	415	(5.3)	431	(5.9)	434	(5.5)	**2.2**	(0.24)
	Netherlands	40.0	(1.1)	570	(3.5)	539	(3.2)	556	(3.8)	**1.6**	(0.15)
	New Zealand	29.4	(0.8)	562	(3.7)	556	(3.9)	561	(4.0)	**1.9**	(0.16)
	Norway	48.8	(1.2)	513	(3.1)	521	(3.4)	507	(3.6)	**1.4**	(0.13)
	Poland	14.5	(0.7)	540	(4.1)	547	(4.2)	561	(4.7)	**1.7**	(0.15)
	Portugal	20.2	(1.0)	486	(6.6)	487	(7.3)	490	(6.0)	**1.5**	(0.13)
	Slovak Republic	20.5	(1.0)	553	(4.1)	516	(3.9)	550	(4.4)	**2.3**	(0.28)
	Spain	30.3	(1.4)	516	(3.0)	507	(3.5)	522	(3.7)	**1.7**	(0.12)
	Sweden	45.3	(1.1)	522	(3.4)	526	(3.2)	520	(3.8)	**1.5**	(0.14)
	Switzerland	38.0	(1.0)	551	(4.7)	520	(4.6)	539	(5.6)	**2.1**	(0.11)
	Turkey	18.5	(1.6)	494	(15.2)	497	(12.4)	499	(13.3)	**2.1**	(0.23)
	United States	36.8	(1.1)	513	(3.7)	521	(3.8)	518	(4.0)	**1.9**	(0.16)
	OECD total	***33.7***	***(0.3)***	***526***	***(1.3)***	***520***	***(1.3)***	***533***	***(1.4)***	***2.4***	***(0.06)***
	OECD average	***33.6***	***(0.2)***	***534***	***(0.8)***	***525***	***(0.7)***	***534***	***(0.8)***	***2.1***	***(0.03)***
Partner countries	Brazil	35.2	(1.2)	366	(7.0)	408	(6.4)	399	(6.2)	1.3	(0.13)
	Hong Kong-China	10.1	(0.8)	575	(9.1)	529	(7.0)	567	(7.6)	**1.5**	(0.13)
	Indonesia	16.1	(0.8)	371	(9.2)	393	(7.6)	411	(7.1)	**1.2**	(0.09)
	Latvia	45.5	(2.0)	491	(4.8)	498	(4.8)	497	(4.9)	**1.7**	(0.26)
	Liechtenstein	40.8	(2.5)	566	(7.5)	547	(7.8)	556	(8.2)	**2.1**	(0.56)
	Macao-China	5.6	(0.7)	522	(12.0)	492	(9.3)	537	(10.3)	1.2	(0.22)
	Russian Federation	29.4	(1.3)	500	(4.8)	475	(4.4)	522	(5.0)	**1.8**	(0.26)
	Serbia	41.2	(1.1)	449	(4.7)	420	(4.3)	451	(4.4)	**1.9**	(0.15)
	Thailand	9.8	(0.7)	475	(8.2)	468	(8.1)	489	(7.5)	**1.6**	(0.18)
	Tunisia	12.8	(0.8)	399	(8.6)	398	(8.4)	415	(8.5)	**1.5**	(0.14)
	Uruguay	38.8	(1.4)	445	(4.5)	464	(4.7)	465	(4.2)	**1.6**	(0.14)
	United Kingdom[1]	29.9	(1.0)	547	(3.7)	543	(4.0)	562	(4.2)	**1.5**	(0.10)

Note: Values that are statistically significant are indicated in bold (see Annex A4).

1. Response rate too low to ensure comparability (see Annex A3).

Table 4.2c *(continued)*

Percentage of students and performance on the mathematics, reading and science scales, by highest level of fathers' education

Results based on students' self-reports

	Difference in performance between students whose father completed upper secondary education and students whose father completed primary or lower secondary education						Difference in performance between students whose father completed tertiary education and those whose father completed upper secondary education					
	Mathematics scale		Reading scale		Science scale		Mathematics scale		Reading scale		Science scale	
	Dif.	S.E.	Dif.	S.E.	Dif.	S.E.	Dif.	S.E.	Dif.	S.E.	Dif.	S.E.
OECD countries												
Australia	**11.2**	(3.0)	4.2	(2.7)	**12.8**	(3.1)	**35.4**	(3.1)	**38.4**	(3.6)	**37.4**	(3.7)
Austria	**39.3**	(7.0)	**49.3**	(7.9)	**38.7**	(7.5)	6.6	(4.1)	**10.8**	(4.6)	**12.4**	(4.6)
Belgium	**34.0**	(4.5)	**30.9**	(5.0)	**31.8**	(4.4)	**28.3**	(3.8)	**25.3**	(4.0)	**29.3**	(3.9)
Canada	**17.9**	(3.1)	**22.4**	(3.4)	**26.1**	(3.6)	**23.0**	(2.3)	**18.2**	(2.4)	**23.8**	(2.5)
Czech Republic	**48.6**	(10.7)	**43.2**	(10.2)	**45.5**	(12.6)	**62.0**	(4.5)	**50.0**	(4.3)	**62.3**	(4.4)
Denmark	**22.2**	(4.6)	**22.1**	(4.3)	**22.0**	(5.0)	**41.0**	(3.8)	**37.2**	(3.3)	**45.6**	(4.5)
Finland	**13.2**	(3.7)	**12.1**	(4.1)	**11.2**	(5.2)	**21.1**	(2.9)	**24.3**	(2.7)	**22.0**	(3.2)
France	**30.5**	(4.7)	**32.3**	(4.9)	**38.3**	(5.6)	**19.0**	(4.1)	**13.8**	(4.5)	**27.8**	(5.6)
Germany	**66.1**	(5.7)	**73.5**	(5.8)	**76.6**	(5.6)	**29.7**	(3.8)	**22.9**	(3.8)	**35.0**	(4.0)
Greece	**31.7**	(3.8)	**38.4**	(4.8)	**34.0**	(4.5)	**15.9**	(5.1)	**11.8**	(5.5)	**16.6**	(5.3)
Hungary	**56.5**	(6.7)	**49.8**	(7.3)	**57.3**	(6.8)	**63.9**	(5.1)	**51.6**	(4.9)	**57.6**	(5.1)
Iceland	**17.6**	(4.6)	**10.5**	(4.8)	8.5	(4.9)	**20.1**	(4.2)	**15.3**	(4.4)	**28.7**	(4.4)
Ireland	**25.1**	(3.7)	**26.8**	(3.7)	**29.3**	(4.1)	**23.8**	(4.1)	**17.1**	(3.9)	**27.1**	(4.4)
Italy	**42.6**	(3.3)	**43.3**	(3.7)	**45.5**	(3.8)	–3.3	(3.4)	6.9	(3.7)	6.6	(4.3)
Japan	**32.4**	(6.4)	**37.6**	(7.4)	**28.9**	(7.0)	**33.9**	(4.8)	**27.9**	(4.7)	**33.6**	(5.1)
Korea	**35.2**	(3.7)	**25.6**	(3.6)	**33.5**	(4.3)	**30.8**	(5.5)	**24.1**	(4.3)	**27.5**	(5.6)
Luxembourg	**37.7**	(5.4)	**49.3**	(4.9)	**45.0**	(5.3)	**23.6**	(4.0)	**19.5**	(4.0)	**25.9**	(4.3)
Mexico	**59.2**	(5.4)	**60.4**	(6.2)	**47.9**	(5.2)	**–11.1**	(4.6)	–9.6	(5.8)	–3.2	(5.4)
Netherlands	**17.8**	(5.1)	**14.0**	(4.7)	**17.9**	(5.8)	**28.6**	(4.1)	**21.1**	(3.7)	**30.9**	(4.9)
New Zealand	**34.4**	(4.5)	**33.0**	(5.4)	**38.2**	(4.9)	**32.2**	(4.2)	**26.4**	(4.8)	**33.3**	(4.7)
Norway	**17.3**	(5.6)	10.2	(6.7)	12.1	(7.3)	**23.2**	(3.8)	**29.5**	(3.8)	**32.7**	(3.8)
Poland	**31.3**	(6.1)	**32.6**	(6.1)	**32.7**	(6.9)	**55.1**	(4.6)	**56.0**	(4.8)	**70.7**	(5.0)
Portugal	**41.8**	(3.9)	**39.1**	(5.1)	**40.4**	(4.7)	–11.3	(6.2)	**–22.9**	(7.2)	–8.4	(6.3)
Slovak Republic	**64.3**	(11.4)	**56.3**	(10.8)	**77.5**	(21.2)	**62.2**	(4.8)	**53.5**	(4.6)	**62.5**	(5.3)
Spain	**19.7**	(3.9)	**17.0**	(4.3)	**20.3**	(4.6)	**27.1**	(3.1)	**21.2**	(3.8)	**32.0**	(4.1)
Sweden	**28.2**	(4.4)	**31.2**	(5.1)	**34.4**	(5.4)	2.5	(4.0)	–0.9	(3.8)	1.5	(5.9)
Switzerland	**51.3**	(4.0)	**49.6**	(4.6)	**60.9**	(4.5)	**8.7**	(4.0)	3.7	(4.1)	7.4	(5.2)
Turkey	**48.2**	(5.3)	**40.8**	(5.7)	**45.3**	(4.8)	**50.2**	(12.3)	**38.0**	(10.6)	**45.6**	(11.5)
United States	**39.4**	(4.9)	**44.0**	(5.1)	**42.7**	(5.3)	**34.5**	(3.6)	**26.5**	(4.3)	**27.4**	(4.5)
OECD total	*57.9*	*(1.8)*	*55.6*	*(1.7)*	*56.3*	*(1.7)*	*29.3*	*(1.5)*	*22.3*	*(1.5)*	*29.1*	*(1.6)*
OECD average	*45.5*	*(1.2)*	*37.8*	*(1.1)*	*43.2*	*(1.0)*	*28.9*	*(0.7)*	*26.3*	*(0.7)*	*29.9*	*(0.8)*
Partner countries												
Brazil	**61.7**	(6.2)	**55.7**	(5.6)	**54.6**	(6.6)	**–37.7**	(6.4)	**–40.8**	(6.4)	**–33.4**	(5.4)
Hong Kong-China	**26.6**	(4.1)	**18.1**	(3.5)	**21.4**	(4.0)	6.3	(7.9)	5.9	(6.5)	13.3	(6.9)
Indonesia	**28.1**	(4.0)	**25.3**	(3.4)	**21.5**	(3.7)	–7.2	(7.3)	–4.4	(6.4)	4.4	(5.9)
Latvia	**30.6**	(8.6)	**25.3**	(9.6)	**40.0**	(9.8)	**9.7**	(4.3)	6.1	(4.4)	8.2	(4.9)
Liechtenstein	**35.5**	(14.2)	**38.4**	(14.5)	**46.9**	(17.9)	**32.1**	(12.3)	16.2	(13.2)	**27.8**	(13.9)
Macao-China	**18.1**	(7.8)	**14.4**	(4.9)	13.4	(7.2)	–19.2	(14.1)	–16.2	(10.6)	3.8	(12.2)
Russian Federation	c	c	c	c	c	c	**40.7**	(4.2)	**44.2**	(3.9)	**42.3**	(4.3)
Serbia	**42.3**	(4.5)	**35.4**	(5.0)	**30.6**	(4.3)	**12.2**	(3.5)	6.3	(3.5)	**17.5**	(3.7)
Thailand	**33.8**	(4.7)	**30.4**	(4.1)	**34.0**	(4.4)	**37.6**	(7.1)	**29.0**	(7.0)	**40.2**	(6.7)
Tunisia	**30.5**	(4.3)	**32.5**	(5.0)	**21.1**	(4.4)	**22.5**	(6.8)	1.9	(7.0)	**18.4**	(6.7)
Uruguay	**36.1**	(6.1)	**39.1**	(7.0)	**35.7**	(5.7)	4.1	(5.7)	**13.6**	(6.9)	**11.4**	(5.3)
United Kingdom[1]	**18.1**	(3.8)	**18.2**	(4.0)	**25.6**	(4.1)	**41.7**	(3.5)	**36.6**	(3.7)	**43.5**	(4.2)

Note: Values that are statistically significant are indicated in bold (see Annex A4).

1. Response rate too low to ensure comparability (see Annex A3).

Table 4.2d

Index of possessions related to "classical" culture in the family home and performance on the mathematics scale, by national quarters of the index

Results based on students' self-reports

		Index of cultural possessions in the family home										Performance on the mathematics scale, by national quarters of the index of cultural possessions in the family home							
		All students		Bottom quarter		Second quarter		Third quarter		Top quarter		Bottom quarter		Second quarter		Third quarter		Top quarter	
		Mean index	S.E.	Mean index	S.E.	Mean index	S.E.	Mean index	S.E.	Mean index	S.E.	Mean score	S.E.	Mean score	S.E.	Mean score	S.E.	Mean score	S.E.
OECD countries	Australia	–0.12	(0.01)	min		–0.64	(0.01)	0.13	(0.01)	1.31	(0.00)	**504**	(2.9)	513	(3.4)	525	(3.0)	**556**	(2.6)
	Austria	–0.05	(0.03)	min		–0.48	(0.01)	0.28	(0.01)	1.29	(0.01)	**476**	(4.3)	490	(3.4)	513	(3.8)	**550**	(3.8)
	Belgium	–0.30	(0.02)	min		–0.94	(0.01)	–0.05	(0.01)	1.08	(0.01)	**497**	(4.3)	510	(3.9)	545	(3.5)	**579**	(2.8)
	Canada	0.00	(0.01)	min		–0.40	(0.01)	0.32	(0.01)	max		**515**	(2.3)	534	(2.4)	538	(2.7)	**557**	(2.7)
	Czech Republic	0.26	(0.02)	–1.00	(0.02)	–0.02	(0.01)	0.71	(0.01)	max		**492**	(3.9)	516	(4.3)	535	(3.8)	**546**	(3.8)
	Denmark	–0.01	(0.03)	min		–0.45	(0.01)	0.35	(0.00)	max		**473**	(3.5)	500	(3.5)	533	(3.1)	**554**	(3.6)
	Finland	0.11	(0.02)	min		–0.28	(0.01)	0.65	(0.01)	max		**520**	(3.1)	538	(2.3)	556	(3.3)	**564**	(3.2)
	France	–0.05	(0.02)	min		–0.44	(0.01)	0.30	(0.01)	1.22	(0.01)	**469**	(4.2)	503	(4.3)	531	(3.5)	**545**	(3.7)
	Germany	0.00	(0.02)	min		–0.44	(0.01)	0.37	(0.01)	max		**488**	(4.6)	497	(4.3)	505	(4.9)	**554**	(3.9)
	Greece	0.23	(0.03)	–0.94	(0.01)	–0.07	(0.01)	0.59	(0.01)	max		**406**	(4.8)	438	(5.3)	459	(4.5)	**477**	(5.5)
	Hungary	0.31	(0.02)	–0.97	(0.02)	0.16	(0.01)	0.69	(0.01)	max		**435**	(4.1)	490	(4.1)	513	(4.2)	**521**	(4.1)
	Iceland	0.79	(0.01)	–0.42	(0.02)	0.90	(0.02)	1.35	(0.00)	max		**491**	(3.4)	518	(4.6)	528	(3.6)	**525**	(3.8)
	Ireland	–0.26	(0.02)	min		–0.85	(0.02)	0.01	(0.01)	1.07	(0.01)	**485**	(3.5)	490	(4.0)	506	(4.3)	**530**	(3.4)
	Italy	0.19	(0.02)	–1.18	(0.01)	–0.08	(0.01)	0.67	(0.01)	max		**435**	(4.0)	462	(4.6)	475	(3.8)	**491**	(4.4)
	Japan	–0.43	(0.02)	min		–1.12	(0.01)	–0.18	(0.01)	0.85	(0.01)	**507**	(5.2)	517	(5.5)	550	(5.2)	**563**	(5.8)
	Korea	0.16	(0.02)	–1.14	(0.01)	–0.11	(0.01)	0.55	(0.01)	max		**508**	(4.0)	533	(4.3)	554	(4.0)	**574**	(5.3)
	Luxembourg	–0.03	(0.01)	min		–0.51	(0.01)	0.31	(0.01)	max		**468**	(2.8)	479	(3.0)	492	(3.0)	**534**	(2.8)
	Mexico	–0.68	(0.03)	min		–1.28	(0.00)	–0.65	(0.02)	0.49	(0.02)	**367**	(4.5)	369	(3.9)	382	(4.6)	**424**	(5.6)
	Netherlands	–0.31	(0.02)	min		–0.78	(0.02)	–0.16	(0.01)	0.96	(0.02)	**518**	(5.1)	531	(4.3)	544	(5.7)	**578**	(4.2)
	New Zealand	–0.18	(0.02)	min		–0.62	(0.01)	0.06	(0.01)	1.11	(0.01)	**497**	(3.7)	513	(3.8)	525	(4.0)	**562**	(3.1)
	Norway	0.15	(0.02)	min		–0.30	(0.01)	0.84	(0.02)	max		**456**	(3.6)	484	(3.1)	514	(3.8)	**528**	(3.8)
	Poland	0.25	(0.02)	–0.84	(0.02)	–0.04	(0.01)	0.53	(0.01)	max		**459**	(4.2)	486	(3.6)	504	(3.8)	**512**	(3.9)
	Portugal	–0.08	(0.03)	min		–0.55	(0.01)	0.27	(0.01)	1.24	(0.01)	**431**	(4.3)	452	(4.3)	477	(3.7)	**505**	(4.2)
	Slovak Republic	0.35	(0.02)	–0.93	(0.02)	0.10	(0.01)	0.88	(0.01)	max		**468**	(5.8)	493	(4.4)	512	(4.6)	**519**	(3.2)
	Spain	0.15	(0.02)	–1.17	(0.01)	–0.11	(0.01)	0.54	(0.01)	max		**453**	(3.4)	479	(3.5)	497	(3.4)	**513**	(3.2)
	Sweden	0.10	(0.02)	–1.26	(0.00)	–0.28	(0.00)	0.59	(0.01)	max		**467**	(3.7)	498	(3.5)	528	(3.2)	**545**	(3.9)
	Switzerland	–0.37	(0.03)	min		–1.02	(0.01)	–0.13	(0.01)	0.95	(0.02)	**518**	(4.3)	517	(5.2)	518	(3.9)	**553**	(5.2)
	Turkey	–0.11	(0.03)	min		–0.51	(0.02)	0.22	(0.01)	1.12	(0.01)	**395**	(5.6)	404	(5.3)	431	(7.7)	**464**	(11.2)
	United States	–0.04	(0.02)	min		–0.57	(0.01)	0.34	(0.01)	max		**450**	(4.0)	466	(4.2)	494	(4.0)	**523**	(3.7)
	OECD total	*–0.10*	*(0.01)*	*–1.28*	*(0.00)*	*–0.62*	*(0.01)*	*0.21*	*(0.01)*	*1.29*	*(0.01)*	*455*	*(1.7)*	*474*	*(1.6)*	*500*	*(1.3)*	*529*	*(1.4)*
	OECD average	*0.00*	*(0.00)*	*–1.28*	*(0.00)*	*–0.45*	*(0.00)*	*0.38*	*(0.02)*	*1.35*	*(0.00)*	*469*	*(1.0)*	*489*	*(0.8)*	*510*	*(0.8)*	*535*	*(0.8)*
Partner countries	Brazil	0.33	(0.02)	-1.28	(0.00)	-0.83	(0.02)	-0.06	(0.01)	0.86	(0.02)	**340**	(5.6)	346	(5.8)	358	(5.6)	**383**	(6.7)
	Hong Kong-China	–0.44	(0.03)	min		–1.04	(0.01)	–0.22	(0.01)	0.78	(0.02)	**528**	(6.0)	534	(6.6)	560	(5.2)	**579**	(6.7)
	Indonesia	–0.65	(0.02)	min		min		–0.51	(0.01)	0.46	(0.02)	**352**	(4.3)	355	(4.4)	364	(4.8)	**370**	(5.0)
	Latvia	0.40	(0.02)	–0.91	(0.02)	0.25	(0.01)	0.92	(0.02)	max		**447**	(4.6)	487	(5.0)	498	(4.6)	**502**	(4.5)
	Liechtenstein	–0.27	(0.05)	min		–0.85	(0.05)	–0.04	(0.03)	1.09	(0.05)	**520**	(11.7)	519	(15.1)	521	(12.0)	**583**	(12.8)
	Macao-China	–0.50	(0.02)	min		–1.16	(0.02)	–0.24	(0.01)	0.69	(0.03)	**518**	(7.6)	522	(7.6)	529	(6.9)	**540**	(5.9)
	Russian Federation	0.48	(0.02)	–0.67	(0.02)	0.38	(0.00)	0.85	(0.01)	max		**436**	(4.4)	479	(4.9)	480	(5.0)	**480**	(5.4)
	Serbia	0.14	(0.03)	min		–0.22	(0.01)	0.73	(0.01)	max		**404**	(4.3)	429	(4.3)	454	(4.5)	**461**	(4.4)
	Thailand	–0.21	(0.02)	min		–0.62	(0.01)	0.05	(0.01)	1.02	(0.01)	**404**	(3.6)	410	(3.3)	418	(4.0)	**435**	(4.6)
	Tunisia	–0.63	(0.02)	min		min		–0.47	(0.01)	0.50	(0.02)	**345**	(3.0)	345	(3.1)	358	(3.4)	**388**	(4.9)
	Uruguay	0.07	(0.02)	–1.21	(0.01)	–0.22	(0.01)	0.38	(0.00)	1.32	(0.00)	**390**	(4.9)	411	(4.2)	432	(4.5)	**456**	(4.7)
	United Kingdom[1]	–0.03	(0.02)	min		–0.61	(0.01)	0.40	(0.01)	max		**479**	(3.1)	492	(3.2)	515	(4.0)	**545**	(4.3)

		Change in the mathematics score per unit of the index of cultural possessions		Increased likelihood of students in the bottom quarter of the index of possessions in the family home related to "classical" culture distribution scoring in the bottom quarter of the national mathematics performance distribution		Explained variance in student performance (r-squared × 100)	
		Effect	S.E.	Ratio	S.E.	%	S.E.
OECD countries	Australia	**19.6**	(1.39)	**1.4**	(0.07)	4.3	(0.55)
	Austria	**28.7**	(1.83)	**1.7**	(0.14)	9.3	(1.08)
	Belgium	**34.8**	(1.89)	**1.8**	(0.09)	10.0	(0.86)
	Canada	**15.4**	(1.23)	**1.5**	(0.06)	3.0	(0.46)
	Czech Republic	**23.9**	(1.73)	**1.8**	(0.10)	5.9	(0.78)
	Denmark	**31.6**	(1.65)	**2.1**	(0.13)	11.7	(1.10)
	Finland	**17.1**	(1.40)	**1.6**	(0.08)	4.3	(0.69)
	France	**30.7**	(2.14)	**2.2**	(0.15)	10.4	(1.27)
	Germany	**24.2**	(1.54)	**1.4**	(0.08)	6.2	(0.76)
	Greece	**31.7**	(2.48)	**2.1**	(0.13)	9.5	(1.32)
	Hungary	**38.1**	(2.07)	**2.5**	(0.16)	14.0	(1.30)
	Iceland	**19.8**	(1.92)	**1.6**	(0.09)	3.3	(0.62)
	Ireland	**19.4**	(1.53)	**1.4**	(0.10)	4.9	(0.72)
	Italy	**21.5**	(1.75)	**1.8**	(0.09)	4.9	(0.77)
	Japan	**25.4**	(2.94)	**1.6**	(0.13)	5.3	(1.02)
	Korea	**26.9**	(2.59)	**1.8**	(0.12)	7.8	(1.26)
	Luxembourg	**24.1**	(1.24)	**1.5**	(0.10)	7.0	(0.69)
	Mexico	**31.5**	(2.56)	**1.4**	(0.12)	9.0	(1.45)
	Netherlands	**26.9**	(2.27)	**1.6**	(0.12)	7.6	(1.17)
	New Zealand	**26.9**	(1.54)	**1.5**	(0.10)	6.8	(0.76)
	Norway	**27.2**	(1.38)	**2.1**	(0.13)	9.7	(0.93)
	Poland	**25.3**	(2.04)	**1.7**	(0.13)	6.0	(0.90)
	Portugal	**29.0**	(1.89)	**2.0**	(0.12)	10.5	(1.22)
	Slovak Republic	**22.5**	(2.33)	**1.8**	(0.10)	5.1	(0.94)
	Spain	**24.5**	(1.54)	**1.9**	(0.11)	7.1	(0.83)
	Sweden	**30.0**	(1.96)	**2.0**	(0.10)	10.0	(1.16)
	Switzerland	**17.0**	(2.03)	**1.1**	(0.08)	2.6	(0.60)
	Turkey	**29.6**	(4.43)	**1.5**	(0.11)	7.1	(1.59)
	United States	**28.5**	(1.49)	**1.8**	(0.12)	9.5	(0.92)
	OECD total	*29.3*	*(0.72)*	*1.8*	*(0.04)*	*8.1*	*(0.33)*
	OECD average	*25.0*	*(0.41)*	*1.7*	*(0.02)*	*6.3*	*(0.17)*
Partner countries	Brazil	**20.8**	(2.43)	**1.3**	(0.10)	3.5	(0.75)
	Hong Kong-China	**24.3**	(2.95)	**1.5**	(0.14)	4.5	(1.07)
	Indonesia	**8.6**	(1.90)	**1.1**	(0.09)	0.7	(0.31)
	Latvia	**23.5**	(1.89)	**2.1**	(0.15)	6.1	(0.97)
	Liechtenstein	**26.1**	(5.52)	**1.2**	(0.33)	6.6	(2.70)
	Macao-China	**9.8**	(3.34)	**1.2**	(0.17)	0.9	(0.63)
	Russian Federation	**21.1**	(1.73)	**1.7**	(0.11)	3.7	(0.59)
	Serbia	**22.7**	(1.66)	**2.0**	(0.13)	7.8	(1.02)
	Thailand	**13.7**	(1.88)	**1.2**	(0.08)	2.4	(0.63)
	Tunisia	**23.4**	(2.52)	**1.2**	(0.08)	5.1	(1.00)
	Uruguay	**26.8**	(2.21)	**1.7**	(0.11)	6.4	(1.00)
	United Kingdom[1]	**24.6**	(1.67)	**1.6**	(0.10)	7.8	(0.96)

Note: Values that are statistically significant are indicated in bold (see Annex A4). "Min" is used for countries with more than 25 per cent of students at the lowest value on this index, which is –1.28. "Max" is used for countries with more than 25 per cent of students at the highest value of this index, which is 1.35.

1. Response rate too low to ensure comparability (see Annex A3).

Table 4.2e
Percentage of students and performance on the mathematics scale, by type of family structure
Results based on students' self-reports

		Students from single-parent families				Students from other types of families				Difference in mathematics performance (single-parent families *minus* students from other types of families)		Increased likelihood of students from single-parent families scoring in the bottom quarter of the national mathematics performance distribution		Effect size (single-parent families *versus* other types of families)	
		% of students	S.E.	Mean score	S.E.	% of students	S.E.	Mean score	S.E.	Dif.	S.E.	Ratio	S.E.	Effect size	S.E.
OECD countries	Australia	20.0	(0.5)	504	(3.0)	80.0	(0.5)	530	(2.2)	**–27**	(2.5)	**1.4**	(0.06)	**–0.28**	0.03
	Austria	15.9	(0.6)	505	(4.6)	84.1	(0.6)	508	(3.3)	–3	(4.2)	1.0	(0.10)	–0.03	0.05
	Belgium	17.0	(0.5)	499	(4.2)	83.0	(0.5)	541	(2.5)	**–42**	(4.0)	**1.6**	(0.08)	**–0.39**	0.04
	Canada	18.6	(0.4)	520	(2.7)	81.4	(0.4)	540	(1.7)	**–20**	(2.6)	**1.3**	(0.07)	**–0.22**	0.03
	Czech Republic	12.8	(0.5)	518	(4.3)	87.2	(0.5)	523	(3.4)	–5	(4.1)	1.0	(0.08)	–0.05	0.04
	Denmark	24.3	(1.1)	495	(3.9)	75.7	(1.1)	521	(2.9)	**–26**	(3.4)	**1.4**	(0.10)	**–0.29**	0.04
	Finland	19.9	(0.7)	538	(3.3)	80.1	(0.7)	546	(1.9)	**–9**	(3.1)	**1.2**	(0.08)	–0.10	0.04
	France	20.3	(0.7)	498	(4.3)	79.7	(0.7)	516	(2.5)	**–18**	(4.2)	**1.3**	(0.10)	–0.20	0.05
	Germany	16.7	(0.6)	504	(5.7)	83.3	(0.6)	514	(3.4)	**–10**	(4.9)	1.2	(0.14)	–0.10	0.05
	Greece	23.4	(1.0)	431	(5.8)	76.6	(1.0)	450	(4.0)	**–19**	(5.2)	**1.3**	(0.10)	–0.20	0.06
	Hungary	19.0	(0.7)	478	(3.6)	81.0	(0.7)	493	(3.0)	**–16**	(3.7)	**1.2**	(0.09)	–0.17	0.04
	Iceland	13.3	(0.6)	509	(4.4)	86.7	(0.6)	517	(1.6)	–8	(4.7)	1.1	(0.10)	–0.09	0.05
	Ireland	15.4	(0.7)	475	(4.2)	84.6	(0.7)	508	(2.5)	**–33**	(4.2)	**1.6**	(0.11)	**–0.39**	0.05
	Italy	15.5	(0.6)	454	(4.5)	84.5	(0.6)	469	(3.1)	**–15**	(3.8)	**1.2**	(0.09)	–0.16	0.04
	Japan	m	m	m	m	m	m	m	m	m	m	m	m	m	m
	Korea	20.3	(0.6)	535	(4.5)	79.7	(0.6)	544	(3.2)	**–9**	(3.4)	**1.2**	(0.08)	–0.10	0.04
	Luxembourg	16.3	(0.5)	478	(3.7)	83.7	(0.5)	497	(1.3)	**–19**	(4.4)	**1.3**	(0.11)	**–0.21**	0.05
	Mexico	33.1	(0.8)	380	(5.1)	66.9	(0.8)	389	(3.4)	**–10**	(3.5)	1.2	(0.11)	–0.11	0.04
	Netherlands	13.7	(0.9)	517	(5.4)	86.3	(0.9)	548	(2.9)	**–31**	(5.3)	**1.5**	(0.14)	**–0.36**	0.06
	New Zealand	18.9	(0.7)	507	(4.1)	81.1	(0.7)	529	(2.4)	**–22**	(4.4)	**1.3**	(0.10)	**–0.22**	0.05
	Norway	27.1	(0.7)	480	(3.2)	72.9	(0.7)	502	(2.7)	**–22**	(3.5)	**1.3**	(0.08)	**–0.25**	0.04
	Poland	11.4	(0.5)	479	(5.2)	88.6	(0.5)	492	(2.5)	**–13**	(4.9)	**1.2**	(0.12)	–0.15	0.05
	Portugal	16.5	(0.6)	458	(5.1)	83.5	(0.6)	468	(3.4)	**–10**	(4.1)	1.2	(0.10)	–0.11	0.05
	Slovak Republic	11.5	(0.5)	496	(5.3)	88.5	(0.5)	500	(3.4)	–4	(4.4)	1.0	(0.09)	–0.04	0.05
	Spain	14.0	(0.5)	475	(4.4)	86.0	(0.5)	487	(2.5)	**–12**	(4.3)	**1.2**	(0.10)	–0.14	0.05
	Sweden	24.0	(0.7)	488	(3.4)	76.0	(0.7)	517	(2.6)	**–29**	(3.2)	**1.5**	(0.08)	**–0.31**	0.03
	Switzerland	20.8	(0.7)	514	(4.4)	79.2	(0.7)	530	(3.5)	**–16**	(3.8)	**1.3**	(0.09)	–0.17	0.04
	Turkey	32.7	(1.3)	421	(7.2)	67.3	(1.3)	426	(7.0)	–5	(4.4)	1.1	(0.08)	–0.05	0.04
	United States	29.4	(0.9)	454	(3.9)	70.6	(0.9)	497	(2.9)	**–43**	(3.5)	**1.8**	(0.11)	**–0.46**	0.04
	OECD total	*23.4*	*(0.3)*	*459*	*(1.8)*	*76.6*	*(0.3)*	*493*	*(1.1)*	*–34*	*(1.5)*	*1.4*	*(0.03)*	*–0.33*	*(0.01)*
	OECD average	*19.4*	*(0.1)*	*481*	*(1.0)*	*80.6*	*(0.1)*	*505*	*(0.6)*	*–24*	*(0.9)*	*1.3*	*(0.02)*	*–0.25*	*(0.01)*
Partner countries	Brazil	26.2	(0.9)	354	(6.8)	73.8	(0.9)	358	(4.8)	–4	(5.4)	1.1	(0.09)	–0.04	0.05
	Hong Kong-China	19.7	(0.7)	535	(5.9)	80.3	(0.7)	555	(4.4)	**–20**	(4.1)	**1.3**	(0.10)	**–0.21**	0.04
	Indonesia	9.9	(0.5)	340	(5.9)	90.1	(0.5)	363	(3.9)	**–23**	(5.0)	**1.4**	(0.13)	**–0.28**	0.06
	Latvia	25.4	(0.9)	480	(4.7)	74.6	(0.9)	485	(3.9)	–6	(4.2)	1.1	(0.10)	–0.06	0.05
	Liechtenstein	17.8	(2.1)	521	(13.3)	82.2	(2.1)	539	(5.2)	–18	(15.7)	1.2	(0.37)	–0.18	0.16
	Macao-China	21.1	(1.3)	521	(6.9)	78.9	(1.3)	529	(3.4)	–8	(8.0)	1.2	(0.17)	–0.09	0.09
	Russian Federation	20.7	(0.6)	466	(4.4)	79.3	(0.6)	471	(4.0)	–5	(3.2)	1.1	(0.09)	–0.06	0.03
	Serbia	14.9	(0.7)	432	(5.0)	85.1	(0.7)	438	(3.9)	–6	(4.4)	1.1	(0.11)	–0.07	0.05
	Thailand	21.7	(0.8)	407	(4.2)	78.3	(0.8)	421	(3.0)	**–13**	(3.5)	**1.3**	(0.13)	–0.16	0.04
	Tunisia	7.3	(0.4)	351	(5.2)	92.7	(0.4)	362	(2.7)	**–10**	(5.2)	1.1	(0.17)	–0.13	0.07
	Uruguay	23.1	(0.6)	416	(4.1)	76.9	(0.6)	424	(3.5)	**–9**	(3.9)	1.1	(0.07)	–0.09	0.04
	United Kingdom[1]	22.2	(0.6)	490	(3.4)	77.8	(0.6)	513	(2.8)	**–24**	(3.4)	**1.4**	(0.10)	**–0.26**	0.04

Note: Values that are statistically significant and effect sizes equal or greater than 0.2 are indicated in bold (see Annex A4).
1. Response rate too low to ensure comparability (see Annex A3).

Table 4.2f
Percentage of students and performance on the mathematics, reading and science scales, by students' nationality and the nationality of their parents
Results based on students' self-reports

		Native students (born in the country of assessment with at least one of their parents born in the same country)								First-generation students (born in the country of assessment but whose parents were born in another country)							
				Performance								Performance					
				Mathematics scale		Reading scale		Science scale				Mathematics scale		Reading scale		Science scale	
		% of students	S.E.	Mean score	S.E.	Mean score	S.E.	Mean score	S.E.	% of students	S.E.	Mean score	S.E.	Mean score	S.E.	Mean score	S.E.
OECD countries	Australia	77.3	(1.1)	527	(2.1)	529	(2.2)	529	(2.1)	11.7	(0.6)	522	(4.7)	525	(4.6)	520	(4.7)
	Austria	86.7	(1.0)	515	(3.3)	501	(3.8)	502	(3.4)	4.1	(0.5)	459	(8.8)	428	(13.5)	434	(9.6)
	Belgium	88.2	(0.9)	545	(2.5)	523	(2.7)	524	(2.6)	6.3	(0.6)	454	(7.5)	439	(7.5)	435	(7.7)
	Canada	79.9	(1.1)	537	(1.6)	534	(1.6)	527	(1.9)	9.2	(0.5)	543	(4.3)	543	(4.2)	519	(5.0)
	Czech Republic	98.7	(0.2)	523	(3.2)	497	(2.7)	529	(3.1)	0.5	(0.1)	c	c	c	c	c	c
	Denmark	93.5	(0.8)	520	(2.5)	497	(2.7)	481	(2.8)	3.5	(0.6)	449	(11.2)	440	(13.8)	396	(13.7)
	Finland	98.1	(0.2)	546	(1.9)	546	(1.6)	550	(1.9)	0.0	(0.0)	c	c	c	c	c	c
	France	85.7	(1.3)	520	(2.4)	505	(2.6)	521	(3.0)	10.8	(1.1)	472	(6.1)	458	(6.9)	465	(7.0)
	Germany	84.6	(1.1)	525	(3.5)	517	(3.5)	529	(3.7)	6.9	(0.8)	432	(9.1)	420	(9.9)	412	(9.6)
	Greece	92.6	(0.6)	449	(3.9)	477	(4.0)	485	(3.8)	0.5	(0.1)	c	c	c	c	c	c
	Hungary	97.7	(0.2)	491	(3.0)	482	(2.6)	505	(2.9)	0.1	(0.0)	c	c	c	c	c	c
	Iceland	99.0	(0.2)	517	(1.4)	494	(1.6)	497	(1.5)	0.2	(0.1)	c	c	c	c	c	c
	Ireland	96.5	(0.3)	503	(2.4)	516	(2.6)	506	(2.7)	1.0	(0.2)	c	c	c	c	c	c
	Italy	97.9	(0.3)	468	(3.0)	478	(3.0)	489	(3.1)	0.4	(0.1)	c	c	c	c	c	c
	Japan	99.9	(0.0)	535	(4.0)	499	(3.9)	548	(4.2)	0.0	(0.0)	c	c	c	c	c	c
	Korea	100.0	(0.0)	543	(3.2)	535	(3.1)	539	(3.5)	0.0	(0.0)	c	c	c	c	c	c
	Luxembourg	66.7	(0.6)	507	(1.3)	500	(1.8)	500	(1.7)	15.8	(0.6)	476	(3.3)	454	(4.0)	464	(3.9)
	Mexico	97.7	(0.3)	392	(3.6)	407	(4.0)	410	(3.4)	0.5	(0.1)	c	c	c	c	c	c
	Netherlands	89.0	(1.4)	551	(3.0)	524	(2.9)	538	(3.2)	7.1	(1.1)	492	(10.3)	475	(8.2)	465	(10.3)
	New Zealand	80.2	(1.1)	528	(2.6)	528	(2.9)	528	(2.7)	6.6	(0.7)	496	(8.4)	506	(8.3)	485	(8.8)
	Norway	94.4	(0.7)	499	(2.3)	505	(2.7)	490	(2.7)	2.3	(0.4)	c	c	c	c	c	c
	Poland	100.0	(0.0)	491	(2.5)	497	(2.8)	499	(2.9)	0.0	(0.0)	c	c	c	c	c	c
	Portugal	95.0	(1.4)	470	(2.9)	481	(3.4)	471	(3.2)	2.3	(0.4)	440	(14.7)	471	(17.8)	457	(17.4)
	Slovak Republic	99.1	(0.2)	499	(3.2)	470	(3.0)	496	(3.6)	0.6	(0.2)	c	c	c	c	c	c
	Spain	96.6	(0.4)	487	(2.4)	483	(2.5)	490	(2.6)	0.6	(0.1)	c	c	c	c	c	c
	Sweden	88.5	(0.9)	517	(2.2)	522	(2.2)	516	(2.6)	5.7	(0.5)	483	(9.8)	502	(8.7)	466	(9.7)
	Switzerland	80.0	(0.9)	543	(3.3)	515	(3.2)	531	(3.5)	8.9	(0.5)	484	(5.0)	462	(5.2)	462	(6.0)
	Turkey	99.0	(0.2)	425	(6.7)	442	(5.7)	434	(5.9)	0.5	(0.2)	c	c	c	c	c	c
	United States	85.6	(1.0)	490	(2.8)	503	(3.1)	499	(2.9)	8.3	(0.7)	468	(7.6)	481	(8.7)	466	(8.9)
	OECD total	*91.5*	*(0.3)*	*494*	*(1.1)*	*493*	*(1.2)*	*502*	*(1.1)*	*4.6*	*(0.2)*	*473*	*(4.0)*	*476*	*(4.5)*	*467*	*(4.6)*
	OECD average	*91.4*	*(0.2)*	*505*	*(0.6)*	*499*	*(0.6)*	*505*	*(0.6)*	*4.0*	*(0.1)*	*481*	*(2.1)*	*475*	*(2.1)*	*469*	*(2.1)*
Partner countries	Brazil	99.2	(0.2)	359	(4.7)	406	(4.5)	392	(4.2)	0.6	(0.2)	c	c	c	c	c	c
	Hong Kong-China	56.7	(1.4)	557	(4.5)	513	(3.7)	545	(4.3)	22.9	(0.9)	570	(4.6)	522	(3.8)	557	(4.3)
	Indonesia	99.7	(0.1)	363	(4.0)	384	(3.3)	396	(3.3)	0.2	(0.1)	c	c	c	c	c	c
	Latvia	90.6	(0.9)	484	(3.8)	492	(3.8)	490	(4.0)	8.3	(0.8)	479	(6.6)	477	(7.0)	486	(7.5)
	Liechtenstein	82.9	(2.0)	545	(5.0)	534	(4.2)	535	(5.7)	7.6	(1.3)	508	(18.1)	503	(16.0)	495	(17.0)
	Macao-China	23.9	(1.4)	528	(5.9)	499	(5.1)	526	(6.9)	57.9	(1.5)	532	(4.1)	497	(2.9)	524	(4.3)
	Russian Federation	86.5	(0.7)	472	(4.4)	446	(4.0)	493	(4.2)	6.4	(0.5)	457	(7.2)	426	(6.9)	463	(7.6)
	Serbia	91.1	(0.6)	439	(3.8)	413	(3.6)	438	(3.6)	3.2	(0.3)	433	(8.0)	410	(8.9)	415	(9.5)
	Thailand	99.9	(0.1)	419	(3.0)	421	(2.8)	430	(2.7)	0.1	(0.1)	c	c	c	c	c	c
	Tunisia	99.7	(0.1)	360	(2.5)	376	(2.8)	385	(2.6)	0.2	(0.1)	c	c	c	c	c	c
	Uruguay	99.2	(0.2)	423	(3.2)	435	(3.4)	439	(2.9)	0.4	(0.1)	c	c	c	c	c	c
	United Kingdom[1]	92.0	(0.8)	510	(2.5)	508	(2.5)	521	(2.7)	5.3	(0.6)	503	(7.1)	509	(8.5)	510	(8.7)

		Non-native students (born in another country and whose parents were also born in another country)								Increased likelihood of non-native students scoring in the bottom quarter of the national mathematics performance distribution	
				Performance							
				Mathematics scale		Reading scale		Science scale			
		% of students	S.E.	Mean score	S.E.	Mean score	S.E.	Mean score	S.E.	Ratio	S.E.
OECD countries	Australia	11.0	(0.7)	525	(4.9)	517	(5.0)	515	(5.5)	**1.1**	(0.09)
	Austria	9.2	(0.7)	452	(6.0)	425	(8.0)	422	(6.4)	**2.1**	(0.18)
	Belgium	5.5	(0.6)	437	(10.8)	407	(11.9)	416	(10.5)	**2.6**	(0.20)
	Canada	10.9	(0.8)	530	(4.7)	515	(4.7)	501	(5.1)	**1.2**	(0.09)
	Czech Republic	0.8	(0.1)	c	c	c	c	c	c	c	c
	Denmark	3.0	(0.4)	455	(10.1)	454	(9.5)	422	(11.0)	**2.1**	(0.31)
	Finland	1.8	(0.2)	c	c	c	c	c	c	c	c
	France	3.5	(0.5)	448	(15.0)	426	(15.3)	433	(17.1)	**2.3**	(0.29)
	Germany	8.5	(0.7)	454	(7.5)	431	(8.9)	444	(8.8)	**2.3**	(0.25)
	Greece	6.9	(0.7)	402	(6.3)	429	(7.6)	433	(6.8)	**1.7**	(0.16)
	Hungary	2.2	(0.2)	c	c	c	c	c	c	c	c
	Iceland	0.8	(0.2)	c	c	c	c	c	c	c	c
	Ireland	2.5	(0.3)	c	c	c	c	c	c	c	c
	Italy	1.7	(0.2)	c	c	c	c	c	c	c	c
	Japan	0.1	(0.0)	c	c	c	c	c	c	c	c
	Korea	a	a	a	a	a	a	a	a	a	a
	Luxembourg	17.4	(0.5)	462	(3.7)	431	(4.4)	441	(4.4)	**1.8**	(0.12)
	Mexico	1.8	(0.2)	c	c	c	c	c	c	c	c
	Netherlands	3.9	(0.4)	472	(8.4)	463	(8.1)	457	(10.6)	**2.6**	(0.29)
	New Zealand	13.3	(0.7)	523	(4.9)	503	(5.3)	511	(5.3)	**1.0**	(0.10)
	Norway	3.4	(0.4)	438	(9.3)	436	(11.5)	399	(11.9)	**2.1**	(0.22)
	Poland	0.0	(0.0)	c	c	c	c	c	c	c	c
	Portugal	2.7	(1.1)	c	c	c	c	c	c	c	c
	Slovak Republic	0.3	(0.1)	c	c	c	c	c	c	c	c
	Spain	2.8	(0.4)	c	c	c	c	c	c	c	c
	Sweden	5.9	(0.7)	425	(9.6)	433	(11.3)	409	(10.9)	**2.5**	(0.20)
	Switzerland	11.1	(0.6)	453	(6.1)	422	(6.3)	429	(6.8)	**2.6**	(0.17)
	Turkey	0.5	(0.1)	c	c	c	c	c	c	c	c
	United States	6.1	(0.4)	453	(7.5)	453	(8.3)	462	(8.3)	**1.6**	(0.17)
	OECD total	*3.9*	*(0.1)*	*456*	*(3.6)*	*448*	*(3.8)*	*454*	*(3.8)*	***1.6***	*(0.08)*
	OECD average	*4.6*	*(0.1)*	*466*	*(2.0)*	*452*	*(1.9)*	*453*	*(1.9)*	***1.6***	*(0.04)*
Partner countries	Brazil	0.2	(0.1)	c	c	c	c	c	c	c	c
	Hong Kong-China	20.4	(1.3)	516	(5.3)	494	(4.8)	511	(5.4)	**1.7**	(0.12)
	Indonesia	0.1	(0.0)	c	c	c	c	c	c	c	c
	Latvia	1.1	(0.2)	c	c	c	c	c	c	c	c
	Liechtenstein	9.4	(1.6)	482	(20.9)	467	(22.5)	469	(25.2)	**2.2**	(0.42)
	Macao-China	18.2	(1.4)	517	(9.2)	499	(7.1)	529	(8.2)	**1.3**	(0.22)
	Russian Federation	7.0	(0.5)	452	(5.9)	413	(7.5)	478	(6.9)	**1.2**	(0.13)
	Serbia	5.6	(0.5)	451	(6.5)	429	(6.5)	445	(6.2)	**0.9**	(0.15)
	Thailand	0.0	(0.0)	c	c	c	c	c	c	c	c
	Tunisia	0.1	(0.0)	c	c	c	c	c	c	c	c
	Uruguay	0.4	(0.1)	c	c	c	c	c	c	c	c
	United Kingdom[1]	2.7	(0.4)	c	c	c	c	c	c	**1.5**	(0.26)

Note: Values that are statistically significant are indicated in bold (see Annex A4).

1. Response rate too low to ensure comparability (see Annex A3).

Table 4.2f *(continued)*

Percentage of students and performance on the mathematics, reading and science scales, by students' nationality and the nationality of their parents

Results based on students' self-reports

		Difference in mathematics performance between native and first-generation students		Difference in mathematics performance between native and non-native students		Difference in mathematics performance between native students and students with immigrant background (first generation or non-native): PISA 2003		Difference in mathematics performance between native students and students with immigrant background (first generation or non-native): PISA 2000		Difference in the index of economic, social and cultural status (ESCS) between native students and students with immigrant background (first generation or non-native)	
		Dif.	S.E.	Dif.	S.E.	Dif.	S.E.	Dif.	S.E.	Dif.	S.E.
OECD countries	Australia	5	(4.7)	2	(4.9)	3	(4.1)	6	(6.8)	**0.10**	(0.03)
	Austria	**56**	(9.3)	**63**	(6.0)	**61**	(5.7)	**80**	(9.2)	**0.59**	(0.05)
	Belgium	**92**	(7.6)	**109**	(10.9)	**100**	(7.0)	**114**	(9.1)	**0.74**	(0.06)
	Canada	–6	(4.4)	7	(4.8)	1	(3.9)	**10**	(3.4)	–0.04	(0.04)
	Czech Republic	c	c	c	c	c	c	c	c	c	c
	Denmark	**70**	(11.1)	**65**	(9.8)	**68**	(8.0)	**73**	(8.5)	**0.65**	(0.09)
	Finland	c	c	c	c	c	c	c	c	c	c
	France	**48**	(6.6)	**72**	(15.0)	**54**	(7.0)	**45**	(7.1)	**0.79**	(0.06)
	Germany	**93**	(9.6)	**71**	(7.9)	**81**	(6.9)	**82**	(7.7)	**1.05**	(0.06)
	Greece	c	c	**47**	(6.7)	**43**	(6.2)	**88**	(17.1)	**0.45**	(0.06)
	Hungary	c	c	c	c	c	c	c	c	c	c
	Iceland	c	c	c	c	c	c	c	c	c	c
	Ireland	c	c	c	c	4	(10.3)	c	c	**–0.36**	(0.10)
	Italy	c	c	c	c	c	c	c	c	**c**	c
	Japan	c	c	c	c	c	c	c	c	c	c
	Korea	c	c	a	a	c	c	a	a	c	c
	Luxembourg	**31**	(3.7)	**45**	(4.1)	**38**	(2.8)	**69**	(4.5)	**0.73**	(0.04)
	Mexico	c	c	c	c	c	c	c	c	c	c
	Netherlands	**59**	(11.1)	**79**	(8.8)	**66**	(9.0)	**90**	(14.9)	**0.69**	(0.08)
	New Zealand	**32**	(9.1)	5	(5.6)	**14**	(6.0)	**16**	(8.1)	0.07	(0.05)
	Norway	c	c	**61**	(9.4)	**52**	(7.6)	**54**	(9.3)	**0.42**	(0.08)
	Poland	c	c	c	c	c	c	c	c	c	c
	Portugal	**30**	(14.2)	c	c	**61**	(19.1)	c	c	–0.03	(0.10)
	Slovak Republic	c	c	c	c	c	c	m	m	c	c
	Spain	c	c	c	c	**45**	(10.5)	c	c	**0.30**	(0.10)
	Sweden	**34**	(9.1)	**92**	(9.7)	**64**	(8.3)	**63**	(7.8)	**0.55**	(0.07)
	Switzerland	**59**	(4.9)	**89**	(6.0)	**76**	(4.5)	**85**	(5.8)	**0.63**	(0.03)
	Turkey	c	c	c	c	c	c	m	m	c	c
	United States	**22**	(7.2)	**36**	(7.5)	**28**	(6.3)	**40**	(11.4)	**0.55**	(0.08)
	OECD total	*22*	***(4.0)***	*38*	***(3.7)***	*29*	***(3.3)***	*36*	***(6.1)***	*0.27*	***(0.04)***
	OECD average	*24*	***(2.0)***	*38*	***(2.0)***	*32*	***(1.6)***	*39*	***(2.4)***	*0.28*	***(0.01)***
Partner countries	Brazil	c	c	c	c	c	c	c	c	c	c
	Hong Kong-China	**–13**	(4.3)	**41**	(4.5)	**12**	(3.6)	**18**	(4.6)	**0.42**	(0.03)
	Indonesia	c	c	c	c	c	c	c	c	c	c
	Latvia	5	(6.2)	c	c	3	(5.7)	5	(10.0)	**–0.15**	(0.05)
	Liechtenstein	37	(18.9)	**62**	(22.7)	**51**	(15.9)	**60**	(20.6)	**0.56**	(0.15)
	Macao-China	–4	(7.9)	11	(10.4)	–1	(7.3)	m	m	**0.30**	(0.07)
	Russian Federation	**14**	(7.2)	**20**	(5.4)	**17**	(4.8)	14	(11.3)	0.03	(0.04)
	Serbia	6	(7.6)	–12	(6.3)	–6	(5.5)	m	m	0.10	(0.05)
	Thailand	c	c	c	c	c	c	c	c	c	c
	Tunisia	c	c	c	c	c	c	m	m	c	c
	Uruguay	c	c	c	c	c	c	m	m	c	c
	United Kingdom[1]	7	(6.3)	c	c	**16**	(6.7)	**35**	(10.5)	**0.21**	(0.07)

Note: Values that are statistically significant are indicated in bold (see Annex A4).

1. Response rate too low to ensure comparability (see Annex A3).

Table 4.2g
Percentage of students and performance on the mathematics, reading and science scales, by language spoken at home
Results based on students' self-reports

		Language spoken at home most of the time IS DIFFERENT from the language of assessment, from other official languages or from other national dialects								Language spoken at home most of the time IS THE SAME as the language of assessment, other official languages or other national dialects							
				Performance								Performance					
				Mathematics scale		Reading scale		Science scale				Mathematics scale		Reading scale		Science scale	
		% of students	S.E.	Mean score	S.E.	Mean score	S.E.	Mean score	S.E.	% of students	S.E.	Mean score	S.E.	Mean score	S.E.	Mean score	S.E.
OECD countries	Australia	8.9	(0.7)	516	(5.8)	510	(5.1)	505	(6.1)	91.1	(0.7)	527	(2.0)	529	(2.1)	529	(2.0)
	Austria	9.0	(0.7)	456	(7.2)	422	(10.4)	427	(7.4)	91.0	(0.7)	513	(3.3)	500	(3.8)	501	(3.4)
	Belgium	4.8	(0.4)	449	(8.4)	429	(10.2)	428	(9.5)	95.2	(0.4)	544	(2.5)	522	(2.8)	523	(2.7)
	Canada	11.2	(0.7)	525	(4.4)	510	(4.6)	492	(5.0)	88.8	(0.7)	538	(1.6)	535	(1.6)	528	(1.9)
	Czech Republic	0.9	(0.2)	c	c	c	c	c	c	99.1	(0.2)	523	(3.2)	496	(2.8)	529	(3.1)
	Denmark	3.9	(0.5)	474	(10.1)	470	(11.3)	443	(13.8)	96.1	(0.5)	517	(2.7)	495	(2.8)	479	(2.9)
	Finland	1.8	(0.2)	c	c	c	c	c	c	98.2	(0.2)	546	(1.9)	546	(1.7)	551	(1.9)
	France	6.1	(0.7)	452	(9.2)	427	(10.6)	440	(11.4)	93.9	(0.7)	518	(2.4)	504	(2.6)	518	(3.0)
	Germany	7.7	(0.6)	434	(6.8)	407	(8.0)	417	(7.4)	92.3	(0.6)	523	(3.3)	515	(3.3)	525	(3.5)
	Greece	3.2	(0.4)	399	(9.4)	406	(11.7)	426	(10.6)	96.8	(0.4)	447	(3.9)	475	(4.0)	484	(3.7)
	Hungary	0.6	(0.1)	c	c	c	c	c	c	99.4	(0.1)	491	(2.9)	483	(2.6)	504	(2.9)
	Iceland	1.6	(0.2)	c	c	c	c	c	c	98.4	(0.2)	517	(1.5)	494	(1.6)	495	(1.5)
	Ireland	0.8	(0.2)	c	c	c	c	c	c	99.2	(0.2)	503	(2.4)	516	(2.6)	506	(2.7)
	Italy	1.6	(0.2)	c	c	c	c	c	c	98.4	(0.2)	469	(3.0)	480	(2.9)	491	(3.1)
	Japan	0.2	(0.1)	c	c	c	c	c	c	99.8	(0.1)	538	(4.1)	502	(3.9)	551	(4.2)
	Korea	0.1	(0.0)	c	c	c	c	c	c	99.9	(0.0)	543	(3.3)	535	(3.1)	539	(3.6)
	Luxembourg	25.0	(0.6)	464	(2.8)	433	(3.3)	446	(3.2)	75.0	(0.6)	506	(1.4)	498	(1.6)	499	(1.7)
	Mexico	1.1	(0.3)	c	c	c	c	c	c	98.9	(0.3)	387	(3.6)	402	(4.0)	406	(3.4)
	Netherlands	4.6	(0.6)	468	(9.7)	458	(8.6)	451	(9.7)	95.4	(0.6)	549	(2.9)	523	(2.8)	535	(3.2)
	New Zealand	9.0	(0.7)	510	(6.8)	474	(6.3)	481	(6.7)	91.0	(0.7)	526	(2.4)	528	(2.7)	526	(2.5)
	Norway	4.5	(0.5)	455	(8.4)	445	(9.6)	415	(10.1)	95.5	(0.5)	499	(2.3)	505	(2.6)	490	(2.8)
	Poland	0.2	(0.1)	c	c	c	c	c	c	99.8	(0.1)	491	(2.5)	497	(2.8)	498	(2.9)
	Portugal	1.4	(0.2)	c	c	c	c	c	c	98.6	(0.2)	468	(3.4)	480	(3.7)	470	(3.5)
	Slovak Republic	1.4	(0.3)	c	c	c	c	c	c	98.6	(0.3)	500	(3.2)	471	(3.0)	498	(3.3)
	Spain	1.7	(0.3)	c	c	c	c	c	c	98.3	(0.3)	485	(2.4)	481	(2.6)	487	(2.6)
	Sweden	6.9	(0.7)	452	(9.8)	462	(10.9)	436	(10.7)	93.1	(0.7)	517	(2.2)	522	(2.1)	515	(2.5)
	Switzerland	9.5	(0.7)	460	(7.1)	428	(6.7)	437	(7.3)	90.5	(0.7)	539	(3.8)	512	(3.7)	527	(4.1)
	Turkey	1.2	(0.6)	c	c	c	c	c	c	98.8	(0.6)	425	(6.7)	442	(5.7)	435	(5.8)
	United States	9.0	(0.7)	444	(6.3)	447	(6.9)	446	(6.9)	91.0	(0.7)	490	(2.9)	503	(3.1)	499	(2.9)
	OECD total	***4.5***	***(0.2)***	***450***	***(3.7)***	***452***	***(4.2)***	***449***	***(4.3)***	***90.7***	***(0.3)***	***494***	***(1.1)***	***492***	***(1.1)***	***499***	***(1.1)***
	OECD average	***4.5***	***(0.1)***	***466***	***(1.9)***	***468***	***(2.0)***	***451***	***(2.1)***	***91.2***	***(0.1)***	***504***	***(0.6)***	***503***	***(0.6)***	***504***	***(0.6)***
Partner countries	Brazil	0.5	(0.1)	c	c	c	c	c	c	99.5	(0.1)	357	(4.8)	403	(4.6)	390	(4.4)
	Hong Kong-China	4.5	(0.4)	488	(9.6)	453	(9.6)	484	(9.6)	95.5	(0.4)	555	(4.4)	514	(3.5)	544	(4.1)
	Indonesia	2.1	(0.3)	c	c	c	c	c	c	97.9	(0.3)	362	(4.0)	383	(3.4)	395	(3.3)
	Latvia	8.3	(1.1)	463	(7.8)	465	(8.5)	468	(8.2)	91.7	(1.1)	487	(3.7)	494	(3.7)	493	(3.9)
	Liechtenstein	18.4	(2.2)	508	(12.0)	506	(10.6)	490	(11.7)	81.6	(2.2)	550	(5.0)	538	(4.8)	542	(5.8)
	Macao-China	4.6	(0.7)	482	(13.8)	464	(10.4)	473	(14.5)	95.4	(0.7)	530	(3.1)	500	(2.3)	528	(3.2)
	Russian Federation	5.4	(1.3)	425	(12.7)	393	(11.2)	433	(11.0)	94.6	(1.3)	471	(4.0)	445	(3.6)	493	(3.8)
	Serbia	1.5	(0.2)	c	c	c	c	c	c	98.5	(0.2)	438	(3.8)	413	(3.6)	438	(3.5)
	Thailand	0.0	(0.0)	a	a	a	a	a	a	100.0	(0.0)	418	(3.0)	420	(2.8)	430	(2.7)
	Tunisia	0.4	(0.1)	c	c	c	c	c	c	99.6	(0.1)	358	(2.6)	374	(2.9)	384	(2.6)
	Uruguay	1.9	(0.4)	c	c	c	c	c	c	98.1	(0.4)	425	(3.3)	436	(3.5)	441	(2.9)
	United Kingdom[1]	3.8	(0.6)	477	(12.1)	471	(12.3)	476	(12.9)	96.2	(0.6)	510	(2.6)	510	(2.6)	521	(2.7)

		Difference in mathematics performance between students who speak at home the language of assessment *versus* students who speak a different language				Increased likelihood of students who do not speak the language of assessment at home scoring in the bottom quarter of the national mathematics performance distribution		Effect size (language spoken at home is the same as the language of assessment *versus* a different language)	
		PISA 2003		PISA 2000					
		Dif.	S.E.	Dif.	S.E.	Ratio	S.E.	Effect size	S.E.
OECD countries	Australia	**12**	(5.6)	**15**	(6.8)	**1.3**	(0.10)	0.12	(0.06)
	Austria	**57**	(7.2)	**80**	(9.6)	**2.0**	(0.19)	**0.63**	(0.08)
	Belgium	**95**	(8.3)	**111**	(11.3)	**2.8**	(0.21)	**0.90**	(0.09)
	Canada	**13**	(4.3)	**14**	(4.2)	**1.2**	(0.10)	0.15	(0.05)
	Czech Republic	c	c	c	c	c	c	c	c
	Denmark	**43**	(10.1)	**74**	(8.7)	**1.7**	(0.23)	**0.48**	(0.11)
	Finland	c	c	c	c	c	c	c	c
	France	**66**	(9.5)	**58**	(8.8)	**2.3**	(0.21)	**0.71**	(0.11)
	Germany	**90**	(6.6)	**110**	(12.4)	**3.1**	(0.23)	**0.95**	(0.08)
	Greece	**48**	(9.4)	c	c	**1.7**	(0.19)	**0.52**	(0.10)
	Hungary	c	c	m	m	c	c	c	c
	Iceland	c	c	c	c	c	c	c	c
	Ireland	c	c	c	c	c	c	c	c
	Italy	c	c	c	c	c	c	c	c
	Japan	c	c	c	c	c	c	c	c
	Korea	c	c	a	a	c	c	c	c
	Luxembourg	**42**	(3.4)	**73**	(6.0)	**2.0**	(0.12)	**0.46**	(0.04)
	Mexico	c	c	c	c	c	c	c	c
	Netherlands	**81**	(9.9)	**84**	(15.9)	**2.7**	(0.35)	**0.95**	(0.13)
	New Zealand	**16**	(7.2)	**34**	(9.9)	**1.3**	(0.14)	0.16	(0.07)
	Norway	**45**	(8.5)	**47**	(11.1)	**1.8**	(0.21)	**0.48**	(0.09)
	Poland	c	c	c	c	c	c	c	c
	Portugal	c	c	31	(21.6)	c	c	c	c
	Slovak Republic	c	c	m	m	c	c	c	c
	Spain	c	c	c	c	c	c	c	c
	Sweden	**65**	(9.3)	**69**	(11.2)	**2.1**	(0.21)	**0.66**	(0.10)
	Switzerland	**79**	(6.7)	**89**	(6.7)	**2.5**	(0.18)	**0.80**	(0.08)
	Turkey	c	c	m	m	c	c	c	c
	United States	**46**	(6.5)	**73**	(10.0)	**1.9**	(0.18)	**0.49**	(0.07)
	OECD total	***43***	***(3.8)***	***57***	***(8.0)***	***1.6***	***(0.09)***	***0.42***	***(0.04)***
	OECD average	***38***	***(1.9)***	***49***	***(3.0)***	***1.6***	***(0.04)***	***0.38***	***(0.02)***
Partner countries	Brazil	c	c	c	c	c	c	c	c
	Hong Kong-China	**67**	(9.0)	**68**	(11.0)	2.1	(0.20)	**0.64**	(0.08)
	Indonesia	c	c	c	c	c	c	c	c
	Latvia	**24**	(7.1)	c	c	**1.4**	(0.17)	**0.27**	(0.08)
	Liechtenstein	**43**	(13.2)	30	(21.6)	1.7	(0.39)	**0.45**	(0.13)
	Macao-China	**48**	(14.7)	m	m	1.6	(0.42)	**0.59**	(0.18)
	Russian Federation	**46**	(12.2)	15	(16.0)	**1.7**	(0.26)	**0.50**	(0.13)
	Serbia	c	c	m	m	c	c	c	c
	Thailand	a	a	c	c	a	a	a	a
	Tunisia	c	c	m	m	c	c	c	c
	Uruguay	c	c	m	m	c	c	c	c
	United Kingdom[1]	**33**	(11.9)	**57**	(14.1)	**1.6**	(0.22)	**0.35**	(0.12)

Note: Values that are statistically significant and effect sizes equal or greater than 0.2 are indicated in bold (see Annex A4).

1. Response rate too low to ensure comparability (see Annex A3).

Table 4.2h

The relationship between place of birth and home language with the economic, social and cultural status of students

Results based on students' self-reports

	Difference in the mathematics score							
	WITHOUT accounting for the economic, social and cultural status of students (ESCS)				WITH accounting for the economic, social and cultural status of students (ESCS)			
	Native students *versus* students with an immigrant background (first generation or non-native students)		Native students *versus* students with an immigrant background (first generation or non-native students) who speak a language at home that is different from the language of instruction		Native students *versus* students with an immigrant background (first generation or non-native)		Native students *versus* students with an immigrant background (first generation or non-native students) who speak a language at home that is different from the language of instruction	
	Difference	S.E.	Difference	S.E.	Difference	S.E.	Difference	S.E.
OECD countries								
Australia	3	(4.1)	8	(6.4)	–1	(3.6)	–4	(6.0)
Austria	**61**	(5.7)	**60**	(7.4)	**36**	(5.3)	**28**	(6.7)
Belgium	**100**	(7.0)	**104**	(8.8)	**60**	(5.9)	**51**	(8.1)
Canada	1	(3.9)	4	(4.6)	1	(3.4)	3	(4.4)
Czech Republic	c	c	c	c	c	c	c	c
Denmark	**68**	(8.0)	c	c	**39**	(7.5)	c	c
Finland	c	c	c	c	c	c	c	c
France	**54**	(7.0)	**69**	(9.8)	**21**	(6.0)	**21**	(8.2)
Germany	**81**	(6.9)	**94**	(7.5)	**35**	(6.5)	**37**	(7.7)
Greece	**43**	(6.2)	c	c	**27**	(6.0)	c	c
Hungary	c	c	c	c	c	c	c	c
Iceland	c	c	c	c	c	c	c	c
Ireland	4	(10.3)	c	c	18	(9.3)	c	c
Italy	c	c	c	c	c	c	c	c
Japan	c	c	c	c	c	c	c	c
Korea	c	c	c	c	c	c	c	c
Luxembourg	**38**	(2.8)	**42**	(3.4)	**13**	(2.9)	**9**	(3.8)
Mexico	c	c	c	c	c	c	c	c
Netherlands	**66**	(9.0)	**85**	(9.3)	**37**	(7.1)	**47**	(9.1)
New Zealand	**14**	(6.0)	14	(7.5)	**11**	(4.7)	6	(6.2)
Norway	**52**	(7.6)	**46**	(9.2)	**34**	(6.7)	**21**	(8.3)
Poland	c	c	c	c	c	c	c	c
Portugal	**61**	(19.1)	**c**	c	**62**	(17.5)	c	c
Slovak Republic	c	c	c	c	c	c	c	c
Spain	**45**	(10.5)	c	c	**36**	(9.1)	c	c
Sweden	**64**	(8.3)	**71**	(9.5)	**41**	(7.1)	**47**	(8.3)
Switzerland	**76**	(4.5)	**84**	(7.1)	**49**	(4.3)	**47**	(6.7)
Turkey	c	c	c	c	c	c	c	c
United States	**28**	(6.3)	**42**	(7.1)	4	(4.8)	6	(6.6)
OECD total	*29*	*(3.3)*	*38*	*(4.2)*	*16*	*(2.6)*	*17*	*(3.7)*
OECD average	*31*	*(1.6)*	*35*	*(2.1)*	*18*	*(1.3)*	*15*	*(1.7)*
Partner countries								
Brazil	c	c	c	c	c	c	c	c
Hong Kong-China	**12**	(3.6)	c	c	–1	(3.7)	c	c
Indonesia	c	c	c	c	c	c	c	c
Latvia	3	(5.7)	c	c	9	(5.2)	c	c
Liechtenstein	**51**	(15.9)	**59**	(26.4)	22	(15.8)	17	(26.2)
Macao-China	–1	(7.4)	**43**	(17.7)	–5	(7.4)	35	(18.3)
Russian Federation	**17**	(4.8)	c	c	**16**	(4.5)	c	c
Serbia	–6	(5.5)	c	c	–9	(5.3)	c	c
Thailand	c	c	c	c	c	c	c	c
Tunisia	c	c	c	c	c	c	c	c
Uruguay	c	c	c	c	c	c	c	c
United Kingdom[1]	**16**	(6.7)	c	c	5	(5.5)	c	c

Note: Values that are statistically significant are indicated in bold (see Annex A4).

1. Response rate too low to ensure comparability (see Annex A3).

Table 4.3a
Relationship between student performance in mathematics and the PISA index of economic, social and cultural status (ESCS) in PISA 2003

		(1) Unadjusted mean score		(2) Mean score if the mean ESCS would be equal in all OECD countries		(3) Strength of the relationship between student performance and the ESCS		(4) Slope of the socio-economic gradient[1]		(5) Length of the projection of the gradient line					
										(5a) 5th percentile of the ESCS		(5b) 95th percentile of the ESCS		(5c) Dif. between 95th and 5th percentile of the ESCS	
		Mean score	S.E.	Mean score	S.E.	Percentage of explained variance in student performance	S.E.	Score point difference associated with one unit on the ESCS	S.E.	Index	S.E.	Index	S.E.	Dif.	S.E.
OECD countries	Australia	524	(2.1)	516	(2.0)	13.7	(1.17)	42	(2.2)	-1.11	(0.04)	1.60	(0.00)	2.71	(0.04)
	Austria	506	(3.3)	505	(2.5)	16.0	(1.54)	43	(2.3)	-1.21	(0.06)	1.53	(0.01)	2.74	(0.06)
	Belgium	529	(2.3)	526	(1.8)	24.1	(1.29)	**55**	(1.7)	-1.44	(0.05)	1.64	(0.04)	3.09	(0.05)
	Canada	532	(1.8)	521	(1.4)	10.5	(0.84)	**34**	(1.4)	-0.90	(0.01)	1.85	(0.02)	2.75	(0.02)
	Czech Republic	516	(3.5)	514	(2.6)	19.5	(1.47)	**51**	(2.1)	-1.03	(0.01)	1.53	(0.03)	2.56	(0.03)
	Denmark	514	(2.7)	506	(2.0)	17.6	(1.39)	44	(2.0)	-1.14	(0.05)	1.58	(0.04)	2.72	(0.07)
	Finland	544	(1.9)	536	(1.7)	10.9	(1.03)	**33**	(1.6)	-1.11	(0.04)	1.63	(0.03)	2.75	(0.05)
	France	511	(2.5)	516	(1.9)	19.6	(1.81)	43	(2.2)	-1.60	(0.09)	1.43	(0.07)	3.03	(0.11)
	Germany	503	(3.3)	505	(2.7)	22.8	(1.47)	47	(1.7)	-1.59	(0.05)	1.85	(0.03)	3.44	(0.06)
	Greece	445	(3.9)	451	(2.7)	15.9	(1.94)	**37**	(2.2)	-1.76	(0.04)	1.55	(0.05)	3.31	(0.06)
	Hungary	490	(2.8)	494	(2.2)	27.0	(1.86)	**55**	(2.3)	-1.44	(0.04)	1.47	(0.03)	2.91	(0.05)
	Iceland	515	(1.4)	496	(1.8)	6.5	(0.86)	**28**	(1.7)	-0.69	(0.03)	1.90	(0.03)	2.59	(0.04)
	Ireland	503	(2.4)	506	(1.8)	16.3	(1.57)	**39**	(2.0)	-1.54	(0.02)	1.40	(0.04)	2.93	(0.04)
	Italy	466	(3.1)	470	(2.9)	13.6	(1.37)	**34**	(2.0)	-1.69	(0.04)	1.68	(0.08)	3.37	(0.09)
	Japan	534	(4.0)	538	(3.6)	11.6	(1.72)	46	(4.1)	-1.21	(0.03)	1.17	(0.06)	2.38	(0.05)
	Korea	542	(3.2)	547	(3.0)	14.2	(1.93)	41	(3.1)	-1.57	(0.03)	1.27	(0.06)	2.84	(0.06)
	Luxembourg	493	(1.0)	487	(1.1)	17.1	(1.02)	**35**	(1.2)	-1.79	(0.02)	1.85	(0.01)	3.64	(0.02)
	Mexico	385	(3.6)	419	(3.5)	17.1	(2.09)	**29**	(1.9)	-3.05	(0.02)	0.92	(0.05)	3.97	(0.05)
	Netherlands	538	(3.1)	539	(2.5)	18.6	(1.70)	45	(2.4)	-1.26	(0.07)	1.52	(0.06)	2.78	(0.09)
	New Zealand	523	(2.3)	516	(2.0)	16.8	(1.21)	44	(1.6)	-1.34	(0.06)	1.64	(0.01)	2.98	(0.06)
	Norway	495	(2.4)	469	(2.4)	14.1	(1.18)	44	(1.7)	-0.64	(0.04)	1.87	(0.00)	2.51	(0.04)
	Poland	490	(2.5)	499	(1.9)	16.7	(1.26)	45	(1.8)	-1.39	(0.04)	1.30	(0.03)	2.69	(0.04)
	Portugal	466	(3.4)	485	(2.5)	17.5	(1.45)	**29**	(1.2)	-2.57	(0.04)	1.68	(0.15)	4.24	(0.16)
	Slovak Republic	498	(3.3)	503	(2.3)	22.3	(1.78)	**53**	(2.6)	-1.28	(0.06)	1.37	(0.04)	2.65	(0.07)
	Spain	485	(2.4)	495	(1.7)	14.0	(1.31)	**33**	(1.7)	-1.90	(0.01)	1.31	(0.03)	3.21	(0.03)
	Sweden	509	(2.6)	499	(1.9)	15.3	(1.34)	42	(2.1)	-1.19	(0.05)	1.66	(0.04)	2.85	(0.06)
	Switzerland	527	(3.4)	530	(2.6)	16.8	(1.21)	47	(2.1)	-1.42	(0.03)	1.29	(0.03)	2.71	(0.04)
	Turkey	423	(6.7)	468	(8.3)	22.3	(3.82)	45	(4.8)	-2.54	(0.08)	1.06	(0.10)	3.59	(0.12)
	United States	483	(2.9)	470	(2.1)	19.0	(1.15)	45	(1.6)	-1.20	(0.06)	1.72	(0.02)	2.92	(0.05)
	OECD total	*489*	*(0.7)*	*493*	*(0.8)*	*22.1*	*(0.62)*	*47*	*(0.7)*	*-1.90*	*(0.02)*	*1.58*	*(0.03)*	*3.49*	*(0.03)*
	OECD average	*500*	*(0.6)*	*501*	*(0.5)*	*20.3*	*(0.34)*	*45*	*(0.4)*	*-1.74*	*(0.02)*	*1.60*	*(0.01)*	*3.34*	*(0.02)*
Partner countries	Brazil	356	(4.8)	390	(5.6)	15.3	(2.43)	**35**	(3.1)	-2.74	(0.02)	0.88	(0.09)	3.62	(0.09)
	Hong Kong-China	550	(4.5)	575	(4.8)	6.5	(1.34)	**31**	(2.9)	-2.02	(0.04)	0.68	(0.06)	2.70	(0.07)
	Indonesia	360	(3.9)	387	(5.9)	7.0	(1.69)	**21**	(2.6)	-2.83	(0.06)	0.52	(0.06)	3.35	(0.07)
	Latvia	483	(3.7)	480	(3.4)	10.5	(1.32)	**38**	(2.3)	-1.08	(0.03)	1.31	(0.05)	2.38	(0.05)
	Liechtenstein	536	(4.1)	536	(4.4)	20.6	(3.59)	55	(5.9)	-1.28	(0.09)	1.28	(0.09)	2.56	(0.12)
	Macao-China	527	(2.9)	540	(3.9)	1.9	(0.92)	**14**	(3.3)	-2.40	(0.14)	0.38	(0.06)	2.77	(0.15)
	Russian Federation	468	(4.2)	472	(3.8)	10.0	(1.09)	**39**	(2.3)	-1.20	(0.03)	1.18	(0.03)	2.37	(0.05)
	Serbia	437	(3.8)	445	(3.2)	14.1	(1.49)	**36**	(2.0)	-1.54	(0.03)	1.33	(0.04)	2.86	(0.04)
	Thailand	417	(3.0)	449	(4.6)	11.4	(1.95)	**27**	(2.6)	-2.46	(0.01)	0.89	(0.05)	3.35	(0.05)
	Tunisia	359	(2.5)	391	(4.7)	13.0	(2.47)	**24**	(2.4)	-3.21	(0.02)	0.86	(0.06)	4.07	(0.06)
	Uruguay	422	(3.3)	436	(2.9)	15.9	(1.69)	**38**	(2.1)	-2.02	(0.03)	1.36	(0.05)	3.37	(0.05)
	United Kingdom[3]	m	m	m	m	m	m	m	m	m	m	m	m	m	m

		(6) ESCS mean		(7) Variability in the ESCS		(8) Index of curvelinearity[2]		(9) Index of skewness in the distribution of the ESCS	(10) Percentage of students that fall within the lowest 15% of the international distribution on the ESCS	
		Mean index	S.E.	Standard deviation	S.E.	Score point difference associated with one unit on the ESCS squared	S.E.	Index	Approximated by the % of students with a value on the PISA index of economic, social and cultural status smaller than -1	S.E.
OECD countries	Australia	0.23	(0.02)	0.83	(0.01)	**4.02**	(1.80)	–0.29	6.6	(0.4)
	Austria	0.06	(0.03)	0.85	(0.01)	–0.83	(1.33)	0.15	9.0	(0.7)
	Belgium	0.15	(0.02)	0.94	(0.01)	–0.57	(0.87)	–0.38	10.4	(0.6)
	Canada	0.15	(0.02)	0.83	(0.01)	0.64	(1.06)	–0.10	3.9	(0.2)
	Czech Republic	0.16	(0.02)	0.80	(0.01)	**–7.17**	(1.48)	0.24	5.7	(0.5)
	Denmark	0.20	(0.03)	0.86	(0.02)	0.90	(1.17)	–0.28	6.9	(0.5)
	Finland	0.25	(0.02)	0.83	(0.01)	0.02	(1.52)	–0.16	6.7	(0.4)
	France	–0.08	(0.03)	0.93	(0.02)	–1.33	(1.33)	–0.27	15.3	(0.9)
	Germany	0.16	(0.02)	0.99	(0.01)	**2.03**	(1.02)	–0.27	9.7	(0.6)
	Greece	–0.15	(0.05)	1.01	(0.02)	2.18	(1.45)	0.09	20.7	(1.2)
	Hungary	–0.07	(0.02)	0.89	(0.01)	**–3.52**	(1.46)	0.16	13.3	(0.7)
	Iceland	0.69	(0.01)	0.81	(0.01)	0.62	(1.62)	–0.34	2.3	(0.2)
	Ireland	–0.08	(0.03)	0.89	(0.02)	–1.13	(1.25)	–0.09	14.6	(0.8)
	Italy	–0.11	(0.02)	1.02	(0.01)	**–5.25**	(1.31)	0.12	21.9	(0.8)
	Japan	–0.08	(0.02)	0.73	(0.01)	–2.51	(2.60)	–0.04	9.3	(0.5)
	Korea	–0.10	(0.02)	0.85	(0.02)	1.75	(1.92)	–0.19	14.6	(0.7)
	Luxembourg	0.18	(0.01)	1.09	(0.01)	**4.00**	(0.96)	–0.43	16.1	(0.5)
	Mexico	–1.13	(0.05)	1.20	(0.02)	–0.07	(0.99)	0.19	57.3	(1.8)
	Netherlands	0.10	(0.02)	0.86	(0.02)	2.24	(1.28)	–0.29	8.8	(0.7)
	New Zealand	0.21	(0.02)	0.91	(0.01)	**4.04**	(1.11)	–0.50	8.8	(0.5)
	Norway	0.61	(0.02)	0.78	(0.01)	–0.63	(1.57)	–0.18	1.9	(0.2)
	Poland	–0.20	(0.02)	0.82	(0.01)	–1.51	(1.43)	0.35	15.3	(0.9)
	Portugal	–0.63	(0.04)	1.27	(0.02)	1.76	(0.84)	0.24	42.1	(1.4)
	Slovak Republic	–0.08	(0.03)	0.83	(0.02)	**–3.65**	(1.82)	0.08	10.5	(1.1)
	Spain	–0.30	(0.04)	1.01	(0.01)	0.38	(1.03)	–0.06	25.7	(1.1)
	Sweden	0.25	(0.02)	0.88	(0.01)	0.01	(1.46)	–0.38	7.3	(0.6)
	Switzerland	–0.06	(0.02)	0.85	(0.01)	–1.77	(1.28)	–0.15	12.8	(0.7)
	Turkey	–0.98	(0.06)	1.10	(0.03)	**9.45**	(2.54)	0.44	54.1	(2.3)
	United States	0.30	(0.03)	0.91	(0.02)	**4.42**	(1.16)	–0.41	8.0	(0.6)
	OECD total	*–0.06*	*(0.01)*	*1.04*	*(0.01)*	*–2.18*	*(0.45)*	*–0.27*	*17.2*	*(0.3)*
	OECD average	*0.00*	*(0.01)*	*1.00*	*(0.00)*	*–2.25*	*(0.28)*	*–0.31*	*15.1*	*(0.2)*
Partner countries	Brazil	–0.95	(0.05)	1.12	(0.02)	**8.15**	(1.63)	0.04	48.1	(1.8)
	Hong Kong-China	–0.76	(0.03)	0.81	(0.02)	–0.45	(2.06)	0.22	40.0	(1.2)
	Indonesia	–1.26	(0.04)	1.00	(0.01)	**7.31**	(1.18)	0.25	62.8	(1.4)
	Latvia	0.12	(0.03)	0.75	(0.01)	–3.44	(2.80)	–0.01	6.4	(0.5)
	Liechtenstein	0.01	(0.04)	0.82	(0.03)	5.81	(6.55)	–0.22	11.3	(1.8)
	Macao-China	–0.90	(0.02)	0.85	(0.02)	1.10	(2.68)	–0.06	44.8	(1.5)
	Russian Federation	–0.09	(0.02)	0.75	(0.01)	0.22	(2.41)	0.21	9.9	(0.6)
	Serbia	–0.23	(0.03)	0.88	(0.01)	0.32	(1.34)	0.24	18.9	(1.0)
	Thailand	–1.18	(0.03)	1.02	(0.02)	**6.41**	(1.30)	0.74	64.2	(1.2)
	Tunisia	–1.34	(0.04)	1.23	(0.02)	**5.76**	(0.96)	0.29	63.1	(1.5)
	Uruguay	–0.35	(0.03)	1.05	(0.01)	**5.01**	(1.26)	0.00	29.2	(1.1)
	United Kingdom[3]	m	m	m	m	m	m	m	m	m

Note: Bold figures represent values that are statistically above or below the average OECD statistics (see Annex A4).

1. Single-level bivariate regression of mathematics performance on the ESCS, the slope is the regression coefficient for the ESCS.
2. Student-level regression of mathematics performance on the ESCS and the squared term of the ESCS, the index of curvelinearity is the regression coefficient for the squared term.
3. Response rate too low to ensure comparability (see Annex A3).

Table 4.3b

Relationship between student performance in mathematics and the PISA index of economic, social and cultural status (ESCS) in PISA 2000

		(1) Unadjusted mean score		(2) Mean score if the mean ESCS would be equal in all OECD countries		(3) Strength of the relationship between student performance and the ESCS		(4) Slope of the socio-economic gradient[1]		(5) ESCS mean		(6) Index of curvilinearity[2]	
						Percentage of explained variance in student performance		Score point difference associated with one unit on the ESCS				Score point difference associated with one unit on the ESCS squared	
		Mean score	S.E.	Mean score	S.E.		S.E.		S.E.	Mean index	S.E.		S.E.
OECD countries	Australia	533	(3.5)	526	(2.7)	17.1	(1.87)	**44**	(2.6)	0.17	(0.03)	2.51	(2.22)
	Austria	515	(2.5)	515	(2.4)	12.4	(1.64)	36	(2.6)	0.01	(0.02)	**–6.28**	(2.22)
	Belgium	520	(3.9)	523	(3.2)	**19.3**	(1.77)	**49**	(2.7)	–0.02	(0.02)	**–4.64**	(1.63)
	Canada	533	(1.4)	521	(1.3)	**9.8**	(0.75)	**30**	(1.2)	0.42	(0.01)	1.40	(0.92)
	Czech Republic	498	(2.8)	501	(2.3)	**21.3**	(1.95)	**59**	(2.8)	–0.04	(0.02)	**–5.89**	(1.82)
	Denmark	514	(2.4)	509	(2.0)	14.4	(1.82)	36	(2.3)	0.20	(0.03)	**–3.96**	(1.83)
	Finland	536	(2.1)	535	(2.0)	**8.7**	(1.08)	**26**	(1.7)	0.04	(0.02)	0.78	(1.76)
	France	517	(2.7)	525	(2.1)	15.5	(1.94)	38	(2.4)	–0.15	(0.03)	0.23	(1.38)
	Germany	490	(2.5)	482	(2.3)	**22.8**	(2.38)	**54**	(2.8)	0.16	(0.02)	–3.68	(2.18)
	Greece	447	(5.6)	449	(4.8)	13.3	(2.35)	37	(3.4)	–0.08	(0.04)	**5.27**	(2.46)
	Hungary	488	(4.0)	492	(2.8)	**26.2**	(2.36)	**60**	(3.1)	–0.05	(0.03)	–2.85	(2.42)
	Iceland	514	(2.3)	502	(2.9)	**6.7**	(1.44)	**24**	(2.6)	0.59	(0.02)	0.78	(1.85)
	Ireland	503	(2.7)	507	(2.1)	13.4	(1.37)	**32**	(1.8)	–0.09	(0.04)	2.93	(1.80)
	Italy	457	(2.9)	462	(2.9)	**7.4**	(1.30)	**25**	(2.2)	–0.17	(0.02)	–2.01	(1.86)
	Japan	557	(5.5)	m	m	m	m	m	m	m	m	m	m
	Korea	547	(2.8)	552	(2.4)	**11.0**	(1.54)	**32**	(2.4)	–0.17	(0.03)	–2.42	(1.82)
	Luxembourg	446	(2.0)	455	(2.0)	17.1	(1.84)	**32**	(1.9)	–0.13	(0.02)	0.00	(1.59)
	Mexico	387	(3.4)	419	(3.7)	17.8	(2.56)	**30**	(2.2)	–1.07	(0.05)	**3.68**	(1.31)
	New Zealand	537	(3.1)	526	(3.0)	16.1	(1.83)	42	(2.6)	0.30	(0.02)	1.97	(1.45)
	Norway	499	(2.8)	484	(3.2)	**10.6**	(1.50)	34	(2.7)	0.49	(0.02)	2.94	(1.71)
	Poland	470	(5.5)	485	(4.9)	14.0	(1.96)	44	(3.6)	–0.23	(0.03)	0.26	(2.58)
	Portugal	454	(4.1)	474	(3.1)	16.7	(2.16)	**34**	(2.1)	–0.58	(0.04)	–1.20	(1.46)
	Spain	476	(3.1)	490	(2.6)	14.6	(1.66)	**33**	(2.0)	–0.39	(0.04)	–1.25	(1.54)
	Sweden	510	(2.5)	498	(2.1)	**12.1**	(1.34)	38	(2.2)	0.34	(0.02)	**6.24**	(1.77)
	Switzerland	529	(4.4)	531	(3.5)	17.1	(1.84)	**44**	(2.3)	0.01	(0.03)	**–4.21**	(1.68)
	United Kingdom	529	(2.5)	525	(2.1)	**18.8**	(1.76)	42	(2.0)	0.16	(0.02)	1.59	(1.85)
	United States	493	(7.6)	490	(4.5)	**23.8**	(2.30)	**50**	(2.8)	0.29	(0.06)	**4.07**	(2.07)
	OECD total	*498*	*(2.1)*	*495*	*(1.3)*	*22.9*	*(0.94)*	*47*	*(1.0)*	*–0.04*	*(0.02)*	***–3.22***	*(0.62)*
	OECD average	*500*	*(0.7)*	*500*	*(0.6)*	*17.9*	*(0.43)*	*42*	*(0.6)*	*0.00*	*(0.01)*	***–3.22***	*(0.32)*
Partner countries	Brazil	334	(3.7)	371	(5.1)	16.7	(2.77)	35	(3.0)	–1.04	(0.04)	**5.94**	(1.74)
	Hong Kong-China	560	3.259	581	(4.0)	**5.7**	(1.57)	**27**	(3.3)	–0.75	(0.03)	–0.31	(2.03)
	Indonesia	367	(4.5)	391	(7.3)	**5.5**	(2.07)	**20**	(4.0)	–1.19	(0.04)	2.77	(2.02)
	Latvia	463	(4.5)	463	(4.3)	**5.6**	(1.33)	**31**	(3.8)	0.05	(0.03)	–2.28	(3.64)
	Liechtenstein	514	(7.0)	520	(6.9)	10.5	(4.73)	33	(8.6)	–0.11	(0.05)	6.62	(4.37)
	Russian Federation	478	(5.5)	480	(4.7)	**7.2**	(1.52)	38	(4.0)	–0.05	(0.03)	–2.78	(3.52)
	Thailand	432	(3.6)	469	(5.6)	**8.6**	(1.90)	**26**	(3.0)	–1.37	(0.04)	**7.25**	(1.46)
	Netherlands[3]	564	(3.6)	565	(3.3)	13.9	(2.83)	36	(3.9)	0.02	(0.03)	–2.67	(3.24)

Note: Bold figures represent values that are statistically above or below the average OECD statistics (see Annex A4).

1. Single-level bivariate regression of mathematics performance on the ESCS, the slope is the regression coefficient for the ESCS.
2. Student-level regression of mathematics performance on the ESCS and the squared term of the ESCS, the index of curvilinearity is the regression coefficient for the squared term.
3. Response rate too low to ensure comparability (see Annex A3, OECD 2001a).

Table 4.4

Index of economic, social and cultural status (ESCS) and performance on the mathematics scale, by national quarters of the index

Results based on students' self-reports

		Index of economic, social and cultural status										Performance on the mathematics scale, by national quarters of the index of economic, social and cultural status							
		All students		Bottom quarter		Second quarter		Third quarter		Top quarter		Bottom quarter		Second quarter		Third quarter		Top quarter	
		Mean index	S.E.	Mean index	S.E.	Mean index	S.E.	Mean index	S.E.	Mean index	S.E.	Mean score	S.E.	Mean score	S.E.	Mean score	S.E.	Mean score	S.E.
OECD countries	Australia	0.23	0.02	–0.85	(0.01)	–0.03	(0.00)	0.53	(0.00)	1.26	(0.01)	**479**	(4.1)	513	(2.3)	537	(2.7)	**572**	(2.9)
	Austria	0.06	0.03	–0.98	(0.02)	–0.26	(0.01)	0.29	(0.01)	1.19	(0.02)	**462**	(4.4)	492	(3.6)	520	(3.1)	**556**	(4.2)
	Belgium	0.15	0.02	–1.07	(0.02)	–0.14	(0.00)	0.51	(0.00)	1.31	(0.01)	**465**	(3.8)	519	(3.0)	555	(2.6)	**599**	(2.7)
	Canada	0.45	0.02	–0.62	(0.01)	0.16	(0.00)	0.76	(0.00)	1.51	(0.01)	**500**	(2.2)	527	(2.2)	544	(2.1)	**574**	(2.7)
	Czech Republic	0.16	0.02	–0.80	(0.01)	–0.15	(0.00)	0.35	(0.01)	1.25	(0.01)	**468**	(3.4)	511	(3.5)	537	(3.7)	**575**	(4.3)
	Denmark	0.20	0.03	–0.89	(0.02)	–0.07	(0.00)	0.49	(0.01)	1.28	(0.02)	**464**	(3.5)	505	(3.3)	526	(3.2)	**565**	(3.6)
	Finland	0.25	0.02	–0.82	(0.01)	–0.04	(0.00)	0.56	(0.00)	1.30	(0.01)	**509**	(2.7)	538	(2.3)	553	(2.6)	**579**	(3.0)
	France	–0.08	0.03	–1.27	(0.02)	–0.37	(0.01)	0.24	(0.01)	1.09	(0.02)	**458**	(4.5)	502	(3.4)	527	(3.0)	**562**	(3.6)
	Germany	0.16	0.02	–1.08	(0.02)	–0.14	(0.01)	0.45	(0.01)	1.42	(0.01)	**452**	(4.1)	494	(3.5)	533	(3.7)	**572**	(3.7)
	Greece	–0.15	0.05	–1.41	(0.01)	–0.53	(0.00)	0.15	(0.01)	1.19	(0.02)	**401**	(4.3)	430	(4.1)	452	(3.9)	**497**	(4.8)
	Hungary	–0.07	0.02	–1.14	(0.02)	–0.42	(0.00)	0.15	(0.01)	1.14	(0.01)	**427**	(4.4)	474	(3.2)	505	(3.4)	**554**	(4.0)
	Iceland	0.69	0.01	–0.39	(0.02)	0.44	(0.01)	1.02	(0.01)	1.69	(0.01)	**485**	(3.0)	513	(2.7)	518	(3.0)	**547**	(2.3)
	Ireland	–0.08	0.03	–1.20	(0.02)	–0.37	(0.01)	0.19	(0.01)	1.06	(0.02)	**458**	(3.8)	494	(2.9)	517	(2.9)	**544**	(3.7)
	Italy	–0.11	0.02	–1.41	(0.01)	–0.49	(0.01)	0.22	(0.01)	1.23	(0.02)	**417**	(4.4)	457	(4.0)	482	(3.5)	**507**	(4.2)
	Japan	–0.08	0.02	–0.99	(0.01)	–0.34	(0.00)	0.15	(0.00)	0.88	(0.01)	**487**	(5.3)	524	(4.4)	549	(4.8)	**576**	(6.1)
	Korea	–0.10	0.03	–1.21	(0.01)	–0.35	(0.00)	0.20	(0.00)	0.96	(0.02)	**497**	(4.2)	533	(3.7)	553	(3.7)	**587**	(6.2)
	Luxembourg	0.18	0.01	–1.31	(0.02)	–0.07	(0.01)	0.63	(0.01)	1.49	(0.01)	**445**	(2.3)	479	(3.1)	506	(2.7)	**546**	(2.9)
	Mexico	–1.13	0.05	–2.61	(0.02)	–1.63	(0.01)	–0.77	(0.01)	0.50	(0.02)	**342**	(4.4)	370	(3.6)	397	(3.7)	**433**	(4.6)
	Netherlands	0.10	0.02	–0.99	(0.03)	–0.19	(0.01)	0.41	(0.01)	1.17	(0.01)	**496**	(5.1)	529	(4.0)	554	(3.4)	**595**	(3.7)
	New Zealand	0.21	0.02	–0.98	(0.02)	–0.02	(0.00)	0.54	(0.01)	1.31	(0.01)	**473**	(3.6)	515	(3.1)	535	(3.2)	**578**	(2.7)
	Norway	0.61	0.02	–0.39	(0.02)	0.33	(0.01)	0.88	(0.01)	1.61	(0.01)	**451**	(3.0)	485	(3.4)	508	(3.5)	**540**	(3.4)
	Poland	–0.20	0.02	–1.16	(0.01)	–0.53	(0.00)	–0.03	(0.01)	0.92	(0.02)	**444**	(4.0)	476	(3.0)	501	(3.2)	**539**	(2.9)
	Portugal	–0.63	0.04	–2.20	(0.01)	–1.15	(0.01)	–0.24	(0.01)	1.08	(0.03)	**425**	(4.3)	453	(3.7)	470	(4.0)	**519**	(3.5)
	Slovak Republic	–0.08	0.03	–1.07	(0.03)	–0.42	(0.00)	0.14	(0.00)	1.02	(0.01)	**438**	(5.2)	486	(2.9)	517	(3.2)	**554**	(4.1)
	Spain	–0.30	0.04	–1.60	(0.01)	–0.65	(0.01)	0.07	(0.01)	0.99	(0.02)	**445**	(3.4)	470	(3.2)	497	(2.7)	**529**	(2.8)
	Sweden	0.25	0.02	–0.87	(0.02)	–0.02	(0.00)	0.57	(0.01)	1.34	(0.01)	**465**	(3.6)	495	(3.1)	522	(3.1)	**557**	(4.1)
	Switzerland	–0.06	0.03	–1.14	(0.02)	–0.31	(0.01)	0.20	(0.00)	1.02	(0.01)	**472**	(3.8)	521	(3.4)	539	(3.4)	**576**	(4.5)
	Turkey	–0.98	0.06	–2.25	(0.02)	–1.45	(0.01)	–0.73	(0.01)	0.52	(0.04)	**380**	(4.5)	397	(4.5)	422	(7.0)	**496**	(12.1)
	United States	0.30	0.03	–0.89	(0.02)	0.01	(0.01)	0.64	(0.01)	1.42	(0.01)	**431**	(3.2)	468	(3.6)	498	(3.1)	**539**	(3.4)
	OECD total	*–0.06*	*0.01*	*–1.42*	*(0.01)*	*–0.36*	*(0.00)*	*0.29*	*(0.00)*	*1.20*	*(0.01)*	*423*	*(1.5)*	*481*	*(1.2)*	*510*	*(1.2)*	*546*	*(1.4)*
	OECD average	*0.00*	*0.01*	*–1.30*	*(0.01)*	*–0.30*	*(0.00)*	*0.34*	*(0.00)*	*1.23*	*(0.00)*	*440*	*(1.0)*	*491*	*(0.7)*	*519*	*(0.6)*	*554*	*(0.8)*
Partner countries	Brazil	0.95	0.05	2.39	(0.02)	–1.36	(0.01)	–0.54	(0.01)	0.49	(0.03)	**319**	(5.1)	339	(5.4)	353	(5.5)	**417**	(7.9)
	Hong Kong-China	–0.76	0.03	–1.75	(0.02)	–1.04	(0.00)	–0.55	(0.00)	0.31	(0.02)	**518**	(5.9)	544	(4.9)	560	(4.7)	**582**	(6.1)
	Indonesia	–1.26	0.04	–2.46	(0.01)	–1.67	(0.01)	–0.99	(0.01)	0.10	(0.02)	**341**	(3.6)	350	(3.4)	357	(4.4)	**393**	(6.7)
	Latvia	0.12	0.03	–0.84	(0.01)	–0.16	(0.01)	0.38	(0.01)	1.08	(0.01)	**448**	(4.3)	474	(4.3)	495	(4.3)	**519**	(5.4)
	Liechtenstein	0.01	0.04	–1.03	(0.05)	–0.25	(0.01)	0.28	(0.02)	1.05	(0.03)	**481**	(9.1)	520	(11.6)	544	(9.5)	**602**	(8.9)
	Macao-China	–0.90	0.02	–2.00	(0.03)	–1.14	(0.01)	–0.61	(0.01)	0.15	(0.03)	**507**	(5.6)	533	(7.0)	526	(6.1)	**544**	(5.6)
	Russian Federation	–0.09	0.02	–0.99	(0.01)	–0.44	(0.00)	0.13	(0.01)	0.92	(0.01)	**435**	(4.6)	457	(4.4)	473	(4.9)	**509**	(4.6)
	Serbia	–0.23	0.03	–1.28	(0.01)	–0.57	(0.00)	–0.01	(0.01)	0.95	(0.02)	**398**	(3.6)	426	(4.3)	444	(4.1)	**480**	(4.7)
	Thailand	–1.18	0.03	–2.27	(0.02)	–1.69	(0.00)	–1.06	(0.01)	0.29	(0.02)	**396**	(3.6)	398	(3.7)	412	(3.7)	**462**	(5.8)
	Tunisia	–1.34	0.04	–2.83	(0.01)	–1.85	(0.01)	–1.01	(0.01)	0.32	(0.03)	**333**	(3.1)	340	(2.9)	358	(3.0)	**404**	(6.3)
	Uruguay	–0.35	0.03	–1.71	(0.01)	–0.73	(0.01)	0.03	(0.01)	1.02	(0.02)	**379**	(4.5)	402	(4.0)	428	(4.2)	**481**	(4.2)
	United Kingdom[1]	0.12	0.02	–1.00	(0.01)	–0.21	(0.00)	0.40	(0.01)	1.30	(0.01)	**461**	(3.1)	492	(2.7)	517	(3.3)	**566**	(3.6)

		Change in the mathematics score per unit of the index of economic, social and cultural status		Increased likelihood of students in the bottom quarter of the ESCS distribution scoring in the bottom quarter of the national mathematics performance distribution		Explained variance in student performance (r-squared × 100)	
		Effect	S.E.	Ratio	S.E.	%	S.E.
OECD countries	Australia	**42.4**	(2.15)	**2.3**	(0.11)	13.7	(1.19)
	Austria	**43.3**	(2.30)	**2.2**	(0.15)	16.0	(1.57)
	Belgium	**55.2**	(1.72)	**3.0**	(0.13)	24.1	(1.32)
	Canada	**34.2**	(1.43)	**2.1**	(0.08)	10.5	(0.82)
	Czech Republic	**51.3**	(2.15)	**2.5**	(0.14)	19.5	(1.44)
	Denmark	**44.4**	(1.96)	**2.4**	(0.14)	17.6	(1.41)
	Finland	**33.1**	(1.63)	**2.0**	(0.08)	10.8	(1.05)
	France	**43.1**	(2.20)	**2.6**	(0.15)	19.6	(1.78)
	Germany	**46.6**	(1.71)	**2.8**	(0.17)	22.8	(1.47)
	Greece	**37.0**	(2.19)	**2.0**	(0.14)	15.9	(1.91)
	Hungary	**54.8**	(2.27)	**2.9**	(0.20)	27.0	(1.81)
	Iceland	**28.2**	(1.74)	**1.7**	(0.10)	6.5	(0.83)
	Ireland	**38.6**	(1.96)	**2.4**	(0.15)	16.2	(1.55)
	Italy	**34.5**	(1.96)	**2.2**	(0.10)	13.6	(1.34)
	Japan	**46.3**	(4.14)	**2.0**	(0.14)	11.6	(1.69)
	Korea	**40.9**	(3.08)	**2.1**	(0.12)	14.2	(1.95)
	Luxembourg	**34.8**	(1.23)	**2.2**	(0.11)	17.1	(1.01)
	Mexico	**29.3**	(1.87)	**2.2**	(0.19)	17.1	(2.06)
	Netherlands	**44.7**	(2.36)	**2.3**	(0.17)	18.6	(1.71)
	New Zealand	**43.7**	(1.62)	**2.4**	(0.14)	16.8	(1.20)
	Norway	**44.0**	(1.72)	**2.1**	(0.12)	14.1	(1.09)
	Poland	**44.8**	(1.81)	**2.2**	(0.12)	16.7	(1.21)
	Portugal	**28.9**	(1.21)	**2.2**	(0.16)	17.5	(1.50)
	Slovak Republic	**53.2**	(2.56)	**2.9**	(0.14)	22.3	(1.85)
	Spain	**32.9**	(1.67)	**2.2**	(0.11)	14.0	(1.33)
	Sweden	**42.1**	(2.06)	**2.1**	(0.10)	15.3	(1.32)
	Switzerland	**47.5**	(2.14)	**2.5**	(0.13)	16.8	(1.27)
	Turkey	**45.1**	(4.82)	**1.8**	(0.16)	22.3	(3.70)
	United States	**45.3**	(1.58)	**2.6**	(0.14)	19.0	(1.20)
	OECD total	*47.1*	*(0.69)*	*2.9*	*(0.07)*	*22.2*	*(0.60)*
	OECD average	*44.8*	*(0.44)*	*2.7*	*(0.03)*	*20.3*	*(0.35)*
Partner countries	Brazil	**35.0**	(3.14)	**1.7**	(0.12)	15.3	(2.39)
	Hong Kong-China	**31.2**	(2.94)	**1.8**	(0.15)	6.5	(1.27)
	Indonesia	**21.3**	(2.63)	**1.3**	(0.08)	7.0	(1.61)
	Latvia	**37.9**	(2.27)	**2.1**	(0.14)	10.5	(1.28)
	Liechtenstein	**55.0**	(5.86)	**3.0**	(0.47)	20.6	(3.71)
	Macao-China	**14.0**	(3.25)	**1.3**	(0.15)	1.9	(0.89)
	Russian Federation	**39.0**	(2.28)	**1.8**	(0.11)	10.0	(1.08)
	Serbia	**36.1**	(1.96)	**2.1**	(0.15)	14.1	(1.45)
	Thailand	**27.0**	(2.57)	**1.3**	(0.11)	11.4	(1.94)
	Tunisia	**24.0**	(2.38)	**1.4**	(0.11)	13.0	(2.43)
	Uruguay	**37.6**	(2.09)	**1.9**	(0.12)	15.9	(1.64)
	United Kingdom[1]	**45.3**	(1.79)	**2.3**	(0.14)	19.7	(1.49)

Note: Values that are statistically significant are indicated in bold (see Annex A4).

1. Response rate too low to ensure comparability (see Annex A3).

Table 4.5

Decomposition of the gradient of the PISA index of economic, social and cultural status (ESCS) into between-school and within-school components[1]

	Overall effect of ESCS[2]		Within-school effects of ESCS[3]				Student variability in the distribution of ESCS					
	(1)		(2)		(3)		(4)		(5)		(6)	
	Score point difference associated with one unit on the ESCS	S.E.	Student-level score point difference associated with one unit of the student-level ESCS	S.E.	Explained within-school variance	S.E.	25th percentile of the student distribution of ESCS	S.E.	75th percentile of the student distribution of ESCS	S.E.	Interquartile range of the distribution of the student-level ESCS	S.E.
OECD countries												
Australia	42	(2.2)	27	(1.0)	5.2	(0.6)	–0.33	(0.02)	0.81	(0.01)	1.14	(0.02)
Austria	43	(2.3)	10	(1.4)	0.9	(0.4)	–0.52	(0.04)	0.63	(0.04)	1.15	(0.03)
Belgium	55	(1.7)	25	(1.0)	6.5	(0.9)	–0.48	(0.03)	0.86	(0.03)	1.34	(0.03)
Canada	34	(1.4)	25	(0.6)	5.9	(0.7)	–0.14	(0.03)	1.06	(0.02)	1.20	(0.03)
Czech Republic	51	(2.1)	22	(1.3)	4.7	(0.7)	–0.38	(0.04)	0.70	(0.03)	1.08	(0.04)
Denmark	44	(2.0)	37	(1.6)	11.6	(1.4)	–0.39	(0.03)	0.80	(0.03)	1.18	(0.02)
Finland	33	(1.6)	33	(1.3)	10.2	(1.2)	–0.36	(0.03)	0.87	(0.02)	1.23	(0.03)
France	w	w	w	w	w	w	w	w	w	w	w	w
Germany	47	(1.7)	17	(1.2)	4.2	(1.2)	–0.45	(0.03)	0.84	(0.04)	1.29	(0.04)
Greece	37	(2.2)	17	(1.3)	3.4	(1.0)	–0.87	(0.04)	0.57	(0.08)	1.44	(0.06)
Hungary	55	(2.3)	14	(1.4)	1.4	(0.8)	–0.69	(0.02)	0.55	(0.06)	1.24	(0.05)
Iceland	28	(1.7)	28	(2.0)	5.1	(0.9)	0.13	(0.01)	1.34	(0.02)	1.21	(0.03)
Ireland	39	(2.0)	29	(1.6)	8.6	(1.2)	–0.69	(0.02)	0.51	(0.04)	1.20	(0.03)
Italy	34	(2.0)	9	(0.7)	1.3	(0.4)	–0.90	(0.02)	0.59	(0.03)	1.48	(0.03)
Japan	46	(4.1)	4	(1.6)	0.2	(0.2)	–0.59	(0.02)	0.43	(0.03)	1.02	(0.03)
Korea	41	(3.1)	13	(1.3)	1.8	(0.6)	–0.64	(0.02)	0.48	(0.06)	1.12	(0.05)
Luxembourg	35	(1.2)	17	(1.3)	4.3	(0.7)	–0.48	(0.02)	0.98	(0.01)	1.46	(0.03)
Mexico	29	(1.9)	6	(0.4)	0.9	(0.3)	–2.02	(0.04)	–0.23	(0.09)	1.79	(0.07)
Netherlands	45	(2.4)	14	(1.2)	3.3	(0.9)	–0.48	(0.03)	0.73	(0.03)	1.22	(0.04)
New Zealand	44	(1.6)	33	(1.5)	9.6	(1.2)	–0.34	(0.01)	0.86	(0.02)	1.20	(0.02)
Norway	44	(1.7)	42	(1.8)	12.1	(1.3)	0.05	(0.03)	1.18	(0.02)	1.12	(0.03)
Poland	45	(1.8)	38	(1.7)	10.8	(1.4)	–0.77	(0.03)	0.26	(0.04)	1.03	(0.03)
Portugal	29	(1.2)	18	(0.9)	7.9	(1.0)	–1.61	(0.05)	0.26	(0.06)	1.87	(0.05)
Slovak Republic	53	(2.6)	24	(1.2)	5.1	(1.1)	–0.64	(0.03)	0.50	(0.03)	1.14	(0.03)
Spain	33	(1.7)	22	(0.9)	5.9	(0.9)	–1.03	(0.04)	0.44	(0.05)	1.47	(0.04)
Sweden	42	(2.1)	38	(1.5)	12.1	(1.5)	–0.32	(0.04)	0.89	(0.03)	1.21	(0.03)
Switzerland	47	(2.1)	28	(1.1)	7.3	(1.0)	–0.60	(0.03)	0.51	(0.04)	1.11	(0.03)
Turkey	45	(4.8)	9	(1.2)	1.1	(0.4)	–1.78	(0.04)	–0.31	(0.08)	1.47	(0.06)
United States	45	(1.6)	31	(1.4)	9.2	(1.2)	–0.32	(0.02)	0.96	(0.04)	1.28	(0.03)
OECD total	***47***	***(0.7)***	–	–	–	–	***–0.70***	***(0.01)***	***0.67***	***(0.02)***	***1.37***	***(0.01)***
OECD average	***45***	***(0.4)***	–	–	–	–	***–0.64***	***(0.01)***	***0.71***	***(0.00)***	***1.35***	***(0.01)***
Partner countries												
Brazil	35	3.141	6	(1.3)	0.5	(0.4)	–1.80	(0.06)	–0.15	(0.06)	1.64	(0.05)
Hong Kong-China	31	(2.9)	5	(1.5)	0.2	(0.3)	–1.28	(0.01)	–0.26	(0.05)	1.02	(0.04)
Indonesia	21	(2.6)	1	(0.7)	0.0	(0.1)	–1.98	(0.05)	–0.57	(0.05)	1.40	(0.05)
Latvia	38	(2.3)	29	(1.7)	6.3	(1.2)	–0.44	(0.03)	0.71	(0.04)	1.15	(0.04)
Liechtenstein	55	(5.9)	16	(5.4)	2.4	(2.4)	–0.48	(0.03)	0.63	(0.06)	1.11	(0.07)
Macao-China	14	(3.3)	6	(3.0)	0.2	(0.6)	–1.46	(0.05)	–0.35	(0.04)	1.12	(0.07)
Russian Federation	39	(2.3)	23	(1.5)	3.7	(0.6)	–0.68	(0.02)	0.49	(0.03)	1.17	(0.03)
Serbia	36	(2.0)	16	(1.4)	3.1	(0.7)	–0.83	(0.04)	0.35	(0.04)	1.18	(0.04)
Thailand	27	(2.6)	8	(1.2)	0.9	(0.4)	–1.94	(0.01)	–0.59	(0.07)	1.34	(0.07)
Tunisia	24	(2.4)	7	(0.9)	1.4	(0.5)	–2.23	(0.05)	–0.49	(0.06)	1.74	(0.05)
Uruguay	38	(2.1)	13	(1.2)	2.2	(0.7)	–1.16	(0.04)	0.46	(0.05)	1.62	(0.05)
United Kingdom[7]	45	(1.8)	31	(1.0)	10.2	(1.0)	–0.50	(0.03)	0.77	(0.04)	1.27	(0.04)

1. In some countries, sub-units within schools were sampled instead of schools as administrative units and this may affect the estimation of school-level effects. In Austria, the Czech Republic, Hungary, Italy and Japan, schools with more than one study programme were split into the units delivering these programmes. In the Netherlands, for schools with both lower and upper secondary programmes, schools were split into units delivering each programme level. In Uruguay and Mexico, schools where instruction is delivered in shifts were split into the corresponding units. In the Flemish part of Belgium, in case of multi-campus schools, implantations (campuses) were sampled whereas in the French part, in case of multi-campus schools the larger administrative units were sampled. In the Slovak Republic, in case of schools with both Slovak and Hungarian as test languages, schools were split into units delivering each language of instruction.
2. Single-level bivariate regression of mathematics performance on the ESCS, the slope is the regression coefficient for the ESCS.
3. Two-level regression of mathematics performance on student ESCS and school mean ESCS: within-school slope for ESCS and explained variance at the student level by the model.
4. Two-level regression of mathematics performance on student ESCS and school mean ESCS: between-school slope for the ESCS and explained variance at the school level by the model.
5. Distribution of the school mean ESCS, percentiles calculated at student-level.
6. The index of inclusion is derived from the intra-class correlation for ESCS as 1-rho.
7. Response rate too low to ensure comparability (see Annex A3).

Table 4.5 *(continued)*

Decomposition of the gradient of the PISA index of economic, social and cultural status (ESCS) into between-school and within-school components[1]

		Between-school effects of ESCS[4]				School variability in the distribution of ESCS[5]						Index of inclusion[6]	
		(7)		(8)		(9)		(10)		(11)		(12)	
		School-level score point difference associated with one unit on the school mean ESCS	S.E.	Explained between-school variance	S.E.	25th percentile of the school mean distribution of ESCS	S.E.	75th percentile of the school mean distribution of ESCS	S.E.	Interquartile range of the distribution of school mean distribution of ESCS	S.E.	Proportion of ESCS variance within schools	S.E.
OECD countries	Australia	57	(3.7)	69.7	(2.6)	–0.11	(0.02)	0.53	(0.03)	0.64	(0.03)	0.74	(0.01)
	Austria	92	(6.5)	63.2	(3.5)	–0.35	(0.02)	0.42	(0.08)	0.77	(0.08)	0.68	(0.02)
	Belgium	97	(4.8)	74.1	(1.4)	–0.21	(0.04)	0.58	(0.03)	0.79	(0.05)	0.68	(0.01)
	Canada	39	(2.7)	46.7	(2.6)	0.17	(0.01)	0.72	(0.02)	0.55	(0.02)	0.82	(0.01)
	Czech Republic	98	(5.2)	73.0	(2.3)	–0.15	(0.02)	0.41	(0.04)	0.56	(0.04)	0.70	(0.02)
	Denmark	31	(4.6)	70.9	(8.8)	–0.03	(0.06)	0.39	(0.04)	0.42	(0.06)	0.81	(0.02)
	Finland	–2	(5.2)	21.8	(11.6)	0.02	(0.02)	0.42	(0.03)	0.40	(0.04)	0.89	(0.01)
	France	w	w	w	w	w	w	w	w	w	w	w	w
	Germany	90	(4.5)	77.5	(2.6)	–0.28	(0.03)	0.66	(0.04)	0.94	(0.06)	0.70	(0.02)
	Greece	60	(5.5)	64.4	(4.8)	–0.66	(0.05)	0.20	(0.12)	0.86	(0.11)	0.71	(0.01)
	Hungary	87	(4.2)	80.4	(3.6)	–0.50	(0.04)	0.35	(0.04)	0.84	(0.05)	0.56	(0.02)
	Iceland	–1	(6.1)	35.2	(15.5)	0.47	(0.00)	0.91	(0.00)	0.45	(0.00)	0.83	(0.03)
	Ireland	42	(4.3)	81.9	(7.1)	–0.30	(0.04)	0.18	(0.04)	0.48	(0.05)	0.79	(0.02)
	Italy	78	(4.5)	53.5	(2.0)	–0.56	(0.07)	0.31	(0.07)	0.87	(0.09)	0.70	(0.01)
	Japan	145	(9.2)	67.4	(1.4)	–0.37	(0.05)	0.22	(0.03)	0.60	(0.06)	0.73	(0.01)
	Korea	88	(6.5)	65.9	(2.5)	–0.49	(0.03)	0.21	(0.09)	0.70	(0.09)	0.70	(0.01)
	Luxembourg	75	(6.8)	88.9	(2.1)	–0.31	(0.00)	0.62	(0.00)	0.92	(0.00)	0.76	(0.01)
	Mexico	49	(1.7)	56.9	(1.6)	–1.65	(0.06)	–0.68	(0.09)	0.97	(0.10)	0.66	(0.01)
	Netherlands	121	(6.9)	74.4	(1.4)	–0.22	(0.04)	0.43	(0.02)	0.65	(0.05)	0.77	(0.02)
	New Zealand	55	(5.2)	75.4	(5.4)	–0.09	(0.04)	0.48	(0.03)	0.57	(0.05)	0.83	(0.01)
	Norway	14	(6.2)	44.1	(11.0)	0.38	(0.02)	0.79	(0.03)	0.42	(0.03)	0.88	(0.01)
	Poland	26	(4.8)	67.7	(5.8)	–0.55	(0.04)	0.10	(0.06)	0.66	(0.08)	0.77	(0.02)
	Portugal	39	(1.5)	56.3	(4.0)	–1.07	(0.08)	–0.29	(0.03)	0.78	(0.09)	0.76	(0.02)
	Slovak Republic	84	(4.3)	75.6	(2.8)	–0.37	(0.04)	0.24	(0.03)	0.61	(0.05)	0.68	(0.02)
	Spain	36	(3.2)	56.9	(3.0)	–0.70	(0.06)	0.09	(0.07)	0.79	(0.09)	0.75	(0.01)
	Sweden	29	(6.0)	52.7	(8.4)	0.04	(0.02)	0.44	(0.07)	0.40	(0.07)	0.88	(0.01)
	Switzerland	74	(5.6)	52.2	(2.0)	–0.35	(0.03)	0.21	(0.06)	0.57	(0.07)	0.81	(0.01)
	Turkey	85	(5.3)	71.1	(3.2)	–1.45	(0.04)	–0.61	(0.08)	0.84	(0.08)	0.63	(0.02)
	United States	55	(4.4)	69.0	(3.0)	0.02	(0.02)	0.59	(0.04)	0.57	(0.04)	0.77	(0.02)
	OECD total	–	–	–	–	*–0.42*	*(0.02)*	*0.39*	*(0.02)*	*0.81*	*(0.02)*	–	–
	OECD average	–	–	–	–	*–0.35*	*(0.01)*	*0.42*	*(0.01)*	*0.77*	*(0.01)*	–	–
Partner countries	Brazil	66	(4.6)	57.9	(2.0)	–1.41	(0.06)	–0.73	(0.08)	0.68	(0.08)	0.63	(0.01)
	Hong Kong-China	102	(10.8)	42.6	(2.6)	–1.06	(0.04)	–0.57	(0.05)	0.49	(0.06)	0.77	(0.02)
	Indonesia	59	(4.2)	41.3	(1.3)	–1.68	(0.05)	–0.95	(0.06)	0.73	(0.06)	0.71	(0.01)
	Latvia	16	(8.4)	38.4	(5.0)	–0.12	(0.05)	0.35	(0.06)	0.47	(0.08)	0.81	(0.02)
	Liechtenstein	123	(29.0)	71.1	(9.1)	–0.35	(0.00)	0.58	(0.00)	0.93	(0.00)	0.79	(0.04)
	Macao-China	37	(13.9)	24.2	(6.3)	–1.19	(0.04)	–0.72	(0.00)	0.47	(0.04)	0.77	(0.03)
	Russian Federation	57	(7.9)	39.7	(5.5)	–0.34	(0.04)	0.11	(0.04)	0.45	(0.05)	0.80	(0.02)
	Serbia	67	(5.8)	63.5	(2.3)	–0.62	(0.02)	0.05	(0.07)	0.67	(0.08)	0.73	(0.01)
	Thailand	45	(4.1)	53.7	(2.9)	–1.62	(0.04)	–0.82	(0.09)	0.80	(0.10)	0.55	(0.02)
	Tunisia	47	(4.3)	54.7	(2.6)	–1.88	(0.07)	–0.93	(0.11)	0.94	(0.13)	0.67	(0.01)
	Uruguay	71	(4.0)	71.3	(2.5)	–0.78	(0.03)	–0.05	(0.08)	0.73	(0.08)	0.64	(0.01)
	United Kingdom[7]	58	(3.8)	72.2	(2.9)	–0.21	(0.05)	0.38	(0.06)	0.58	(0.06)	0.82	(0.01)

1. In some countries, sub-units within schools were sampled instead of schools as administrative units and this may affect the estimation of school-level effects. In Austria, the Czech Republic, Hungary, Italy and Japan, schools with more than one study programme were split into the units delivering these programmes. In the Netherlands, for schools with both lower and upper secondary programmes, schools were split into units delivering each programme level. In Uruguay and Mexico, schools where instruction is delivered in shifts were split into the corresponding units. In the Flemish part of Belgium, in case of multi-campus schools, implantations (campuses) were sampled whereas in the French part, in case of multi-campus schools the larger administrative units were sampled. In the Slovak Republic, in case of schools with both Slovak and Hungarian as test languages, schools were split into units delivering each language of instruction.
2. Single-level bivariate regression of mathematics performance on the index of economic, social and cultural status (ESCS), the slope is the regression coefficient for the ESCS.
3. Two-level regression of mathematics performance on student ESCS and school mean ESCS: within-school slope for ESCS and explained variance at the student level by the model.
4. Two-level regression of mathematics performance on student ESCS and school mean ESCS: between-school slope for ESCS and explained variance at the school level by the model.
5. Distribution of the school mean ESCS, percentiles calculated at student-level.
6. The index of inclusion is derived from the intra-class correlation for ESCS as 1-rho.
7. Response rate too low to ensure comparability (see Annex A3).

Table 4.6
Relationship between parents' years of schooling and performance in mathematics

		Unadjusted mean score in mathematics		Mean score if the mean years of the highest number of years of schooling of mother and father would be equal in all OECD countries		Years of schooling (highest between the mother and father)		Explained variance of student performance (r-squared x 100)	
		Mean score	S.E.	Mean score	S.E.	Score point difference associated with one year of parents' schooling	S.E.	Percentage	S.E.
OECD countries	Australia	524	(2.1)	526	(2.0)	8.1	(0.9)	4.2	(0.80)
	Austria	506	(3.3)	507	(2.9)	7.4	(0.8)	4.9	(1.00)
	Belgium	529	(2.3)	534	(2.0)	9.7	(0.5)	8.3	(0.90)
	Canada	532	(1.8)	526	(1.5)	6.8	(0.4)	3.9	(0.50)
	Czech Republic	516	(3.5)	512	(2.8)	15.2	(0.9)	11.9	(1.40)
	Denmark	514	(2.7)	508	(2.3)	8.8	(0.7)	7.2	(1.00)
	Finland	544	(1.9)	541	(1.8)	6.5	(0.5)	3.5	(0.60)
	France	511	(2.5)	523	(2.2)	8.6	(0.6)	8.1	(1.10)
	Germany	503	(3.3)	516	(3.0)	8.2	(0.5)	11.3	(1.30)
	Greece	445	(3.9)	445	(3.3)	6.8	(0.7)	6.4	(1.10)
	Hungary	490	(2.8)	496	(2.4)	15.6	(0.8)	18.7	(1.60)
	Iceland	515	(1.4)	506	(1.6)	6.6	(0.5)	3.6	(0.60)
	Ireland	503	(2.4)	508	(2.1)	8.3	(0.6)	7.2	(1.00)
	Italy	466	(3.1)	469	(3.0)	6.2	(0.5)	5.8	(0.90)
	Japan	534	(4.0)	527	(4.1)	10.0	(1.6)	5.7	(1.60)
	Korea	542	(3.2)	546	(3.3)	7.0	(0.7)	6.6	(1.20)
	Luxembourg	493	(1.0)	496	(1.2)	5.4	(0.3)	7.6	(0.80)
	Mexico	385	(3.6)	403	(3.8)	5.1	(0.5)	8.9	(1.40)
	Netherlands	538	(3.1)	548	(2.7)	8.1	(0.7)	6.4	(1.20)
	New Zealand	523	(2.3)	527	(2.1)	6.9	(0.5)	5.7	(0.90)
	Norway	495	(2.4)	484	(2.4)	8.4	(0.7)	3.6	(0.60)
	Poland	490	(2.5)	497	(2.1)	12.1	(0.9)	8.0	(1.00)
	Portugal	466	(3.4)	483	(3.4)	4.2	(0.3)	7.7	(1.20)
	Slovak Republic	498	(3.3)	494	(2.9)	12.9	(1.0)	10.8	(1.40)
	Spain	485	(2.4)	498	(2.3)	5.8	(0.4)	6.7	(0.90)
	Sweden	509	(2.6)	510	(2.3)	6.9	(0.6)	4.1	(0.70)
	Switzerland	527	(3.4)	537	(3.2)	10.5	(0.6)	9.0	(0.90)
	Turkey	423	(6.7)	462	(9.5)	9.3	(1.2)	14.1	(2.80)
	United States	483	(2.9)	480	(2.5)	8.9	(0.5)	6.1	(0.80)
	OECD total	*500*	*(0.6)*	*505*	*(0.6)*	*9.1*	*(0.1)*	*10.3*	*(0.30)*
	OECD average	*489*	*(0.7)*	*495*	*(0.9)*	*10.1*	*(0.2)*	*12.1*	*(0.50)*
Partner countries	Brazil	356	(4.8)	367	(5.1)	4.0	(0.5)	4.2	(1.00)
	Hong Kong-China	550	(4.5)	564	(5.4)	3.8	(0.8)	1.7	(0.60)
	Indonesia	360	(3.9)	369	(5.1)	2.7	(0.6)	2.1	(0.80)
	Latvia	483	(3.7)	477	(3.7)	5.3	(0.9)	1.7	(0.50)
	Liechtenstein	536	(4.1)	548	(4.6)	11.1	(1.7)	9.5	(3.20)
	Macao-China	527	(2.9)	533	(3.5)	1.7	(0.8)	0.7	(0.60)
	Russian Federation	468	(4.2)	466	(4.0)	12.4	(1.1)	4.3	(0.70)
	Serbia	437	(3.8)	439	(3.5)	7.8	(0.7)	5.0	(0.90)
	Thailand	417	(3.0)	441	(4.5)	5.8	(0.7)	7.3	(1.50)
	Tunisia	359	(2.5)	374	(4.0)	3.8	(0.6)	5.3	(1.40)
	Uruguay	422	(3.3)	429	(3.1)	7.1	(0.6)	7.5	(1.20)
	United Kingdom[1]	508	(2.4)	512	(2.5)	9.2	(0.7)	7.3	(1.10)

1. Response rate too low to ensure comparability (see Annex A3).

Table 5.1a

Index of teacher support in mathematics lessons and student performance on the mathematics scale, by national quarters of the index

Results based on students' self-reports

		Index of teacher support in mathematics lessons															
		All students		Males		Females		Gender difference (M – F)		Bottom quarter		Second quarter		Third quarter		Top quarter	
		Mean index	S.E.	Mean index	S.E.	Mean index	S.E.	Dif.	S.E.	Mean index	S.E.	Mean index	S.E.	Mean index	S.E.	Mean index	S.E.
OECD countries	Australia	0.25	(0.02)	0.21	(0.02)	0.29	(0.02)	**–0.08**	(0.02)	–1.01	(0.01)	–0.05	(0.00)	0.54	(0.00)	1.52	(0.01)
	Austria	–0.39	(0.03)	–0.26	(0.04)	–0.53	(0.04)	**0.27**	(0.04)	–1.71	(0.02)	–0.66	(0.01)	–0.06	(0.01)	0.85	(0.02)
	Belgium	–0.11	(0.02)	–0.13	(0.02)	–0.09	(0.03)	–0.05	(0.03)	–1.36	(0.01)	–0.41	(0.00)	0.16	(0.00)	1.16	(0.01)
	Canada	0.27	(0.01)	0.23	(0.02)	0.31	(0.02)	**–0.08**	(0.02)	–0.96	(0.01)	–0.03	(0.00)	0.56	(0.00)	1.51	(0.01)
	Czech Republic	–0.16	(0.03)	–0.12	(0.03)	–0.19	(0.04)	0.07	(0.04)	–1.30	(0.02)	–0.42	(0.01)	0.11	(0.00)	0.98	(0.02)
	Denmark	0.14	(0.02)	0.16	(0.02)	0.12	(0.03)	0.04	(0.03)	–0.88	(0.02)	–0.12	(0.01)	0.34	(0.01)	1.24	(0.02)
	Finland	0.08	(0.02)	0.09	(0.02)	0.07	(0.02)	0.02	(0.02)	–1.02	(0.02)	–0.15	(0.00)	0.32	(0.01)	1.15	(0.01)
	France	–0.17	(0.02)	–0.16	(0.03)	–0.18	(0.03)	0.03	(0.03)	–1.42	(0.02)	–0.44	(0.01)	0.12	(0.01)	1.05	(0.02)
	Germany	–0.29	(0.03)	–0.21	(0.03)	–0.36	(0.03)	**0.15**	(0.03)	–1.62	(0.02)	–0.57	(0.01)	0.05	(0.01)	1.00	(0.02)
	Greece	–0.06	(0.03)	–0.04	(0.03)	–0.08	(0.03)	0.04	(0.03)	–1.19	(0.03)	–0.31	(0.01)	0.18	(0.00)	1.09	(0.02)
	Hungary	–0.08	(0.03)	–0.07	(0.03)	–0.10	(0.04)	0.03	(0.04)	–1.34	(0.02)	–0.36	(0.01)	0.18	(0.01)	1.19	(0.02)
	Iceland	0.20	(0.01)	0.17	(0.02)	0.23	(0.02)	–0.06	(0.03)	–0.92	(0.02)	–0.04	(0.01)	0.43	(0.01)	1.33	(0.02)
	Ireland	0.00	(0.03)	–0.01	(0.04)	0.01	(0.04)	–0.02	(0.05)	–1.42	(0.02)	–0.29	(0.01)	0.37	(0.01)	1.34	(0.02)
	Italy	–0.12	(0.02)	–0.11	(0.03)	–0.12	(0.04)	0.01	(0.04)	–1.47	(0.03)	–0.40	(0.01)	0.20	(0.01)	1.19	(0.02)
	Japan	–0.34	(0.02)	–0.34	(0.02)	–0.34	(0.03)	0.00	(0.03)	–1.39	(0.02)	–0.53	(0.00)	–0.07	(0.00)	0.64	(0.02)
	Korea	–0.22	(0.02)	–0.23	(0.02)	–0.21	(0.02)	–0.01	(0.02)	–1.08	(0.01)	–0.46	(0.00)	–0.04	(0.00)	0.69	(0.02)
	Luxembourg	–0.30	(0.01)	–0.28	(0.02)	–0.32	(0.02)	0.04	(0.03)	–1.75	(0.02)	–0.54	(0.01)	0.05	(0.01)	1.06	(0.02)
	Mexico	0.48	(0.02)	0.45	(0.02)	0.51	(0.03)	**–0.06**	(0.03)	–0.79	(0.01)	0.12	(0.00)	0.76	(0.01)	1.85	(0.01)
	Netherlands	–0.27	(0.03)	–0.24	(0.03)	–0.30	(0.03)	**0.06**	(0.03)	–1.38	(0.02)	–0.51	(0.01)	–0.01	(0.01)	0.81	(0.02)
	New Zealand	0.16	(0.02)	0.17	(0.02)	0.15	(0.03)	0.01	(0.03)	–1.07	(0.02)	–0.11	(0.01)	0.42	(0.01)	1.41	(0.02)
	Norway	–0.11	(0.02)	–0.07	(0.03)	–0.15	(0.02)	**0.07**	(0.03)	–1.21	(0.02)	–0.34	(0.00)	0.12	(0.00)	0.98	(0.02)
	Poland	–0.18	(0.02)	–0.22	(0.03)	–0.14	(0.03)	**–0.09**	(0.03)	–1.31	(0.02)	–0.47	(0.00)	0.07	(0.00)	0.99	(0.02)
	Portugal	0.27	(0.03)	0.20	(0.03)	0.33	(0.03)	**–0.13**	(0.04)	–1.00	(0.02)	–0.05	(0.01)	0.53	(0.01)	1.59	(0.02)
	Slovak Republic	–0.10	(0.03)	–0.03	(0.03)	–0.17	(0.03)	**0.14**	(0.04)	–1.28	(0.02)	–0.40	(0.01)	0.15	(0.01)	1.12	(0.02)
	Spain	–0.07	(0.02)	–0.11	(0.03)	–0.03	(0.03)	**–0.08**	(0.03)	–1.34	(0.03)	–0.35	(0.00)	0.20	(0.01)	1.22	(0.02)
	Sweden	0.20	(0.02)	0.22	(0.02)	0.17	(0.02)	0.06	(0.03)	–0.92	(0.02)	–0.08	(0.00)	0.41	(0.01)	1.37	(0.02)
	Switzerland	0.01	(0.02)	0.08	(0.03)	–0.07	(0.03)	**0.16**	(0.04)	–1.20	(0.02)	–0.24	(0.01)	0.29	(0.00)	1.19	(0.02)
	Turkey	0.41	(0.03)	0.35	(0.04)	0.48	(0.04)	**–0.13**	(0.04)	–0.85	(0.02)	0.04	(0.01)	0.66	(0.01)	1.80	(0.01)
	United States	0.34	(0.02)	0.29	(0.03)	0.39	(0.03)	**–0.10**	(0.03)	–0.98	(0.02)	0.01	(0.01)	0.64	(0.01)	1.70	(0.01)
	OECD total	***0.07***	***(0.01)***	***0.06***	***(0.01)***	***0.09***	***(0.01)***	***–0.03***	***(0.01)***	***–1.20***	***(0.01)***	***–0.25***	***(0.00)***	***0.33***	***(0.00)***	***1.40***	***(0.01)***
	OECD average	***0.00***	***(0.00)***	***0.00***	***(0.01)***	***0.00***	***(0.01)***	***0.01***	***(0.01)***	***–1.24***	***(0.01)***	***–0.29***	***(0.00)***	***0.27***	***(0.01)***	***1.26***	***(0.01)***
Partner countries	Brazil	0.56	(0.02)	0.50	(0.03)	0.60	(0.03)	**–0.10**	(0.04)	–0.65	(0.02)	0.19	(0.01)	0.87	(0.01)	1.82	(0.01)
	Hong Kong-China	0.03	(0.02)	0.01	(0.02)	0.06	(0.02)	–0.05	(0.03)	–0.97	(0.02)	–0.24	(0.01)	0.21	(0.00)	1.14	(0.02)
	Indonesia	0.39	(0.01)	0.39	(0.02)	0.40	(0.02)	–0.01	(0.02)	–0.50	(0.01)	0.10	(0.00)	0.56	(0.01)	1.41	(0.02)
	Latvia	0.05	(0.03)	0.05	(0.03)	0.06	(0.03)	0.00	(0.03)	–0.94	(0.02)	–0.19	(0.01)	0.28	(0.01)	1.08	(0.02)
	Liechtenstein	–0.07	(0.05)	0.09	(0.06)	–0.25	(0.08)	**0.34**	(0.10)	–1.34	(0.08)	–0.28	(0.02)	0.23	(0.02)	1.11	(0.06)
	Macao-China	–0.05	(0.03)	0.02	(0.04)	–0.08	(0.03)	0.06	(0.05)	–0.98	(0.02)	–0.30	(0.01)	0.13	(0.01)	0.95	(0.04)
	Russian Federation	0.26	(0.02)	0.24	(0.02)	0.28	(0.03)	–0.04	(0.03)	–0.79	(0.01)	–0.05	(0.00)	0.45	(0.01)	1.41	(0.01)
	Serbia	–0.17	(0.03)	–0.06	(0.04)	–0.28	(0.04)	**0.22**	(0.05)	–1.55	(0.02)	–0.55	(0.01)	0.11	(0.01)	1.30	(0.02)
	Thailand	0.67	(0.02)	0.54	(0.03)	0.77	(0.03)	**–0.23**	(0.04)	–0.46	(0.01)	0.29	(0.01)	0.93	(0.01)	1.90	(0.01)
	Tunisia	0.24	(0.02)	0.28	(0.03)	0.20	(0.03)	**0.08**	(0.03)	–1.08	(0.02)	–0.07	(0.01)	0.56	(0.01)	1.56	(0.01)
	Uruguay	0.32	(0.03)	0.31	(0.04)	0.34	(0.03)	–0.02	(0.04)	–1.00	(0.03)	0.00	(0.01)	0.64	(0.01)	1.65	(0.01)
	United Kingdom[1]	0.18	(0.02)	0.18	(0.03)	0.18	(0.03)	0.01	(0.03)	–1.14	(0.02)	–0.11	(0.01)	0.48	(0.01)	1.48	(0.01)

		Performance on the mathematics scale, by national quarters of the index of teacher support							
		Bottom quarter		Second quarter		Third quarter		Top quarter	
		Mean score	S.E.	Mean score	S.E.	Mean score	S.E.	Mean score	S.E.
OECD countries	Australia	**512**	(3.2)	518	(3.24)	535	(2.56)	**539**	(2.8)
	Austria	**516**	(3.4)	514	(4.57)	506	(4.53)	**495**	(5.2)
	Belgium	**544**	(3.5)	540	(2.93)	540	(3.52)	**531**	(3.7)
	Canada	**526**	(2.5)	535	(2.25)	541	(2.30)	**543**	(2.9)
	Czech Republic	525	(4.2)	527	(4.38)	523	(4.23)	517	(4.5)
	Denmark	**504**	(4.2)	517	(3.42)	524	(3.99)	**521**	(4.1)
	Finland	**538**	(3.1)	543	(3.60)	547	(3.51)	**550**	(3.2)
	France	515	(3.6)	518	(3.49)	513	(3.72)	507	(4.3)
	Germany	**523**	(4.6)	523	(4.36)	511	(5.01)	**497**	(4.6)
	Greece	**458**	(4.6)	444	(4.63)	444	(4.94)	**442**	(4.8)
	Hungary	492	(3.7)	488	(4.20)	493	(4.53)	491	(4.7)
	Iceland	**501**	(3.1)	515	(3.37)	521	(3.07)	**528**	(3.1)
	Ireland	504	(3.5)	507	(3.86)	509	(3.03)	495	(4.1)
	Italy	**484**	(3.8)	477	(3.66)	464	(4.20)	**441**	(5.1)
	Japan	**515**	(5.9)	540	(4.52)	542	(5.49)	**544**	(5.8)
	Korea	**532**	(3.9)	545	(3.74)	546	(4.14)	**547**	(4.9)
	Luxembourg	**507**	(2.3)	499	(2.92)	496	(3.16)	**478**	(3.3)
	Mexico	391	(3.9)	385	(4.00)	388	(5.33)	388	(4.4)
	Netherlands	543	(4.1)	550	(3.73)	540	(4.80)	547	(4.2)
	New Zealand	**518**	(3.9)	523	(3.54)	533	(3.79)	**528**	(3.4)
	Norway	**478**	(3.6)	494	(4.19)	507	(3.99)	**512**	(3.3)
	Poland	492	(3.5)	493	(3.76)	491	(3.25)	488	(3.8)
	Portugal	**475**	(3.9)	462	(5.82)	470	(4.68)	**459**	(4.1)
	Slovak Republic	**517**	(4.2)	507	(4.40)	494	(3.71)	**477**	(4.4)
	Spain	487	(3.5)	487	(3.72)	490	(3.39)	483	(3.6)
	Sweden	**502**	(3.6)	510	(3.84)	513	(3.42)	**517**	(4.5)
	Switzerland	**541**	(6.7)	531	(4.43)	525	(3.84)	**515**	(4.1)
	Turkey	417	(8.4)	427	(7.21)	432	(8.13)	428	(9.2)
	United States	**472**	(4.1)	478	(3.79)	498	(3.94)	**492**	(3.7)
	OECD total	***496***	***(1.3)***	***498***	***(1.35)***	***492***	***(1.55)***	***481***	***(1.6)***
	OECD average	***505***	***(0.8)***	***506***	***(0.71)***	***503***	***(0.87)***	***496***	***(1.0)***
Partner countries	Brazil	**373**	(5.7)	367	(6.36)	357	(5.33)	**342**	(5.5)
	Hong Kong-China	**533**	(5.6)	550	(4.70)	556	(6.16)	**564**	(5.3)
	Indonesia	**374**	(5.9)	360	(4.22)	360	(4.76)	**351**	(3.4)
	Latvia	486	(4.6)	484	(4.58)	486	(5.08)	479	(5.1)
	Liechtenstein	546	(10.4)	521	(10.44)	532	(10.23)	543	(9.8)
	Macao-China	527	(7.1)	530	(7.67)	527	(6.65)	526	(6.2)
	Russian Federation	464	(5.0)	469	(5.10)	473	(5.19)	473	(4.8)
	Serbia	**457**	(4.8)	451	(4.15)	438	(4.31)	**413**	(4.8)
	Thailand	**413**	(4.0)	412	(3.69)	421	(4.11)	**423**	(3.6)
	Tunisia	**373**	(3.4)	358	(3.41)	354	(3.38)	**359**	(3.9)
	Uruguay	**440**	(4.9)	428	(4.19)	428	(4.79)	**407**	(4.2)
	United Kingdom[1]	**496**	(3.7)	500	(3.43)	518	(3.51)	**520**	(4.1)

Note: Values that are statistically significant are indicated in bold (see Annex A4).

1. Response rate too low to ensure comparability (see Annex A3).

Table 5.1a *(continued)*

Index of teacher support in mathematics lessons and student performance on the mathematics scale, by national quarters of the index

Results based on students' self-reports

		Change in the mathematics score per unit of the index of teacher support		Increased likelihood of students in the bottom quarter of this index scoring in the bottom quarter of the national mathematics performance distribution		Explained variance in student performance (r-squared × 100)	
		Effect	S.E.	Ratio	S.E.	Percentage	S.E.
OECD countries	Australia	**10.8**	(1.43)	**1.3**	(0.06)	1.3	(0.35)
	Austria	**–8.4**	(1.91)	**0.7**	(0.07)	0.9	(0.39)
	Belgium	**–6.0**	(1.61)	**0.9**	(0.06)	0.3	(0.19)
	Canada	**6.3**	(1.08)	**1.2**	(0.05)	0.5	(0.17)
	Czech Republic	**–5.1**	(2.11)	0.9	(0.07)	0.3	(0.21)
	Denmark	**6.7**	(2.05)	**1.2**	(0.08)	0.4	(0.25)
	Finland	**4.4**	(1.83)	**1.1**	(0.06)	0.2	(0.19)
	France	**–5.2**	(1.93)	0.9	(0.08)	0.3	(0.26)
	Germany	**–10.9**	(1.93)	**0.7**	(0.06)	1.4	(0.51)
	Greece	**–6.4**	(2.07)	**0.8**	(0.06)	0.4	(0.27)
	Hungary	–0.3	(2.14)	0.9	(0.08)	0.0	(0.05)
	Iceland	**9.5**	(1.87)	**1.4**	(0.09)	0.9	(0.37)
	Ireland	–2.9	(1.81)	0.9	(0.07)	0.1	(0.17)
	Italy	**–16.3**	(1.67)	**0.6**	(0.05)	3.3	(0.61)
	Japan	**12.9**	(3.27)	**1.4**	(0.10)	1.2	(0.59)
	Korea	**7.5**	(2.56)	**1.2**	(0.07)	0.4	(0.24)
	Luxembourg	**–9.8**	(1.30)	**0.7**	(0.05)	1.5	(0.39)
	Mexico	–1.6	(1.41)	1.0	(0.07)	0.0	(0.07)
	Netherlands	0.3	(2.21)	1.0	(0.09)	0.0	(0.04)
	New Zealand	**3.9**	(1.62)	1.1	(0.08)	0.2	(0.14)
	Norway	**14.0**	(1.93)	**1.4**	(0.09)	1.9	(0.52)
	Poland	–2.9	(1.86)	1.0	(0.06)	0.1	(0.12)
	Portugal	**–5.5**	(1.76)	**0.8**	(0.07)	0.4	(0.26)
	Slovak Republic	**–16.0**	(1.83)	**0.7**	(0.07)	2.7	(0.59)
	Spain	–1.1	(1.55)	0.9	(0.07)	0.0	(0.07)
	Sweden	**4.5**	(1.81)	**1.2**	(0.08)	0.2	(0.16)
	Switzerland	**–10.3**	(2.97)	**0.7**	(0.06)	1.0	(0.57)
	Turkey	3.8	(3.54)	1.1	(0.09)	0.1	(0.26)
	United States	**7.9**	(1.27)	**1.2**	(0.06)	0.8	(0.25)
	OECD total	*–5.9*	*(0.58)*	*0.9*	*(0.02)*	*0.4*	*(0.07)*
	OECD average	*–4.2*	*(0.36)*	*0.9*	*(0.01)*	*0.2*	*(0.03)*
Partner countries	Brazil	**–12.2**	(2.36)	**0.8**	(0.06)	1.4	(0.54)
	Hong Kong-China	**12.0**	(2.29)	**1.4**	(0.08)	1.1	(0.40)
	Indonesia	**–10.7**	(2.35)	0.9	(0.07)	1.0	(0.45)
	Latvia	–3.8	(2.39)	0.9	(0.06)	0.1	(0.17)
	Liechtenstein	–6.5	(4.57)	**0.6**	(0.18)	0.4	(0.63)
	Macao-China	–4.1	(4.45)	0.9	(0.12)	0.2	(0.32)
	Russian Federation	**3.9**	(1.98)	1.1	(0.08)	0.1	(0.15)
	Serbia	**–15.6**	(1.74)	**0.7**	(0.06)	4.4	(0.91)
	Thailand	**4.4**	(1.65)	**1.2**	(0.08)	0.2	(0.18)
	Tunisia	**–5.2**	(1.64)	**0.7**	(0.06)	0.4	(0.29)
	Uruguay	**–11.4**	(1.78)	**0.7**	(0.06)	1.5	(0.45)
	United Kingdom[1]	**9.7**	(1.41)	**1.2**	(0.08)	1.2	(0.36)

Note: Values that are statistically significant are indicated in bold (see Annex A4).

1. Response rate too low to ensure comparability (see Annex A3).

Table 5.1b
Teacher support in PISA 2003 (mathematics) and PISA 2000 (language of instruction)
Results based on students' self-reports

		Percentage of students reporting that the following happens in every or most lessons:									
		The teacher shows an interest in every student's learning				The teacher gives extra help when students need it		The teacher helps student with their learning			
		PISA 2003		PISA 2000		PISA 2003		PISA 2003		PISA 2000	
		%	S.E.	%	S.E.	%	S.E.	%	S.E.	%	S.E.
OECD countries	Australia	**63.7**	(0.6)	**72.5**	(0.9)	78.4	(0.6)	**84.9**	(0.4)	**77.6**	(0.8)
	Austria	49.1	(1.1)	49.5	(1.2)	58.6	(1.3)	**45.1**	(1.3)	**32.8**	(1.1)
	Belgium	**49.0**	(0.8)	**43.6**	(1.0)	64.6	(0.8)	**66.3**	(0.8)	**38.6**	(1.0)
	Canada	**62.9**	(0.6)	**69.3**	(0.6)	80.1	(0.5)	**86.4**	(0.4)	**75.8**	(0.5)
	Czech Republic	47.1	(1.2)	47.9	(1.0)	75.4	(1.2)	**59.4**	(1.2)	**24.7**	(1.1)
	Denmark	**57.3**	(1.0)	**63.2**	(1.0)	68.5	(1.0)	**84.6**	(0.7)	**69.0**	(1.0)
	Finland	54.3	(0.9)	52.9	(1.1)	77.3	(0.8)	**86.5**	(0.7)	**67.0**	(0.9)
	France	**47.7**	(0.8)	**56.3**	(1.2)	62.6	(0.9)	**66.4**	(0.8)	**43.4**	(1.0)
	Germany	43.5	(1.0)	41.5	(1.0)	59.3	(1.2)	**59.1**	(1.1)	**34.7**	(0.8)
	Greece	**43.3**	(1.4)	**70.7**	(0.9)	62.2	(1.3)	**73.6**	(1.1)	**70.8**	(0.9)
	Hungary	**53.6**	(1.2)	**59.4**	(1.0)	63.8	(1.1)	**71.8**	(1.1)	**52.3**	(0.9)
	Iceland	**65.7**	(0.8)	**53.8**	(0.7)	69.2	(0.6)	**89.4**	(0.5)	**75.5**	(0.7)
	Ireland	**61.5**	(1.2)	**70.5**	(1.1)	61.8	(1.2)	**75.4**	(0.8)	**61.8**	(1.2)
	Italy	**56.5**	(0.9)	m	m	48.8	(0.9)	**69.9**	(0.8)	m	m
	Japan	49.6	(1.0)	51.8	(1.3)	62.3	(0.9)	**73.2**	(0.8)	**54.5**	(1.5)
	Korea	**57.9**	(0.9)	**31.2**	(1.1)	55.8	(1.0)	**78.5**	(0.7)	**41.3**	(1.1)
	Luxembourg	**53.4**	(0.7)	**47.0**	(0.9)	60.9	(0.7)	**48.7**	(0.7)	**33.2**	(0.8)
	Mexico	**80.8**	(0.6)	**72.4**	(1.3)	67.9	(0.9)	**78.0**	(0.8)	**63.5**	(1.1)
	Netherlands	**48.6**	(1.1)	**38.0**	(1.1)	66.3	(1.1)	**49.1**	(1.1)	**39.2**	(1.4)
	New Zealand	**63.1**	(1.0)	**69.9**	(1.0)	76.6	(0.8)	**83.9**	(0.7)	**77.1**	(0.9)
	Norway	**54.6**	(1.0)	**49.6**	(1.1)	59.7	(1.0)	**80.7**	(0.8)	**71.0**	(1.0)
	Poland	**51.3**	(1.1)	**39.9**	(1.2)	61.4	(1.1)	**61.7**	(1.0)	**37.1**	(1.1)
	Portugal	**67.1**	(1.2)	**83.7**	(0.8)	73.4	(1.1)	82.0	(0.9)	79.8	(0.8)
	Slovak Republic	57.4	(0.9)	a	a	58.0	(1.1)	64.9	(1.0)	a	a
	Spain	64.7	(0.8)	62.8	(1.0)	48.2	(1.0)	**71.9**	(0.8)	**63.5**	(1.3)
	Sweden	**68.9**	(0.8)	**65.3**	(1.0)	70.2	(0.9)	**87.4**	(0.6)	**77.5**	(0.8)
	Switzerland	**54.6**	(1.0)	**57.7**	(1.2)	72.9	(0.7)	**66.6**	(0.8)	**47.7**	(1.1)
	Turkey	77.2	(1.1)	a	a	74.2	(1.1)	82.3	(0.9)	a	a
	United States	69.3	(0.8)	70.0	(1.5)	78.0	(0.8)	**84.2**	(0.8)	**73.9**	(1.2)
	OECD total	*61.1*	*(0.3)*	*58.2*	*(0.5)*	*67.9*	*(0.3)*	*75.6*	*(0.3)*	*59.1*	*(0.5)*
	OECD average	*57.9*	*(0.2)*	*56.7*	*(0.2)*	*66.3*	*(0.2)*	*73.2*	*(0.1)*	*57.4*	*(0.2)*
Partner countries	Brazil	**80.9**	(0.8)	**74.8**	(0.9)	70.8	(0.9)	**86.4**	(0.8)	**77.0**	(1.0)
	Hong Kong-China	**62.2**	(0.9)	**57.4**	(0.9)	66.6	(0.9)	**74.1**	(0.7)	**57.5**	(0.9)
	Indonesia	**63.7**	(0.8)	**55.2**	(0.8)	66.3	(0.8)	**81.0**	(0.6)	**68.0**	(0.9)
	Latvia	**50.5**	(1.8)	**10.6**	(1.3)	71.5	(1.1)	**82.5**	(0.9)	**54.1**	(1.5)
	Liechtenstein	54.8	(2.7)	52.9	(2.8)	71.9	(2.4)	**62.8**	(2.8)	**42.7**	(2.5)
	Macao-China	60.3	(1.6)	a	a	57.5	(1.5)	68.2	(1.6)	a	a
	Russian Federation	**67.1**	(0.9)	**57.0**	(0.9)	73.8	(0.8)	**80.1**	(0.7)	**72.4**	(0.8)
	Serbia	53.5	(1.1)	a	a	48.9	(1.1)	54.1	(1.0)	a	a
	Thailand	**84.7**	(0.8)	**76.4**	(1.2)	77.4	(0.8)	**88.2**	(0.6)	**67.4**	(0.9)
	Tunisia	70.8	(0.9)	a	a	61.6	(0.9)	77.2	(0.8)	a	a
	Uruguay	76.8	(1.1)	a	a	51.3	(1.3)	80.9	(1.0)	a	a
	United Kingdom[1]	m	m	m	m	m	m	m	m	m	m

		Percentage of students reporting that the following happens in every or most lessons:							
		The teacher continues teaching until all students understand				The teacher gives students an opportunity to express their opinions			
		PISA 2003		PISA 2000		PISA 2003		PISA 2000	
		%	S.E.	%	S.E.	%	S.E.	%	S.E.
OECD countries	Australia	71.8	(0.8)	72.3	(0.9)	**62.9**	(0.6)	**78.1**	(0.9)
	Austria	**50.6**	(1.3)	**57.6**	(1.3)	**52.1**	(1.2)	**68.7**	(1.2)
	Belgium	**63.6**	(0.9)	**59.4**	(0.8)	**52.9**	(0.7)	**57.8**	(1.0)
	Canada	**71.2**	(0.5)	**68.8**	(0.5)	**62.3**	(0.6)	**74.2**	(0.5)
	Czech Republic	**51.2**	(1.2)	**41.8**	(1.1)	57.1	(1.3)	58.0	(1.2)
	Denmark	**72.5**	(1.0)	**68.2**	(1.1)	**69.0**	(0.9)	**77.9**	(0.9)
	Finland	61.0	(0.8)	59.9	(1.0)	**61.7**	(0.9)	**72.8**	(1.1)
	France	**62.2**	(1.0)	**57.9**	(1.0)	**50.0**	(0.9)	**62.2**	(1.1)
	Germany	54.0	(1.1)	53.6	(0.9)	**53.4**	(1.1)	**63.1**	(1.0)
	Greece	**58.6**	(1.1)	**63.4**	(1.0)	**71.3**	(0.9)	**79.6**	(0.8)
	Hungary	**54.9**	(1.2)	**59.8**	(1.0)	**61.7**	(1.2)	**72.1**	(0.9)
	Iceland	**77.8**	(0.8)	**72.0**	(0.6)	**59.1**	(0.8)	**51.2**	(0.9)
	Ireland	**68.1**	(1.0)	**64.7**	(1.0)	**49.6**	(1.1)	**67.1**	(1.0)
	Italy	61.0	(0.9)	63.0	(1.1)	**61.4**	(0.8)	**72.6**	(0.9)
	Japan	49.8	(1.0)	50.7	(1.5)	**46.6**	(1.2)	**61.3**	(1.3)
	Korea	39.5	(0.9)	40.9	(1.2)	**49.1**	(0.9)	**43.6**	(1.2)
	Luxembourg	57.1	(0.7)	58.2	(0.8)	58.8	(0.7)	59.6	(0.8)
	Mexico	**69.7**	(0.9)	**64.6**	(1.2)	**73.1**	(0.7)	**79.9**	(1.0)
	Netherlands	**60.4**	(1.2)	**65.2**	(1.4)	**53.6**	(1.1)	**57.6**	(1.3)
	New Zealand	67.9	(0.9)	67.9	(1.0)	**59.0**	(1.0)	**74.1**	(1.0)
	Norway	60.4	(1.0)	60.4	(1.1)	**57.7**	(1.1)	**63.3**	(1.4)
	Poland	54.8	(1.1)	44.9	(1.4)	**54.6**	(1.0)	**62.6**	(1.5)
	Portugal	71.2	(1.0)	69.2	(0.9)	**67.5**	(1.1)	**78.1**	(0.8)
	Slovak Republic	52.3	(1.2)	a	a	59.9	(1.0)	a	a
	Spain	64.7	(1.0)	66.4	(1.2)	**59.7**	(0.8)	**64.0**	(1.2)
	Sweden	70.8	(0.9)	69.4	(1.0)	**61.7**	(0.9)	**71.9**	(0.9)
	Switzerland	**60.5**	(1.5)	**66.9**	(1.2)	68.7	(0.8)	69.0	(0.9)
	Turkey	68.0	(1.3)	a	a	69.9	(1.1)	a	a
	United States	**71.4**	(0.9)	**67.6**	(1.2)	**63.0**	(0.8)	**70.5**	(1.4)
	OECD total	*63.1*	*(0.3)*	*60.9*	*(0.4)*	*59.0*	*(0.3)*	*67.5*	*(0.4)*
	OECD average	*62.3*	*(0.2)*	*61.9*	*(0.2)*	*59.5*	*(0.2)*	*67.4*	*(0.2)*
Partner countries	Brazil	**81.0**	(0.7)	**70.8**	(1.2)	**75.8**	(1.0)	**71.9**	(1.0)
	Hong Kong-China	**68.5**	(0.9)	**53.0**	(0.8)	60.3	(1.0)	62.1	(1.0)
	Indonesia	**78.0**	(0.7)	**64.5**	(1.1)	**81.0**	(0.9)	**77.3**	(0.9)
	Latvia	**63.2**	(1.0)	**55.1**	(1.5)	64.3	(1.2)	61.2	(1.6)
	Liechtenstein	**59.8**	(2.6)	**71.2**	(2.7)	65.5	(2.4)	70.0	(2.1)
	Macao-China	63.6	(1.8)	a	a	56.9	(1.7)	a	a
	Russian Federation	**66.6**	(1.0)	**62.4**	(1.1)	70.6	(0.8)	70.2	(0.9)
	Serbia	51.0	(1.2)	a	a	55.3	(1.0)	a	a
	Thailand	**82.6**	(0.8)	**59.5**	(1.3)	78.9	(1.0)	79.2	(0.9)
	Tunisia	70.0	(0.9)	a	a	62.5	(1.1)	a	a
	Uruguay	74.8	(1.0)	a	a	72.6	(0.9)	a	a
	United Kingdom[1]	m	m	m	m	m	m	m	m

Note: Values that are statistically significant are indicated in bold (see Annex A4).
1. Response rate too low to ensure comparability (see Annex A3).

Table 5.2a
Index of principals' perception of student-related factors affecting school climate and student performance on the mathematics scale, by national quarters of the index

Results based on reports from school principals and reported proportionate to the number of 15-year-olds enrolled in the school

		Index of student-related factors affecting school climate										Performance on the mathematics scale, by national quarters of the index of student-related factors affecting school climate							
		All students		Bottom quarter		Second quarter		Third quarter		Top quarter		Bottom quarter		Second quarter		Third quarter		Top quarter	
		Mean index	S.E.	Mean index	S.E.	Mean index	S.E.	Mean index	S.E.	Mean index	S.E.	Mean score	S.E.	Mean score	S.E.	Mean score	S.E.	Mean score	S.E.
OECD countries	Australia	–0.02	(0.05)	–1.10	(0.04)	–0.36	(0.02)	0.15	(0.02)	1.25	(0.09)	**500**	(4.3)	507	(5.3)	535	(4.5)	**555**	(6.3)
	Austria	–0.02	(0.06)	–1.10	(0.06)	–0.28	(0.02)	0.23	(0.03)	1.08	(0.07)	491	(10.3)	503	(9.4)	512	(8.5)	514	(8.9)
	Belgium	0.37	(0.06)	–1.06	(0.05)	0.00	(0.02)	0.76	(0.02)	1.77	(0.05)	461	(8.9)	521	(6.5)	555	(6.9)	**581**	(6.1)
	Canada	–0.42	(0.04)	–1.45	(0.05)	–0.70	(0.01)	–0.21	(0.01)	0.67	(0.04)	**517**	(3.5)	533	(3.8)	531	(3.6)	**548**	(3.1)
	Czech Republic	0.19	(0.04)	–0.69	(0.04)	–0.05	(0.02)	0.39	(0.01)	1.11	(0.04)	**497**	(7.6)	514	(8.9)	526	(6.4)	**528**	(8.5)
	Denmark	0.26	(0.05)	–0.60	(0.04)	–0.01	(0.02)	0.44	(0.01)	1.22	(0.07)	**501**	(6.0)	517	(5.2)	519	(4.6)	**520**	(5.3)
	Finland	–0.10	(0.05)	–0.90	(0.04)	–0.28	(0.02)	0.15	(0.01)	0.62	(0.05)	**536**	(3.2)	541	(4.1)	552	(2.9)	**548**	(3.7)
	France	w	w	w	w	w	w	w	w	w	w	w	w	w	w	w	w	w	w
	Germany	–0.08	(0.06)	–1.33	(0.09)	–0.30	(0.02)	0.22	(0.02)	1.10	(0.07)	**439**	(8.7)	501	(9.2)	531	(7.2)	**541**	(7.8)
	Greece	–0.36	(0.18)	–2.35	(0.10)	–0.88	(0.07)	0.39	(0.05)	1.39	(0.12)	435	(11.7)	438	(11.6)	446	(7.6)	459	(10.3)
	Hungary	0.32	(0.08)	–1.16	(0.11)	0.06	(0.04)	0.78	(0.03)	1.62	(0.08)	**455**	(9.5)	473	(8.7)	502	(6.9)	**532**	(6.6)
	Iceland	0.06	(0.00)	–1.04	(0.00)	–0.25	(0.00)	0.27	(0.00)	1.27	(0.01)	**510**	(3.2)	512	(3.5)	519	(3.2)	**522**	(3.2)
	Ireland	–0.29	(0.09)	–1.39	(0.11)	–0.54	(0.02)	–0.08	(0.02)	0.85	(0.10)	**487**	(7.2)	498	(5.3)	514	(5.8)	**516**	(4.9)
	Italy	0.00	(0.06)	–1.18	(0.04)	–0.32	(0.03)	0.25	(0.02)	1.25	(0.06)	**435**	(6.8)	461	(7.1)	473	(7.5)	**496**	(9.5)
	Japan	0.47	(0.07)	–0.78	(0.06)	0.16	(0.03)	0.73	(0.03)	1.76	(0.08)	**468**	(7.9)	522	(10.1)	554	(8.1)	**592**	(8.3)
	Korea	0.95	(0.13)	–1.10	(0.18)	0.69	(0.04)	1.63	(0.04)	2.58	(0.01)	**506**	(9.5)	528	(9.2)	560	(8.1)	**575**	(8.2)
	Luxembourg	–0.14	(0.00)	–0.88	(0.01)	–0.47	(0.00)	0.07	(0.00)	0.74	(0.01)	**486**	(2.3)	478	(2.5)	491	(2.4)	**518**	(2.6)
	Mexico	0.23	(0.07)	–1.09	(0.05)	–0.10	(0.03)	0.57	(0.02)	1.54	(0.06)	**370**	(5.5)	384	(6.3)	391	(9.0)	**398**	(7.4)
	Netherlands	–0.19	(0.07)	–1.17	(0.07)	–0.43	(0.02)	0.03	(0.01)	0.80	(0.11)	**487**	(8.8)	527	(9.9)	568	(9.7)	**564**	(11.2)
	New Zealand	–0.38	(0.04)	–1.35	(0.06)	–0.62	(0.02)	–0.08	(0.02)	0.52	(0.05)	**505**	(5.7)	516	(5.5)	532	(5.4)	**546**	(4.7)
	Norway	–0.15	(0.05)	–0.99	(0.05)	–0.36	(0.02)	0.04	(0.02)	0.69	(0.05)	493	(4.6)	494	(4.6)	491	(3.8)	499	(5.7)
	Poland	–0.04	(0.06)	–1.10	(0.07)	–0.25	(0.02)	0.19	(0.02)	1.00	(0.06)	487	(5.5)	490	(4.5)	491	(5.6)	492	(5.0)
	Portugal	–0.12	(0.07)	–1.15	(0.08)	–0.34	(0.02)	0.10	(0.02)	0.89	(0.08)	**446**	(10.3)	480	(5.9)	464	(6.2)	**473**	(6.5)
	Slovak Republic	0.32	(0.05)	–0.76	(0.07)	0.13	(0.02)	0.60	(0.02)	1.30	(0.06)	**477**	(8.5)	490	(6.9)	506	(8.3)	**520**	(5.6)
	Spain	–0.01	(0.07)	–1.29	(0.07)	–0.40	(0.02)	0.18	(0.02)	1.46	(0.09)	**468**	(5.1)	475	(6.6)	482	(4.2)	**516**	(4.9)
	Sweden	–0.08	(0.05)	–1.00	(0.06)	–0.29	(0.02)	0.16	(0.01)	0.79	(0.05)	**499**	(5.8)	508	(3.5)	512	(6.2)	**517**	(5.3)
	Switzerland	0.00	(0.08)	–0.94	(0.05)	–0.28	(0.02)	0.12	(0.02)	1.10	(0.09)	522	(9.6)	523	(7.8)	527	(8.3)	534	(9.0)
	Turkey	–0.35	(0.14)	–2.27	(0.10)	–0.88	(0.08)	0.34	(0.05)	1.41	(0.10)	417	(12.1)	409	(11.3)	416	(12.6)	453	(18.3)
	United States	–0.26	(0.06)	–1.31	(0.06)	–0.50	(0.02)	–0.06	(0.02)	0.84	(0.08)	**471**	(7.7)	482	(6.1)	483	(5.7)	**505**	(6.8)
	OECD total	*0.01*	*(0.02)*	*–1.28*	*(0.02)*	*–0.33*	*(0.01)*	*0.28*	*(0.01)*	*1.36*	*(0.03)*	*459*	*(2.9)*	*483*	*(2.5)*	*496*	*(2.7)*	*517*	*(2.8)*
	OECD average	*0.00*	*(0.01)*	*–1.23*	*(0.02)*	*–0.30*	*(0.01)*	*0.26*	*(0.01)*	*1.27*	*(0.02)*	*475*	*(1.9)*	*496*	*(1.3)*	*509*	*(1.6)*	*519*	*(1.7)*
Partner countries	Brazil	–0.17	(0.10)	–1.83	(0.08)	–0.66	(0.05)	0.33	(0.03)	1.47	(0.06)	**341**	(8.8)	351	(10.4)	349	(9.9)	**387**	(11.9)
	Hong Kong-China	0.37	(0.13)	–2.06	(0.16)	0.11	(0.05)	1.10	(0.04)	2.33	(0.06)	**540**	(9.7)	519	(10.0)	546	(13.4)	**594**	(7.5)
	Indonesia	–1.76	(0.13)	–3.41	(0.04)	–2.59	(0.03)	–1.64	(0.06)	0.59	(0.10)	363	(8.8)	358	(7.1)	349	(7.8)	371	(7.9)
	Latvia	–0.12	(0.08)	–1.33	(0.12)	–0.36	(0.02)	0.20	(0.02)	1.00	(0.07)	483	(6.6)	475	(5.4)	489	(7.5)	487	(8.5)
	Liechtenstein	c	c	c	c	c	c	c	c	c	c	c	c	c	c	c	c	c	c
	Macao-China	–0.56	(0.01)	–2.59	(0.01)	–1.34	(0.02)	0.00	(0.01)	1.71	(0.01)	532	(5.2)	520	(8.4)	518	(4.8)	538	(4.6)
	Russian Federation	–1.05	(0.11)	–2.92	(0.09)	–1.46	(0.06)	–0.37	(0.04)	0.57	(0.07)	**447**	(9.1)	468	(6.5)	466	(8.1)	**492**	(7.2)
	Serbia	–0.63	(0.09)	–1.80	(0.08)	–0.91	(0.02)	–0.37	(0.03)	0.54	(0.07)	**423**	(6.4)	430	(8.3)	444	(9.0)	**450**	(9.5)
	Thailand	0.30	(0.07)	–0.67	(0.07)	0.06	(0.02)	0.56	(0.02)	1.26	(0.07)	412	(6.2)	424	(6.3)	418	(6.3)	413	(7.2)
	Tunisia	–1.21	(0.11)	–2.92	(0.08)	–1.76	(0.04)	–0.74	(0.06)	0.59	(0.09)	**370**	(7.5)	359	(8.2)	360	(7.0)	348	(7.3)
	Uruguay	0.52	(0.07)	–0.85	(0.09)	0.25	(0.02)	0.87	(0.02)	1.81	(0.06)	**398**	(8.1)	423	(10.3)	418	(7.6)	**450**	(7.2)
	United Kingdom[1]	–0.20	(0.05)	–1.28	(0.05)	–0.51	(0.02)	0.08	(0.02)	0.90	(0.10)	**468**	(5.2)	502	(4.1)	524	(5.0)	**542**	(5.8)

		Change in the mathematics score per unit of the index of student-related factors affecting school climate		Increased likelihood of students in the bottom quarter of this index scoring in the bottom quarter of the national mathematics performance distribution		Explained variance in student performance (r-squared × 100)	
		Effect	S.E.	Ratio	S.E.	Percentage	S.E.
OECD countries	Australia	**22.5**	(3.08)	**1.5**	(0.12)	4.9	(1.20)
	Austria	**10.7**	(4.95)	1.2	(0.20)	1.0	(1.04)
	Belgium	**42.1**	(3.34)	**2.7**	(0.28)	17.7	(2.62)
	Canada	**14.3**	(1.90)	**1.4**	(0.08)	2.0	(0.57)
	Czech Republic	**19.1**	(6.44)	**1.4**	(0.20)	2.0	(1.37)
	Denmark	**9.8**	(4.40)	**1.3**	(0.13)	0.7	(0.59)
	Finland	**8.8**	(2.80)	**1.2**	(0.08)	0.4	(0.27)
	France	w	w	w	w	w	w
	Germany	**40.4**	(4.37)	**2.8**	(0.34)	14.7	(3.06)
	Greece	7.0	(4.23)	1.2	(0.23)	1.2	(1.48)
	Hungary	**21.2**	(5.62)	**1.8**	(0.27)	6.4	(3.02)
	Iceland	**5.1**	(1.79)	**1.2**	(0.08)	0.3	(0.19)
	Ireland	**11.8**	(3.33)	1.3	(0.19)	1.6	(0.92)
	Italy	**25.5**	(3.91)	**1.7**	(0.21)	6.3	(1.93)
	Japan	**48.1**	(4.06)	**2.8**	(0.36)	22.4	(3.48)
	Korea	**18.7**	(3.44)	**1.9**	(0.31)	8.7	(3.10)
	Luxembourg	**16.9**	(1.61)	**1.2**	(0.08)	1.4	(0.27)
	Mexico	**9.9**	(3.86)	**1.3**	(0.12)	1.4	(1.09)
	Netherlands	**39.6**	(7.27)	**2.5**	(0.42)	12.0	(4.08)
	New Zealand	**19.2**	(3.68)	**1.4**	(0.13)	2.2	(0.86)
	Norway	2.2	(4.08)	1.1	(0.10)	0.0	(0.12)
	Poland	2.9	(3.35)	1.0	(0.10)	0.1	(0.17)
	Portugal	8.0	(5.73)	**1.6**	(0.27)	0.6	(0.81)
	Slovak Republic	**19.5**	(5.21)	**1.4**	(0.19)	3.1	(1.57)
	Spain	**17.5**	(2.58)	**1.4**	(0.13)	4.6	(1.62)
	Sweden	**9.4**	(4.13)	1.2	(0.11)	0.5	(0.46)
	Switzerland	8.4	(5.70)	1.1	(0.14)	0.5	(0.65)
	Turkey	10.3	(6.27)	1.0	(0.18)	2.0	(2.38)
	United States	**17.9**	(3.89)	1.3	(0.17)	2.7	(1.24)
	OECD total	*22.9*	*(1.32)*	*1.5*	*(0.07)*	*5.3*	*(0.65)*
	OECD average	*18.9*	*(0.99)*	*1.5*	*(0.04)*	*3.6*	*(0.38)*
Partner countries	Brazil	**13.0**	(4.53)	1.2	(0.18)	2.8	(1.95)
	Hong Kong-China	**9.6**	(3.25)	1.2	(0.20)	2.8	(1.79)
	Indonesia	2.0	(2.65)	1.0	(0.14)	0.2	(0.51)
	Latvia	2.2	(3.88)	1.0	(0.10)	0.1	(0.22)
	Liechtenstein	c	c	c	c	c	c
	Macao-China	2.5	(1.45)	1.0	(0.10)	0.3	(0.28)
	Russian Federation	**10.6**	(3.16)	**1.5**	(0.21)	2.5	(1.48)
	Serbia	**13.2**	(4.99)	1.3	(0.17)	2.1	(1.52)
	Thailand	1.3	(5.00)	1.0	(0.12)	0.0	(0.27)
	Tunisia	–4.1	(2.97)	0.8	(0.12)	0.5	(0.72)
	Uruguay	**17.4**	(3.69)	**1.5**	(0.19)	3.4	(1.37)
	United Kingdom[1]	**33.4**	(3.50)	**2.0**	(0.16)	10.3	(1.96)

Note: Values that are statistically significant are indicated in bold (see Annex A4). The scale was inverted so that positive and high values represent a positive school climate with regard to student-related factors.
1. Response rate too low to ensure comparability (see Annex A3).

Table 5.2b

Student-related factors affecting school climate in PISA 2003 and PISA 2000

Results based on reports from school principals and reported proportionate to the number of 15-year-olds enrolled in the school

	Percentage of students in schools where the principals report that the following hinders students' learning to some extent or a lot											
	Student absenteeism				Disruption of classes by students				Students skipping classes			
	PISA 2003		PISA 2000		PISA 2003		PISA 2000		PISA 2003		PISA 2000	
	%	S.E.	%	S.E.	%	S.E.	%	S.E.	%	S.E.	%	S.E.
OECD countries												
Australia	**51.8**	(2.8)	**41.8**	(3.4)	37.1	(3.0)	36.4	(3.6)	19.8	(2.2)	20.3	(3.0)
Austria	53.0	(4.0)	57.8	(3.8)	38.4	(4.2)	45.1	(4.1)	42.5	(3.8)	46.3	(4.1)
Belgium	**33.8**	(2.7)	**25.8**	(2.6)	**26.3**	(2.4)	**34.8**	(3.2)	21.2	(2.4)	22.3	(2.7)
Canada	**65.5**	(2.6)	**56.9**	(1.8)	34.0	(2.7)	28.4	(1.8)	**57.6**	(2.4)	**45.0**	(1.8)
Czech Republic	**64.7**	(3.2)	**54.3**	(3.7)	**36.2**	(2.9)	**27.6**	(2.9)	24.2	(2.8)	22.0	(2.8)
Denmark	**39.4**	(3.7)	**19.7**	(2.5)	**41.7**	(3.2)	**20.7**	(3.2)	**14.4**	(2.3)	**6.8**	(1.7)
Finland	**56.1**	(3.7)	**72.9**	(3.9)	**38.5**	(3.8)	**60.0**	(4.4)	**34.1**	(3.8)	**58.4**	(3.9)
France	w	w	w	w	w	w	w	w	w	w	w	w
Germany	34.6	(3.0)	34.7	(3.1)	50.7	(3.5)	55.3	(3.5)	25.4	(3.1)	26.1	(2.8)
Greece	**65.7**	(5.6)	**83.4**	(3.5)	52.1	(5.9)	55.3	(4.8)	**46.5**	(5.2)	**65.9**	(3.9)
Hungary	56.3	(3.3)	60.4	(3.7)	41.6	(3.8)	45.7	(3.7)	26.0	(3.9)	30.6	(3.7)
Iceland	**38.2**	(0.2)	**48.3**	(0.2)	**62.0**	(0.2)	**57.5**	(0.2)	**27.8**	(0.2)	**40.0**	(0.2)
Ireland	63.1	(4.4)	68.2	(4.4)	46.8	(4.2)	46.0	(3.9)	21.4	(3.8)	23.3	(3.7)
Italy	67.8	(3.3)	65.2	(3.9)	40.8	(3.3)	41.7	(3.9)	63.3	(3.2)	62.6	(3.6)
Japan	38.5	(3.8)	39.0	(4.3)	12.6	(2.6)	8.8	(2.4)	22.5	(3.0)	18.0	(3.1)
Korea	17.4	(3.0)	19.7	(2.7)	17.8	(3.1)	16.7	(2.9)	12.9	(2.9)	14.2	(2.7)
Luxembourg	**39.2**	(0.1)	**41.3**	(0.2)	**45.2**	(0.1)	**68.0**	(0.0)	**25.1**	(0.1)	**24.7**	(0.0)
Mexico	44.4	(2.9)	53.1	(4.2)	26.7	(3.3)	30.3	(4.2)	32.3	(3.4)	32.6	(3.4)
Netherlands	**43.2**	(4.3)	**29.9**	(4.5)	43.3	(4.3)	34.1	(5.4)	30.1	(4.0)	21.6	(4.1)
New Zealand	**63.4**	(2.9)	**50.6**	(3.2)	**41.3**	(3.0)	**31.3**	(3.5)	**38.0**	(2.9)	**28.2**	(3.2)
Norway	37.0	(3.7)	35.7	(3.5)	73.8	(3.6)	69.0	(3.3)	20.3	(3.0)	21.1	(3.3)
Poland	**46.9**	(3.6)	**60.0**	(5.0)	**39.9**	(4.2)	**23.1**	(3.5)	44.6	(3.6)	55.4	(4.9)
Portugal	61.2	(4.1)	62.1	(4.0)	**34.6**	(4.1)	**62.4**	(4.3)	**50.0**	(4.0)	**70.1**	(3.7)
Slovak Republic	61.4	(3.3)	a	a	39.9	(3.6)	a	a	a	a	a	a
Spain	44.2	(3.2)	37.0	(3.3)	59.3	(2.9)	63.6	(3.8)	38.4	(3.2)	37.2	(3.4)
Sweden	48.5	(4.1)	42.9	(4.2)	50.4	(3.8)	46.8	(4.1)	28.2	(3.3)	28.6	(3.8)
Switzerland	27.2	(4.2)	25.6	(3.3)	51.7	(4.2)	48.5	(3.9)	10.7	(2.0)	14.5	(2.7)
Turkey	69.9	(4.6)	a	a	45.7	(4.9)	a	a	44.6	(4.6)	a	a
United States	**69.0**	(3.1)	**58.2**	(4.2)	27.2	(2.7)	19.2	(4.0)	35.7	(3.2)	31.2	(4.1)
OECD total	*48.9*	*(0.9)*	*48.0*	*(1.3)*	*31.4*	*(0.9)*	*30.1*	*(1.2)*	*30.6*	*(0.9)*	*30.3*	*(1.2)*
OECD average	*48.4*	*(0.6)*	*47.7*	*(0.7)*	*40.0*	*(0.6)*	*41.3*	*(0.8)*	*30.3*	*(0.6)*	*32.4*	*(0.6)*
Partner countries												
Brazil	50.8	(3.6)	56.0	(3.4)	44.5	(3.6)	47.7	(3.6)	45.0	(3.9)	51.8	(3.6)
Hong Kong-China	27.3	(3.5)	25.6	(3.7)	31.3	(3.7)	29.2	(3.9)	**20.8**	(3.4)	**8.4**	(2.5)
Indonesia	**79.9**	(3.2)	**44.2**	(4.8)	**78.9**	(3.6)	**21.0**	(4.1)	**72.2**	(3.6)	**36.4**	(3.9)
Latvia	**79.1**	(3.4)	**66.5**	(4.7)	24.4	(3.8)	24.2	(3.9)	57.2	(4.2)	68.6	(4.2)
Liechtenstein	c	c	c	c	c	c	c	c	c	c	c	c
Macao-China	61.9	(0.3)	a	a	54.5	(0.3)	a	a	51.2	(0.3)	a	a
Russian Federation	90.5	(2.2)	86.5	(2.0)	41.4	(3.7)	43.2	(3.5)	85.9	(2.5)	86.4	(2.6)
Serbia	90.2	(2.7)	a	a	45.3	(4.0)	a	a	81.6	(3.6)	a	a
Thailand	**45.4**	(3.8)	**58.6**	(4.1)	**18.8**	(2.5)	**28.5**	(3.9)	**18.8**	(3.3)	**29.9**	(3.8)
Tunisia	83.9	(3.2)	a	a	78.2	(3.3)	a	a	66.9	(4.0)	a	a
Uruguay	57.6	(3.4)	a	a	12.1	(2.5)	a	a	42.0	(4.1)	a	a
United Kingdom[1]	m	m	m	m	m	m	m	m	m	m	m	m

	Percentage of students in schools where the principals report that the following hinders students' learning to some extent or a lot											
	Students lacking respect for teachers				Student use of alcohol or illegal drugs				Students intimidating or bullying other students			
	PISA 2003		PISA 2000		PISA 2003		PISA 2000		PISA 2003		PISA 2000	
	%	S.E.	%	S.E.	%	S.E.	%	S.E.	%	S.E.	%	S.E.
OECD countries												
Australia	21.8	(2.4)	26.3	(3.7)	5.8	(1.3)	3.8	(1.3)	23.8	(2.6)	21.0	(3.0)
Austria	17.1	(3.1)	17.4	(3.2)	8.6	(2.2)	4.5	(1.5)	14.8	(2.5)	16.5	(3.0)
Belgium	**17.6**	(2.3)	**25.7**	(3.2)	7.3	(1.9)	7.0	(1.7)	14.1	(2.4)	13.4	(2.0)
Canada	24.8	(2.4)	19.6	(1.4)	**32.0**	(2.1)	**21.7**	(1.8)	**18.1**	(2.0)	11.1	(1.1)
Czech Republic	16.4	(2.4)	13.9	(2.4)	1.9	(0.9)	1.6	(0.9)	2.1	(0.9)	a	a
Denmark	**12.5**	(2.3)	**6.4**	(1.9)	0.8	(0.6)	0.7	(0.5)	6.9	(1.7)	3.1	(1.2)
Finland	**12.4**	(2.5)	**24.6**	(3.7)	3.8	(1.6)	5.4	(1.9)	**7.4**	(2.0)	13.9	(2.5)
France	w	w	w	w	w	w	w	w	w	w	w	w
Germany	22.2	(3.2)	20.4	(2.4)	9.0	(1.8)	4.1	(1.8)	**24.0**	(2.9)	16.1	(2.5)
Greece	**47.3**	(5.4)	**62.5**	(4.3)	**31.3**	(5.7)	**57.5**	(4.6)	**23.4**	(5.3)	45.7	(5.0)
Hungary	14.0	(3.2)	18.7	(2.6)	5.7	(2.0)	5.6	(1.7)	8.2	(2.3)	7.8	(1.8)
Iceland	**22.1**	(0.2)	**25.7**	(0.2)	**5.2**	(0.1)	**15.0**	(0.1)	**24.6**	(0.1)	23.0	(0.1)
Ireland	22.8	(4.2)	31.3	(4.0)	**24.1**	(4.0)	**9.6**	(2.7)	20.8	(3.6)	16.5	(3.5)
Italy	17.0	(2.8)	19.0	(3.0)	0.7	(0.3)	1.1	(0.8)	7.8	(1.7)	4.1	(1.6)
Japan	31.7	(3.2)	29.1	(4.2)	0.7	(0.7)	a	a	7.3	(2.3)	4.9	(1.8)
Korea	23.4	(3.6)	28.7	(4.4)	**13.1**	(3.2)	**1.7**	(1.2)	**13.5**	(3.2)	3.5	(1.5)
Luxembourg	**15.8**	(0.1)	**17.0**	(0.0)	**8.7**	(0.0)	**11.6**	(0.0)	15.2	(0.0)	27.2	(0.0)
Mexico	13.5	(1.8)	15.8	(2.5)	7.8	(1.1)	11.1	(2.6)	24.0	(3.2)	18.8	(3.3)
Netherlands	28.4	(4.3)	27.6	(4.8)	7.1	(2.9)	7.0	(2.3)	21.8	(3.9)	27.0	(4.8)
New Zealand	24.4	(3.1)	18.7	(2.7)	20.1	(2.4)	15.1	(2.5)	15.0	(2.6)	10.2	(2.4)
Norway	35.5	(3.8)	42.9	(3.5)	3.4	(1.4)	3.0	(1.5)	12.2	(2.7)	19.0	(3.2)
Poland	**20.8**	(3.2)	**11.1**	(3.1)	9.6	(2.3)	13.5	(3.3)	7.5	(2.2)	8.6	(2.8)
Portugal	**16.0**	(3.0)	**32.7**	(4.4)	2.7	(1.3)	3.2	(1.7)	9.3	(2.6)	10.8	(2.9)
Slovak Republic	12.4	(1.9)	a	a	3.9	(1.8)	a	a	5.1	(1.3)	a	a
Spain	33.8	(3.4)	28.1	(3.4)	4.7	(1.4)	4.9	(1.9)	13.2	(2.4)	17.6	(3.8)
Sweden	25.2	(3.4)	26.6	(3.6)	4.6	(1.6)	2.4	(1.2)	**16.6**	(2.6)	9.3	(2.4)
Switzerland	17.4	(3.6)	16.6	(2.8)	**19.3**	(2.8)	**10.8**	(2.3)	24.4	(3.9)	24.0	(3.5)
Turkey	37.1	(5.0)	a	a	22.3	(3.9)	a	a	32.0	(4.7)	a	a
United States	22.1	(2.8)	26.4	(4.3)	21.3	(3.1)	17.3	(3.3)	**14.2**	(2.4)	7.3	(2.4)
OECD total	*22.5*	*(0.8)*	*23.9*	*(1.3)*	*11.4*	*(0.8)*	*9.0*	*(0.8)*	*14.9*	*(0.8)*	*10.3*	*(0.8)*
OECD average	*22.0*	*(0.6)*	*24.1*	*(0.6)*	*9.9*	*(0.4)*	*8.8*	*(0.4)*	*14.8*	*(0.4)*	*14.1*	*(0.5)*
Partner countries												
Brazil	29.7	(3.5)	32.2	(3.4)	20.8	(3.1)	14.6	(2.5)	26.0	(3.9)	24.5	(3.1)
Hong Kong-China	27.8	(3.5)	22.1	(3.5)	**17.8**	(3.3)	**1.6**	(1.1)	**24.8**	(3.3)	9.8	(2.7)
Indonesia	**68.5**	(3.5)	**29.7**	(4.0)	**67.4**	(4.0)	**22.6**	(4.4)	**63.8**	(3.8)	17.8	(3.4)
Latvia	14.2	(3.1)	13.4	(3.2)	**10.7**	(2.7)	**1.4**	(1.2)	**7.5**	(2.3)	0.2	(0.2)
Liechtenstein	c	c	c	c	c	c	c	c	c	c	c	c
Macao-China	56.2	(0.2)	a	a	39.2	(0.3)	a	a	31.8	(0.3)	a	a
Russian Federation	48.8	(4.0)	54.6	(3.6)	41.3	(4.3)	35.4	(3.0)	40.7	(4.0)	32.7	(3.4)
Serbia	33.7	(4.0)	a	a	24.3	(3.7)	a	a	12.1	(2.8)	a	a
Thailand	8.0	(2.2)	11.9	(2.7)	**1.8**	(1.0)	**6.8**	(2.0)	4.1	(1.5)	10.8	(3.8)
Tunisia	58.1	(4.2)	a	a	45.1	(3.8)	a	a	42.6	(4.0)	a	a
Uruguay	16.7	(2.5)	a	a	7.4	(2.0)	a	a	11.5	(2.0)	a	a
United Kingdom[1]	m	m	m	m	m	m	m	m	m	m	m	m

Note: Values that are statistically significant are indicated in bold (see Annex A4).

1. Response rate too low to ensure comparability (see Annex A3).

Table 5.3a

Index of disciplinary climate in mathematics lessons and student performance on the mathematics scale, by national quarters of the index

Results based on students' self-reports

		Index of disciplinary climate in mathematics lessons										Performance on the mathematics scale by national quarters of the index of disciplinary climate							
		All students		Bottom quarter		Second quarter		Third quarter		Top quarter		Bottom quarter		Second quarter		Third quarter		Top quarter	
		Mean index	S.E.	Mean index	S.E.	Mean index	S.E.	Mean index	S.E.	Mean index	S.E.	Mean score	S.E.	Mean score	S.E.	Mean score	S.E.	Mean score	S.E.
OECD countries	Australia	–0.01	(0.02)	–1.29	(0.01)	–0.34	(0.00)	0.25	(0.00)	1.32	(0.01)	**498**	(2.6)	514	(2.77)	532	(2.82)	**560**	(3.1)
	Austria	0.21	(0.03)	–1.21	(0.02)	–0.23	(0.01)	0.55	(0.01)	1.74	(0.02)	**480**	(4.9)	492	(4.12)	520	(4.04)	**540**	(4.9)
	Belgium	0.04	(0.02)	–1.26	(0.01)	–0.31	(0.01)	0.31	(0.01)	1.42	(0.02)	**508**	(3.7)	526	(3.76)	549	(2.83)	**573**	(3.2)
	Canada	0.02	(0.01)	–1.18	(0.01)	–0.27	(0.00)	0.25	(0.00)	1.27	(0.01)	**515**	(2.5)	528	(2.31)	542	(2.26)	**560**	(2.4)
	Czech Republic	–0.01	(0.03)	–1.27	(0.02)	–0.30	(0.01)	0.27	(0.01)	1.24	(0.02)	**502**	(5.0)	514	(4.12)	528	(4.04)	**548**	(4.6)
	Denmark	–0.08	(0.02)	–1.18	(0.02)	–0.33	(0.01)	0.18	(0.00)	1.03	(0.02)	**505**	(3.8)	509	(3.89)	521	(4.02)	**532**	(4.0)
	Finland	–0.15	(0.02)	–1.25	(0.01)	–0.43	(0.00)	0.09	(0.00)	0.99	(0.02)	**533**	(3.0)	539	(3.33)	546	(2.50)	**561**	(2.8)
	France	–0.13	(0.03)	–1.48	(0.02)	–0.50	(0.01)	0.15	(0.01)	1.32	(0.02)	**498**	(4.1)	505	(3.81)	517	(4.29)	**535**	(4.1)
	Germany	0.30	(0.03)	–1.14	(0.02)	–0.11	(0.01)	0.67	(0.01)	1.79	(0.02)	**483**	(5.2)	503	(4.76)	531	(4.08)	**539**	(4.1)
	Greece	–0.22	(0.03)	–1.21	(0.01)	–0.50	(0.01)	0.00	(0.00)	0.82	(0.02)	**436**	(4.1)	435	(4.04)	450	(5.00)	**467**	(5.6)
	Hungary	0.17	(0.03)	–1.06	(0.02)	–0.13	(0.01)	0.45	(0.01)	1.42	(0.02)	**470**	(4.3)	475	(4.17)	497	(4.25)	**522**	(4.5)
	Iceland	–0.15	(0.01)	–1.22	(0.02)	–0.39	(0.01)	0.11	(0.00)	0.90	(0.02)	**501**	(3.2)	512	(3.30)	523	(2.59)	**529**	(2.9)
	Ireland	0.27	(0.03)	–1.22	(0.02)	–0.09	(0.01)	0.67	(0.01)	1.70	(0.02)	**482**	(4.0)	498	(3.99)	509	(3.52)	**526**	(4.0)
	Italy	–0.10	(0.03)	–1.40	(0.02)	–0.47	(0.01)	0.23	(0.01)	1.23	(0.02)	**452**	(4.6)	455	(4.22)	471	(4.17)	**487**	(4.4)
	Japan	0.44	(0.03)	–0.72	(0.02)	0.15	(0.01)	0.75	(0.01)	1.60	(0.02)	**489**	(5.7)	530	(5.36)	551	(5.00)	**572**	(5.1)
	Korea	0.12	(0.02)	–0.89	(0.01)	–0.11	(0.01)	0.28	(0.01)	1.18	(0.01)	**521**	(4.3)	540	(3.80)	554	(4.22)	**554**	(4.3)
	Luxembourg	–0.21	(0.02)	–1.49	(0.02)	–0.58	(0.01)	0.02	(0.01)	1.23	(0.02)	**477**	(2.8)	485	(3.15)	503	(2.69)	**516**	(3.0)
	Mexico	0.00	(0.02)	–1.11	(0.02)	–0.26	(0.01)	0.23	(0.00)	1.15	(0.01)	**365**	(4.4)	386	(4.27)	398	(4.28)	**411**	(4.5)
	Netherlands	–0.13	(0.03)	–1.26	(0.03)	–0.41	(0.01)	0.13	(0.01)	1.03	(0.02)	**532**	(4.2)	535	(5.15)	547	(4.50)	**566**	(4.0)
	New Zealand	–0.17	(0.02)	–1.43	(0.02)	–0.47	(0.01)	0.12	(0.01)	1.12	(0.02)	**501**	(3.9)	518	(3.27)	530	(3.45)	**555**	(3.6)
	Norway	–0.24	(0.02)	–1.26	(0.02)	–0.46	(0.01)	0.00	(0.00)	0.77	(0.02)	**483**	(3.7)	493	(3.51)	507	(4.08)	**509**	(3.9)
	Poland	0.10	(0.04)	–1.15	(0.02)	–0.20	(0.01)	0.37	(0.01)	1.38	(0.02)	**479**	(4.3)	480	(4.32)	491	(3.55)	**514**	(3.4)
	Portugal	0.01	(0.02)	–1.09	(0.02)	–0.27	(0.01)	0.26	(0.01)	1.15	(0.02)	**437**	(5.0)	459	(5.28)	478	(3.99)	**493**	(3.8)
	Slovak Republic	–0.10	(0.02)	–1.25	(0.02)	–0.37	(0.00)	0.17	(0.01)	1.07	(0.02)	**484**	(4.6)	496	(4.58)	500	(4.17)	**517**	(3.5)
	Spain	–0.04	(0.03)	–1.22	(0.02)	–0.38	(0.01)	0.21	(0.00)	1.24	(0.02)	**465**	(3.8)	478	(3.46)	493	(2.83)	**511**	(3.7)
	Sweden	–0.05	(0.03)	–1.13	(0.02)	–0.31	(0.01)	0.16	(0.01)	1.10	(0.03)	**491**	(4.1)	507	(2.98)	516	(3.14)	**527**	(4.3)
	Switzerland	0.10	(0.03)	–1.17	(0.02)	–0.28	(0.01)	0.36	(0.01)	1.49	(0.02)	**502**	(6.5)	516	(4.20)	542	(4.20)	**552**	(4.1)
	Turkey	–0.12	(0.03)	–1.26	(0.02)	–0.37	(0.00)	0.13	(0.00)	1.02	(0.02)	**397**	(6.1)	413	(5.89)	433	(7.05)	**470**	(11.1)
	United States	0.12	(0.02)	–1.14	(0.02)	–0.19	(0.01)	0.40	(0.01)	1.44	(0.02)	**445**	(3.9)	478	(3.59)	499	(3.81)	**518**	(3.3)
	OECD total	*0.09*	*(0.01)*	*–1.17*	*(0.01)*	*–0.23*	*(0.00)*	*0.35*	*(0.00)*	*1.38*	*(0.01)*	*461*	*(1.6)*	*482*	*(1.43)*	*500*	*(1.26)*	*526*	*(1.3)*
	OECD average	*0.00*	*(0.01)*	*–1.23*	*(0.00)*	*–0.33*	*(0.00)*	*0.23*	*(0.00)*	*1.28*	*(0.00)*	*480*	*(0.9)*	*493*	*(0.84)*	*508*	*(0.77)*	*530*	*(0.8)*
Partner countries	Brazil	–0.35	(0.02)	–1.27	(0.01)	–0.59	(0.01)	–0.16	(0.00)	0.62	(0.02)	**336**	(5.3)	352	(4.79)	371	(5.50)	**387**	(7.0)
	Hong Kong-China	0.15	(0.03)	–0.97	(0.03)	–0.01	(0.00)	0.25	(0.01)	1.33	(0.02)	**523**	(6.8)	543	(4.77)	553	(4.63)	**585**	(4.3)
	Indonesia	0.07	(0.02)	–1.05	(0.01)	–0.25	(0.01)	0.26	(0.01)	1.30	(0.02)	**341**	(5.0)	364	(4.78)	379	(4.93)	**367**	(4.1)
	Latvia	0.30	(0.04)	–0.91	(0.02)	–0.04	(0.01)	0.57	(0.01)	1.60	(0.02)	**466**	(6.1)	476	(4.66)	488	(4.06)	**506**	(5.0)
	Liechtenstein	0.23	(0.05)	–1.18	(0.06)	–0.19	(0.02)	0.54	(0.02)	1.79	(0.05)	**499**	(10.1)	512	(10.76)	550	(10.61)	**581**	(10.0)
	Macao-China	0.09	(0.02)	–0.82	(0.03)	–0.01	(0.01)	0.22	(0.01)	0.98	(0.03)	**517**	(6.1)	518	(7.18)	519	(5.96)	**556**	(6.8)
	Russian Federation	0.50	(0.04)	–0.81	(0.02)	0.12	(0.01)	0.82	(0.01)	1.85	(0.02)	**439**	(5.0)	461	(5.13)	477	(4.57)	**502**	(4.6)
	Serbia	–0.09	(0.02)	–1.27	(0.02)	–0.35	(0.01)	0.19	(0.01)	1.08	(0.02)	**420**	(4.0)	436	(4.80)	445	(4.39)	**462**	(4.4)
	Thailand	0.00	(0.03)	–1.04	(0.02)	–0.22	(0.01)	0.19	(0.00)	1.08	(0.04)	**390**	(3.7)	410	(3.89)	426	(4.07)	**443**	(3.9)
	Tunisia	–0.08	(0.03)	–1.22	(0.01)	–0.46	(0.00)	0.13	(0.01)	1.23	(0.02)	**347**	(3.5)	355	(3.29)	369	(3.40)	**373**	(5.1)
	Uruguay	–0.03	(0.02)	–1.23	(0.02)	–0.35	(0.01)	0.25	(0.01)	1.21	(0.02)	**404**	(4.6)	417	(4.55)	440	(4.32)	**451**	(4.9)
	United Kingdom[1]	-0.01	(0.03)	-1.42	(0.02)	-0.36	(0.01)	0.33	(0.01)	1.41	(0.02)	**475**	(3.6)	493	(3.45)	518	(3.21)	**549**	(4.4)

		Change in the mathematics score per unit of the index of disciplinary climate		Increased likelihood of students in the bottom quarter of this index scoring in the bottom quarter of the national mathematics performance distribution		Explained variance in student performance (r-squared × 100)	
		Effect	S.E.	Ratio	S.E.	Percentage	S.E.
OECD countries	Australia	**21.0**	(1.07)	**1.6**	(0.06)	5.3	(0.49)
	Austria	**19.3**	(2.03)	**1.6**	(0.11)	5.9	(1.23)
	Belgium	**23.5**	(1.57)	**1.6**	(0.09)	5.9	(0.71)
	Canada	**17.3**	(0.92)	**1.5**	(0.06)	3.7	(0.40)
	Czech Republic	**16.7**	(2.05)	**1.6**	(0.10)	3.3	(0.79)
	Denmark	**10.4**	(2.07)	**1.2**	(0.08)	1.1	(0.43)
	Finland	**10.4**	(1.50)	**1.3**	(0.06)	1.3	(0.36)
	France	**12.1**	(1.83)	**1.3**	(0.09)	2.2	(0.62)
	Germany	**18.6**	(1.73)	**1.8**	(0.13)	5.0	(0.89)
	Greece	**14.1**	(2.95)	**1.1**	(0.07)	1.5	(0.62)
	Hungary	**20.3**	(2.30)	**1.4**	(0.09)	4.6	(0.98)
	Iceland	**12.6**	(1.71)	**1.4**	(0.09)	1.5	(0.40)
	Ireland	**15.5**	(1.60)	**1.6**	(0.11)	4.5	(0.91)
	Italy	**12.5**	(1.79)	**1.2**	(0.08)	1.8	(0.50)
	Japan	**32.7**	(2.91)	**2.2**	(0.16)	9.3	(1.72)
	Korea	**14.7**	(2.17)	**1.5**	(0.09)	1.8	(0.47)
	Luxembourg	**13.9**	(1.40)	**1.4**	(0.08)	2.8	(0.54)
	Mexico	**18.9**	(2.05)	**1.6**	(0.09)	4.1	(0.81)
	Netherlands	**12.4**	(2.36)	**1.3**	(0.09)	1.7	(0.61)
	New Zealand	**17.9**	(1.60)	**1.6**	(0.10)	3.5	(0.61)
	Norway	**11.8**	(1.85)	**1.4**	(0.08)	1.2	(0.38)
	Poland	**13.5**	(1.98)	**1.3**	(0.08)	2.3	(0.67)
	Portugal	**23.7**	(2.08)	**1.8**	(0.10)	5.8	(0.89)
	Slovak Republic	**13.6**	(1.59)	**1.3**	(0.08)	1.8	(0.39)
	Spain	**16.9**	(1.67)	**1.5**	(0.09)	3.6	(0.75)
	Sweden	**15.4**	(2.09)	**1.4**	(0.09)	2.2	(0.60)
	Switzerland	**17.3**	(2.56)	**1.6**	(0.13)	3.5	(1.09)
	Turkey	**30.0**	(4.37)	**1.5**	(0.10)	7.1	(1.60)
	United States	**25.8**	(1.40)	**1.9**	(0.10)	7.9	(0.83)
	OECD total	*23.4*	*(0.65)*	*1.7*	*(0.04)*	*5.4*	*(0.27)*
	OECD average	*18.3*	*(0.38)*	*1.5*	*(0.02)*	*3.4*	*(0.13)*
Partner countries	Brazil	**23.9**	(3.19)	**1.5**	(0.09)	3.5	(0.90)
	Hong Kong-China	**23.1**	(2.26)	**1.7**	(0.10)	4.7	(0.84)
	Indonesia	**10.7**	(1.94)	**1.5**	(0.08)	1.6	(0.55)
	Latvia	**15.2**	(2.25)	**1.4**	(0.10)	2.9	(0.82)
	Liechtenstein	**27.4**	(4.70)	**2.2**	(0.33)	10.3	(3.43)
	Macao-China	**18.7**	(4.28)	**1.5**	(0.18)	2.5	(1.10)
	Russian Federation	**21.7**	(2.02)	**1.7**	(0.12)	6.2	(1.05)
	Serbia	**16.9**	(1.85)	**1.6**	(0.09)	3.7	(0.77)
	Thailand	**22.6**	(1.94)	**1.7**	(0.10)	5.6	(0.99)
	Tunisia	**10.2**	(2.36)	**1.5**	(0.08)	1.5	(0.68)
	Uruguay	**18.6**	(2.02)	**1.5**	(0.09)	3.4	(0.71)
	United Kingdom[1]	**24.7**	(1.48)	**1.8**	(0.11)	9.1	(1.06)

Note: Values that are statistically significant are indicated in bold (see Annex A4). The scale was inverted so that positive and high values represent a positive student perception of disciplinary climate.
1. Response rate too low to ensure comparability (see Annex A3).

Table 5.3b
Disciplinary climate in PISA 2003 (mathematics) and PISA 2000 (language of instruction)
Results based on students' self-reports

Percentage of students reporting that the following happens in every or most lessons:

		Students don't listen to what the teacher says				There is noise and disorder				The teacher has to wait a long time for students to quieten down			
		PISA 2003		PISA 2000		PISA 2003		PISA 2000		PISA 2003		PISA 2000	
		%	S.E.	%	S.E.	%	S.E.	%	S.E.	%	S.E.	%	S.E.
OECD countries	Australia	**33.5**	(0.7)	**21.3**	(0.9)	**41.8**	(0.8)	**33.5**	(0.7)	31.9	(0.7)	31.4	(1.0)
	Austria	**30.9**	(1.0)	**21.0**	(0.8)	**27.2**	(1.1)	**30.9**	(1.0)	33.0	(1.2)	32.0	(1.3)
	Belgium	**27.6**	(0.7)	**24.1**	(0.9)	**37.4**	(0.9)	**27.6**	(0.7)	34.1	(0.8)	35.4	(1.3)
	Canada	**28.9**	(0.5)	**22.9**	(0.4)	**38.8**	(0.7)	**28.9**	(0.5)	**27.8**	(0.6)	**35.2**	(0.6)
	Czech Republic	**36.0**	(1.2)	**26.1**	(1.0)	33.7	(1.4)	36.0	(1.2)	33.6	(1.4)	32.3	(1.4)
	Denmark	**32.1**	(0.9)	**19.7**	(0.9)	**43.2**	(1.3)	**32.1**	(0.9)	27.6	(1.2)	27.7	(1.2)
	Finland	**36.2**	(0.9)	**30.0**	(0.9)	**48.2**	(1.1)	**36.2**	(0.9)	**34.8**	(1.1)	**39.5**	(1.2)
	France	**33.1**	(0.8)	**27.9**	(0.9)	**45.5**	(1.1)	**33.1**	(0.8)	38.0	(1.1)	35.6	(1.1)
	Germany	22.2	(0.8)	24.1	(0.8)	**25.3**	(1.0)	**22.2**	(0.8)	**31.5**	(1.1)	**36.2**	(1.1)
	Greece	**35.0**	(1.3)	**29.7**	(1.0)	**43.0**	(1.4)	**35.0**	(1.3)	**35.3**	(1.3)	**43.2**	(1.2)
	Hungary	**27.7**	(1.1)	**22.5**	(1.1)	28.5	(1.1)	27.7	(1.1)	**29.8**	(1.3)	**34.3**	(1.5)
	Iceland	**30.6**	(0.7)	**20.0**	(0.7)	**40.8**	(0.8)	**30.6**	(0.7)	**36.1**	(0.8)	**33.8**	(0.7)
	Ireland	**32.2**	(0.9)	**25.1**	(0.9)	31.6	(1.2)	32.2	(0.9)	**25.4**	(1.0)	**29.2**	(1.2)
	Italy	36.7	(1.0)	35.5	(1.1)	**41.7**	(1.3)	**36.7**	(1.0)	**38.6**	(1.2)	**48.6**	(1.3)
	Japan	19.1	(0.9)	17.4	(1.2)	16.9	(1.0)	19.1	(0.9)	**13.7**	(0.8)	**9.5**	(0.9)
	Korea	**27.3**	(0.9)	**32.1**	(1.1)	a	a	27.3	(0.9)	18.9	(0.7)	17.5	(0.9)
	Luxembourg	**35.2**	(0.7)	**25.6**	(0.8)	**48.4**	(0.8)	**35.2**	(0.7)	**42.8**	(0.8)	**31.6**	(0.7)
	Mexico	**28.5**	(0.7)	**19.6**	(0.8)	26.8	(0.8)	28.5	(0.7)	26.3	(1.0)	29.0	(1.1)
	Netherlands	**27.2**	(1.0)	**20.8**	(1.1)	**41.6**	(1.3)	**27.2**	(1.0)	36.3	(1.3)	39.0	(1.7)
	New Zealand	**38.4**	(0.7)	**23.6**	(0.9)	**47.4**	(0.9)	**38.4**	(0.7)	**37.1**	(0.9)	**33.5**	(1.0)
	Norway	**34.0**	(0.9)	**27.6**	(1.0)	**41.2**	(1.2)	**34.0**	(0.9)	**35.9**	(1.1)	**42.2**	(1.6)
	Poland	**33.1**	(1.2)	**20.2**	(1.0)	**26.9**	(1.3)	**33.1**	(1.2)	30.4	(1.3)	26.7	(1.4)
	Portugal	**28.1**	(0.8)	**20.6**	(0.7)	**35.1**	(1.1)	**28.1**	(0.8)	**30.2**	(1.0)	**25.2**	(0.9)
	Slovak Republic	39.1	(0.9)	a	a	34.2	(0.9)	39.1	(0.9)	34.1	(0.9)	a	a
	Spain	**29.6**	(1.0)	**25.0**	(0.9)	**35.1**	(1.2)	**29.6**	(1.0)	**35.7**	(1.2)	**40.8**	(1.5)
	Sweden	**25.9**	(0.9)	**29.2**	(0.9)	**35.9**	(1.2)	**25.9**	(0.9)	**32.7**	(1.1)	**43.4**	(1.3)
	Switzerland	**27.6**	(0.9)	**18.4**	(0.8)	**32.7**	(1.1)	**27.6**	(0.9)	**32.4**	(1.0)	**27.7**	(1.1)
	Turkey	23.9	(1.1)	a	a	32.8	(1.1)	23.9	(1.1)	35.5	(1.1)	a	a
	United States	**32.0**	(0.8)	**26.2**	(1.1)	34.0	(0.9)	32.0	(0.8)	26.1	(0.8)	27.5	(1.3)
	OECD total	*29.3*	*(0.3)*	*24.2*	*(0.4)*	*32.7*	*(0.4)*	*29.3*	*(0.3)*	*28.4*	*(0.3)*	*28.8*	*(0.4)*
	OECD average	*30.9*	*(0.2)*	*24.2*	*(0.2)*	*36.5*	*(0.2)*	*30.9*	*(0.2)*	*32.0*	*(0.2)*	*32.9*	*(0.2)*
Partner countries	Brazil	34.6	(1.1)	29.5	(0.9)	**38.0**	(1.1)	34.6	(1.1)	38.2	(1.0)	36.8	(1.4)
	Hong Kong-China	**20.5**	(0.8)	**27.8**	(1.0)	**17.3**	(0.8)	**20.5**	(0.8)	18.9	(0.9)	21.0	(0.8)
	Indonesia	**25.2**	(0.8)	**15.7**	(0.9)	**32.3**	(0.9)	**25.2**	(0.8)	**37.5**	(1.0)	**51.3**	(1.1)
	Latvia	**26.7**	(1.0)	**19.0**	(1.0)	**20.0**	(1.2)	**26.7**	(1.0)	20.4	(1.1)	19.4	(1.1)
	Liechtenstein	**26.2**	(2.5)	**14.9**	(2.0)	27.8	(2.1)	26.2	(2.5)	**33.0**	(2.5)	**25.4**	(1.9)
	Macao-China	18.4	(1.3)	a	a	15.5	(1.1)	18.4	(1.3)	17.5	(1.1)	a	a
	Russian Federation	**21.9**	(0.9)	**16.3**	(0.6)	**16.0**	(0.9)	**21.9**	(0.9)	18.5	(1.0)	19.2	(0.9)
	Serbia	33.4	(0.9)	a	a	32.0	(1.1)	33.4	(0.9)	28.5	(1.2)	a	a
	Thailand	**22.2**	(0.9)	**12.8**	(0.6)	**26.7**	(0.9)	**22.2**	(0.9)	**31.8**	(1.0)	**19.5**	(0.9)
	Tunisia	25.7	(0.7)	a	a	36.7	(1.1)	25.7	(0.7)	36.4	(1.2)	a	a
	Uruguay	32.1	(1.0)	a	a	37.4	(1.3)	32.1	(1.0)	32.0	(1.0)	a	a
	United Kingdom[1]	m	m	m	m	m	m	m	m	m	m	m	m

Percentage of students reporting that the following happens in every or most lessons:

		Students cannot work well				Students don't start working for a long time after the lesson begins			
		PISA 2003		PISA 2000		PISA 2003		PISA 2000	
		%	S.E.	%	S.E.	%	S.E.	%	S.E.
OECD countries	Australia	19.7	(0.7)	18.4	(1.0)	26.7	(0.6)	25.9	(0.9)
	Austria	**26.7**	(1.0)	**20.5**	(0.8)	30.4	(0.9)	30.0	(1.1)
	Belgium	**19.4**	(0.6)	**15.0**	(0.7)	33.1	(0.8)	31.2	(0.9)
	Canada	17.7	(0.4)	16.7	(0.3)	31.0	(0.6)	29.6	(0.5)
	Czech Republic	**24.7**	(0.9)	**17.3**	(0.7)	**24.9**	(1.0)	**21.2**	(0.8)
	Denmark	**19.7**	(0.9)	**17.2**	(0.8)	**26.9**	(0.9)	**22.8**	(1.0)
	Finland	**18.8**	(0.7)	**15.2**	(0.6)	**32.0**	(0.9)	**21.8**	(0.8)
	France	**24.9**	(0.9)	**15.2**	(0.6)	**41.9**	(0.9)	**37.4**	(0.9)
	Germany	25.5	(0.8)	23.7	(0.7)	25.6	(0.9)	27.6	(0.8)
	Greece	**28.7**	(1.2)	**40.1**	(1.0)	**39.3**	(1.1)	**34.8**	(0.8)
	Hungary	**22.3**	(0.8)	**25.7**	(1.1)	18.8	(0.9)	16.7	(0.9)
	Iceland	**25.2**	(0.7)	**16.4**	(0.7)	**26.1**	(0.7)	**20.0**	(0.7)
	Ireland	**19.2**	(0.9)	**16.6**	(0.9)	**21.2**	(0.8)	**25.2**	(0.9)
	Italy	**24.9**	(1.0)	**22.2**	(0.8)	**32.5**	(1.0)	**29.3**	(0.9)
	Japan	**24.8**	(1.0)	**21.4**	(1.1)	15.5	(1.0)	17.9	(1.2)
	Korea	**17.9**	(0.7)	**21.3**	(0.9)	20.9	(0.8)	22.9	(0.9)
	Luxembourg	**39.3**	(0.8)	**22.1**	(0.7)	**35.3**	(0.8)	**27.7**	(0.7)
	Mexico	**24.0**	(0.7)	**17.6**	(0.7)	**34.3**	(1.0)	**19.5**	(0.8)
	Netherlands	19.1	(0.9)	16.6	(1.0)	38.5	(1.1)	36.9	(1.5)
	New Zealand	22.8	(0.7)	22.2	(0.8)	**31.3**	(0.8)	**26.4**	(0.9)
	Norway	**28.3**	(1.0)	**23.3**	(0.9)	36.1	(1.0)	33.5	(1.2)
	Poland	**21.4**	(1.0)	**13.9**	(0.8)	22.3	(0.9)	20.2	(1.1)
	Portugal	**22.4**	(0.9)	**19.9**	(0.8)	27.2	(1.1)	24.9	(0.8)
	Slovak Republic	25.1	(0.7)	a	a	28.4	(0.7)	a	a
	Spain	**23.9**	(1.0)	**18.6**	(0.8)	34.5	(1.1)	35.4	(1.0)
	Sweden	**19.9**	(0.9)	**22.9**	(0.9)	28.4	(1.2)	31.5	(1.1)
	Switzerland	**25.9**	(0.9)	**18.7**	(0.7)	**31.1**	(0.9)	**23.2**	(1.0)
	Turkey	30.9	(1.3)	a	a	31.0	(1.3)	a	a
	United States	18.9	(0.7)	18.5	(1.0)	26.9	(0.8)	25.1	(1.0)
	OECD total	*22.3*	*(0.3)*	*19.3*	*(0.3)*	*27.9*	*(0.3)*	*25.3*	*(0.3)*
	OECD average	*23.5*	*(0.2)*	*19.8*	*(0.1)*	*29.3*	*(0.2)*	*26.5*	*(0.1)*
Partner countries	Brazil	**29.7**	(0.8)	**24.8**	(0.8)	**63.0**	(1.0)	**39.7**	(1.2)
	Hong Kong-China	**19.5**	(0.8)	**29.0**	(0.9)	**19.8**	(0.8)	**34.0**	(0.9)
	Indonesia	**21.6**	(0.7)	**14.3**	(0.8)	**29.6**	(0.8)	**20.5**	(0.9)
	Latvia	18.3	(1.0)	17.0	(0.9)	**20.6**	(1.1)	**16.3**	(1.0)
	Liechtenstein	28.2	(2.4)	21.1	(2.3)	**25.0**	(2.1)	**15.2**	(1.9)
	Macao-China	20.6	(1.5)	a	a	19.7	(1.2)	a	a
	Russian Federation	18.8	(0.8)	17.0	(0.7)	15.1	(0.8)	13.7	(0.8)
	Serbia	27.3	(0.9)	a	a	28.5	(0.9)	a	a
	Thailand	**23.4**	(0.9)	**14.9**	(0.8)	**27.9**	(1.0)	**10.8**	(0.8)
	Tunisia	32.6	(0.9)	a	a	51.6	(1.0)	a	a
	Uruguay	24.0	(1.0)	a	a	31.1	(1.0)	a	a
	United Kingdom[1]	m	m	m	m	m	m	m	m

Note: Values that are statistically significant are indicated in bold (see Annex A4). The scale was inverted so that positive and high values represent a positive student perception of disciplinary climate.
1. Response rate too low to ensure comparability (see Annex A3).

Table 5.4a

Index of principals' perceptions of teacher-related factors affecting school climate and student performance on the mathematics scale, by national quarters of the index

Results based on reports from school principals and reported proportionate to the number of 15-year-olds enrolled in the school

	Index of principals' perceptions of teacher-related factors affecting school climate										Performance on the mathematics scale by national quarters of the index of principals' perceptions of teacher-related factors affecting school climate							
	All students		Bottom quarter		Second quarter		Third quarter		Top quarter		Bottom quarter		Second quarter		Third quarter		Top quarter	
	Mean index	S.E.	Mean index	S.E.	Mean index	S.E.	Mean index	S.E.	Mean index	S.E.	Mean score	S.E.	Mean score	S.E.	Mean score	S.E.	Mean score	S.E.
OECD countries																		
Australia	–0.16	(0.05)	–1.15	(0.04)	–0.45	(0.01)	–0.02	(0.01)	0.99	(0.08)	**502**	(4.6)	516	(5.6)	533	(5.2)	**547**	(5.2)
Austria	0.24	(0.07)	–0.88	(0.05)	–0.09	(0.03)	0.51	(0.02)	1.41	(0.09)	508	(8.8)	502	(9.2)	507	(8.0)	503	(8.9)
Belgium	0.30	(0.05)	–0.80	(0.04)	–0.02	(0.02)	0.51	(0.02)	1.50	(0.07)	**512**	(9.0)	523	(8.7)	538	(7.7)	**545**	(7.7)
Canada	0.03	(0.05)	–0.98	(0.03)	–0.25	(0.01)	0.19	(0.01)	1.15	(0.05)	**524**	(3.4)	531	(3.6)	533	(4.0)	**541**	(3.5)
Czech Republic	0.19	(0.04)	–0.68	(0.04)	–0.07	(0.01)	0.32	(0.02)	1.20	(0.06)	519	(6.5)	515	(7.6)	527	(9.6)	502	(8.1)
Denmark	0.42	(0.06)	–0.53	(0.07)	0.05	(0.02)	0.58	(0.03)	1.60	(0.08)	**508**	(5.1)	511	(6.7)	518	(4.1)	**522**	(4.8)
Finland	0.08	(0.05)	–0.80	(0.06)	–0.12	(0.02)	0.30	(0.02)	0.95	(0.06)	541	(3.5)	544	(3.8)	548	(3.6)	544	(3.8)
France	w	w	w	w	w	w	w	w	w	w	w	w	w	w	w	w	w	w
Germany	–0.03	(0.06)	–0.84	(0.04)	–0.25	(0.02)	0.13	(0.01)	0.84	(0.06)	495	(8.6)	507	(10.0)	527	(10.2)	484	(9.3)
Greece	–0.32	(0.21)	–2.74	(0.17)	–0.78	(0.09)	0.47	(0.04)	1.77	(0.12)	441	(11.1)	432	(12.3)	447	(8.0)	459	(11.1)
Hungary	0.39	(0.09)	–0.94	(0.11)	0.19	(0.03)	0.69	(0.02)	1.62	(0.08)	485	(10.0)	509	(8.9)	479	(9.0)	489	(9.7)
Iceland	0.34	(0.00)	–0.67	(0.01)	0.07	(0.00)	0.56	(0.01)	1.40	(0.01)	511	(3.6)	523	(3.8)	513	(3.2)	514	(3.8)
Ireland	–0.15	(0.08)	–1.19	(0.07)	–0.47	(0.02)	0.11	(0.03)	0.94	(0.11)	**488**	(6.6)	502	(6.2)	515	(5.2)	**509**	(6.7)
Italy	0.05	(0.07)	–1.21	(0.09)	–0.30	(0.02)	0.30	(0.03)	1.43	(0.09)	469	(6.3)	467	(8.0)	472	(8.8)	458	(9.7)
Japan	–0.21	(0.07)	–1.27	(0.04)	–0.51	(0.02)	–0.03	(0.02)	0.99	(0.13)	**491**	(8.5)	521	(10.4)	536	(11.6)	**588**	(8.2)
Korea	0.36	(0.10)	–1.12	(0.10)	0.07	(0.03)	0.65	(0.02)	1.85	(0.08)	533	(9.1)	529	(9.2)	550	(6.8)	557	(8.8)
Luxembourg	–0.32	(0.00)	–1.02	(0.00)	–0.52	(0.00)	–0.25	(0.00)	0.51	(0.01)	**499**	(3.0)	509	(2.9)	487	(3.6)	**478**	(2.2)
Mexico	–0.27	(0.09)	–1.82	(0.06)	–0.76	(0.04)	0.08	(0.03)	1.42	(0.09)	378	(6.0)	380	(5.2)	391	(7.2)	394	(9.2)
Netherlands	–0.69	(0.06)	–1.52	(0.07)	–0.93	(0.02)	–0.51	(0.02)	0.20	(0.07)	512	(10.7)	547	(10.1)	552	(10.2)	535	(12.0)
New Zealand	–0.16	(0.05)	–1.15	(0.05)	–0.41	(0.02)	0.08	(0.02)	0.83	(0.07)	**500**	(6.5)	525	(5.1)	532	(5.7)	**541**	(5.5)
Norway	–0.34	(0.06)	–1.15	(0.06)	–0.60	(0.01)	–0.17	(0.02)	0.55	(0.06)	498	(4.6)	492	(3.8)	493	(4.7)	494	(5.5)
Poland	0.38	(0.08)	–0.72	(0.08)	0.09	(0.02)	0.57	(0.02)	1.60	(0.08)	490	(5.6)	496	(5.0)	494	(5.8)	480	(5.8)
Portugal	–0.36	(0.06)	–1.24	(0.04)	–0.60	(0.02)	–0.19	(0.02)	0.60	(0.06)	464	(7.2)	456	(8.3)	470	(7.9)	474	(7.1)
Slovak Republic	0.51	(0.05)	–0.56	(0.06)	0.28	(0.02)	0.74	(0.02)	1.59	(0.06)	496	(8.4)	513	(7.6)	487	(6.5)	497	(10.4)
Spain	0.29	(0.08)	–0.93	(0.04)	–0.14	(0.03)	0.55	(0.03)	1.69	(0.09)	478	(7.4)	487	(5.9)	482	(4.0)	494	(6.1)
Sweden	0.13	(0.06)	–0.83	(0.07)	–0.16	(0.02)	0.33	(0.01)	1.16	(0.10)	505	(5.0)	502	(4.8)	516	(6.7)	514	(4.4)
Switzerland	0.39	(0.05)	–0.54	(0.06)	0.07	(0.01)	0.57	(0.03)	1.48	(0.09)	**543**	(6.7)	532	(7.5)	521	(6.7)	**509**	(8.7)
Turkey	–0.84	(0.13)	–2.43	(0.13)	–1.39	(0.05)	–0.43	(0.04)	0.90	(0.16)	424	(13.2)	414	(9.8)	426	(14.3)	430	(20.4)
United States	–0.03	(0.06)	–1.03	(0.04)	–0.31	(0.02)	0.18	(0.02)	1.02	(0.07)	**470**	(6.5)	487	(6.4)	483	(8.5)	**501**	(6.1)
OECD total	*–0.07*	*(0.02)*	*–1.28*	*(0.02)*	*–0.37*	*(0.01)*	*0.16*	*(0.01)*	*1.20*	*(0.03)*	*463*	*(3.0)*	*492*	*(2.8)*	*499*	*(2.8)*	*500*	*(2.8)*
OECD average	*0.00*	*(0.01)*	*–1.21*	*(0.02)*	*–0.31*	*(0.00)*	*0.26*	*(0.01)*	*1.26*	*(0.02)*	*483*	*(1.7)*	*502*	*(1.6)*	*510*	*(1.4)*	*505*	*(1.7)*
Partner countries																		
Brazil	0.18	(0.10)	–1.59	(0.07)	–0.17	(0.04)	0.62	(0.04)	1.86	(0.08)	348	(10.3)	353	(10.7)	367	(13.6)	361	(10.8)
Hong Kong-China	–0.35	(0.10)	–2.28	(0.14)	–0.54	(0.06)	0.29	(0.02)	1.12	(0.08)	546	(9.3)	539	(11.8)	545	(12.7)	568	(9.4)
Indonesia	–2.11	(0.11)	–3.84	(0.05)	–2.75	(0.02)	–1.98	(0.04)	0.12	(0.13)	369	(9.0)	357	(6.2)	350	(8.5)	364	(8.0)
Latvia	0.27	(0.08)	–0.82	(0.09)	–0.03	(0.02)	0.46	(0.02)	1.46	(0.09)	480	(6.2)	483	(7.3)	485	(7.4)	486	(8.4)
Liechtenstein	c	c	c	c	c	c	c	c	c	c	c	c	c	c	c	c	c	c
Macao-China	–0.88	(0.01)	–2.41	(0.01)	–1.69	(0.01)	–0.53	(0.01)	1.11	(0.01)	525	(6.5)	529	(9.0)	524	(4.8)	532	(3.8)
Russian Federation	–0.67	(0.09)	–2.18	(0.05)	–1.11	(0.04)	–0.24	(0.03)	0.87	(0.11)	**458**	(8.0)	452	(7.9)	478	(6.8)	**485**	(9.4)
Serbia	–0.26	(0.08)	–1.44	(0.05)	–0.67	(0.03)	0.08	(0.03)	0.98	(0.09)	429	(7.2)	441	(10.4)	426	(6.1)	451	(8.8)
Thailand	0.01	(0.09)	–1.07	(0.06)	–0.34	(0.02)	0.20	(0.02)	1.25	(0.11)	**405**	(6.1)	412	(5.3)	422	(6.9)	**429**	(8.8)
Tunisia	–1.36	(0.08)	–2.53	(0.06)	–1.78	(0.03)	–1.07	(0.03)	–0.04	(0.08)	363	(7.9)	364	(7.6)	353	(7.1)	356	(8.2)
Uruguay	–0.47	(0.10)	–1.91	(0.08)	–0.98	(0.04)	–0.09	(0.03)	1.09	(0.08)	427	(9.4)	412	(10.5)	413	(8.3)	436	(7.7)
United Kingdom[1]	–0.20	(0.06)	–1.24	(0.04)	–0.53	(0.02)	0.03	(0.02)	0.94	(0.10)	**488**	(5.5)	496	(5.6)	517	(5.6)	**535**	(6.9)

	Change in the mathematics score per unit of the index of principals' perceptions of teacher-related factors affecting school climate		Increased likelihood of students in the bottom quarter of this index scoring in the bottom quarter of the national mathematics performance distribution		Explained variance in student performance (r-squared × 100)	
	Effect	S.E.	Ratio	S.E.	Percentage	S.E.
OECD countries						
Australia	**19.1**	(2.94)	**1.5**	(0.12)	2.9	(0.90)
Austria	–0.8	(4.72)	1.0	(0.14)	0.0	(0.16)
Belgium	**14.6**	(4.91)	1.3	(0.19)	1.5	(1.05)
Canada	**8.3**	(1.97)	**1.2**	(0.08)	0.7	(0.32)
Czech Republic	–8.2	(5.53)	0.9	(0.13)	0.4	(0.70)
Denmark	5.1	(3.41)	1.2	(0.11)	0.2	(0.33)
Finland	1.7	(3.10)	1.1	(0.07)	0.0	(0.09)
France	w	w	w	w	w	w
Germany	–3.4	(8.81)	1.1	(0.17)	0.1	(0.40)
Greece	4.7	(3.79)	1.1	(0.21)	0.8	(1.27)
Hungary	–3.6	(5.95)	1.1	(0.20)	0.2	(0.59)
Iceland	2.4	(1.88)	1.1	(0.08)	0.1	(0.08)
Ireland	**10.3**	(4.23)	**1.4**	(0.17)	1.1	(0.94)
Italy	–6.1	(4.98)	0.9	(0.14)	0.4	(0.78)
Japan	**39.5**	(4.47)	**1.9**	(0.25)	13.3	(2.72)
Korea	**9.8**	(4.83)	1.1	(0.21)	1.5	(1.42)
Luxembourg	**–6.3**	(1.57)	0.9	(0.06)	0.2	(0.10)
Mexico	**6.8**	(3.32)	1.0	(0.12)	1.0	(0.92)
Netherlands	16.4	(9.35)	**1.6**	(0.32)	1.6	(1.86)
New Zealand	**19.7**	(3.78)	**1.6**	(0.17)	2.6	(0.98)
Norway	–1.3	(3.84)	0.9	(0.08)	0.0	(0.09)
Poland	–3.0	(3.92)	1.0	(0.09)	0.1	(0.26)
Portugal	5.8	(5.36)	1.1	(0.17)	0.2	(0.44)
Slovak Republic	–5.0	(4.97)	1.0	(0.15)	0.2	(0.45)
Spain	5.2	(3.40)	1.2	(0.14)	0.4	(0.51)
Sweden	4.6	(3.55)	1.1	(0.11)	0.2	(0.26)
Switzerland	**–17.2**	(4.38)	**0.8**	(0.09)	2.0	(1.09)
Turkey	4.3	(7.39)	1.0	(0.19)	0.3	(1.20)
United States	**15.5**	(3.94)	**1.3**	(0.15)	1.8	(0.90)
OECD total	*14.7*	*(1.67)*	*1.5*	*(0.07)*	*3.6*	*(0.53)*
OECD average	*9.5*	*(1.03)*	*1.4*	*(0.04)*	*0.9*	*(0.19)*
Partner countries						
Brazil	5.6	(4.78)	1.1	(0.19)	0.6	(1.04)
Hong Kong-China	4.7	(3.88)	1.1	(0.20)	0.4	(0.73)
Indonesia	–1.0	(2.50)	0.9	(0.13)	0.0	(0.20)
Latvia	3.6	(3.76)	1.0	(0.11)	0.1	(0.27)
Liechtenstein	c	c	c	c	c	c
Macao-China	3.0	(1.70)	1.0	(0.13)	0.2	(0.28)
Russian Federation	**10.5**	(3.56)	**1.3**	(0.14)	1.9	(1.28)
Serbia	5.9	(4.37)	1.2	(0.17)	0.5	(0.68)
Thailand	7.0	(4.23)	1.2	(0.13)	0.6	(0.84)
Tunisia	–3.4	(4.72)	1.0	(0.14)	0.2	(0.48)
Uruguay	4.0	(3.56)	0.9	(0.17)	0.2	(0.41)
United Kingdom[1]	**20.3**	(4.28)	**1.4**	(0.13)	3.7	(1.52)

Note: Values that are statistically significant are indicated in bold (see Annex A4). The scale was inverted so that positive and high values represent a positive student perception of disciplinary climate.
1. Response rate too low to ensure comparability (see Annex A3).

Table 5.4b
Teacher-related factors affecting school climate in PISA 2003 and PISA 2000

Results based on reports from school principals and reported proportionate to the number of 15-year-olds enrolled in the school

		Percentage of students in schools where the principals report that the following hinders students' learning to some extent or a lot															
		Teachers' low expectations of students				Poor student-teacher relations				Teachers not meeting individual students' needs				Teacher absenteeism			
		PISA 2003		PISA 2000		PISA 2003		PISA 2000		PISA 2003		PISA 2000		PISA 2003		PISA 2000	
		%	S.E.	%	S.E.	%	S.E.	%	S.E.	%	S.E.	%	S.E.	%	S.E.	%	S.E.
OECD countries	Australia	31.4	(2.8)	27.0	(3.7)	14.6	(1.9)	10.0	(2.2)	48.1	(3.3)	45.1	4.0	**15.8**	(2.2)	**8.0**	(2.4)
	Austria	15.7	(3.5)	11.9	(2.3)	9.4	(2.3)	5.6	(1.6)	21.4	(2.9)	18.9	2.9	14.0	(2.9)	9.7	(2.3)
	Belgium	8.2	(1.6)	10.0	(1.9)	9.0	(1.7)	13.2	(2.2)	21.8	(3.0)	26.8	2.8	22.3	(2.6)	24.4	(3.2)
	Canada	10.8	(1.6)	10.0	(1.1)	**12.2**	(1.6)	**7.9**	(0.9)	**32.8**	(2.5)	**22.6**	1.5	8.0	(1.4)	6.3	(0.7)
	Czech Republic	**8.8**	(1.9)	**3.9**	(1.3)	**7.0**	(1.3)	**3.3**	(1.1)	**13.1**	(2.1)	**5.6**	1.5	**22.7**	(2.5)	**6.8**	(1.7)
	Denmark	9.1	(2.0)	4.2	(1.9)	**4.9**	(1.7)	**0.7**	(0.5)	**18.9**	(2.7)	**7.7**	2.1	**14.0**	(2.6)	**5.3**	(1.7)
	Finland	6.7	(1.8)	11.1	(2.7)	14.0	(2.6)	11.3	(2.3)	34.6	(3.5)	34.1	4.2	20.4	(3.2)	16.6	(3.1)
	France	w	w	w	w	w	w	w	w	w	w	w	w	w	w	w	w
	Germany	9.5	(2.1)	15.1	(2.6)	13.9	(2.6)	11.1	(2.3)	31.1	(3.4)	29.0	3.6	23.2	(3.3)	25.9	(3.4)
	Greece	45.2	(5.1)	47.5	(4.7)	**40.8**	(5.6)	**62.3**	(4.3)	**43.0**	(6.0)	**66.9**	4.1	**39.9**	(5.6)	**67.2**	(4.0)
	Hungary	9.1	(2.6)	10.4	(2.3)	16.5	(3.4)	12.0	(3.0)	23.0	(3.6)	19.3	3.1	21.4	(3.5)	17.2	(2.8)
	Iceland	**14.4**	(0.1)	**15.9**	(0.1)	**8.2**	(0.1)	**9.8**	(0.1)	**39.5**	(0.2)	**27.2**	0.1	**32.2**	(0.2)	**14.5**	(0.1)
	Ireland	29.5	(4.0)	31.4	(3.9)	15.5	(3.5)	13.1	(2.8)	**47.4**	(4.8)	**31.4**	4.0	29.8	(4.0)	27.0	(3.7)
	Italy	**12.4**	(2.3)	**20.0**	(3.0)	34.3	(3.2)	26.9	(3.7)	27.9	(3.3)	22.8	3.6	10.4	(2.3)	12.0	(2.5)
	Japan	31.7	(3.6)	22.5	(3.5)	23.4	(3.4)	14.8	(3.0)	**33.9**	(4.1)	**20.4**	3.7	3.7	(1.6)	4.1	(1.8)
	Korea	31.9	(4.0)	27.2	(4.2)	14.1	(3.2)	8.4	(2.4)	28.0	(3.2)	26.4	4.3	10.9	(2.9)	4.6	(1.9)
	Luxembourg	**8.8**	(0.0)	**8.8**	(0.0)	**28.9**	(0.1)	**21.6**	(0.2)	**56.2**	(0.1)	**49.7**	0.0	**5.0**	(0.0)	**14.5**	(0.2)
	Mexico	40.7	(3.6)	39.8	(4.4)	23.7	(2.9)	16.6	(3.2)	35.2	(3.1)	28.9	3.8	26.6	(3.1)	32.1	(3.7)
	Netherlands	38.9	(4.8)	28.4	(4.1)	20.1	(3.5)	13.4	(3.5)	55.9	(4.8)	50.6	5.5	45.6	(3.9)	45.4	(5.4)
	New Zealand	**39.7**	(3.2)	**28.8**	(3.2)	**17.6**	(2.9)	**7.1**	(2.1)	**46.1**	(3.4)	**35.2**	3.5	**7.9**	(1.8)	**3.5**	(1.2)
	Norway	20.4	(3.3)	14.5	(3.2)	22.3	(3.4)	21.5	(3.4)	71.5	(3.9)	66.3	4.0	24.5	(3.5)	20.0	(3.4)
	Poland	12.1	(2.7)	15.7	(3.7)	10.3	(2.5)	4.7	(2.3)	18.9	(3.1)	23.0	4.4	10.3	(2.5)	11.7	(3.6)
	Portugal	**44.5**	(4.6)	**28.6**	(3.8)	15.9	(3.0)	14.5	(3.3)	44.6	(4.5)	48.2	3.8	29.5	(4.1)	25.7	(4.2)
	Slovak Republic	17.0	(2.8)	a	a	6.9	(2.1)	a	a	10.2	(1.8)	a	a	18.8	(2.9)	a	a
	Spain	21.1	(3.0)	16.5	(2.6)	9.7	(2.4)	7.4	(2.1)	**20.6**	(3.3)	**30.6**	3.6	12.8	(2.6)	8.1	(2.2)
	Sweden	11.5	(2.6)	7.0	(2.1)	10.9	(2.2)	10.4	(2.7)	32.6	(3.4)	38.3	4.4	15.7	(2.8)	21.2	(3.2)
	Switzerland	7.8	(1.8)	7.5	(2.2)	10.8	(2.0)	11.6	(2.2)	20.5	(2.8)	21.7	3.1	4.8	(1.4)	3.9	(1.5)
	Turkey	60.8	(4.7)	a	a	58.1	(4.8)	a	a	46.3	(4.1)	a	a	37.4	(3.9)	a	a
	United States	24.3	(3.3)	18.9	(4.3)	14.1	(2.5)	9.8	(3.2)	32.1	(3.0)	24.5	4.0	13.3	(2.3)	13.1	(3.5)
	OECD total	*25.1*	*(0.9)*	*21.2*	*(1.3)*	*17.5*	*(1.0)*	*12.5*	*(0.9)*	*31.0*	*(1.0)*	*28.4*	*1.1*	*16.1*	*(0.8)*	*14.7*	*(1.0)*
	OECD average	*22.1*	*(0.5)*	*18.7*	*(0.5)*	*16.7*	*(0.6)*	*13.2*	*(0.5)*	*33.3*	*(0.6)*	*32.2*	*0.7*	*18.9*	*(0.6)*	*16.9*	*(0.5)*
Partner countries	Brazil	27.5	(3.3)	19.3	(3.2)	**19.0**	(3.2)	**7.4**	(1.9)	26.9	(3.5)	20.4	2.9	27.0	(3.5)	25.7	(3.2)
	Hong Kong-China	**43.4**	(3.9)	**28.7**	(3.9)	23.7	(3.2)	16.0	(3.1)	**43.7**	(3.8)	**30.3**	3.7	**21.0**	(3.5)	**8.9**	(2.6)
	Indonesia	**75.1**	(2.8)	**24.0**	(3.9)	**73.3**	(3.9)	**24.1**	(5.3)	**75.6**	(3.2)	**35.8**	4.1	**78.4**	(3.1)	**32.1**	(4.1)
	Latvia	12.7	(2.7)	8.5	(2.5)	15.3	(3.5)	7.5	(2.6)	24.5	(4.0)	16.3	3.2	6.8	(1.7)	3.7	(1.7)
	Liechtenstein	c	c	c	c	c	c	c	c	c	c	c	c	c	c	c	c
	Macao-China	59.2	(0.3)	a	a	44.1	(0.3)	a	a	60.3	(0.2)	a	a	37.4	(0.3)	a	a
	Russian Federation	52.3	(4.4)	50.5	(3.9)	44.9	(3.9)	40.9	(4.3)	39.8	(3.5)	49.6	3.6	51.2	(4.2)	43.8	(3.9)
	Serbia	32.9	(4.0)	a	a	20.6	(3.7)	a	a	45.1	(4.0)	a	a	20.3	(3.7)	a	a
	Thailand	38.0	(4.0)	33.8	(4.2)	13.0	(2.7)	16.3	(2.9)	36.5	(4.0)	47.7	4.3	11.8	(2.9)	13.8	(2.4)
	Tunisia	83.9	(3.1)	a	a	66.2	(4.0)	a	a	74.6	(3.7)	a	a	73.7	(3.4)	a	a
	Uruguay	49.7	(4.3)	a	a	21.8	(3.6)	a	a	33.5	(4.2)	a	a	64.1	(3.2)	a	a
	United Kingdom[1]	m	m	m	m	m	m	m	m	m	m	m	m	m	m	m	m

		Percentage of students in schools where the principals report that the following hinders students learning to some extent or a lot											
		Staff resisting change				Teachers being too strict with students				Students not being encouraged to achieve their full potential			
		PISA 2003		PISA 2000		PISA 2003		PISA 2000		PISA 2003		PISA 2000	
		%	S.E.	%	S.E.	%	S.E.	%	S.E.	%	S.E.	%	S.E.
OECD countries	Australia	34.1	(3.0)	37.8	(3.7)	**7.5**	(1.6)	**2.1**	(1.0)	18.6	(2.3)	25.2	(3.5)
	Austria	16.5	(2.9)	14.9	(2.4)	7.2	(2.0)	6.6	(2.1)	22.0	(3.6)	19.3	(3.4)
	Belgium	26.6	(2.6)	32.8	(2.4)	3.1	(1.2)	5.2	(1.6)	15.0	(2.3)	20.5	(2.8)
	Canada	32.8	(2.2)	30.7	(1.9)	**8.4**	(1.4)	**4.2**	(0.8)	15.9	(1.8)	14.3	(1.3)
	Czech Republic	10.2	(2.2)	7.5	(2.1)	**9.9**	(2.0)	**4.2**	(1.4)	20.3	(2.7)	18.8	(2.8)
	Denmark	16.1	(2.8)	9.4	(2.2)	2.6	(1.1)	0.5	(0.5)	6.9	(2.0)	4.9	(1.6)
	Finland	13.4	(2.4)	18.5	(3.5)	5.8	(1.7)	a	a	16.3	(3.2)	19.9	(3.1)
	France	w	w	w	w	w	w	w	w	w	w	w	w
	Germany	24.6	(3.2)	22.4	(2.7)	2.9	(1.2)	4.9	(1.6)	23.0	(3.3)	19.0	(3.1)
	Greece	**31.5**	(4.9)	**48.0**	(4.4)	**23.4**	(5.1)	**42.5**	(4.6)	**29.1**	(5.4)	**60.8**	(4.7)
	Hungary	**4.5**	(1.2)	**10.8**	(2.5)	12.0	(2.8)	16.2	(2.9)	**22.6**	(3.8)	**36.6**	(3.9)
	Iceland	**12.9**	(0.1)	**19.8**	(0.1)	**1.3**	(0.1)	**0.6**	(0.0)	**11.3**	(0.1)	**12.8**	(0.1)
	Ireland	27.8	(3.9)	19.3	(3.4)	8.7	(2.5)	10.8	(3.0)	21.0	(3.8)	15.9	(3.0)
	Italy	36.7	(3.5)	41.9	(3.6)	13.3	(2.5)	14.1	(2.9)	24.7	(3.3)	31.7	(4.0)
	Japan	**41.5**	(4.4)	**19.4**	(3.4)	**20.6**	(3.6)	**3.5**	(1.8)	37.1	(3.9)	30.2	(4.0)
	Korea	**17.3**	(3.2)	**7.5**	(2.5)	**7.7**	(2.3)	**1.3**	(0.9)	27.0	(4.0)	17.5	(3.5)
	Luxembourg	**18.9**	(0.1)	**26.9**	(0.2)	**13.8**	(0.0)	**6.9**	(0.0)	**36.8**	(0.1)	**57.5**	(0.2)
	Mexico	40.4	(3.4)	47.0	(3.9)	27.4	(3.1)	18.7	(3.1)	45.7	(3.6)	54.1	(4.0)
	Netherlands	60.1	(4.6)	57.3	(5.6)	**18.2**	(3.6)	**8.1**	(3.1)	40.4	(4.3)	34.4	(5.3)
	New Zealand	23.4	(3.3)	23.9	(3.1)	6.2	(1.8)	4.6	(1.6)	23.8	(2.8)	21.4	(2.9)
	Norway	35.1	(3.6)	27.7	(3.7)	3.5	(1.5)	1.4	(1.0)	23.7	(3.5)	17.2	(3.1)
	Poland	10.0	(2.4)	18.1	(4.2)	4.9	(1.7)	12.0	(3.4)	**18.5**	(3.4)	**33.1**	(4.3)
	Portugal	43.6	(4.7)	43.7	(4.6)	2.0	(1.2)	2.1	(1.2)	35.0	(4.3)	30.6	(4.0)
	Slovak Republic	7.5	(1.6)	a	a	5.8	(1.2)	a	a	12.1	(2.2)	a	a
	Spain	26.6	(3.4)	29.6	(3.5)	6.9	(2.1)	4.1	(1.4)	21.1	(2.6)	26.8	(3.0)
	Sweden	31.4	(3.4)	37.9	(3.6)	2.2	(1.1)	0.6	(0.9)	**16.0**	(3.0)	**28.5**	(4.1)
	Switzerland	22.6	(3.1)	22.5	(3.4)	2.8	(1.0)	1.2	(0.6)	11.5	(2.1)	14.5	(2.5)
	Turkey	46.4	(4.7)	a	a	34.3	(4.5)	a	a	62.5	(4.7)	a	a
	United States	34.0	(3.4)	23.9	(5.3)	5.0	(1.5)	1.7	(1.0)	13.5	(2.5)	15.5	(3.8)
	OECD total	*29.7*	*(1.1)*	*27.1*	*(1.6)*	*10.5*	*(0.7)*	*6.4*	*(0.5)*	*24.2*	*(1.0)*	*26.1*	*(1.3)*
	OECD average	*25.7*	*(0.5)*	*27.0*	*(0.7)*	*9.1*	*(0.4)*	*6.8*	*(0.4)*	*23.2*	*(0.6)*	*26.1*	*(0.6)*
Partner countries	Brazil	24.1	(3.2)	16.8	(2.7)	12.8	(2.6)	7.2	(2.0)	27.8	(3.4)	28.9	(3.3)
	Hong Kong-China	**31.1**	(3.5)	**15.8**	(3.1)	**19.6**	(3.4)	**5.1**	(1.7)	**39.9**	(3.5)	**22.9**	(3.6)
	Indonesia	**61.0**	(3.6)	**16.6**	(3.8)	**71.8**	(3.6)	**23.7**	(4.2)	**74.2**	(3.0)	**29.6**	(4.4)
	Latvia	**12.2**	(2.9)	**5.2**	(1.9)	6.5	(2.2)	5.5	(2.0)	**24.1**	(4.0)	**9.2**	(2.7)
	Liechtenstein	c	c	c	c	c	c	c	c	c	c	c	c
	Macao-China	47.9	(0.3)	a	a	45.1	(0.2)	a	a	56.0	(0.3)	a	a
	Russian Federation	38.5	(3.7)	30.0	(4.1)	55.5	(3.4)	55.2	(3.8)	41.6	(3.7)	47.1	(3.4)
	Serbia	41.3	(4.0)	a	a	20.5	(3.7)	a	a	44.5	(4.4)	a	a
	Thailand	9.8	(2.3)	8.6	(2.2)	25.8	(3.8)	25.2	(3.6)	17.1	(3.1)	22.1	(3.2)
	Tunisia	45.5	(4.0)	a	a	45.1	(4.4)	a	a	59.7	(3.6)	a	a
	Uruguay	40.8	(3.8)	a	a	20.6	(4.0)	a	a	46.8	(4.8)	a	a
	United Kingdom[1]	m	m	m	m	m	m	m	m	m	m	m	m

Note: Values that are statistically significant are indicated in bold (see Annex A4).
1. Response rate too low to ensure comparability (see Annex A3).

Table 5.5a

Index of principals' perceptions of teachers' morale and commitment and student performance on the mathematics scale, by national quarters of the index

Results based on reports from school principals and reported proportionate to the number of 15-year-olds enrolled in the school

		Index of school principals' perceptions of teachers' morale and commitment										Performance on the mathematics scale by national quarters of the index of school principals' perceptions of teachers' morale and commitment							
		All students		Bottom quarter		Second quarter		Third quarter		Top quarter		Bottom quarter		Second quarter		Third quarter		Top quarter	
		Mean index	S.E.	Mean index	S.E.	Mean index	S.E.	Mean index	S.E.	Mean index	S.E.	Mean score	S.E.	Mean score	S.E.	Mean score	S.E.	Mean score	S.E.
OECD countries	Australia	0.18	(0.06)	–0.89	(0.06)	–0.38	(0.03)	0.49	(0.02)	1.51	(0.03)	**510**	(5.2)	514	(4.71)	529	(5.08)	**545**	(4.6)
	Austria	0.49	(0.07)	–0.74	(0.06)	0.16	(0.04)	0.90	(0.02)	1.63	(0.01)	513	(9.0)	499	(7.82)	508	(8.97)	500	(9.3)
	Belgium	–0.39	(0.05)	–1.43	(0.04)	–0.58	(0.00)	–0.32	(0.03)	0.77	(0.06)	**488**	(8.7)	521	(5.97)	543	(4.73)	**566**	(5.9)
	Canada	0.13	(0.05)	–0.99	(0.05)	–0.42	(0.02)	0.49	(0.02)	1.44	(0.03)	526	(3.6)	528	(3.18)	540	(3.14)	537	(4.3)
	Czech Republic	–0.17	(0.05)	–1.06	(0.05)	–0.57	(0.00)	0.24	(0.00)	0.72	(0.05)	521	(6.9)	514	(8.03)	517	(8.18)	512	(8.9)
	Denmark	0.31	(0.06)	–0.64	(0.04)	–0.17	(0.05)	0.67	(0.02)	1.38	(0.04)	514	(4.8)	510	(5.39)	513	(4.49)	522	(4.6)
	Finland	0.30	(0.06)	–0.79	(0.06)	0.10	(0.03)	0.57	(0.01)	1.33	(0.05)	541	(3.3)	542	(3.62)	544	(3.08)	550	(3.9)
	France	w	w	w	w	w	w	w	w	w	w	w	w	w	w	w	w	w	w
	Germany	0.04	(0.06)	–1.07	(0.07)	–0.37	(0.04)	0.41	(0.03)	1.18	(0.05)	488	(9.0)	504	(8.21)	517	(9.28)	504	(9.7)
	Greece	0.09	(0.12)	–1.47	(0.07)	–0.26	(0.06)	0.65	(0.02)	1.45	(0.06)	**424**	(7.4)	423	(9.67)	466	(6.96)	**466**	(9.3)
	Hungary	0.10	(0.08)	–1.04	(0.07)	–0.18	(0.05)	0.50	(0.02)	1.14	(0.05)	477	(9.4)	493	(5.77)	495	(6.92)	500	(9.4)
	Iceland	0.62	(0.00)	–0.64	(0.01)	0.45	(0.00)	1.04	(0.01)	1.65	(0.00)	**510**	(3.6)	511	(4.03)	520	(3.09)	**521**	(3.6)
	Ireland	0.25	(0.09)	–0.98	(0.07)	–0.31	(0.04)	0.65	(0.04)	1.65	(0.00)	494	(6.4)	503	(5.28)	514	(5.49)	504	(4.6)
	Italy	–0.61	(0.05)	–1.84	(0.04)	–0.64	(0.01)	–0.51	(0.01)	0.54	(0.06)	472	(6.3)	456	(6.59)	459	(6.45)	478	(9.5)
	Japan	–0.39	(0.09)	–1.79	(0.07)	–0.78	(0.04)	–0.15	(0.06)	1.17	(0.06)	**489**	(8.6)	517	(7.98)	539	(9.10)	**592**	(8.5)
	Korea	–0.42	(0.08)	–1.80	(0.07)	–0.62	(0.01)	–0.26	(0.06)	0.99	(0.07)	**511**	(9.4)	540	(6.43)	545	(6.84)	**573**	(8.7)
	Luxembourg	–0.39	(0.00)	–1.11	(0.01)	–0.57	(0.00)	–0.41	(0.01)	0.54	(0.00)	**489**	(3.1)	493	(4.01)	490	(3.31)	**500**	(2.3)
	Mexico	–0.02	(0.07)	–1.47	(0.09)	–0.57	(0.00)	0.45	(0.03)	1.51	(0.03)	378	(6.8)	376	(5.87)	386	(8.11)	398	(8.9)
	Netherlands	–0.18	(0.06)	–0.81	(0.07)	–0.57	(0.00)	–0.18	(0.05)	0.82	(0.08)	**521**	(8.4)	531	(6.72)	544	(8.52)	**552**	(10.3)
	New Zealand	0.17	(0.07)	–0.89	(0.08)	–0.25	(0.04)	0.45	(0.02)	1.37	(0.04)	**515**	(5.4)	522	(4.45)	527	(5.03)	**533**	(6.6)
	Norway	0.05	(0.07)	–0.95	(0.07)	–0.49	(0.02)	0.35	(0.02)	1.31	(0.05)	495	(5.0)	495	(4.59)	496	(3.79)	491	(5.9)
	Poland	0.08	(0.07)	–1.05	(0.07)	–0.21	(0.04)	0.47	(0.02)	1.10	(0.05)	483	(4.5)	493	(4.17)	495	(5.37)	489	(5.9)
	Portugal	–0.42	(0.08)	–1.54	(0.05)	–0.58	(0.00)	–0.22	(0.05)	0.66	(0.05)	470	(6.8)	458	(8.56)	460	(6.15)	475	(6.5)
	Slovak Republic	–0.17	(0.06)	–1.19	(0.04)	–0.57	(0.00)	0.08	(0.03)	0.99	(0.06)	492	(6.4)	498	(6.76)	509	(6.38)	494	(9.4)
	Spain	–0.35	(0.06)	–1.42	(0.06)	–0.57	(0.00)	–0.22	(0.04)	0.81	(0.06)	**467**	(7.1)	482	(4.86)	493	(3.61)	**500**	(6.5)
	Sweden	0.49	(0.06)	–0.59	(0.04)	0.29	(0.01)	0.78	(0.02)	1.50	(0.03)	507	(4.6)	500	(4.62)	510	(5.13)	519	(5.3)
	Switzerland	0.21	(0.07)	–0.92	(0.05)	–0.20	(0.05)	0.64	(0.02)	1.31	(0.05)	529	(7.2)	530	(5.95)	519	(10.16)	528	(7.5)
	Turkey	–0.37	(0.11)	–1.97	(0.09)	–0.74	(0.04)	–0.02	(0.06)	1.24	(0.07)	399	(7.9)	428	(9.74)	434	(14.44)	433	(17.6)
	United States	0.23	(0.07)	–1.05	(0.08)	–0.22	(0.04)	0.65	(0.02)	1.55	(0.02)	475	(6.0)	482	(5.87)	484	(8.03)	**498**	(6.6)
	OECD total	*–0.03*	*(0.02)*	*–1.32*	*(0.02)*	*–0.55*	*(0.00)*	*0.41*	*(0.01)*	*1.34*	*(0.02)*	*472*	*(2.7)*	*485*	*(2.48)*	*496*	*(3.17)*	*501*	*(2.7)*
	OECD average	*0.00*	*(0.01)*	*–1.17*	*(0.02)*	*–0.51*	*(0.01)*	*0.39*	*(0.01)*	*1.27*	*(0.01)*	*484*	*(1.5)*	*498*	*(1.36)*	*507*	*(1.40)*	*510*	*(1.6)*
Partner countries	Brazil	–0.12	(0.09)	–1.46	(0.13)	–0.57	(0.00)	0.33	(0.02)	1.21	(0.05)	**340**	(10.3)	359	(9.11)	358	(11.64)	**372**	(10.2)
	Hong Kong-China	–0.37	(0.07)	–1.48	(0.08)	–0.57	(0.00)	–0.23	(0.05)	0.83	(0.07)	**522**	(8.0)	543	(7.82)	566	(7.60)	**571**	(15.5)
	Indonesia	0.59	(0.07)	–0.89	(0.09)	0.30	(0.03)	1.30	(0.03)	1.66	(0.00)	366	(7.6)	357	(7.86)	357	(5.77)	361	(5.9)
	Latvia	0.15	(0.08)	–0.76	(0.06)	–0.26	(0.04)	0.39	(0.03)	1.22	(0.07)	479	(6.6)	483	(5.37)	484	(6.70)	487	(8.2)
	Liechtenstein	c	c	c	c	c	c	c	c	c	c	c	c	c	c	c	c	c	c
	Macao-China	–0.63	(0.00)	–1.71	(0.01)	–0.58	(0.00)	–0.57	(0.00)	0.35	(0.04)	**503**	(5.3)	532	(7.49)	529	(7.93)	**546**	(6.0)
	Russian Federation	–0.21	(0.06)	–1.19	(0.05)	–0.57	(0.00)	–0.11	(0.04)	1.02	(0.07)	**452**	(5.5)	462	(7.18)	467	(6.31)	**493**	(7.4)
	Serbia	–0.52	(0.08)	–1.79	(0.07)	–0.84	(0.04)	–0.23	(0.05)	0.77	(0.07)	440	(7.3)	429	(5.58)	432	(6.08)	445	(8.9)
	Thailand	–0.18	(0.10)	–1.46	(0.09)	–0.57	(0.00)	–0.06	(0.04)	1.36	(0.06)	**406**	(4.2)	413	(5.35)	420	(5.93)	**430**	(8.0)
	Tunisia	0.06	(0.08)	–1.22	(0.09)	–0.57	(0.00)	0.48	(0.04)	1.53	(0.04)	**342**	(5.3)	352	(6.34)	374	(9.15)	**366**	(6.2)
	Uruguay	–0.13	(0.06)	–1.04	(0.06)	–0.57	(0.00)	0.01	(0.04)	1.10	(0.06)	417	(6.3)	426	(6.38)	416	(7.41)	430	(7.1)
	United Kingdom[1]	0.25	(0.07)	–0.91	(0.07)	–0.26	(0.04)	0.64	(0.02)	1.55	(0.02)	**492**	(4.6)	504	(4.28)	511	(6.86)	**528**	(7.5)

		Change in the mathematics score per unit of the index of school principals' perceptions of teachers' morale and commitment		Increased likelihood of students in the bottom quarter of this index scoring in the bottom quarter of the national mathematics performance distribution		Explained variance in student performance (r-squared × 100)	
		Effect	S.E.	Ratio	S.E.	Percentage	S.E.
OECD countries	Australia	**14.3**	(3.16)	**1.3**	(0.10)	2.1	(0.85)
	Austria	–2.4	(5.77)	0.9	(0.15)	0.1	(0.34)
	Belgium	**33.4**	(5.18)	**2.0**	(0.20)	7.2	(1.99)
	Canada	**5.7**	(2.10)	1.1	(0.07)	0.4	(0.31)
	Czech Republic	–4.3	(7.03)	0.9	(0.13)	0.1	(0.55)
	Denmark	3.9	(2.84)	1.0	(0.10)	0.1	(0.18)
	Finland	**5.0**	(2.48)	1.1	(0.07)	0.3	(0.25)
	France	w	w	w	w	w	w
	Germany	7.4	(5.87)	1.3	(0.18)	0.4	(0.69)
	Greece	**16.2**	(4.11)	1.3	(0.19)	4.0	(1.91)
	Hungary	8.6	(7.01)	1.2	(0.20)	0.7	(1.35)
	Iceland	**5.4**	(2.05)	1.1	(0.07)	0.3	(0.22)
	Ireland	5.4	(3.11)	**1.3**	(0.14)	0.4	(0.55)
	Italy	1.5	(4.50)	0.9	(0.12)	0.0	(0.18)
	Japan	**34.3**	(4.11)	**1.8**	(0.26)	15.6	(3.55)
	Korea	**21.9**	(4.46)	**1.8**	(0.28)	6.3	(2.50)
	Luxembourg	**4.9**	(1.64)	1.1	(0.07)	0.1	(0.10)
	Mexico	**6.9**	(3.47)	1.1	(0.15)	0.9	(0.91)
	Netherlands	**18.1**	(8.90)	1.4	(0.22)	2.0	(2.05)
	New Zealand	**8.8**	(3.65)	1.1	(0.12)	0.7	(0.57)
	Norway	–1.5	(2.75)	1.0	(0.08)	0.0	(0.11)
	Poland	5.6	(3.27)	1.1	(0.10)	0.3	(0.37)
	Portugal	3.0	(4.69)	0.8	(0.16)	0.1	(0.30)
	Slovak Republic	1.8	(5.43)	1.1	(0.12)	0.0	(0.30)
	Spain	**14.1**	(4.04)	**1.4**	(0.17)	2.0	(1.15)
	Sweden	**6.5**	(3.24)	1.1	(0.10)	0.3	(0.30)
	Switzerland	–0.7	(4.52)	1.0	(0.10)	0.0	(0.16)
	Turkey	10.5	(6.34)	1.4	(0.21)	1.6	(1.82)
	United States	**8.5**	(3.09)	1.2	(0.14)	0.9	(0.63)
	OECD total	*11.4*	*(1.48)*	*1.3*	*(0.06)*	*1.4*	*(0.35)*
	OECD average	*11.1*	*(0.94)*	*1.3*	*(0.03)*	*1.2*	*(0.21)*
Partner countries	Brazil	**12.7**	(5.70)	1.2	(0.19)	**1.9**	**(1.89)**
	Hong Kong-China	**22.2**	(7.56)	**1.6**	(0.26)	**4.3**	**(3.01)**
	Indonesia	–1.0	(3.43)	0.9	(0.12)	**0.0**	**(0.17)**
	Latvia	5.2	(4.73)	1.1	(0.14)	**0.2**	**(0.45)**
	Liechtenstein	c	c	c	c	**c**	**c**
	Macao-China	**21.1**	(2.61)	**1.4**	(0.16)	**4.3**	**(1.02)**
	Russian Federation	**18.3**	(4.17)	1.2	(0.12)	**3.1**	**(1.47)**
	Serbia	3.4	(4.38)	0.9	(0.14)	**0.2**	**(0.52)**
	Thailand	**9.7**	(3.11)	1.1	(0.11)	**1.8**	**(1.13)**
	Tunisia	**8.8**	(2.88)	**1.3**	(0.13)	**1.4**	**(0.90)**
	Uruguay	4.9	(3.99)	1.1	(0.13)	**0.2**	**(0.31)**
	United Kingdom[1]	**13.4**	(2.90)	**1.3**	(0.12)	**2.1**	**(0.87)**

Note: Values that are statistically significant are indicated in bold (see Annex A4).
1. Response rate too low to ensure comparability (see Annex A3).

Table 5.5b
Principals' perceptions of teachers' morale and commitment in PISA 2003 and PISA 2000

Results based on reports from school principals and reported proportionate to the number of 15-year-olds enrolled in the school

		Percentage of students in schools where the principals agree or strongly agree with the following statements about the teachers in the school															
		The morale of teachers in this school is high				Teachers work with enthusiasm				Teachers take pride in this school				Teachers value academic achievement			
		PISA 2003		PISA 2000		PISA 2003		PISA 2000		PISA 2003		PISA 2000		PISA 2003		PISA 2000	
		%	S.E.	%	S.E.	%	S.E.	%	S.E.	%	S.E.	%	S.E.	%	S.E.	%	S.E.
OECD countries	Australia	90.1	(1.8)	85.7	(2.7)	96.9	(1.6)	95.5	(1.7)	97.5	(1.0)	95.6	(1.9)	99.8	(0.2)	98.7	(0.9)
	Austria	98.2	(1.0)	98.5	(1.1)	98.8	(0.9)	98.1	(1.1)	97.1	(1.6)	99.2	(0.4)	99.0	(0.8)	100.0	(0.0)
	Belgium	87.4	(2.1)	85.5	(2.6)	**93.4**	(1.4)	**97.1**	(1.1)	95.0	(1.1)	91.8	(2.3)	**90.5**	(1.6)	**95.6**	(1.7)
	Canada	**87.7**	(1.7)	**78.0**	(1.9)	95.3	(1.1)	93.7	(1.0)	97.5	(0.7)	97.4	(0.6)	99.0	(0.4)	99.1	(0.3)
	Czech Republic	96.4	(1.2)	93.7	(1.6)	85.7	(2.5)	81.4	(2.6)	**96.9**	(1.1)	**91.6**	(1.7)	99.3	(0.5)	99.3	(0.6)
	Denmark	98.8	(0.9)	97.9	(1.1)	**100.0**	(0.0)	**94.8**	(1.4)	**99.2**	(0.5)	**94.3**	(1.7)	97.6	(0.7)	98.0	(1.0)
	Finland	**97.9**	(1.1)	**89.2**	(2.8)	96.2	(1.2)	95.7	(1.6)	95.9	(1.3)	91.8	(2.2)	99.4	(0.6)	100.0	(0.0)
	France	w	w	w	w	w	w	w	w	w	w	w	w	w	w	w	w
	Germany	96.6	(1.4)	95.4	(1.8)	96.1	(1.2)	93.8	(1.3)	89.6	(2.0)	83.9	(2.6)	97.4	(1.2)	98.1	(0.4)
	Greece	87.1	(3.3)	92.2	(3.5)	83.7	(3.6)	88.6	(3.6)	**87.3**	(3.0)	**97.5**	(1.3)	99.3	(0.7)	98.8	(1.2)
	Hungary	96.4	(1.8)	92.8	(2.0)	86.6	(3.0)	78.9	(3.3)	**95.9**	(1.6)	**88.7**	(2.4)	**100.0**	(0.0)	**92.9**	(1.9)
	Iceland	**98.7**	(0.0)	**96.0**	(0.1)	**98.8**	(0.0)	**95.3**	(0.1)	**98.4**	(0.0)	**94.9**	(0.1)	**99.0**	(0.0)	**97.1**	(0.0)
	Ireland	87.6	(2.6)	88.2	(3.0)	96.8	(1.6)	97.0	(0.9)	95.0	(1.8)	96.0	(1.7)	98.8	(0.9)	99.3	(0.7)
	Italy	**75.4**	(2.4)	**53.2**	(4.1)	**81.2**	(2.8)	**66.7**	(3.7)	**87.4**	(2.0)	**94.8**	(1.6)	**94.0**	(1.4)	**98.0**	(1.1)
	Japan	90.1	(2.5)	85.5	(3.1)	93.6	(1.9)	93.7	(2.2)	79.7	(3.0)	85.5	(2.8)	**75.4**	(3.2)	**91.0**	(2.6)
	Korea	80.2	(3.4)	61.6	(4.2)	**93.4**	(2.0)	**85.3**	(3.3)	85.2	(3.1)	77.0	(3.7)	86.8	(2.7)	87.0	(2.5)
	Luxembourg	**92.2**	(0.0)	**100.0**	(0.0)	**92.2**	(0.0)	**94.7**	(0.0)	**85.6**	(0.0)	**84.1**	(0.0)	100.0	(0.0)	100.0	(0.0)
	Mexico	91.1	(1.9)	91.3	(2.1)	89.9	(1.9)	93.7	(1.9)	**87.2**	(2.7)	**93.9**	(1.9)	92.4	(1.9)	95.4	(1.6)
	Netherlands	98.2	(1.0)	92.5	(3.1)	100.0	(0.0)	96.7	(2.3)	96.7	(1.6)	91.3	(3.4)	96.9	(1.5)	98.7	(1.2)
	New Zealand	91.2	(2.0)	87.6	(2.5)	97.9	(1.1)	95.8	(1.7)	97.8	(1.1)	98.0	(1.2)	97.3	(1.2)	98.6	(1.0)
	Norway	98.2	(1.1)	95.5	(2.0)	94.8	(1.7)	95.0	(1.7)	91.1	(2.3)	87.2	(2.9)	100.0	(0.0)	98.8	(0.9)
	Poland	**81.4**	(3.1)	**33.5**	(4.4)	96.9	(1.1)	92.7	(2.6)	94.9	(1.8)	94.0	(2.3)	99.4	(0.6)	95.3	(2.6)
	Portugal	70.7	(4.1)	64.9	(4.1)	84.6	(3.3)	76.0	(3.4)	**96.6**	(1.3)	**86.3**	(3.1)	98.6	(1.0)	95.1	(1.9)
	Slovak Republic	98.0	(0.9)	a	a	81.5	(2.4)	a	a	94.5	(1.7)	a	a	99.0	(0.6)	a	a
	Spain	79.0	(2.9)	73.3	(3.1)	**89.8**	(2.5)	**82.2**	(2.9)	93.4	(1.8)	90.7	(2.4)	97.0	(1.1)	95.1	(1.2)
	Sweden	**99.5**	(0.5)	**95.5**	(1.7)	**99.5**	(0.5)	**92.8**	(2.1)	95.9	(1.5)	92.2	(2.1)	99.0	(0.7)	99.3	(0.7)
	Switzerland	94.2	(1.5)	95.8	(1.3)	99.3	(0.1)	98.0	(1.2)	**93.9**	(1.7)	**87.0**	(2.8)	98.2	(0.5)	99.1	(0.9)
	Turkey	81.6	(3.4)	a	a	81.0	(3.9)	a	a	84.5	(3.0)	a	a	83.7	(3.4)	a	a
	United States	88.5	(2.4)	85.1	(3.2)	95.3	(1.3)	95.1	(3.0)	96.5	(1.1)	96.1	(2.3)	99.4	(0.5)	96.0	(2.3)
	OECD total	*82.4*	*(0.7)*	*80.4*	*(1.1)*	*87.0*	*(0.5)*	*91.9*	*(0.8)*	*85.5*	*(0.6)*	*91.3*	*(0.9)*	*87.9*	*(0.5)*	*95.4*	*(0.7)*
	OECD average	*87.2*	*(0.4)*	*84.5*	*(0.6)*	*89.7*	*(0.4)*	*91.4*	*(0.4)*	*90.0*	*(0.4)*	*91.6*	*(0.5)*	*93.1*	*(0.2)*	*97.1*	*(0.3)*
Partner countries	Brazil	**89.9**	(2.7)	**69.1**	(3.6)	83.2	(3.2)	80.2	(3.0)	93.7	(2.4)	91.9	(2.4)	94.1	(2.3)	94.5	(2.1)
	Hong Kong-China	85.9	(2.8)	81.8	(3.6)	94.8	(1.8)	96.5	(1.6)	87.1	(2.4)	83.0	(3.4)	94.9	(1.5)	95.5	(1.5)
	Indonesia	97.6	(1.1)	96.8	(1.8)	93.9	(1.6)	96.8	(1.8)	96.1	(1.5)	96.4	(1.9)	99.1	(0.6)	95.8	(2.3)
	Latvia	**98.9**	(0.8)	**56.3**	(5.0)	**97.9**	(1.1)	**83.5**	(4.1)	98.2	(1.0)	95.6	(1.8)	95.8	(1.7)	98.9	(0.5)
	Liechtenstein	c	c	c	c	c	c	c	c	c	c	c	c	c	c	c	c
	Macao-China	82.4	(0.2)	a	a	96.7	(0.1)	a	a	83.4	(0.2)	a	a	91.7	(0.1)	a	a
	Russian Federation	93.4	(1.8)	91.3	(1.8)	86.8	(2.0)	87.5	(2.6)	**97.4**	(1.5)	**90.4**	(2.3)	98.1	(0.8)	97.2	(1.0)
	Serbia	87.3	(2.9)	a	a	65.0	(3.5)	a	a	84.9	(2.9)	a	a	95.1	(2.0)	a	a
	Thailand	88.8	(2.7)	83.3	(3.2)	86.8	(3.1)	85.3	(3.4)	92.4	(2.3)	93.0	(2.5)	91.0	(2.6)	94.8	(1.8)
	Tunisia	93.2	(2.1)	a	a	90.3	(2.2)	a	a	95.2	(1.5)	a	a	91.7	(2.4)	a	a
	Uruguay	98.0	(0.7)	a	a	91.3	(2.1)	a	a	95.0	(1.4)	a	a	98.0	(1.1)	a	a
	United Kingdom[1]	m	m	m	m	m	m	m	m	m	m	m	m	m	m	m	m

Note: Values that are statistically significant are indicated in bold (see Annex A4).
1. Response rate too low to ensure comparability (see Annex A3).

Table 5.6a

Index of principals' perceptions of students' morale and commitment and student performance on the mathematics scale, by national quarters of the index

Results based on reports from school principals and reported proportionate to the number of 15-year-olds enrolled in the school

		Index of school principals' perceptions of students' morale and commitment										Performance on the mathematics scale, by national quarters of the index of school principals' perceptions of students' morale and commitment							
		All students		Bottom quarter		Second quarter		Third quarter		Top quarter		Bottom quarter		Second quarter		Third quarter		Top quarter	
		Mean index	S.E.	Mean index	S.E.	Mean index	S.E.	Mean index	S.E.	Mean index	S.E.	Mean score	S.E.	Mean score	S.E.	Mean score	S.E.	Mean score	S.E.
OECD countries	Australia	0.47	(0.05)	–0.73	(0.06)	0.02	(0.00)	0.67	(0.02)	1.93	(0.07)	**500**	(4.2)	511	(5.7)	523	(3.9)	**562**	(5.9)
	Austria	0.12	(0.06)	–1.20	(0.06)	–0.09	(0.03)	0.54	(0.02)	1.25	(0.05)	**475**	(8.4)	508	(8.9)	520	(6.9)	**519**	(7.0)
	Belgium	–0.26	(0.04)	–1.26	(0.03)	–0.45	(0.03)	0.02	(0.00)	0.67	(0.05)	**475**	(9.0)	536	(7.6)	554	(6.4)	**559**	(7.1)
	Canada	0.43	(0.05)	–0.58	(0.05)	0.02	(0.00)	0.59	(0.01)	1.69	(0.06)	**517**	(2.9)	530	(3.0)	533	(4.1)	**551**	(3.5)
	Czech Republic	–0.40	(0.05)	–1.21	(0.03)	–0.77	(0.02)	–0.17	(0.02)	0.54	(0.04)	**499**	(8.0)	517	(5.7)	516	(8.7)	**531**	(7.6)
	Denmark	0.16	(0.06)	–0.79	(0.07)	0.02	(0.00)	0.29	(0.03)	1.14	(0.08)	**499**	(5.4)	517	(4.1)	517	(4.7)	**525**	(6.4)
	Finland	0.03	(0.06)	–1.03	(0.06)	–0.19	(0.03)	0.24	(0.03)	1.09	(0.08)	**533**	(4.1)	544	(3.4)	547	(3.0)	**554**	(3.8)
	France	w	w	w	w	w	w	w	w	w	w	w	w	w	w	w	w	w	w
	Germany	–0.46	(0.07)	–1.56	(0.05)	–0.89	(0.02)	–0.20	(0.03)	0.83	(0.06)	**461**	(8.9)	516	(8.8)	517	(8.2)	**520**	(9.8)
	Greece	0.00	(0.13)	–1.47	(0.10)	–0.46	(0.06)	0.49	(0.04)	1.43	(0.14)	**424**	(9.0)	431	(7.7)	450	(8.0)	**475**	(9.2)
	Hungary	–0.44	(0.08)	–1.58	(0.06)	–0.94	(0.02)	–0.26	(0.04)	1.03	(0.06)	**450**	(6.5)	480	(6.2)	512	(9.4)	**522**	(9.6)
	Iceland	0.18	(0.00)	–0.98	(0.01)	0.02	(0.00)	0.36	(0.01)	1.33	(0.01)	507	(3.2)	518	(3.1)	521	(3.9)	516	(3.1)
	Ireland	0.33	(0.07)	–0.73	(0.09)	0.05	(0.01)	0.66	(0.03)	1.35	(0.06)	**482**	(5.0)	496	(6.1)	523	(5.0)	**512**	(5.1)
	Italy	–0.06	(0.07)	–1.35	(0.06)	–0.33	(0.04)	0.31	(0.03)	1.15	(0.07)	**435**	(6.2)	468	(7.3)	477	(7.8)	**482**	(8.0)
	Japan	0.28	(0.10)	–1.60	(0.09)	–0.09	(0.04)	0.75	(0.04)	2.09	(0.07)	**479**	(9.1)	509	(7.9)	555	(12.8)	**594**	(6.7)
	Korea	–0.11	(0.09)	–1.76	(0.08)	–0.44	(0.06)	0.28	(0.04)	1.49	(0.10)	**491**	(8.4)	537	(6.9)	560	(6.7)	**581**	(9.2)
	Luxembourg	–0.58	(0.00)	–1.27	(0.00)	–0.89	(0.00)	–0.30	(0.00)	0.13	(0.00)	**470**	(2.5)	483	(2.5)	488	(3.1)	**532**	(2.7)
	Mexico	0.36	(0.06)	–0.99	(0.05)	0.08	(0.01)	0.73	(0.02)	1.63	(0.06)	**372**	(6.8)	380	(6.2)	387	(9.6)	**399**	(7.2)
	Netherlands	–0.15	(0.07)	–1.22	(0.07)	–0.23	(0.04)	0.03	(0.00)	0.82	(0.08)	**497**	(9.5)	535	(7.8)	551	(9.2)	**564**	(9.3)
	New Zealand	0.37	(0.06)	–0.66	(0.08)	0.02	(0.00)	0.53	(0.02)	1.57	(0.06)	**508**	(5.0)	520	(5.0)	527	(6.4)	**543**	(6.0)
	Norway	–0.12	(0.05)	–1.22	(0.05)	–0.23	(0.04)	0.21	(0.03)	0.77	(0.05)	491	(4.4)	493	(4.2)	496	(4.6)	497	(4.9)
	Poland	–0.04	(0.07)	–1.22	(0.04)	–0.29	(0.04)	0.31	(0.03)	1.04	(0.05)	**476**	(4.8)	495	(4.8)	496	(4.2)	**493**	(6.7)
	Portugal	–0.10	(0.08)	–1.16	(0.06)	–0.22	(0.04)	0.15	(0.02)	0.83	(0.06)	450	(8.9)	472	(6.8)	471	(6.7)	472	(7.8)
	Slovak Republic	–0.38	(0.07)	–1.43	(0.05)	–0.74	(0.02)	–0.19	(0.03)	0.85	(0.07)	**479**	(7.7)	494	(5.2)	512	(7.1)	**511**	(10.9)
	Spain	–0.45	(0.06)	–1.46	(0.05)	–0.87	(0.01)	–0.18	(0.03)	0.69	(0.04)	**459**	(4.8)	474	(4.8)	499	(5.1)	**510**	(6.3)
	Sweden	0.26	(0.07)	–0.91	(0.07)	0.05	(0.01)	0.58	(0.01)	1.33	(0.07)	**498**	(5.7)	510	(6.2)	508	(4.5)	**521**	(5.8)
	Switzerland	–0.05	(0.08)	–1.11	(0.03)	–0.21	(0.03)	0.14	(0.02)	0.98	(0.06)	**512**	(8.0)	519	(5.8)	530	(5.2)	**544**	(9.4)
	Turkey	–0.11	(0.11)	–1.63	(0.07)	–0.53	(0.03)	0.27	(0.05)	1.44	(0.10)	**400**	(6.0)	405	(7.8)	426	(12.9)	**462**	(21.9)
	United States	0.36	(0.07)	–0.78	(0.07)	0.02	(0.00)	0.56	(0.02)	1.65	(0.10)	**462**	(5.9)	486	(4.6)	491	(5.8)	**504**	(7.5)
	OECD total	*0.13*	*(0.02)*	*–1.27*	*(0.02)*	*–0.12*	*(0.01)*	*0.41*	*(0.01)*	*1.51*	*(0.03)*	*464*	*(2.7)*	*487*	*(2.4)*	*492*	*(2.4)*	*512*	*(3.2)*
	OECD average	*0.00*	*(0.01)*	*–1.28*	*(0.01)*	*–0.24*	*(0.01)*	*0.25*	*(0.01)*	*1.26*	*(0.02)*	*473*	*(1.5)*	*500*	*(1.4)*	*507*	*(1.5)*	*518*	*(1.6)*
Partner countries	Brazil	0.04	(0.10)	–1.41	(0.12)	–0.23	(0.03)	0.36	(0.03)	1.43	(0.08)	**331**	(8.7)	353	(9.5)	364	(11.2)	**381**	(13.0)
	Hong Kong-China	–0.17	(0.08)	–1.39	(0.06)	–0.45	(0.05)	0.13	(0.02)	1.05	(0.07)	**488**	(8.7)	551	(10.1)	565	(6.9)	**598**	(8.7)
	Indonesia	1.30	(0.07)	–0.21	(0.05)	0.95	(0.04)	1.86	(0.04)	2.59	(0.00)	364	(9.9)	355	(9.0)	360	(7.9)	362	(6.4)
	Latvia	–0.18	(0.06)	–1.03	(0.03)	–0.55	(0.01)	0.02	(0.00)	0.82	(0.07)	**469**	(7.6)	478	(6.9)	493	(7.2)	**494**	(6.3)
	Liechtenstein	c	c	c	c	c	c	c	c	c	c	c	c	c	c	c	c	c	c
	Macao-China	–0.02	(0.00)	–1.05	(0.02)	–0.30	(0.01)	0.21	(0.01)	1.05	(0.01)	**498**	(6.3)	531	(8.9)	532	(7.5)	**548**	(6.1)
	Russian Federation	–0.10	(0.05)	–1.12	(0.04)	–0.33	(0.03)	0.19	(0.03)	0.86	(0.03)	**438**	(7.4)	464	(6.0)	483	(6.0)	**488**	(8.0)
	Serbia	–0.89	(0.08)	–2.08	(0.07)	–1.32	(0.02)	–0.67	(0.04)	0.50	(0.06)	**422**	(6.7)	426	(7.0)	439	(7.7)	**461**	(8.2)
	Thailand	1.09	(0.08)	–0.30	(0.08)	0.64	(0.03)	1.50	(0.03)	2.51	(0.02)	408	(6.0)	418	(6.7)	423	(7.0)	420	(8.4)
	Tunisia	0.33	(0.09)	–1.28	(0.08)	0.02	(0.03)	0.73	(0.02)	1.86	(0.09)	353	(7.3)	352	(6.9)	358	(6.5)	371	(9.7)
	Uruguay	–0.21	(0.07)	–1.45	(0.10)	–0.55	(0.02)	0.12	(0.03)	1.05	(0.05)	414	(8.0)	432	(7.3)	416	(7.6)	427	(7.0)
	United Kingdom[1]	0.41	(0.08)	–0.73	(0.06)	0.02	(0.00)	0.56	(0.03)	1.78	(0.10)	**486**	(4.3)	502	(5.3)	508	(5.4)	**541**	(7.0)

		Change in the mathematics score per unit of the index of school principals' perceptions of students' morale and commitment		Increased likelihood of students in the bottom quarter of this index scoring in the bottom quarter of the national mathematics performance distribution		Explained variance in student performance (r-squared × 100)	
		Effect	S.E.	Ratio	S.E.	Percentage	S.E.
OECD countries	Australia	**21.9**	(3.03)	**1.5**	(0.10)	6.1	(1.62)
	Austria	**19.7**	(4.02)	**1.7**	(0.20)	4.2	(1.70)
	Belgium	**45.6**	(5.73)	**2.3**	(0.25)	10.3	(2.50)
	Canada	**14.2**	(1.79)	**1.4**	(0.07)	2.4	(0.63)
	Czech Republic	**16.4**	(6.65)	1.3	(0.19)	1.5	(1.14)
	Denmark	**14.3**	(3.37)	**1.3**	(0.14)	1.6	(0.74)
	Finland	**9.2**	(2.64)	**1.3**	(0.09)	0.9	(0.50)
	France	w	w	w	w	w	w
	Germany	**21.1**	(5.61)	**2.0**	(0.27)	3.8	(1.97)
	Greece	**17.0**	(4.50)	**1.5**	(0.21)	4.5	(2.42)
	Hungary	**27.9**	(4.52)	**1.9**	(0.24)	9.4	(3.09)
	Iceland	**4.9**	(1.57)	**1.1**	(0.07)	0.2	(0.15)
	Ireland	**17.8**	(3.39)	**1.5**	(0.15)	3.2	(1.18)
	Italy	**15.4**	(4.51)	**1.7**	(0.20)	2.5	(1.46)
	Japan	**32.9**	(2.79)	**2.3**	(0.34)	21.1	(3.49)
	Korea	**28.4**	(3.21)	**2.5**	(0.33)	15.1	(3.31)
	Luxembourg	**38.8**	(1.80)	**1.6**	(0.09)	6.0	(0.54)
	Mexico	**8.7**	(3.06)	1.3	(0.17)	1.1	(0.72)
	Netherlands	**31.9**	(5.75)	**1.9**	(0.32)	7.6	(2.64)
	New Zealand	**14.2**	(3.20)	**1.3**	(0.13)	1.8	(0.78)
	Norway	2.9	(2.90)	1.0	(0.09)	0.1	(0.14)
	Poland	**6.9**	(3.30)	**1.3**	(0.11)	0.4	(0.44)
	Portugal	**12.0**	(6.06)	1.4	(0.26)	1.2	(1.13)
	Slovak Republic	**14.3**	(5.90)	**1.4**	(0.18)	1.9	(1.56)
	Spain	**25.7**	(3.22)	**1.6**	(0.14)	6.1	(1.66)
	Sweden	**11.9**	(3.68)	**1.2**	(0.12)	1.3	(0.81)
	Switzerland	**16.6**	(5.46)	**1.2**	(0.12)	1.8	(1.20)
	Turkey	**20.2**	(7.85)	1.3	(0.19)	5.4	(4.02)
	United States	**17.2**	(3.33)	**1.6**	(0.15)	3.3	(1.31)
	OECD total	*18.2*	*(1.32)*	*1.4*	*(0.06)*	*3.6*	*(0.53)*
	OECD average	*18.2*	*(0.86)*	*1.5*	*(0.04)*	*3.3*	*(0.32)*
Partner countries	Brazil	**18.7**	(4.85)	1.4	(0.21)	4.4	(2.44)
	Hong Kong-China	**43.4**	(4.68)	**2.9**	(0.43)	17.1	(3.79)
	Indonesia	0.5	(3.61)	1.0	(0.15)	0.0	(0.23)
	Latvia	**14.3**	(5.70)	1.3	(0.17)	1.4	(1.06)
	Liechtenstein	c	c	c	c	c	c
	Macao-China	**21.3**	(2.89)	**1.7**	(0.22)	4.2	(1.12)
	Russian Federation	**24.8**	(5.02)	**1.7**	(0.20)	4.2	(1.72)
	Serbia	**14.1**	(3.77)	1.3	(0.17)	2.9	(1.52)
	Thailand	4.6	(3.45)	1.0	(0.12)	0.4	(0.63)
	Tunisia	4.0	(3.67)	1.1	(0.16)	0.4	(0.64)
	Uruguay	3.5	(3.76)	1.1	(0.16)	0.1	(0.27)
	United Kingdom[1]	**20.1**	(2.92)	**1.5**	(0.14)	5.0	(1.25)

Note: Values that are statistically significant are indicated in bold (see Annex A4).
1. Response rate too low to ensure comparability (see Annex A3).

Table 5.6b
Principals' perceptions of students' morale and commitment
Results based on reports from school principals and reported proportionate to the number of 15-year-olds enrolled in the school

		Percentage of students in schools where the principals agree or strongly agree with the following statements about the students in the school													
		Students enjoy being in school		Students work with enthusiasm		Students take pride in this school		Students value academic achievement		Students are cooperative and respectful		Students value the education they can receive in this school		Students do their best to learn as much as possible	
		%	S.E.	%	S.E.	%	S.E.	%	S.E.	%	S.E.	%	S.E.	%	S.E.
OECD countries	Australia	99.2	(0.5)	90.1	(1.6)	93.9	(1.3)	90.1	(1.4)	98.1	(0.8)	95.6	(1.1)	85.2	(2.3)
	Austria	97.4	(1.2)	85.4	(3.2)	90.1	(2.1)	82.1	(2.9)	93.3	(1.9)	90.7	(2.3)	71.8	(3.4)
	Belgium	98.8	(0.6)	75.7	(2.9)	86.5	(2.4)	77.0	(2.2)	91.7	(1.3)	89.3	(1.8)	67.5	(2.4)
	Canada	99.1	(0.5)	93.6	(1.0)	94.2	(1.2)	94.0	(1.2)	96.5	(0.9)	95.5	(1.0)	89.5	(1.5)
	Czech Republic	91.4	(1.9)	49.3	(3.4)	92.0	(2.0)	94.1	(1.5)	93.4	(1.9)	86.2	(2.2)	51.4	(3.7)
	Denmark	98.6	(0.8)	92.5	(2.0)	94.9	(1.5)	86.8	(2.3)	93.3	(1.8)	95.2	(1.6)	83.8	(2.8)
	Finland	99.2	(0.8)	89.7	(2.2)	86.9	(2.6)	94.2	(1.9)	96.8	(1.4)	89.7	(2.4)	64.3	(3.8)
	France	w	w	w	w	w	w	w	w	w	w	w	w	w	w
	Germany	98.7	(0.7)	63.4	(3.4)	71.1	(3.2)	63.2	(3.4)	88.2	(2.5)	87.8	(2.5)	40.3	(3.5)
	Greece	78.3	(3.9)	65.0	(4.3)	89.3	(3.2)	90.4	(2.0)	93.1	(2.4)	85.5	(3.5)	59.8	(5.2)
	Hungary	93.5	(2.0)	52.7	(3.6)	92.7	(2.4)	59.4	(3.9)	83.8	(2.9)	89.7	(2.6)	32.2	(3.2)
	Iceland	99.8	(0.0)	93.3	(0.1)	94.8	(0.1)	89.2	(0.1)	94.6	(0.1)	86.4	(0.1)	73.2	(0.1)
	Ireland	98.8	(0.8)	83.0	(3.0)	93.8	(1.8)	92.6	(2.2)	98.2	(1.1)	93.1	(2.1)	83.7	(3.1)
	Italy	79.5	(2.7)	64.2	(3.7)	87.8	(2.3)	96.3	(1.3)	86.2	(2.2)	94.7	(1.4)	66.7	(3.3)
	Japan	98.5	(1.0)	76.4	(3.1)	81.2	(2.9)	78.5	(3.4)	89.6	(2.5)	82.2	(3.0)	66.6	(3.6)
	Korea	86.0	(2.6)	64.7	(3.9)	81.2	(2.9)	72.5	(3.3)	93.1	(1.9)	81.3	(3.2)	70.2	(3.8)
	Luxembourg	100.0	(0.0)	40.2	(0.1)	87.6	(0.0)	81.3	(0.0)	92.6	(0.0)	94.4	(0.0)	44.8	(0.1)
	Mexico	95.1	(1.0)	89.3	(1.8)	96.1	(0.9)	89.5	(2.1)	88.3	(2.5)	88.3	(2.4)	83.4	(2.3)
	Netherlands	94.8	(1.9)	87.2	(3.1)	86.4	(3.2)	89.7	(2.7)	88.6	(2.5)	90.8	(2.5)	66.9	(3.9)
	New Zealand	100.0	(0.0)	91.5	(1.9)	96.1	(1.5)	90.2	(2.2)	97.5	(1.1)	95.6	(1.5)	83.8	(2.6)
	Norway	100.0	(0.0)	77.1	(3.1)	81.9	(2.7)	91.2	(2.2)	93.5	(1.7)	86.5	(2.8)	68.9	(3.5)
	Poland	97.5	(1.3)	65.1	(3.7)	96.2	(1.6)	95.3	(1.5)	89.1	(2.7)	87.2	(2.6)	70.9	(3.4)
	Portugal	100.0	(0.0)	76.0	(3.8)	95.0	(2.4)	88.0	(2.1)	91.4	(2.3)	85.7	(3.4)	59.9	(4.3)
	Slovak Republic	89.4	(1.9)	59.5	(3.2)	89.4	(1.6)	93.4	(1.6)	87.9	(2.0)	91.5	(1.6)	34.7	(3.6)
	Spain	96.7	(0.8)	54.2	(3.6)	92.1	(2.0)	77.4	(3.2)	80.7	(2.8)	88.7	(2.1)	34.6	(4.1)
	Sweden	98.3	(1.0)	88.2	(2.3)	85.2	(2.6)	92.9	(1.8)	96.5	(1.2)	89.6	(2.3)	85.4	(2.8)
	Switzerland	98.3	(1.0)	79.8	(2.6)	79.2	(2.8)	91.5	(3.2)	96.4	(0.9)	89.6	(3.3)	76.8	(3.7)
	Turkey	87.9	(2.8)	57.0	(4.3)	88.9	(2.2)	75.3	(3.9)	89.2	(3.0)	86.7	(2.7)	64.1	(5.1)
	United States	98.5	(0.8)	89.4	(2.1)	95.2	(1.4)	92.3	(1.8)	95.9	(1.5)	94.2	(1.7)	84.0	(2.3)
	OECD total	***89.6***	***(0.4)***	***73.4***	***(0.8)***	***83.6***	***(0.6)***	***79.8***	***(0.6)***	***85.9***	***(0.6)***	***83.9***	***(0.6)***	***67.3***	***(0.9)***
	OECD average	***92.3***	***(0.3)***	***72.8***	***(0.6)***	***86.2***	***(0.4)***	***83.1***	***(0.4)***	***89.0***	***(0.4)***	***86.7***	***(0.4)***	***64.9***	***(0.6)***
Partner countries	Brazil	94.1	(2.0)	83.7	(3.1)	91.6	(2.1)	76.7	(3.4)	86.7	(3.0)	87.8	(2.8)	66.3	(3.9)
	Hong Kong-China	99.3	(0.7)	71.1	(3.8)	85.8	(3.2)	74.5	(4.0)	93.6	(2.3)	94.8	(1.9)	57.4	(4.1)
	Indonesia	98.4	(0.7)	95.8	(1.0)	99.4	(0.3)	99.0	(0.7)	98.6	(0.6)	98.8	(0.7)	94.3	(1.2)
	Latvia	100.0	(0.0)	72.0	(4.0)	98.6	(0.8)	94.7	(1.9)	90.8	(2.5)	95.6	(1.8)	39.4	(4.4)
	Liechtenstein	c	c	c	c	c	c	c	c	c	c	c	c	c	c
	Macao-China	97.4	(0.2)	75.5	(0.3)	94.5	(0.1)	96.9	(0.1)	96.5	(0.1)	95.7	(0.1)	55.3	(0.2)
	Russian Federation	98.1	(1.5)	56.5	(4.1)	96.8	(1.5)	89.1	(2.5)	87.7	(2.5)	98.2	(0.5)	80.7	(3.0)
	Serbia	44.8	(4.0)	40.3	(4.5)	74.5	(3.4)	69.4	(3.9)	68.6	(4.0)	87.0	(2.5)	38.6	(4.3)
	Thailand	99.5	(0.5)	87.9	(2.7)	97.9	(1.6)	99.4	(0.6)	99.6	(0.4)	99.1	(0.7)	94.7	(1.9)
	Tunisia	98.0	(1.1)	75.8	(3.3)	94.4	(1.6)	84.3	(2.6)	85.1	(2.7)	82.4	(2.9)	78.0	(3.0)
	Uruguay	91.5	(2.5)	71.5	(4.0)	89.7	(2.5)	78.1	(3.3)	93.0	(1.9)	85.8	(2.9)	52.5	(3.1)
	United Kingdom[1]	m	m	m	m	m	m	m	m	m	m	m	m	m	m

1. Response rate too low to ensure comparability (see Annex A3).

Table 5.7
Strength of the relationship between the student and school socio-economic context, and school climate factors on student performance in mathematics

		Percentage of variance in mathematics performance that is attributable to:		
		Between-school variance accounted for by student and school socio-economic context	Between-school variance accounted for by school climate factors, after accounting for the impact of student and school socio-economic context	Joint variance explained by student and school socio-economic context as well as school climate factors
OECD countries	Australia	35.5	4.2	37.7
	Austria	51.1	2.5	18.0
	Belgium	28.5	7.5	49.4
	Canada	31.6	6.6	15.8
	Czech Republic	50.1	1.5	25.1
	Denmark	58.2	4.7	15.0
	Finland	13.3	10.2	13.3
	France	w	w	w
	Germany	34.2	6.1	34.3
	Greece	60.8	1.9	8.0
	Hungary	65.9	2.3	15.4
	Iceland	40.2	8.5	2.1
	Ireland	65.7	4.1	19.8
	Italy	41.5	3.7	19.1
	Japan	32.5	4.6	47.6
	Korea	39.1	7.4	31.4
	Luxembourg	75.7	2.1	15.3
	Mexico	51.3	6.2	13.4
	Netherlands	44.9	1.4	33.5
	New Zealand	55.5	2.8	25.4
	Norway	41.0	6.3	9.5
	Poland	56.7	3.2	16.1
	Portugal	44.8	8.2	11.7
	Slovak Republic	49.4	1.9	25.6
	Spain	31.9	6.5	29.3
	Sweden	43.7	1.6	21.0
	Switzerland	51.6	8.3	12.1
	Turkey	55.1	4.0	18.3
	United States	52.4	3.9	22.2
	OECD average	***46.1***	***4.7***	***22.0***
Partner countries	Brazil	m	m	m
	Hong Kong-China	26.7	15.6	26.3
	Indonesia	42.7	5.6	3.1
	Latvia	42.6	2.7	8.8
	Liechtenstein	c	c	c
	Macao-China	31.1	21.0	2.0
	Russian Federation	26.1	10.3	15.2
	Serbia	40.9	8.6	24.8
	Thailand	49.7	3.6	6.5
	Tunisia	50.5	4.0	5.2
	Uruguay	50.6	6.8	21.2
	United Kingdom[1]	35.2	5.6	33.0

Note: The estimates are based on the combined impact of the socio-economic and climate variables at the school level. Socio-economic context is measured by: the index of economic, social and cultural status, the student's place of birth and the language spoken at their home, the number of books at the student's home, the index of possessions related to "classical" culture in the family home, the student's gender, the school-level average index of economic, social and cultural status, the school location (rural/urban), and the school type (public/private). School climate is measured by: the index of student-teacher relations, the index of student's sense of belonging at school, the index of teacher support, the index of disciplinary climate, the index of students' morale and commitment, the index of teachers' morale and commitment, the index of teacher-related factors affecting school climate, and the index of student-related factors affecting school climate (see Annex A1). The analysis is undertaken for the combined OECD student population, with countries given equal weight. The resulting international model is then applied to each country to estimate the effects at the country level.

1. Response rate too low to ensure comparability (see Annex A3).

Table 5.8
School admittance policies
Results based on reports from school principals and reported proportionate to the number of 15-year-olds enrolled in the school

Percentage of students in schools where the principals consider the following statements as a "prerequisite" or a "high priority" for admittance at school

		Residence in a particular area		Students' academic records		Recommendations of feeder schools		Parents' endorsement of the instructional or religious philosophy of the school		Students' needs or desires for a special programme		Attendance of other family members at the school	
		%	S.E.	%	S.E.	%	S.E.	%	S.E.	%	S.E.	%	S.E.
OECD countries	Australia	40.8	(2.2)	7.9	(1.5)	16.0	(2.4)	28.3	(1.8)	27.5	(3.1)	43.5	(2.9)
	Austria	26.2	(2.7)	52.5	(3.0)	5.0	(1.9)	9.8	(2.6)	39.3	(3.6)	13.7	(2.6)
	Belgium	0.8	(0.6)	27.0	(2.4)	6.6	(1.8)	38.3	(2.9)	37.9	(2.8)	4.6	(1.4)
	Canada	75.3	(1.6)	13.1	(1.6)	18.2	(2.1)	16.5	(2.0)	30.9	(2.4)	12.2	(1.5)
	Czech Republic	22.8	(2.0)	51.3	(2.6)	2.4	(1.1)	12.6	(2.5)	12.9	(2.4)	5.5	(1.5)
	Denmark	59.3	(3.2)	4.0	(1.1)	4.6	(1.5)	17.0	(2.4)	14.0	(2.6)	19.6	(2.7)
	Finland	67.2	(3.3)	3.3	(1.5)	3.7	(1.6)	5.2	(1.8)	10.2	(2.4)	5.5	(1.7)
	France	w	w	w	w	w	w	w	w	w	w	w	w
	Germany	54.9	(2.9)	23.9	(2.7)	49.6	(3.4)	6.0	(1.7)	19.6	(3.3)	11.6	(2.2)
	Greece	64.6	(4.0)	1.3	(1.3)	1.7	(1.4)	2.5	(1.6)	12.9	(3.3)	15.1	(3.7)
	Hungary	8.8	(1.7)	75.0	(3.3)	8.0	(2.3)	23.3	(3.6)	64.2	(3.7)	15.5	(2.7)
	Iceland	93.1	(0.1)	a	a	3.0	(0.1)	1.8	(0.1)	1.1	(0.0)	0.2	(0.0)
	Ireland	41.7	(3.7)	4.1	(1.7)	7.0	(2.0)	25.7	(3.6)	10.0	(2.7)	38.0	(4.0)
	Italy	7.2	(2.0)	7.7	(2.0)	9.1	(2.1)	6.9	(1.8)	51.2	(3.6)	13.1	(2.6)
	Japan	29.7	(3.6)	88.1	(2.6)	36.7	(4.5)	10.6	(2.3)	38.1	(3.5)	3.3	(1.5)
	Korea	30.6	(4.0)	56.6	(3.9)	12.3	(2.6)	6.9	(2.1)	14.3	(3.0)	0.8	(0.9)
	Luxembourg	15.0	(0.0)	49.6	(0.1)	13.1	(0.0)	14.2	(0.0)	11.9	(0.0)	24.0	(0.1)
	Mexico	14.5	(2.6)	36.0	(3.4)	12.1	(2.9)	10.3	(2.5)	13.4	(2.2)	12.5	(2.2)
	Netherlands	6.5	(2.1)	70.0	(4.4)	84.2	(3.6)	17.3	(3.5)	16.7	(3.3)	3.2	(1.7)
	New Zealand	42.5	(2.8)	12.5	(2.4)	14.0	(2.4)	14.2	(1.9)	22.5	(2.9)	32.9	(3.0)
	Norway	73.8	(3.5)	a	a	2.6	(1.3)	0.9	(0.7)	2.2	(1.1)	2.5	(0.9)
	Poland	82.2	(2.7)	26.6	(2.8)	12.7	(1.9)	12.4	(2.4)	12.4	(2.5)	8.2	(2.1)
	Portugal	58.7	(4.0)	0.7	(0.5)	1.3	(0.9)	8.9	(2.2)	41.7	(4.4)	29.9	(3.6)
	Slovak Republic	11.1	(1.8)	49.7	(3.2)	2.6	(0.9)	6.8	(1.6)	23.7	(3.0)	3.3	(0.8)
	Spain	71.5	(3.0)	2.6	(1.1)	1.7	(0.8)	11.2	(2.2)	12.4	(2.4)	37.6	(3.4)
	Sweden	62.3	(3.4)	4.5	(1.2)	2.5	(1.2)	8.5	(2.0)	11.7	(1.7)	9.5	(2.2)
	Switzerland	78.2	(3.0)	53.0	(4.1)	41.1	(3.6)	1.4	(0.6)	23.1	(3.8)	5.0	(2.2)
	Turkey	27.3	(4.0)	11.8	(2.8)	3.4	(1.6)	1.1	(1.0)	7.2	(2.0)	3.5	(1.6)
	United States	79.3	(2.7)	15.9	(2.3)	16.6	(2.2)	8.8	(1.6)	23.7	(3.3)	7.9	(2.0)
	OECD total	***46.7***	***(1.0)***	***28.0***	***(0.7)***	***17.6***	***(0.8)***	***9.8***	***(0.5)***	***21.0***	***(1.0)***	***11.4***	***(0.6)***
	OECD average	***43.2***	***(0.6)***	***25.5***	***(0.4)***	***13.3***	***(0.4)***	***11.5***	***(0.4)***	***20.5***	***(0.5)***	***14.1***	***(0.4)***
Partner countries	Brazil	19.3	(3.1)	7.9	(2.1)	1.7	(1.0)	9.1	(2.2)	7.2	(1.9)	0.5	(0.4)
	Hong Kong-China	6.9	(2.1)	76.3	(3.6)	22.2	(4.1)	19.8	(3.8)	3.2	(1.5)	12.0	(2.6)
	Indonesia	22.7	(3.2)	60.8	(3.9)	24.3	(3.1)	39.8	(3.1)	19.7	(2.7)	8.2	(1.8)
	Latvia	19.6	(3.5)	16.6	(3.0)	1.3	(0.9)	17.6	(3.6)	46.1	(4.3)	7.0	(1.7)
	Liechtenstein	c	c	c	c	c	c	c	c	c	c	c	c
	Macao-China	2.0	(0.1)	71.1	(0.2)	65.5	(0.2)	9.4	(0.2)	5.7	(0.1)	16.2	(0.2)
	Russian Federation	34.0	(3.2)	15.0	(3.1)	5.1	(1.6)	12.8	(2.4)	12.3	(2.5)	11.3	(3.1)
	Serbia	6.2	(2.2)	93.2	(2.2)	4.9	(1.9)	5.2	(1.4)	49.5	(4.1)	0.6	(0.4)
	Thailand	39.6	(3.6)	40.1	(3.6)	51.0	(4.3)	44.4	(4.4)	44.9	(4.2)	17.2	(3.0)
	Tunisia	75.5	(3.4)	28.7	(3.4)	13.9	(3.1)	a	a	a	a	19.9	(3.0)
	Uruguay	19.8	(3.2)	8.8	(2.0)	3.2	(1.1)	6.3	(1.4)	8.3	(1.6)	7.7	(1.8)
	United Kingdom[1]	62.2	(3.3)	9.2	(1.8)	7.1	(1.7)	17.2	(2.4)	6.8	(1.9)	40.3	(3.5)

1. Response rate too low to ensure comparability (see Annex A3).

Table 5.9

Methods of assessment and student performance in mathematics

Results based on reports from school principals and reported proportionate to the number of 15-year-olds enrolled in the school

	Standardized tests															
	2 times a year or less				At least 3 times a year											
	% of students		Math. performance		% of students		Math. performance		Performance dif.		Correlation[1]		Explained variance (r-squared × 100)	
	%	S.E.	Score	S.E.	%	S.E.	Score	S.E.	Dif.	S.E.	Coef.	S.E.	%	S.E.
OECD countries														
Australia	88.7	(2.0)	526	(2.3)	11.3	(2.0)	511	(8.1)	–15	(8.6)	–0.03	(0.03)	0.1	(0.19)
Austria	88.1	(2.6)	503	(4.0)	11.9	(2.6)	522	(14.0)	20	(15.5)	0.04	(0.06)	0.1	(0.60)
Belgium	90.5	(1.9)	529	(3.4)	9.5	(1.9)	546	(16.1)	16	(17.8)	0.06	(0.05)	0.3	(0.60)
Canada	87.4	(1.5)	533	(2.1)	12.6	(1.5)	532	(6.8)	0	(7.3)	0.01	(0.02)	0.0	(0.03)
Czech Republic	90.7	(1.7)	517	(3.6)	9.3	(1.7)	508	(13.9)	–9	(14.1)	0.02	(0.05)	0.1	(0.25)
Denmark	83.6	(3.0)	513	(2.9)	16.4	(3.0)	523	(7.6)	9	(8.1)	0.01	(0.03)	0.0	(0.12)
Finland	83.5	(2.9)	544	(2.0)	16.5	(2.9)	544	(4.9)	0	(5.1)	0.01	(0.02)	0.0	(0.07)
France	w	w	w	w	w	w	w	w	w	w	w	w	w	w
Germany	93.7	(1.5)	506	(3.7)	6.3	(1.5)	486	(14.8)	–20	(16.1)	–0.06	(0.04)	0.4	(0.52)
Greece	68.1	(5.8)	437	(5.0)	32.0	(5.8)	466	(7.3)	**30**	(9.2)	**0.14**	(0.05)	1.9	(1.36)
Hungary	81.1	(3.4)	495	(4.1)	18.9	(3.4)	471	(12.8)	–24	(15.1)	–0.13	(0.07)	1.6	(1.75)
Iceland	85.4	(0.1)	515	(1.8)	14.6	(0.1)	521	(4.4)	6	(5.1)	0.02	(0.02)	0.0	(0.09)
Ireland	89.5	(2.8)	504	(2.9)	10.5	(2.8)	496	(10.7)	–9	(11.7)	0.00	(0.04)	0.0	(0.13)
Italy	61.8	(3.4)	474	(5.0)	38.2	(3.4)	450	(7.0)	**–25**	(10.1)	**–0.13**	(0.05)	1.6	(1.26)
Japan	75.9	(3.4)	525	(5.8)	24.1	(3.4)	566	(7.8)	**41**	(11.1)	**0.14**	(0.06)	2.0	(1.59)
Korea	41.3	(3.8)	516	(6.9)	58.7	(3.8)	560	(4.8)	**44**	(9.1)	**0.25**	(0.05)	**6.4**	(2.55)
Luxembourg	89.3	(0.0)	500	(1.1)	10.7	(0.0)	438	(3.3)	**–62**	(3.6)	**–0.23**	(0.01)	**5.2**	(0.59)
Mexico	59.4	(3.4)	392	(5.4)	40.6	(3.4)	375	(6.5)	–16	(8.7)	–0.07	(0.05)	0.6	(0.71)
Netherlands	55.8	(4.4)	543	(6.2)	44.2	(4.4)	530	(8.5)	–13	(13.0)	**–0.17**	(0.06)	2.9	(2.03)
New Zealand	48.4	(3.3)	527	(3.5)	51.6	(3.3)	523	(3.6)	–5	(5.1)	–0.04	(0.03)	0.1	(0.21)
Norway	70.3	(3.5)	493	(2.7)	29.7	(3.5)	498	(4.4)	6	(5.2)	0.04	(0.02)	0.2	(0.21)
Poland	79.9	(3.0)	489	(2.8)	20.1	(3.0)	494	(6.7)	5	(7.6)	0.04	(0.03)	0.1	(0.25)
Portugal	100.0	(0.0)	466	(3.4)	a	a	a	a	a	a	–0.02	(0.05)	0.1	(0.30)
Slovak Republic	83.5	(3.2)	496	(4.0)	16.5	(3.2)	508	(10.2)	12	(11.9)	0.05	(0.05)	0.3	(0.57)
Spain	63.6	(3.3)	490	(3.5)	36.4	(3.3)	477	(5.4)	**–14**	(6.7)	–0.02	(0.04)	0.1	(0.21)
Sweden	59.0	(4.1)	509	(3.2)	41.0	(4.1)	507	(3.9)	–2	(4.8)	–0.03	(0.03)	0.1	(0.19)
Switzerland	88.9	(2.4)	528	(4.0)	11.1	(2.4)	512	(6.7)	–15	(7.9)	–0.01	(0.03)	0.0	(0.10)
Turkey	57.4	(5.0)	417	(9.0)	42.6	(5.0)	432	(12.8)	15	(16.5)	0.11	(0.09)	1.2	(2.09)
United States	78.7	(2.8)	487	(3.7)	21.3	(2.8)	481	(6.6)	–6	(7.7)	–0.02	(0.03)	0.0	(0.11)
OECD total	*74.8*	*(0.9)*	*491*	*(1.6)*	*25.2*	*(0.9)*	*483*	*(3.1)*	*–8*	*(3.9)*	*–0.06*	*(0.02)*	*0.3*	*(0.22)*
OECD average	*77.0*	*(0.6)*	*501*	*(0.9)*	*23.0*	*(0.6)*	*496*	*(2.1)*	*–5*	*(2.5)*	*–0.03*	*(0.01)*	*0.1*	*(0.08)*
Partner countries														
Brazil	66.9	(3.4)	349	(6.7)	33.1	(3.4)	371	(9.1)	22	(12.7)	0.08	(0.07)	0.7	(1.25)
Hong Kong-China	m	m	m	m	m	m	m	m	m	m	m	m	m	m
Indonesia	83.9	(2.9)	362	(4.3)	16.1	(2.9)	352	(10.1)	–9	(10.8)	–0.02	(0.05)	0.0	(0.27)
Latvia	50.6	(4.0)	491	(4.9)	49.4	(4.0)	477	(5.3)	–14	(7.5)	**–0.12**	(0.04)	1.5	(0.95)
Liechtenstein	c	c	c	c	c	c	c	c	c	c	c	c	c	c
Macao-China	m	m	m	m	m	m	m	m	m	m	m	m	m	m
Russian Federation	73.2	(3.9)	467	(5.4)	26.8	(3.9)	474	(9.0)	7	(11.1)	0.08	(0.05)	0.6	(0.73)
Serbia	93.2	(2.4)	438	(4.0)	6.8	(2.4)	426	(15.0)	–12	(15.9)	–0.02	(0.05)	0.0	(0.25)
Thailand	96.4	(1.4)	417	(3.1)	3.6	(1.4)	418	(18.9)	1	(19.4)	0.05	(0.04)	0.2	(0.39)
Tunisia	43.2	(4.1)	349	(5.6)	56.8	(4.1)	364	(4.6)	15	(8.9)	0.09	(0.06)	0.7	(1.06)
Uruguay	93.6	(2.1)	423	(3.7)	6.4	(2.1)	428	(14.0)	5	(15.6)	0.00	(0.04)	0.0	(0.15)
United Kingdom[2]	89.1	(2.2)	511	(3.1)	10.9	(2.2)	496	(6.6)	**–15**	(7.5)	**–0.07**	(0.04)	0.5	(0.57)

	Student portfolios													
	2 times a year or less				At least 3 times a year									
	% of students		Math. performance		% of students		Math. performance		Performance dif.		Correlation[1]		Explained variance (r-squared × 100)	
	%	S.E.	Score	S.E.	%	S.E.	Score	S.E.	Dif.	S.E.	Coef.	S.E.	%	S.E.
OECD countries														
Australia	59.6	(2.7)	519	(3.5)	40.4	(2.7)	534	(4.6)	**14**	(6.7)	0.04	(0.03)	0.2	(0.22)
Austria	56.5	(4.0)	511	(4.9)	43.5	(4.0)	494	(7.3)	–17	(10.3)	**0.15**	(0.05)	2.3	(1.60)
Belgium	57.5	(3.0)	532	(5.4)	42.5	(3.0)	526	(6.7)	–6	(10.6)	0.06	(0.04)	0.4	(0.49)
Canada	61.4	(2.3)	535	(2.5)	38.6	(2.3)	529	(3.3)	–5	(4.4)	**0.06**	(0.02)	0.3	(0.27)
Czech Republic	34.6	(3.0)	515	(7.5)	65.4	(3.0)	516	(5.5)	1	(10.6)	**0.10**	(0.04)	1.0	(0.80)
Denmark	18.1	(2.9)	512	(6.8)	81.9	(2.9)	515	(3.0)	3	(7.4)	0.05	(0.03)	0.3	(0.32)
Finland	83.7	(3.1)	544	(2.0)	16.3	(3.1)	546	(5.3)	2	(5.7)	0.02	(0.02)	0.0	(0.10)
France	w	w	w	w	w	w	w	w	w	w	w	w	w	w
Germany	47.1	(3.7)	517	(7.4)	52.9	(3.7)	494	(6.0)	**–23**	(11.5)	–0.01	(0.05)	0.0	(0.21)
Greece	83.0	(4.1)	449	(4.5)	17.0	(4.1)	431	(15.7)	–18	(17.6)	0.07	(0.06)	0.4	(0.73)
Hungary	52.6	(4.2)	486	(5.9)	47.4	(4.2)	496	(6.1)	11	(10.4)	0.10	(0.06)	0.9	(1.17)
Iceland	19.7	(0.2)	518	(3.9)	80.3	(0.2)	515	(1.7)	–3	(4.3)	–0.01	(0.02)	0.0	(0.05)
Ireland	86.7	(3.0)	505	(3.2)	13.3	(3.0)	495	(6.1)	–10	(7.7)	0.05	(0.04)	0.3	(0.37)
Italy	24.0	(2.8)	477	(8.2)	76.0	(2.8)	462	(4.1)	–15	(10.3)	0.01	(0.05)	0.0	(0.22)
Japan	15.4	(3.3)	546	(19.2)	84.6	(3.3)	533	(5.2)	–14	(21.7)	**0.12**	(0.05)	1.3	(1.07)
Korea	55.6	(4.7)	547	(6.6)	44.4	(4.7)	538	(7.1)	–10	(11.9)	0.00	(0.01)	0.0	(0.02)
Luxembourg	59.0	(0.1)	523	(1.3)	41.0	(0.1)	449	(1.8)	**–73**	(2.3)	**0.09**	(0.01)	0.8	(0.21)
Mexico	24.8	(2.7)	391	(5.1)	75.2	(2.7)	382	(5.0)	–8	(7.4)	0.03	(0.05)	0.1	(0.31)
Netherlands	83.6	(3.3)	536	(4.6)	16.4	(3.3)	537	(14.2)	1	(16.9)	0.02	(0.08)	0.0	(0.59)
New Zealand	60.3	(3.5)	528	(3.8)	39.7	(3.5)	522	(4.4)	–5	(6.4)	0.01	(0.03)	0.0	(0.08)
Norway	76.6	(3.7)	494	(3.0)	23.4	(3.7)	495	(3.9)	1	(5.0)	–0.02	(0.02)	0.0	(0.10)
Poland	73.3	(3.4)	491	(3.0)	26.7	(3.4)	488	(5.4)	–3	(6.4)	0.01	(0.03)	0.0	(0.11)
Portugal	79.4	(3.6)	467	(4.3)	20.6	(3.6)	465	(8.5)	–2	(10.2)	**–0.11**	(0.05)	1.2	(1.19)
Slovak Republic	56.3	(3.6)	498	(5.3)	43.7	(3.6)	498	(4.6)	0	(7.4)	**0.13**	(0.04)	1.8	(1.13)
Spain	4.0	(1.0)	477	(12.7)	96.0	(1.0)	485	(2.8)	8	(13.7)	0.01	(0.04)	0.0	(0.19)
Sweden	86.9	(2.8)	507	(3.0)	13.1	(2.8)	517	(5.5)	10	(6.4)	–0.03	(0.04)	0.1	(0.29)
Switzerland	82.3	(2.4)	530	(4.9)	17.7	(2.4)	516	(9.2)	–13	(12.2)	–0.05	(0.05)	0.3	(0.51)
Turkey	68.0	(4.2)	418	(8.4)	32.0	(4.2)	433	(12.6)	15	(15.6)	**0.22**	(0.08)	5.0	(3.68)
United States	67.7	(3.3)	485	(4.4)	32.3	(3.3)	488	(5.5)	3	(7.6)	**0.09**	(0.04)	0.7	(0.60)
OECD total	*51.1*	*(1.1)*	*493*	*(2.3)*	*48.9*	*(1.1)*	*484*	*(2.4)*	*–9*	*(4.1)*	*0.06*	*(0.02)*	*0.3*	*(0.18)*
OECD average	*56.7*	*(0.6)*	*503*	*(1.0)*	*43.3*	*(0.6)*	*495*	*(1.3)*	*–9*	*(1.9)*	*0.09*	*(0.01)*	*0.8*	*(0.14)*
Partner countries														
Brazil	5.6	(1.8)	367	(30.8)	94.4	(1.8)	356	(5.0)	–11	(31.0)	0.08	(0.05)	0.7	(0.86)
Hong Kong-China	83.5	(3.4)	554	(5.8)	16.5	(3.4)	534	(14.4)	–20	(16.8)	0.04	(0.06)	0.1	(0.51)
Indonesia	72.2	(3.4)	354	(3.9)	27.8	(3.4)	373	(9.9)	19	(10.3)	0.01	(0.07)	0.0	(0.37)
Latvia	28.7	(3.7)	480	(6.1)	71.3	(3.7)	485	(4.6)	5	(7.8)	–0.04	(0.05)	0.2	(0.35)
Liechtenstein	c	c	c	c	c	c	c	c	c	c	c	c	c	c
Macao-China	57.5	(0.3)	519	(3.8)	42.5	(0.3)	544	(4.3)	**25**	(5.9)	**0.15**	(0.03)	2.2	(0.91)
Russian Federation	57.7	(4.5)	466	(5.6)	42.3	(4.5)	472	(6.7)	6	(8.7)	0.02	(0.04)	0.1	(0.26)
Serbia	94.1	(1.5)	439	(3.9)	5.9	(1.5)	407	(10.7)	**–32**	(11.3)	–0.03	(0.06)	0.1	(0.41)
Thailand	62.6	(4.0)	419	(4.3)	37.4	(4.0)	415	(5.9)	–4	(8.1)	0.05	(0.05)	0.3	(0.46)
Tunisia	59.1	(4.1)	352	(4.1)	40.9	(4.1)	369	(6.3)	17	(8.9)	0.04	(0.05)	0.2	(0.41)
Uruguay	75.2	(2.4)	431	(4.3)	24.8	(2.4)	394	(8.3)	**–37**	(10.4)	–0.02	(0.04)	0.0	(0.24)
United Kingdom[2]	68.2	(3.4)	510	(3.7)	31.8	(3.4)	505	(4.5)	–5	(6.3)	**0.12**	(0.04)	1.5	(0.98)

Note: Values that are statistically significant are indicated in bold (see Annex A4).

1. Correlation between the frequency of assessment using this method and performance in mathematics.
2. Response rate too low to ensure comparability (see Annex A3).

Table 5.9 *(continued – 1)*

Methods of assessment and student performance in mathematics

Results based on reports from school principals and reported proportionate to the number of 15-year-olds enrolled in the school

		Judgemental ratings													
		2 times a year or less				At least 3 times a year									
		% of students		Math. performance		% of students		Math. performance		Performance dif.		Correlation[1]		Explained variance (r-squared × 100)	
		%	S.E.	Score	S.E.	%	S.E.	Score	S.E.	Dif.	S.E.	Coef.	S.E.	%	S.E.
OECD countries	Australia	23.8	(2.5)	527	(6.1)	76.2	(2.5)	523	(2.8)	–4	(7.4)	0.02	(0.03)	0.0	(0.16)
	Austria	4.6	(2.1)	493	(10.3)	95.4	(2.1)	505	(3.7)	12	(11.9)	0.04	(0.06)	0.2	(0.39)
	Belgium	9.5	(1.9)	521	(18.0)	90.5	(1.9)	531	(3.2)	9	(19.5)	**0.09**	(0.04)	0.7	(0.67)
	Canada	26.2	(2.1)	535	(4.3)	73.8	(2.1)	531	(2.0)	–3	(4.7)	–0.01	(0.02)	0.0	(0.09)
	Czech Republic	18.3	(2.6)	536	(11.8)	81.7	(2.6)	511	(4.3)	–25	(13.5)	**–0.12**	(0.05)	1.4	(1.06)
	Denmark	45.0	(3.7)	510	(3.6)	55.0	(3.7)	519	(3.7)	9	(5.2)	0.06	(0.03)	0.3	(0.36)
	Finland	44.1	(3.8)	545	(3.0)	55.9	(3.8)	544	(2.7)	–1	(4.2)	–0.01	(0.02)	0.0	(0.05)
	France	w	w	w	w	w	w	w	w	w	w	w	w	w	w
	Germany	10.5	(2.2)	508	(14.4)	89.5	(2.2)	505	(4.0)	–4	(16.1)	–0.07	(0.06)	0.4	(0.84)
	Greece	43.8	(5.1)	449	(7.1)	56.2	(5.1)	441	(5.5)	–8	(9.7)	0.04	(0.06)	0.1	(0.41)
	Hungary	17.5	(3.0)	503	(11.2)	82.5	(3.0)	488	(4.0)	–15	(13.4)	–0.05	(0.06)	0.3	(0.70)
	Iceland	8.5	(0.1)	512	(5.8)	91.5	(0.1)	517	(1.6)	4	(6.0)	–0.02	(0.02)	0.0	(0.08)
	Ireland	27.3	(4.0)	496	(6.0)	72.7	(4.0)	506	(3.1)	9	(7.3)	0.02	(0.04)	0.0	(0.20)
	Italy	15.0	(2.7)	481	(12.8)	85.0	(2.7)	463	(3.5)	–18	(14.3)	–0.09	(0.05)	0.8	(0.95)
	Japan	20.2	(3.6)	561	(13.3)	79.8	(3.6)	527	(5.6)	**–33**	(16.4)	–0.07	(0.07)	0.5	(1.05)
	Korea	33.4	(4.0)	553	(7.3)	66.6	(4.0)	536	(5.0)	–16	(10.3)	–0.07	(0.06)	0.5	(0.84)
	Luxembourg	15.6	(0.0)	550	(2.7)	84.4	(0.0)	483	(1.1)	**–67**	(3.0)	**–0.27**	(0.01)	7.1	(0.62)
	Mexico	44.6	(3.1)	396	(6.9)	55.4	(3.1)	376	(4.5)	**–20**	(8.3)	–0.08	(0.04)	0.6	(0.62)
	Netherlands	47.9	(4.3)	533	(8.2)	52.1	(4.3)	539	(6.3)	6	(12.7)	–0.05	(0.06)	0.3	(0.78)
	New Zealand	33.7	(2.9)	534	(5.1)	66.3	(2.9)	518	(2.9)	**–16**	(6.1)	**–0.08**	(0.03)	0.7	(0.57)
	Norway	21.1	(3.3)	497	(5.4)	78.9	(3.3)	493	(2.7)	–4	(6.0)	–0.02	(0.03)	0.1	(0.14)
	Poland	86.8	(2.9)	488	(2.8)	13.2	(2.9)	504	(8.8)	15	(9.5)	0.05	(0.03)	0.3	(0.34)
	Portugal	0.6	(0.6)	c	c	99.4	(0.6)	466	(3.4)	c	c	c	c	c	c
	Slovak Republic	5.1	(1.6)	513	(27.3)	94.9	(1.6)	498	(3.4)	–15	(27.8)	0.02	(0.05)	0.0	(0.24)
	Spain	11.7	(2.2)	495	(7.9)	88.3	(2.2)	483	(3.0)	–12	(8.8)	–0.01	(0.04)	0.0	(0.15)
	Sweden	11.0	(2.6)	520	(10.9)	89.0	(2.6)	507	(2.5)	–13	(11.0)	–0.03	(0.04)	0.1	(0.27)
	Switzerland	15.5	(2.3)	562	(10.1)	84.5	(2.3)	520	(3.9)	**–42**	(11.4)	**–0.14**	(0.05)	2.1	(1.39)
	Turkey	57.9	(4.8)	429	(8.9)	42.1	(4.8)	415	(9.7)	–14	(13.2)	0.00	(0.08)	0.0	(0.44)
	United States	4.9	(1.5)	495	(7.4)	95.1	(1.5)	485	(3.3)	–9	(8.1)	0.01	(0.03)	0.0	(0.12)
	OECD total	*24.0*	*(0.8)*	*485*	*(3.1)*	*76.0*	*(0.8)*	*490*	*(1.5)*	*5*	*(4.0)*	*0.01*	*(0.01)*	*0.0*	*(0.03)*
	OECD average	*25.3*	*(0.5)*	*501*	*(1.8)*	*74.7*	*(0.5)*	*499*	*(0.9)*	*–2*	*(2.2)*	*–0.02*	*(0.01)*	*0.0*	*(0.04)*
Partner countries	Brazil	9.7	(2.2)	403	(24.2)	90.3	(2.2)	353	(5.0)	**–50**	(24.7)	**–0.13**	(0.06)	1.8	(1.71)
	Hong Kong-China	64.7	(4.2)	555	(7.4)	35.3	(4.2)	539	(7.9)	–16	(12.1)	–0.04	(0.05)	0.2	(0.54)
	Indonesia	46.6	(3.4)	350	(5.8)	53.4	(3.4)	369	(5.8)	**19**	(8.6)	0.08	(0.05)	0.6	(0.75)
	Latvia	7.5	(2.4)	495	(10.8)	92.5	(2.4)	482	(3.7)	–13	(11.1)	–0.05	(0.04)	0.2	(0.37)
	Liechtenstein	c	c	c	c	c	c	c	c	c	c	c	c	c	c
	Macao-China	37.4	(0.2)	521	(4.5)	62.6	(0.2)	534	(2.8)	13	(5.3)	**0.06**	(0.03)	0.4	(0.38)
	Russian Federation	31.7	(2.9)	459	(6.4)	68.3	(2.9)	473	(5.0)	14	(7.8)	0.02	(0.05)	0.1	(0.32)
	Serbia	4.4	(1.7)	446	(23.4)	95.6	(1.7)	436	(3.8)	–9	(23.9)	–0.04	(0.06)	0.2	(0.53)
	Thailand	70.1	(3.4)	415	(4.1)	29.9	(3.4)	420	(7.3)	5	(9.4)	0.04	(0.05)	0.1	(0.58)
	Tunisia	29.6	(3.9)	355	(7.5)	70.4	(3.9)	360	(3.9)	5	(9.9)	0.01	(0.05)	0.0	(0.23)
	Uruguay	5.8	(1.8)	405	(22.6)	94.2	(1.8)	423	(3.6)	18	(23.7)	–0.08	(0.05)	0.6	(0.76)
	United Kingdom[2]	25.7	(3.6)	512	(7.5)	74.3	(3.6)	508	(3.3)	–4	(8.9)	0.00	(0.04)	0.0	(0.15)

		Teacher developed tests													
		2 times a year or less				At least 3 times a year									
		% of students		Math. performance		% of students		Math. performance		Performance dif.		Correlation[1]		Explained variance (r-squared × 100)	
		%	S.E.	Score	S.E.	%	S.E.	Score	S.E.	Dif.	S.E.	Coef.	S.E.	%	S.E.
OECD countries	Australia	3.8	(1.3)	514	(16.1)	96.2	(1.3)	525	(2.3)	11	(16.8)	0.05	(0.03)	0.2	(0.28)
	Austria	7.7	(2.2)	460	(10.7)	92.3	(2.2)	510	(3.7)	**50**	(11.5)	**–0.11**	(0.05)	1.1	(1.01)
	Belgium	9.1	(1.6)	516	(9.3)	90.9	(1.6)	532	(3.1)	16	(10.7)	**–0.12**	(0.05)	1.4	(1.19)
	Canada	1.0	(0.5)	c	c	99.0	(0.5)	533	(1.8)	c	c	c	c	c	c
	Czech Republic	6.7	(1.6)	488	(12.3)	93.3	(1.6)	518	(3.8)	**30**	(13.4)	–0.07	(0.06)	0.4	(0.59)
	Denmark	34.7	(3.3)	512	(4.6)	65.3	(3.3)	515	(3.5)	3	(5.9)	0.04	(0.03)	0.2	(0.28)
	Finland	0.0	(0.0)	c	c	100.0	(0.0)	544	(1.9)	c	c	c	c	c	c
	France	w	w	w	w	w	w	w	w	w	w	w	w	w	w
	Germany	4.0	(1.5)	524	(29.3)	96.0	(1.5)	504	(3.5)	–20	(30.0)	–0.10	(0.05)	0.9	(0.96)
	Greece	8.0	(2.5)	437	(13.6)	92.0	(2.5)	446	(4.3)	9	(14.7)	–0.04	(0.07)	0.2	(0.64)
	Hungary	1.5	(0.9)	c	c	98.5	(0.9)	491	(3.0)	c	c	c	c	c	c
	Iceland	5.0	(0.1)	523	(7.7)	95.0	(0.1)	515	(1.5)	–8	(7.9)	–0.03	(0.02)	0.1	(0.12)
	Ireland	25.6	(4.2)	504	(6.2)	74.4	(4.2)	503	(3.2)	–1	(7.7)	–0.04	(0.04)	0.2	(0.35)
	Italy	6.6	(1.8)	481	(16.7)	93.4	(1.8)	466	(3.2)	–16	(17.8)	**–0.11**	(0.05)	1.3	(1.18)
	Japan	0.7	(0.7)	c	c	99.3	(0.7)	534	(4.0)	c	c	c	c	c	c
	Korea	2.4	(1.4)	c	c	97.6	(1.4)	542	(3.4)	c	c	c	c	c	c
	Luxembourg	15.7	(0.1)	495	(2.8)	84.3	(0.1)	493	(1.1)	–3	(3.1)	**–0.39**	(0.01)	15.3	(0.87)
	Mexico	11.8	(2.0)	380	(7.1)	88.2	(2.0)	385	(4.4)	5	(8.6)	0.00	(0.05)	0.0	(0.17)
	Netherlands	0.5	(0.5)	c	c	99.5	(0.5)	539	(3.8)	c	c	c	c	c	c
	New Zealand	4.6	(1.4)	518	(12.3)	95.4	(1.4)	525	(2.5)	7	(12.6)	–0.01	(0.04)	0.0	(0.12)
	Norway	a	a	a	a	100.0	(0.0)	494	(2.4)	a	a	0.02	(0.02)	0.1	(0.14)
	Poland	6.6	(1.8)	499	(10.9)	93.4	(1.8)	490	(2.8)	–9	(12.0)	0.01	(0.03)	0.0	(0.10)
	Portugal	a	a	a	a	100.0	(0.0)	466	(3.4)	a	a	0.00	(0.05)	0.0	(0.23)
	Slovak Republic	6.9	(1.4)	473	(12.7)	93.1	(1.4)	500	(3.6)	27	(13.7)	0.00	(0.04)	0.0	(0.14)
	Spain	a	a	a	a	100.0	(0.0)	485	(2.7)	a	a	–0.02	(0.03)	0.0	(0.13)
	Sweden	3.8	(1.5)	532	(24.3)	96.2	(1.5)	507	(2.2)	–25	(23.9)	0.02	(0.02)	0.1	(0.13)
	Switzerland	2.2	(0.7)	c	c	97.8	(0.7)	526	(3.6)	c	c	c	c	c	c
	Turkey	60.0	(4.5)	410	(7.5)	40.0	(4.5)	447	(13.2)	**37**	(15.6)	0.11	(0.07)	1.3	(1.63)
	United States	0.5	(0.5)	c	c	99.5	(0.5)	486	(3.2)	c	c	c	c	c	c
	OECD total	*7.1*	*(0.4)*	*444*	*(5.0)*	*92.9*	*(0.4)*	*492*	*(1.2)*	***48***	*(5.1)*	***–0.07***	*(0.02)*	*0.4*	*(0.22)*
	OECD average	*8.5*	*(0.3)*	*471*	*(3.0)*	*91.5*	*(0.3)*	*503*	*(0.6)*	***32***	*(3.0)*	***–0.06***	*(0.01)*	*0.3*	*(0.10)*
Partner countries	Brazil	3.4	(1.2)	345	(26.1)	96.6	(1.2)	357	(5.1)	12	(26.5)	–0.04	(0.07)	0.2	(0.63)
	Hong Kong-China	5.9	(2.0)	579	(25.7)	94.1	(2.0)	549	(5.2)	–30	(27.6)	–0.05	(0.05)	0.3	(0.63)
	Indonesia	22.5	(3.3)	360	(10.0)	77.5	(3.3)	360	(4.7)	1	(11.8)	0.09	(0.05)	0.8	(1.03)
	Latvia	3.3	(1.3)	469	(26.8)	96.7	(1.3)	484	(3.6)	16	(27.1)	0.03	(0.04)	0.1	(0.26)
	Liechtenstein	c	c	c	c	c	c	c	c	c	c	c	c	c	c
	Macao-China	2.4	(0.0)	c	c	97.6	(0.0)	529	(3.1)	c	c	c	c	c	c
	Russian Federation	5.4	(1.8)	480	(20.2)	94.6	(1.8)	468	(4.4)	–12	(21.1)	0.05	(0.05)	0.3	(0.55)
	Serbia	32.9	(4.0)	442	(8.3)	67.1	(4.0)	435	(4.4)	–8	(9.7)	**–0.09**	(0.04)	0.9	(0.80)
	Thailand	21.7	(3.4)	407	(6.9)	78.3	(3.4)	420	(3.5)	14	(8.0)	0.00	(0.05)	0.0	(0.22)
	Tunisia	12.6	(2.4)	343	(10.5)	87.4	(2.4)	361	(3.0)	18	(11.4)	0.07	(0.06)	0.5	(0.72)
	Uruguay	0.8	(0.5)	c	c	99.2	(0.5)	422	(3.3)	c	c	c	c	c	c
	United Kingdom[2]	18.4	(2.7)	489	(6.6)	81.6	(2.7)	513	(3.1)	**24**	(7.5)	–0.05	(0.04)	0.3	(0.41)

Note: Values that are statistically significant are indicated in bold (see Annex A4).

1. Correlation between the frequency of assessment using this method and performance in mathematics.
2. Response rate too low to ensure comparability (see Annex A3).

Table 5.9 *(continued – 2)*

Methods of assessment and student performance in mathematics

Results based on reports from school principals and reported proportionate to the number of 15-year-olds enrolled in the school

		Student assignments / projects / homework														
		2 times a year or less				At least 3 times a year										
		% of students		Math. performance		% of students		Math. performance		Performance dif.		Correlation[1]		Explained variance (r-squared × 100)	
		%	S.E.	Score	S.E.	%	S.E.	Score	S.E.	Dif.	S.E.	Coef.	S.E.	%	S.E.
OECD countries	Australia	1.8	(0.8)	c	c	98.2	(0.8)	525	(2.2)	c	c	c	c	c	c
	Austria	11.0	(2.4)	466	(14.8)	89.0	(2.4)	510	(4.0)	**44**	(16.2)	0.09	(0.05)	0.8	(0.92)
	Belgium	5.0	(1.4)	481	(22.9)	95.0	(1.4)	533	(2.5)	**52**	(23.2)	**0.12**	(0.04)	1.4	(1.05)
	Canada	2.1	(0.7)	c	c	97.9	(0.7)	532	(1.8)	c	c	c	c	c	c
	Czech Republic	8.1	(2.1)	538	(16.6)	91.9	(2.1)	514	(4.1)	–24	(18.2)	–0.08	(0.05)	0.7	(0.69)
	Denmark	12.0	(2.1)	515	(7.2)	88.0	(2.1)	515	(2.8)	0	(7.7)	0.01	(0.03)	0.0	(0.06)
	Finland	11.6	(2.5)	540	(3.6)	88.4	(2.5)	545	(2.1)	5	(4.1)	0.03	(0.02)	0.1	(0.11)
	France	w	w	w	w	w	w	w	w	w	w	w	w	w	w
	Germany	9.6	(2.1)	511	(14.7)	90.4	(2.1)	504	(3.9)	–7	(16.3)	–0.06	(0.05)	0.4	(0.68)
	Greece	85.3	(4.3)	447	(4.5)	14.7	(4.3)	435	(18.2)	–12	(20.1)	–0.01	(0.08)	0.0	(0.55)
	Hungary	1.2	(0.8)	c	c	98.8	(0.8)	490	(3.0)	c	c	c	c	c	c
	Iceland	4.0	(0.1)	499	(9.5)	96.0	(0.1)	516	(1.5)	17	(9.6)	–0.03	(0.02)	0.1	(0.12)
	Ireland	5.5	(1.8)	519	(15.1)	94.5	(1.8)	503	(2.7)	–16	(15.7)	–0.05	(0.04)	0.2	(0.37)
	Italy	10.0	(1.9)	497	(12.5)	90.0	(1.9)	462	(3.4)	**–35**	(13.8)	–0.10	(0.05)	0.9	(0.94)
	Japan	18.0	(3.4)	513	(16.2)	82.0	(3.4)	539	(5.3)	26	(19.1)	**0.19**	(0.07)	3.6	(2.61)
	Korea	34.6	(4.2)	536	(8.7)	65.4	(4.2)	545	(5.5)	10	(12.5)	0.03	(0.05)	0.1	(0.39)
	Luxembourg	12.4	(0.0)	528	(2.8)	87.6	(0.0)	488	(1.1)	**–40**	(3.0)	**–0.10**	(0.01)	1.1	(0.23)
	Mexico	25.0	(3.0)	390	(6.5)	75.0	(3.0)	383	(4.8)	–7	(8.3)	0.00	(0.05)	0.0	(0.17)
	Netherlands	10.1	(2.4)	526	(19.9)	89.9	(2.4)	538	(4.4)	12	(22.4)	0.03	(0.06)	0.1	(0.46)
	New Zealand	8.4	(2.0)	517	(10.1)	91.6	(2.0)	526	(2.6)	8	(10.8)	–0.02	(0.03)	0.1	(0.17)
	Norway	5.0	(1.5)	487	(9.8)	95.0	(1.5)	495	(2.4)	7	(9.9)	0.03	(0.02)	0.1	(0.14)
	Poland	4.2	(1.6)	498	(8.3)	95.8	(1.6)	490	(2.6)	–9	(8.4)	0.01	(0.03)	0.0	(0.07)
	Portugal	7.7	(2.4)	483	(13.7)	92.3	(2.4)	465	(3.8)	–18	(14.8)	–0.10	(0.05)	1.0	(1.04)
	Slovak Republic	15.2	(2.3)	510	(8.8)	84.8	(2.3)	497	(3.9)	–13	(10.2)	–0.07	(0.04)	0.5	(0.61)
	Spain	2.9	(1.1)	c	c	97.1	(1.1)	485	(2.8)	c	c	c	c	c	c
	Sweden	5.4	(1.9)	532	(15.5)	94.6	(1.9)	507	(2.4)	–26	(15.4)	–0.05	(0.03)	0.3	(0.36)
	Switzerland	14.7	(2.3)	548	(8.4)	85.3	(2.3)	523	(4.2)	**–25**	(10.0)	**–0.15**	(0.04)	2.4	(1.24)
	Turkey	64.5	(4.6)	417	(8.4)	35.5	(4.6)	436	(14.2)	19	(17.4)	0.10	(0.07)	1.1	(1.59)
	United States	0.5	(0.5)	c	c	99.5	(0.5)	486	(3.2)	c	c	c	c	c	c
	OECD total	***13.0***	***(0.6)***	***466***	***(5.4)***	***87.0***	***(0.6)***	***492***	***(1.5)***	**27**	***(6.2)***	**0.06**	***(0.02)***	**0.3**	***(0.19)***
	OECD average	***14.1***	***(0.4)***	***477***	***(3.0)***	***85.9***	***(0.4)***	***503***	***(0.8)***	**26**	***(3.3)***	**0.07**	***(0.01)***	**0.5**	***(0.11)***
Partner countries	Brazil	3.4	(1.4)	371	(48.0)	96.6	(1.4)	357	(4.6)	–14	(47.3)	–0.02	(0.08)	0.0	(0.60)
	Hong Kong-China	25.1	(3.8)	542	(14.4)	74.9	(3.8)	553	(5.3)	11	(16.6)	0.07	(0.07)	0.4	(0.98)
	Indonesia	8.2	(2.0)	352	(13.9)	91.8	(2.0)	361	(4.4)	8	(15.9)	0.02	(0.05)	0.0	(0.23)
	Latvia	11.9	(2.8)	488	(13.5)	88.1	(2.8)	482	(3.8)	–6	(14.0)	–0.01	(0.05)	0.0	(0.20)
	Liechtenstein	c	c	c	c	c	c	c	c	c	c	c	c	c	c
	Macao-China	16.0	(0.1)	513	(6.7)	84.0	(0.1)	530	(3.3)	**17**	(7.9)	**0.07**	(0.03)	0.5	(0.46)
	Russian Federation	21.8	(3.2)	485	(7.4)	78.2	(3.2)	464	(4.7)	**–21**	(8.7)	–0.05	(0.04)	0.3	(0.46)
	Serbia	60.0	(4.2)	440	(5.8)	40.0	(4.2)	434	(5.4)	–6	(8.6)	–0.04	(0.04)	0.2	(0.33)
	Thailand	16.3	(3.0)	413	(7.2)	83.7	(3.0)	418	(3.3)	4	(7.8)	0.01	(0.04)	0.0	(0.14)
	Tunisia	36.5	(4.1)	346	(5.7)	63.5	(4.1)	366	(4.6)	**20**	(9.0)	**0.12**	(0.05)	1.4	(1.27)
	Uruguay	15.2	(3.4)	461	(8.4)	84.8	(3.4)	416	(3.5)	**–45**	(9.4)	**–0.21**	(0.04)	4.3	(1.55)
	United Kingdom[2]	6.2	(1.7)	479	(13.5)	93.8	(1.7)	511	(2.7)	**31**	(13.9)	**0.07**	(0.04)	0.5	(0.53)

Note: Values that are statistically significant are indicated in bold (see Annex A4).

1. Correlation between the frequency of assessment using this method and performance in mathematics.
2. Response rate too low to ensure comparability (see Annex A3).

Table 5.10
Use of assessment results and student performance in mathematics
Results based on reports from school principals and reported proportionate to the number of 15-year-olds enrolled in the school

		Inform parents about their child's progress									
		Schools that use this method				Schools that do not use this method					
		% of students		Math. performance		% of students		Math. performance		Performance difference	
		%	S.E.	Score	S.E.	%	S.E.	Score	S.E.	Dif.	S.E.
OECD countries	Australia	100.0	(0.0)	524	(2.2)	a	a	a	a	a	a
	Austria	91.5	(2.3)	512	(3.5)	7.8	(2.2)	442	(6.2)	**70**	(7.2)
	Belgium	98.8	(0.7)	531	(2.6)	0.4	(0.4)	c	c	**c**	c
	Canada	97.7	(0.7)	532	(1.8)	0.6	(0.3)	c	c	c	c
	Czech Republic	97.6	(1.0)	516	(3.7)	1.7	(0.9)	c	c	c	c
	Denmark	66.8	(3.5)	517	(3.3)	32.0	(3.5)	509	(5.0)	8	(6.2)
	Finland	100.0	(0.0)	544	(1.9)	0.0	c	c	c	c	c
	France	w	w	w	w	w	w	w	w	w	w
	Germany	94.1	(1.5)	503	(3.6)	3.9	(1.4)	539	(21.2)	–36	(22.3)
	Greece	96.2	(2.0)	443	(4.0)	3.4	(2.0)	505	(7.7)	**–62**	(8.4)
	Hungary	97.3	(1.2)	491	(3.0)	0.9	(0.9)	c	c	**c**	c
	Iceland	98.8	(0.0)	515	(1.6)	0.3	c	c	c	c	c
	Ireland	99.3	(0.7)	504	(2.6)	0.7		c	c	**c**	c
	Italy	94.8	(1.5)	466	(3.2)	4.0	(1.3)	468	(22.9)	–2	(23.8)
	Japan	97.6	(1.2)	535	(4.2)	1.7	(1.0)	c	c	c	c
	Korea	94.7	(1.9)	544	(3.6)	4.5	(1.8)	525	(23.6)	19	(24.7)
	Luxembourg	99.8	(0.0)	493	(1.0)	a	a	a	a	a	a
	Mexico	96.0	(0.9)	385	(4.0)	3.2	(0.9)	384	(13.9)	0	(14.5)
	Netherlands	96.8	(1.4)	538	(3.8)	0.5	c	c	c	**c**	c
	New Zealand	98.4	(1.0)	524	(2.4)	1.6	(1.0)	c	c	c	c
	Norway	100.0	(0.0)	494	(2.4)	a	a	a	a	a	a
	Poland	98.0	(1.1)	490	(2.5)	2.0	(1.1)	c	c	c	c
	Portugal	98.8	(0.7)	467	(3.5)	1.2	(0.7)	c	c	**c**	c
	Slovak Republic	98.7	(0.7)	498	(3.4)	1.3	(0.7)	c	c	c	c
	Spain	99.6	(0.3)	485	(2.7)	0.3	c	c	c	**c**	c
	Sweden	95.8	(1.6)	508	(2.3)	3.6	(1.5)	530	(22.8)	–22	(22.8)
	Switzerland	92.6	(1.8)	524	(4.2)	5.8	(1.5)	574	(16.1)	**–50**	(17.9)
	Turkey	84.6	(3.0)	426	(7.3)	15.2	(2.9)	409	(17.2)	17	(18.3)
	United States	97.7	(1.0)	486	(3.2)	1.6	(0.8)	c	c	c	c
	OECD total	*96.0*	*(0.4)*	*489*	*(1.2)*	*3.2*	*(0.3)*	*460*	*(8.9)*	*29*	*(9.1)*
	OECD average	*95.1*	*(0.3)*	*500*	*(0.7)*	*4.2*	*(0.3)*	*483*	*(5.4)*	*18*	*(5.3)*
Partner countries	Brazil	86.7	(2.7)	360	(5.0)	12.0	(2.6)	336	(15.2)	25	(15.0)
	Hong Kong-China	98.7	(0.9)	551	(4.7)	1.3	(0.9)	c	c	**c**	c
	Indonesia	85.3	(2.8)	362	(4.6)	10.4	(2.3)	347	(12.1)	14	(14.2)
	Latvia	100.0	(0.0)	483	(3.7)	a	a	a	a	a	a
	Liechtenstein	c	c	c	c	c	c	c	c	c	c
	Macao-China	96.5	(0.1)	528	(3.0)	3.5	(0.1)	496	(13.7)	**32**	(14.1)
	Russian Federation	100.0	(0.0)	468	(4.7)	a	a	a	a	a	a
	Serbia	91.9	(2.2)	438	(4.1)	7.2	(2.2)	430	(15.5)	8	(16.6)
	Thailand	89.0	(2.5)	419	(3.4)	10.3	(2.6)	405	(9.5)	14	(10.8)
	Tunisia	73.6	(3.5)	364	(4.1)	24.7	(3.3)	347	(7.3)	16	(10.3)
	Uruguay	93.6	(1.7)	423	(3.6)	5.7	(1.7)	417	(14.5)	6	(15.9)
	United Kingdom[1]	97.9	(1.0)	509	(2.6)	a	a	a	a	a	a

		Make decisions about students' retention or promotion									
		Schools that use this method				Schools that do not use this method					
		% of students		Math. performance		% of students		Math. performance		Performance difference	
		%	S.E.	Score	S.E.	%	S.E.	Score	S.E.	Dif.	S.E.
OECD countries	Australia	61.0	(2.9)	524	(2.7)	38.2	(2.9)	525	(3.8)	–1	(4.7)
	Austria	92.0	(2.4)	511	(3.5)	6.7	(2.3)	435	(10.1)	**75**	(10.6)
	Belgium	98.1	(0.8)	532	(2.7)	0.9	(0.6)	c	c	**c**	c
	Canada	93.0	(1.1)	533	(1.9)	4.4	(0.9)	525	(7.1)	7	(7.6)
	Czech Republic	91.2	(1.9)	517	(3.8)	8.2	(1.9)	502	(18.4)	15	(19.4)
	Denmark	3.8	(0.9)	508	(13.4)	95.6	(1.1)	515	(2.7)	–7	(13.8)
	Finland	94.0	(1.3)	545	(2.0)	4.7	(0.9)	533	(9.1)	11	(9.4)
	France	w	w	w	w	w	w	w	w	w	w
	Germany	93.6	(1.6)	507	(3.7)	3.6	(1.2)	451	(32.9)	55	(33.1)
	Greece	99.4	(0.5)	445	(3.9)	0.6	(0.5)	c	c	**c**	c
	Hungary	92.9	(2.0)	493	(3.3)	5.2	(1.9)	457	(20.3)	36	(21.1)
	Iceland	14.6	(0.1)	508	(3.8)	83.8	(0.2)	517	(1.7)	**–9**	(4.0)
	Ireland	43.3	(4.1)	500	(4.0)	55.9	(4.2)	505	(3.8)	–5	(6.0)
	Italy	81.8	(2.9)	474	(3.8)	16.0	(2.7)	423	(11.3)	**51**	(12.9)
	Japan	88.9	(2.6)	530	(4.6)	10.4	(2.5)	560	(18.5)	–30	(20.1)
	Korea	24.4	(3.7)	542	(9.5)	74.0	(3.8)	543	(4.3)	–1	(11.7)
	Luxembourg	99.8	(0.0)	493	(1.0)	a	a	a	a	a	a
	Mexico	91.5	(1.9)	388	(3.9)	7.0	(1.8)	351	(11.6)	**37**	(12.6)
	Netherlands	94.1	(1.9)	540	(3.9)	3.1	(1.5)	436	(28.2)	**104**	(29.3)
	New Zealand	77.0	(2.9)	527	(3.0)	21.8	(2.7)	518	(5.8)	9	(7.2)
	Norway	m	m	m	m	m	m	m	m	m	m
	Poland	84.2	(2.8)	491	(2.7)	15.8	(2.8)	487	(7.4)	4	(8.1)
	Portugal	96.6	(1.6)	466	(3.6)	3.4	(1.6)	453	(29.3)	13	(30.3)
	Slovak Republic	96.0	(1.2)	499	(3.5)	3.3	(1.0)	493	(15.2)	5	(16.2)
	Spain	99.5	(0.3)	485	(2.7)	0.5	(0.3)	c	c	c	c
	Sweden	38.9	(4.1)	512	(3.9)	61.0	(4.0)	507	(3.7)	4	(5.7)
	Switzerland	94.9	(1.5)	527	(3.7)	4.8	(1.5)	502	(20.5)	25	(21.4)
	Turkey	70.2	(4.3)	426	(8.4)	28.6	(4.1)	408	(11.9)	18	(15.1)
	United States	75.2	(2.8)	480	(4.2)	23.3	(2.7)	502	(5.9)	–22	(7.6)
	OECD total	*79.2*	*(0.9)*	*486*	*(1.5)*	*19.4*	*(0.9)*	*499*	*(3.3)*	***–13***	*(4.0)*
	OECD average	*78.9*	*(0.4)*	*499*	*(0.8)*	*20.1*	*(0.4)*	*504*	*(1.7)*	***–6***	*(1.9)*
Partner countries	Brazil	82.3	(2.6)	363	(6.1)	16.4	(2.4)	327	(9.3)	**36**	(12.2)
	Hong Kong-China	96.3	(1.5)	550	(4.8)	3.7	(1.5)	559	(16.9)	–9	(18.1)
	Indonesia	81.1	(2.7)	360	(4.6)	15.2	(2.5)	360	(11.4)	0	(12.9)
	Latvia	94.1	(2.7)	485	(3.7)	5.9	(2.7)	455	(19.5)	30	(19.3)
	Liechtenstein	c	c	c	c	c	c	c	c	c	c
	Macao-China	96.5	(0.1)	528	(3.0)	3.5	(0.1)	496	(13.7)	**32**	(14.1)
	Russian Federation	96.7	(1.3)	467	(4.3)	3.3	(1.3)	517	(14.0)	**–51**	(14.6)
	Serbia	87.1	(2.5)	436	(4.1)	11.1	(2.4)	446	(14.2)	–10	(15.2)
	Thailand	71.7	(4.0)	420	(3.9)	28.0	(3.9)	410	(5.9)	9	(7.6)
	Tunisia	83.4	(2.9)	362	(3.4)	15.6	(2.9)	342	(8.8)	21	(10.7)
	Uruguay	90.4	(2.4)	423	(3.7)	9.4	(2.4)	421	(13.4)	1	(14.6)
	United Kingdom[1]	66.5	(3.4)	509	(3.2)	30.9	(3.3)	508	(5.6)	2	(6.8)

Note: Values that are statistically significant are indicated in bold (see Annex A4).
1. Response rate too low to ensure comparability (see Annex A3).

Table 5.10 *(continued – 1)*

Use of assessment results and student performance in mathematics

Results based on reports from school principals and reported proportionate to the number of 15-year-olds enrolled in the school

		Group students for instructional purposes									
		Schools that use this method				Schools that do not use this method					
		% of students		Math. performance		% of students		Math. performance		Performance difference	
		%	S.E.	Score	S.E.	%	S.E.	Score	S.E.	Dif.	S.E.
OECD countries	Australia	77.6	(2.6)	526	(2.8)	22.1	(2.6)	519	(6.6)	6	(8.0)
	Austria	31.0	(2.3)	453	(6.4)	66.6	(2.3)	528	(3.7)	**–75**	(7.5)
	Belgium	19.4	(2.3)	508	(10.3)	78.3	(2.7)	536	(3.5)	**–29**	(12.4)
	Canada	69.0	(2.2)	534	(2.3)	26.8	(2.0)	528	(4.2)	6	(5.1)
	Czech Republic	35.1	(3.2)	515	(7.9)	64.6	(3.3)	517	(4.5)	–2	(9.8)
	Denmark	14.0	(2.6)	503	(7.8)	85.4	(2.7)	516	(2.8)	–14	(8.3)
	Finland	17.1	(3.0)	547	(5.3)	82.9	(3.0)	544	(2.0)	3	(5.6)
	France	w	w	w	w	w	w	w	w	w	w
	Germany	35.1	(3.0)	457	(6.2)	62.9	(2.9)	531	(4.8)	**–74**	(8.2)
	Greece	10.9	(2.1)	441	(11.6)	87.8	(2.2)	446	(4.3)	–5	(12.7)
	Hungary	34.2	(3.5)	513	(7.5)	63.9	(3.5)	479	(4.6)	**34**	(10.5)
	Iceland	54.9	(0.2)	514	(1.9)	43.0	(0.2)	517	(2.6)	–3	(3.2)
	Ireland	78.1	(3.3)	502	(3.1)	21.9	(3.3)	507	(7.5)	–5	(8.9)
	Italy	49.9	(3.8)	461	(5.8)	47.1	(3.9)	470	(5.5)	–9	(9.7)
	Japan	44.4	(4.5)	545	(7.8)	54.9	(4.4)	524	(8.3)	21	(13.6)
	Korea	61.6	(4.0)	545	(5.1)	36.8	(3.9)	538	(7.2)	7	(10.3)
	Luxembourg	29.6	(0.1)	460	(1.9)	70.2	(0.1)	507	(1.3)	**–47**	(2.4)
	Mexico	58.7	(3.2)	384	(4.9)	40.1	(3.2)	385	(7.4)	–1	(9.3)
	Netherlands	86.2	(2.9)	536	(4.2)	11.0	(2.6)	541	(15.8)	–5	(18.1)
	New Zealand	72.7	(3.0)	523	(3.3)	26.0	(3.0)	530	(5.8)	–6	(7.5)
	Norway	37.8	(4.0)	490	(3.9)	62.2	(4.0)	497	(2.9)	–7	(4.8)
	Poland	33.0	(4.1)	495	(5.8)	67.0	(4.1)	488	(2.7)	7	(6.7)
	Portugal	26.1	(3.8)	466	(7.9)	73.9	(3.8)	466	(4.3)	0	(9.7)
	Slovak Republic	54.5	(3.8)	500	(4.8)	44.8	(3.8)	497	(6.2)	3	(8.8)
	Spain	47.4	(3.5)	476	(4.0)	52.2	(3.5)	494	(3.7)	**–18**	(5.7)
	Sweden	44.6	(4.0)	508	(3.6)	54.0	(3.9)	510	(3.8)	–2	(5.5)
	Switzerland	27.1	(3.1)	513	(5.6)	69.2	(3.5)	532	(5.5)	**–19**	(8.7)
	Turkey	49.1	(4.3)	421	(9.6)	47.6	(4.2)	422	(8.9)	–2	(12.9)
	United States	64.8	(3.3)	487	(4.4)	33.5	(3.2)	483	(6.2)	3	(8.1)
	OECD total	***54.0***	***(1.1)***	***487***	***(1.9)***	***44.4***	***(1.1)***	***490***	***(2.3)***	***–3***	***(3.5)***
	OECD average	***43.4***	***(0.6)***	***498***	***(1.1)***	***54.9***	***(0.6)***	***501***	***(1.1)***	***–3***	***(1.7)***
Partner countries	Brazil	42.6	(3.9)	348	(7.1)	52.7	(4.0)	363	(8.4)	–15	(11.9)
	Hong Kong-China	63.3	(4.2)	537	(7.5)	36.7	(4.2)	571	(8.0)	**–34**	(12.9)
	Indonesia	44.6	(3.6)	359	(6.5)	51.5	(3.9)	361	(5.1)	–3	(8.3)
	Latvia	39.9	(4.2)	492	(5.8)	59.7	(4.3)	478	(4.7)	**15**	(7.3)
	Liechtenstein	c	c	c	c	c	c	c	c	c	c
	Macao-China	38.9	(0.2)	539	(3.8)	50.8	(0.2)	521	(3.6)	**18**	(5.4)
	Russian Federation	54.6	(4.0)	472	(5.8)	43.5	(3.8)	465	(6.9)	7	(9.2)
	Serbia	18.9	(3.4)	437	(10.3)	78.5	(3.6)	436	(4.4)	1	(11.9)
	Thailand	77.2	(3.5)	421	(3.8)	22.8	(3.5)	404	(6.8)	**17**	(8.3)
	Tunisia	42.6	(4.2)	365	(5.5)	55.1	(4.2)	355	(4.2)	10	(8.2)
	Uruguay	28.2	(3.1)	413	(6.6)	69.0	(3.0)	426	(4.5)	–13	(8.9)
	United Kingdom[1]	91.7	(1.9)	508	(2.7)	6.2	(1.6)	521	(15.4)	–13	(15.8)

		Compare the school to district or national performance									
		Schools that use this method				Schools that do not use this method					
		% of students		Math. performance		% of students		Math. performance		Performance difference	
		%	S.E.	Score	S.E.	%	S.E.	Score	S.E.	Dif.	S.E.
OECD countries	Australia	54.8	(2.4)	521	(3.0)	44.9	(2.4)	528	(3.7)	–8	(5.0)
	Austria	12.2	(2.7)	505	(11.0)	85.9	(2.8)	505	(3.9)	0	(12.2)
	Belgium	9.5	(2.2)	566	(12.9)	89.7	(2.2)	527	(3.2)	**39**	(14.2)
	Canada	67.8	(2.2)	533	(2.4)	28.9	(2.1)	533	(3.7)	0	(4.7)
	Czech Republic	49.8	(3.3)	521	(5.2)	49.8	(3.3)	510	(6.6)	11	(9.4)
	Denmark	5.9	(1.7)	527	(7.2)	93.6	(1.8)	514	(2.9)	14	(7.8)
	Finland	56.0	(4.0)	546	(2.6)	43.4	(4.1)	542	(2.7)	4	(3.8)
	France	w	w	w	w	w	w	w	w	w	w
	Germany	20.7	(3.1)	521	(11.1)	76.8	(3.1)	500	(4.2)	21	(12.8)
	Greece	12.1	(2.8)	465	(12.4)	86.8	(2.7)	443	(4.5)	22	(14.0)
	Hungary	84.3	(2.8)	489	(3.8)	13.2	(2.6)	503	(14.7)	–14	(16.8)
	Iceland	82.5	(0.1)	516	(1.7)	15.6	(0.1)	512	(3.7)	4	(4.1)
	Ireland	17.2	(3.2)	507	(7.6)	82.8	(3.2)	503	(3.1)	5	(9.0)
	Italy	31.8	(3.3)	472	(7.0)	65.3	(3.5)	463	(4.2)	9	(9.2)
	Japan	17.7	(3.4)	563	(10.9)	81.5	(3.5)	527	(5.6)	**36**	(14.0)
	Korea	61.0	(3.6)	562	(4.5)	37.4	(3.7)	511	(7.3)	**52**	(9.1)
	Luxembourg	21.8	(0.0)	486	(2.3)	78.0	(0.0)	495	(1.2)	**–9**	(2.8)
	Mexico	53.9	(3.1)	391	(4.3)	43.2	(3.0)	379	(7.2)	12	(8.5)
	Netherlands	61.3	(4.1)	551	(5.9)	35.3	(4.0)	510	(8.9)	**42**	(12.8)
	New Zealand	86.1	(2.4)	525	(2.6)	13.3	(2.3)	520	(6.6)	5	(7.4)
	Norway	63.8	(3.6)	498	(2.9)	36.2	(3.6)	487	(3.9)	**11**	(4.7)
	Poland	71.1	(3.7)	493	(3.1)	28.9	(3.7)	484	(4.3)	9	(5.3)
	Portugal	32.9	(4.2)	467	(8.8)	67.1	(4.2)	465	(4.0)	2	(10.5)
	Slovak Republic	45.1	(3.7)	499	(6.3)	53.3	(3.6)	498	(5.0)	2	(9.0)
	Spain	18.1	(2.1)	490	(7.0)	81.2	(2.1)	484	(2.9)	6	(7.7)
	Sweden	72.5	(3.1)	508	(2.6)	26.8	(3.1)	510	(5.7)	–2	(6.1)
	Switzerland	18.3	(1.9)	540	(8.4)	80.3	(2.2)	523	(4.5)	16	(10.4)
	Turkey	58.0	(4.4)	429	(9.8)	40.8	(4.3)	410	(10.7)	19	(15.7)
	United States	89.8	(2.1)	484	(3.3)	9.2	(1.9)	497	(9.9)	–12	(10.1)
	OECD total	***56.5***	***(0.9)***	***489***	***(1.9)***	***41.9***	***(0.9)***	***488***	***(2.1)***	***1***	***(3.2)***
	OECD average	***45.8***	***(0.5)***	***504***	***(1.1)***	***52.7***	***(0.5)***	***496***	***(1.0)***	***9***	***(1.6)***
Partner countries	Brazil	36.3	(3.4)	352	(7.2)	60.5	(3.6)	359	(7.6)	–7	(11.4)
	Hong Kong-China	22.7	(4.0)	537	(16.7)	77.3	(4.0)	554	(4.8)	–17	(18.6)
	Indonesia	48.5	(3.7)	371	(4.9)	47.4	(3.8)	349	(5.5)	**23**	(7.0)
	Latvia	79.3	(4.1)	481	(3.5)	20.1	(4.1)	495	(9.5)	–15	(9.6)
	Liechtenstein	c	c	c	c	c	c	c	c	c	c
	Macao-China	2.8	(0.1)	c	c	87.0	(0.1)	c	c	c	c
	Russian Federation	69.2	(4.2)	466	(4.8)	29.8	(4.1)	474	(8.4)	–7	(9.4)
	Serbia	41.9	(4.1)	438	(6.2)	56.3	(4.0)	436	(5.3)	2	(8.6)
	Thailand	59.3	(3.6)	423	(4.8)	40.7	(3.6)	408	(5.6)	15	(8.5)
	Tunisia	71.9	(3.7)	361	(3.8)	26.4	(3.6)	357	(6.9)	4	(9.2)
	Uruguay	17.8	(3.1)	408	(9.8)	80.6	(3.2)	425	(3.8)	–17	(11.4)
	United Kingdom[1]	86.6	(2.1)	505	(3.0)	10.8	(1.8)	545	(12.1)	**–40**	(13.1)

Note: Values that are statistically significant are indicated in bold (see Annex A4).

1. Response rate too low to ensure comparability (see Annex A3).

Table 5.10 *(continued – 2)*

Use of assessment results and student performance in mathematics

Results based on reports from school principals and reported proportionate to the number of 15-year-olds enrolled in the school

	Monitor the school's progress from year to year									
	Schools that use this method				Schools that do not use this method					
	% of students		Math. performance		% of students		Math. performance		Performance difference	
	%	S.E.	Score	S.E.	%	S.E.	Score	S.E.	Dif.	S.E.
OECD countries										
Australia	76.5	(2.7)	519	(2.7)	23.5	(2.7)	542	(4.3)	**–23**	(5.3)
Austria	57.6	(3.8)	503	(5.4)	39.8	(3.9)	508	(6.9)	–5	(10.0)
Belgium	37.0	(2.8)	538	(7.2)	61.3	(2.8)	526	(5.0)	13	(10.8)
Canada	77.1	(1.9)	534	(2.1)	19.9	(1.7)	528	(4.7)	5	(5.4)
Czech Republic	85.2	(2.4)	516	(4.4)	14.3	(2.4)	516	(12.7)	–1	(15.0)
Denmark	8.4	(2.0)	525	(12.0)	91.0	(2.1)	513	(2.7)	12	(12.1)
Finland	65.0	(4.1)	547	(2.4)	35.0	(4.1)	539	(2.9)	7	(3.8)
France	w	w	w	w	w	w	w	w	w	w
Germany	43.2	(3.2)	493	(7.9)	54.8	(3.1)	513	(6.3)	–20	(12.6)
Greece	35.2	(5.7)	451	(8.8)	63.8	(5.7)	441	(4.5)	10	(10.6)
Hungary	93.9	(1.6)	492	(3.1)	4.2	(1.4)	460	(32.5)	32	(33.5)
Iceland	87.0	(0.1)	515	(1.8)	11.8	(0.1)	519	(4.9)	–4	(5.5)
Ireland	49.1	(3.9)	505	(3.4)	50.1	(4.0)	502	(4.7)	2	(6.5)
Italy	67.2	(3.0)	460	(4.8)	29.7	(3.0)	480	(6.6)	**–20**	(9.8)
Japan	47.3	(4.4)	551	(7.4)	52.0	(4.5)	518	(7.4)	**33**	(12.2)
Korea	57.6	(4.0)	561	(5.9)	40.8	(3.9)	516	(6.2)	**45**	(9.5)
Luxembourg	26.0	(0.1)	494	(2.0)	73.8	(0.1)	493	(1.2)	1	(2.5)
Mexico	90.4	(1.6)	386	(4.3)	8.8	(1.6)	367	(8.6)	19	(10.5)
Netherlands	61.4	(4.1)	539	(6.0)	35.7	(4.1)	533	(7.5)	5	(11.7)
New Zealand	95.1	(1.7)	524	(2.4)	4.3	(1.6)	530	(15.8)	–6	(16.2)
Norway	67.7	(3.3)	497	(2.7)	32.3	(3.3)	488	(4.1)	**10**	(4.6)
Poland	96.6	(1.5)	491	(2.5)	3.4	(1.5)	462	(11.2)	**29**	(11.5)
Portugal	78.5	(3.1)	465	(4.2)	21.5	(3.1)	469	(6.9)	–3	(8.5)
Slovak Republic	94.6	(1.6)	497	(3.5)	5.0	(1.5)	520	(12.0)	–23	(12.7)
Spain	68.0	(3.2)	482	(3.7)	31.1	(3.1)	492	(5.0)	–11	(6.8)
Sweden	84.1	(2.8)	509	(2.7)	14.4	(2.7)	506	(8.3)	4	(9.0)
Switzerland	24.3	(4.4)	537	(9.8)	73.2	(4.5)	520	(4.2)	17	(10.8)
Turkey	75.4	(3.4)	420	(7.8)	23.4	(3.2)	423	(12.8)	–3	(15.2)
United States	92.3	(1.8)	485	(3.3)	6.5	(1.6)	499	(15.2)	–14	(15.5)
OECD total	*75.1*	*(0.9)*	*484*	*(1.6)*	*23.6*	*(0.9)*	*501*	*(2.7)*	*–17*	*(3.5)*
OECD average	*69.3*	*(0.5)*	*498*	*(1.0)*	*29.5*	*(0.5)*	*503*	*(1.3)*	*–5*	*(1.7)*
Partner countries										
Brazil	73.8	(3.3)	364	(6.8)	23.7	(3.6)	340	(11.9)	24	(15.5)
Hong Kong-China	90.0	(2.6)	552	(5.3)	9.4	(2.5)	533	(22.3)	19	(24.2)
Indonesia	82.2	(2.8)	362	(4.8)	13.3	(2.6)	347	(10.1)	15	(12.4)
Latvia	99.2	(0.6)	484	(3.7)	0.8	(0.6)	c	c	c	c
Liechtenstein	c	c	c	c	c	c	c	c	c	c
Macao-China	81.4	(0.2)	528	(3.4)	18.6	(0.2)	523	(5.9)	5	(7.0)
Russian Federation	96.7	(1.3)	469	(4.2)	3.1	(1.3)	464	(23.1)	4	(23.5)
Serbia	75.4	(3.6)	442	(4.2)	22.9	(3.5)	421	(8.6)	**20**	(9.8)
Thailand	88.0	(3.0)	418	(3.4)	12.0	(3.0)	413	(10.0)	5	(11.1)
Tunisia	80.5	(3.4)	361	(3.8)	17.9	(3.3)	355	(9.7)	6	(12.2)
Uruguay	75.6	(3.9)	420	(4.6)	23.2	(3.9)	433	(9.0)	–13	(11.5)
United Kingdom[1]	94.7	(1.5)	508	(2.8)	2.6	(1.0)	c	c	c	c

	Make judgements about teachers' effectiveness									
	Schools that use this method				Schools that do not use this method					
	% of students		Math. performance		% of students		Math. performance		Performance difference	
	%	S.E.	Score	S.E.	%	S.E.	Score	S.E.	Dif.	S.E.
OECD countries										
Australia	34.0	(2.9)	525	(4.7)	66.0	(2.9)	524	(3.2)	1	(6.4)
Austria	35.0	(3.4)	503	(6.7)	63.2	(3.4)	506	(5.1)	–3	(9.5)
Belgium	19.1	(2.3)	562	(9.0)	79.3	(2.5)	523	(3.7)	**40**	(11.0)
Canada	30.4	(2.3)	537	(3.6)	66.5	(2.4)	530	(2.1)	7	(4.2)
Czech Republic	61.4	(3.4)	514	(5.1)	38.2	(3.4)	519	(6.4)	–5	(9.1)
Denmark	3.7	(1.4)	508	(9.2)	95.7	(1.5)	515	(2.7)	–7	(9.2)
Finland	31.9	(3.5)	548	(3.3)	67.3	(3.4)	542	(2.3)	6	(4.0)
France	w	w	w	w	w	w	w	w	w	w
Germany	11.5	(2.3)	518	(14.7)	86.0	(2.4)	503	(4.1)	15	(16.4)
Greece	15.0	(4.3)	475	(11.8)	83.9	(4.2)	440	(4.0)	**34**	(12.6)
Hungary	74.5	(3.6)	488	(4.4)	22.3	(3.4)	503	(11.5)	–15	(14.3)
Iceland	30.3	(0.2)	515	(2.8)	67.7	(0.2)	516	(1.9)	–1	(3.4)
Ireland	16.7	(3.2)	510	(8.4)	81.9	(3.3)	502	(2.8)	7	(9.2)
Italy	22.5	(3.1)	459	(10.1)	73.9	(3.3)	468	(3.6)	–9	(11.7)
Japan	81.0	(3.3)	537	(4.6)	18.3	(3.3)	518	(15.9)	19	(17.7)
Korea	53.6	(4.2)	549	(5.1)	44.8	(4.3)	534	(7.0)	15	(10.1)
Luxembourg	20.9	(0.0)	482	(2.2)	78.9	(0.0)	496	(1.1)	**–14**	(2.5)
Mexico	76.2	(3.1)	390	(3.8)	22.4	(3.1)	366	(10.7)	**24**	(11.1)
Netherlands	40.3	(4.2)	544	(7.7)	55.2	(4.3)	532	(6.5)	12	(12.4)
New Zealand	51.6	(3.5)	527	(4.1)	45.9	(3.3)	522	(4.2)	5	(6.6)
Norway	19.5	(3.0)	498	(5.8)	80.5	(3.0)	493	(2.7)	5	(6.6)
Poland	73.2	(3.2)	492	(2.9)	26.8	(3.2)	485	(5.9)	7	(6.8)
Portugal	34.3	(4.3)	461	(8.4)	64.4	(4.4)	468	(4.8)	–7	(11.1)
Slovak Republic	73.6	(2.8)	493	(4.4)	24.5	(2.6)	516	(7.2)	**–23**	(9.3)
Spain	35.6	(3.5)	482	(5.0)	63.5	(3.5)	487	(3.8)	–6	(7.0)
Sweden	21.2	(3.1)	517	(7.7)	78.7	(3.1)	507	(2.8)	11	(8.5)
Switzerland	36.2	(3.5)	522	(6.7)	62.3	(3.4)	527	(5.3)	–5	(9.6)
Turkey	33.1	(4.4)	418	(10.7)	64.7	(4.2)	423	(8.0)	–5	(12.9)
United States	53.9	(3.1)	478	(4.3)	44.7	(3.0)	494	(4.9)	**–16**	(6.3)
OECD total	*53.0*	*(1.0)*	*487*	*(1.8)*	*45.5*	*(1.0)*	*490*	*(2.0)*	*–3*	*(3.0)*
OECD average	*43.9*	*(0.6)*	*500*	*(1.2)*	*54.4*	*(0.6)*	*500*	*(1.0)*	*0*	*(1.8)*
Partner countries										
Brazil	54.2	(3.5)	365	(8.1)	43.4	(3.3)	348	(7.4)	17	(11.8)
Hong Kong-China	63.1	(4.0)	550	(7.4)	35.6	(4.0)	549	(8.6)	1	(13.1)
Indonesia	84.2	(3.0)	361	(4.7)	12.2	(2.4)	354	(10.1)	7	(12.0)
Latvia	86.5	(2.8)	485	(4.2)	13.5	(2.8)	471	(8.1)	15	(9.7)
Liechtenstein	c	c	c	c	c	c	c	c	c	c
Macao-China	73.2	(0.2)	533	(2.9)	16.6	(0.2)	510	(5.0)	**23**	(5.8)
Russian Federation	98.7	(0.8)	467	(4.2)	1.3	(0.8)	c	c	c	c
Serbia	50.0	(4.4)	442	(5.9)	48.0	(4.4)	432	(5.8)	9	(8.9)
Thailand	70.6	(3.6)	420	(4.1)	29.4	(3.6)	411	(6.0)	9	(8.0)
Tunisia	61.7	(3.7)	360	(4.5)	36.6	(3.6)	358	(6.1)	2	(9.3)
Uruguay	40.1	(4.4)	418	(7.3)	58.4	(4.4)	426	(5.1)	–8	(10.2)
United Kingdom[1]	83.2	(2.5)	509	(2.8)	13.7	(2.2)	512	(9.1)	–4	(9.7)

Note: Values that are statistically significant are indicated in bold (see Annex A4).

1. Response rate too low to ensure comparability (see Annex A3).

Table 5.10 *(continued – 3)*

Use of assessment results and student performance in mathematics

Results based on reports from school principals and reported proportionate to the number of 15-year-olds enrolled in the school

		Identify aspects of instruction or the curriculum that could be improved									
		Schools that use this method				Schools that do not use this method					
		% of students		Math. performance		% of students		Math. performance		Performance difference	
		%	S.E.	Score	S.E.	%	S.E.	Score	S.E.	Dif.	S.E.
OECD countries	Australia	80.6	(2.5)	527	(2.5)	18.3	(2.5)	510	(7.4)	**18**	(8.3)
	Austria	63.9	(3.6)	501	(4.9)	33.5	(3.7)	510	(8.6)	–9	(11.2)
	Belgium	64.5	(3.0)	532	(4.6)	33.1	(3.0)	529	(7.3)	3	(10.5)
	Canada	81.9	(2.0)	533	(2.0)	15.5	(1.7)	528	(6.4)	5	(6.9)
	Czech Republic	88.2	(2.1)	515	(3.9)	11.3	(2.1)	524	(9.6)	–9	(10.7)
	Denmark	45.9	(3.8)	518	(3.8)	52.4	(3.8)	510	(3.8)	8	(5.3)
	Finland	65.1	(3.6)	545	(2.2)	34.2	(3.6)	543	(3.6)	1	(4.3)
	France	w	w	w	w	w	w	w	w	w	w
	Germany	43.6	(3.8)	485	(6.9)	53.8	(3.8)	520	(6.1)	**–35**	(10.9)
	Greece	40.0	(5.2)	458	(7.5)	58.7	(5.1)	438	(4.9)	**20**	(9.8)
	Hungary	90.7	(2.4)	489	(3.6)	6.1	(2.1)	509	(24.5)	–19	(26.1)
	Iceland	95.8	(0.0)	516	(1.6)	3.3	(0.0)	497	(8.7)	**19**	(8.8)
	Ireland	41.5	(4.3)	504	(4.7)	57.0	(4.3)	503	(4.0)	1	(7.1)
	Italy	81.8	(2.8)	463	(3.8)	15.9	(2.9)	474	(12.1)	–11	(14.1)
	Japan	78.3	(3.4)	535	(5.5)	21.0	(3.4)	527	(13.3)	8	(16.4)
	Korea	88.8	(2.8)	544	(3.8)	9.7	(2.7)	526	(17.4)	18	(18.8)
	Luxembourg	62.8	(0.1)	484	(1.2)	37.0	(0.1)	509	(1.8)	**–25**	(2.2)
	Mexico	87.9	(2.2)	387	(4.2)	10.6	(2.2)	371	(9.8)	15	(10.7)
	Netherlands	69.0	(4.0)	535	(5.3)	27.1	(3.8)	538	(9.9)	–3	(13.2)
	New Zealand	95.2	(1.4)	525	(2.3)	4.2	(1.2)	520	(12.0)	5	(11.8)
	Norway	69.7	(3.5)	493	(2.6)	29.7	(3.5)	498	(4.6)	–5	(5.0)
	Poland	87.8	(2.8)	489	(2.7)	12.2	(2.8)	499	(9.4)	–10	(9.9)
	Portugal	83.6	(3.3)	464	(3.8)	15.5	(3.2)	473	(12.0)	–9	(13.2)
	Slovak Republic	87.6	(2.3)	499	(3.9)	10.8	(2.2)	496	(9.2)	2	(10.8)
	Spain	87.8	(2.4)	486	(3.0)	11.4	(2.3)	481	(7.5)	5	(8.5)
	Sweden	80.1	(2.9)	510	(2.9)	19.1	(3.0)	503	(5.9)	7	(6.8)
	Switzerland	51.3	(3.6)	524	(4.7)	47.5	(3.5)	529	(7.2)	–5	(9.6)
	Turkey	33.2	(3.8)	420	(13.4)	64.6	(3.6)	422	(8.3)	–1	(16.8)
	United States	90.9	(1.9)	487	(3.3)	7.9	(1.9)	468	(14.1)	19	(14.6)
	OECD total	*78.9*	*(0.8)*	*489*	*(1.4)*	*19.6*	*(0.8)*	*488*	*(3.6)*	*1*	*(4.2)*
	OECD average	*74.3*	*(0.5)*	*501*	*(0.8)*	*24.3*	*(0.5)*	*497*	*(1.9)*	*4*	*(2.3)*
Partner countries	Brazil	90.9	(2.2)	358	(5.2)	7.8	(2.0)	347	(23.3)	11	(24.3)
	Hong Kong-China	96.3	(1.3)	551	(4.9)	3.1	(1.2)	525	(36.4)	25	(37.1)
	Indonesia	75.9	(3.5)	361	(4.9)	20.4	(3.0)	356	(8.2)	6	(10.3)
	Latvia	96.7	(1.4)	483	(3.8)	3.3	(1.4)	488	(13.1)	–5	(13.9)
	Liechtenstein	c	c	c	c	c	c	c	c	c	c
	Macao-China	97.5	(0.1)	528	(2.9)	2.5	(0.1)	c	c	c	c
	Russian Federation	98.8	(0.7)	468	(4.2)	1.2	(0.7)	c	c	c	c
	Serbia	62.8	(3.8)	439	(5.0)	34.7	(4.0)	434	(7.5)	6	(9.7)
	Thailand	76.9	(3.8)	423	(3.6)	23.1	(3.8)	398	(6.8)	**24**	(7.9)
	Tunisia	70.7	(3.3)	364	(4.1)	27.6	(3.2)	347	(5.8)	17	(8.7)
	Uruguay	68.2	(3.7)	421	(4.8)	31.0	(3.7)	425	(7.6)	–4	(10.2)
	United Kingdom[1]	88.2	(2.4)	508	(2.8)	8.3	(2.1)	529	(16.2)	–22	(16.9)

		Compare the school with other schools									
		Schools that use this method				Schools that do not use this method					
		% of students		Math. performance		% of students		Math. performance		Performance difference	
		%	S.E.	Score	S.E.	%	S.E.	Score	S.E.	Dif.	S.E.
OECD countries	Australia	38.5	(2.7)	518	(4.7)	61.0	(2.7)	528	(3.2)	–11	(6.5)
	Austria	36.7	(3.9)	494	(8.1)	60.0	(3.8)	511	(5.3)	–17	(11.2)
	Belgium	6.8	(1.7)	547	(14.0)	92.0	(1.7)	529	(2.9)	18	(15.1)
	Canada	50.7	(2.3)	533	(3.1)	45.0	(2.4)	533	(3.0)	–1	(4.7)
	Czech Republic	55.3	(3.7)	513	(4.8)	44.7	(3.7)	520	(7.4)	–7	(10.0)
	Denmark	2.9	(1.2)	c	c	96.0	(1.5)	514	(2.7)	c	c
	Finland	34.7	(3.4)	545	(3.5)	64.7	(3.5)	544	(2.0)	1	(3.9)
	France	w	w	w	w	w	w	w	w	w	w
	Germany	16.7	(2.6)	494	(13.0)	80.8	(2.6)	507	(3.7)	–13	(14.2)
	Greece	15.7	(3.0)	473	(6.8)	83.2	(3.0)	440	(4.4)	**32**	(8.3)
	Hungary	75.0	(3.3)	493	(4.2)	21.8	(3.1)	482	(11.2)	11	(13.7)
	Iceland	64.3	(0.2)	513	(2.0)	33.8	(0.2)	521	(2.6)	**–9**	(3.4)
	Ireland	8.8	(2.6)	518	(11.2)	91.2	(2.6)	502	(2.5)	17	(11.8)
	Italy	28.3	(3.1)	462	(8.6)	68.9	(3.3)	467	(3.7)	–5	(10.3)
	Japan	11.6	(2.8)	570	(8.5)	87.0	(3.0)	528	(5.0)	**42**	(11.0)
	Korea	54.0	(3.8)	558	(5.0)	44.4	(3.9)	524	(7.3)	**34**	(9.9)
	Luxembourg	10.3	(0.0)	434	(3.9)	89.5	(0.0)	500	(1.0)	**–66**	(4.2)
	Mexico	49.6	(3.5)	390	(4.6)	48.7	(3.4)	379	(6.4)	11	(7.9)
	Netherlands	45.2	(4.3)	552	(7.8)	50.9	(4.4)	525	(7.2)	**26**	(13.3)
	New Zealand	72.2	(3.3)	525	(3.2)	26.0	(3.2)	522	(5.1)	3	(6.8)
	Norway	47.1	(3.8)	501	(3.3)	52.9	(3.8)	488	(3.1)	**13**	(4.2)
	Poland	62.3	(3.6)	491	(3.5)	37.7	(3.6)	489	(3.9)	3	(5.4)
	Portugal	22.1	(3.4)	484	(6.7)	77.0	(3.5)	460	(4.7)	**24**	(9.4)
	Slovak Republic	47.1	(3.1)	499	(6.1)	51.7	(3.2)	497	(4.9)	2	(8.7)
	Spain	17.0	(2.1)	487	(9.8)	82.1	(2.1)	485	(2.6)	2	(10.2)
	Sweden	63.7	(3.4)	508	(3.1)	34.6	(3.5)	509	(4.1)	0	(4.9)
	Switzerland	15.7	(3.6)	546	(9.7)	82.8	(3.6)	521	(4.1)	**25**	(9.6)
	Turkey	58.2	(4.5)	431	(9.3)	40.7	(4.4)	406	(9.2)	25	(13.1)
	United States	79.4	(2.8)	484	(3.4)	19.5	(2.8)	492	(7.9)	–8	(8.5)
	OECD total	*50.0*	*(1.0)*	*486*	*(2.1)*	*48.3*	*(1.1)*	*491*	*(1.8)*	*–6*	*(3.1)*
	OECD average	*40.4*	*(0.6)*	*501*	*(1.3)*	*57.9*	*(0.6)*	*499*	*(1.0)*	*2*	*(1.8)*
Partner countries	Brazil	22.6	(2.8)	376	(10.4)	74.5	(3.1)	351	(6.4)	25	(13.2)
	Hong Kong-China	18.8	(3.1)	545	(19.9)	80.5	(3.2)	551	(4.4)	–6	(21.2)
	Indonesia	74.5	(2.9)	363	(4.8)	22.0	(2.8)	350	(8.1)	13	(10.1)
	Latvia	65.0	(4.2)	485	(4.4)	34.8	(4.2)	480	(6.7)	5	(7.9)
	Liechtenstein	c	c	c	c	c	c	c	c	c	c
	Macao-China	12.7	(0.1)	523	(7.2)	75.0	(0.2)	530	(2.7)	–7	(7.8)
	Russian Federation	80.9	(3.3)	464	(4.9)	18.6	(3.2)	486	(7.7)	**–22**	(9.3)
	Serbia	49.3	(4.2)	435	(5.5)	49.0	(4.1)	439	(6.0)	–5	(8.6)
	Thailand	56.8	(4.0)	422	(4.7)	43.2	(4.0)	410	(5.8)	12	(8.6)
	Tunisia	70.1	(3.5)	363	(3.6)	27.6	(3.3)	351	(6.8)	13	(9.0)
	Uruguay	10.4	(2.4)	395	(12.9)	88.7	(2.4)	426	(3.7)	**–31**	(14.1)
	United Kingdom[1]	81.4	(2.3)	505	(3.2)	15.1	(2.0)	537	(9.1)	**–32**	(10.1)

Note: Values that are statistically significant are indicated in bold (see Annex A4).

1. Response rate too low to ensure comparability (see Annex A3).

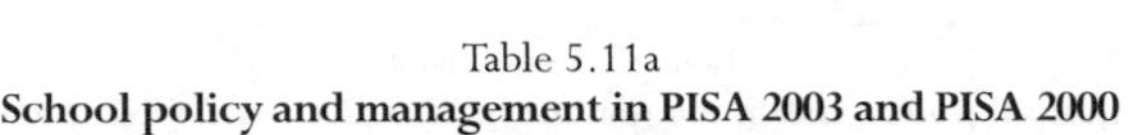

Table 5.11a
School policy and management in PISA 2003 and PISA 2000
Results based on reports from school principals and reported proportionate to the number of 15-year-olds enrolled in the school

	Percentage of students in schools where the principals report that schools have responsibility for the following aspects of school policy and management											
	Appointing teachers				Dismissing teachers				Establishing teachers' starting salaries			
	PISA 2003		PISA 2000		PISA 2003		PISA 2000		PISA 2003		PISA 2000	
	%	S.E.	%	S.E.	%	S.E.	%	S.E.	%	S.E.	%	S.E.
OECD countries												
Australia	61.7	(2.0)	59.7	(2.2)	47.5	(2.0)	47.3	(3.1)	20.0	(2.0)	18.1	(2.2)
Austria	**22.2**	(2.6)	**14.6**	(2.9)	8.2	(2.1)	5.3	(1.7)	0.4	(0.3)	0.7	(0.5)
Belgium	**83.1**	(1.3)	**95.9**	(1.3)	**83.9**	(2.0)	**95.0**	(1.4)	a	a	**6.6**	(1.7)
Canada	81.0	(1.8)	81.7	(1.2)	**54.9**	(2.2)	**60.6**	(1.7)	32.0	(1.8)	33.7	(1.8)
Czech Republic	98.3	(1.1)	96.5	(1.2)	**98.3**	(1.1)	**94.8**	(1.3)	68.9	(3.2)	70.4	(3.1)
Denmark	97.4	(1.2)	97.0	(1.3)	64.5	(3.6)	56.8	(3.2)	**21.4**	(2.8)	**13.2**	(2.5)
Finland	**69.9**	(3.5)	**35.1**	(3.8)	**35.5**	(3.6)	**21.3**	(3.3)	**10.1**	(2.2)	**1.1**	(0.8)
France	w	w	w	w	w	w	w	w	w	w	w	w
Germany	**17.6**	(2.7)	**10.1**	(2.3)	6.3	(1.7)	3.5	(1.3)	1.7	(1.0)	2.0	(0.9)
Greece	m	m	m	m	m	m	m	m	m	m	m	m
Hungary	100.0	(0.0)	100.0	(0.0)	97.9	(1.2)	98.5	(1.0)	38.0	(4.0)	41.0	(4.3)
Iceland	**100.0**	(0.0)	**99.5**	(0.0)	**99.6**	(0.0)	**98.8**	(0.1)	**18.5**	(0.1)	**4.0**	(0.1)
Ireland	85.7	(1.8)	87.9	(2.5)	70.2	(3.0)	73.3	(3.0)	3.8	(1.7)	4.3	(1.7)
Italy	7.5	(1.9)	10.3	(2.1)	7.7	(1.7)	10.9	(2.6)	2.1	(0.9)	1.1	(0.8)
Japan	**28.6**	(1.1)	**33.1**	(1.9)	28.6	(1.1)	32.5	(2.0)	**26.5**	(1.8)	**32.5**	(2.0)
Korea	33.2	(4.0)	32.3	(4.1)	17.7	(3.2)	22.1	(4.0)	15.5	(3.1)	14.6	(3.1)
Luxembourg	m	m	m	m	m	m	m	m	m	m	m	m
Mexico	**75.4**	(2.9)	**57.1**	(3.4)	**65.8**	(3.2)	**47.9**	(3.8)	**47.3**	(3.2)	**25.8**	(3.1)
Netherlands	99.5	(0.5)	100.0	(0.0)	99.3	(0.6)	100.0	(0.0)	**88.3**	(2.5)	**71.5**	(5.0)
New Zealand	100.0	(0.0)	100.0	(0.0)	99.2	(0.8)	99.2	(0.8)	18.7	(2.5)	17.2	(2.4)
Norway	64.2	(3.8)	a	a	46.1	(4.1)	a	a	0.7	(0.6)	a	a
Poland	100.0	(0.0)	a	a	99.2	(0.6)	a	a	21.4	(3.2)	a	a
Portugal	8.1	(1.7)	12.7	(2.1)	7.4	(1.5)	8.7	(1.2)	0.9	(0.5)	0.9	(0.7)
Slovak Republic	99.6	(0.4)	a	a	100.0	(0.0)	a	a	60.0	(3.7)	a	a
Spain	36.0	(1.5)	37.7	(2.5)	36.2	(1.5)	38.7	(2.6)	6.3	(1.2)	9.2	(2.2)
Sweden	99.5	(0.5)	99.0	(0.8)	83.0	(2.9)	82.8	(3.2)	70.8	(3.5)	61.8	(3.6)
Switzerland	92.9	(3.0)	92.6	(1.7)	85.1	(3.1)	82.0	(2.3)	13.5	(2.7)	12.7	(2.7)
Turkey	7.4	(2.2)	a	a	5.4	(1.9)	a	a	5.5	(2.0)	a	a
United States	98.2	(0.8)	97.1	(0.9)	93.8	(1.7)	97.7	(1.2)	68.9	(3.1)	76.2	(4.9)
OECD total	*64.3*	*(0.6)*	*58.4*	*(0.9)*	*58.0*	*(0.7)*	*53.0*	*(0.9)*	*37.9*	*(1.0)*	*36.6*	*(1.4)*
OECD average	*64.0*	*(0.5)*	*61.5*	*(0.4)*	*55.9*	*(0.5)*	*53.6*	*(0.5)*	*25.6*	*(0.5)*	*23.4*	*(0.5)*
Partner countries												
Brazil	38.6	(3.1)	39.2	(2.7)	36.7	(3.1)	32.7	(2.9)	**17.4**	(2.7)	**9.8**	(1.7)
Hong Kong-China	91.2	(0.8)	91.2	(1.5)	**92.4**	(1.2)	**86.9**	(2.3)	27.9	(3.7)	26.1	(3.6)
Indonesia	**49.8**	(3.0)	**73.4**	(4.2)	**52.8**	(3.1)	**65.0**	(5.2)	**51.6**	(3.1)	**64.5**	(4.0)
Latvia	99.2	(0.7)	100.0	(0.0)	100.0	(0.0)	99.0	(1.0)	**37.4**	(4.6)	**24.9**	(4.2)
Liechtenstein	c	c	c	c	c	c	c	c	c	c	c	c
Macao-China	97.5	(0.1)	a	a	97.5	(0.1)	a	a	95.6	(0.1)	a	a
Russian Federation	99.3	(0.5)	99.6	(0.4)	99.3	(0.5)	98.5	(0.7)	48.6	(3.9)	41.2	(3.2)
Serbia	98.6	(1.0)	a	a	96.9	(1.5)	a	a	23.4	(3.7)	a	a
Thailand	26.2	(2.7)	30.4	(3.0)	41.0	(4.0)	43.8	(3.7)	22.4	(2.7)	26.5	(2.7)
Tunisia	1.4	(0.5)	a	a	1.5	(1.3)	a	a	28.5	(4.0)	a	a
Uruguay	19.6	(1.6)	a	a	21.0	(1.7)	a	a	20.0	(1.6)	a	a
United Kingdom[1]	m	m	m	m	m	m	m	m	m	m	m	m

	Percentage of students in schools where the principals report that schools have responsibility for the following aspects of school policy and management											
	Determining teachers' salary increases				Formulating the school budget				Deciding on budget allocations within the school			
	PISA 2003		PISA 2000		PISA 2003		PISA 2000		PISA 2003		PISA 2000	
	%	S.E.	%	S.E.	%	S.E.	%	S.E.	%	S.E.	%	S.E.
OECD countries												
Australia	20.4	(1.9)	18.7	(2.6)	**89.4**	(1.6)	**95.7**	(1.5)	99.6	(0.4)	99.6	(0.2)
Austria	0.4	(0.3)	0.7	(0.5)	14.5	(2.5)	13.7	(2.7)	93.9	(2.1)	92.5	(2.0)
Belgium	a	a	6.9	(1.8)	**81.4**	(1.4)	**97.8**	(1.0)	**93.5**	(1.5)	**99.2**	(0.6)
Canada	33.6	(1.9)	34.0	(1.7)	75.2	(1.9)	77.3	(1.4)	97.3	(0.7)	98.7	(0.3)
Czech Republic	67.8	(3.4)	73.3	(3.1)	83.2	(2.1)	83.1	(2.6)	**95.5**	(1.6)	**99.1**	(0.6)
Denmark	**25.7**	(2.9)	**15.3**	(2.7)	90.8	(2.1)	89.3	(2.2)	99.5	(0.5)	97.9	(1.0)
Finland	**5.9**	(1.7)	**1.7**	(1.0)	**79.8**	(3.1)	**56.1**	(3.9)	99.9	(0.0)	98.7	(0.9)
France	w	w	w	w	w	w	w	w	w	w	w	w
Germany	6.5	(1.9)	11.0	(2.2)	9.1	(2.2)	12.8	(2.0)	95.9	(1.4)	95.6	(1.3)
Greece	m	m	m	m	m	m	m	m	m	m	m	m
Hungary	46.5	(4.3)	50.4	(4.3)	**87.1**	(2.5)	**60.6**	(4.1)	96.7	(1.4)	92.2	(2.3)
Iceland	**34.3**	(0.2)	**7.4**	(0.1)	**93.6**	(0.1)	**75.9**	(0.2)	**98.1**	(0.0)	**87.1**	(0.1)
Ireland	3.0	(1.5)	5.4	(2.2)	77.0	(3.1)	79.1	(3.1)	**94.8**	(1.9)	**100.0**	(0.0)
Italy	1.9	(0.8)	1.0	(0.8)	m	m	93.7	(2.4)	98.5	(0.6)	m	m
Japan	29.1	(1.4)	32.5	(2.0)	47.4	(3.4)	50.4	(3.3)	94.0	(1.5)	91.2	(2.9)
Korea	7.7	(2.5)	7.0	(2.4)	92.1	(2.4)	88.0	(2.5)	96.1	(1.7)	94.7	(1.7)
Luxembourg	m	m	m	m	m	m	m	m	m	m	m	m
Mexico	**43.9**	(3.2)	**27.7**	(3.1)	**84.3**	(1.7)	**67.6**	(4.2)	85.4	(1.8)	77.3	(3.7)
Netherlands	**72.5**	(4.0)	**45.3**	(5.6)	99.5	(0.5)	100.0	(0.0)	98.8	(0.8)	100.0	(0.0)
New Zealand	31.8	(3.2)	40.8	(3.3)	98.9	(0.8)	97.7	(1.1)	99.4	(0.6)	100.0	(0.0)
Norway	9.7	(2.3)	a	a	72.6	(3.5)	a	a	98.2	(1.1)	a	a
Poland	13.1	(2.7)	a	a	30.4	(3.3)	a	a	90.3	(2.3)	a	a
Portugal	0.9	(0.5)	0.9	(0.7)	83.2	(3.8)	88.9	(2.9)	87.3	(3.6)	94.9	(2.0)
Slovak Republic	56.4	(3.6)	a	a	84.5	(2.8)	a	a	95.6	(1.4)	a	a
Spain	6.7	(1.2)	9.0	(2.2)	86.4	(2.0)	89.7	(2.5)	99.0	(0.7)	98.2	(1.3)
Sweden	**85.0**	(2.6)	**73.6**	(3.6)	87.9	(2.3)	85.1	(3.1)	98.8	(0.8)	99.4	(0.6)
Switzerland	12.1	(3.3)	14.8	(3.0)	64.2	(3.0)	**54.3**	(3.3)	**93.8**	(1.4)	**86.9**	(2.9)
Turkey	5.0	(1.8)	a	a	50.6	(4.7)	a	a	68.4	(4.9)	a	a
United States	68.4	(3.2)	74.3	(5.1)	84.6	(2.5)	**95.9**	(1.9)	**93.8**	(1.7)	**98.7**	(1.0)
OECD total	*37.7*	*(1.0)*	*37.0*	*(1.5)*	*67.8*	*(0.8)*	*75.1*	*(1.0)*	*93.3*	*(0.7)*	*93.3*	*(0.6)*
OECD average	*26.6*	*(0.5)*	*25.9*	*(0.5)*	*71.2*	*(0.5)*	*76.1*	*(0.6)*	*95.2*	*(0.4)*	*94.5*	*(0.3)*
Partner countries												
Brazil	12.4	(2.4)	9.5	(1.7)	58.8	(3.5)	55.3	(3.4)	**84.2**	(2.6)	**74.8**	(2.8)
Hong Kong-China	13.9	(2.8)	8.1	(1.8)	97.5	(0.8)	93.7	(2.1)	98.9	(0.8)	97.9	(1.2)
Indonesia	54.7	(3.1)	64.3	(5.3)	97.2	(1.1)	96.9	(1.7)	97.3	(0.8)	97.4	(0.9)
Latvia	45.7	(4.6)	35.0	(5.2)	78.9	(3.0)	**33.0**	(4.5)	87.0	(2.6)	89.0	(3.8)
Liechtenstein	c	c	c	c	c	c	c	c	c	c	c	c
Macao-China	97.5	(0.1)	a	a	100.0	(0.0)	a	a	100.0	(0.0)	a	a
Russian Federation	51.2	(4.1)	46.9	(3.3)	48.5	(4.3)	47.4	(4.0)	70.2	(3.7)	70.1	(3.8)
Serbia	29.2	(3.7)	a	a	27.2	(4.2)	a	a	97.3	(1.3)	a	a
Thailand	97.7	(2.5)	95.4	(1.9)	80.1	(3.6)	75.9	(3.2)	**97.2**	(1.2)	**89.6**	(1.9)
Tunisia	a	a	a	a	32.5	(3.8)	a	a	97.9	(1.2)	a	a
Uruguay	20.1	(1.7)	a	a	28.0	(2.4)	a	a	50.4	(4.3)	a	a
United Kingdom[1]	m	m	m	m	m	m	m	m	m	m	m	m

Note: Values that are statistically significant are indicated in bold (see Annex A4).
1. Response rate too low to ensure comparability (see Annex A3).

Table 5.11a *(continued)*

School policy and management in PISA 2003 and PISA 2000

Results based on reports from school principals and reported proportionate to the number of 15-year-olds enrolled in the school

		Percentage of students in schools where the principals report that schools have responsibility for the following aspects of school policy and management											
		Establishing student disciplinary policies				Establishing student assessment policies				Approving students for admittance to school			
		PISA 2003		PISA 2000		PISA 2003		PISA 2000		PISA 2003		PISA 2000	
		%	S.E.	%	S.E.	%	S.E.	%	S.E.	%	S.E.	%	S.E.
OECD countries	Australia	98.4	(0.8)	99.6	(0.2)	97.4	(0.8)	98.8	(0.6)	91.2	(1.6)	93.5	(1.6)
	Austria	97.4	(1.2)	96.4	(1.6)	76.9	(3.0)	69.3	(3.5)	73.1	(3.2)	74.6	(2.9)
	Belgium	97.1	(1.0)	98.7	(0.9)	**93.9**	(1.4)	**99.6**	(0.4)	89.9	(2.0)	94.7	(1.7)
	Canada	99.0	(0.5)	98.5	(0.5)	92.1	(1.3)	94.1	(1.0)	89.3	(1.4)	89.2	(1.0)
	Czech Republic	100.0	(0.0)	99.5	(0.5)	98.3	(1.0)	99.6	(0.3)	**96.1**	(1.2)	**89.2**	(1.7)
	Denmark	97.9	(1.1)	98.9	(0.8)	83.2	(2.7)	86.9	(2.4)	82.6	(2.9)	87.1	(2.6)
	Finland	**99.9**	(0.0)	**95.6**	(1.9)	**99.0**	(0.7)	**89.0**	(2.6)	**71.1**	(3.7)	**53.8**	(4.0)
	France	w	w	w	w	w	w	w	w	w	w	w	w
	Germany	95.5	(1.4)	95.3	(1.4)	**87.5**	(2.9)	**79.3**	(2.8)	79.4	(2.8)	79.3	(3.0)
	Greece	m	m	m	m	m	m	m	m	m	m	m	m
	Hungary	100.0	(0.0)	100.0	(0.0)	100.0	(0.0)	98.1	(1.0)	99.7	(0.1)	98.7	(0.7)
	Iceland	**100.0**	(0.0)	**99.5**	(0.0)	**100.0**	(0.0)	**98.5**	(0.1)	**80.6**	(0.1)	**74.2**	(0.1)
	Ireland	100.0	(0.0)	99.4	(0.6)	97.3	(1.4)	98.7	(0.9)	95.9	(1.9)	95.2	(2.0)
	Italy	99.9	(0.1)	100.0	(0.0)	99.8	(0.2)	100.0	(0.0)	90.3	(1.8)	m	m
	Japan	100.0	(0.0)	99.6	(0.4)	100.0	(0.0)	100.0	(0.0)	100.0	(0.0)	100.0	(0.0)
	Korea	100.0	(0.0)	100.0	(0.0)	99.3	(0.5)	98.8	(0.1)	93.1	(2.3)	96.5	(1.4)
	Luxembourg	m	m	m	m	m	m	m	m	m	m	m	m
	Mexico	99.5	(0.2)	99.3	(0.7)	95.7	(1.4)	92.2	(2.5)	81.2	(2.3)	85.9	(2.3)
	Netherlands	99.5	(0.5)	100.0	(0.0)	98.8	(0.9)	100.0	(0.0)	99.2	(0.6)	100.0	(0.0)
	New Zealand	100.0	(0.0)	100.0	(0.0)	**97.3**	(1.0)	**100.0**	(0.0)	**87.4**	(2.0)	**94.4**	(1.2)
	Norway	87.4	(2.6)	a	a	61.9	(3.7)	a	a	24.0	(3.4)	a	a
	Poland	100.0	(0.0)	a	a	100.0	(0.0)	a	a	97.4	(1.3)	a	a
	Portugal	**55.1**	(4.3)	**91.7**	(2.2)	**53.3**	(4.2)	**88.4**	(2.6)	82.5	(3.3)	85.0	(3.1)
	Slovak Republic	99.1	(0.6)	a	a	89.2	(2.0)	a	a	96.3	(1.2)	a	a
	Spain	98.8	(0.9)	99.1	(0.8)	96.2	(1.4)	96.6	(1.5)	**72.8**	(2.9)	**89.3**	(2.4)
	Sweden	100.0	(0.0)	100.0	(0.0)	97.4	(1.3)	96.7	(1.5)	63.1	(3.6)	54.1	(4.0)
	Switzerland	99.7	(0.1)	97.7	(1.2)	78.3	(2.5)	74.6	(3.6)	73.3	(4.1)	81.7	(3.0)
	Turkey	98.9	(1.1)	a	a	92.2	(3.0)	a	a	76.8	(3.6)	a	a
	United States	96.5	(1.1)	98.5	(0.9)	88.3	(2.1)	93.2	(2.2)	**76.8**	(2.9)	**88.9**	(2.6)
	OECD total	*97.1*	*(0.3)*	*98.6*	*(0.3)*	*92.6*	*(0.6)*	*94.0*	*(0.7)*	*83.7*	*(0.9)*	*85.4*	*(0.8)*
	OECD average	*93.8*	*(0.3)*	*94.5*	*(0.2)*	*85.2*	*(0.3)*	*89.4*	*(0.4)*	*84.0*	*(0.5)*	*83.7*	*(0.5)*
Partner countries	Brazil	96.3	(1.4)	97.9	(0.7)	86.8	(2.6)	90.7	(1.8)	80.7	(2.9)	79.1	(3.3)
	Hong Kong-China	100.0	(0.0)	100.0	(0.0)	100.0	(0.0)	100.0	(0.0)	97.3	(1.3)	97.3	(1.3)
	Indonesia	99.4	(0.6)	100.0	(0.0)	98.5	(1.0)	100.0	(0.0)	**95.0**	(1.6)	**99.7**	(0.3)
	Latvia	97.6	(1.8)	99.9	(0.1)	86.8	(3.7)	77.3	(4.6)	99.4	(0.5)	98.0	(1.3)
	Liechtenstein	c	c	c	c	c	c	c	c	c	c	c	c
	Macao-China	100.0	(0.0)	.	.	97.4	(0.0)	a	a	100.0	(0.0)	a	a
	Russian Federation	99.6	(0.4)	100.0	(0.0)	98.4	(0.8)	99.6	(0.4)	100.0	(0.0)	99.2	(0.6)
	Serbia	98.8	(0.9)	a	a	96.7	(1.5)	a	a	43.9	(4.6)	a	a
	Thailand	100.0	(0.0)	98.4	(1.0)	**100.0**	(0.0)	**94.9**	(1.5)	99.0	(0.8)	98.4	(1.0)
	Tunisia	91.2	(2.6)	a	a	38.0	(4.2)	a	a	70.0	(3.4)	a	a
	Uruguay	73.8	(3.7)	a	a	62.8	(4.1)	a	a	41.8	(3.4)	a	a
	United Kingdom[1]	m	m	m	m	m	m	m	m	m	m	m	m

		Percentage of students in schools where the principals report that schools have responsibility for the following aspects of school policy and management											
		Choosing which textbooks are used				Determining course content				Deciding which courses are offered			
		PISA 2003		PISA 2000		PISA 2003		PISA 2000		PISA 2003		PISA 2000	
		%	S.E.	%	S.E.	%	S.E.	%	S.E.	%	S.E.	%	S.E.
OECD countries	Australia	99.3	(0.5)	99.7	(0.2)	79.3	(2.5)	84.4	(3.2)	97.2	(1.0)	95.9	(1.8)
	Austria	98.8	(1.0)	99.3	(0.7)	61.3	(3.8)	54.0	(3.6)	55.2	(3.8)	56.8	(3.7)
	Belgium	98.1	(0.8)	98.5	(0.6)	55.0	(2.4)	58.6	(3.7)	67.3	(3.0)	60.7	(3.6)
	Canada	88.8	(0.8)	89.1	(0.9)	45.3	(2.2)	48.9	(1.8)	89.0	(1.5)	89.8	(1.1)
	Czech Republic	99.9	(0.1)	100.0	(0.0)	74.6	(3.0)	81.9	(2.9)	**72.7**	(3.0)	**81.5**	(2.8)
	Denmark	99.7	(0.2)	100.0	(0.0)	**76.0**	(3.3)	**89.8**	(1.9)	76.3	(2.9)	76.8	(2.6)
	Finland	100.0	(0.0)	100.0	(0.0)	92.0	(1.8)	91.4	(2.3)	**99.8**	(0.0)	**94.7**	(2.0)
	France	w	w	w	w	w	w	w	w	w	w	w	w
	Germany	98.5	(0.9)	95.5	(1.7)	**47.7**	(3.1)	**34.9**	(3.3)	**68.0**	(3.7)	**35.1**	(3.4)
	Greece	m	m	m	m	m	m	m	m	m	m	m	m
	Hungary	100.0	(0.0)	99.6	(0.4)	**80.3**	(2.9)	**97.0**	(1.3)	**82.1**	(2.7)	**98.4**	(1.0)
	Iceland	**99.6**	(0.0)	**98.7**	(0.0)	**85.5**	(0.1)	**78.8**	(0.2)	**85.0**	(0.1)	**61.6**	(0.2)
	Ireland	100.0	(0.0)	100.0	(0.0)	38.1	(3.9)	36.9	(4.1)	95.7	(1.7)	97.4	(1.3)
	Italy	100.0	(0.0)	100.0	(0.0)	**84.4**	(2.5)	**93.2**	(2.9)	m	m	21.6	(4.0)
	Japan	95.5	(2.0)	99.3	(0.7)	100.0	(0.0)	99.3	(0.7)	98.5	(1.1)	97.8	(1.3)
	Korea	100.0	(0.0)	99.4	(0.6)	99.1	(0.9)	99.4	(0.6)	**98.4**	(1.1)	**93.2**	(2.3)
	Luxembourg	m	m	m	m	m	m	m	m	m	m	m	m
	Mexico	84.4	(2.5)	81.3	(3.0)	**70.0**	(3.3)	**58.8**	(4.1)	**71.4**	(3.3)	**58.2**	(3.4)
	Netherlands	99.5	(0.5)	100.0	(0.0)	96.7	(2.0)	91.7	(3.2)	97.3	(1.8)	94.9	(2.4)
	New Zealand	100.0	(0.0)	100.0	(0.0)	**94.4**	(1.8)	**87.2**	(2.7)	**98.9**	(0.1)	**99.9**	(0.1)
	Norway	98.3	(1.0)	a	a	47.8	(3.8)	a	a	25.1	(3.3)	a	a
	Poland	100.0	(0.0)	a	a	100.0	(0.0)	a	a	46.2	(4.0)	a	a
	Portugal	100.0	(0.0)	100.0	(0.0)	**36.4**	(3.6)	**20.3**	(3.4)	51.2	(4.4)	54.2	(4.5)
	Slovak Republic	94.1	(1.5)	a	a	64.6	(3.2)	a	a	67.5	(3.4)	a	a
	Spain	100.0	(0.0)	99.6	(0.4)	**65.1**	(3.5)	**86.0**	(2.9)	56.9	(3.5)	54.4	(3.8)
	Sweden	100.0	(0.0)	100.0	(0.0)	92.5	(1.8)	87.6	(2.8)	76.6	(3.4)	76.2	(3.7)
	Switzerland	57.1	(3.1)	50.7	(4.1)	**39.0**	(3.4)	**29.5**	(3.5)	38.5	(4.5)	34.2	(3.4)
	Turkey	96.9	(1.9)	a	a	35.9	(4.9)	a	a	46.6	(4.6)	a	a
	United States	93.8	(1.6)	92.2	(3.0)	80.5	(2.6)	84.0	(4.3)	95.5	(1.3)	97.3	(1.3)
	OECD total	*94.4*	*(0.5)*	*94.7*	*(0.8)*	*76.6*	*(0.8)*	*76.9*	*(1.3)*	*81.9*	*(0.7)*	*77.0*	*(0.7)*
	OECD average	*89.8*	*(0.2)*	*91.7*	*(0.2)*	*66.8*	*(0.5)*	*69.2*	*(0.6)*	*70.3*	*(0.5)*	*70.9*	*(0.6)*
Partner countries	Brazil	98.3	(0.8)	99.7	(0.3)	88.1	(2.5)	90.3	(2.2)	61.2	(3.8)	57.1	(3.4)
	Hong Kong-China	100.0	(0.0)	100.0	(0.0)	98.0	(1.2)	97.5	(1.3)	99.3	(0.7)	99.7	(0.3)
	Indonesia	98.0	(1.0)	98.3	(0.7)	**97.8**	(0.9)	**80.1**	(3.4)	93.1	(2.4)	96.2	(1.5)
	Latvia	95.7	(1.9)	99.4	(0.6)	**56.1**	(4.4)	**75.9**	(5.0)	**74.3**	(3.7)	**90.1**	(3.5)
	Liechtenstein	c	c	c	c	c	c	c	c	c	c	c	c
	Macao-China	100.0	(0.0)	a	a	100.0	(0.0)	a	a	97.5	(0.1)	a	a
	Russian Federation	**92.3**	(2.1)	**97.4**	(1.0)	**83.4**	(2.9)	**94.5**	(1.4)	93.1	(2.2)	95.5	(1.3)
	Serbia	38.8	(4.4)	a	a	16.0	(3.5)	a	a	11.4	(2.9)	a	a
	Thailand	99.0	(0.7)	97.7	(0.9)	**98.9**	(0.8)	**92.6**	(2.1)	98.4	(1.1)	98.2	(1.0)
	Tunisia	2.7	(1.3)	a	a	11.0	(2.7)	a	a	16.1	(3.0)	a	a
	Uruguay	62.4	(3.7)	a	a	26.3	(2.8)	a	a	28.9	(2.1)	a	a
	United Kingdom[1]	m	m	m	m	m	m	m	m	m	m	m	m

Note: Values that are statistically significant are indicated in bold (see Annex A4).

1. Response rate too low to ensure comparability (see Annex A3).

Table 5.11b
Relationship between student performance in mathematics and aspects of school policy and management in PISA 2003 and PISA 2000

	Cross country correlation with country average achievement on the combined mathematical scale (OECD countries)		Cross country correlation with country average achievement on the combined mathematical scale (all PISA countries)	
	PISA 2003	PISA 2000	PISA 2003	PISA 2000
Appointing teachers	0.4	0.2	0.5	0.3
Dismissing teachers	0.3	0.1	0.4	0.2
Establishing teachers' starting salaries	0.1	–0.1	0.1	0.0
Determining teachers' salary increases	0.1	–0.1	0.0	–0.2
Formulating the school budget	0.1	–0.1	0.2	0.1
Deciding on budget allocations within the school	0.6	0.4	0.4	0.4
Establishing student disciplinary policies	0.4	0.2	0.2	0.1
Establishing student assessment policies	0.1	0.0	0.2	0.1
Approving students for admittance to school	0.1	0.0	0.2	0.0
Choosing which textbooks are used	0.1	0.1	0.3	0.0
Determining course content	0.3	0.2	0.3	0.1
Deciding which cou rses are offered	0.3	0.4	0.4	0.3

Table 5.12
Involvement of stakeholders in decision-making at school
Results based on reports from school principals and reported proportionate to the number of 15-year-olds enrolled in the school

Percentage of students in schools where the principals report that the following stakeholders exert a direct influence on decision-making about **staffing**

		Regional or national education authorities (*e.g.* inspectorates)		The school's governing board		Employers		Parent groups		Teacher groups		Student groups		External examination board	
		%	S.E.	%	S.E.	%	S.E.	%	S.E.	%	S.E.	%	S.E.	%	S.E.
OECD countries	Australia	67.8	(2.2)	20.6	(2.4)	21.3	(2.5)	2.7	(1.1)	22.8	(2.6)	1.2	(0.5)	2.3	(0.7)
	Austria	94.0	(2.0)	3.4	(1.6)	4.7	(1.8)	1.3	(1.2)	22.8	(3.2)	1.3	(0.8)	a	a
	Belgium	64.2	(2.9)	60.3	(2.9)	2.4	(1.0)	2.4	(1.0)	40.3	(2.3)	1.4	(0.6)	0.6	(0.4)
	Canada	52.9	(2.3)	57.6	(2.4)	6.5	(1.2)	5.8	(1.2)	37.7	(2.1)	0.4	(0.1)	1.1	(0.4)
	Czech Republic	52.3	(3.7)	5.1	(1.7)	38.6	(3.3)	a	a	3.0	(1.1)	a	a	a	a
	Denmark	36.4	(3.8)	72.1	(3.3)	4.1	(1.3)	4.2	(1.4)	28.4	(3.0)	5.1	(1.7)	4.1	(1.4)
	Finland	88.3	(2.6)	52.4	(4.2)	2.8	(1.3)	42.4	(4.0)	1.6	(1.0)	1.1	(0.8)	25.0	(3.1)
	France	w	w	w	w	w	w	w	w	w	w	w	w	w	w
	Germany	89.6	(2.0)	28.2	(2.8)	2.1	(1.4)	8.4	(1.9)	19.8	(2.6)	2.7	(1.1)	1.9	(1.0)
	Greece	88.8	(3.0)	9.1	(3.0)	15.9	(3.9)	3.6	(1.7)	14.5	(4.0)	2.7	(1.5)	8.7	(3.7)
	Hungary	26.3	(3.4)	77.1	(3.4)	3.3	(1.4)	1.5	(1.3)	26.6	(3.7)	0.3	c	38.4	(4.1)
	Iceland	32.0	(0.1)	35.5	(0.2)	a	a	a	a	4.0	(0.1)	a	a	0.3	.
	Ireland	95.4	(1.8)	51.7	(4.4)	2.9	(1.5)	a	a	13.0	(3.0)	a	a	12.5	(2.8)
	Italy	91.1	(2.0)	15.8	(2.4)	20.9	(2.8)	a	a	4.7	(1.3)	a	a	2.2	(1.2)
	Japan	71.9	(1.8)	22.0	(2.4)	20.7	(3.6)	a	a	2.1	(1.2)	a	a	a	a
	Korea	24.9	(4.1)	24.7	(3.4)	6.2	(1.7)	26.6	(3.9)	28.9	(3.6)	14.5	(3.1)	7.2	(1.8)
	Luxembourg	85.9	(0.1)	51.2	(0.1)	10.6	(0.0)	a	a	8.9	(0.1)	a	a	22.8	(0.1)
	Mexico	50.8	(3.2)	31.9	(3.3)	29.2	(3.2)	14.0	(2.3)	45.5	(3.3)	13.3	(1.9)	16.9	(2.9)
	Netherlands	40.7	(4.1)	66.8	(4.2)	4.6	(1.7)	4.4	(1.6)	54.3	(4.4)	3.8	(1.6)	1.0	(0.8)
	New Zealand	78.8	(2.9)	73.0	(3.0)	1.7	(0.9)	2.7	(1.2)	52.3	(3.5)	1.3	(0.9)	4.6	(1.3)
	Norway	17.4	(2.9)	10.2	(2.4)	72.8	(3.4)	0.7	c	83.1	(2.9)	0.7	(0.7)	1.3	(1.0)
	Poland	21.7	(3.2)	1.6	(0.9)	55.8	(3.7)	4.1	(1.6)	29.5	(3.8)	0.7	c	1.4	(1.0)
	Portugal	92.8	(1.5)	28.0	(3.0)	5.4	(2.0)	0.6	(0.6)	2.7	(1.4)	a	a	a	a
	Slovak Republic	37.2	(3.0)	23.3	(2.7)	30.3	(3.6)	0.1	c	30.3	(4.1)	0.5	(0.4)	10.8	(2.5)
	Spain	65.3	(3.0)	18.1	(2.6)	24.1	(2.3)	4.0	(1.0)	11.2	(2.2)	0.2	(0.1)	1.6	(0.8)
	Sweden	10.6	(2.3)	11.0	(2.4)	74.4	(3.1)	4.3	(1.5)	61.1	(3.5)	5.6	(1.8)	0.6	c
	Switzerland	42.2	(4.2)	79.6	(3.4)	54.6	(3.5)	0.5	(0.4)	5.0	(1.7)	c	c	1.9	(1.1)
	Turkey	59.0	(4.5)	33.4	(4.1)	11.4	(3.3)	24.0	(4.4)	29.7	(4.7)	16.7	(3.4)	8.7	(2.4)
	United States	45.2	(2.8)	76.1	(2.8)	26.1	(3.3)	11.8	(2.1)	32.4	(3.4)	3.2	(1.2)	7.7	(1.7)
	OECD total	***55.9***	***(1.0)***	***42.9***	***(0.9)***	***21.0***	***(1.0)***	***8.6***	***(0.7)***	***25.0***	***(1.0)***	***4.3***	***(0.4)***	***6.0***	***(0.5)***
	OECD average	***57.3***	***(0.5)***	***39.0***	***(0.5)***	***19.5***	***(0.4)***	***7.3***	***(0.3)***	***22.2***	***(0.4)***	***2.8***	***(0.2)***	***8.1***	***(0.3)***
Partner countries	Brazil	73.6	(3.1)	17.8	(2.6)	6.5	(1.7)	3.4	(1.3)	9.6	(1.9)	4.5	(1.3)	5.9	(1.8)
	Hong Kong-China	32.4	(4.2)	72.1	(3.3)	10.6	(2.4)	0.7	c	2.0	(1.2)	0.8	(0.8)	1.4	(1.0)
	Indonesia	65.6	(3.5)	13.8	(2.5)	2.7	(1.4)	1.9	(0.9)	9.6	(2.2)	1.7	(1.0)	5.8	(2.1)
	Latvia	34.5	(4.3)	66.3	(4.4)	40.8	(4.5)	38.1	(4.6)	18.9	(4.0)	3.1	(1.0)	53.7	(4.5)
	Liechtenstein	c	c	c	c	c	c	c	c	c	c	c	c	c	c
	Macao-China	31.1	(0.2)	66.4	(0.2)	3.6	(0.1)	2.0	(0.1)	4.3	(0.1)	3.0	(0.0)	1.6	(0.1)
	Russian Federation	76.1	(3.2)	13.9	(2.8)	11.2	(2.6)	1.0	(0.6)	10.5	(2.4)	0.3	(0.3)	5.0	(2.0)
	Serbia	31.8	(3.9)	88.9	(2.9)	16.0	(3.2)	21.3	(3.2)	14.9	(3.1)	6.7	(1.8)	10.0	(2.6)
	Thailand	66.8	(3.4)	49.4	(4.0)	31.8	(3.4)	21.9	(3.3)	23.1	(2.9)	10.1	(2.4)	43.0	(3.9)
	Tunisia	84.4	(3.0)	1.7	(1.0)	24.9	(3.5)	0.7	(0.7)	6.0	(2.0)	0.7	(0.7)	4.8	(1.8)
	Uruguay	81.8	(2.1)	14.9	(1.7)	2.8	(1.0)	9.8	(2.5)	5.0	(1.7)	1.8	(1.0)	2.8	(1.6)
	United Kingdom[1]	44.2	(3.4)	85.1	(2.3)	5.0	(1.1)	0.4	(0.2)	23.1	(2.6)	3.4	(1.4)	1.3	(0.8)

Percentage of students in schools where the principals report that the following stakeholders exert a direct influence on decision-making about **budgeting**

		Regional or national education authorities (*e.g.* inspectorates)		The school's governing board		Employers		Parent groups		Teacher groups		Student groups		External examination board	
		%	S.E.	%	S.E.	%	S.E.	%	S.E.	%	S.E.	%	S.E.	%	S.E.
OECD countries	Australia	59.2	(2.9)	67.5	(2.6)	19.0	(2.6)	24.3	(2.6)	25.6	(2.3)	4.8	(1.1)	1.0	(0.6)
	Austria	67.4	(3.1)	20.5	(3.4)	1.5	(1.1)	10.1	(2.3)	14.6	(2.8)	0.5	(0.5)	a	a
	Belgium	55.9	(2.8)	68.9	(2.9)	1.1	(0.8)	3.9	(1.2)	24.7	(2.9)	3.8	(1.1)	a	a
	Canada	68.9	(1.9)	74.0	(2.3)	4.8	(1.1)	23.8	(2.1)	19.7	(2.1)	6.6	(0.9)	1.7	(0.6)
	Czech Republic	60.4	(3.8)	11.9	(2.2)	37.2	(3.4)	2.2	(1.0)	6.5	(1.5)	a	a	a	a
	Denmark	40.0	(3.4)	92.3	(1.8)	1.4	(0.8)	7.9	(1.7)	65.1	(3.3)	19.3	(3.0)	0.4	c
	Finland	96.9	(1.3)	53.3	(3.9)	4.8	(1.7)	32.2	(4.0)	4.5	(1.6)	0.4	c	40.2	(3.5)
	France	w	w	w	w	w	w	w	w	w	w	w	w	w	w
	Germany	25.5	(3.1)	93.3	(1.7)	0.5	c	25.3	(2.8)	2.5	(1.1)	9.8	(2.0)	a	a
	Greece	55.7	(5.2)	49.0	(4.3)	12.7	(3.8)	13.6	(3.6)	3.8	(2.7)	2.9	(1.5)	a	a
	Hungary	64.9	(3.8)	62.3	(3.9)	3.8	(1.4)	2.1	(1.4)	31.5	(4.0)	7.6	(2.2)	62.5	(3.3)
	Iceland	96.4	(0.1)	72.2	(0.2)	0.4	c	2.9	(0.0)	1.8	(0.1)	1.5	(0.0)	a	a
	Ireland	77.8	(3.3)	71.3	(3.2)	a	a	3.8	(1.7)	3.6	(1.3)	a	a	3.9	(1.8)
	Italy	30.2	(3.1)	90.0	(2.2)	17.3	(2.9)	23.3	(3.2)	17.6	(2.4)	17.7	(3.1)	0.0	(0.0)
	Japan	63.2	(3.2)	28.2	(2.3)	15.2	(3.2)	10.7	(2.0)	4.2	(1.5)	8.4	(2.2)	2.6	(0.9)
	Korea	40.1	(3.9)	69.4	(4.1)	10.3	(2.4)	18.9	(2.7)	29.9	(3.6)	11.9	(2.9)	7.2	(2.3)
	Luxembourg	65.6	(0.1)	76.1	(0.1)	10.6	(0.0)	15.0	(0.0)	14.3	(0.0)	15.0	(0.0)	a	a
	Mexico	38.1	(2.9)	24.3	(2.5)	13.9	(2.2)	34.9	(3.2)	7.5	(1.4)	7.8	(2.1)	6.5	(1.4)
	Netherlands	79.4	(3.3)	74.9	(3.5)	1.8	(1.0)	9.6	(2.7)	59.9	(4.1)	a	a	2.1	(1.5)
	New Zealand	64.8	(3.3)	96.5	(1.2)	5.6	(1.9)	13.0	(2.4)	16.5	(2.5)	6.0	(1.3)	7.8	(1.5)
	Norway	36.4	(3.8)	58.6	(3.8)	92.9	(2.0)	16.4	(3.0)	62.3	(3.8)	11.0	(2.4)	0.7	c
	Poland	23.8	(3.4)	16.5	(2.9)	49.4	(4.3)	37.3	(3.7)	16.0	(3.1)	2.6	(1.3)	a	a
	Portugal	90.2	(2.5)	82.2	(3.7)	0.4	(0.4)	6.0	(1.6)	4.2	(1.6)	2.0	(1.1)	a	a
	Slovak Republic	96.7	(1.1)	40.2	(3.3)	3.9	(1.5)	19.4	(3.3)	16.9	(3.3)	a	a	2.8	(1.2)
	Spain	52.4	(3.6)	81.1	(2.4)	23.1	(2.1)	28.7	(3.0)	9.2	(2.3)	8.1	(2.6)	1.2	(0.7)
	Sweden	9.7	(2.0)	40.7	(3.6)	83.4	(2.7)	8.0	(1.9)	52.5	(3.9)	5.2	(1.6)	0.6	c
	Switzerland	59.5	(3.6)	74.9	(2.7)	53.8	(4.2)	0.7	(0.6)	5.1	(1.9)	0.1	c	2.3	(1.2)
	Turkey	25.4	(3.3)	36.3	(4.6)	28.0	(4.6)	25.4	(4.2)	7.2	(2.3)	8.5	(2.7)	4.3	(1.8)
	United States	74.5	(2.7)	88.7	(2.1)	28.5	(3.5)	23.7	(3.0)	36.1	(3.5)	4.3	(1.4)	7.1	(1.8)
	OECD total	***54.5***	***(0.9)***	***64.1***	***(0.7)***	***19.3***	***(1.0)***	***20.9***	***(1.0)***	***18.2***	***(0.9)***	***6.5***	***(0.6)***	***4.8***	***(0.5)***
	OECD average	***58.0***	***(0.6)***	***61.4***	***(0.5)***	***18.5***	***(0.5)***	***15.2***	***(0.4)***	***17.0***	***(0.4)***	***5.4***	***(0.3)***	***7.2***	***(0.3)***
Partner countries	Brazil	61.6	(3.6)	57.7	(3.3)	2.6	(1.1)	31.2	(3.4)	17.6	(2.7)	13.5	(2.0)	3.3	(1.0)
	Hong Kong-China	47.1	(4.2)	89.7	(2.7)	15.0	(3.4)	13.9	(2.8)	27.3	(3.7)	1.4	(1.0)	4.0	(1.7)
	Indonesia	39.3	(3.5)	82.5	(2.7)	31.8	(3.5)	80.3	(3.0)	10.2	(2.0)	22.2	(3.3)	8.9	(2.1)
	Latvia	72.9	(3.3)	71.8	(4.1)	54.0	(4.5)	29.6	(4.1)	23.5	(4.0)	a	a	64.2	(3.7)
	Liechtenstein	c	c	c	c	c	c	c	c	c	c	c	c	c	c
	Macao-China	43.3	(0.2)	70.9	(0.2)	10.4	(0.1)	0.3	c	a	a	4.3	(0.1)	a	a
	Russian Federation	92.2	(2.3)	18.9	(3.0)	23.3	(3.4)	30.9	(3.3)	8.0	(2.7)	2.2	(1.3)	6.0	(2.1)
	Serbia	86.0	(3.1)	65.6	(4.0)	8.6	(2.3)	15.7	(3.0)	19.2	(3.0)	4.9	(1.1)	3.5	(1.6)
	Thailand	72.4	(3.6)	69.9	(3.8)	33.3	(4.2)	30.7	(3.5)	32.1	(3.2)	13.6	(3.0)	42.5	(3.8)
	Tunisia	18.7	(3.1)	85.4	(2.8)	6.1	(2.0)	2.3	(1.2)	2.8	(1.4)	1.9	(1.1)	0.7	(0.7)
	Uruguay	80.5	(1.9)	13.1	(1.5)	1.0	(0.6)	16.1	(3.1)	4.4	(2.1)	1.1	(0.8)	0.5	(0.3)
	United Kingdom[1]	76.9	(2.8)	90.4	(1.9)	4.4	(1.1)	3.4	(1.3)	11.1	(2.2)	1.5	(0.8)	4.8	(1.5)

1. Response rate too low to ensure comparability (see Annex A3).

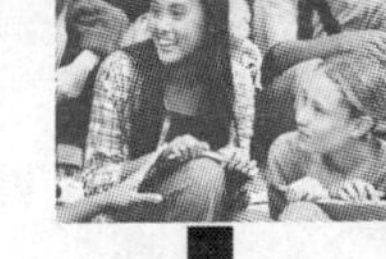

Table 5.12 *(continued)*
Involvement of stakeholders in decision-making at school
Results based on reports from school principals and reported proportionate to the number of 15-year-olds enrolled in the school

Percentage of students in schools where the principals report that the following stakeholders exert a direct influence on decision-making about **instructional content**

		Regional or national education authorities (*e.g.* inspectorates)		The school's governing board		Employers		Parent groups		Teacher groups		Student groups		External examination board	
		%	S.E.	%	S.E.	%	S.E.	%	S.E.	%	S.E.	%	S.E.	%	S.E.
OECD countries	Australia	82.5	(2.7)	11.8	(2.1)	21.1	(2.3)	12.6	(1.9)	74.3	(2.5)	14.2	(2.0)	71.6	(2.8)
	Austria	66.4	(4.0)	35.4	(3.6)	20.2	(2.7)	7.6	(2.2)	63.8	(3.6)	14.1	(2.6)	a	a
	Belgium	81.8	(2.1)	16.0	(2.4)	13.7	(1.9)	7.0	(1.5)	27.0	(3.0)	6.6	(1.5)	6.6	(1.4)
	Canada	92.9	(1.1)	19.2	(1.8)	11.4	(1.5)	8.4	(1.1)	47.6	(2.0)	5.3	(0.9)	25.6	(2.0)
	Czech Republic	56.9	(3.4)	4.5	(1.6)	28.5	(2.9)	16.4	(2.7)	24.8	(3.5)	7.6	(1.9)	14.2	(2.3)
	Denmark	75.3	(3.4)	44.6	(3.7)	4.5	(1.7)	12.5	(2.4)	86.8	(2.5)	48.6	(3.7)	14.4	(2.7)
	Finland	67.6	(3.3)	21.8	(3.1)	54.0	(3.8)	83.9	(2.8)	43.7	(4.2)	9.0	(2.2)	79.4	(2.6)
	France	w	w	w	w	w	w	w	w	w	w	w	w	w	w
	Germany	83.1	(2.6)	2.3	(0.7)	6.5	(1.8)	22.1	(2.7)	7.2	(1.8)	16.8	(2.5)	3.6	(1.3)
	Greece	92.1	(2.3)	2.7	(1.6)	3.8	(1.8)	4.8	(3.0)	8.9	(3.6)	5.4	(3.1)	2.0	(1.2)
	Hungary	64.2	(3.7)	64.3	(3.7)	29.1	(3.2)	22.5	(3.5)	86.1	(2.5)	26.9	(3.8)	33.6	(3.9)
	Iceland	20.1	(0.1)	1.2	(0.1)	10.2	(0.1)	5.8	(0.1)	7.5	(0.1)	6.2	(0.1)	6.8	(0.1)
	Ireland	79.9	(3.3)	12.6	(2.7)	10.9	(2.8)	2.4	(1.4)	38.1	(4.9)	4.2	(1.7)	71.4	(4.2)
	Italy	45.8	(3.7)	44.3	(3.6)	8.7	(2.0)	16.6	(3.0)	35.4	(3.3)	20.1	(3.0)	6.4	(1.5)
	Japan	49.0	(4.4)	12.8	(2.7)	15.6	(2.7)	12.3	(2.8)	6.9	(2.2)	6.4	(2.1)	6.5	(2.2)
	Korea	26.3	(3.7)	13.5	(2.7)	29.5	(3.8)	25.0	(3.9)	53.3	(4.3)	28.1	(4.1)	13.6	(3.1)
	Luxembourg	90.6	(0.0)	20.4	(0.1)	8.8	(0.0)	7.2	(0.0)	53.4	(0.1)	a	a	13.4	(0.0)
	Mexico	63.4	(3.2)	38.5	(3.2)	6.9	(1.4)	8.0	(1.4)	34.5	(3.1)	15.3	(2.4)	28.1	(2.9)
	Netherlands	48.3	(4.5)	15.4	(3.3)	6.0	(2.3)	17.1	(3.2)	59.6	(3.8)	14.1	(3.2)	13.1	(3.2)
	New Zealand	87.3	(2.2)	10.8	(2.4)	10.3	(2.2)	13.5	(2.5)	41.4	(3.3)	11.5	(2.1)	54.7	(3.2)
	Norway	87.8	(2.6)	12.1	(2.5)	5.6	(1.7)	11.4	(2.5)	13.0	(2.8)	19.6	(3.3)	4.8	(1.5)
	Poland	28.7	(3.7)	26.1	(3.4)	8.5	(2.1)	49.1	(3.8)	14.3	(2.9)	21.4	(3.3)	19.7	(2.9)
	Portugal	84.6	(2.9)	11.4	(2.4)	7.2	(2.2)	2.4	(1.2)	64.8	(4.3)	2.6	(1.3)	18.8	(3.3)
	Slovak Republic	38.1	(3.4)	41.3	(3.5)	11.2	(1.9)	34.5	(3.1)	71.2	(4.0)	20.6	(2.6)	76.8	(3.2)
	Spain	83.9	(2.2)	25.0	(2.9)	7.5	(1.8)	7.1	(1.8)	26.9	(3.4)	2.2	(0.8)	11.4	(2.1)
	Sweden	61.8	(3.7)	16.0	(2.9)	26.6	(3.0)	25.9	(2.9)	45.8	(3.7)	63.5	(3.5)	4.0	(1.5)
	Switzerland	77.2	(3.0)	14.1	(3.2)	11.9	(1.6)	2.3	(0.8)	45.1	(3.4)	10.5	(2.9)	9.0	(1.8)
	Turkey	47.0	(5.0)	24.7	(3.9)	17.5	(3.3)	20.6	(4.2)	34.4	(4.1)	31.0	(4.1)	17.3	(3.6)
	United States	80.0	(2.4)	51.6	(3.3)	37.7	(3.7)	30.9	(3.2)	69.1	(3.6)	16.3	(2.2)	29.5	(3.3)
	OECD total	***64.9***	***(1.0)***	***28.1***	***(0.9)***	***19.9***	***(1.1)***	***20.4***	***(0.9)***	***38.8***	***(1.0)***	***16.4***	***(0.7)***	***24.8***	***(0.9)***
	OECD average	***65.8***	***(0.6)***	***20.9***	***(0.4)***	***16.6***	***(0.4)***	***18.8***	***(0.5)***	***40.3***	***(0.6)***	***18.3***	***(0.5)***	***27.6***	***(0.5)***
Partner countries	Brazil	41.8	(3.8)	49.9	(3.6)	12.0	(2.4)	23.7	(3.0)	43.8	(3.7)	25.7	(3.5)	24.0	(2.8)
	Hong Kong-China	55.2	(4.6)	33.7	(4.1)	15.0	(3.2)	31.7	(3.9)	61.9	(4.2)	24.6	(3.8)	62.4	(4.1)
	Indonesia	49.6	(3.5)	11.9	(2.7)	7.3	(2.2)	7.2	(2.0)	62.5	(3.8)	28.0	(3.1)	27.5	(3.4)
	Latvia	29.5	(3.8)	21.5	(4.1)	27.0	(3.9)	86.5	(2.7)	34.8	(4.2)	88.3	(2.7)	68.2	(4.5)
	Liechtenstein	c	c	c	c	c	c	c	c	c	c	c	c	c	c
	Macao-China	36.2	(0.2)	39.9	(0.3)	12.5	(0.1)	29.8	(0.2)	43.8	(0.2)	22.1	(0.1)	35.6	(0.2)
	Russian Federation	69.5	(3.5)	73.6	(3.0)	25.1	(3.6)	40.9	(3.9)	81.9	(2.6)	40.7	(4.5)	51.9	(3.0)
	Serbia	87.0	(2.7)	1.3	(0.9)	51.8	(4.3)	9.5	(2.3)	59.0	(4.3)	22.9	(3.8)	38.8	(4.1)
	Thailand	36.8	(3.8)	57.6	(4.2)	12.3	(2.6)	65.8	(3.8)	81.3	(3.1)	65.4	(3.7)	57.6	(3.7)
	Tunisia	59.4	(4.0)	3.5	(1.6)	7.5	(2.2)	9.3	(2.7)	19.6	(3.5)	15.3	(3.1)	11.6	(2.3)
	Uruguay	90.8	(2.4)	8.4	(2.0)	1.6	(1.2)	a	a	30.7	(3.4)	2.1	(1.5)	6.5	(2.3)
	United Kingdom[1]	57.8	(3.1)	15.1	(2.4)	18.5	(3.1)	9.5	(2.0)	15.4	(2.4)	17.0	(2.3)	80.7	(2.7)

Percentage of students in schools where the principals report that the following stakeholders exert a direct influence on decision-making about **assessment practices**

		Regional or national education authorities (*e.g.* inspectorates)		The school's governing board		Employers		Parent groups		Teacher groups		Student groups		External examination board	
		%	S.E.	%	S.E.	%	S.E.	%	S.E.	%	S.E.	%	S.E.	%	S.E.
OECD countries	Australia	75.6	(3.2)	11.5	(2.1)	19.1	(2.0)	14.6	(2.1)	74.3	(2.7)	12.6	(2.0)	82.9	(2.3)
	Austria	43.3	(4.0)	11.1	(2.6)	2.2	(1.3)	4.0	(1.5)	53.7	(3.9)	10.8	(2.6)	a	a
	Belgium	41.4	(3.0)	22.2	(2.5)	17.0	(2.7)	13.6	(2.4)	39.6	(3.0)	34.4	(2.8)	18.6	(2.2)
	Canada	79.9	(1.8)	30.4	(2.2)	12.9	(1.5)	11.8	(1.5)	58.8	(2.5)	7.4	(1.2)	42.1	(2.5)
	Czech Republic	44.4	(3.7)	3.6	(1.4)	18.8	(2.8)	18.9	(2.7)	19.4	(3.0)	10.2	(2.3)	18.1	(2.6)
	Denmark	51.7	(3.6)	45.4	(3.9)	3.5	(1.3)	5.8	(1.7)	78.1	(3.1)	25.1	(2.9)	30.6	(3.6)
	Finland	66.8	(3.8)	17.6	(3.0)	55.6	(3.9)	79.0	(2.9)	28.5	(3.7)	26.0	(3.4)	85.4	(2.6)
	France	w	w	w	w	w	w	w	w	w	w	w	w	w	w
	Germany	80.5	(2.9)	6.4	(1.5)	8.2	(2.4)	11.9	(2.2)	12.4	(2.3)	8.2	(1.8)	11.9	(2.1)
	Greece	87.9	(2.7)	14.3	(3.0)	3.8	(1.8)	5.8	(3.1)	11.9	(3.9)	6.0	(3.2)	6.7	(2.1)
	Hungary	32.3	(3.8)	85.5	(2.8)	30.9	(3.1)	67.2	(3.4)	91.9	(2.2)	79.9	(3.1)	31.9	(4.1)
	Iceland	27.4	(0.2)	14.3	(0.1)	3.9	(0.1)	13.3	(0.1)	2.7	(0.1)	4.5	(0.1)	29.9	(0.2)
	Ireland	60.4	(4.3)	18.8	(3.3)	15.1	(3.4)	13.2	(2.9)	53.5	(4.4)	5.9	(1.9)	76.9	(3.7)
	Italy	12.8	(2.4)	49.8	(3.7)	5.9	(1.5)	7.9	(1.8)	34.3	(3.5)	11.6	(2.5)	32.6	(3.6)
	Japan	34.0	(4.2)	14.7	(2.9)	12.3	(2.4)	4.7	(1.7)	6.2	(1.6)	2.0	(1.2)	2.1	(1.2)
	Korea	36.9	(3.7)	5.9	(2.0)	16.3	(3.2)	13.3	(3.0)	43.4	(4.3)	17.3	(3.1)	33.6	(3.7)
	Luxembourg	74.5	(0.0)	48.9	(0.1)	4.1	(0.0)	5.9	(0.0)	55.2	(0.1)	10.8	(0.0)	38.4	(0.1)
	Mexico	46.4	(3.2)	49.9	(3.2)	9.4	(2.2)	6.2	(1.0)	32.1	(2.8)	15.1	(2.3)	42.4	(3.0)
	Netherlands	46.1	(5.0)	7.5	(2.5)	7.0	(2.5)	6.6	(2.4)	38.8	(4.0)	16.9	(3.5)	77.9	(3.9)
	New Zealand	84.8	(2.3)	8.3	(1.9)	2.6	(1.2)	5.6	(1.8)	51.5	(3.3)	5.3	(1.3)	98.2	(1.0)
	Norway	71.9	(3.3)	10.6	(2.2)	22.5	(3.3)	18.2	(3.0)	29.4	(3.7)	31.2	(3.4)	20.7	(3.0)
	Poland	26.8	(3.4)	35.0	(3.7)	9.2	(1.8)	78.5	(3.3)	8.5	(2.1)	81.9	(3.1)	22.2	(3.3)
	Portugal	47.6	(4.3)	49.1	(4.4)	18.3	(3.2)	26.6	(3.5)	91.2	(2.2)	19.2	(3.6)	51.1	(4.1)
	Slovak Republic	16.8	(2.0)	27.5	(2.9)	1.2	(0.7)	46.4	(3.5)	68.8	(3.8)	33.7	(3.4)	79.2	(2.8)
	Spain	50.4	(3.7)	26.5	(3.1)	7.7	(1.8)	7.8	(2.1)	27.6	(3.5)	10.3	(2.3)	24.8	(2.6)
	Sweden	53.0	(3.9)	1.7	(1.0)	10.3	(2.2)	6.5	(1.9)	37.7	(3.6)	14.2	(2.6)	11.1	(2.4)
	Switzerland	64.6	(3.9)	35.2	(4.2)	19.8	(3.5)	1.9	(0.8)	39.5	(4.1)	2.8	(1.3)	19.2	(3.2)
	Turkey	59.3	(4.6)	33.3	(4.3)	15.6	(3.5)	17.7	(3.2)	19.8	(3.5)	20.5	(3.5)	41.3	(4.6)
	United States	82.3	(2.7)	40.8	(2.9)	24.8	(3.1)	11.1	(2.1)	57.1	(3.7)	8.5	(2.1)	40.0	(3.6)
	OECD total	***57.4***	***(1.0)***	***28.9***	***(1.0)***	***15.2***	***(0.9)***	***15.4***	***(0.7)***	***35.8***	***(1.1)***	***15.4***	***(0.7)***	***35.5***	***(1.0)***
	OECD average	***52.6***	***(0.7)***	***25.2***	***(0.5)***	***16.1***	***(0.5)***	***21.9***	***(0.4)***	***40.9***	***(0.6)***	***21.8***	***(0.4)***	***40.5***	***(0.6)***
Partner countries	Brazil	34.3	(4.0)	55.0	(3.3)	7.9	(2.0)	28.3	(3.4)	44.7	(3.7)	26.8	(3.5)	38.1	(3.8)
	Hong Kong-China	51.7	(4.8)	32.3	(4.2)	7.3	(2.2)	37.1	(4.1)	57.7	(4.3)	21.8	(3.6)	74.8	(3.8)
	Indonesia	38.8	(3.2)	15.9	(3.0)	8.0	(1.5)	9.2	(2.4)	50.4	(3.6)	20.8	(3.1)	56.6	(3.7)
	Latvia	35.1	(4.2)	17.0	(3.1)	37.5	(4.5)	92.0	(2.8)	53.7	(4.5)	92.4	(2.3)	64.2	(4.1)
	Liechtenstein	c	c	c	c	c	c	c	c	c	c	c	c	c	c
	Macao-China	39.0	(0.3)	43.1	(0.2)	8.2	(0.0)	25.2	(0.2)	42.3	(0.2)	27.6	(0.2)	42.2	(0.2)
	Russian Federation	40.5	(3.8)	56.5	(3.8)	15.3	(3.2)	12.5	(2.7)	68.0	(3.6)	26.9	(3.9)	61.2	(3.9)
	Serbia	43.3	(4.2)	2.8	(1.4)	89.5	(2.8)	42.9	(4.2)	53.2	(4.2)	52.5	(4.2)	42.4	(3.6)
	Thailand	43.5	(4.4)	50.2	(3.7)	12.0	(3.4)	51.3	(4.3)	66.3	(4.0)	48.1	(4.2)	84.8	(2.5)
	Tunisia	40.8	(4.2)	19.1	(3.1)	16.2	(3.1)	24.2	(3.8)	17.4	(3.0)	14.6	(3.0)	54.6	(4.0)
	Uruguay	70.6	(3.8)	14.4	(2.5)	1.2	(0.5)	0.6	c	29.8	(3.4)	1.3	(0.7)	15.0	(3.2)
	United Kingdom[1]	60.3	(3.0)	16.4	(2.6)	5.1	(1.5)	13.0	(2.3)	27.7	(3.1)	9.7	(2.1)	86.4	(2.8)

1. Response rate too low to ensure comparability (see Annex A3).

Table 5.13
Strength of the relationship between student and school socio-economic context, and school policies and practices on student performance in mathematics

		Between-school variance accounted for by student and school socio-economic context	Between-school variance accounted for by school policies and practices, after accounting for the impact of student and school socio-economic context	Joint variance explained by student and school socio-economic context as well as school policies and practices
OECD countries	Australia	58.1	0.4	15.1
	Austria	32.3	6.7	36.8
	Belgium	42.8	4.6	35.2
	Canada	43.5	0.3	3.9
	Czech Republic	60.5	0.5	14.6
	Denmark	73.3	1.3	-0.1
	Finland	33.2	-1.0	-6.6
	France	w	w	w
	Germany	40.8	3.8	27.7
	Greece	61.9	-0.3	6.9
	Hungary	61.1	-0.7	20.2
	Iceland	34.5	-3.7	7.8
	Ireland	62.2	0.3	23.3
	Italy	52.4	3.3	8.2
	Japan	62.9	1.8	17.1
	Korea	43.1	7.4	27.5
	Luxembourg	71.1	3.7	19.8
	Mexico	52.5	2.0	12.1
	Netherlands	44.9	1.6	33.5
	New Zealand	73.6	-0.6	7.3
	Norway	41.2	0.7	9.3
	Poland	66.9	1.3	5.9
	Portugal	29.8	7.5	26.8
	Slovak Republic	52.9	0.2	22.1
	Spain	47.4	1.0	13.8
	Sweden	58.7	9.6	6.0
	Switzerland	46.0	5.4	17.6
	Turkey	60.9	0.6	12.6
	United States	72.1	-0.2	2.5
	OECD average	*53.1*	*2.0*	*15.0*
Partner countries	Brazil	m	m	m
	Hong Kong-China	40.4	3.5	12.6
	Indonesia	34.7	4.4	11.2
	Latvia	29.8	3.9	21.6
	Liechtenstein	c	c	c
	Macao-China	21.9	-6.3	11.1
	Russian Federation	32.8	0.0	8.6
	Serbia	60.8	1.8	5.0
	Thailand	44.2	0.8	12.1
	Tunisia	56.7	0.7	-1.0
	Uruguay	29.6	0.7	42.2
	United Kingdom[1]	59.4	2.0	8.8

Note: The estimates are based on the combined impact of socio-economic and policy and practice variables at the school level. Socio-economic context is measured by: the index of economic, social and cultural status, the student's place of birth and the language spoken at their home, the number of books at the student's home, the index of possessions related to "classical" culture in the family home, the student's gender, the school-level average index of economic, social and cultural status, the school location (rural/urban), and the school type (public/private). School policies and practices are measured by: academic selectivity of schools, the estimated times per year standardised tests are used, the estimated times per year teacher-developed tests are used, the use of ability grouping for all classes, the school offerings of extension activities, the number of decisions made at the school level regarding staffing and budgeting, and the number of decisions made at the school level regarding curriculum and assessment (see Annex A1).

The analysis is undertaken for the combined OECD student population, with countries given equal weight. The resulting international model is then applied to each country to estimate the effects at the country level.

1. Response rate too low to ensure comparability (see Annex A3).

Table 5.14
Student learning time
Students' reports of the average number of hours spent on the following "out-of and in-school" activities during each school week, for all subjects and for mathematics

Time in hours per week for all subjects

		"In-school" activities						"Out-of-school" activities							
		Instructional time		Remedial classes		Enrichment classes		Homework or other study set by their teachers		Working with a tutor		Attending out-of-school classes		Other study	
		Mean	S.E.	Mean	S.E.	Mean	S.E.	Mean	S.E.	Mean	S.E.	Mean	S.E.	Mean	S.E.
OECD countries	Australia	24.1	(0.11)	0.6	(0.04)	0.5	(0.04)	5.7	(0.10)	0.3	(0.02)	0.3	(0.02)	1.4	(0.03)
	Austria	27.2	(0.34)	0.2	(0.02)	0.5	(0.03)	4.0	(0.11)	0.3	(0.02)	0.2	(0.02)	2.1	(0.08)
	Belgium	26.9	(0.08)	0.2	(0.01)	0.3	(0.02)	6.2	(0.12)	0.1	(0.01)	0.3	(0.02)	0.5	(0.03)
	Canada	23.6	(0.10)	1.0	(0.05)	0.9	(0.05)	5.6	(0.10)	0.3	(0.01)	0.5	(0.02)	1.3	(0.04)
	Czech Republic	23.6	(0.07)	0.3	(0.02)	0.4	(0.02)	3.8	(0.11)	0.3	(0.02)	0.7	(0.04)	1.0	(0.05)
	Denmark	22.2	(0.21)	0.2	(0.03)	0.1	(0.02)	5.4	(0.09)	0.1	(0.01)	0.3	(0.02)	0.8	(0.04)
	Finland	22.6	(0.05)	0.2	(0.02)	1.9	(0.07)	3.7	(0.07)	0.1	(0.01)	0.3	(0.02)	0.9	(0.03)
	France	24.8	(0.21)	0.6	(0.03)	0.2	(0.02)	6.8	(0.11)	0.4	(0.02)	0.2	(0.02)	0.5	(0.03)
	Germany	22.6	(0.10)	0.1	(0.01)	0.6	(0.03)	6.3	(0.10)	0.5	(0.02)	0.1	(0.02)	1.4	(0.05)
	Greece	23.5	(0.07)	1.8	(0.10)	1.3	(0.06)	8.3	(0.20)	2.3	(0.10)	5.3	(0.22)	2.4	(0.07)
	Hungary	23.9	(0.10)	0.5	(0.03)	0.4	(0.03)	10.0	(0.18)	0.6	(0.02)	0.6	(0.03)	2.2	(0.06)
	Iceland	26.1	(0.08)	0.5	(0.02)	0.7	(0.02)	4.6	(0.06)	0.4	(0.02)	0.3	(0.02)	0.6	(0.03)
	Ireland	27.4	(0.14)	0.6	(0.05)	0.3	(0.03)	7.7	(0.15)	0.3	(0.02)	0.5	(0.04)	2.7	(0.08)
	Italy	26.4	(0.25)	1.1	(0.04)	0.5	(0.03)	10.5	(0.20)	0.6	(0.03)	0.7	(0.03)	1.0	(0.04)
	Japan	23.8	(0.24)	1.1	(0.11)	0.8	(0.05)	3.8	(0.21)	0.1	(0.01)	0.5	(0.06)	2.0	(0.10)
	Korea	30.3	(0.27)	4.9	(0.22)	1.9	(0.11)	3.5	(0.12)	1.3	(0.06)	3.8	(0.15)	4.2	(0.14)
	Luxembourg	24.1	(0.08)	0.3	(0.02)	0.4	(0.05)	6.1	(0.07)	0.5	(0.02)	0.8	(0.04)	2.5	(0.06)
	Mexico	24.2	(0.34)	4.1	(0.21)	3.0	(0.15)	5.8	(0.14)	2.5	(0.14)	3.0	(0.13)	3.6	(0.13)
	Netherlands	23.9	(0.16)	0.2	(0.03)	0.8	(0.06)	5.7	(0.13)	0.2	(0.02)	m	m	m	m
	New Zealand	23.5	(0.11)	1.2	(0.09)	0.5	(0.03)	4.5	(0.08)	0.3	(0.02)	0.3	(0.02)	1.6	(0.05)
	Norway	22.1	(0.11)	0.3	(0.02)	0.2	(0.02)	4.8	(0.11)	0.1	(0.01)	0.2	(0.02)	0.8	(0.05)
	Poland	23.0	(0.08)	0.7	(0.03)	1.2	(0.04)	8.1	(0.16)	0.4	(0.02)	1.1	(0.04)	m	m
	Portugal	25.1	(0.35)	0.4	(0.03)	0.3	(0.05)	4.9	(0.12)	0.9	(0.04)	0.4	(0.03)	1.6	(0.08)
	Slovak Republic	23.5	(0.12)	0.6	(0.04)	0.5	(0.03)	8.4	(0.15)	0.6	(0.02)	0.3	(0.02)	0.7	(0.03)
	Spain	26.4	(0.14)	0.4	(0.02)	0.2	(0.02)	7.4	(0.13)	1.1	(0.03)	1.5	(0.05)	1.9	(0.05)
	Sweden	22.5	(0.22)	0.3	(0.03)	0.1	(0.01)	3.9	(0.10)	0.2	(0.03)	0.2	(0.02)	0.8	(0.05)
	Switzerland	24.1	(0.31)	0.3	(0.03)	0.2	(0.02)	4.6	(0.13)	0.2	(0.01)	0.7	(0.05)	0.7	(0.04)
	Turkey	23.1	(0.33)	2.7	(0.10)	2.2	(0.08)	5.9	(0.19)	1.8	(0.09)	4.1	(0.20)	5.8	(0.19)
	United States	22.2	(0.29)	1.4	(0.07)	1.6	(0.09)	5.7	(0.14)	0.3	(0.02)	0.4	(0.03)	1.5	(0.05)
	OECD total	*23.9*	*(0.09)*	*1.2*	*(0.03)*	*1.1*	*(0.02)*	*5.9*	*(0.05)*	*0.4*	*(0.01)*	*0.8*	*(0.02)*	*1.8*	*(0.03)*
	OECD average	*24.4*	*(0.04)*	*0.8*	*(0.01)*	*0.7*	*(0.01)*	*5.9*	*(0.03)*	*0.5*	*(0.01)*	*0.9*	*(0.02)*	*1.6*	*(0.02)*
Partner countries	Brazil	19.0	(0.19)	1.1	(0.07)	0.8	(0.07)	4.9	(0.13)	0.6	(0.04)	2.1	(0.08)	2.2	(0.12)
	Hong Kong-China	26.5	(0.23)	1.2	(0.07)	0.6	(0.05)	6.8	(0.20)	0.7	(0.04)	0.8	(0.04)	0.9	(0.06)
	Indonesia	m	m	m	m	m	m	m	m	m	m	m	m	m	m
	Latvia	23.9	(0.22)	1.3	(0.06)	1.0	(0.05)	9.4	(0.20)	0.6	(0.03)	1.9	(0.09)	2.1	(0.12)
	Liechtenstein	27.1	(0.18)	0.2	(0.03)	0.2	(0.04)	4.4	(0.18)	0.1	(0.03)	0.4	(0.06)	0.8	(0.14)
	Macao-China	26.9	(0.15)	1.3	(0.11)	0.9	(0.08)	7.8	(0.20)	0.6	(0.07)	0.6	(0.07)	1.2	(0.12)
	Russian Federation	23.8	(0.21)	2.0	(0.06)	1.3	(0.07)	12.7	(0.28)	0.5	(0.03)	1.5	(0.06)	3.7	(0.12)
	Serbia	23.7	(0.14)	0.3	(0.03)	0.3	(0.03)	5.3	(0.22)	0.8	(0.04)	0.3	(0.03)	2.9	(0.10)
	Thailand	30.5	(0.18)	0.9	(0.06)	0.8	(0.04)	6.9	(0.19)	0.5	(0.03)	1.1	(0.08)	0.3	(0.02)
	Tunisia	27.6	(0.19)	1.4	(0.06)	m	m	4.9	(0.16)	m	m	1.4	(0.07)	2.4	(0.10)
	Uruguay	21.6	(0.30)	0.5	(0.04)	0.3	(0.03)	6.8	(0.13)	1.5	(0.06)	0.9	(0.05)	2.1	(0.07)
	United Kingdom[1]	24.6	(0.09)	0.5	(0.02)	0.6	(0.02)	6.0	(0.10)	0.2	(0.01)	0.5	(0.02)	1.3	(0.10)

Time in hours per week for mathematics

		"In-school" activities						"Out-of-school" activities									
		Instructional time		Remedial classes		Enrichment classes		Homework or other study set by their teachers		Working with a tutor		Attending out-of-school classes		Other study		Instructional weeks in years	
		Mean	S.E.	Mean	S.E.	Mean	S.E.	Mean	S.E.	Mean	S.E.	Mean	S.E.	Mean	S.E.	Mean	S.E.
OECD countries	Australia	3.8	(0.03)	0.2	(0.01)	0.2	(0.02)	2.3	(0.04)	0.2	(0.01)	0.1	(0.01)	0.1	(0.01)	39.4	(0.1)
	Austria	2.8	(0.07)	0.1	(0.01)	0.1	(0.01)	1.7	(0.04)	0.1	(0.01)	0.0	(0.00)	0.1	(0.01)	36.7	(0.8)
	Belgium	3.3	(0.03)	0.1	(0.01)	0.1	(0.01)	2.2	(0.04)	0.1	(0.01)	0.1	(0.01)	0.1	(0.01)	36.2	(0.2)
	Canada	3.7	(0.03)	0.4	(0.02)	0.3	(0.02)	2.8	(0.05)	0.2	(0.01)	0.1	(0.01)	0.1	(0.01)	38.6	(0.2)
	Czech Republic	2.8	(0.04)	0.1	(0.01)	0.0	(0.01)	1.7	(0.04)	0.1	(0.01)	0.1	(0.01)	0.1	(0.01)	41.0	(0.2)
	Denmark	3.4	(0.04)	0.1	(0.01)	0.0	(0.01)	2.6	(0.04)	0.0	(0.01)	0.1	(0.01)	0.1	(0.02)	39.6	(0.1)
	Finland	2.6	(0.04)	0.1	(0.01)	0.3	(0.02)	1.5	(0.03)	0.0	(0.01)	0.0	(0.00)	0.0	(0.00)	38.1	(0.0)
	France	3.5	(0.03)	0.3	(0.02)	0.1	(0.01)	2.5	(0.05)	0.2	(0.02)	0.1	(0.01)	0.1	(0.01)	m	m
	Germany	3.0	(0.03)	0.1	(0.01)	0.1	(0.01)	2.6	(0.05)	0.3	(0.02)	0.0	(0.01)	0.1	(0.01)	39.7	(0.2)
	Greece	3.1	(0.03)	0.8	(0.05)	0.5	(0.02)	3.3	(0.07)	0.9	(0.04)	1.7	(0.09)	0.4	(0.02)	34.3	(0.2)
	Hungary	2.7	(0.03)	0.2	(0.02)	0.1	(0.01)	3.3	(0.05)	0.2	(0.01)	0.3	(0.02)	0.2	(0.01)	36.6	(0.1)
	Iceland	4.2	(0.02)	0.3	(0.02)	0.2	(0.01)	2.3	(0.03)	0.2	(0.01)	0.1	(0.01)	0.1	(0.01)	36.7	(0.0)
	Ireland	3.2	(0.03)	0.2	(0.02)	0.1	(0.01)	2.8	(0.05)	0.2	(0.02)	0.1	(0.01)	0.1	(0.02)	33.1	(0.2)
	Italy	3.6	(0.05)	0.4	(0.02)	0.1	(0.01)	3.5	(0.07)	0.3	(0.02)	0.1	(0.01)	0.1	(0.01)	33.5	(0.2)
	Japan	3.6	(0.07)	0.5	(0.04)	0.4	(0.02)	2.0	(0.10)	0.1	(0.01)	0.3	(0.03)	0.1	(0.01)	38.9	(0.3)
	Korea	4.1	(0.06)	1.4	(0.07)	0.7	(0.04)	1.8	(0.06)	0.7	(0.04)	1.4	(0.06)	0.4	(0.02)	35.6	(0.3)
	Luxembourg	3.3	(0.03)	0.2	(0.01)	0.1	(0.02)	2.3	(0.04)	0.3	(0.02)	0.1	(0.01)	0.2	(0.02)	36.0	(0.0)
	Mexico	3.9	(0.08)	2.2	(0.05)	2.0	(0.05)	3.2	(0.07)	1.8	(0.08)	1.9	(0.11)	2.1	(0.11)	23.9	(0.7)
	Netherlands	2.5	(0.04)	0.1	(0.01)	0.3	(0.02)	1.9	(0.05)	0.1	(0.01)	m	m	0.1	(0.01)	38.1	(0.2)
	New Zealand	4.0	(0.03)	0.4	(0.02)	0.2	(0.02)	1.7	(0.03)	0.1	(0.01)	0.1	(0.01)	0.1	(0.01)	36.0	(0.1)
	Norway	2.8	(0.07)	0.2	(0.01)	0.1	(0.01)	1.8	(0.04)	0.1	(0.01)	0.0	(0.01)	0.1	(0.01)	38.0	(0.0)
	Poland	3.4	(0.03)	0.3	(0.02)	0.2	(0.02)	4.1	(0.08)	0.2	(0.02)	0.2	(0.01)	0.2	(0.01)	38.3	(0.2)
	Portugal	3.3	(0.05)	0.2	(0.02)	0.1	(0.01)	2.0	(0.04)	0.5	(0.03)	0.2	(0.01)	0.2	(0.02)	35.4	(0.2)
	Slovak Republic	3.3	(0.05)	0.3	(0.03)	0.1	(0.02)	3.2	(0.06)	0.1	(0.01)	0.1	(0.01)	0.2	(0.01)	39.2	(0.3)
	Spain	2.9	(0.02)	0.2	(0.01)	0.1	(0.01)	2.9	(0.05)	0.6	(0.02)	0.6	(0.03)	0.4	(0.02)	35.4	(0.2)
	Sweden	2.8	(0.04)	0.1	(0.01)	0.1	(0.01)	1.3	(0.03)	0.1	(0.01)	0.0	(0.01)	0.1	(0.01)	36.6	(0.1)
	Switzerland	3.3	(0.09)	0.1	(0.01)	0.1	(0.01)	1.9	(0.04)	0.1	(0.01)	0.0	(0.01)	0.1	(0.02)	39.2	(0.1)
	Turkey	3.3	(0.05)	1.5	(0.06)	1.2	(0.06)	2.8	(0.07)	1.1	(0.07)	1.8	(0.08)	1.2	(0.06)	35.7	(0.3)
	United States	3.7	(0.06)	0.5	(0.03)	0.5	(0.02)	2.8	(0.05)	0.2	(0.01)	0.1	(0.01)	0.2	(0.02)	36.0	(0.0)
	OECD total	*3.5*	*(0.02)*	*0.5*	*(0.01)*	*0.4*	*(0.01)*	*2.6*	*(0.02)*	*0.3*	*(0.01)*	*0.3*	*(0.01)*	*0.2*	*(0.01)*	*36.1*	*(0.1)*
	OECD average	*3.3*	*(0.01)*	*0.3*	*(0.00)*	*0.2*	*(0.00)*	*2.4*	*(0.01)*	*0.2*	*(0.00)*	*0.3*	*(0.01)*	*0.2*	*(0.00)*	*36.7*	*(0.0)*
Partner countries	Brazil	3.5	(0.07)	0.6	(0.04)	0.5	(0.04)	2.4	(0.06)	0.5	(0.04)	0.6	(0.04)	0.5	(0.04)	40.6	(0.2)
	Hong Kong-China	4.5	(0.06)	0.3	(0.03)	0.2	(0.02)	3.1	(0.09)	0.4	(0.02)	0.3	(0.02)	0.1	(0.01)	35.4	(0.4)
	Indonesia	3.9	(0.08)	m	m	m	m	m	m	m	m	m	m	m	m	40.0	(0.4)
	Latvia	3.6	(0.05)	0.6	(0.02)	0.3	(0.02)	3.7	(0.08)	0.3	(0.02)	0.2	(0.02)	0.3	(0.02)	34.9	(0.1)
	Liechtenstein	3.6	(0.03)	0.1	(0.02)	0.1	(0.02)	1.7	(0.08)	0.1	(0.02)	0.0	(0.01)	0.1	(0.04)	39.0	(0.0)
	Macao-China	4.5	(0.05)	0.6	(0.05)	0.3	(0.06)	4.3	(0.11)	0.3	(0.04)	0.2	(0.03)	0.1	(0.02)	39.2	(0.0)
	Russian Federation	3.5	(0.07)	1.2	(0.05)	0.6	(0.03)	5.0	(0.10)	0.4	(0.02)	0.4	(0.03)	0.4	(0.03)	35.0	(0.2)
	Serbia	2.7	(0.04)	0.1	(0.02)	0.1	(0.01)	2.4	(0.07)	0.5	(0.03)	0.1	(0.01)	0.2	(0.02)	37.1	(0.1)
	Thailand	3.7	(0.05)	0.5	(0.02)	0.3	(0.02)	4.0	(0.11)	0.3	(0.02)	0.6	(0.04)	0.1	(0.01)	39.7	(0.1)
	Tunisia	4.2	(0.02)	0.9	(0.03)	m	m	2.8	(0.08)	m	m	0.9	(0.04)	0.7	(0.04)	31.9	(0.3)
	Uruguay	3.0	(0.06)	0.2	(0.02)	0.1	(0.02)	2.8	(0.05)	0.5	(0.03)	0.3	(0.03)	0.2	(0.02)	33.9	(0.2)
	United Kingdom[1]	3.4	(0.03)	0.2	(0.01)	0.2	(0.01)	2.0	(0.04)	0.1	(0.01)	0.1	(0.01)	0.1	(0.01)	37.8	(0.1)

1. Response rate too low to ensure comparability (see Annex A3).

Table 5.15

Index of teacher shortage and student performance on the mathematics scale, by national quarters of the index

Results based on reports from school principals and reported proportionate to the number of 15-year-olds enrolled in the school

		Index of teacher shortage										Performance on the mathematics scale by national quarters of the index of teacher shortage							
		All students		Bottom quarter		Second quarter		Third quarter		Top quarter		Bottom quarter		Second quarter		Third quarter		Top quarter	
		Mean index	S.E.	Mean index	S.E.	Mean index	S.E.	Mean index	S.E.	Mean index	S.E.	Mean score	S.E.	Mean score	S.E.	Mean score	S.E.	Mean score	S.E.
OECD countries	Australia	0.09	(0.05)	–1.13	(0.02)	–0.14	(0.02)	0.48	(0.02)	1.14	(0.03)	**547**	(4.4)	527	(4.3)	509	(4.2)	**513**	(5.9)
	Austria	–0.58	(0.06)	–1.21	(0.00)	–1.15	(0.01)	–0.37	(0.02)	0.40	(0.06)	**527**	(7.0)	523	(6.6)	472	(7.8)	**498**	(7.7)
	Belgium	0.25	(0.06)	–1.07	(0.02)	–0.03	(0.03)	0.62	(0.02)	1.47	(0.08)	**558**	(6.8)	537	(7.1)	524	(8.7)	**502**	(7.5)
	Canada	–0.21	(0.04)	–1.21	(0.00)	–0.63	(0.02)	0.12	(0.01)	0.89	(0.04)	537	(4.3)	539	(3.1)	525	(3.2)	529	(4.1)
	Czech Republic	0.08	(0.03)	–0.58	(0.04)	–0.06	(0.01)	0.23	(0.01)	0.73	(0.03)	**555**	(8.4)	530	(6.8)	500	(5.5)	**479**	(7.6)
	Denmark	–0.32	(0.05)	–1.20	(0.00)	–0.52	(0.01)	–0.06	(0.02)	0.51	(0.07)	523	(5.4)	517	(5.9)	504	(4.8)	514	(5.3)
	Finland	–0.56	(0.04)	–1.21	(0.00)	–0.99	(0.03)	–0.36	(0.02)	0.33	(0.05)	542	(2.7)	545	(3.2)	550	(3.7)	541	(3.2)
	France	w	w	w	w	w	w	w	w	w	w	w	w	w	w	w	w	w	w
	Germany	0.15	(0.06)	–1.01	(0.04)	–0.10	(0.02)	0.47	(0.02)	1.22	(0.07)	**537**	(8.4)	525	(7.2)	482	(9.6)	**468**	(9.1)
	Greece	0.21	(0.16)	–1.21	(0.00)	–0.75	(0.07)	0.53	(0.07)	2.25	(0.16)	447	(10.2)	446	(7.1)	430	(10.0)	451	(10.0)
	Hungary	–0.37	(0.05)	–1.21	(0.00)	–0.68	(0.03)	–0.07	(0.02)	0.47	(0.03)	**509**	(9.6)	493	(9.5)	482	(7.8)	**479**	(8.1)
	Iceland	0.08	(0.00)	–1.06	(0.01)	–0.15	(0.00)	0.45	(0.00)	1.09	(0.00)	518	(3.1)	520	(3.8)	509	(4.1)	515	(3.4)
	Ireland	–0.28	(0.07)	–1.21	(0.00)	–0.72	(0.04)	0.06	(0.03)	0.73	(0.04)	510	(5.3)	503	(5.2)	499	(6.6)	502	(5.7)
	Italy	0.08	(0.07)	–1.16	(0.01)	–0.15	(0.04)	0.44	(0.01)	1.18	(0.08)	452	(8.6)	475	(7.6)	486	(7.6)	452	(6.5)
	Japan	–0.04	(0.10)	–1.21	(0.00)	–0.68	(0.03)	0.16	(0.05)	1.58	(0.14)	**557**	(9.7)	537	(7.4)	525	(10.5)	**517**	(12.1)
	Korea	–0.64	(0.06)	–1.21	(0.00)	–1.20	(0.00)	–0.54	(0.04)	0.40	(0.07)	539	(6.9)	538	(7.3)	553	(8.0)	538	(8.2)
	Luxembourg	0.57	(0.00)	–0.99	(0.01)	0.52	(0.00)	1.12	(0.00)	1.62	(0.00)	**509**	(2.4)	495	(2.5)	493	(2.2)	**476**	(2.2)
	Mexico	0.41	(0.07)	–0.94	(0.05)	0.16	(0.03)	0.76	(0.01)	1.66	(0.07)	400	(10.4)	384	(7.0)	376	(7.5)	379	(5.4)
	Netherlands	0.19	(0.06)	–0.82	(0.06)	–0.04	(0.03)	0.44	(0.02)	1.19	(0.08)	**565**	(10.5)	539	(9.2)	545	(10.5)	**497**	(11.2)
	New Zealand	0.33	(0.04)	–0.76	(0.05)	0.14	(0.02)	0.62	(0.02)	1.31	(0.03)	**540**	(5.8)	532	(4.4)	516	(6.2)	**509**	(5.9)
	Norway	0.04	(0.05)	–0.88	(0.05)	–0.09	(0.02)	0.38	(0.01)	0.77	(0.06)	505	(4.8)	484	(5.1)	496	(4.0)	493	(4.8)
	Poland	0.05	(0.08)	–0.99	(0.04)	–0.22	(0.02)	0.19	(0.02)	1.24	(0.14)	498	(5.9)	482	(5.0)	489	(5.5)	491	(5.4)
	Portugal	–0.51	(0.06)	–1.21	(0.00)	–0.95	(0.04)	–0.38	(0.02)	0.49	(0.10)	473	(5.3)	473	(4.6)	456	(8.1)	461	(9.6)
	Slovak Republic	–0.19	(0.03)	–1.07	(0.03)	–0.30	(0.02)	–0.01	(0.01)	0.63	(0.05)	**523**	(5.2)	511	(7.6)	486	(6.3)	**473**	(8.7)
	Spain	–0.46	(0.08)	–1.21	(0.00)	–1.20	(0.00)	–0.51	(0.03)	1.07	(0.21)	**490**	(4.3)	490	(4.5)	487	(5.1)	**473**	(5.8)
	Sweden	0.07	(0.07)	–1.06	(0.03)	–0.18	(0.02)	0.31	(0.02)	1.19	(0.11)	518	(5.2)	504	(6.0)	507	(6.1)	507	(3.8)
	Switzerland	–0.33	(0.07)	–1.21	(0.00)	–0.88	(0.04)	–0.02	(0.02)	0.78	(0.10)	523	(6.1)	526	(6.3)	534	(10.5)	523	(9.9)
	Turkey	1.78	(0.09)	0.47	(0.11)	1.36	(0.03)	2.16	(0.06)	3.13	(0.02)	440	(17.8)	420	(11.7)	409	(13.0)	425	(12.9)
	United States	–0.20	(0.06)	–1.21	(0.00)	–0.73	(0.04)	0.19	(0.02)	0.95	(0.06)	**507**	(5.9)	494	(5.8)	475	(5.9)	**469**	(7.1)
	OECD total	***0.04***	***(0.02)***	***–1.20***	***(0.00)***	***–0.41***	***(0.01)***	***0.34***	***(0.01)***	***1.43***	***(0.03)***	***512***	***(3.1)***	***503***	***(2.7)***	***484***	***(2.8)***	***457***	***(3.2)***
	OECD average	***0.00***	***(0.01)***	***–1.20***	***(0.00)***	***–0.39***	***(0.01)***	***0.28***	***(0.01)***	***1.31***	***(0.02)***	***514***	***(1.7)***	***510***	***(1.7)***	***499***	***(1.6)***	***476***	***(1.9)***
Partner countries	Brazil	0.20	(0.09)	–1.21	(0.00)	–0.48	(0.05)	0.62	(0.04)	1.86	(0.10)	**382**	(10.7)	371	(10.7)	339	(9.8)	**335**	(8.3)
	Hong Kong-China	–0.22	(0.06)	–1.20	(0.00)	–0.48	(0.02)	0.02	(0.02)	0.80	(0.06)	560	(10.5)	563	(9.3)	538	(9.3)	540	(13.7)
	Indonesia	1.28	(0.10)	–0.06	(0.08)	0.76	(0.03)	1.56	(0.05)	2.88	(0.05)	353	(7.3)	356	(9.4)	363	(8.4)	368	(7.9)
	Latvia	–0.14	(0.05)	–0.97	(0.05)	–0.32	(0.03)	0.10	(0.02)	0.65	(0.06)	475	(7.0)	482	(6.0)	488	(6.7)	490	(7.4)
	Liechtenstein	c	c	c	c	c	c	c	c	c	c	c	c	c	c	c	c	c	c
	Macao-China	0.29	(0.00)	–0.70	(0.01)	0.13	(0.00)	0.56	(0.01)	1.17	(0.01)	529	(4.6)	515	(5.3)	541	(8.2)	524	(5.5)
	Russian Federation	0.36	(0.09)	–0.92	(0.05)	0.10	(0.02)	0.66	(0.03)	1.60	(0.13)	469	(11.5)	468	(6.8)	463	(6.4)	469	(7.6)
	Serbia	–0.34	(0.05)	–1.20	(0.00)	–0.52	(0.01)	–0.10	(0.02)	0.47	(0.05)	438	(8.6)	444	(8.0)	441	(7.7)	427	(7.4)
	Thailand	0.28	(0.09)	–1.00	(0.05)	0.01	(0.04)	0.58	(0.02)	1.54	(0.11)	**440**	(8.6)	414	(6.3)	406	(5.4)	**408**	(7.2)
	Tunisia	0.18	(0.06)	–0.85	(0.06)	0.08	(0.02)	0.52	(0.01)	0.97	(0.03)	368	(9.2)	370	(8.0)	352	(7.2)	344	(6.2)
	Uruguay	0.55	(0.08)	–0.87	(0.06)	0.35	(0.03)	1.02	(0.02)	1.70	(0.06)	**441**	(8.1)	414	(8.6)	414	(8.4)	**420**	(7.5)
	United Kingdom[1]	0.26	(0.06)	–1.09	(0.03)	–0.03	(0.03)	0.63	(0.02)	1.52	(0.06)	**535**	(5.6)	510	(5.4)	505	(6.5)	**486**	(5.6)

		Change in the mathematics score per unit of the index of teacher shortage		Increased likelihood of students in the top quarter of this index scoring in the bottom quarter of the national mathematics performance distribution		Explained variance in student performance (r-squared × 100)	
		Effect	S.E.	Ratio	S.E.	Percentage	S.E.
OECD countries	Australia	**–16.5**	(2.78)	**1.2**	(0.11)	2.3	(0.78)
	Austria	**–22.8**	(7.22)	1.2	(0.16)	3.0	(1.77)
	Belgium	**–23.4**	(3.97)	**1.6**	(0.18)	4.6	(1.47)
	Canada	**–5.4**	(2.41)	1.1	(0.08)	0.3	(0.25)
	Czech Republic	**–58.4**	(8.57)	**1.8**	(0.24)	10.2	(2.95)
	Denmark	–5.6	(3.72)	1.0	(0.09)	0.2	(0.24)
	Finland	–0.5	(3.03)	1.1	(0.07)	0.0	(0.05)
	France	w	w	w	w	w	w
	Germany	**–28.4**	(6.75)	**1.7**	(0.22)	6.0	(2.47)
	Greece	–1.2	(3.93)	0.8	(0.17)	0.0	(0.38)
	Hungary	**–19.1**	(8.10)	1.2	(0.15)	1.8	(1.54)
	Iceland	–3.1	(1.89)	1.0	(0.07)	0.1	(0.09)
	Ireland	–5.1	(4.03)	1.0	(0.13)	0.2	(0.36)
	Italy	1.8	(5.10)	1.2	(0.15)	0.0	(0.31)
	Japan	–9.9	(5.07)	1.4	(0.25)	1.3	(1.40)
	Korea	0.3	(6.98)	1.0	(0.18)	0.0	(0.24)
	Luxembourg	**–11.0**	(1.09)	**1.4**	(0.08)	1.5	(0.29)
	Mexico	–6.1	(3.40)	1.0	(0.12)	0.5	(0.56)
	Netherlands	**–26.8**	(8.58)	**2.0**	(0.42)	5.4	(3.54)
	New Zealand	**–16.0**	(3.44)	**1.4**	(0.15)	1.7	(0.76)
	Norway	–5.1	(3.47)	0.9	(0.09)	0.1	(0.18)
	Poland	–3.8	(3.41)	1.0	(0.10)	0.2	(0.30)
	Portugal	–6.9	(6.28)	1.1	(0.18)	0.4	(0.72)
	Slovak Republic	**–30.2**	(5.78)	**1.6**	(0.21)	4.6	(1.68)
	Spain	–4.8	(3.38)	1.2	(0.13)	0.4	(0.49)
	Sweden	–4.0	(2.66)	1.0	(0.09)	0.2	(0.22)
	Switzerland	–0.6	(4.63)	1.1	(0.15)	0.0	(0.15)
	Turkey	–6.3	(8.69)	1.0	(0.19)	0.4	(1.20)
	United States	**–18.8**	(3.48)	**1.4**	(0.16)	3.2	(1.23)
	OECD total	***–19.6***	***(1.59)***	***1.8***	***(0.08)***	***3.9***	***(0.63)***
	OECD average	***–15.8***	***(0.99)***	***1.5***	***(0.04)***	***2.5***	***(0.32)***
Partner countries	Brazil	**–17.5**	(3.96)	1.2	(0.17)	4.6	(2.16)
	Hong Kong-China	–10.9	(8.03)	1.3	(0.25)	0.7	(1.11)
	Indonesia	2.2	(3.40)	**0.7**	(0.11)	0.1	(0.34)
	Latvia	9.9	(5.83)	0.8	(0.12)	0.5	(0.66)
	Liechtenstein	c	c	c	c	c	c
	Macao-China	**–6.6**	(3.10)	1.2	(0.13)	0.3	(0.33)
	Russian Federation	–2.3	(5.14)	0.9	(0.13)	0.1	(0.33)
	Serbia	–7.2	(6.53)	1.2	(0.18)	0.3	(0.57)
	Thailand	**–13.3**	(3.85)	1.2	(0.14)	2.7	(1.52)
	Tunisia	–8.6	(6.42)	1.3	(0.16)	0.6	(0.88)
	Uruguay	**–9.9**	(4.00)	1.0	(0.15)	1.0	(0.72)
	United Kingdom[1]	**–17.4**	(2.52)	**1.5**	(0.13)	3.6	(1.05)

Note: Values that are statistically significant are indicated in bold (see Annex A4).

1. Response rate too low to ensure comparability (see Annex A3).

Table 5.16
Monitoring practices of mathematics teachers
Results based on reports from school principals and reported proportionate to the number of 15-year-olds enrolled in the school

		Percentage of students in schools where the principals report that they monitored the practice of mathematics teachers in the preceding year through the following methods							
		Principal or senior staff observations of lessons				Observations of classes by inspectors or other persons external to the school			
		Percentage of students in schools where the principals report using this method		Difference in mathematics performance for students in schools using and not using this method		Percentage of students in schools where the principals report using this method		Difference in mathematics performance for students in schools using and not using this method	
		%	S.E.	Difference	S.E.	%	S.E.	Difference	S.E.
OECD countries	Australia	63.4	(2.6)	7	(5.4)	7.8	(1.9)	**24**	(7.1)
	Austria	77.9	(3.3)	–1	(12.4)	37.1	(3.4)	1	(9.5)
	Belgium	57.8	(3.2)	10	(10.7)	47.5	(3.1)	19	(10.7)
	Canada	86.9	(1.2)	–3	(6.0)	10.1	(1.2)	–6	(6.9)
	Czech Republic	99.3	(0.4)	c	c	31.5	(2.9)	–4	(10.2)
	Denmark	63.0	(3.3)	1	(5.3)	11.3	(2.3)	6	(8.0)
	Finland	34.4	(3.4)	2	(3.8)	3.8	(1.6)	17	(9.9)
	France	w	w	w	w	w	w	w	w
	Germany	69.4	(3.3)	**44**	(10.5)	25.7	(2.8)	6	(12.2)
	Greece	7.2	(3.4)	5	(27.0)	16.1	(4.1)	–4	(13.9)
	Hungary	95.8	(1.5)	0	(34.3)	26.0	(3.9)	11	(12.1)
	Iceland	46.7	(0.2)	**–8**	(3.4)	1.8	(0.1)	c	c
	Ireland	6.6	(2.3)	6	(11.0)	4.7	(1.6)	16	(9.0)
	Italy	16.1	(2.8)	12	(9.5)	1.2	(0.8)	c	c
	Japan	55.9	(4.4)	13	(12.6)	15.1	(3.0)	26	(15.3)
	Korea	90.1	(2.6)	27	(15.6)	61.9	(3.4)	9	(10.1)
	Luxembourg	42.2	(0.1)	**9**	(2.6)	7.3	(0.0)	**72**	(4.3)
	Mexico	72.1	(2.6)	–9	(9.7)	36.3	(3.2)	**–25**	(8.6)
	Netherlands	58.4	(4.8)	17	(14.8)	33.3	(4.3)	21	(14.1)
	New Zealand	94.3	(1.7)	3	(16.5)	52.4	(3.2)	6	(6.2)
	Norway	25.9	(3.3)	**15**	(5.2)	6.9	(2.2)	2	(14.5)
	Poland	97.4	(1.3)	c	c	13.7	(2.6)	**32**	(6.6)
	Portugal	4.9	(1.6)	18	(12.8)	9.6	(2.8)	–8	(12.4)
	Slovak Republic	97.8	(1.0)	c	c	24.6	(3.0)	11	(11.5)
	Spain	14.8	(2.6)	**19**	(6.0)	14.1	(2.5)	7	(6.1)
	Sweden	58.4	(3.4)	5	(4.7)	15.7	(2.4)	**27**	(9.8)
	Switzerland	41.8	(4.3)	**29**	(7.9)	58.8	(4.0)	**–19**	(7.5)
	Turkey	89.3	(2.6)	3	(17.4)	39.5	(4.3)	–12	(16.0)
	United States	99.7	(0.3)	c	c	37.2	(3.6)	**–23**	(7.8)
	OECD total	***75.1***	***(0.8)***	***7***	***(3.2)***	***30.2***	***(1.1)***	***–8***	***(3.4)***
	OECD average	***60.7***	***(0.5)***	***12***	***(1.4)***	***24.5***	***(0.6)***	***6***	***(1.8)***
Partner countries	Brazil	49.6	(3.7)	4	(13.3)	11.5	(2.2)	–7	(12.4)
	Hong Kong-China	92.2	(2.4)	–24	(19.0)	26.2	(3.5)	2	(16.9)
	Indonesia	91.6	(2.2)	**55**	(12.5)	75.0	(3.4)	1	(13.1)
	Latvia	99.5	(0.5)	c	c	41.4	(4.9)	–8	(7.6)
	Liechtenstein	c	c	c	c	c	c	c	c
	Macao-China	95.0	(0.0)	c	c	29.9	(0.3)	–2	(5.5)
	Russian Federation	100.0	(0.0)	a	a	73.8	(3.3)	8	(8.6)
	Serbia	88.0	(3.1)	–4	(14.9)	25.4	(3.7)	–8	(9.6)
	Thailand	87.1	(2.7)	17	(11.4)	49.3	(3.7)	14	(7.8)
	Tunisia	74.2	(3.6)	0	(10.4)	80.4	(3.4)	**20**	(10.0)
	Uruguay	92.4	(1.6)	–20	(20.1)	51.9	(3.7)	16	(9.3)
	United Kingdom[1]	91.3	(1.6)	**–32**	(9.5)	61.1	(3.4)	**–22**	(6.7)

		Percentage of students in schools where the principals report that they monitored the practice of mathematics teachers in the preceding year through the following methods							
		Tests or assessments of student achievement				Teacher peer review (of lessons plans, assessment instruments, lessons)			
		Percentage of students in schools where the principals report using this method		Difference in mathematics performance for students in schools using and not using this method		Percentage of students in schools where the principals report using this method		Difference in mathematics performance for students in schools using and not using this method	
		%	S.E.	Difference	S.E.	%	S.E.	Difference	S.E.
OECD countries	Australia	58.7	(3.1)	–1	(6.1)	65.0	(3.3)	2	(6.8)
	Austria	25.3	(3.7)	–9	(11.1)	78.5	(3.6)	–18	(10.1)
	Belgium	40.9	(3.0)	5	(8.8)	61.7	(3.0)	**23**	(9.6)
	Canada	a	a	a	a	a	a	a	a
	Czech Republic	73.4	(3.1)	6	(12.0)	63.0	(2.9)	–17	(9.2)
	Denmark	12.8	(2.6)	5	(8.2)	31.1	(3.5)	3	(6.0)
	Finland	47.2	(3.8)	0	(3.5)	35.0	(3.8)	1	(3.6)
	France	w	w	w	w	w	w	w	w
	Germany	61.6	(3.2)	16	(13.4)	25.3	(3.1)	–12	(12.2)
	Greece	34.5	(5.7)	13	(11.0)	4.6	(1.9)	–30	(23.3)
	Hungary	62.6	(4.1)	2	(11.1)	83.1	(3.0)	–19	(15.4)
	Iceland	80.3	(0.2)	–1	(4.2)	12.6	(0.1)	–6	(4.8)
	Ireland	42.0	(4.3)	–6	(6.2)	9.2	(2.7)	8	(5.1)
	Italy	44.4	(3.8)	1	(10.5)	84.0	(2.8)	21	(12.7)
	Japan	56.9	(4.0)	8	(14.2)	51.2	(4.3)	22	(13.0)
	Korea	70.6	(3.2)	5	(10.3)	73.2	(3.7)	4	(12.5)
	Luxembourg	58.9	(0.1)	**–36**	(2.2)	27.2	(0.1)	**–25**	(2.6)
	Mexico	92.2	(1.6)	**29**	(12.9)	62.8	(3.3)	13	(9.2)
	Netherlands	54.1	(4.2)	**30**	(12.2)	52.0	(4.9)	–3	(13.5)
	New Zealand	73.0	(3.1)	3	(6.1)	91.2	(2.2)	8	(12.0)
	Norway	49.1	(3.9)	2	(4.7)	35.3	(3.8)	4	(5.2)
	Poland	94.9	(1.8)	14	(11.5)	71.9	(3.6)	**15**	(5.3)
	Portugal	32.9	(4.7)	3	(10.9)	58.0	(4.7)	1	(10.5)
	Slovak Republic	70.1	(3.0)	11	(9.0)	87.9	(2.2)	15	(11.4)
	Spain	71.9	(3.2)	7	(7.3)	39.1	(3.5)	3	(6.2)
	Sweden	41.4	(4.0)	**13**	(5.6)	21.3	(3.0)	10	(8.7)
	Switzerland	42.7	(3.6)	5	(12.5)	45.7	(3.9)	**20**	(7.9)
	Turkey	72.3	(4.2)	19	(16.9)	77.0	(4.0)	14	(16.7)
	United States	89.2	(2.2)	**–23**	(11.6)	59.6	(3.2)	7	(7.2)
	OECD total	***73.3***	***(0.9)***	***–12***	***(4.2)***	***59.7***	***(1.2)***	***1***	***(3.6)***
	OECD average	***58.5***	***(0.7)***	***–2***	***(1.8)***	***53.7***	***(0.7)***	***0***	***(1.9)***
Partner countries	Brazil	75.4	(3.3)	8	(13.4)	53.8	(3.3)	26	(12.3)
	Hong Kong-China	82.4	(3.5)	–31	(19.0)	86.0	(2.8)	–11	(19.3)
	Indonesia	91.3	(1.9)	12	(16.2)	66.9	(4.0)	17	(10.3)
	Latvia	94.8	(2.3)	0	(12.5)	97.5	(1.3)	c	c
	Liechtenstein	c	c	c	c	c	c	c	c
	Macao-China	87.5	(0.1)	**27**	(6.0)	95.5	(0.2)	**49**	(10.2)
	Russian Federation	95.5	(1.6)	15	(8.6)	98.4	(1.0)	c	c
	Serbia	22.7	(3.7)	15	(12.8)	58.8	(4.4)	2	(9.8)
	Thailand	91.1	(2.0)	**24**	(10.7)	85.4	(2.5)	8	(10.1)
	Tunisia	79.0	(3.6)	–10	(11.2)	60.1	(4.0)	2	(8.4)
	Uruguay	50.7	(4.0)	2	(9.7)	63.2	(3.2)	9	(8.6)
	United Kingdom[1]	90.8	(1.9)	–14	(18.7)	88.3	(2.0)	**–33**	(9.7)

Note: Values that are statistically significant are indicated in bold (see Annex A4).
1. Response rate too low to ensure comparability (see Annex A3).

Table 5.17

Index of the quality of the schools' physical infrastructure and student performance on the mathematics scale, by national quarters of the index

Results based on reports from school principals and reported proportionate to the number of 15-year-olds enrolled in the school

		Index of the quality of the schools' physical infrastructure										Performance on the mathematics scale by national quarters of the index of the quality of the schools' physical infrastructure							
		All students		Bottom quarter		Second quarter		Third quarter		Top quarter		Bottom quarter		Second quarter		Third quarter		Top quarter	
		Mean index	S.E.	Mean index	S.E.	Mean index	S.E.	Mean index	S.E.	Mean index	S.E.	Mean score	S.E.	Mean score	S.E.	Mean score	S.E.	Mean score	S.E.
OECD countries	Australia	0.18	(0.05)	–0.90	(0.06)	–0.08	(0.01)	0.40	(0.02)	1.32	(0.03)	**517**	(4.9)	514	(5.8)	525	(4.7)	**541**	(5.2)
	Austria	0.13	(0.10)	–1.38	(0.09)	–0.14	(0.04)	0.57	(0.03)	1.49	(0.00)	500	(10.4)	515	(9.3)	514	(9.0)	493	(11.5)
	Belgium	0.08	(0.06)	–1.19	(0.07)	–0.23	(0.02)	0.37	(0.02)	1.38	(0.02)	526	(8.8)	536	(9.1)	521	(7.7)	534	(6.4)
	Canada	0.19	(0.04)	–0.90	(0.04)	–0.12	(0.01)	0.42	(0.02)	1.34	(0.02)	537	(3.8)	529	(3.4)	531	(3.4)	533	(4.4)
	Czech Republic	0.57	(0.05)	–0.43	(0.05)	0.27	(0.02)	0.95	(0.03)	1.49	(0.00)	521	(8.8)	524	(9.0)	500	(8.4)	518	(7.8)
	Denmark	–0.17	(0.07)	–1.20	(0.08)	–0.49	(0.02)	0.06	(0.02)	0.95	(0.07)	516	(5.7)	513	(4.7)	517	(5.5)	511	(5.6)
	Finland	–0.24	(0.08)	–1.40	(0.08)	–0.59	(0.03)	0.08	(0.02)	0.95	(0.06)	542	(4.7)	550	(3.4)	542	(3.2)	543	(3.4)
	France	w	w	w	w	w	w	w	w	w	w	w	w	w	w	w	w	w	w
	Germany	0.14	(0.08)	–1.33	(0.08)	–0.12	(0.03)	0.56	(0.03)	1.46	(0.01)	506	(11.1)	493	(9.1)	499	(8.9)	514	(10.9)
	Greece	–0.42	(0.14)	–1.99	(0.08)	–0.86	(0.03)	–0.06	(0.05)	1.21	(0.08)	431	(10.1)	452	(7.3)	445	(7.9)	452	(10.9)
	Hungary	–0.18	(0.08)	–1.40	(0.08)	–0.40	(0.03)	0.16	(0.02)	0.94	(0.06)	490	(7.7)	496	(9.7)	468	(8.6)	509	(9.1)
	Iceland	0.33	(0.00)	–0.94	(0.01)	0.02	(0.00)	0.75	(0.01)	1.49	(0.00)	**510**	(3.4)	517	(3.8)	513	(3.8)	**522**	(3.3)
	Ireland	–0.28	(0.10)	–1.62	(0.08)	–0.64	(0.03)	–0.01	(0.03)	1.17	(0.06)	513	(5.8)	501	(4.5)	501	(5.3)	498	(8.0)
	Italy	–0.03	(0.07)	–1.28	(0.08)	–0.36	(0.02)	0.20	(0.02)	1.33	(0.04)	**443**	(8.0)	470	(8.8)	480	(5.1)	**471**	(8.7)
	Japan	–0.09	(0.10)	–1.45	(0.09)	–0.39	(0.04)	0.25	(0.02)	1.24	(0.05)	533	(10.9)	543	(12.5)	529	(9.2)	532	(11.3)
	Korea	0.57	(0.06)	–0.43	(0.07)	0.32	(0.02)	0.92	(0.03)	1.49	(0.00)	**523**	(8.9)	531	(7.3)	544	(9.0)	**571**	(7.5)
	Luxembourg	–0.15	(0.00)	–1.09	(0.00)	–0.40	(0.01)	0.03	(0.00)	0.87	(0.00)	**467**	(2.2)	469	(2.8)	505	(2.6)	**532**	(2.3)
	Mexico	–0.10	(0.06)	–1.38	(0.06)	–0.55	(0.02)	0.25	(0.02)	1.29	(0.03)	**375**	(6.4)	365	(6.1)	379	(5.8)	**419**	(8.2)
	Netherlands	0.28	(0.09)	–1.03	(0.12)	–0.01	(0.02)	0.67	(0.03)	1.49	(0.00)	534	(11.3)	528	(9.4)	549	(10.3)	536	(8.8)
	New Zealand	0.25	(0.05)	–0.69	(0.05)	–0.03	(0.01)	0.40	(0.02)	1.33	(0.04)	518	(5.3)	525	(5.5)	522	(5.5)	532	(6.7)
	Norway	–0.50	(0.06)	–1.58	(0.07)	–0.72	(0.01)	–0.31	(0.02)	0.60	(0.07)	489	(4.7)	495	(4.6)	498	(5.4)	495	(4.4)
	Poland	0.29	(0.07)	–0.80	(0.08)	0.02	(0.02)	0.60	(0.02)	1.32	(0.03)	494	(5.9)	482	(5.2)	491	(4.4)	493	(5.3)
	Portugal	0.03	(0.07)	–1.08	(0.06)	–0.23	(0.02)	0.32	(0.02)	1.13	(0.05)	463	(10.3)	465	(7.1)	472	(6.7)	464	(8.0)
	Slovak Republic	–0.31	(0.05)	–1.29	(0.06)	–0.57	(0.02)	–0.05	(0.02)	0.68	(0.05)	**515**	(8.0)	496	(7.5)	493	(6.6)	**487**	(6.1)
	Spain	0.13	(0.07)	–1.23	(0.09)	–0.13	(0.03)	0.50	(0.02)	1.39	(0.02)	**483**	(6.9)	470	(5.5)	485	(4.3)	**502**	(4.6)
	Sweden	0.03	(0.06)	–1.04	(0.06)	–0.29	(0.02)	0.26	(0.02)	1.20	(0.05)	503	(6.5)	509	(6.1)	508	(5.5)	516	(3.8)
	Switzerland	0.39	(0.06)	–0.61	(0.09)	0.06	(0.02)	0.60	(0.02)	1.49	(0.00)	530	(7.2)	520	(7.8)	525	(8.2)	531	(9.9)
	Turkey	–1.11	(0.10)	–2.31	(0.00)	–1.61	(0.04)	–0.79	(0.02)	0.26	(0.09)	424	(14.0)	412	(13.9)	417	(8.6)	441	(15.6)
	United States	0.29	(0.06)	–0.84	(0.07)	–0.03	(0.02)	0.54	(0.03)	1.48	(0.00)	482	(6.8)	474	(6.3)	488	(6.5)	501	(6.9)
	OECD total	*0.06*	*(0.02)*	*–1.27*	*(0.02)*	*–0.24*	*(0.01)*	*0.39*	*(0.01)*	*1.34*	*(0.01)*	*473*	*(3.3)*	*488*	*(2.6)*	*490*	*(2.7)*	*504*	*(2.5)*
	OECD average	*0.00*	*(0.01)*	*–1.29*	*(0.01)*	*–0.31*	*(0.01)*	*0.32*	*(0.01)*	*1.28*	*(0.01)*	*485*	*(1.9)*	*500*	*(1.6)*	*502*	*(1.4)*	*512*	*(1.6)*
Partner countries	Brazil	–0.06	(0.09)	–1.59	(0.09)	–0.44	(0.03)	0.32	(0.03)	1.48	(0.00)	352	(13.5)	342	(7.0)	347	(8.2)	389	(13.3)
	Hong Kong-China	–0.01	(0.07)	–1.08	(0.07)	–0.24	(0.02)	0.27	(0.02)	1.03	(0.07)	564	(10.3)	541	(10.5)	556	(9.5)	541	(14.4)
	Indonesia	–0.53	(0.08)	–1.67	(0.07)	–0.88	(0.02)	–0.18	(0.03)	0.60	(0.06)	**370**	(6.1)	370	(8.7)	354	(7.8)	**346**	(7.7)
	Latvia	0.06	(0.07)	–0.95	(0.05)	–0.14	(0.02)	0.33	(0.02)	1.01	(0.07)	489	(7.5)	483	(5.8)	478	(5.7)	483	(8.7)
	Liechtenstein	c	c	c	c	c	c	c	c	c	c	c	c	c	c	c	c	c	c
	Macao-China	–0.25	(0.00)	–1.38	(0.01)	–0.53	(0.00)	–0.02	(0.00)	0.95	(0.01)	538	(6.7)	523	(8.3)	529	(4.9)	520	(5.1)
	Russian Federation	–0.10	(0.10)	–1.44	(0.07)	–0.50	(0.03)	0.24	(0.03)	1.31	(0.05)	460	(8.2)	468	(8.2)	464	(9.1)	478	(10.5)
	Serbia	–0.22	(0.07)	–1.24	(0.06)	–0.50	(0.03)	0.10	(0.02)	0.77	(0.06)	437	(8.9)	443	(7.7)	433	(6.6)	436	(7.2)
	Thailand	0.00	(0.08)	–1.22	(0.07)	–0.27	(0.02)	0.26	(0.02)	1.25	(0.06)	412	(8.7)	409	(5.2)	424	(8.2)	423	(6.2)
	Tunisia	–0.34	(0.07)	–1.41	(0.06)	–0.58	(0.02)	–0.16	(0.01)	0.78	(0.10)	344	(5.4)	366	(7.2)	375	(9.2)	351	(8.4)
	Uruguay	–0.65	(0.07)	–1.88	(0.07)	–0.99	(0.03)	–0.38	(0.03)	0.67	(0.06)	**408**	(7.6)	411	(10.0)	412	(7.2)	**457**	(8.9)
	United Kingdom[1]	–0.25	(0.07)	–1.34	(0.06)	–0.63	(0.02)	–0.04	(0.02)	1.01	(0.06)	511	(6.9)	501	(5.3)	509	(6.5)	513	(6.3)

		Change in the mathematics score per unit of the index of the quality of the schools' physical infrastructure		Increased likelihood of students in the bottom quarter of this index scoring in the bottom quarter of the national mathematics performance distribution		Explained variance in student performance (r-squared × 100)	
		Effect	S.E.	Ratio	S.E.	Percentage	S.E.
OECD countries	Australia	**11.4**	(3.22)	1.2	(0.11)	1.1	(0.60)
	Austria	–4.2	(5.34)	1.1	(0.19)	0.2	(0.59)
	Belgium	–1.2	(3.81)	1.0	(0.14)	0.0	(0.10)
	Canada	–1.4	(2.34)	0.9	(0.06)	0.0	(0.08)
	Czech Republic	–3.2	(5.62)	0.9	(0.14)	0.1	(0.28)
	Denmark	0.0	(3.20)	1.0	(0.10)	0.0	(0.08)
	Finland	–0.8	(2.09)	1.0	(0.08)	0.0	(0.06)
	France	w	w	w	w	w	w
	Germany	4.0	(5.26)	1.0	(0.19)	0.2	(0.52)
	Greece	5.3	(4.77)	1.2	(0.21)	0.5	(0.89)
	Hungary	6.3	(5.43)	0.8	(0.14)	0.4	(0.75)
	Iceland	**4.7**	(1.78)	1.1	(0.08)	0.3	(0.18)
	Ireland	–6.1	(3.89)	**0.8**	(0.11)	0.6	(0.77)
	Italy	**11.4**	(4.51)	**1.6**	(0.22)	1.4	(1.09)
	Japan	–2.1	(6.00)	1.0	(0.18)	0.1	(0.37)
	Korea	**24.3**	(6.40)	**1.5**	(0.20)	4.2	(2.17)
	Luxembourg	**36.4**	(1.32)	**1.5**	(0.08)	**9.5**	(0.63)
	Mexico	**14.9**	(3.94)	1.2	(0.17)	3.3	(1.80)
	Netherlands	6.5	(6.58)	1.3	(0.27)	0.5	(1.03)
	New Zealand	5.0	(4.17)	1.2	(0.13)	0.2	(0.27)
	Norway	2.4	(2.64)	1.1	(0.10)	0.1	(0.11)
	Poland	1.0	(3.72)	1.0	(0.09)	0.0	(0.11)
	Portugal	2.8	(6.37)	1.1	(0.22)	0.1	(0.44)
	Slovak Republic	**–13.9**	(4.92)	**0.7**	(0.12)	1.4	(1.05)
	Spain	**10.3**	(3.16)	1.0	(0.12)	1.4	(0.85)
	Sweden	4.8	(3.25)	1.1	(0.13)	0.2	(0.27)
	Switzerland	0.2	(5.19)	0.9	(0.10)	0.0	(0.14)
	Turkey	7.8	(8.82)	1.0	(0.21)	0.6	(1.36)
	United States	**9.5**	(4.03)	1.0	(0.13)	0.8	(0.72)
	OECD total	***11.7***	*(1.68)*	***1.4***	*(0.07)*	***1.3***	*(0.37)*
	OECD average	***10.2***	*(1.02)*	***1.3***	*(0.03)*	***1.0***	*(0.20)*
Partner countries	Brazil	**12.8**	(6.05)	1.1	(0.16)	2.2	(2.20)
	Hong Kong-China	–10.9	(7.80)	0.7	(0.17)	0.8	(1.19)
	Indonesia	–8.0	(4.21)	**0.8**	(0.11)	0.8	(0.90)
	Latvia	–1.0	(5.74)	0.9	(0.12)	0.0	(0.19)
	Liechtenstein	c	c	c	c	c	c
	Macao-China	–3.2	(3.01)	0.9	(0.11)	0.1	(0.24)
	Russian Federation	5.3	(4.51)	1.0	(0.15)	0.4	(0.71)
	Serbia	–1.9	(5.59)	1.1	(0.17)	0.0	(0.34)
	Thailand	6.2	(4.94)	1.0	(0.14)	0.5	(0.89)
	Tunisia	5.3	(4.71)	1.2	(0.13)	0.3	(0.57)
	Uruguay	**20.8**	(4.25)	1.2	(0.17)	**4.4**	(1.73)
	United Kingdom[1]	3.1	(3.49)	1.0	(0.12)	0.1	(0.21)

Note: Values that are statistically significant are indicated in bold (see Annex A4). The scale was inverted so that positive and high values indicate that the schools' physical infrastructure is perceived less of a problem than on OECD average.

1. Response rate too low to ensure comparability (see Annex A3).

Table 5.18
Index of the quality of the schools' educational resources and student performance on the mathematics scale, by national quarters of the index

Results based on reports from school principals and reported proportionate to the number of 15-year-olds enrolled in the school

		Index of the quality of the schools' educational resources										Performance on the mathematics scale, by quarters of the index of the quality of the schools' educational resources							
		All students		Bottom quarter		Second quarter		Third quarter		Top quarter		Bottom quarter		Second quarter		Third quarter		Top quarter	
		Mean index	S.E.	Mean index	S.E.	Mean index	S.E.	Mean index	S.E.	Mean index	S.E.	Mean score	S.E.	Mean score	S.E.	Mean score	S.E.	Mean score	S.E.
OECD countries	Australia	0.57	(0.07)	–0.57	(0.03)	0.16	(0.02)	0.73	(0.02)	1.97	(0.04)	**517**	(5.1)	509	(6.49)	526	(4.87)	**545**	(4.6)
	Austria	0.35	(0.08)	–0.78	(0.07)	0.06	(0.03)	0.56	(0.02)	1.56	(0.08)	503	(9.6)	517	(8.82)	503	(9.59)	497	(8.1)
	Belgium	0.19	(0.06)	–0.98	(0.07)	–0.18	(0.02)	0.43	(0.02)	1.49	(0.06)	**523**	(7.3)	519	(9.09)	534	(9.42)	**544**	(8.2)
	Canada	–0.04	(0.04)	–1.07	(0.04)	–0.39	(0.01)	0.12	(0.01)	1.17	(0.06)	530	(3.3)	528	(3.51)	532	(4.48)	540	(4.3)
	Czech Republic	–0.05	(0.06)	–0.83	(0.03)	–0.33	(0.01)	0.08	(0.01)	0.89	(0.08)	512	(6.6)	519	(7.33)	524	(8.60)	509	(10.1)
	Denmark	0.04	(0.07)	–0.89	(0.05)	–0.21	(0.02)	0.19	(0.01)	1.05	(0.10)	**501**	(5.8)	517	(4.69)	521	(4.70)	**518**	(5.3)
	Finland	–0.02	(0.06)	–0.83	(0.06)	–0.25	(0.02)	0.13	(0.01)	0.85	(0.09)	546	(3.9)	546	(3.88)	542	(3.17)	543	(3.6)
	France	w	w	w	w	w	w	w	w	w	w	w	w	w	w	w	w	w	w
	Germany	0.20	(0.07)	–0.88	(0.06)	–0.09	(0.02)	0.32	(0.02)	1.46	(0.08)	**479**	(11.0)	502	(8.69)	519	(11.26)	**513**	(10.9)
	Greece	–0.46	(0.12)	–1.76	(0.14)	–0.79	(0.04)	–0.16	(0.03)	0.87	(0.15)	**430**	(9.4)	446	(11.19)	437	(10.80)	**467**	(8.8)
	Hungary	0.09	(0.08)	–0.93	(0.07)	–0.15	(0.01)	0.25	(0.02)	1.19	(0.09)	**481**	(8.3)	487	(9.38)	476	(10.51)	**519**	(10.0)
	Iceland	0.30	(0.00)	–0.78	(0.00)	–0.07	(0.00)	0.42	(0.00)	1.62	(0.01)	512	(3.2)	520	(3.56)	513	(3.53)	518	(3.1)
	Ireland	–0.06	(0.08)	–1.05	(0.06)	–0.35	(0.03)	0.05	(0.02)	1.12	(0.12)	503	(5.4)	508	(5.84)	501	(6.02)	501	(7.5)
	Italy	0.14	(0.07)	–1.08	(0.08)	–0.16	(0.02)	0.38	(0.02)	1.40	(0.07)	**440**	(9.3)	469	(9.12)	478	(7.33)	**477**	(8.4)
	Japan	0.01	(0.10)	–1.24	(0.11)	–0.35	(0.03)	0.22	(0.02)	1.39	(0.11)	521	(12.8)	534	(11.92)	554	(9.66)	527	(12.8)
	Korea	0.57	(0.05)	–0.33	(0.06)	0.29	(0.02)	0.65	(0.02)	1.67	(0.07)	**522**	(9.3)	549	(8.15)	546	(7.70)	**552**	(7.7)
	Luxembourg	0.15	(0.00)	–0.55	(0.00)	–0.04	(0.00)	0.38	(0.00)	0.80	(0.00)	**518**	(2.6)	465	(3.51)	508	(3.03)	**481**	(2.6)
	Mexico	–0.40	(0.09)	–1.83	(0.06)	–0.83	(0.02)	–0.11	(0.03)	1.16	(0.11)	**369**	(6.9)	375	(5.68)	388	(5.52)	**406**	(10.1)
	Netherlands	0.51	(0.06)	–0.50	(0.07)	0.18	(0.03)	0.68	(0.02)	1.67	(0.08)	**509**	(11.2)	551	(10.43)	532	(10.45)	**554**	(9.0)
	New Zealand	0.27	(0.06)	–0.80	(0.04)	–0.17	(0.02)	0.38	(0.02)	1.68	(0.06)	**502**	(5.9)	533	(5.22)	527	(6.18)	**536**	(5.9)
	Norway	–0.29	(0.05)	–1.02	(0.04)	–0.48	(0.01)	–0.19	(0.01)	0.51	(0.08)	493	(4.7)	496	(4.34)	494	(4.64)	495	(4.7)
	Poland	–0.66	(0.06)	–1.67	(0.08)	–0.88	(0.02)	–0.48	(0.02)	0.41	(0.09)	**481**	(5.5)	486	(5.19)	496	(4.91)	**498**	(6.1)
	Portugal	–0.05	(0.07)	–1.05	(0.06)	–0.35	(0.02)	0.07	(0.02)	1.12	(0.11)	470	(7.0)	456	(8.85)	472	(9.26)	466	(7.0)
	Slovak Republic	–0.76	(0.06)	–1.64	(0.05)	–0.95	(0.01)	–0.56	(0.02)	0.12	(0.07)	**480**	(8.0)	502	(8.19)	503	(6.58)	**509**	(7.0)
	Spain	–0.13	(0.07)	–1.36	(0.06)	–0.44	(0.03)	0.19	(0.03)	1.09	(0.07)	**467**	(7.5)	485	(7.15)	494	(4.64)	**494**	(6.0)
	Sweden	0.06	(0.07)	–0.97	(0.08)	–0.25	(0.02)	0.28	(0.02)	1.19	(0.09)	511	(4.4)	501	(5.20)	504	(5.40)	520	(5.1)
	Switzerland	0.53	(0.07)	–0.46	(0.11)	0.28	(0.01)	0.63	(0.02)	1.68	(0.08)	525	(9.3)	511	(7.54)	530	(5.88)	539	(10.6)
	Turkey	–1.37	(0.09)	–2.52	(0.11)	–1.70	(0.02)	–1.15	(0.03)	–0.13	(0.12)	403	(12.8)	430	(11.31)	427	(11.56)	434	(14.6)
	United States	0.53	(0.08)	–0.77	(0.05)	0.03	(0.02)	0.77	(0.03)	2.10	(0.03)	**471**	(6.2)	488	(6.73)	478	(7.27)	**507**	(7.9)
	OECD total	*0.06*	*(0.03)*	*–1.28*	*(0.03)*	*–0.32*	*(0.01)*	*0.30*	*(0.01)*	*1.54*	*(0.03)*	*458*	*(3.4)*	*488*	*(3.09)*	*504*	*(2.48)*	*506*	*(3.4)*
	OECD average	*0.00*	*(0.01)*	*–1.21*	*(0.02)*	*–0.31*	*(0.00)*	*0.23*	*(0.01)*	*1.28*	*(0.02)*	*476*	*(1.8)*	*501*	*(1.73)*	*507*	*(1.46)*	*515*	*(1.8)*
Partner countries	Brazil	–0.81	(0.09)	–2.37	(0.06)	–1.36	(0.03)	–0.44	(0.03)	0.94	(0.13)	**321**	(8.3)	337	(8.03)	365	(9.65)	**405**	(12.2)
	Hong Kong-China	0.34	(0.07)	–0.75	(0.09)	0.08	(0.02)	0.46	(0.02)	1.56	(0.09)	561	(8.9)	535	(15.05)	542	(11.05)	564	(10.3)
	Indonesia	–0.67	(0.08)	–2.17	(0.08)	–1.12	(0.03)	–0.17	(0.03)	0.77	(0.06)	**367**	(6.7)	363	(8.69)	366	(7.39)	**345**	(6.8)
	Latvia	–0.47	(0.06)	–1.42	(0.06)	–0.68	(0.02)	–0.24	(0.02)	0.46	(0.07)	484	(7.5)	481	(7.06)	478	(5.88)	490	(7.6)
	Liechtenstein	c	c	c	c	c	c	c	c	c	c	c	c	c	c	c	c	c	c
	Macao-China	–0.14	(0.00)	–1.11	(0.01)	–0.35	(0.01)	0.00	(0.01)	0.91	(0.01)	529	(4.7)	529	(7.67)	521	(8.73)	529	(4.6)
	Russian Federation	–1.14	(0.07)	–2.30	(0.08)	–1.39	(0.03)	–0.86	(0.02)	–0.02	(0.08)	**448**	(7.5)	464	(7.45)	479	(7.00)	**484**	(10.7)
	Serbia	–0.77	(0.07)	–1.66	(0.07)	–1.02	(0.02)	–0.58	(0.02)	0.15	(0.10)	445	(8.8)	439	(7.70)	431	(7.09)	435	(7.9)
	Thailand	–0.60	(0.10)	–2.01	(0.07)	–1.04	(0.04)	–0.31	(0.03)	0.99	(0.17)	**395**	(6.3)	407	(5.56)	423	(8.76)	**443**	(8.6)
	Tunisia	–0.46	(0.07)	–1.58	(0.06)	–0.79	(0.03)	–0.26	(0.03)	0.78	(0.09)	**336**	(4.5)	352	(6.89)	380	(7.76)	**367**	(8.7)
	Uruguay	–0.93	(0.09)	–2.36	(0.09)	–1.34	(0.02)	–0.66	(0.03)	0.65	(0.09)	**423**	(8.7)	406	(8.19)	410	(7.88)	**450**	(7.9)
	United Kingdom[1]	–0.07	(0.06)	–1.15	(0.08)	–0.39	(0.02)	0.09	(0.02)	1.18	(0.08)	**497**	(7.1)	503	(5.49)	502	(5.66)	**532**	(5.1)

		Change in the mathematics score per unit of the index of the quality of the schools' educational resources		Increased likelihood of students in the bottom quarter of this index scoring in the bottom quarter of the national mathematics performance distribution		Explained variance in student performance (r-squared × 100)	
		Effect	S.E.	Ratio	S.E.	Percentage	S.E.
OECD countries	Australia	**13.5**	(2.40)	1.2	(0.10)	**1.9**	(0.69)
	Austria	–1.6	(5.77)	1.0	(0.18)	0.0	(0.34)
	Belgium	7.6	(4.11)	1.0	(0.13)	0.4	(0.48)
	Canada	**5.7**	(2.13)	1.1	(0.07)	0.3	(0.28)
	Czech Republic	1.4	(6.74)	1.0	(0.15)	0.0	(0.24)
	Denmark	6.0	(4.12)	**1.3**	(0.12)	0.3	(0.38)
	Finland	0.2	(2.74)	0.9	(0.07)	0.0	(0.05)
	France	w	w	w	w	w	w
	Germany	11.0	(6.45)	**1.6**	(0.25)	1.0	(1.16)
	Greece	9.3	(5.75)	1.2	(0.21)	1.1	(1.34)
	Hungary	11.1	(7.27)	1.1	(0.18)	1.0	(1.28)
	Iceland	1.5	(1.46)	1.0	(0.07)	0.0	(0.04)
	Ireland	–1.8	(4.09)	1.0	(0.12)	0.0	(0.19)
	Italy	**14.4**	(4.22)	**1.7**	(0.25)	2.2	(1.23)
	Japan	5.6	(6.20)	1.2	(0.24)	0.4	(0.88)
	Korea	**14.7**	(4.63)	**1.5**	(0.19)	1.6	(1.03)
	Luxembourg	**–18.9**	(2.04)	**0.6**	(0.04)	**1.3**	(0.27)
	Mexico	**15.1**	(3.29)	**1.4**	(0.20)	**4.4**	(2.10)
	Netherlands	**14.5**	(6.62)	**1.7**	(0.33)	1.9	(1.65)
	New Zealand	**11.0**	(3.01)	**1.5**	(0.16)	1.2	(0.63)
	Norway	1.6	(3.68)	1.0	(0.08)	0.0	(0.08)
	Poland	5.9	(3.14)	1.1	(0.10)	0.3	(0.30)
	Portugal	1.5	(4.19)	0.9	(0.15)	0.0	(0.19)
	Slovak Republic	10.3	(7.37)	**1.4**	(0.18)	0.6	(0.84)
	Spain	**11.2**	(4.16)	**1.5**	(0.17)	1.5	(1.12)
	Sweden	3.8	(2.59)	0.9	(0.08)	0.1	(0.17)
	Switzerland	6.6	(5.39)	1.1	(0.15)	0.4	(0.64)
	Turkey	16.5	(9.67)	1.4	(0.25)	2.3	(2.72)
	United States	**11.0**	(3.48)	**1.4**	(0.14)	1.7	(1.08)
	OECD total	*17.2*	*(1.78)*	*1.7*	*(0.09)*	*3.4*	*(0.70)*
	OECD average	*15.9*	*(1.04)*	*1.5*	*(0.04)*	*2.5*	*(0.34)*
Partner countries	Brazil	**26.3**	(3.69)	**1.6**	(0.20)	**12.0**	(3.38)
	Hong Kong-China	6.1	(6.45)	0.7	(0.16)	0.3	(0.61)
	Indonesia	**–6.5**	(2.75)	0.9	(0.11)	0.9	(0.79)
	Latvia	2.7	(5.27)	1.0	(0.13)	0.1	(0.22)
	Liechtenstein	c	c	c	c	c	c
	Macao-China	4.0	(2.60)	1.1	(0.10)	0.2	(0.21)
	Russian Federation	**17.5**	(4.18)	**1.4**	(0.18)	**3.1**	(1.51)
	Serbia	–7.0	(4.67)	0.9	(0.14)	0.4	(0.56)
	Thailand	**16.7**	(3.88)	**1.4**	(0.16)	**5.8**	(2.39)
	Tunisia	**10.2**	(4.35)	**1.3**	(0.13)	1.3	(1.07)
	Uruguay	**11.0**	(3.84)	0.9	(0.16)	1.7	(1.15)
	United Kingdom[1]	**13.0**	(3.34)	**1.3**	(0.13)	**1.8**	(0.91)

Note: Values that are statistically significant are indicated in bold (see Annex A4). The scale was inverted so that positive and high values indicate that the schools' educational resources is perceived less of a problem than on OECD average.

1. Response rate too low to ensure comparability (see Annex A3).

Table 5.19
Percentage of students and student performance on the mathematics and reading scales, by type of school
Results based on reports from school principals and reported proportionate to the number of 15-year-olds enrolled in the school

		Government or public schools[1]				
			Performance on the mathematics scale		Performance on the reading scale	
	% of students	S.E.	Mean score	S.E.	Mean score	S.E.
OECD countries						
Australia	w	w	w	w	w	w
Austria	92.0	(1.9)	504	(3.4)	487	(3.9)
Belgium	w	w	w	w	w	w
Canada	94.2	(0.7)	529	(1.8)	526	(1.8)
Czech Republic	93.3	(1.7)	517	(3.8)	488	(3.7)
Denmark	77.8	(2.5)	515	(3.1)	494	(3.1)
Finland	93.3	(1.6)	545	(1.8)	544	(1.6)
France	w	w	w	w	w	w
Germany	92.2	(1.7)	497	(3.7)	485	(3.8)
Greece	97.4	(1.9)	442	(3.6)	470	(4.0)
Hungary	88.9	(2.5)	489	(3.6)	481	(3.3)
Iceland	99.5	(0.1)	515	(1.6)	492	(1.8)
Ireland	41.6	(1.6)	486	(3.8)	492	(4.3)
Italy	96.1	(1.2)	468	(3.1)	477	(3.3)
Japan	73.0	(1.7)	544	(4.7)	508	(4.8)
Korea	42.3	(3.7)	527	(6.1)	520	(5.3)
Luxembourg	85.9	(0.1)	498	(1.1)	481	(1.6)
Mexico	86.7	(1.9)	375	(3.5)	388	(3.9)
Netherlands	23.3	(4.2)	516	(14.0)	493	(12.2)
New Zealand	95.4	(0.6)	522	(2.3)	519	(2.6)
Norway	99.1	(0.7)	494	(2.4)	498	(2.7)
Poland	99.2	(0.4)	489	(2.5)	496	(2.9)
Portugal	93.7	(1.3)	465	(3.6)	477	(3.9)
Slovak Republic	87.4	(2.7)	495	(3.7)	466	(3.4)
Spain	64.2	(1.5)	472	(3.4)	466	(3.6)
Sweden	95.7	(0.5)	509	(2.6)	513	(2.5)
Switzerland	95.3	(1.0)	528	(3.8)	499	(3.5)
Turkey	99.0	(1.0)	420	(6.6)	438	(5.8)
United States	94.3	(1.0)	483	(3.6)	495	(4.0)
OECD total	*85.5*	*(0.5)*	*483*	*(1.5)*	*483*	*(1.5)*
OECD average	*83.5*	*(0.4)*	*494*	*(0.8)*	*489*	*(0.8)*
Partner countries						
Brazil	87.4	(2.3)	342	(6.2)	390	(5.8)
Hong Kong-China	93.1	(0.9)	552	(4.5)	511	(3.7)
Indonesia	51.4	(2.3)	373	(4.9)	393	(4.6)
Latvia	99.0	(0.7)	485	(3.7)	492	(3.7)
Liechtenstein	c	c	c	c	c	c
Macao-China	5.0	(0.1)	483	(9.3)	466	(5.8)
Russian Federation	99.7	(0.2)	468	(4.3)	441	(4.0)
Serbia	100.0	(0.0)	436	(3.9)	411	(3.8)
Thailand	88.0	(1.2)	416	(3.0)	419	(2.7)
Tunisia	m	m	m	m	m	m
Uruguay	85.9	(0.8)	409	(3.7)	420	(3.8)
United Kingdom[4]	93.8	(0.5)	503	(2.6)	502	(2.6)

		Government-dependent private schools[2]				
			Performance on the mathematics scale		Performance on the reading scale	
	% of students	S.E.	Mean score	S.E.	Mean score	S.E.
OECD countries						
Australia	w	w	w	w	w	w
Austria	6.7	(1.6)	518	(12.6)	530	(12.0)
Belgium	w	w	w	w	w	w
Canada	3.8	(0.6)	573	(10.8)	560	(9.9)
Czech Republic	5.8	(1.6)	505	(13.5)	491	(11.9)
Denmark	21.7	(2.6)	511	(6.3)	490	(7.1)
Finland	6.7	(1.6)	539	(12.2)	537	(10.7)
France	w	w	w	w	w	w
Germany	7.5	(1.8)	566	(12.7)	564	(14.6)
Greece	0.0	(0.0)	a	a	a	a
Hungary	9.8	(2.3)	504	(16.8)	493	(16.9)
Iceland	0.0	(0.0)	a	a	a	a
Ireland	57.6	(1.8)	516	(3.3)	533	(3.1)
Italy	0.4	(0.2)	c	c	c	c
Japan	0.6	(0.6)	c	c	c	c
Korea	36.0	(4.1)	532	(7.5)	528	(6.3)
Luxembourg	14.1	(0.1)	463	(2.9)	469	(3.3)
Mexico	0.1	(0.1)	c	c	c	c
Netherlands	76.7	(4.2)	541	(4.5)	517	(4.3)
New Zealand	0.0	(0.0)	a	a	a	a
Norway	0.9	(0.7)	c	c	c	c
Poland	0.4	(0.4)	c	c	c	c
Portugal	4.2	(1.2)	459	(8.5)	462	(12.9)
Slovak Republic	12.6	(2.7)	523	(9.3)	496	(8.2)
Spain	28.1	(2.1)	505	(4.2)	501	(4.8)
Sweden	4.3	(0.5)	516	(11.0)	531	(9.8)
Switzerland	0.9	(0.7)	c	c	c	c
Turkey	0.0	(0.0)	a	a	a	a
United States	0.0	(0.0)	a	a	a	a
OECD total	*6.4*	*(0.3)*	*532*	*(2.9)*	*522*	*(3.1)*
OECD average	*12.8*	*(0.3)*	*526*	*(1.7)*	*516*	*(1.8)*
Partner countries						
Brazil	0.0	(0.0)	a	a	a	a
Hong Kong-China	6.5	(1.1)	518	(29.2)	487	(23.3)
Indonesia	4.1	(1.5)	326	(19.3)	354	(17.0)
Latvia	0.0	(0.0)	a	a	a	a
Liechtenstein	c	c	c	c	c	c
Macao-China	49.3	(0.2)	528	(3.5)	499	(2.4)
Russian Federation	0.0	(0.0)	a	a	a	a
Serbia	0.0	(0.0)	a	a	a	a
Thailand	6.0	(1.1)	419	(18.8)	428	(13.7)
Tunisia	m	m	m	m	m	m
Uruguay	0.0	(0.0)	a	a	a	a
United Kingdom[4]	0.9	(0.9)	c	c	c	c

Note: Values that are statistically significant are indicated in bold (see Annex A4). The scale was inverted so that positive and high values indicate that the schools' educational resources are perceived less of a problem than on OECD average.
1. Government or public schools: schools which are directly controlled or managed by: *i)* a public education authority or agency; or *ii)* by a government agency directly or by a governing body, most of whose members are either appointed by a public authority or elected by public franchise.
2. Government-dependent private schools: schools which receive 50 per cent or more of their core funding (funding that support the basic educational services of the institution) from government agencies.
3. Government-independent private schools: schools which receive less than 50 per cent of their core funding (funding that support the basic educational services of the institution) from government agencies.
4. Response rate too low to ensure comparability (see Annex A3).

Table 5.19 *(continued)*

Percentage of students and student performance on the mathematics and reading scales, by type of school

Results based on reports from school principals and reported proportionate to the number of 15-year-olds enrolled in the school

		Government-independent private schools[3]					
				Performance on the mathematics scale		Performance on the reading scale	
		% of students	S.E.	Mean score	S.E.	Mean score	S.E.
OECD countries	Australia	w	w	w	w	w	w
	Austria	1.3	(0.6)	c	c	c	c
	Belgium	w	w	w	w	w	w
	Canada	1.9	(0.3)	c	c	c	c
	Czech Republic	0.9	(0.5)	c	c	c	c
	Denmark	0.5	(0.5)	c	c	c	c
	Finland	0.0	(0.0)	a	a	a	a
	France	w	w	w	w	w	w
	Germany	0.4	(0.4)	c	c	c	c
	Greece	2.6	(1.9)	c	c	c	c
	Hungary	1.2	(0.8)	c	c	c	c
	Iceland	0.5	(0.1)	c	c	c	c
	Ireland	0.9	(0.9)	c	c	c	c
	Italy	3.5	(1.3)	452	(35.4)	478	(23.0)
	Japan	26.4	(1.8)	513	(7.5)	478	(7.2)
	Korea	21.7	(3.4)	593	(9.6)	573	(7.9)
	Luxembourg	0.0	(0.0)	a	a	a	a
	Mexico	13.2	(1.9)	430	(8.9)	454	(6.6)
	Netherlands	0.0	(0.0)	a	a	a	a
	New Zealand	4.6	(0.6)	579	(17.1)	583	(17.8)
	Norway	0.0	(0.0)	a	a	a	a
	Poland	0.4	(0.3)	c	c	c	c
	Portugal	2.1	(1.2)	c	c	c	c
	Slovak Republic	0.0	(0.0)	a	a	a	a
	Spain	7.7	(1.7)	520	(9.7)	515	(9.4)
	Sweden	0.0	(0.0)	a	a	a	a
	Switzerland	3.8	(0.7)	497	(23.2)	487	(9.7)
	Turkey	1.0	(1.0)	c	c	c	c
	United States	5.7	(1.0)	507	(9.1)	531	(9.6)
	OECD total	8.0	(0.5)	515	(4.9)	506	(4.3)
	OECD average	3.8	(0.2)	530	(5.2)	520	(4.4)
Partner countries	Brazil	12.6	(2.3)	454	(11.3)	487	(9.2)
	Hong Kong-China	0.4	(0.3)	c	c	c	c
	Indonesia	44.5	(2.6)	345	(7.0)	368	(6.1)
	Latvia	1.0	(0.7)	c	c	c	c
	Liechtenstein	c	c	c	c	c	c
	Macao-China	45.8	(0.2)	529	(5.2)	498	(3.8)
	Russian Federation	0.3	(0.2)	c	c	c	c
	Serbia	0.0	(0.0)	a	a	a	a
	Thailand	6.0	(1.6)	428	(13.7)	430	(14.3)
	Tunisia	m	m	m	m	m	m
	Uruguay	14.1	(0.8)	501	(6.1)	524	(6.1)
	United Kingdom[4]	5.3	(0.9)	589	(9.0)	583	(12.2)

		Difference in performance on the mathematics scale between public and private schools (government-dependent and government-independent)		The index of economic, social and cultural status						Difference in performance on the mathematics scales between public and private schools after accounting for the index of economic, social and cultural status of:			
				Public schools		Private schools (government-dependent and government-independent)		Difference		Students		Students and schools	
		Dif. (Pub. - Priv.)	S.E.	Mean index	S.E.	Mean index	S.E.	Dif. (Pub. - Priv.)	S.E.	Dif. (Pub. - Priv.)	S.E.	Dif. (Pub. - Priv.)	S.E.
OECD countries	Australia	w	w	w	w	w	w	w	w	w	w	w	w
	Austria	–18	(12.0)	0.04	(0.03)	0.29	(0.11)	**–0.25**	(0.12)	–5	(10.4)	–3	(2.7)
	Belgium	w	w	w	w	w	w	w	w	w	w	w	w
	Canada	**–41**	(8.3)	0.42	(0.02)	0.88	(0.07)	**–0.46**	(0.07)	**–26**	(6.1)	–4	(3.2)
	Czech Republic	3	(13.5)	0.16	(0.02)	0.25	(0.12)	–0.09	(0.13)	14	(9.8)	**29**	(4.4)
	Denmark	4	(7.1)	0.20	(0.03)	0.22	(0.06)	–0.03	(0.07)	5	(5.2)	**7**	(3.1)
	Finland	5	(12.3)	0.23	(0.02)	0.47	(0.13)	–0.24	(0.13)	13	(10.7)	**16**	(6.8)
	France	w	w	w	w	w	w	w	w	w	w	w	w
	Germany	**–66**	(13.7)	0.10	(0.03)	0.82	(0.07)	**–0.71**	(0.08)	**–30**	(10.5)	**14**	(2.5)
	Greece	c	c	–0.20	(0.04)	c	c	c	c	c	c	c	c
	Hungary	–17	(18.1)	–0.09	(0.03)	0.13	(0.11)	–0.21	(0.13)	–5	(12.7)	**16**	(4.7)
	Iceland	c	c	0.68	(0.01)	c	c	c	c	c	c	c	c
	Ireland	**–31**	(5.0)	–0.30	(0.03)	0.10	(0.04)	**–0.40**	(0.06)	**–16**	(3.9)	–2	(2.5)
	Italy	22	(22.4)	–0.12	(0.03)	0.14	(0.07)	**–0.26**	(0.07)	32	(22.3)	**27**	(4.1)
	Japan	**31**	(8.6)	–0.12	(0.02)	0.08	(0.05)	**–0.20**	(0.05)	**40**	(6.8)	**64**	(1.3)
	Korea	**–28**	(10.1)	–0.31	(0.05)	0.05	(0.04)	**–0.36**	(0.07)	–14	(8.2)	**9**	(1.9)
	Luxembourg	**35**	(3.3)	0.22	(0.02)	–0.02	(0.04)	**0.24**	(0.04)	**28**	(3.6)	**16**	(3.9)
	Mexico	**–55**	(9.8)	–1.32	(0.05)	–0.16	(0.13)	**–1.16**	(0.14)	**–26**	(8.0)	**17**	(2.1)
	Netherlands	–25	(16.4)	0.02	(0.07)	0.09	(0.03)	–0.07	(0.09)	–10	(10.5)	–2	(2.0)
	New Zealand	**–57**	(17.3)	0.19	(0.02)	0.89	(0.13)	**–0.69**	(0.13)	**–25**	(12.2)	5	(4.7)
	Norway	c	c	0.60	(0.02)	c	c	c	c	c	c	c	c
	Poland	c	c	–0.21	(0.02)	c	c	c	c	c	c	c	c
	Portugal	–19	(16.9)	–0.65	(0.04)	–0.34	(0.32)	–0.31	(0.32)	–11	(10.3)	1	(5.2)
	Slovak Republic	**–27**	(10.3)	–0.11	(0.03)	0.10	(0.07)	**–0.21**	(0.08)	**–16**	(8.1)	–3	(1.8)
	Spain	**–36**	(5.4)	–0.52	(0.05)	0.06	(0.06)	**–0.58**	(0.08)	**–19**	(4.3)	–3	(1.6)
	Sweden	–8	(11.3)	0.24	(0.03)	0.59	(0.10)	**–0.35**	(0.10)	7	(7.9)	**16**	(5.1)
	Switzerland	21	(22.3)	–0.09	(0.03)	0.27	(0.08)	**–0.35**	(0.09)	39	(21.3)	**72**	(7.0)
	Turkey	c	c	–1.03	(0.06)	c	c	c	c	c	c	c	c
	United States	**–24**	(9.9)	0.29	(0.03)	0.70	(0.09)	**–0.41**	(0.09)	–4	(8.4)	**12**	(5.2)
	OECD total	**–40**	(3.4)	**–0.12**	(0.01)	**0.20**	(0.02)	**–0.33**	(0.03)	**–24**	(2.9)	**–8**	(0.5)
	OECD average	**–33**	(1.7)	**–0.04**	(0.01)	**0.17**	(0.02)	**–0.22**	(0.02)	**–24**	(1.4)	**–9**	(0.7)
Partner countries	Brazil	–112	(13.5)	–1.14	(0.05)	0.35	(0.08)	–1.49	(0.10)	–74	(13.8)	9	(4.0)
	Hong Kong-China	32	(28.0)	–0.78	(0.03)	–0.49	(0.25)	–0.29	(0.25)	41	(21.2)	**82**	(3.3)
	Indonesia	**29**	(8.1)	–1.21	(0.06)	–1.31	(0.06)	0.10	(0.08)	**27**	(7.2)	**13**	(1.2)
	Latvia	c	c	0.11	(0.03)	c	c	c	c	c	c	c	c
	Liechtenstein	c	c	c	c	c	c	c	c	c	c	c	c
	Macao-China	**–46**	(10.2)	1.41	(0.12)	–0.87	(0.02)	**–0.53**	(0.12)	**–40**	(11.0)	–21	(11.4)
	Russian Federation	c	c	–0.10	(0.02)	c	c	c	c	c	c	c	c
	Serbia	a	a	–0.23	(0.03)	a	a	a	a	a	a	a	a
	Thailand	–7	(12.7)	–1.23	(0.03)	–0.84	(0.08)	**–0.39**	(0.09)	3	(12.1)	**18**	(2.2)
	Tunisia	m	m	m	m	m	m	m	m	m	m	m	m
	Uruguay	**–92**	(6.8)	–0.52	(0.03)	0.72	(0.06)	**1.24**	(0.07)	**–54**	(6.8)	7	(4.6)
	United Kingdom[4]	**–87**	(8.3)	0.07	(0.02)	0.99	(0.06)	**–0.92**	(0.06)	**–50**	(7.6)	1	(2.5)

Note: Values that are statistically significant are indicated in bold (see Annex A4). The scale was inverted so that positive and high values indicate that the schools' educational resources are perceived less of a problem than on OECD average.

1. Government or public schools: schools which are directly controlled or managed by: *i)* a public education authority or agency; or *ii)* by a government agency directly or by a governing body, most of whose members are either appointed by a public authority or elected by public franchise.
2. Government-dependent private schools: schools which receive more than 50 per cent of their core funding (funding that support the basic educational services of the institution) from government agencies.
3. Government-independent private schools: schools which receive less than 50 per cent of their core funding (funding that support the basic educational services of the institution) from government agencies.
4. Response rate too low to ensure comparability (see Annex A3).

Table 5.20
Strength of the relationship between student and school socio-economic context, and school resources on student performance in mathematics

		Percentage of variance in mathematics performance that is attributable to:		
		Between-school variance accounted for by student and school socio-economic context	Between-school variance accounted for by school resources after accounting for the impact of student and school socio-economic context	Joint variance explained by student and school socio-economic context as well as school resources
OECD countries	Australia	44.7	2.0	28.6
	Austria	36.7	3.8	32.4
	Belgium	34.4	6.5	43.6
	Canada	38.1	5.9	9.2
	Czech Republic	38.4	2.7	36.7
	Denmark	49.8	6.0	23.3
	Finland	17.4	–1.9	9.1
	France	w	w	w
	Germany	36.3	5.5	32.1
	Greece	63.9	1.7	4.9
	Hungary	68.5	0.7	12.7
	Iceland	38.8	–31.1	3.5
	Ireland	61.9	0.0	23.6
	Italy	52.6	3.1	8.0
	Japan	54.9	1.3	25.2
	Korea	47.6	0.7	22.9
	Luxembourg	77.2	–0.2	13.8
	Mexico	52.5	–0.1	12.2
	Netherlands	37.2	1.9	41.2
	New Zealand	51.6	2.8	29.3
	Norway	47.3	6.6	3.1
	Poland	62.7	1.6	10.1
	Portugal	31.0	6.5	25.5
	Slovak Republic	54.7	0.9	20.3
	Spain	42.5	3.0	18.7
	Sweden	48.2	5.1	16.6
	Switzerland	52.3	1.1	11.3
	Turkey	57.8	0.1	15.6
	United States	60.6	0.2	14.0
	OECD average	*49.1*	*1.4*	*19.0*
Partner countries	Brazil	m	m	m
	Hong Kong-China	25.4	20.1	27.6
	Indonesia	32.8	1.2	13.1
	Latvia	26.0	1.2	25.4
	Liechtenstein	c	c	c
	Macao-China	23.4	12.3	9.7
	Russian Federation	22.2	5.3	19.1
	Serbia	63.9	1.0	1.9
	Thailand	11.3	4.1	45.0
	Tunisia	30.5	3.0	25.2
	Uruguay	43.4	6.0	28.4
	United Kingdom[1]	65.2	3.2	3.0

Note: The estimates are based on the combined impact of socio-economic and school resource variables. Socio-economic context is measured by: the index of economic, social and cultural status, the student's place of birth and the language spoken at their home, the number of books at the student's home, the index of possessions related to "classical" culture in the family home, the student's gender, the school-level average index of economic, social and cultural status, the school location (rural/urban), and the school type (public/private). School resource variables include: class size, school size, school size squared, the student-teacher ratio, the index of the quality of the school's educational resources, and the index of teacher shortage (see Annex A1). The analysis is undertaken for the combined OECD student population, with countries given equal weight. The resulting international model is then applied to each country to estimate the effects at the country level.

1. Response rate too low to ensure comparability (see Annex A3).

Table 5.21a

Effects of student-level and school-level factors on performance on the mathematics scale, for all OECD countries combined

		Model 1		Model 2		Model 3		Model 4		Model 5	
Intercept		**502**	**(6.0)**	**507**	**(5.0)**	**506**	**(5.0)**	**499**	**(5.0)**	**501**	**(7.2)**
Student characteristics											
Student is female				**–14.8**	**(1.32)**	**–15.0**	**(1.39)**	**–15.3**	**(1.40)**		
Student is foreign-born				**–12.1**	**(3.04)**	**–12.2**	**(3.02)**	**–12.3**	**(2.97)**		
Students speaks a foreign language most of the time or always at home				**–10.1**	**(2.28)**	**–10.1**	**(2.21)**	**–10.2**	**(2.18)**		
Student attended pre-primary education for one year or more				**8.4**	**(1.84)**	**7.9**	**(1.83)**	**8.0**	**(1.82)**		
Index of economic, social and cultural status	1 = OECD Std Dev			**24.1**	**(1.55)**	**22.0**	**(1.70)**	**22.0**	**(1.70)**		
School-level average index of economic, social and cultural status	1 = OECD Std Dev					**63.3**	**(5.35)**	**52.9**	**(4.34)**		
School characteristics											
School is located in a rural area (less than 3 000 inhabitants)								**8.7**	**(1.86)**	–2.6	(3.16)
School is public								**7.3**	**(3.49)**	**–11.3**	**(3.90)**
School size[1]	100 students							**1.7**	**(0.26)**	**4.7**	**(0.53)**
School size squared[1]								**0.0**	**(0.01)**	**–0.1**	**(0.01)**
School resources											
Student teacher ratio[1]	Students per teacher							0.0	(0.43)	0.7	(0.88)
Student-teacher ratio squared[1]								0.0	(0.01)	0.0	(0.01)
Index of the quality of the school's educational resources	1 = OECD Std Dev							**1.7**	**(0.81)**	**2.4**	**(1.22)**
Index of teacher shortage	1 = OECD Std Dev							**–1.2**	**(0.82)**	**–3.7**	**(1.38)**
School climate											
Index of principals' perceptions of students' morale and commitment	1 = OECD Std Dev							**2.5**	**(0.63)**	**10.2**	**(0.84)**
Index of principals' perceptions of teachers' morale and commitment	1 = OECD Std Dev							–0.8	(0.61)	–1.0	(0.71)
Index of principals' perceptions of teacher-related factors affecting school climate	1 = OECD Std Dev							–0.6	(0.90)	–1.4	(1.26)
Index of disciplinary climate	1 = OECD Std Dev							**27.1**	**(1.64)**	**41.1**	**(3.37)**
Index of students' sense of belonging at school	1 = OECD Std Dev							2.8	(3.07)	**14.6**	**(4.74)**
Poor student-teacher relations	Lowest rating for all questions							**–74.4**	**(17.06)**	–51.0	(42.23)
School policy and practice											
Academic record or feeder school recommendation is a high priority or a pre-requisite for student admittance								**11.6**	**(3.16)**	**17.9**	**(4.97)**
Academic record or feeder school recommendation NOT considered for student admittance								1.8	(1.47)	–1.1	(1.94)
Estimated times per year that standardised testing is used[1]	One additional time per year							–0.4	(0.38)	**–0.9**	**(0.45)**
Estimated times per year teacher-developed tests are used[1]	One additional time per year							0.3	(0.14)	**0.7**	**(0.25)**
Ability grouping is used for all classes								–2.1	(1.62)	–3.5	(2.06)
No ability grouping in mathematics classes is used within schools								**5.4**	**(2.07)**	**8.6**	**(3.38)**
School is offering extension courses (0 = none, 1 = either remedial or enrichment, 2 = both)	One additional activity							0.6	(0.72)	2.6	(1.35)
School is offering mathematics-related activities (0 = none, 1, 2, 3 = number of activities offered)	One additional activity							**2.4**	**(1.19)**	**6.7**	**(2.24)**
Number of decisions made at the school level regarding staffing and budgeting								**–1.6**	**(0.54)**	0.3	(0.70)
Number of decisions made at the school level regarding curriculum and assessment								0.3	(0.67)	–0.9	(1.07)
Percentage of variance explained											
Between countries				33.2		44.2		53.6		22.4	
Between schools within countries				32.2		63.6		71.4		36.0	
Between students within schools				7.5		7.5		7.6		0.0	
Percentage of variance											
Between countries		10									
Between schools within countries		28									
Between students within schools		61									

Note: Values that are statistically significant are indicated in bold (see Annex A4). These models treated missing values by adding a dummy indicator for missing.

1. Variable centered around country mean.

Table 5.21b

Effects of student-level and school-level factors on performance on the mathematics scale

	Student characteristics											
	Student is a female		Student is foreign-born		Student speaks a foreign language most of the time or always at home		Student attended pre-primary education for one year or more		Index of economic, social and cultural status (1 unit increase)		School-level average index of economic, social and cultural status (1 unit increase)	
	Effect	S.E.	Effect	S.E.	Effect	S.E.	Effect	S.E.	Effect	S.E.	Effect	S.E.
OECD countries												
Australia	**–8.25**	(1.61)	–2.43	(2.54)	0.21	(3.04)	**4.50**	(1.53)	**25.66**	(1.05)	**42.86**	(4.96)
Austria	**–18.45**	(2.45)	**–19.60**	(4.44)	**–16.02**	(4.80)	–3.75	(2.62)	**7.03**	(1.44)	**41.64**	(7.57)
Belgium	**–25.48**	(1.78)	**–23.38**	(3.40)	**–27.40**	(4.28)	**38.76**	(3.53)	**21.34**	(1.04)	**51.72**	(5.19)
Canada	**–14.72**	(0.98)	**–5.89**	(1.95)	**–10.31**	(1.97)	**13.74**	(1.04)	**24.60**	(0.66)	**25.53**	(3.20)
Czech Republic	**–22.88**	(1.91)	–3.04	(8.05)	2.51	(10.10)	2.14	(2.16)	**20.88**	(1.29)	**72.60**	(6.26)
Denmark	**–16.30**	(2.58)	**–24.55**	(6.11)	–5.01	(7.36)	**16.16**	(2.78)	**35.47**	(1.68)	**25.66**	(5.19)
Finland	**–9.64**	(2.04)	**–23.28**	(8.04)	**–46.00**	(10.76)	3.23	(2.22)	**32.63**	(1.31)	–2.05	(6.17)
France	w	w	w	w	w	w	w	w	w	w	w	w
Germany	**–29.81**	(2.06)	–6.01	(4.05)	**–19.99**	(4.60)	**17.35**	(2.86)	**12.44**	(1.26)	**66.12**	(5.74)
Greece	**–24.44**	(2.31)	–3.71	(4.74)	9.91	(7.60)	**7.97**	(2.44)	**15.28**	(1.35)	**63.74**	(7.02)
Hungary	**–24.16**	(2.08)	–3.39	(5.97)	–14.48	(12.77)	7.73	(4.11)	**12.38**	(1.42)	**70.99**	(5.62)
Iceland	**15.67**	(3.00)	–0.97	(6.56)	**–35.05**	(12.34)	–2.62	(4.90)	**28.02**	(2.05)	3.90	(8.82)
Ireland	**–17.85**	(2.81)	–0.94	(5.05)	–15.02	(14.85)	**–14.35**	(2.69)	**28.63**	(1.57)	**36.06**	(4.95)
Italy	**–23.45**	(1.48)	**–9.58**	(4.42)	6.24	(6.22)	**9.43**	(1.92)	**7.44**	(0.75)	**70.66**	(5.11)
Japan	**–17.88**	(2.27)	11.27	(17.70)	**–114.40**	(22.33)	**20.24**	(5.96)	**3.76**	(1.61)	**106.09**	(11.53)
Korea	**–16.57**	(2.75)	29.95	(21.74)	**–86.41**	(27.68)	**–6.40**	(2.87)	**13.43**	(1.35)	**60.76**	(8.29)
Luxembourg	**–23.33**	(2.52)	**–9.03**	(3.53)	**–10.71**	(3.59)	**13.28**	(2.98)	**14.11**	(1.33)	20.86	(16.75)
Mexico	**–15.94**	(0.77)	**–36.98**	(2.85)	**–19.79**	(4.49)	**7.98**	(0.85)	**5.31**	(0.41)	**40.33**	(2.19)
Netherlands	**–13.16**	(1.92)	**–18.45**	(4.75)	**–17.74**	(5.27)	**18.95**	(4.18)	**12.30**	(1.25)	**85.38**	(9.94)
New Zealand	**–9.70**	(2.90)	–4.14	(4.14)	–8.00	(5.51)	**11.09**	(2.98)	**32.33**	(1.58)	**46.15**	(7.42)
Norway	**–7.69**	(2.65)	**–25.45**	(7.00)	–4.14	(7.84)	**12.04**	(3.34)	**39.50**	(1.84)	**18.20**	(7.43)
Poland	**–6.16**	(2.43)	–20.88	(59.40)	–37.94	(29.98)	**6.78**	(2.60)	**37.19**	(1.72)	**31.43**	(7.59)
Portugal	**–16.19**	(2.09)	**–9.12**	(4.50)	8.42	(9.57)	–0.24	(2.15)	**17.60**	(0.96)	**19.90**	(4.76)
Slovak Republic	**–24.54**	(1.78)	–1.87	(7.61)	**–22.35**	(8.66)	3.92	(2.00)	**22.40**	(1.22)	**78.12**	(5.35)
Spain	**–12.20**	(1.53)	**–20.44**	(4.00)	4.56	(6.16)	**18.66**	(2.12)	**20.64**	(0.88)	**29.45**	(4.06)
Sweden	**–6.84**	(2.49)	**–40.71**	(5.50)	**–15.45**	(6.19)	**6.85**	(2.61)	**34.78**	(1.55)	**14.99**	(5.97)
Switzerland	**–25.18**	(1.69)	**–31.14**	(2.87)	**–23.79**	(3.54)	–0.49	(1.99)	**23.22**	(1.13)	**62.90**	(5.60)
Turkey	**–21.51**	(2.14)	–17.44	(10.09)	–12.20	(9.68)	**10.23**	(4.03)	**8.71**	(1.19)	**64.76**	(6.88)
United States	**–10.65**	(2.24)	–4.45	(5.01)	3.55	(4.96)	**–18.07**	(3.75)	**30.31**	(1.44)	**37.29**	(4.98)
Partner countries												
Brazil	**–19.25**	(2.27)	–5.07	(18.64)	–27.34	(16.34)	**10.34**	(2.43)	**4.74**	(1.31)	**47.72**	(6.59)
Hong Kong-China	**–19.45**	(2.41)	**–10.01**	(2.86)	**–27.30**	(5.27)	**38.13**	(3.60)	1.52	(1.51)	**66.64**	(10.23)
Indonesia	**–8.97**	(1.20)	–16.39	(12.66)	–7.98	(4.15)	**5.17**	(1.55)	0.65	(0.69)	**46.26**	(4.40)
Latvia	**–8.42**	(2.29)	**18.20**	(6.99)	**–11.60**	(4.59)	0.49	(2.39)	**28.42**	(1.67)	**27.69**	(10.37)
Russian Federation	**–17.13**	(2.06)	**–12.30**	(3.35)	**–12.73**	(5.61)	**12.01**	(2.49)	**21.03**	(1.49)	**38.82**	(10.17)
Serbia	**–21.07**	(2.38)	**9.50**	(3.99)	**–25.89**	(8.68)	–1.34	(2.29)	**15.29**	(1.40)	**58.65**	(6.93)
Thailand	2.25	(1.99)	25.24	(31.50)	0.00	a	**7.05**	(2.29)	**7.04**	(1.21)	**34.71**	(7.02)
Tunisia	**–21.85**	(1.82)	**–16.86**	(7.87)	20.23	(15.72)	3.73	(2.30)	**6.66**	(0.93)	**37.80**	(5.69)
Uruguay	**–19.14**	(2.08)	–8.94	(5.42)	**–17.02**	(7.88)	**11.15**	(2.29)	**11.37**	(1.19)	**55.23**	(7.02)
United Kingdom[1]	**–12.53**	(1.67)	**–9.95**	(3.76)	–1.07	(4.58)	**5.34**	(1.78)	**30.13**	(1.01)	**46.84**	(4.60)

	School characteristics							
	School is located in a rural area, defined as communities with a population of less than 3 000 inhabitants		Government or public school		Index of school size (per 100 students)		Index of school size squared (per 100 students)	
	Effect	S.E.	Effect	S.E.	Effect	S.E.	Effect	S.E.
OECD countries								
Australia	7.87	(7.28)	0.00	a	2.18	(1.75)	–0.11	(0.08)
Austria	–12.56	(8.21)	10.52	(10.66)	3.13	(1.70)	–0.04	(0.06)
Belgium	–13.37	(13.89)	–3.97	(5.62)	3.16	(2.42)	–0.15	(0.14)
Canada	**8.85**	(3.35)	–5.53	(4.95)	1.83	(0.96)	–0.02	(0.04)
Czech Republic	5.32	(8.75)	**27.08**	(9.08)	1.31	(2.40)	–0.08	(0.12)
Denmark	10.25	(6.10)	–0.34	(6.94)	6.85	(5.19)	–0.45	(0.51)
Finland	10.21	(5.94)	13.63	(7.75)	3.90	(4.40)	–0.06	(0.44)
France	w	w	w	w	w	w	w	w
Germany	11.83	(10.98)	5.75	(10.68)	**5.86**	(1.91)	**–0.26**	(0.09)
Greece	5.83	(14.58)	–30.15	(128.86)	–2.03	(11.36)	–0.32	(1.38)
Hungary	–7.82	(12.63)	7.48	(8.78)	4.41	(3.22)	–0.17	(0.22)
Iceland	–6.15	(10.19)	**70.67**	(33.15)	–3.56	(6.98)	0.11	(0.70)
Ireland	–3.25	(4.61)	–0.26	(4.85)	1.90	(3.01)	–0.14	(0.19)
Italy	12.51	(21.49)	**33.50**	(12.68)	1.05	(2.23)	–0.03	(0.13)
Japan	0.00	a	34.10	(22.64)	3.48	(3.03)	–0.11	(0.11)
Korea	–19.69	(23.31)	**13.36**	(6.17)	–0.55	(3.64)	0.08	(0.15)
Luxembourg	0.00	a	**60.57**	(22.15)	–1.27	(3.48)	–0.04	(0.08)
Mexico	**–8.05**	(3.43)	**10.61**	(4.39)	0.25	(0.36)	0.01	(0.01)
Netherlands	8.60	(27.26)	7.65	(8.46)	1.74	(2.47)	–0.04	(0.10)
New Zealand	9.93	(8.61)	5.39	(12.34)	–0.39	(1.53)	0.03	(0.05)
Norway	2.09	(5.63)	–35.02	(19.41)	3.55	(9.79)	–0.36	(1.40)
Poland	4.44	(6.68)	0.79	(21.48)	1.85	(3.90)	–0.07	(0.31)
Portugal	0.87	(9.73)	–12.31	(13.44)	**5.98**	(1.89)	**–0.15**	(0.07)
Slovak Republic	–2.05	(7.17)	–1.35	(6.22)	1.14	(3.45)	–0.05	(0.26)
Spain	8.14	(8.08)	2.72	(8.03)	1.29	(1.41)	–0.06	(0.06)
Sweden	3.28	(4.71)	12.48	(9.03)	–1.13	(2.26)	0.15	(0.14)
Switzerland	8.19	(4.95)	**48.78**	(12.04)	1.61	(0.93)	–0.02	(0.02)
Turkey	36.48	(32.64)	4.99	(31.05)	2.41	(1.39)	–0.05	(0.04)
United States	**19.61**	(7.20)	10.97	(9.43)	1.80	(0.99)	–0.04	(0.03)
Partner countries								
Brazil	–11.55	(11.16)	17.68	(14.65)	1.34	(0.92)	–0.02	(0.02)
Hong Kong-China	0.00	a	**55.79**	(16.20)	4.35	(16.25)	–0.05	(0.77)
Indonesia	–4.02	(5.50)	–0.36	(9.32)	**1.98**	(0.78)	**–0.03**	(0.01)
Latvia	10.41	(8.52)	**79.07**	(27.34)	3.47	(4.10)	–0.10	(0.24)
Russian Federation	5.63	(11.84)	54.93	(43.46)	1.09	(2.99)	–0.02	(0.15)
Serbia	0.00	a	0.00	a	0.54	(1.88)	0.03	(0.08)
Thailand	–4.78	(8.10)	19.45	(11.61)	–0.49	(1.09)	0.03	(0.02)
Tunisia	1.46	(14.47)	0.00	a	4.23	(2.47)	–0.10	(0.09)
Uruguay	10.57	(11.19)	0.72	(16.56)	**6.94**	(2.53)	–0.22	(0.13)
United Kingdom[1]	–6.44	(6.00)	–6.94	(11.04)	1.66	(1.76)	–0.04	(0.07)

Note: Values that are statistically significant are indicated in bold (see Annex A4). These models treated missing values by adding a dummy indicator for missing.
1. Response rate too low to ensure comparability (see Annex A3).

Table 5.21b *(continued – 1)*

Effects of student-level and school-level factors on performance on the mathematics scale

		School resources							
		Student-teacher ratio (1 student per teacher)		Student-teacher staff ratio squared		Index of the quality of the school's educational resources (1 unit change)		Index of teacher shortage (1 unit change)	
		Effect	S.E.	Effect	S.E.	Effect	S.E.	Effect	S.E.
OECD countries	Australia	1.67	(7.20)	0.03	(0.27)	1.00	(1.86)	2.23	(2.07)
	Austria	0.75	(2.00)	–0.01	(0.04)	2.39	(2.90)	–4.32	(3.81)
	Belgium	2.96	(4.05)	–0.03	(0.18)	**5.92**	(2.18)	**–5.59**	(2.25)
	Canada	**3.57**	(1.47)	**–0.09**	(0.04)	1.62	(1.24)	1.40	(1.31)
	Czech Republic	2.85	(2.14)	**–0.13**	(0.06)	0.73	(3.59)	**–16.26**	(4.92)
	Denmark	4.54	(4.42)	–0.18	(0.20)	4.17	(2.69)	–4.70	(3.11)
	Finland	4.26	(5.82)	–0.25	(0.29)	–0.10	(2.42)	0.51	(2.60)
	France	w	w	w	w	w	w	w	w
	Germany	–7.79	(5.99)	0.22	(0.17)	4.74	(2.95)	–0.97	(3.40)
	Greece	–9.34	(7.57)	0.52	(0.35)	–1.83	(4.35)	1.44	(3.06)
	Hungary	–2.40	(1.49)	0.07	(0.04)	1.18	(3.27)	5.46	(4.60)
	Iceland	–5.10	(9.13)	0.22	(0.42)	–0.34	(3.21)	–3.45	(3.52)
	Ireland	2.38	(2.08)	–0.04	(0.03)	–2.23	(2.04)	2.92	(2.44)
	Italy	–0.57	(1.35)	0.00	(0.02)	**10.29**	(2.61)	1.43	(3.19)
	Japan	–1.84	(4.66)	0.09	(0.17)	–1.95	(3.28)	–1.05	(3.09)
	Korea	14.00	(7.37)	**–0.44**	(0.22)	–1.35	(3.67)	5.30	(3.96)
	Luxembourg	15.46	(27.00)	–0.94	(1.35)	10.37	(7.52)	**–13.21**	(5.04)
	Mexico	0.00	a	0.00	a	–0.31	(1.15)	1.13	(1.20)
	Netherlands	4.77	(5.32)	–0.14	(0.16)	2.68	(3.85)	–5.49	(4.56)
	New Zealand	1.52	(4.95)	–0.02	(0.14)	4.20	(2.65)	–0.19	(3.09)
	Norway	–7.70	(10.17)	0.26	(0.48)	5.05	(3.11)	–1.65	(2.94)
	Poland	0.95	(3.46)	–0.03	(0.13)	–0.19	(2.75)	–2.28	(2.44)
	Portugal	–1.22	(1.41)	0.02	(0.02)	–2.62	(3.07)	–5.13	(3.36)
	Slovak Republic	2.04	(2.92)	–0.09	(0.09)	4.55	(2.67)	–3.59	(3.35)
	Spain	1.07	(1.44)	–0.04	(0.03)	2.14	(1.96)	–1.89	(1.69)
	Sweden	–1.83	(1.84)	0.08	(0.05)	–1.03	(2.31)	1.34	(2.13)
	Switzerland	–0.12	(1.20)	0.00	(0.03)	0.03	(2.27)	1.43	(2.57)
	Turkey	–0.83	(1.13)	0.00	(0.02)	1.53	(4.22)	–2.28	(3.81)
	United States	–0.71	(1.50)	0.03	(0.04)	1.42	(2.34)	0.91	(2.93)
Partner countries	Brazil	–0.80	(0.98)	0.01	(0.01)	5.11	(3.02)	–0.68	(2.89)
	Hong Kong-China	–4.75	(16.07)	0.36	(0.46)	2.44	(4.10)	3.39	(5.06)
	Indonesia	0.00	a	0.00	a	0.47	(2.08)	–0.33	(2.01)
	Latvia	–7.85	(6.77)	0.36	(0.25)	–1.53	(3.70)	7.61	(4.67)
	Russian Federation	–0.89	(1.42)	0.00	(0.03)	**8.17**	(3.42)	5.13	(3.29)
	Serbia	0.00	a	0.00	a	3.27	(3.34)	3.66	(4.25)
	Thailand	1.44	(1.51)	0.02	(0.02)	–2.69	(3.60)	–0.86	(3.30)
	Tunisia	–16.26	(10.30)	0.29	(0.25)	–0.06	(3.52)	4.57	(5.00)
	Uruguay	–0.81	(1.03)	0.01	(0.02)	–2.35	(2.58)	0.64	(2.88)
	United Kingdom[1]	–1.36	(5.70)	0.07	(0.20)	–0.23	(1.88)	–2.56	(1.85)

		School climate											
		Index of principals' perceptions of students' morale and commitment (1 unit change)		Index of principals' perceptions of teachers' morale and commitment (1 unit change)		Index of principals' perceptions of teacher-related factors affecting school climate (1 unit change)		School-level average index of disciplinary climate (1 unit change)		School-level index of sense of belonging at school (1 unit change)		Poor student-teacher relations	
		Effect	S.E.	Effect	S.E.	Effect	S.E.	Effect	S.E.	Effect	S.E.	Effect	S.E.
OECD countries	Australia	**5.03**	(1.80)	–3.68	(1.92)	2.61	(2.25)	**20.73**	(5.23)	–11.56	(6.80)	**–254.14**	(61.02)
	Austria	–3.99	(3.39)	–0.06	(3.28)	2.91	(3.32)	**27.15**	(5.57)	5.74	(8.17)	–73.88	(50.53)
	Belgium	–1.21	(2.98)	4.96	(2.62)	–1.77	(2.51)	**24.04**	(5.59)	**23.58**	(9.58)	–83.97	(58.90)
	Canada	**3.15**	(1.33)	–2.16	(1.24)	**3.62**	(1.40)	**23.32**	(2.92)	–2.85	(3.62)	**–164.24**	(32.55)
	Czech Republic	–2.11	(3.40)	0.55	(3.23)	–2.51	(3.54)	**20.32**	(5.03)	–8.38	(9.20)	–51.88	(51.51)
	Denmark	–0.25	(2.61)	–1.91	(2.57)	–1.87	(2.60)	**21.31**	(5.78)	–0.76	(6.88)	–90.76	(57.10)
	Finland	**4.47**	(2.21)	0.54	(2.24)	–0.59	(2.46)	5.89	(4.95)	**–22.90**	(8.14)	**–164.11**	(60.53)
	France	w	w	w	w	w	w	w	w	w	w	w	w
	Germany	4.32	(3.13)	–3.06	(3.29)	–3.38	(4.74)	**29.09**	(6.45)	–16.72	(9.99)	–37.54	(58.45)
	Greece	–2.94	(3.81)	4.41	(3.78)	1.00	(2.52)	**34.11**	(12.91)	–7.69	(12.38)	–54.66	(67.72)
	Hungary	–2.14	(3.34)	–1.88	(3.34)	1.31	(2.55)	**21.04**	(5.23)	11.39	(6.92)	69.43	(52.43)
	Iceland	0.80	(3.03)	1.68	(3.26)	–0.52	(3.24)	10.20	(5.48)	9.37	(8.64)	–63.33	(51.74)
	Ireland	3.79	(2.48)	1.64	(2.00)	**5.60**	(2.46)	**14.47**	(4.69)	**–19.77**	(8.58)	–2.11	(46.86)
	Italy	3.82	(3.05)	–2.21	(3.18)	–1.46	(2.93)	**19.54**	(5.92)	–2.94	(8.86)	–61.82	(56.74)
	Japan	–0.19	(3.22)	–0.43	(3.80)	7.71	(4.51)	**32.08**	(7.21)	15.86	(16.19)	–49.66	(55.92)
	Korea	**8.54**	(3.47)	1.05	(3.69)	0.91	(2.59)	**46.19**	(10.73)	13.08	(14.66)	–102.10	(105.50)
	Luxembourg	12.36	(8.84)	–4.18	(5.84)	–5.55	(5.92)	12.03	(20.01)	**64.07**	(28.63)	–41.43	(138.47)
	Mexico	–0.86	(1.22)	1.03	(1.23)	1.43	(1.30)	**29.50**	(3.31)	**9.67**	(3.75)	**–169.29**	(38.88)
	Netherlands	3.37	(4.65)	–6.09	(4.99)	7.27	(5.67)	10.79	(11.01)	12.59	(16.75)	–219.29	(114.66)
	New Zealand	–2.61	(2.87)	–2.61	(2.74)	4.73	(3.22)	**24.71**	(7.10)	–14.85	(9.95)	–25.72	(72.63)
	Norway	–2.42	(2.71)	–1.46	(2.32)	0.00	(3.20)	**18.10**	(6.76)	–0.21	(7.09)	–55.71	(35.65)
	Poland	0.93	(2.57)	–1.73	(2.69)	–0.36	(2.51)	**16.50**	(5.52)	4.90	(9.50)	17.93	(52.41)
	Portugal	–1.33	(3.65)	–2.48	(3.05)	–0.39	(3.66)	**65.24**	(8.80)	18.84	(11.46)	157.00	(138.27)
	Slovak Republic	–0.15	(2.47)	–2.33	(2.50)	–1.82	(2.37)	**22.39**	(5.10)	–11.43	(8.43)	–62.53	(42.24)
	Spain	**6.34**	(2.42)	–0.89	(2.39)	–1.06	(2.00)	**20.49**	(4.28)	9.70	(5.49)	–9.33	(36.52)
	Sweden	**5.21**	(2.24)	1.68	(2.60)	–1.65	(2.57)	5.88	(5.60)	–1.41	(7.90)	**–178.54**	(66.44)
	Switzerland	1.73	(2.50)	3.44	(2.43)	**–12.66**	(2.90)	**23.60**	(4.57)	**20.17**	(6.01)	–27.17	(43.55)
	Turkey	–1.55	(3.94)	–0.80	(3.36)	–1.55	(2.93)	**63.11**	(11.11)	26.79	(17.79)	–2.13	(83.57)
	United States	1.71	(2.70)	–1.65	(2.49)	3.54	(3.32)	**30.98**	(5.64)	0.00	a	**–148.06**	(54.62)
								24.7					
Partner countries	Brazil	1.45	(3.25)	–2.22	(3.69)	–2.93	(2.85)	**55.49**	(10.73)	–9.68	(10.01)	–205.56	(127.58)
	Hong Kong-China	**12.34**	(4.64)	–1.01	(4.37)	–1.26	(2.69)	**49.36**	(12.89)	–8.51	(21.54)	18.86	(107.55)
	Indonesia	2.16	(2.30)	–2.41	(2.52)	–1.06	(1.40)	**17.01**	(6.58)	**22.53**	(10.86)	**–563.94**	(135.27)
	Latvia	3.60	(4.23)	0.09	(3.63)	1.87	(3.20)	**16.46**	(6.20)	**40.32**	(14.42)	–15.39	(107.82)
	Russian Federation	1.08	(4.62)	6.61	(3.77)	**5.26**	(2.57)	**33.93**	(7.48)	–15.05	(11.35)	93.50	(110.92)
	Serbia	3.06	(2.93)	**–7.68**	(3.15)	3.27	(3.02)	**60.22**	(9.62)	–3.10	(11.33)	49.59	(71.59)
	Thailand	–3.05	(2.82)	4.18	(3.02)	2.50	(3.54)	**31.75**	(10.63)	–0.76	(12.36)	**–647.60**	(261.44)
	Tunisia	–0.84	(2.89)	**7.96**	(2.99)	–0.15	(3.02)	**44.18**	(11.54)	–5.45	(11.17)	32.17	(68.46)
	Uruguay	0.24	(3.04)	–4.17	(3.52)	1.61	(2.84)	**35.81**	(6.85)	–2.87	(10.05)	–170.66	(89.76)
	United Kingdom[1]	1.36	(2.05)	–1.54	(2.03)	1.13	(2.54)	**17.99**	(4.49)	–2.75	(6.73)	**–113.54**	(48.89)

Note: Values that are statistically significant are indicated in bold (see Annex A4). These models treated missing values by adding a dummy indicator for missing.
1. Response rate too low to ensure comparability (see Annex A3).

Table 5.21b *(continued – 2)*
Effects of student-level and school-level factors on performance on the mathematics scale

	School policy and practice									
	Academic record or feeder school recommendation is a high priority or a pre-requisite for student admittance		Academic record or feeder school recommendation NOT considered for student admittance		Estimated times per year that standardised testing is used (1 additional time per year)		Estimated times per year that teacher-developed tests are used (1 additional time per year)		Ability grouping is used for all classes	
	Effect	**S.E.**	**Effect**	**S.E.**	**Effect**	**S.E.**	**Effect**	**S.E.**	**Effect**	**S.E.**
OECD countries										
Australia	2.72	(3.99)	0.20	(3.40)	**–2.94**	(0.92)	–0.47	(0.44)	3.06	(3.04)
Austria	11.07	(7.46)	–18.88	(9.75)	2.20	(1.84)	1.28	(0.73)	–4.54	(10.57)
Belgium	7.16	(4.56)	2.24	(4.65)	–0.48	(0.90)	0.64	(0.52)	2.23	(5.07)
Canada	–4.46	(2.70)	–0.13	(2.48)	–0.08	(0.76)	0.67	(0.43)	1.63	(2.13)
Czech Republic	**15.78**	(5.55)	**–19.42**	(6.64)	–1.27	(1.70)	0.55	(0.67)	9.53	(7.85)
Denmark	**–16.88**	(8.57)	–5.77	(4.23)	–0.44	(1.25)	0.95	(0.75)	0.10	(5.04)
Finland	**15.34**	(7.60)	6.72	(4.30)	0.90	(1.86)	0.23	(0.56)	0.12	(5.44)
France	w	w	w	w	w	w	w	w	w	w
Germany	**17.72**	(6.03)	–1.13	(6.88)	–2.73	(1.41)	0.31	(0.67)	–7.85	(7.07)
Greece	18.57	(29.91)	9.07	(8.47)	0.23	(1.16)	–1.89	(1.12)	–9.94	(16.11)
Hungary	**22.85**	(7.57)	–13.75	(9.45)	–2.16	(1.62)	0.87	(0.85)	–1.48	(7.08)
Iceland	30.48	(16.13)	10.47	(8.19)	0.86	(2.83)	–0.39	(0.89)	–1.97	(6.70)
Ireland	5.39	(5.95)	–0.87	(3.91)	0.91	(1.16)	–0.27	(0.56)	5.60	(3.89)
Italy	–12.59	(7.95)	5.16	(5.34)	**–1.91**	(0.81)	0.21	(0.72)	**–16.43**	(6.30)
Japan	8.80	(8.71)	11.61	(34.32)	0.52	(1.51)	–0.35	(1.94)	5.41	(9.60)
Korea	6.64	(8.38)	2.15	(9.25)	**5.35**	(1.67)	2.44	(5.57)	2.19	(8.44)
Luxembourg	**31.02**	(8.84)	6.26	(21.14)	**–8.42**	(2.47)	**2.11**	(0.98)	**–39.25**	(16.17)
Mexico	1.35	(2.59)	**–7.16**	(2.88)	–0.61	(0.38)	–0.41	(0.34)	0.53	(2.68)
Netherlands	16.17	(11.68)	30.48	(22.28)	–0.39	(1.06)	–1.58	(1.29)	1.47	(7.06)
New Zealand	2.59	(6.37)	6.71	(5.04)	0.75	(0.56)	–1.05	(0.65)	–3.75	(4.24)
Norway	**29.79**	(13.10)	5.73	(5.65)	2.16	(1.45)	–0.68	(0.68)	4.67	(5.58)
Poland	–1.94	(5.45)	1.16	(5.10)	1.43	(1.11)	0.20	(0.58)	4.01	(4.58)
Portugal	–14.74	(20.65)	–2.45	(6.41)	–3.14	(4.36)	–0.87	(0.95)	–1.83	(5.62)
Slovak Republic	**16.34**	(4.82)	6.17	(5.70)	0.61	(1.23)	–0.28	(0.58)	2.71	(4.79)
Spain	–1.42	(9.19)	6.74	(5.36)	–0.23	(0.53)	0.11	(0.57)	–0.72	(3.68)
Sweden	**23.11**	(9.01)	3.10	(4.79)	–0.86	(1.05)	0.03	(0.59)	1.21	(3.67)
Switzerland	7.73	(5.25)	–0.37	(5.91)	0.63	(0.96)	0.68	(0.68)	**–11.56**	(4.28)
Turkey	11.87	(11.23)	–2.00	(7.45)	–0.13	(1.58)	0.80	(1.31)	8.50	(7.53)
United States	2.03	(6.06)	4.05	(5.49)	–0.69	(1.48)	2.16	(1.40)	–1.76	(4.33)
Partner countries										
Brazil	**30.76**	(12.26)	7.09	(7.99)	–0.95	(0.75)	1.27	(0.91)	–11.46	(7.19)
Hong Kong-China	7.98	(8.82)	–37.85	(37.41)	0.00	a	0.27	(0.90)	–7.50	(7.86)
Indonesia	0.10	(5.39)	–3.21	(8.43)	–1.60	(1.19)	0.08	(0.57)	–7.06	(5.95)
Latvia	**23.15**	(7.37)	–1.47	(7.40)	–1.50	(1.02)	0.66	(0.87)	3.27	(5.94)
Russian Federation	–0.40	(8.77)	0.14	(6.37)	0.14	(1.09)	–0.67	(0.94)	–6.66	(6.12)
Serbia	–6.63	(11.15)	–1.11	(25.85)	–0.04	(1.66)	–0.64	(1.11)	–3.11	(6.17)
Thailand	–2.75	(6.63)	6.76	(10.14)	0.54	(3.76)	0.41	(0.69)	–9.69	(6.46)
Tunisia	6.82	(6.88)	2.70	(7.42)	**1.81**	(0.89)	–1.10	(0.85)	–4.67	(9.78)
Uruguay	5.53	(8.86)	5.01	(6.87)	–0.45	(1.62)	1.17	(1.33)	–4.62	(6.91)
United Kingdom[1]	**28.56**	(5.61)	**11.47**	(4.30)	0.72	(0.96)	0.66	(0.45)	–3.44	(3.98)

	School policy and practice									
	No ability grouping in mathematics classes is used within schools		School is offering extension courses (0 = none, 1 = either remedial or enrichment, 2 = both) (1 additional activity)		School is offering mathematics-related activities (0 = none, 1, 2, 3 = number of activities offered (1 additional activity)		Number of decisions made at the school level regarding staffing and budgeting		Number of decisions made at the school level regarding curriculum and assessment	
	Effect	**S.E.**	**Effect**	**S.E.**	**Effect**	**S.E.**	**Effect**	**S.E.**	**Effect**	**S.E.**
OECD countries										
Australia	9.90	(8.31)	–0.78	(3.57)	2.35	(2.62)	–0.77	(1.13)	–2.67	(2.76)
Austria	**30.92**	(12.73)	5.69	(4.38)	4.28	(5.43)	–1.13	(3.24)	–3.62	(2.56)
Belgium	–5.01	(4.56)	2.34	(2.91)	**14.03**	(4.09)	2.69	(2.34)	4.20	(2.19)
Canada	–4.74	(4.83)	–0.47	(1.84)	0.83	(1.40)	–0.80	(0.69)	1.57	(1.11)
Czech Republic	6.28	(5.29)	4.07	(4.07)	–1.05	(2.97)	–1.17	(1.95)	–1.98	(2.87)
Denmark	–7.87	(4.79)	3.67	(3.99)	6.91	(6.35)	0.14	(1.92)	–3.96	(2.36)
Finland	2.00	(3.34)	–0.20	(2.59)	0.12	(3.03)	–0.27	(1.44)	0.50	(4.47)
France	w	w	w	w	w	w	w	w	w	w
Germany	11.05	(6.67)	–2.43	(3.67)	2.08	(4.11)	–1.99	(2.98)	–3.71	(2.47)
Greece	–4.68	(10.62)	4.16	(7.06)	2.44	(7.17)	–27.76	(45.95)	0.00	a
Hungary	5.54	(6.47)	–0.92	(4.60)	**7.05**	(3.41)	2.35	(2.39)	–0.64	(4.05)
Iceland	–4.39	(7.07)	0.42	(5.20)	–1.48	(5.99)	1.43	(3.12)	–0.54	(2.95)
Ireland	3.74	(11.35)	–6.51	(3.36)	0.45	(3.25)	–0.55	(1.78)	–4.61	(3.12)
Italy	0.54	(5.57)	–3.80	(4.82)	**7.20**	(2.89)	–2.45	(2.91)	**–9.31**	(4.22)
Japan	9.42	(6.93)	2.02	(4.59)	4.46	(5.47)	–1.41	(4.41)	–13.09	(12.82)
Korea	1.08	(5.96)	6.75	(4.91)	–0.78	(3.51)	0.92	(2.28)	5.43	(13.47)
Luxembourg	–12.96	(8.93)	–23.72	(12.49)	3.71	(4.99)	88.60	(68.06)	0.00	a
Mexico	0.02	(2.84)	**5.07**	(1.67)	**2.91**	(1.47)	1.00	(0.71)	**–2.40**	(1.10)
Netherlands	9.26	(14.09)	–2.43	(4.85)	**20.23**	(7.19)	0.75	(4.19)	6.00	(12.76)
New Zealand	43.21	(25.69)	5.97	(7.20)	–9.24	(5.25)	–3.22	(3.00)	6.58	(5.15)
Norway	11.26	(9.54)	1.21	(3.05)	2.25	(3.71)	–2.36	(1.76)	–1.15	(1.74)
Poland	8.58	(5.83)	1.91	(3.30)	–7.35	(4.91)	–3.48	(2.06)	4.79	(4.28)
Portugal	3.09	(6.53)	7.50	(6.19)	–3.88	(3.39)	2.60	(3.76)	–1.75	(2.33)
Slovak Republic	9.31	(5.54)	0.98	(3.01)	**5.62**	(2.65)	–1.30	(1.73)	1.01	(1.90)
Spain	4.12	(7.01)	0.82	(3.05)	**6.43**	(2.88)	0.51	(2.24)	1.24	(2.18)
Sweden	–7.89	(7.83)	0.41	(3.66)	3.68	(3.35)	–0.29	(1.76)	2.09	(2.98)
Switzerland	9.74	(5.40)	–1.19	(2.62)	7.05	(4.21)	2.46	(1.68)	0.84	(1.46)
Turkey	–2.43	(9.21)	–3.07	(4.43)	2.65	(6.10)	–5.50	(3.16)	0.04	(3.61)
United States	1.94	(12.75)	3.66	(4.15)	–1.92	(2.11)	0.87	(1.67)	2.07	(2.69)
Partner countries										
Brazil	2.13	(9.15)	5.68	(5.79)	1.56	(4.53)	**6.14**	(2.52)	3.42	(3.35)
Hong Kong-China	15.70	(9.57)	–4.22	(5.18)	3.37	(4.60)	0.98	(3.27)	–14.44	(14.99)
Indonesia	2.26	(6.49)	5.09	(4.30)	**12.44**	(3.09)	–0.57	(2.20)	3.16	(4.45)
Latvia	7.22	(9.88)	**12.15**	(6.14)	0.96	(4.13)	1.60	(2.86)	–0.88	(3.07)
Russian Federation	–0.17	(11.84)	6.39	(7.87)	–0.76	(3.98)	2.11	(2.00)	–2.28	(4.51)
Serbia	–13.61	(7.43)	1.15	(4.34)	5.11	(4.23)	0.16	(2.77)	–2.02	(3.45)
Thailand	8.89	(8.16)	2.05	(5.85)	1.19	(3.85)	1.24	(2.64)	–5.87	(8.89)
Tunisia	–7.33	(9.84)	–4.30	(7.54)	–5.85	(3.90)	6.82	(3.81)	–2.82	(3.34)
Uruguay	6.57	(7.06)	4.04	(4.92)	3.22	(3.77)	1.57	(2.46)	0.42	(2.72)
United Kingdom[1]	–10.32	(20.16)	–0.70	(2.24)	–0.26	(1.69)	**–3.80**	(1.26)	1.99	(4.95)

Note: Values that are statistically significant are indicated in bold (see Annex A4). These models treated missing values by adding a dummy indicator for missing.
1. Response rate too low to ensure comparability (see Annex A3).

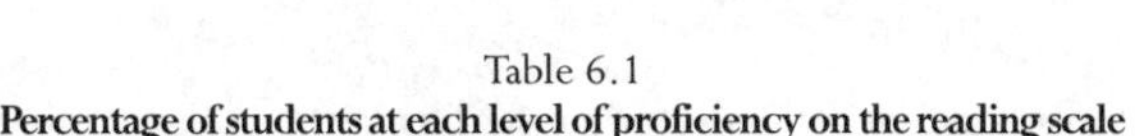

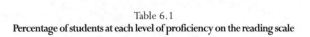

Table 6.1
Percentage of students at each level of proficiency on the reading scale

		Proficiency levels											
		Below Level 1 (below 335 score points)		Level 1 (from 335 to 407 score points)		Level 2 (from 408 to 480 score points)		Level 3 (from 481 to 552 score points)		Level 4 (from 553 to 625 score points)		Level 5 (above 625 score points)	
		%	S.E.	%	S.E.	%	S.E.	%	S.E.	%	S.E.	%	S.E.
OECD countries	Australia	3.6	(0.4)	8.2	(0.4)	18.3	(0.6)	28.4	(0.8)	26.9	(0.8)	14.6	(0.7)
	Austria	7.3	(0.8)	13.4	(1.0)	22.6	(1.0)	27.4	(1.0)	21.0	(1.0)	8.3	(0.8)
	Belgium	7.8	(0.7)	10.0	(0.6)	18.2	(0.6)	26.0	(0.8)	25.4	(0.8)	12.5	(0.5)
	Canada	2.3	(0.2)	7.3	(0.5)	18.3	(0.6)	31.0	(0.7)	28.6	(0.6)	12.6	(0.5)
	Czech Republic	6.5	(0.9)	12.9	(0.9)	24.7	(1.0)	30.3	(1.3)	19.3	(1.1)	6.4	(0.6)
	Denmark	4.6	(0.6)	11.9	(0.7)	24.9	(1.1)	33.4	(1.1)	20.0	(1.0)	5.2	(0.5)
	Finland	1.1	(0.2)	4.6	(0.4)	14.6	(0.6)	31.7	(0.8)	33.4	(0.7)	14.7	(0.7)
	France	6.3	(0.7)	11.2	(0.7)	22.8	(0.8)	29.7	(1.1)	22.5	(0.9)	7.4	(0.6)
	Germany	9.3	(0.8)	13.0	(0.9)	19.8	(0.8)	26.3	(0.8)	21.9	(1.0)	9.6	(0.6)
	Greece	10.2	(0.8)	15.0	(0.8)	25.0	(1.2)	27.3	(1.1)	16.8	(1.2)	5.7	(0.7)
	Hungary	6.1	(0.7)	14.4	(0.9)	26.7	(0.9)	30.2	(1.1)	17.6	(1.1)	4.9	(0.6)
	Iceland	6.7	(0.6)	11.8	(0.7)	23.9	(0.8)	29.7	(1.0)	20.9	(0.8)	7.1	(0.6)
	Ireland	2.7	(0.5)	8.3	(0.7)	21.2	(1.2)	32.4	(1.3)	26.2	(1.2)	9.3	(0.7)
	Italy	9.1	(0.9)	14.8	(0.8)	24.9	(0.8)	28.3	(1.0)	17.8	(0.7)	5.2	(0.3)
	Japan	7.4	(0.8)	11.6	(0.8)	20.9	(1.0)	27.2	(1.1)	23.2	(1.1)	9.7	(0.9)
	Korea	1.4	(0.3)	5.4	(0.6)	16.8	(1.0)	33.5	(1.2)	30.8	(1.1)	12.2	(1.1)
	Luxembourg	8.7	(0.4)	14.0	(0.7)	24.2	(0.7)	28.7	(1.0)	19.1	(0.9)	5.2	(0.4)
	Mexico	24.9	(1.5)	27.1	(1.2)	27.5	(1.0)	15.6	(1.0)	4.3	(0.6)	0.5	(0.1)
	Netherlands	2.1	(0.5)	9.4	(0.9)	23.4	(1.1)	30.7	(1.3)	25.6	(1.1)	8.8	(0.7)
	New Zealand	4.8	(0.5)	9.7	(0.6)	18.5	(0.9)	26.3	(0.9)	24.3	(0.9)	16.3	(0.8)
	Norway	6.4	(0.6)	11.8	(0.8)	21.4	(1.2)	29.0	(1.0)	21.5	(0.8)	10.0	(0.7)
	Poland	5.3	(0.5)	11.5	(0.7)	24.4	(0.8)	30.0	(0.9)	20.7	(0.9)	8.0	(0.6)
	Portugal	7.6	(0.9)	14.4	(0.9)	25.9	(1.0)	30.5	(1.1)	17.9	(1.0)	3.8	(0.5)
	Slovak Republic	8.0	(0.8)	16.9	(1.0)	28.4	(1.0)	27.7	(1.1)	15.4	(0.7)	3.5	(0.4)
	Spain	7.4	(0.7)	13.7	(0.7)	26.1	(0.7)	29.6	(0.8)	18.2	(0.9)	5.0	(0.5)
	Sweden	3.9	(0.5)	9.4	(0.7)	20.7	(1.0)	29.9	(1.5)	24.8	(1.2)	11.4	(0.7)
	Switzerland	5.4	(0.5)	11.3	(0.7)	22.7	(1.1)	30.9	(1.4)	21.9	(0.9)	7.9	(0.8)
	Turkey	12.5	(1.2)	24.3	(1.5)	30.9	(1.4)	20.8	(1.4)	7.7	(1.1)	3.8	(1.2)
	United States	6.5	(0.7)	12.9	(0.9)	22.7	(1.1)	27.8	(1.0)	20.8	(0.9)	9.3	(0.7)
	OECD total	***8.1***	***(0.3)***	***13.6***	***(0.3)***	***22.9***	***(0.4)***	***27.2***	***(0.4)***	***20.1***	***(0.3)***	***8.1***	***(0.2)***
	OECD average	***6.7***	***(0.1)***	***12.4***	***(0.2)***	***22.8***	***(0.2)***	***28.7***	***(0.2)***	***21.3***	***(0.2)***	***8.3***	***(0.1)***
Partner countries	Brazil	26.9	(1.6)	23.1	(1.2)	25.2	(1.0)	16.5	(1.0)	6.3	(0.7)	1.9	(0.5)
	Hong Kong-China	3.4	(0.7)	8.6	(0.8)	20.0	(1.0)	35.1	(1.2)	27.1	(1.2)	5.7	(0.5)
	Indonesia	26.0	(1.5)	37.2	(1.2)	27.3	(1.1)	8.2	(0.9)	1.2	(0.3)	0.1	(0.1)
	Latvia	5.0	(0.6)	13.0	(1.0)	25.6	(1.2)	30.8	(1.3)	19.5	(1.3)	6.0	(0.7)
	Liechtenstein	2.5	(1.0)	7.9	(1.7)	18.7	(3.2)	30.3	(2.9)	27.6	(2.7)	13.0	(2.5)
	Macao-China	1.0	(0.3)	8.7	(1.3)	27.8	(1.9)	41.4	(1.7)	19.4	(1.6)	1.7	(0.5)
	Russian Federation	12.8	(1.1)	21.3	(1.0)	30.4	(1.0)	24.5	(1.1)	9.3	(0.8)	1.7	(0.3)
	Serbia	17.1	(1.1)	29.6	(1.3)	33.3	(1.1)	16.4	(1.1)	3.5	(0.6)	0.2	(0.1)
	Thailand	13.5	(1.0)	30.5	(1.2)	34.3	(1.0)	17.0	(0.9)	4.1	(0.6)	0.5	(0.1)
	Tunisia	33.7	(1.3)	29.0	(0.9)	23.6	(0.9)	10.9	(0.8)	2.5	(0.4)	0.3	(0.1)
	Uruguay	20.2	(1.0)	19.6	(0.8)	23.9	(0.8)	19.8	(0.9)	11.2	(0.8)	5.3	(0.7)
	United Kingdom[1]	m	m	m	m	m	m	m	m	m	m	m	m

1. Response rate too low to ensure comparability (see Annex A3).

Table 6.2
Mean score and variation in student performance on the reading scale

	All students				Percentiles											
	Mean score		Standard deviation		5th		10th		25th		75th		90th		95th	
	Mean	S.E.	S.D.	S.E.	Score	S.E.	Score	S.E.	Score	S.E.	Score	S.E.	Score	S.E.	Score	S.E.
OECD countries																
Australia	525	(2.1)	97	(1.5)	352	(4.8)	395	(3.6)	464	(3.0)	594	(2.5)	644	(2.7)	673	(3.1)
Austria	491	(3.8)	103	(2.3)	313	(7.5)	354	(6.3)	423	(4.9)	565	(4.2)	617	(3.7)	646	(4.7)
Belgium	507	(2.6)	110	(2.1)	300	(8.4)	355	(6.6)	440	(4.2)	587	(2.1)	635	(2.1)	662	(2.6)
Canada	528	(1.7)	89	(0.9)	373	(3.1)	410	(3.1)	472	(2.3)	590	(2.1)	636	(2.1)	663	(2.5)
Czech Republic	489	(3.5)	96	(2.4)	320	(9.5)	362	(6.9)	428	(4.7)	555	(4.0)	607	(3.8)	636	(4.0)
Denmark	492	(2.8)	88	(1.8)	338	(6.6)	376	(4.6)	438	(4.0)	553	(3.0)	600	(2.7)	627	(3.9)
Finland	543	(1.6)	81	(1.1)	400	(4.8)	437	(3.1)	494	(2.4)	599	(1.7)	641	(2.2)	666	(2.5)
France	496	(2.7)	97	(2.2)	320	(7.7)	367	(7.0)	436	(4.0)	565	(2.8)	614	(2.7)	641	(3.3)
Germany	491	(3.4)	109	(2.3)	295	(6.0)	341	(6.8)	419	(5.6)	572	(3.4)	624	(3.2)	652	(3.9)
Greece	472	(4.1)	105	(2.0)	288	(6.2)	333	(6.2)	406	(5.2)	546	(4.4)	599	(4.4)	631	(5.4)
Hungary	482	(2.5)	92	(1.8)	324	(6.0)	361	(4.2)	422	(3.3)	546	(3.3)	597	(3.4)	625	(5.0)
Iceland	492	(1.6)	98	(1.4)	316	(6.4)	362	(4.8)	431	(2.3)	560	(2.2)	612	(2.8)	640	(3.6)
Ireland	515	(2.6)	87	(1.7)	364	(7.3)	401	(4.6)	460	(3.8)	577	(2.8)	622	(3.0)	647	(3.3)
Italy	476	(3.0)	101	(2.2)	295	(8.6)	341	(6.8)	411	(4.4)	547	(2.5)	598	(2.1)	627	(2.6)
Japan	498	(3.9)	106	(2.5)	310	(7.3)	355	(6.5)	431	(5.4)	574	(3.7)	624	(4.8)	652	(4.7)
Korea	534	(3.1)	83	(2.0)	393	(6.0)	428	(5.2)	484	(4.1)	590	(2.8)	634	(4.1)	660	(5.0)
Luxembourg	479	(1.5)	100	(1.0)	302	(3.8)	344	(2.9)	416	(2.8)	551	(1.9)	601	(2.1)	627	(2.7)
Mexico	400	(4.1)	95	(1.9)	238	(6.1)	274	(5.5)	335	(4.9)	467	(4.3)	521	(6.1)	552	(5.5)
Netherlands	513	(2.9)	85	(2.0)	369	(6.4)	400	(5.2)	454	(4.5)	576	(3.2)	621	(2.9)	645	(4.2)
New Zealand	522	(2.5)	105	(1.5)	338	(6.2)	381	(4.4)	453	(3.5)	596	(2.8)	652	(2.9)	682	(3.4)
Norway	500	(2.8)	102	(1.8)	321	(6.1)	364	(4.7)	434	(3.8)	571	(3.6)	625	(3.9)	656	(3.9)
Poland	497	(2.9)	96	(1.8)	330	(6.3)	374	(5.0)	436	(3.6)	563	(3.1)	616	(3.4)	645	(4.4)
Portugal	478	(3.7)	93	(2.1)	311	(6.6)	351	(7.1)	418	(5.2)	544	(3.5)	592	(3.5)	617	(3.9)
Slovak Republic	469	(3.1)	93	(2.0)	310	(5.7)	348	(5.8)	408	(4.6)	535	(3.2)	587	(3.0)	613	(3.5)
Spain	481	(2.6)	95	(1.5)	313	(5.8)	354	(4.9)	421	(3.4)	548	(2.8)	597	(2.8)	625	(3.1)
Sweden	514	(2.4)	96	(1.9)	349	(6.0)	390	(4.3)	453	(3.4)	582	(2.9)	631	(2.9)	660	(3.6)
Switzerland	499	(3.3)	95	(1.9)	330	(5.8)	373	(5.6)	439	(4.5)	565	(3.7)	615	(3.9)	643	(5.0)
Turkey	441	(5.8)	95	(4.1)	291	(6.1)	324	(5.3)	377	(5.7)	500	(6.6)	562	(11.4)	608	(19.4)
United States	495	(3.2)	101	(1.4)	319	(6.6)	361	(5.2)	429	(4.1)	568	(3.6)	622	(3.5)	651	(4.5)
OECD total	*488*	*(1.2)*	*104*	*(0.7)*	*305*	*(2.2)*	*349*	*(2.2)*	*420*	*(1.8)*	*562*	*(1.2)*	*616*	*(1.2)*	*646*	*(1.3)*
OECD average	*494*	*(0.6)*	*100*	*(0.4)*	*318*	*(1.4)*	*361*	*(1.3)*	*430*	*(1.0)*	*565*	*(0.6)*	*617*	*(0.6)*	*646*	*(0.7)*
Partner countries																
Brazil	403	(4.6)	111	(2.3)	214	(7.3)	256	(7.5)	328	(5.5)	479	(5.1)	542	(5.2)	581	(6.9)
Hong Kong-China	510	(3.7)	85	(2.7)	355	(9.9)	397	(6.7)	461	(5.1)	569	(2.8)	608	(2.9)	630	(3.0)
Indonesia	382	(3.4)	76	(1.8)	254	(5.3)	282	(4.9)	332	(3.7)	433	(4.0)	478	(4.6)	506	(6.1)
Latvia	491	(3.7)	90	(1.7)	335	(6.4)	372	(5.3)	431	(4.9)	554	(3.5)	603	(4.6)	632	(4.6)
Liechtenstein	525	(3.6)	90	(3.4)	365	(15.0)	405	(11.7)	467	(9.1)	588	(5.7)	636	(11.8)	661	(14.3)
Macao-China	498	(2.2)	67	(1.9)	381	(6.2)	409	(5.1)	455	(3.5)	544	(4.4)	583	(3.7)	601	(4.3)
Russian Federation	442	(3.9)	93	(1.8)	281	(6.9)	319	(6.1)	381	(5.4)	506	(3.9)	558	(4.4)	588	(4.7)
Serbia	412	(3.6)	81	(1.6)	274	(5.0)	306	(4.6)	358	(4.0)	467	(4.0)	516	(4.8)	542	(5.9)
Thailand	420	(2.8)	78	(1.5)	293	(4.9)	322	(3.4)	366	(3.1)	472	(3.6)	520	(4.5)	550	(5.3)
Tunisia	375	(2.8)	96	(1.8)	216	(4.7)	251	(3.8)	310	(3.2)	441	(3.5)	497	(4.3)	530	(5.5)
Uruguay	434	(3.4)	121	(2.0)	224	(5.8)	272	(6.0)	355	(4.4)	518	(4.4)	587	(4.5)	628	(6.1)
United Kingdom[1]	m	m	m	m	m	m	m	m	m	m	m	m	m	m	m	m

1. Response rate too low to ensure comparability (see Annex A3).

Table 6.3
Mean score on the reading scale, by gender

		Males				Females							
		Mean score		Standard deviation		Mean score		Standard deviation		Difference (M – F)		Effect size	
		Mean	**S.E.**	**S.D.**	**S.E.**	**Mean**	**S.E.**	**S.D..**	**S.E.**	**Score dif.**	**S.E.**	**Effect size**	**S.E.**
OECD countries	Australia	506	(2.8)	100	(1.7)	545	(2.6)	90	(2.0)	**–39**	(3.6)	**–0.41**	(0.04)
	Austria	467	(4.5)	105	(2.7)	514	(4.2)	95	(2.5)	**–47**	(5.2)	**–0.47**	(0.05)
	Belgium	489	(3.8)	114	(2.9)	526	(3.3)	103	(2.5)	**–37**	(5.1)	**–0.34**	(0.05)
	Canada	514	(2.0)	93	(1.2)	546	(1.8)	83	(1.1)	**–32**	(2.0)	**–0.36**	(0.02)
	Czech Republic	473	(4.1)	95	(2.8)	504	(4.4)	93	(3.4)	**–31**	(4.9)	**–0.33**	(0.06)
	Denmark	479	(3.3)	90	(2.2)	505	(3.0)	85	(2.3)	**–25**	(2.9)	**–0.29**	(0.03)
	Finland	521	(2.2)	82	(1.6)	565	(2.0)	73	(1.5)	**–44**	(2.7)	**–0.56**	(0.03)
	France	476	(3.8)	100	(2.8)	514	(3.2)	90	(2.1)	**–38**	(4.5)	**–0.40**	(0.04)
	Germany	471	(4.2)	111	(3.0)	513	(3.9)	102	(2.3)	**–42**	(4.6)	**–0.39**	(0.04)
	Greece	453	(5.1)	110	(2.6)	490	(4.0)	96	(2.4)	**–37**	(4.1)	**–0.36**	(0.04)
	Hungary	467	(3.2)	93	(2.0)	498	(3.0)	88	(2.5)	**–31**	(3.8)	**–0.34**	(0.04)
	Iceland	464	(2.3)	100	(2.0)	522	(2.2)	87	(1.9)	**–58**	(3.5)	**–0.62**	(0.04)
	Ireland	501	(3.3)	87	(2.2)	530	(3.7)	83	(2.1)	**–29**	(4.6)	**–0.34**	(0.05)
	Italy	455	(5.1)	105	(3.0)	495	(3.4)	92	(1.8)	**–39**	(6.0)	**–0.40**	(0.06)
	Japan	487	(5.5)	111	(3.5)	509	(4.1)	99	(2.8)	**–22**	(5.4)	**–0.21**	(0.05)
	Korea	525	(3.7)	83	(2.3)	547	(4.3)	80	(3.0)	**–21**	(5.6)	**–0.26**	(0.07)
	Luxembourg	463	(2.6)	103	(1.7)	496	(1.8)	93	(1.5)	**–33**	(3.4)	**–0.34**	(0.03)
	Mexico	389	(4.6)	96	(2.3)	410	(4.6)	93	(2.7)	**–21**	(4.4)	**–0.23**	(0.05)
	Netherlands	503	(3.7)	86	(2.3)	524	(3.2)	83	(2.4)	**–21**	(3.9)	**–0.25**	(0.05)
	New Zealand	508	(3.1)	107	(1.8)	535	(3.3)	100	(2.2)	**–28**	(4.4)	**–0.27**	(0.04)
	Norway	475	(3.4)	105	(2.5)	525	(3.4)	93	(2.1)	**–49**	(3.7)	**–0.49**	(0.04)
	Poland	477	(3.6)	100	(2.2)	516	(3.2)	88	(1.9)	**–40**	(3.7)	**–0.42**	(0.04)
	Portugal	459	(4.3)	97	(2.3)	495	(3.7)	85	(2.3)	**–36**	(3.3)	**–0.40**	(0.04)
	Slovak Republic	453	(3.8)	93	(2.1)	486	(3.3)	89	(2.6)	**–33**	(3.5)	**–0.36**	(0.04)
	Spain	461	(3.8)	99	(1.8)	500	(2.5)	88	(1.9)	**–39**	(3.9)	**–0.42**	(0.04)
	Sweden	496	(2.8)	96	(2.4)	533	(2.9)	91	(2.1)	**–37**	(3.2)	**–0.39**	(0.03)
	Switzerland	482	(4.4)	96	(2.7)	517	(3.1)	90	(1.9)	**–35**	(4.7)	**–0.38**	(0.05)
	Turkey	426	(6.8)	99	(4.6)	459	(6.1)	87	(4.2)	**–33**	(5.8)	**–0.36**	(0.07)
	United States	479	(3.7)	104	(2.1)	511	(3.5)	96	(1.8)	**–32**	(3.3)	**–0.32**	(0.03)
	OECD total	*472*	*(1.4)*	*106*	*(0.9)*	*503*	*(1.3)*	*99*	*(0.8)*	*–31*	*(1.4)*	*–0.30*	*(0.01)*
	OECD average	*477*	*(0.7)*	*103*	*(0.5)*	*511*	*(0.7)*	*95*	*(0.4)*	*–34*	*(0.8)*	*–0.35*	*(0.01)*
Partner countries	Brazil	384	(5.8)	116	(2.9)	419	(4.1)	105	(2.9)	**–35**	(3.9)	**–0.31**	(0.04)
	Hong Kong-China	494	(5.3)	91	(3.4)	525	(3.5)	75	(2.4)	**–32**	(5.5)	**–0.38**	(0.06)
	Indonesia	369	(3.4)	75	(1.9)	394	(3.9)	75	(2.0)	**–24**	(2.8)	**–0.32**	(0.03)
	Latvia	470	(4.5)	93	(2.6)	509	(3.7)	83	(1.8)	**–39**	(4.2)	**–0.44**	(0.05)
	Liechtenstein	517	(7.2)	93	(4.9)	534	(6.5)	85	(4.9)	–17	(11.9)	–0.20	(0.13)
	Macao-China	491	(3.6)	69	(2.6)	504	(2.8)	64	(2.2)	–13	(4.8)	–0.20	(0.07)
	Russian Federation	428	(4.7)	98	(2.3)	456	(3.7)	86	(1.8)	**–29**	(3.9)	**–0.31**	(0.04)
	Serbia	390	(3.7)	83	(2.0)	433	(3.9)	74	(1.9)	**–43**	(3.9)	**–0.55**	(0.05)
	Thailand	396	(3.7)	78	(2.2)	439	(3.0)	72	(1.8)	**–43**	(4.1)	**–0.57**	(0.06)
	Tunisia	362	(3.3)	95	(2.2)	387	(3.3)	95	(2.1)	**–25**	(3.6)	**–0.27**	(0.04)
	Uruguay	414	(4.5)	125	(2.7)	453	(3.7)	114	(2.4)	**–39**	(4.7)	**–0.33**	(0.04)
	United Kingdom[1]	m	m	m	m	m	m	m	m	m	m	m	m

Note: Values that are statistically significant and effect sizes equal or greater than 0.2 are indicated in bold (see Annex A4).
1. Response rate too low to ensure comparability (see Annex A3).

Table 6.4
Percentage of students scoring below 400 points and above 600 points on the reading scale

	Percentage of students scoring below 400 points on the reading scale						Increased likelihood for males to score below 400 points on the reading scale		Percentage of students scoring above 600 points on the reading scale						Increased likelihood for females to score above 600 points on the reading scale	
	All students		Males		Females				All students		Males		Females			
	%	S.E.	%	S.E.	%	S.E.	Ratio	S.E.	%	S.E.	%	S.E.	%	S.E.	Ratio	S.E.
OECD countries																
Australia	10.8	(0.6)	15.2	(0.7)	6.2	(0.7)	**2.4**	(0.28)	22.6	(0.8)	17.3	(1.0)	28.1	(1.1)	**1.6**	(0.11)
Austria	19.0	(1.2)	26.3	(1.7)	11.7	(1.1)	**2.2**	(0.23)	14.3	(1.0)	9.9	(0.9)	18.7	(1.5)	**1.9**	(0.21)
Belgium	16.5	(0.9)	20.9	(1.4)	11.7	(1.0)	**1.8**	(0.20)	20.4	(0.7)	16.3	(0.9)	24.8	(1.1)	**1.5**	(0.11)
Canada	8.4	(0.5)	12.0	(0.6)	4.7	(0.4)	**2.5**	(0.23)	21.0	(0.8)	17.5	(0.8)	26.4	(1.0)	**1.5**	(0.08)
Czech Republic	17.5	(1.4)	21.4	(1.7)	13.6	(1.7)	**1.6**	(0.21)	11.5	(0.8)	8.4	(0.8)	14.7	(1.2)	**1.7**	(0.18)
Denmark	14.7	(0.9)	18.5	(1.3)	11.0	(1.1)	**1.7**	(0.20)	10.1	(0.7)	7.6	(0.9)	12.5	(0.9)	**1.7**	(0.21)
Finland	5.0	(0.4)	7.9	(0.7)	2.2	(0.3)	**3.7**	(0.65)	24.4	(0.8)	16.1	(1.1)	32.5	(1.2)	**2.0**	(0.16)
France	16.0	(1.0)	21.8	(1.7)	10.8	(1.0)	**2.0**	(0.21)	13.4	(0.8)	9.3	(0.9)	17.2	(1.1)	**1.8**	(0.21)
Germany	20.7	(1.2)	26.2	(1.5)	14.9	(1.3)	**1.8**	(0.15)	16.0	(0.9)	12.0	(1.0)	20.2	(1.4)	**1.7**	(0.17)
Greece	23.2	(1.3)	30.5	(1.8)	16.4	(1.2)	**1.9**	(0.13)	9.9	(0.9)	8.0	(1.0)	11.7	(1.0)	**1.5**	(0.16)
Hungary	18.6	(1.0)	23.5	(1.3)	13.2	(1.2)	**1.8**	(0.17)	9.3	(0.8)	6.9	(0.9)	11.9	(1.0)	**1.7**	(0.23)
Iceland	16.9	(0.7)	24.8	(1.0)	8.4	(0.9)	**3.0**	(0.35)	12.5	(0.8)	7.3	(1.0)	18.2	(1.2)	**2.5**	(0.41)
Ireland	9.7	(0.8)	12.8	(1.2)	6.7	(0.9)	**1.9**	(0.29)	16.4	(1.0)	12.0	(1.1)	20.8	(1.7)	**1.7**	(0.21)
Italy	21.8	(1.2)	28.7	(2.2)	15.4	(1.2)	**1.9**	(0.20)	9.6	(0.4)	7.1	(0.6)	11.9	(0.7)	**1.7**	(0.17)
Japan	17.5	(1.3)	21.5	(1.7)	13.7	(1.5)	**1.6**	(0.17)	16.3	(1.1)	14.7	(1.8)	17.8	(1.0)	1.2	(0.15)
Korea	5.8	(0.7)	7.3	(0.9)	3.6	(0.7)	**2.0**	(0.47)	20.7	(1.3)	17.8	(1.4)	25.0	(2.0)	**1.4**	(0.15)
Luxembourg	20.8	(0.8)	26.4	(1.4)	15.5	(0.8)	**1.7**	(0.14)	10.2	(0.5)	8.0	(0.8)	12.3	(0.7)	**1.5**	(0.19)
Mexico	49.0	(1.8)	54.0	(2.2)	44.3	(2.0)	**1.2**	(0.06)	1.2	(0.2)	0.9	(0.3)	1.4	(0.3)	1.5	(0.49)
Netherlands	9.9	(1.1)	12.4	(1.4)	7.4	(1.1)	**1.7**	(0.27)	16.3	(1.0)	13.5	(1.2)	19.2	(1.4)	**1.4**	(0.15)
New Zealand	13.1	(0.8)	16.4	(1.1)	9.9	(1.2)	**1.7**	(0.24)	23.6	(0.9)	19.9	(1.1)	27.4	(1.5)	**1.4**	(0.10)
Norway	16.6	(0.9)	23.3	(1.2)	9.9	(1.0)	**2.4**	(0.24)	16.0	(0.9)	10.7	(0.9)	21.4	(1.3)	**2.0**	(0.17)
Poland	15.0	(1.0)	21.2	(1.5)	8.8	(1.0)	**2.4**	(0.29)	13.7	(0.7)	10.1	(0.7)	17.4	(1.0)	**1.7**	(0.14)
Portugal	19.9	(1.5)	27.4	(2.1)	13.2	(1.3)	**2.1**	(0.18)	8.1	(0.8)	6.1	(0.9)	9.8	(1.2)	**1.6**	(0.31)
Slovak Republic	22.4	(1.4)	28.2	(1.8)	16.3	(1.4)	**1.7**	(0.13)	7.2	(0.5)	4.9	(0.6)	9.6	(0.9)	**2.0**	(0.29)
Spain	19.1	(0.9)	25.7	(1.5)	12.7	(0.7)	**2.0**	(0.17)	9.4	(0.6)	6.8	(0.8)	11.8	(0.9)	**1.8**	(0.25)
Sweden	11.9	(0.8)	15.9	(1.1)	7.8	(0.7)	**2.0**	(0.18)	18.6	(0.9)	13.4	(1.1)	23.8	(1.3)	**1.8**	(0.16)
Switzerland	15.1	(1.1)	19.5	(1.6)	10.5	(0.9)	**1.9**	(0.19)	13.9	(1.1)	10.3	(1.4)	17.8	(1.4)	**1.7**	(0.26)
Turkey	33.7	(2.3)	41.2	(2.9)	24.6	(2.3)	**1.7**	(0.15)	5.5	(1.4)	5.0	(1.5)	6.2	(1.5)	1.2	(0.26)
United States	17.5	(1.0)	22.3	(1.2)	12.7	(1.1)	**1.7**	(0.14)	15.0	(0.9)	11.8	(1.2)	18.3	(1.2)	**1.5**	(0.18)
OECD total	*19.9*	*(0.4)*	*24.7*	*(0.6)*	*15.1*	*(0.4)*	*1.6*	*(0.05)*	*13.7*	*(0.3)*	*10.8*	*(0.3)*	*16.5*	*(0.4)*	*1.5*	*(0.05)*
OECD average	*17.3*	*(0.2)*	*22.3*	*(0.3)*	*12.3*	*(0.2)*	*1.8*	*(0.03)*	*14.1*	*(0.2)*	*10.8*	*(0.2)*	*17.5*	*(0.2)*	*1.6*	*(0.03)*
Partner countries																
Brazil	47.1	(1.7)	54.1	(2.2)	41.0	(1.7)	**1.3**	(0.05)	2.1	(0.5)	3.0	(0.8)	1.3	(0.4)	1.3	(0.37)
Hong Kong-China	10.6	(1.2)	15.3	(1.9)	5.9	(0.9)	**2.6**	(0.44)	12.4	(0.9)	9.7	(1.2)	15.1	(1.3)	**1.6**	(0.25)
Indonesia	59.6	(1.8)	66.0	(1.8)	53.3	(2.3)	**1.2**	(0.05)	0.2	(0.1)	0.1	(0.1)	0.3	(0.2)	3.4	(3.46)
Latvia	16.0	(1.2)	22.4	(1.8)	10.1	(1.0)	**2.2**	(0.24)	10.7	(0.9)	7.6	(1.0)	13.6	(1.2)	**1.8**	(0.23)
Liechtenstein	9.2	(1.6)	11.5	(2.8)	6.7	(2.0)	1.7	(0.80)	20.9	(1.9)	18.5	(3.0)	23.5	(3.1)	1.3	(0.31)
Macao-China	8.2	(1.2)	10.6	(1.6)	6.0	(1.6)	1.8	(0.56)	5.2	(1.0)	4.9	(1.4)	5.6	(1.5)	1.2	(0.52)
Russian Federation	31.3	(1.8)	38.2	(2.2)	24.5	(1.7)	**1.6**	(0.09)	3.7	(0.5)	3.1	(0.6)	4.3	(0.7)	1.4	(0.37)
Serbia	43.2	(1.9)	54.9	(2.2)	31.8	(2.1)	**1.7**	(0.11)	0.7	(0.2)	0.4	(0.2)	1.0	(0.3)	2.2	(1.05)
Thailand	40.4	(1.5)	53.9	(2.2)	29.2	(1.5)	**1.8**	(0.10)	1.3	(0.3)	0.7	(0.2)	1.7	(0.6)	2.5	(1.30)
Tunisia	59.6	(1.3)	65.3	(1.4)	54.1	(1.5)	**1.2**	(0.03)	0.7	(0.2)	0.6	(0.2)	0.7	(0.3)	1.2	(0.53)
Uruguay	37.4	(1.2)	43.9	(1.7)	31.2	(1.4)	**1.4**	(0.07)	8.2	(0.7)	6.3	(0.8)	9.9	(0.9)	**1.6**	(0.21)
United Kingdom[1]	m	m	m	m	m	m	m	m	m	m	m	m	m	m	m	m

Note: Values that are statistically significant are indicated in bold (see Annex A4).
1. Response rate too low to ensure comparability (see Annex A3).

Table 6.5
Percentage of students at each level of proficiency on the reading scale, by gender

Males – Proficiency levels

		Below Level 1 (below 335 score points)		Level 1 (from 335 to 407 score points)		Level 2 (from 408 to 480 score points)		Level 3 (from 481 to 552 score points)		Level 4 (from 553 to 625 score points)		Level 5 (above 625 score points)	
		%	S.E.	%	S.E.	%	S.E.	%	S.E.	%	S.E.	%	S.E.
OECD countries	Australia	5.5	(0.6)	11.0	(0.7)	21.2	(0.9)	28.1	(0.9)	23.4	(0.8)	10.7	(0.8)
	Austria	11.2	(1.2)	17.0	(1.4)	24.0	(1.4)	25.4	(1.4)	17.0	(1.1)	5.3	(0.7)
	Belgium	10.5	(1.0)	11.9	(0.9)	20.1	(1.0)	25.2	(1.1)	23.0	(0.9)	9.4	(0.7)
	Canada	3.6	(0.3)	9.8	(0.6)	20.3	(0.6)	30.5	(0.9)	25.6	(1.0)	10.3	(0.7)
	Czech Republic	8.1	(1.2)	15.4	(1.2)	27.6	(1.3)	28.5	(1.3)	15.9	(1.1)	4.6	(0.7)
	Denmark	6.1	(0.8)	14.4	(1.0)	26.9	(1.2)	32.0	(1.6)	16.9	(1.3)	3.8	(0.5)
	Finland	1.8	(0.3)	7.2	(0.7)	19.7	(0.9)	34.0	(1.2)	28.5	(1.4)	8.8	(0.8)
	France	9.3	(1.3)	14.2	(1.1)	24.6	(1.3)	28.4	(1.5)	18.8	(1.0)	4.6	(0.7)
	Germany	12.5	(1.2)	15.5	(1.1)	22.1	(1.2)	25.2	(1.1)	17.7	(1.3)	7.0	(0.9)
	Greece	14.8	(1.3)	17.8	(1.1)	24.5	(1.6)	24.4	(1.6)	14.1	(1.4)	4.5	(0.7)
	Hungary	8.2	(0.9)	17.4	(1.4)	28.2	(1.4)	27.9	(1.2)	14.9	(1.1)	3.4	(0.7)
	Iceland	10.7	(1.1)	16.2	(1.4)	26.8	(1.3)	27.7	(1.3)	14.9	(0.9)	3.7	(0.7)
	Ireland	3.6	(0.7)	10.7	(1.1)	24.1	(1.4)	32.4	(1.7)	22.9	(1.6)	6.3	(0.8)
	Italy	13.4	(1.7)	17.6	(1.3)	25.7	(1.2)	24.9	(1.5)	14.7	(1.2)	3.7	(0.4)
	Japan	9.9	(1.1)	13.3	(1.1)	20.6	(1.5)	26.7	(1.4)	20.4	(1.3)	9.0	(1.5)
	Korea	1.7	(0.4)	6.6	(0.8)	18.5	(1.4)	33.7	(1.3)	29.6	(1.4)	9.8	(1.0)
	Luxembourg	12.1	(0.8)	16.5	(1.2)	25.4	(1.3)	25.8	(1.5)	16.4	(1.1)	3.9	(0.5)
	Mexico	29.2	(1.9)	27.7	(1.7)	25.3	(1.5)	13.7	(1.1)	3.6	(0.6)	0.4	(0.2)
	Netherlands	2.7	(0.7)	11.6	(1.3)	25.3	(1.4)	30.0	(1.6)	23.6	(1.6)	6.9	(0.8)
	New Zealand	6.4	(0.6)	11.5	(0.8)	20.3	(1.1)	26.1	(1.3)	22.1	(1.1)	13.6	(0.8)
	Norway	9.9	(1.0)	14.9	(1.0)	24.0	(1.4)	27.8	(1.4)	17.1	(1.3)	6.2	(0.7)
	Poland	8.4	(0.9)	15.0	(1.1)	25.8	(1.1)	28.0	(1.4)	17.0	(1.3)	5.7	(0.6)
	Portugal	11.5	(1.3)	17.9	(1.5)	26.8	(1.4)	26.1	(1.5)	14.7	(1.1)	2.9	(0.5)
	Slovak Republic	10.6	(1.0)	20.4	(1.2)	29.2	(1.3)	25.2	(1.3)	12.5	(1.1)	2.1	(0.3)
	Spain	10.9	(1.0)	17.0	(1.0)	27.7	(1.1)	26.8	(1.2)	14.0	(1.1)	3.6	(0.6)
	Sweden	5.3	(0.9)	12.4	(0.9)	23.4	(1.2)	29.9	(1.8)	21.1	(1.2)	7.8	(0.7)
	Switzerland	7.5	(0.8)	13.7	(1.1)	25.1	(1.9)	30.4	(2.6)	17.8	(1.8)	5.5	(1.0)
	Turkey	17.1	(1.8)	27.0	(2.0)	28.6	(1.5)	17.4	(1.8)	6.5	(1.1)	3.5	(1.2)
	United States	8.8	(0.8)	15.5	(0.9)	24.0	(1.1)	26.4	(1.2)	18.1	(1.0)	7.1	(0.8)
	OECD total	*10.7*	*(0.4)*	*15.9*	*(0.4)*	*23.8*	*(0.4)*	*25.9*	*(0.4)*	*17.4*	*(0.4)*	*6.3*	*(0.3)*
	OECD average	*9.2*	*(0.2)*	*15.0*	*(0.2)*	*24.3*	*(0.3)*	*27.3*	*(0.3)*	*18.1*	*(0.2)*	*6.1*	*(0.2)*
Partner countries	Brazil	33.1	(2.0)	23.8	(1.6)	22.3	(1.5)	14.0	(1.4)	5.0	(0.8)	1.7	(0.5)
	Hong Kong-China	5.7	(1.2)	11.4	(1.2)	21.6	(1.3)	33.6	(1.6)	23.7	(1.6)	4.0	(0.7)
	Indonesia	30.9	(1.8)	38.5	(1.5)	23.9	(1.5)	6.0	(0.7)	0.7	(0.2)	0.0	c
	Latvia	7.9	(1.3)	17.1	(1.6)	27.7	(1.4)	27.9	(1.5)	15.2	(1.6)	4.1	(0.9)
	Liechtenstein	3.6	(1.6)	9.0	(3.0)	19.2	(4.4)	30.2	(4.6)	26.6	(4.0)	11.3	(3.7)
	Macao-China	1.4	(0.5)	10.8	(1.9)	29.9	(3.2)	39.0	(2.8)	17.1	(2.1)	1.8	(0.9)
	Russian Federation	17.3	(1.5)	23.4	(1.1)	28.6	(1.4)	21.3	(1.3)	8.0	(0.9)	1.4	(0.3)
	Serbia	25.0	(1.6)	33.2	(1.7)	28.0	(1.4)	11.3	(1.3)	2.3	(0.6)	0.2	(0.1)
	Thailand	21.3	(1.7)	35.9	(1.6)	28.5	(1.3)	11.3	(1.1)	2.8	(0.6)	0.2	(0.1)
	Tunisia	38.8	(1.7)	29.4	(1.3)	21.3	(1.2)	8.4	(0.8)	2.0	(0.6)	0.2	(0.1)
	Uruguay	25.9	(1.6)	20.4	(1.4)	23.0	(1.4)	17.2	(1.0)	9.4	(1.4)	4.1	(0.8)
	United Kingdom[1]	m	m	m	m	m	m	m	m	m	m	m	m

Females – Proficiency levels

		Below Level 1 (below 335 score points)		Level 1 (from 335 to 407 score points)		Level 2 (from 408 to 480 score points)		Level 3 (from 481 to 552 score points)		Level 4 (from 553 to 625 score points)		Level 5 (above 625 score points)	
		%	S.E.	%	S.E.	%	S.E.	%	S.E.	%	S.E.	%	S.E.
OECD countries	Australia	1.7	(0.3)	5.4	(0.6)	15.2	(0.8)	28.6	(1.1)	30.5	(1.2)	18.6	(1.1)
	Austria	3.4	(0.6)	9.7	(1.1)	21.1	(1.3)	29.4	(1.5)	25.0	(1.7)	11.3	(1.3)
	Belgium	4.9	(0.7)	8.0	(0.6)	16.1	(0.9)	26.8	(1.2)	28.1	(1.1)	16.0	(0.8)
	Canada	1.1	(0.2)	4.5	(0.4)	14.9	(0.8)	31.0	(0.9)	32.3	(0.9)	16.2	(0.7)
	Czech Republic	4.7	(1.2)	10.2	(1.1)	21.7	(1.3)	32.1	(2.3)	22.9	(1.7)	8.3	(0.8)
	Denmark	3.2	(0.7)	9.5	(0.8)	23.1	(1.5)	34.8	(1.3)	23.0	(1.1)	6.5	(0.8)
	Finland	0.3	(0.1)	2.1	(0.4)	9.5	(1.0)	29.3	(1.4)	38.3	(1.4)	20.5	(1.3)
	France	3.6	(0.6)	8.5	(0.8)	21.2	(1.2)	30.9	(1.3)	25.9	(1.4)	9.9	(0.8)
	Germany	5.9	(0.7)	10.4	(1.1)	17.6	(1.1)	27.5	(1.1)	26.3	(1.3)	12.3	(1.0)
	Greece	6.0	(0.7)	12.5	(1.0)	25.4	(1.5)	29.9	(1.4)	19.4	(1.4)	6.8	(0.9)
	Hungary	3.7	(0.7)	11.2	(1.4)	25.0	(1.6)	32.8	(1.6)	20.7	(1.6)	6.5	(0.8)
	Iceland	2.4	(0.4)	7.1	(0.8)	20.7	(1.3)	31.8	(1.4)	27.3	(1.4)	10.7	(0.9)
	Ireland	1.8	(0.5)	5.9	(0.7)	18.2	(1.4)	32.3	(1.6)	29.5	(1.6)	12.3	(1.1)
	Italy	5.0	(0.7)	12.2	(1.0)	24.1	(1.0)	31.4	(1.1)	20.7	(1.0)	6.5	(0.5)
	Japan	5.1	(0.8)	10.0	(1.0)	21.1	(1.5)	27.7	(1.7)	25.8	(1.3)	10.3	(0.9)
	Korea	0.8	(0.3)	3.6	(0.7)	14.4	(1.3)	33.0	(1.7)	32.5	(1.7)	15.6	(1.8)
	Luxembourg	5.5	(0.6)	11.7	(0.9)	23.1	(1.5)	31.4	(1.1)	21.8	(1.3)	6.5	(0.6)
	Mexico	20.8	(1.6)	26.6	(1.4)	29.7	(1.4)	17.4	(1.2)	5.0	(0.8)	0.6	(0.2)
	Netherlands	1.5	(0.6)	7.1	(1.0)	21.4	(1.5)	31.4	(1.8)	27.8	(1.5)	10.8	(1.0)
	New Zealand	3.2	(0.6)	7.9	(1.1)	16.8	(1.5)	26.5	(1.3)	26.6	(1.4)	19.0	(1.4)
	Norway	2.7	(0.5)	8.6	(0.9)	18.7	(1.4)	30.3	(1.2)	25.9	(1.2)	13.7	(1.0)
	Poland	2.3	(0.4)	7.9	(0.8)	23.1	(1.2)	32.0	(1.1)	24.4	(1.3)	10.3	(0.9)
	Portugal	4.0	(0.8)	11.1	(1.1)	25.1	(1.2)	34.4	(1.3)	20.8	(1.3)	4.6	(0.9)
	Slovak Republic	5.3	(0.8)	13.2	(1.2)	27.5	(1.5)	30.4	(1.7)	18.5	(1.0)	5.0	(0.5)
	Spain	4.0	(0.6)	10.5	(0.9)	24.5	(0.9)	32.3	(1.1)	22.3	(1.0)	6.3	(0.6)
	Sweden	2.4	(0.5)	6.3	(0.7)	17.9	(1.2)	29.9	(2.0)	28.4	(1.8)	15.0	(1.0)
	Switzerland	3.1	(0.5)	8.7	(0.9)	20.1	(1.1)	31.4	(1.2)	26.3	(1.3)	10.4	(1.0)
	Turkey	6.8	(1.1)	21.0	(2.1)	33.7	(2.2)	25.1	(1.9)	9.2	(1.7)	4.2	(1.3)
	United States	4.1	(0.7)	10.3	(1.2)	21.3	(1.3)	29.3	(1.5)	23.6	(1.2)	11.4	(0.9)
	OECD total	*5.5*	*(0.3)*	*11.3*	*(0.4)*	*22.0*	*(0.5)*	*28.5*	*(0.5)*	*22.8*	*(0.5)*	*10.0*	*(0.3)*
	OECD average	*4.1*	*(0.1)*	*9.7*	*(0.2)*	*21.2*	*(0.2)*	*30.0*	*(0.2)*	*24.4*	*(0.3)*	*10.6*	*(0.2)*
Partner countries	Brazil	21.5	(1.7)	22.5	(1.7)	27.8	(1.3)	18.7	(1.1)	7.5	(0.8)	2.1	(0.6)
	Hong Kong-China	1.2	(0.3)	5.8	(0.8)	18.4	(1.4)	36.6	(1.8)	30.6	(1.6)	7.4	(0.8)
	Indonesia	21.3	(1.6)	36.0	(1.7)	30.7	(1.6)	10.4	(1.2)	1.6	(0.5)	0.1	c
	Latvia	2.4	(0.5)	9.2	(0.9)	23.7	(1.6)	33.5	(1.9)	23.5	(1.6)	7.7	(0.9)
	Liechtenstein	1.3	(1.1)	6.7	(2.4)	18.1	(4.2)	30.4	(4.6)	28.7	(3.9)	14.7	(2.9)
	Macao-China	0.7	(0.3)	6.7	(1.4)	25.9	(2.6)	43.7	(2.9)	21.6	(2.4)	1.6	(0.7)
	Russian Federation	8.3	(1.0)	19.1	(1.1)	32.1	(1.3)	27.7	(1.3)	10.7	(0.9)	2.1	(0.4)
	Serbia	9.4	(1.2)	26.0	(1.8)	38.3	(1.4)	21.3	(1.5)	4.6	(1.0)	0.3	(0.2)
	Thailand	7.2	(0.9)	26.0	(1.4)	39.1	(1.5)	21.8	(1.2)	5.3	(0.8)	0.7	(0.3)
	Tunisia	28.8	(1.4)	28.6	(1.2)	25.9	(1.1)	13.4	(1.1)	3.0	(0.5)	0.3	(0.2)
	Uruguay	14.8	(1.2)	18.8	(1.2)	24.8	(1.4)	22.2	(1.3)	13.0	(1.1)	6.3	(0.9)
	United Kingdom[1]	m	m	m	m	m	m	m	m	m	m	m	m

1. Response rate too low to ensure comparability (see Annex A3).

Table 6.6
Mean score and variation in student performance on the science scale

		All students				Percentiles											
		Mean score		Standard deviation		5th		10th		25th		75th		90th		95th	
		Mean	S.E.	S.D.	S.E.	Score	S.E.	Score	S.E.	Score	S.E.	Score	S.E.	Score	S.E.	Score	S.E.
OECD countries	Australia	525	(2.1)	102	(1.5)	351	(4.2)	391	(3.4)	457	(3.1)	596	(2.7)	652	(2.9)	686	(3.7)
	Austria	491	(3.4)	97	(1.5)	327	(6.6)	363	(4.1)	423	(4.1)	561	(4.0)	615	(4.1)	644	(4.4)
	Belgium	509	(2.5)	107	(1.8)	320	(6.1)	364	(5.0)	436	(3.8)	588	(2.4)	640	(2.5)	668	(2.6)
	Canada	519	(2.0)	99	(1.0)	352	(3.9)	389	(3.3)	452	(2.7)	588	(2.4)	644	(3.0)	676	(2.9)
	Czech Republic	523	(3.4)	101	(1.7)	356	(5.8)	391	(4.3)	453	(4.2)	594	(3.9)	652	(4.7)	686	(4.5)
	Denmark	475	(3.0)	102	(1.7)	306	(6.4)	343	(4.7)	407	(3.9)	547	(3.6)	605	(3.4)	638	(4.4)
	Finland	548	(1.9)	91	(1.1)	393	(3.5)	429	(2.6)	488	(2.8)	611	(2.2)	662	(2.9)	691	(3.5)
	France	511	(3.0)	111	(2.2)	321	(6.7)	363	(5.5)	435	(4.4)	591	(3.4)	651	(3.2)	682	(4.5)
	Germany	502	(3.6)	111	(2.1)	307	(7.1)	351	(5.6)	427	(5.8)	584	(4.0)	640	(3.6)	672	(3.5)
	Greece	481	(3.8)	101	(1.6)	315	(5.8)	349	(5.0)	412	(4.5)	552	(4.0)	610	(4.6)	643	(4.9)
	Hungary	503	(2.8)	97	(2.0)	340	(5.9)	375	(4.1)	437	(3.1)	572	(3.9)	628	(5.5)	658	(4.6)
	Iceland	495	(1.5)	96	(1.4)	331	(5.9)	369	(4.0)	432	(2.8)	562	(2.7)	616	(3.6)	647	(3.6)
	Ireland	505	(2.7)	93	(1.3)	348	(6.1)	384	(4.8)	442	(3.7)	572	(3.0)	625	(3.3)	652	(3.4)
	Italy	486	(3.1)	108	(2.0)	303	(7.3)	344	(6.3)	415	(4.9)	563	(2.8)	622	(2.7)	656	(3.9)
	Japan	548	(4.1)	109	(2.7)	357	(7.0)	402	(6.0)	475	(6.1)	624	(4.2)	682	(6.0)	715	(7.9)
	Korea	538	(3.5)	101	(2.2)	365	(6.3)	405	(5.0)	473	(4.8)	609	(4.3)	663	(4.7)	695	(5.8)
	Luxembourg	483	(1.5)	103	(1.1)	309	(4.2)	347	(2.6)	413	(2.9)	556	(2.4)	614	(3.1)	645	(2.9)
	Mexico	405	(3.5)	87	(2.2)	264	(5.1)	295	(4.8)	347	(3.5)	462	(4.2)	517	(5.3)	551	(6.8)
	Netherlands	524	(3.1)	99	(2.2)	363	(6.6)	394	(5.6)	451	(5.3)	599	(4.0)	653	(4.1)	682	(4.3)
	New Zealand	521	(2.4)	104	(1.4)	347	(3.9)	382	(4.1)	448	(3.9)	596	(3.3)	653	(3.9)	687	(3.2)
	Norway	484	(2.9)	104	(1.8)	312	(5.3)	349	(4.6)	414	(4.0)	557	(3.8)	616	(4.6)	651	(6.1)
	Poland	498	(2.9)	102	(1.4)	333	(5.3)	367	(3.5)	426	(4.3)	570	(3.5)	630	(4.1)	666	(6.3)
	Portugal	468	(3.5)	93	(1.7)	310	(5.9)	346	(6.2)	405	(5.0)	533	(3.4)	587	(3.7)	618	(4.5)
	Slovak Republic	495	(3.7)	102	(3.1)	331	(7.0)	367	(6.0)	428	(4.6)	566	(3.6)	625	(3.8)	657	(3.9)
	Spain	487	(2.6)	100	(1.5)	318	(5.8)	355	(4.0)	421	(3.4)	557	(3.1)	613	(3.1)	644	(3.8)
	Sweden	506	(2.7)	107	(1.8)	327	(6.5)	368	(4.0)	435	(3.5)	581	(4.0)	642	(4.0)	673	(4.8)
	Switzerland	513	(3.7)	108	(1.9)	328	(5.8)	369	(4.6)	440	(4.5)	588	(4.6)	648	(5.9)	683	(6.8)
	Turkey	434	(5.9)	96	(4.7)	295	(5.0)	321	(4.7)	367	(4.9)	492	(8.4)	560	(12.8)	609	(20.0)
	United States	491	(3.1)	102	(1.3)	322	(5.4)	359	(4.4)	420	(3.8)	564	(3.3)	622	(4.3)	654	(3.5)
	OECD total	*496*	*(1.1)*	*109*	*(0.7)*	*316*	*(1.9)*	*353*	*(1.6)*	*419*	*(1.7)*	*574*	*(1.4)*	*636*	*(1.5)*	*670*	*(1.7)*
	OECD average	*500*	*(0.6)*	*105*	*(0.4)*	*324*	*(1.2)*	*362*	*(1.1)*	*427*	*(1.0)*	*575*	*(0.8)*	*634*	*(0.9)*	*668*	*(1.0)*
Partner countries	Brazil	390	(4.3)	98	(2.6)	235	(7.6)	268	(5.2)	323	(4.8)	452	(5.4)	520	(7.6)	560	(7.9)
	Hong Kong-China	539	(4.3)	94	(2.8)	373	(9.8)	412	(8.6)	478	(6.9)	608	(3.5)	653	(3.9)	680	(4.3)
	Indonesia	395	(3.2)	68	(1.9)	285	(4.5)	310	(4.0)	350	(3.0)	438	(3.8)	483	(5.5)	512	(6.2)
	Latvia	489	(3.9)	93	(1.5)	336	(5.6)	370	(5.0)	425	(4.6)	553	(5.1)	609	(4.9)	642	(5.7)
	Liechtenstein	525	(4.3)	103	(4.4)	351	(17.3)	389	(8.7)	450	(5.7)	598	(9.1)	659	(10.4)	690	(13.5)
	Macao-China	525	(3.0)	88	(3.0)	375	(7.9)	410	(7.7)	465	(5.3)	587	(4.0)	635	(6.2)	663	(9.5)
	Russian Federation	489	(4.1)	100	(1.5)	324	(5.6)	359	(5.4)	422	(4.8)	558	(4.5)	617	(4.0)	652	(5.0)
	Serbia	436	(3.5)	83	(1.6)	305	(4.5)	332	(3.9)	380	(3.9)	492	(4.4)	544	(5.2)	576	(6.4)
	Thailand	429	(2.7)	81	(1.6)	303	(3.6)	329	(3.4)	373	(2.9)	480	(3.5)	537	(4.4)	571	(5.6)
	Tunisia	385	(2.6)	87	(1.8)	244	(4.6)	274	(3.8)	325	(2.7)	444	(3.3)	498	(5.0)	530	(6.2)
	Uruguay	438	(2.9)	109	(1.8)	257	(3.9)	296	(4.4)	363	(4.0)	516	(4.5)	579	(5.0)	613	(5.3)
	United Kingdom[1]	m	m	m	m	m	m	m	m	m	m	m	m	m	m	m	m

1. Response rate too low to ensure comparability (see Annex A3).

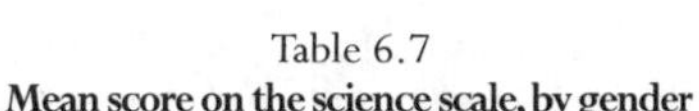

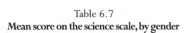

Table 6.7
Mean score on the science scale, by gender

	Males				Females							
	Mean score		Standard deviation		Mean score		Standard deviation		Difference (M – F)		Effect size	
	Mean	S.E.	S.D.	S.E.	Mean	S.E.	S.D..	S.E.	Score dif.	S.E.	Effect size	S.E.
OECD countries												
Australia	525	(2.9)	107	(1.8)	525	(2.8)	97	(1.9)	0	(3.8)	0.00	(0.04)
Austria	490	(4.3)	102	(2.1)	492	(4.2)	92	(1.9)	–3	(5.0)	–0.03	(0.05)
Belgium	509	(3.6)	111	(2.5)	509	(3.5)	103	(2.2)	0	(5.0)	0.00	(0.05)
Canada	527	(2.3)	104	(1.3)	516	(2.2)	95	(1.3)	**11**	(2.6)	0.11	(0.03)
Czech Republic	526	(4.3)	101	(2.0)	520	(4.1)	100	(2.5)	6	(4.9)	0.06	(0.05)
Denmark	484	(3.6)	103	(2.3)	467	(3.2)	100	(2.2)	**17**	(3.2)	0.17	(0.03)
Finland	545	(2.6)	95	(1.5)	551	(2.2)	86	(1.6)	**–6**	(2.8)	–0.07	(0.03)
France	511	(4.1)	115	(2.9)	511	(3.5)	107	(2.4)	0	(4.8)	0.00	(0.04)
Germany	506	(4.5)	114	(3.1)	500	(4.2)	108	(2.4)	6	(4.8)	0.05	(0.04)
Greece	487	(4.8)	105	(2.0)	475	(3.9)	96	(1.9)	**12**	(4.2)	0.12	(0.04)
Hungary	503	(3.3)	101	(2.3)	504	(3.3)	94	(2.3)	–1	(3.7)	–0.01	(0.04)
Iceland	490	(2.4)	100	(1.9)	500	(2.4)	91	(1.8)	**–10**	(3.8)	–0.11	(0.04)
Ireland	506	(3.1)	94	(1.9)	504	(3.9)	92	(1.8)	2	(4.5)	0.02	(0.05)
Italy	490	(5.2)	114	(3.4)	484	(3.6)	101	(1.6)	6	(6.3)	0.05	(0.06)
Japan	550	(6.0)	116	(3.5)	546	(4.1)	103	(3.0)	4	(6.0)	0.04	(0.05)
Korea	546	(4.7)	102	(2.6)	527	(5.5)	98	(2.9)	**18**	(7.0)	0.18	(0.07)
Luxembourg	489	(2.5)	108	(1.7)	477	(1.9)	98	(2.0)	**13**	(3.3)	0.12	(0.03)
Mexico	410	(3.9)	89	(2.3)	400	(4.2)	84	(3.0)	**9**	(4.1)	0.11	(0.05)
Netherlands	527	(4.2)	100	(2.4)	522	(3.6)	97	(2.6)	5	(4.7)	0.05	(0.05)
New Zealand	529	(3.0)	107	(1.8)	513	(3.4)	101	(2.3)	**16**	(4.2)	0.15	(0.04)
Norway	485	(3.5)	108	(2.4)	483	(3.3)	99	(2.1)	2	(3.6)	0.02	(0.03)
Poland	501	(3.2)	106	(1.8)	494	(3.4)	99	(1.9)	**7**	(3.3)	0.07	(0.03)
Portugal	471	(4.0)	98	(2.1)	465	(3.6)	89	(1.9)	**6**	(3.2)	0.07	(0.03)
Slovak Republic	502	(4.3)	104	(3.0)	487	(3.9)	100	(3.9)	**15**	(3.7)	0.15	(0.04)
Spain	489	(3.9)	105	(1.8)	485	(2.6)	96	(2.2)	4	(3.9)	0.04	(0.04)
Sweden	509	(3.1)	108	(2.4)	504	(3.5)	105	(2.4)	5	(3.6)	0.05	(0.03)
Switzerland	518	(5.0)	110	(2.2)	508	(3.9)	105	(2.4)	**10**	(5.0)	0.10	(0.05)
Turkey	434	(6.7)	98	(5.3)	434	(6.4)	93	(4.6)	0	(5.8)	0.01	(0.06)
United States	494	(3.5)	105	(2.0)	489	(3.5)	98	(1.9)	5	(3.3)	0.05	(0.03)
OECD total	*499*	*(1.3)*	*112*	*(0.9)*	*493*	*(1.3)*	*106*	*(0.8)*	*6*	*(1.5)*	*0.05*	*(0.01)*
OECD average	*503*	*(0.7)*	*109*	*(0.5)*	*497*	*(0.8)*	*102*	*(0.4)*	*6*	*(0.9)*	*0.05*	*(0.01)*
Partner countries												
Brazil	393	(5.3)	102	(3.5)	387	(4.3)	95	(2.6)	6	(3.9)	0.06	(0.04)
Hong Kong-China	538	(6.1)	100	(3.7)	541	(4.2)	87	(2.7)	–3	(6.0)	–0.04	(0.06)
Indonesia	396	(3.1)	67	(1.8)	394	(3.8)	69	(2.4)	1	(2.7)	0.02	(0.04)
Latvia	487	(5.1)	97	(2.4)	491	(3.9)	89	(2.1)	–4	(4.7)	–0.04	(0.05)
Liechtenstein	538	(7.7)	108	(6.7)	512	(7.3)	96	(5.3)	**26**	(12.5)	**0.25**	(0.12)
Macao-China	529	(5.0)	88	(1.9)	521	(4.0)	88	(2.7)	8	(6.8)	0.09	(0.08)
Russian Federation	494	(5.3)	105	(2.0)	485	(4.0)	94	(1.8)	**9**	(4.3)	0.09	(0.04)
Serbia	434	(3.7)	86	(2.2)	439	(4.2)	79	(2.1)	–5	(3.8)	–0.06	(0.05)
Thailand	425	(3.7)	83	(2.0)	433	(3.1)	80	(2.0)	–8	(4.2)	–0.10	(0.05)
Tunisia	380	(2.7)	89	(2.1)	390	(3.0)	86	(2.3)	**–10**	(2.6)	–0.11	(0.03)
Uruguay	441	(3.7)	113	(2.0)	436	(3.6)	105	(2.5)	4	(4.4)	0.04	(0.04)
United Kingdom[1]	m	m	m	m	m	m	m	m	m	m	m	m

Note: Values that are statistically significant and effect sizes equal or greater than 0.2 are indicated in bold (see Annex A4).

1. Response rate too low to ensure comparability (see Annex A3).

Table 6.8

Percentage of students scoring below 400 points and above 600 points on the science scale

	Percentage of students scoring below 400 points on the reading scale						Increased likelihood for males to score below 400 points on the science scale		Percentage of students scoring above 600 points on the reading scale						Increased likelihood for males to score above 600 points on the science scale	
	All students		Males		Females				All students		Males		Females			
	%	S.E.	%	S.E.	%	S.E.	Ratio	S.E.	%	S.E.	%	S.E.	%	S.E.	Ratio	S.E.
OECD countries																
Australia	11.6	(0.6)	12.9	(0.7)	10.2	(0.8)	**1.3**	(0.11)	23.7	(0.8)	24.9	(1.2)	22.5	(1.0)	1.1	(0.07)
Austria	18.5	(1.2)	20.2	(1.6)	16.7	(1.4)	1.2	(0.12)	13.4	(1.0)	14.9	(1.4)	12.0	(1.2)	1.2	(0.17)
Belgium	16.5	(0.9)	17.5	(1.3)	15.4	(1.2)	1.1	(0.12)	20.9	(0.8)	22.5	(1.2)	19.1	(0.9)	**1.2**	(0.08)
Canada	12.0	(0.6)	11.5	(0.6)	11.6	(0.7)	1.0	(0.06)	21.0	(0.8)	25.3	(1.1)	19.3	(1.0)	**1.3**	(0.09)
Czech Republic	11.6	(0.9)	11.2	(1.1)	12.1	(1.2)	0.9	(0.12)	23.2	(1.2)	24.2	(1.6)	22.1	(1.3)	1.1	(0.08)
Denmark	22.7	(1.2)	20.6	(1.5)	24.7	(1.3)	0.8	(0.06)	10.8	(0.7)	12.4	(0.8)	9.3	(0.9)	**1.3**	(0.14)
Finland	5.7	(0.4)	6.9	(0.6)	4.6	(0.5)	**1.5**	(0.21)	29.2	(0.9)	29.2	(1.4)	29.2	(1.0)	1.0	(0.06)
France	16.6	(1.0)	17.7	(1.5)	15.6	(1.1)	1.1	(0.11)	22.5	(1.1)	23.6	(1.2)	21.5	(1.5)	1.1	(0.08)
Germany	18.8	(1.1)	19.0	(1.4)	18.2	(1.4)	1.1	(0.10)	19.9	(1.1)	21.9	(1.3)	18.0	(1.4)	**1.2**	(0.11)
Greece	21.7	(1.2)	21.0	(1.6)	22.3	(1.3)	0.9	(0.08)	12.1	(1.0)	14.6	(1.3)	9.8	(1.2)	**1.5**	(0.19)
Hungary	14.8	(0.8)	15.5	(1.1)	14.0	(1.1)	1.1	(0.10)	16.4	(1.3)	17.3	(1.6)	15.4	(1.3)	1.1	(0.09)
Iceland	16.2	(0.7)	18.7	(1.0)	13.5	(1.0)	**1.4**	(0.13)	13.4	(0.7)	13.4	(1.1)	13.4	(0.9)	1.0	(0.11)
Ireland	13.1	(0.9)	13.4	(1.3)	12.8	(1.2)	1.0	(0.13)	15.8	(0.9)	16.5	(1.0)	15.2	(1.4)	1.1	(0.11)
Italy	21.2	(1.2)	21.6	(1.9)	20.9	(1.6)	1.0	(0.12)	14.5	(0.6)	16.4	(1.0)	12.7	(0.8)	**1.3**	(0.11)
Japan	9.7	(0.9)	11.0	(1.1)	8.4	(1.1)	1.3	(0.18)	33.4	(1.5)	35.8	(2.4)	31.2	(1.5)	1.1	(0.09)
Korea	9.2	(0.8)	8.6	(1.1)	10.0	(1.2)	0.9	(0.14)	28.1	(1.5)	31.2	(1.8)	23.4	(2.2)	**1.3**	(0.14)
Luxembourg	21.4	(0.9)	21.1	(1.1)	21.8	(1.4)	1.0	(0.09)	12.9	(0.6)	15.8	(1.0)	10.0	(0.9)	**1.6**	(0.18)
Mexico	48.7	(1.9)	46.7	(2.2)	50.5	(2.0)	0.9	(0.04)	1.4	(0.3)	1.8	(0.5)	1.0	(0.3)	1.8	(0.82)
Netherlands	11.1	(1.2)	10.6	(1.3)	11.6	(1.4)	0.9	(0.11)	24.5	(1.2)	25.5	(1.8)	23.4	(1.3)	1.1	(0.09)
New Zealand	13.5	(0.7)	12.5	(0.9)	14.6	(1.2)	0.9	(0.10)	23.7	(1.1)	27.0	(1.3)	20.3	(1.4)	**1.3**	(0.09)
Norway	21.3	(1.0)	22.0	(1.4)	20.5	(1.3)	1.1	(0.09)	12.9	(0.9)	13.9	(1.0)	11.9	(1.0)	1.2	(0.09)
Poland	17.7	(0.9)	17.9	(1.1)	17.4	(1.2)	1.0	(0.08)	16.4	(0.8)	18.1	(1.0)	14.7	(1.0)	**1.2**	(0.09)
Portugal	23.5	(1.6)	23.9	(1.8)	23.1	(1.6)	1.0	(0.07)	7.5	(0.6)	9.1	(0.8)	6.0	(0.7)	**1.5**	(0.20)
Slovak Republic	16.9	(1.3)	16.1	(1.5)	17.6	(1.6)	0.9	(0.10)	15.1	(0.9)	17.3	(1.2)	12.8	(1.0)	**1.4**	(0.11)
Spain	19.1	(0.8)	19.6	(1.3)	18.7	(1.0)	1.1	(0.09)	12.7	(0.8)	14.5	(1.2)	11.1	(0.9)	**1.3**	(0.14)
Sweden	16.1	(0.8)	15.7	(1.1)	16.6	(1.0)	0.9	(0.08)	19.5	(1.0)	20.3	(1.1)	18.7	(1.4)	1.1	(0.08)
Switzerland	15.6	(1.0)	15.3	(1.2)	15.8	(1.1)	1.0	(0.08)	21.4	(1.4)	23.6	(2.3)	19.0	(1.4)	1.2	(0.14)
Turkey	38.6	(2.3)	38.9	(2.5)	38.3	(3.0)	1.0	(0.08)	5.7	(1.5)	6.2	(1.7)	5.0	(1.4)	1.3	(0.26)
United States	19.3	(1.1)	19.1	(1.2)	19.4	(1.2)	1.0	(0.06)	14.7	(0.9)	16.3	(1.1)	13.1	(1.2)	1.2	(0.12)
OECD total	***19.9***	***(0.4)***	***20.0***	***(0.5)***	***19.9***	***(0.5)***	***1.0***	***(0.02)***	***17.7***	***(0.3)***	***19.4***	***(0.4)***	***16.1***	***(0.4)***	***1.2***	***(0.03)***
OECD average	***17.9***	***(0.2)***	***18.0***	***(0.3)***	***17.7***	***(0.2)***	***1.0***	***(0.02)***	***17.6***	***(0.2)***	***19.3***	***(0.2)***	***16.0***	***(0.2)***	***1.2***	***(0.02)***
Partner countries																
Brazil	56.2	(1.8)	55.3	(2.1)	56.9	(2.1)	1.0	(0.03)	2.1	(0.5)	3.0	(0.8)	1.3	(0.4)	2.3	(0.68)
Hong Kong-China	8.2	(1.2)	10.3	(1.7)	6.0	(0.9)	**1.7**	(0.30)	27.8	(1.4)	29.0	(2.0)	26.6	(1.7)	1.1	(0.10)
Indonesia	54.4	(2.0)	54.3	(2.0)	54.6	(2.3)	1.0	(0.03)	0.2	(0.1)	0.2	(0.1)	0.3	(0.2)	0.6	(0.30)
Latvia	17.2	(1.2)	18.7	(1.7)	15.8	(1.5)	1.2	(0.14)	11.5	(1.0)	12.4	(1.4)	10.7	(1.3)	1.2	(0.19)
Liechtenstein	12.1	(1.7)	11.0	(2.5)	13.3	(2.7)	0.8	(0.28)	24.2	(2.5)	30.7	(4.5)	17.3	(3.0)	1.8	(0.46)
Macao-China	8.5	(1.2)	7.7	(1.5)	9.3	(1.5)	0.8	(0.19)	19.9	(1.4)	20.9	(2.3)	18.9	(2.3)	1.1	(0.21)
Russian Federation	18.6	(1.3)	18.7	(1.7)	18.4	(1.4)	1.0	(0.10)	13.5	(1.0)	16.0	(1.4)	11.0	(1.0)	**1.5**	(0.14)
Serbia	33.6	(1.6)	35.5	(1.7)	31.7	(2.2)	1.1	(0.08)	2.7	(0.5)	3.0	(0.6)	2.3	(0.6)	1.3	(0.34)
Thailand	37.6	(1.4)	40.0	(2.0)	35.6	(1.6)	1.1	(0.07)	2.5	(0.4)	2.6	(0.5)	2.4	(0.6)	1.1	(0.35)
Tunisia	57.5	(1.4)	60.3	(1.5)	54.8	(1.8)	**1.1**	(0.03)	0.7	(0.2)	0.8	(0.4)	0.6	(0.2)	1.3	(0.78)
Uruguay	36.3	(1.2)	36.1	(1.5)	36.4	(1.6)	1.0	(0.05)	6.6	(0.7)	7.9	(0.9)	5.4	(0.8)	**1.5**	(0.21)
United Kingdom[1]	m	m	m	m	m	m	m	m	m	m	m	m	m	m	m	m

Note: Values that are statistically significant are indicated in bold (see Annex A4).

1. Response rate too low to ensure comparability (see Annex A3).

Annex B2: Performance differences between regions within countries

Adjudicated regions

Data for which adherence to the PISA sampling standards and international comparability was internationally adjudicated.

Non-adjudicated regions

Data for which adherence to the PISA sampling standards at sub-national levels was assessed by the countries concerned.

In these countries, adherence to the PISA sampling standards and international comparability was internationally adjudicated only for the combined set of all sub-national entities.

Table B2.1 (see Table 2.5a, Annex A1)

Percentage of students at each level of proficiency on the mathematics scale

	Proficiency levels													
	Below Level 1 (below 358 score points)		Level 1 (from 358 to 420 score points)		Level 2 (from 421 to 482 score points)		Level 3 (from 483 to 544 score points)		Level 4 (from 545 to 606 score points)		Level 5 (from 607 to 668 score points)		Level 6 (above 668 score points)	
	%	S.E.	%	S.E.	%	S.E.	%	S.E.	%	S.E.	%	S.E.	%	S.E.
Adjudicated regions														
Italy (Provincia Autonoma di Bolzano)	1.8	(0.5)	7.0	(1.0)	17.2	(1.8)	27.8	(2.4)	25.9	(1.8)	15.0	(1.4)	5.3	(1.1)
Italy (Provincia Autonoma di Trento)	1.0	(0.3)	3.9	(0.9)	13.5	(1.8)	29.8	(2.4)	29.8	(1.9)	16.9	(1.5)	5.1	(1.3)
Italy (Regione Lombardia)	4.5	(1.3)	9.8	(2.0)	18.9	(1.6)	26.8	(2.0)	23.2	(1.7)	12.0	(1.8)	4.8	(1.0)
Italy (Regione Piemonte)	6.6	(1.1)	12.4	(1.4)	23.7	(1.8)	29.2	(2.0)	19.2	(1.6)	7.1	(1.2)	1.9	(0.5)
Italy (Regione Toscana)	6.7	(1.1)	14.8	(1.3)	23.0	(1.3)	27.2	(1.6)	19.7	(1.4)	7.2	(0.9)	1.5	(0.4)
Italy (Regione Veneto)	3.7	(0.8)	10.7	(1.4)	21.6	(1.8)	29.5	(1.6)	22.1	(1.8)	9.3	(1.1)	3.1	(0.8)
Spain (Basque Country)	4.7	(0.5)	11.6	(0.8)	23.7	(0.9)	28.7	(1.1)	21.6	(1.2)	8.2	(0.7)	1.5	(0.3)
Spain (Castile and Leon)	4.8	(1.0)	11.4	(1.1)	23.0	(1.5)	28.3	(1.7)	21.7	(1.6)	8.9	(1.2)	1.9	(0.6)
Spain (Catalonia)	6.1	(0.9)	13.3	(1.3)	24.2	(1.1)	28.5	(1.7)	17.6	(1.7)	8.0	(1.1)	2.2	(0.6)
United Kingdom (Scotland)	2.8	(0.5)	8.5	(0.7)	19.2	(1.1)	28.2	(1.4)	25.1	(1.1)	12.2	(0.8)	3.9	(0.4)
Non-adjudicated regions														
Belgium (Flemish Community)	4.8	(0.4)	6.6	(0.5)	13.0	(0.7)	18.7	(0.9)	22.7	(0.8)	21.9	(0.9)	12.4	(0.6)
Belgium (French Community)	10.3	(1.2)	12.9	(0.9)	19.8	(1.0)	21.9	(1.1)	18.9	(1.1)	11.7	(0.8)	4.5	(0.7)
Belgium (German-speaking Community)	6.4	(0.9)	11.3	(1.1)	19.0	(1.4)	23.2	(1.8)	20.9	(1.5)	13.7	(1.3)	5.4	(0.8)
Finland (Finnish speaking)	1.4	(0.2)	5.3	(0.4)	15.8	(0.6)	27.7	(0.7)	26.1	(0.9)	16.8	(0.7)	6.8	(0.5)
Finland (Swedish speaking)	1.9	(0.6)	5.8	(0.7)	19.1	(1.5)	27.5	(1.9)	26.3	(2.0)	15.0	(1.8)	4.3	(0.9)
United Kingdom (Northern Ireland)	5.4	(0.7)	11.1	(0.8)	19.3	(0.9)	25.3	(1.2)	22.2	(1.0)	12.1	(0.8)	4.6	(0.5)
United Kingdom (Wales)	6.6	(2.5)	13.0	(4.3)	23.2	(5.2)	26.9	(3.5)	20.0	(3.5)	9.0	(3.0)	1.3	(1.2)

Table B2.2 (see Table 2.5b, Annex A1)

Percentage of students at each level of proficiency on the mathematics scale, by gender

	Males – Proficiency levels													
	Below Level 1 (below 358 score points)		Level 1 (from 358 to 420 score points)		Level 2 (from 421 to 482 score points)		Level 3 (from 483 to 544 score points)		Level 4 (from 545 to 606 score points)		Level 5 (from 607 to 668 score points)		Level 6 (above 668 score points)	
	%	S.E.	%	S.E.	%	S.E.	%	S.E.	%	S.E.	%	S.E.	%	S.E.
Adjudicated regions														
Italy (Provincia Autonoma di Bolzano)	1.1	(0.5)	5.4	(1.2)	14.6	(3.0)	24.9	(3.7)	27.3	(2.5)	18.4	(1.9)	8.2	(1.9)
Italy (Provincia Autonoma di Trento)	0.6	(0.2)	2.2	(0.8)	8.3	(1.8)	24.4	(2.8)	33.2	(2.8)	22.3	(3.2)	9.1	(2.5)
Italy (Regione Lombardia)	6.0	(2.4)	10.6	(3.7)	16.5	(2.1)	23.8	(2.6)	22.5	(2.8)	13.6	(2.5)	7.0	(1.6)
Italy (Regione Piemonte)	6.8	(1.6)	11.1	(2.2)	21.1	(2.0)	28.1	(2.1)	21.0	(2.5)	9.2	(1.4)	2.7	(0.9)
Italy (Regione Toscana)	6.5	(1.6)	13.9	(2.4)	20.6	(2.0)	27.2	(2.9)	20.3	(2.0)	9.3	(1.5)	2.2	(0.6)
Italy (Regione Veneto)	4.9	(1.6)	11.0	(2.3)	19.2	(1.8)	27.2	(2.1)	22.0	(2.3)	11.0	(1.7)	4.7	(1.3)
Spain (Basque Country)	5.9	(0.8)	12.5	(1.4)	22.0	(1.4)	25.9	(1.4)	21.8	(1.6)	9.5	(1.1)	2.3	(0.4)
Spain (Castile and Leon)	5.3	(1.2)	9.8	(1.4)	21.3	(1.6)	27.8	(2.7)	22.5	(2.5)	10.5	(1.6)	2.8	(0.9)
Spain (Catalonia)	5.3	(1.1)	11.6	(1.7)	23.2	(1.4)	27.9	(2.2)	18.9	(1.9)	9.9	(2.1)	3.2	(1.1)
United Kingdom (Scotland)	2.8	(0.7)	8.3	(1.1)	18.4	(1.5)	27.2	(2.0)	25.5	(1.6)	13.4	(1.0)	4.5	(0.6)
Non-adjudicated regions														
Belgium (Flemish Community)	4.3	(0.5)	6.8	(0.8)	12.3	(1.1)	17.1	(1.0)	21.4	(1.1)	23.0	(1.5)	15.1	(1.2)
Belgium (French Community)	11.3	(1.7)	13.6	(1.6)	18.5	(1.5)	20.3	(1.5)	18.4	(1.5)	12.2	(1.1)	5.7	(1.0)
Belgium (German-speaking Community)	7.7	(1.7)	11.8	(2.0)	19.6	(2.1)	21.7	(2.3)	20.6	(2.2)	12.3	(1.9)	6.3	(1.2)
Finland (Finnish speaking)	1.5	(0.3)	5.8	(0.6)	15.3	(0.8)	25.9	(0.9)	25.3	(1.2)	17.8	(1.1)	8.4	(0.9)
Finland (Swedish speaking)	2.2	(0.9)	5.3	(1.2)	17.7	(2.0)	26.4	(2.6)	26.7	(2.5)	16.7	(2.5)	5.0	(1.1)
United Kingdom (Northern Ireland)	6.2	(1.2)	10.6	(1.3)	18.1	(1.4)	24.9	(1.7)	21.5	(1.7)	13.4	(1.5)	5.3	(0.8)
United Kingdom (Wales)	6.9	(3.7)	12.9	(4.4)	22.7	(6.8)	28.8	(7.3)	18.8	(5.5)	8.3	(3.8)	1.6	(1.5)

	Females – Proficiency levels													
	Below Level 1 (below 358 score points)		Level 1 (from 358 to 420 score points)		Level 2 (from 421 to 482 score points)		Level 3 (from 483 to 544 score points)		Level 4 (from 545 to 606 score points)		Level 5 (from 607 to 668 score points)		Level 6 (above 668 score points)	
	%	S.E.	%	S.E.	%	S.E.	%	S.E.	%	S.E.	%	S.E.	%	S.E.
Adjudicated regions														
Italy (Provincia Autonoma di Bolzano)	2.4	(0.8)	8.4	(1.4)	19.5	(2.0)	30.4	(2.2)	24.6	(2.2)	12.0	(1.8)	2.7	(0.8)
Italy (Provincia Autonoma di Trento)	1.3	(0.5)	5.4	(1.3)	17.9	(2.4)	34.3	(4.1)	27.0	(2.4)	12.3	(1.9)	1.7	(0.8)
Italy (Regione Lombardia)	2.9	(0.9)	9.0	(1.9)	21.4	(2.3)	29.7	(2.3)	24.0	(2.2)	10.3	(2.0)	2.6	(1.0)
Italy (Regione Piemonte)	6.4	(1.4)	13.5	(2.2)	25.9	(2.8)	30.2	(2.9)	17.6	(2.1)	5.3	(1.3)	1.2	(0.4)
Italy (Regione Toscana)	6.8	(1.7)	15.7	(2.0)	25.7	(2.0)	27.2	(2.0)	19.0	(2.3)	4.9	(0.9)	0.7	(0.4)
Italy (Regione Veneto)	2.4	(0.9)	10.4	(1.8)	24.2	(2.7)	31.8	(2.6)	22.1	(3.0)	7.6	(1.5)	1.5	(0.6)
Spain (Basque Country)	3.5	(0.5)	10.8	(0.9)	25.4	(1.3)	31.4	(1.3)	21.3	(1.3)	6.9	(0.9)	0.7	(0.3)
Spain (Castile and Leon)	4.4	(1.2)	12.8	(1.6)	24.5	(2.4)	28.8	(2.3)	20.9	(1.7)	7.4	(1.5)	1.1	(0.8)
Spain (Catalonia)	6.9	(1.4)	14.8	(2.1)	25.2	(1.7)	29.1	(2.5)	16.4	(2.5)	6.3	(1.2)	1.4	(0.5)
United Kingdom (Scotland)	2.8	(0.6)	8.7	(1.3)	20.1	(1.6)	29.2	(1.5)	24.8	(1.4)	11.0	(1.1)	3.3	(0.6)
Non-adjudicated regions														
Belgium (Flemish Community)	5.3	(0.8)	6.5	(0.9)	13.6	(0.9)	20.3	(1.3)	24.0	(1.2)	20.8	(1.0)	9.6	(0.7)
Belgium (French Community)	9.2	(1.6)	12.0	(1.2)	21.4	(1.6)	23.8	(1.5)	19.4	(1.5)	11.1	(1.0)	3.0	(0.7)
Belgium (German-speaking Community)	5.2	(1.4)	10.8	(1.9)	18.5	(2.6)	24.7	(2.8)	21.2	(2.3)	15.0	(1.8)	4.6	(1.2)
Finland (Finnish speaking)	1.3	(0.3)	4.8	(0.6)	16.4	(0.8)	29.5	(1.2)	26.9	(1.3)	15.9	(0.9)	5.2	(0.6)
Finland (Swedish speaking)	1.7	(0.6)	6.2	(1.1)	20.4	(2.0)	28.6	(2.6)	26.0	(2.7)	13.4	(2.2)	3.7	(1.2)
United Kingdom (Northern Ireland)	4.6	(0.7)	11.5	(1.2)	20.5	(1.4)	25.8	(1.6)	23.0	(1.7)	10.8	(1.1)	3.8	(0.7)
United Kingdom (Wales)	6.4	(3.7)	13.1	(5.4)	23.8	(5.5)	24.7	(5.6)	21.3	(6.4)	9.8	(3.6)	1.0	

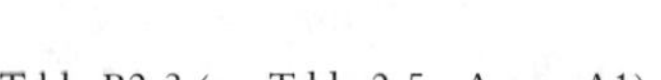

Table B2.3 (see Table 2.5c, Annex A1)

Mean score, variation and gender differences in student performance on the mathematics scale

	All students				Gender differences					
	Mean score		Standard deviation		Males		Females		Difference (M – F)	
	Mean	**S.E.**	**S.D.**	**S.E.**	**Mean score**	**S.E.**	**Mean score**	**S.E.**	**Score dif.**	**S.E.**
Adjudicated regions										
Italy (Provincia Autonoma di Bolzano)	536	(4.8)	85	(2.3)	552	(5.8)	522	(4.6)	**30**	(4.5)
Italy (Provincia Autonoma di Trento)	547	(3.0)	78	(2.6)	570	(3.8)	528	(3.9)	**42**	(5.1)
Italy (Regione Lombardia)	519	(7.3)	93	(4.1)	523	(14.1)	516	(6.4)	6	(16.3)
Italy (Regione Piemonte)	494	(4.9)	88	(3.1)	502	(6.3)	487	(6.1)	15	(8.3)
Italy (Regione Toscana)	492	(4.3)	87	(2.4)	499	(8.1)	484	(6.0)	15	(11.4)
Italy (Regione Veneto)	511	(5.5)	85	(2.8)	515	(9.6)	507	(6.6)	8	(12.4)
Spain (Basque Country)	502	(2.8)	82	(1.1)	502	(3.9)	501	(3.1)	1	(4.1)
Spain (Castile and Leon)	503	(4.0)	85	(2.7)	509	(5.6)	498	(4.7)	11	(6.4)
Spain (Catalonia)	494	(4.7)	88	(2.0)	504	(5.6)	486	(5.8)	**18**	(6.2)
United Kingdom (Scotland)	524	(2.3)	84	(1.7)	527	(3.3)	520	(2.9)	7	(4.1)
Non-adjudicated regions										
Belgium (Flemish Community)	553	(2.1)	105	(1.4)	561	(3.6)	546	(3.6)	**15**	(5.8)
Belgium (French Community)	498	(4.3)	108	(3.1)	498	(6.2)	497	(5.3)	1	(7.8)
Belgium (German-speaking Community)	515	(3.0)	100	(2.4)	512	(5.0)	518	(4.2)	–6	(6.9)
Finland (Finnish speaking)	545	(2.0)	84	(1.1)	549	(2.6)	541	(2.2)	**7**	(2.8)
Finland (Swedish speaking)	534	(2.3)	81	(1.6)	538	(3.7)	531	(3.3)	8	(5.2)
United Kingdom (Northern Ireland)	515	(2.8)	94	(2.0)	517	(5.3)	513	(4.0)	4	(7.5)
United Kingdom (Wales)	498	(10.8)	85	(3.1)	497	(10.0)	499	(14.1)	–2	(11.3)

	Percentiles											
	5th		10th		25th		75th		90th		95th	
	Score	**S.E.**	**Score**	**S.E.**	**Score**	**S.E.**	**Score**	**S.E.**	**Score**	**S.E.**	**Score**	**S.E.**
Adjudicated regions												
Italy (Provincia Autonoma di Bolzano)	394	(7.1)	426	(5.9)	479	(5.1)	596	(5.7)	645	(7.2)	672	(9.6)
Italy (Provincia Autonoma di Trento)	421	(7.3)	451	(8.5)	498	(6.0)	599	(5.3)	644	(5.8)	669	(6.9)
Italy (Regione Lombardia)	364	(14.4)	400	(12.0)	459	(10.4)	582	(7.4)	636	(8.5)	668	(9.3)
Italy (Regione Piemonte)	345	(7.9)	381	(8.0)	438	(5.7)	553	(6.0)	602	(7.6)	632	(7.9)
Italy (Regione Toscana)	346	(7.7)	376	(7.8)	432	(6.6)	552	(4.4)	601	(4.8)	631	(5.0)
Italy (Regione Veneto)	370	(8.8)	401	(7.6)	455	(6.5)	568	(6.3)	619	(6.7)	650	(8.1)
Spain (Basque Country)	361	(5.2)	395	(3.8)	447	(3.4)	560	(3.6)	606	(3.3)	631	(3.7)
Spain (Castile and Leon)	359	(10.7)	395	(7.2)	448	(5.3)	562	(4.3)	611	(5.1)	639	(6.7)
Spain (Catalonia)	349	(6.9)	381	(6.2)	438	(5.7)	552	(6.1)	608	(6.2)	640	(8.9)
United Kingdom (Scotland)	380	(6.0)	413	(4.8)	468	(3.4)	583	(2.5)	631	(4.1)	660	(4.3)
Non-adjudicated regions												
Belgium (Flemish Community)	360	(5.9)	411	(4.9)	485	(3.7)	631	(2.6)	679	(3.0)	707	(2.8)
Belgium (French Community)	309	(11.9)	355	(9.3)	427	(6.2)	575	(4.8)	633	(5.0)	665	(6.5)
Belgium (German-speaking Community)	343	(14.0)	384	(5.3)	447	(6.1)	587	(3.8)	642	(5.6)	673	(6.6)
Finland (Finnish speaking)	407	(3.9)	439	(3.0)	489	(2.4)	603	(2.4)	652	(3.0)	681	(3.3)
Finland (Swedish speaking)	401	(7.3)	433	(4.7)	478	(3.8)	591	(3.6)	638	(5.7)	665	(6.8)
United Kingdom (Northern Ireland)	354	(5.5)	389	(5.1)	450	(4.7)	580	(3.5)	634	(5.1)	666	(4.1)
United Kingdom (Wales)	349	(17.6)	383	(18.4)	436	(16.2)	561	(13.9)	607	(16.9)	634	(16.6)

Note: Values that are statistically significant are indicated in bold (see Annex A4).

Table B2.4 (see Table 6.1, Annex A1)

Percentage of students at each level of proficiency on the reading scale

	Proficiency levels											
	Below Level 1 (below 335 score points)		Level 1 (from 335 to 407 score points)		Level 2 (from 408 to 480 score points)		Level 3 (from 481 to 552 score points)		Level 4 (from 553 to 625 score points)		Level 5 (above 625 score points)	
	%	**S.E.**	**%**	**S.E.**	**%**	**S.E.**	**%**	**S.E.**	**%**	**S.E.**	**%**	**S.E.**
Adjudicated regions												
Italy (Provincia Autonoma di Bolzano)	1.5	(0.5)	5.4	(1.0)	14.7	(1.2)	30.3	(1.9)	30.7	(2.1)	17.4	(2.5)
Italy (Provincia Autonoma di Trento)	0.6	(0.2)	3.1	(0.6)	13.8	(1.2)	36.7	(2.1)	35.5	(1.9)	10.3	(1.4)
Italy (Regione Lombardia)	3.8	(1.3)	7.7	(1.6)	20.1	(1.8)	31.9	(2.0)	27.3	(2.0)	9.2	(1.2)
Italy (Regione Piemonte)	4.8	(0.7)	9.9	(1.1)	21.6	(1.7)	34.4	(2.0)	22.4	(1.7)	6.9	(1.1)
Italy (Regione Toscana)	7.1	(1.8)	11.7	(1.4)	22.6	(1.8)	30.6	(2.2)	20.8	(2.1)	7.2	(0.9)
Italy (Regione Veneto)	3.0	(1.0)	8.5	(1.5)	20.5	(1.8)	32.8	(2.1)	26.9	(2.1)	8.2	(1.2)
Spain (Basque Country)	5.3	(0.5)	11.8	(0.8)	22.8	(1.0)	30.8	(1.0)	22.6	(1.3)	6.6	(0.6)
Spain (Castile and Leon)	4.4	(0.9)	10.4	(1.0)	23.9	(1.4)	32.1	(1.8)	23.2	(1.7)	5.9	(0.8)
Spain (Catalonia)	6.2	(0.7)	13.0	(1.4)	26.5	(1.7)	31.9	(1.8)	18.1	(1.6)	4.3	(0.9)
United Kingdom (Scotland)	2.6	(0.4)	8.2	(0.8)	21.2	(1.0)	33.0	(1.2)	26.0	(1.0)	9.0	(0.7)
Non-adjudicated regions												
Belgium (Flemish Community)	4.5	(0.4)	7.9	(0.6)	15.8	(0.8)	25.8	(0.8)	29.5	(0.9)	16.6	(0.7)
Belgium (French Community)	12.3	(1.4)	12.8	(1.1)	21.3	(1.0)	26.2	(1.2)	20.1	(1.2)	7.3	(0.9)
Belgium (German-speaking Community)	6.6	(1.0)	13.6	(1.4)	19.2	(1.5)	27.7	(2.5)	23.5	(2.0)	9.5	(1.3)
Finland (Finnish speaking)	1.1	(0.2)	4.6	(0.4)	14.4	(0.6)	31.4	(0.8)	33.5	(0.8)	15.0	(0.8)
Finland (Swedish speaking)	1.2	(0.4)	5.5	(0.8)	17.6	(1.5)	35.0	(1.9)	31.0	(1.4)	9.7	(0.9)
United Kingdom (Northern Ireland)	4.0	(0.6)	9.4	(0.6)	20.5	(1.3)	28.1	(1.6)	25.3	(1.3)	12.7	(0.9)
United Kingdom (Wales)	5.7	(2.2)	12.6	(3.4)	22.9	(3.6)	28.2	(3.9)	22.9	(4.1)	7.6	(2.9)

Table B2.5 (see Tables 6.2 and 6.3, Annex A1)
Mean score, variation and gender differences in student performance on the reading scale

	All students				Gender differences					
	Mean score		Standard deviation		Males		Females		Difference (M – F)	
	Mean	**S.E.**	**S.D.**	**S.E.**	**Mean score**	**S.E.**	**Mean score**	**S.E.**	**Score dif.**	**S.E.**
Adjudicated regions										
Italy (Provincia Autonoma di Bolzano)	544	(5.4)	88	(2.5)	524	(7.0)	562	(5.1)	**–37**	(5.4)
Italy (Provincia Autonoma di Trento)	542	(2.2)	71	(2.3)	532	(3.8)	551	(3.2)	**–19**	(5.4)
Italy (Regione Lombardia)	515	(6.9)	92	(5.6)	490	(11.9)	541	(5.4)	**–51**	(14.2)
Italy (Regione Piemonte)	501	(4.0)	93	(3.5)	478	(6.8)	522	(5.5)	**–44**	(8.5)
Italy (Regione Toscana)	492	(6.7)	100	(3.8)	464	(9.2)	523	(7.3)	**–59**	(12.2)
Italy (Regione Veneto)	514	(6.3)	87	(4.4)	494	(9.9)	535	(6.8)	**–42**	(12.5)
Spain (Basque Country)	497	(2.9)	93	(1.4)	474	(4.2)	519	(2.9)	**–45**	(4.4)
Spain (Castile and Leon)	499	(3.9)	89	(2.7)	480	(5.3)	517	(4.5)	**–37**	(5.9)
Spain (Catalonia)	483	(4.5)	91	(2.3)	461	(5.0)	502	(6.0)	**–42**	(7.4)
United Kingdom (Scotland)	516	(2.5)	86	(1.7)	504	(3.2)	527	(3.4)	**–24**	(4.4)
Non-adjudicated regions										
Belgium (Flemish Community)	530	(2.1)	101	(1.4)	516	(3.6)	544	(3.5)	**–28**	(5.8)
Belgium (French Community)	477	(5.0)	114	(3.6)	456	(6.9)	501	(6.0)	**–45**	(8.9)
Belgium (German-speaking Community)	499	(2.7)	102	(2.7)	471	(4.8)	525	(4.9)	**–54**	(8.1)
Finland (Finnish speaking)	544	(1.7)	81	(1.2)	522	(2.3)	566	(2.1)	**–44**	(2.8)
Finland (Swedish speaking)	530	(2.4)	78	(2.3)	508	(3.9)	549	(2.9)	**–41**	(5.0)
United Kingdom (Northern Ireland)	517	(3.1)	98	(2.7)	500	(5.3)	533	(4.3)	**–33**	(7.8)
United Kingdom (Wales)	496	(12.4)	95	(4.8)	475	(11.2)	519	(12.3)	**–44**	(8.9)

	Percentiles											
	5th		10th		25th		75th		90th		95th	
	Score	**S.E.**	**Score**	**S.E.**	**Score**	**S.E.**	**Score**	**S.E.**	**Score**	**S.E.**	**Score**	**S.E.**
Adjudicated regions												
Italy (Provincia Autonoma di Bolzano)	393	(10.3)	431	(8.6)	490	(6.0)	603	(7.0)	652	(10.5)	680	(8.7)
Italy (Provincia Autonoma di Trento)	422	(8.1)	453	(5.2)	499	(2.7)	589	(3.9)	626	(6.0)	650	(5.7)
Italy (Regione Lombardia)	355	(20.5)	401	(12.2)	462	(10.0)	577	(4.5)	623	(5.6)	650	(6.3)
Italy (Regione Piemonte)	337	(8.7)	380	(8.4)	448	(6.4)	564	(5.2)	610	(6.6)	638	(6.1)
Italy (Regione Toscana)	310	(18.2)	358	(15.6)	431	(10.6)	561	(6.4)	611	(6.6)	641	(7.5)
Italy (Regione Veneto)	361	(15.1)	399	(12.1)	460	(9.4)	575	(5.8)	617	(5.3)	643	(6.2)
Spain (Basque Country)	331	(6.8)	372	(5.2)	437	(5.1)	563	(3.4)	610	(3.1)	636	(3.3)
Spain (Castile and Leon)	340	(12.1)	383	(8.3)	445	(5.1)	563	(4.5)	607	(4.8)	632	(6.0)
Spain (Catalonia)	323	(7.3)	364	(6.7)	426	(5.7)	547	(5.3)	594	(6.3)	621	(5.7)
United Kingdom (Scotland)	365	(7.2)	403	(5.2)	461	(3.5)	577	(3.2)	621	(3.5)	646	(3.9)
Non-adjudicated regions												
Belgium (Flemish Community)	341	(4.7)	391	(4.3)	468	(3.8)	603	(2.3)	648	(2.5)	674	(3.0)
Belgium (French Community)	265	(14.0)	316	(11.4)	407	(8.6)	560	(4.5)	611	(4.7)	638	(5.2)
Belgium (German-speaking Community)	319	(11.6)	358	(8.9)	428	(5.9)	575	(5.9)	623	(5.8)	648	(7.2)
Finland (Finnish speaking)	400	(5.2)	438	(3.3)	495	(2.7)	600	(1.8)	642	(2.5)	666	(2.6)
Finland (Swedish speaking)	393	(6.0)	426	(6.2)	481	(3.7)	584	(4.0)	624	(4.3)	649	(5.9)
United Kingdom (Northern Ireland)	348	(7.2)	388	(5.3)	453	(4.5)	586	(4.3)	637	(3.5)	667	(4.0)
United Kingdom (Wales)	330	(22.1)	367	(15.2)	433	(20.8)	568	(12.9)	616	(13.3)	640	(13.6)

Note: Values that are statistically significant are indicated in bold (see Annex A4).

Table B2.6 (see Table 6.5, Annex A1)

Percentage of students at each level of proficiency on the reading scale, by gender

	Males – Proficiency levels											
	Below Level 1 (below 335 score points)		Level 1 (from 335 to 407 score points)		Level 2 (from 408 to 480 score points)		Level 3 (from 481 to 552 score points)		Level 4 (from 553 to 625 score points)		Level 5 (above 625 score points)	
	%	S.E.	%	S.E.	%	S.E.	%	S.E.	%	S.E.	%	S.E.
Adjudicated regions												
Italy (Provincia Autonoma di Bolzano)	2.7	(0.9)	8.3	(1.8)	17.4	(2.2)	32.3	(2.4)	26.5	(2.5)	12.8	(2.6)
Italy (Provincia Autonoma di Trento)	0.9	(0.4)	4.8	(1.1)	16.1	(2.0)	37.7	(2.8)	31.9	(2.6)	8.5	(2.2)
Italy (Regione Lombardia)	6.8	(2.3)	11.7	(2.7)	24.5	(3.0)	28.1	(2.9)	22.6	(3.4)	6.2	(1.4)
Italy (Regione Piemonte)	7.8	(1.5)	13.1	(1.7)	25.5	(2.2)	32.6	(2.8)	17.0	(2.1)	4.0	(1.0)
Italy (Regione Toscana)	11.0	(2.9)	15.3	(2.1)	26.2	(2.6)	29.2	(3.0)	14.5	(2.1)	3.8	(0.9)
Italy (Regione Veneto)	5.2	(1.7)	12.6	(2.3)	23.8	(2.2)	30.1	(2.8)	22.1	(2.7)	6.2	(1.4)
Spain (Basque Country)	8.7	(0.9)	16.3	(1.1)	24.8	(1.4)	27.5	(1.2)	18.1	(1.9)	4.5	(0.9)
Spain (Castile and Leon)	7.4	(1.6)	13.3	(1.5)	27.1	(2.8)	29.4	(2.4)	18.2	(2.1)	4.6	(1.0)
Spain (Catalonia)	9.4	(1.1)	17.0	(2.6)	29.8	(3.0)	28.9	(2.3)	11.9	(1.6)	3.0	(1.1)
United Kingdom (Scotland)	3.6	(0.7)	10.4	(1.2)	22.8	(1.3)	33.1	(1.9)	23.3	(1.7)	6.9	(0.9)
Non-adjudicated regions												
Belgium (Flemish Community)	5.6	(0.6)	9.2	(1.0)	18.5	(1.4)	26.1	(1.2)	27.7	(1.3)	12.8	(0.9)
Belgium (French Community)	16.7	(2.1)	15.1	(1.7)	22.0	(1.8)	23.9	(1.7)	17.2	(1.3)	5.1	(0.9)
Belgium (German-speaking Community)	9.2	(1.5)	18.6	(2.2)	23.6	(2.4)	26.0	(2.4)	17.3	(2.1)	5.2	(1.5)
Finland (Finnish speaking)	1.8	(0.3)	7.2	(0.7)	19.6	(1.0)	33.8	(1.2)	28.6	(1.4)	9.0	(0.8)
Finland (Swedish speaking)	2.4	(0.9)	7.9	(1.5)	22.6	(2.8)	36.6	(3.2)	25.6	(2.0)	5.0	(1.2)
United Kingdom (Northern Ireland)	6.1	(1.2)	11.5	(1.3)	22.8	(1.5)	27.2	(1.5)	22.3	(1.5)	10.0	(1.1)
United Kingdom (Wales)	9.1	(3.5)	15.1	(4.6)	24.2	(5.8)	29.9	(5.1)	15.3	(4.1)	6.5	(3.4)

	Females – Proficiency levels											
	Below Level 1 (below 335 score points)		Level 1 (from 335 to 407 score points)		Level 2 (from 408 to 480 score points)		Level 3 (from 481 to 552 score points)		Level 4 (from 553 to 625 score points)		Level 5 (above 625 score points)	
	%	S.E.	%	S.E.	%	S.E.	%	S.E.	%	S.E.	%	S.E.
Adjudicated regions												
Italy (Provincia Autonoma di Bolzano)	0.4	(0.2)	2.8	(0.7)	12.3	(1.5)	28.6	(2.4)	34.5	(2.8)	21.4	(2.9)
Italy (Provincia Autonoma di Trento)	0.3	(0.2)	1.6	(0.5)	11.8	(2.3)	35.9	(2.7)	38.6	(3.0)	11.8	(1.7)
Italy (Regione Lombardia)	0.7	(0.5)	3.5	(1.2)	15.5	(2.0)	35.8	(2.3)	32.1	(2.4)	12.3	(1.8)
Italy (Regione Piemonte)	2.2	(0.7)	7.0	(1.5)	18.2	(2.1)	36.0	(2.6)	27.2	(2.6)	9.5	(1.7)
Italy (Regione Toscana)	2.8	(0.9)	7.6	(1.7)	18.5	(2.3)	32.0	(2.6)	28.0	(3.0)	11.1	(1.8)
Italy (Regione Veneto)	0.7	(0.3)	4.2	(1.2)	17.1	(2.6)	35.7	(2.6)	32.0	(3.0)	10.4	(2.1)
Spain (Basque Country)	2.0	(0.6)	7.4	(0.9)	20.7	(1.3)	34.1	(1.5)	27.1	(1.4)	8.7	(1.0)
Spain (Castile and Leon)	1.7	(0.8)	7.8	(1.3)	21.1	(2.5)	34.6	(2.4)	27.7	(2.5)	7.0	(1.2)
Spain (Catalonia)	3.4	(1.1)	9.6	(1.7)	23.8	(2.3)	34.5	(2.7)	23.4	(2.4)	5.3	(1.2)
United Kingdom (Scotland)	1.6	(0.5)	6.1	(0.8)	19.7	(1.4)	32.9	(1.9)	28.7	(1.7)	11.0	(1.1)
Non-adjudicated regions												
Belgium (Flemish Community)	3.4	(0.4)	6.5	(0.7)	13.0	(0.9)	25.4	(1.2)	31.4	(1.2)	20.4	(1.2)
Belgium (French Community)	7.1	(1.5)	10.2	(1.3)	20.5	(1.6)	28.8	(1.9)	23.5	(1.9)	9.8	(1.4)
Belgium (German-speaking Community)	4.1	(1.5)	8.8	(2.2)	15.0	(2.1)	29.2	(3.6)	29.4	(3.1)	13.5	(2.1)
Finland (Finnish speaking)	0.4	(0.1)	2.0	(0.4)	9.2	(1.0)	29.1	(1.4)	38.4	(1.4)	21.0	(1.4)
Finland (Swedish speaking)	0.1		3.4	(0.9)	13.1	(1.8)	33.6	(2.9)	35.9	(2.4)	13.9	(1.4)
United Kingdom (Northern Ireland)	1.9	(0.5)	7.3	(0.9)	18.1	(2.0)	29.0	(2.5)	28.2	(2.2)	15.4	(1.3)
United Kingdom (Wales)	2.0	(1.7)	10.0	(6.3)	21.5	(3.9)	26.3	(5.8)	31.3	(4.9)	8.9	(3.9)

Table B2.7 (see Tables 6.6 and 6.7, Annex A1)

Mean score, variation and gender differences in student performance on the science scale

	All students				Gender differences					
	Mean score		Standard deviation		Males		Females		Difference (M – F)	
	Mean	**S.E.**	**S.D.**	**S.E.**	**Mean score**	**S.E.**	**Mean score**	**S.E.**	**Score dif.**	**S.E.**
Adjudicated regions										
Italy (Provincia Autonoma di Bolzano)	533	(5.5)	92	(3.0)	536	(7.0)	529	(5.1)	7	(5.3)
Italy (Provincia Autonoma di Trento)	566	(2.9)	85	(2.7)	582	(4.8)	553	(4.3)	**29**	(7.0)
Italy (Regione Lombardia)	540	(7.5)	100	(5.6)	533	(14.5)	548	(5.9)	–15	(16.7)
Italy (Regione Piemonte)	522	(5.2)	100	(3.6)	527	(6.7)	517	(6.5)	10	(8.7)
Italy (Regione Toscana)	513	(5.7)	106	(3.1)	509	(9.7)	519	(7.5)	–10	(13.4)
Italy (Regione Veneto)	533	(6.0)	92	(3.2)	525	(9.8)	542	(7.0)	–17	(12.3)
Spain (Basque Country)	484	(3.1)	95	(1.3)	481	(4.4)	487	(3.2)	–6	(4.6)
Spain (Castile and Leon)	502	(4.8)	98	(4.8)	506	(6.3)	498	(5.2)	9	(6.2)
Spain (Catalonia)	502	(4.0)	92	(2.2)	505	(5.1)	500	(5.3)	5	(6.8)
United Kingdom (Scotland)	514	(2.7)	100	(1.7)	518	(3.7)	510	(4.0)	8	(5.5)
Non-adjudicated regions										
Belgium (Flemish Community)	529	(2.1)	101	(1.5)	533	(3.5)	525	(3.7)	8	(5.8)
Belgium (French Community)	483	(4.6)	110	(3.2)	479	(6.6)	487	(5.9)	–8	(8.6)
Belgium (German-speaking Community)	492	(2.8)	101	(2.7)	486	(4.4)	498	(5.0)	–13	(7.6)
Finland (Finnish speaking)	550	(2.0)	91	(1.1)	546	(2.7)	553	(2.3)	**–7**	(2.9)
Finland (Swedish speaking)	524	(2.7)	90	(2.0)	525	(4.0)	523	(3.8)	2	(5.6)
United Kingdom (Northern Ireland)	524	(3.0)	105	(2.2)	524	(5.6)	524	(4.5)	0	(8.1)
United Kingdom (Wales)	511	(11.3)	98	(4.2)	506	(12.5)	516	(12.8)	–10	(12.5)

	Percentiles											
	5th		10th		25th		75th		90th		95th	
	Score	**S.E.**	**Score**	**S.E.**	**Score**	**S.E.**	**Score**	**S.E.**	**Score**	**S.E.**	**Score**	**S.E.**
Adjudicated regions												
Italy (Provincia Autonoma di Bolzano)	380	(8.0)	412	(7.9)	471	(6.7)	597	(8.1)	650	(9.5)	680	(10.1)
Italy (Provincia Autonoma di Trento)	421	(8.1)	458	(7.7)	513	(4.6)	623	(5.0)	669	(5.4)	699	(7.9)
Italy (Regione Lombardia)	367	(20.1)	414	(14.2)	481	(10.5)	609	(6.3)	658	(8.3)	689	(8.4)
Italy (Regione Piemonte)	347	(9.9)	388	(9.1)	461	(6.5)	588	(6.8)	643	(5.8)	677	(9.1)
Italy (Regione Toscana)	330	(13.3)	375	(12.7)	447	(8.1)	587	(5.6)	643	(7.7)	675	(7.4)
Italy (Regione Veneto)	378	(10.0)	413	(9.2)	472	(8.2)	597	(6.5)	651	(7.1)	679	(5.9)
Spain (Basque Country)	326	(5.1)	359	(4.9)	419	(4.1)	551	(3.8)	605	(4.3)	637	(4.4)
Spain (Castile and Leon)	345	(11.9)	383	(6.6)	441	(5.9)	568	(4.9)	621	(4.9)	649	(5.8)
Spain (Catalonia)	348	(7.5)	385	(5.7)	440	(5.0)	568	(4.9)	618	(6.4)	647	(8.0)
United Kingdom (Scotland)	348	(6.6)	383	(4.5)	445	(4.2)	585	(3.3)	641	(3.6)	675	(3.8)
Non-adjudicated regions												
Belgium (Flemish Community)	351	(5.1)	390	(4.1)	463	(3.3)	602	(2.5)	651	(2.6)	677	(2.8)
Belgium (French Community)	291	(11.7)	334	(8.6)	407	(6.4)	565	(5.5)	620	(4.8)	651	(6.0)
Belgium (German-speaking Community)	322	(10.0)	357	(7.5)	420	(5.8)	568	(6.5)	619	(5.9)	647	(5.7)
Finland (Finnish speaking)	395	(4.0)	431	(2.9)	490	(2.9)	612	(2.4)	663	(3.2)	692	(3.6)
Finland (Swedish speaking)	373	(7.5)	407	(5.8)	464	(4.8)	589	(4.3)	639	(4.5)	666	(6.5)
United Kingdom (Northern Ireland)	345	(7.8)	386	(5.0)	452	(4.3)	598	(4.8)	657	(4.0)	689	(4.7)
United Kingdom (Wales)	341	(18.9)	375	(16.3)	443	(18.9)	581	(13.8)	640	(15.7)	669	(16.1)

Note: Values that are statistically significant are indicated in bold (see Annex A4).

Table B2.8 (see Table 4.2a, Annex A1)

International socio-economic index of occupational status (HISEI) and performance on the mathematics scale, by national quarters of the index

Results based on students' self-reports

	International socio-economic index of occupational status (highest of the father's or mother's)										Performance on the mathematics scale, by national quarters of the international socio-economic index of occupational status							
	All students		Bottom quarter		Second quarter		Third quarter		Top quarter		Bottom quarter		Second quarter		Third quarter		Top quarter	
	Mean index	S.E.	Mean index	S.E.	Mean index	S.E.	Mean index	S.E.	Mean index	S.E.	Mean score	S.E.	Mean score	S.E.	Mean score	S.E.	Mean score	S.E.
Adjudicated regions																		
Italy (Provincia Autonoma di Bolzano)	49.7	(0.6)	29.3	(0.3)	44.8	(0.26)	54.4	(0.2)	70.5	(0.4)	**523**	(5.2)	536	(8.9)	529	(5.9)	**562**	(7.9)
Italy (Provincia Autonoma di Trento)	48.6	(0.6)	27.9	(0.3)	41.8	(0.29)	51.9	(0.2)	72.9	(0.6)	542	(5.9)	543	(5.5)	550	(5.5)	558	(6.2)
Italy (Regione Lombardia)	49.6	(0.7)	29.8	(0.2)	45.0	(0.22)	52.5	(0.1)	71.0	(0.6)	**485**	(10.9)	518	(8.7)	524	(5.3)	**557**	(9.8)
Italy (Regione Piemonte)	47.0	(0.9)	28.4	(0.2)	40.6	(0.26)	50.8	(0.1)	68.3	(0.8)	**463**	(7.0)	485	(5.0)	507	(6.1)	**524**	(8.9)
Italy (Regione Toscana)	48.0	(0.9)	28.5	(0.2)	42.0	(0.27)	51.6	(0.1)	69.8	(0.7)	**457**	(7.5)	490	(5.1)	506	(5.3)	**517**	(5.1)
Italy (Regione Veneto)	46.3	(0.9)	28.1	(0.3)	39.8	(0.21)	49.8	(0.1)	67.5	(0.6)	**496**	(6.7)	505	(6.5)	512	(7.4)	**533**	(5.8)
Spain (Basque Country)	45.2	(0.8)	25.6	(0.2)	35.5	(0.12)	49.5	(0.1)	70.2	(0.4)	**472**	(3.9)	494	(4.0)	512	(3.3)	**533**	(3.6)
Spain (Castile and Leon)	43.3	(1.0)	25.9	(0.3)	33.8	(0.19)	48.2	(0.2)	65.5	(0.8)	**476**	(7.0)	497	(7.1)	508	(6.8)	**535**	(6.1)
Spain (Catalonia)	47.8	(1.1)	29.1	(0.2)	40.1	(0.25)	52.5	(0.1)	69.6	(0.7)	**462**	(6.1)	486	(6.0)	509	(4.2)	**527**	(6.7)
United Kingdom (Scotland)	51.0	(0.4)	30.6	(0.2)	45.7	(0.14)	55.3	(0.2)	72.4	(0.3)	**493**	(4.1)	514	(4.2)	534	(3.4)	**565**	(3.5)
Non-adjudicated regions																		
Belgium (Flemish Community)	51.0	(0.4)	29.2	(0.2)	45.3	(0.19)	56.8	(0.2)	72.8	(0.2)	**505**	(5.0)	554	(3.7)	581	(3.4)	**611**	(2.8)
Belgium (French Community)	50.0	(0.7)	28.8	(0.2)	43.4	(0.18)	55.9	(0.2)	72.0	(0.2)	**451**	(5.7)	494	(5.7)	519	(4.4)	**561**	(5.9)
Belgium (German-speaking Community)	50.7	(0.6)	29.0	(0.4)	44.0	(0.33)	57.0	(0.4)	72.9	(0.5)	**467**	(6.3)	503	(6.3)	537	(6.7)	**571**	(7.8)
Finland (Finnish speaking)	50.1	(0.4)	28.6	(0.1)	43.2	(0.17)	56.2	(0.1)	72.3	(0.2)	**516**	(3.0)	537	(3.2)	553	(3.1)	**577**	(3.1)
Finland (Swedish speaking)	52.8	(0.5)	30.2	(0.3)	46.4	(0.29)	60.5	(0.3)	74.0	(0.4)	**503**	(5.1)	528	(4.7)	546	(6.4)	**561**	(4.9)
United Kingdom (Northern Ireland)	47.9	(0.5)	27.5	(0.2)	39.6	(0.13)	53.5	(0.1)	71.1	(0.3)	**478**	(4.0)	504	(4.0)	536	(3.5)	**565**	(4.3)
United Kingdom (Wales)	49.3	(0.8)	29.1	(0.7)	41.7	(0.75)	55.1	(0.5)	71.7	(1.1)	**478**	(16.5)	491	(22.3)	494	(7.9)	**542**	(17.7)

	Change in the mathematics score per 16.4 units of the international socio-economic index of occupational status		Increased likelihood of students in the bottom quarter of the HISEI index distribution scoring in the bottom quarter of the national mathematics performance distribution		Explained variance in student performance (r-squared × 100)	
	Effect	S.E.	Ratio	S.E.	%	S.E.
Adjudicated regions						
Italy (Provincia Autonoma di Bolzano)	**12.8**	(3.02)	**1.3**	(0.16)	2.1	(0.97)
Italy (Provincia Autonoma di Trento)	**6.9**	(2.87)	1.1	(0.14)	0.9	(0.70)
Italy (Regione Lombardia)	**27.0**	(5.05)	**1.9**	(0.22)	7.9	(2.49)
Italy (Regione Piemonte)	**24.7**	(2.92)	**1.8**	(0.19)	7.4	(1.70)
Italy (Regione Toscana)	**22.2**	(3.22)	**1.9**	(0.19)	6.4	(1.71)
Italy (Regione Veneto)	**15.9**	(2.58)	**1.3**	(0.14)	3.1	(0.98)
Spain (Basque Country)	**21.4**	(1.78)	**1.9**	(0.14)	7.8	(1.30)
Spain (Castile and Leon)	**21.8**	(3.75)	**1.7**	(0.23)	6.5	(1.88)
Spain (Catalonia)	**23.8**	(2.47)	**1.9**	(0.19)	7.1	(1.42)
United Kingdom (Scotland)	**28.4**	(1.91)	**2.1**	(0.15)	11.0	(1.40)
Non-adjudicated regions						
Belgium (Flemish Community)	**38.8**	(2.13)	**2.7**	(0.17)	16.55	(1.56)
Belgium (French Community)	**39.3**	(2.93)	**2.3**	(0.16)	15.0	(1.95)
Belgium (German-speaking Community)	**35.1**	(3.50)	**2.3**	(0.27)	13.7	(2.79)
Finland (Finnish speaking)	**21.9**	(1.35)	**1.7**	(0.08)	7.3	(0.87)
Finland (Swedish speaking)	**20.5**	(2.53)	**2.1**	(0.23)	7.0	(1.70)
United Kingdom (Northern Ireland)	**32.2**	(1.90)	**2.1**	(0.12)	13.2	(1.35)
United Kingdom (Wales)	**23.0**	(6.11)	1.6	(0.53)	7.7	(3.86)

Note: Values that are statistically significant are indicated in bold (see Annex A4).

Table B2.9 (see Table 4.4, Annex A1)

Index of economic, social and cultural status (ESCS) and performance on the mathematics scale, by national quarters of the index

Results based on students' self-reports

	Index of economic, social and cultural status										Performance on the mathematics scale, by national quarters of the index of economic, social and cultural status							
	All students		Bottom quarter		Second quarter		Third quarter		Top quarter		Bottom quarter		Second quarter		Third quarter		Top quarter	
	Mean index	S.E.	Mean index	S.E.	Mean index	S.E.	Mean index	S.E.	Mean index	S.E.	Mean score	S.E.	Mean score	S.E.	Mean score	S.E.	Mean score	S.E.
Adjudicated regions																		
Italy (Provincia Autonoma di Bolzano)	0.1	(0.0)	–1.0	(0.0)	–0.2	(0.01)	0.4	(0.0)	1.3	(0.0)	**513**	(6.1)	535	(5.3)	538	(7.1)	**560**	(8.2)
Italy (Provincia Autonoma di Trento)	0.1	(0.0)	–1.0	(0.0)	–0.3	(0.01)	0.4	(0.0)	1.4	(0.0)	**532**	(6.8)	548	(5.6)	550	(6.4)	**561**	(6.3)
Italy (Regione Lombardia)	0.1	(0.0)	–1.1	(0.1)	–0.2	(0.01)	0.4	(0.0)	1.3	(0.0)	**485**	(9.2)	509	(6.7)	527	(8.7)	**559**	(9.0)
Italy (Regione Piemonte)	0.0	(0.1)	–1.2	(0.0)	–0.4	(0.01)	0.3	(0.0)	1.2	(0.0)	**459**	(6.6)	483	(5.8)	507	(6.2)	**528**	(8.3)
Italy (Regione Toscana)	0.0	(0.1)	–1.2	(0.0)	–0.3	(0.01)	0.4	(0.0)	1.3	(0.0)	**451**	(5.9)	485	(6.7)	507	(5.2)	**524**	(5.0)
Italy (Regione Veneto)	–0.1	(0.1)	–1.3	(0.0)	–0.5	(0.01)	0.2	(0.0)	1.2	(0.0)	**485**	(6.6)	505	(7.8)	517	(7.3)	**537**	(6.2)
Spain (Basque Country)	–0.1	(0.0)	–1.3	(0.0)	–0.4	(0.01)	0.2	(0.0)	1.1	(0.0)	**471**	(4.1)	489	(3.6)	511	(3.6)	**538**	(3.4)
Spain (Castile and Leon)	–0.2	(0.1)	–1.4	(0.0)	–0.5	(0.01)	0.1	(0.0)	1.0	(0.0)	**462**	(6.3)	497	(5.8)	514	(5.3)	**540**	(5.2)
Spain (Catalonia)	–0.1	(0.1)	–1.4	(0.0)	–0.4	(0.01)	0.2	(0.0)	1.1	(0.0)	**452**	(5.2)	486	(4.8)	505	(5.6)	**535**	(6.0)
United Kingdom (Scotland)	0.1	(0.0)	–1.1	(0.0)	–0.2	(0.01)	0.4	(0.0)	1.2	(0.0)	**482**	(4.0)	509	(3.2)	536	(3.1)	**573**	(3.2)
Non-adjudicated regions																		
Belgium (Flemish Community)	0.2	(0.0)	–1.0	(0.0)	–0.1	(0.01)	0.5	(0.0)	1.3	(0.0)	**495**	(5.3)	545	(3.5)	581	(3.1)	**618**	(2.8)
Belgium (French Community)	0.1	(0.0)	–1.2	(0.0)	–0.2	(0.01)	0.5	(0.0)	1.3	(0.0)	**433**	(5.6)	481	(4.6)	523	(4.8)	**570**	(5.5)
Belgium (German-speaking Community)	0.1	(0.0)	–1.0	(0.0)	–0.2	(0.01)	0.5	(0.0)	1.3	(0.0)	**474**	(6.5)	495	(6.5)	527	(6.9)	**571**	(6.9)
Finland (Finnish speaking)	0.2	(0.0)	–0.8	(0.0)	0.0	(0.01)	0.6	(0.0)	1.3	(0.0)	**509**	(2.9)	538	(2.6)	554	(2.8)	**580**	(3.0)
Finland (Swedish speaking)	0.3	(0.0)	–0.8	(0.0)	0.0	(0.01)	0.6	(0.0)	1.3	(0.0)	**498**	(5.3)	527	(5.0)	537	(5.1)	**575**	(4.5)
United Kingdom (Northern Ireland)	0.0	(0.0)	–1.1	(0.0)	–0.4	(0.01)	0.2	(0.0)	1.2	(0.0)	**466**	(4.6)	499	(4.3)	530	(3.7)	**572**	(3.5)
United Kingdom (Wales)	0.2	(0.1)	–0.9	(0.0)	–0.2	(0.02)	0.5	(0.1)	1.4	(0.1)	**481**	(15.3)	475	(15.2)	500	(15.0)	**547**	(16.8)

	Change in the mathematics score per unit of the index of economic, social and cultural status		Increased likelihood of students in the bottom quarter of the ESCS distribution scoring in the bottom quarter of the national mathematics performance distribution		Explained variance in student performance (r-squared × 100)	
	Effect	S.E.	Ratio	S.E.	%	S.E.
Adjudicated regions						
Italy (Provincia Autonoma di Bolzano)	**21.3**	(3.94)	**1.60**	(0.20)	4.8	(1.62)
Italy (Provincia Autonoma di Trento)	**12.9**	(3.54)	**1.41**	(0.20)	2.4	(1.24)
Italy (Regione Lombardia)	**30.8**	(4.19)	**1.95**	(0.18)	10.1	(2.59)
Italy (Regione Piemonte)	**29.7**	(3.25)	**1.96**	(0.15)	10.6	(2.17)
Italy (Regione Toscana)	**29.8**	(3.09)	**2.11**	(0.21)	11.0	(2.18)
Italy (Regione Veneto)	**21.3**	(3.11)	**1.68**	(0.19)	5.6	(1.43)
Spain (Basque Country)	**28.8**	(2.05)	**2.01**	(0.12)	10.7	(1.46)
Spain (Castile and Leon)	**32.2**	(3.70)	**2.14**	(0.22)	13.0	(2.52)
Spain (Catalonia)	**33.3**	(2.41)	**2.43**	(0.20)	13.8	(1.97)
United Kingdom (Scotland)	**39.0**	(1.88)	**2.48**	(0.16)	18.1	(1.43)
Non-adjudicated regions						
Belgium (Flemish Community)	**53.3**	(2.31)	**2.95**	(0.22)	23.5	(1.94)
Belgium (French Community)	**54.0**	(2.90)	**3.10**	(0.20)	25.5	(2.17)
Belgium (German-speaking Community)	**42.3**	(3.79)	**2.09**	(0.24)	15.5	(2.73)
Finland (Finnish speaking)	**33.1**	(1.73)	**1.97**	(0.09)	10.8	(1.10)
Finland (Swedish speaking)	**34.2**	(3.02)	**2.39**	(0.24)	12.1	(2.08)
United Kingdom (Northern Ireland)	**46.3**	(2.10)	**2.34**	(0.17)	19.9	(1.46)
United Kingdom (Wales)	**34.7**	(7.00)	**2.23**	(0.36)	13.6	(4.83)

Note: Values that are statistically significant are indicated in bold (see Annex A4).

Table B2.10 (see Table 5.1a, Annex A1)

Index of teacher support in mathematics lessons and student performance on the mathematics scale, by national quarters of the index

Results based on students' self-reports

	Index of teacher support in mathematics lessons										Performance on the mathematics scale, by national quarters of the index of teacher support							
	All students		Bottom quarter		Second quarter		Third quarter		Top quarter		Bottom quarter		Second quarter		Third quarter		Top quarter	
	Mean index	S.E.	Mean index	S.E.	Mean index	S.E.	Mean index	S.E.	Mean index	S.E.	Mean score	S.E.	Mean score	S.E.	Mean score	S.E.	Mean score	S.E.
Adjudicated regions																		
Italy (Provincia Autonoma di Bolzano)	–0.44	(0.04)	–1.71	(0.05)	–0.74	(0.01)	–0.11	(0.01)	0.79	(0.03)	537	(10.4)	538	(5.8)	545	(6.5)	525	(4.9)
Italy (Provincia Autonoma di Trento)	–0.32	(0.03)	–1.58	(0.06)	–0.58	(0.01)	–0.02	(0.01)	0.91	(0.03)	545	(5.3)	554	(6.4)	550	(5.6)	543	(6.5)
Italy (Regione Lombardia)	–0.26	(0.05)	–1.50	(0.04)	–0.54	(0.01)	0.04	(0.01)	0.94	(0.03)	518	(9.5)	525	(8.7)	524	(9.6)	513	(10.9)
Italy (Regione Piemonte)	–0.22	(0.07)	–1.55	(0.05)	–0.47	(0.01)	0.12	(0.01)	1.01	(0.03)	**503**	(8.2)	503	(5.4)	488	(6.6)	**484**	(7.0)
Italy (Regione Toscana)	–0.30	(0.04)	–1.60	(0.03)	–0.55	(0.01)	0.06	(0.01)	0.91	(0.03)	497	(7.1)	496	(5.2)	491	(7.1)	484	(6.8)
Italy (Regione Veneto)	–0.32	(0.06)	–1.57	(0.04)	–0.59	(0.01)	0.01	(0.01)	0.89	(0.03)	522	(8.1)	508	(6.4)	511	(6.9)	503	(7.2)
Spain (Basque Country)	–0.10	(0.03)	–1.26	(0.03)	–0.37	(0.01)	0.13	(0.01)	1.11	(0.02)	498	(4.5)	503	(3.6)	508	(4.5)	501	(3.2)
Spain (Castile and Leon)	–0.26	(0.07)	–1.68	(0.05)	–0.58	(0.01)	0.05	(0.01)	1.19	(0.03)	513	(6.7)	502	(5.4)	503	(5.8)	498	(6.4)
Spain (Catalonia)	–0.03	(0.05)	–1.18	(0.05)	–0.30	(0.01)	0.18	(0.01)	1.20	(0.04)	492	(6.4)	497	(5.6)	498	(7.5)	495	(7.0)
United Kingdom (Scotland)	0.19	(0.03)	–1.14	(0.03)	–0.07	(0.01)	0.52	(0.01)	1.46	(0.02)	**515**	(3.6)	516	(4.8)	532	(4.0)	**535**	(4.1)
Non-adjudicated regions																		
Belgium (Flemish Community)	–0.14	(0.02)	–1.37	(0.02)	–0.43	(0.01)	0.15	(0.01)	1.11	(0.02)	561	(4.1)	562	(3.4)	565	(3.6)	563	(4.5)
Belgium (French Community)	–0.07	(0.03)	–1.33	(0.03)	–0.38	(0.01)	0.19	(0.01)	1.23	(0.02)	**521**	(5.9)	511	(4.6)	506	(5.8)	**490**	(6.2)
Belgium (German-speaking Community)	–0.42	(0.03)	–1.73	(0.04)	–0.72	(0.01)	–0.10	(0.01)	0.88	(0.04)	518	(6.1)	529	(6.2)	520	(7.7)	502	(7.7)
Finland (Finnish speaking)	0.08	(0.02)	–1.02	(0.02)	–0.14	(0.00)	0.32	(0.01)	1.15	(0.02)	**539**	(3.3)	543	(3.1)	549	(3.5)	**550**	(3.4)
Finland (Swedish speaking)	0.02	(0.02)	–1.04	(0.03)	–0.21	(0.01)	0.25	(0.01)	1.10	(0.03)	530	(4.3)	531	(5.3)	538	(5.5)	539	(6.5)
United Kingdom (Northern Ireland)	0.19	(0.03)	–1.14	(0.02)	–0.12	(0.01)	0.50	(0.01)	1.51	(0.02)	515	(3.8)	514	(5.5)	522	(4.5)	517	(4.3)
United Kingdom (Wales)	0.20	(0.11)	–1.17	(0.11)	–0.05	(0.02)	0.54	(0.02)	1.54	(0.06)	496	(16.8)	488	(13.7)	511	(12.2)	500	(17.9)

	Change in the mathematics score per unit of the index of teacher support		Increased likelihood of students in the bottom quarter of this index scoring in the bottom quarter of the national mathematics performance distribution		Explained variance in student performance (r-squared × 100)	
	Effect	S.E.	Ratio	S.E.	%	S.E.
Adjudicated regions						
Italy (Provincia Autonoma di Bolzano)	–5.4	(3.70)	0.9	(0.14)	–3.6	(3.78)
Italy (Provincia Autonoma di Trento)	–1.7	(3.03)	0.9	(0.12)	–2.4	(3.19)
Italy (Regione Lombardia)	–3.5	(4.20)	0.9	(0.11)	–3.1	(2.85)
Italy (Regione Piemonte)	**–9.2**	(3.27)	0.9	(0.12)	–3.8	(3.22)
Italy (Regione Toscana)	–5.2	(2.91)	**0.8**	(0.08)	–5.4	(2.22)
Italy (Regione Veneto)	–6.4	(3.38)	0.8	(0.13)	–3.9	(3.59)
Spain (Basque Country)	1.6	(1.74)	1.1	(0.10)	3.2	(2.37)
Spain (Castile and Leon)	–4.8	(3.22)	**0.7**	(0.11)	–9.4	(3.54)
Spain (Catalonia)	0.5	(2.80)	1.1	(0.13)	3.2	(2.93)
United Kingdom (Scotland)	**7.7**	(2.03)	1.1	(0.09)	3.1	(2.09)
Non-adjudicated regions						
Belgium (Flemish Community)	0.7	(2.08)	0.9	(0.07)	–2.5	(1.77)
Belgium (French Community)	**–12.5**	(2.57)	**0.8**	(0.07)	–6.5	(1.99)
Belgium (German-speaking Community)	–5.8	(3.47)	0.9	(0.12)	–2.9	(3.26)
Finland (Finnish speaking)	**4.4**	(1.93)	1.1	(0.06)	2.8	(1.51)
Finland (Swedish speaking)	3.4	(3.62)	1.0	(0.13)	–0.8	(3.49)
United Kingdom (Northern Ireland)	0.9	(1.88)	1.0	(0.08)	0.1	(2.07)
United Kingdom (Wales)	4.9	(7.41)	0.9	(0.31)	–2.1	(8.20)

Note: Values that are statistically significant are indicated in bold (see Annex A4).

Table B2.11 (see Table 5.2a, Annex A1)

Index of principals' perceptions of student-related factors affecting school climate and student performance on the mathematics scale, by national quarters of the index

Results based on reports from school principals and reported proportionate to the number of 15-year-olds enrolled in the school

	Index of student-related factors affecting school climate										Performance on the mathematics scale, by national quarters of the index of student-related factors affecting school climate							
	All students		Bottom quarter		Second quarter		Third quarter		Top quarter		Bottom quarter		Second quarter		Third quarter		Top quarter	
	Mean index	S.E.	Mean index	S.E.	Mean index	S.E.	Mean index	S.E.	Mean index	S.E.	Mean score	S.E.	Mean score	S.E.	Mean score	S.E.	Mean score	S.E.
Adjudicated regions																		
Italy (Provincia Autonoma di Bolzano)	–0.15	(0.06)	–1.05	(0.01)	–0.29	(0.01)	0.01	(0.02)	0.75	(0.06)	540	(4.9)	523	(6.3)	524	(6.2)	558	(12.2)
Italy (Provincia Autonoma di Trento)	0.41	(0.02)	–1.02	(0.02)	0.08	(0.04)	0.76	(0.02)	1.85	(0.02)	**546**	(4.9)	555	(9.4)	563	(6.1)	**525**	(5.6)
Italy (Regione Lombardia)	0.33	(0.11)	–0.96	(0.06)	–0.10	(0.04)	0.70	(0.06)	1.68	(0.16)	**480**	(7.2)	511	(24.1)	534	(13.1)	**553**	(16.6)
Italy (Regione Piemonte)	0.11	(0.12)	–1.00	(0.12)	–0.12	(0.05)	0.46	(0.05)	1.11	(0.08)	**465**	(11.6)	497	(11.5)	505	(11.6)	**509**	(7.9)
Italy (Regione Toscana)	–0.10	(0.11)	–1.04	(0.12)	–0.30	(0.03)	0.14	(0.02)	0.81	(0.13)	**457**	(13.2)	490	(14.4)	519	(9.3)	**495**	(13.9)
Italy (Regione Veneto)	0.31	(0.13)	–0.86	(0.14)	–0.07	(0.05)	0.68	(0.05)	1.50	(0.16)	**472**	(12.8)	526	(14.5)	520	(10.6)	**526**	(8.6)
Spain (Basque Country)	0.59	(0.09)	–0.73	(0.08)	0.20	(0.03)	0.83	(0.03)	2.08	(0.08)	**488**	(5.2)	500	(5.8)	506	(5.8)	**513**	(5.0)
Spain (Castile and Leon)	–0.16	(0.13)	–1.34	(0.12)	–0.54	(0.05)	0.17	(0.05)	1.05	(0.08)	**493**	(8.6)	494	(8.5)	507	(9.0)	**518**	(7.5)
Spain (Catalonia)	0.50	(0.18)	–0.76	(0.14)	–0.04	(0.04)	0.81	(0.07)	1.98	(0.15)	481	(9.5)	486	(9.9)	502	(7.8)	509	(11.4)
United Kingdom (Scotland)	–0.11	(0.06)	–0.99	(0.06)	–0.35	(0.03)	0.09	(0.01)	0.79	(0.10)	**500**	(5.6)	520	(4.4)	532	(7.3)	**544**	(5.7)
Non-adjudicated regions																		
Belgium (Flemish Community)	0.76	(0.07)	–0.54	(0.09)	0.42	(0.03)	1.13	(0.03)	2.03	(0.05)	**489**	(10.0)	553	(9.9)	568	(7.2)	**597**	(7.1)
Belgium (French Community)	–0.15	(0.10)	–1.31	(0.07)	–0.61	(0.03)	0.16	(0.04)	1.16	(0.11)	**459**	(14.7)	467	(13.3)	530	(10.1)	**543**	(7.9)
Belgium (German-speaking Community)	0.10	(0.00)	–0.55	(0.00)	–0.03	(0.01)	0.39	(0.00)	0.58	(0.01)	**425**	(6.2)	537	(7.0)	554	(6.1)	**545**	(6.0)
Finland (Finnish speaking)	–0.11	(0.05)	–0.91	(0.04)	–0.30	(0.02)	0.15	(0.01)	0.62	(0.05)	**536**	(3.4)	542	(4.2)	553	(3.3)	**548**	(3.8)
Finland (Swedish speaking)	0.05	(0.00)	–0.47	(0.01)	–0.01	(0.01)	0.09	(0.00)	0.59	(0.01)	**517**	(5.7)	533	(5.7)	545	(6.2)	**541**	(4.2)
United Kingdom (Northern Ireland)	0.05	(0.05)	–1.01	(0.06)	–0.28	(0.02)	0.29	(0.03)	1.22	(0.09)	**457**	(7.6)	495	(8.7)	538	(9.1)	**569**	(8.2)
United Kingdom (Wales)	–0.09	(0.25)	–0.87	(0.07)	–0.62	(0.07)	–0.03	(0.24)	1.21	(0.11)	480	(16.6)	524	(13.2)	491	(10.7)	497	(13.3)

	Change in the mathematics score per unit of the index of student-related factors affecting school climate		Increased likelihood of students in the bottom quarter of this index scoring in the bottom quarter of the national mathematics performance distribution		Explained variance in student performance (r-squared × 100)	
	Effect	S.E.	Ratio	S.E.	%	S.E.
Adjudicated regions						
Italy (Provincia Autonoma di Bolzano)	12.3	(8.65)	0.9	(0.13)	1.0	(1.42)
Italy (Provincia Autonoma di Trento)	–2.4	(2.48)	1.0	(0.13)	0.1	(0.28)
Italy (Regione Lombardia)	**29.7**	(5.99)	1.9	(0.47)	10.9	(4.24)
Italy (Regione Piemonte)	**22.7**	(5.97)	1.8	(0.42)	4.7	(2.73)
Italy (Regione Toscana)	**26.6**	(7.79)	1.9	(0.50)	5.2	(3.25)
Italy (Regione Veneto)	**16.8**	(5.82)	**2.1**	(0.43)	3.6	(2.30)
Spain (Basque Country)	**7.3**	(2.39)	**1.3**	(0.15)	0.9	(0.68)
Spain (Castile and Leon)	**10.7**	(4.17)	1.3	(0.21)	1.4	(1.10)
Spain (Catalonia)	10.7	(5.53)	1.2	(0.22)	1.8	(1.83)
United Kingdom (Scotland)	**22.9**	(3.67)	**1.6**	(0.17)	**3.9**	(1.37)
Non-adjudicated regions						
Belgium (Flemish Community)	**40.3**	(4.12)	**2.8**	(0.41)	15.3	(3.34)
Belgium (French Community)	**36.8**	(6.64)	**1.9**	(0.40)	11.1	(3.76)
Belgium (German-speaking Community)	**103.2**	(6.97)	**4.8**	(0.53)	22.3	(2.55)
Finland (Finnish speaking)	**9.0**	(2.91)	**1.2**	(0.08)	0.4	(0.29)
Finland (Swedish speaking)	**11.6**	(5.50)	**1.5**	(0.18)	0.4	(0.40)
United Kingdom (Northern Ireland)	**47.5**	(5.28)	**2.3**	(0.25)	20.5	(3.34)
United Kingdom (Wales)	1.9	(9.47)	1.8	(0.69)	0.0	(0.67)

Note: Values that are statistically significant are indicated in bold (see Annex A4).

Table B2.12 (see Table 5.3a, Annex A1)

Index of disciplinary climate and student performance on the mathematics scale, by national quarters of the index

Results based on students' self-reports

	Index of disciplinary climate in mathematics lessons										Performance on the mathematics scale, by national quarters of the index of disciplinary climate							
	All students		Bottom quarter		Second quarter		Third quarter		Top quarter		Bottom quarter		Second quarter		Third quarter		Top quarter	
	Mean index	S.E.	Mean index	S.E.	Mean index	S.E.	Mean index	S.E.	Mean index	S.E.	Mean score	S.E.	Mean score	S.E.	Mean score	S.E.	Mean score	S.E.
Adjudicated regions																		
Italy (Provincia Autonoma di Bolzano)	0.09	(0.04)	–1.30	(0.03)	–0.33	(0.01)	0.37	(0.01)	1.63	(0.05)	**525**	(6.2)	524	(5.8)	535	(7.3)	**560**	(7.7)
Italy (Provincia Autonoma di Trento)	0.08	(0.03)	–1.35	(0.04)	–0.26	(0.02)	0.44	(0.02)	1.48	(0.03)	**530**	(7.3)	546	(7.0)	559	(5.7)	**557**	(6.2)
Italy (Regione Lombardia)	–0.04	(0.07)	–1.41	(0.03)	–0.43	(0.02)	0.31	(0.01)	1.36	(0.03)	**493**	(9.9)	507	(10.7)	526	(8.1)	**554**	(8.8)
Italy (Regione Piemonte)	–0.17	(0.04)	–1.50	(0.03)	–0.51	(0.01)	0.18	(0.01)	1.14	(0.04)	**479**	(7.0)	487	(5.9)	497	(6.8)	**516**	(7.3)
Italy (Regione Toscana)	–0.28	(0.05)	–1.50	(0.04)	–0.65	(0.01)	0.03	(0.01)	1.01	(0.03)	**472**	(6.5)	483	(8.7)	499	(5.7)	**516**	(5.7)
Italy (Regione Veneto)	–0.14	(0.05)	–1.43	(0.02)	–0.50	(0.01)	0.19	(0.01)	1.18	(0.03)	**491**	(8.9)	502	(7.2)	520	(6.6)	**531**	(6.3)
Spain (Basque Country)	0.00	(0.03)	–1.18	(0.03)	–0.31	(0.01)	0.23	(0.01)	1.26	(0.02)	**488**	(5.0)	495	(4.5)	507	(3.4)	**520**	(3.7)
Spain (Castile and Leon)	–0.01	(0.05)	–1.30	(0.03)	–0.36	(0.01)	0.25	(0.01)	1.36	(0.04)	**489**	(7.3)	492	(5.9)	510	(5.6)	**525**	(5.2)
Spain (Catalonia)	–0.04	(0.05)	–1.16	(0.02)	–0.33	(0.01)	0.20	(0.01)	1.15	(0.04)	**466**	(6.0)	491	(6.9)	504	(6.5)	**522**	(6.4)
United Kingdom (Scotland)	0.19	(0.04)	–1.26	(0.02)	–0.17	(0.01)	0.56	(0.01)	1.62	(0.03)	**487**	(4.4)	515	(4.0)	536	(3.9)	**561**	(3.6)
Non-adjudicated regions																		
Belgium (Flemish Community)	0.17	(0.03)	–1.16	(0.02)	–0.16	(0.01)	0.44	(0.01)	1.54	(0.02)	**539**	(3.5)	553	(3.8)	571	(3.4)	**588**	(4.1)
Belgium (French Community)	–0.13	(0.04)	–1.36	(0.02)	–0.50	(0.01)	0.13	(0.01)	1.23	(0.03)	**478**	(6.0)	495	(5.8)	513	(4.6)	**545**	(5.1)
Belgium (German-speaking Community)	–0.05	(0.03)	–1.33	(0.05)	–0.39	(0.01)	0.18	(0.01)	1.34	(0.04)	**490**	(7.9)	506	(6.9)	518	(6.2)	**556**	(6.8)
Finland (Finnish speaking)	–0.16	(0.02)	–1.26	(0.01)	–0.44	(0.01)	0.08	(0.00)	0.97	(0.02)	**534**	(3.2)	539	(3.4)	545	(3.0)	**562**	(3.5)
Finland (Swedish speaking)	0.03	(0.03)	–1.08	(0.03)	–0.23	(0.01)	0.24	(0.01)	1.19	(0.03)	**516**	(5.2)	534	(5.1)	539	(4.8)	**550**	(5.7)
United Kingdom (Northern Ireland)	0.23	(0.03)	–1.13	(0.03)	–0.11	(0.01)	0.55	(0.01)	1.63	(0.02)	**485**	(5.2)	510	(5.0)	524	(4.2)	**549**	(3.8)
United Kingdom (Wales)	–0.04	(0.21)	–1.38	(0.06)	–0.45	(0.05)	0.29	(0.03)	1.40	(0.07)	**467**	(13.8)	487	(13.5)	504	(14.6)	**537**	(15.5)

	Change in the mathematics score per unit of the index of disciplinary climate		Increased likelihood of students in the bottom quarter of this index scoring in the bottom quarter of the national mathematics performance distribution		Explained variance in student performance (r-squared × 100)	
	Effect	S.E.	Ratio	S.E.	%	S.E.
Adjudicated regions						
Italy (Provincia Autonoma di Bolzano)	**12.1**	(2.52)	1.1	(0.13)	2.7	(1.12)
Italy (Provincia Autonoma di Trento)	**10.0**	(3.12)	1.4	(0.21)	2.1	(1.26)
Italy (Regione Lombardia)	**20.2**	(5.16)	**1.7**	(0.23)	5.8	(2.62)
Italy (Regione Piemonte)	**14.0**	(3.13)	1.3	(0.18)	2.8	(1.35)
Italy (Regione Toscana)	**16.1**	(3.13)	**1.7**	(0.23)	3.5	(1.40)
Italy (Regione Veneto)	**15.1**	(3.83)	**1.4**	(0.20)	3.3	(1.65)
Spain (Basque Country)	**11.1**	(2.40)	**1.5**	(0.11)	1.7	(0.73)
Spain (Castile and Leon)	**11.7**	(2.94)	**1.4**	(0.13)	2.2	(1.11)
Spain (Catalonia)	**21.5**	(2.66)	**1.7**	(0.22)	5.2	(1.32)
United Kingdom (Scotland)	**23.9**	(2.05)	**2.0**	(0.17)	10.5	(1.72)
Non-adjudicated regions						
Belgium (Flemish Community)	**17.4**	(1.76)	**1.4**	(0.08)	3.6	(0.72)
Belgium (French Community)	**24.5**	(2.40)	**1.7**	(0.13)	6.4	(1.11)
Belgium (German-speaking Community)	**22.8**	(3.21)	**1.8**	(0.24)	5.9	(1.62)
Finland (Finnish speaking)	**10.4**	(1.62)	**1.3**	(0.07)	1.3	(0.39)
Finland (Swedish speaking)	**12.1**	(3.14)	**1.5**	(0.17)	1.8	(0.90)
United Kingdom (Northern Ireland)	**20.4**	(2.16)	**1.8**	(0.14)	5.7	(1.07)
United Kingdom (Wales)	**23.7**	(4.75)	1.9	(0.77)	9.6	(3.76)

Note: Values that are statistically significant are indicated in bold (see Annex A4).

Table B2.13 (see Table 5.4a, Annex A1)

Index of principals' perceptions of teacher-related factors affecting school climate and student performance on the mathematics scale, by national quarters of the index

Results based on reports from school principals and reported proportionate to the number of 15-year-olds enrolled in the school

	Index of teacher-related factors affecting school climate										Performance on the mathematics scale, by national quarters of the index of teacher-related factors affecting school climate							
	All students		Bottom quarter		Second quarter		Third quarter		Top quarter		Bottom quarter		Second quarter		Third quarter		Top quarter	
	Mean index	S.E.	Mean index	S.E.	Mean index	S.E.	Mean index	S.E.	Mean index	S.E.	Mean score	S.E.	Mean score	S.E.	Mean score	S.E.	Mean score	S.E.
Adjudicated regions																		
Italy (Provincia Autonoma di Bolzano)	–0.20	(0.09)	–1.23	(0.04)	–0.53	(0.01)	0.01	(0.01)	0.96	(0.15)	523	(5.0)	529	(5.3)	551	(8.6)	542	(15.4)
Italy (Provincia Autonoma di Trento)	–0.03	(0.01)	–0.82	(0.01)	–0.19	(0.01)	0.13	(0.00)	0.77	(0.04)	**549**	(5.5)	556	(5.4)	560	(10.0)	**525**	(4.9)
Italy (Regione Lombardia)	0.12	(0.12)	–1.05	(0.04)	–0.26	(0.06)	0.42	(0.05)	1.36	(0.15)	540	(14.0)	526	(13.1)	523	(17.1)	490	(21.5)
Italy (Regione Piemonte)	0.29	(0.12)	–0.84	(0.12)	0.06	(0.05)	0.56	(0.03)	1.38	(0.13)	504	(12.4)	491	(10.8)	487	(13.6)	493	(13.2)
Italy (Regione Toscana)	–0.10	(0.13)	–1.25	(0.08)	–0.43	(0.04)	0.15	(0.07)	1.15	(0.20)	495	(15.1)	498	(18.4)	495	(12.0)	479	(12.7)
Italy (Regione Veneto)	–0.04	(0.13)	–1.26	(0.15)	–0.37	(0.05)	0.20	(0.03)	1.29	(0.20)	510	(10.5)	516	(10.3)	526	(8.3)	492	(16.3)
Spain (Basque Country)	0.28	(0.08)	–0.89	(0.06)	–0.04	(0.03)	0.47	(0.03)	1.57	(0.10)	492	(6.5)	506	(5.9)	506	(5.1)	502	(5.7)
Spain (Castile and Leon)	0.31	(0.17)	–0.91	(0.06)	–0.27	(0.04)	0.70	(0.06)	1.71	(0.17)	510	(11.4)	511	(9.9)	504	(8.4)	488	(6.9)
Spain (Catalonia)	0.26	(0.15)	–0.97	(0.16)	–0.07	(0.04)	0.49	(0.07)	1.60	(0.15)	491	(8.2)	499	(8.4)	492	(10.0)	495	(10.9)
United Kingdom (Scotland)	–0.09	(0.07)	–1.08	(0.06)	–0.39	(0.03)	0.08	(0.04)	1.04	(0.12)	**502**	(6.3)	523	(4.2)	528	(6.0)	**543**	(5.8)
Non-adjudicated regions																		
Belgium (Flemish Community)	0.62	(0.07)	–0.43	(0.06)	0.29	(0.02)	0.87	(0.02)	1.75	(0.08)	540	(11.3)	561	(10.6)	556	(9.0)	550	(9.5)
Belgium (French Community)	–0.12	(0.09)	–1.05	(0.06)	–0.37	(0.02)	0.10	(0.02)	0.86	(0.13)	494	(14.7)	490	(12.3)	513	(13.6)	502	(12.9)
Belgium (German-speaking Community)	–0.27	(0.00)	–0.84	(0.01)	–0.34	(0.01)	–0.03	(0.01)	0.12	(0.00)	551	(5.1)	455	(9.3)	491	(8.5)	564	(8.1)
Finland (Finnish speaking)	0.09	(0.06)	–0.81	(0.07)	–0.12	(0.02)	0.31	(0.02)	0.97	(0.06)	541	(3.7)	545	(4.0)	549	(3.7)	545	(4.0)
Finland (Swedish speaking)	0.03	(0.00)	–0.71	(0.01)	–0.12	(0.01)	0.20	(0.00)	0.73	(0.01)	536	(5.5)	532	(5.4)	536	(5.5)	532	(5.2)
United Kingdom (Northern Ireland)	0.09	(0.05)	–0.88	(0.05)	–0.19	(0.02)	0.27	(0.02)	1.17	(0.09)	**465**	(7.3)	506	(8.4)	525	(11.2)	**563**	(9.8)
United Kingdom (Wales)	0.22	(0.32)	–1.19	(0.34)	–0.30	(0.11)	0.52	(0.18)	1.90	(0.47)	505	(5.1)	500	(30.6)	494	(12.9)	493	(14.1)

	Change in the mathematics score per unit of the index of teacher-related factors affecting school climate		Increased likelihood of students in the bottom quarter of this index scoring in the bottom quarter of the national mathematics performance distribution		Explained variance in student performance (r-squared × 100)	
	Effect	S.E.	Ratio	S.E.	%	S.E.
Adjudicated regions						
Italy (Provincia Autonoma di Bolzano)	13.1	(7.26)	1.1	(0.15)	1.8	(2.17)
Italy (Provincia Autonoma di Trento)	–7.2	(4.06)	1.2	(0.18)	0.4	(0.40)
Italy (Regione Lombardia)	–19.5	(11.35)	**0.6**	(0.20)	3.9	(4.44)
Italy (Regione Piemonte)	2.7	(9.45)	0.9	(0.22)	0.1	(0.81)
Italy (Regione Toscana)	–7.3	(7.70)	1.0	(0.37)	0.7	(1.53)
Italy (Regione Veneto)	–4.0	(6.55)	1.0	(0.19)	0.2	(0.83)
Spain (Basque Country)	3.0	(3.14)	1.2	(0.13)	0.1	(0.34)
Spain (Castile and Leon)	–8.1	(5.18)	0.9	(0.18)	1.0	(1.27)
Spain (Catalonia)	1.6	(6.78)	1.0	(0.19)	0.0	(0.50)
United Kingdom (Scotland)	**16.3**	(3.85)	**1.5**	(0.17)	2.8	(1.31)
Non-adjudicated regions						
Belgium (Flemish Community)	2.7	(7.09)	1.3	(0.23)	0.0	(0.44)
Belgium (French Community)	5.5	(11.16)	1.2	(0.29)	0.2	(0.97)
Belgium (German-speaking Community)	1.9	(7.42)	**0.4**	(0.07)	0.0	(0.09)
Finland (Finnish speaking)	1.8	(3.26)	1.1	(0.08)	0.0	(0.11)
Finland (Swedish speaking)	–2.6	(4.49)	0.9	(0.12)	0.0	(0.15)
United Kingdom (Northern Ireland)	**41.8**	(5.79)	**2.2**	(0.26)	13.1	(2.91)
United Kingdom (Wales)	–4.8	(3.40)	0.8	(0.37)	0.5	(0.86)

Note: Values that are statistically significant are indicated in bold (see Annex A4).

Table B2.14 (see Table 5.5a, Annex A1)

Index of principals' perceptions of teachers' morale and commitment and student performance on the mathematics scale, by national quarters of the index

Results based on reports from school principals and reported proportionate to the number of 15-year-olds enrolled in the school

	Index of school principals' perceptions of teachers' morale and commitment										Performance on the mathematics scale, by national quarters of the index of school principals' perceptions of teachers' morale and commitment							
	All students		Bottom quarter		Second quarter		Third quarter		Top quarter		Bottom quarter		Second quarter		Third quarter		Top quarter	
	Mean index	S.E.	Mean index	S.E.	Mean index	S.E.	Mean index	S.E.	Mean index	S.E.	Mean score	S.E.	Mean score	S.E.	Mean score	S.E.	Mean score	S.E.
Adjudicated regions																		
Italy (Provincia Autonoma di Bolzano)	–0.10	(0.07)	–0.94	(0.08)	–0.57	(0.00)	0.15	(0.03)	0.96	(0.02)	**525**	(6.7)	522	(5.7)	538	(4.3)	**560**	(14.3)
Italy (Provincia Autonoma di Trento)	–0.63	(0.00)	–1.39	(0.03)	–0.58	(0.00)	–0.57	(0.00)	0.03	(0.02)	546	(5.1)	542	(7.3)	545	(6.9)	557	(6.1)
Italy (Regione Lombardia)	–0.48	(0.12)	–1.53	(0.11)	–0.58	(0.00)	–0.31	(0.07)	0.51	(0.07)	504	(14.8)	515	(15.5)	528	(12.2)	531	(13.7)
Italy (Regione Piemonte)	–0.70	(0.09)	–1.53	(0.05)	–0.78	(0.06)	–0.57	(0.00)	0.07	(0.12)	494	(13.8)	488	(8.2)	487	(9.2)	507	(11.1)
Italy (Regione Toscana)	–0.75	(0.13)	–2.00	(0.10)	–0.91	(0.09)	–0.56	(0.00)	0.50	(0.14)	502	(10.5)	491	(11.7)	477	(14.4)	497	(15.0)
Italy (Regione Veneto)	–0.84	(0.13)	–1.93	(0.06)	–1.21	(0.04)	–0.57	(0.00)	0.35	(0.19)	496	(11.7)	506	(8.7)	523	(11.9)	519	(13.0)
Spain (Basque Country)	–0.29	(0.08)	–1.35	(0.06)	–0.57	(0.00)	–0.16	(0.06)	0.93	(0.07)	**488**	(5.0)	505	(4.7)	504	(5.7)	**510**	(6.4)
Spain (Castile and Leon)	–0.34	(0.11)	–1.48	(0.08)	–0.57	(0.00)	–0.01	(0.07)	0.71	(0.13)	487	(6.8)	517	(8.7)	509	(8.8)	499	(8.1)
Spain (Catalonia)	–0.37	(0.14)	–1.37	(0.09)	–0.57	(0.00)	–0.27	(0.09)	0.72	(0.16)	**478**	(10.3)	488	(6.4)	498	(7.4)	**514**	(9.6)
United Kingdom (Scotland)	0.23	(0.10)	–0.90	(0.08)	–0.19	(0.06)	0.48	(0.05)	1.53	(0.04)	514	(5.7)	525	(5.2)	531	(5.7)	525	(4.9)
Non-adjudicated regions																		
Belgium (Flemish Community)	–0.13	(0.06)	–1.01	(0.08)	–0.57	(0.00)	–0.03	(0.04)	1.07	(0.08)	**532**	(8.2)	535	(7.6)	574	(7.5)	**566**	(8.9)
Belgium (French Community)	–0.73	(0.07)	–1.62	(0.05)	–0.96	(0.04)	–0.57	(0.00)	0.22	(0.07)	**460**	(11.6)	493	(9.4)	504	(10.7)	**542**	(8.2)
Belgium (German-speaking Community)	–0.48	(0.00)	–1.48	(0.04)	–0.57	(0.00)	–0.40	(0.02)	0.55	(0.01)	**505**	(6.7)	490	(11.4)	497	(9.3)	**569**	(6.5)
Finland (Finnish speaking)	0.31	(0.06)	–0.80	(0.07)	0.12	(0.02)	0.58	(0.01)	1.33	(0.05)	542	(3.6)	544	(4.0)	543	(3.5)	551	(4.1)
Finland (Swedish speaking)	0.24	(0.00)	–0.59	(0.00)	–0.21	(0.02)	0.42	(0.01)	1.33	(0.01)	536	(5.6)	533	(6.8)	531	(5.5)	538	(4.9)
United Kingdom (Northern Ireland)	0.52	(0.08)	–0.83	(0.10)	0.24	(0.03)	1.02	(0.04)	1.65	(0.00)	**483**	(6.9)	507	(8.9)	514	(10.4)	**556**	(8.4)
United Kingdom (Wales)	0.30	(0.32)	–0.58	(0.00)	–0.36	(0.14)	0.72	(0.08)	1.42	(0.18)	513	(19.1)	516	(15.8)	482	(21.2)	480	(7.5)

	Change in the mathematics score per unit of the index of school principals' perceptions of teachers' morale and commitment		Increased likelihood of students in the bottom quarter of this index scoring in the bottom quarter of the national mathematics performance distribution		Explained variance in student performance (r-squared × 100)	
	Effect	S.E.	Ratio	S.E.	%	S.E.
Adjudicated regions						
Italy (Provincia Autonoma di Bolzano)	**23.2**	(6.51)	1.2	(0.28)	4.8	(2.56)
Italy (Provincia Autonoma di Trento)	2.1	(3.56)	1.0	(0.17)	0.0	(0.13)
Italy (Regione Lombardia)	11.0	(10.08)	1.3	(0.37)	0.9	(1.66)
Italy (Regione Piemonte)	6.3	(10.69)	1.3	(0.24)	0.2	(0.92)
Italy (Regione Toscana)	–2.5	(7.20)	0.8	(0.20)	0.1	(0.78)
Italy (Regione Veneto)	11.0	(8.23)	1.3	(0.29)	1.5	(2.30)
Spain (Basque Country)	**8.3**	(3.39)	**1.3**	(0.14)	0.8	(0.69)
Spain (Castile and Leon)	2.4	(4.69)	1.4	(0.21)	0.1	(0.31)
Spain (Catalonia)	**15.9**	(7.04)	1.4	(0.29)	2.4	(2.04)
United Kingdom (Scotland)	4.2	(3.20)	1.2	(0.14)	0.2	(0.36)
Non-adjudicated regions						
Belgium (Flemish Community)	**18.3**	(6.64)	**1.4**	(0.18)	2.3	(1.63)
Belgium (French Community)	**42.5**	(7.59)	**2.0**	(0.28)	8.5	(3.11)
Belgium (German-speaking Community)	**21.2**	(3.36)	1.1	(0.20)	3.0	(0.93)
Finland (Finnish speaking)	**5.2**	(2.60)	1.0	(0.08)	0.3	(0.27)
Finland (Swedish speaking)	–1.1	(3.11)	0.9	(0.13)	0.0	(0.12)
United Kingdom (Northern Ireland)	**25.8**	(4.54)	**1.7**	(0.20)	7.3	(2.36)
United Kingdom (Wales)	**–18.0**	(6.02)	0.6	(0.25)	3.3	(2.24)

Note: Values that are statistically significant are indicated in bold (see Annex A4).

Table B2.15 (see Table 5.6a, Annex A1)

Index of principals' perceptions of students' morale and commitment and student performance on the mathematics scale, by national quarters of the index

Results based on reports from school principals and reported proportionate to the number of 15-year-olds enrolled in the school

	Index of school principals' perceptions of students' morale and commitment										Performance on the mathematics scale, by national quarters of the index of school principals' perceptions of students' morale and commitment							
	All students		Bottom quarter		Second quarter		Third quarter		Top quarter		Bottom quarter		Second quarter		Third quarter		Top quarter	
	Mean index	S.E.	Mean index	S.E.	Mean index	S.E.	Mean index	S.E.	Mean index	S.E.	Mean score	S.E.	Mean score	S.E.	Mean score	S.E.	Mean score	S.E.
Adjudicated regions																		
Italy (Provincia Autonoma di Bolzano)	–0.20	(0.01)	–1.13	(0.01)	–0.53	(0.02)	0.03	(0.01)	0.83	(0.00)	**515**	(5.0)	523	(7.6)	549	(13.5)	**559**	(4.4)
Italy (Provincia Autonoma di Trento)	0.10	(0.02)	–0.93	(0.04)	–0.06	(0.02)	0.29	(0.02)	1.10	(0.01)	554	(8.6)	557	(5.8)	532	(4.8)	546	(5.3)
Italy (Regione Lombardia)	0.14	(0.12)	–1.17	(0.10)	–0.04	(0.04)	0.62	(0.03)	1.14	(0.05)	492	(15.1)	507	(10.4)	561	(16.0)	517	(24.5)
Italy (Regione Piemonte)	–0.13	(0.12)	–1.10	(0.07)	–0.47	(0.10)	0.20	(0.06)	0.84	(0.09)	493	(12.3)	496	(9.4)	491	(7.9)	495	(13.6)
Italy (Regione Toscana)	–0.20	(0.10)	–1.28	(0.08)	–0.51	(0.05)	0.10	(0.04)	0.89	(0.10)	**468**	(12.9)	491	(19.8)	501	(10.0)	**514**	(12.6)
Italy (Regione Veneto)	0.03	(0.13)	–1.41	(0.08)	–0.28	(0.11)	0.56	(0.06)	1.24	(0.08)	**479**	(12.7)	507	(12.9)	516	(13.7)	**542**	(9.8)
Spain (Basque Country)	–0.42	(0.08)	–1.41	(0.05)	–0.78	(0.02)	–0.15	(0.03)	0.68	(0.07)	**485**	(4.6)	504	(5.5)	506	(5.0)	**511**	(6.2)
Spain (Castile and Leon)	–0.69	(0.09)	–1.47	(0.07)	–1.05	(0.02)	–0.46	(0.07)	0.22	(0.07)	**482**	(9.7)	491	(9.8)	515	(8.4)	**526**	(8.9)
Spain (Catalonia)	–0.05	(0.12)	–1.09	(0.07)	–0.34	(0.08)	0.26	(0.07)	0.99	(0.08)	**475**	(11.2)	498	(6.6)	490	(6.8)	**516**	(10.7)
United Kingdom (Scotland)	0.34	(0.09)	–0.56	(0.09)	0.02	(0.00)	0.35	(0.04)	1.55	(0.15)	**514**	(6.0)	519	(7.0)	525	(6.5)	**537**	(6.5)
Non-adjudicated regions																		
Belgium (Flemish Community)	–0.13	(0.06)	–1.14	(0.04)	–0.17	(0.04)	0.03	(0.00)	0.75	(0.08)	**513**	(10.4)	569	(6.7)	564	(8.0)	**570**	(9.2)
Belgium (French Community)	–0.41	(0.07)	–1.39	(0.05)	–0.72	(0.04)	–0.11	(0.03)	0.57	(0.05)	**434**	(11.9)	506	(14.0)	524	(10.6)	**539**	(9.4)
Belgium (German-speaking Community)	–0.54	(0.00)	–1.36	(0.01)	–0.63	(0.01)	–0.19	(0.01)	0.02	(0.00)	**438**	(6.3)	529	(6.4)	528	(6.7)	**565**	(6.5)
Finland (Finnish speaking)	0.02	(0.07)	–1.03	(0.06)	–0.18	(0.03)	0.24	(0.03)	1.08	(0.08)	**534**	(4.9)	543	(4.0)	548	(4.3)	**555**	(4.0)
Finland (Swedish speaking)	0.07	(0.00)	–1.00	(0.00)	–0.26	(0.01)	0.24	(0.01)	1.31	(0.01)	529	(5.1)	538	(6.1)	528	(5.9)	542	(5.3)
United Kingdom (Northern Ireland)	0.64	(0.06)	–0.53	(0.08)	0.10	(0.02)	0.90	(0.05)	2.09	(0.07)	**466**	(7.8)	482	(6.6)	530	(9.2)	**582**	(6.4)
United Kingdom (Wales)	0.42	(0.14)	0.01	(0.00)	0.02	(0.00)	0.64	(0.11)	1.00	(0.07)	492	(18.2)	481	(16.8)	521	(13.8)	498	(14.3)

	Change in the mathematics score per unit of the index of school principals' perceptions of students' morale and commitment		Increased likelihood of students in the bottom quarter of this index scoring in the bottom quarter of the national mathematics performance distribution		Explained variance in student performance (r-squared × 100)	
	Effect	S.E.	Ratio	S.E.	%	S.E.
Adjudicated regions						
Italy (Provincia Autonoma di Bolzano)	**27.2**	(3.08)	**1.5**	(0.18)	6.0	(1.33)
Italy (Provincia Autonoma di Trento)	**–10.5**	(3.69)	1.0	(0.20)	1.1	(0.77)
Italy (Regione Lombardia)	18.8	(11.50)	1.6	(0.51)	3.4	(4.19)
Italy (Regione Piemonte)	–0.9	(9.67)	1.1	(0.25)	0.0	(0.64)
Italy (Regione Toscana)	**23.2**	(7.87)	1.6	(0.42)	5.2	(3.39)
Italy (Regione Veneto)	**22.3**	(6.82)	1.8	(0.43)	7.3	(4.01)
Spain (Basque Country)	**12.6**	(3.08)	**1.4**	(0.14)	1.6	(0.84)
Spain (Castile and Leon)	**26.6**	(7.62)	**1.7**	(0.25)	4.6	(2.53)
Spain (Catalonia)	**17.2**	(7.41)	1.5	(0.34)	2.5	(2.22)
United Kingdom (Scotland)	**10.9**	(3.26)	1.2	(0.14)	1.4	(0.81)
Non-adjudicated regions						
Belgium (Flemish Community)	**32.5**	(8.16)	**1.9**	(0.32)	5.3	(2.76)
Belgium (French Community)	**50.7**	(6.90)	**2.7**	(0.42)	13.3	(3.62)
Belgium (German-speaking Community)	**81.7**	(5.02)	**4.1**	(0.49)	20.8	(2.22)
Finland (Finnish speaking)	**9.5**	(2.82)	**1.2**	(0.10)	0.9	(0.54)
Finland (Swedish speaking)	4.7	(3.01)	1.2	(0.15)	0.3	(0.35)
United Kingdom (Northern Ireland)	**42.9**	(3.01)	**2.2**	(0.24)	23.4	(2.47)
United Kingdom (Wales)	**18.1**	(17.93)	1.3	(0.57)	0.9	(1.67)

Note: Values that are statistically significant are indicated in bold (see Annex A4).

Table B2.16 (see Table 5.15, Annex A1)

Index of teacher shortage and student performance on the mathematics scale, by national quarters of the index

Results based on reports from school principals and reported proportionate to the number of 15-year-olds enrolled in the school

	Index of teacher shortage										Performance on the mathematics scale, by national quarters of the index of teacher shortage							
	All students		Bottom quarter		Second quarter		Third quarter		Top quarter		Bottom quarter		Second quarter		Third quarter		Top quarter	
	Mean index	S.E.	Mean index	S.E.	Mean index	S.E.	Mean index	S.E.	Mean index	S.E.	Mean score	S.E.	Mean score	S.E.	Mean score	S.E.	Mean score	S.E.
Adjudicated regions																		
Italy (Provincia Autonoma di Bolzano)	0.22	(0.08)	–0.78	(0.08)	–0.03	(0.02)	0.46	(0.00)	1.22	(0.07)	**568**	(11.1)	532	(5.01)	531	(3.85)	**515**	(7.5)
Italy (Provincia Autonoma di Trento)	0.08	(0.01)	–1.13	(0.01)	0.09	(0.02)	0.46	(0.01)	0.88	(0.02)	552	(4.8)	520	(6.52)	574	(6.00)	544	(5.5)
Italy (Regione Lombardia)	0.28	(0.10)	–0.58	(0.12)	0.15	(0.03)	0.45	(0.00)	1.10	(0.19)	535	(15.5)	515	(13.29)	534	(16.04)	493	(18.3)
Italy (Regione Piemonte)	–0.27	(0.10)	–1.21	(0.00)	–0.68	(0.05)	–0.03	(0.04)	0.84	(0.11)	474	(11.7)	498	(11.85)	507	(6.84)	496	(16.0)
Italy (Regione Toscana)	0.28	(0.12)	–0.98	(0.08)	0.31	(0.03)	0.55	(0.02)	1.22	(0.16)	480	(13.8)	513	(10.05)	502	(12.45)	467	(20.3)
Italy (Regione Veneto)	0.30	(0.09)	–0.63	(0.13)	0.27	(0.02)	0.51	(0.02)	1.03	(0.10)	495	(14.0)	533	(9.39)	511	(14.56)	507	(8.0)
Spain (Basque Country)	–0.26	(0.10)	–1.21	(0.00)	–1.20	(0.00)	–0.47	(0.04)	1.85	(0.18)	498	(5.2)	498	(5.41)	508	(6.18)	503	(5.5)
Spain (Castile and Leon)	–0.50	(0.15)	–1.21	(0.00)	–1.19	(0.01)	–0.52	(0.01)	0.93	(0.36)	500	(7.4)	502	(7.06)	519	(12.18)	492	(10.9)
Spain (Catalonia)	–0.51	(0.15)	–1.21	(0.00)	–1.06	(0.05)	–0.37	(0.06)	0.59	(0.30)	494	(9.4)	502	(7.99)	499	(6.60)	482	(7.4)
United Kingdom (Scotland)	–0.14	(0.09)	–1.21	(0.00)	–0.69	(0.07)	0.32	(0.03)	1.01	(0.07)	**537**	(5.5)	527	(5.56)	524	(4.38)	**507**	(6.2)
Non-adjudicated regions																		
Belgium (Flemish Community)	–0.15	(0.07)	–1.21	(0.00)	–0.62	(0.03)	0.18	(0.02)	1.03	(0.09)	**571**	(8.5)	557	(7.27)	550	(9.96)	**538**	(11.5)
Belgium (French Community)	0.80	(0.08)	–0.19	(0.11)	0.62	(0.02)	0.94	(0.02)	1.84	(0.14)	507	(11.2)	490	(13.26)	515	(12.76)	481	(15.9)
Belgium (German-speaking Community)	0.56	(0.00)	–0.14	(0.00)	0.27	(0.01)	0.56	(0.00)	1.54	(0.01)	**543**	(6.6)	532	(6.47)	531	(6.08)	**454**	(5.6)
Finland (Finnish speaking)	–0.58	(0.05)	–1.21	(0.00)	–1.03	(0.03)	–0.39	(0.02)	0.29	(0.05)	543	(3.8)	543	(3.53)	551	(4.00)	542	(3.6)
Finland (Swedish speaking)	–0.12	(0.00)	–1.03	(0.01)	–0.21	(0.01)	0.15	(0.00)	0.60	(0.01)	520	(6.2)	539	(6.75)	546	(5.22)	532	(4.4)
United Kingdom (Northern Ireland)	–0.32	(0.06)	–1.21	(0.00)	–0.78	(0.03)	–0.05	(0.04)	0.77	(0.04)	515	(6.9)	533	(7.09)	519	(10.15)	493	(10.3)
United Kingdom (Wales)	–0.65	(0.37)	–1.21	(0.00)	–1.20	(0.00)	–0.76	(0.06)	0.58	(0.50)	493	(16.6)	490	(18.73)	509	(24.32)	500	(20.4)

	Change in the mathematics score per unit of the index of teacher shortage		Increased likelihood of students in the bottom quarter of this index scoring in the bottom quarter of the national mathematics performance distribution		Explained variance in student performance (r-squared × 100)	
	Effect	S.E.	Ratio	S.E.	%	S.E.
Adjudicated regions						
Italy (Provincia Autonoma di Bolzano)	**–23.8**	(6.66)	**0.6**	(0.12)	4.8	(2.91)
Italy (Provincia Autonoma di Trento)	1.0	(3.22)	1.0	(0.15)	0.0	(0.14)
Italy (Regione Lombardia)	–19.7	(13.15)	0.7	(0.24)	2.4	(2.89)
Italy (Regione Piemonte)	10.2	(10.87)	1.4	(0.29)	0.9	(2.32)
Italy (Regione Toscana)	–5.5	(10.08)	1.3	(0.33)	0.3	(1.34)
Italy (Regione Veneto)	2.1	(11.43)	1.3	(0.32)	0.0	(0.66)
Spain (Basque Country)	0.5	(2.20)	1.1	(0.11)	0.0	(0.11)
Spain (Castile and Leon)	1.0	(3.76)	1.1	(0.17)	0.0	(0.19)
Spain (Catalonia)	–7.0	(4.83)	1.1	(0.20)	0.4	(0.55)
United Kingdom (Scotland)	**–12.2**	(3.57)	**0.7**	(0.10)	1.7	(1.01)
Non-adjudicated regions						
Belgium (Flemish Community)	**–14.0**	(5.90)	**0.7**	(0.12)	1.5	(1.30)
Belgium (French Community)	–12.2	(8.95)	0.7	(0.16)	0.9	(1.36)
Belgium (German-speaking Community)	**–60.9**	(4.27)	**0.6**	(0.08)	16.2	(2.17)
Finland (Finnish speaking)	–0.3	(3.32)	1.0	(0.08)	0.0	(0.05)
Finland (Swedish speaking)	7.7	(4.01)	**1.3**	(0.15)	0.4	(0.36)
United Kingdom (Northern Ireland)	**–12.6**	(6.41)	1.0	(0.14)	1.1	(1.13)
United Kingdom (Wales)	5.2	(6.92)	1.3	(0.71)	0.3	(0.73)

Note: Values that are statistically significant are indicated in bold (see Annex A4).

Table B2.17 (see Table 5.17, Annex A1)

Index of the quality of the schools' physical infrastructure and student performance on the mathematics scale, by national quarters of the index

Results based on reports from school principals and reported proportionate to the number of 15-year-olds enrolled in the school

	Index of the quality of the schools' physical infrastructure										Performance on the mathematics scale by national quarters of the index of the quality of the schools' physical infrastructure							
	All students		Bottom quarter		Second quarter		Third quarter		Top quarter		Bottom quarter		Second quarter		Third quarter		Top quarter	
	Mean index	S.E.	Mean index	S.E.	Mean index	S.E.	Mean index	S.E.	Mean index	S.E.	Mean score	S.E.	Mean score	S.E.	Mean score	S.E.	Mean score	S.E.
Adjudicated regions																		
Italy (Provincia Autonoma di Bolzano)	0.33	(0.06)	–0.88	(0.13)	0.14	(0.02)	0.72	(0.01)	1.34	(0.01)	538	(14.5)	528	(8.8)	548	(4.6)	531	(5.2)
Italy (Provincia Autonoma di Trento)	0.32	(0.05)	–0.76	(0.03)	0.27	(0.03)	0.52	(0.01)	1.25	(0.03)	543	(5.6)	546	(8.9)	556	(6.7)	546	(3.8)
Italy (Regione Lombardia)	0.12	(0.12)	–0.99	(0.19)	–0.09	(0.02)	0.25	(0.04)	1.31	(0.09)	489	(18.8)	524	(12.0)	537	(13.5)	528	(15.0)
Italy (Regione Piemonte)	0.05	(0.15)	–1.22	(0.10)	–0.27	(0.04)	0.40	(0.07)	1.31	(0.09)	484	(18.5)	505	(9.6)	491	(9.1)	497	(14.7)
Italy (Regione Toscana)	–0.19	(0.09)	–1.03	(0.09)	–0.42	(0.05)	–0.07	(0.02)	0.76	(0.12)	499	(13.3)	491	(12.9)	492	(14.2)	485	(14.0)
Italy (Regione Veneto)	–0.19	(0.15)	–1.51	(0.17)	–0.37	(0.03)	–0.07	(0.03)	1.21	(0.13)	494	(11.4)	517	(11.8)	515	(14.5)	518	(13.7)
Spain (Basque Country)	0.23	(0.08)	–1.20	(0.12)	–0.08	(0.03)	0.71	(0.04)	1.49	(0.00)	**492**	(4.9)	502	(6.6)	505	(6.5)	**508**	(6.3)
Spain (Castile and Leon)	0.28	(0.14)	–1.05	(0.18)	–0.10	(0.05)	0.80	(0.07)	1.49	(0.00)	500	(10.1)	499	(10.7)	504	(8.9)	509	(9.3)
Spain (Catalonia)	0.44	(0.11)	–0.58	(0.11)	0.20	(0.02)	0.70	(0.05)	1.45	(0.02)	495	(7.3)	482	(8.6)	491	(8.6)	510	(12.2)
United Kingdom (Scotland)	0.14	(0.08)	–0.92	(0.09)	–0.23	(0.02)	0.38	(0.05)	1.33	(0.05)	523	(6.7)	525	(5.0)	527	(6.1)	521	(7.0)
Non-adjudicated regions																		
Belgium (Flemish Community)	0.26	(0.08)	–0.98	(0.12)	–0.04	(0.02)	0.57	(0.03)	1.49	(0.00)	553	(8.9)	558	(9.8)	554	(11.0)	547	(9.7)
Belgium (French Community)	–0.14	(0.10)	–1.26	(0.11)	–0.54	(0.03)	0.08	(0.03)	1.17	(0.08)	**524**	(9.8)	497	(11.6)	489	(13.9)	**479**	(10.9)
Belgium (German-speaking Community)	–1.22	(0.00)	–2.31	(0.00)	–1.54	(0.02)	–0.87	(0.01)	–0.16	(0.01)	**464**	(6.3)	566	(7.3)	518	(6.8)	**513**	(5.3)
Finland (Finnish speaking)	–0.25	(0.08)	–1.41	(0.09)	–0.61	(0.03)	0.08	(0.02)	0.95	(0.07)	543	(4.6)	551	(3.8)	543	(3.4)	543	(3.5)
Finland (Swedish speaking)	–0.14	(0.00)	–1.21	(0.01)	–0.37	(0.01)	0.14	(0.00)	0.91	(0.02)	531	(6.1)	539	(6.2)	534	(5.5)	533	(5.3)
United Kingdom (Northern Ireland)	–0.18	(0.09)	–1.54	(0.08)	–0.48	(0.03)	0.18	(0.02)	1.12	(0.06)	512	(10.1)	517	(10.6)	514	(10.8)	516	(9.9)
United Kingdom (Wales)	0.03	(0.15)	–0.77	(0.34)	–0.11	(0.06)	0.36	(0.07)	0.67	(0.11)	504	(5.2)	492	(23.4)	513	(13.0)	482	(11.6)

	Change in the mathematics score per unit of the index of the quality of the schools' physical infrastructure		Increased likelihood of students in the bottom quarter of this index scoring in the bottom quarter of the national mathematics performance distribution		Explained variance in student performance (r-squared × 100)	
	Effect	S.E.	Ratio	S.E.	%	S.E.
Adjudicated regions						
Italy (Provincia Autonoma di Bolzano)	1.3	(5.36)	1.2	(0.20)	0.0	(0.30)
Italy (Provincia Autonoma di Trento)	3.6	(3.04)	1.1	(0.13)	0.2	(0.23)
Italy (Regione Lombardia)	12.1	(9.36)	1.7	(0.53)	1.3	(1.98)
Italy (Regione Piemonte)	6.1	(10.13)	1.4	(0.43)	0.5	(1.56)
Italy (Regione Toscana)	–4.9	(10.18)	0.9	(0.29)	0.2	(0.96)
Italy (Regione Veneto)	9.5	(6.31)	1.3	(0.27)	1.3	(1.81)
Spain (Basque Country)	**5.1**	(2.48)	1.2	(0.12)	0.4	(0.44)
Spain (Castile and Leon)	2.8	(4.84)	1.1	(0.25)	0.1	(0.48)
Spain (Catalonia)	7.1	(7.15)	1.0	(0.17)	0.4	(0.85)
United Kingdom (Scotland)	–2.1	(4.32)	1.1	(0.15)	0.1	(0.31)
Non-adjudicated regions						
Belgium (Flemish Community)	–0.7	(5.71)	0.9	(0.16)	0.0	(0.23)
Belgium (French Community)	**–16.5**	(5.39)	**0.6**	(0.11)	2.2	(1.43)
Belgium (German-speaking Community)	**15.2**	(3.72)	**2.7**	(0.31)	1.6	(0.80)
Finland (Finnish speaking)	–0.8	(2.20)	1.0	(0.08)	0.0	(0.07)
Finland (Swedish speaking)	1.2	(2.94)	1.2	(0.20)	0.0	(0.12)
United Kingdom (Northern Ireland)	1.7	(5.38)	1.0	(0.18)	0.0	(0.36)
United Kingdom (Wales)	–5.9	(9.81)	0.9	(0.36)	0.2	(0.56)

Note: Values that are statistically significant are indicated in bold (see Annex A4).

Table B2.18 (see Table 5.18, Annex A1)

Index of the quality of the schools' educational resources and student performance on the mathematics scale, by national quarters of the index

Results based on reports from school principals and reported proportionate to the number of 15-year-olds enrolled in the school

	Index of the quality of the schools' educational resources										Performance on the mathematics scale by national quarters of the index of the quality of the schools' educational resources							
	All students		Bottom quarter		Second quarter		Third quarter		Top quarter		Bottom quarter		Second quarter		Third quarter		Top quarter	
	Mean index	S.E.	Mean index	S.E.	Mean index	S.E.	Mean index	S.E.	Mean index	S.E.	Mean score	S.E.	Mean score	S.E.	Mean score	S.E.	Mean score	S.E.
Adjudicated regions																		
Italy (Provincia Autonoma di Bolzano)	0.65	(0.05)	–0.43	(0.10)	0.33	(0.01)	0.90	(0.02)	1.81	(0.01)	527	(18.5)	548	(5.1)	521	(6.3)	550	(3.6)
Italy (Provincia Autonoma di Trento)	0.90	(0.01)	**–0.02**	(0.01)	0.59	(0.02)	0.93	(0.01)	**2.11**	(0.01)	537	(5.1)	548	(9.7)	551	(4.7)	553	(4.8)
Italy (Regione Lombardia)	0.17	(0.11)	–0.66	(0.16)	–0.04	(0.03)	0.34	(0.03)	1.04	(0.13)	479	(19.5)	536	(12.4)	547	(15.5)	515	(15.5)
Italy (Regione Piemonte)	0.35	(0.18)	–1.14	(0.20)	0.01	(0.05)	0.74	(0.06)	1.78	(0.09)	484	(17.6)	508	(10.7)	485	(8.3)	500	(14.5)
Italy (Regione Toscana)	0.21	(0.11)	**–0.73**	(0.08)	–0.09	(0.05)	0.37	(0.03)	**1.29**	(0.14)	453	(17.8)	494	(13.8)	515	(13.0)	499	(9.9)
Italy (Regione Veneto)	0.25	(0.14)	**–1.16**	(0.13)	–0.15	(0.07)	0.48	(0.07)	**1.83**	(0.14)	490	(10.2)	509	(13.9)	514	(16.6)	531	(13.3)
Spain (Basque Country)	0.13	(0.09)	**–1.24**	(0.08)	–0.28	(0.04)	0.44	(0.03)	**1.61**	(0.10)	491	(4.9)	494	(6.3)	505	(6.0)	518	(5.1)
Spain (Castile and Leon)	–0.39	(0.11)	–1.32	(0.15)	–0.71	(0.03)	–0.21	(0.03)	0.67	(0.21)	501	(9.2)	497	(8.8)	509	(12.1)	505	(8.1)
Spain (Catalonia)	0.30	(0.10)	–0.58	(0.06)	0.06	(0.02)	0.52	(0.03)	1.22	(0.14)	490	(8.4)	490	(9.4)	497	(12.1)	500	(9.6)
United Kingdom (Scotland)	0.53	(0.09)	–0.44	(0.05)	0.06	(0.02)	0.64	(0.04)	1.87	(0.09)	514	(6.5)	529	(8.7)	528	(6.5)	525	(6.2)
Non-adjudicated regions																		
Belgium (Flemish Community)	0.51	(0.08)	–0.55	(0.06)	0.20	(0.02)	0.70	(0.03)	1.69	(0.07)	528	(11.0)	561	(10.0)	561	(9.3)	562	(10.7)
Belgium (French Community)	–0.25	(0.10)	**–1.30**	(0.09)	–0.59	(0.02)	–0.10	(0.03)	**1.00**	(0.13)	531	(13.5)	510	(10.9)	497	(13.5)	457	(15.7)
Belgium (German-speaking Community)	–0.03	(0.00)	**–0.67**	(0.01)	–0.22	(0.00)	–0.12	(0.01)	**0.88**	(0.01)	523	(5.3)	489	(9.5)	482	(12.1)	566	(7.4)
Finland (Finnish speaking)	–0.02	(0.06)	–0.84	(0.06)	–0.25	(0.02)	0.15	(0.01)	0.86	(0.09)	546	(4.3)	547	(4.4)	542	(3.6)	543	(3.7)
Finland (Swedish speaking)	–0.06	(0.00)	–0.60	(0.01)	–0.32	(0.00)	–0.10	(0.00)	0.80	(0.01)	539	(6.0)	537	(6.1)	525	(5.4)	536	(6.0)
United Kingdom (Northern Ireland)	0.39	(0.11)	**–0.78**	(0.08)	–0.09	(0.03)	0.50	(0.04)	**1.92**	(0.08)	496	(9.4)	511	(9.6)	520	(11.7)	533	(11.9)
United Kingdom (Wales)	0.08	(0.21)	–0.76	(0.05)	–0.26	(0.18)	0.28	(0.02)	1.09	(0.31)	481	(17.0)	503	(12.8)	505	(22.0)	503	(20.4)

	Change in the mathematics score per unit of the index of the quality of the schools' educational resource		Increased likelihood of students in the bottom quarter of this index scoring in the bottom quarter of the national mathematics performance distribution		Explained variance in student performance (r-squared × 100)	
	Effect	S.E.	Ratio	S.E.	%	S.E.
Adjudicated regions						
Italy (Provincia Autonoma di Bolzano)	7.8	(5.40)	1.4	(0.25)	0.7	(1.02)
Italy (Provincia Autonoma di Trento)	5.5	(3.28)	1.3	(0.19)	0.4	(0.39)
Italy (Regione Lombardia)	10.7	(12.41)	2.2	(0.67)	0.7	(1.56)
Italy (Regione Piemonte)	5.9	(8.90)	1.4	(0.38)	0.6	(1.88)
Italy (Regione Toscana)	19.0	(11.44)	**2.3**	(0.63)	3.1	(3.53)
Italy (Regione Veneto)	**13.1**	(5.83)	1.6	(0.34)	3.1	(2.77)
Spain (Basque Country)	**10.5**	(2.03)	**1.3**	(0.13)	2.0	(0.82)
Spain (Castile and Leon)	–1.1	(5.67)	1.1	(0.22)	0.0	(0.25)
Spain (Catalonia)	2.5	(7.08)	1.0	(0.18)	0.0	(0.38)
United Kingdom (Scotland)	2.2	(3.91)	1.3	(0.16)	0.1	(0.22)
Non-adjudicated regions						
Belgium (Flemish Community)	**13.5**	(6.83)	**1.5**	(0.27)	1.3	(1.32)
Belgium (French Community)	**–24.8**	(8.86)	**0.5**	(0.16)	4.5	(2.97)
Belgium (German-speaking Community)	**34.1**	(4.09)	**0.7**	(0.09)	4.4	(1.03)
Finland (Finnish speaking)	0.3	(2.86)	0.9	(0.07)	0.0	(0.05)
Finland (Swedish speaking)	–3.3	(4.55)	0.9	(0.14)	0.1	(0.20)
United Kingdom (Northern Ireland)	**13.1**	(6.15)	1.3	(0.19)	2.1	(1.89)
United Kingdom (Wales)	2.4	(11.96)	1.8	(0.70)	0.1	(0.95)

Note: Values that are statistically significant are indicated in bold (see Annex A4).

Table B2.19 (see Table A3.1, Annex A3)

PISA target populations and samples

	Population and sample information						
	(1)	(2)	(3)	(4)	(5)	(6)	(7)
	Total population of 15-year-olds	Total enrolled population of 15-year-olds at grade 7 or above	Total in national desired target population	Total school-level exclusions	Total in national desired target population after school exclusions and before within-school exclusions	Percentage of all school-level exclusions	Number of participating students
Adjudicated regions							
Italy (Provincia Autonoma di Bolzano)	4 908	4 087	4 087	9	4077.88	0.22	1 264
Italy (Provincia Autonoma di Trento)	4 534	4 199	4 199	77	4122.15	1.83	1 030
Italy (Regione Lombardia)	76 269	74 994	74 994	252	74741.89	0.34	1 545
Italy (Regione Piemonte)	33 340	33 242	33 242	185	33056.81	0.56	1 565
Italy (Regione Toscana)	27 111	29 208	29 208	161	29047.23	0.55	1 509
Italy (Regione Veneto)	37 843	36 388	36 388	242	36145.53	0.67	1 538
Spain (Basque Country)	18 160	17 753	17 753	15	17738.00	0.08	3 885
Spain (Castile and Leon)	24 210	21 580	21 580	109	21471.00	0.51	1 490
Spain (Catalonia)	62 946	61 829	61 829	576	61253.00	0.93	1 516
United Kingdom (Scotland)	65 913	63 950	63 950	917	63033.00	1.43	2 723

	Population and sample information					Coverage indices		
	(8)	(9)	(10)	(11)	(12)	(13)	(14)	(15)
	Weighted number of participating students	Number of excluded students	Weighted number of excluded students	Within-school exclusion rate (%)	Overall exclusion rate (%)	Coverage index 1: Coverage of national desired population	Coverage index 2: Coverage of national enrolled population	Coverage index 3: Percentage of enrolled population
Adjudicated regions								
Italy (Provincia Autonoma di Bolzano)	3 464	25	67	1.90	2.11	0.98	0.98	0.83
Italy (Provincia Autonoma di Trento)	3 324	20	73	2.16	3.95	0.96	0.96	0.93
Italy (Regione Lombardia)	63 916	38	2 037	3.09	3.41	0.97	0.97	0.98
Italy (Regione Piemonte)	30 107	27	522	1.70	2.25	0.98	0.98	1.00
Italy (Regione Toscana)	25 722	21	346	1.33	1.87	0.98	0.98	1.08
Italy (Regione Veneto)	30 854	22	416	1.33	1.99	0.98	0.98	0.96
Spain (Basque Country)	16 978	56	252	1.46	1.55	0.98	0.98	0.98
Spain (Castile and Leon)	18 224	95	1 057	5.48	5.96	0.94	0.94	0.89
Spain (Catalonia)	50 484	61	1 847	3.53	4.43	0.96	0.96	0.98
United Kingdom (Scotland)	58 559	39	715	1.21	2.62	0.97	0.97	0.97

Table B2.20 (see Table A3.2, Annex A3)
Exclusions

	Student exclusions (unweighted)				
	(1) Number of excluded students with disability (Code 1)	(2) Number of excluded students with disability (Code 2)	(3) Number of excluded students because of language (Code 3)	(4) Number of excluded students for other reasons (Code 4)	(5) Total number of excluded students
Adjudicated regions					
Italy (Provincia Autonoma di Bolzano)	1	20	4	0	25
Italy (Provincia Autonoma di Trento)	5	4	11	0	20
Italy (Regione Lombardia)	4	16	18	0	38
Italy (Regione Piemonte)	2	11	14	0	27
Italy (Regione Toscana)	5	9	7	0	21
Italy (Regione Veneto)	0	16	6	0	22
Spain (Basque Country)	5	44	7	0	56
Spain (Castile and Leon)	1	75	19	0	95
Spain (Catalonia)	3	46	12	0	61
United Kingdom (Scotland)	1	36	2	0	39

	Student exclusions (weighted)				
	(6) Weighted number of excluded students with disability (Code 1)	(7) Weighted number of excluded students with disability (Code 2)	(8) Weighted number of excluded students because of language (Code 3)	(9) Weighted number of excluded students for other reasons (Code 4)	(10) Total weighted number of excluded students
Adjudicated regions					
Italy (Provincia Autonoma di Bolzano)	9	46	11	0	67
Italy (Provincia Autonoma di Trento)	15	9	50	0	73
Italy (Regione Lombardia)	130	802	1 105	0	2 037
Italy (Regione Piemonte)	56	212	254	0	522
Italy (Regione Toscana)	75	128	143	0	346
Italy (Regione Veneto)	0	298	118	0	416
Spain (Basque Country)	28	186	38	0	252
Spain (Castile and Leon)	7	844	206	0	1 057
Spain (Catalonia)	91	1 372	385	0	1 847
United Kingdom (Scotland)	19	660	35	0	715

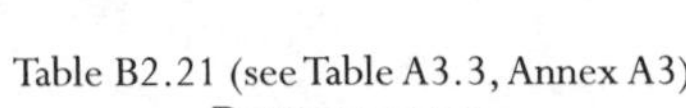

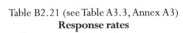

Table B2.21 (see Table A3.3, Annex A3)
Response rates

	Initial sample – before school replacement				
	(1) Weighted school participation rate before replacement (%)	(2) Number of responding schools (weighted by enrolment)	(3) Number of schools sampled (responding and non-responding, weighted by enrolment)	(4) Number of responding schools (unweighted)	(5) Number of responding and non-responding schools (unweighted)
Adjudicated regions					
Italy (Provincia Autonoma di Bolzano)	100.00	3 967	3 967	43	43
Italy (Provincia Autonoma di Trento)	100.00	3 962	3 962	33	33
Italy (Regione Lombardia)	100.00	72 657	72 657	52	52
Italy (Regione Piemonte)	96.12	32 249	33 552	55	57
Italy (Regione Toscana)	95.93	27 120	28 272	50	52
Italy (Regione Veneto)	97.97	34 344	35 056	51	52
Spain (Basque Country)	98.58	17 803	18 059	139	141
Spain (Castile and Leon)	98.45	20 625	20 950	50	51
Spain (Catalonia)	97.95	58 385	59 609	49	50
United Kingdom (Scotland)	78.32	49 198	62 814	84	108
	Final sample – after school replacement				
	(6) Weighted school participation rate after replacement (%)	(7) Number of responding schools (weighted by enrolment)	(8) Number of schools sampled (responding and non-responding, weighted by enrolment)	(9) Number of responding schools (unweighted)	(10) Number of responding and non-responding schools (unweighted)
Adjudicated regions					
Italy (Provincia Autonoma di Bolzano)	100.00	3 967	3 967	43	43
Italy (Provincia Autonoma di Trento)	100.00	3 962	3 962	33	33
Italy (Regione Lombardia)	100.00	72 657	72 657	52	52
Italy (Regione Piemonte)	100.00	33 552	33 552	57	57
Italy (Regione Toscana)	100.00	28 272	28 272	52	52
Italy (Regione Veneto)	100.00	35 056	35 056	52	52
Spain (Basque Country)	100.00	18 047	18 047	141	141
Spain (Castile and Leon)	100.00	20 911	20 911	51	51
Spain (Catalonia)	100.00	59 609	59 609	50	50
United Kingdom (Scotland)	88.89	55 737	62 794	96	108
	Student exclusions (weighted)				
	(11) Weighted student participation rate after replacement (%)	(12) Number of students assessed (weighted)	(13) Number of students sampled (assessed and absent, weighted)	(14) Number of students assessed (unweighted)	(15) Number of students sampled (assessed and absent, unweighted)
Adjudicated regions					
Italy (Provincia Autonoma di Bolzano)	96.13	3 331	3 464	1 264	1 318
Italy (Provincia Autonoma di Trento)	95.97	3 190	3 324	1 030	1 078
Italy (Regione Lombardia)	95.48	61 024	63 916	1 545	1 620
Italy (Regione Piemonte)	94.15	28 344	30 107	1 565	1 661
Italy (Regione Toscana)	93.04	23 931	25 722	1 509	1 617
Italy (Regione Veneto)	93.84	28 954	30 854	1 538	1 640
Spain (Basque Country)	95.38	16 195	16 978	3 885	4 072
Spain (Castile and Leon)	93.28	17 000	18 224	1 490	1 600
Spain (Catalonia)	92.95	46 922	50 484	1 516	1 634
United Kingdom (Scotland)	85.14	44 308	52 042	2 692	3 160

Annex C

THE DEVELOPMENT AND IMPLEMENTATION OF PISA – A COLLABORATIVE EFFORT

Annex C: The development and implementation of PISA – a collaborative effort

Introduction

PISA is a collaborative effort, bringing together scientific expertise from the participating countries, steered jointly by their governments on the basis of shared, policy-driven interests.

A PISA Governing Board on which each country is represented determines, in the context of OECD objectives, the policy priorities for PISA and oversees adherence to these priorities during the implementation of the programme. This includes the setting of priorities for the development of indicators, for the establishment of the assessment instruments and for the reporting of the results.

Experts from participating countries also serve on working groups that are charged with linking policy objectives with the best internationally available technical expertise. By participating in these expert groups, countries ensure that the instruments are internationally valid and take into account the cultural and educational contexts in OECD Member countries, the assessment materials have strong measurement properties, and the instruments place an emphasis on authenticity and educational validity.

Through National Project Managers, participating countries implement PISA at the national level subject to the agreed administration procedures. National Project Managers play a vital role in ensuring that the implementation of the survey is of high quality, and verify and evaluate the survey results, analyses, reports and publications.

The design and implementation of the surveys, within the framework established by the PISA Governing Board, is the responsibility of an international consortium, referred to as the PISA Consortium, led by the Australian Council for Educational Research (ACER). Other partners in this consortium include the Netherlands National Institute for Educational Measurement (Citogroep), The National Institute for Educational Research in Japan (NIER), the Educational Testing Service in the United States (ETS), and WESTAT in the United States.

The OECD Secretariat has overall managerial responsibility for the programme, monitors its implementation on a day-to-day basis, acts as the secretariat for the PISA Governing Board, builds consensus among countries and serves as the interlocutor between the PISA Governing Board and the international consortium charged with the implementation of the activities. The OECD Secretariat also produces the indicators and analyses and prepares the international reports and publications in co-operation with the PISA consortium and in close consultation with Member countries both at the policy level (PISA Governing Board) and at the level of implementation (National Project Managers).

The following lists the members of the various PISA bodies and the individual experts and consultants who have contributed to PISA.

Members of the PISA Governing Board

Chair: Ryo Watanabe

Australia: Wendy Whitham

Austria: Helmut Bachmann and Jürgen Horschinegg

Belgium: Dominique Barthélémy, Christiane Blondin and Liselotte van de Perre

Brazil: Eliezer Pacheco

Canada: Satya Brink and Dianne Pennock

Czech Republic: Jan Koucky

Denmark: Jørgen Balling Rasmussen

Finland: Jari Rajanen

France: Gérard Bonnet

Germany: Hans Konrad Koch, Elfriede Ohrnberger and Botho Priebe

Greece: Vassilis Koulaidis

Hong Kong-China: Esther Ho Sui Chu

Hungary: Péter Vári

Iceland: Júlíus K. Björnsson

Indonesia: Bahrul Hayat

Ireland: Gerry Shiel

Italy: Giacomo Elias and Angela Vegliante

Japan: Ryo Watanabe

Korea: Kye Young Lee

Latvia: Andris Kangro

Luxembourg: Michel Lanners

Macao-China: Lam Fat Lo

Mexico: Felipe Martínez Rizo

Netherlands: Jules L. Peschar

New Zealand: Lynne Whitney

Norway: Alette Schreiner

Poland: Stanislaw Drzazdzewski

Portugal: Glória Ramalho
Russian Federation: Galina Kovalyova
Serbia: Dragica Pavlovic Babic
Slovak Republic: Vladimir Repas
Spain: Guillermo Gil and Carme Amorós Basté
Sweden: Anita Wester
Switzerland: Katrin Holenstein and Heinz Rhyn
Thailand: Sunee Klainin
Tunisia: Néjib Ayed
Turkey: Sevki Karaca and Ruhi Kilç
United Kingdom: Lorna Bertrand and Liz Levy
United States: Mariann Lemke and Elois Scott
Uruguay: Pedro Ravela
Special Advisor: Eugene Owen

PISA 2003 National Project Managers

Australia: John Cresswell and Sue Thomson
Austria: Günter Haider and Claudia Reiter
Belgium: Luc van de Poele
Brazil: Mariana Migliari
Canada: Tamara Knighton and Dianne Pennock
Czech Republic: Jana Paleckova
Denmark: Jan Mejding
Finland: Jouni Välijärvi
France: Anne-Laure Monnier
Germany: Manfred Prenzel
Greece: Vassilia Hatzinikita
Hong Kong-China: Esther Ho Sui Chu
Hungary: Péter Vári
Iceland: Almar Midvik Halldorsson
Indonesia: Bahrul Hayat
Ireland: Judith Cosgrove
Italy: Maria Teresa Siniscalco
Japan: Ryo Watanabe
Korea: Mee-Kyeong Lee
Latvia: Andris Kangro
Luxembourg: Iris Blanke
Macao-China: Lam Fat Lo
Mexico: Rafael Vidal
Netherlands: Erna Gille
New Zealand: Fiona Sturrock
Norway: Marit Kjaernsli
Poland: Michal Federowicz
Portugal: Lídia Padinha
Russian Federation: Galina Kovalyova
Serbia: Dragica Pavlovic Babic
Slovak Republic: Paulina Korsnakova
Spain: Guillermo Gil
Sweden: Karin Taube
Switzerland: Huguette McCluskey
Thailand: Sunee Klainin
Tunisia: Néjib Ayed
Turkey: Sevki Karaca
United Kingdom: Rachael Harker, Graham Thorpe
United States: Mariann Lemke
Uruguay: Pedro Ravela

OECD Secretariat

Andreas Schleicher (overall co-ordination of PISA and Member country relations)
Miyako Ikeda (project management)
Claire Shewbridge (project management)
Claudia Tamassia (project management)
Sophie Vayssettes (statistical support)
Juliet Evans (administrative support)
Kate Lancaster (editorial support)

PISA Expert Groups

Mathematics Expert Group

Jan de Lange (Chair) (Utrecht University, The Netherlands)
Werner Blum (Chair) (University of Kassel, Germany)
Vladimir Burjan (National Institute for Education, Slovak Republic)
Sean Close (St Patrick's College, Ireland)
John Dossey (Consultant, United States of America)
Mary Lindquist (Columbus State University, United States of America)
Zbigniew Marciniak (Warsaw University, Poland)
Mogens Niss (Roskilde University, Denmark)
Kyung-Mee Park (Hongik University, Korea)
Luis Rico (University of Granada, Spain)
Yoshinori Shimizu (Tokyo Gakugei University, Japan)

Reading Expert Group

Irwin Kirsch (Chair) (Educational Testing Service, United States)
Marilyn Binkley (National Center for Educational Statistics, United States)
Alan Davies (University of Edinburgh, United Kingdom)
Stan Jones (Statistics Canada, Canada)
John de Jong (Language Testing Services, The Netherlands)
Dominique Lafontaine (Université de Liège Sart Tilman, Belgium)
Pirjo Linnakylä (University of Jyväskylä, Finland)
Martine Rémond (Institut National de Recherche Pédagogique, France)

Science Expert Group

Wynne Harlen (Chair) (University of Bristol, United Kingdom)

Peter Fensham (Monash University, Australia)

Raul Gagliardi (University of Geneva, Switzerland)

Svein Lie (University of Oslo, Norway)

Manfred Prenzel (Universität Kiel, Germany)

Senta A. Raizen (National Center for Improving Science Education (NCISE), United States)

Donghee Shin (KICE, Korea)

Elizabeth Stage (University of California, United States)

PISA Technical Advisory Group

Keith Rust (Chair) (Westat)

Ray Adams (ACER, Australia)

Pierre Foy (Statistics Canada, Canada)

Aletta Grisay (Belgium)

Larry Hedges (The University of Chicago, United States)

Eugene Johnson (American Institutes for Research, United States)

John de Jong (Language Testing Services, The Netherlands)

Irwin Kirsch (Educational Testing Service, United States)

Steve May (Ministry of Education, New Zealand)

Christian Monseur (HallStat SPRL, Belgium)

Norman Verhelst (Citogroep, The Netherlands)

J. Douglas Willms (University of New Brunswick, Canada)

PISA Consortium

Australian Council for Educational Research

Ray Adams (Project Director of the PISA Consortium)

Alla Berezner (data management, data analysis)

Eveline Gerbhardt (data processing, data analysis)

Marten Koomen (management)

Dulce Lay (data processing)

Le Tu Luc (data processing)

Greg Macaskill (data processing)

Barry McCrae (science instruments, test development mathematics and problem solving)

Martin Murphy (field operations and sampling)

Van Nguyen (data processing)

Alla Routitsky (data processing)

Wolfram Schulz (Coordinator questionnaire development. data processing, data analysis)

Ross Turner (Coordinator test development)

Maurice Walker (sampling, data processing, questionnaire development)

Margaret Wu (test development mathematics and problem solving, data analysis)

John Cresswell (test development science)

Juliette Mendelovits (test development reading)

Joy McQueen (test development reading)

Beatrice Halleux (translation quality control)

Westat

Nancy Caldwell (Director of the PISA Consortium for field operations and quality monitoring)

Ming Chen (weighting)

Fran Cohen (weighting)

Susan Fuss (weighting)

Brice Hart (weighting)

Sharon Hirabayashi (weighting)

Sheila Krawchuk (sampling and weighting)

Christian Monseur (consultant) (weighting)

Phu Nguyen (weighting)

Mats Nyfjall (weighting)

Merl Robinson (field operations and quality monitoring)

Keith Rust (Director of the PISA Consortium for sampling and weighting)

Leslie Wallace (weighting)

Erin Wilson (weighting)

Citogroep

Steven Bakker (science test development)

Bart Bossers (reading test development)

Truus Decker (mathematics test development)

Erna van Hest (reading test development and quality monitoring)

Kees Lagerwaard (mathematics test development)

Gerben van Lent (mathematics test development)

Ico de Roo (science test development)

Maria van Toor (office support and quality monitoring)

Norman Verhelst (technical advice, data analysis)

Educational Testing Service

Irwin Kirsch (reading test development)

Other experts

Cordula Artelt (questionnaire development)

Aletta Grisay (technical advice, data analysis, translation, questionnaire development)

Donald Hirsch (editorial review)